AA

Big Easy Read
BRITAIN

Scale 1:160,000
or 2.52 miles to 1 inch

17th edition June 2021 © AA Media Limited 2021
Original edition printed 1991.

All cartography in this atlas edited, designed and produced by the Mapping Services Department of AA Media Limited (A05783).

This atlas contains Ordnance Survey data © Crown copyright and database right 2021. Contains public sector information licensed under the Open Government Licence v3.0. Distances and journey times contains data available from openstreetmap.org © under the Open Database License found at opendatacommons.org

Published by AA Media Limited, whose registered office is Grove House, Lutyens Close, Basingstoke, Hampshire RG24 8AG, UK. Registered number 06112600.

ISBN: 978 0 7495 8262 3 (spiral bound)
ISBN: 978 0 7495 8261 6 (paperback)

A CIP catalogue record for this book is available from The British Library.

Disclaimer: The contents of this atlas are believed to be correct at the time of the latest revision, it will not contain any subsequent amended, new or temporary information including diversions and traffic control or enforcement systems. The publishers cannot be held responsible or liable for any loss or damage occasioned to any person acting or refraining from action as a result of any use or reliance on material in this atlas, nor for any errors, omissions or changes in such material. This does not affect your statutory rights.

The publishers would welcome information to correct any errors or omissions and to keep this atlas up to date. Please write to the Atlas Editor, AA Media Limited, Grove House, Lutyens Close, Basingstoke, Hampshire RG24 8AG, UK.
E-mail: roadatlasfeedback@aamediagroup.co.uk

Acknowledgements: AA Media Limited would like to thank the following for information used in the creation of this atlas:
Cadw, English Heritage, Forestry Commission, Historic Scotland, National Trust and National Trust for Scotland, RSPB, The Wildlife Trust, Scottish Natural Heritage, Natural England, The Countryside Council for Wales. Award winning beaches from 'Blue Flag' and 'Keep Scotland Beautiful' (summer 2019 data): for latest information visit *www.blueflag.org* and *www.keepscotlandbeautiful.org*. Road signs are © Crown Copyright 2021. Reproduced under the terms of the Open Government Licence.
Printed by Elcograf S.p.A, Italy

Contents

Map pages	inside front cover
Route planning	**II–XII**
Route planner	II–V
Caravan and camping sites in Britain	VI–VII
Traffic signs and road markings	VIII–IX
Ferries and port plans	X–XII
Motorways	**XIII–XVI**
Restricted junctions	XIII
M25 London Orbital motorway	XIV
M6 Toll motorway	XV
Smart motorways	XVI
Atlas symbols	**1**
Road maps 1:160,000 scale	**2–152**
Channel Islands 1:113,000 scale	12–13
Isle of Man 1:200,000 scale	102
Orkney and Shetland Islands 1:605,000 scale	147
Western Isles 1:528,000 scale	152

Ferry ports

Aberdeen Harbour..........*XII*	Harwich International	Liverpool Docks............*XII*	Port of Tyne..................*XII*
Calais ....*X*	Port ....*XII*	Newhaven Harbour ....*XI*	Portsmouth Harbour.......*X*
Channel Tunnel..............*XI*	Heysham Harbour ....*XII*	Pembroke Dock ....*XII*	Southampton, Port of......*X*
Dover, Port of ....*XI*	Holyhead Harbour ....*XII*	Plymouth, Port of ....*X*	
Fishguard Harbour..........*XII*	Hull, Port of ....*XII*	Poole, Port of ....*X*	

Town plans

Aberdeen...................133	Durham 154	London.......................156	St Andrews.................125
Aberystwyth 48	Edinburgh...................154	Manchester 156	Salisbury.....................157
Bath 153	Exeter.............................9	Middlesbrough 93	Scarborough 93
Birmingham.................153	Glasgow 155	Milton Keynes 156	Sheffield 157
Blackpool 82	Great Yarmouth 71	Newcastle upon	Shrewsbury 157
Bradford 153	Harrogate 155	Tyne.......................101	Southampton 158
Bristol.........................153	Inverness....................155	Newquay........................3	Southend-on-Sea..........35
Cambridge 153	Ipswich.........................47	Norwich.......................156	Stratford-upon-Avon....158
Canterbury 153	Kingston upon Hull......155	Nottingham 156	Sunderland..................101
Cardiff.........................154	Leeds 155	Oxford 157	Swansea 26
Chester 154	Leicester.....................155	Peterborough 157	Swindon 158
Coventry......................154	Lincoln........................156	Plymouth 4	Wolverhampton 158
Derby 154	Liverpool.......................74	Portsmouth 157	Worcester....................158
Dundee 125	Llandudno 73	Ramsgate.......................35	York.............................158

Tourist sites with satnav friendly postcodes	**159**
London district map	**160–161**
Index to place names	**162–192**
County, administrative area map	162
Place name index	162–192
Distances and journey times	**inside back cover**

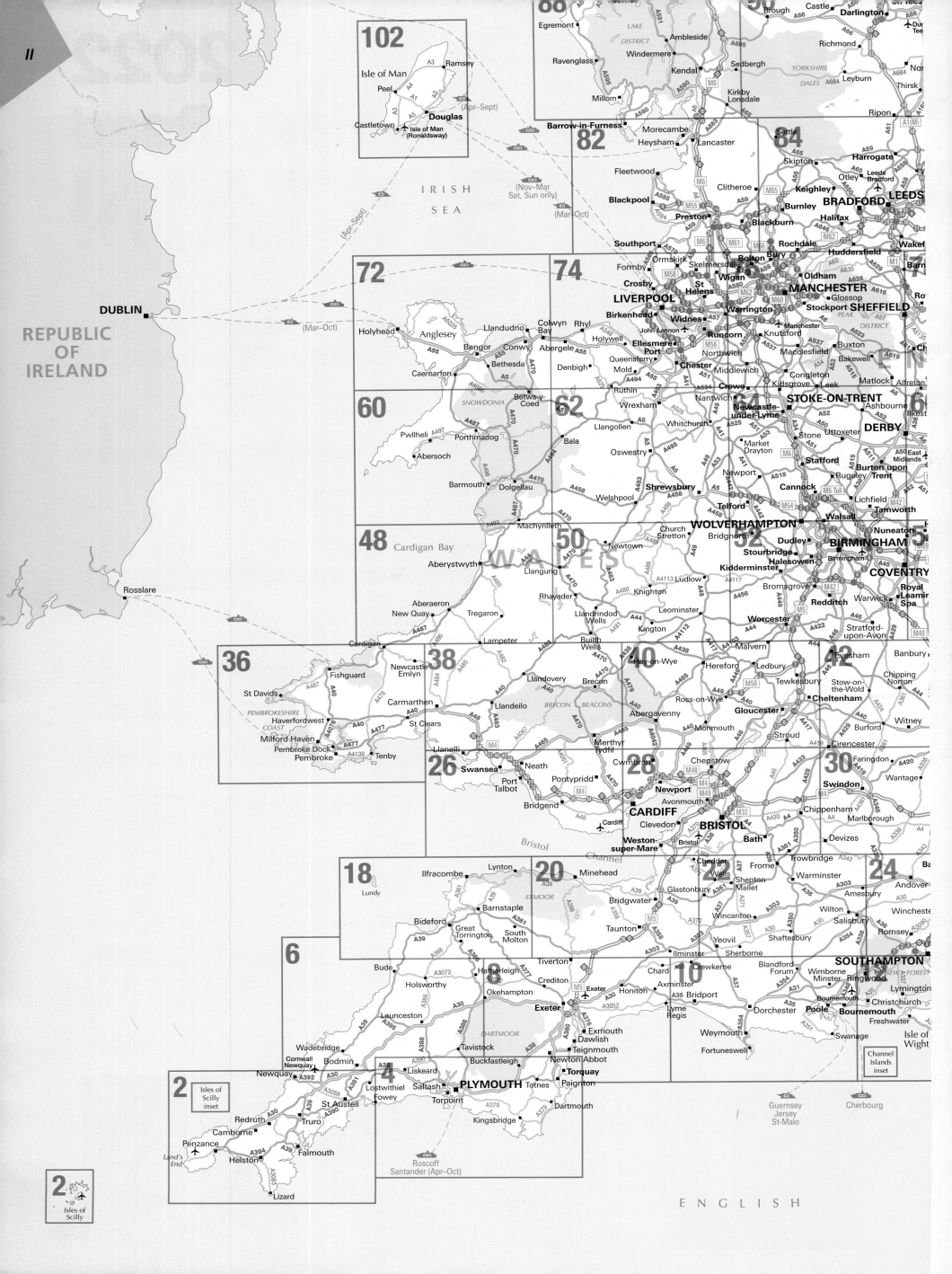

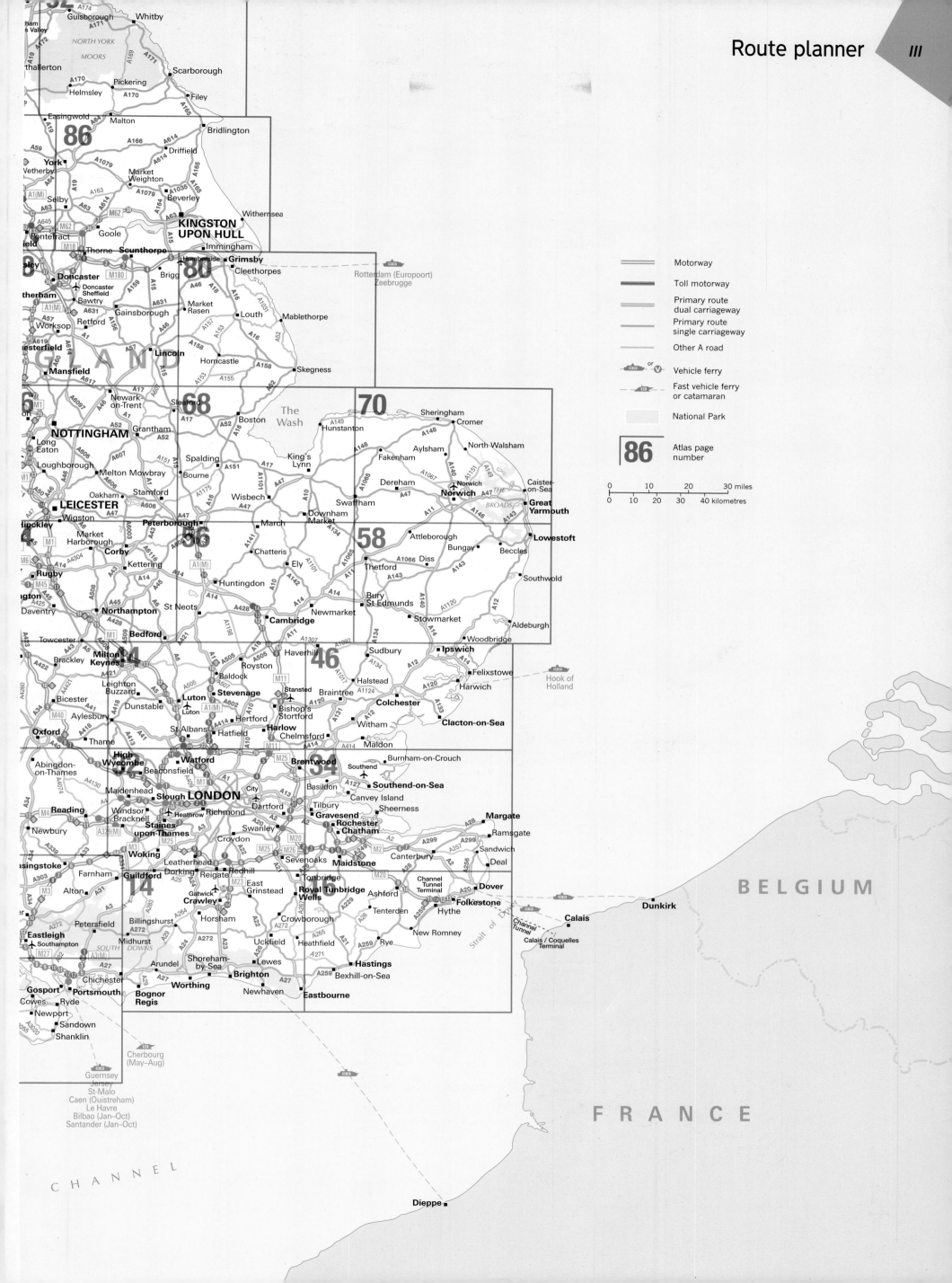

Motorway

Toll motorway

Primary route
dual carriageway

Primary route
single carriageway

Other A road

Vehicle ferry

Fast vehicle ferry
or catamaran

National Park

86 Atlas page
number

0   10   20   30 miles
0   10   20   30   40 kilometres

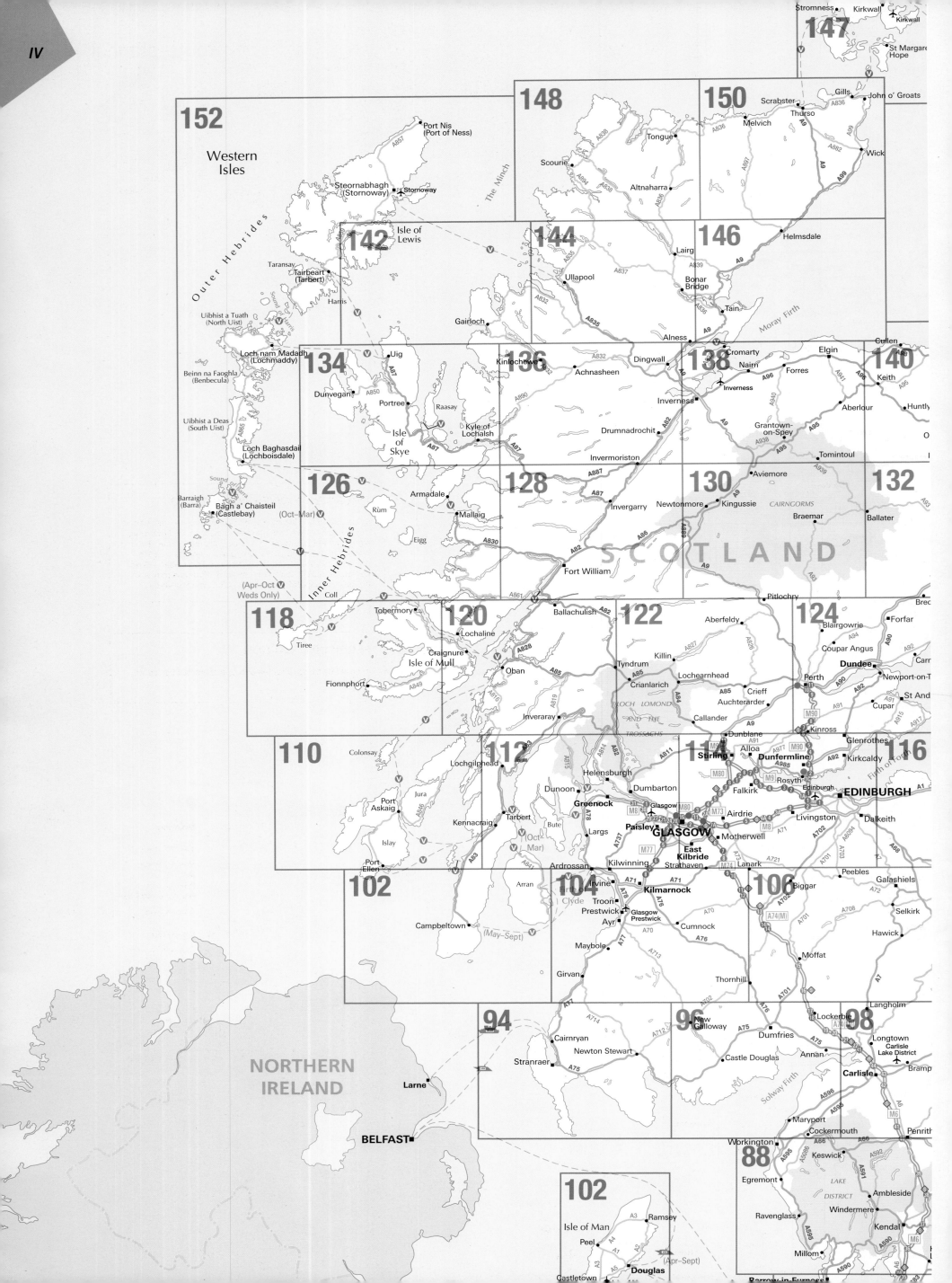

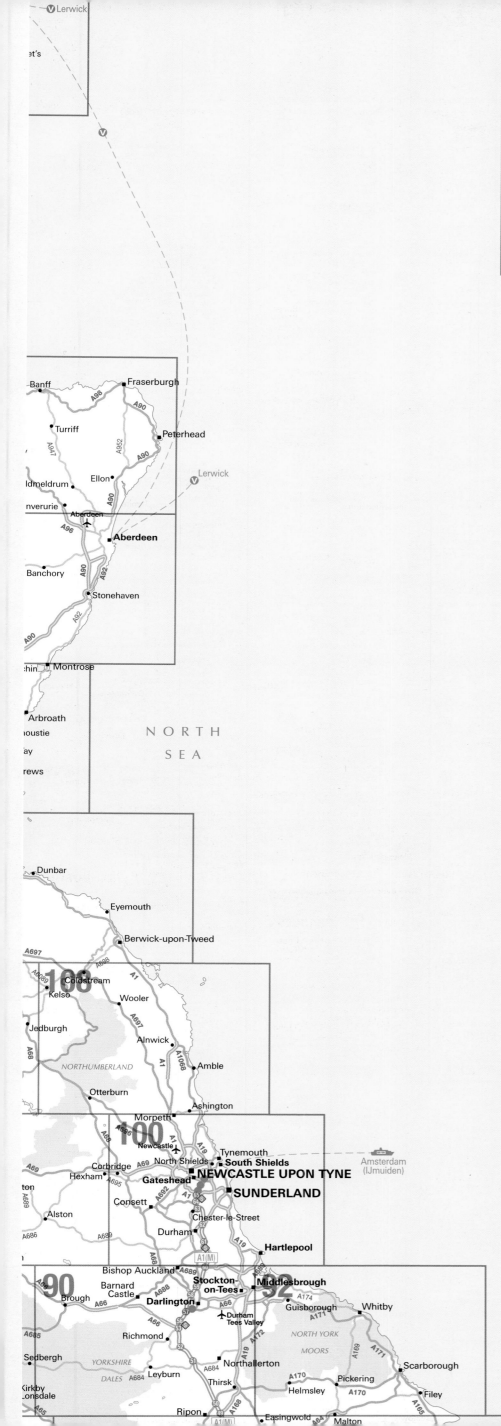

147
Orkney Islands

Papa Westray
North Ronaldsay
Westray
Rousay
Eday
Sanday
Mainland
Stronsay
Shapinsay
Lerwick
Stromness
Kirkwall
Hoy
St Margaret's Hope
South Ronaldsay
Aberdeen
Scrabster
Gills

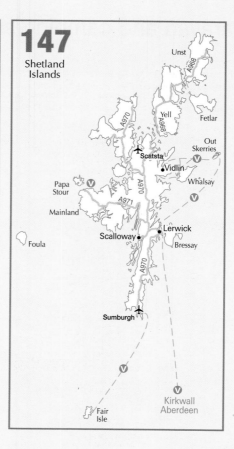

147
Shetland Islands

Unst
Yell
Fetlar
Out Skerries
Papa Stour
Scatsta
Vidlin
Whalsay
Mainland
Scalloway
Lerwick
Bressay
Foula
Sumburgh
Fair Isle
Kirkwall Aberdeen

EMERGENCY DIVERSION ROUTES

In an emergency it may be necessary to close a section of motorway or other main road to traffic, so a temporary sign may advise drivers to follow a diversion route. To help drivers navigate the route, black symbols on yellow patches may be permanently displayed on existing direction signs, including motorway signs. Symbols may also be used on separate signs with yellow backgrounds.

FERRY INFORMATION

Information on ferry routes and operators can be found on pages *X–XII*.

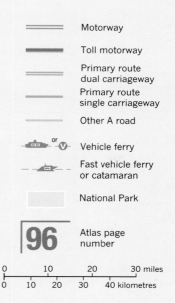

═══	Motorway
═══	Toll motorway
═══	Primary route dual carriageway
───	Primary route single carriageway
───	Other A road
⛴ or Ⓥ	Vehicle ferry
⛴	Fast vehicle ferry or catamaran
▨	National Park
96	Atlas page number

0   10   20   30 miles
0 10 20 30 40 kilometres

Caravan and camping sites in Britain

These pages list the top 300 AA-inspected Caravan and Camping (C & C) sites in the Pennant rating scheme. **Five Pennant Premier sites are shown in green,** Four Pennant sites are shown in blue.

Listings include addresses, telephone numbers and websites together with page and grid references to locate the sites in the atlas. The total number of touring pitches is also included for each site, together with the type of pitch available.
The following abbreviations are used: **C = Caravan CV = Campervan T = Tent**

To discover more AA-rated caravan and camping sites not included on these pages please visit **RatedTrips.com**

ENGLAND

Alders Caravan Park
Home Farm, Alne, York
YO61 1RY
Tel: 01347 838722 85 P2
alderscaravanpark.co.uk
Total Pitches: 91 (C, CV & T)

Andrewshayes Holiday Park
Dalwood, Axminster
EX13 7DY
Tel: 01404 831225 9 N5
andrewshayes.co.uk
Total Pitches: 230 (C, CV & T)

Ayr Holiday Park
St Ives, Cornwall
TR26 1EJ
Tel: 01736 795855 2 E6
ayrholidaypark.co.uk
Total Pitches: 40 (C, CV & T)

Back of Beyond Touring Park
234 Ringwood Road, St Leonards, Dorset
BH24 2SB
Tel: 01202 876968 11 Q4
backofbeyondtouringpark.co.uk
Total Pitches: 83 (C, CV & T)

Bagwell Farm Touring Park
Knights in the Bottom, Chickerell, Weymouth
DT3 4EA
Tel: 01305 782575 10 G8
bagwellfarm.co.uk
Total Pitches: 320 (C, CV & T)

Bardsea Leisure Park
Priory Road, Ulverston
LA12 9QE
Tel: 01229 584712 89 J11
bardsealeisure.co.uk
Total Pitches: 171 (C & CV)

Bath Chew Valley Caravan Park
Ham Lane, Bishop Sutton
BS39 5TZ
Tel: 01275 332127 29 J10
bathchewvalley.co.uk
Total Pitches: 45 (C, CV & T)

Bay View Farm C & C Park
Croyde, Devon
EX33 1PN
Tel: 01271 890501 19 J6
bayviewfarm.co.uk
Total Pitches: 75 (C, CV & T)

Bay View Holiday Park
Bolton le Sands, Carnforth
LA5 9TN
Tel: 01524 732854 83 L1
holgates.co.uk
Total Pitches: 202 (C, CV & T)

Beacon Cottage Farm Touring Park
Beacon Drive, St Agnes
TR5 0NU
Tel: 01872 552347 2 H4
beaconcottagefarmholidays.co.uk
Total Pitches: 70 (C, CV & T)

Beaconsfield Farm Caravan Park
Battlefield, Shrewsbury
SY4 4AA
Tel: 01939 210370 63 N8
beaconsfieldholidaypark.co.uk
Total Pitches: 95 (C & CV)

Beech Croft Farm
Beech Croft, Blackwell in the Peak, Buxton
SK17 9TQ
Tel: 01298 85330 77 L9
beechcroftfarm.co.uk
Total Pitches: 30 (C, CV & T)

Beehive Woodland Lakes
Rosliston, Swadlincote, Derbyshire
DE12 8HZ
Tel: 01283 763981 65 N9
beehivefarm-woodlandlakes.co.uk
Total Pitches: 50 (C, CV & T)

Bellingham C & C Club Site
Brown Rigg, Bellingham
NE48 2JY
Tel: 01434 220175 99 N2
campingandcaravanningclub.co.uk/bellingham
Total Pitches: 68 (C, CV & T)

Beverley Park C & C Park
Goodrington Road, Paignton
TQ4 7JE
Tel: 01803 843887 5 Q5
beverley-holidays.co.uk
Total Pitches: 149 (C, CV & T)

Blue Rose Caravan Country Park
Star Carr Lane, Brandesburton
YO25 8RU
Tel: 01964 543366 87 L6
bluerosepark.com
Total Pitches: 114 (C & CV)

Briarfields Motel & Touring Park
Gloucester Road, Cheltenham
GL51 0SX
Tel: 01242 235324 41 P7
briarfields.net
Total Pitches: 72 (C, CV & T)

Broadhembury C & C Park
Steeds Lane, Kingsnorth, Ashford
TN26 1NQ
Tel: 01233 620859 16 H3
broadhembury.co.uk
Total Pitches: 120 (C, CV & T)

Burnham-on-Sea Holiday Village
Marine Drive, Burnham-on-Sea
TA8 1LA
Tel: 01278 783391 21 M4
haven.com/burnhamonsea
Total Pitches: 781 (C, CV & T)

Burrowhayes Farm C & C Site & Riding Stables
West Luccombe, Porlock, Minehead
TA24 8HT
Tel: 01643 862463 20 D4
burrowhayes.co.uk
Total Pitches: 139 (C, CV & T)

Burton Constable Holiday Park & Arboretum
Old Lodges, Sproatley, Hull
HU11 4LJ
Tel: 01964 562508 87 M8
burtonconstableholidaypark.co.uk
Total Pitches: 500 (C, CV & T)

Caister-on-Sea Holiday Park
Ormesby Road, Caister-on-Sea, Great Yarmouth
NR30 5NH
Tel: 01493 728931 71 Q9
haven.com/caister
Total Pitches: 949 (C & CV)

Caistor Lakes Leisure Park
99a Brigg Road, Caistor
LN7 6RX
Tel: 01472 859626 80 B3
caistorlakes.co.uk
Total Pitches: 36 (C & CV)

Cakes & Ale
Abbey Lane, Theberton, Leiston
IP16 4TE
Tel: 01728 831655 59 N8
cakesandale.co.uk
Total Pitches: 255 (C, CV & T)

Calloose C & C Park
Leedstown, Hayle
TR27 5ET
Tel: 01736 850431 2 F7
calloose.co.uk
Total Pitches: 134 (C, CV & T)

Camping Caradon Touring Park
Trelawne, Looe
PL13 2NA
Tel: 01503 272388 4 C6
campingcaradon.co.uk
Total Pitches: 75 (C, CV & T)

Capesthorne Hall
Congleton Road, Siddington, Macclesfield
SK11 9JY
Tel: 01625 861221 76 F9
capesthorne.com/caravan-park
Total Pitches: 50 (C & CV)

Carlyon Bay C & C Park
Bethesda, Cypress Avenue, Carlyon Bay
PL25 3RE
Tel: 01726 812735 3 P4
carlyonbay.net
Total Pitches: 180 (C, CV & T)

Carnon Downs C & C Park
Carnon Downs, Truro
TR3 6JJ
Tel: 01872 862283 3 K6
carnon-downs-caravanpark.co.uk
Total Pitches: 152 (C, CV & T)

Cartref C & C
Cartref, Ford Heath, Shrewsbury, Shropshire
SY5 9GD
Tel: 01743 821688 63 L10
cartrefcaravansite.co.uk
Total Pitches: 44 (C, CV & T)

Carvynick Holiday Park
Summercourt, Newquay
TR8 5AF
Tel: 01872 510716 3 L3
carvynick.co.uk
Total Pitches: 47 (C, CV & T)

Castlerigg Hall C & C Park
Castlerigg Hall, Keswick
CA12 4TE
Tel: 017687 74499 89 J2
castlerigg.co.uk
Total Pitches: 105 (C, CV & T)

Cheddar Mendip Heights C & C Club Site
Townsend, Priddy, Wells
BA5 3BP
Tel: 01749 870241 22 C3
campingandcaravanningclub.co.uk/cheddar
Total Pitches: 92 (C, CV & T)

Clippesby Hall
Hall Lane, Clippesby, Great Yarmouth
NR29 3BL
Tel: 01493 367800 71 N9
clippesbyhall.com
Total Pitches: 120 (C, CV & T)

Cofton Holidays
Starcross, Dawlish
EX6 8RP
Tel: 01626 890111 8 H8
coftonholidays.co.uk
Total Pitches: 532 (C, CV & T)

Concierge Camping
Ratham Estate, Ratham Lane, West Ashling, Chichester
PO18 8DL
Tel: 01243 573118 13 P3
conciergecamping.co.uk
Total Pitches: 15 (C & CV)

Coombe Touring Park
Race Plain, Netherhampton, Salisbury
SP2 8PN
Tel: 01722 328451 23 N7
coombecaravanpark.co.uk
Total Pitches: 56 (C, CV & T)

Corfe Castle C & C Club Site
Bucknowle, Wareham
BH20 5PQ
Tel: 01929 480280 11 M8
campingandcaravanningclub.co.uk/corfecastle
Total Pitches: 80 (C, CV & T)

Cornish Farm Touring Park
Shoreditch, Taunton
TA3 7BS
Tel: 01823 327746 21 K9
cornishfarm.com
Total Pitches: 50 (C, CV & T)

Cosawes Park
Perranarworthal, Truro
TR3 7QS
Tel: 01872 863724 3 J7
cosawes.co.uk
Total Pitches: 59 (C, CV & T)

Cote Ghyll C & C Park
Osmotherley, Northallerton
DL6 3AH
Tel: 01609 883425 91 Q7
coteghyll.com
Total Pitches: 95 (C, CV & T)

Country View Holiday Park
Sand Road, Sand Bay, Weston-super-Mare
BS22 9UJ
Tel: 01934 627595 28 D9
cvhp.co.uk
Total Pitches: 255 (C, CV & T)

Crealy Theme Park & Resort
Sidmouth Road, Clyst St Mary, Exeter
EX5 1DR
Tel: 01395 234888 9 J6
crealy.co.uk
Total Pitches: 127 (C, CV & T)

Crows Nest Caravan Park
Gristhorpe, Filey
YO14 9PS
Tel: 01723 582206 93 M10
crowsnestcaravanpark.com
Total Pitches: 263 (C, CV & T)

Deepdale Backpackers & Camping
Deepdale Farm, Burnham Deepdale
PE31 8DD
Tel: 01485 210256 69 Q3
deepdalebackpackers.co.uk
Total Pitches: 80 (CV & T)

Diamond C & C Park
Islip Road, Bletchingdon, Oxfordshire
OX5 3DR
Tel: 01869 350909 43 L8
diamondpark.co.uk
Total Pitches: 37 (C, CV & T)

Dibles Park
Dibles Road, Warsash, Southampton, Hampshire
SO31 9SA
Tel: 01489 575232 12 H3
diblespark.co.uk
Total Pitches: 60 (C, CV & T)

Dornafield
Dornafield Farm, Two Mile Oak, Newton Abbot
TQ12 6DD
Tel: 01803 812732 5 P3
dornafield.com
Total Pitches: 135 (C, CV & T)

East Fleet Farm Touring Park
Chickerell, Weymouth
DT3 4DW
Tel: 01305 785768 10 G9
eastfleet.co.uk
Total Pitches: 400 (C, CV & T)

Eastham Hall Holiday Park
Saltcotes Road, Lytham St Annes, Lancashire
FY8 4LS
Tel: 01253 737907 83 J9
easthamhall.co.uk
Total Pitches: 274 (C & CV)

Eden Valley Holiday Park
Lanlivery, Nr Lostwithiel
PL30 5BU
Tel: 01208 872277 3 Q3
edenvalleyholidaypark.co.uk
Total Pitches: 94 (C, CV & T)

Exe Valley Caravan Site
Mill House, Bridgetown, Dulverton
TA22 9JR
Tel: 01643 851432 20 E7
exevalleycamping.co.uk
Total Pitches: 48 (C, CV & T)

Eye Kettleby Lakes
Eye Kettleby, Melton Mowbray
LE14 2TN
Tel: 01664 565900 67 J9
eyekettlebylakes.com
Total Pitches: 130 (C, CV & T)

Fen Farm Caravan Site
Moore Lane, East Mersea, Mersea Island, Colchester, Essex
CO5 8FE
Tel: 01206 383275 47 J9
fenfarm.co.uk
Total Pitches: 180 (C, CV & T)

Fernwood Caravan Park
Lyneal, Ellesmere, Shropshire
SY12 0QF
Tel: 01948 710221 63 M5
fernwoodpark.co.uk
Total Pitches: 225 (C & CV)

Fields End Water Caravan Park & Fishery
Benwick Road, Doddington, March
PE15 0TY
Tel: 01354 740199 56 G2
fieldsendwater.co.uk
Total Pitches: 52 (C, CV & T)

Fishpool Farm Caravan Park
Fishpool Road, Delamere, Northwich, Cheshire
CW8 2HP
Tel: 01606 883970 75 P10
fishpoolfarmcaravanpark.co.uk
Total Pitches: 51 (C, CV & T)

Flower of May Holiday Park
Lebberston Cliff, Filey, Scarborough
YO11 3NU
Tel: 01723 584311 93 M10
flowerofmay.com
Total Pitches: 503 (C, CV & T)

Freshwater Beach Holiday Park
Burton Bradstock, Bridport
DT6 4PT
Tel: 01308 897317 10 D7
freshwaterbeach.co.uk
Total Pitches: 750 (C, CV & T)

Glenfield Caravan Park
Blackmoor Lane, Bardsey, Leeds
LS17 9DZ
Tel: 01937 574657 85 M7
glenfieldcaravanpark.co.uk
Total Pitches: 31 (C, CV & T)

Globe Vale Holiday Park
Radnor, Redruth
TR16 4BH
Tel: 01209 891183 2 H5
globevale.co.uk
Total Pitches: 195 (C, CV & T)

Glororum Caravan Park
Glororum Farm, Bamburgh
NE69 7AW
Tel: 01670 860256 109 K3
northumbrianleisure.co.uk
Total Pitches: 213 (C & CV)

Golden Cap Holiday Park
Seatown, Chideock, Bridport
DT6 6JX
Tel: 01308 422139 10 C6
wdlh.co.uk
Total Pitches: 345 (C, CV & T)

Golden Coast Holiday Park
Station Road, Woolacombe
EX34 7HW
Tel: 01271 872302 19 J5
woolacombe.com
Total Pitches: 431 (C, CV & T)

Golden Sands Holiday Park
Quebec Road, Mablethorpe
LN12 1QJ
Tel: 01507 477871 81 J6
haven.com/goldensands
Total Pitches: 1672 (C, CV & T)

Golden Square C & C Park
Oswaldkirk, Helmsley
YO62 5YQ
Tel: 01439 788269 92 C10
goldensquarecaravanpark.com
Total Pitches: 150 (C, CV & T)

Golden Valley C & C Park
Coach Road, Ripley, Derbyshire
DE55 4ES
Tel: 01773 513881 66 C2
goldenvalleycaravanpark.co.uk
Total Pitches: 47 (C, CV & T)

Goosewood Holiday Park
Sutton-on-the-Forest, York
YO61 1ET
Tel: 01347 810829 86 B3
flowerofmay.com
Total Pitches: 145 (C & CV)

Green Acres Caravan Park
High Knells, Houghton, Carlisle
CA6 4JW
Tel: 01228 675418 98 E6
caravanpark-cumbria.com
Total Pitches: 35 (C, CV & T)

Greenhill Farm C & C Park
Greenhill Farm, New Road, Landford, Salisbury
SP5 2AZ
Tel: 01794 324117 24 D9
greenhillfarm.co.uk
Total Pitches: 160 (C, CV & T)

Greenhills Holiday Park
Crowhill Lane, Bakewell, Derbyshire
DE45 1PX
Tel: 01629 813052 77 M10
greenhillsholidaypark.co.uk
Total Pitches: 245 (C, CV & T)

Grouse Hill Caravan Park
Flask Bungalow Farm, Fylingdales, Robin Hood's Bay
YO22 4QH
Tel: 01947 880543 93 J7
grousehill.co.uk
Total Pitches: 192 (C, CV & T)

Gunvenna Holiday Park
St Minver, Wadebridge
PL27 6QN
Tel: 01208 862405 6 D9
gunvenna.com
Total Pitches: 121 (C, CV & T)

Haggerston Castle Holiday Park
Beal, Berwick-upon-Tweed
TD15 2PA
Tel: 01289 381333 108 G1
haven.com/haggerstoncastle
Total Pitches: 1340 (C & CV)

Harbury Fields
Harbury Fields Farm, Harbury, Nr Leamington Spa
CV33 9JN
Tel: 01926 612457 54 B8
harburyfields.co.uk
Total Pitches: 59 (C & CV)

Harford Bridge Holiday Park
Peter Tavy, Tavistock
PL19 9LS
Tel: 01822 810349 7 P9
harfordbridge.co.uk
Total Pitches: 198 (C, CV & T)

Haw Wood Farm Caravan Park
Hinton, Saxmundham
IP17 3QT
Tel: 01502 359550 59 N6
hawwoodfarm.co.uk
Total Pitches: 115 (C, CV & T)

Heathfield Farm Camping
Heathfield Road, Freshwater, Isle of Wight
PO40 9SH
Tel: 01983 407822 12 E7
heathfieldcamping.co.uk
Total Pitches: 75 (C, CV & T)

Heathland Beach Holiday Park
London Road, Kessingland
NR33 7PJ
Tel: 01502 740337 59 Q3
heathlandbeach.co.uk
Total Pitches: 263 (C, CV & T)

Hele Valley Holiday Park
Hele Bay, Ilfracombe
EX34 9RD
Tel: 01271 862460 19 K4
helevalley.co.uk
Total Pitches: 133 (C, CV & T)

Hendra Holiday Park
Newquay
TR8 4NY
Tel: 01637 875778 3 K2
hendra-holidays.com
Total Pitches: 865 (C, CV & T)

Herding Hill Farm Touring & Camping Site
Shield Hill, Haltwhistle, Northumberland
NE49 9NW
Tel: 01434 320175 99 K5
herdinghillfarm.co.uk
Total Pitches: 22 (C, CV & T)

Highfield Farm Touring Park
Long Road, Comberton, Cambridge
CB23 7DG
Tel: 01223 262308 56 H9
highfieldfarmtouringpark.co.uk
Total Pitches: 120 (C, CV & T)

Highlands End Holiday Park
Eype, Bridport, Dorset
DT6 6AR
Tel: 01308 422139 10 C6
wdlh.co.uk
Total Pitches: 357 (C, CV & T)

Hill of Oaks & Blakeholme
Windermere
LA12 8NR
Tel: 015395 31578 89 K9
hillofoaks.co.uk
Total Pitches: 263 (C & CV)

Hillside Caravan Park
Canvas Farm, Moor Road, Knayton, Thirsk
YO7 4BR
Tel: 01845 537349 91 Q9
hillsidecaravanpark.co.uk
Total Pitches: 52 (C & CV)

Holiday Resort Unity
Coast Road, Brean Sands, Brean
TA8 2RB
Tel: 01278 751235 21 L3
hru.co.uk
Total Pitches: 1114 (C, CV & T)

Hollins Farm C & C
Far Arnside, Carnforth
LA5 0SL
Tel: 01524 701767 89 M11
holgates.co.uk
Total Pitches: 14 (C, CV & T)

Hylton Caravan Park
Eden Street, Silloth
CA7 4AY
Tel: 016973 32666 97 M7
stanwix.com
Total Pitches: 303 (C, CV & T)

Island Lodge C & C Site
Stumpy Post Cross, Kingsbridge
TQ7 4BL
Tel: 01548 852956 5 M7
islandlodgesite.co.uk
Total Pitches: 30 (C, CV & T)

Isle of Avalon Touring Caravan Park
Godney Road, Glastonbury
BA6 9AF
Tel: 01458 833618 22 C5
avaloncaravanpark.co.uk
Total Pitches: 120 (C, CV & T)

Jasmine Caravan Park
Cross Lane, Snainton, Scarborough
YO13 9BE
Tel: 01723 859240 93 J10
jasminepark.co.uk
Total Pitches: 84 (C, CV & T)

Kennford International Holiday Park
Kennford, Exeter
EX6 7YN
Tel: 01392 833046 8 G7
kennfordinternational.co.uk
Total Pitches: 87 (C, CV & T)

King's Lynn C & C Park
New Road, North Runcton, King's Lynn
PE33 0RA
Tel: 01553 840004 69 M9
kl-cc.co.uk
Total Pitches: 170 (C, CV & T)

Kloofs Caravan Park
Sandhurst Lane, Bexhill
TN39 4RG
Tel: 01424 842839 16 C9
kloofs.com
Total Pitches: 125 (C, CV & T)

Kneps Farm Holiday Park
River Road, Stanah, Thornton-Cleveleys, Blackpool
FY5 5LR
Tel: 01253 823632 83 J6
knepsfarm.co.uk
Total Pitches: 86 (C & CV)

Knight Stainforth Hall Caravan & Campsite
Stainforth, Settle
BD24 0DP
Tel: 01729 822200 84 B2
knightstainforth.co.uk
Total Pitches: 160 (C, CV & T)

Ladycross Plantation Caravan Park
Egton, Whitby
YO21 1UA
Tel: 01947 895502 92 G5
ladycrossplantation.co.uk
Total Pitches: 130 (C & CV)

Lady's Mile Holiday Park
Dawlish, Devon
EX7 0LX
Tel: 01626 863411 8 H9
ladysmile.co.uk
Total Pitches: 692 (C, CV & T)

Lakeland Leisure Park
Moor Lane, Flookburgh
LA11 7LT
Tel: 01539 558556 89 K12
haven.com/lakeland
Total Pitches: 977 (C, CV & T)

Lamb Cottage Caravan Park
Dalefords Lane, Whitegate, Northwich
CW8 2BN
Tel: 01606 882302 75 Q10
lambcottage.co.uk
Total Pitches: 71 (C & CV)

Langstone Manor C & C Park
Moortown, Tavistock
PL19 9JZ
Tel: 01822 613371 7 P10
langstonemanor.co.uk
Total Pitches: 76 (C, CV & T)

Lanyon Holiday Park
Loscombe Lane, Four Lanes, Redruth
TR16 6LP
Tel: 01209 313474 2 H7
lanyonholidaypark.co.uk
Total Pitches: 74 (C, CV & T)

Lickpenny Caravan Site
Lickpenny Lane, Tansley, Matlock
DE4 5GF
Tel: 01629 583040 77 Q11
lickpennycaravanpark.co.uk
Total Pitches: 80 (C & CV)

Lime Tree Park
Dukes Drive, Buxton
SK17 9RP
Tel: 01298 22988 77 K9
limetreeparkbuxton.com
Total Pitches: 149 (C, CV & T)

Lincoln Farm Park Oxfordshire
High Street, Standlake
OX29 7RH
Tel: 01865 300239 43 J11
lincolnfarmpark.co.uk
Total Pitches: 90 (C, CV & T)

Littlesea Holiday Park
Lynch Lane, Weymouth
DT4 9DT
Tel: 01305 774414 10 G9
haven.com/littlesea
Total Pitches: 861 (C, CV & T)

Long Acres Touring Park
Station Road, Old Leake, Boston
PE22 9RF
Tel: 01205 871555 68 G2
long-acres.co.uk
Total Pitches: 40 (C, CV & T)

Long Hazel Park
High Street, Sparkford, Yeovil, Somerset
BA22 7JH
Tel: 01963 440002 22 E8
longhazelpark.co.uk
Total Pitches: 52 (C, CV & T)

Longnor Wood Holiday Park
Newtown, Longnor, Nr Buxton
SK17 0NG
Tel: 01298 83648 77 K11
longnorwood.co.uk
Total Pitches: 50 (C, CV & T)

Lowther Holiday Park
Eamont Bridge, Penrith
CA10 2JB
Tel: 01768 863631 89 N1
lowther-holidaypark.co.uk
Total Pitches: 180 (C, CV & T)

Manor Wood Country Caravan Park
Manor Wood, Coddington, Chester
CH3 9EN
Tel: 01829 782990 63 M1
cheshire-caravan-sites.co.uk
Total Pitches: 66 (C, CV & T)

Marton Mere Holiday Village
Mythop Road, Blackpool
FY4 4XN
Tel: 01253 767544 82 H8
haven.com/martonmere
Total Pitches: 782 (C & CV)

Mayfield Park
Cheltenham Road, Cirencester
GL7 7BH
Tel: 01285 831301 42 B10
mayfieldpark.co.uk
Total Pitches: 105 (C, CV & T)

Meadow Lakes Holiday Park
Hewas Water, St Austell, Cornwall
PL26 7JG
Tel: 01726 882540 3 N5
meadow-lakes.co.uk
Total Pitches: 232 (C, CV & T)

Meadowbank Holidays
Stour Way, Christchurch
BH23 2PQ
Tel: 01202 483597 12 B6
meadowbank-holidays.co.uk
Total Pitches: 221 (C & CV)

Middlewood Farm Holiday Park
Middlewood Lane, Fylingthorpe, Robin Hood's Bay, Whitby
YO22 4UF
Tel: 01947 880414 93 J6
middlewoodfarm.com
Total Pitches: 144 (C, CV & T)

Mill Park Touring C & C Park
Mill Lane, Berrynarbor, Ilfracombe, Devon
EX34 9SH
Tel: 01271 882647 19 L4
millpark.com
Total Pitches: 160 (C, CV & T)

Minnows Touring Park
Holbrook Lane, Sampford Peverell
EX16 7EN
Tel: 01884 821770 20 G10
minnowstouringpark.co.uk
Total Pitches: 60 (C, CV & T)

Monkey Tree Holiday Park
Hendra Croft, Scotland Road, Newquay
TR8 5QR
Tel: 01872 572032 3 K4
monkeytreeholidaypark.co.uk
Total Pitches: 700 (C, CV & T)

Moon & Sixpence
Newbourn Road, Waldringfield, Woodbridge
IP12 4PP
Tel: 01473 736650 47 N3
moonandsixpence.co.uk
Total Pitches: 275 (C & CV)

Moss Wood Caravan Park
Crimbles Lane, Cockerham
LA2 0ES
Tel: 01524 791041 83 L5
mosswood.co.uk
Total Pitches: 168 (C & CV)

Naburn Lock Caravan Park
Naburn
YO19 4RU
Tel: 01904 728697 86 B6
naburnlock.co.uk
Total Pitches: 115 (C, CV & T)

New Lodge Farm C & C Site
New Lodge Farm, Bulwick, Corby
NN17 3DU
Tel: 01780 450493 55 N2
newlodgefarm.com
Total Pitches: 72 (C, CV & T)

Newberry Valley Park
Woodlands, Combe Martin
EX34 0AT
Tel: 01271 882334 19 L4
newberryvalleypark.co.uk
Total Pitches: 112 (C, CV & T)

Newlands Holidays
Charmouth, Bridport
DT6 6RB
Tel: 01297 560259 10 B6
newlandsholidays.co.uk
Total Pitches: 330 (C, CV & T)

Ninham Country Holidays
Ninham, Shanklin, Isle of Wight
PO37 7PL
Tel: 01983 864243 13 J8
ninham-holidays.co.uk
Total Pitches: 141 (C, CV & T)

North Morte Farm C & C Park
North Morte Road, Mortehoe, Woolacombe
EX34 7EG
Tel: 01271 870381 19 J4
northmortefarm.co.uk
Total Pitches: 253 (C, CV & T)

Northam Farm Caravan & Touring Park
Brean, Burnham-on-Sea
TA8 2SE
Tel: 01278 751244 21 M2
northamfarm.co.uk
Total Pitches: 350 (C, CV & T)

Oakdown Country Holiday Park
Gatedown Lane, Weston, Sidmouth
EX10 0PT
Tel: 01297 680387 9 M7
oakdown.co.uk
Total Pitches: 170 (C, CV & T)

Old Hall Caravan Park
Capernwray, Carnforth
LA6 1AD
Tel: 01524 733276 83 M1
oldhallcaravanpark.co.uk
Total Pitches: 298 (C & CV)

Old Oaks Touring & Glamping
Wick Farm, Wick, Glastonbury
BA6 8JS
Tel: 01458 831437 22 C5
theoldoaks.co.uk
Total Pitches: 100 (C, CV & T)

Orchard Farm Holiday Village
Stonegate, Hunmanby, Filey, North Yorkshire
YO14 0PU
Tel: 01723 891582 93 M11
orchardfarmholidayvillage.co.uk
Total Pitches: 137 (C, CV & T)

Ord House Country Park
East Ord, Berwick-upon-Tweed
TD15 2NS
Tel: 01289 305288 117 L11
maguirescountryparks.co.uk
Total Pitches: 344 (C, CV & T)

Otterington Park
Station Farm, South Otterington, Northallerton, North Yorkshire
DL7 9JB
Tel: 01609 780656 91 P9
otteringtonpark.com
Total Pitches: 67 (C, CV & T)

Oxon Hall Touring Park
Welshpool Road, Shrewsbury
SY3 5FB
Tel: 01743 340868 63 M9
morris-leisure.co.uk
Total Pitches: 165 (C, CV & T)

Park Cliffe C & C Estate
Birks Road, Tower Wood, Windermere
LA23 3PG
Tel: 015395 31344 89 L8
parkcliffe.co.uk
Total Pitches: 126 (C, CV & T)

Parkers Farm Holiday Park
Higher Mead Farm, Ashburton, Devon
TQ13 7LJ
Tel: 01364 654869 8 E10
parkersfarmholidays.co.uk
Total Pitches: 118 (C, CV & T)

Park Foot C & C Park
Howtown Road, Pooley Bridge
CA10 2NA
Tel: 017684 86309 89 M2
parkfootullswater.co.uk
Total Pitches: 454 (C, CV & T)

Parkland C & C Site
Sorley Green Cross, Kingsbridge
TQ7 4AF
Tel: 01548 852723 5 M7
parklandsite.co.uk
Total Pitches: 50 (C, CV & T)

Pebble Bank Caravan Park
Camp Road, Wyke Regis, Weymouth
DT4 9HF
Tel: 01305 774844 10 G9
pebblebank.co.uk
Total Pitches: 120 (C, CV & T)

Perran Sands Holiday Park
Perranporth, Truro
TR6 0AQ
Tel: 01872 573551 3 J3
haven.com/perransands
Total Pitches: 1012 (C, CV & T)

Petwood Caravan Park
Off Stixwould Road, Woodhall Spa
LN10 6QH
Tel: 01526 354799 80 D11
petwoodcaravanpark.com
Total Pitches: 98 (C, CV & T)

Plough Lane Touring Caravan Site
Plough Lane, Chippenham, Wiltshire
SN15 5PS
Tel: 01249 750146 29 Q7
ploughlane.co.uk
Total Pitches: 52 (C & CV)

Polladras Holiday Park
Carleen, Breage, Helston
TR13 9NX
Tel: 01736 762220 2 F8
polladrasholidaypark.co.uk
Total Pitches: 42 (C, CV & T)

Polmanter Touring Park
Halsetown, St Ives
TR26 3LX
Tel: 01736 795640 2 E7
polmanter.com
Total Pitches: 270 (C, CV & T)

Porthtowan Tourist Park
Mile Hill, Porthtowan, Truro
TR4 8TY
Tel: 01209 890256 2 H5
porthtowantouristpark.co.uk
Total Pitches: 80 (C, CV & T)

Primrose Valley Holiday Park
Filey
YO14 9RF
Tel: 01723 513771 93 M11
haven.com/primrosevalley
Total Pitches: 1549 (C & CV)

Quantock Orchard Caravan Park
Flaxpool, Crowcombe, Taunton
TA4 4AW
Tel: 01984 618618 21 J6
quantock-orchard.co.uk
Total Pitches: 75 (C, CV & T)

Ranch Caravan Park
Station Road, Honeybourne, Evesham
WR11 7PR
Tel: 01386 830744 42 C3
ranch.co.uk
Total Pitches: 338 (C & CV)

Ripley Caravan Park
Knaresborough Road, Ripley, Harrogate
HG3 3AU
Tel: 01423 770050 85 L3
ripleycaravanpark.com
Total Pitches: 135 (C, CV & T)

River Dart Country Park
Holne Park, Ashburton
TQ13 7NP
Tel: 01364 652511 5 M3
riverdart.co.uk
Total Pitches: 170 (C, CV & T)

River Valley Holiday Park
London Apprentice, St Austell
PL26 7AP
Tel: 01726 73533 3 N4
rivervalleyholidaypark.co.uk
Total Pitches: 85 (C, CV & T)

Riverside C & C Park
Marsh Lane, North Molton Road,
South Molton
EX36 3HQ
Tel: 01769 579269 19 P8
exmoorriverside.co.uk
Total Pitches: 61 (C, CV & T)

Riverside Caravan Park
High Bentham, Lancaster
LA2 7FJ
Tel: 015242 61272 83 P1
riversidecaravanpark.co.uk
Total Pitches: 267 (C & CV)

Riverside Meadows Country Caravan Park
Ure Bank Top, Ripon
HG4 1JD
Tel: 01765 602964 91 N12
flowerofmay.com
Total Pitches: 349 (C)

Robin Hood C & C Park
Green Dyke Lane, Slingsby
YO62 4AP
Tel: 01653 628391 92 E11
robinhoodcaravanpark.co.uk
Total Pitches: 66 (C, CV & T)

Rose Farm Touring & Camping Park
Stepshort, Belton, Nr Great Yarmouth
NR31 9JS
Tel: 01493 738292 71 P11
rosefarmtouringpark.co.uk
Total Pitches: 147 (C, CV & T)

Rosedale Abbey Caravan Park
Rosedale Abbey, Pickering
YO18 8SA
Tel: 01751 417272 92 E7
rosedaleabbeycaravanpark.co.uk
Total Pitches: 141 (C, CV & T)

Ross Park
Park Hill Farm, Ipplepen,
Newton Abbot
TQ12 5TT
Tel: 01803 812983 5 P3
rossparkcaravanpark.co.uk
Total Pitches: 110 (C, CV & T)

Rudding Holiday Park
Follifoot, Harrogate
HG3 1JH
Tel: 01423 870439 85 L4
ruddingholidaypark.co.uk
Total Pitches: 143 (C, CV & T)

Run Cottage Touring Park
Alderton Road, Hollesley, Woodbridge
IP12 3RQ
Tel: 01394 411309 47 P3
runcottage.co.uk
Total Pitches: 47 (C, CV & T)

Rutland C & C
Park Lane, Greetham, Oakham
LE15 7FN
Tel: 01572 813520 67 M9
rutlandcaravanandcamping.co.uk
Total Pitches: 130 (C, CV & T)

St Helens in the Park
Wykeham, Scarborough
YO13 9QD
Tel: 01723 862771 93 K10
sthelenscaravanpark.co.uk
Total Pitches: 260 (C, CV & T)

St Ives Bay Holiday Park
73 Loggans Road,
Upton Towans, Hayle
TR27 5BH
Tel: 01736 752274 2 F6
stivesbay.co.uk
Total Pitches: 507 (C, CV & T)

Salcombe Regis C & C Park
Salcombe Regis, Sidmouth
EX10 0JH
Tel: 01395 514303 9 M7
salcombe-regis.co.uk
Total Pitches: 110 (C, CV & T)

Sand le Mere Holiday Village
Southfield Lane, Tunstall
HU12 0JF
Tel: 01964 670403 87 P9
sand-le-mere.co.uk
Total Pitches: 89 (C & CV)

Searles Leisure Resort
South Beach Road, Hunstanton
PE36 5BB
Tel: 01485 534211 69 M4
searles.co.uk
Total Pitches: 413 (C, CV & T)

Seaview Gorran Haven Holiday Park
Boswinger, Mevagissey
PL26 6LL
Tel: 01726 843425 3 N6
seaviewinternational.com
Total Pitches: 240 (C, CV & T)

Seaview Holiday Park
Preston, Weymouth
DT3 6DZ
Tel: 01305 832271 10 H8
haven.com/seaview
Total Pitches: 347 (C, CV & T)

Severn Gorge Park
Bridgnorth Road, Tweedale, Telford
TF7 4JB
Tel: 01952 684789 64 D11
severngorgepark.co.uk
Total Pitches: 132 (C & CV)

Shamba Holidays
East Moors Lane, St Leonards, Ringwood
BH24 2SB
Tel: 01202 873302 11 Q4
shambaholidays.co.uk
Total Pitches: 150 (C, CV & T)

Shrubbery Touring Park
Rousdon, Lyme Regis
DT7 3XW
Tel: 01297 442227 9 P6
shrubberypark.co.uk
Total Pitches: 122 (C, CV & T)

Silverdale Caravan Park
Middlebarrow Plain, Cove Road, Silverdale,
Nr Carnforth
LA5 0SH
Tel: 01524 701508 89 M11
holgates.co.uk
Total Pitches: 427 (C, CV & T)

Skelwith Fold Caravan Park
Ambleside, Cumbria
LA22 0HX
Tel: 015394 32277 89 K6
skelwith.com
Total Pitches: 470 (C & CV)

Skirlington Leisure Park
Driffield, Skipsea
YO25 8SY
Tel: 01262 468213 87 M5
skirlington.com
Total Pitches: 930 (C & CV)

Sleningford Watermill Caravan Camping Park
North Stainley, Ripon
HG4 3HQ
Tel: 01765 635201 91 M11
sleningfordwatermill.co.uk
Total Pitches: 135 (C, CV & T)

Somers Wood Caravan Park
Somers Road, Meriden
CV7 7PL
Tel: 01676 522978 53 N4
somerswood.co.uk
Total Pitches: 48 (C & CV)

South Lytchett Manor C & C Park
Dorchester Road, Lytchett Minster, Poole
BH16 6JB
Tel: 01202 622577 11 M6
southlytchettmanor.co.uk
Total Pitches: 154 (C, CV & T)

South Meadows Caravan Park
South Road, Belford
NE70 7DP
Tel: 01668 213326 109 J3
southmeadows.co.uk
Total Pitches: 186 (C, CV & T)

Stanmore Hall Touring Park
Stourbridge Road, Bridgnorth
WV15 6DT
Tel: 01746 761761 52 D2
morris-leisure.co.uk
Total Pitches: 129 (C, CV & T)

Stanwix Park Holiday Centre
Greenrow, Silloth
CA7 4HH
Tel: 016973 32666 97 M7
stanwix.com
Total Pitches: 337 (C, CV & T)

Stowford Farm Meadows
Berry Down, Combe Martin
EX34 0PW
Tel: 01271 882476 19 L5
stowford.co.uk
Total Pitches: 700 (C, CV & T)

Stroud Hill Park
Fen Road, Pidley, St Ives
PE28 3DE
Tel: 01487 741333 56 G5
stroudhillpark.co.uk
Total Pitches: 60 (C, CV & T)

Sumners Ponds Fishery & Campsite
Chapel Road, Barns Green, Horsham
RH13 0PR
Tel: 01403 732539 14 G5
sumnersponds.co.uk
Total Pitches: 90 (C, CV & T)

Swiss Farm Touring & Camping
Marlow Road, Henley-on-Thames
RG9 2HY
Tel: 01491 573419 31 Q6
swissfarmhenley.co.uk
Total Pitches: 148 (C, CV & T)

Tanner Farm Touring C & C Park
Tanner Farm, Goudhurst Road, Marden
TN12 9ND
Tel: 01622 832399 16 C3
tannerfarmpark.co.uk
Total Pitches: 122 (C, CV & T)

Tattershall Lakes Country Park
Sleaford Road, Tattershall
LN4 4LR
Tel: 01526 348800 80 D12
awayresorts.co.uk/tattershall-lakes
Total Pitches: 690 (C, CV & T)

Tehidy Holiday Park
Harris Mill, Illogan, Portreath
TR16 4JQ
Tel: 01209 216489 2 H6
tehidy.co.uk
Total Pitches: 52 (C, CV & T)

Tencreek Holiday Park
Polperro Road, Looe
PL13 2JR
Tel: 01503 262447 4 C6
dolphinholidays.co.uk
Total Pitches: 355 (C, CV & T)

Teversal C & C Club Site
Silverhill Lane, Teversal
NG17 3JJ
Tel: 01623 551838 78 D11
campingandcaravanningclub.co.uk/teversal
Total Pitches: 136 (C, CV & T)

The Laurels Holiday Park
Padstow Road, Whitecross,
Wadebridge
PL27 7JQ
Tel: 01208 813341 6 D10
thelaurelsholidaypark.co.uk
Total Pitches: 30 (C, CV & T)

The Old Brick Kilns
Little Barney Lane, Barney, Fakenham
NR21 0NL
Tel: 01328 878305 70 E5
old-brick-kilns.co.uk
Total Pitches: 65 (C, CV & T)

The Orchards Holiday Caravan Park
Main Road, Newbridge, Yarmouth,
Isle of Wight
PO41 0TS
Tel: 01983 531331 12 G7
orchards-holiday-park.co.uk
Total Pitches: 225 (C, CV & T)

The Quiet Site
Ullswater, Watermillock
CA11 0LS
Tel: 07768 727016 89 L2
thequietsite.co.uk
Total Pitches: 151 (C, CV & T)

Thornwick Bay Holiday Village
North Marine Road, Flamborough
YO15 1AU
Tel: 01262 850569 93 P12
haven.com/parks/yorkshire/thornwick-bay
Total Pitches: 225 (C, CV & T)

Thorpe Park Holiday Centre
Cleethorpes
DN35 0PW
Tel: 01472 813395 80 F2
haven.com/thorpepark
Total Pitches: 1491 (C, CV & T)

Treago Farm Caravan Site
Crantock, Newquay
TR8 5QS
Tel: 01637 830277 3 J2
treagofarm.co.uk
Total Pitches: 100 (C, CV & T)

Treloy Touring Park
Newquay
TR8 4JN
Tel: 01637 872063 3 L2
treloy.co.uk
Total Pitches: 223 (C, CV & T)

Trencreek Holiday Park
Hillcrest, Higher Trencreek, Newquay
TR8 4NS
Tel: 01637 874210 3 K2
trencreekholidaypark.co.uk
Total Pitches: 200 (C, CV & T)

Trethem Mill Touring Park
St Just-in-Roseland, Nr St Mawes, Truro
TR2 5JF
Tel: 01872 580504 3 L7
trethem.com
Total Pitches: 84 (C, CV & T)

Trevalgan Touring Park
Trevalgan, St Ives
TR26 3BJ
Tel: 01736 791892 2 D6
trevalgantouringpark.co.uk
Total Pitches: 135 (C, CV & T)

Trevarth Holiday Park
Blackwater, Truro
TR4 8HR
Tel: 01872 560266 3 J5
trevarth.co.uk
Total Pitches: 50 (C, CV & T)

Trevedra Farm C & C Site
Sennen, Penzance
TR19 7BE
Tel: 01736 871818 2 B9
trevedrafarm.co.uk
Total Pitches: 100 (C, CV & T)

Trevella Park
Crantock, Newquay
TR8 5EW
Tel: 01637 830308 3 K3
trevella.co.uk
Total Pitches: 290 (C, CV & T)

Trevornick
Holywell Bay, Newquay
TR8 5PW
Tel: 01637 830531 3 J3
trevornick.co.uk
Total Pitches: 600 (C, CV & T)

Truro C & C Park
Truro
TR4 8QN
Tel: 01872 560274 3 J5
trurocaravanandcampingpark.co.uk
Total Pitches: 100 (C, CV & T)

Tudor C & C
Shepherds Patch, Slimbridge,
Gloucester
GL2 7BP
Tel: 01453 890483 41 L11
tudorcaravanpark.com
Total Pitches: 75 (C, CV & T)

Twitchen House Holiday Park
Mortehoe Station Road, Mortehoe,
Woolacombe
EX34 7ES
Tel: 01271 872302 19 J4
woolacombe.com
Total Pitches: 569 (C, CV & T)

Two Mills Touring Park
Yarmouth Road, North Walsham
NR28 9NA
Tel: 01692 405829 71 K6
twomills.co.uk
Total Pitches: 81 (C, CV & T)

Ulwell Cottage Caravan Park
Ulwell Cottage, Ulwell, Swanage
BH19 3DG
Tel: 01929 422823 11 N8
ulwellcottagepark.co.uk
Total Pitches: 219 (C, CV & T)

Upper Lynstone Caravan Park
Lynstone, Bude
EX23 0LP
Tel: 01288 352017 7 J4
upperlynstone.co.uk
Total Pitches: 106 (C, CV & T)

Vale of Pickering Caravan Park
Carr House Farm, Allerston, Pickering
YO18 7PQ
Tel: 01723 859280 92 H10
valeofpickering.co.uk
Total Pitches: 120 (C, CV & T)

Waldegraves Holiday Park
Mersea Island, Colchester
CO5 8SE
Tel: 01206 382898 47 J9
waldegraves.co.uk
Total Pitches: 30 (C, CV & T)

Waleswood C &C Park
Delves Lane, Waleswood, Wales Bar,
Wales, South Yorkshire
S26 5RN
Tel: 07825 125328 78 D7
waleswood.co.uk
Total Pitches: 163 (C, CV & T)

Warcombe Farm C & C Park
Station Road, Mortehoe, Woolacombe
EX34 7EJ
Tel: 01271 870690 19 J4
warcombefarm.co.uk
Total Pitches: 250 (C, CV & T)

Wareham Forest Tourist Park
North Trigon, Wareham
BH20 7NZ
Tel: 01929 551393 11 L6
warehamforest.co.uk
Total Pitches: 200 (C, CV & T)

Waren C & C Park
Waren Mill, Bamburgh
NE70 7EE
Tel: 01668 214366 109 J3
meadowhead.co.uk
Total Pitches: 458 (C, CV & T)

Warren Farm Holiday Centre
Brean Sands, Brean,
Burnham-on-Sea
TA8 2RP
Tel: 01278 751227 28 D11
warrenfarm.co.uk
Total Pitches: 975 (C, CV & T)

Watergate Bay Touring Park
Watergate Bay, Tregurrian
TR8 4AD
Tel: 01637 860387 6 B11
watergatebaytouringpark.co.uk
Total Pitches: 173 (C, CV & T)

Waterrow Touring Park
Wiveliscombe, Taunton
TA4 2AZ
Tel: 01984 623464 20 G8
waterrowpark.co.uk
Total Pitches: 44 (C, CV & T)

Wayfarers C & C Park
Relubbus Lane, St Hilary, Penzance
TR20 9EF
Tel: 01736 763326 2 E8
wayfarerspark.co.uk
Total Pitches: 35 (C, CV & T)

Wells Touring Park
Haybridge, Wells
BA5 1AJ
Tel: 01749 676869 22 C4
wellstouringpark.co.uk
Total Pitches: 84(C & CV)

Westbrook Park
Little Hereford, Herefordshire
SY8 4AU
Tel: 01584 711280 51 P7
westbrookpark.co.uk
Total Pitches: 59 (C, CV & T)

Wheathill Touring Park
Wheathill, Bridgnorth
WV16 6QT
Tel: 01584 823456 51 Q4
wheathillpark.co.uk
Total Pitches: 50 (C & CV)

Whitefield Forest Touring Park
Brading Road, Ryde,
Isle of Wight
PO33 1QL
Tel: 01983 617069 13 K7
whitefieldforest.co.uk
Total Pitches: 90 (C, CV & T)

Whitehill Country Park
Stoke Road, Paignton, Devon
TQ4 7PF
Tel: 01803 782338 5 P5
whitehill-park.co.uk
Total Pitches: 325 (C, CV & T)

Whitemead Caravan Park
East Burton Road, Wool
BH20 6HG
Tel: 01929 462241 11 K7
whitemeadcaravanpark.co.uk
Total Pitches: 105 (C, CV & T)

Willowbank Holiday Home & Touring Park
Coastal Road, Ainsdale, Southport
PR8 3ST
Tel: 01704 571566 75 K2
willowbankcp.co.uk
Total Pitches: 315 (C & CV)

Willow Valley Holiday Park
Bush, Bude, Cornwall
EX23 9LB
Tel: 01288 353104 7 J3
willowvalley.co.uk
Total Pitches: 44 (C, CV & T)

Wilson House Holiday Park
Lancaster Road,
Out Rawcliffe, Preston, Lancashire
PR3 6BN
Tel: 07807 560685 83 K6
whhp.co.uk
Total Pitches: 40 (C & CV)

Wolds View Touring Park
115 Brigg Road, Caistor
LN7 6RX
Tel: 01472 851099 80 B3
woldsviewtouringpark.co.uk
Total Pitches: 60 (C, CV & T)

Wood Farm C & C Park
Axminster Road, Charmouth
DT6 6BT
Tel: 01297 560697 9 Q6
woodfarm.co.uk
Total Pitches: 267 (C, CV & T)

Wooda Farm Holiday Park
Poughill, Bude
EX23 9HJ
Tel: 01288 352069 7 J3
wooda.co.uk
Total Pitches: 255 (C, CV & T)

Woodclose Caravan Park
High Casterton, Kirkby Lonsdale
LA6 2SE
Tel: 01524 271597 89 Q11
woodclosepark.com
Total Pitches: 117 (C & CV)

Woodhall Country Park
Stixwold Road, Woodhall Spa
LN10 6UJ
Tel: 01526 353710 80 D10
woodhallcountrypark.co.uk
Total Pitches: 120 (C, CV & T)

Woodland Springs Adult Touring Park
Venton, Drewsteignton
EX6 6PG
Tel: 01647 231695 8 D6
woodlandsprings.co.uk
Total Pitches: 81 (C, CV & T)

Woodlands Grove C & C Park
Blackawton, Dartmouth
TQ9 7DQ
Tel: 01803 712598 5 N6
woodlandsgrove.com
Total Pitches: 350 (C, CV & T)

Woodovis Park
Gulworthy, Tavistock
PL19 8NY
Tel: 01822 832968 7 N10
woodovis.com
Total Pitches: 89 (C, CV & T)

Yeatheridge Farm Caravan Park
East Worlington, Crediton, Devon
EX17 4TN
Tel: 01884 860330 8 E3
yeatheridge.co.uk
Total Pitches: 122 (C, CV & T)

York Meadows Caravan Park
York Road, Sheriff Hutton, York,
North Yorkshire
YO60 6QP
Tel: 01347 878508 86 B2
yorkmeadowscaravanpark.com
Total Pitches: 60 (C, CV & T)

SCOTLAND

Anwoth Caravan Site
Gatehouse of Fleet, Castle Douglas,
Dumfries & Galloway
DG7 2JU
Tel: 01557 814333 96 C7
swalwellholidaygroup.co.uk
Total Pitches: 72 (C, CV & T)

Auchenlarie Holiday Park
Gatehouse of Fleet
DG7 2EX
Tel: 01556 506200 95 P8
swalwellholidaygroup.co.uk
Total Pitches: 451 (C, CV & T)

Banff Links Caravan Park
Inverboyndie, Banff,
Aberdeenshire
AB45 2JJ
Tel: 01261 812228 140 G3
banfflinkscaravanpark.co.uk
Total Pitches: 93 (C, CV & T)

Beecraigs C & C Site
Beecraigs Country Park,
The Visitor Centre, Linlithgow
EH49 6PL
Tel: 01506 284516 115 J6
westlothian.gov.uk/stay-at-beecraigs
Total Pitches: 38 (C, CV & T)

Belhaven Bay C & C Park
Belhaven Bay, Dunbar,
East Lothian
EH42 1TS
Tel: 01368 865956 116 F5
meadowhead.co.uk
Total Pitches: 119 (C, CV & T)

Blair Castle Caravan Park
Blair Atholl, Pitlochry
PH18 5SR
Tel: 01796 481263 130 F11
blaircastlecaravanpark.co.uk
Total Pitches: 325 (C, CV & T)

Brighouse Bay Holiday Park
Brighouse Bay, Borgue,
Kirkcudbright
DG6 4TS
Tel: 01557 870267 96 D9
gillespie-leisure.co.uk
Total Pitches: 418 (C, CV & T)

Cairnsmill Holiday Park
Largo Road, St Andrews
KY16 8NN
Tel: 01334 473604 125 K10
cairnsmill.co.uk
Total Pitches: 256 (C, CV & T)

Craig Tara Holiday Park
Ayr
KA7 4LB
Tel: 0800 975 7579 104 E6
haven.com/craigtara
Total Pitches: 1144 (C & CV)

Craigtoun Meadows Holiday Park
Mount Melville, St Andrews
KY16 8PQ
Tel: 01334 475959 125 J10
craigtounmeadows.co.uk
Total Pitches: 257 (C, CV & T)

Crossburn Caravan Park
Edinburgh Road, Peebles,
Scottish Borders
EH45 8ED
Tel: 01721 720501 106 H2
crossburn-caravans.com
Total Pitches: 132 (C, CV & T)

Faskally Caravan Park
Pitlochry
PH16 5LA
Tel: 01796 472007 130 G12
faskally.co.uk
Total Pitches: 430 (C, CV & T)

Glen Nevis C & C Park
Glen Nevis, Fort William
PH33 6SX
Tel: 01397 702191 128 F10
glen-nevis.co.uk
Total Pitches: 415 (C, CV & T)

Hoddom Castle Caravan Park
Hoddom, Lockerbie
DG11 1AS
Tel: 01576 300251 97 N4
hoddomcastle.co.uk
Total Pitches: 265 (C, CV & T)

Huntly Castle Caravan Park
The Meadow, Huntly
AB54 4UJ
Tel: 01466 794999 140 E8
huntlycastle.co.uk
Total Pitches: 130 (C, CV & T)

Invercoe C & C Park
Ballachulish, Glencoe
PH49 4HP
Tel: 01855 811210 121 L1
invercoe.co.uk
Total Pitches: 66 (C, CV & T)

Linwater Caravan Park
West Clifton, East Calder
EH53 0HT
Tel: 0131 333 3326 115 K7
linwater.co.uk
Total Pitches: 64 (C, CV & T)

Loch Ken Holiday Park
Parton, Castle Douglas,
Dumfries & Galloway
DG7 3NE
Tel: 01644 470282 96 E4
lochkenholidaypark.co.uk
Total Pitches: 75 (C, CV & T)

Lomond Woods Holiday Park
Old Luss Road, Balloch,
Loch Lomond
G83 8QP
Tel: 01389 755000 113 M5
woodleisure.co.uk/our-parks/lomond-woods
Total Pitches: 153 (C & CV)

Milton of Fonab Caravan Park
Bridge Road, Pitlochry
PH16 5NA
Tel: 01796 472882 123 N1
fonab.co.uk
Total Pitches: 188 (C, CV & T)

Sands of Luce Holiday Park
Sands of Luce, Sandhead, Stranraer
DG9 9JN
Tel: 01776 830456 94 G8
sandsofluce.com
Total Pitches: 350 (C, CV & T)

Seal Shore Camping and Touring Site
Kildonan, Isle of Arran,
North Ayrshire
KA27 8SE
Tel: 01770 820320 103 Q5
campingarran.com
Total Pitches: 47 (C, CV & T)

Seaward Holiday Park
Dhoon Bay, Kirkudbright
DG6 4TJ
Tel: 01557 870267 96 D8
gillespie-leisure.co.uk
Total Pitches: 84 (C, CV & T)

Seton Sands Holiday Village
Longniddry
EH32 0QF
Tel: 01875 813333 116 A6
haven.com/setonsands
Total Pitches: 640 (C & CV)

Shieling Holidays Mull
Craignure, Isle of Mull,
Argyll & Bute
PA65 6AY
Tel: 01680 812496 120 D5
shielingholidays.co.uk
Total Pitches: 106 (C, CV & T)

Silver Sands Holiday Park
Covesea, West Beach,
Lossiemouth
IV31 6SP
Tel: 01343 813262 147 M11
silver-sands.co.uk
Total Pitches: 340 (C, CV & T)

Skye C & C Club Site
Loch Greshornish, Borve, Arnisort,
Edinbane, Isle of Skye
IV51 9PS
Tel: 01470 582230 134 F5
campingandcaravanningclub.co.uk/skye
Total Pitches: 107 (C, CV & T)

Thurston Manor Leisure Park
Innerwick, Dunbar
EH42 1SA
Tel: 01368 840643 116 G6
thurstonmanor.co.uk
Total Pitches: 690 (C & CV)

Witches Craig C & C Park
Blairlogie, Stirling
FK9 5PX
Tel: 01786 474947 114 E2
witchescraig.co.uk
Total Pitches: 60 (C, CV & T)

WALES

Bodnant Caravan Park
Nebo Road, Llanrwst, Conwy Valley,
Conwy
LL26 0SD
Tel: 01492 640248 73 P11
bodnant-caravan-park.co.uk
Total Pitches: 56 (C, CV & T)

Bron Derw Touring Caravan Park
Llanrwst
LL26 0YT
Tel: 01492 640494 73 N11
bronderw-wales.co.uk
Total Pitches: 48 (C & CV)

Bron-Y-Wendon Caravan Park
Wern Road, Llanddulas,
Colwyn Bay
LL22 8HG
Tel: 01492 512903 74 B8
bronywendon.co.uk
Total Pitches: 130 (C & CV)

Bryn Gloch C & C Park
Betws Garmon, Caernarfon
LL54 7YY
Tel: 01286 650216 73 J12
campwales.co.uk
Total Pitches: 177 (C, CV & T)

Caerfai Bay Caravan & Tent Park
Caerfai Bay, St Davids, Haverfordwest
SA62 6QT
Tel: 01437 720274 36 E5
caerfaibay.co.uk
Total Pitches: 136 (C, CV & T)

Cenarth Falls Holiday Park
Cenarth, Newcastle Emlyn
SA38 9JS
Tel: 01239 710345 37 P2
cenarth-holipark.co.uk
Total Pitches: 119 (C, CV & T)

Creampots Touring C & C Park
Broadway, Broad Haven, Haverfordwest,
Pembrokeshire
SA62 3TU
Tel: 01437 781776 36 G8
creampots.co.uk
Total Pitches: 73 (C, CV & T)

Daisy Bank Caravan Park
Snead, Montgomery
SY15 6EB
Tel: 01588 620471 51 K2
daisy-bank.co.uk
Total Pitches: 87 (C, CV & T)

Deucoch Touring & Camping Park
Sarn Bach, Abersoch, Gwynedd
LL53 7LD
Tel: 01758 713293 60 E7
deucoch.com
Total Pitches: 70 (C, CV & T)

Dinlle Caravan Park
Dinas Dinlle, Caernarfon
LL54 5TW
Tel: 01286 830324 72 G12
thornleyleisure.co.uk
Total Pitches: 349 (C, CV & T)

Eisteddfa
Eisteddfa Lodge, Pentrefelin, Criccieth
LL52 0PT
Tel: 01766 522696 61 J4
eisteddfapark.co.uk
Total Pitches: 116 (C, CV & T)

Fforest Fields C & C Park
Hundred House, Builth Wells
LD1 5RT
Tel: 01982 570406 50 F10
fforestfields.co.uk
Total Pitches: 122 (C, CV & T)

Fishguard Bay Resort
Garn Gelli, Fishguard
SA65 9ET
Tel: 01348 811415 37 J3
fishguardbay.com
Total Pitches: 102 (C, CV & T)

Greenacres Holiday Park
Black Rock Sands, Morfa Bychan,
Porthmadog
LL49 9YF
Tel: 01766 512781 61 J5
haven.com/greenacres
Total Pitches: 945 (C & CV)

Hafan y Môr Holiday Park
Pwllheli
LL53 6HJ
Tel: 01758 612112 60 G5
haven.com/hafanymor
Total Pitches: 875 (C & CV)

Hendre Mynach Touring C & C Park
Llanaber Road, Barmouth
LL42 1YR
Tel: 01341 280262 61 K8
hendremynach.co.uk
Total Pitches: 241 (C, CV & T)

Home Farm Caravan Park
Marian-glas,
Isle of Anglesey
LL73 8PH
Tel: 01248 410614 72 H7
homefarm-anglesey.co.uk
Total Pitches: 186 (C, CV & T)

Islawrffordd Caravan Park
Talybont, Barmouth
LL43 2AQ
Tel: 01341 247269 61 K8
islawrffordd.co.uk
Total Pitches: 306 (C & CV)

Kiln Park Holiday Centre
Marsh Road, Tenby
SA70 8RB
Tel: 01834 844121 37 M10
haven.com/kilnpark
Total Pitches: 849 (C, CV & T)

Pencelli Castle C & C Park
Pencelli, Brecon
LD3 7LX
Tel: 01874 665451 39 P7
pencelli-castle.com
Total Pitches: 80 (C, CV & T)

Penisar Mynydd Caravan Park
Caerwys Road, Rhuallt, St Asaph
LL17 0TY
Tel: 01745 582227 74 F8
penisarmynydd.co.uk
Total Pitches: 71 (C, CV & T)

Plassey Holiday Park
The Plassey, Eyton, Wrexham
LL13 0SP
Tel: 01978 780277 63 K3
plassey.com
Total Pitches: 123 (C, CV & T)

Pont Kemys C & C Park
Chainbridge, Abergavenny
NP7 9DS
Tel: 01873 880688 40 D10
pontkemys.com
Total Pitches: 65 (C, CV & T)

Presthaven Sands Holiday Park
Gronant, Prestatyn
LL19 9TT
Tel: 01745 856471 74 F7
haven.com/presthavensands
Total Pitches: 1102 (C & CV)

Red Kite Touring Park
Van Road, Llanidloes
SY18 6NG
Tel: 01686 412122 50 C4
redkitetouringpark.co.uk
Total Pitches: 66 (C & CV)

Riverside Camping
Seiont Nurseries, Pont Rug, Caernarfon
LL55 2BB
Tel: 01286 678781 72 H11
riversidecamping.co.uk
Total Pitches: 73 (C, CV & T)

The Trotting Mare Caravan Park
Overton, Wrexham
LL13 0LE
Tel: 01978 711963 63 L4
thetrottingmare.co.uk
Total Pitches: 65 (C, CV & T)

Trawsdir Touring C & C Park
Llanaber, Barmouth
LL42 1RR
Tel: 01341 280999 61 K8
barmouthholidays.co.uk
Total Pitches: 80 (C, CV & T)

Tyddyn Isaf Caravan Park
Lligwy Bay, Dulas,
Isle of Anglesey
LL70 9PQ
Tel: 01248 410203 72 H6
tyddynisaf.co.uk
Total Pitches: 136 (C, CV & T)

White Tower Caravan Park
Llandwrog, Caernarfon
LL54 5UH
Tel: 01286 830649 72 G12
whitetowerpark.co.uk
Total Pitches: 126 (C & CV)

Traffic signs

Signs giving orders

**Signs with red circles are mostly prohibitive.
Plates below signs qualify their message**

 Entry to 20mph zone

 End of 20mph zone

40 Maximum speed

National speed limit applies

School crossing patrol

STOP — Stop and give way

GIVE WAY — Give way to traffic on major road

STOP/GO — Manually operated temporary STOP and GO signs

GO

No entry for vehicular traffic

No vehicles except bicycles being pushed

No cycling

No motor vehicles

No buses (over 8 passenger seats)

No overtaking

No towed caravans

No vehicles carrying explosives

32'6" No vehicle or combination of vehicles over length shown

4.4 m 14'6 No vehicles over height shown

2.0m 6'6" No vehicles over width shown

Give way to oncoming vehicles — Give priority to vehicles from opposite direction

No right turn

No left turn

No U-turns

7.5T Except for loading — No goods vehicles over maximum gross weight shown (in tonnes) except for loading and unloading

WEAK BRIDGE 18T mgw — No vehicles over maximum gross weight shown (in tonnes)

P Permit holders only — Parking restricted to permit holders

RED ROUTE No stopping at any time except buses — No stopping during period indicated except for buses

URBAN CLEARWAY Monday to Friday am 8.00 - 9.30 pm 4.30 - 6.30 — No stopping during times shown except for as long as necessary to set down or pick up passengers

No waiting

No stopping (Clearway)

Signs with blue circles but no red border mostly give positive instruction.

Ahead only

Turn left ahead (right if symbol reversed)

Turn left (right if symbol reversed)

Keep left (right if symbol reversed)

Vehicles may pass either side to reach same destination

Mini-roundabout (roundabout circulation – give way to vehicles from the immediate right)

Route to be used by pedal cycles only

Segregated pedal cycle and pedestrian route

30 Minimum speed

End of minimum speed

Only Buses and cycles only

Only Trams only

TRAMWAY LOOK BOTH WAYS Pedestrian crossing point over tramway

One-way traffic (note: compare circular 'Ahead only' sign)

With-flow bus and cycle lane

Contraflow bus lane

With-flow pedal cycle lane

Warning signs

Mostly triangular

STOP 100 yds Distance to 'STOP' line ahead

Dual carriageway ends

Road narrows on right (left if symbol reversed)

Road narrows on both sides

GIVE WAY 50 yds Distance to 'Give Way' line ahead

Crossroads

Junction on bend ahead

T-junction with priority over vehicles from the right

Staggered junction

Traffic merging from left ahead

The priority through route is indicated by the broader line.

Double bend first to left (symbol may be reversed)

Bend to right (or left if symbol reversed)

Roundabout

Uneven road

REDUCE SPEED NOW Plate below some signs

Two-way traffic crosses one-way road

Two-way traffic straight ahead

Opening or swing bridge ahead

Low-flying aircraft or sudden aircraft noise

Falling or fallen rocks

Traffic signals not in use

Traffic signals

Slippery road

10% Steep hill downwards

20% Steep hill upwards

Gradients may be shown as a ratio i.e. 20% = 1:5

Tunnel ahead

Trams crossing ahead

Level crossing with barrier or gate ahead

Level crossing without barrier or gate ahead

Level crossing without barrier

Patrol School crossing patrol ahead (some signs have amber lights which flash when crossings are in use)

Frail (or blind or disabled if shown) pedestrians likely to cross road ahead

No footway for 400 yds Pedestrians in road ahead

Zebra crossing

Safe height 16'-6" Overhead electric cable; plate indicates maximum height of vehicles which can pass safely

14'-6" 4.4m Available width of headroom indicated

Sharp deviation of route to left (or right if chevrons reversed)

STOP when lights show Light signals ahead at level crossing, airfield or bridge

Red STOP Green Clear IF NO LIGHT - PHONE CROSSING OPERATOR Miniature warning lights at level crossings

Cattle

Wild animals

Wild horses or ponies

Accompanied horses or ponies

Cycle route ahead

Ice Risk of ice

Queues likely Traffic queues likely ahead

Humps for ½ mile Distance over which road humps extend

Hidden dip Other danger; plate indicates nature of danger

Soft verges for 2 miles — Soft verges

Side winds

Hump bridge

Ford Worded warning sign

Quayside or river bank

Risk of grounding

Direction signs

Mostly rectangular
Signs on motorways - blue backgrounds

 Nottingham 23 M1 — At a junction leading directly into a motorway (junction number may be shown on a black background)

Nottingham A 52 25 ½ m — On approaches to junctions (junction number on black background)

M1 The NORTH Sheffield 32 Leeds 59 — Route confirmatory sign after junction

A 404 Marlow Birmingham, Oxford M 40 4 ½ m — Downward pointing arrows mean 'Get in lane' The left-hand lane leads to a different destination from the other lanes.

A 46 (M 69) Leicester, Coventry (E) The NORTH WEST, Birmingham, Coventry (N) M 6 2 ½ m — The panel with the inclined arrow indicates the destinations which can be reached

Signs on primary routes - green backgrounds

PARK STREET ROUNDABOUT Birmingham Bourne 1 M 15 (M1) (M 14) Penderton A 105 Walsham A 1183 Nutfield A 1183 — On approaches to junctions

Lampton Axtley A11 1 mile — At the junction

A 46 The SOUTH Nottingham 17 Leicester 32 (M 1 South) 35 — Route confirmatory sign after junction

TURPIN'S CROSSROADS Biggleswick A 11 Lampton (M 11) Dorfield A 123 Axtley B 1991 Steam railway — On approaches to junctions

Swansea Abertawe A 483 — On approach to a junction in Wales (bilingual)

Blue panels indicate that the motorway starts at the junction ahead.
Motorways shown in brackets can also be reached along the route indicated.
White panels indicate local or non-primary routes leading from the junction ahead.
Brown panels show the route to tourist attractions.
The name of the junction may be shown at the top of the sign.
The aircraft symbol indicates the route to an airport.
A symbol may be included to warn of a hazard or restriction along that route.

Port Lever Hartley A 666 Ring road Ring road Maverton A 6604 Doncastle A 6604 — Primary route forming part of a ring road

R

Signs on non-primary and local routes - black borders

HANGMAN'S CROSSROADS Axtley B 1234 (M11) Lampton A11 Townley A11 — On approaches to junctions

(A1(M)) 8 Barnes 10 Mackstone 2½ Elkington 1 A404 (A41) Millington Green (A4011) 3

Market Walborough B 486 7 — At the junction

WC — Direction to toilets with access for the disabled

Green panels indicate that the primary route starts at the junction ahead.
Route numbers on a blue background show the direction to a motorway.
Route numbers on a green background show the direction to a primary route.

Signs on non-primary and local routes - black borders

150 yds — Picnic site

Wrest Park — Ancient monument in the care of English Heritage

P Saturday only — Direction to a car park

Zoo — Tourist attraction

300 yds — Direction to camping and caravan site

(A33) (M1) — Advisory route for lorries

4 — Route for pedal cycles forming part of a network

Marton 3 — Recommended route for pedal cycles to place shown

Public library Council offices — Route for pedestrians

Emergency diversion routes

■ ▲ ◆ ● — Symbols showing emergency diversion route for motorway and other main road traffic

Northtown — Diversion route

In an emergency it may be necessary to close a section of motorway or other main road to traffic, so a temporary sign may advise drivers to follow a diversion route. To help drivers navigate the route, black symbols on yellow patches may be permanently displayed on existing direction signs, including motorway signs. Symbols may also be used on separate signs with yellow backgrounds.

Note: The signs shown in this road atlas are those most commonly in use and are not all drawn to the same scale. In Scotland and Wales bilingual versions of some signs are used, showing both English and Gaelic or Welsh spellings. Some older designs of signs may still be seen on the roads. A comprehensive explanation of the signing system illustrating the vast majority of road signs can be found in the AA's handbook *Know Your Road Signs*. Where there is a reference to a rule number, this refers to *The Highway Code*.

 THE HIGHWAY CODE / KNOW YOUR ROAD SIGNS

Information signs

All rectangular

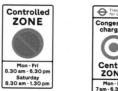

Entrance to controlled parking zone

Entrance to congestion charging zone

Greater London Low Emission Zone (LEZ)

Advance warning of restriction or prohibition ahead

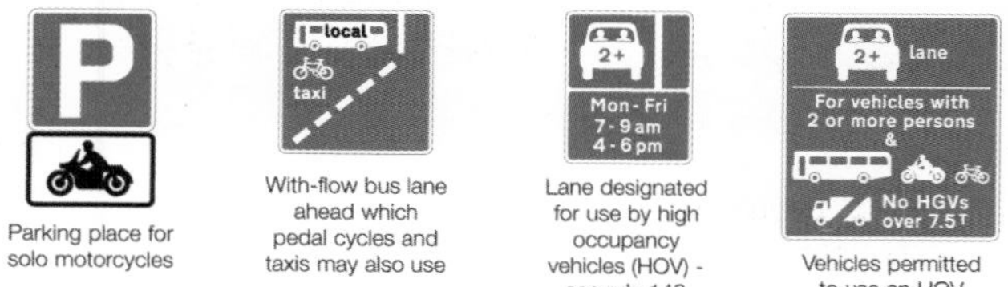

Parking place for solo motorcycles

With-flow bus lane ahead which pedal cycles and taxis may also use

Lane designated for use by high occupancy vehicles (HOV) - see rule 142

Vehicles permitted to use an HOV lane ahead

End of motorway

Start of motorway and point from which motorway regulations apply

Appropriate traffic lanes at junction ahead

Traffic on the main carriageway coming from right has priority over joining traffic

Additional traffic joining from left ahead. Traffic on main carriageway has priority over joining traffic from right hand lane of slip road

Traffic in right hand lane of slip road joining the main carriageway has priority over left hand lane

'Countdown' markers at exit from motorway (each bar represents 100 yards to the exit). Green-backed markers may be used on primary routes and white-backed markers with black bars on other routes. At approaches to concealed level crossings white-backed markers with red bars may be used. Although these will be erected at equal distances the bars do not represent 100 yard intervals.

GOOD FOOD
Puddleworth services
½ m
LPG
Petrol

Motorway service area sign showing the operator's name

Priority over oncoming vehicles

Traffic has priority over oncoming vehicles

H A&E not 24 hrs

Hospital ahead with Accident and Emergency facilities

i Tourist information

Tourist information point

T

No through road for vehicles

Recommended route for pedal cycles

Home Zone Entry

Area in which cameras are used to enforce traffic regulations

Bus lane

Bus lane on road at junction ahead

*Home Zone Entry – You are entering an area where people could be using the whole street for a range of activities. You should drive slowly and carefully and be prepared to stop to allow people time to move out of the way.

Roadworks signs

Road works

Loose chippings

SLOW WET TAR
Temporary hazard at roadworks

800 yards
Temporary lane closure (the number and position of arrows and red bars may be varied according to lanes open and closed)

Slow-moving or stationary works vehicle blocking a traffic lane. Pass in the direction shown by the arrow.

50 ¾ mile ahead
Mandatory speed limit ahead

Delays possible until Mar 08
1 mile
Roadworks 1 mile ahead

Sorry for any delay
End Authority name
End of roadworks and any temporary restrictions including speed limits

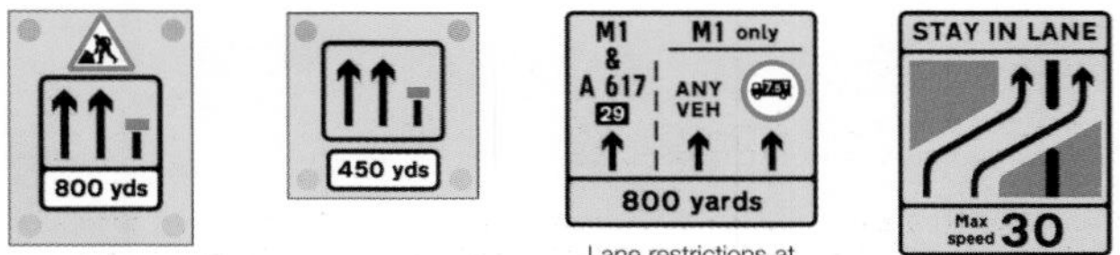

800 yds
Signs used on the back of slow-moving or stationary works vehicle warning of a lane closed ahead by a works vehicle. There are no cones on the road.

450 yds
Lane restrictions at roadworks ahead

M1 & A 617 29 | M1 only ANY VEH
800 yards
Lane restrictions at roadworks ahead

STAY IN LANE
Max speed 30
One lane crossover at contraflow roadworks

Road markings

Across the carriageway

Stop line at signals or police control

Stop line at 'Stop' sign

Stop line for pedestrians at a level crossing

Give way to traffic on major road (can also be used at mini roundabouts)

Give way to traffic from the right at a roundabout

Give way to traffic from the right at a mini-roundabout

Along the carriageway

Edge line

Centre line See Rule 127

Hazard warning line See Rule 127

Double white lines See Rules 128 and 129

See Rule 130

Lane line See Rule 131

Along the edge of the carriageway

Waiting restrictions

Waiting restrictions indicated by yellow lines apply to the carriageway, pavement and verge. You may stop to load or unload (unless there are also loading restrictions as described below) or while passengers board or alight. Double yellow lines mean no waiting at any time, unless there are signs that specifically indicate seasonal restrictions. The times at which the restrictions apply for other road markings are shown on nearby plates or on entry signs to controlled parking zones. If no days are shown on the signs, the restrictions are in force every day including Sundays and Bank Holidays. White bay markings and upright signs (see below) indicate where parking is allowed.

No waiting at any time

8 am - 6 pm →
No waiting during times shown on sign

P Mon - Sat 8 am - 7 pm 20 mins No return within 40 mins
Waiting is limited to the duration specified during the days and times shown

Red Route stopping controls

Red lines are used on some roads instead of yellow lines. In London the double and single red lines used on Red Routes indicate that stopping to park, load/unload or to board and alight from a vehicle (except for a licensed taxi or if you hold a Blue Badge) is prohibited. The red lines apply to the carriageway, pavement and verge. The times that the red line prohibitions apply are shown on nearby signs, but the double red line ALWAYS means no stopping at any time. On Red Routes you may stop to park, load/unload in specially marked boxes and adjacent signs specify the times and purposes and duration allowed. A box MARKED IN RED indicates that it may only be available for the purpose specified for part of the day (e.g. between busy peak periods). A box MARKED IN WHITE means that it is available throughout the day.

RED AND SINGLE YELLOW LINES CAN ONLY GIVE A GUIDE TO THE RESTRICTIONS AND CONTROLS IN FORCE AND SIGNS, NEARBY OR AT A ZONE ENTRY, MUST BE CONSULTED.

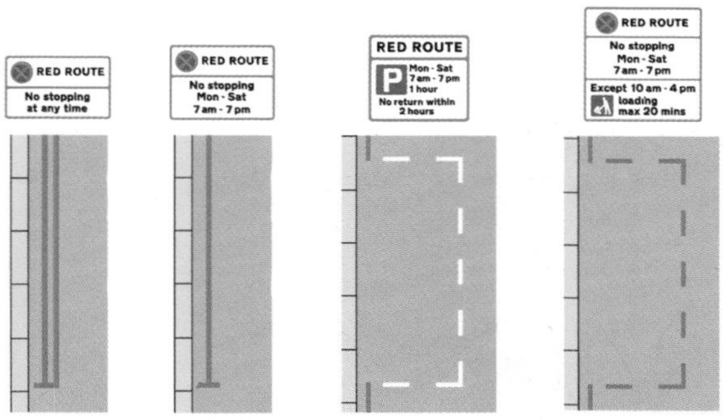

RED ROUTE No stopping at any time

RED ROUTE No stopping Mon - Sat 7am - 7pm

RED ROUTE Mon - Sat 7am - 7pm P No return within 2 hours

RED ROUTE No stopping Mon - Sat 7am - 7pm Except 10 am - 4 pm loading max 20 mins

No stopping at any time

No stopping during times shown on sign

Parking is limited to the duration specified during the days and times shown

Only loading may take place at the times shown for up to a maximum duration of 20 mins

On the kerb or at the edge of the carriageway

Loading restrictions on roads other than Red Routes

Yellow marks on the kerb or at the edge of the carriageway indicate that loading or unloading is prohibited at the times shown on the nearby black and white plates. You may stop while passengers board or alight. If no days are indicated on the signs the restrictions are in force every day including Sundays and Bank Holidays.

ALWAYS CHECK THE TIMES SHOWN ON THE PLATES.

Lengths of road reserved for vehicles loading and unloading are indicated by a white 'bay' marking with the words 'Loading Only' and a sign with the white on blue 'trolley' symbol. This sign also shows whether loading and unloading is restricted to goods vehicles and the times at which the bay can be used. If no times or days are shown it may be used at any time. Vehicles may not park here if they are not loading or unloading.

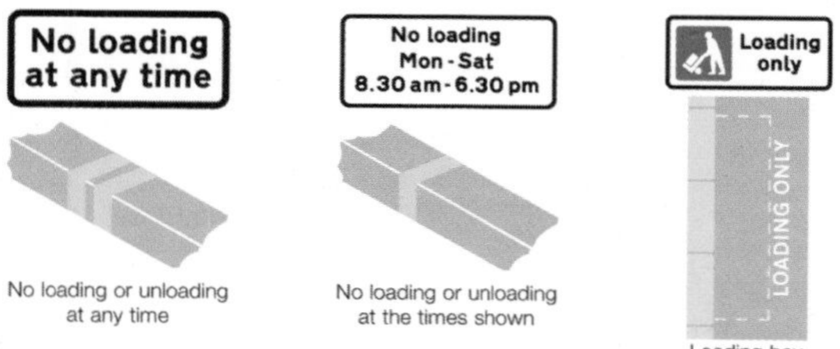

No loading at any time

No loading Mon - Sat 8.30 am - 6.30 pm

Loading only

No loading or unloading at any time

No loading or unloading at the times shown

Loading bay

Other road markings

SCHOOL KEEP CLEAR

Keep entrance clear of stationary vehicles, even if picking up or setting down children

Warning of 'Give Way' just ahead

DOCTOR
Parking space reserved for vehicles named

BUS STOP
See Rule 243

BUS LANE
See Rule 141

Box junction - See Rule 174

KEEP CLEAR
Do not block that part of the carriageway indicated

CITY | A3 | YORK ST
Indication of traffic lanes

Light signals controlling traffic

Traffic Light Signals

RED means 'Stop'. Wait behind the stop line on the carriageway

RED AND AMBER also means 'Stop'. Do not pass through or start until GREEN shows

GREEN means you may go on if the way is clear. Take special care if you intend to turn left or right and give way to pedestrians who are crossing

AMBER means 'Stop' at the stop line. You may go on only if the AMBER appears after you have crossed the stop line or are so close to it that to pull up might cause an accident

A GREEN ARROW may be provided in addition to the full green signal if movement in a certain direction is allowed before or after the full green phase. If the way is clear you may go but only in the direction shown by the arrow. You may do this whatever other lights may be showing. White light signals may be provided for trams

Flashing red lights

Alternately flashing red lights mean YOU MUST STOP

At level crossings, lifting bridges, airfields, fire stations, etc.

Motorway signals

You MUST NOT proceed further in this lane

Change lane

Fog
Reduced visibility ahead

Lane ahead closed

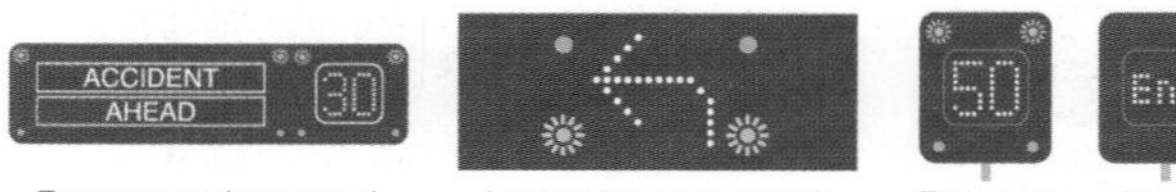

ACCIDENT AHEAD 30
Temporary maximum speed advised and information message

Leave motorway at next exit

50
Temporary maximum speed advised

End
End of restriction

Lane control signals

Green arrow – lane available to traffic facing the sign
Red crosses – lane closed to traffic facing the sign
White diagonal arrow – change lanes in direction shown

Channel hopping and the Isle of Wight

For business or pleasure, hopping on a ferry across to France, the Channel Islands or Isle of Wight has never been easier.

The vehicle ferry services listed in the table give you all the options, together with detailed port plans to help you navigate to and from the ferry terminals. Simply choose your preferred route, not forgetting the fast sailings (see). Bon voyage!

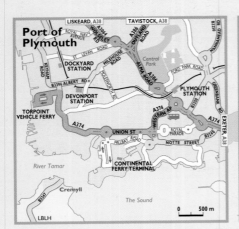

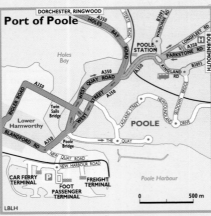

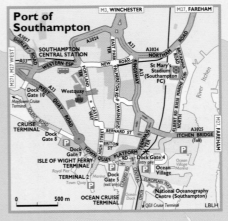

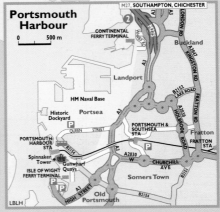

ENGLISH CHANNEL AND ISLE OF WIGHT FERRY CROSSINGS

From	To	Journey time	Operator website
Dover	Calais	1 hr 30 mins	dfdsseaways.co.uk
Dover	Calais	1 hr 30 mins	poferries.com
Dover	Dunkirk	2 hrs	dfdsseaways.co.uk
Folkestone	Calais (Coquelles)	35 mins	eurotunnel.com
Lymington	Yarmouth (IOW)	40 mins	wightlink.co.uk
Newhaven	Dieppe	4 hrs	dfdsseaways.co.uk
Plymouth	Roscoff	6–8 hrs	brittany-ferries.co.uk
Poole	Cherbourg	4 hrs 30 mins	brittany-ferries.co.uk
Poole	Guernsey	3 hrs	condorferries.co.uk
Poole	Jersey	4 hrs 30 mins	condorferries.co.uk
Poole	St-Malo	7–12 hrs (via Channel Is.)	condorferries.co.uk
Portsmouth	Caen (Ouistreham)	6–7 hrs	brittany-ferries.co.uk
Portsmouth	Cherbourg	3 hrs (May–Aug)	brittany-ferries.co.uk
Portsmouth	Fishbourne (IOW)	45 mins	wightlink.co.uk
Portsmouth	Guernsey	7 hrs	condorferries.co.uk
Portsmouth	Jersey	8–11 hrs	condorferries.co.uk
Portsmouth	Le Havre	5 hrs 30 mins	brittany-ferries.co.uk
Portsmouth	St-Malo	9–11 hrs	brittany-ferries.co.uk
Southampton	East Cowes (IOW)	1 hr	redfunnel.co.uk

The information listed is provided as a guide only, as services are liable to change at short notice and are weather dependent. Services shown are for vehicle ferries only, operated by conventional ferry unless indicated as a fast ferry service ( ). Please check sailings before planning your journey.

Travelling further afield? For ferry services to Northern Spain see *brittany-ferries.co.uk*.

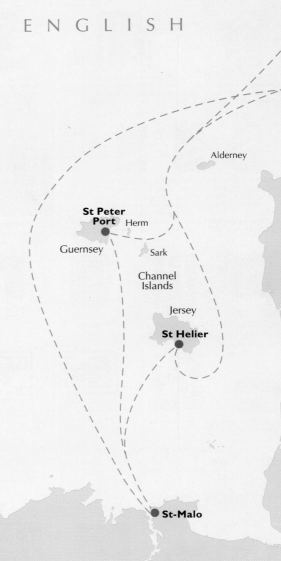

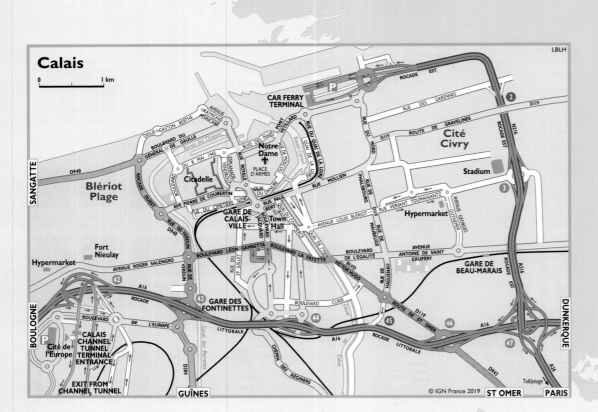

© IGN France 2019

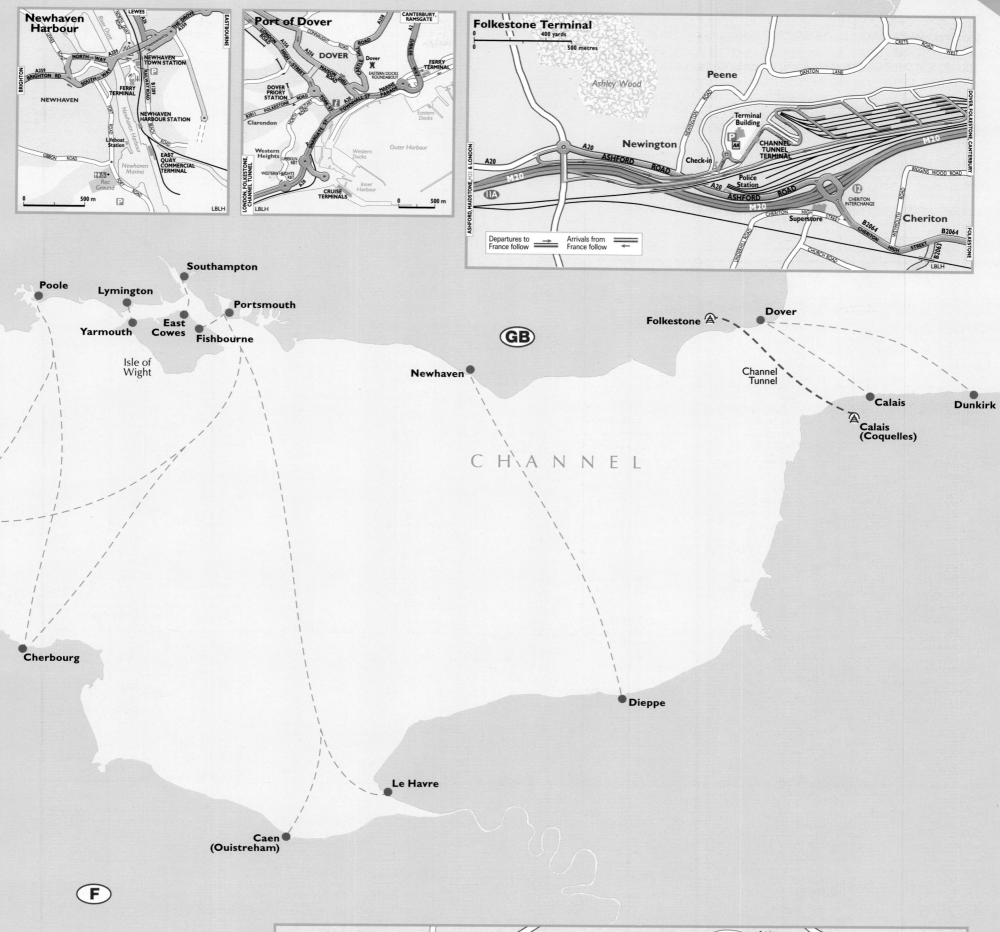

Newhaven Harbour

Port of Dover

Folkestone Terminal

Departures to France follow → Arrivals from France follow →

Poole
Lymington
Southampton
Yarmouth
East Cowes
Fishbourne
Portsmouth
Isle of Wight

GB

Newhaven

Folkestone
Dover
Channel Tunnel
Calais
Calais (Coquelles)
Dunkirk

CHANNEL

Cherbourg

Dieppe

Le Havre

Caen (Ouistreham)

F

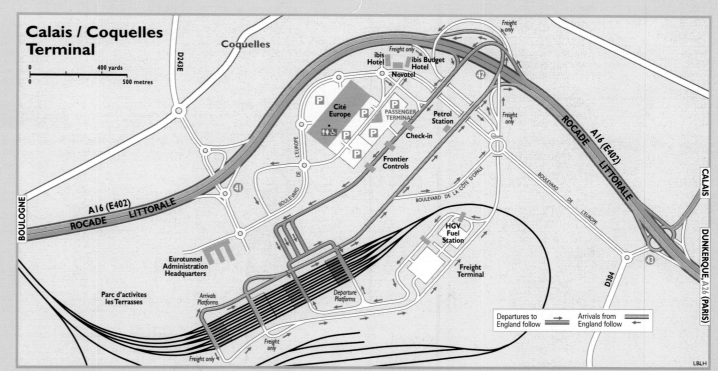

Calais / Coquelles Terminal

Coquelles

Departures to England follow → Arrivals from England follow →

Scotland, North Sea and Irish Sea ferries

SCOTLAND FERRIES

From	To	Journey time	Operator website
Scottish Islands/west coast of Scotland			
Gourock	Dunoon	20 mins	western-ferries.co.uk
Glenelg	Skye	20 mins (Easter–Oct)	skyeferry.co.uk

Numerous and varied sailings from the west coast of Scotland to Scottish islands are provided by Caledonian MacBrayne. Please visit calmac.co.uk for all ferry information, including those of other operators.

From	To	Journey time	Operator website
Orkney Islands			
Aberdeen	Kirkwall	6 hrs	northlinkferries.co.uk
Gills	St Margaret's Hope	1 hr	pentlandferries.co.uk
Scrabster	Stromness	1 hr 30 mins	northlinkferries.co.uk
Lerwick	Kirkwall	5 hrs 30 mins	northlinkferries.co.uk

Inter-island services are operated by Orkney Ferries. Please see orkneyferries.co.uk for details.

From	To	Journey time	Operator website
Shetland Islands			
Aberdeen	Lerwick	12 hrs 30 mins	northlinkferries.co.uk
Kirkwall	Lerwick	7 hrs 45 mins	northlinkferries.co.uk

Inter-island services are operated by Shetland Island Council Ferries. Please see shetland.gov.uk/ferries for details.

Please note that some smaller island services are day and weather dependent. Reservations are required for some routes. Book and confirm sailing schedules by contacting the operator.

NORTH SEA FERRY CROSSINGS

From	To	Journey time	Operator website
Harwich	Hook of Holland	7–8 hrs	stenaline.co.uk
Kingston upon Hull	Rotterdam (Europoort)	12 hrs	poferries.com
Kingston upon Hull	Zeebrugge	12 hrs	poferries.com
Newcastle upon Tyne	Amsterdam (IJmuiden)	15 hrs 30 mins	dfdsseaways.co.uk

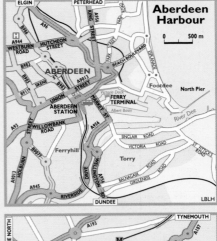

Aberdeen Harbour

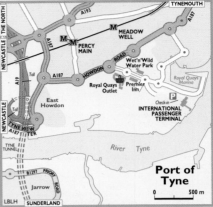

Port of Tyne

Port of Hull

Harwich International Port

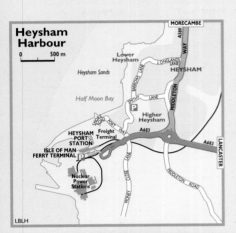

Heysham Harbour

Liverpool Docks

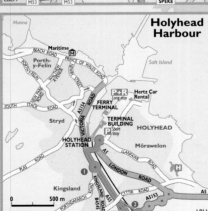

Holyhead Harbour

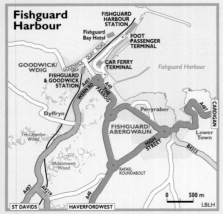

Fishguard Harbour

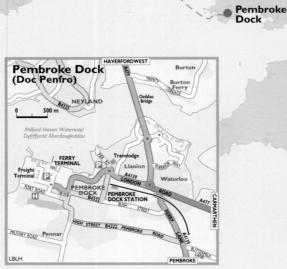

Pembroke Dock (Doc Penfro)

IRISH SEA FERRY CROSSINGS

From	To	Journey time	Operator website
Cairnryan	Belfast	2 hrs 15 mins	stenaline.co.uk
Cairnryan	Larne	2 hrs	poferries.com
Douglas	Belfast	2 hrs 45 mins (April–Sept)	steam-packet.com
Douglas	Dublin	2 hrs 55 mins (April–Sept)	steam-packet.com
Fishguard	Rosslare	3 hrs 15 mins	stenaline.co.uk
Heysham	Douglas	3 hrs 45 mins	steam-packet.com
Holyhead	Dublin	2 hrs (Mar–Oct)	irishferries.com
Holyhead	Dublin	3 hrs 15 mins	irishferries.com
Holyhead	Dublin	3 hrs 15 mins	stenaline.co.uk
Liverpool	Douglas	2 hrs 45 mins (Mar–Oct)	steam-packet.com
Liverpool	Douglas	8 hrs–8 hrs 30 mins	poferries.com
Liverpool (Birkenhead)	Belfast	8 hrs	stenaline.co.uk
Liverpool (Birkenhead)	Douglas	4 hrs 15 mins (Nov–Mar Sat, Sun only)	steam-packet.com
Pembroke Dock	Rosslare	4 hrs	irishferries.com

The information listed is provided as a guide only, as services are liable to change at short notice and are weather dependent. Services shown are for vehicle ferries only, operated by conventional ferry unless indicated as a fast ferry service. Please check sailings before planning your journey.

Restricted junctions

Motorway and primary route junctions which have access or exit restrictions are shown on the map pages thus:

M1 London - Leeds

Junction	Northbound	Southbound
2	Access only from A1 *(northbound)*	Exit only to A1 *(southbound)*
4	Access only from A41 *(northbound)*	Exit only to A41 *(southbound)*
6A	Access only from M25 (no link from A405)	Exit only to M25 (no link from A405)
7	Access only from A414	Exit only to A414
17	Exit only to M45	Access only from M45
19	Exit only to M6 *(northbound)*	Exit only to A14 *(southbound)*
21A	Exit only, no access	Access only, no exit
24A	Access only, no exit	Access only from A50 *(eastbound)*
35A	Exit only, no access	Access only, no exit
43	Exit only to M621	Access only from M621
48	Exit only to A1(M) *(northbound)*	Access only from A1(M) *(southbound)*

M2 Rochester - Faversham

Junction	Westbound	Eastbound
1	No exit to A2 *(eastbound)*	No access from A2 *(westbound)*

M3 Sunbury - Southampton

Junction	Northeastbound	Southwestbound
8	Access only from A303, no exit	Exit only to A303, no access
10	Exit only, no access	Access only, no exit
14	Access from M27 only, no exit	No access to M27 *(westbound)*

M4 London - South Wales

Junction	Westbound	Eastbound
1	Access only from A4 *(westbound)*	Exit only to A4 *(eastbound)*
2	Access only from A4 *(westbound)*	Access only from A4 *(eastbound)*
21	Exit only to M48	Access only from M48
23	Access only from M48	Exit only to M48
25	Exit only, no access	Access only, no exit
25A	Exit only, no access	Access only, no exit
29	Exit only to A48(M)	Access only from A48(M)
38	Exit only, no access	No restriction
39	Access only, no exit	No access or exit
42	Exit only to A483	Access only from A483

M5 Birmingham - Exeter

Junction	Northeastbound	Southwestbound
10	Access only, no exit	Exit only, no access
11A	Access only from A417 *(westbound)*	Exit only to A417 *(eastbound)*
18A	Exit only to M49	Access only from M49
18	Exit only, no access	Access only, no exit

M6 Toll Motorway

Junction	Northwestbound	Southeastbound
T1	Access only, no exit	No access or exit
T2	No access or exit	Exit only, no access
T5	Access only, no exit	Exit only to A5148 *(northbound)*, no access
T7	Exit only, no access	Access only, no exit
T8	Exit only, no access	Access only, no exit

M6 Rugby - Carlisle

Junction	Northbound	Southbound
3A	Exit only to M6 Toll	Access only from M6 Toll
4	Exit only to M42 *(southbound)* & A446	Exit only to A446
4A	Access only from M42 *(southbound)*	Exit only to M42
5	Exit only, no access	Access only, no exit
10A	Exit only to M54	Access only from M54
11A	Access only from M6 Toll	Exit only to M6 Toll
with M56 (jct 20A)	No restriction	Access only from M56 *(eastbound)*
20	Exit only to M56 *(westbound)*	Access only from M56 *(eastbound)*
24	Access only, no exit	Exit only, no access
25	Exit only, no access	Access only, no exit
30	Access only from M61	Exit only to M61
31A	Exit only, no access	Access only, no exit
45	Exit only, no access	Access only, no exit

M8 Edinburgh - Bishopton

Junction	Westbound	Eastbound
6	Exit only, no access	Access only, no exit
6A	Access only, no exit	Exit only, no access
7	Access only, no exit	Exit only, no access
7A	Exit only, no access	Access only from A725 *(northbound)*, no exit
8	No access from M73 *(southbound)* or from A8 *(eastbound)* & A89	No exit to M73 *(northbound)* or to A8 *(westbound)* & A89
9	Access only, no exit	Exit only, no access
13	Access only from M80 *(southbound)*	Exit only to M80 *(northbound)*
14	Access only, no exit	Exit only, no access
16	Exit only to A804	Access only from A879
17	Exit only to A82	No restriction
18	Access only from A82 *(eastbound)*	Exit only to A814
19	No access from A814 *(westbound)*	Exit only to A814 *(westbound)*
20	Exit only, no access	Access only, no exit
21	Access only, no exit	Exit only to A8
22	Exit only to M77 *(southbound)*	Access only from M77 *(northbound)*
23	Exit only to B768	Access only from B768
25	No access or exit from or to A8	No access or exit from or to A8
25A	Exit only, no access	Access only, no exit
28	Exit only, no access	Access only, no exit
28A	Exit only to A737	Access only from A737
29A	Exit only to A8	Access only, no exit

M9 Edinburgh - Dunblane

Junction	Northwestbound	Southeastbound
2	Access only, no exit	Exit only, no access
3	Exit only, no access	Access only, no exit
6	Access only, no exit	Exit only to A905
8	Exit only to M876 *(southwestbound)*	Access only from M876 *(northeastbound)*

M11 London - Cambridge

Junction	Northbound	Southbound
4	Access only from A406 *(eastbound)*	Exit only to A406
5	Exit only, no access	Access only, no exit
8A	Exit only, no access	No direct access, use jct 8
9	Exit only to A11	Access only from A11
13	Exit only, no access	Access only, no exit
14	Exit only, no access	Access only, no exit

M20 Swanley - Folkestone

Junction	Northwestbound	Southeastbound
2	Staggered junction; follow signs - access only	Staggered junction; follow signs - exit only
3	Exit only to M26 *(westbound)*	Access only from M26 *(eastbound)*
5	Access only from A20	For access follow signs - exit only to A20
6	No restriction	For exit follow signs
11A	Access only, no exit	Exit only, no access

M23 Hooley - Crawley

Junction	Northbound	Southbound
7	Exit only to A23 *(northbound)*	Access only from A23 *(southbound)*
10A	Access only, no exit	Exit only, no access

M25 London Orbital Motorway

Junction	Clockwise	Anticlockwise
1B	No direct access, use slip road to jct 2 Exit only	Access only, no exit
5	No exit to M26 *(eastbound)*	No access from M26
19	Exit only, no access	Access only, no exit
21	Access only from M1 *(southbound)* Exit only to M1 *(northbound)*	Access only from M1 *(southbound)* Exit only to M1 *(northbound)*
31	No exit (use slip road via jct 30), access only	No access (use slip road via jct 30), exit only

M26 Sevenoaks - Wrotham

Junction	Westbound	Eastbound
with M25 (jct 5)	Exit only to clockwise M25 *(westbound)*	Access only from anticlockwise M25 *(eastbound)*
with M20 (jct 3)	Access only from M20 *(northwestbound)*	Exit only to M20 *(southeastbound)*

M27 Cadnam - Portsmouth

Junction	Westbound	Eastbound
4	Staggered junction; follow signs - access only from M3 *(southbound)*. Exit only to M3 *(northbound)*	Staggered junction; follow signs - access only from M3 *(southbound)*. Exit only to M3 *(northbound)*
10	Exit only, no access	Access only, no exit
12	Staggered junction; follow signs - exit only to M275 *(southbound)*	Staggered junction; follow signs - access only from M275 *(northbound)*

M40 London - Birmingham

Junction	Northwestbound	Southeastbound
3	Exit only, no access	Access only, no exit
7	Exit only, no access	Access only, no exit
8	Exit only to M40/A40	Access only from M40/A40
13	Exit only, no access	Access only, no exit
14	Access only, no exit	Exit only, no access
16	Access only, no exit	Exit only, no access

M42 Bromsgrove - Measham

Junction	Northeastbound	Southwestbound
1	Access only, no exit	Exit only, no access
7	Exit only to M6 *(northwestbound)*	Access only from M6 *(northwestbound)*
7A	Exit only to M6 *(southeastbound)*	No access or exit
8	Access only from M6 *(southeastbound)*	Exit only to M6 *(northwestbound)*

M45 Coventry - M1

Junction	Westbound	Eastbound
Dunchurch (unnumbered)	Access only from A45	Exit only, no access
with M1 (jct 17)	Access only from M1 *(northbound)*	Exit only to M1 *(southbound)*

M48 Chepstow

Junction	Westbound	Eastbound
21	Access only from M4 *(westbound)*	Exit only to M4 *(eastbound)*
23	No exit to M4 *(eastbound)*	No access from M4 *(westbound)*

M53 Mersey Tunnel - Chester

Junction	Northbound	Southbound
11	Access only from M56 *(westbound)* Exit only to M56 *(eastbound)*	Access only from M56 *(westbound)* Exit only to M56 *(eastbound)*

M54 Telford - Birmingham

Junction	Westbound	Eastbound
with M6 (jct 10A)	Access only from M6 *(northbound)*	Exit only to M6 *(southbound)*

M56 Chester - Manchester

Junction	Westbound	Eastbound
1	Access only from M60 *(westbound)*	Exit only to M60 *(eastbound)* & A34 *(northbound)*
2	Exit only, no access	Access only, no exit
3	Access only, no exit	Exit only, no access
4	Exit only, no access	Access only, no exit
7	Exit only, no access	No restriction
8	Access only, no exit	No access or exit
9	No exit to M6 *(southbound)*	No access from M6 *(northbound)*
15	Exit only to M53	Access only from M53
16	No access or exit	No restriction

M57 Liverpool Outer Ring Road

Junction	Northwestbound	Southeastbound
3	Access only, no exit	Exit only, no access
5	Access only from A580 *(westbound)*	Exit only, no access

M60 Manchester Orbital

Junction	Clockwise	Anticlockwise
2	Access only, no exit	Exit only, no access
3	No access from M56	Access only from A34 *(northbound)*
4	Access only from A34 *(northbound)*. Exit only to M56	Access only from M56 *(eastbound)*. Exit only to A34 *(southbound)*
5	Access and exit only from and to A5103 *(northbound)*	Access and exit only from and to A5103 *(southbound)*
7	No direct access, use slip road to jct 8. Exit only to A56	Access only from A56. No exit, use jct 8
14	Access from A580 *(eastbound)*	Exit only to A580 *(westbound)*
16	Access only, no exit	Exit only, no access
20	Exit only, no access	Access only, no exit
22	No restriction	Exit only, no access
25	Exit only, no access	No restriction
26	No restriction	Exit only, no access
27	Access only, no exit	Exit only, no access

M61 Manchester - Preston

Junction	Northwestbound	Southeastbound
3	No access or exit	Exit only, no access
with M6 (jct 30)	Exit only to M6 *(northbound)*	Access only from M6 *(southbound)*

M62 Liverpool - Kingston upon Hull

Junction	Westbound	Eastbound
23	Access only, no exit	Exit only, no access
32A	No access to A1(M) *(southbound)*	No restriction

M65 Preston - Colne

Junction	Northeastbound	Southwestbound
9	Exit only, no access	Access only, no exit
11	Access only, no exit	Exit only, no access

M66 Bury

Junction	Northbound	Southbound
with A56	Exit only to A56 *(northbound)*	Access only from A56 *(southbound)*
1	Exit only, no access	Access only, no exit

M67 Hyde Bypass

Junction	Westbound	Eastbound
1A	Access only, no exit	Exit only, no access
2	Exit only, no access	Access only, no exit

M69 Coventry - Leicester

Junction	Northbound	Southbound
2	Access only, no exit	Exit only, no access

M73 East of Glasgow

Junction	Northbound	Southbound
1	No exit to A74 & A721	No exit to A74 & A721
2	No access from or exit to A89. No access from *(eastbound)*	No access from or exit to A89. No exit to M8 *(westbound)*

M74 and A74(M) Glasgow - Gretna

Junction	Northbound	Southbound
3	Exit only, no access	Access only, no exit
3A	Access only, no exit	Exit only, no access
4	No access from A74 & A721	Access only, no exit to A74 & A721
7	Access only, no exit	Exit only, no access
9	No access or exit	Exit only, no access
10	No restriction	Access only, no exit
11	Access only, no exit	Exit only, no access
12	Exit only, no access	Access only, no exit
18	Exit only, no access	Access only, no exit

M77 Glasgow - Kilmarnock

Junction	Northbound	Southbound
with M8 (jct 22)	No exit to M8 *(westbound)*	No access from M8 *(eastbound)*
4	Access only, no exit	Exit only, no access
6	Access only, no exit	Exit only, no access
7	Access only, no exit	No restriction
8	Exit only, no access	Exit only, no access

M80 Glasgow - Stirling

Junction	Northbound	Southbound
4A	Exit only, no access	Access only, no exit
6A	Access only, no exit	Exit only, no access
8	Exit only to M876 *(northeastbound)*	Access only from M876 *(southwestbound)*

M90 Edinburgh - Perth

Junction	Northbound	Southbound
1	No exit, access only	Exit only to A90 *(eastbound)*
2A	Exit only to A92 *(eastbound)*	Access only from A92 *(westbound)*
7	Access only, no exit	Exit only, no access
8	Exit only, no access	Access only, no exit
10	No access from A912. No exit to A912 *(southbound)*	No access from A912 *(northbound)* No exit to A912

M180 Doncaster - Grimsby

Junction	Westbound	Eastbound
1	Access only, no exit	Exit only, no access

M606 Bradford Spur

Junction	Northbound	Southbound
2	Exit only, no access	No restriction

M621 Leeds - M1

Junction	Clockwise	Anticlockwise
2A	Access only, no exit	Exit only, no access
4	No exit or access	No restriction
5	Access only, no exit	Exit only, no access
6	Exit only, no access	Access only, no exit
with M1 (jct 43)	Exit only to M1 *(southbound)*	Access only from M1 *(northbound)*

M876 Bonnybridge - Kincardine Bridge

Junction	Northeastbound	Southwestbound
with M80 (jct 5)	Access only from M80 *(northeastbound)*	Exit only to M80 *(southwestbound)*
with M9 (jct 8)	Exit only to M9 *(eastbound)*	Access only from M9 *(westbound)*

A1(M) South Mimms - Baldock

Junction	Northbound	Southbound
2	Exit only, no access	Access only, no exit
3	No restriction	Exit only, no access
5	Access only, no exit	No access or exit

A1(M) Pontefract - Bedale

Junction	Northbound	Southbound
41	No access to M62 *(eastbound)*	No restriction
43	Access only from M1 *(northbound)*	Exit only to M1 *(southbound)*

A1(M) Scotch Corner - Newcastle upon Tyne

Junction	Northbound	Southbound
57	Exit only to A66(M) *(eastbound)*	Access only from A66(M) *(westbound)*
65	No access Exit only to A194(M) & A1 *(northbound)*	No exit Access only from A194(M) & A1 *(southbound)*

A3(M) Horndean - Havant

Junction	Northbound	Southbound
1	Access only from A3	Exit only to A3
4	Exit only, no access	Access only, no exit

A38(M) Birmingham, Victoria Road (Park Circus)

Junction	Northbound	Southbound
with B4132	No exit	No access

A48(M) Cardiff Spur

Junction	Westbound	Eastbound
29	Access only from M4 *(westbound)*	Exit only to M4 *(eastbound)*
29A	Exit only to A48 *(westbound)*	Access only from A48 *(eastbound)*

A57(M) Manchester, Brook Street (A34)

Junction	Westbound	Eastbound
with A34	No exit	No access

A58(M) Leeds, Park Lane and Westgate

Junction	Northbound	Southbound
with A58	No restriction	No access

A64(M) Leeds, Clay Pit Lane (A58)

Junction	Westbound	Eastbound
with A58	No exit (to Clay Pit Lane)	No access (from Clay Pit Lane)

A66(M) Darlington Spur

Junction	Westbound	Eastbound
with A1(M) (jct 57)	Exit only to A1(M) *(southbound)*	Access only from A1(M) *(northbound)*

A74(M) Gretna - Abington

Junction	Northbound	Southbound
18	Exit only, no access	Access only, no exit

A194(M) Newcastle upon Tyne

Junction	Northbound	Southbound
with A1(M) (jct 65)	Access only from A1(M) *(northbound)*	Exit only to A1(M) *(southbound)*

A12 M25 - Ipswich

Junction	Northeastbound	Southwestbound
13	Access only, no exit	No restriction
14	Exit only, no access	Access only, no exit
20A	Exit only, no access	Access only, no exit
20B	Access only, no exit	Exit only, no access
21	No restriction	Access only, no exit
23	Exit only, no access	Access only, no exit
24	Access only, no exit	Exit only, no access
27	Exit only, no access	Access only, no exit
Dedham & Stratford St Mary (unnumbered)	Exit only	Access only

A14 M1 - Felixstowe

Junction	Westbound	Eastbound
with M1/M6 (jct19)	Exit only to M6 and M1 *(northbound)*	Access only from M6 and M1 *(southbound)*
4	Exit only, no access	Access only, no exit
21	Access only, no exit	Exit only, no access
22	Exit only, no access	Access only from A1 *(southbound)*
23	Access only, no exit	Exit only, no access
26	No restriction	Access only, no exit
34	Access only, no exit	Exit only, no access
36	Exit only to A11, access only from A1303	Access only from A11
38	Access only from A11	Exit only to A11
39	Exit only, no access	Access only, no exit
61	Access only, no exit	Exit only, no access

A55 Holyhead - Chester

Junction	Westbound	Eastbound
8A	Exit only, no access	Access only, no exit
23A	Access only, no exit	Exit only, no access
24A	Exit only, no access	No access or exit
27A	No restriction	No access or exit
33A	Exit only, no access	No access or exit
33B	Exit only, no access	Access only, no exit
36A	Exit only to A5104	Access only from A5104

Refer also to atlas pages 32–33. In October 2021 the Ultra Low Emission Zone is due to be extended. For further information visit **tfl.gov.uk/ULEZ**

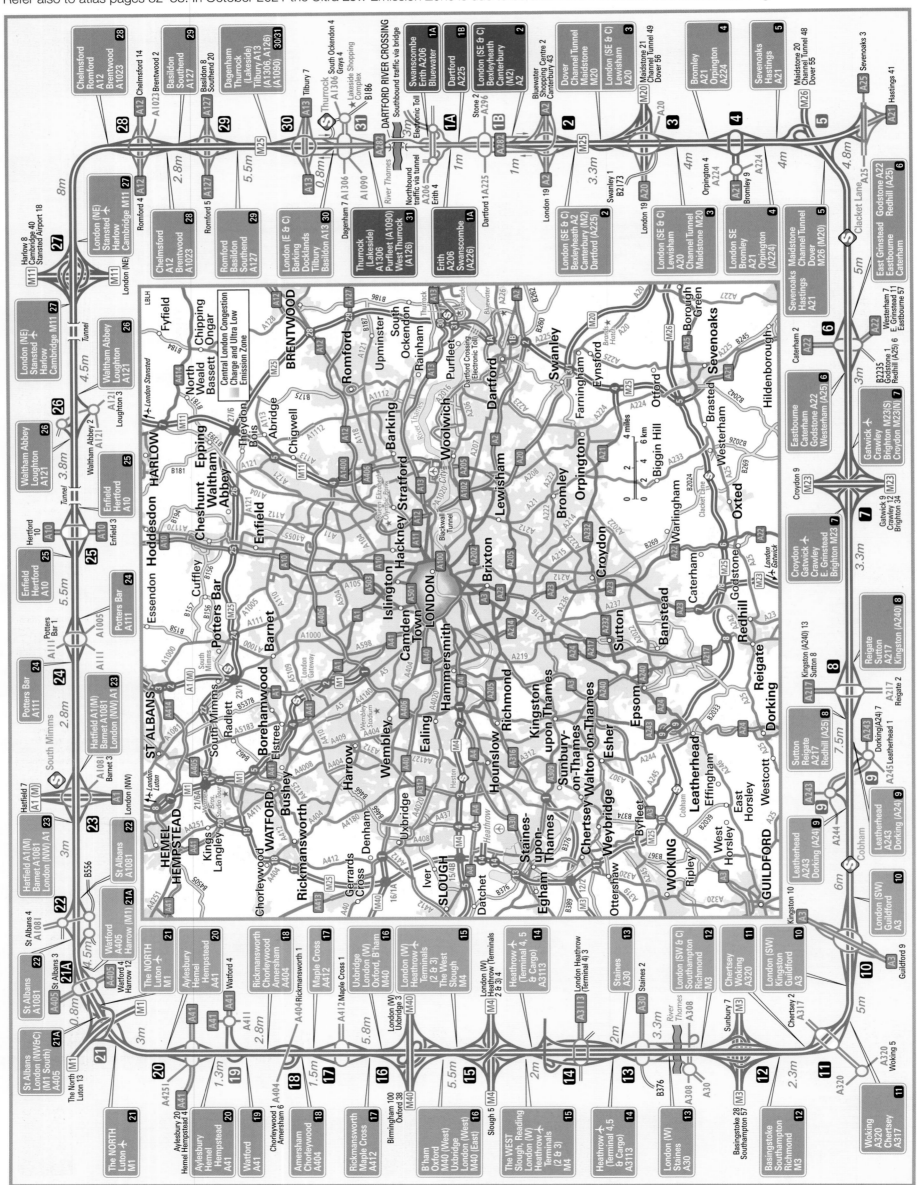

Refer also to atlas pages 53, 64–65

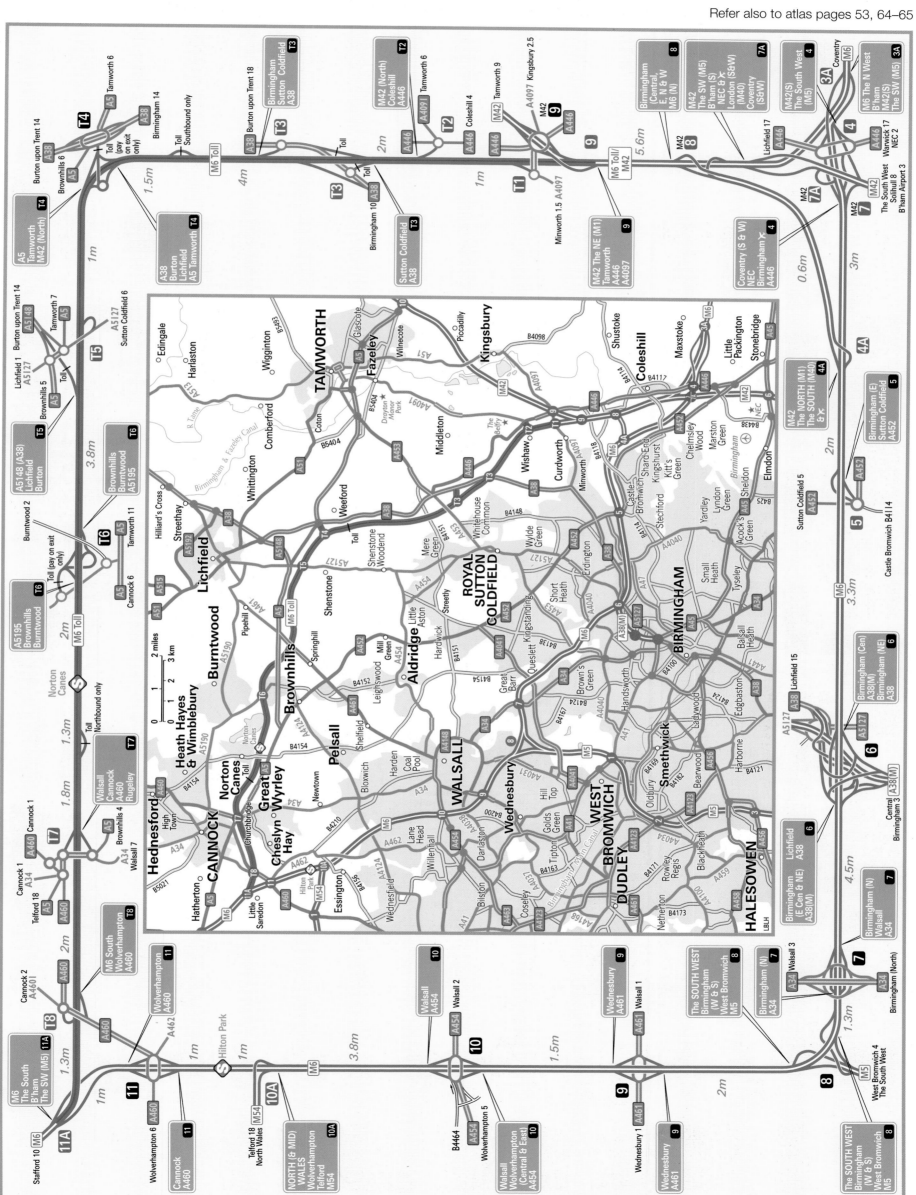

Smart motorways

Since Britain's first motorway (the Preston Bypass) opened in 1958, motorways have changed significantly. A vast increase in car journeys over the last 62 years has meant that motorways quickly filled to capacity. To combat this, the recent development of **smart motorways** uses technology to monitor and actively manage traffic flow and congestion.

How they work

Smart motorways utilise various active traffic management methods, monitored through a regional traffic control centre:

- Traffic flow is monitored using CCTV
- Speed limits are changed to smooth traffic flow and reduce stop-start driving
- Capacity of the motorway can be increased by either temporarily or permanently opening the hard shoulder to traffic
- Warning signs and messages alert drivers to hazards and traffic jams ahead
- Lanes can be closed in the case of an accident or emergency by displaying a red X sign

- Emergency refuge areas are located regularly along the motorway where there is no hard shoulder available

The map shows the main motorway network with the three different types of smart motorway in operation or planned to open over the next five years:

Controlled motorway — Variable speed limits without hard shoulder (the hard shoulder is used in emergencies only)

Hard shoulder running — Variable speed limits with part-time hard shoulder (the hard shoulder is open to traffic at busy times when signs permit)

All lane running — Variable speed limits with hard shoulder as permanent running lane (there is no hard shoulder); this is standard for all new motorway schemes since 2013

Standard motorway

Quick tips

- Never drive in a lane closed by a red X
- Keep to the speed limit shown on the gantries
- A solid white line indicates the hard shoulder – do not drive in it unless directed or in the case of an emergency
- A broken white line indicates a normal running lane
- Exit the smart motorway where possible if your vehicle is in difficulty. In an emergency, move onto the hard shoulder where there is one, or the nearest emergency refuge area
- Put on your hazard lights if you break down

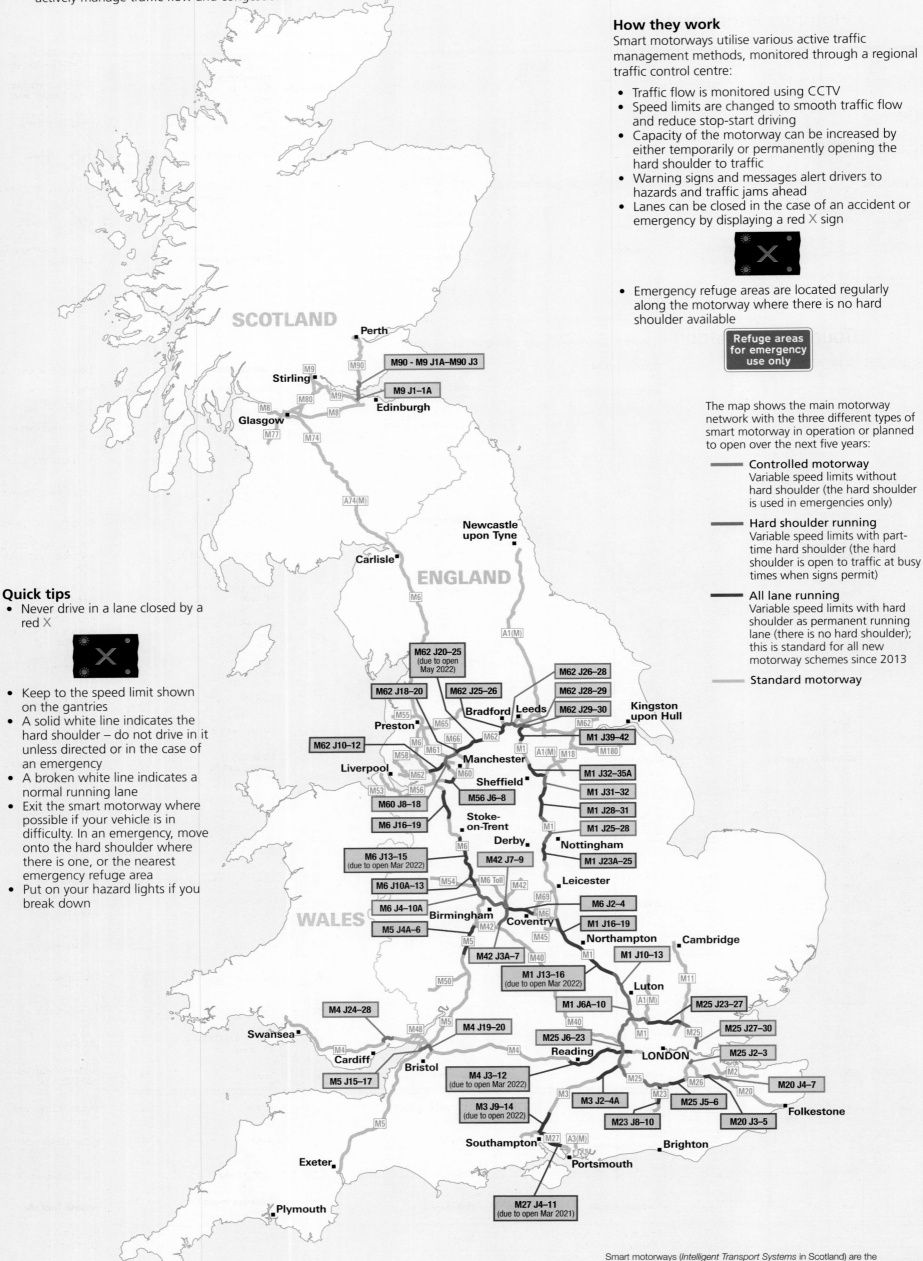

Smart motorways (*Intelligent Transport Systems* in Scotland) are the responsibility of Highways England, Transport Scotland and Transport for Wales

Motoring information

M4	Motorway with number	
Toll T4	Toll motorway with toll station	
6	Motorway junction with and without number	
5	Restricted motorway junctions	
Fleet S R Todhills	Motorway service area, rest area	
	Motorway and junction under construction	
A3	Primary route single/dual carriageway	
1	Primary route junction with and without number	
3	Restricted primary route junctions	
S	Primary route service area	
BATH	Primary route destination	
A1123	Other A road single/dual carriageway	
B2070	B road single/dual carriageway	
	Minor road more than 4 metres wide, less than 4 metres wide	
	Roundabout	
	Interchange/junction	

Narrow primary/other A/B road with passing places (Scotland)	
Road under construction	
Road tunnel	
Toll	Road toll, steep gradient (arrows point downhill)
5	Distance in miles between symbols
or	Vehicle ferry (all year, seasonal)
	Fast vehicle ferry or catamaran
or P P	Passenger ferry (all year, seasonal)

Railway line, in tunnel	
X	Railway station, tram stop, level crossing
	Preserved or tourist railway
✈	Airport (major/minor)
H	Heliport
F	International freight terminal
H	24-hour Accident & Emergency hospital
C	Crematorium

P•R	Park and Ride (at least 6 days per week)
	City, town, village or other built-up area
628 ▲	Height in metres
637 Lecht Summit	Mountain pass
	Snow gates (on main routes)
	National boundary
	County or administrative boundary

Touring information   To avoid disappointment, check opening times before visiting

Scenic route	Industrial interest	RSPB site	Cave or cavern	National Trust site
Tourist Information Centre	Aqueduct or viaduct	National Nature Reserve (England, Scotland, Wales)	Windmill, monument or memorial	National Trust for Scotland site
Tourist Information Centre (seasonal)	Vineyard	Local nature reserve	Beach (award winning)	English Heritage site
Visitor or heritage centre	Brewery or distillery	Wildlife Trust reserve	Lighthouse	Historic Scotland site
Picnic site	Garden	Forest drive	Golf course	Cadw (Welsh heritage) site
Caravan site (AA inspected)	Arboretum	National trail	Football stadium	Other place of interest
Camping site (AA inspected)	Country park	Viewpoint	County cricket ground	Boxed symbols indicate attractions within urban area
Caravan & camping site (AA inspected)	Showground	Waterfall	Rugby Union national stadium	World Heritage Site (UNESCO)
Abbey, cathedral or priory	Theme park	Hill-fort	International athletics stadium	National Park and National Scenic Area (Scotland)
Ruined abbey, cathedral or priory	Farm or animal centre	Roman antiquity	Horse racing, show jumping	Forest Park
Castle	Zoological or wildlife collection	Prehistoric monument	Motor-racing circuit	Sandy beach
Historic house or building	Bird collection	Battle site with year 1066	Air show venue	Heritage coast
Museum or art gallery	Aquarium	Preserved or tourist railway	Ski slope (natural, artificial)	Major shopping centre

Town plans

2 Motorway and junction	Railway station	Toilet, with facilities for the less able	Tourist Information Centre	Abbey, chapel, church
4 Primary road single/dual carriageway and numbered junction	Tramway	Building of interest	Visitor or heritage centre	Synagogue
37 A road single/dual carriageway and numbered junction	London Underground station	Ruined building	Post Office	Mosque
B road single/dual carriageway	London Overground station	City wall	Public library	Golf course
Local road single/dual carriageway	Rail interchange	Cliff lift	Shopping centre	Racecourse
Other road single/dual carriageway, minor road	Docklands Light Railway (DLR) station	Escarpment	Shopmobility	Nature reserve
One-way, gated/closed road	Light rapid transit system station	River/canal, lake	Theatre or performing arts centre	Aquarium
Restricted access road	Airport, heliport	Lock, weir	Cinema	World Heritage Site (UNESCO)
Pedestrian area	Railair terminal	Park/sports ground	Museum	English Heritage site
Footpath	P•R Park and Ride (at least 6 days per week)	Cemetery	Castle	Historic Scotland site
Road under construction	P P Car park, with electric charging point	Woodland	Castle mound	Cadw (Welsh heritage) site
Road tunnel	Bus/coach station	Built-up area	Monument, memorial, statue	National Trust site
Level crossing	H H Hospital, 24-hour Accident & Emergency hospital	Beach	Viewpoint	National Trust Scotland site

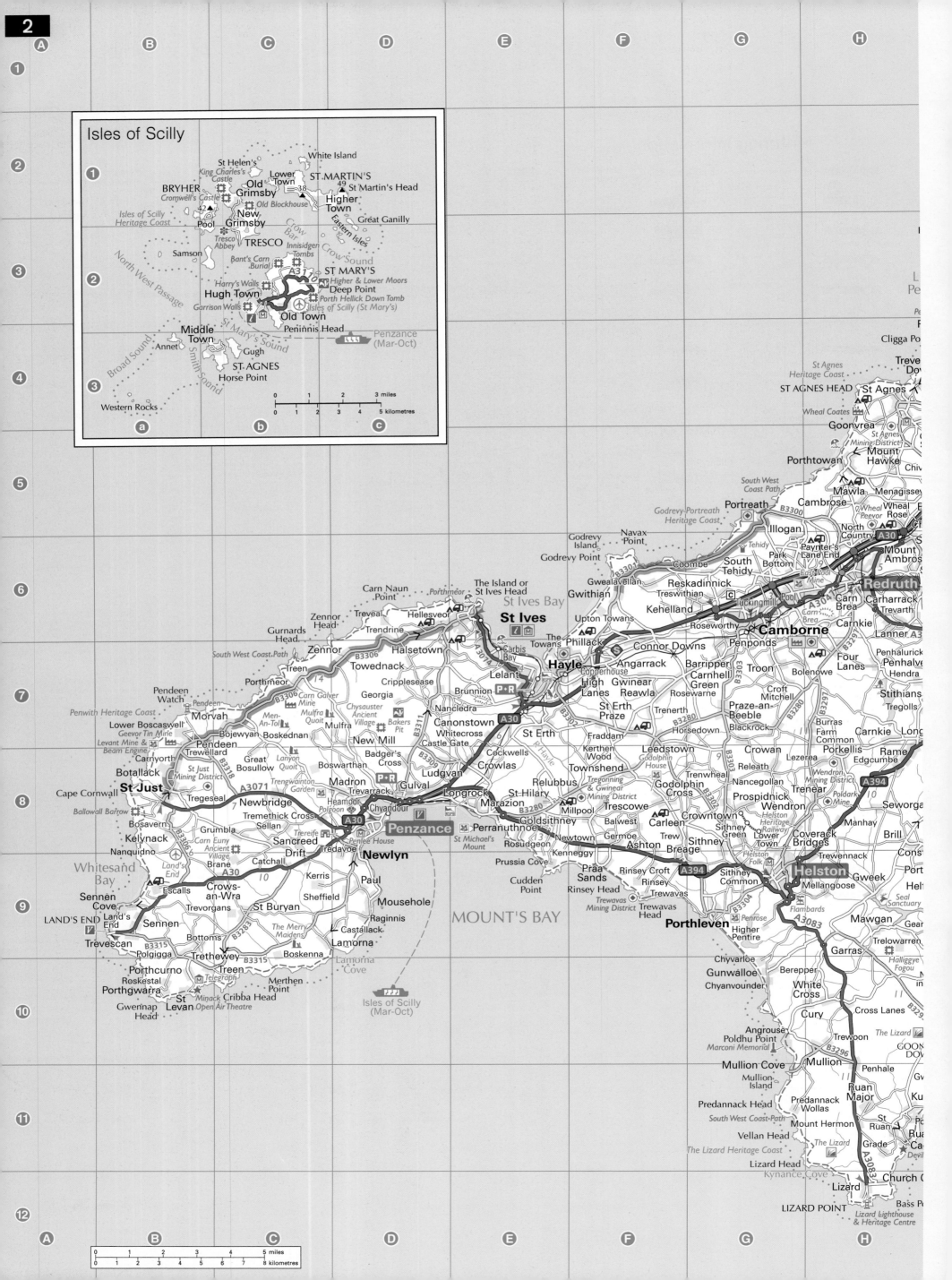

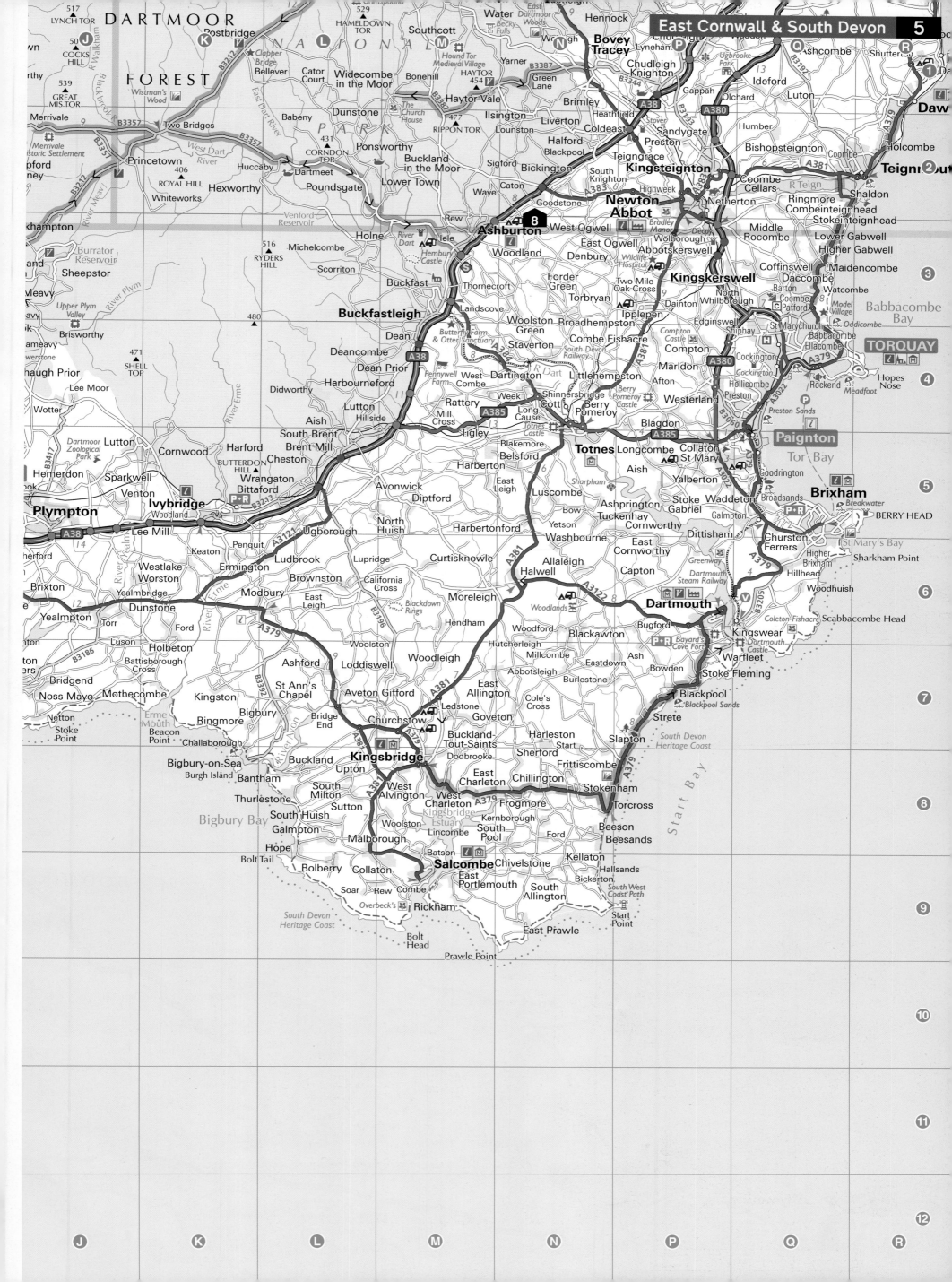

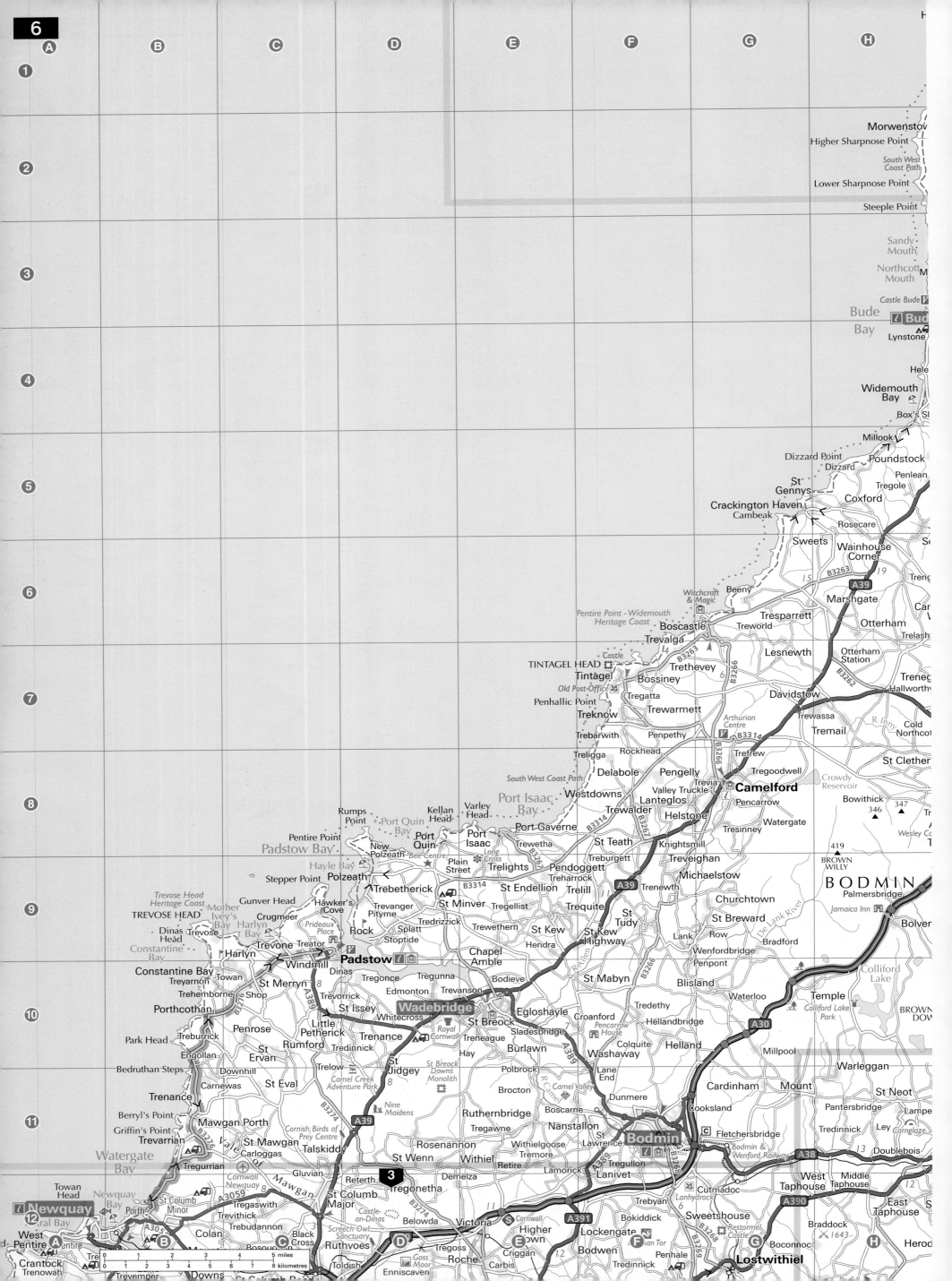

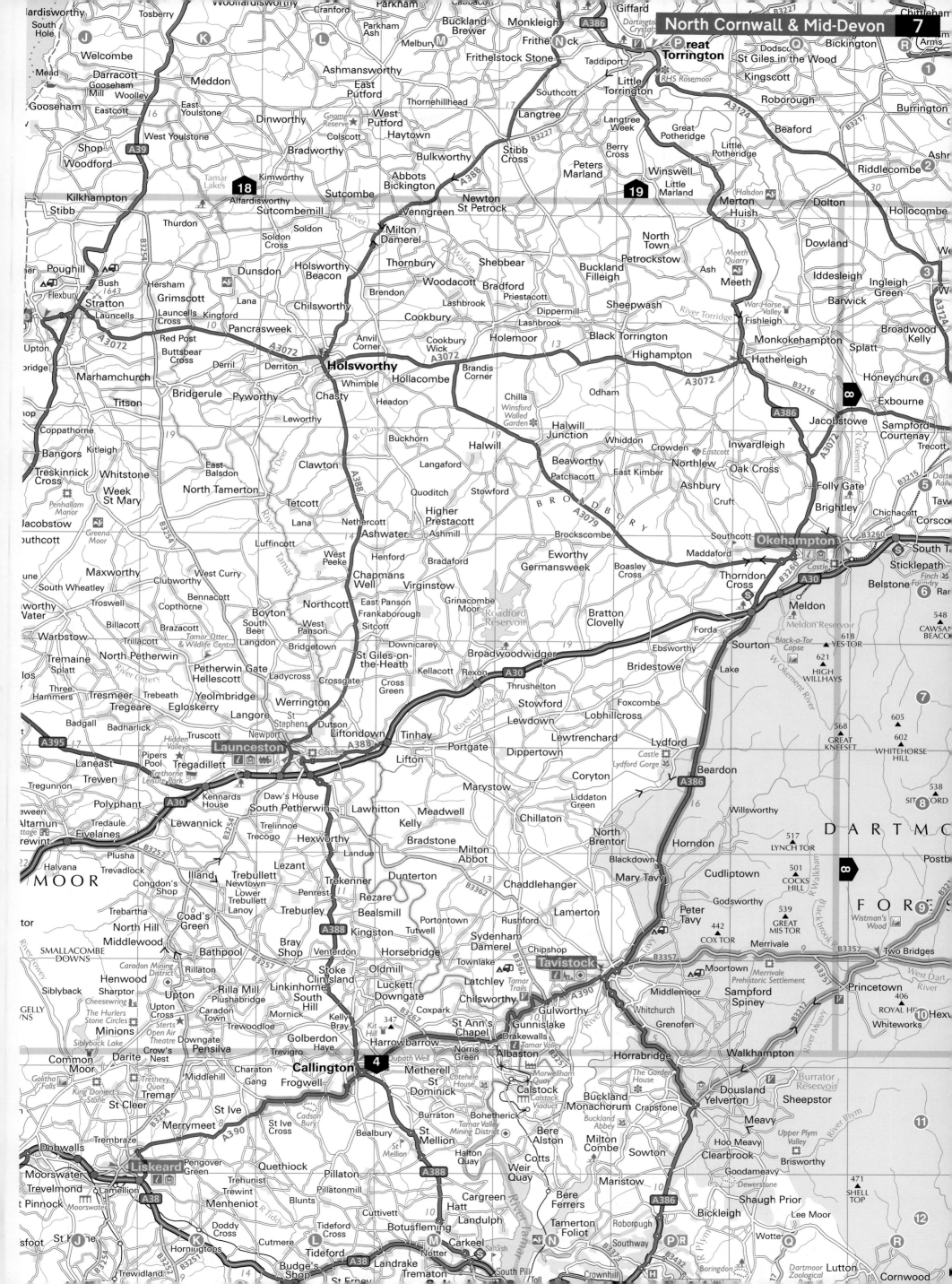

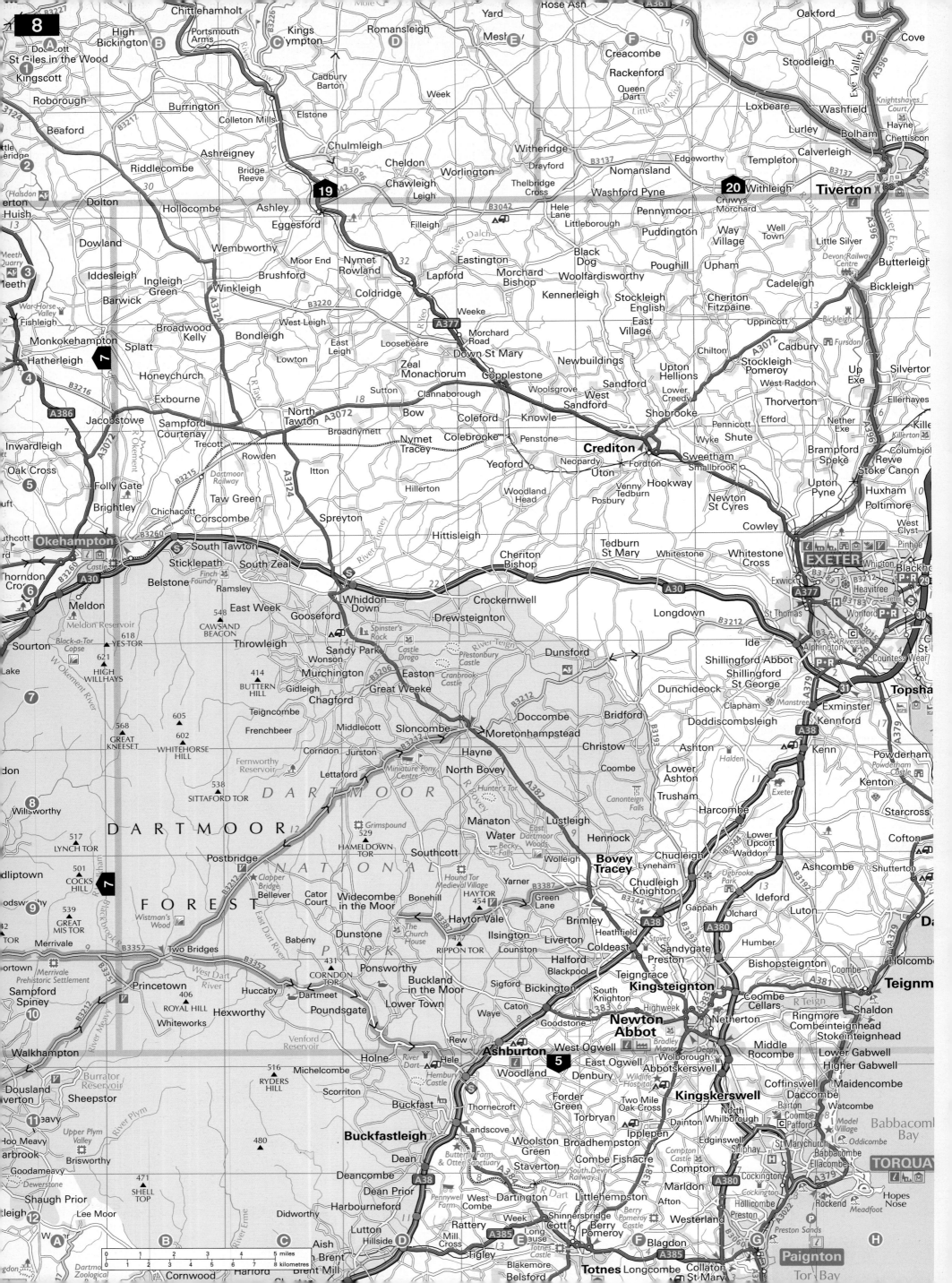

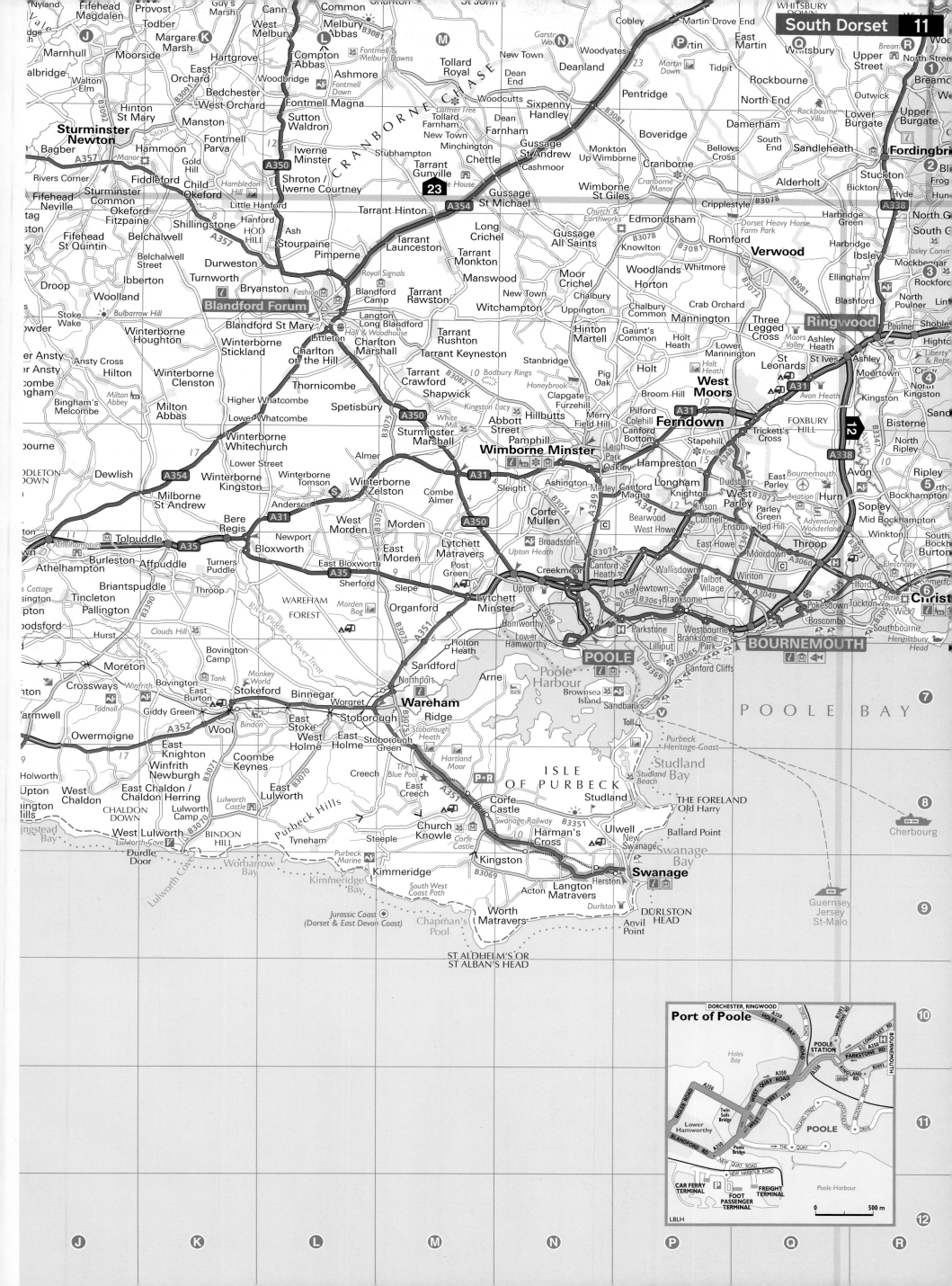

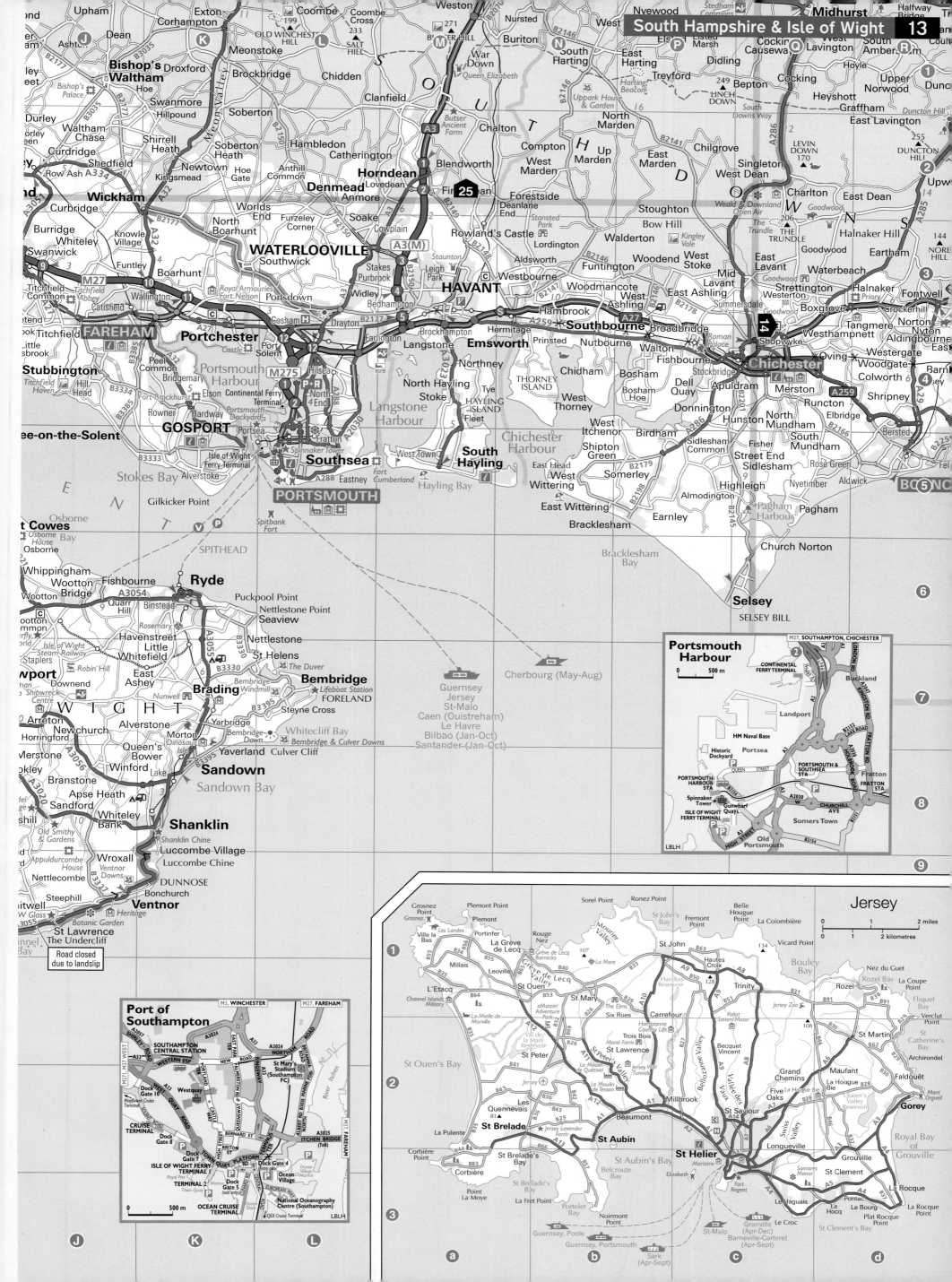

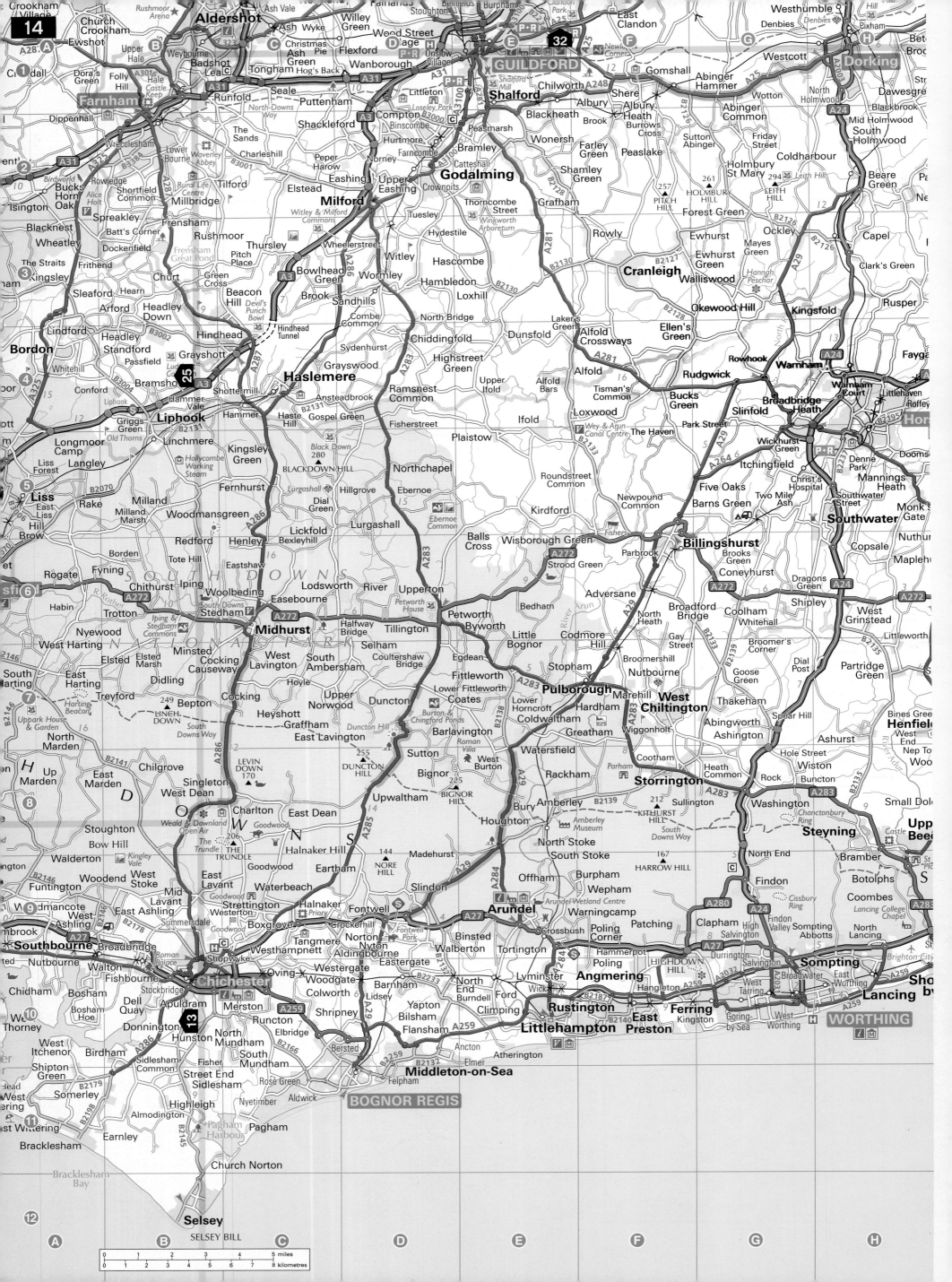

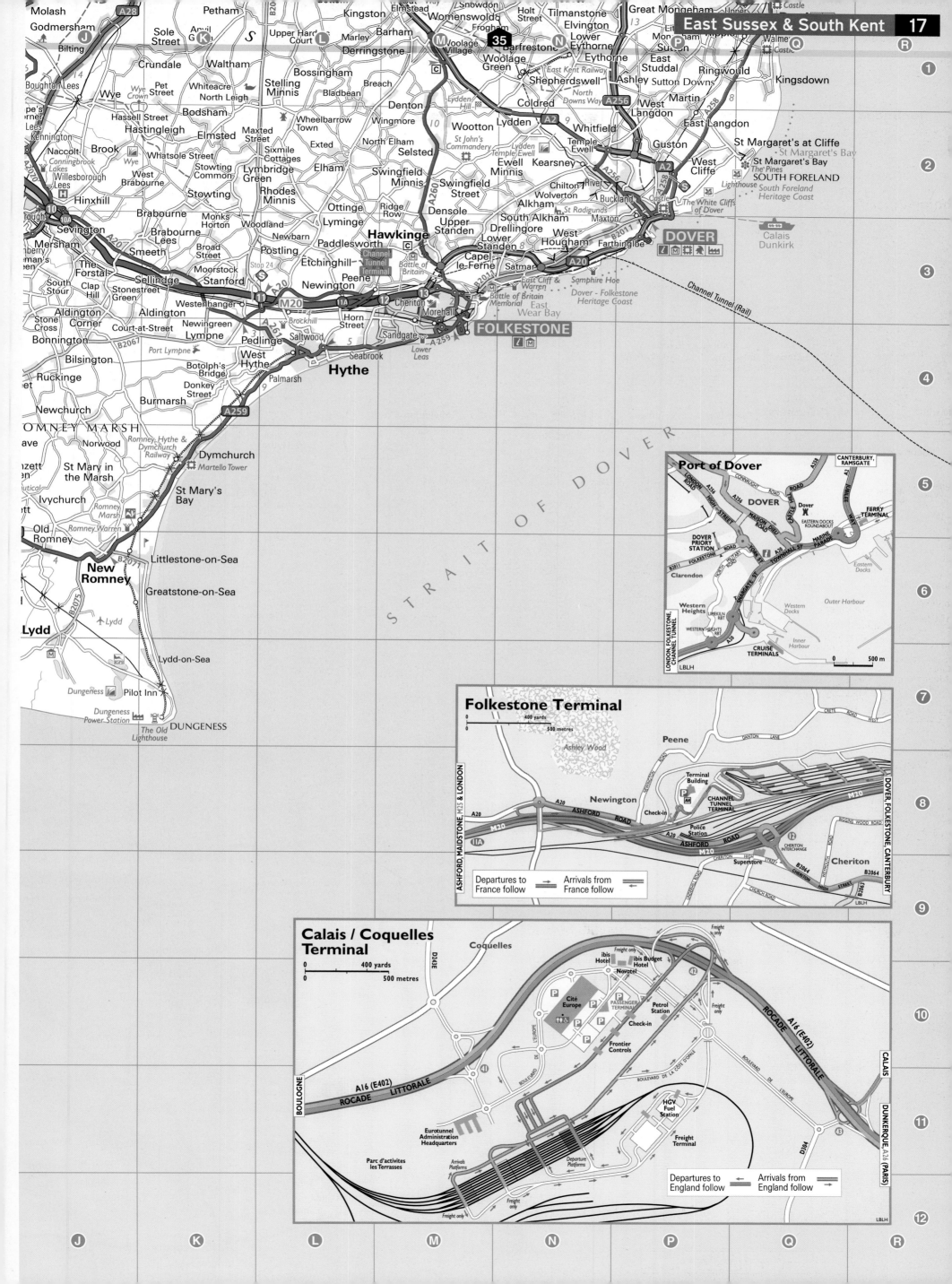

A · **B** · **C** · **D** · **E** · **F** · **G** · **H**

North West Point

Lundy Heritage Coast LUNDY

▲142

Marine Reserve
Shutter Point Surf Point

Ⓟ Bideford (Apr-Oct)
Ilfracombe (Apr-Oct)

Baggy Point Putsboro

Croyde Bay
Croyde Bay

Morte Point

Wool...

Mo...
Ba...

North Devon Heritage Coast

Lundy Ⓟ (Apr-Oct)

Northam Burrows

B A R N S T A P L E

O R

B I D E F O R D   B A Y

Westward Ho!

Shipload Bay
HARTLAND POINT
Titchberry Brownsham
Abbotsham
Damehole Point *Hartland Abbey & Gardens*
Ⓜ Stoke Velly Clovelly
Hartland Quay Hartland
Hartland Heritage Coast
Fairy Cross Ford
Buck's Mills Woodtown Yeo Vale
Speke's Mill Mouth Milford
Higher Clovelly Horns Cross Littleha...
Goldworthy Salt...
Docton Mill
Elmscott Philham Buck's Cross
Milky Way
Hardisworthy Edistone Woolfardisworthy Cabbacott
South Hole Tosberry Cranford Parkham Buckland Brewer Monk...
Parkham Ash Fri...
Mead Melbury Frithelstock St...
Welcombe Darracott Ashmansworthy
Gooseham Mill Woolley Meddon East Putford
Gooseham Eastcott East Youlstone Thornehillhead 17
Morwenstow 16 Dinworthy West Putford
Higher Sharpnose Point West Youlstone Colscott Haytown Lan...
Gnome Reserve ★
South West Coast Path Shop Bradworthy Bulkworthy Stibb Cross
Woodford Kimworthy Abbots Bickington
Lower Sharpnose Point Sutcombe Newton St Petrock
Tamar Lakes Alfardisworthy Sutcombemill Venngreen
Kilkhampton ■7 River Milton Damerel
Steeple Point Stibb Thurdon Soldon
Soldon Cross Thornbury Shebbear
Sandy Mouth Holsworthy Beacon Woodacott Bradford
Dunsdon Brendon Lashbrook Priesta...
Northcott Mouth Maer Poughill Bush Hersham Lana Chilsworthy Cookbury
1643 Grimscott
Ⓟ Stratton Launcells Kingford Anvil Corner
Castle Bude Flexbury Cross Pancrasweek Cookbury Wick Holemoo...
Bude Launcells 10 Cookbury La...
Bude Bay Lynstone Red Post Holsworthy
Upton Buttsbear Derril Derriton A3072
Helebridge Cross Hollacombe Brandis Corner
Widemouth Marhamchurch Bridgerule Pyworthy Whimble Chasty Chilla...
Bay

0 1 2 3 4 5 miles
0 1 2 3 4 5 6 7 8 kilometres

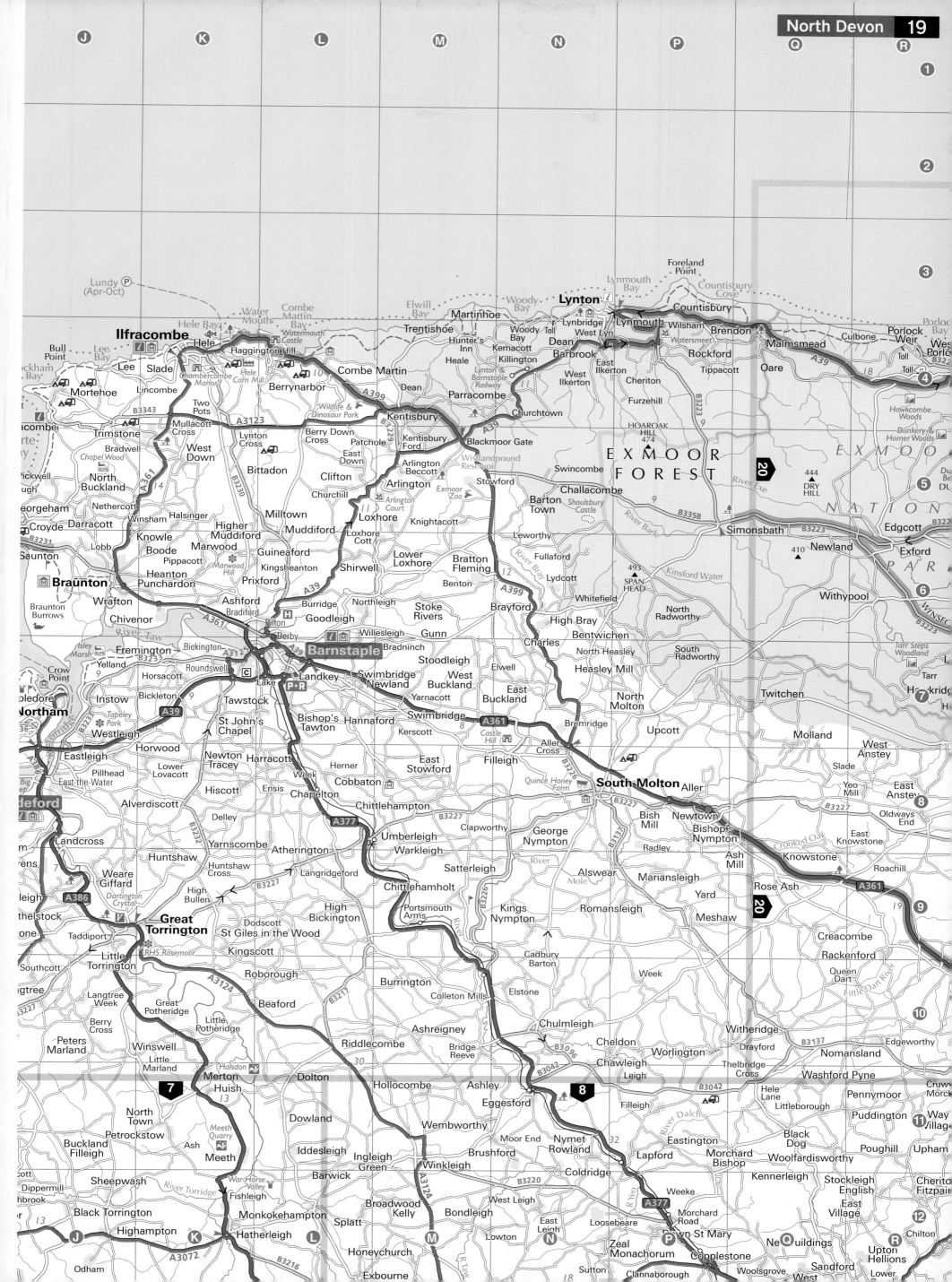

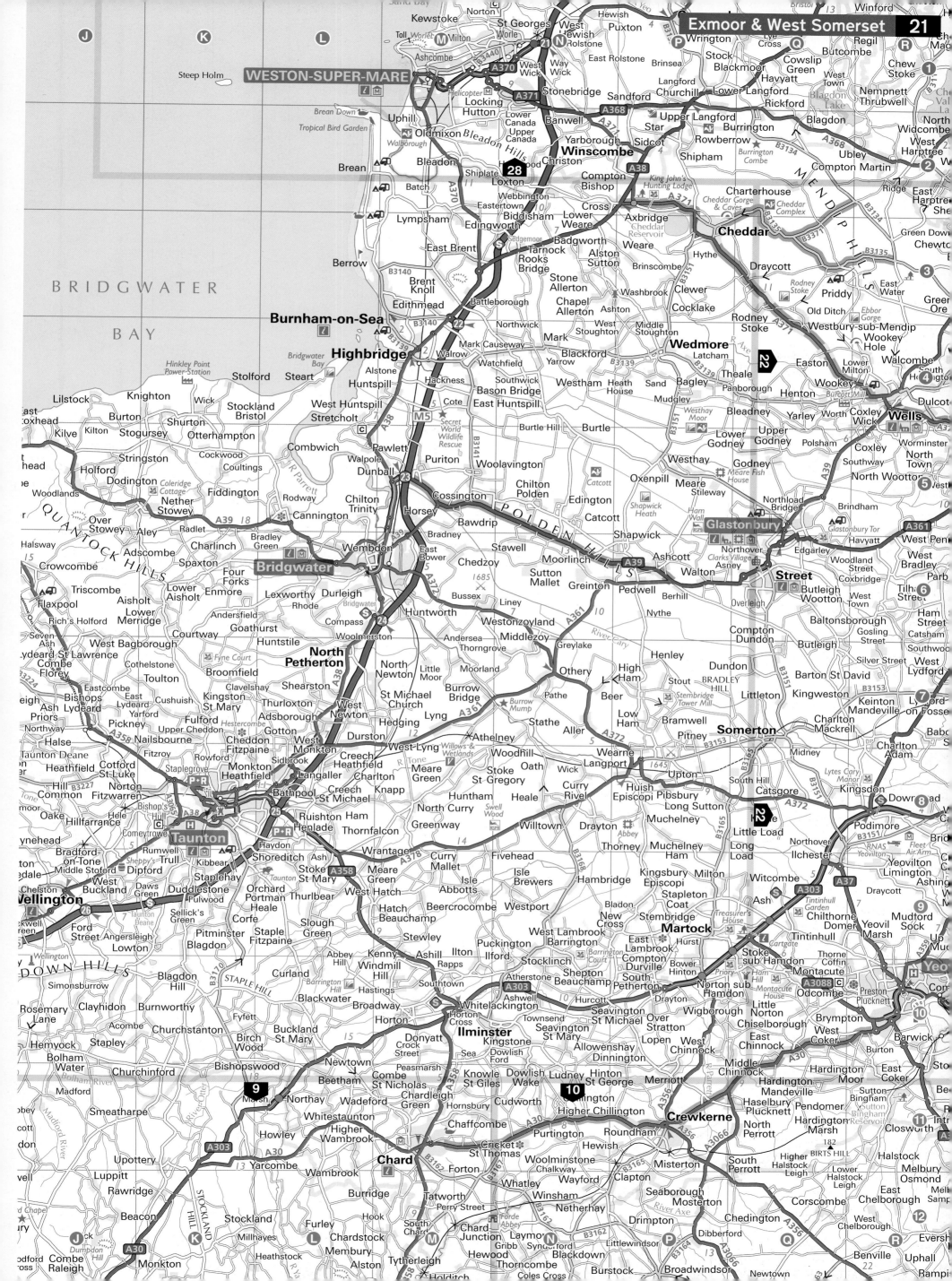

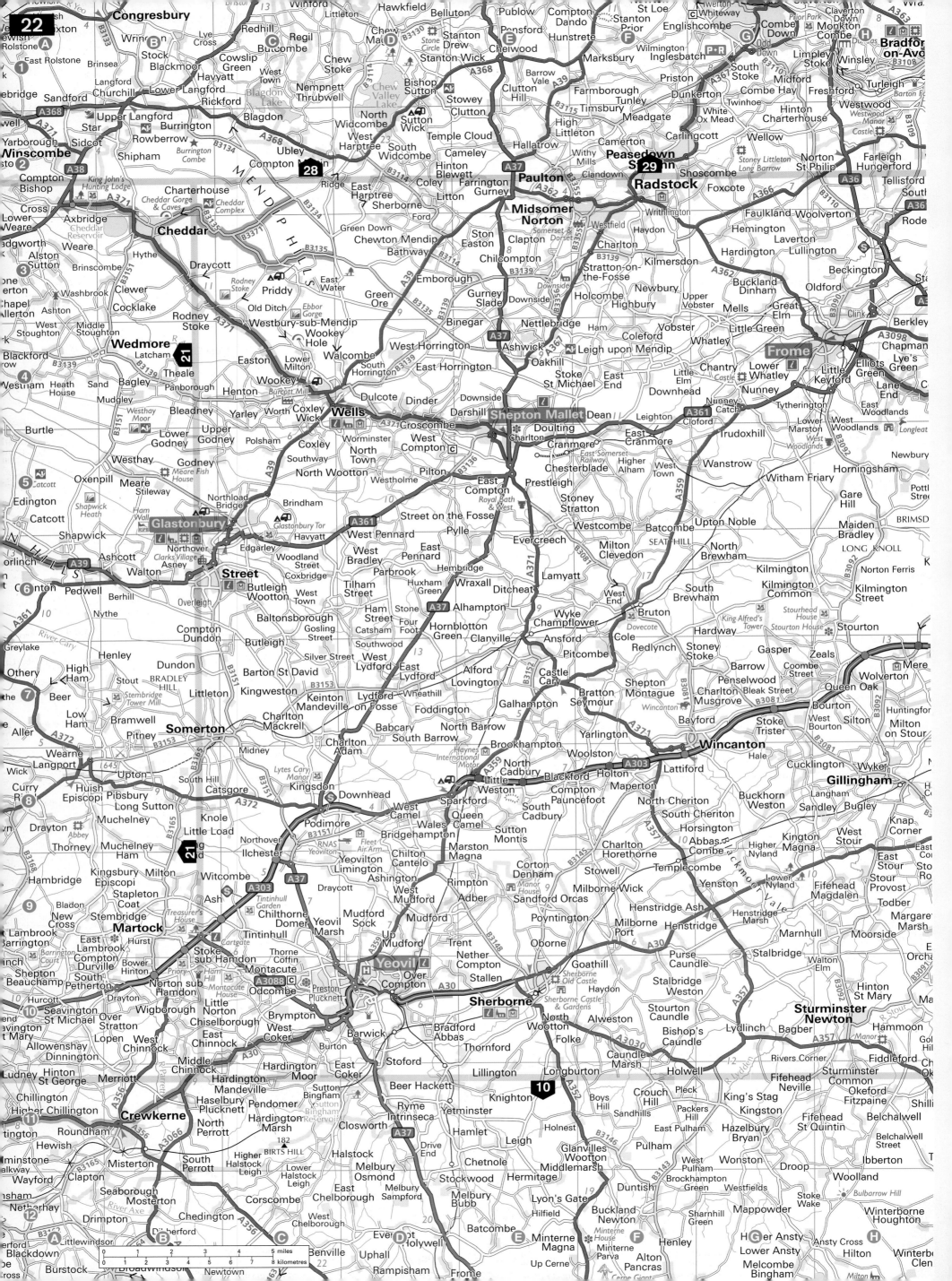

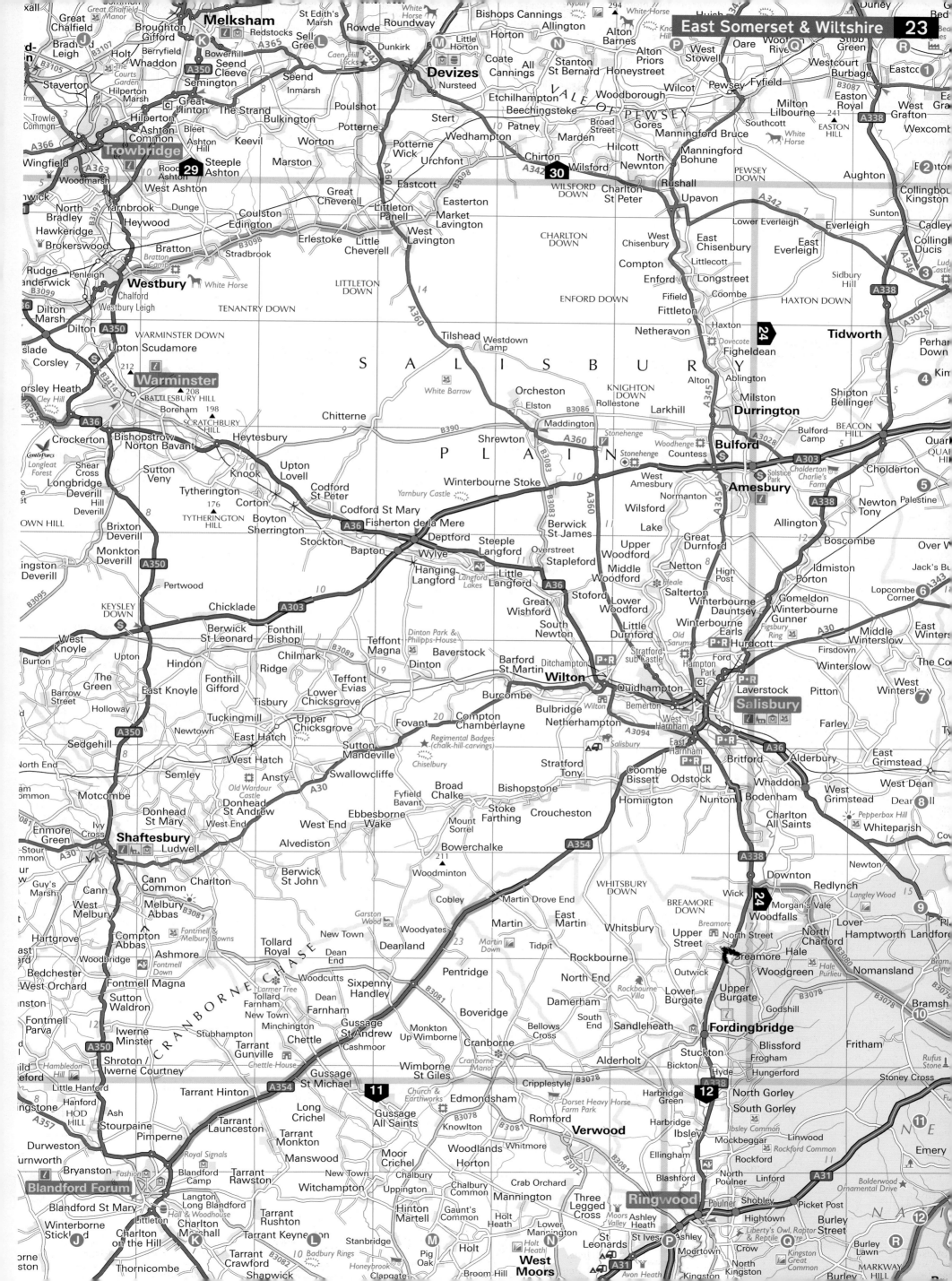

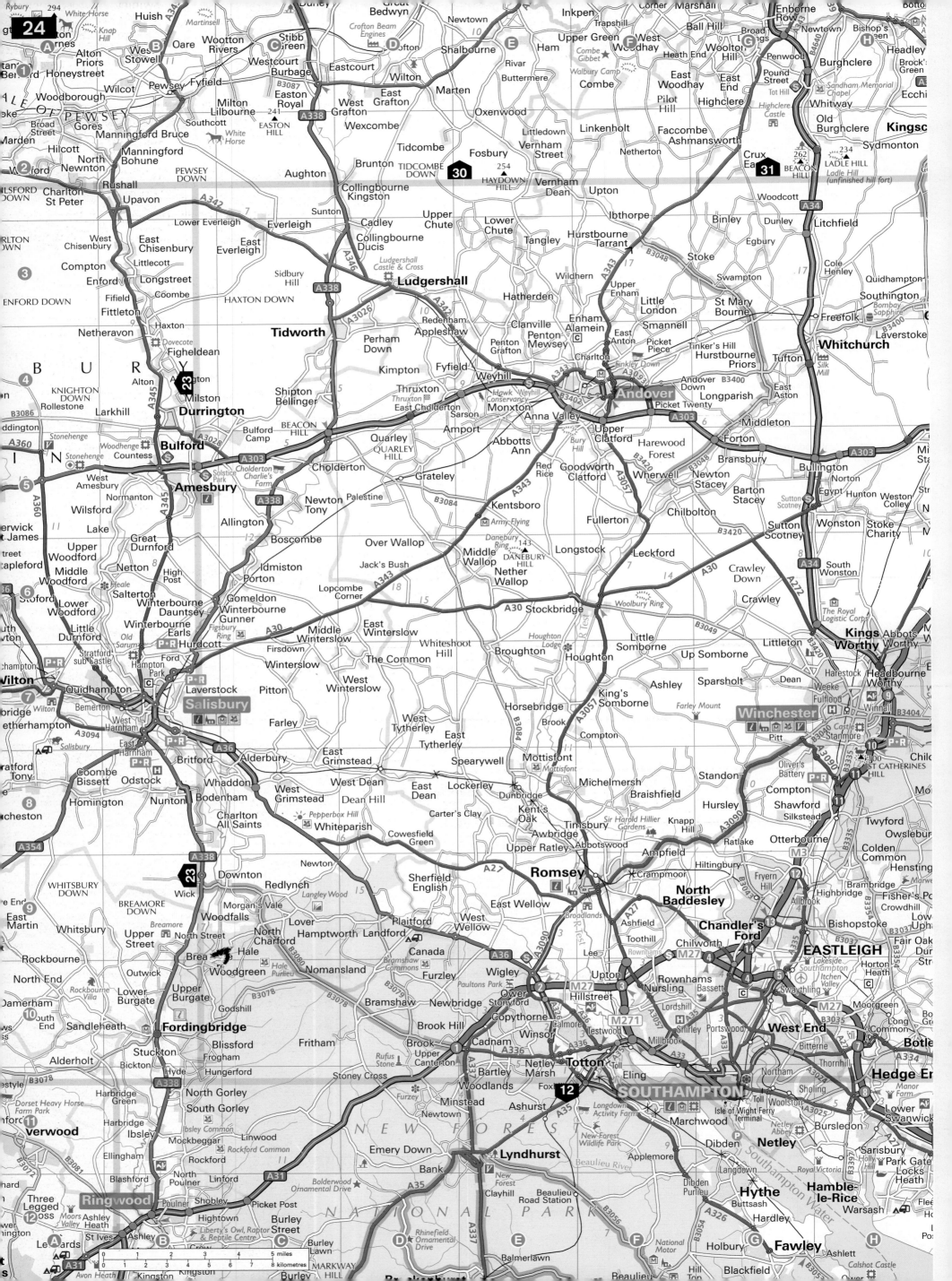

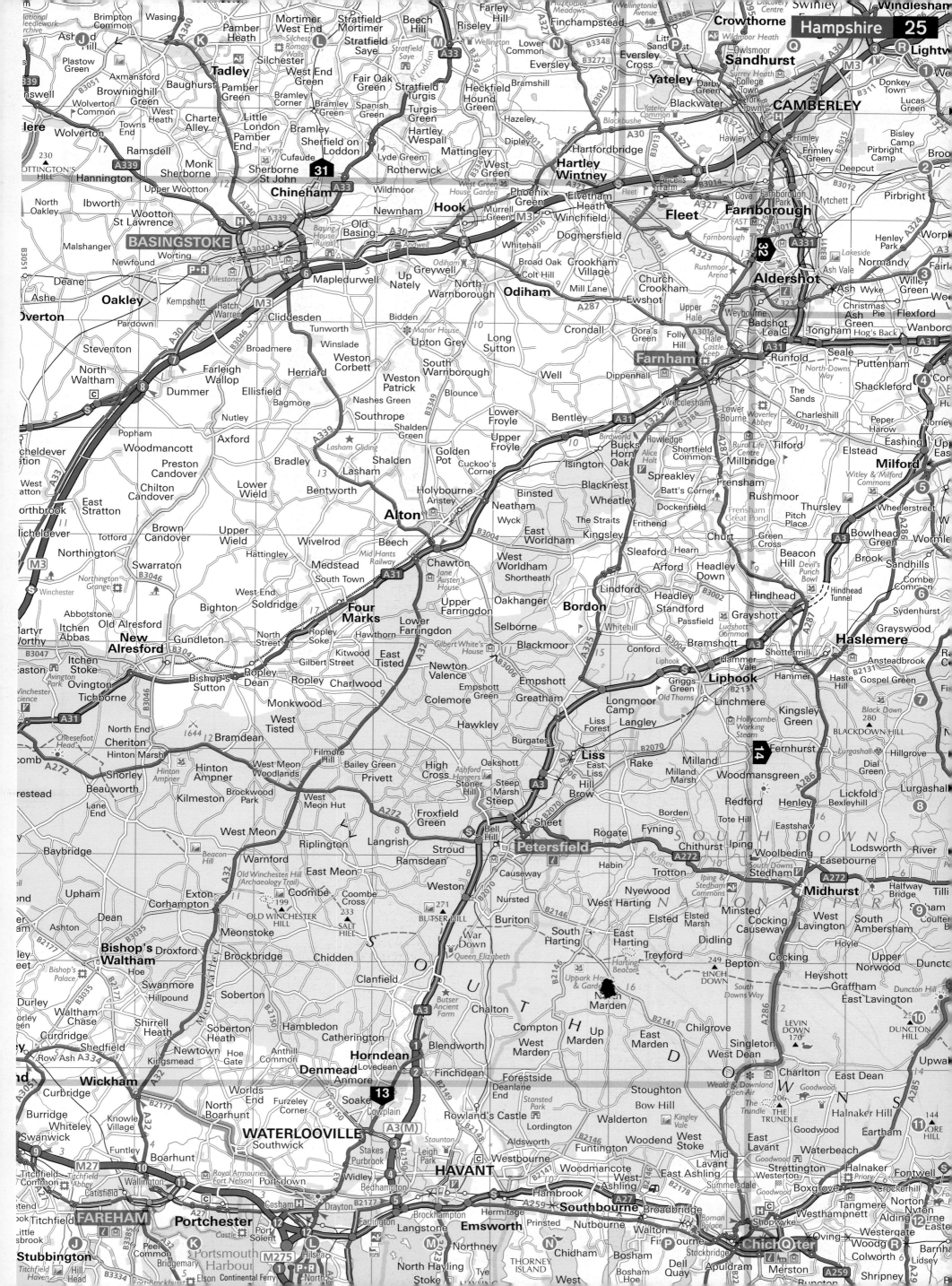

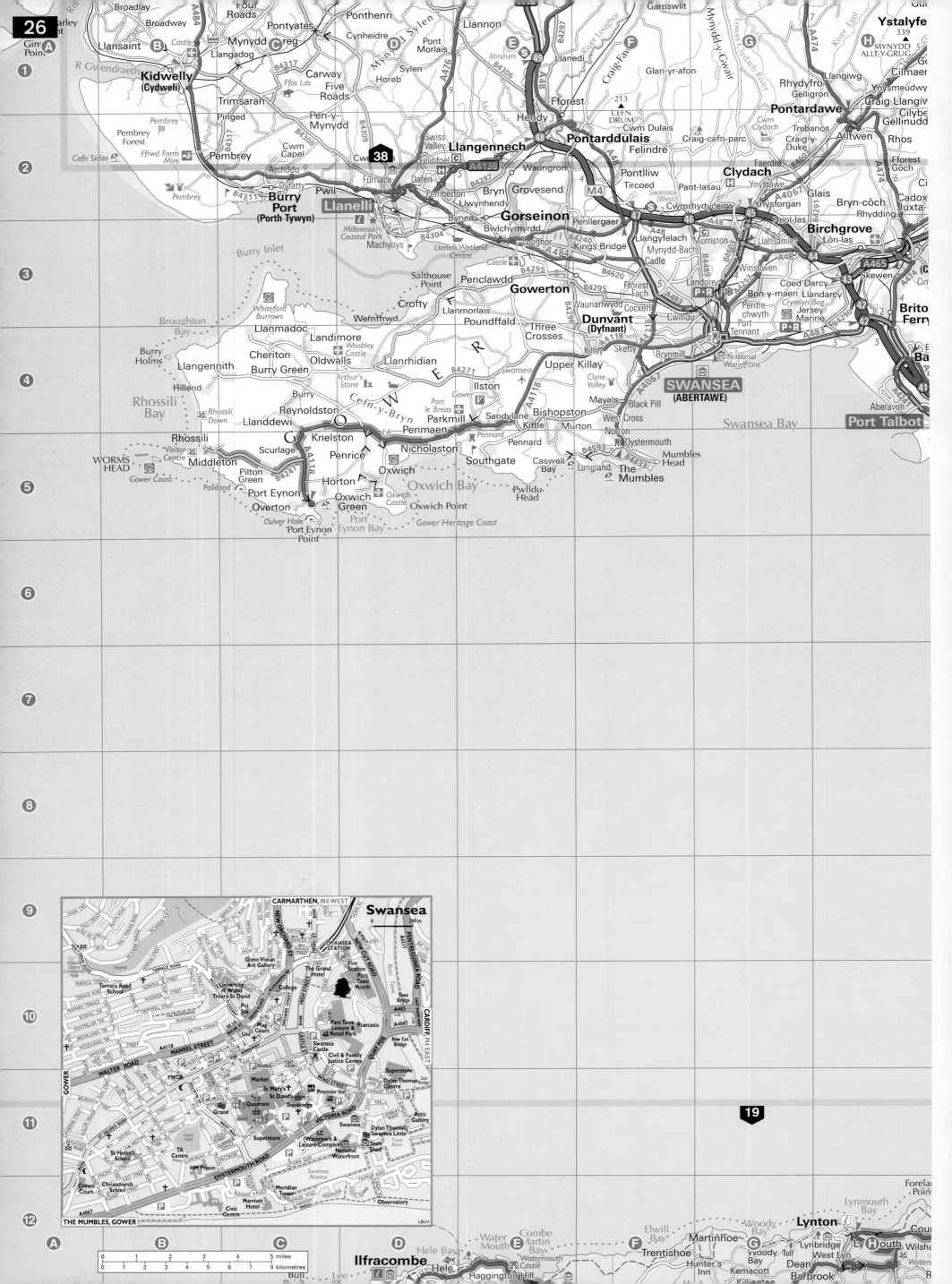

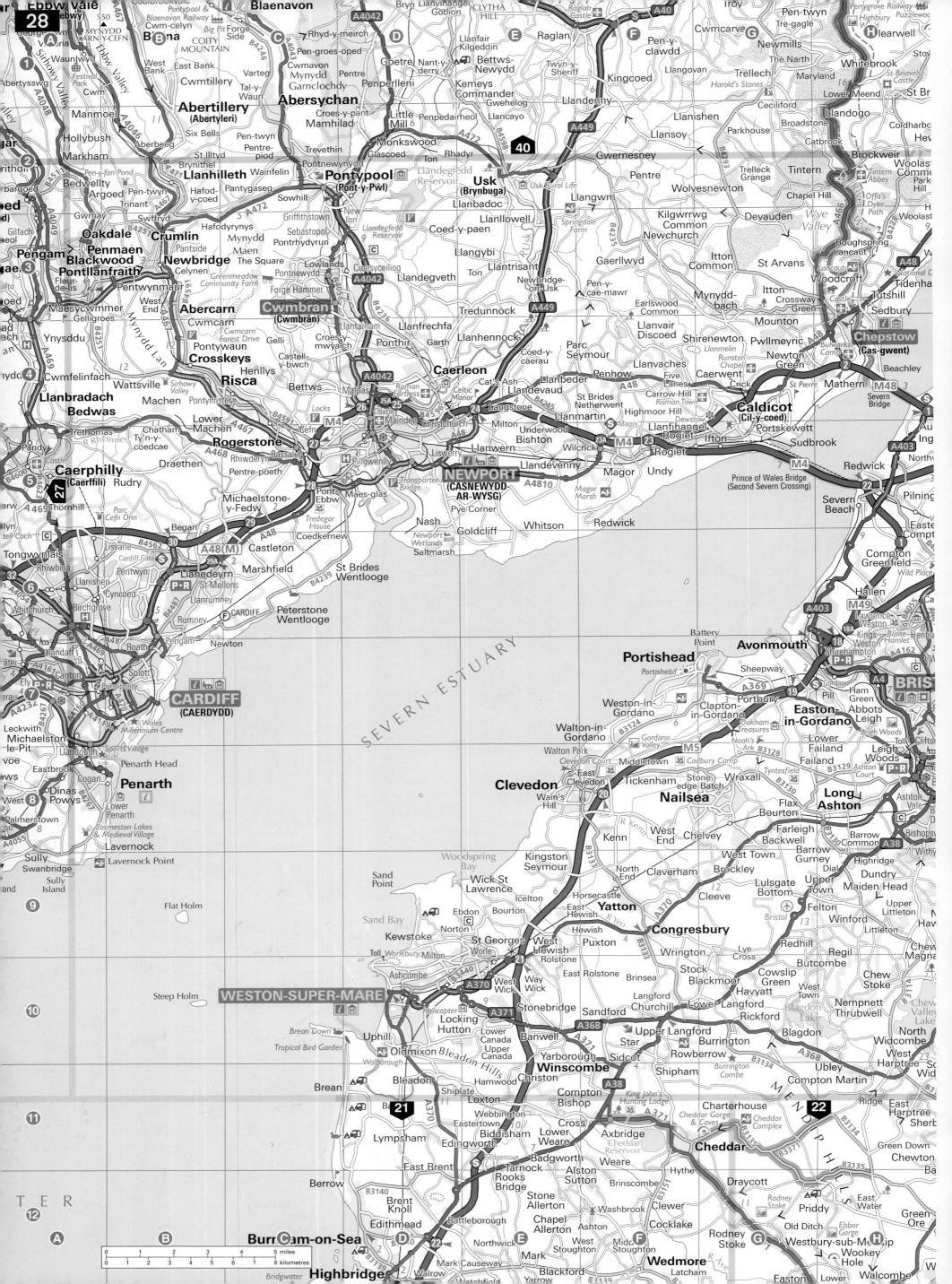

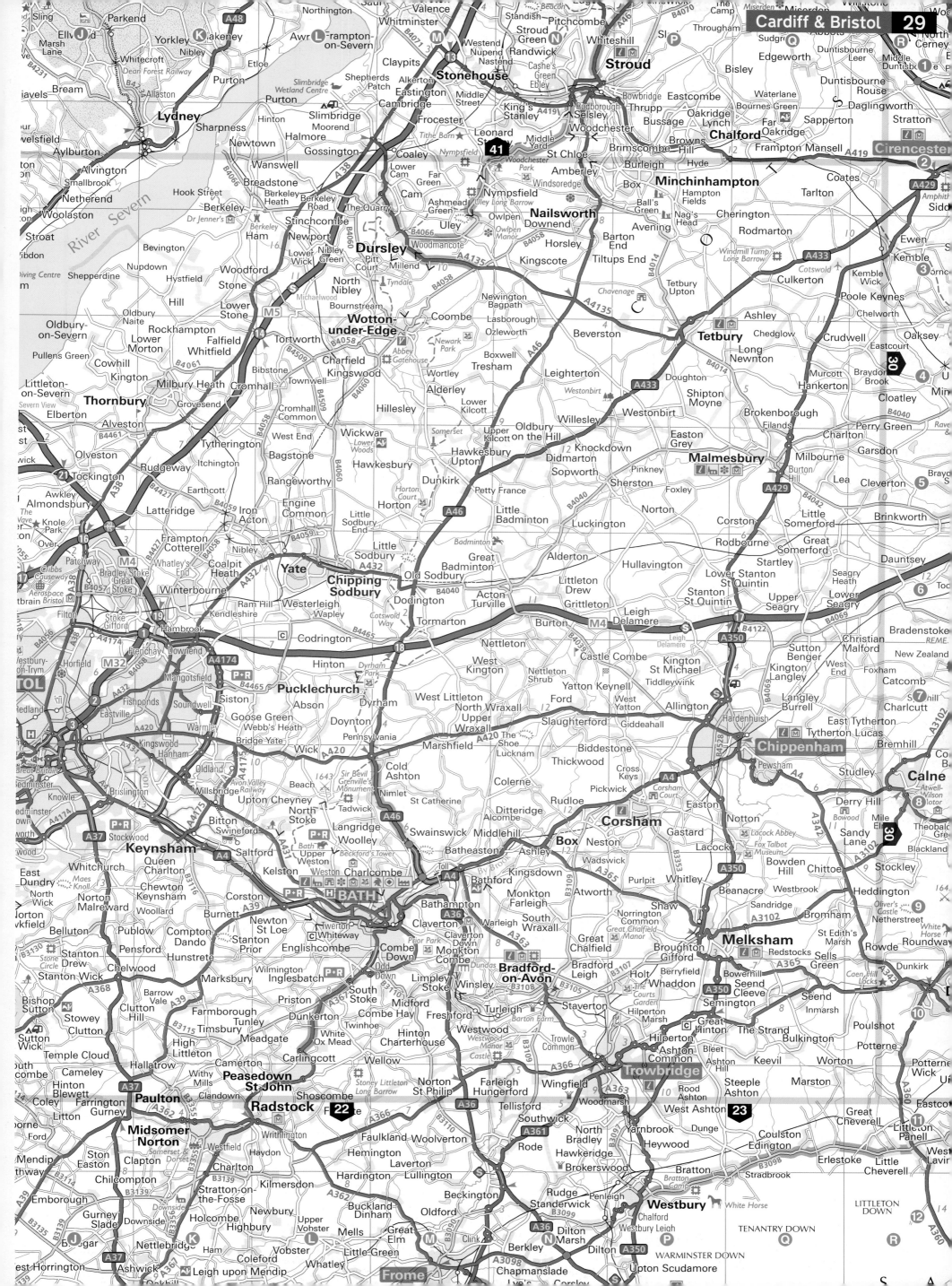

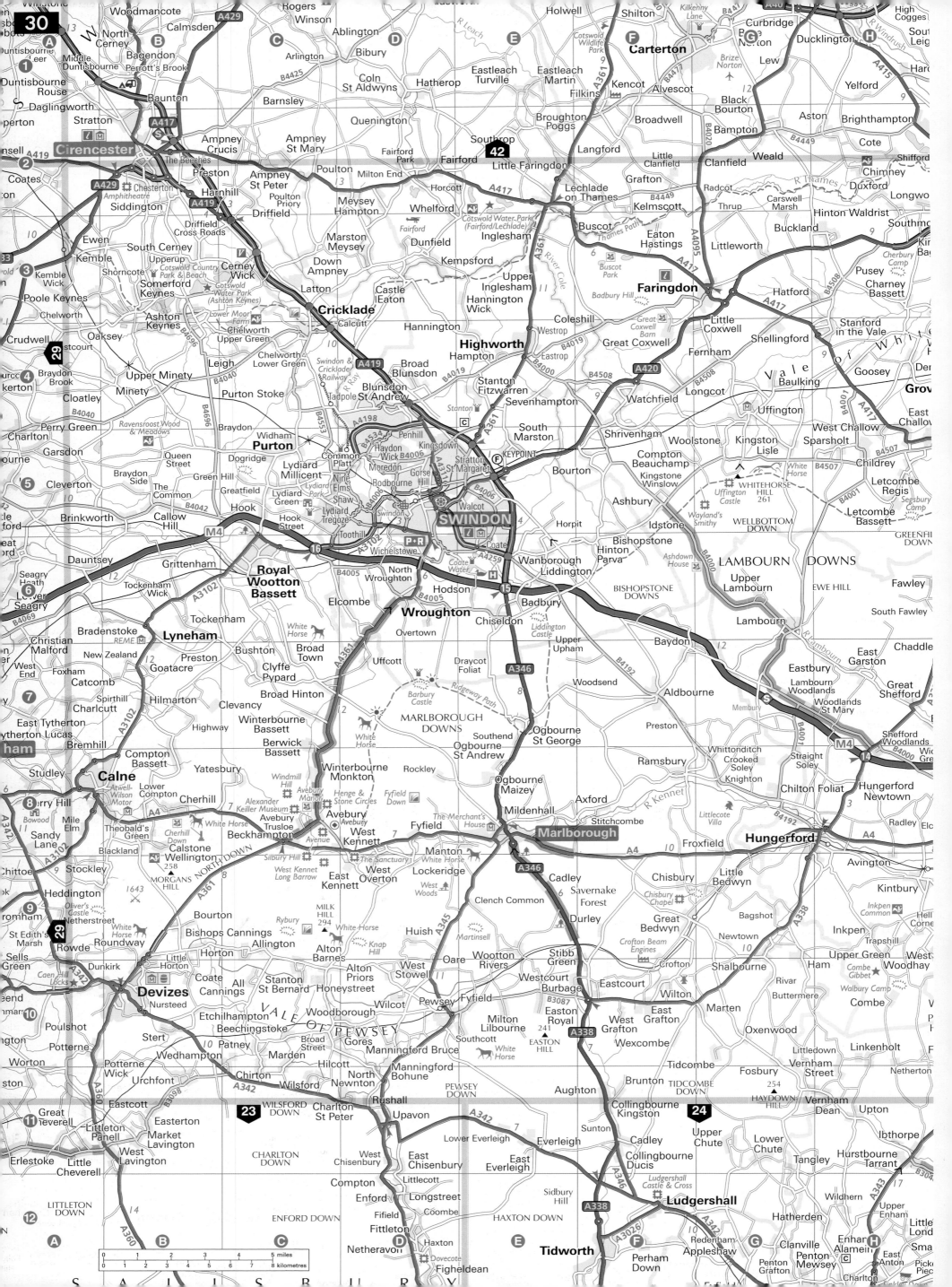

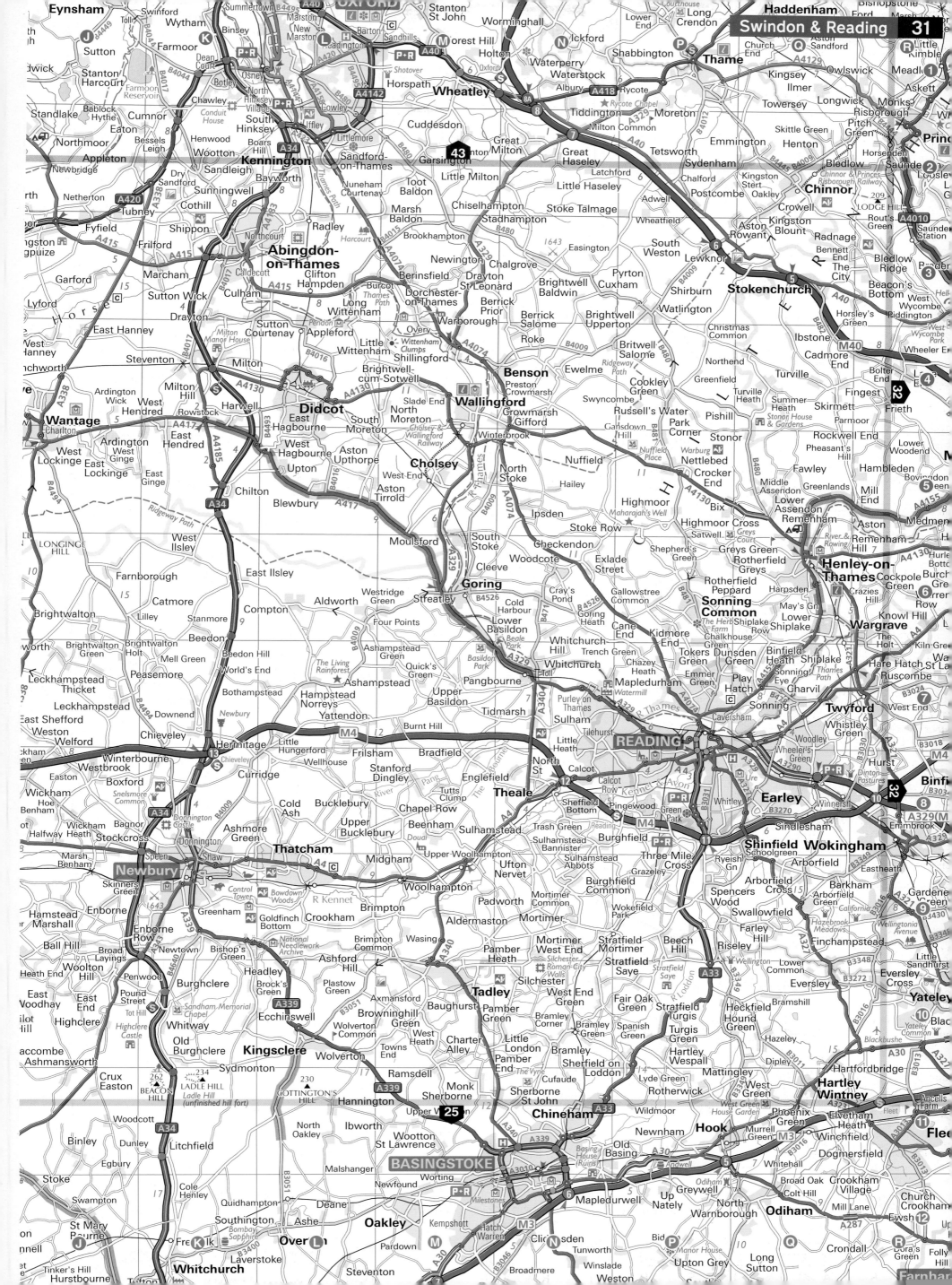

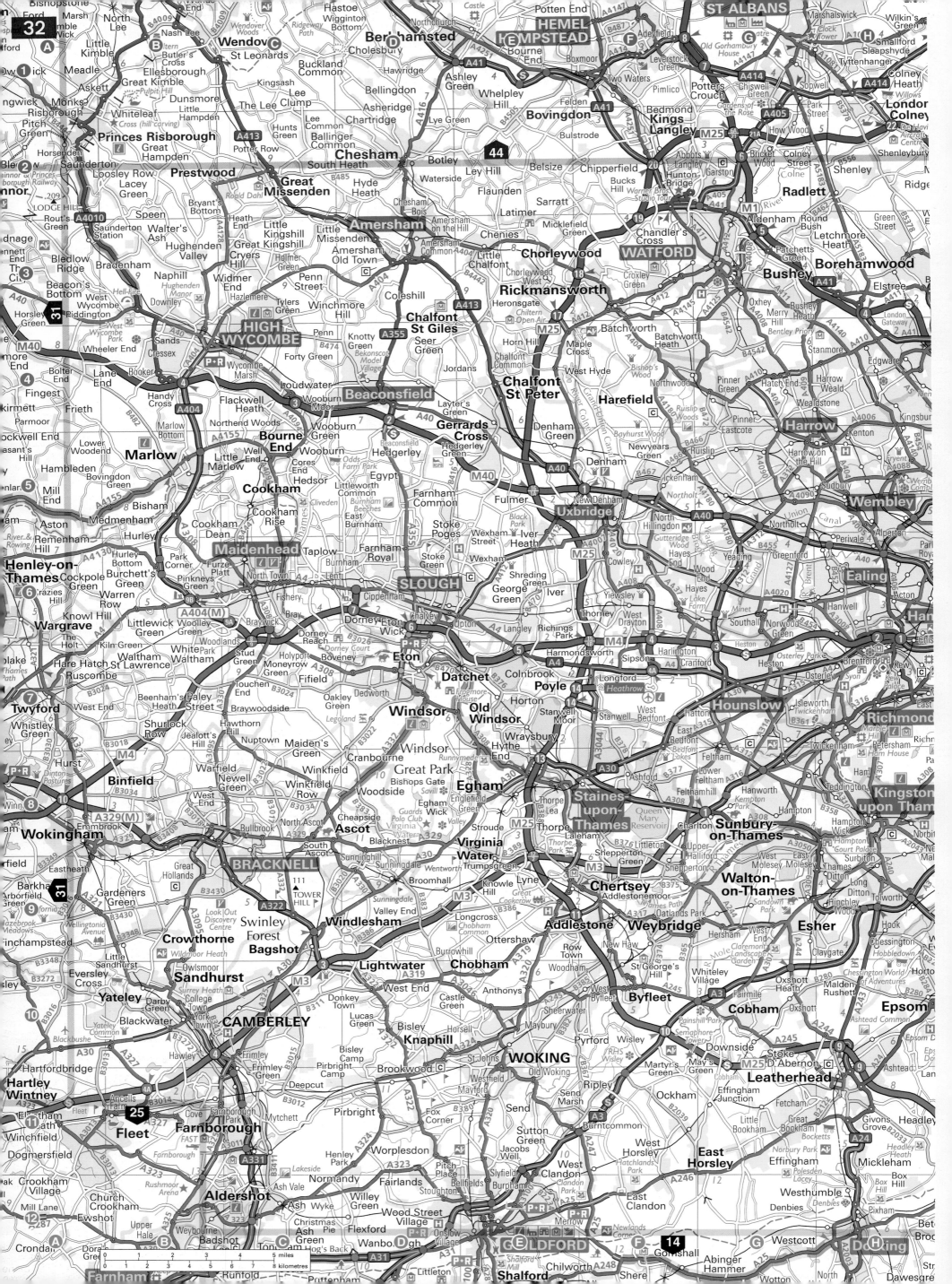

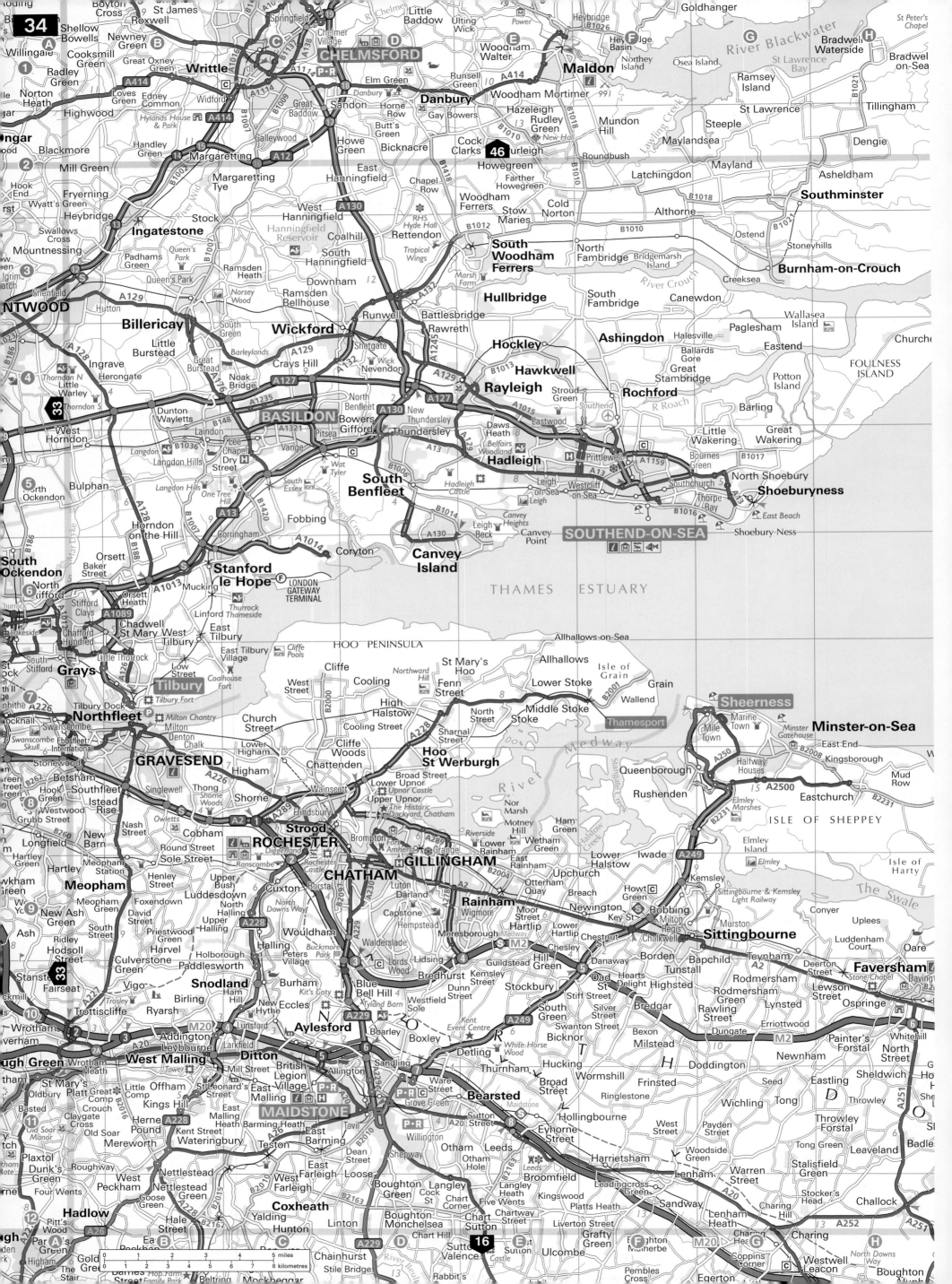

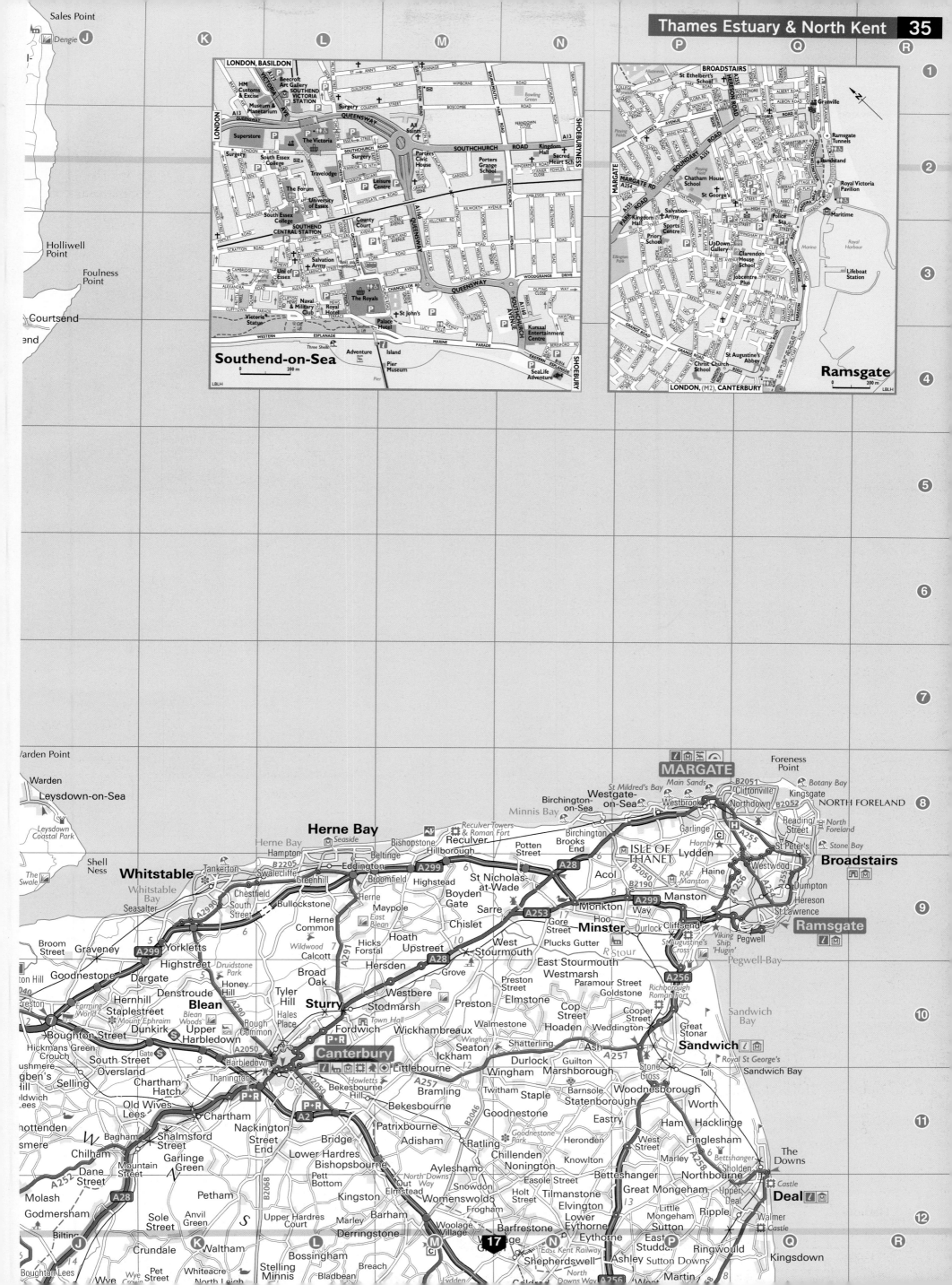

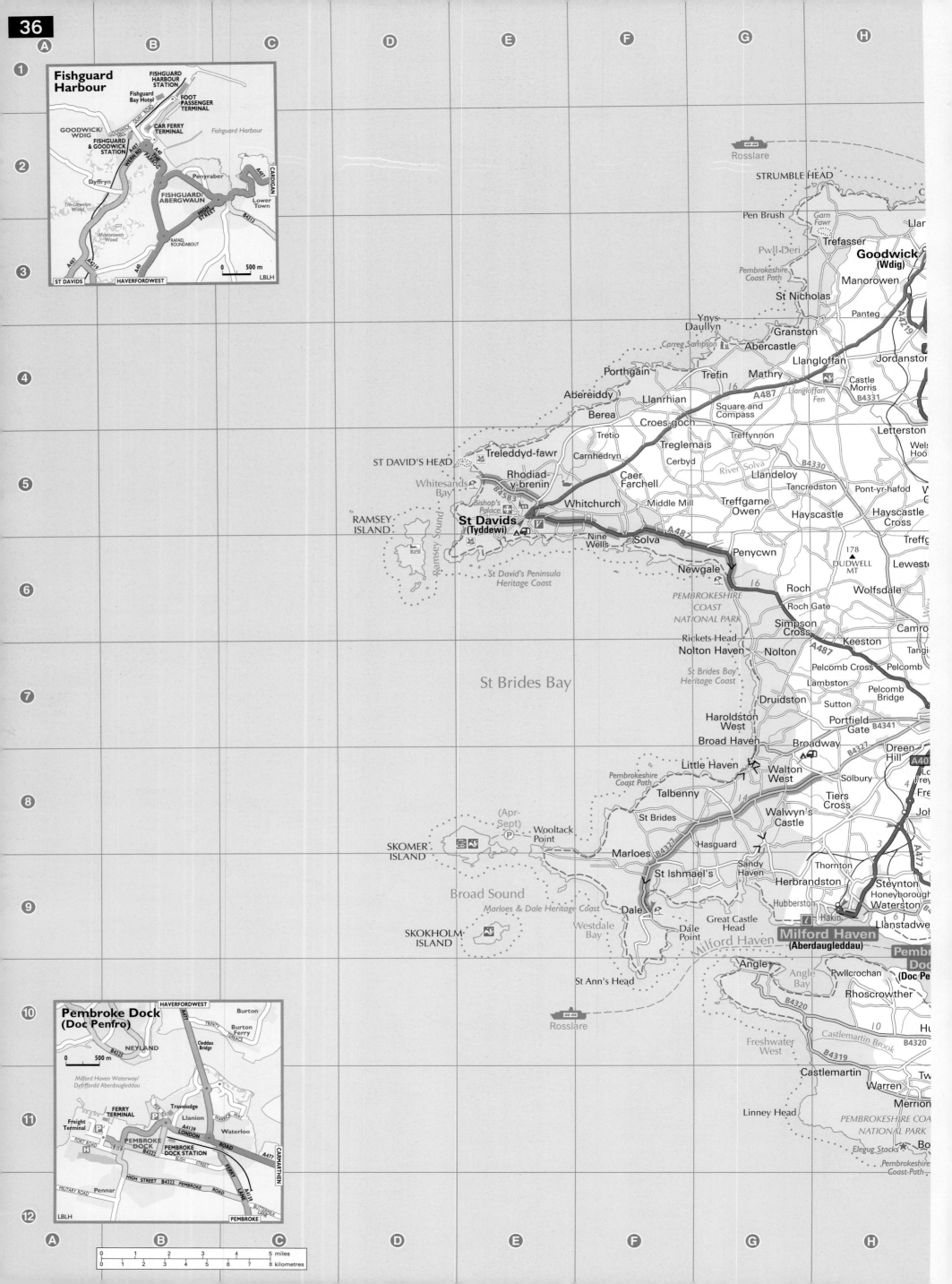

Fishguard Harbour

FISHGUARD HARBOUR STATION
FISHGUARD BAY HOTEL
FOOT PASSENGER TERMINAL
CAR FERRY TERMINAL
Fishguard Harbour
GOODWICK/WDIG
FISHGUARD & GOODWICK STATION
Penyraber
Lower Town
Dyffryn
Tre-Llewelyn Wood
FISHGUARD ABERGWAUN
HIGH STREET
Manorowen Wood
RAFAEL ROUNDABOUT
ST DAVIDS
HAVERFORDWEST
0 500 m
LBLH

Pembroke Dock (Doc Penfro)

HAVERFORDWEST
Burton
Burton Ferry
NEYLAND
Cleddau Bridge
0 500 m
Milford Haven Waterway/ Dyfrffordd Aberdaugleddau
FERRY TERMINAL
Travelodge
Llanion
Freight Terminal
A4139 LONDON
Waterloo
PEMBROKE DOCK
PEMBROKE DOCK STATION
FERRY LANE
HIGH STREET B4322 PEMBROKE ROAD
CARMARTHEN
MILITARY ROAD
Pennar
PEMBROKE
LBLH

Rosslare
STRUMBLE HEAD
Pen Brush
Garn Fawr
Trefasser
Pwll-Deri
Goodwick (Wdig)
Pembrokeshire Coast Path
Manorowen
St Nicholas
Panteg
Ynys Daullyn
Granston
Carreg Sampson
Abercastle
Llangloffan
Jordanston
Porthgain
Trefin
Mathry
Abereiddy
Llanrhian
16
A487
Llangloffan Fen
Castle Morris
B4331
Berea
Croes-goch
Square and Compass
Letterston
Tretio
Treffynnon
Wels... Hoo...
ST DAVID'S HEAD
Treleddyd-fawr
Carnhedryn
Cerbyd
River Solva
B4330
Whitesands Bay
Rhodiad-y-brenin
Caer Farchell
Llandeloy
Treffgarne Owen
Treff...
Bishop's Palace
Whitchurch
Middle Mill
Tancredston
Pont-yr-hafod
V... G...
St Davids (Tyddewi)
A487
Hayscastle
Hayscastle Cross
Hayscastle
RAMSEY ISLAND
Ramsey Sound
Nine Wells
Solva
Penycwn
178 DUDWELL MT
Lewest...
RSPB
Treff...
St David's Peninsula Heritage Coast
Newgale
16
Roch
Wolfsdale
PEMBROKESHIRE COAST NATIONAL PARK
Roch Gate
Simpson Cross
Camro...
Rickets Head
Keeston
Nolton Haven
Nolton
Tangi...
A487
St Brides Bay
Pelcomb Cross
Pelcomb
Lambston
Pelcomb Bridge
St Brides Bay Heritage Coast
Druidston
Sutton
St Brides Bay
Haroldston West
Portfield Gate
B4341
Broadway
Broad Haven
Dreen Hill
A40
Little Haven
Walton West
Sölbury
Lo... Frey...
Pembrokeshire Coast Path
Talbenny
14
Tiers Cross
Fre...
St Brides
Walwyn's Castle
Joh...
(Apr-Sept)
Wooltack Point
Marloes
B4327
Hasguard
Thornton
A477
SKOMER ISLAND
St Ishmael's
Sandy Haven
Herbrandston
Steynton
Broad Sound
Dale
Hubberston
Honeyborough
Waterston
Marloes & Dale Heritage Coast
Great Castle Head
Milford Haven (Aberdaugleddau)
Hakin
Llanstadwe...
SKOKHOLM ISLAND
Westdale Bay
Dale Point
Milford Haven
Pemb... Do...
(Doc Pe...
St Ann's Head
Angle
Angle Bay
Pwllcrochan
Rhoscrowther
Rosslare
Castlemartin Brook
B4320
Freshwater West
B4319
Castlemartin
Tw...
Linney Head
PEMBROKESHIRE COAST NATIONAL PARK
Warren
Merrion
Elegug Stacks
Bo...
Pembrokeshire Coast-Path
Hu...

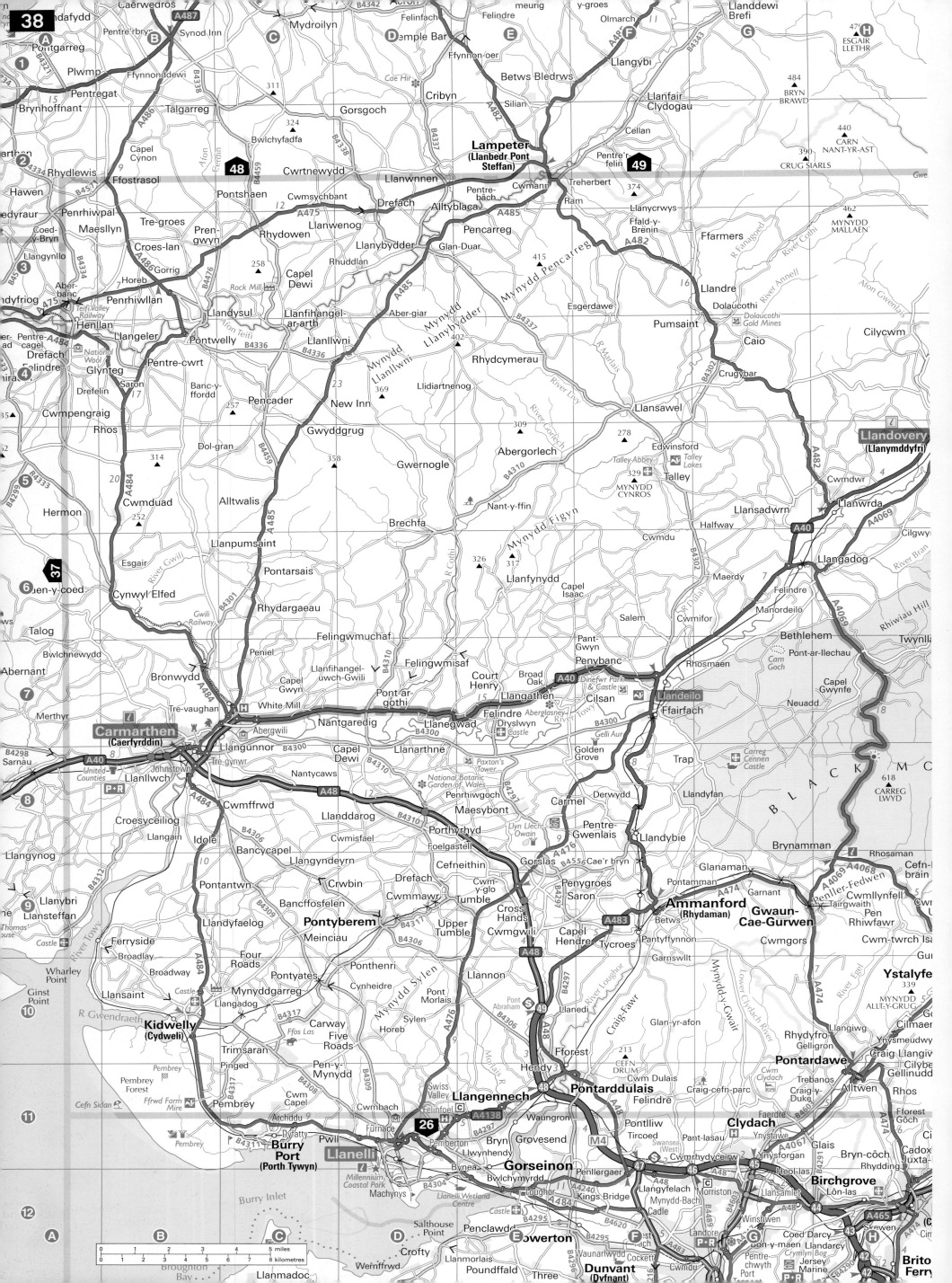

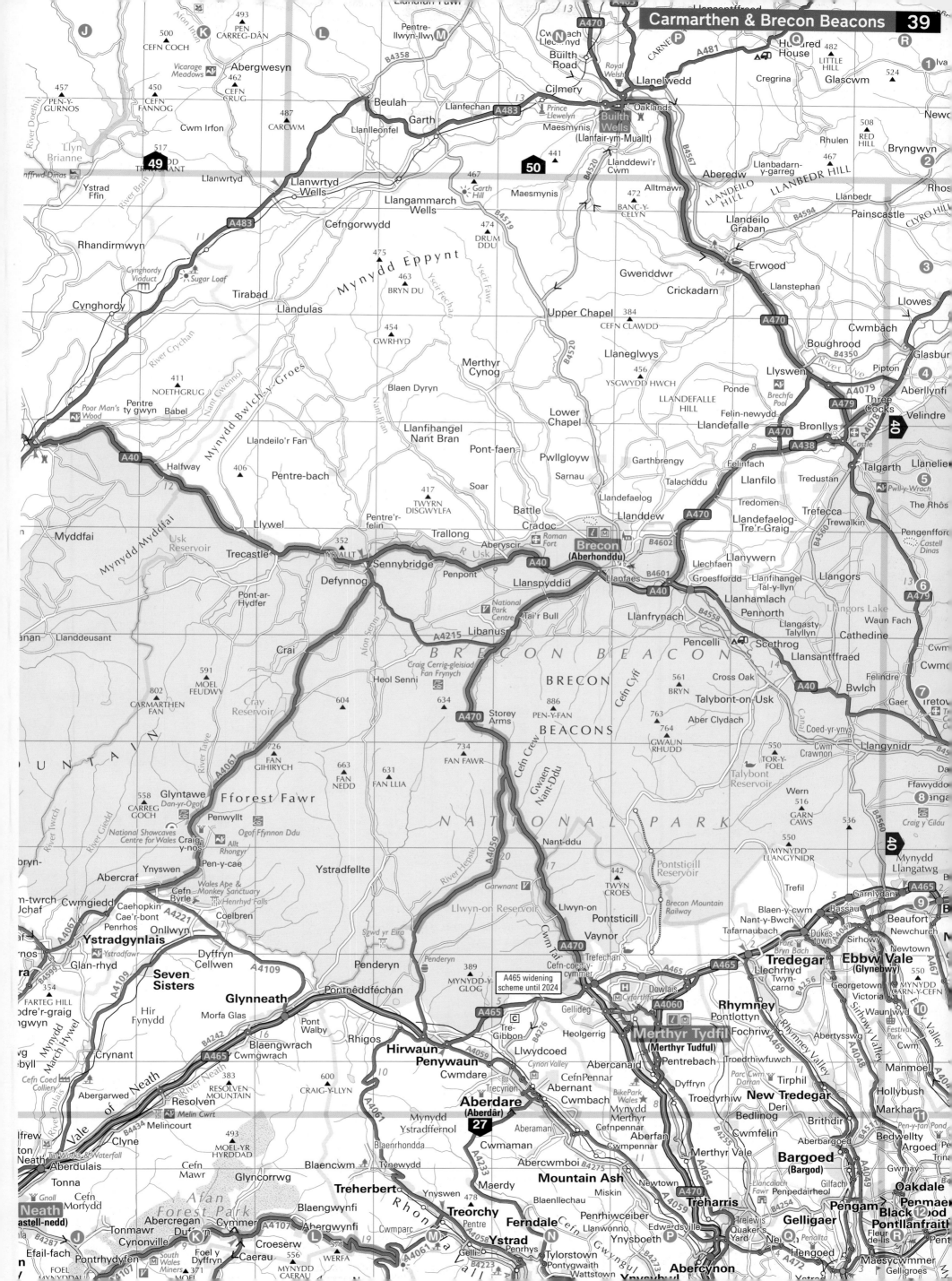

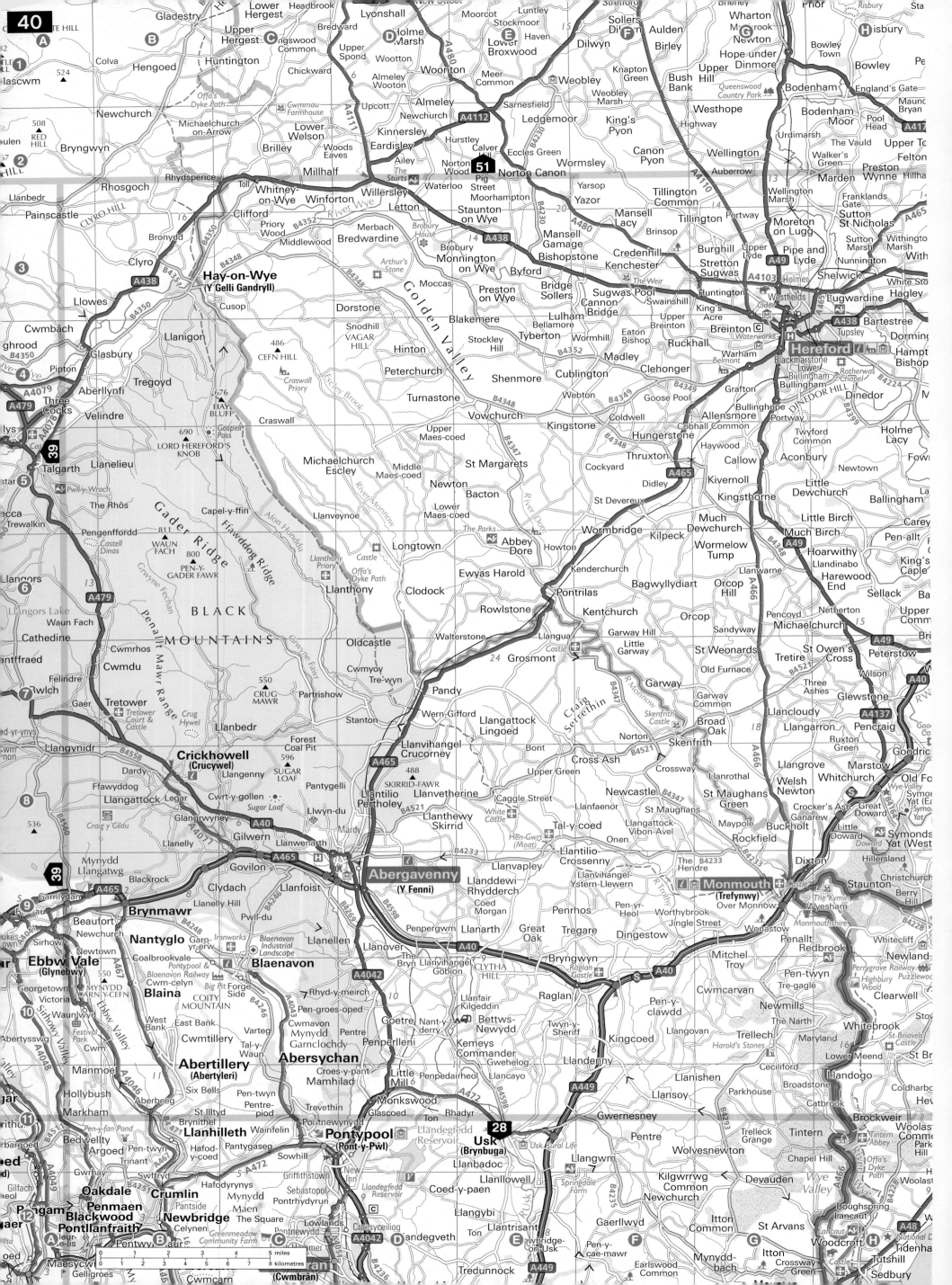

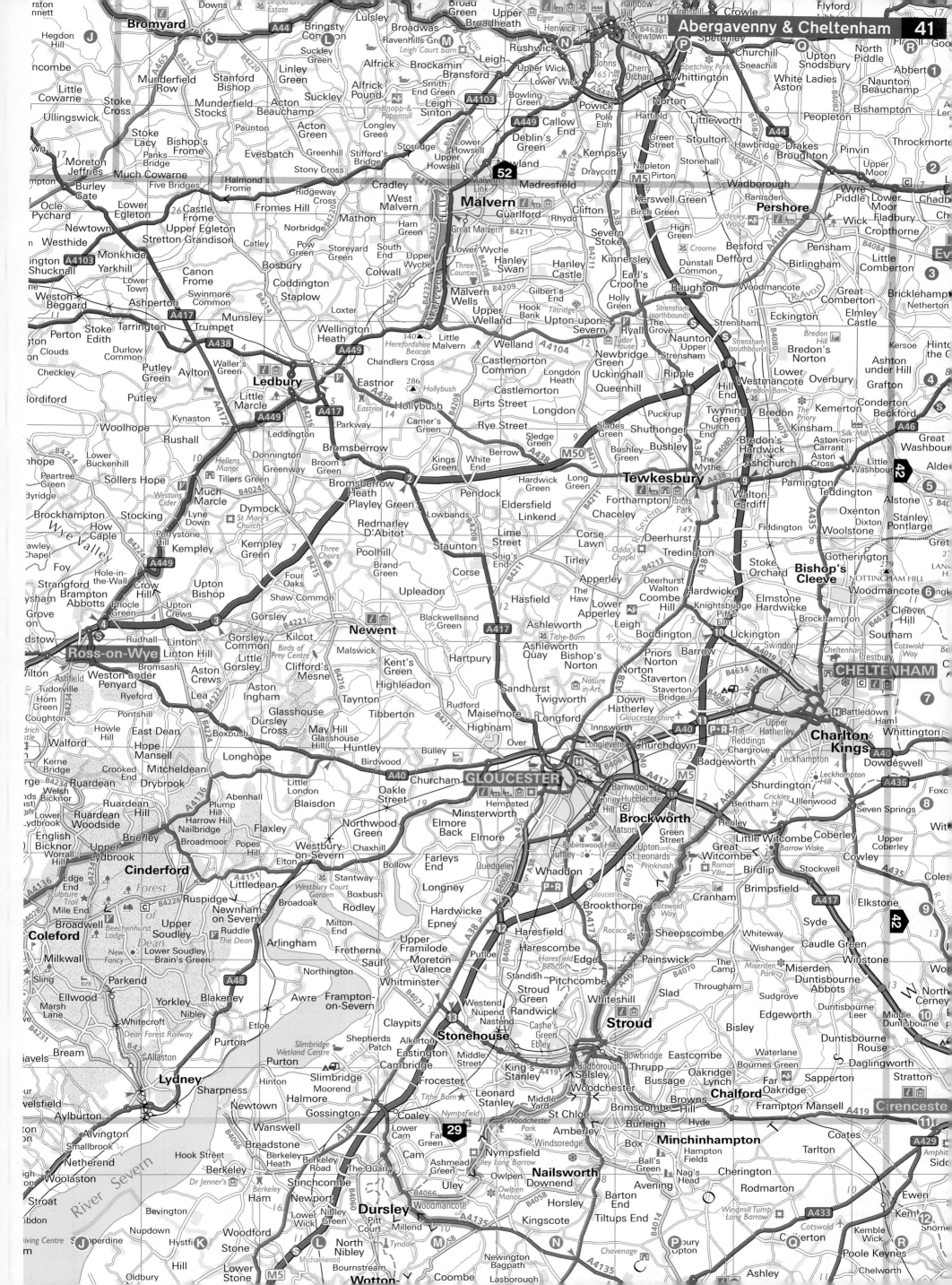

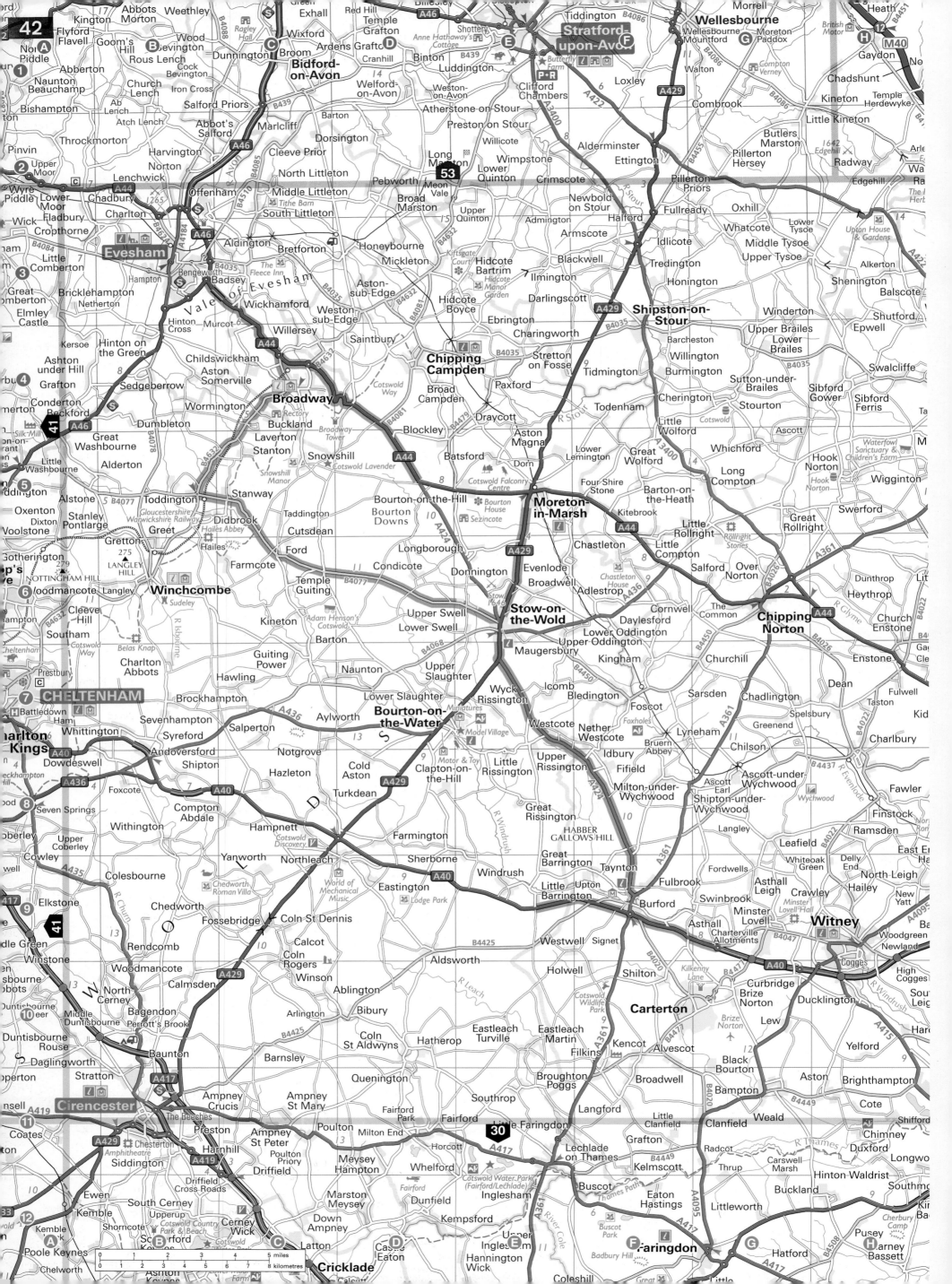

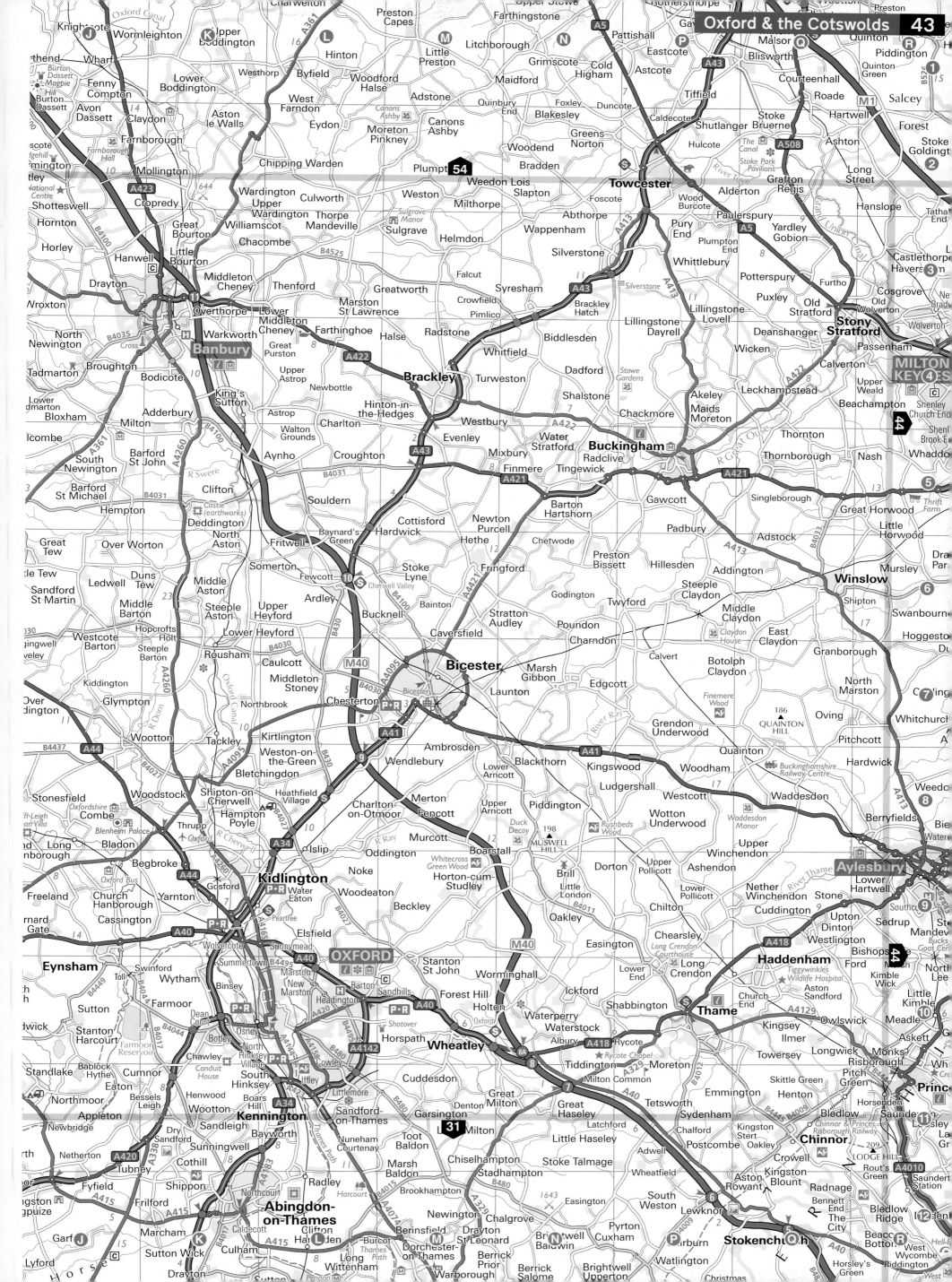

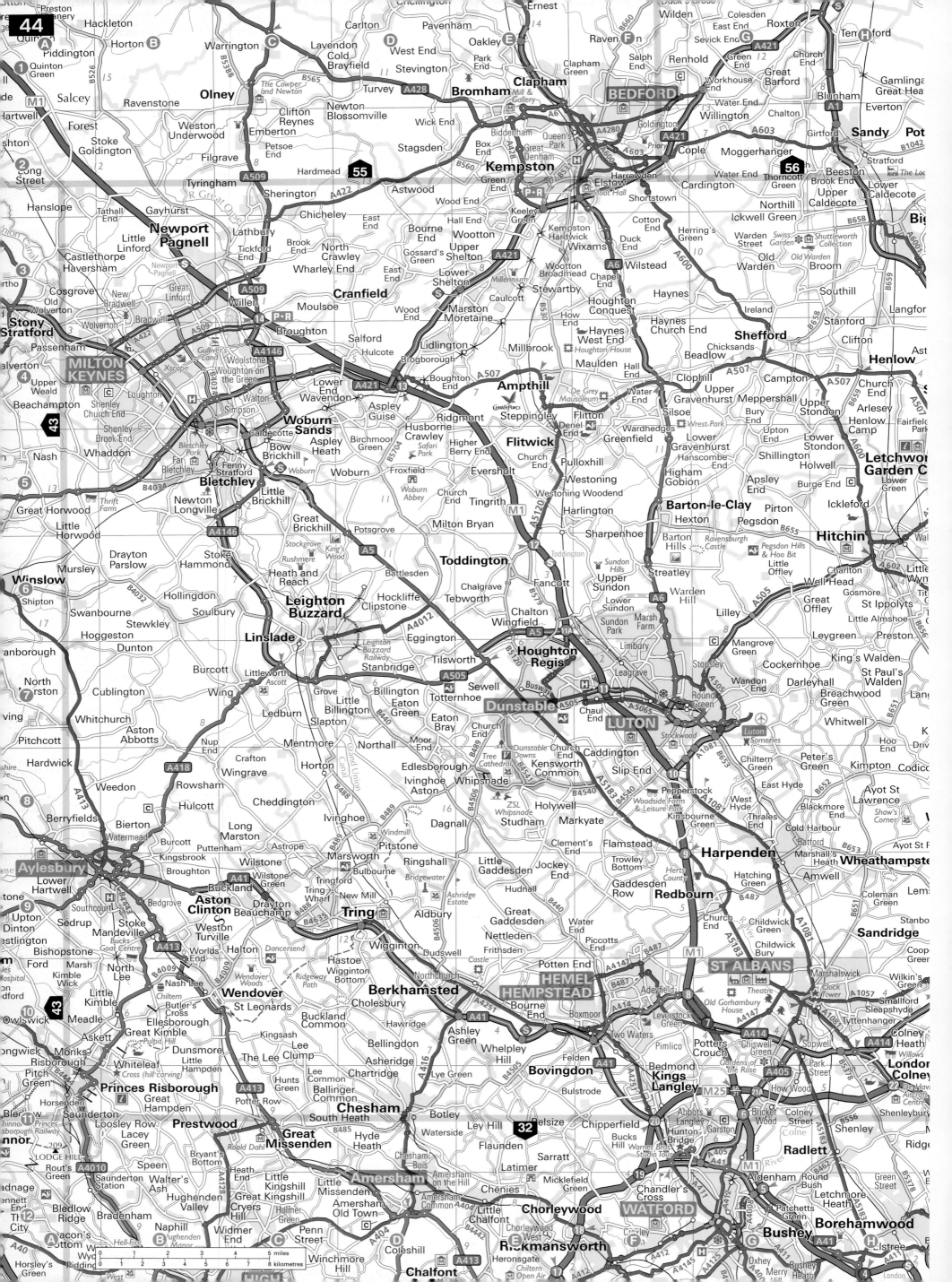

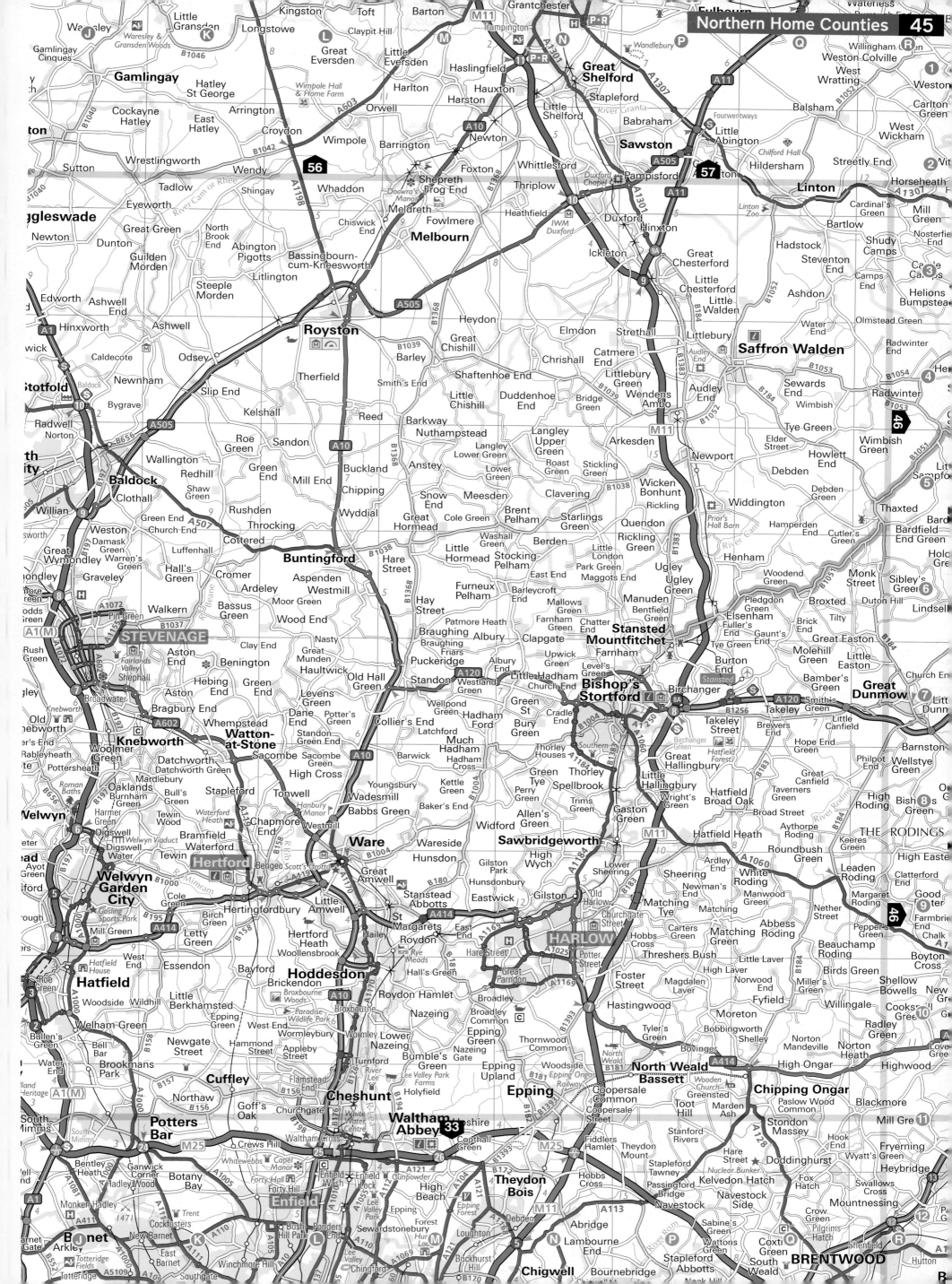

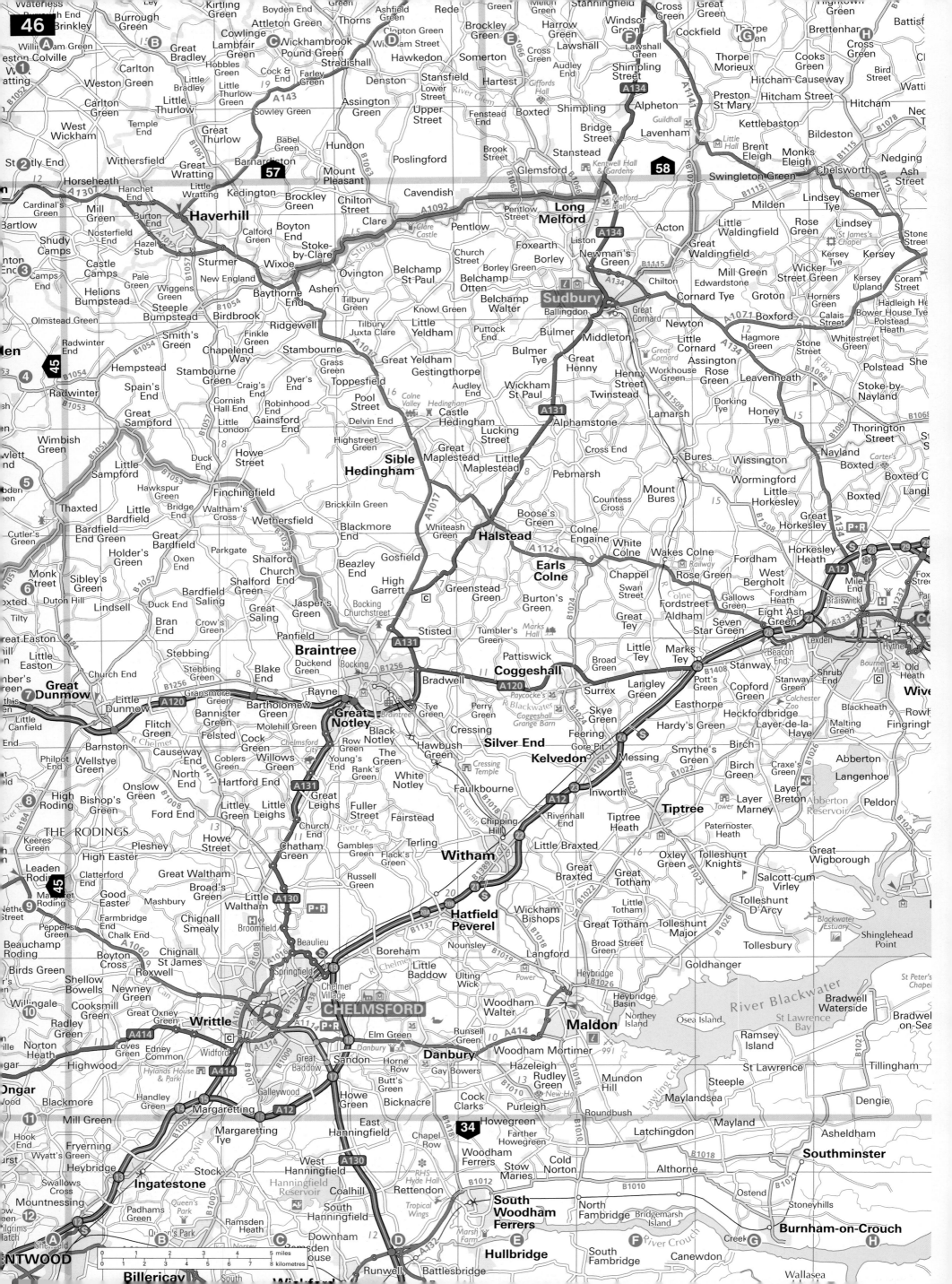

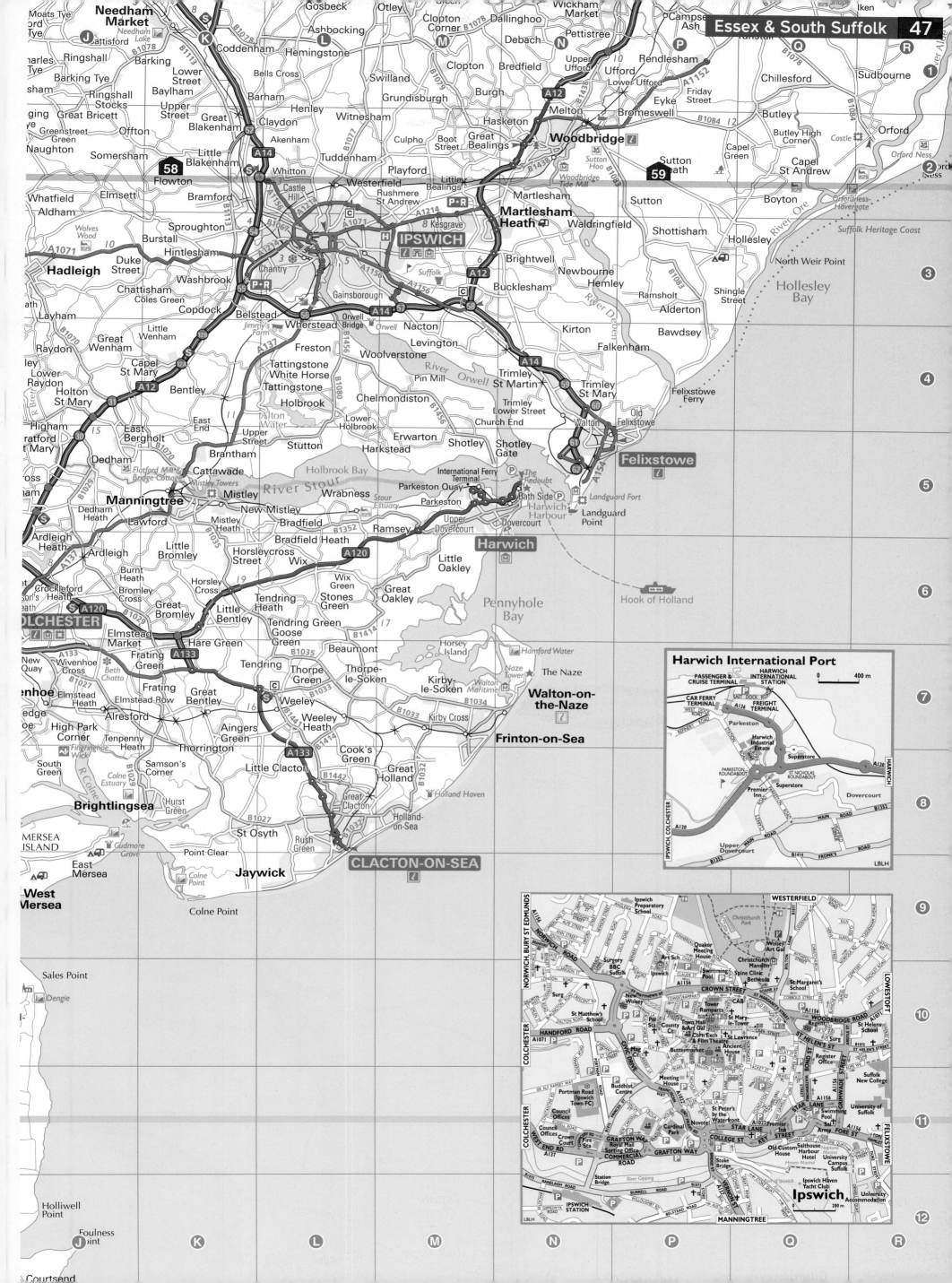

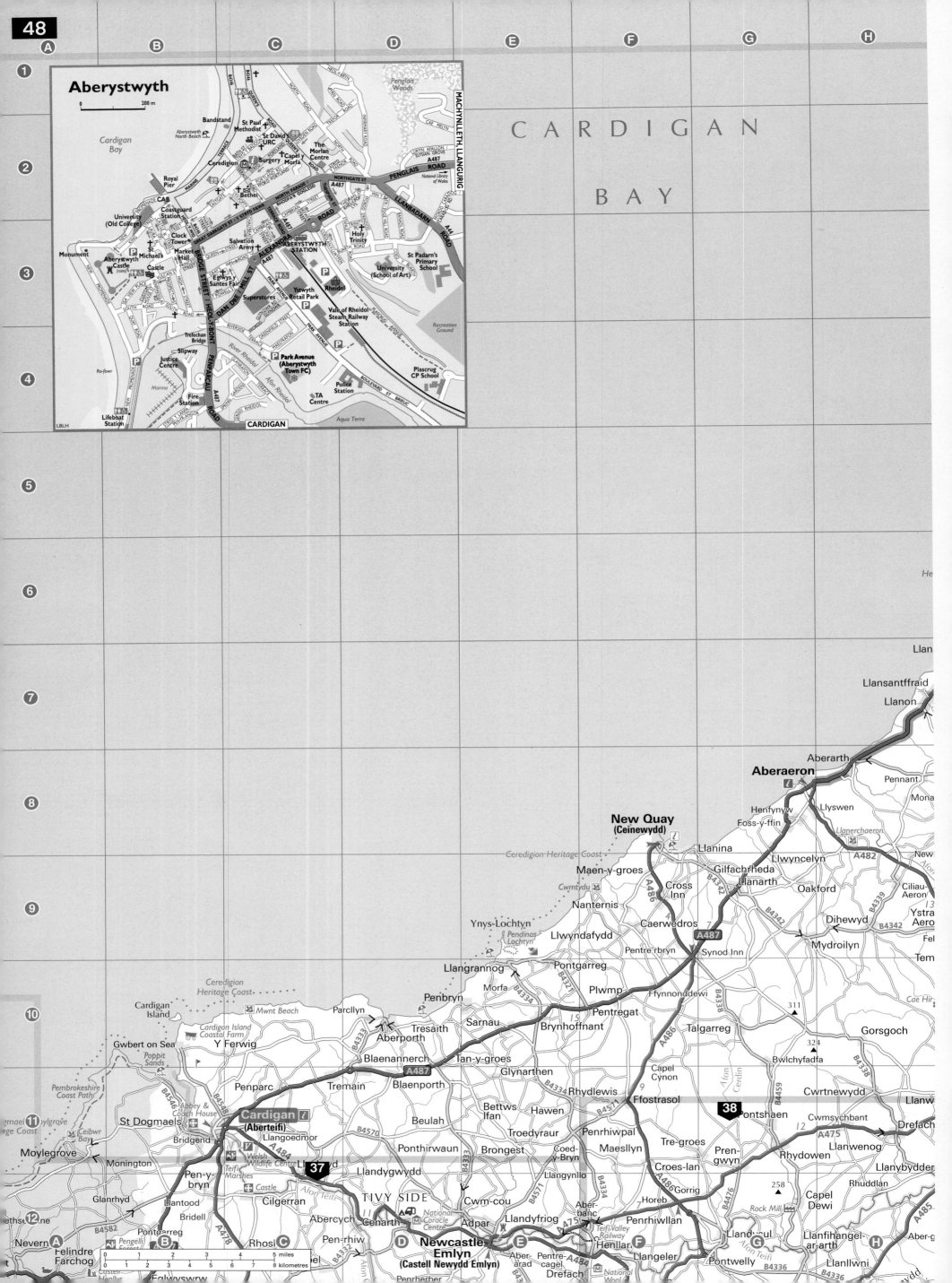

Aberystwyth

0   200 m

Cardigan Bay

CARDIGAN BAY

CARDIGAN BAY

Aberarth
Pennant
Aberaeron
Henfynyw
Llyswen
Mona
Foss-y-ffin
Llanerchaeron

New Quay
(Ceinewydd)
Llanina
Llwyncelyn
A482
New
Maen-y-groes
Gilfachrheda
Llanarth
Oakford
Ciliau-
Aeron
Cwmtydu
Cross
Inn
B4342
Nanternis
Caerwedros
Synod Inn
Mydroilyn
Dihewyd
Ystra
Aero
Ynys-Lochtyn
Pentre'rbryn
A487
Fel
Pendinas
Lochtyn
Llwyndafydd
Tem
Llangrannog
Pontgarreg
Morfa
Plwmp
Ffynnonddewi
Cae Hir
Penbryn
Pentregat
311
Ceredigion
Heritage Coast
Cardigan Island
Sarnau
Brynhoffnant
Talgarreg
Gorsgoch
Mwnt Beach
Parcllyn
Cardigan Island
Coastal Farm
Tresaith
324
Bwlchyfadfa
Gwbert on Sea
Y Ferwig
Aberporth
Capel
Cynon
Poppit Sands
Blaenannerch
Tan-y-groes
Glynarthen
Rhydlewis
Cwrtnewydd
Pembrokeshire
Coast Path
Penparc
Tremain
Blaenporth
A487
Ffostrasol
38
Llanw
St Dogmaels
Bettws
Ifan
Hawen
Penrhiwpal
Pontshaen
Cwmsychbant
Drefach
Cardigan
(Aberteifi)
Beulah
Troedyraur
Tre-groes
A475
Llanwenog
Bridgend
Llangoedmor
Ponthirwaun
Coed-
y-Bryn
Maesllyn
Prengwyn
Rhydowen
Llanybydder
Moylegrove
Monington
Pen-y-
bryn
Llandygwydd
Croes-lan
Rhuddlan
37
Llangynllo
Ceibwr Bay
Glanrhyd
Llantood
Cilgerran
TIVY SIDE
Cwm-cou
Gorrig
258
Capel
Dewi
Bridell
Rock Mill
Nevern
B4582
Pontgarreg
Rhosl
Aber-
banc
Horeb
Penrhiwllan
Llanfihangel-
ar-arth
Aber
Felindre
Farchog
A478
Pen-rhiw
Newcastle
Emlyn
(Castell Newydd Emlyn)
Adpar
Aber-
arad
Pentre-
cagal
Henllan
Llandyfriog
Teifi Valley
Railway
A484
Pontwelly
Llangeler
Drefach
Egwlyswrw
B4332
Cenarth
Abercych

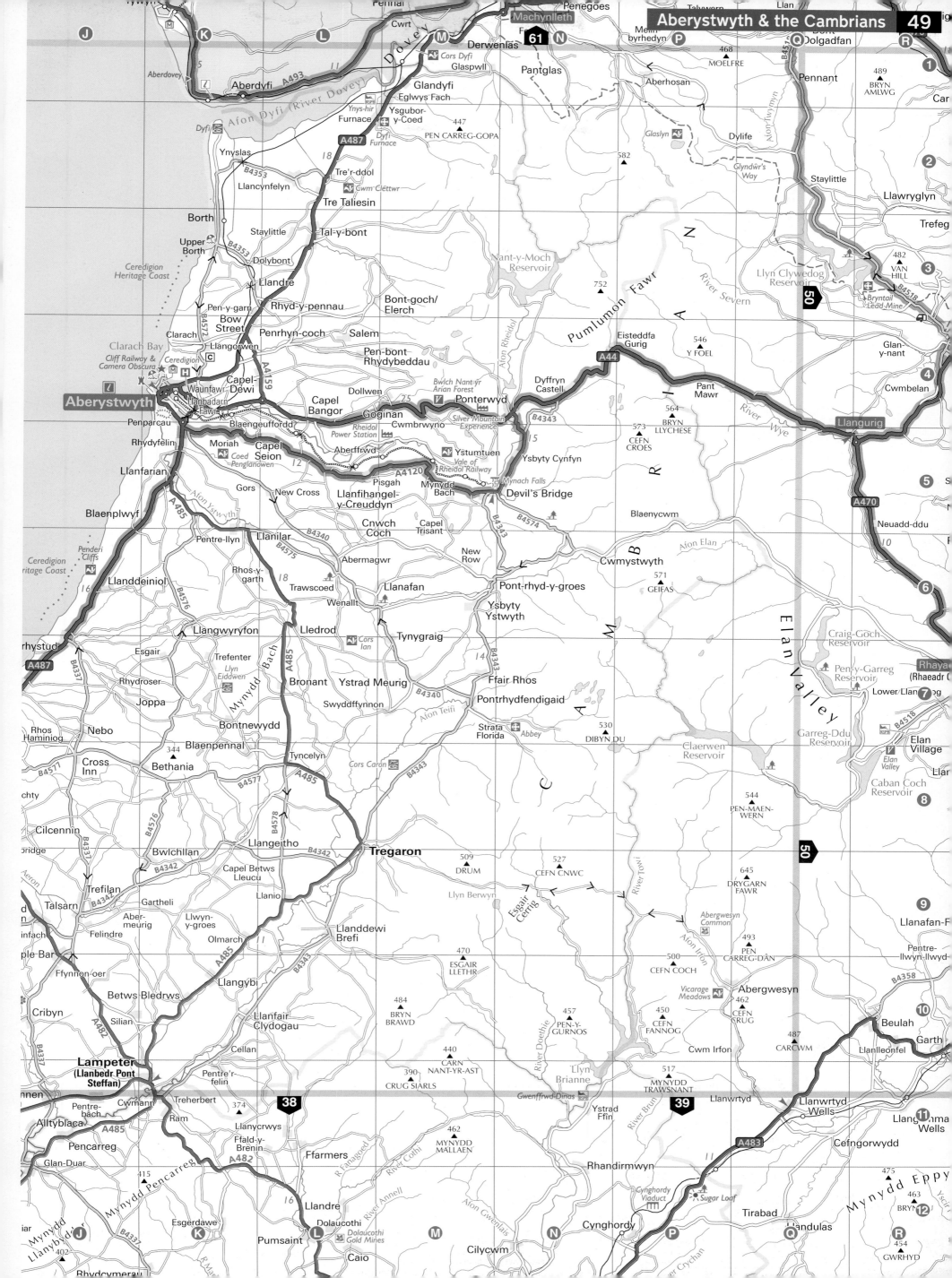

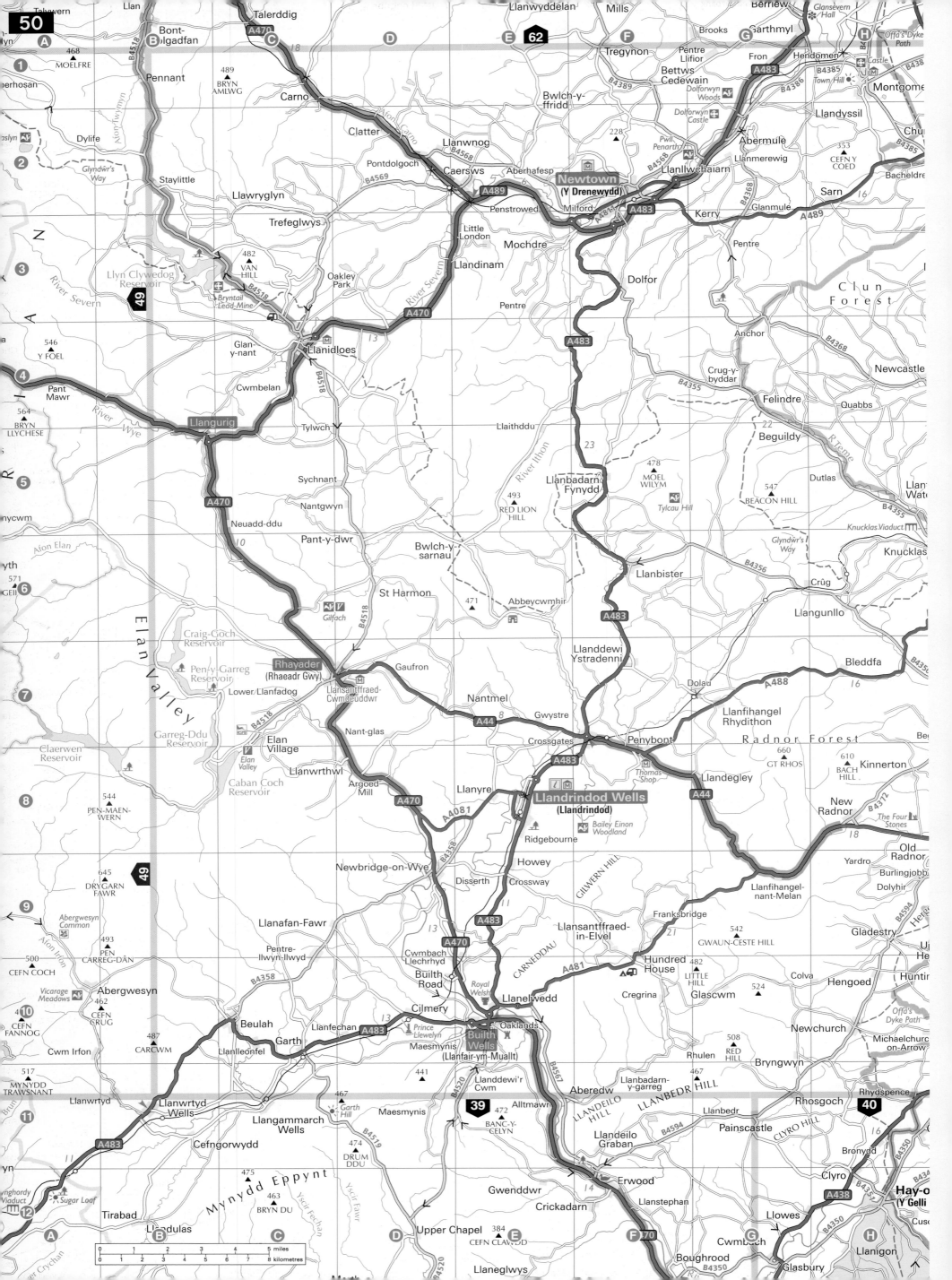

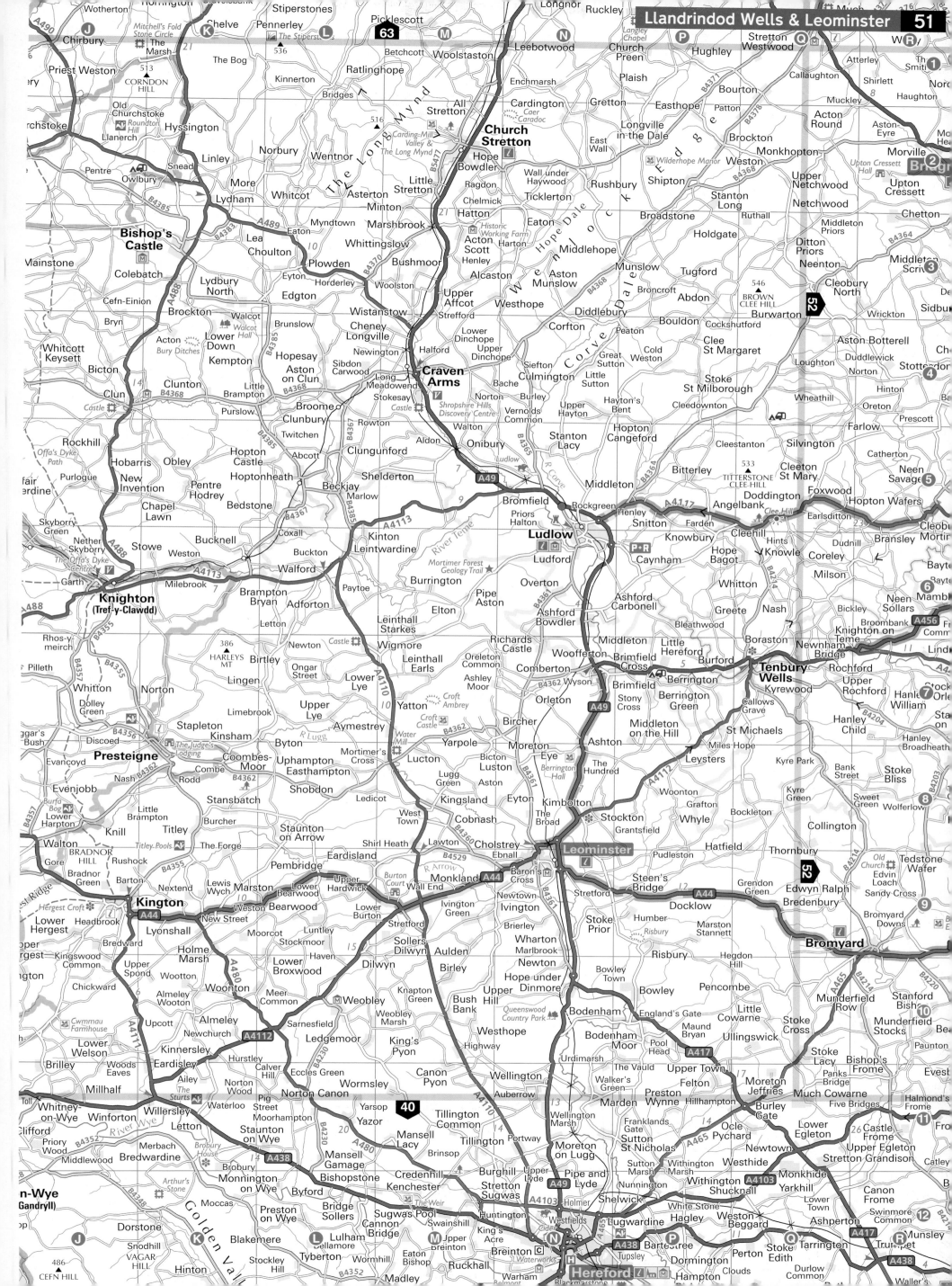

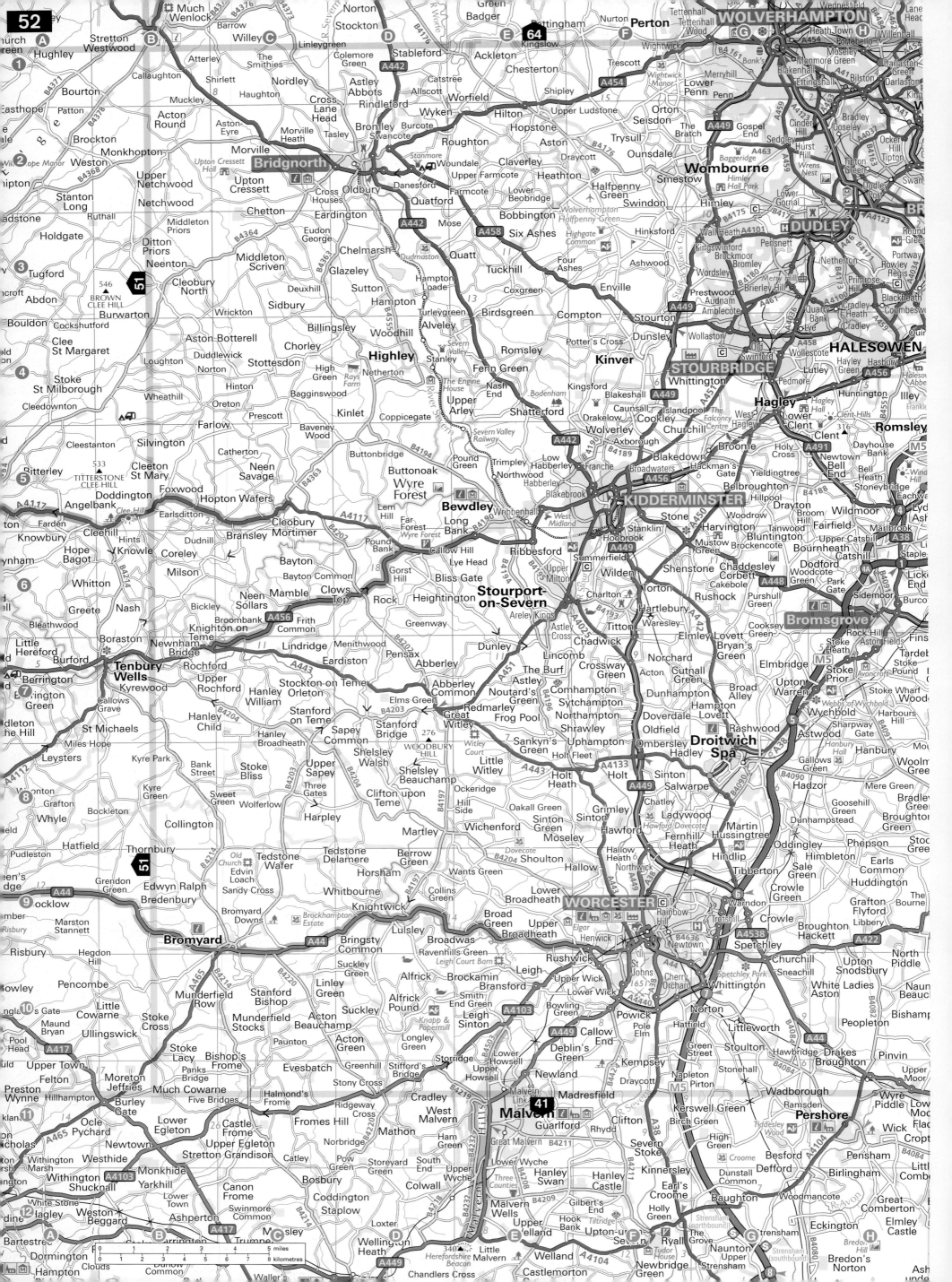

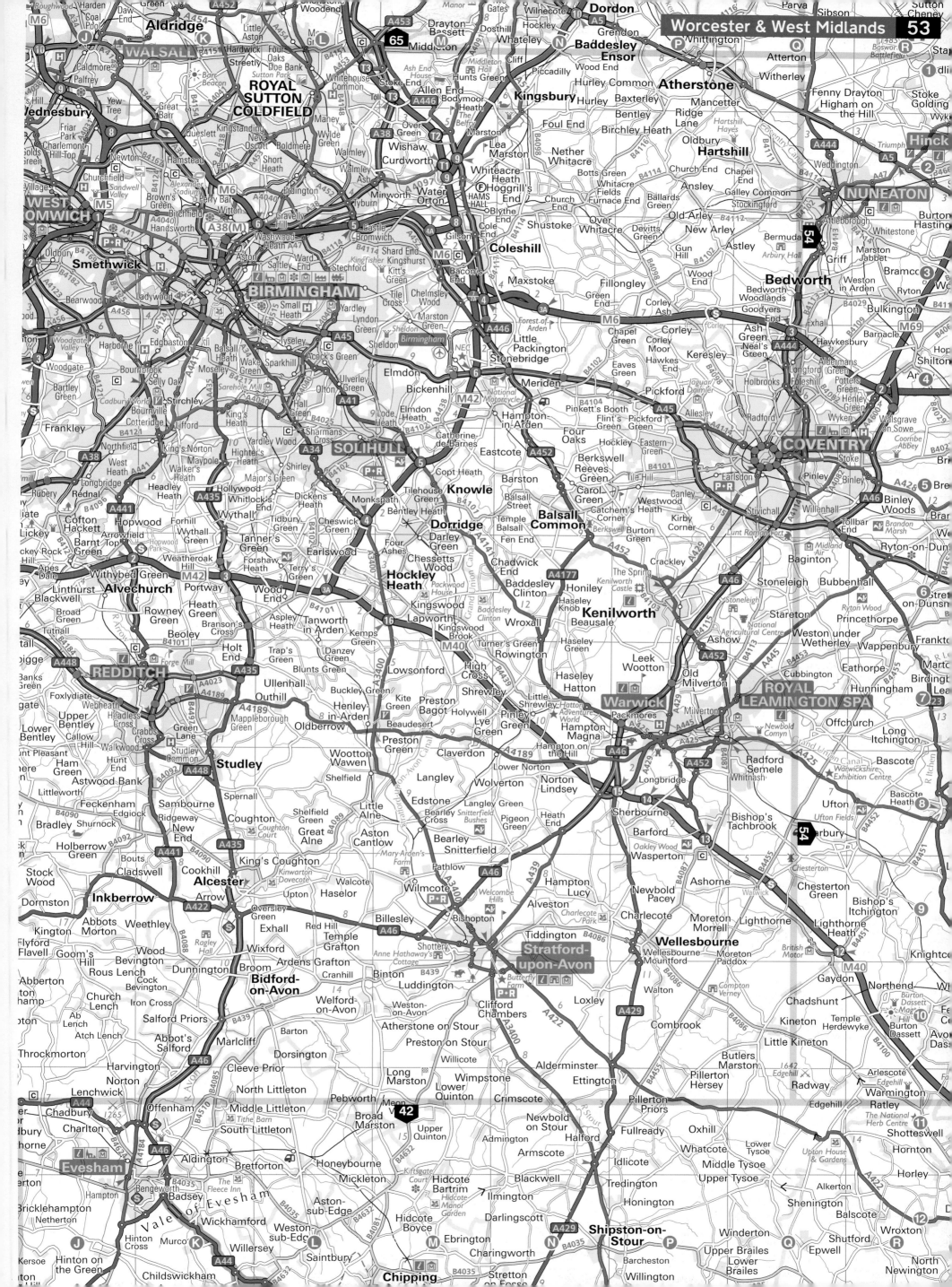

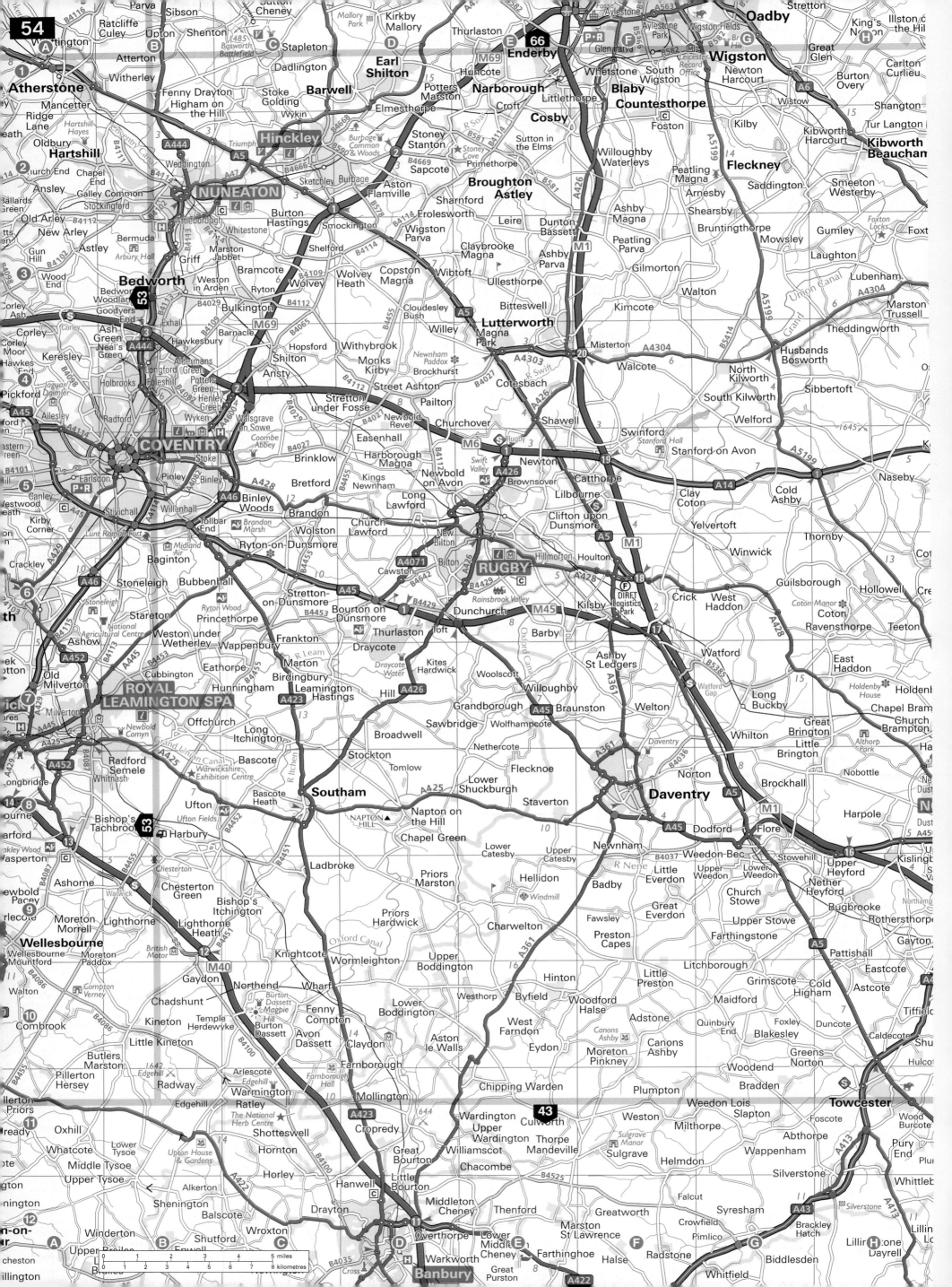

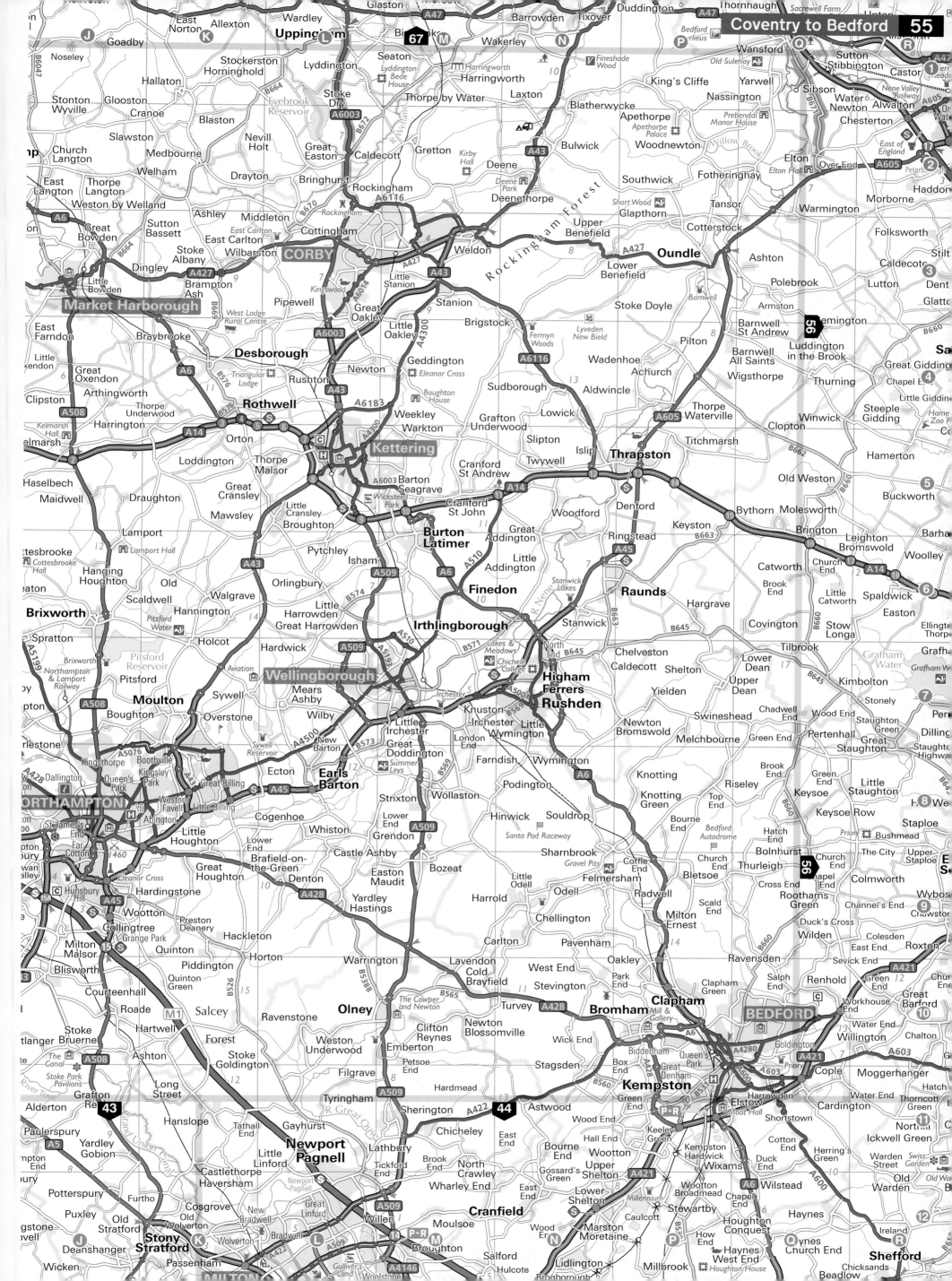

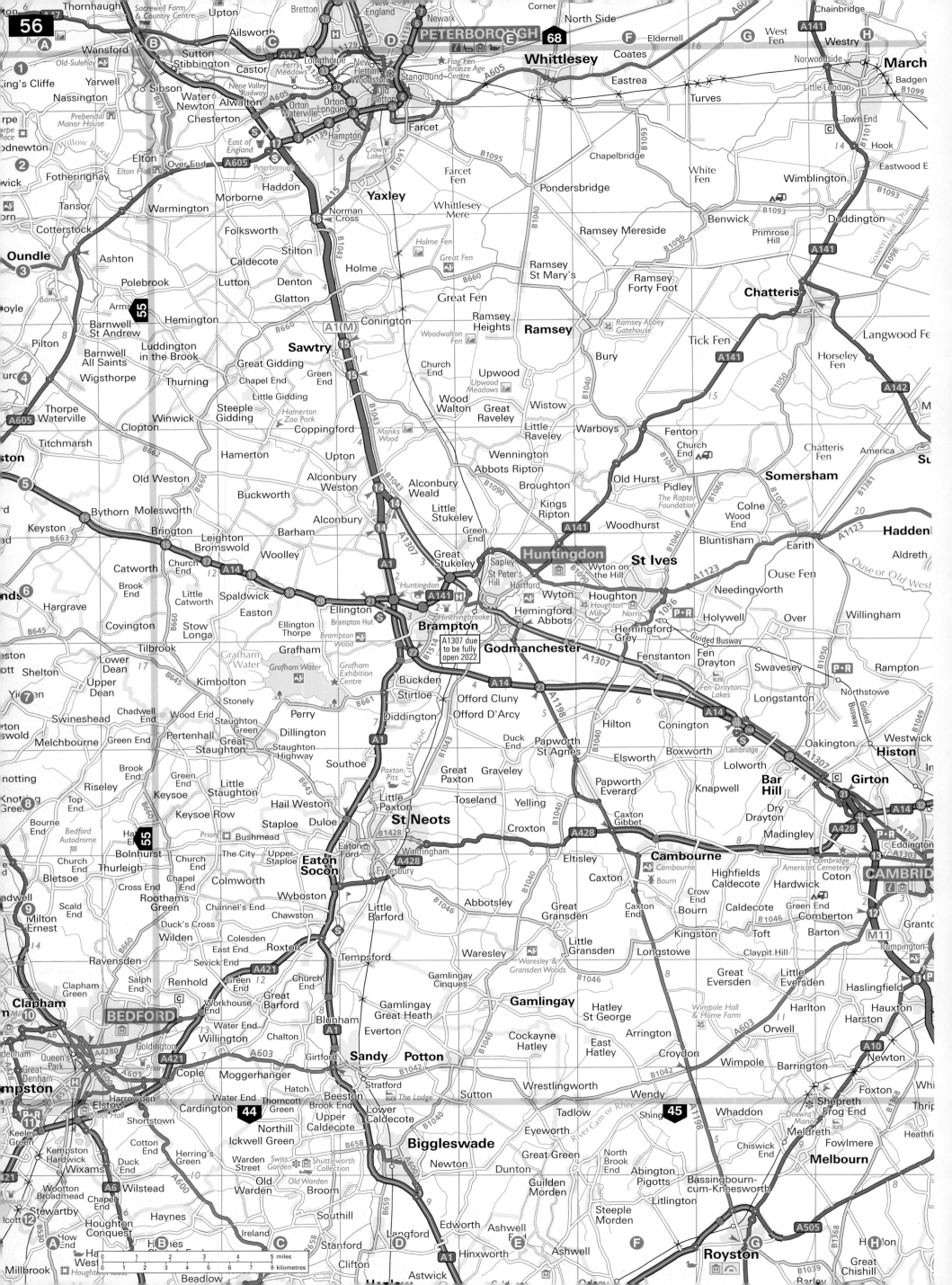

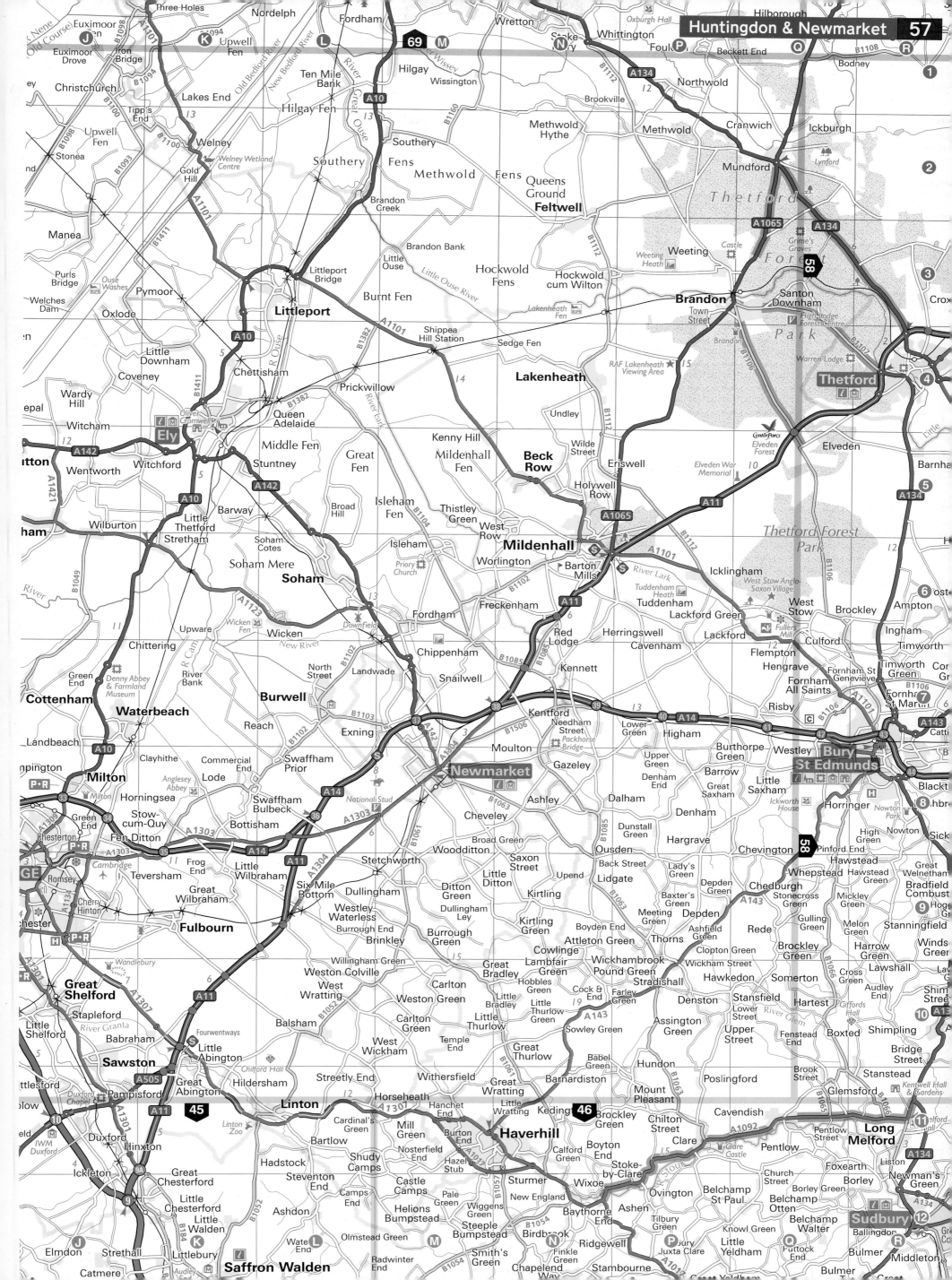

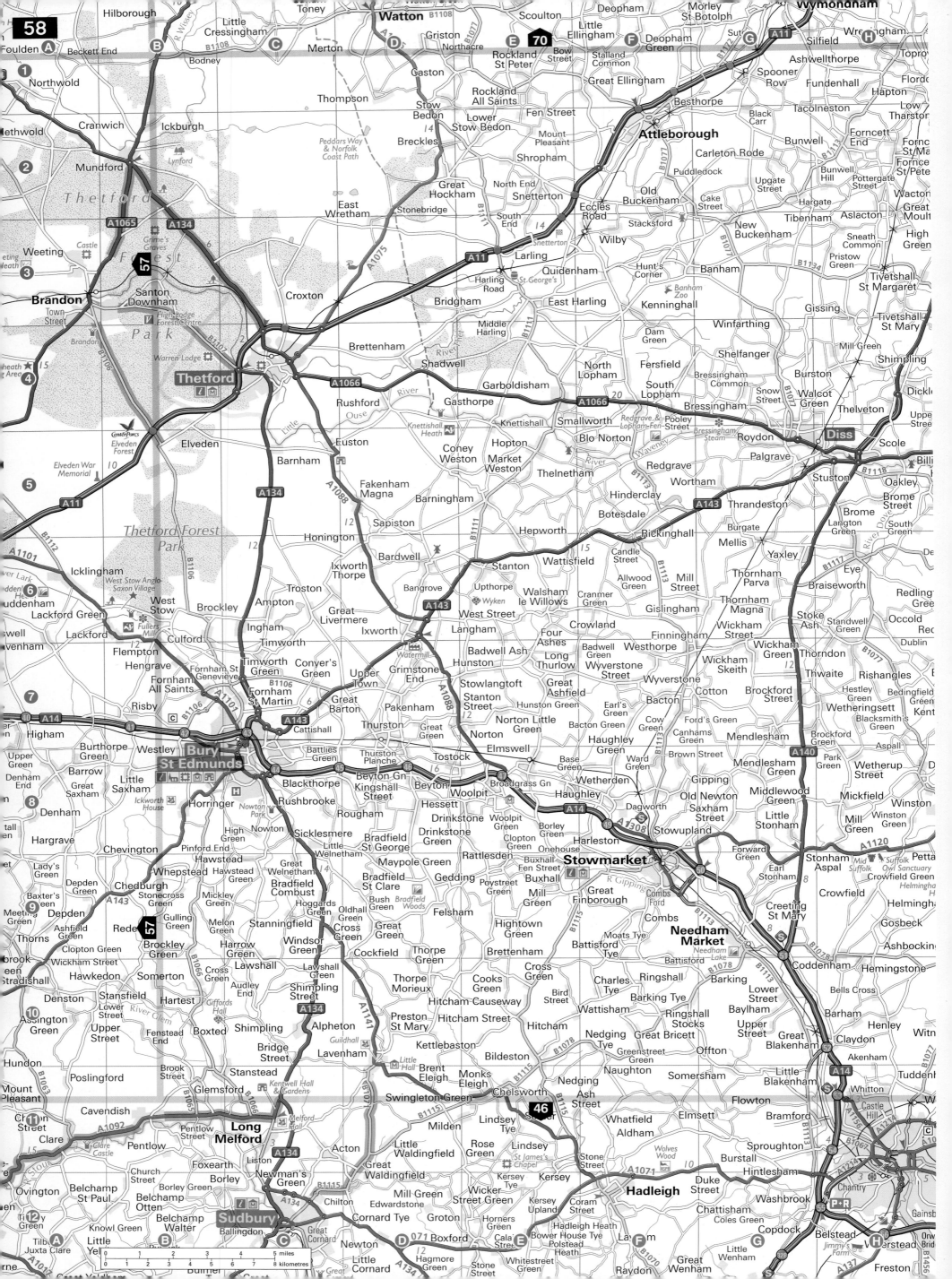

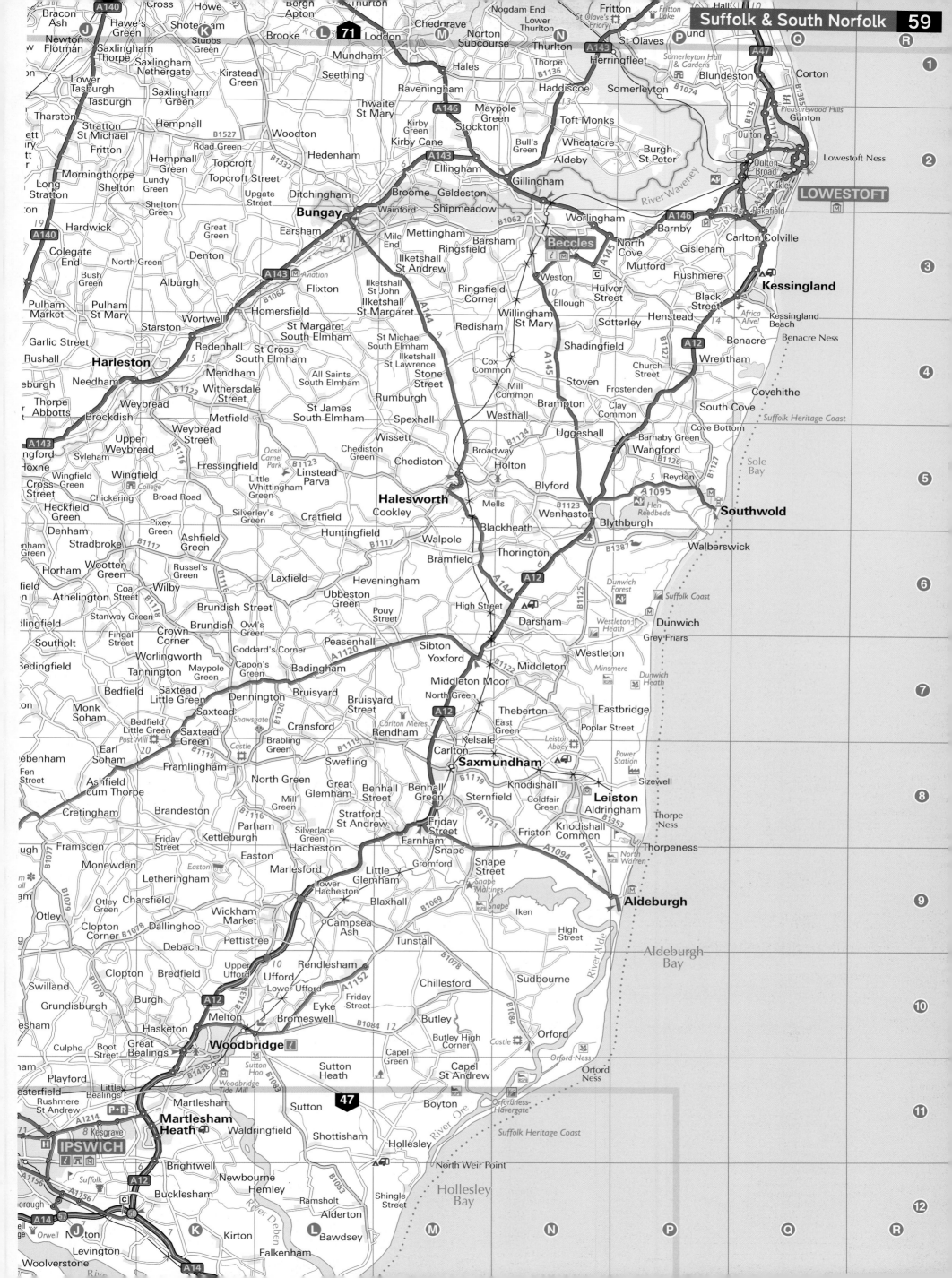

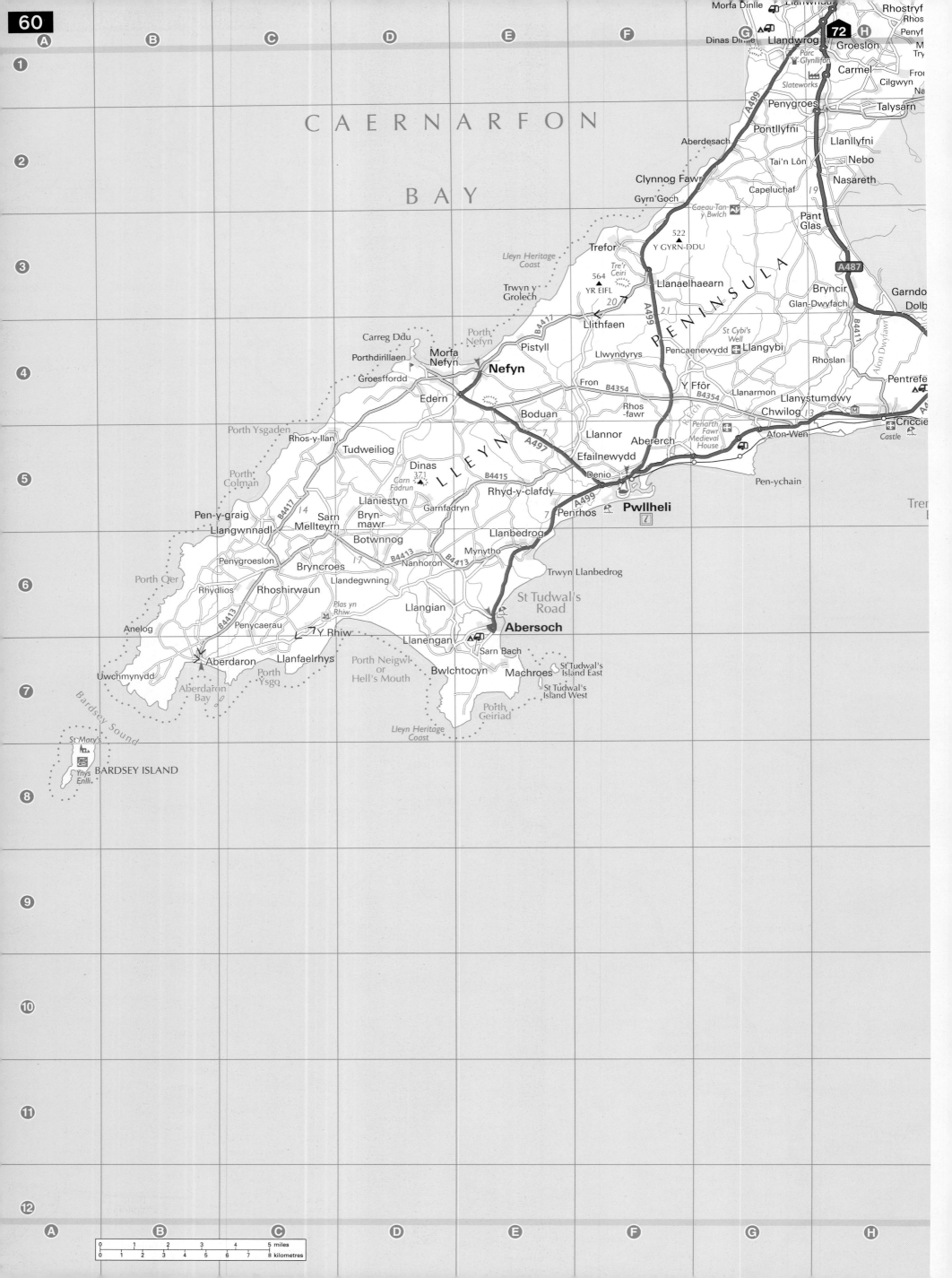

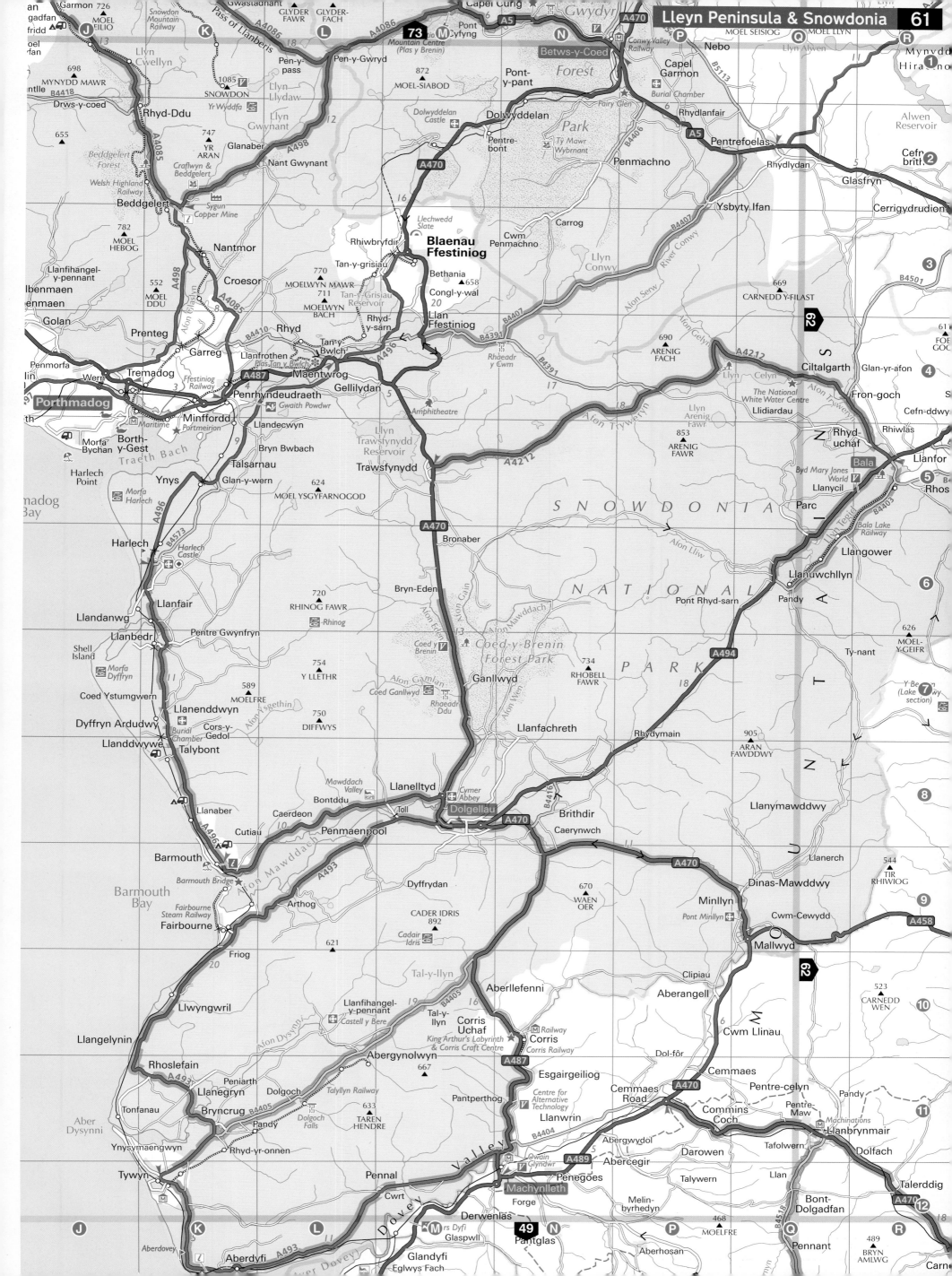

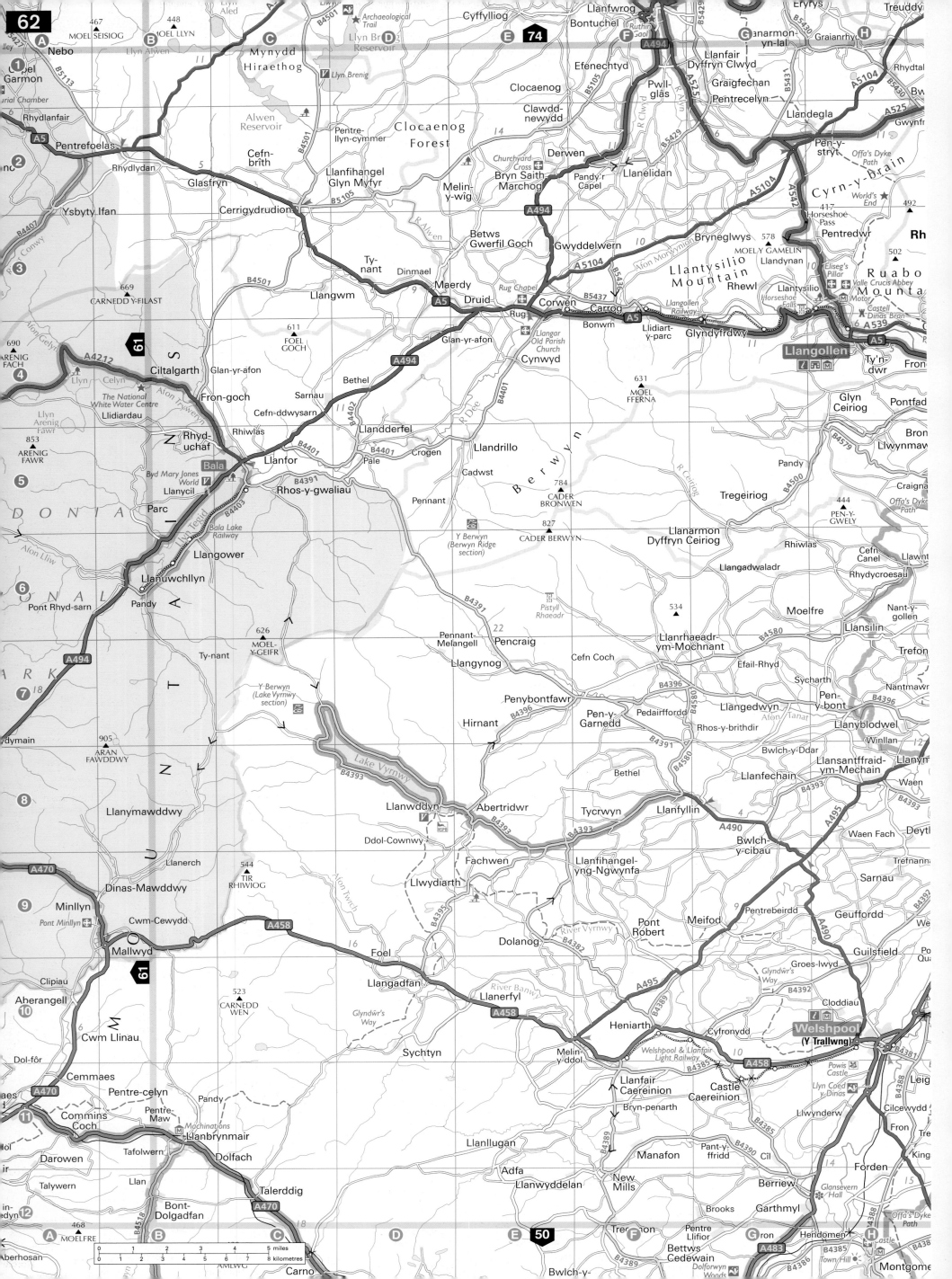

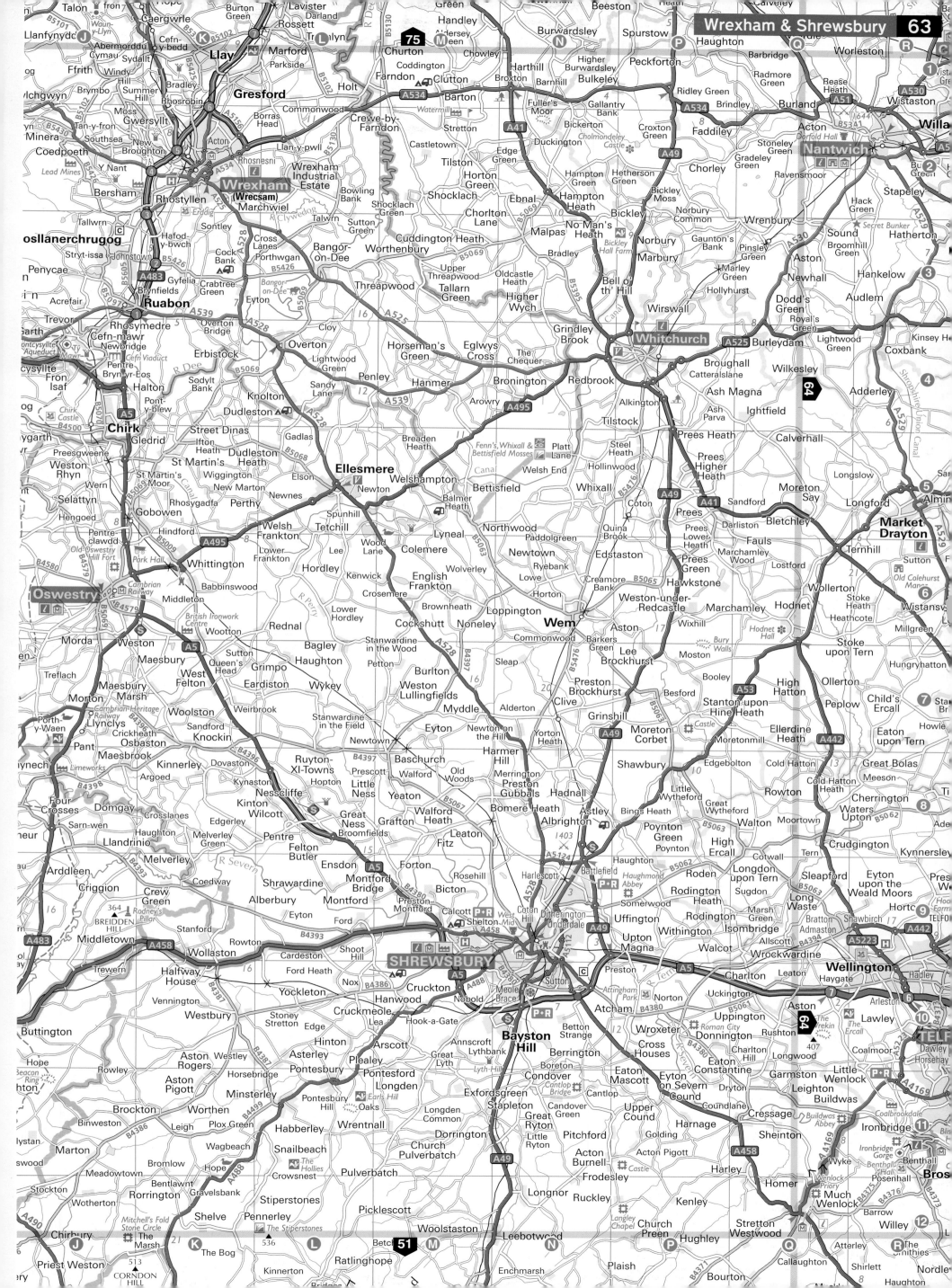

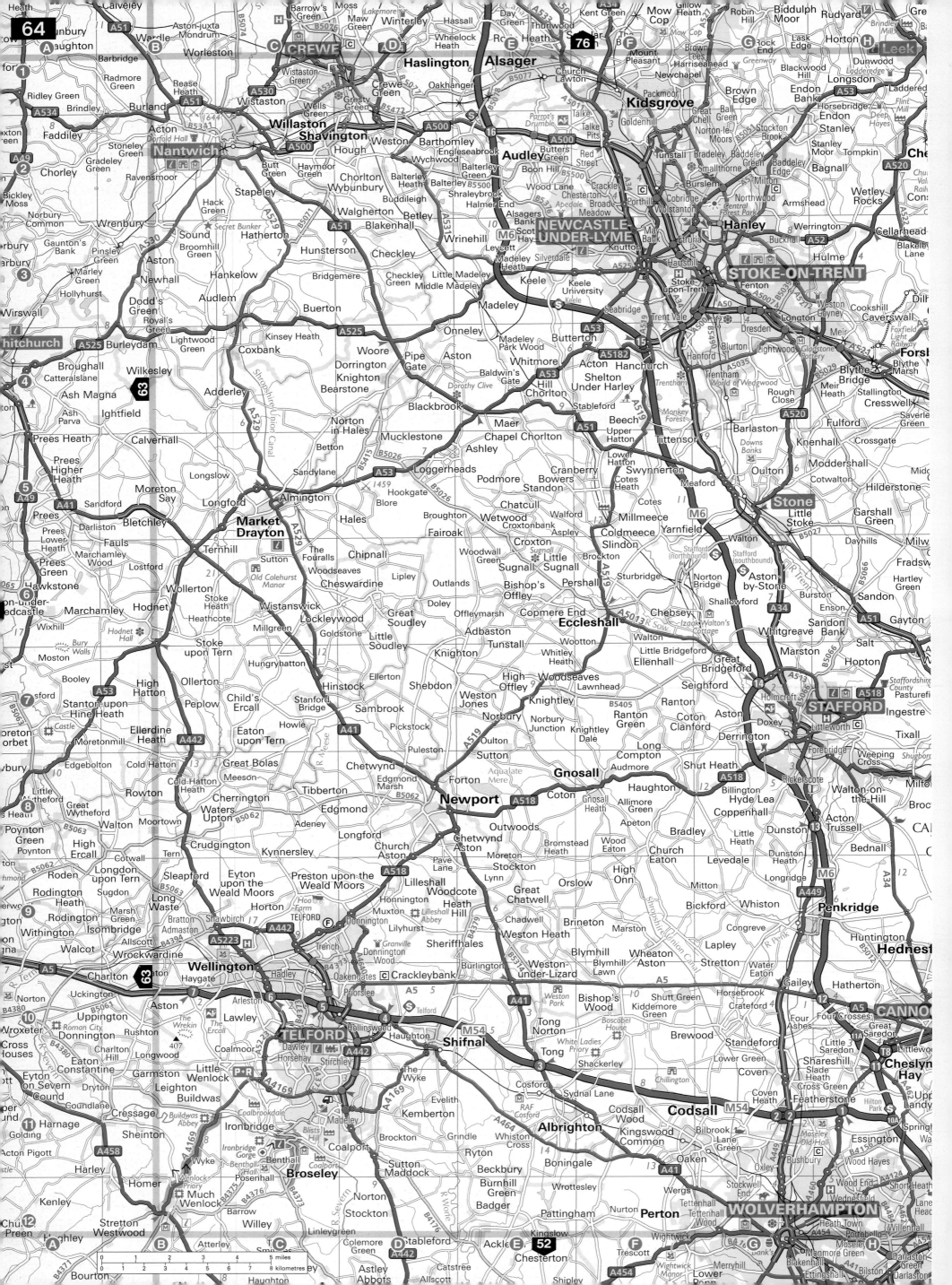

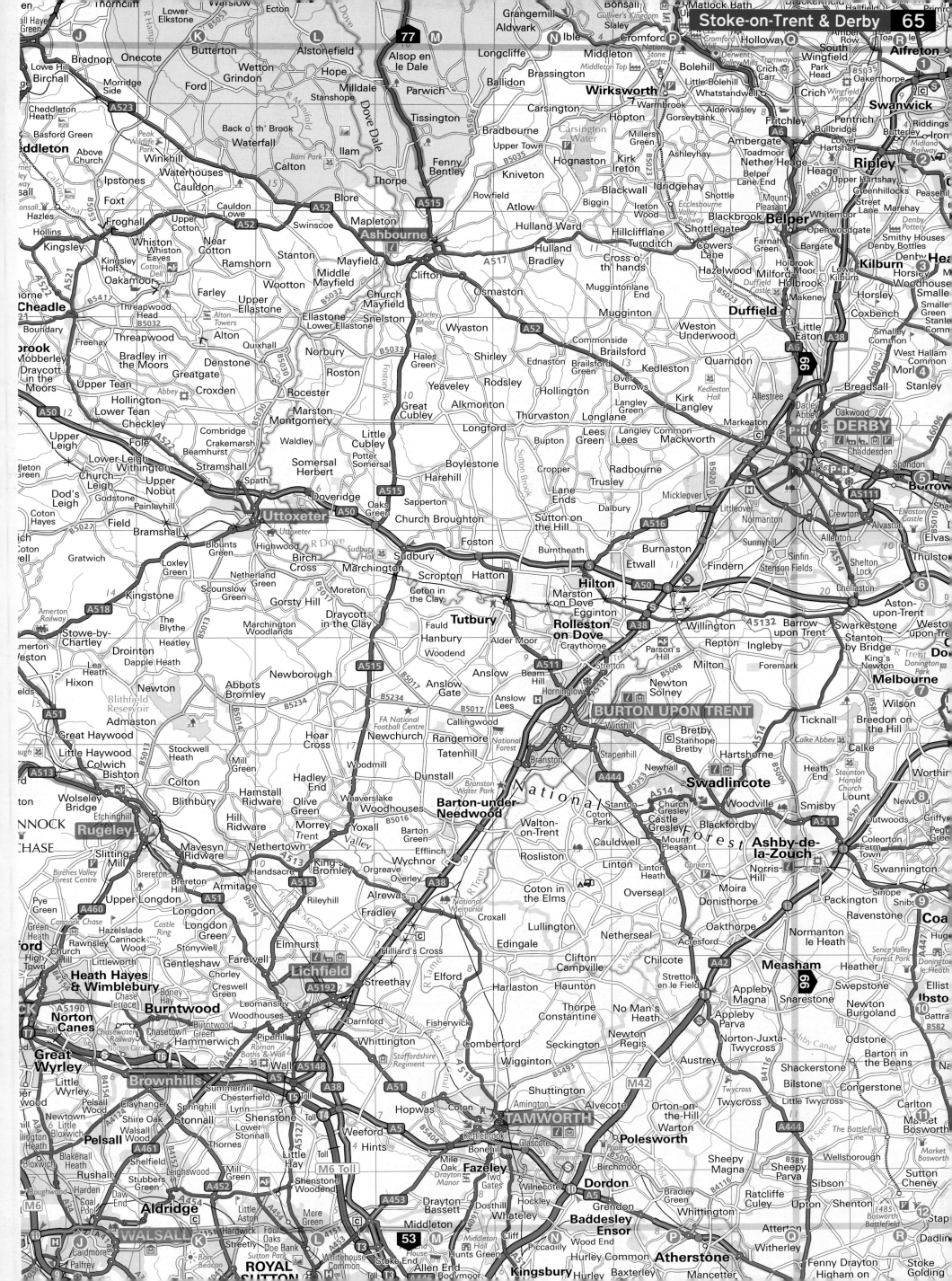

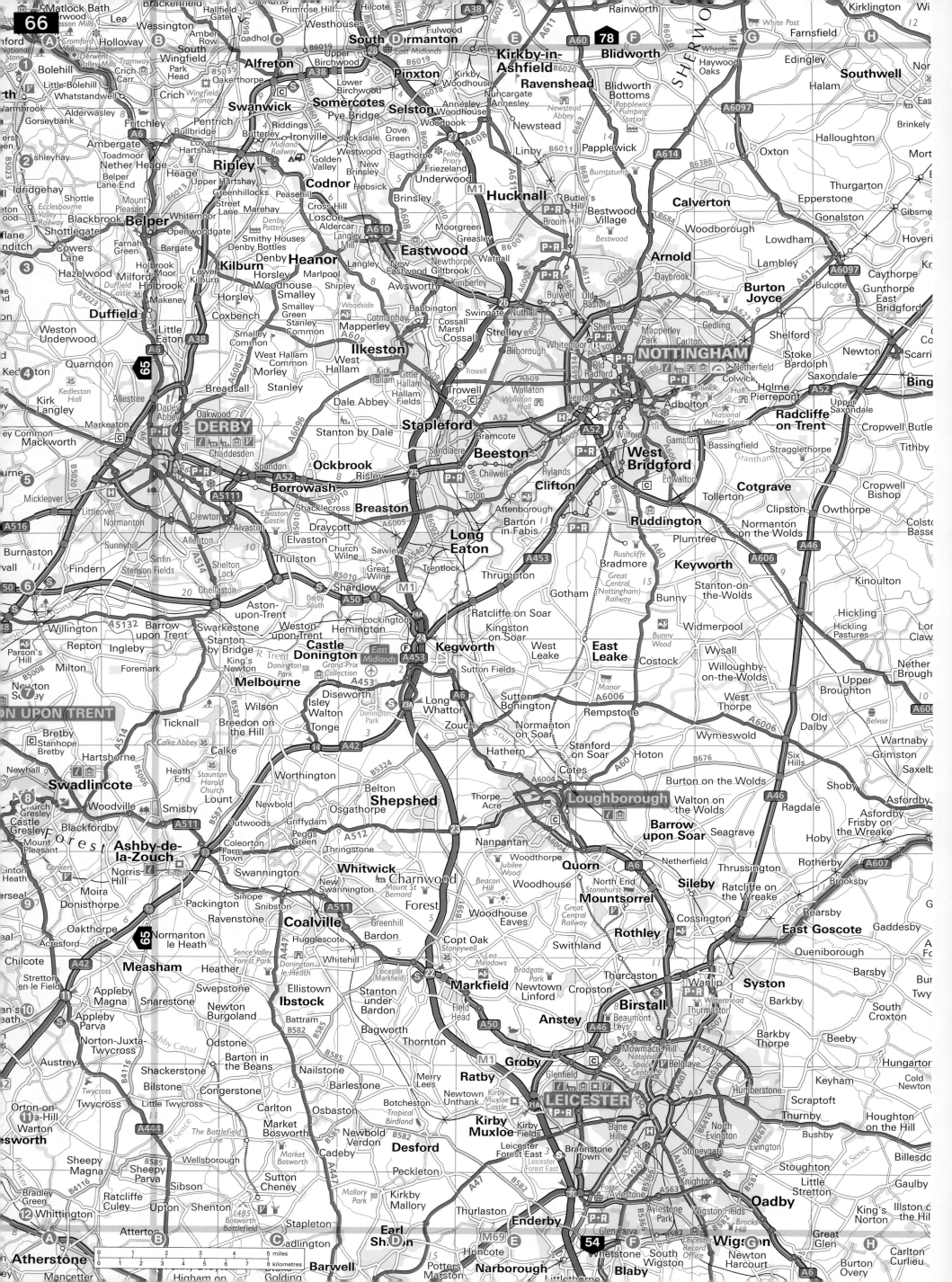

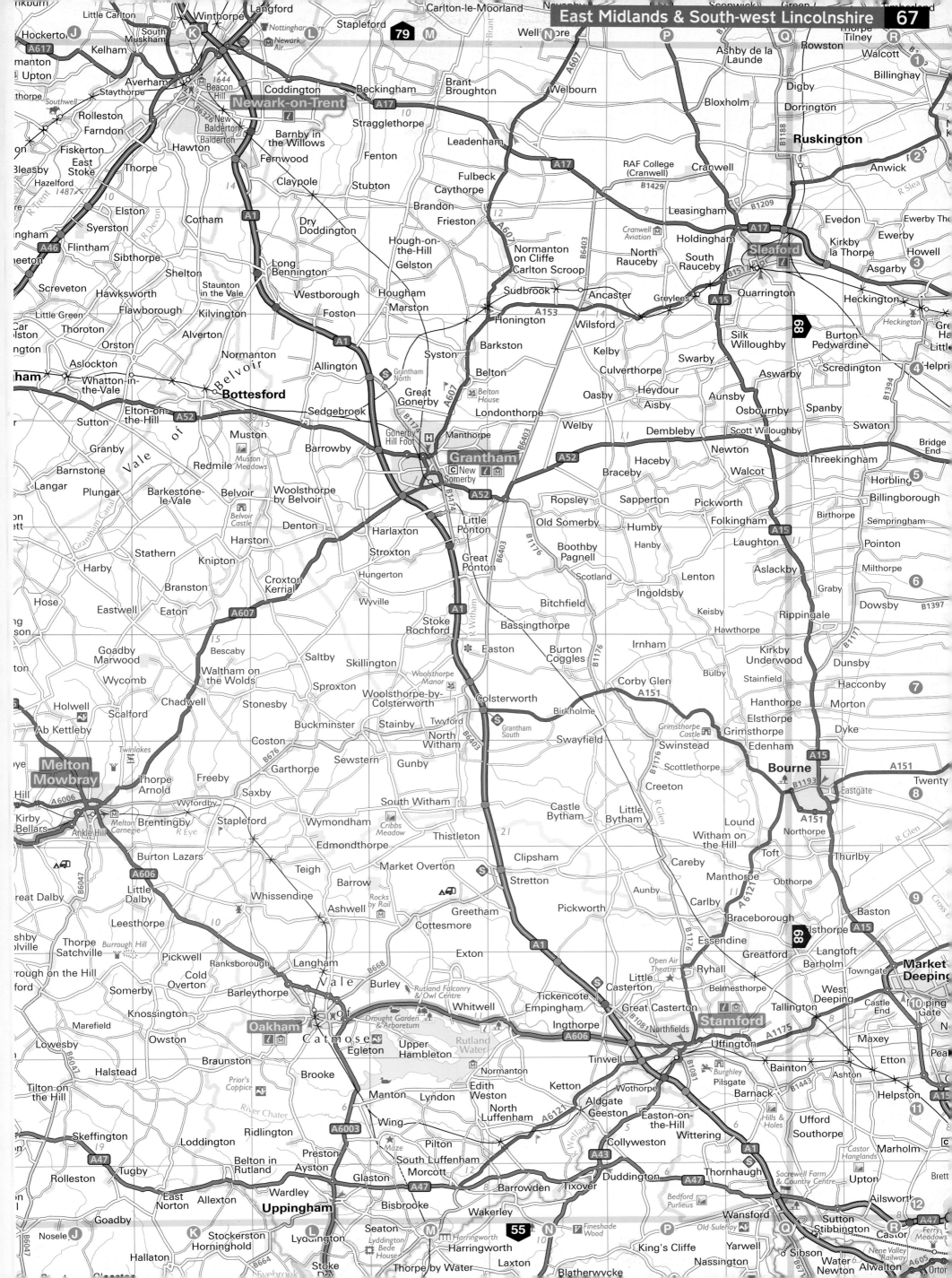

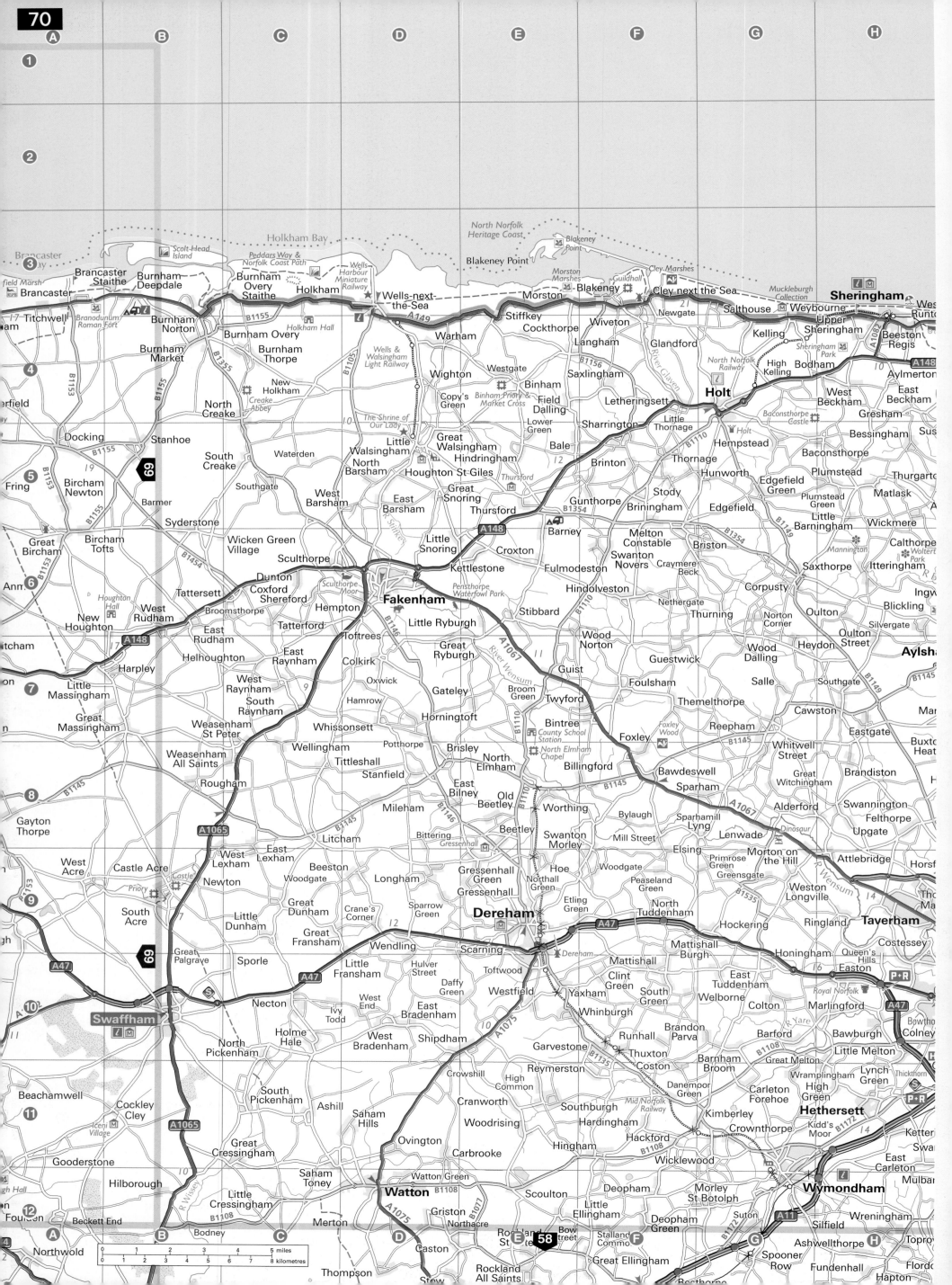

Great Yarmouth

NORWICH   CAISTER

East Runton
Cromer
Overstrand
Felbrigg
Sidestrand
Northrepps
Crossdale Street
Trimingham
Metton
Gimingham
Roughton
Hanworth
Southrepps
Mundesley
Stow Mill
Alby Hill
Thorpe Market
Lower Street
Paston
borough
Trunch
Knapton
Bacton
Bradfield
Old Hall Street
Edingthorpe
Walcott
Antingham
Suffield
Swafield
Pollard Street
Colby
Edingthorpe Green
Happisburgh
North Walsham
Witton
Ridlington
Banningham
Spa Common
Ridlington Street
Whimpwell Green
Felmingham
Tungate
Meeting House Hill
Crostwight
Happisburgh Common
Eccles on Sea
Hempstead
Tuttington
Norfolk Motorcycle
Honing
Lessingham
Ingham Corner
Skeyton Corner
Westwick
Bengate
Briggate
East Ruston
Ingham
Sea Palling
Burgh next Aylsham
Skeyton
Worstead
Stalham
Waxham
Bure Valley Railway
Dilham
Stalham Green
Swanton Abbott
Sloley
Frankfort
Low Street
Hickling
Horsey Corner
Oxnead
Lamas
Scottow
Fairstead
Smallburgh
Barton Turf
Sutton
Hickling Green
Horsey
Brampton
Badersfield
Little Hautbois
Pennygate
Wood Street
Hickling Heath
Hill Common
Horsey Windpump
Westgate Street
Buxton
Sco Ruston
Tunstead
Crowgate Street
Neatishead
Catfield
Hickling Broad
Stratton Strawless
St James
Crostwick
Irstead
Catfield Common
Martham Broad
East Somerton
Waterloo
Horstead
Coltishall
Threehammer Common
Sharp Green
Potter Heigham
West Somerton
Winterton-on-Sea
Hainford
Belaugh
Hoveton
Wroxham Barns
Ludham
Martham
Hemsby Hole
Frettenham
Wroxham
BeWILDerwood
RAF Radar
Johnson Street
Bastwick
Cess
Hemsby
Newton St Faith
Upper Street
Horning
Upper Street
Repps
Ormesby Broad
Newport
Horsham St Faith
Crostwick
Thurne
Rollesby
Ormesby St Michael
Scratby
Spixworth
Rackheath
Salhouse
Ranworth
Broads Wildlife Centre
Clippesby
Fleggburgh/Burgh St Margaret
California
New Rackheath
Ranworth Broad
Pilson Green
Billockby
Ormesby St Margaret
Caister-on-Sea
NORWICH
Little Plumstead
Panxworth
South Walsham
Cargate Green
Thrigby
Filby
Mautby
Caister Roman Fort
Sprowston
Thorpe End
Fairhaven
Town Green
Upton
Thrigby Hall
West End
West Caister
Great Plumstead
Blofield Heath
Burlingham Green
North Burlingham
Acle
Stokesby
Runham
Thorpe St Andrew
Witton
Hemblington
Stracey Arms Windpump
NORWICH
Blofield
Lingwood
Damgate
Runham
Brundall
Beighton
Tunstall
GREAT YARMOUTH
Postwick
Strumpshaw
South Burlingham
Moulton St Mary
THE BROADS
Norfolk Ski Centre
Buckenham
Halvergate
Berney Marshes
River Yare
Southtown
Trowse Newton
Surlingham
Southwood
Freethorpe
Burgh Castle
GREAT YARMOUTH
Arminghall
Hassingham
Freethorpe Common
Berney Arms Windmill
Gorleston-on-Sea
Caister St Edmund
Framingham Pigot
Bramerton
Rockland St Mary
Cantley
Wickhampton
Burgh Castle
Keswick
Framingham Earl
Claxton
Southwood
Belton
Bradwell
Dunston
Yelverton
Carleton St Peter
Limpenhoe
Witton Green
Caister Roman
Upper Stoke
Ashby St Mary
Langley Street
Pettitts Animal Adventure Park
Browston Green
Poringland
Hellington
Reedham
Hobland Hall
Stoke Holy Cross
Mill Common
Hardley Street
Howe
Alpington
Bergh Apton
Thurton
Chedgrave
Fritton
Swainsthorpe
Shotesham
Brooke
Loddon
Norton Subcourse
Fritton Lake
Hopton on Sea
Bracon Ash
Hawe's Green
Stubbs
Nogdam End
Lower Thurlton
St Olave's Priory
Newton Flotma
Saxlingham Thorpe
Mundham
Thurlton
St Olaves
Leyton Hall
Blundeston
Lower Tasburgh
Saxlingham Nethergate
Kirstead Green
Hales
Thorpe
Herringfleet
Corton
Seething
Haddiscoe
Somerleyton
Raveningham

Llandudno

(inset town map)

Great Orme Tramway
TABOR HILL
Great Orme
The Grand Hotel
Llandudno Pier
PLAS ROAD
HILL TERRACE
North Shore Beach
HILL PARADE
The Old Bank Gallery
War Memorial
SOUTH PARADE
Travelodge
MOSTYN STREET
A546
GLODDAETH
A546
Town Hall
St John's
The Promenade
Llandudno Bay
Victoria
Our Lady Star of the Sea
THE PARADE
Holy Trinity
Medical Centre
LLANDUDNO STATION
Mostyn Gallery
MOSTYN BROADWAY
Swimming Pool
Venue Cymru
B5115
Police Station
Magistrates' Court
CILCH-Y-TUDOR
Fire & Ambulance Station
St Paul's
MOSTYN AVE
Ysgol Tudno
Superstore
CAE CAU
CLARENCE CRESCENT
CLYD
Ysgol Ffordd Dyffryn
CONWAY
Ysgol Morfa Rhianedd
Ysgol John Bright
Ysgol Craig Y Don
CLARENCE DRIVE
B5115
Coach
Llandudno FC
A55, BETWS-Y-COED
LBLH

0   200 m

Seawatch Centre
Moelfre
Benllech
Red Wharf Bay
Red Wharf Bay
Llanddona
Pentraeth
Llanfaes
Llangoed
Beaumaris
Beaumaris Castle
Courthouse
Llansadwrn
Llandegfan
Menai Bridge (Porthaethwy)
Bangor
Penrhyn Castle
Llandygai
Britannia Bridge
Penrhosgarnedd
Capel-y-graig
Waen-wen
Glasinfryn
Rhyd-y-groes
Pentir
Tregarth
Bethesda
Gerlan
Seion
Llanddeiniolen
Waen-pentir
Mynydd Llandygai
Rachub
Llanllechid
Saron
Penisarwaun
Rhiwlas
Ogwen Bank
Zip World Penrhyn Quarry
Llanrug
Rhiwen
Deiniolen
Cwm-y-glo
Brynrefail
Gallt-y-foel
CARNEDD DAFYDD
Llanberis Lake Railway
Llanberis
Electric Mountain
National Slate Museum
Dolbadarn Castle
Nant Peris
Gwastadnant
Snowdon Mountain Railway
Pass of Llanberis
Pen-y-pass
Pen-y-Gwryd

Puffin Island
Penmon Priory
Black Point
Caim
Penmon
Toll
GREAT ORME'S HEAD
Great Orme Heritage Coast
Great Orme Tramway
Little Ormes Head
Penrhyn Bay
Penrhynside
Conwy Bay
Llandudno
Deganwy
Llanrhos
Rhôs-on-Sea
Colwyn Bay (Bae Colwyn)
Abergele Roads
Llandrillo-yn-Rhos
Pydew
Dwygyfylchi
Tywyn
Esgyryn
Mochdre
Old Colwyn
Abergele
Conwy
Capelulo
Conwy Castle
Llandudno Junction
Llanelian-yn-Rhos
Llanddulas
Llysfaen
Rhyd-y-foel
Penmaenmawr
Penmaenan
Llansanffraid Glan Conwy
Bryn-y-Maen
Llanfairfechan
Henryd
A470
Dolwen
Nant-y-pandy
Gorddinog
SNOWDONIA
TAL-Y-FAN
Rowen
Ty'n-y-Groes
Graig
Dawn
Betws-yn-Rhos
Abergwyngregyn
Caerhun
Eglwysbach
Trofarth
Spinnies Abergowen
Coedydd Aber
Castell
Pentre'r Felin
Llanfair Talhaiarn
Tal-y-bont
Llanbedr-y-Cennin
Tal-y-Cafn
River Elwy
Llanllechid
MOEL WINION
Aber Falls
Tal-y-bont
NATIONAL
Vale of Conwy
Hafodunos
Langernyw
Afon Anafon
Pont Dolgarrog
Dolgarrog
Maenan
Mynydd Llandygai
Afon Caseg
Ogwen Bank
PARK
Llyn Eigiau
Llanddoged
Pandy Tudur
Gwytherin
Afon Dulyn
Afon Ddu
Trefriw Woollen Mills
Trefriw
Pentre-tafarn-y-fedw
Llansannan
CARNEDD LLEWELYN
Llyn Cowlyd
Llanrhychwyn
Llanrwst
Melin-y-coed
Y DROSGL
FOEL-FRAS
Adventure Parc Snowdonia
Cors Bodgynydd
Y GARN
Llyn Ogwen
Llyn Crafnant
Llyn Geirionydd
Uchaf Chapel
Llyn Aled
Pont Pen-y-benglog
The Ugly House (Ty Hyll)
Swallow Falls (Rhaeadr Ewynnol)
Conwy Valley Railway
Y TRYFAN
GLYDER FAWR
GLYDER FACH
Capel Curig
Pont Cyfyng
Gwydyr Forest
National Mountain Centre (Plas y Brenin)
A5
A470
Betws-y-Coed
Nebo
Capel Garmon
MOEL SEISIOG
MOEL LLYN
Llyn Alwen
MOEL EILIO
MOEL SIABOD
Burial Chamber
MYNYDD MAWR
Llyn Cwellyn
Pont-y-pant
Waunfawr
Betws Garmon

61
74

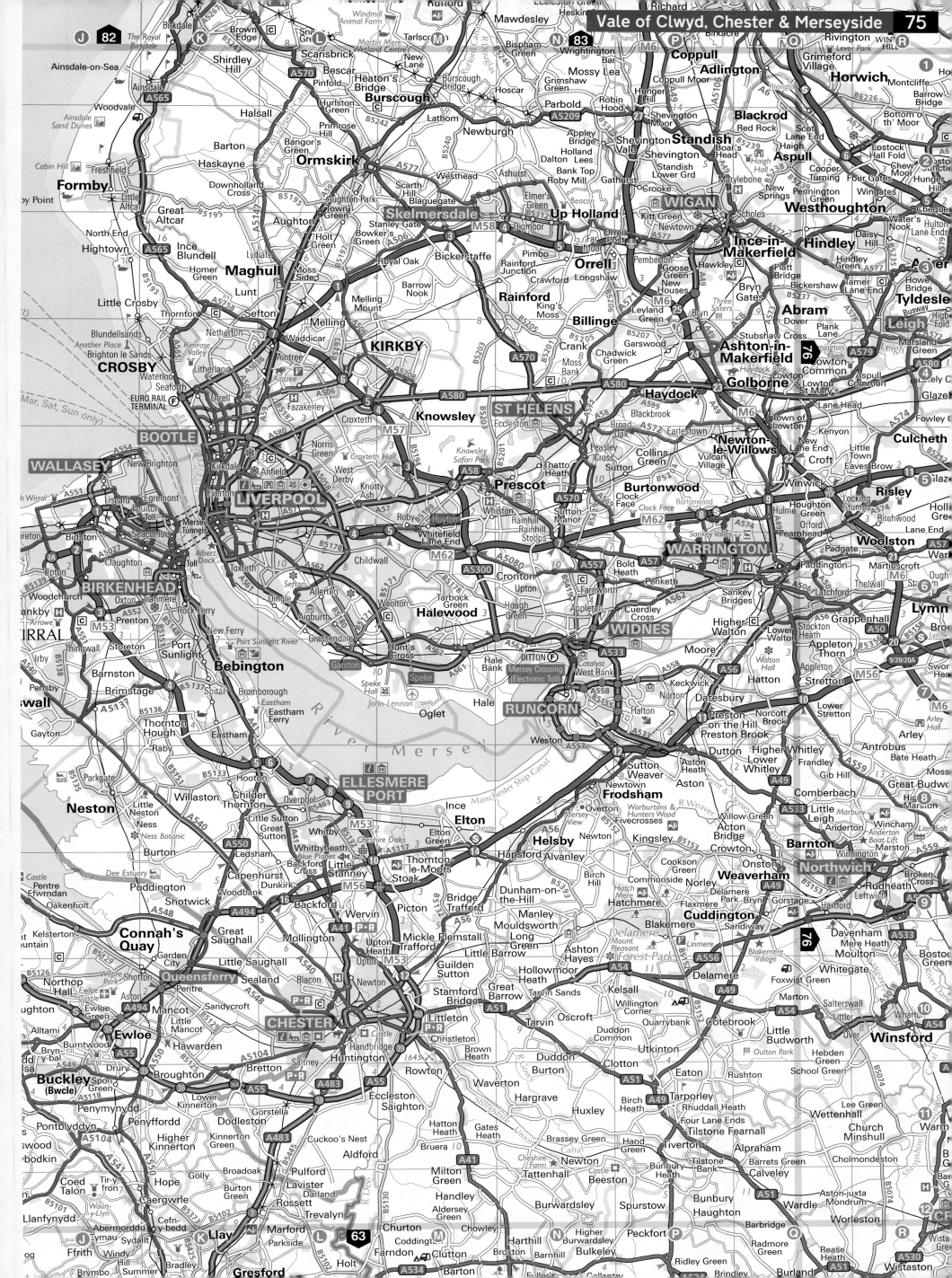

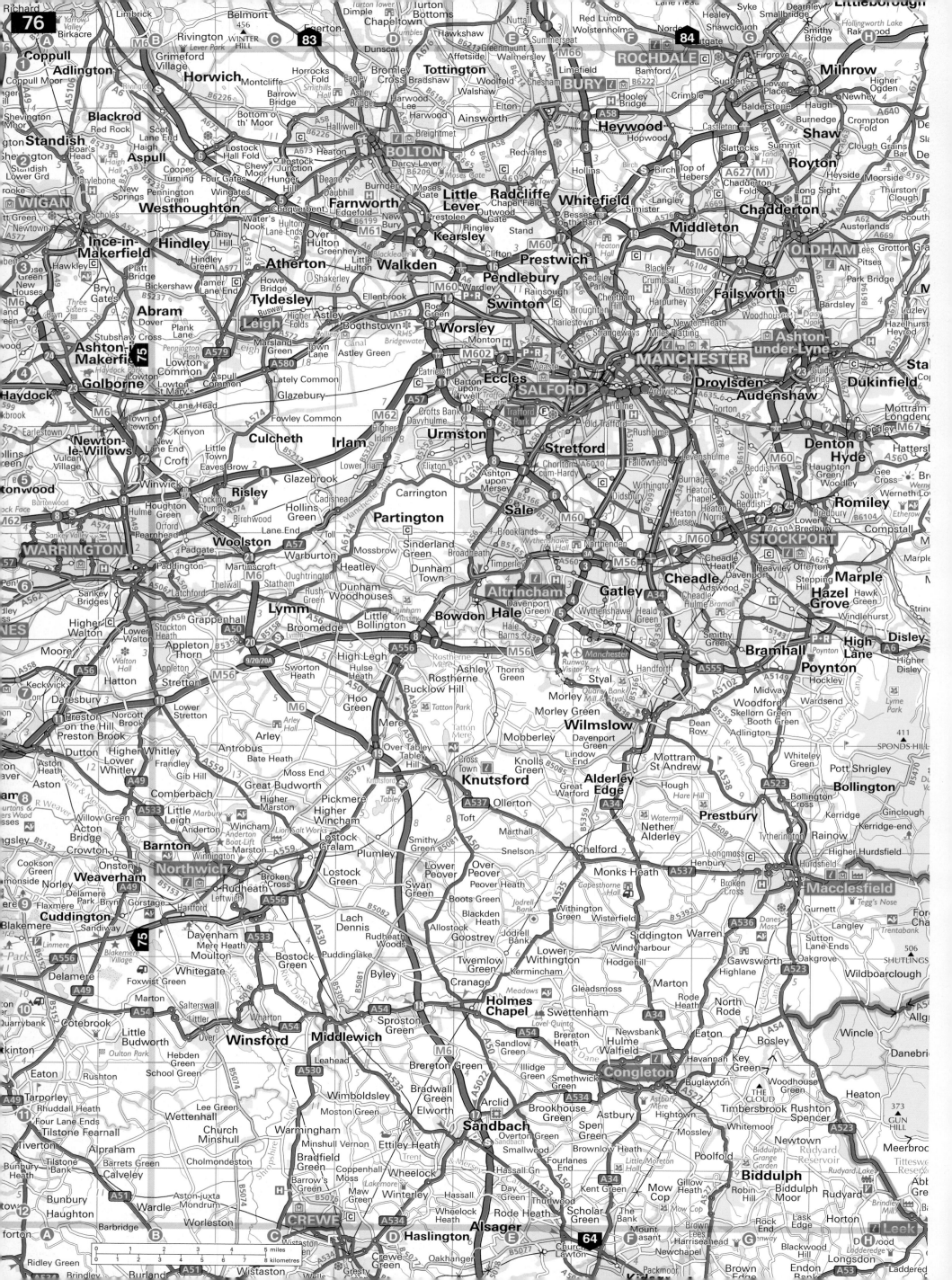

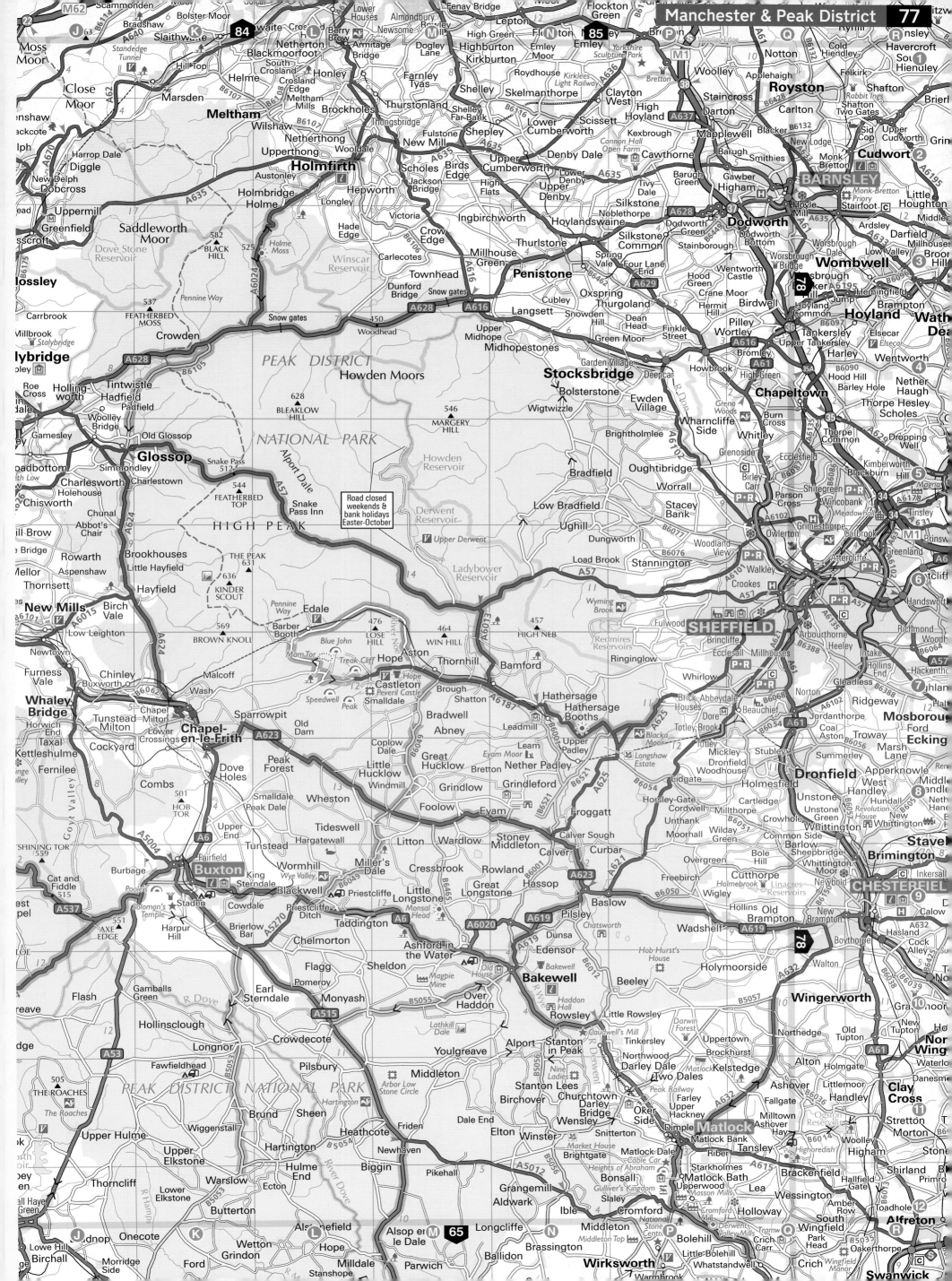

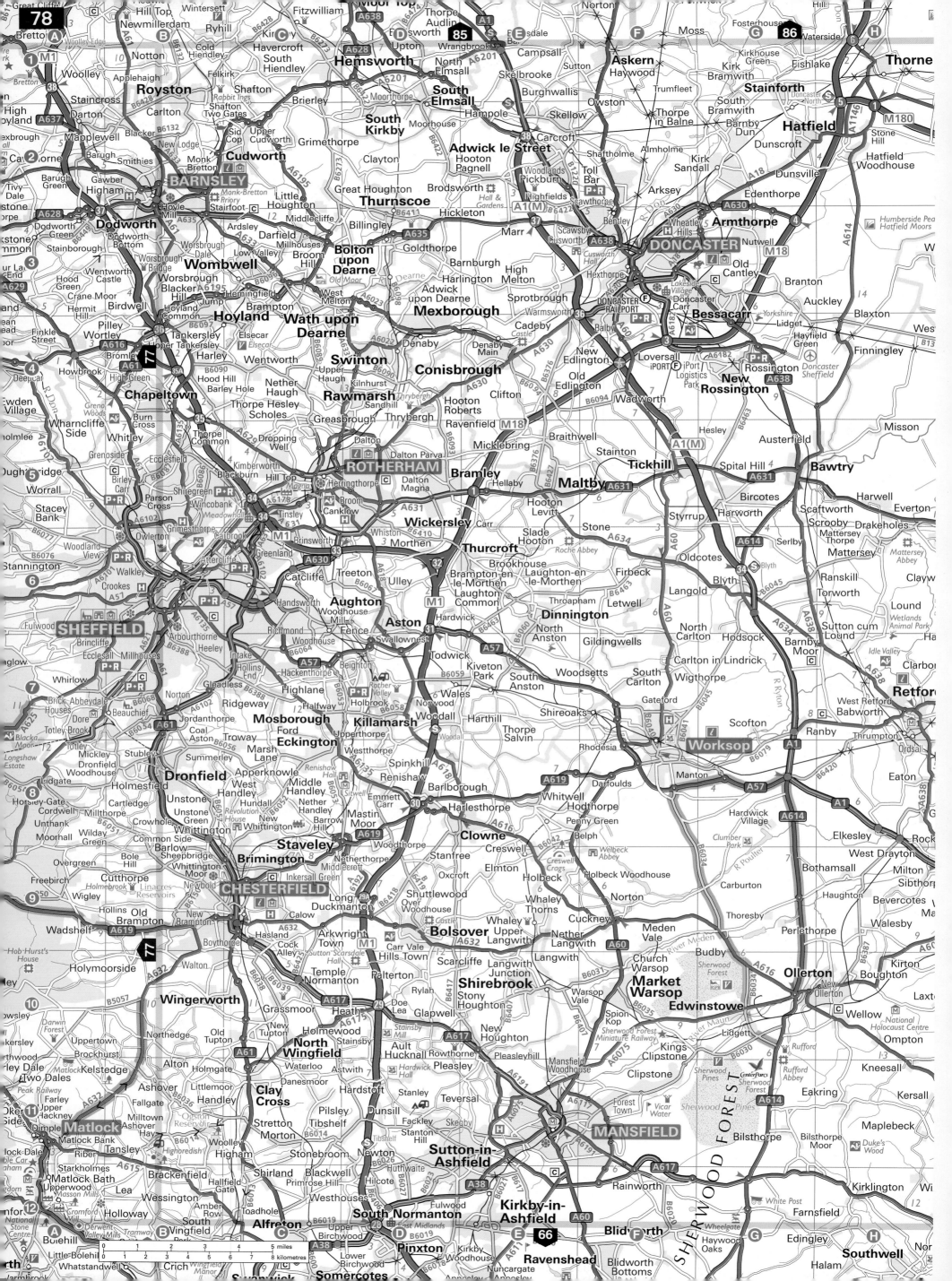

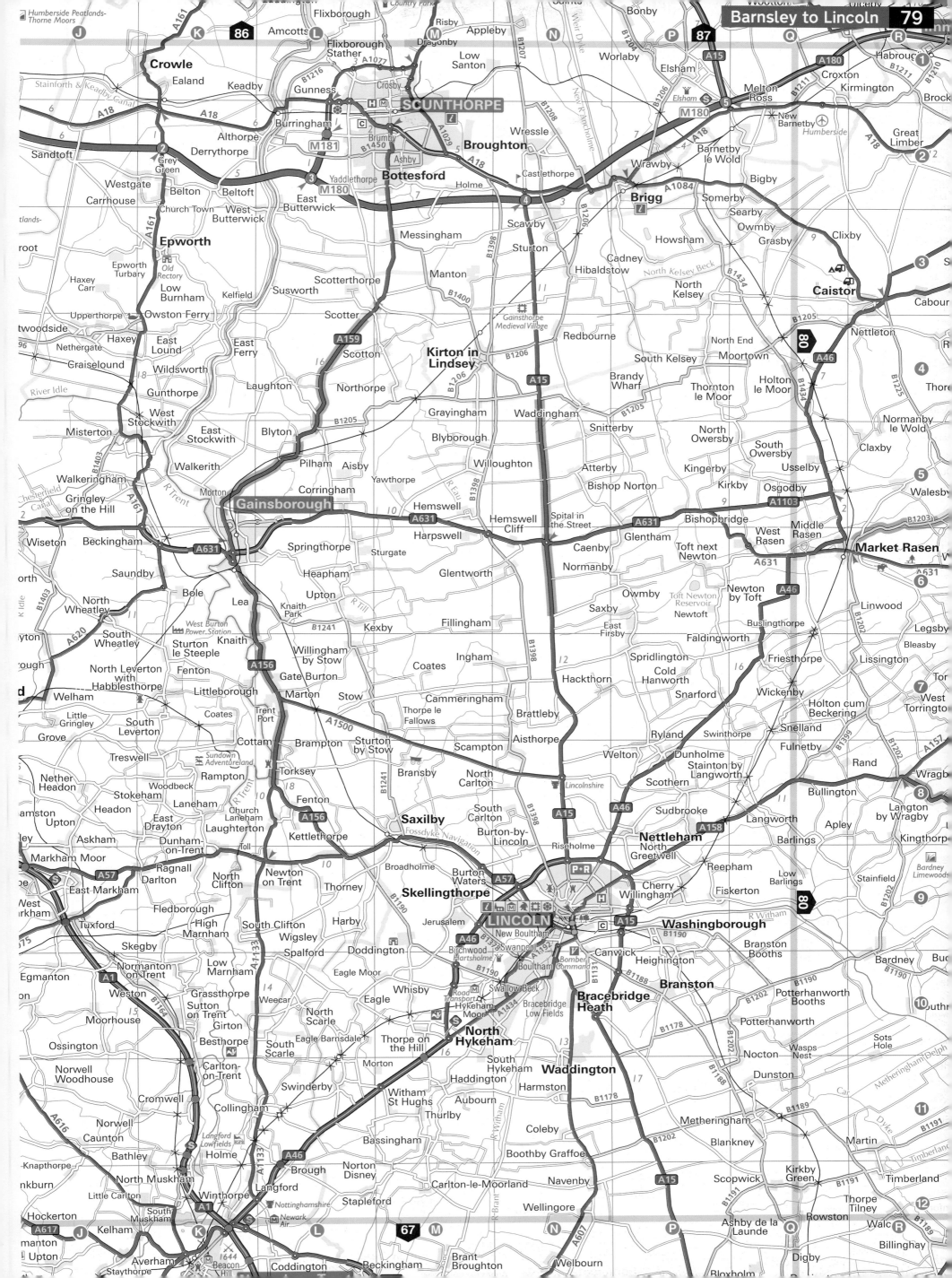

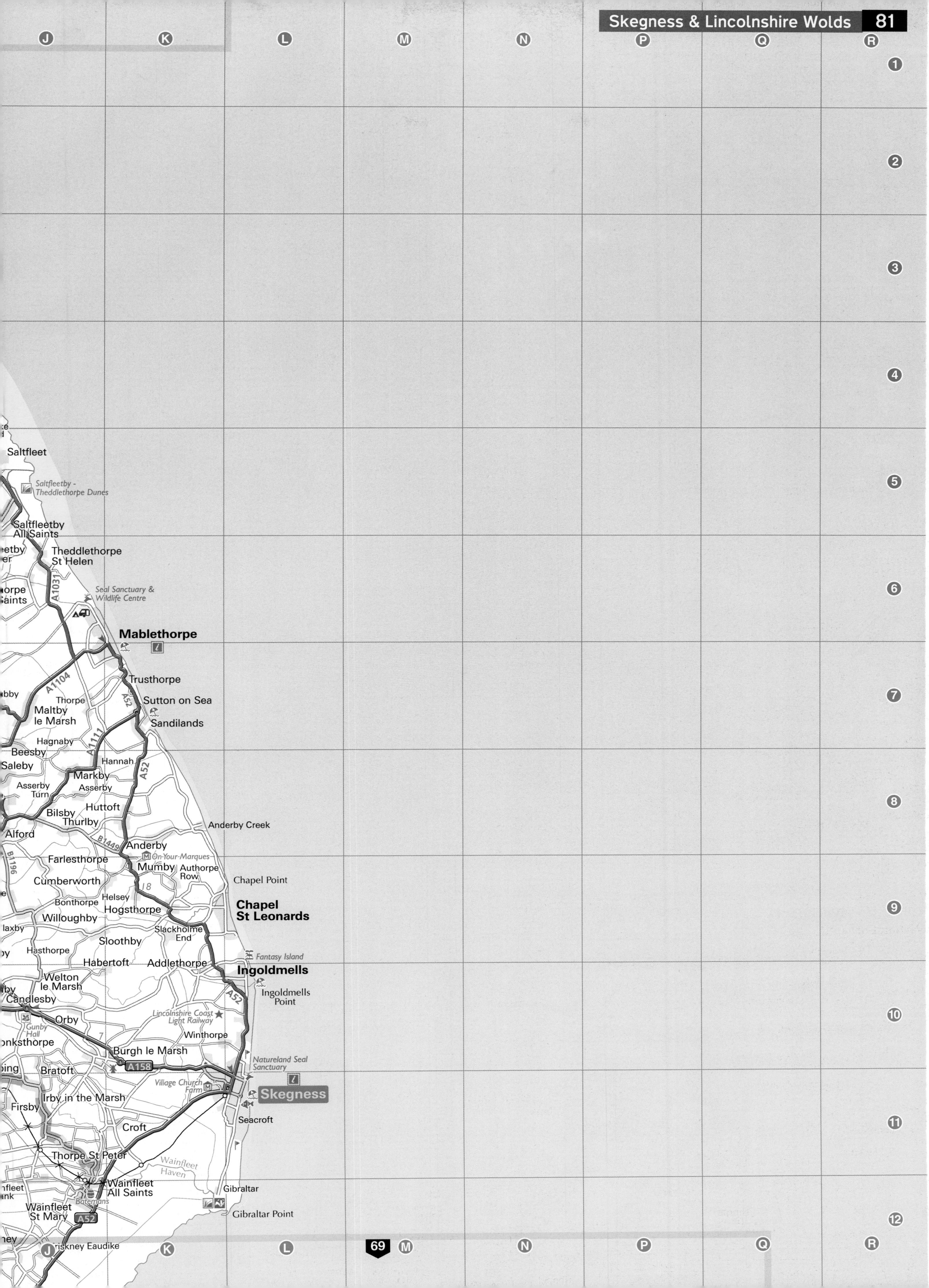

J K L M N P Q R

1
2
3
4
5
6
7
8
9
10
11
12

Saltfleet

Saltfleetby -
Theddlethorpe Dunes

Saltfleetby
All Saints

etby
er

Theddlethorpe
St Helen

orpe
aints

Seal Sanctuary &
Wildlife Centre

A1031

Mablethorpe

Trusthorpe

A1104

Thorpe

Sutton on Sea

Maltby
le Marsh

A52

Sandilands

Hagnaby

A1111

Beesby
Saleby

Hannah

Markby

A52

Asserby
Turn

Asserby

Bilsby

Huttoft

Thurlby

Anderby Creek

Alford

B1449

Anderby

B1196

Farlesthorpe

On-Your-Marques

Mumby

Authorpe
Row

Chapel Point

Cumberworth

18

Bonthorpe

Helsey

**Chapel
St Leonards**

Willoughby

Hogsthorpe

laxby

Sloothby

Slackholme
End

Hasthorpe

Fantasy Island

Habertoft

Addlethorpe

Ingoldmells

Welton
le Marsh

A52

Ingoldmells
Point

Candlesby

Orby

Lincolnshire Coast
Light Railway

Gunby
Hall

7

Winthorpe

nksthorpe

Burgh le Marsh

Natureland Seal
Sanctuary

A158

ping

Bratoft

Village Church
Farm

Skegness

Irby in the Marsh

Firsby

Seacroft

Croft

Thorpe St Peter

Wainfleet
Haven

fleet
ank

Wainfleet
All Saints

Gibraltar

Wainfleet
St Mary

A52

Gibraltar Point

ney

riskney Eaudike

J K L M N P Q R

Heysham Harbour

0   500 m

MORECAMBE
Lower Heysham
HEYSHAM
Heysham Sands
Half Moon Bay
Higher Heysham
HEYSHAM PORT STATION
Freight Terminal
ISLE OF MAN FERRY TERMINAL
Nuclear Power Stations
LANCASTER
A683
LBLH

88

ISLE OF WALNEY

Douglas

DALTON-in-Furness
Urswick
Scales
Baycliff
89
BARROW-IN-FURNESS
Furness Abbey
Hawc
Newton
Staintor with Adgarley
Aldingham
North Scale
Dendron
Gleaston
Watermill
Vickerstown
Roose
Leece
Newbiggin
Barrow Island
Walney
Biggar
Roosebeck
Roa Island
Rampside
Sheep Island
Piel Castle
Foulney Island
Piel Island
Hilpsford Point
South Walney
Piel Bar

Fleetwood
Rossall Point

Cleveleys

Thornto
Norcross
Little Bispham
Churchtow
Norbreck
Bispham
Carlet
Waroreck
North Shore
Normos
Hoohill
BLACKPOOL
Model Vi
Great
Marton
South Shore
Common
Edge
St Anne's
Royal Lytham & St Annes Ansc
Fairhaven
Lytham St Annes

SOUTHPORT
Pleasureland
P R
Birkdale
The Royal Birkdale
Ainsdale-on-Sea
Ainsdale

Blackpool

0   200 m

FLEETWOOD
BLACKPOOL NORTH STATION
LANCASTER
Metropole Hotel
PROMENADE
Grundy Art Gallery
Superstore
Sports Barn
Council Offices
GEORGE STREET
Sacred Heart
Jobcentre Plus
BUCHANAN ST
North Pier
Travelodge
St John the Evangelist
CEDAR SQUARE
TALBOT ROAD
DICKSON RD
CHURCH STREET
PRESTON STREET
A583
St John's School
Salvation Army
Grand
Winter Gardens
Medical Centre
Meeting House
Tower Festival Headland
The Blackpool Tower & Ballroom
Houndshill
Council Offices
Register Office
St John Ambulance
Spiritualist
ALBERT ROAD
CORONATION STREET
Kingdom Hall
Blackpool & Fylde College
Coral Island
Lifeboat Station
Sea Life
Market
Police Station
County Court
PALATINE
CENTRAL DRIVE
Blackpool & Fylde College
Madame Tussauds Blackpool
Magistrates' Court
Central Pier
LBLH
LYTHAM ST ANNES
PRESTON, (M55)

0   1   2   3   4   5 miles
0 1 2 3 4 5 6 7 8 kilometres

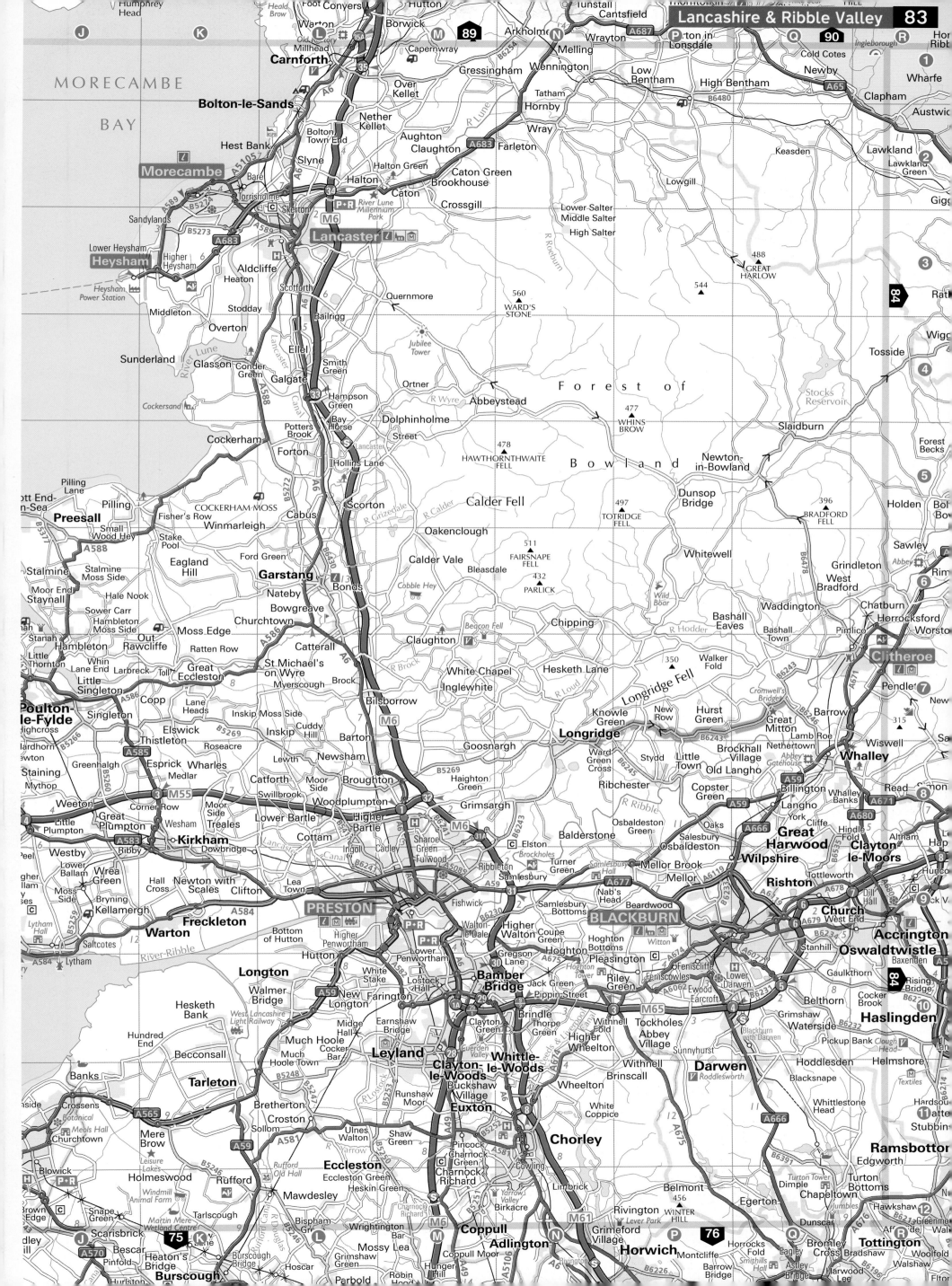

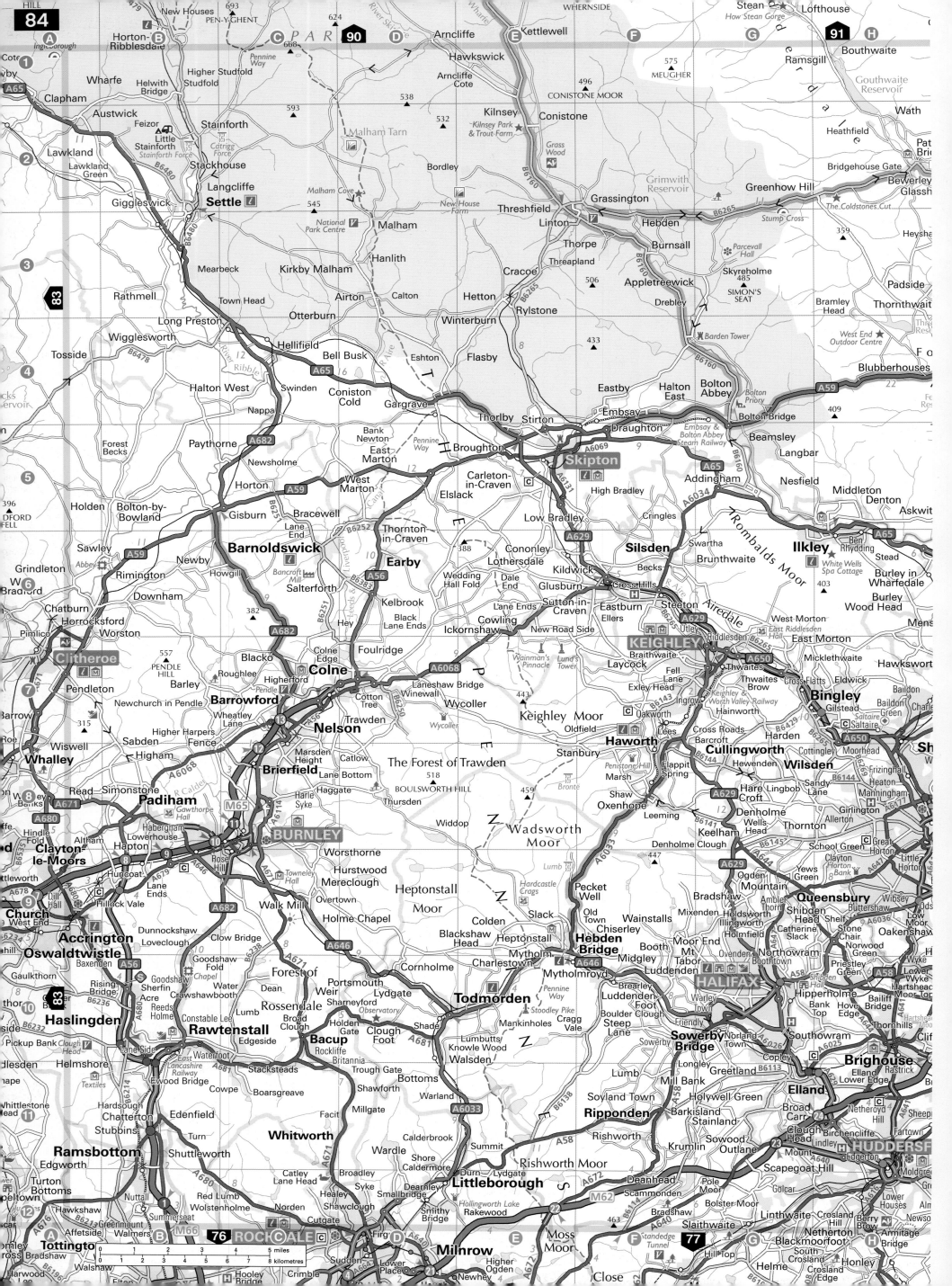

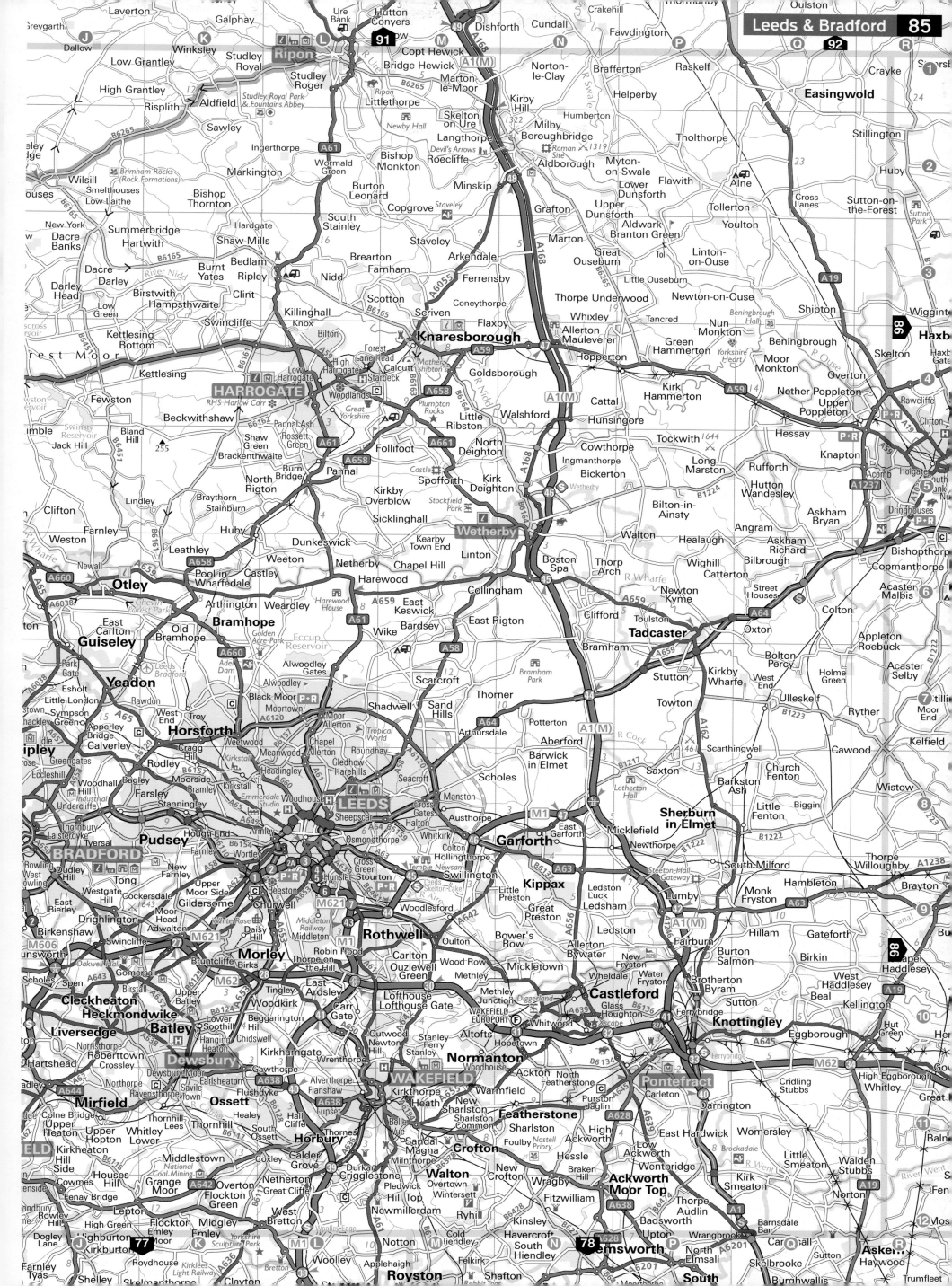

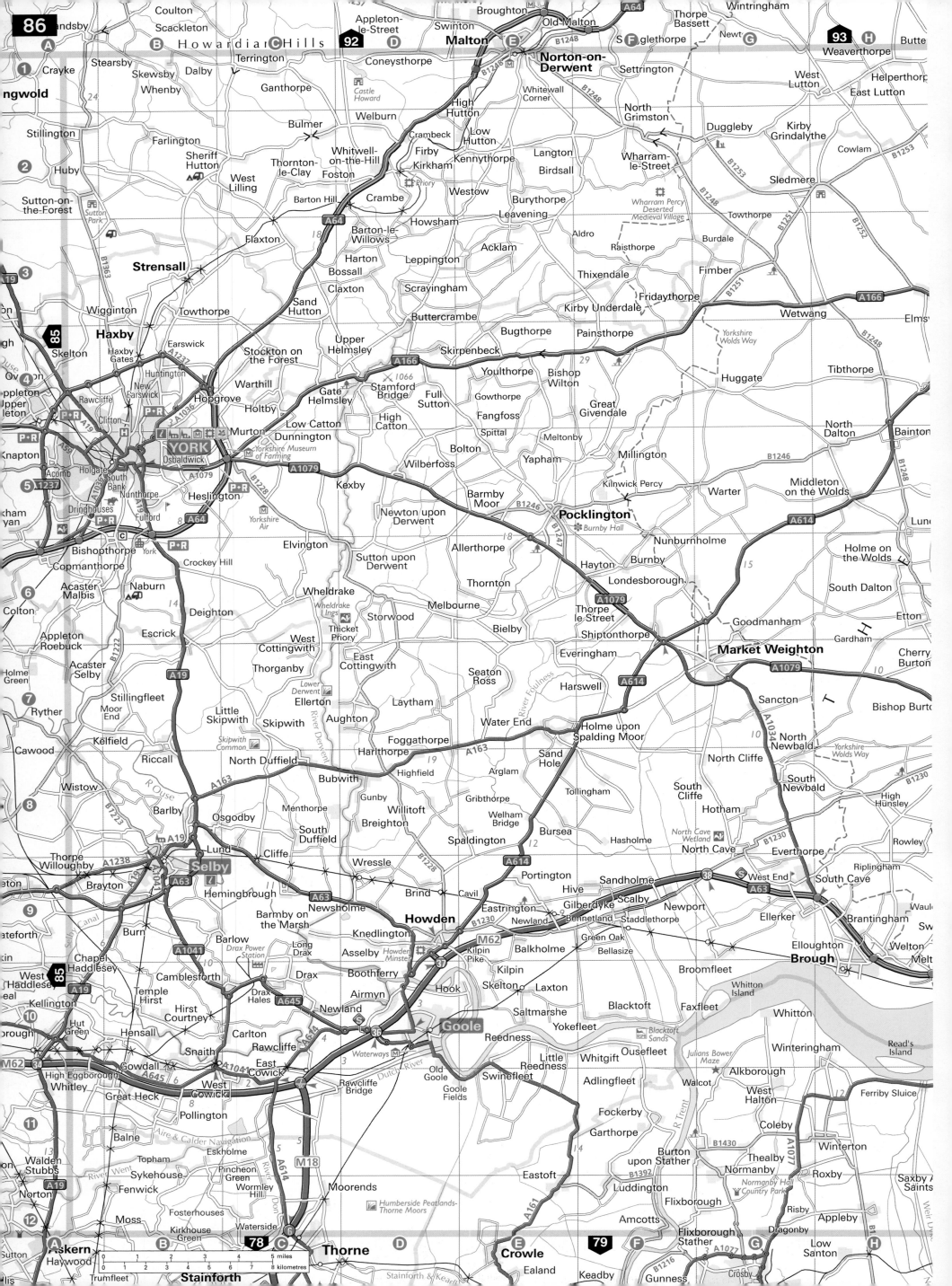

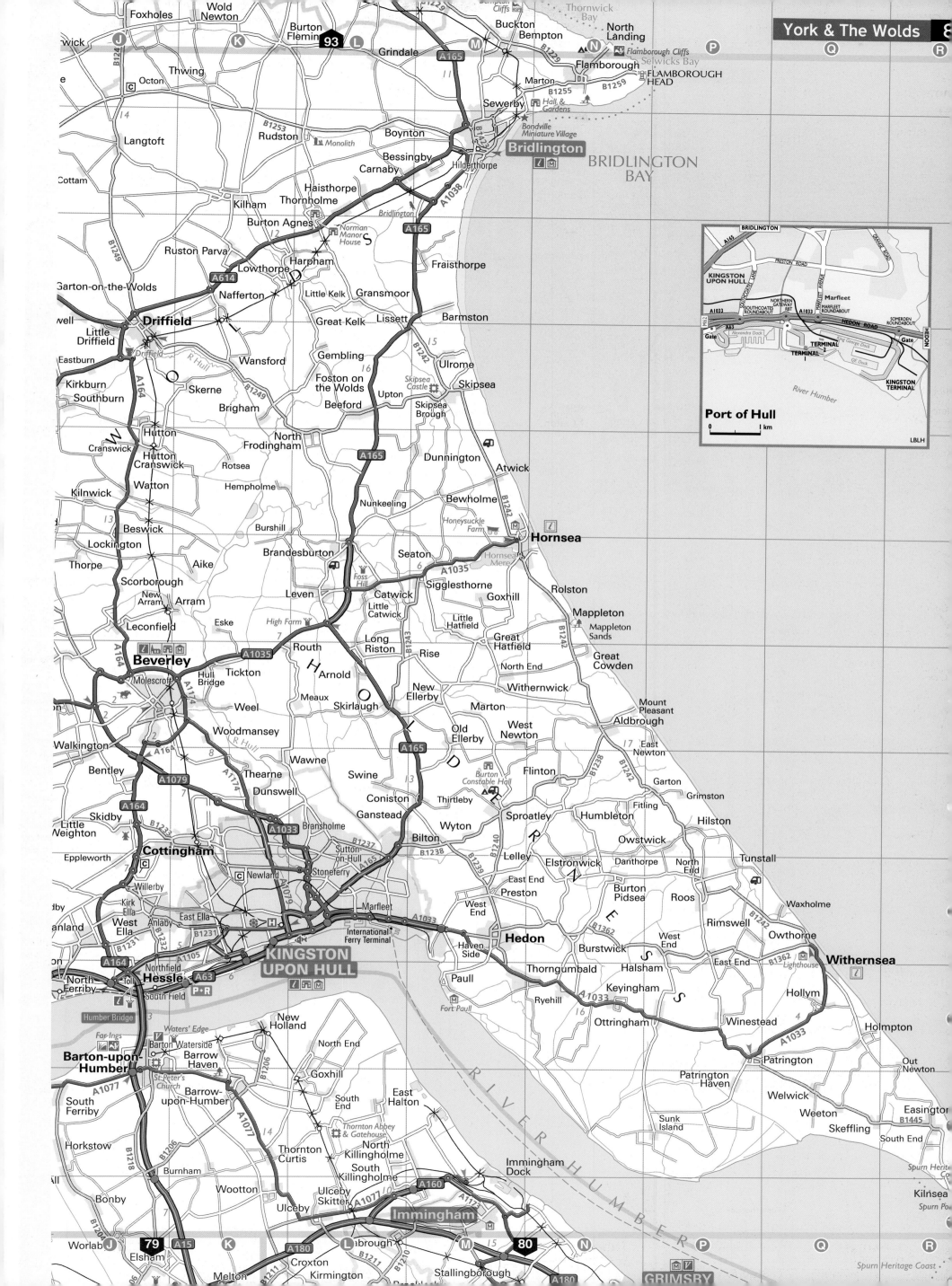

Port of Hull

BRIDLINGTON
KINGSTON UPON HULL
SOUTHCOATES ROUNDABOUT
NORTHERN GATEWAY RBT
Alexandra Dock
King George Dock
QE Dock
Marfleet
MARFLEET ROUNDABOUT
SOMERDEN ROUNDABOUT
HEDON ROAD
HEDON
KINGSTON TERMINAL
TERMINAL 1
TERMINAL 2
Gate
Gate
PRESTON ROAD
GRANGE ROAD
MARFLEET AVENUE
SOUTHCOATES LANE
River Humber
A165
A1033
A63
M62
LBLH
0   km

Foxholes
Wold Newton
Burton Fleming
93
Grindale
Buckton
Bempton
North Landing
Flamborough Cliffs
Flamborough
FLAMBOROUGH HEAD
Selwicks Bay
Thwing
Octon
Langtoft
Rudston
Monolith
Boynton
Bessingby
Carnaby
Hilderthorpe
Sewerby
Hall & Gardens
Bondville Miniature Village
Bridlington
BRIDLINGTON BAY
Cottam
Kilham
Haisthorpe
Thornholme
Burton Agnes
Norman Manor House
Bridlington
Fraisthorpe
Garton-on-the-Wolds
Ruston Parva
Lowthorpe
Harpham
Little Kelk
Gransmoor
Barmston
Driffield
Nafferton
Little Driffield
Great Kelk
Lissett
Eastburn
Wansford
Gembling
Ulrome
Skipsea
Kirkburn
Southburn
Skerne
Foston on the Wolds
Beeford
Upton
Skipsea Castle
Skipsea Brough
Brigham
Hutton
Hutton Cranswick
Rotsea
Hempholme
Dunnington
Atwick
Cranswick
Watton
Kilnwick
Nunkeeling
Bewholme
Honeysuckle Farm
Beswick
Burshill
Brandesburton
Seaton
Hornsea
Hornsea Mere
Lockington
Thorpe
Aike
Foss Hill
A1035
Sigglesthorne
Goxhill
Rolston
Scorborough
New Arram
Arram
Leven
Catwick
Little Catwick
Little Hatfield
Mappleton
Mappleton Sands
Leconfield
Eske
High Farm
Long Riston
Rise
Great Hatfield
North End
Great Cowden
Beverley
Molescroft
Routh
Arnold
New Ellerby
Withernwick
Mount Pleasant
Tickton
Hull Bridge
Meaux
Skirlaugh
Marton
Aldbrough
Weel
Woodmansey
Swine
Old Ellerby
West Newton
East Newton
Walkington
Wawne
Coniston
Thirtleby
Flinton
Garton
Grimston
Bentley
Thearne
Dunswell
Ganstead
Wyton
Burton Constable Hall
Sproatley
Humbleton
Fitling
Hilston
Skidby
Little Weighton
Bransholme
Bilton
Lelley
Elstronwick
Danthorpe
North End
Owstwick
Tunstall
Eppleworth
Newland
Sutton-on-Hull
Stoneferry
East End
Preston
Burton Pidsea
Roos
Cottingham
Willerby
Marfleet
West End
Keyingham
Rimswell
Waxholme
Kirk Ella
West Ella
East Ella
Anlaby
International Ferry Terminal
KINGSTON UPON HULL
Haven Side
Hedon
Burstwick
Halsham
East End
Withernsea
North Ferriby
Hessle
Toll
South Field
P+R
Humber Bridge
Paull
Fort Paull
Thorngumbald
Ryehill
Ottringham
Winestead
Hollym
Holmpton
Far Ings
Waters' Edge
Barton Waterside
Barrow Haven
North End
Goxhill
Patrington
Barton-upon-Humber
St Peter's Church
Barrow-upon-Humber
South End
East Halton
Patrington Haven
Welwick
Weeton
Skeffling
South Ferriby
Horkstow
Bonby
Burnham
Wootton
Thornton Curtis
Thornton Abbey & Gatehouse
North Killingholme
South Killingholme
Immingham Dock
Sunk Island
Out Newton
Kilnsea
Spurn Point
RIVER HUMBER
Worlaby
79
Elsham
Melton
Croxton
Kirmington
Immingham
80
Stallingborough
GRIMSBY
Ulceby Skitter
Ulceby
Bonby
Easington
South End
Spurn Heritage Coast

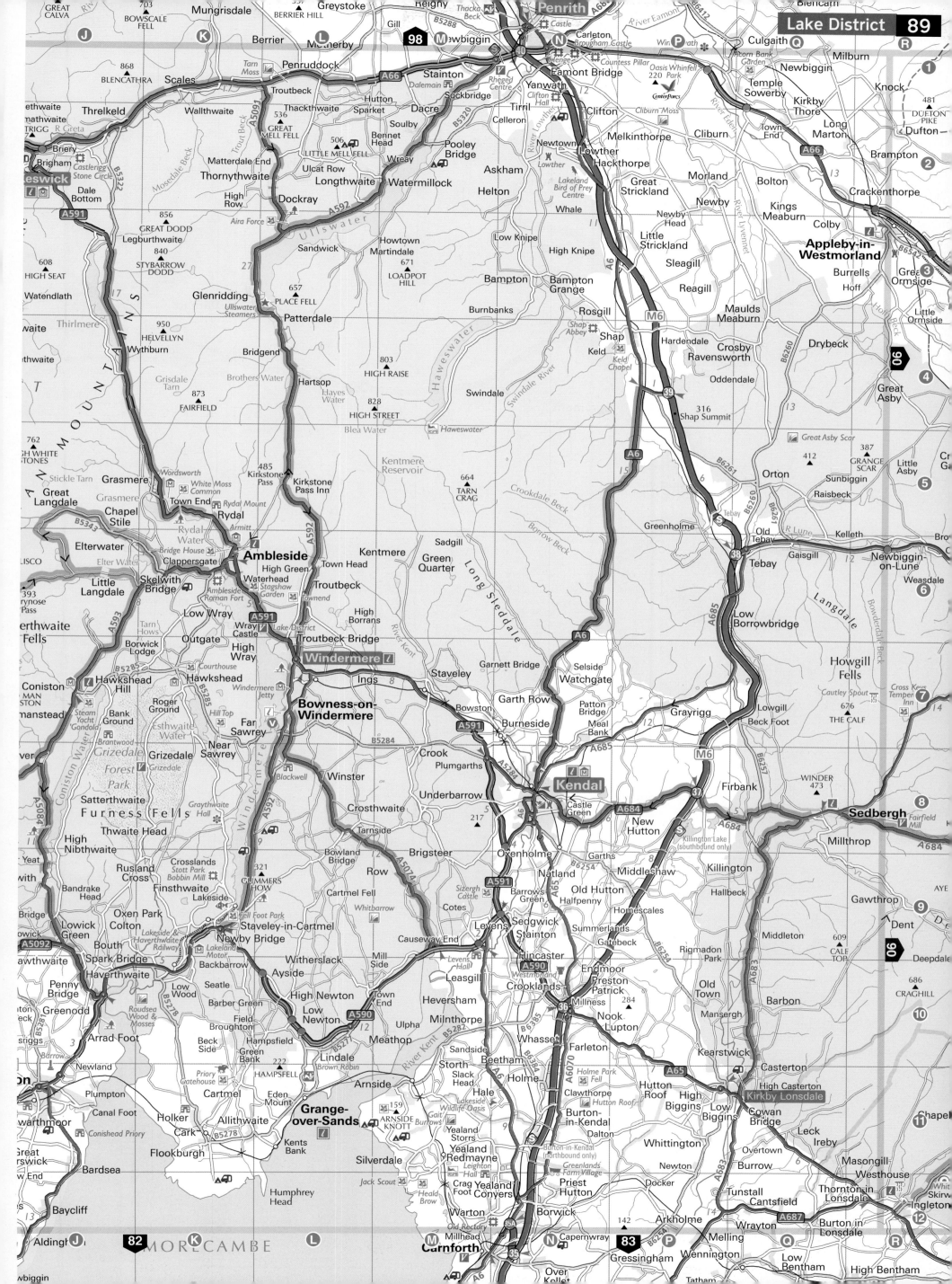

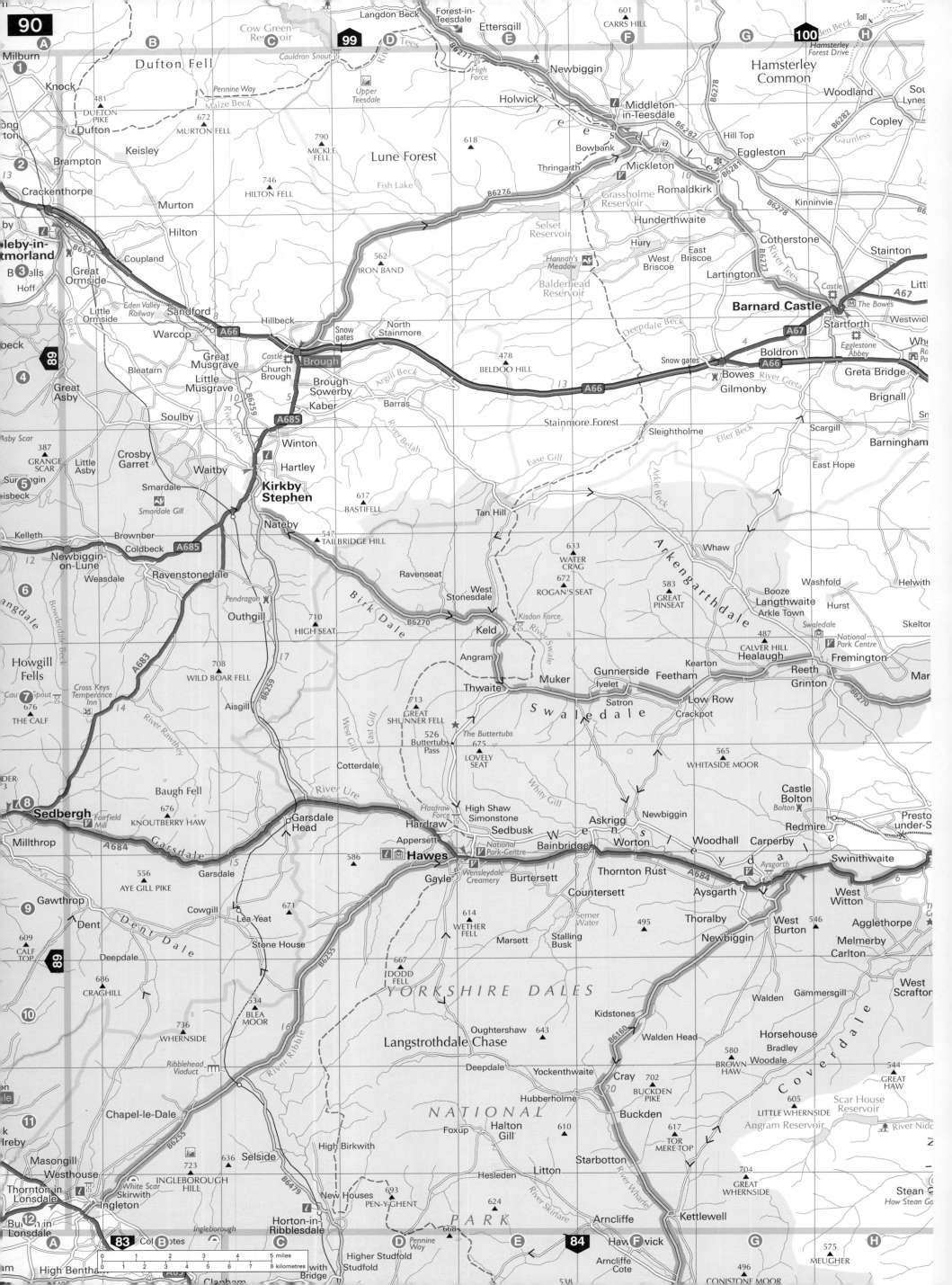

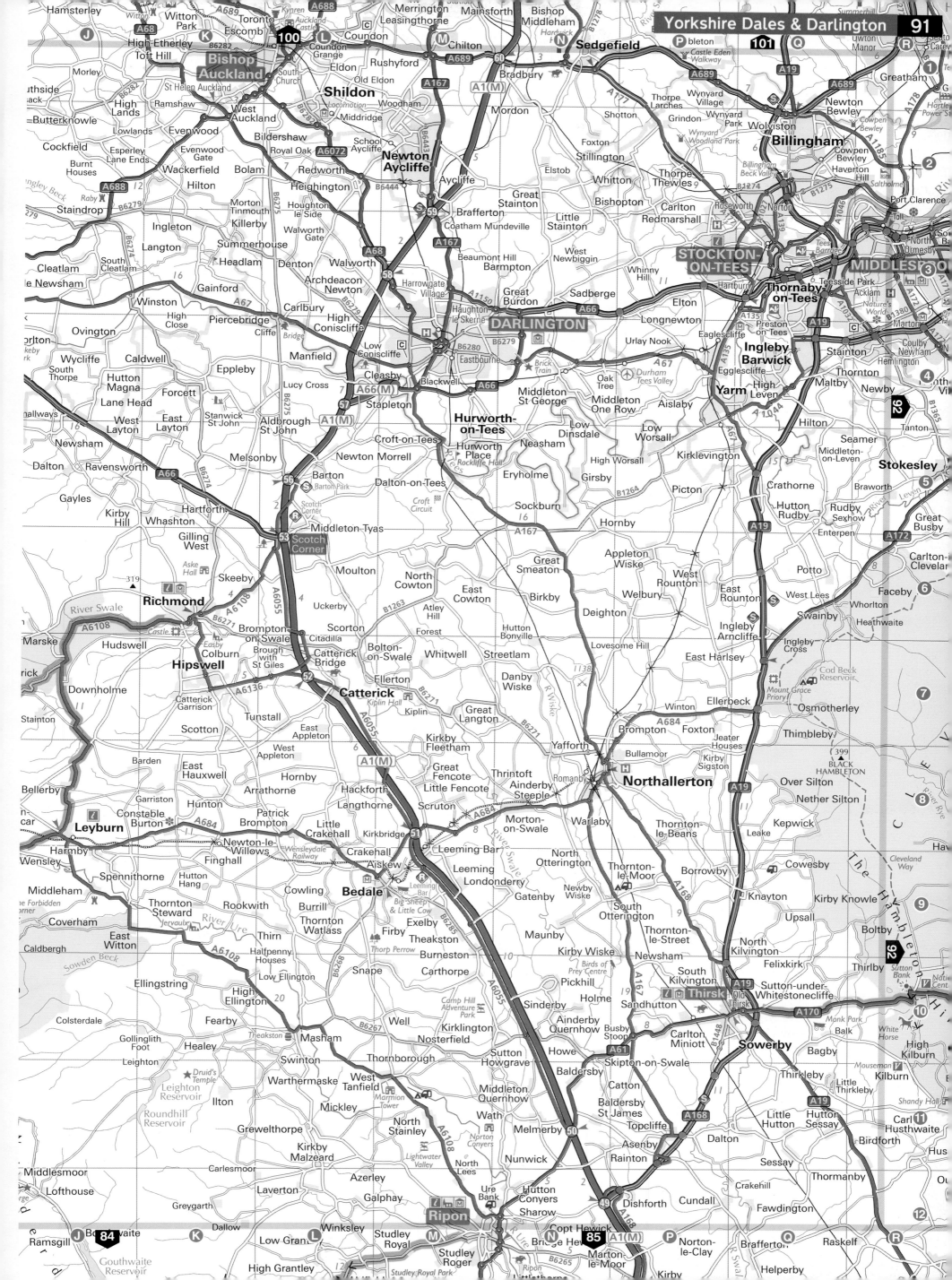

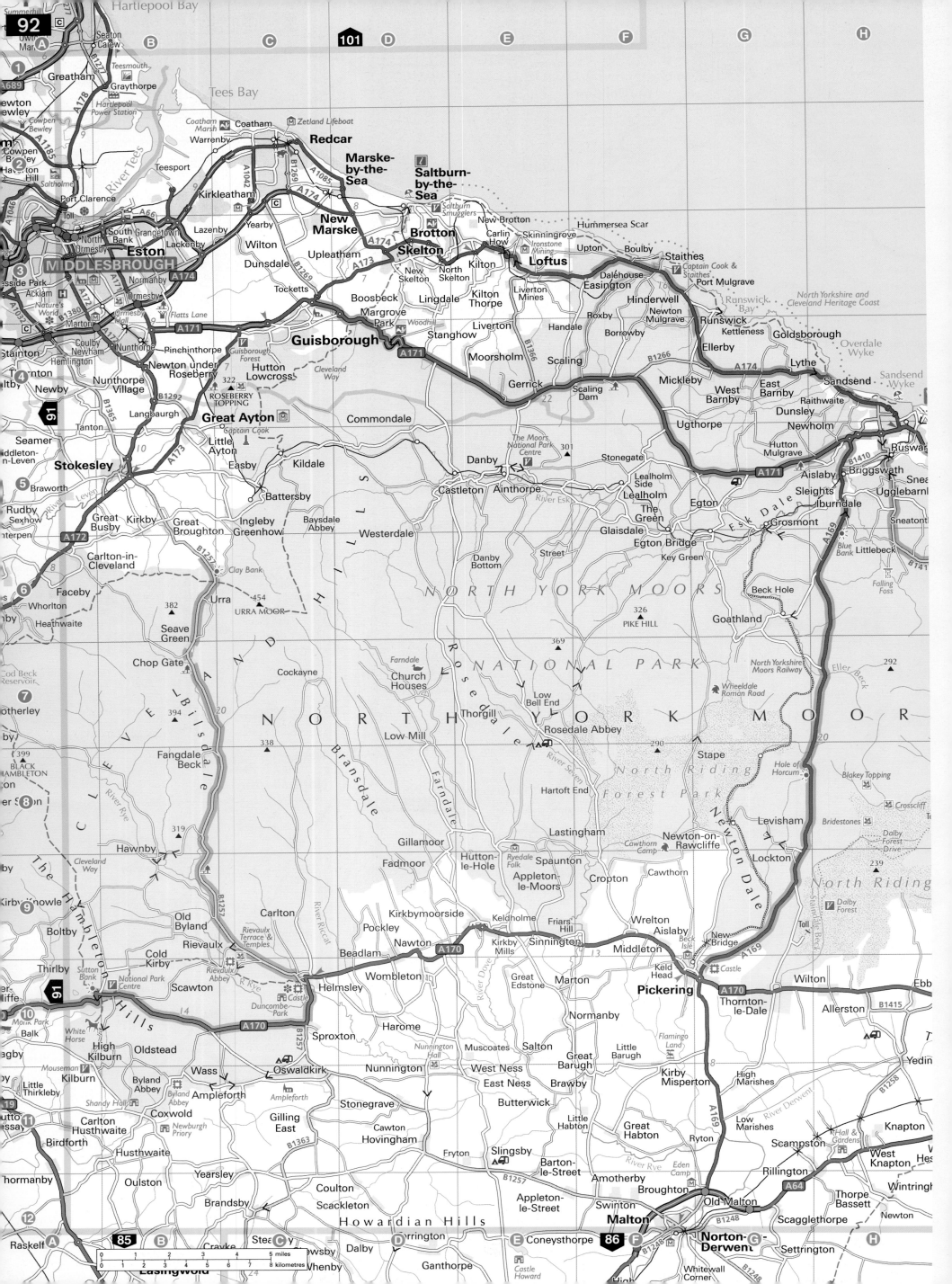

Middlesbrough

Whitby

Scarborough

Whitby
Saltwick Bay
Abbey
Stainsacre
High Hawsker
Low Hawsker
Raw
Robin Hood's Bay
Fylingthorpe
Robin Hood's Bay
Old Peak or South Cheek
Ravenscar
A171
Staintondale
Shire Horse Centre
Hayburn Wyke
Harwood Dale
Cloughton Newlands
Cloughton Wyke
Cloughton
Bickley
Broxa
Silpho
Suffield
Burniston
Cromer Point
Langdale End
Hackness
Cleveland Way
Forest Park
Wrench Green
Everley
Scalby
Newby
North Bay Railway
Castle
Sawdon
Forge Valley Wood
Falsgrave
Scarborough
Ruston
Snainton
Wykeham
Hutton Buscel
East Ayton
West Ayton
A170
Oliver's Mount
Brompton-by-Sawdon
Irton Seamer
Eastfield
Osgodby
Cayton Bay
The Wyke
Crossgates
Cayton
High Killerby
Filey Brigg
Lebberston
Gristhorpe
Filey
Willerby
Folkton
Muston
Filey Bay
Sherburn
Staxton
Flixton
West Flotmanby
Ganton
Potter Brompton
Fordon
Hunmanby
Flamborough Head Heritage Coast
East Heslerton
Reighton
Speeton
Bempton Cliffs
Thornwick Bay
Foxholes
Wold Newton
Burton Fleming
Buckton
Bempton
North Landing
Weaverthorpe
Grindale
Flamborough
Selwicks Bay
West Lutton
Helperthorpe
Thwing
Marton
FLAMBOROUGH HEAD
East Lutton
Octon
Hall

A   B   C   D   E   F   G   104   H

1
2
3
4
5
6
7
8
9
10
11
12

Bennane Head
Colmonell

Ballantrae
Heronsford
Water of Tig

Belfast
Currarie
Port
BENERAIRD
437

Larne
321
CARLOCK HILL
ALTIMEG HILL
387

Milleur
Point

Corsewall Point
Glenwhilly
Laggang
Standing S

Lady
Bay
Glen App
A77

Barnhills
Portencalzie
Penwhirn
Reservoir

THE RHINS
B738

Kirkcolm
A718
Cairnryan
17
Braid Fell
New
Luce

Loch
Connell
Ervie
Low
Barbeth
B798
6
Low
Salchrie
Beoch Burn

Knocknain
Leswalt
B7043
Loch Ryan
Innermessan
A751
A77
Black Loch
104
CRAIG
FELL

Balgracie
Castle of
St John
White
Loch
Castle
Kennedy
Chlenry

Auchnotteroch
Stranraer
Aird
Castle Kennedy
Glenluce Abb

Portslogan
B738
Glenwhan
Dunragit
Glenluce

Broadsea Bay
A75
10

Black Head
Dunskey
Lochans
CAIRN
PAT
181
8
Kildrochet House
Piltanton Burn
Whitecrook
B7084

Portpatrick
A77
14
B7077
Ringdoo
Point
Milto

OF GALLOWAY
A716
19
B7084
Luce Sands
Stairhave

Stoneykirk
North
Milmain
18
Au
Mull of Si

Sandhead

Cairngarroch
Kirkmadrine
Stones

Money Head

High Ardwell
Ardwell
Ardwell Bay

Chapel Rossan

Drumbreddon
Balgowan
L U C E

Logan

Port Logan Bay

Port Logan
B7065
A716

Garrochtrie
Kilstay

Clanyard Bay

Laggantalluch Head
Kirkmaiden
Drummore

Barncorkrie
High
Drummore
Cailiness Point

Damnaglaur
Maryport
B7041

Cardryne

Cardrain

West
Cairngaan
MULL OF GALLOWAY

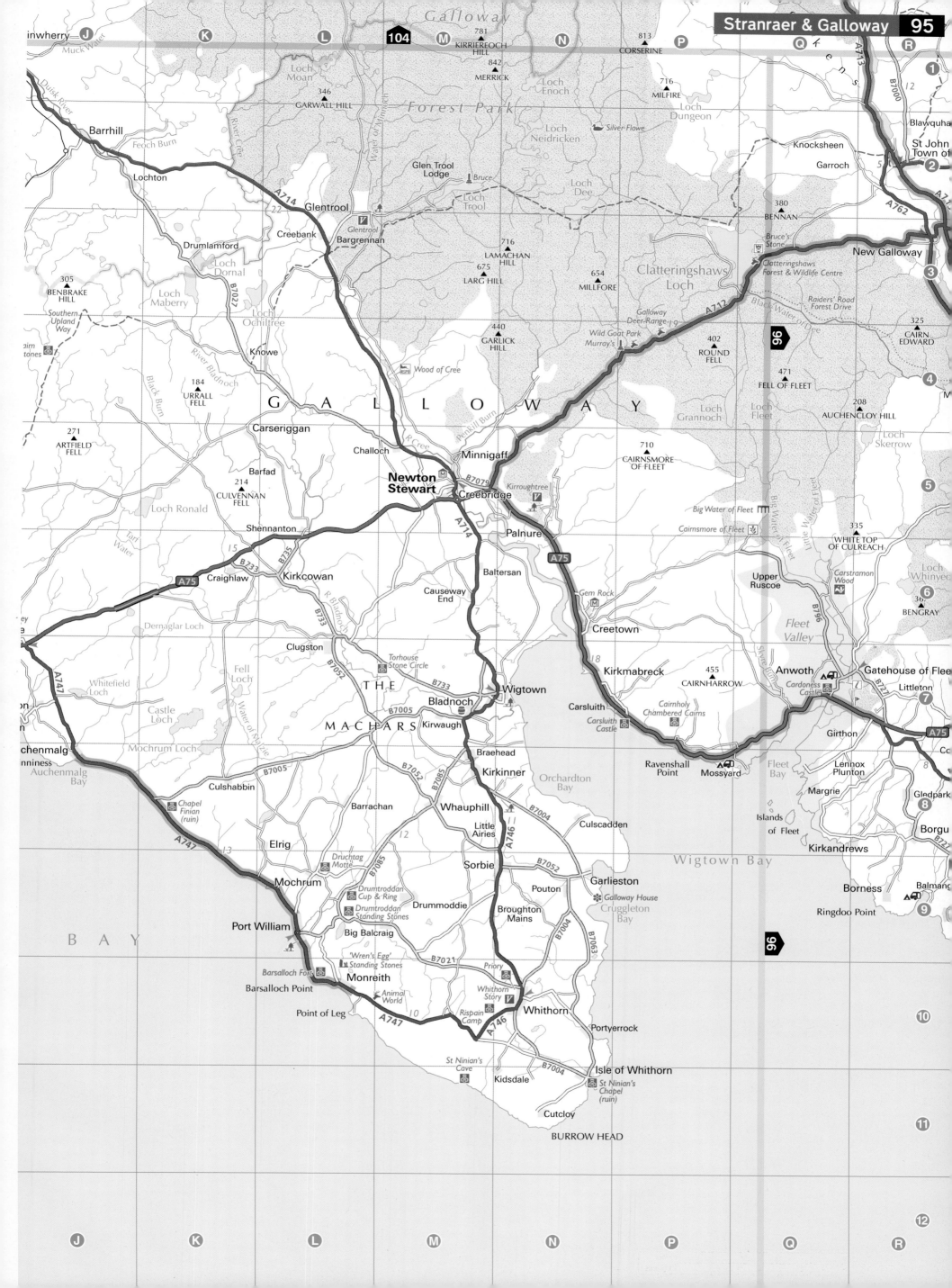

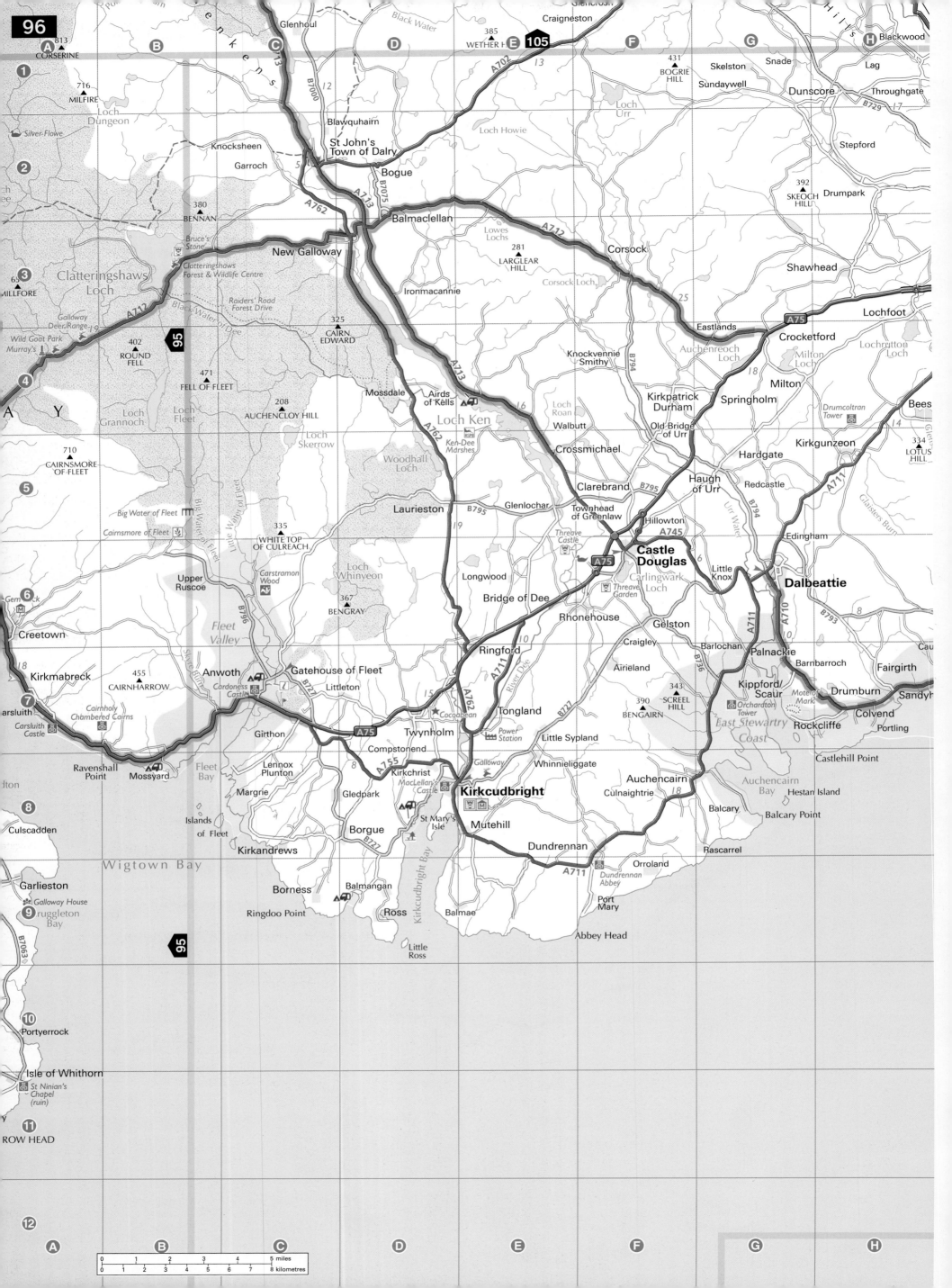

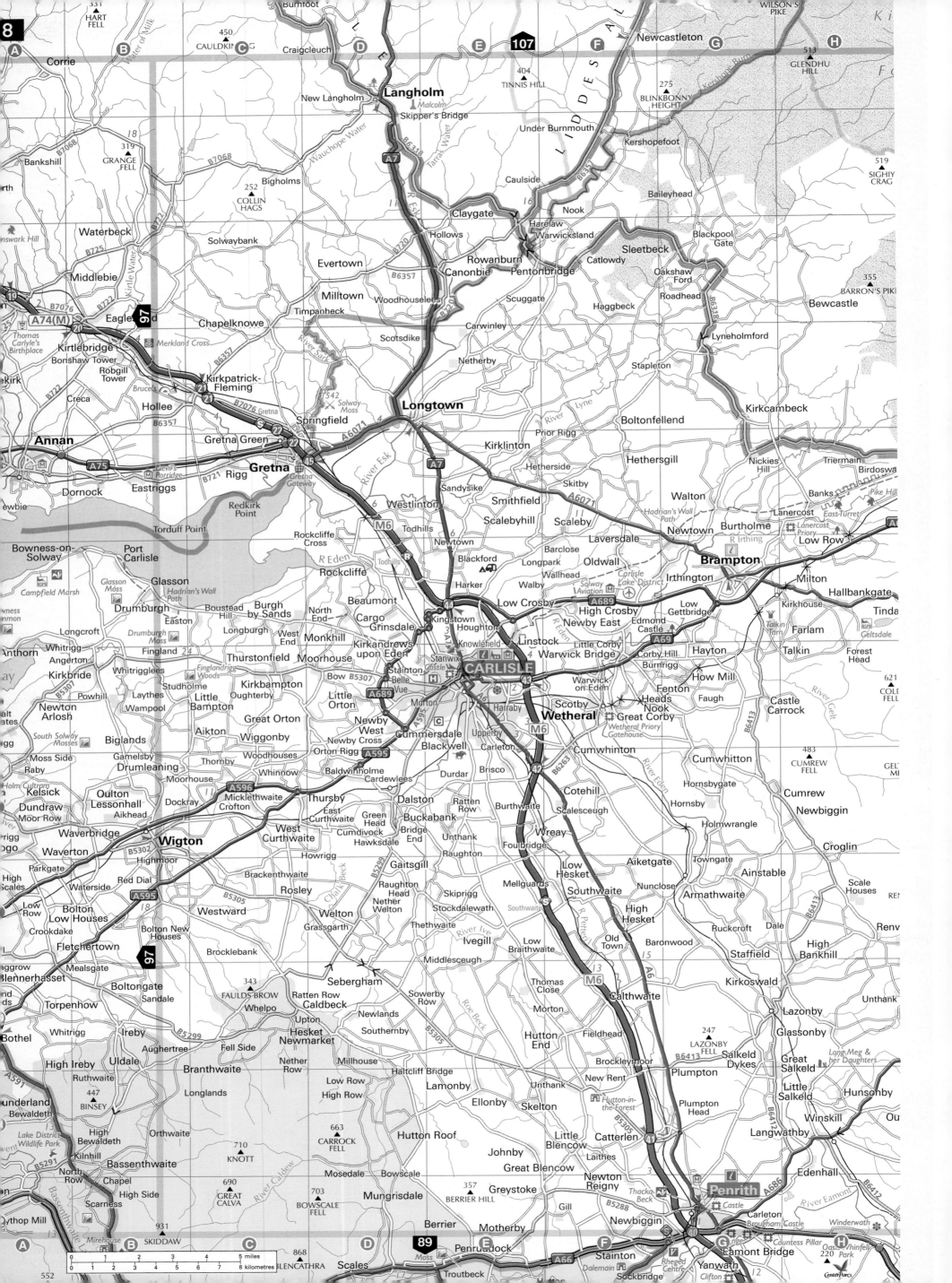

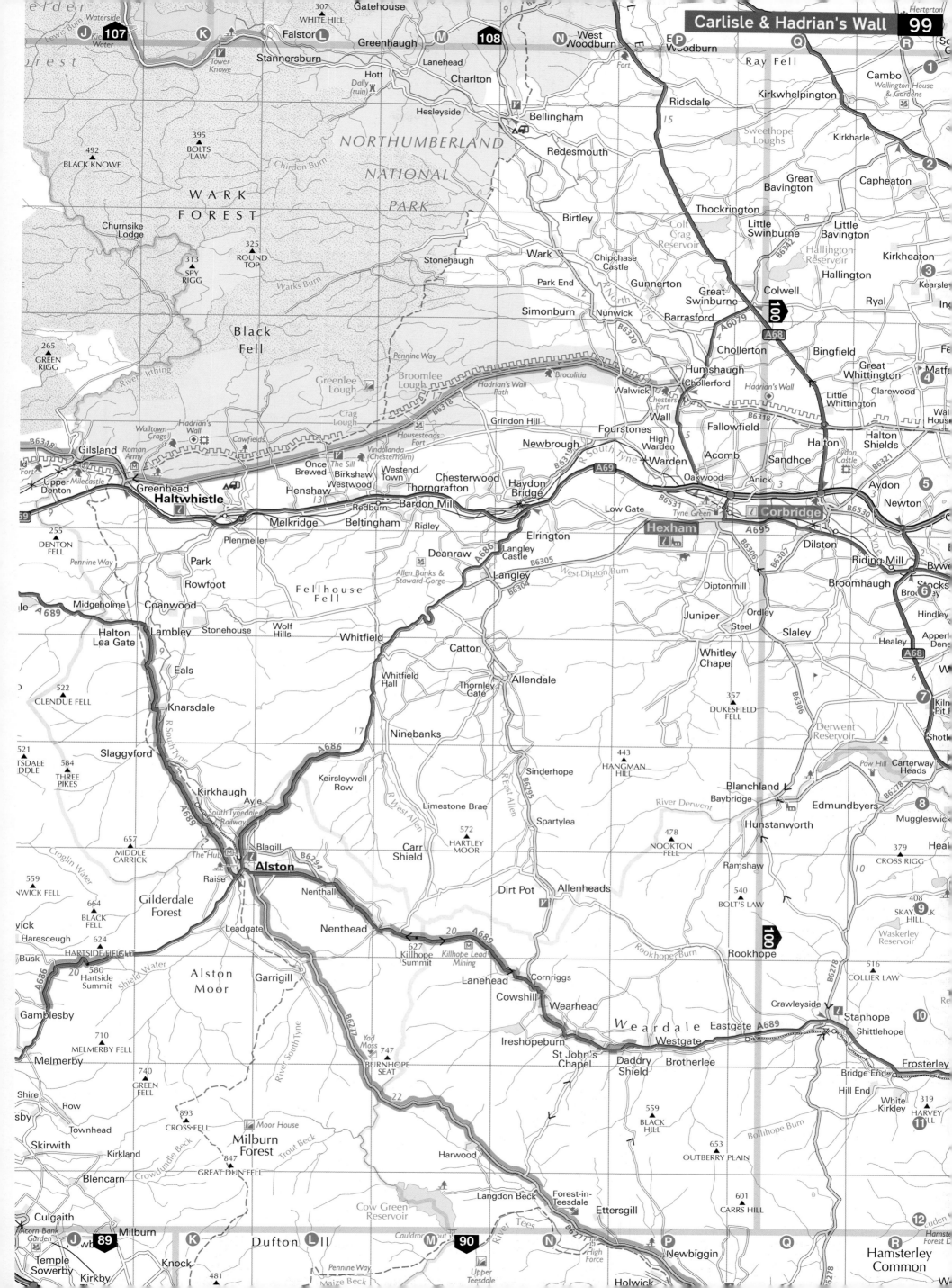

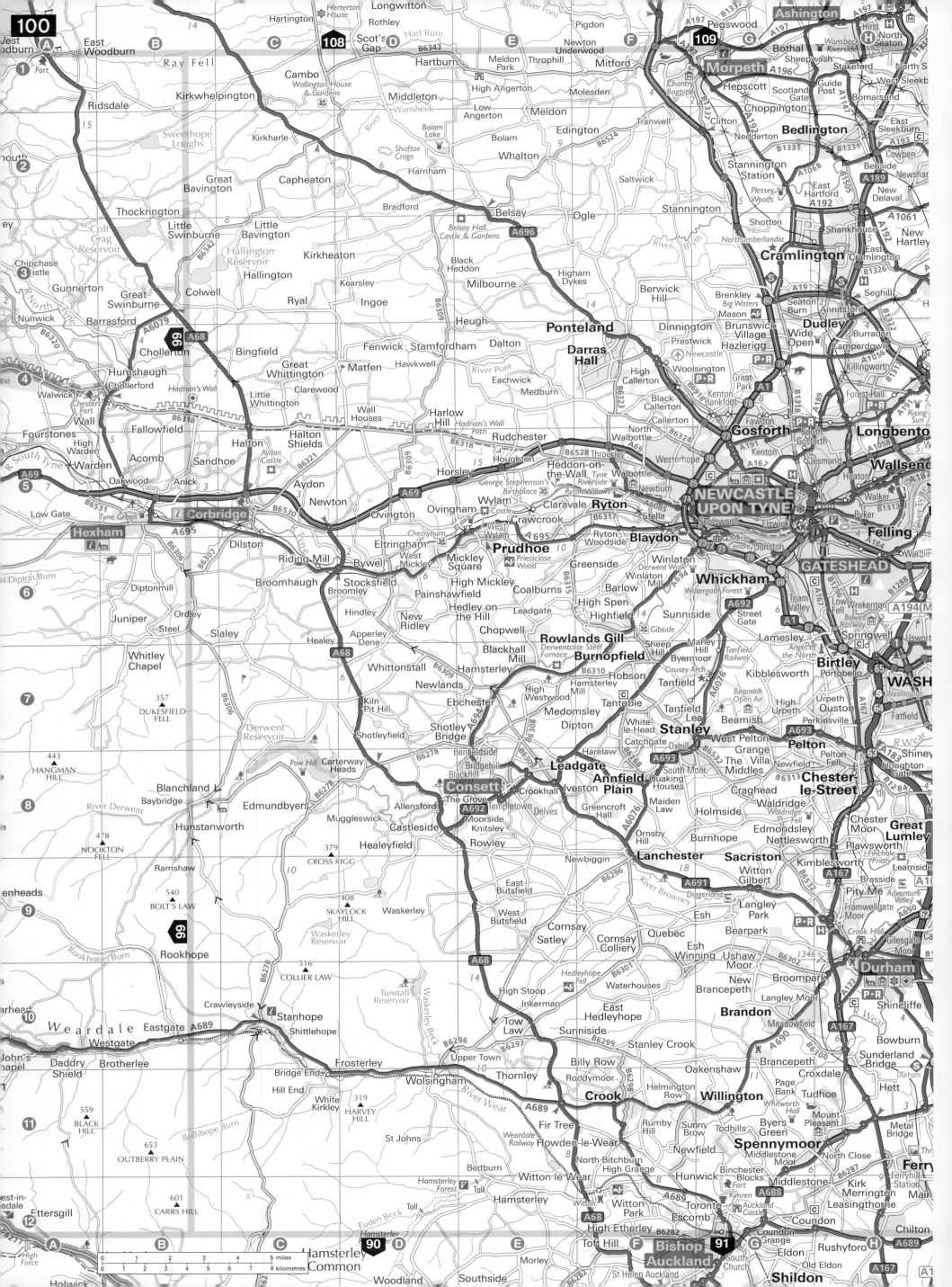

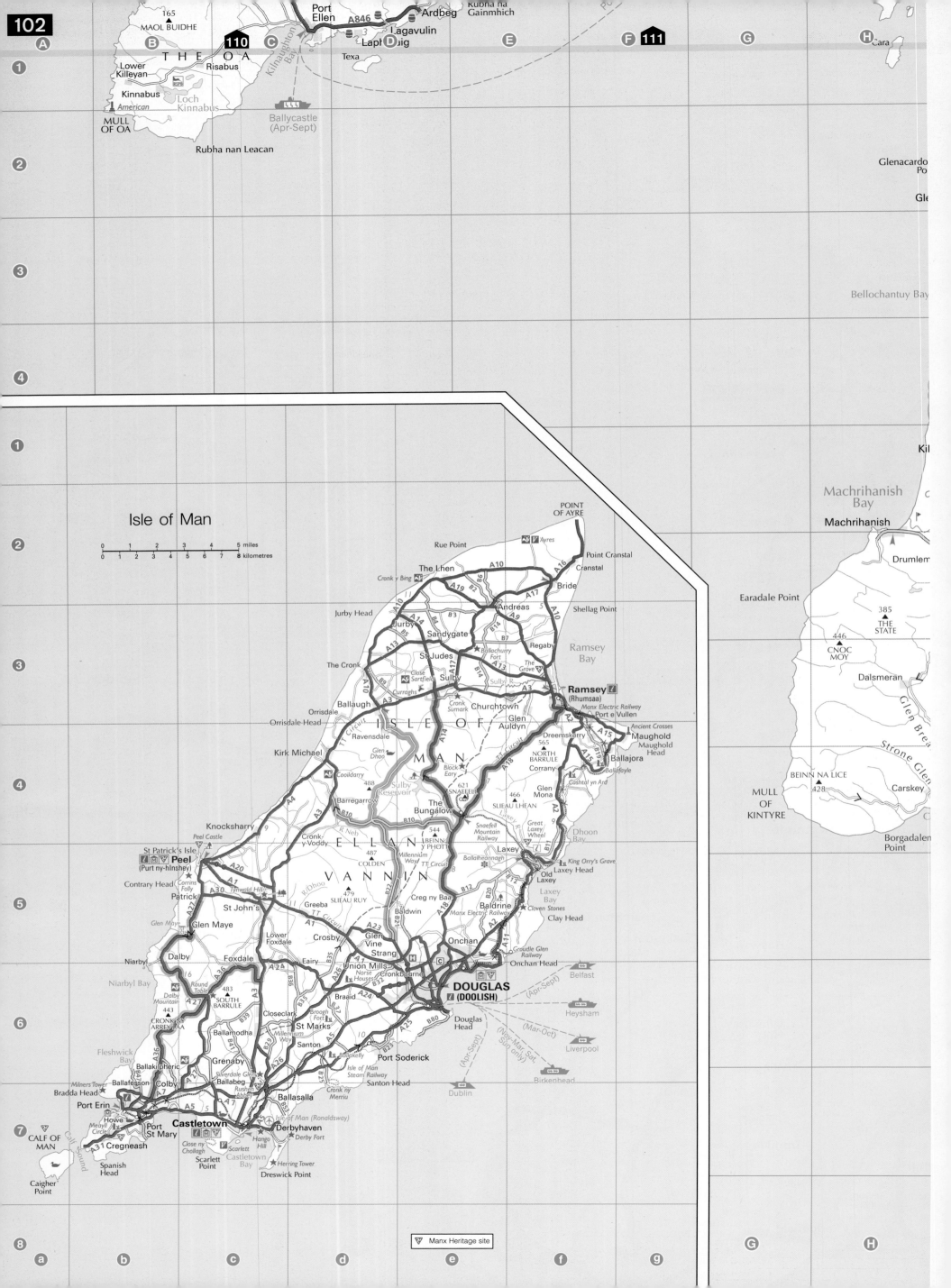

Tayinloan
111
J
K
L
Grogport
Barmollack
M
Pirnmill
Penrioch
N
112
orth Arran
P
CAISTEAL ABHAIL
Q
R
Corrie

A83
354
CRUACH
NAN GABHAR
Whitefarland
715
BEINN
BHARRAIN
Glen Iorsa
874
GOATFELL
Merkland Point
6

Muasdale
B842
39
Imachar
792
BEINN
NUIS
Glen Rosa
Brodick Castle, Garden
& Country Park

Belloch
Barr Water
Carradale Water
Carradale
Port Righ
Carradale House
Balliekine
Iorsa Water
A R R A N
Brodick
Bay
Brodick
Strathwhillan

enbarr
Clan
MacAlister
Carradale Village
Bridgend
Dippen
Waterfoot
Auchagallon
Stone Circle
Machrie
Corriegills
104

Cleongart
454
BEINN-AN TUIRC
Torrisdale
Carradale
Point
Machrie
Bay
Machrie Moor
Stone Circles
512
A'CHRUACH
Clauchlands
Point

319
408
BORD
MOR
Carradale
Bay
Tormore
503
BEINN BHREAC
Lamlash
H
Margnaheglish

Bellochantuy
Saddell
Saddell Water
Moss Farm Road
Stone Circle
A841
Lamlash
Bay
Holy Island

Z
Saddell
Saddell Bay
Balmichael
Cordon

Lussa Loch
396
SGREADAN
HILL
Ugadale
Torbeg
Shiskine
B880
Glen Scorrodale
Auchencairn
Kingscross
Knockenkelly

Tangy Loch
Drumadoon
Point
Blackwaterfoot
Carn Ban
Whiting Bay
V

Glen Lussa
Peninver
Ardnacross
Bay
Drumadoon
Bay
Kilpatrick
Kilpatrick Dun
Glenashdale
Whiting
Bay

kenzie
A83
Kilmichael
Brown Head
Corriecravie
Kilmory Water
Dippin
Largymore
Largybeg
Dippin Head

Campbeltown
Torr a' Chaisteal Fort
Sliddery
Bennan
Dippin

Campbeltown
Campbeltown
Loch
Island Davaar
Lagg
Torrylin
Cairn
Kilmory
Kildonan
Pladda
(May-Sept, Sat only)

B842
Stewarton
Kilkerran
Ballycastle
(Apr-Sept)
Bennan Head
Campbeltown-Ardrossan (May-Sept)
V

6
B843
Kildalloig
352
BEINN GHUILEAN
Achinhoan

Conie Glen
Glen Kerran
Ru Stafnish

10
Cattadale
Polliwilline Bay

ckerie
Macharioch
Southend
Dunaverty
Sound of Sanda
Sheep Island
Sanda Island

arskey Bay
104

Ailsa
Craig
340

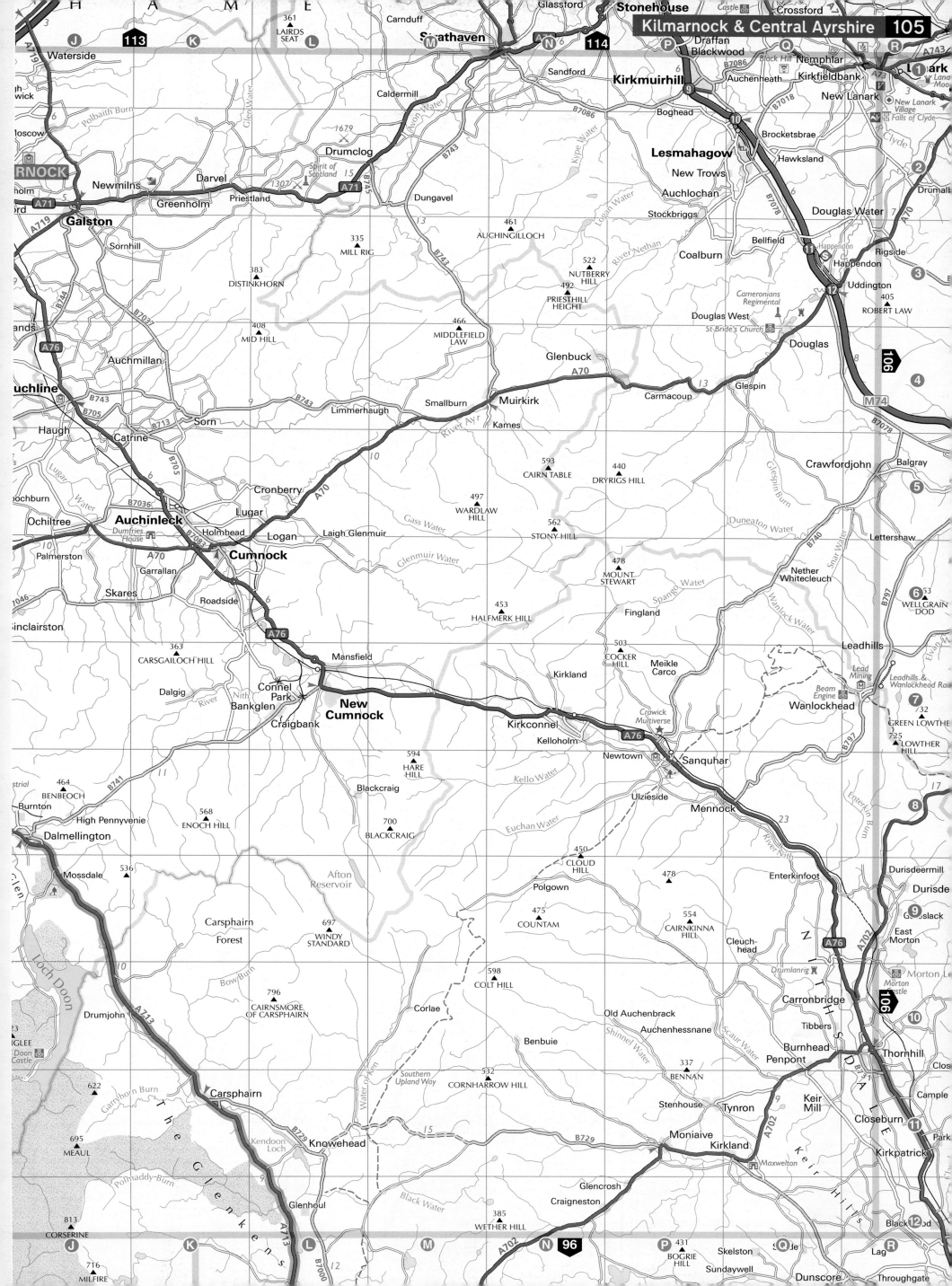

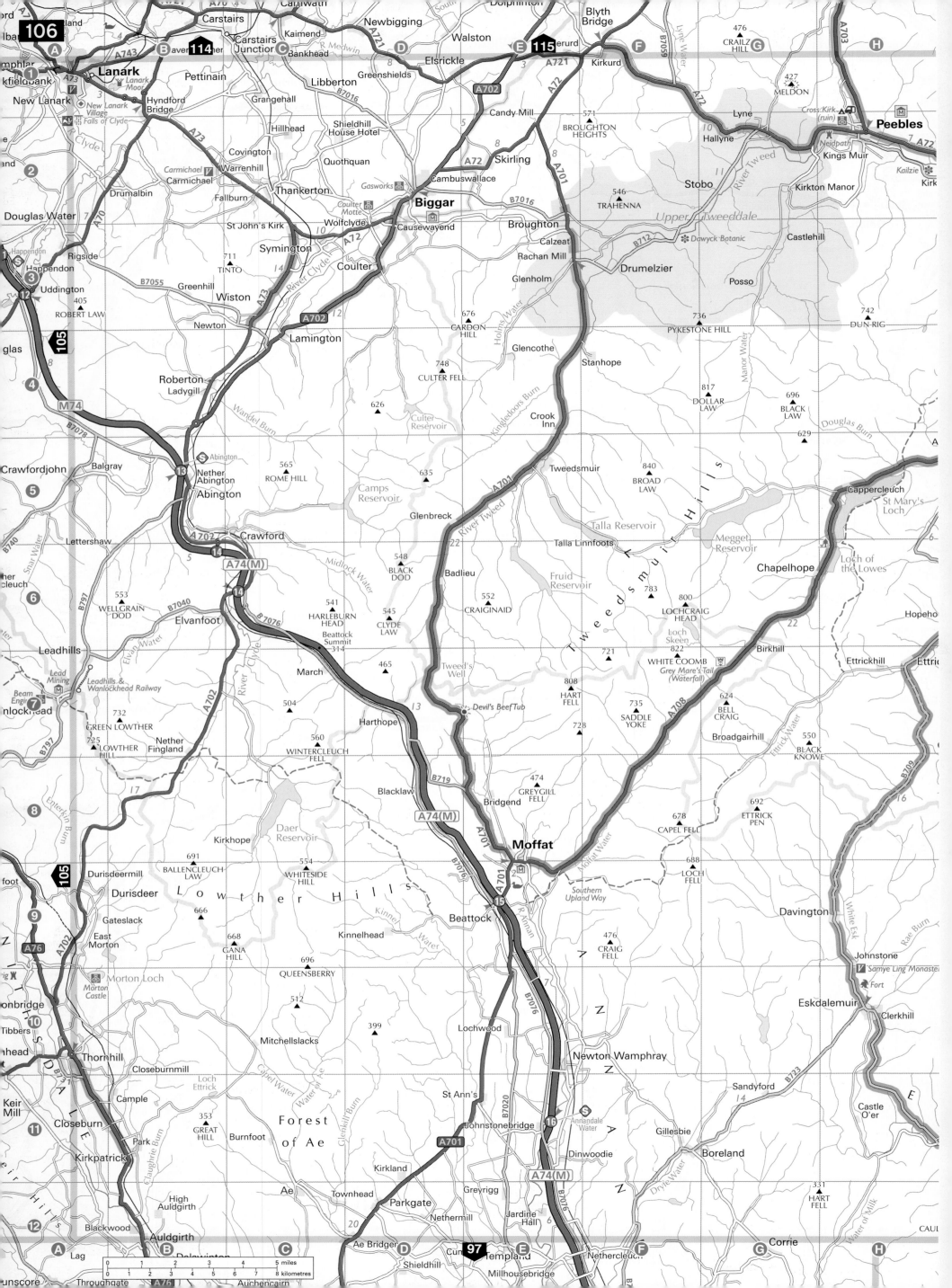

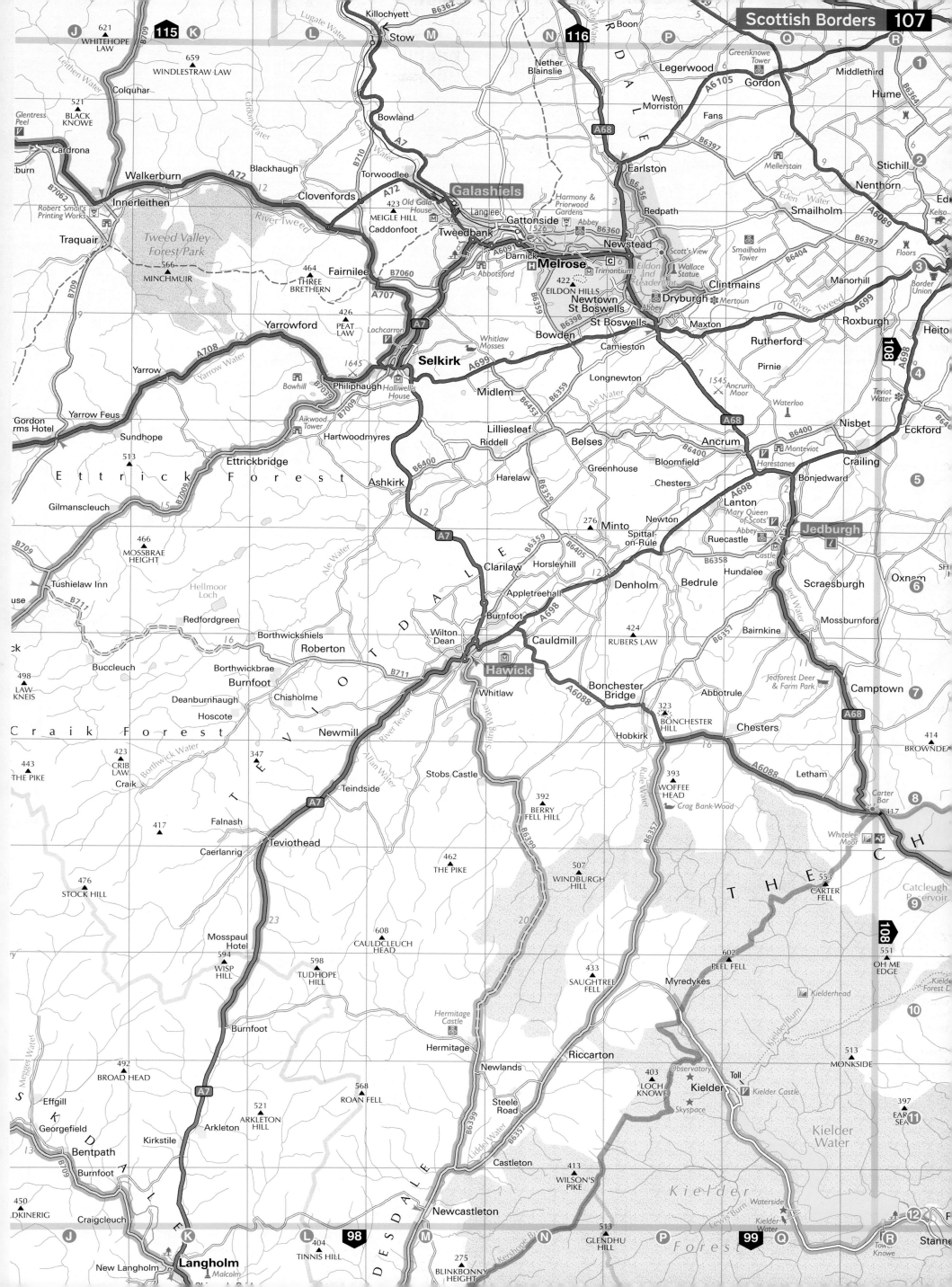

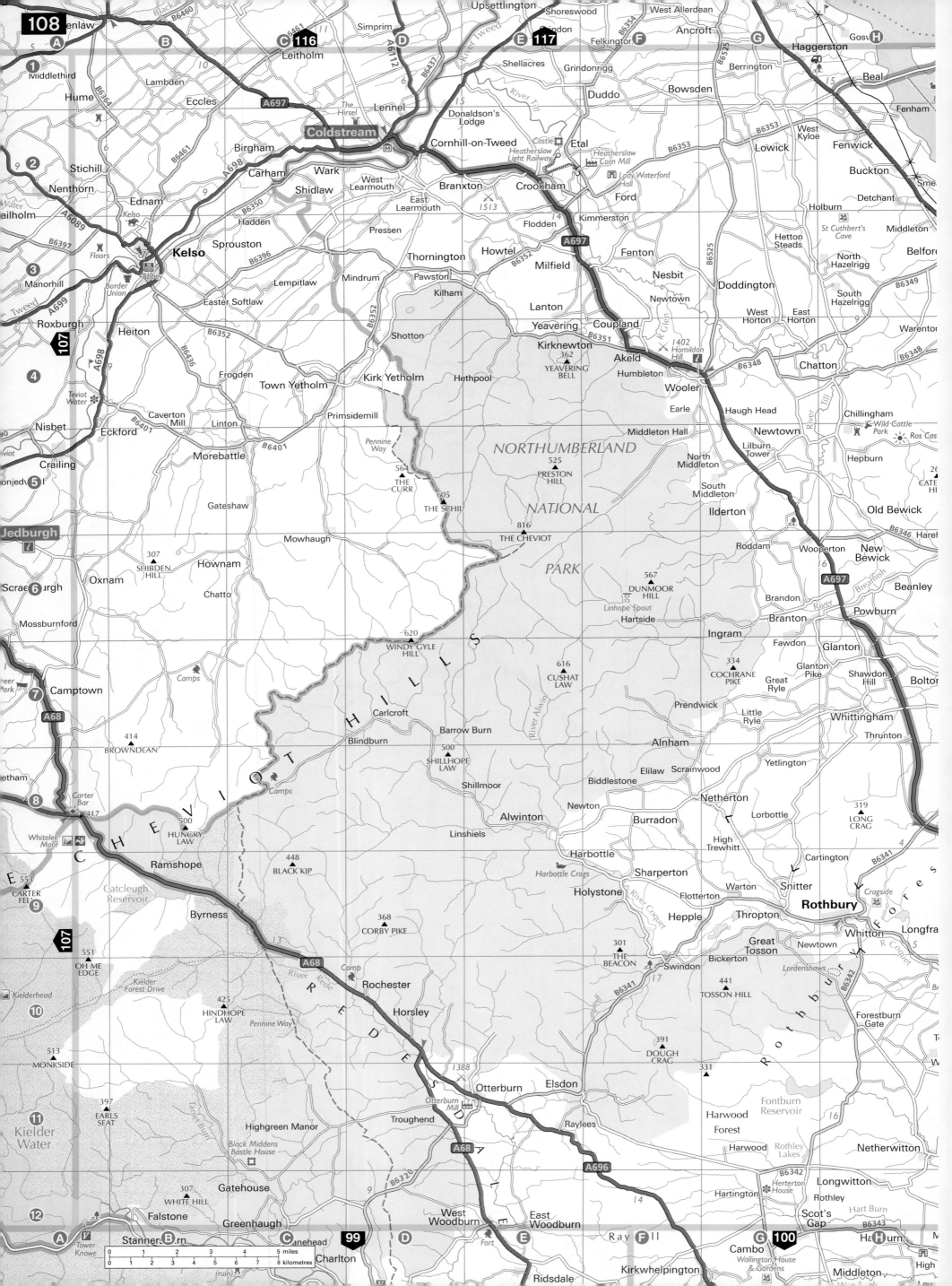

HOLY ISLAND
Holy
Island
Lindisfarne Priory
Lindisfarne Castle
Castle Point
Guile Point

Causeway flooded at high tide

FARNE ISLANDS
Longstone
Staple Sound
Inner Sound

North Northumberland Heritage Coast

afield
Elwick
Ross
Low Middleton
Easington
Waren Mill
Budle
Budle Bay
Bamburgh
New Shoreston
Outchester
Spindlestone
Burton
Bradford
Bellshill
Lucker
Adderstone
Warenford
Newham
Newstead
Chathill
Tughall
Ellingham
Preston
Brunton
Pele Tower
Doxford
Brownieside
North Charlton
Fallodon
West Ditchburn
South Charlton
Eglingham
Rock
Rennington
Stamford
Broxfield
Littlehoughton
Longhoughton
East Bolton
River Aln
Abberwick
Alnwick
Broome Park
Hawkhill
Lesbury
Aln Valley Railway
Bilton
Hipsburn
Alnmouth

Seahouses
North Sunderland
Elford
Beadnell
Swinhoe
Beadnell Bay
High Newton-by-the-Sea
Low Newton-by-the-Sea
Embleton & Newton Links
Embleton
Embleton Bay
Dunstan Steads
Dunstanburgh Castle
Dunstan
Craster
Cullernose Point
Howick
Howick Hall
Boulmer
Seaton Point
Alnmouth Bay

Castle
Edlingham
GLANTLEES HILL
260
Newton-on-the-Moor
Bilton Banks
High Buston
Shilbottle
Low Buston
Birling
Warkworth Castle & Hermitage
Warkworth
Amble
Coquet Island
Swarland
Old Swarland
North End
Guyzance
Gloster Hill
North Togston
Acklington
Togston
Radcliffe
High Hauxley
Felton
East Thirston
Broomhill
West Thirston
Eshott
South Broomhill
Hadston
Red Row
Druridge Bay
Pauperhaugh
Weldon Bridge
rinkburn Priory
Helm
West Chevington
Druridge
Druridge Bay
North Northumberland Heritage Coast
Causey Park
Stobswood
Widdrington
Longhorsley
Causey Park Bridge
Earsdon
Widdrington Station
Cresswell
Stanton
Fenrother
Tritlington
Ulgham
Linton
Ellington
Lynemouth
Hebron
Longhirst
Woodhorn
Beacon Point
Pigdon
Longhirst
Woodhorn Demesne
Newton Underwood
Pegswood
Ashington
Hirst
North Seaton
Newbiggin-by-the-Sea
Meldon Park
Thro
Mitford
Bothal
epwash
Wansbeck Riverside
North Seaton Colliery
Angerton
Molesden
Morpeth
Hepscott
Stakeford
West Sleekburn
Stanton
Pigdon
Guide Post
Bomarsund
Scotland Gate
Choppington

A B C D E F G H

① ② ③ ④ ⑤ ⑥ ⑦ ⑧ ⑨ ⑩ ⑪ ⑫

COLONSAY

Kilchattan

Colonsay

Garvard

Oronsay

Dubh Eilean

ORONSAY

Nave Island
Ardnave
Point
Gortantaoid
Point

Tòn Mhòr

Kilnave

Eilean Mòr
Sanaigmore

Rubha Lamanais

Loch
Gòrr

Lecht Gruinart

Loch Gruinart

Gleann Mòr

Saligo Bay

B8018

B8017

Gruinart

B8017

Loch
Gorm

B8018

Coul Point

Sunderland

Kilchoman

A847

Bridgend

Machir
Bay

Bruichladdich

Loch
Indaal

Gartacho

Kilchiaran Bay

RHINNS OF ISLAY

Bowmore

River Laggan

I'S

Port
Charlotte

231
BEINN TART A'MHILL

Lossit Bay

Nerabus

Laggan
Point

Dùich R.

B8016

A846

Rubha na
Faing

A847

Portnahaven

Port Wemyss

Orsay

RHINNS
POINT

Laggan
Bay

Islay

Glenegedale

Rubha Mòr

Kintra

165
MAOL BUIDHE

P.
E.

A B C D E F G H

THE OA

Lov
Killeyan

Risabus

Kinnabus

Kilnaughton
Bay

American

Loch

0 1 2 3 4 5 miles
0 1 2 3 4 5 6 7 8 kilometres

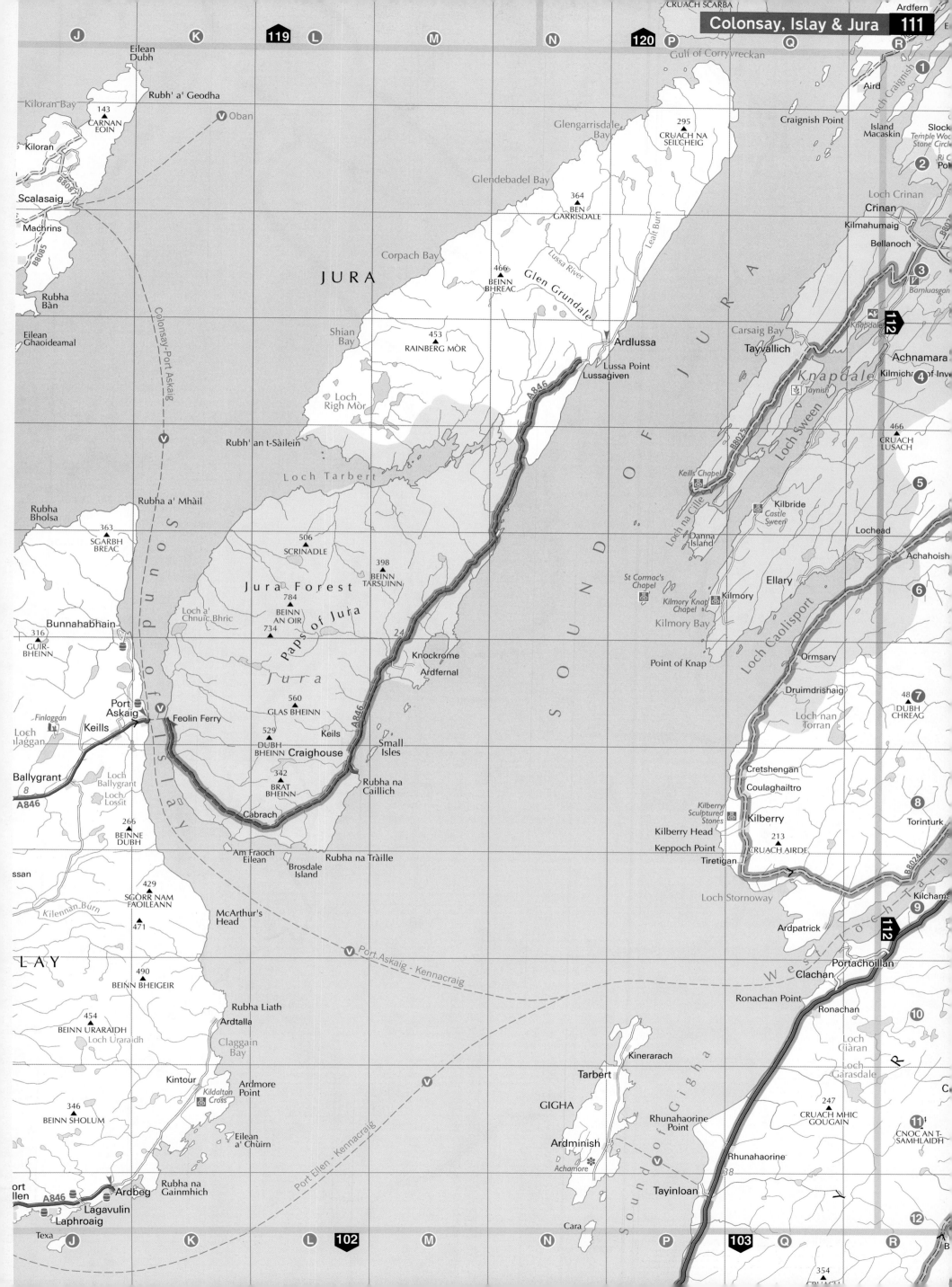

CRUACH SCARBA
Ardfern

J
K
119
L
M
N
120
P
Q
R

1
Gulf of Corryvreckan
Aird
Loch Craignish

Eilean
Dubh
Rubh' a' Geodha
Oban
Glengarrisdale
Bay
Craignish Point
Island
Macaskin
Slock

Kiloran Bay
143
CARNAN
EOIN
295
CRUACH NA
SEILCHEIG
Temple Woo
Stone Circle

2
Loch Crinan

Kiloran
B8085
Glendebadel Bay
Ri C
Po

Scalasaig
364
BEN
GARRISDALE
Crinan
Kilmahumaig

Machrins
B8085
Corpach Bay
JURA
466
BEINN
BHREAC
Glen Grundale
Lussa River
Leall Burn
Bellanoch

3
Barnluasgan

Rubha
Bàn
Shian
Bay
453
RAINBERG MÒR
Ardlussa
Carsaig Bay
Knapdale
Tayvallich
Achnamara

4
Kilmich
of Inve

Eilean
Ghaoideamal
Lussa Point
Lussagiven
S
O
U
N
D
Taynish

Rubh' an t-Sàilein
Loch Right Mòr
Keills Chapel
Loch na Cille

Rubha a' Mhàil
Loch Tarbert
Danna
Island
Kilbride
Castle
Sween
Lochead

5

Rubha
Bholsa
363
SGARBH
BREAC
506
SCRINADLE
St Cormac's
Chapel
Kilmory
Kilmory Knap
Chapel
Achahoish

Bunnahabhain
316
GUIR-
BHEINN
Jura Forest
398
BEINN
TARSUINN
O
F
Kilmory Bay
Ellary
466
CRUACH
LUSACH

6

Loch a'
Chnuic Bhric
784
BEINN
AN OIR
Point of Knap
Loch Caolisport

734
Paps of Jura
24
J
U
R
A
Loch nan
Torran
Ormsary

Port
Askaig
560
GLAS BHEINN
Knockrome
Ardfernal
Druimdrishaig
48
DUBH
CHREAG

7

Finlaggan
Feolin Ferry
Keils
Keills
Small
Isles
Cretshengan

Ballygrant
8
529
DÙBH
BHEINN
Craighouse
Coulaghailtro
Kilberry
Sculptured
Stones
Kilberry

8
Torinturk

A846
342
BRAT
BHEINN
Rubha na
Caillich
213
CRUACH AIRDE
Loch
Ballygrant
Loch
Lossit

266
BEINNE
DUBH
Cabrach
Kilberry Head
Keppoch Point
Tiretigan

Am Fraoch
Eilean
Brosdale
Island
Rubha na Tràille
Loch Stornoway
Kilcham

9
112

429
SGÒRR NAM
FAOILEANN
McArthur's
Head
Ardpatrick

Kilennan Burn
471
Port Askaig - Kennacraig
Clachan
Portachoillan

LAY
Ronachan Point

490
BEINN BHEIGEIR
Ronachan

10
Loch
Ciàran

Rubha Liath
Ardtalla
Loch
Garasdale

454
BEINN URARAIDH
Loch Uraraidh
Claggain
Bay
Kinerarach

Kintour
Tarbert
Rhunahaorine
Point

Ardmore
Point
Kildalton
Cross
GIGHA
247
CRUACH MHIC
GOUGAIN

346
BEINN SHOLUM
Eilean
a' Chùirn
Ardminish
Rhunahaorine

11
CNOC AN T-
SAMHLAIDH

Port
Ellen
A846
Ardbeg
Rubha na
Gainmhich
Achamore
Tayinloan

Lagavulin
Laphroaig
Cara
38

Texa

12

J
K
102
L
M
N
P
103
Q
R
354

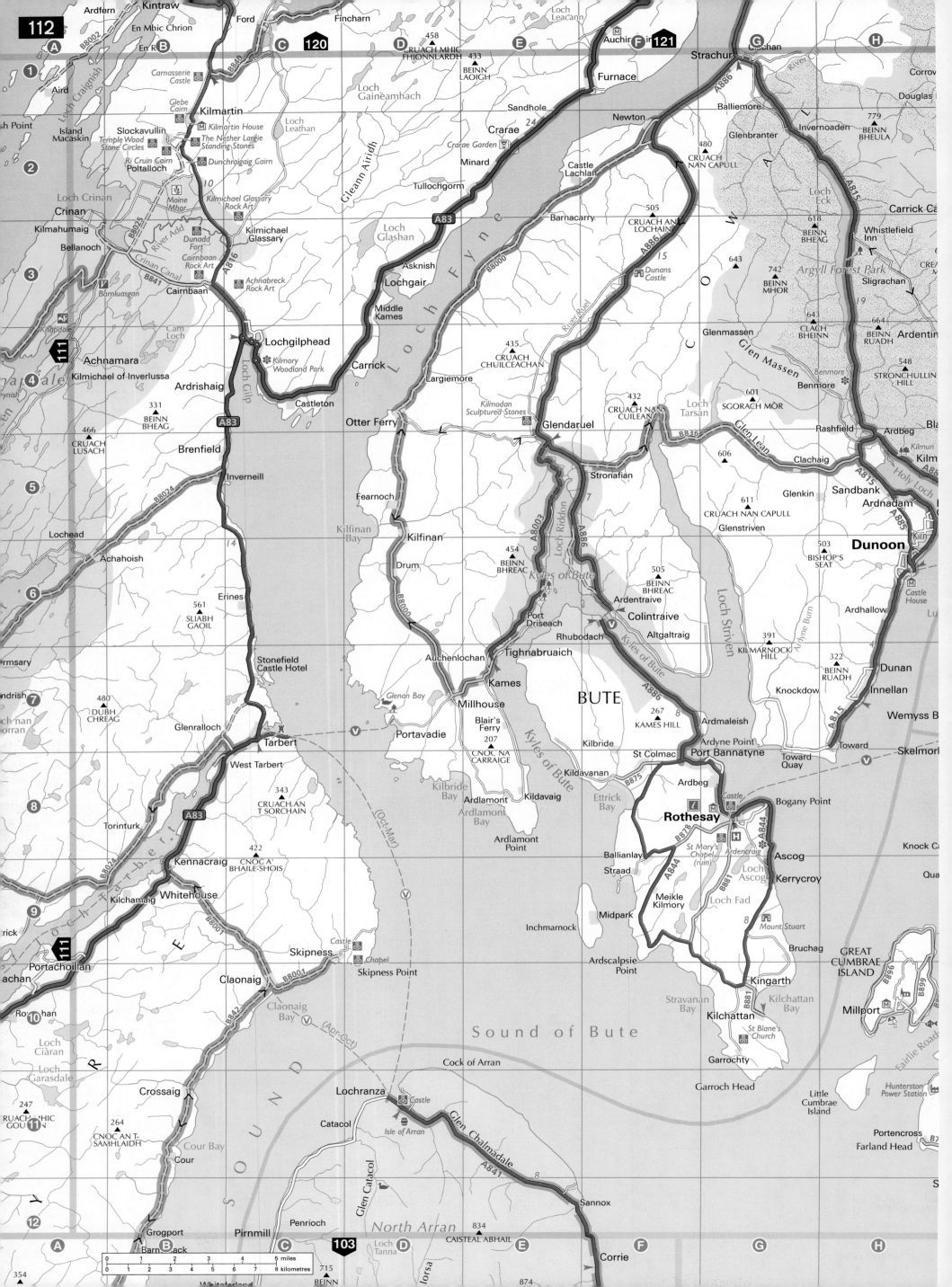

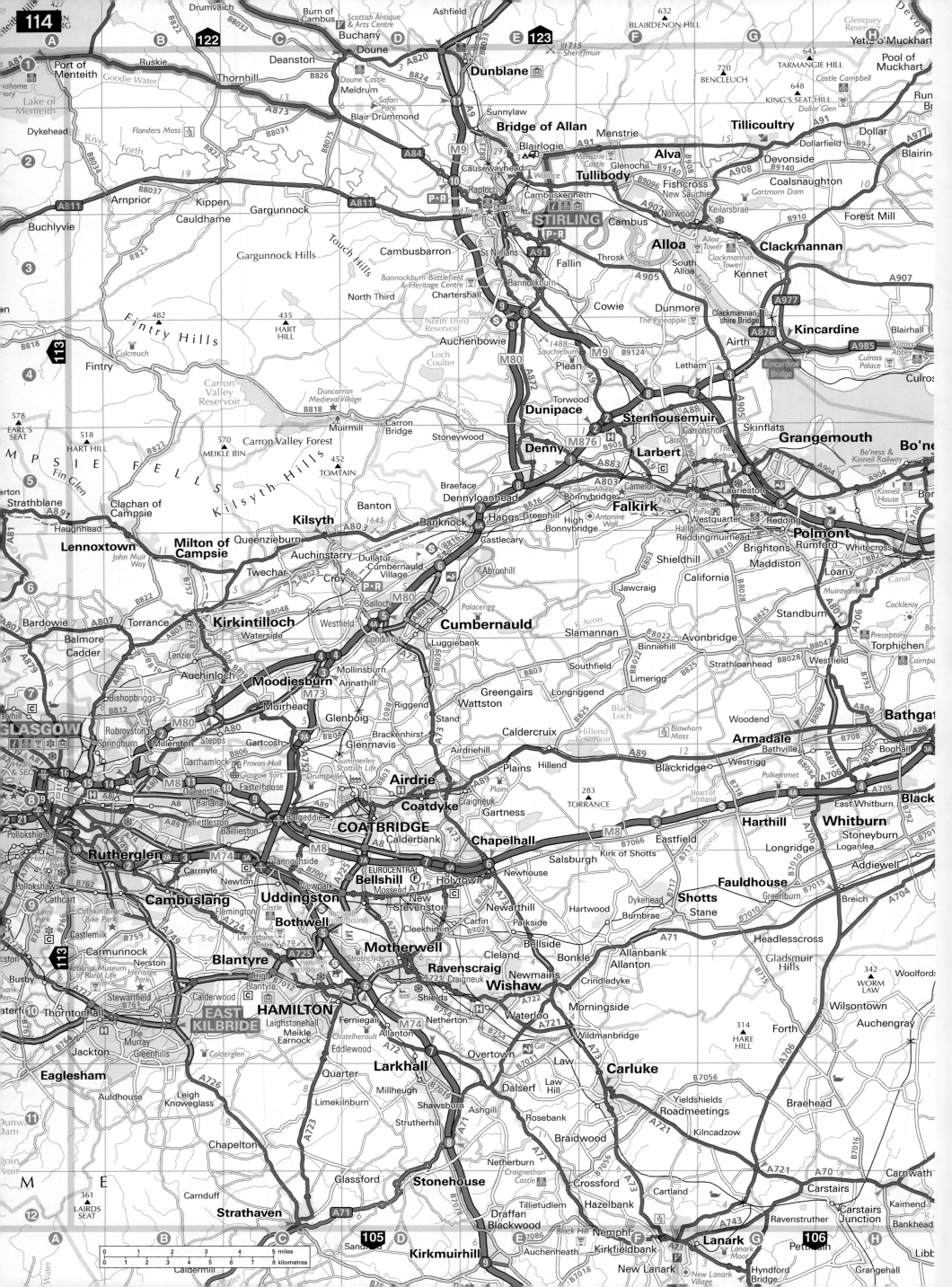

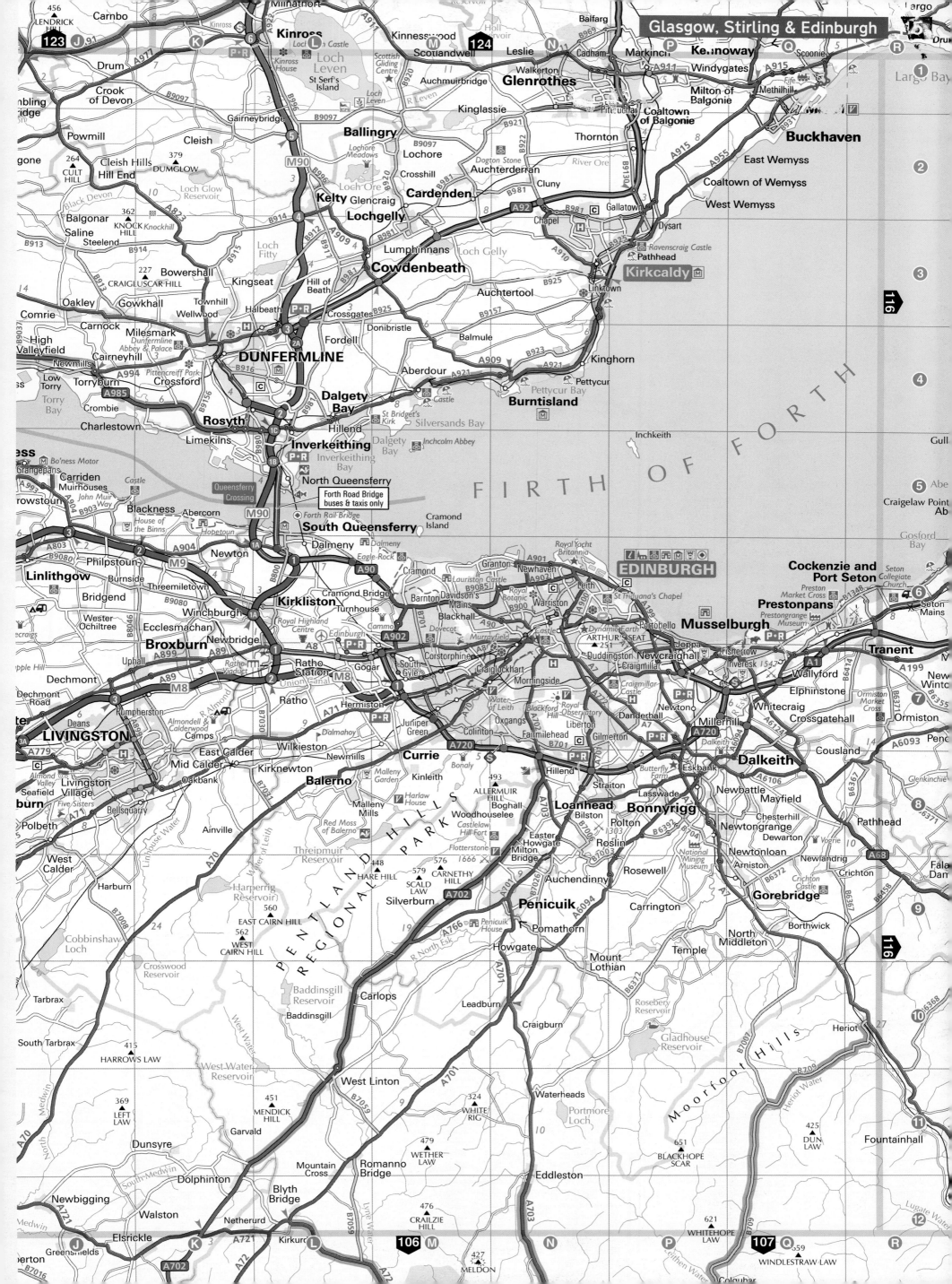

FIRTH OF FORTH

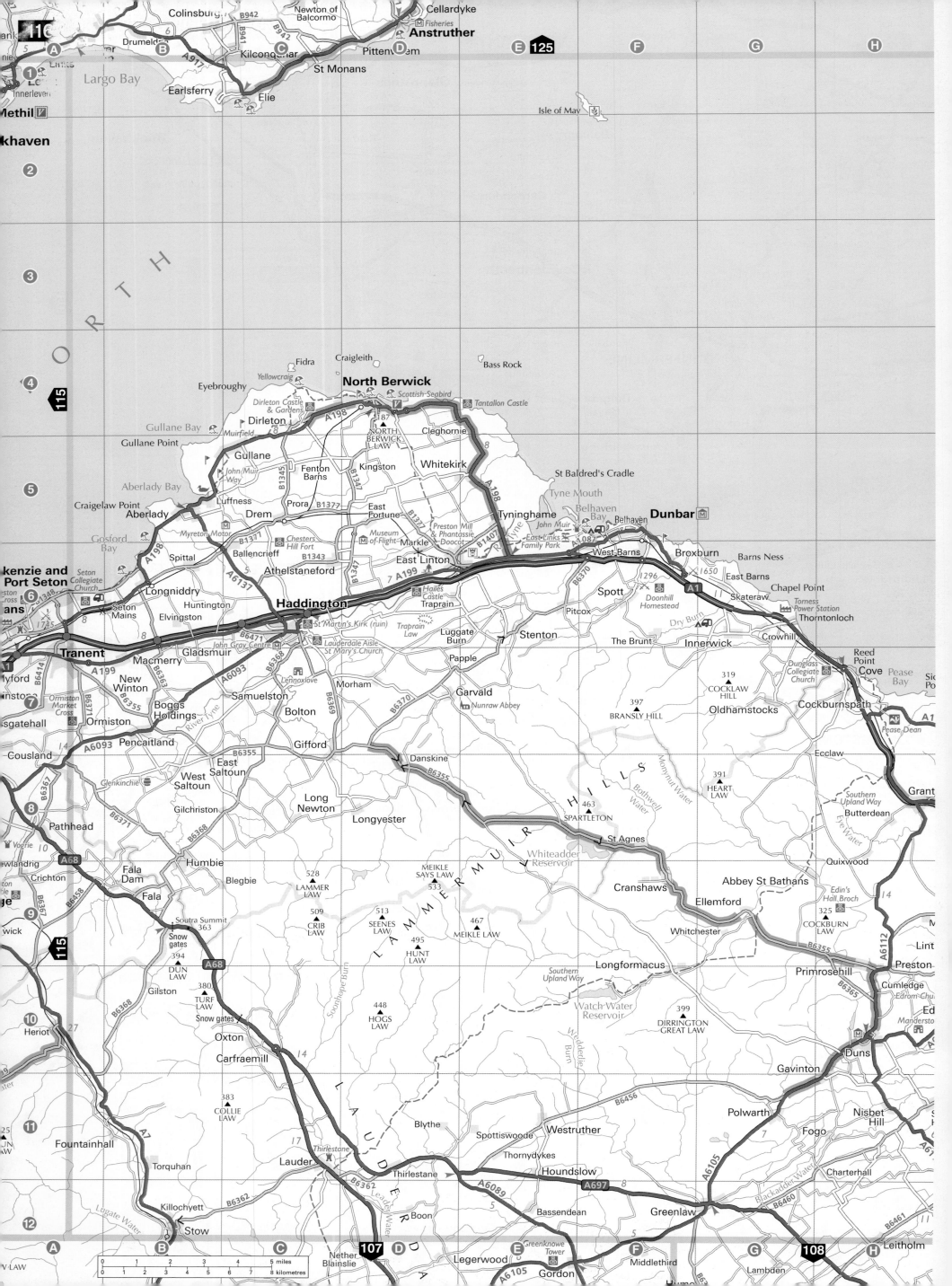

J   K   L   M   N   P   Q   R

① ② ③ ④ ⑤ ⑥ ⑦ ⑧ ⑨ ⑩ ⑪ ⑫

car
int
Fast Castle Head

107
196
BROWN
RIG
Coldingham
Loch
ST ABB'S HEAD

shouse
St Abbs

Coldingham
B6438
A1107
22
Coldingham
Bay

Houndwood
Cairncross
Eyemouth

Heugh
Head

262
HORSELEY HILL
Reston
Ayton
Burnmouth

B6438
Auchencrow

A1
B6355

Marygold
Lamberton

law
B6355
B6437
Marshall Meadows Bay

Chirnside
Foulden
North Northumberland
Heritage Coast

rch
15
Chirnsidebridge
1333

rom
B6105
Broadhaugh
Edington
Whiteadder Water
A6105
Berwick-upon-Tweed

Allanton
Hutton
Foulden
Tithe Barn
Castle

Blackadder
B6460
Paxton
Town
Ramparts
Barracks &
Main Guard

Sinclair's
Hill
Whitsome
Hilton
B6461
Paxton
Tweedmouth

Horndean
13
Loanend
East
Ord
Spittal
Huds
Head

2
Ladykirk
B6470
Horncliffe
Murton
Unthank
Scremerston

Swinton
Norham
Castle
Thornton
A1

Upsettlington
Shoreswood
West Allerdean
Cheswick

Simprim
Grindon
Ancroft
Causeway
flooded at
high tide
Goswick

The
Kennel

Kellacres
Grindonrigg
Berrington
Beal
Holy
Island
Lindisfarne
Lindisfarne
Castle

Duddo
Bowsden

River Tweed

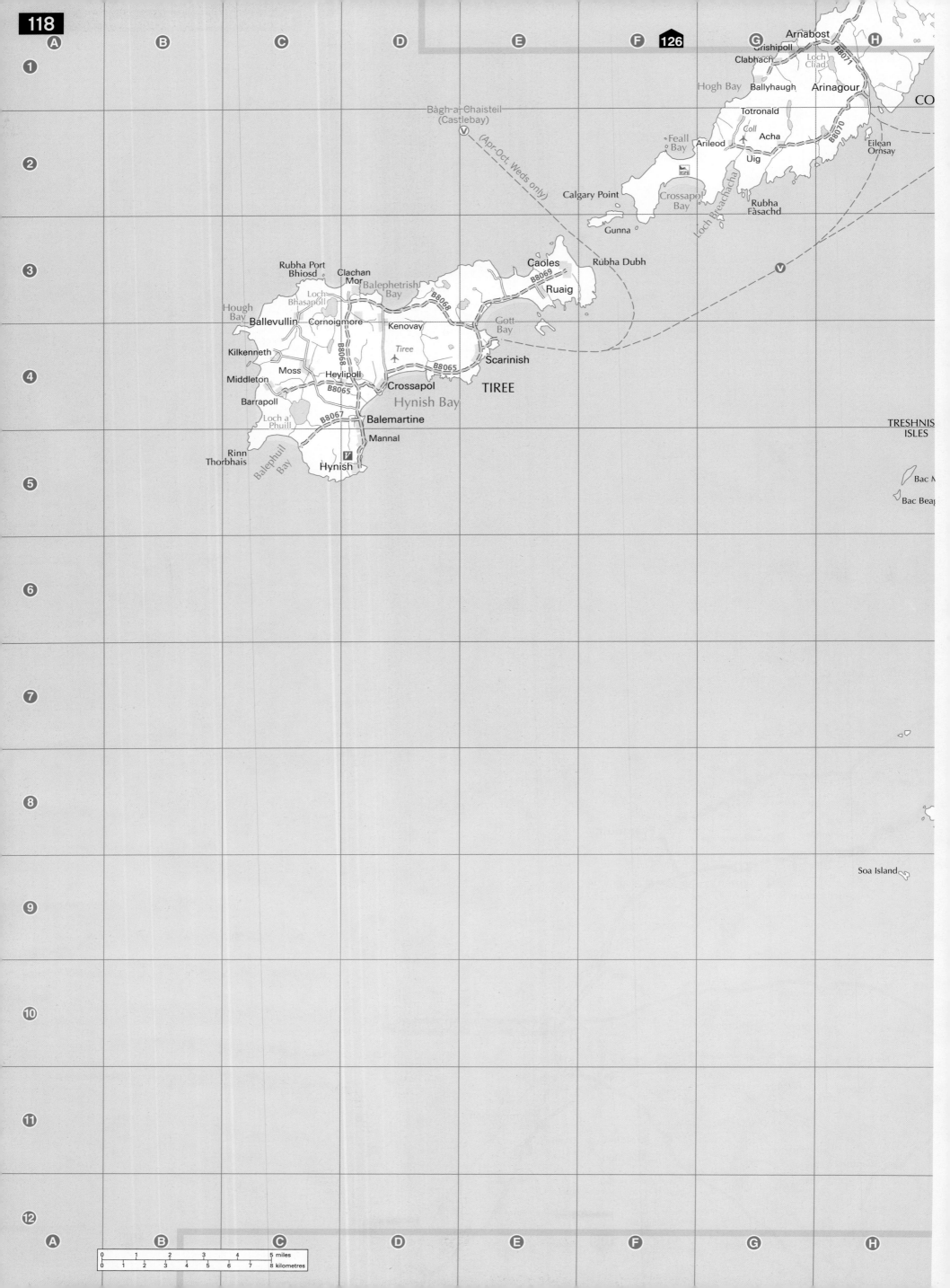

A B C D E F 126 G H
1
2

Bàgh-a-Chaisteil
(Castlebay)
V

(Apr-Oct, Weds only)

Arnabost
Grishipoll
Clabhach
Loch
Cliad
B8071

Hogh Bay   Ballyhaugh   Arinagour

CO

Totronald

Coll

Feall
Bay   Arileod   Acha
Uig

B8070

Eilean
Ornsay

3

Rubha Port
Bhiosd   Clachan
Mor
Hough
Bay
Loch
Bhasapoll
Ballevullin   Cornoigmore
Balephetrish
Bay
B8068

Kenovay

Tiree

Caoles
B8069
Ruaig

Rubha Dubh

Calgary Point   Crossapol
Bay

Gunna

Loch Breachacha

Rubha
Fàsachd

V

4

Kilkenneth
Moss   Heylipoll
B8068
Middleton
Barrapoll   B8065
Loch a
Phuill   B8067

Scarinish
Gott
Bay
B8065   TIREE
Crossapol
Hynish Bay
Balemartine
Mannal

TRESHNISH
ISLES

5

Rinn
Thorbhais   Balephuil
Bay   V
Hynish

Bac M
Bac Beag

6
7
8

Soa Island

9
10
11
12

A B C D E F G H

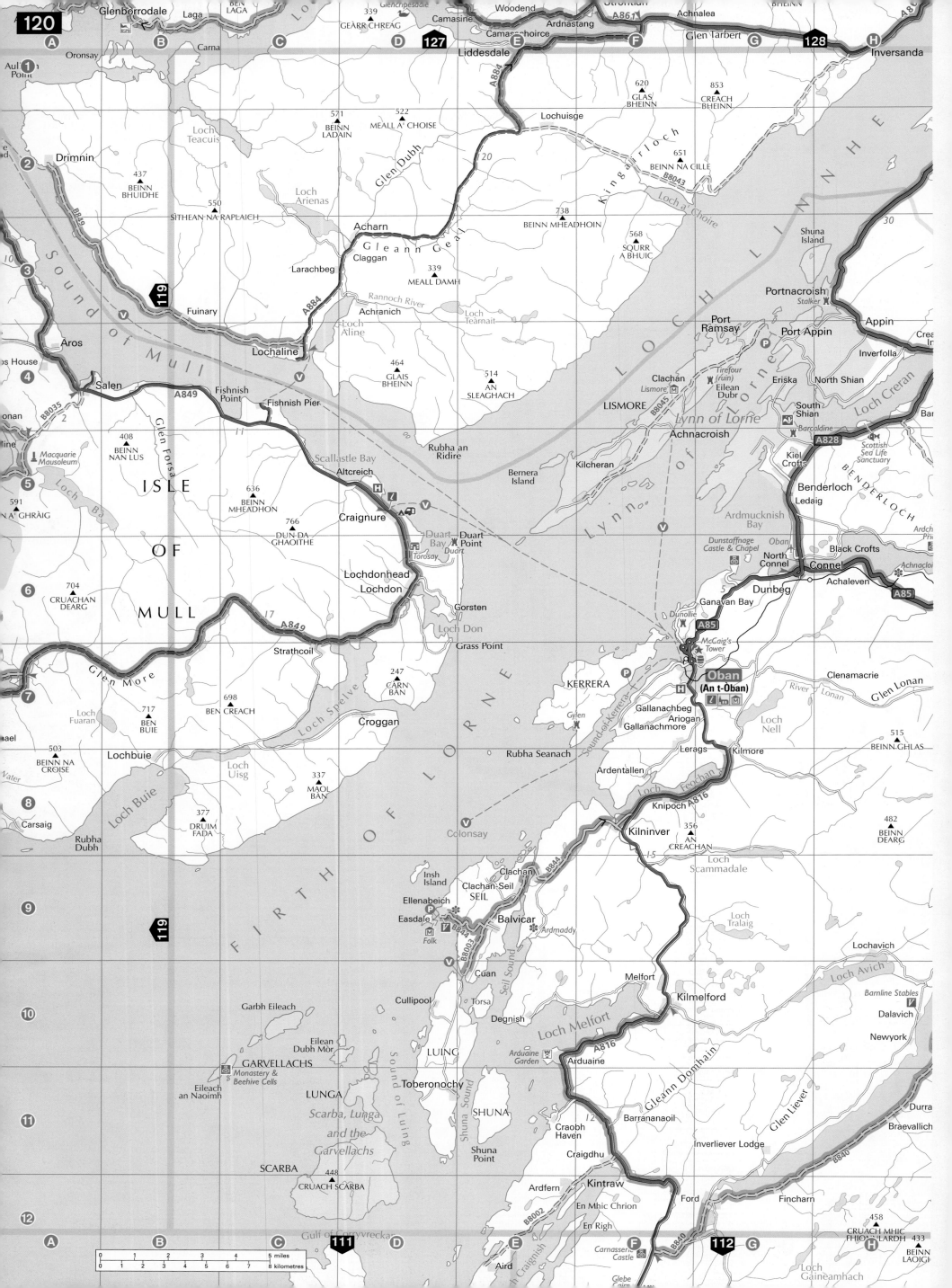

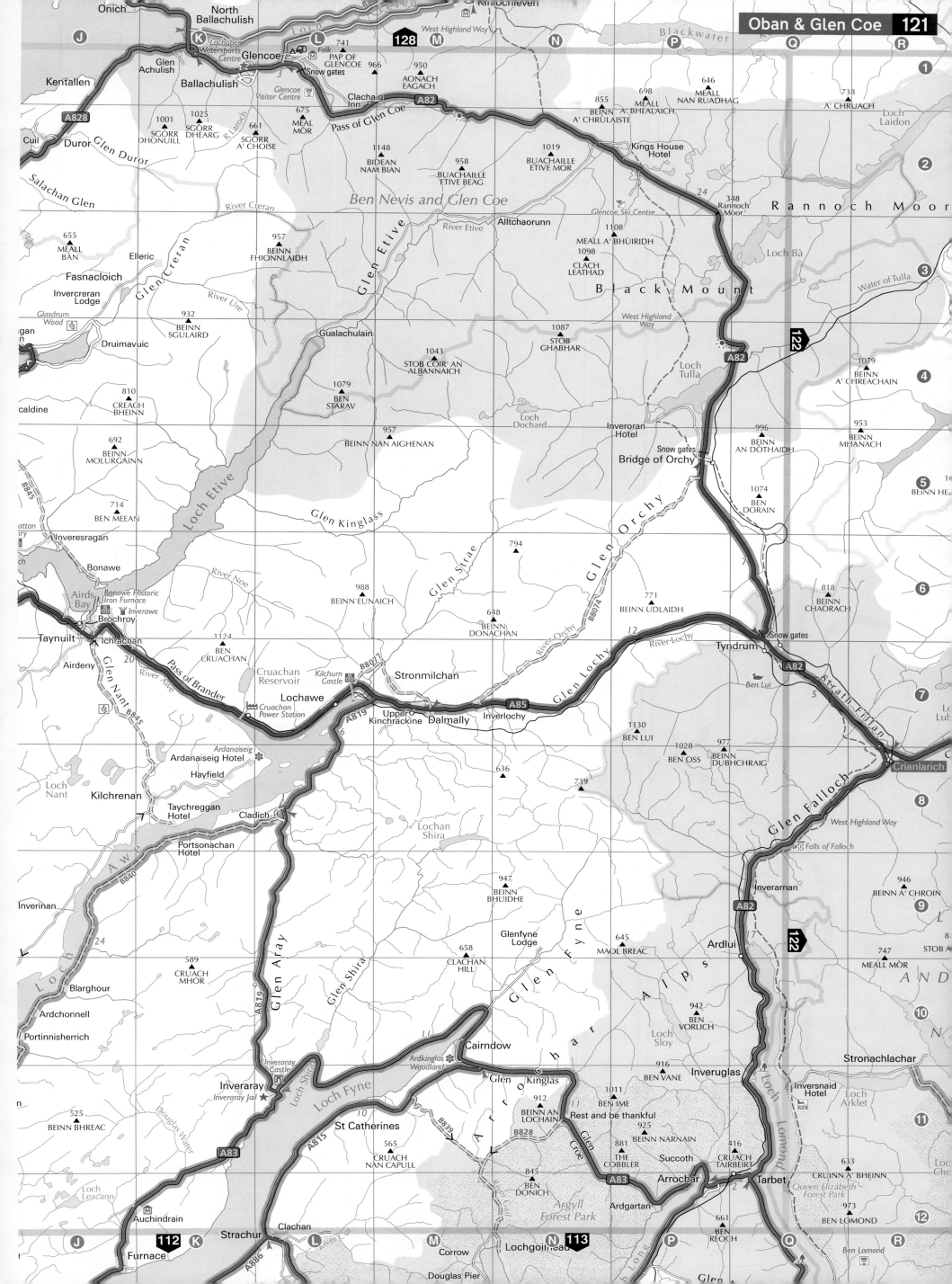

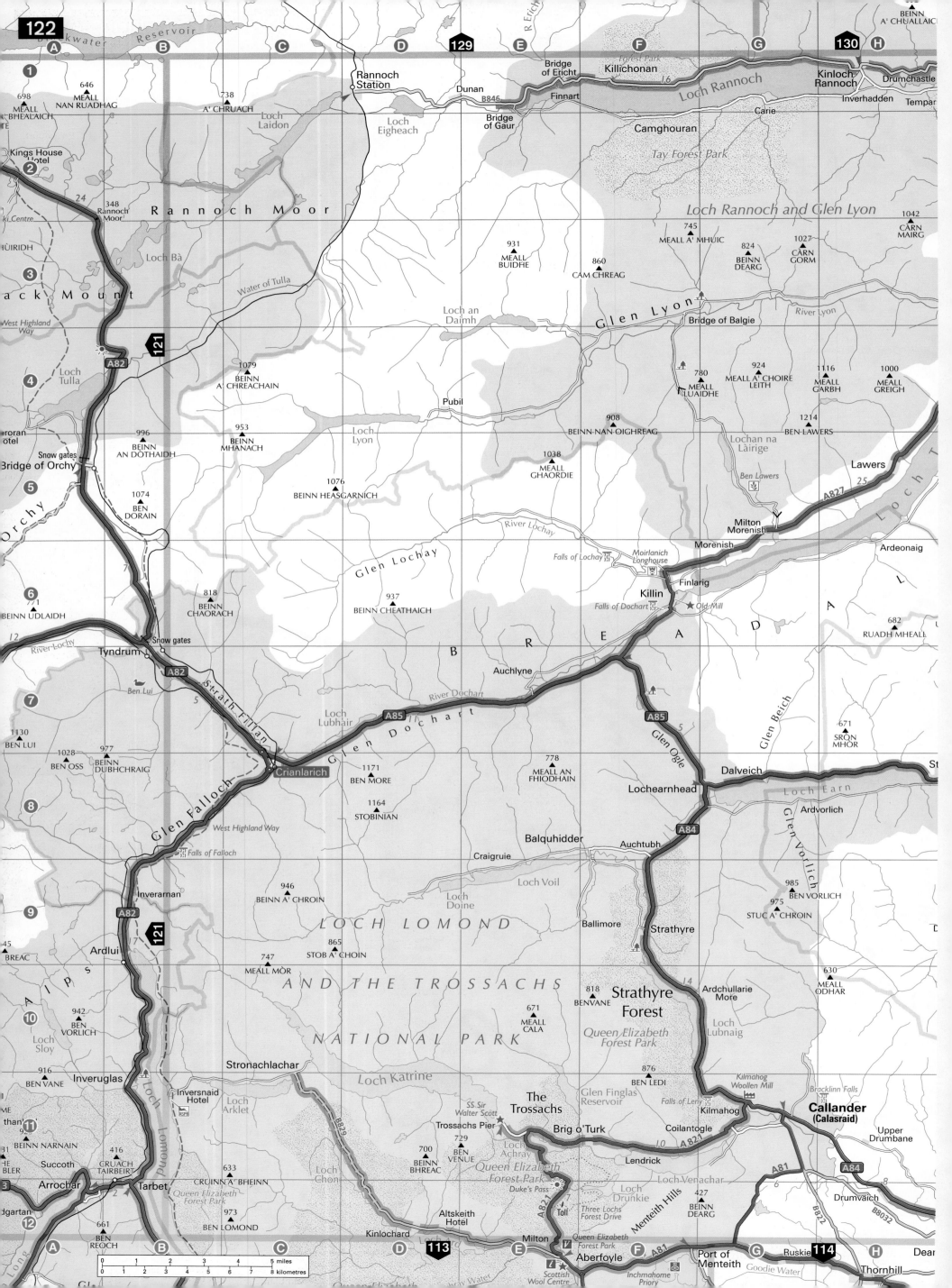

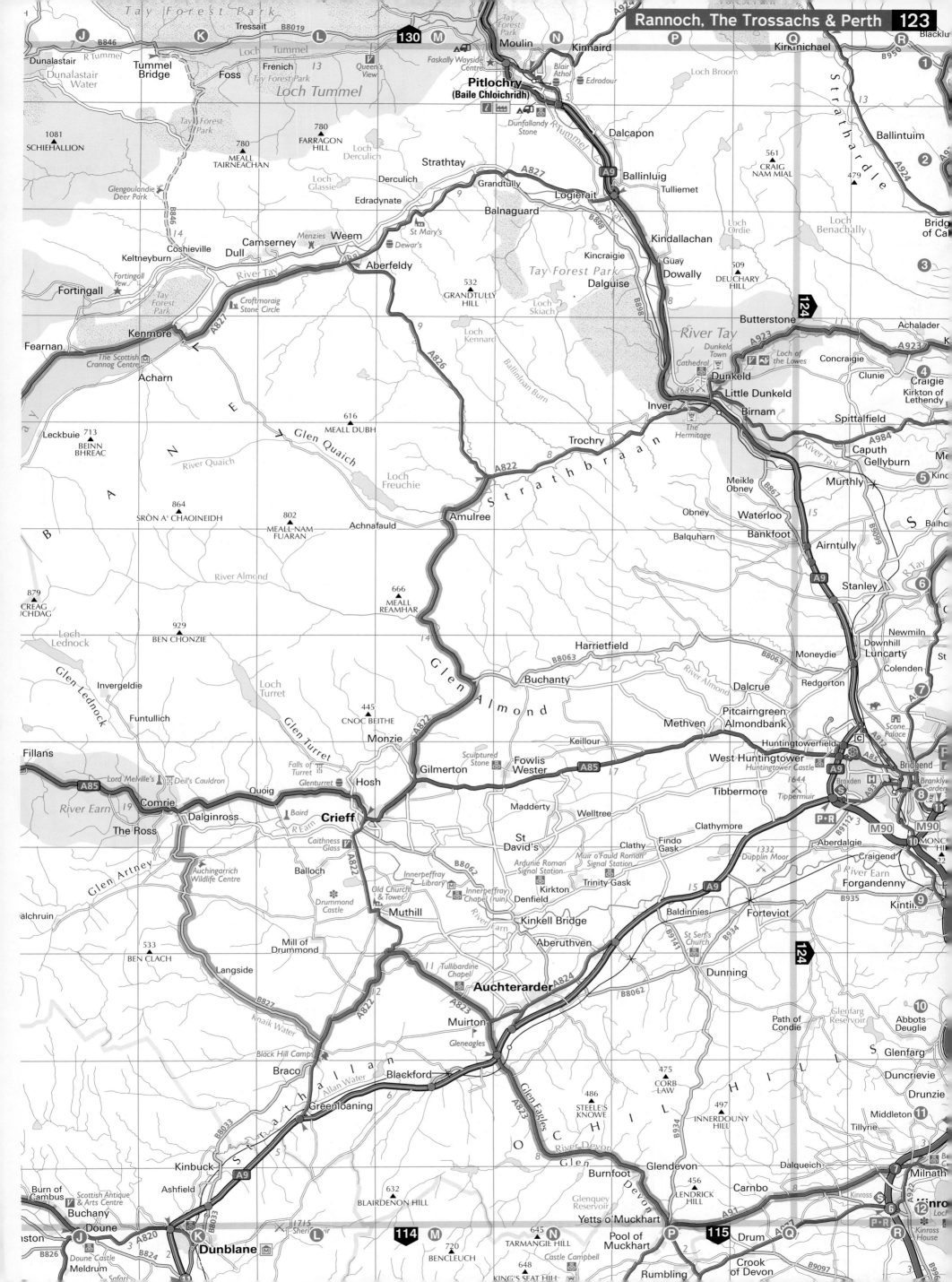

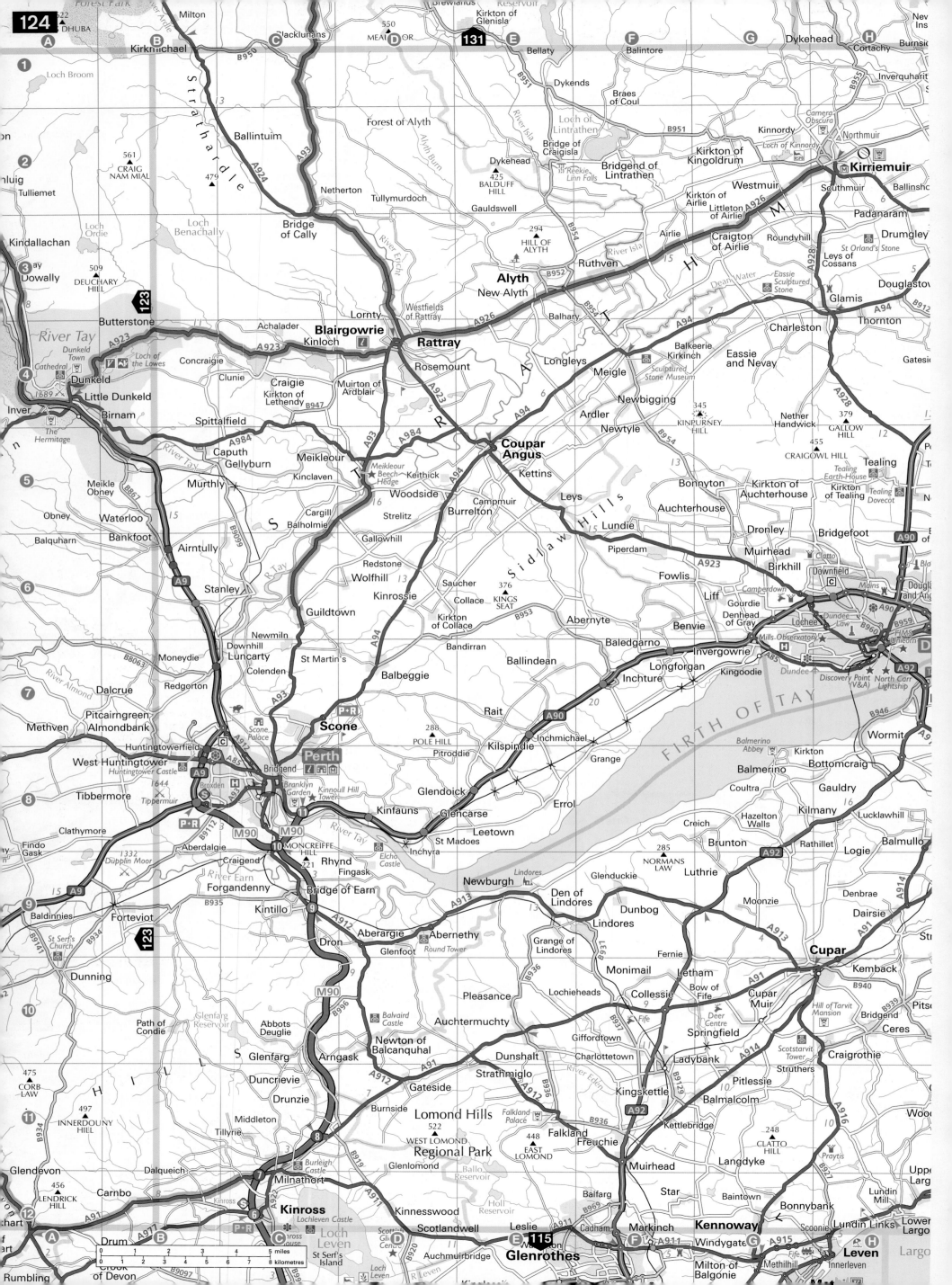

GARS
BHEINN

225

CEANN NA BEINNE

Rubha an Dùnain

Soay Sound

139
BEINN
BHREAC

Mol-chlach

SOAY

Rubh'
Aonghais

Rubh'
Aonghais

CUILLIN SOUND

Loch Baghasdail
(Lochboisdale)

210
CÀRN A' GHAILL

CANNA

Garrisdale Point

A'Chill

Canna
Harbour

Sanday

Kilmory
Bay

Rubha
Shamhnan
Insir

Sound of Canna

302
MULLACH
MÒR

A' Bhrideanach

570
ORVAL

Rubha
na Roinne

Kinloch

Loch Scresort

Oigh-sgeir

RÙM

810
ASKIVAL

Harris
Bay

763
SGÙRR NAN
GILLEAN

The Small Isles

All vehicles must have
the relevant island
permit prior to travel
to The Small Isles.
Services are seasonal,
day & weather dependent.

Rubha nam
Meirleach

Sound of Rùm

Bay of
Laig

Rubha an
Fhasaidh

Laig

CRU

EIGG

393
AN SGURR

Sound of Eigg

Eilean
nan Each

MUCK

Port Mòr

Sanna Point

Sanna

Sanna
Bay

Achnaha

Ardnamurchan
Point

Portuairk

Achosnich

B8007

Bàgh a' Chaisteil
(Castlebay)
Loch Baghasdail
(Lochboisdale)
(Oct-Mar)

342
BEINN
NA SEILG

Eilean Mòr

Rubha
Mòr

Rubha
Sgor-innis

Ormsaigmore

Bousd

Sorisdale

Cliad
Bay

B8072

Arnabost

Grishipoll

Clab ch

118

B8071

Ardmore
Point

Coll - Oban

Sorne
Point

Arinagour

119

Quinish Point

Glengorm Castle

COLL

0 1 2 3 4 5 miles
0 1 2 3 4 5 6 7 8 kilometres

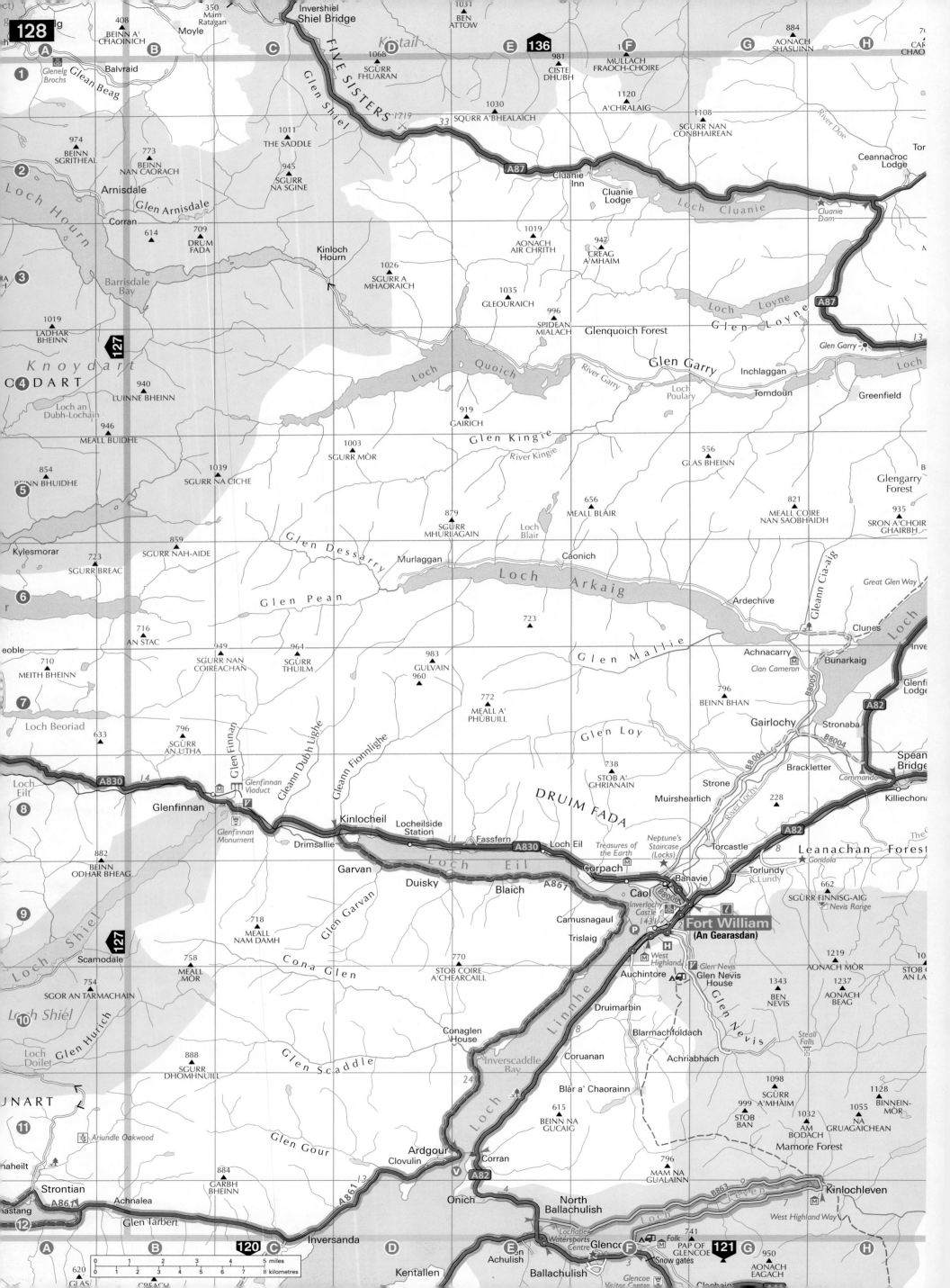

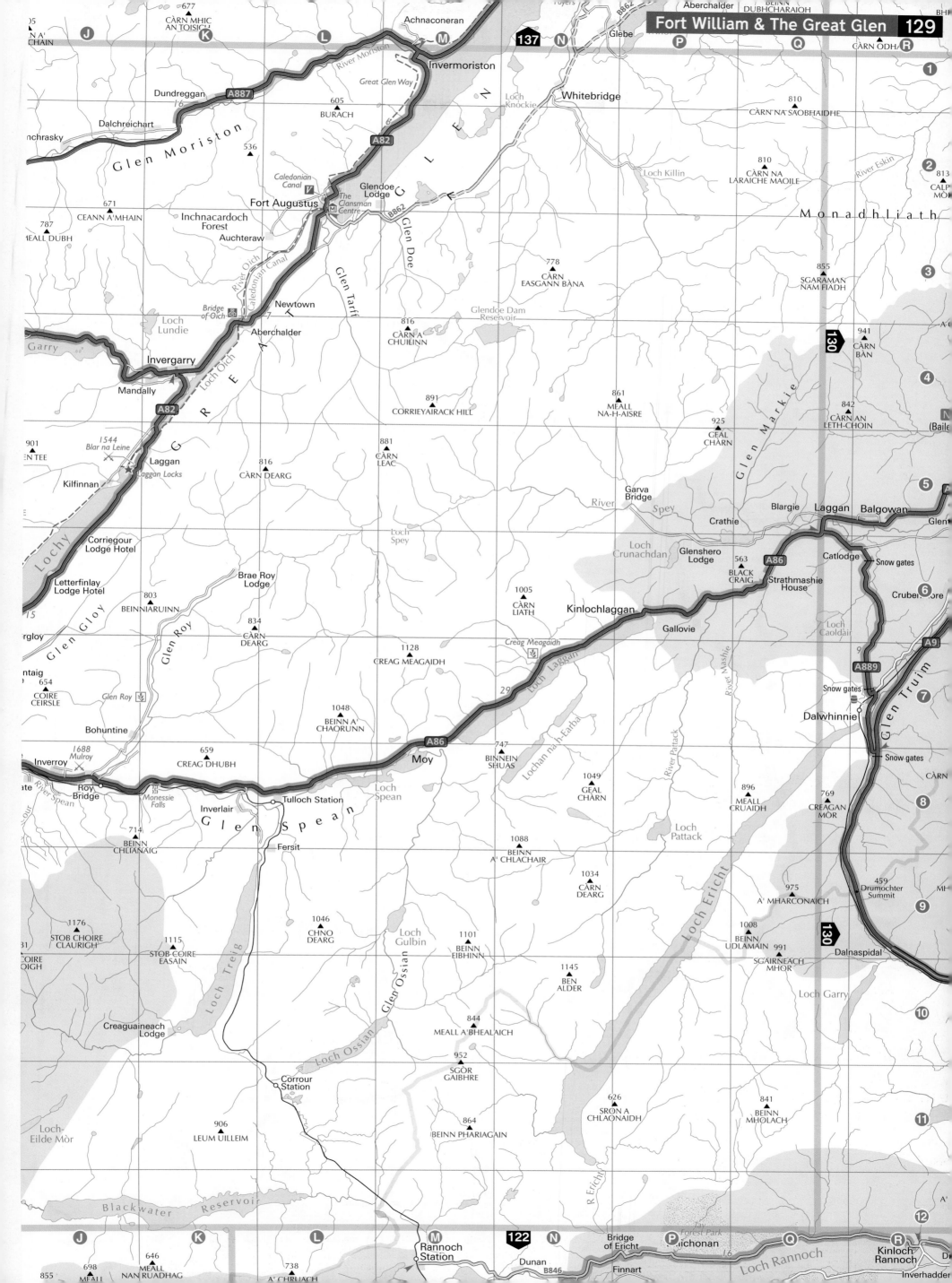

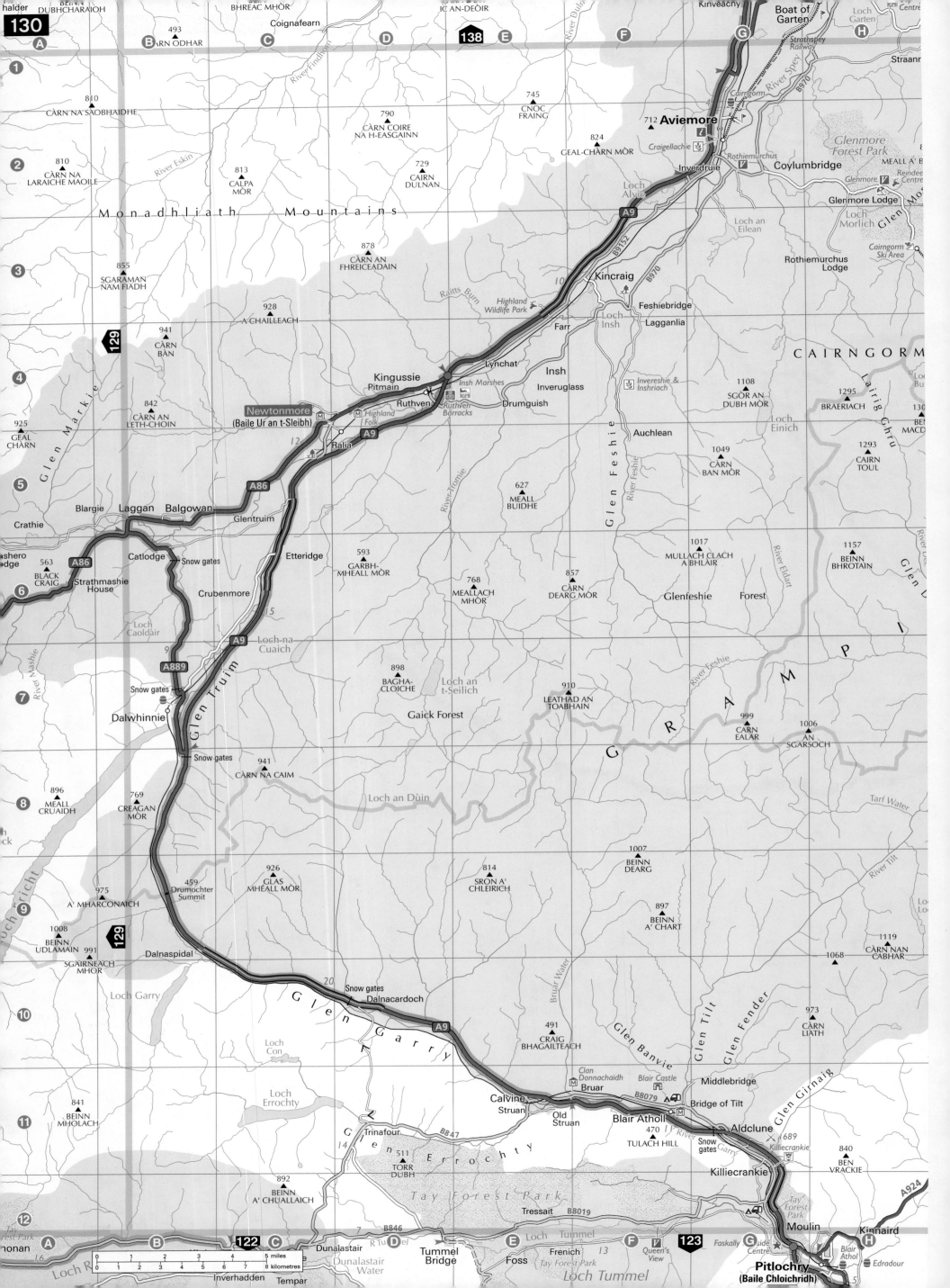

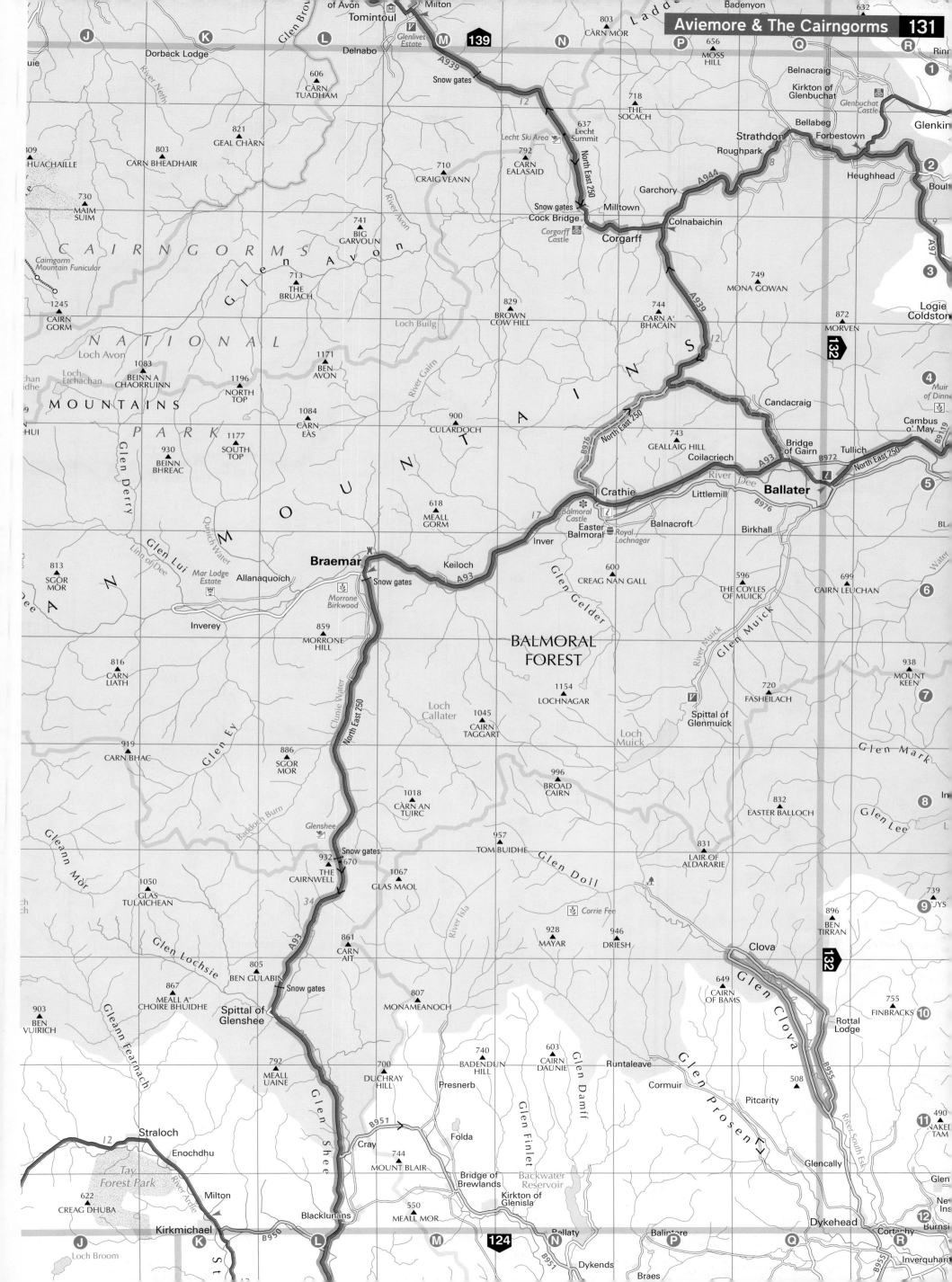

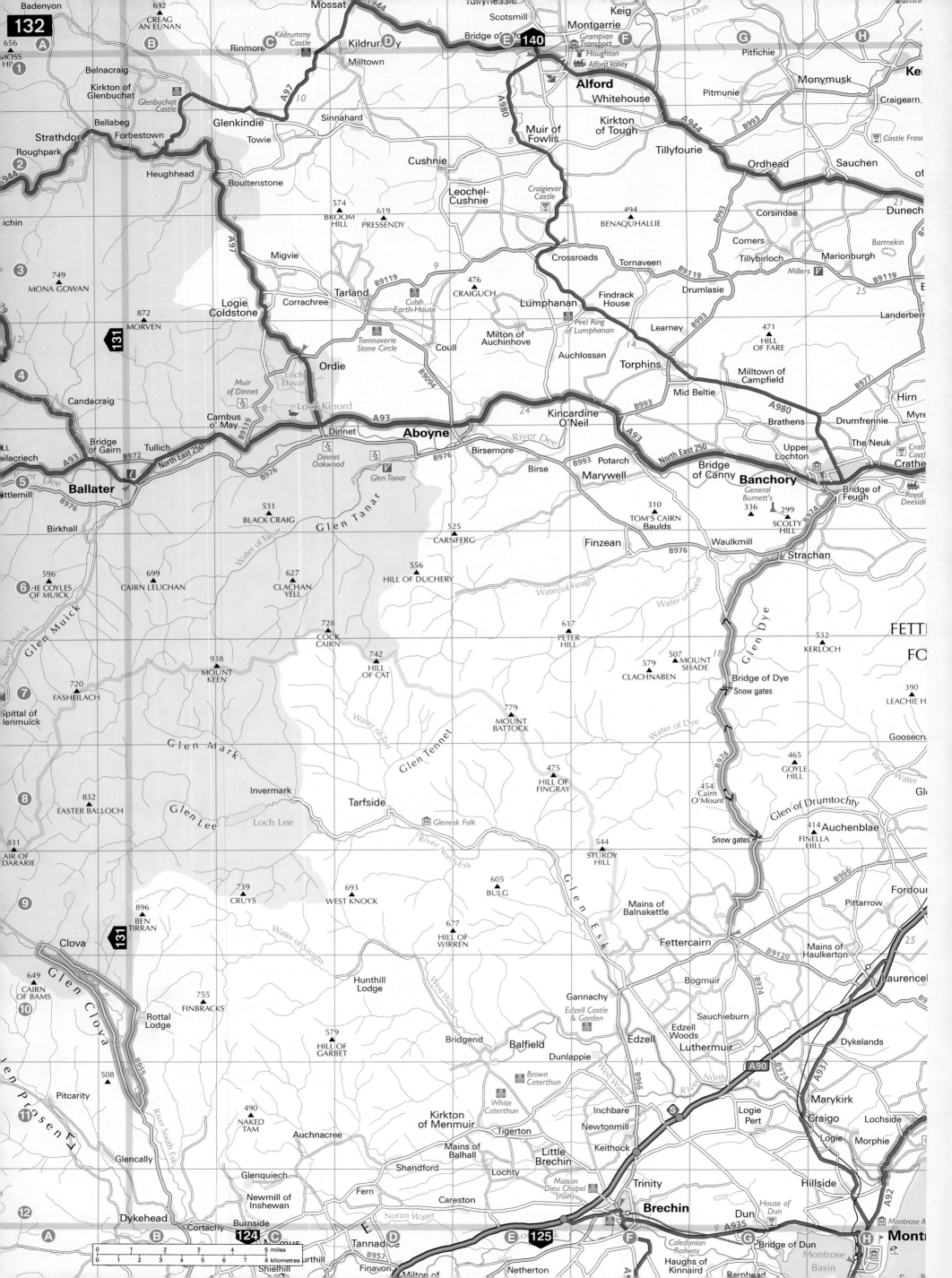

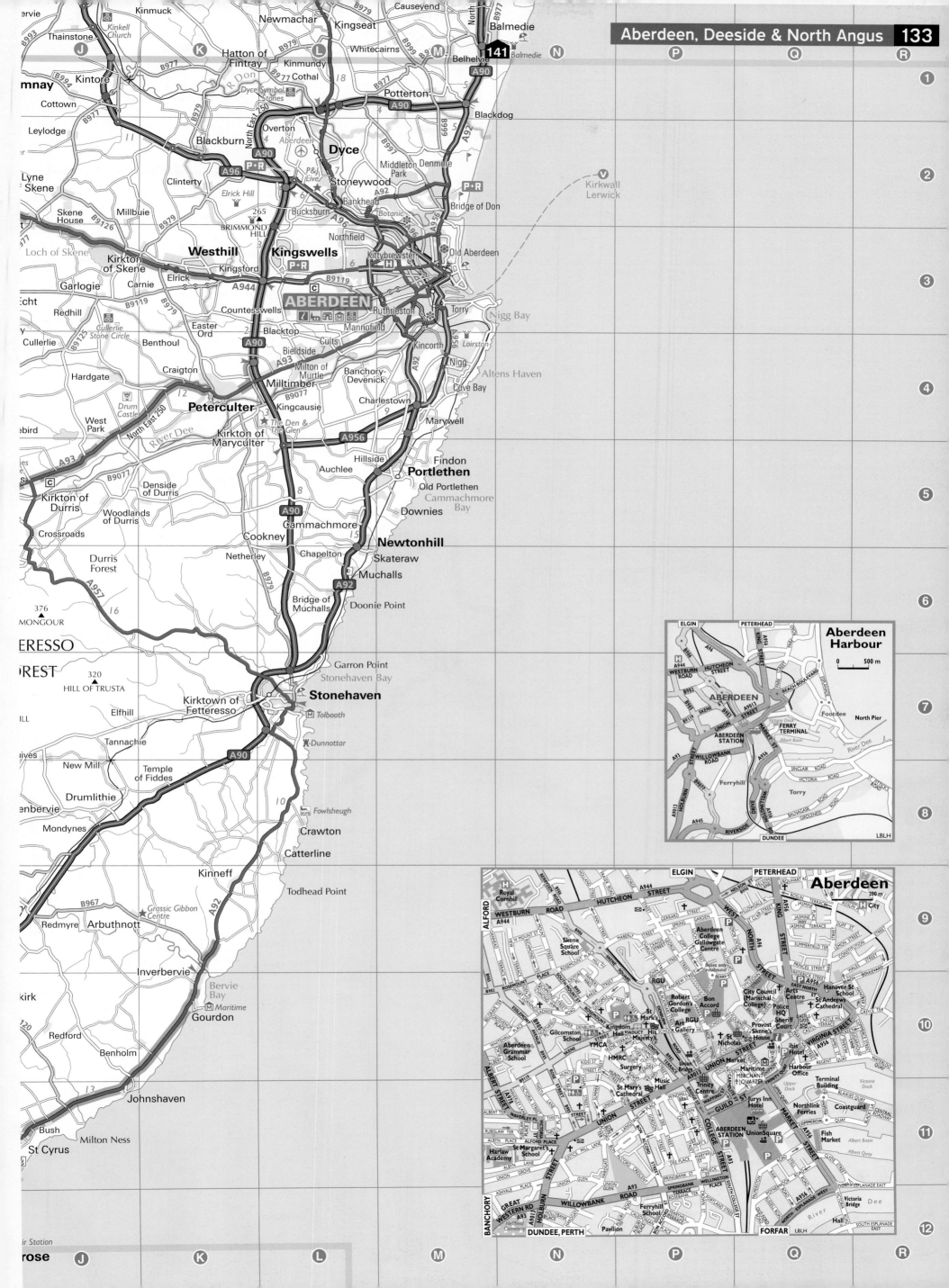

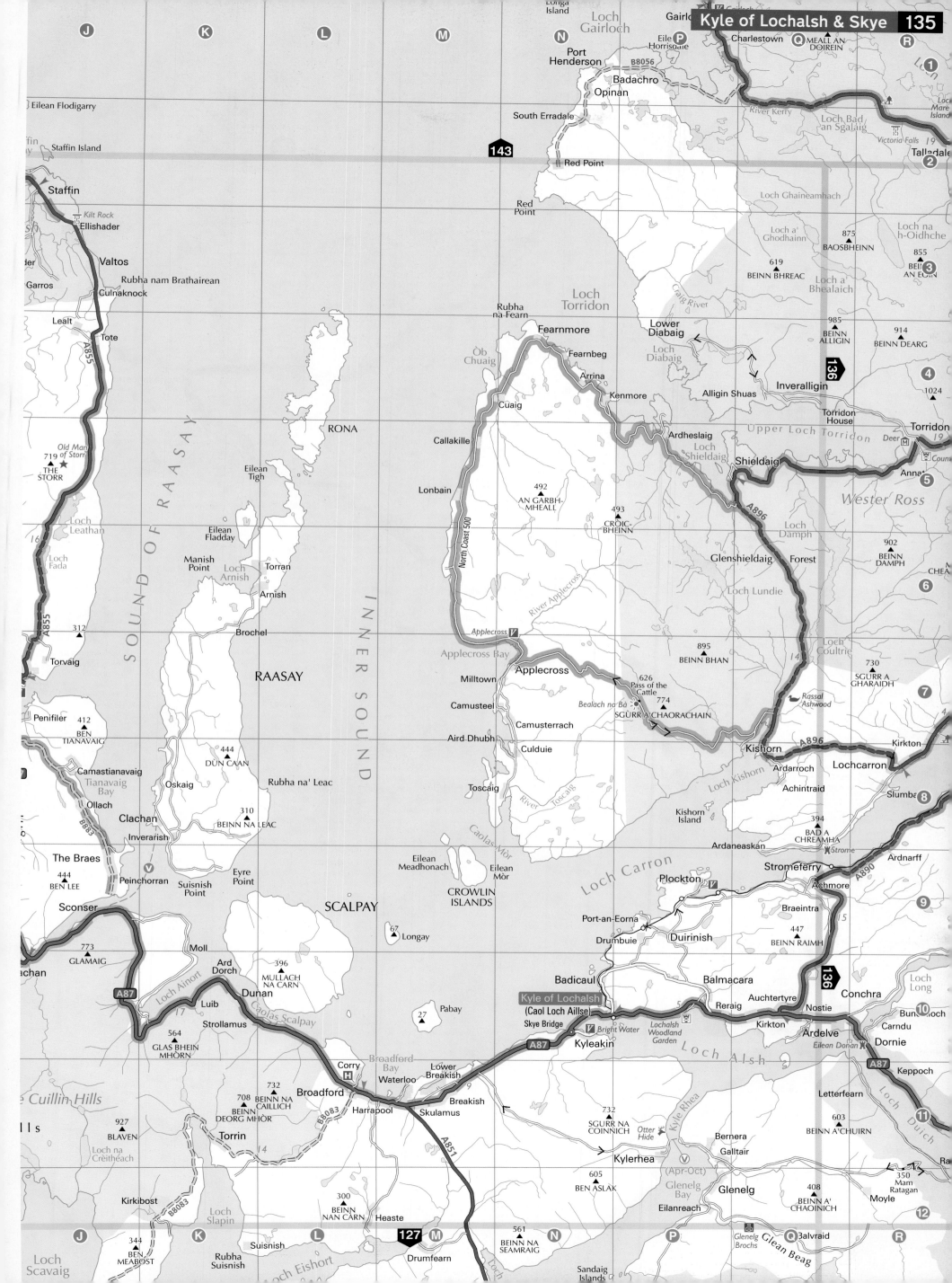

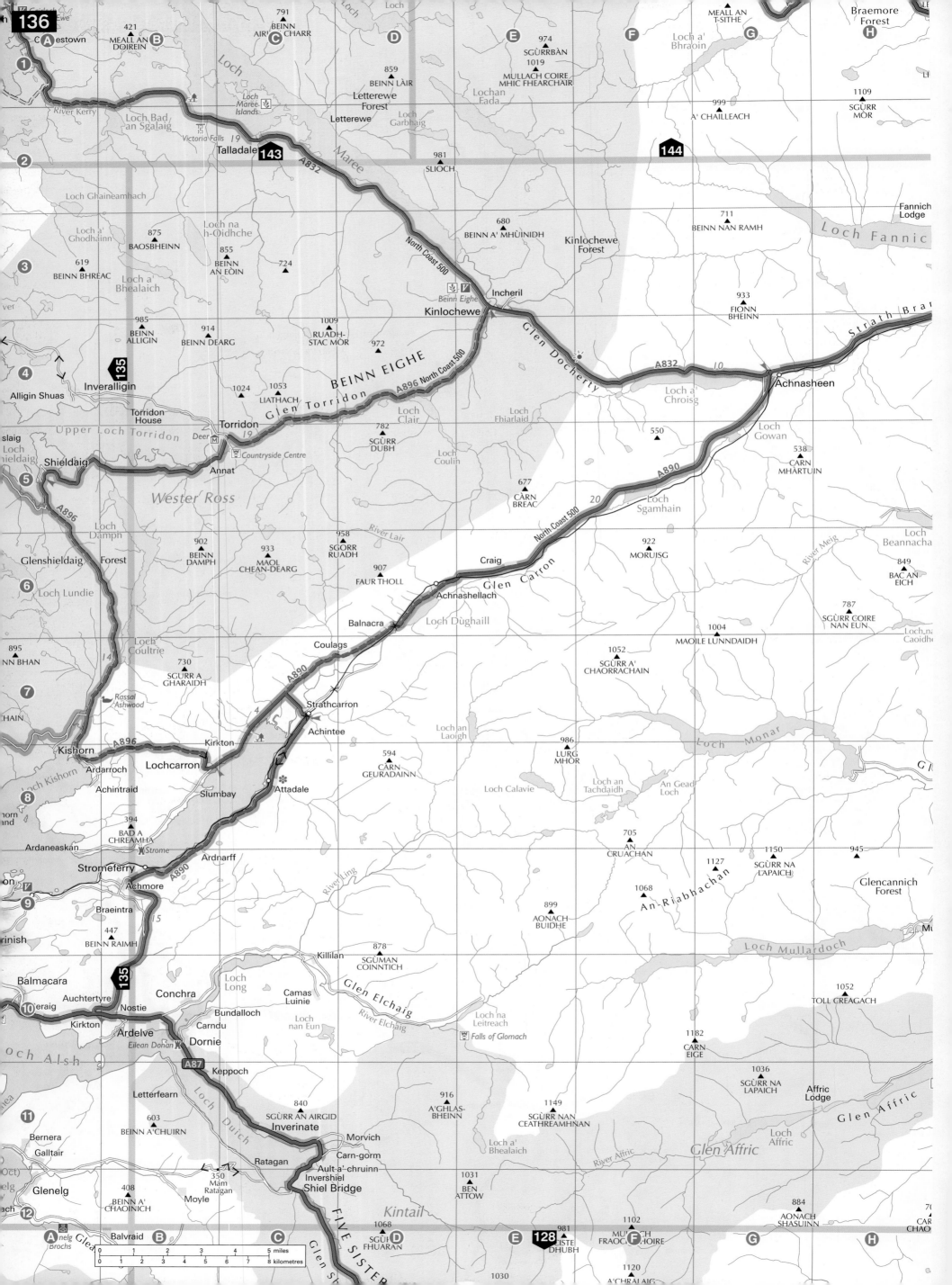

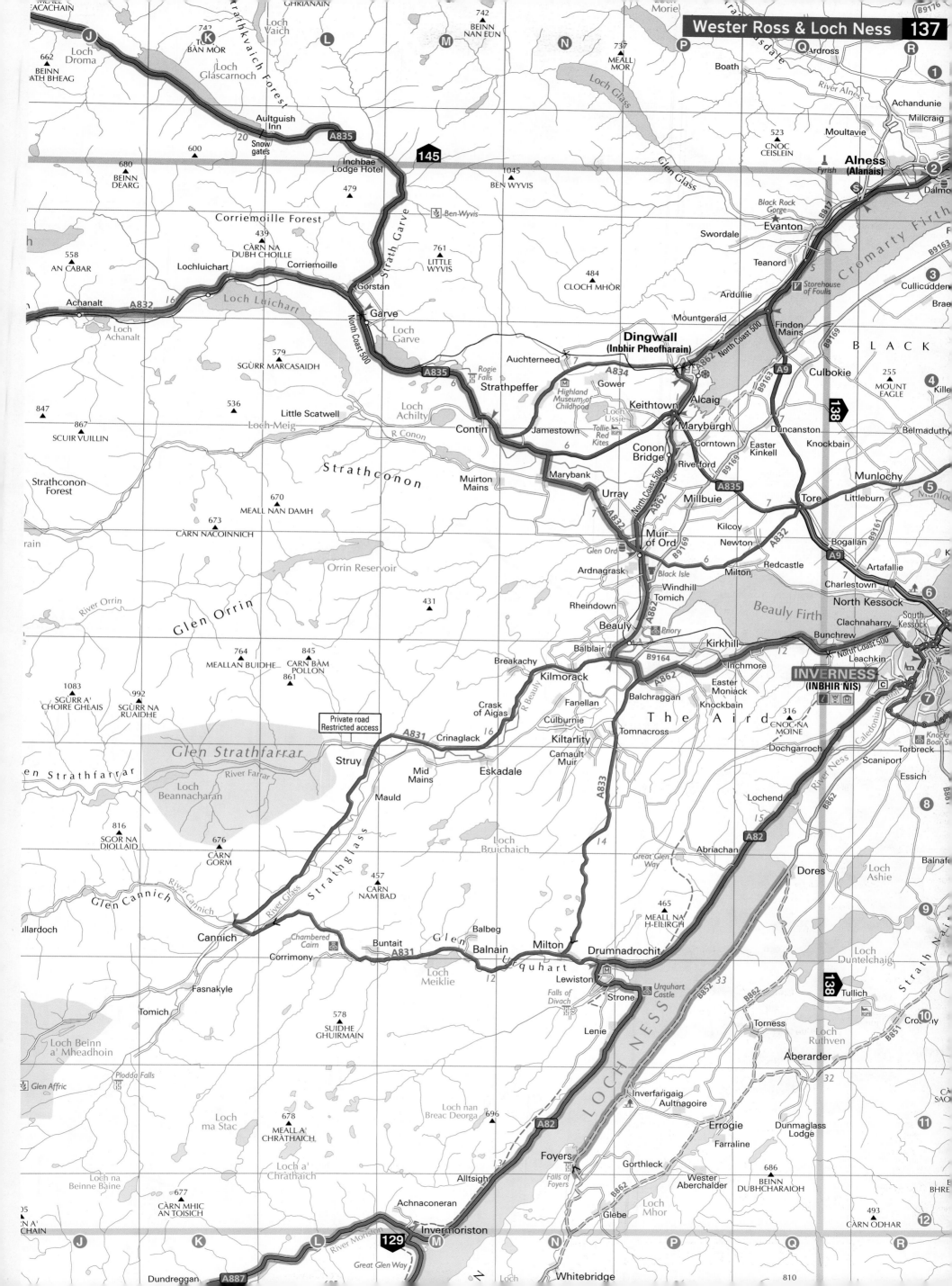

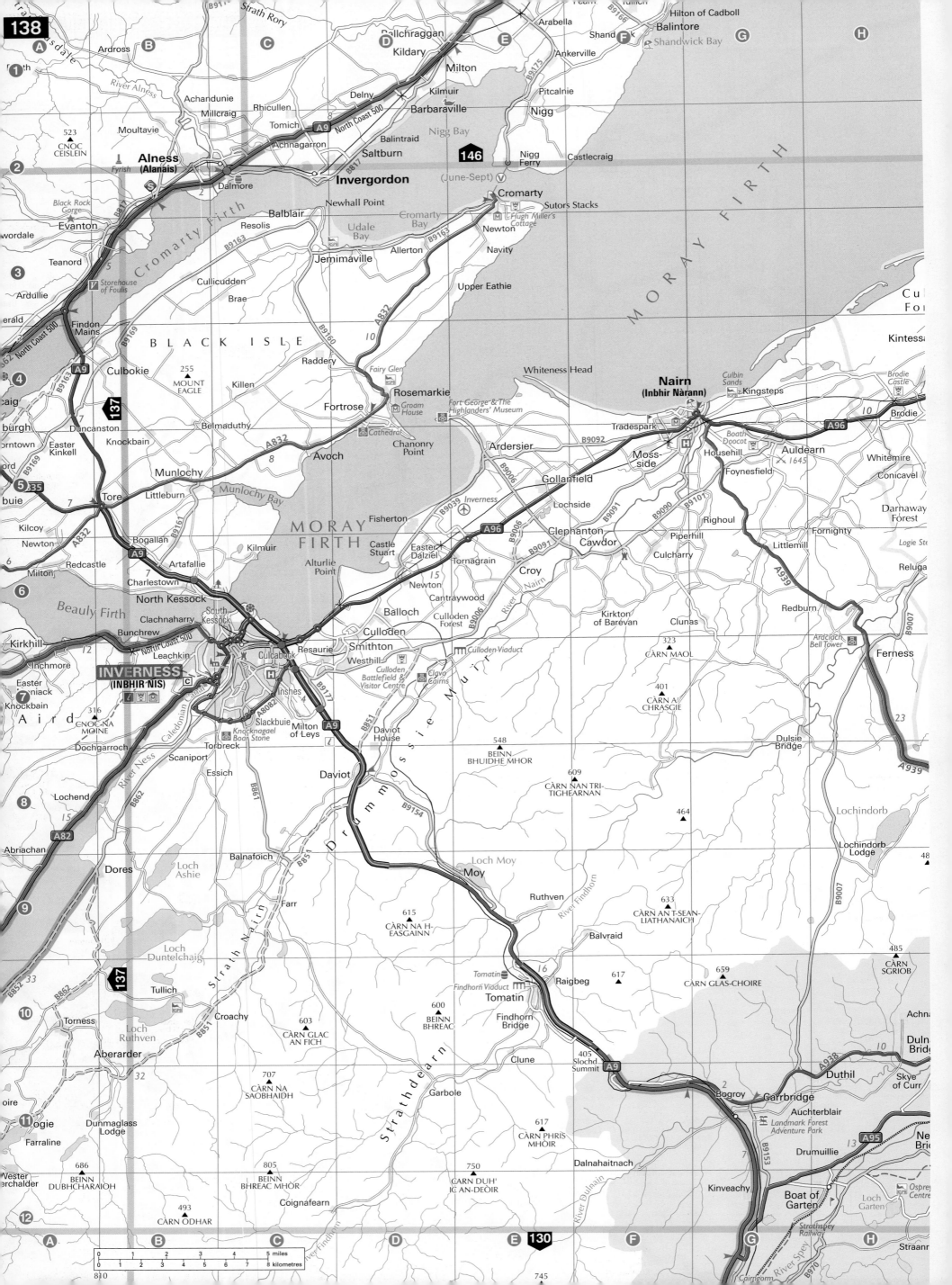

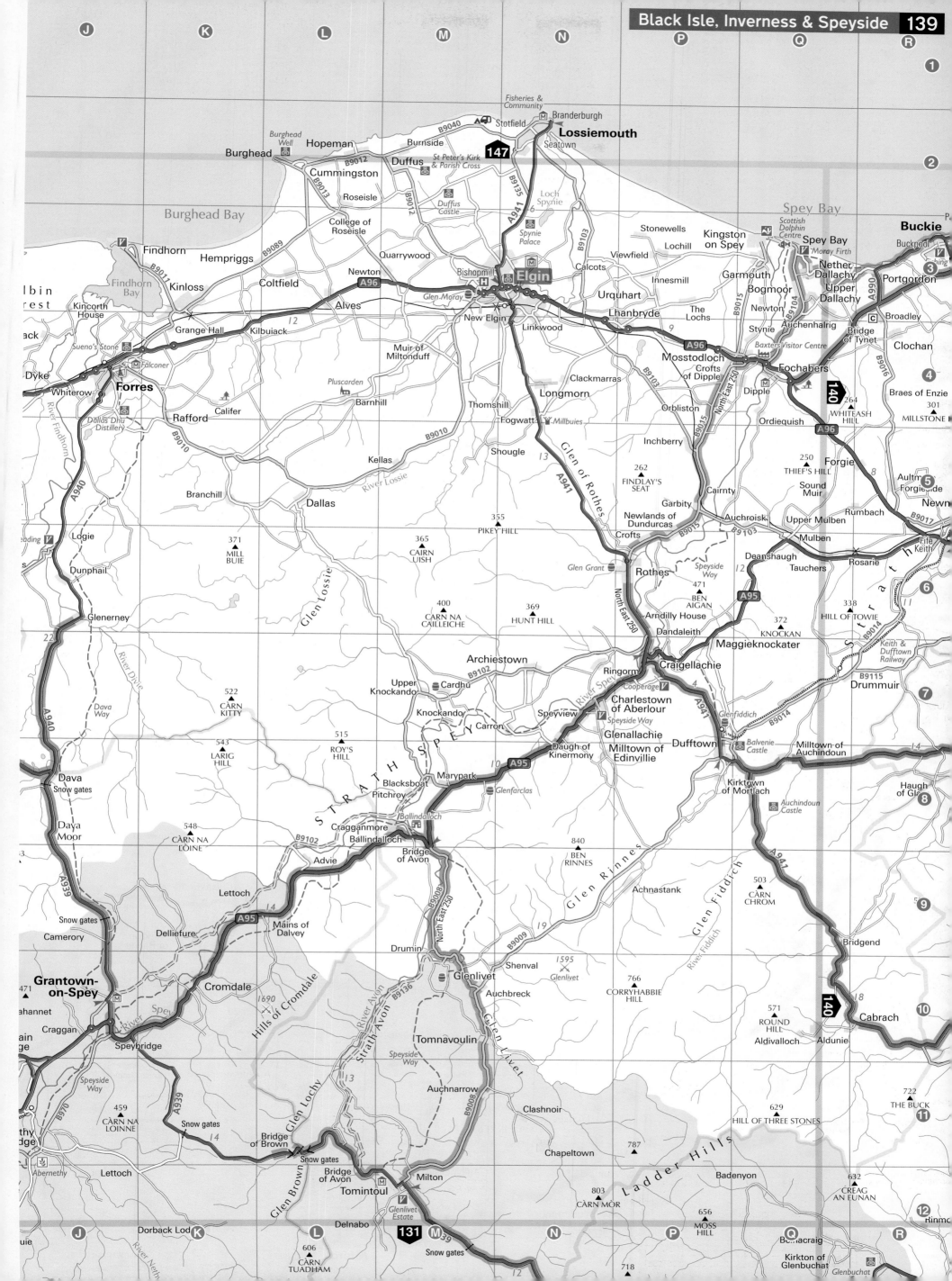

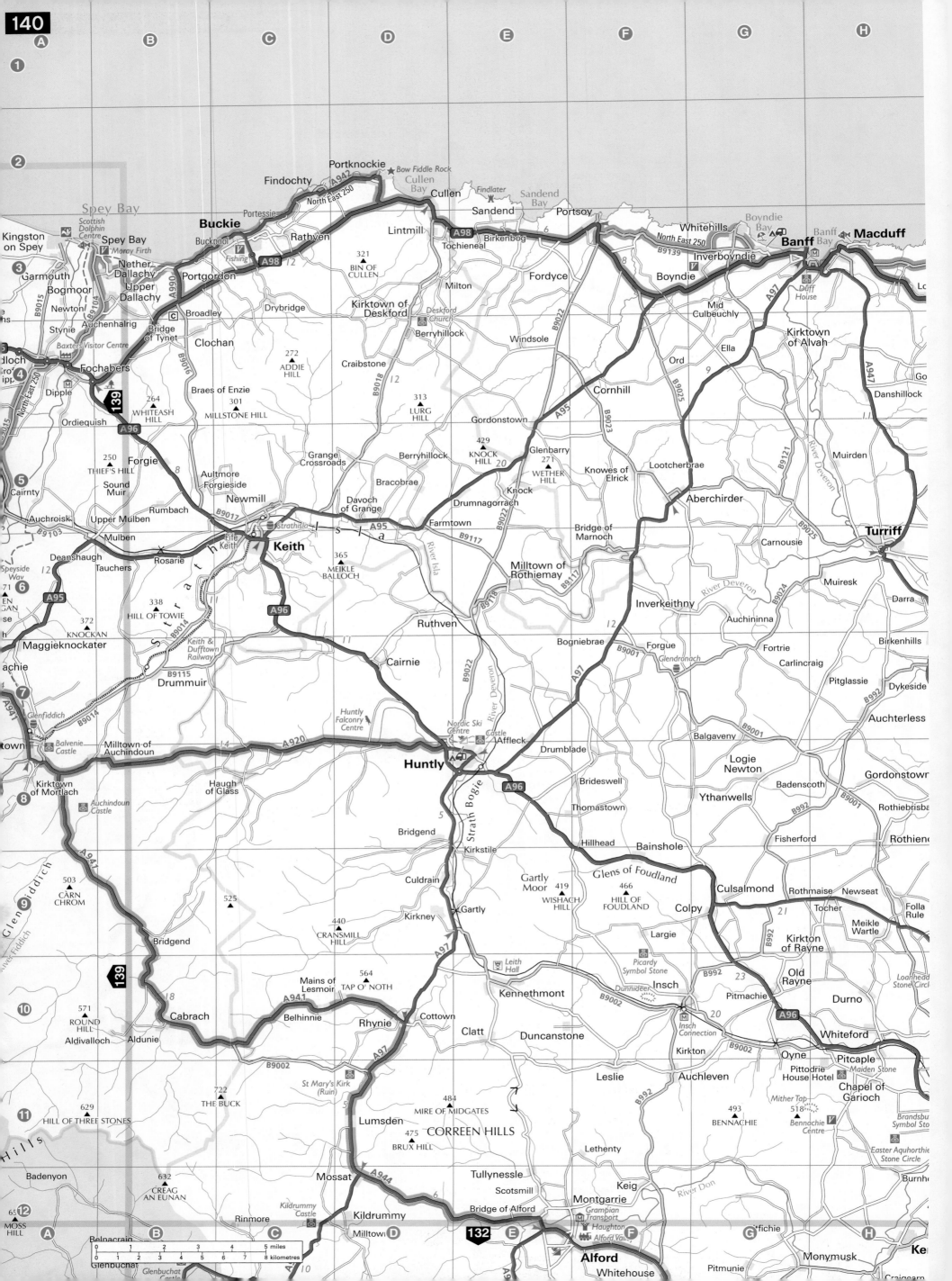

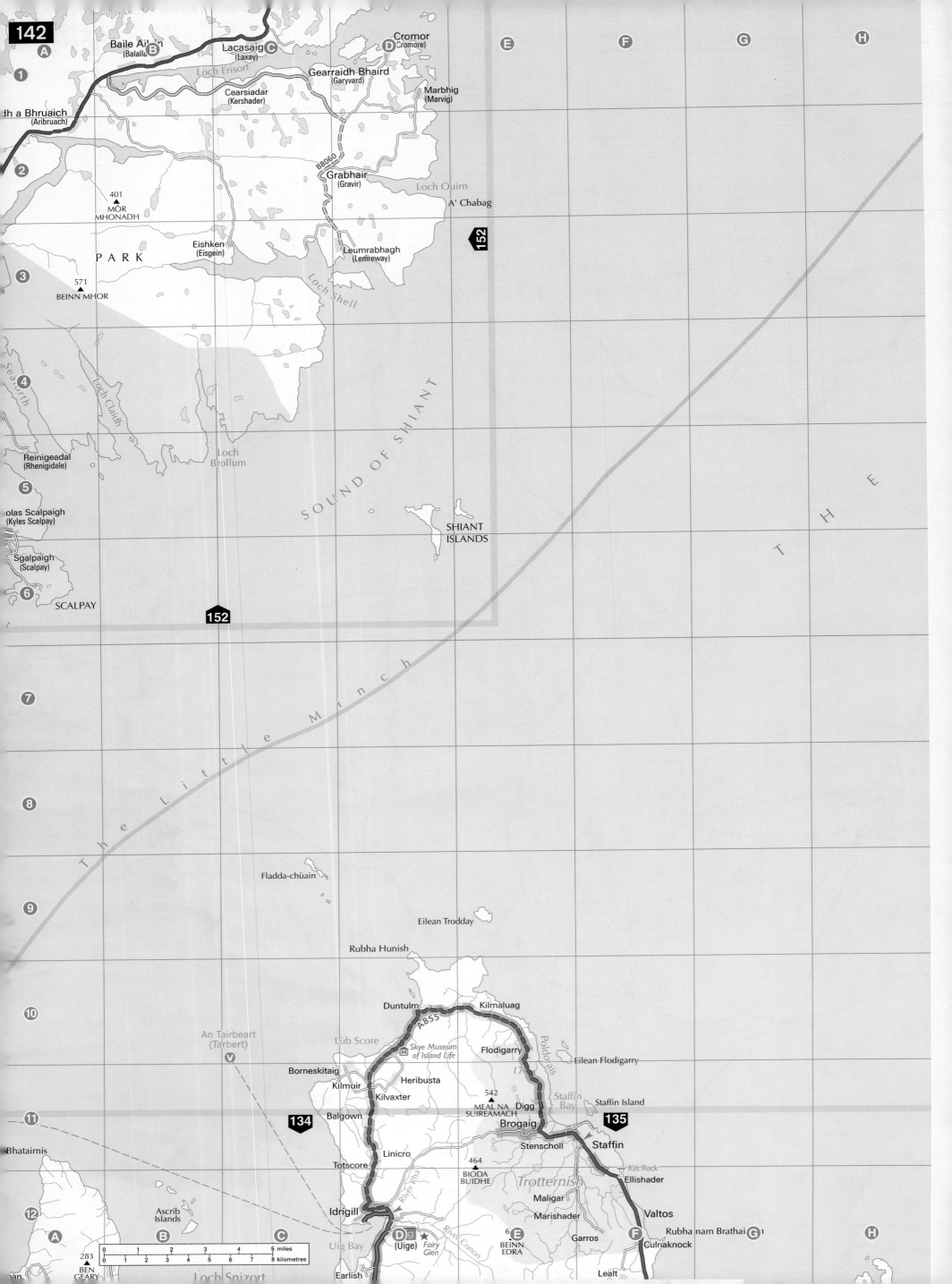

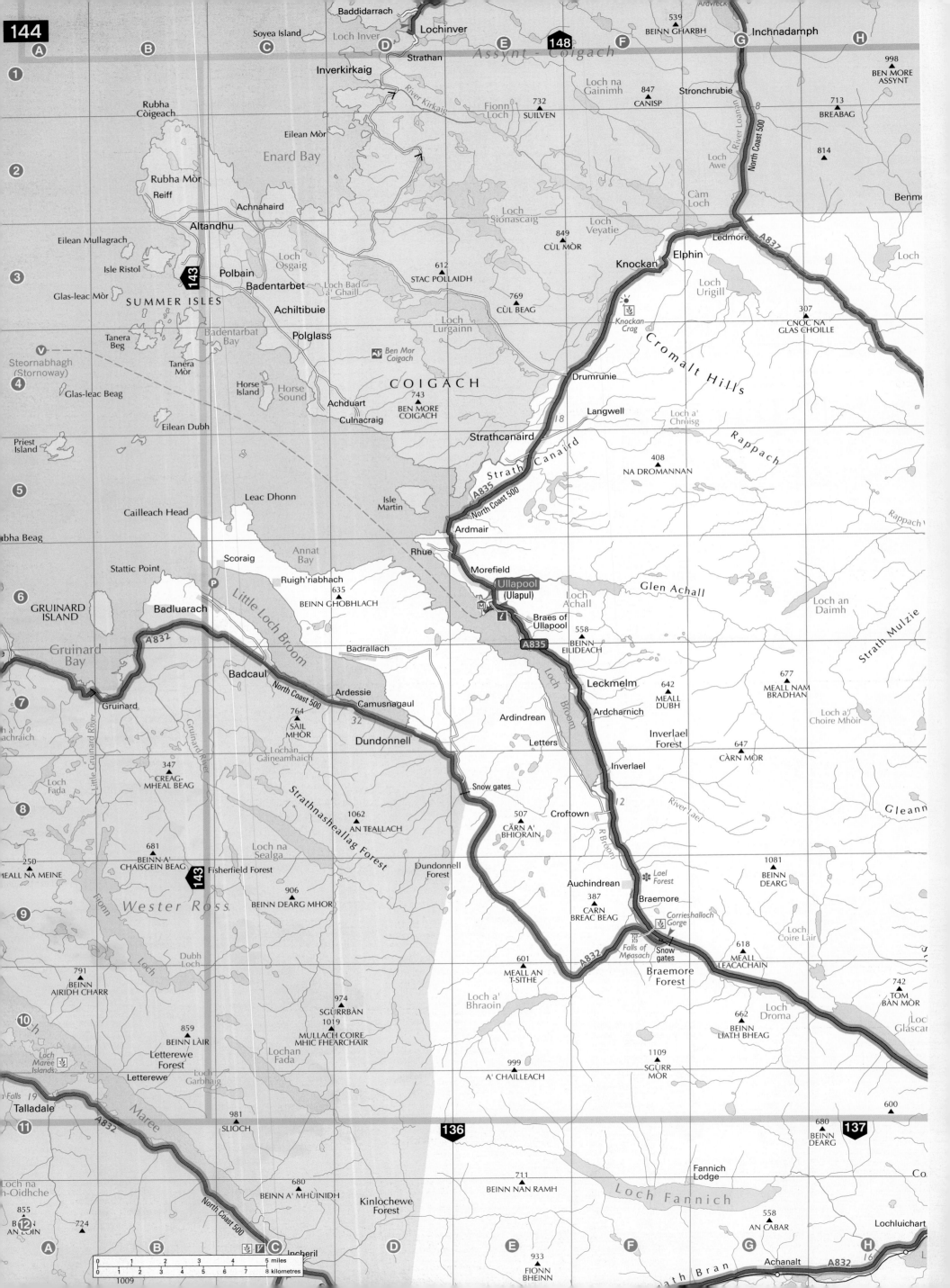

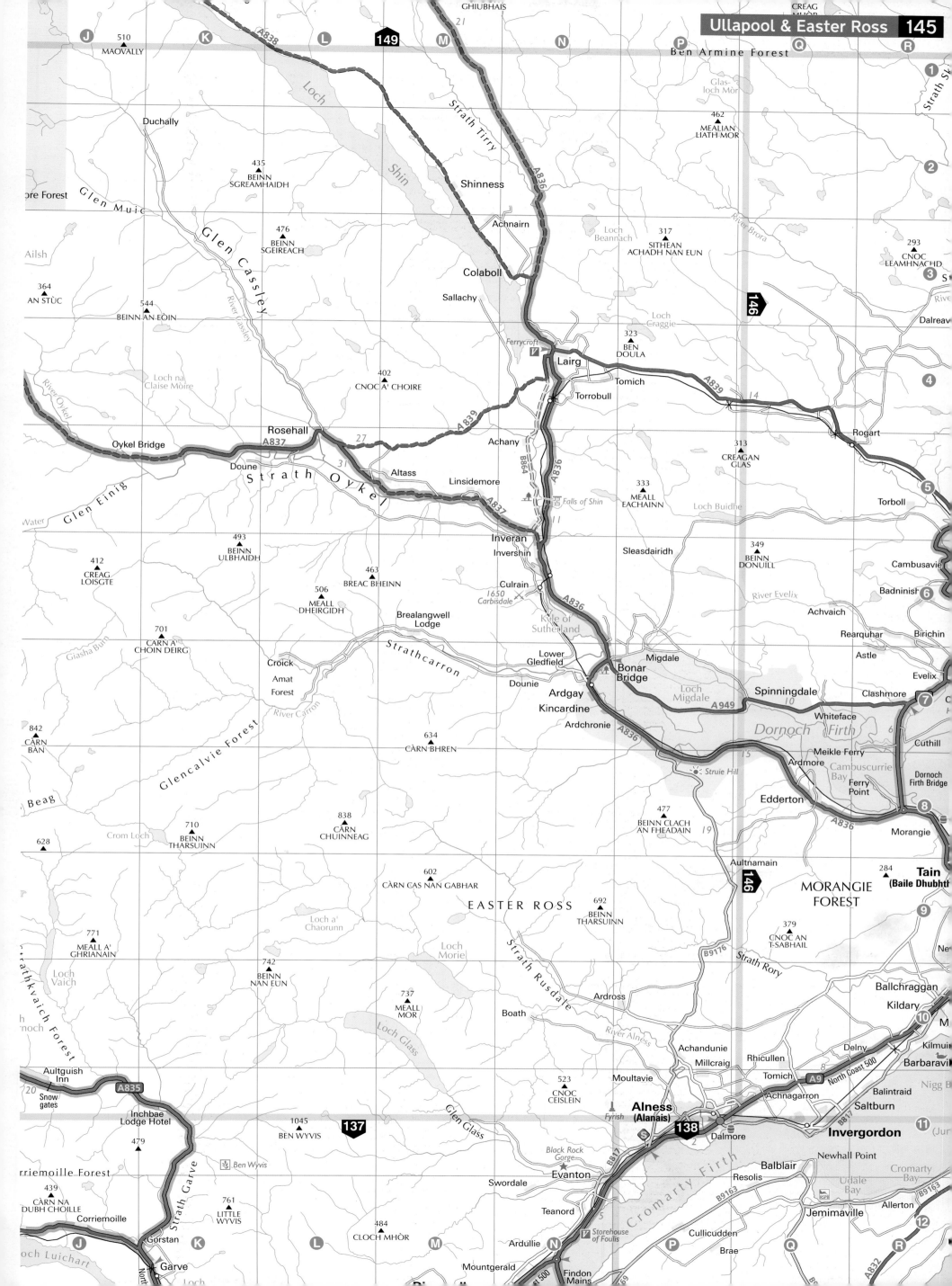

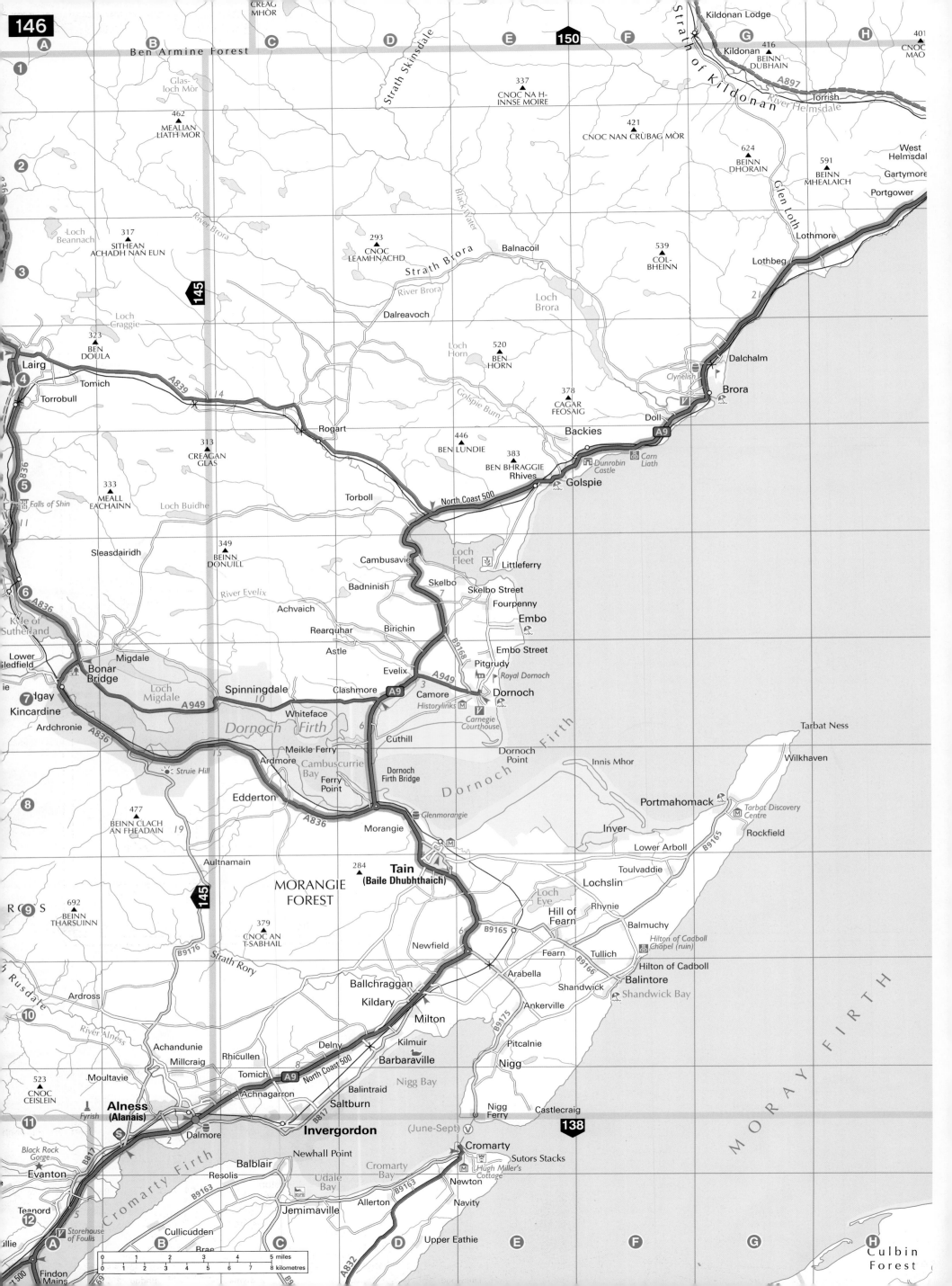

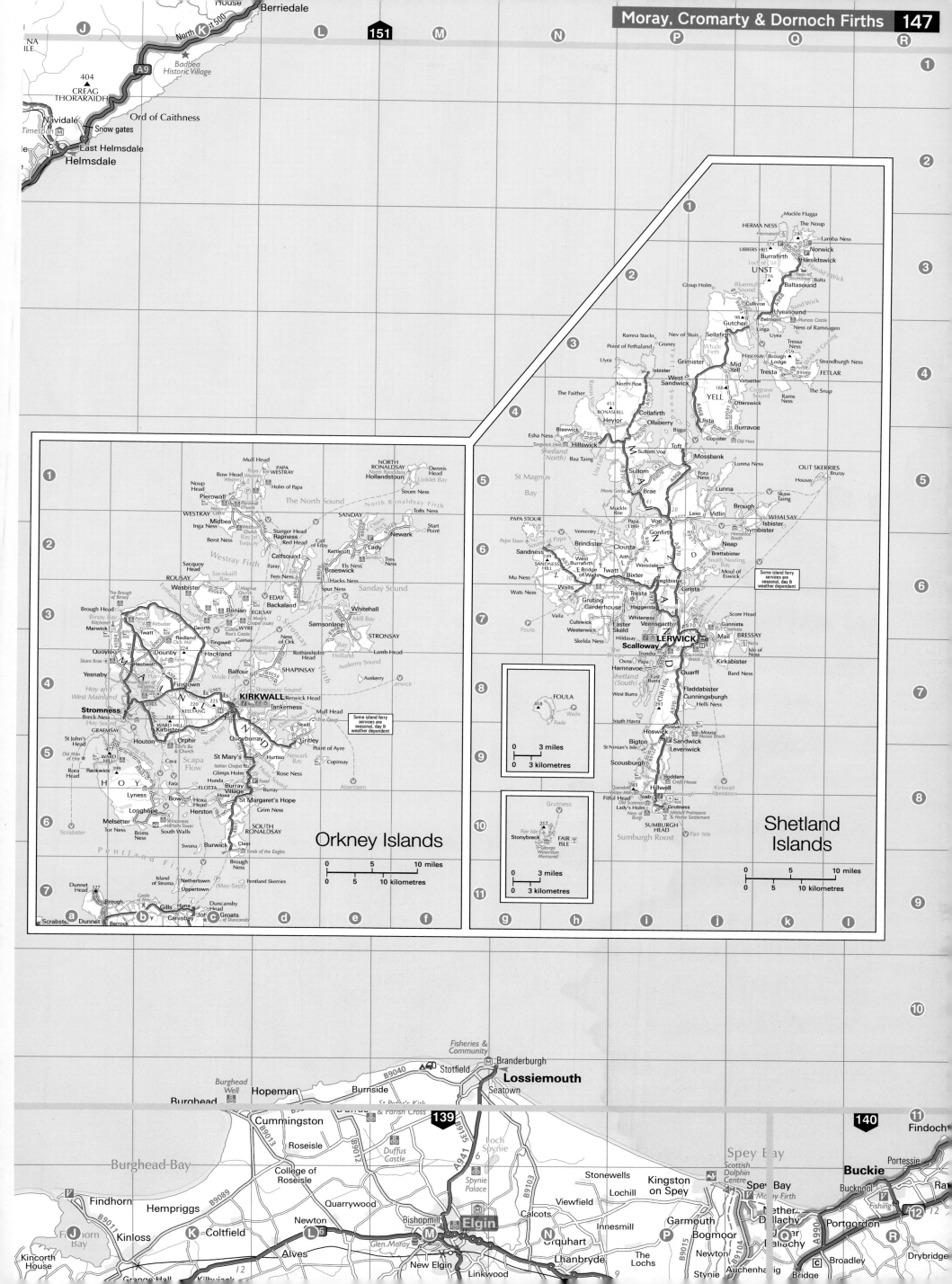

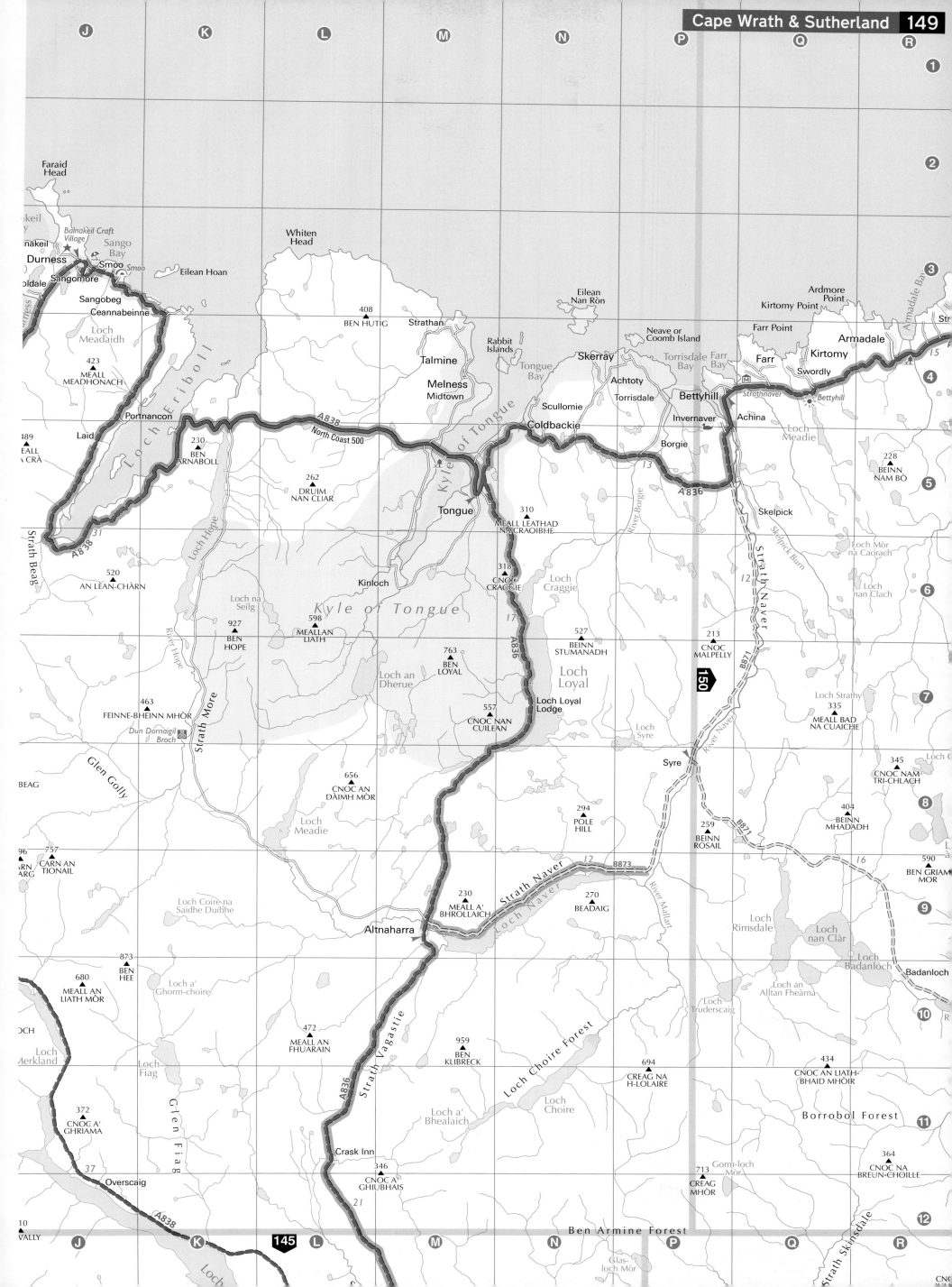

J   K   L   M   N   P   Q   R

Faraid
Head

Balnakeil Craft
Village

Sango
Bay

Durness
Sangomore   Smoo   Smoo   Eilean Hoan
Sangobeg
Ceannabeinne

Loch
Meadaidh

423
MEALL
MEADHONACH

Portnancon

489
EALL
A CRÀ   Laid

Loch Eriboll   North Coast 500   A838

230
BEN
ARNABOLL

262
DRUIM
NAN CLIAR

Strath Beag   31   A838

520
AN LEAN-CHÀRN

Loch Hope

Loch na
Seilg

927
BEN
HOPE

598
MEALLAN
LIATH

Whiten
Head

408
BEN HUTIG   Strathan

Talmine

Melness
Midtown

Rabbit
Islands

Tongue
Bay

Kyle of Tongue

Tongue

Kinloch

Kyle of Tongue

Loch an
Dherue

763
BEN
LOYAL

Eilean
Nan Ròn

Skerray
Achtoty
Torrisdale

Scullomie

Coldbackie

310
MEALL LEATHAD
NA CRAOIBHE

318
CNOC
CRAGGIE

Loch
Craggie

527
BEINN
STUMANADH

Loch
Loyal

Neave or
Coomb Island

Torrisdale Farr
Bay   Bay

Farr

Bettyhill

Invernaver

Borgie

13   River Borgie   A836

17   A836

557
CNOC NAN
CUILEAN

Loch Loyal
Lodge

Ardmore
Point
Kirtomy Point   Farr Point

Armadale
Farr   Kirtomy
Swordly

Achina   Strathnaver   Bettyhill

Loch
Meadie

228
BEINN
NAM BÒ

Skelpick

Strath Naver   Skelpick Burn

213
CNOC
MALPELLY

Loch Mòr
na Caorach
Loch
nan Clach

12   B871

Loch Strathy

335
MEALL BAD
NA CUAICHE

Armadale Bay

15

14

5

6

7

Glen Golly

BEAG

463
FEINNE-BHEINN MHÒR

Dun Dornaigil
Broch

Strath More

656
CNOC AN
DÀIMH MÒR

Loch
Meadie

294
POLE
HILL

Loch
Syre

Syre

River Naver   B871

259
BEINN
ROSAIL

345
CNOC NAM
TRI-CHLACH

404
BEINN
MHADADH

8

96
RN
ARG   757
CARN AN
TIONAIL

Loch Coire na
Saidhe Duibhe

230
MEALL A'
BHROLLAICH

Strath Naver

270
BEADAIG

12   B873   River Mallart   16   590
BEN GRIAM
MÒR

9

Loch
Merkland

Loch
Fiag

680
MEALL AN
LIATH MÒR

873
BEN
HEE

Loch a'
Ghorm-choire

Altnaharra

Loch Naver

Loch
Rimsdale

Loch
nan Clàr

Loch
Badanloch   Badanloch

10

472
MEALL AN
FHUARAIN

Strath Vagastie

959
BEN KLIBRECK

Loch Choire Forest

694
CREAG NA
H-LOLAIRE

Loch an
Alltan Fhearna

Loch
Truderscaig

434
CNOC AN LIATH
BHAID MHÒR

11

OCH

372
CNOC A'
GHRIAMA

37   Overscaig

Glen Fiag

A836

Crask Inn

346
CNOC A'
GHIUBHAIS

21

Loch a'
Bhealaich

Loch
Choire

713
CREAG
MHÒR

Gorm-loch
Mòr

Borrobol Forest

364
CNOC NA
BREUN-CHOILLE

12

A838   145   Ben Armine Forest

Glas-
loch Mòr

Strath Skinsdale

J   K   L   M   N   P   Q   R

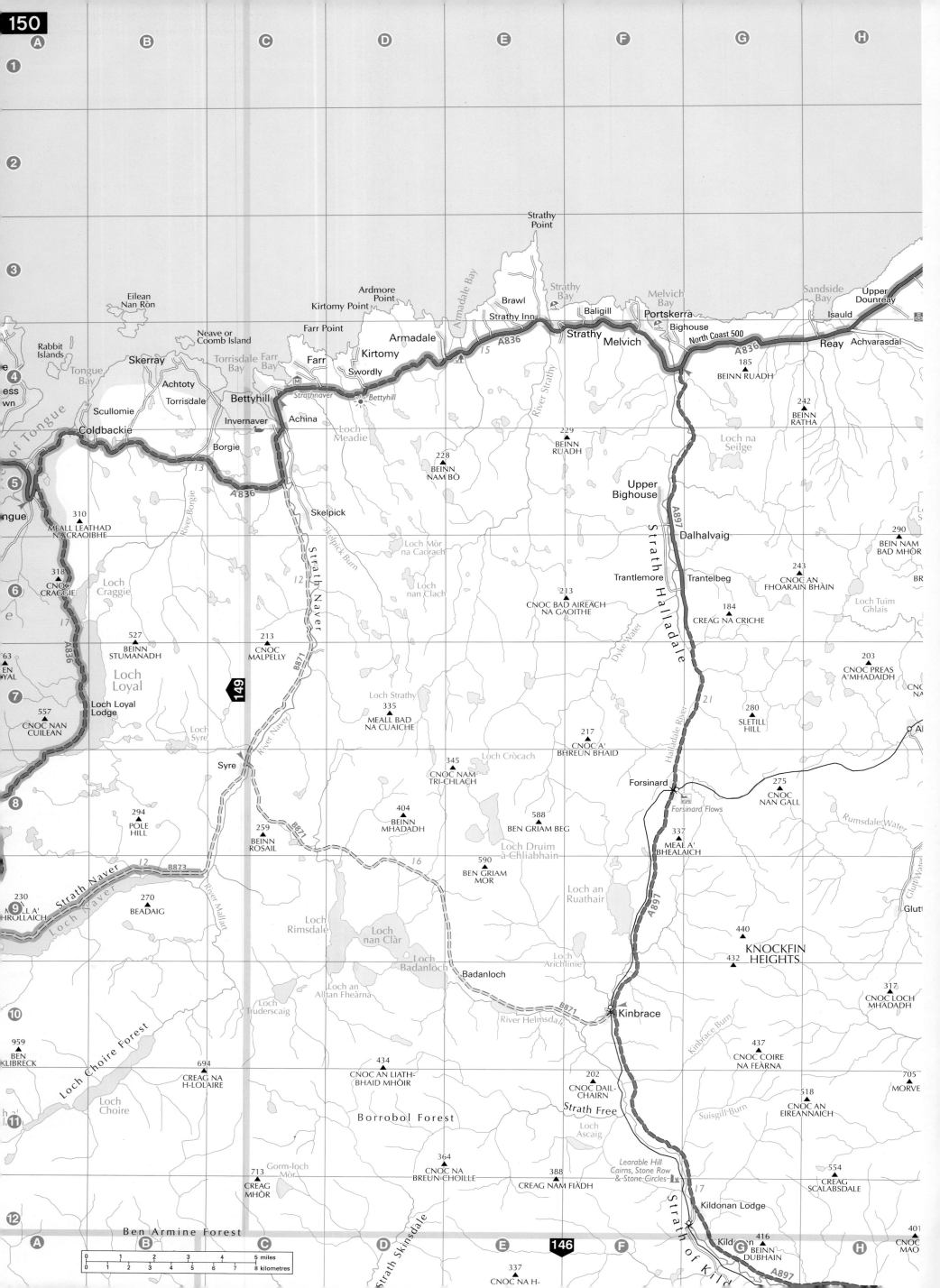

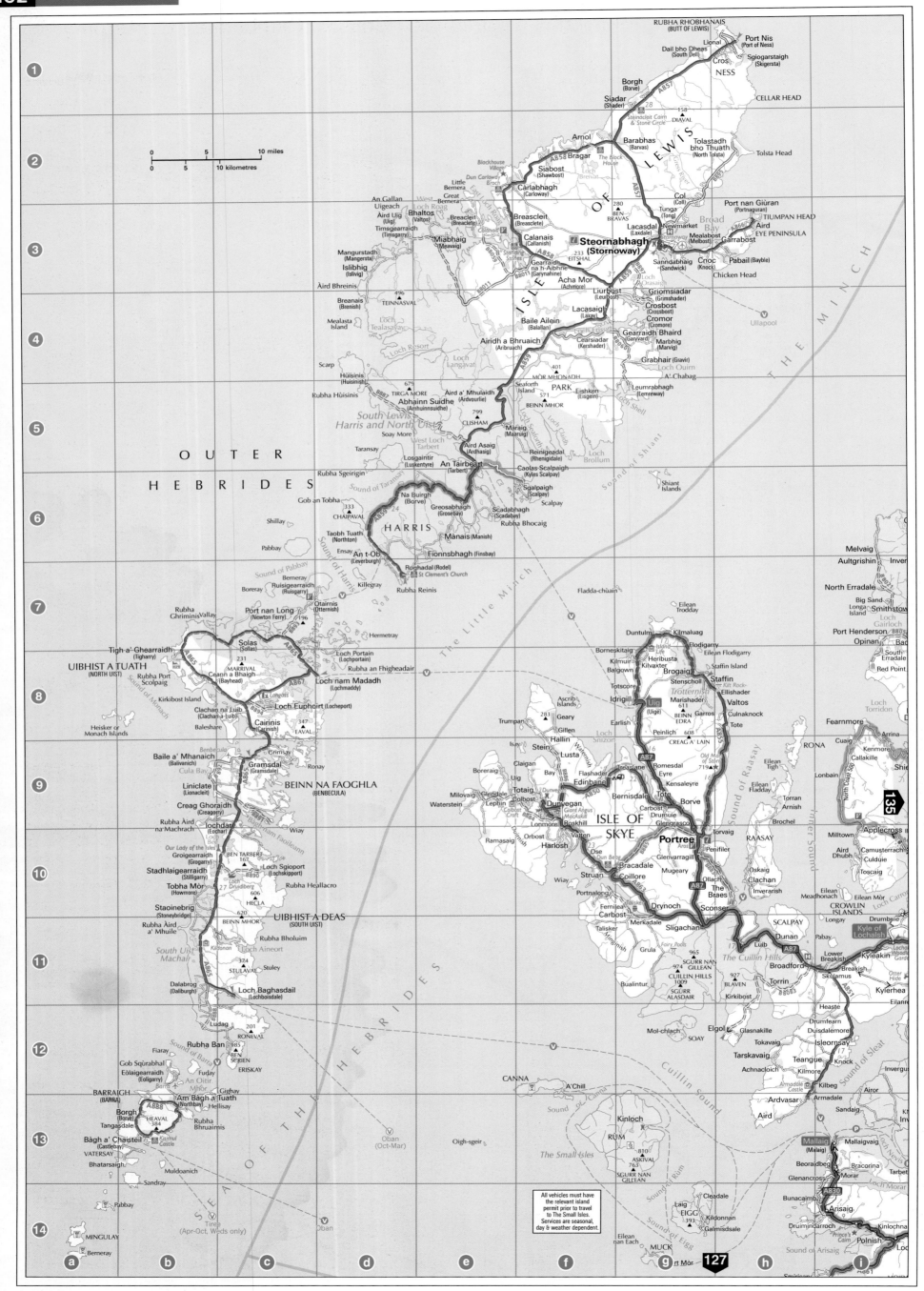

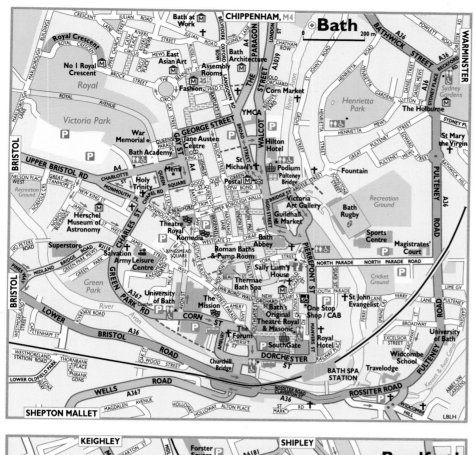

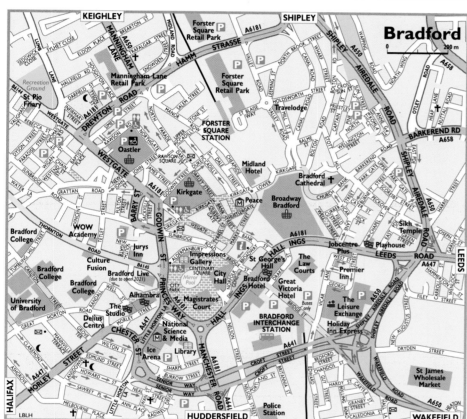

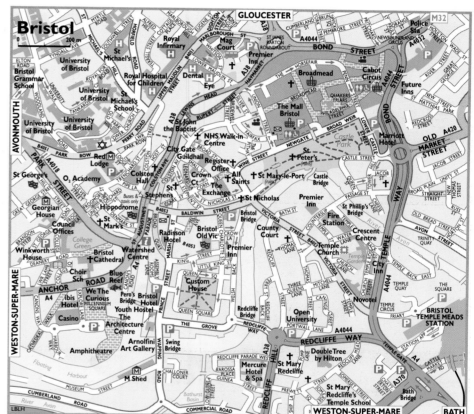

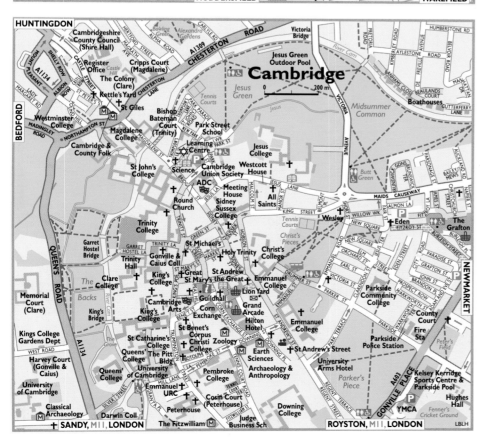

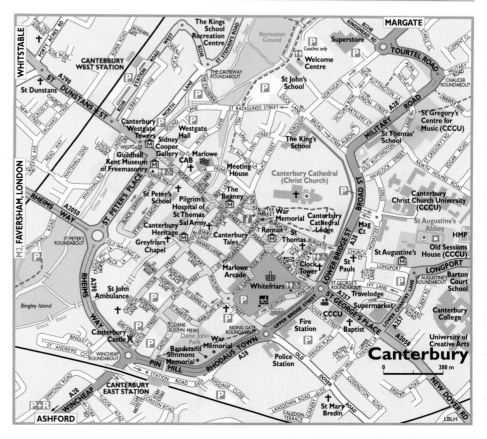

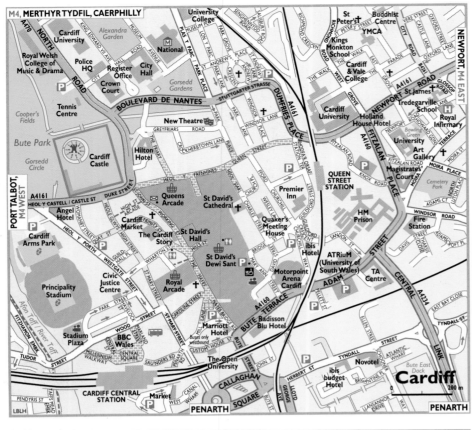

Cardiff

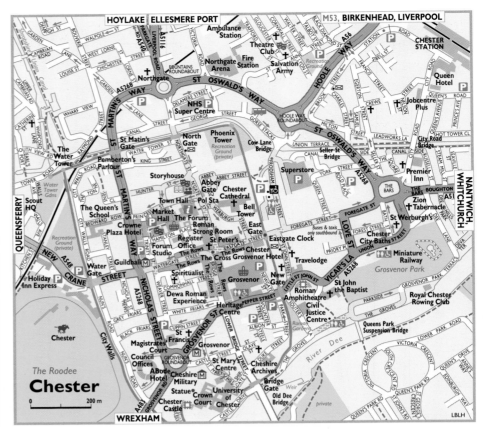

Chester

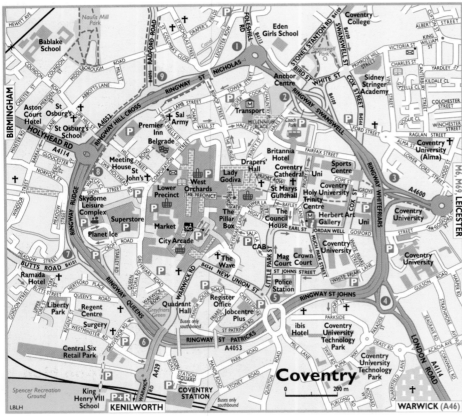

Coventry

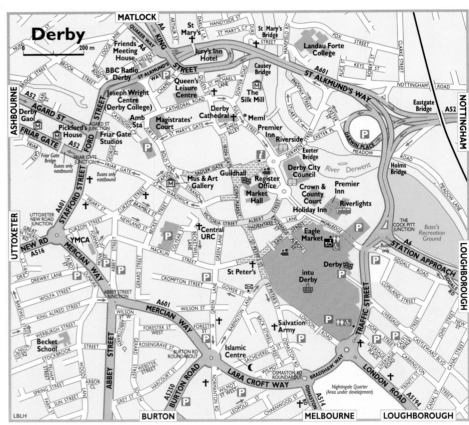

Derby

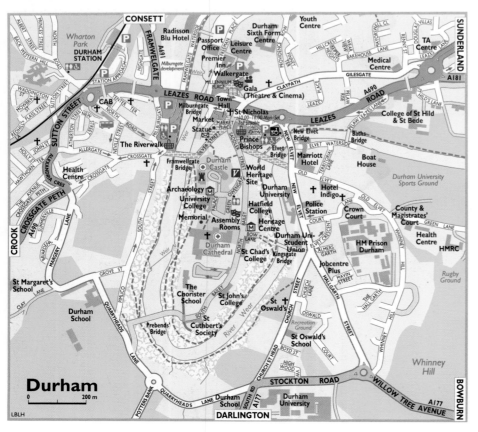

Durham

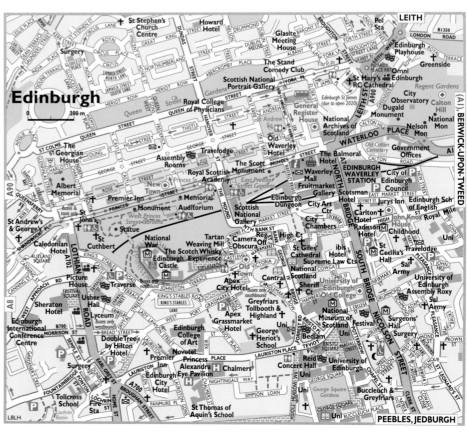

Edinburgh

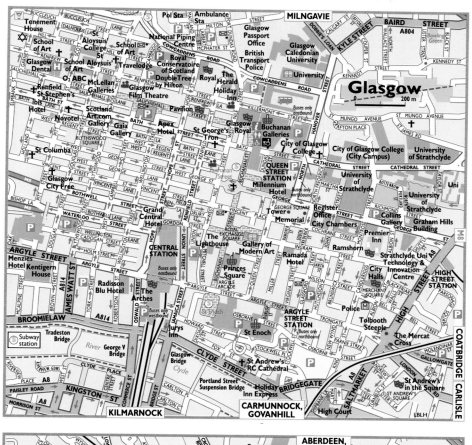

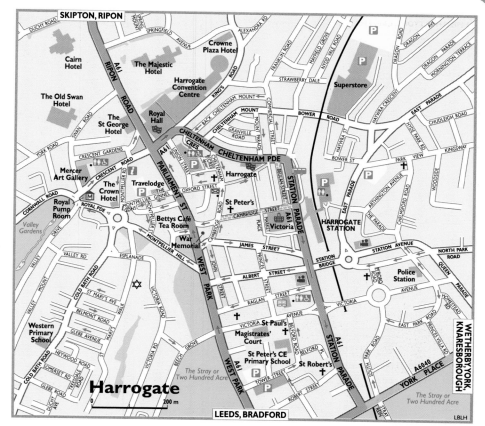

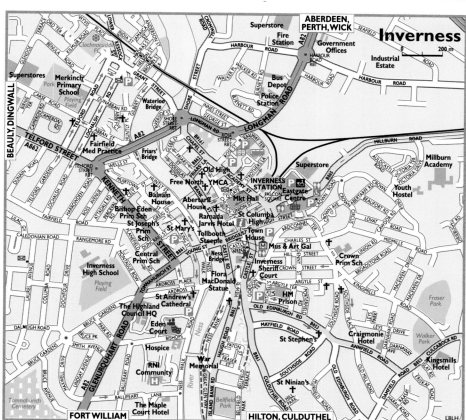

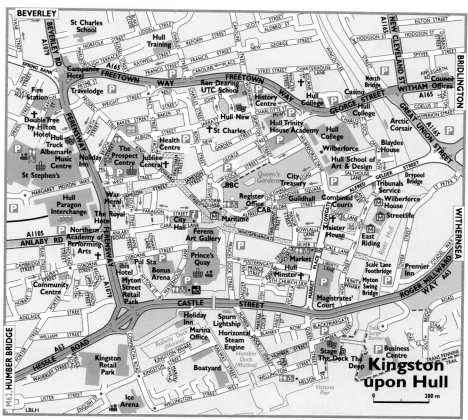

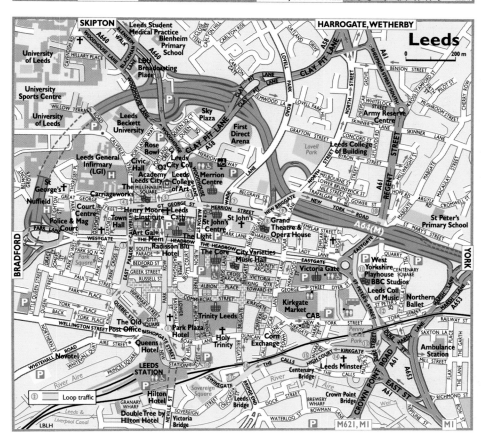

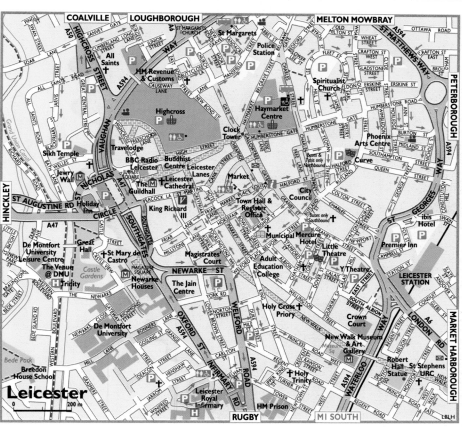

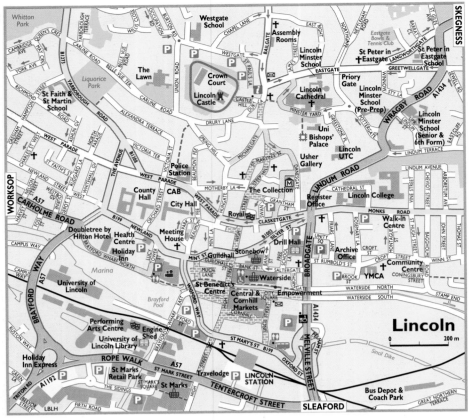

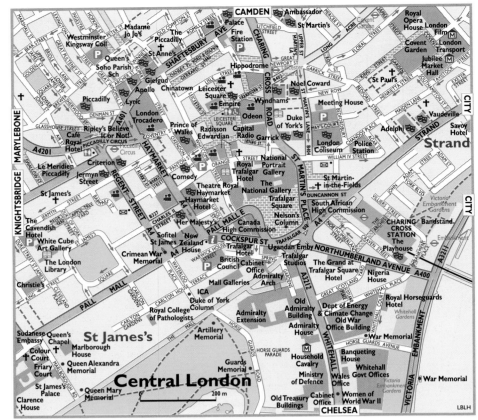

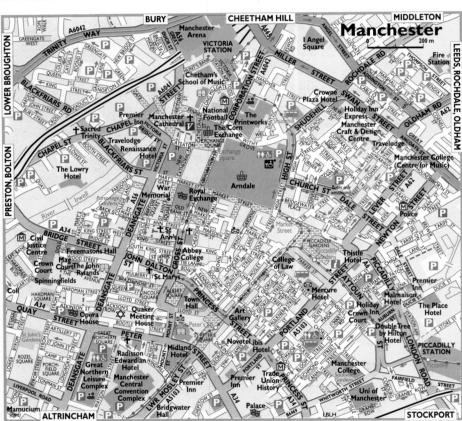

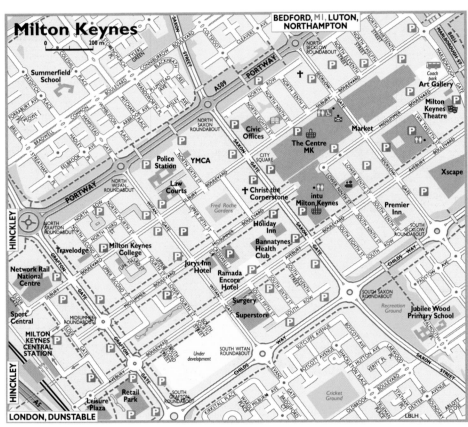

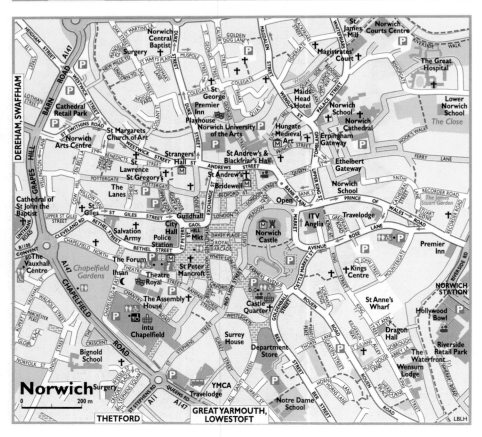

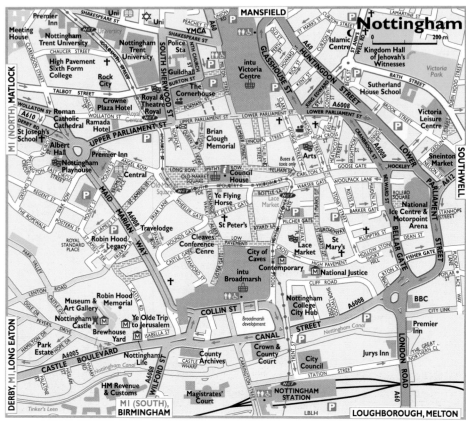

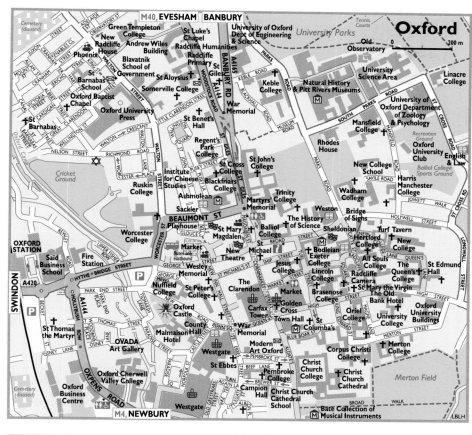

Oxford

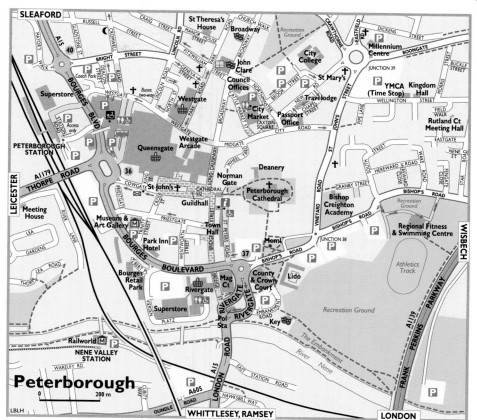

Peterborough

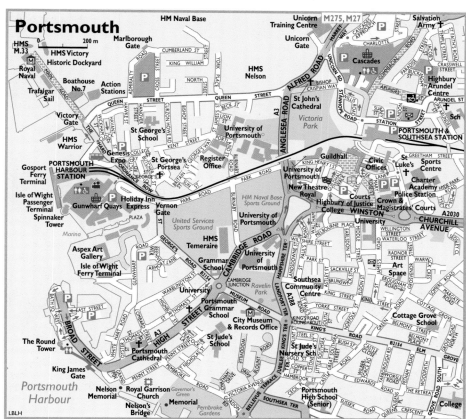

Portsmouth

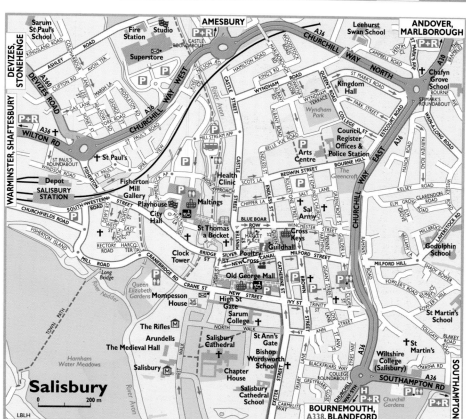

Salisbury

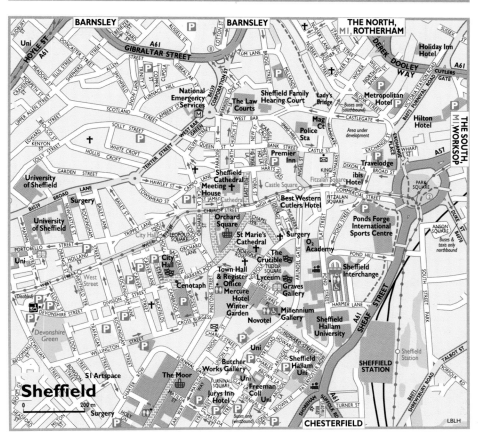

Sheffield

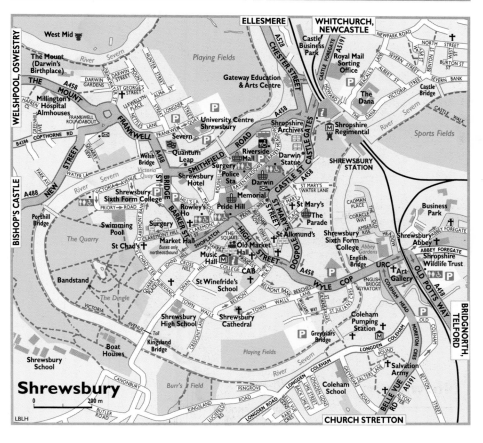

Shrewsbury

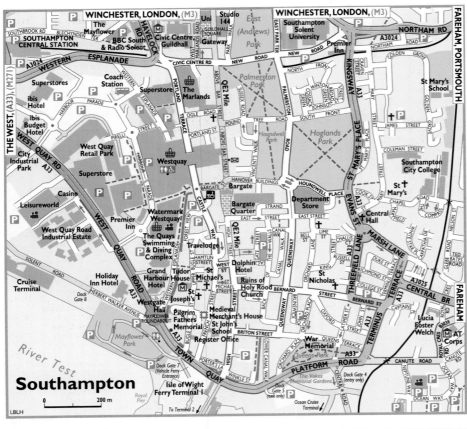

Southampton

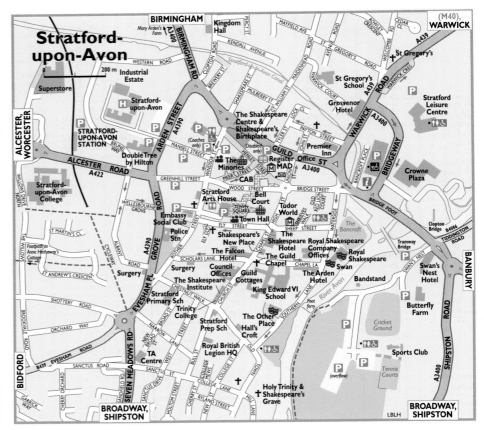

Stratford-upon-Avon

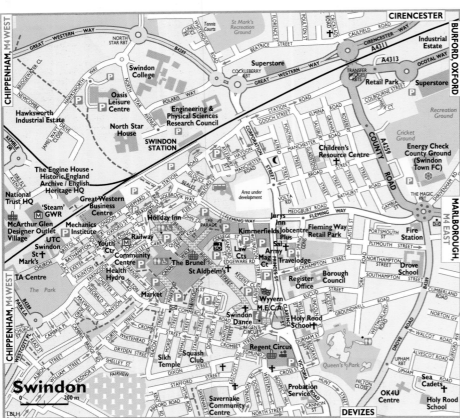

Swindon

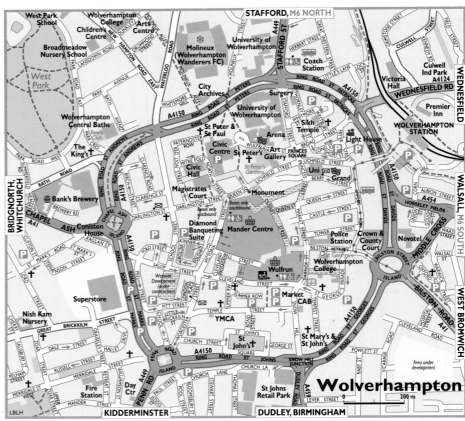

Wolverhampton

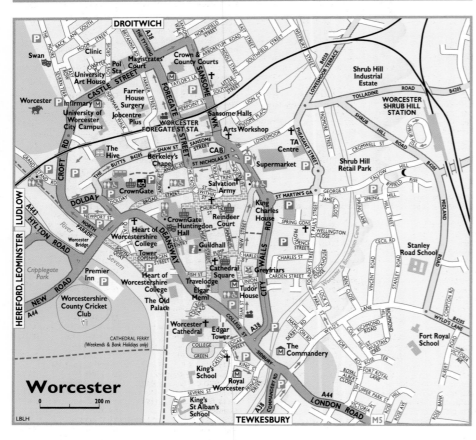

Worcester

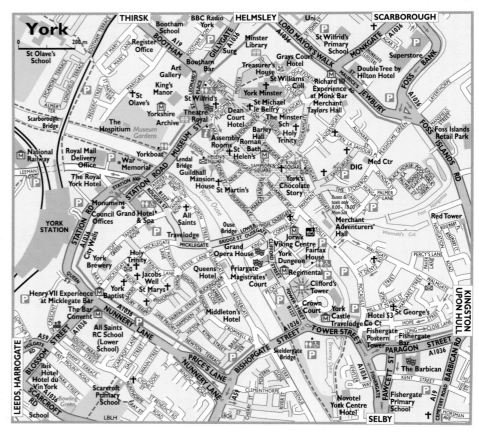

York

ENGLAND

- **Acorn Bank Garden** CA10 1SP Cumb 89 Q1
- **Aldborough Roman Site** YO51 9ES N York 85 N2
- **Alfriston Clergy House** BN26 5TL E Susx 15 P10
- **Alton Towers** ST10 4DB Staffs 65 K3
- **Anglesey Abbey** CB25 9EJ Cambs 57 K8
- **Anne Hathaway's Cottage** CV37 9HH Warwks 53 M9
- **Antony House** PL11 2QA Cnwll 4 F5
- **Appuldurcombe House** PO38 3EW IoW 13 J9
- **Apsley House** W1J 7NT Gt Lon 33 K6
- **Arlington Court** EX31 4LP Devon 19 M5
- **Ascott** LU7 0PS Bucks 44 C7
- **Ashby-de-la-Zouch Castle** LE65 1BR Leics 66 B9
- **Athelhampton House & Gardens** DT2 7LG Dorset 11 J6
- **Attingham Park** SY4 4TP Shrops 63 P10
- **Audley End House & Gardens** CB11 4JF Essex 45 P4
- **Avebury Manor & Garden** SN8 1RF Wilts 30 C8
- **Baconsthorpe Castle** NR25 6LN Norfk 70 G4
- **Baddesley Clinton Hall** B93 0DQ Warwks 53 M6
- **Bamburgh Castle** NE69 7DF Nthumb 109 K3
- **Barnard Castle** DL12 8PR Dur 90 H3
- **Barrington Court** TA19 0NQ Somset 21 N9
- **Basildon Park** RG8 9NR W Berk 31 M7
- **Bateman's** TN19 7DS E Susx 16 B6
- **Battle of Britain Memorial Flight Visitor Centre** LN4 4SY Lincs 80 E12
- **Beamish Museum** DH9 0RG Dur 100 G7
- **Beatrix Potter Gallery** LA22 0NS Cumb 89 K7
- **Beaulieu** SO42 7ZN Hants 12 F4
- **Belton House** NG32 2LS Lincs 67 M4
- **Belvoir Castle** NG32 1PE Leics 67 K5
- **Bembridge Windmill** PO35 5SQ IoW 13 L7
- **Beningbrough Hall & Gardens** YO30 1DD N York 85 Q3
- **Benthall Hall** TF12 5RX Shrops 64 C11
- **Berkeley Castle** GL13 9PJ Gloucs 29 L3
- **Berrington Hall** HR6 0DW Herefs 51 N8
- **Berry Pomeroy Castle** TQ9 6LJ Devon 5 P4
- **Beth Chatto Gardens** CO7 7DB Essex 47 J7
- **Biddulph Grange Garden** ST8 7SD Staffs 76 G11
- **Bishop's Waltham Palace** SO32 1DH Hants 25 J10
- **Blackpool Zoo** FY3 8PP Bpool 82 H8
- **Blenheim Palace** OX20 1PX Oxon 43 J8
- **Blickling Estate** NR11 6NF Norfk 70 H6
- **Blue John Cavern** S33 8WA Derbys 77 L7
- **Bodiam Castle** TN32 5UA E Susx 16 D6
- **Bolsover Castle** S44 6PR Derbys 78 D9
- **Boscobel House** ST19 9AR Staffs 64 F10
- **Bovington Tank Museum** BH20 6JG Dorset 11 K7
- **Bowes Castle** DL12 9LD Dur 90 G4
- **Bradford Industrial Museum** BD2 3HP W York 85 J8
- **Bradley Manor** TQ12 6BN Devon 8 F10
- **Bramber Castle** BN44 3WW W Susx 14 H8
- **Brinkburn Priory** NE65 8AR Nthumb 109 J10
- **Bristol Zoo Gardens** BS8 3HA Bristl 28 H7
- **Brockhampton Estate** WR6 5TB Herefs 52 C9
- **Brough Castle** CA17 4EJ Cumb 90 C4
- **Buckfast Abbey** TQ11 0EE Devon 5 M3
- **Buckingham Palace** SW1A 1AA Gt Lon 33 K6
- **Buckland Abbey** PL20 6EY Devon 4 G3
- **Buscot Park** SN7 8BU Oxon 30 F3
- **Byland Abbey** YO61 4BD N York 92 B11
- **Cadbury World** B30 1JR Birm 53 K4
- **Calke Abbey** DE73 7LE Derbys 66 B7
- **Canons Ashby House** NN11 3SD Nhants 54 F10
- **Canterbury Cathedral** CT1 2EH Kent 35 L10
- **Carisbrooke Castle** PO30 1XY IoW 12 H7
- **Carlyle's House** SW3 5HL Gt Lon 33 K7
- **Castle Drogo** EX6 6PB Devon 8 D7
- **Castle Howard** YO60 7DA N York 86 D1
- **Castle Rising Castle** PE31 6AH Norfk 69 M7
- **Charlecote Park** CV35 9ER Warwks 53 N9
- **Chartwell** TN16 1PS Kent 33 N12
- **Chastleton House** GL56 0SU Oxon 42 F6
- **Chatsworth** DE45 1PP Derbys 77 N9
- **Chedworth Roman Villa** GL54 3LJ Gloucs 42 B9
- **Chessington World of Adventures** KT9 2NE Gt Lon 32 H10
- **Chester Cathedral** CH1 2HU Ches W 75 L10
- **Chester Zoo** CH2 1EU Ches W 75 L9
- **Chesters Roman Fort & Museum** NE46 4EU Nthumb 99 P4
- **Chiswick House & Gardens** W4 2RP Gt Lon 32 H7
- **Chysauster Ancient Village** TR20 8XA Cnwll 2 D7
- **Claremont Landscape Garden** KT10 9JG Surrey 32 G9
- **Claydon House** MK18 2EY Bucks 43 P6
- **Cleeve Abbey** TA23 0PS Somset 20 G5
- **Clevedon Court** BS21 6QU N Som 28 F8
- **Cliveden** SL6 0JA Bucks 32 C5
- **Clouds Hill** BH20 7NQ Dorset 11 K6
- **Clumber Park** S80 3AZ Notts 78 G8
- **Colchester Zoo** CO3 0SL Essex 46 G7
- **Coleridge Cottage** TA5 1NQ Somset 21 K5
- **Coleton Fishacre** TQ6 0EQ Devon 5 Q6
- **Compton Castle** TQ3 1TA Devon 5 P4
- **Conisbrough Castle** DN12 3BU Donc 78 E4
- **Corbridge Roman Town** NE45 5NT Nthumb 100 C5
- **Corfe Castle** BH20 5EZ Dorset 11 M8
- **Corsham Court** SN13 0BZ Wilts 29 P8
- **Cotehele** PL12 6TA Cnwll 4 F3
- **Coughton Court** B49 5JA Warwks 53 K8
- **Courts Garden** BA14 6RR Wilts 29 P10
- **Cragside** NE65 7PX Nthumb 108 H9
- **Crealy Theme Park** EX5 1DR Devon 9 J7
- **Crich Tramway Village** DE4 5DP Derbys 65 Q1
- **Croft Castle** HR6 9PW Herefs 51 M7
- **Croome Park** WR8 9DW Worcs 41 P3
- **Deddington Castle** OX15 0TE Oxon 43 K5
- **Didcot Railway Centre** OX11 7NJ Oxon 31 L4
- **Dover Castle** CT16 1HU Kent 17 P2
- **Drayton Manor Theme Park** B78 3SA Staffs 65 M12
- **Dudmaston Estate** WV15 6QN Shrops 52 D3
- **Dunham Massey** WA14 4SJ Traffd 76 D6
- **Dunstanburgh Castle** NE66 3TT Nthumb 109 L5
- **Dunster Castle** TA24 6SL Somset 20 F5
- **Durham Cathedral** DH1 3EH Dur 100 H10
- **Dyrham Park** SN14 8HY S Glos 29 L7
- **East Riddlesden Hall** BD20 5EL Brad 84 G7
- **Eden Project** PL24 2SG Cnwll 3 P4
- **Eltham Palace & Gardens** SE9 5QE Gt Lon 33 M7
- **Emmetts Garden** TN14 6BA Kent 33 N12
- **Exmoor Zoo** EX31 4SG Devon 19 M5
- **Farleigh Hungerford Castle** BA2 7RS Somset 29 N10
- **Farnborough Hall** OX17 1DU Warwks 54 C10
- **Felbrigg Hall** NR11 8PR Norfk 71 J4
- **Fenton House & Garden** NW3 6SP Gt Lon 33 J5
- **Finch Foundry** EX20 2NW Devon 8 C6
- **Finchale Priory** DH1 5SH Dur 100 H9
- **Fishbourne Roman Palace** PO19 3QR W Susx 13 P4
- **Flamingo Land** YO17 6UX N York 92 F10
- **Forde Abbey** TA20 4LU Somset 9 Q4
- **Fountains Abbey & Studley Royal** HG4 3DY N York 85 K1
- **Gawthorpe Hall** BB12 8UA Lancs 84 B8
- **Gisborough Priory** TS14 6HG R & Cl 92 C3
- **Glendurgan Garden** TR11 5JZ Cnwll 3 J9
- **Goodrich Castle** HR9 6HY Herefs 41 J7
- **Great Chalfield Manor & Garden** SN12 8NH Wilts 29 P9
- **Great Coxwell Barn** SN7 7LZ Oxon 30 F3
- **Greenway** TQ5 0ES Devon 5 P6
- **Haddon Hall** DE45 1LA Derbys 77 N10
- **Hailes Abbey** GL54 5PB Gloucs 42 B6
- **Ham House & Garden** TW10 7RS Gt Lon 32 H8
- **Hampton Court Palace** KT8 9AU Gt Lon 32 H8
- **Hanbury Hall** WR9 7EA Worcs 52 H8
- **Hardwick Hall** S44 5QJ Derbys 78 D11
- **Hardy's Cottage** DT2 8QJ Dorset 10 H6
- **Hare Hill** SK10 4PY Ches E 76 G8
- **Hatchlands Park** GU4 7RT Surrey 32 F12
- **Heale Gardens** SP4 6NU Wilts 23 P6
- **Helmsley Castle** YO62 5AB N York 92 C10
- **Hereford Cathedral** HR1 2NG Herefs 40 G4
- **Hergest Croft Gardens** HR5 3EG Herefs 51 J9
- **Hever Castle & Gardens** TN8 7NG Kent 15 N2
- **Hidcote Manor Garden** GL55 6LR Gloucs 42 E3
- **Hill Top** LA22 0LF Cumb 89 K7
- **Hinton Ampner** SO24 0LA Hants 25 K8
- **Holkham Hall** NR23 1AB Norfk 70 C4
- **Housesteads Roman Fort** NE47 6NN Nthumb 99 M4
- **Howletts Wild Animal Park** CT4 5EL Kent 35 M11
- **Hughenden Manor** HP14 4LA Bucks 32 B3
- **Hurst Castle** SO41 0TP Hants 12 E7
- **Hylands House & Park** CM2 8WQ Essex 46 B11
- **Ickworth** IP29 5QE Suffk 58 B8
- **Ightham Mote** TN15 0NT Kent 33 Q11
- **Ironbridge Gorge Museums** TF8 7DQ Wrekin 64 C11
- **Kedleston Hall** DE22 5JH Derbys 65 P4
- **Kenilworth Castle & Elizabethan Garden** CV8 1NE Warwks 53 P6
- **Kenwood House** NW3 7JR Gt Lon 33 K5
- **Killerton** EX5 3LE Devon 8 H5
- **King John's Hunting Lodge** BS26 2AP Somset 21 P2
- **Kingston Lacy** BH21 4EA Dorset 11 N4
- **Kirby Hall** NN17 3EN Nhants 55 M2
- **Knightshayes Court** EX16 7RQ Devon 20 E10
- **Knole House** TN13 1HU Kent 33 P11
- **Knowsley Safari Park** L34 4AN Knows 75 M5
- **Lacock Abbey** SN15 2LG Wilts 29 Q8
- **Lamb House** TN31 7ES E Susx 16 G7
- **Lanhydrock House** PL30 5AD Cnwll 3 Q2
- **Launceston Castle** PL15 7DR Cnwll 7 L8
- **Leeds Castle** ME17 1PB Kent 34 E11
- **Legoland** SL4 4AY W&M 32 D7
- **Lindisfarne Castle** TD15 2SH Nthumb 109 J1
- **Lindisfarne Priory** TD15 2RX Nthumb 109 J1
- **Little Moreton Hall** CW12 4SD Ches E 76 F11
- **Liverpool Cathedral** L1 7AZ Lpool 75 K6
- **London Zoo ZSL** NW1 4RY Gt Lon 33 K6
- **Longleat** BA12 7NW Wilts 22 H5
- **Loseley Park** GU3 1HS Surrey 14 D1
- **Ludgershall Castle** SP11 9QR Wilts 24 D3
- **Lydford Castle** EX20 4BH Devon 7 P8
- **Lyme Park, House & Garden** SK12 2NX Ches E 76 H7
- **Lytes Cary Manor** TA11 7HU Somset 22 C8
- **Lyveden New Bield** PE8 5AT Nhants 55 N4
- **Maiden Castle** DT2 9PP Dorset 10 G7
- **Mapledurham Estate** RG4 7TR Oxon 31 N7
- **Marble Hill House** TW1 2NL Gt Lon 32 H7
- **Marwell Zoo** SO21 1JH Hants 24 H9
- **Melford Hall** CO10 9AA Suffk 46 F2
- **Merseyside Maritime Museum** L3 4AQ Lpool 75 K6
- **Minster Lovell Hall** OX29 0RR Oxon 42 G9
- **Mompesson House** SP1 2EL Wilts 23 P7
- **Monk Bretton Priory** S71 5QD Barns 78 B2
- **Montacute House** TA15 6XP Somset 22 C10
- **Morwellham Quay** PL19 8JL Devon 4 G3
- **Moseley Old Hall** WV10 7HY Staffs 64 H11
- **Mottisfont** SO51 0LP Hants 24 E8
- **Mottistone Manor Garden** PO30 4ED IoW 12 G8
- **Mount Grace Priory** DL6 3JG N York 91 Q7
- **National Maritime Museum** SE10 9NF Gt Lon 33 M7
- **National Motorcycle Museum** B92 0ED Solhll 53 M4
- **National Portrait Gallery** WC2H 0HE Gt Lon 33 K6
- **National Railway Museum** YO26 4XJ York 86 B5
- **National Space Centre** LE4 5NS C Leic 66 F10
- **Natural History Museum** SW7 5BD Gt Lon 33 K6
- **Needles Old Battery** PO39 0JH IoW 12 E8
- **Nene Valley Railway** PE8 6LR Cambs 56 C1
- **Netley Abbey** SO31 5FB Hants 12 G3
- **Newark Air Museum** NG24 2NY Notts 79 L12
- **Newtown Old Town Hall** PO30 4PA IoW 12 G6
- **North Leigh Roman Villa** OX29 6QB Oxon 43 J8
- **Norwich Cathedral** NR1 4DH Norfk 71 J10
- **Nostell Priory** WF4 1QE Wakefd 85 N11
- **Nunnington Hall** YO62 5UY N York 92 D11
- **Nymans House** RH17 6EB W Susx 15 K5
- **Old Royal Naval College** SE10 9NN Gt Lon 33 M7
- **Old Sarum** SP1 3SD Wilts 23 P7
- **Old Wardour Castle** SP3 6RR Wilts 23 K8
- **Oliver Cromwell's House** CB7 4HF Cambs 57 K4
- **Orford Castle** IP12 2ND Suffk 59 N10
- **Ormesby Hall** TS3 0SR R & Cl 92 B3
- **Osborne House** PO32 6JX IoW 13 J6
- **Osterley Park & House** TW7 4RB Gt Lon 32 G7
- **Overbeck's** TQ8 8LW Devon 5 M9
- **Oxburgh Hall** PE33 9PS Norfk 69 P12
- **Packwood House** B94 6AT Warwks 53 M6
- **Paignton Zoo** TQ4 7EU Torbay 5 P5
- **Paycocke's House & Garden** CO6 1NS Essex 46 E7
- **Peckover House & Garden** PE13 1JR Cambs 69 J10
- **Pendennis Castle** TR11 4LP Cnwll 3 K8
- **Petworth House & Park** GU28 0AE W Susx 14 D6
- **Pevensey Castle** BN24 5LE E Susx 16 B10
- **Peveril Castle** S33 8WQ Derbys 77 L7
- **Polesden Lacey** RH5 6BD Surrey 32 G11
- **Portland Castle** DT5 1AZ Dorset 10 G10
- **Portsmouth Historic Dockyard** PO1 3LJ C Port 13 L5
- **Powderham Castle** EX6 8JQ Devon 8 H8
- **Prior Park Landscape Garden** BA2 5AH BaNES 29 M9
- **Prudhoe Castle** NE42 6NA Nthumb 100 E5
- **Quarry Bank Mill & Styal** SK9 4LA Ches E 76 F7
- **Quebec House** TN16 1TD Kent 33 N11
- **Ramsey Abbey Gatehouse** PE26 1DH Cambs 56 F4
- **Reculver Towers & Roman Fort** CT6 6SU Kent 35 M8
- **Red House** DA6 8JF Gt Lon 33 N7
- **Restormel Castle** PL22 0EE Cnwll 3 Q2
- **Richborough Roman Fort** CT13 9JW Kent 35 P10
- **Richmond Castle** DL10 4QW N York 91 K6
- **Roche Abbey** S66 8NW Rothm 78 E6
- **Rochester Castle** ME1 1SW Medway 34 C8
- **Rockbourne Roman Villa** SP6 3PG Hants 23 P10
- **Roman Baths & Pump Room** BA1 1LZ BaNES 29 M9
- **Royal Botanic Gardens, Kew** TW9 3AB Gt Lon 32 H7
- **Royal Observatory Greenwich** SE10 8XJ Gt Lon 33 M7
- **Rufford Old Hall** L40 1SG Lancs 83 L12
- **Runnymede** SL4 2JJ W & M 32 E8
- **Rushton Triangular Lodge** NN14 1RP Nhants 55 L4
- **Rycote Chapel** OX9 2PA Oxon 43 P10
- **St Leonard's Tower** ME19 6PE Kent 34 B11
- **St Michael's Mount** TR17 0HT Cnwll 2 E8
- **St Paul's Cathedral** EC4M 8AD Gt Lon 33 L6
- **Salisbury Cathedral** SP1 2EJ Wilts 23 P7
- **Saltram** PL7 1UH C Plym 4 H5
- **Sandham Memorial Chapel** RG20 9JT Hants 31 K10
- **Sandringham House & Grounds** PE35 6EH Norfk 69 N6
- **Saxtead Green Post Mill** IP13 9QQ Suffk 59 K8
- **Scarborough Castle** YO11 1HY N York 93 L9
- **Science Museum** SW7 2DD Gt Lon 33 K6
- **Scotney Castle** TN3 8JN Kent 16 B4
- **Shaw's Corner** AL6 9BX Herts 44 H8
- **Sheffield Park & Garden** TN22 3QX E Susx 15 M6
- **Sherborne Old Castle** DT9 3SA Dorset 22 E10
- **Sissinghurst Castle Garden** TN17 2AB Kent 16 E3
- **Sizergh Castle & Garden** LA8 8AE Cumb 89 M9
- **Smallhythe Place** TN30 7NG Kent 16 F5
- **Snowshill Manor & Garden** WR12 7JU Gloucs 42 C5
- **Souter Lighthouse** SR6 7NH S Tyne 101 K5
- **Speke Hall, Garden & Estate** L24 1XD Lpool 75 M7
- **Spinnaker Tower, Emirates** PO1 3TT C Port 13 L5
- **Stokesay Castle** SY7 9AH Shrops 51 M4
- **Stonehenge** SP4 7DE Wilts 23 P5
- **Stourhead** BA12 6QD Wilts 22 H6
- **Stowe Gardens** MK18 5EQ Bucks 43 P4
- **Sudbury Hall** DE6 5HT Derbys 65 M6
- **Sulgrave Manor** OX17 2SD Nhants 43 M3
- **Sunnycroft** TF1 2DR Wrekin 64 C10
- **Sutton Hoo** IP12 3DJ Suffk 59 K10
- **Sutton House** E9 6JQ Gt Lon 33 L5
- **Tate Britain** SW1P 4RG Gt Lon 33 K6
- **Tate Liverpool** L3 4BB Lpool 75 K6
- **Tate Modern** SE1 9TG Gt Lon 33 K6
- **Tattershall Castle** LN4 4LR Lincs 80 D12
- **Tatton Park** WA16 6QN Ches E 76 D7
- **The British Library** NW1 2DB Gt Lon 33 K6
- **The British Museum** WC1B 3DG Gt Lon 33 K6
- **The Lost Gardens of Heligan** PL26 6EN Cnwll 3 N5
- **The Lowry** M50 3AZ Salfd 76 E4
- **The National Gallery** WC2N 5DN Gt Lon 33 K6
- **The Vyne** RG24 9HL Hants 31 N11
- **The Weir Garden** HR4 7QF Herefs 40 F3
- **Thornton Abbey & Gatehouse** DN39 6TU N Linc 87 L11
- **Thorpe Park** KT16 8PN Surrey 32 E8
- **Tilbury Fort** RM18 7NR Thurr 34 B7
- **Tintagel Castle** PL34 0HE Cnwll 6 F7
- **Tintinhull Garden** BA22 8PZ Somset 22 C9
- **Totnes Castle** TQ9 5NU Devon 5 N4
- **Tower of London** EC3N 4AB Gt Lon 33 L6
- **Townend** LA23 1LB Cumb 89 L6
- **Treasurer's House** YO1 7JL York 86 B5
- **Trelissick Garden** TR3 6QL Cnwll 3 K6
- **Trengwainton Garden** TR20 8RZ Cnwll 2 C8
- **Trerice** TR8 4PG Cnwll 3 L3
- **Twycross Zoo** CV9 3PX Leics 65 P11
- **Upnor Castle** ME2 4XG Medway 34 D8
- **Uppark House & Garden** GU31 5QR W Susx 25 N10
- **Upton House & Garden** OX15 6HT Warwks 42 H3
- **Victoria & Albert Museum** SW7 2RL Gt Lon 33 K6
- **Waddesdon Manor** HP18 0JH Bucks 43 Q8
- **Wakehurst Place** RH17 6TN W Susx 15 L4
- **Wall Roman Site** WS14 0AW Staffs 65 L11
- **Wallington** NE61 4AR Nthumb 100 C1
- **Walmer Castle & Gardens** CT14 7LJ Kent 35 Q12
- **Warkworth Castle & Hermitage** NE65 0UJ Nthumb 109 L8
- **Warner Bros. Studio Tour London** WD25 7LR Herts 32 F2
- **Warwick Castle** CV34 4QU Warwks 53 P7
- **Washington Old Hall** NE38 7LE Sundld 101 J7
- **Waterperry Gardens** OX33 1LG Oxon 43 N10
- **Weeting Castle** IP27 0RQ Norfk 57 P3
- **Wenlock Priory** TF13 6HS Shrops 64 B12
- **West Midland Safari & Leisure Park** DY12 1LF Worcs 52 E5
- **West Wycombe Park** HP14 3AJ Bucks 32 B3
- **Westbury Court Garden** GL14 1PD Gloucs 41 L9
- **Westminster Abbey** SW1P 3PA Gt Lon 33 K6
- **Westonbirt Arboretum** GL8 8QS Gloucs 29 N4
- **Westwood Manor** BA15 2AF Wilts 29 N10
- **Whipsnade Zoo ZSL** LU6 2LF C Beds 44 E8
- **Whitby Abbey** YO22 4JT N York 93 J4
- **Wicksteed Park** NN15 6NJ Nhants 55 L5
- **Wightwick Manor & Gardens** WV6 8EE Wolves 52 F1
- **Wimpole Estate** SG8 0BW Cambs 56 F10
- **Winchester Cathedral** SO23 9LS Hants 24 H7
- **Winchester City Mill** SO23 0EJ Hants 24 H7
- **Windsor Castle** SL4 1NJ W & M 32 D7
- **Winkworth Arboretum** GU8 4AD Surrey 14 E3
- **Wisley RHS Garden** GU23 6QB Surrey 32 F10
- **Woburn Safari Park** MK17 9QN C Beds 44 D5
- **Wookey Hole Caves** BA5 1BA Somset 22 C4
- **Woolsthorpe Manor** NG33 5PD Lincs 67 M7
- **Wordsworth House** CA13 9RX Cumb 97 M12
- **Wrest Park** MK45 4HR C Beds 44 F4
- **Wroxeter Roman City** SY5 6PR Shrops 63 P10
- **WWT Arundel Wetland Centre** BN18 9PB W Susx 14 E9
- **WWT Slimbridge Wetland Centre** GL2 7BT Gloucs 41 L10
- **Yarmouth Castle** PO41 0PB IoW 12 F7
- **York Minster** YO1 7HH York 86 B5

SCOTLAND

- **Aberdour Castle** KY3 0SL Fife 115 M4
- **Alloa Tower** FK10 1PP Clacks 114 G3
- **Arbroath Abbey** DD11 1EG Angus 125 M4
- **Arduaine Garden** PA34 4XQ Ag & B 120 E10
- **Bachelors' Club** KA5 5RB S Ayrs 104 H4
- **Balmoral Castle Grounds** AB35 5TB Abers 131 N5
- **Balvenie Castle** AB55 4DH Moray 139 P7
- **Bannockburn Battlefield & Heritage Centre** FK7 0LJ Stirlg 114 E3
- **Blackness Castle** EH49 7NH Falk 115 J5
- **Blair Castle** PH18 5TL P & K 130 F11
- **Bothwell Castle** G71 8BL S Lans 114 C9
- **Branklyn Garden** PH2 7BB P & K 124 C8
- **Brodick Castle, Garden & Country Park** KA27 8HY N Ayrs 103 Q2
- **Brodie Castle** IV36 2TE Moray 138 H4
- **Broughton House & Garden** DG6 4JX D & G 96 D8
- **Burleigh Castle** KY13 9GG P & K 124 C11
- **Caerlaverock Castle** DG1 4RU D & G 97 L5
- **Cardoness Castle** DG7 2EH D & G 96 C7
- **Castle Campbell & Garden** FK14 7PP Clacks 114 H1
- **Castle Fraser, Garden & Estate** AB51 7LD Abers 132 H2
- **Castle Kennedy Gardens** DG9 8SL D & G 94 G6
- **Castle Menzies** PH15 2JD P & K 123 L3
- **Corgarff Castle** AB36 8YP Abers 131 N3
- **Craigievar Castle** AB33 8JF Abers 132 E2
- **Craigmillar Castle** EH16 4SY C Edin 115 P7
- **Crarae Garden** PA32 8YA Ag & B 112 E2
- **Crathes Castle & Garden** AB31 5QJ Abers 132 H5
- **Crichton Castle** EH37 5XA Mdloth 115 Q9
- **Crossraguel Abbey** KA19 8HQ S Ayrs 104 E8
- **Culloden Battlefield** IV2 5EU Highld 138 D7
- **Culross Palace** KY12 8JH Fife 114 H4
- **Culzean Castle & Country Park** KA19 8LE S Ayrs 104 D8
- **Dallas Dhu Distillery** IV36 2RR Moray 139 J4
- **David Livingstone Centre** G72 9BY S Lans 114 C9
- **Dirleton Castle & Garden** EH39 5ER E Loth 116 C4
- **Doune Castle** FK16 6EA Stirlg 114 D1
- **Drum Castle, Garden & Estate** AB31 5EY Abers 133 J4
- **Dryburgh Abbey** TD6 0RQ Border 107 P3
- **Duff House** AB45 3SX Abers 140 H3
- **Dumbarton Castle** G82 1JJ W Duns 113 M6
- **Dundrennan Abbey** DG6 4QH D & G 96 F9
- **Dunnottar Castle** AB39 2TL Abers 133 L7
- **Dunstaffnage Castle & Chapel** PA37 1PZ Ag & B 120 G6
- **Edinburgh Castle** EH1 2NG C Edin 115 N6
- **Edinburgh Zoo RZSS** EH12 6TS C Edin 115 M6
- **Edzell Castle & Garden** DD9 7UE Angus 132 F10
- **Eilean Donan Castle** IV40 8DX Highld 136 B10
- **Elgin Cathedral** IV30 1HU Moray 139 N3
- **Falkland Palace & Garden** KY15 7BU Fife 124 E11
- **Fort George** IV2 7TE Highld 138 D4
- **Fyvie Castle** AB53 8JS Abers 141 J8
- **Georgian House** EH2 4DR C Edin 115 N6
- **Gladstone's Land** EH1 2NT C Edin 115 N6
- **Glamis Castle** DD8 1RJ Angus 124 H3
- **Glasgow Botanic Gardens** G12 0UE C Glas 113 Q8
- **Glasgow Cathedral** G4 0QZ C Glas 114 A8
- **Glasgow Science Centre** G51 1EA C Glas 113 Q8
- **Glen Grant Distillery** AB38 7BS Moray 139 N6
- **Glenluce Abbey** DG8 0AF D & G 94 H6
- **Greenbank Garden** G76 8RB E Rens 113 Q10
- **Haddo House** AB41 7EQ Abers 141 L9
- **Harmony Garden** TD6 9LJ Border 107 N3
- **Hermitage Castle** TD9 0LU Border 107 M10
- **Highland Wildlife Park RZSS** PH21 1NL Highld 130 E3
- **Hill House** G84 9AJ Ag & B 113 L4
- **Hill of Tarvit Mansion & Garden** KY15 5PB Fife 124 H10
- **Holmwood** G44 3YG C Glas 113 R9
- **House of Dun** DD10 9LQ Angus 132 G12
- **House of the Binns** EH49 7NA W Loth 115 J6
- **Huntingtower Castle** PH1 3JL P & K 124 B8
- **Huntly Castle** AB54 4SH Abers 140 E7
- **Hutchesons' Hall** G1 1EJ C Glas 114 A8
- **Inchmahome Priory** FK8 3RA Stirlg 113 Q1
- **Inveresk Lodge Garden** EH21 7TE E Loth 115 Q7
- **Inverewe Garden & Estate** IV22 2LG Highld 143 M8
- **Inverlochy Castle** PH33 6SN Highld 128 F9
- **Kellie Castle & Garden** KY10 2RF Fife 125 K11
- **Kildrummy Castle** AB33 8RA Abers 132 C1
- **Killiecrankie** PH16 5LG P & K 130 G11
- **Leith Hall Garden & Estate** AB54 4NQ Abers 140 E10
- **Linlithgow Palace** EH49 7AL W Loth 115 J6
- **Lochleven Castle** KY13 8UF P & K 124 C12
- **Logan Botanic Garden** DG9 9ND D & G 94 F9
- **Malleny Garden** EH14 7AF C Edin 115 L8
- **Melrose Abbey** TD6 9LG Border 107 N3
- **National Museum of Scotland** EH1 1JF C Edin 115 N6
- **Newark Castle** PA14 5NH Inver 113 L6
- **Palace of Holyroodhouse** EH8 8DX C Edin 115 N6
- **Pitmedden Garden** AB41 7PD Abers 141 L10
- **Preston Mill** EH40 3DS E Loth 116 E6
- **Priorwood Garden** TD6 9PX Border 107 N3
- **Robert Smail's Printing Works** EH44 6HA Border 107 J2
- **Rothesay Castle** PA20 0DA Ag & B 112 G8
- **Royal Botanic Garden Edinburgh** EH3 5LR C Edin 115 N6
- **Royal Yacht Britannia** EH6 6JJ C Edin 115 N6
- **St Andrews Aquarium** KY16 9AS Fife 125 K9
- **Scone Palace** PH2 6BD P & K 124 C7
- **Smailholm Tower** TD5 7PG Border 107 Q3
- **Souter Johnnie's Cottage** KA19 8HY S Ayrs 104 D8
- **Stirling Castle** FK8 1EJ Stirlg 114 E2
- **Sweetheart Abbey** DG2 8BU D & G 97 K5
- **Tantallon Castle** EH39 5PN E Loth 116 E4
- **Tenement House** G3 6QN C Glas 113 R8
- **The Burrell Collection** G43 1AT C Glas 113 Q9
- **The Falkirk Wheel** FK1 4RS Falk 114 F5
- **The Hunterian Museum** G12 8QQ C Glas 113 Q8
- **Threave Castle** DG7 1TJ D & G 96 E6
- **Threave Garden** DG7 1RX D & G 96 F6
- **Tolquhon Castle** AB41 7LP Abers 141 L10
- **Traquair House** EH44 6PW Border 107 J3
- **Urquhart Castle** IV63 6XJ Highld 137 P10
- **Weaver's Cottage** PA10 2JG Rens 113 M8
- **Whithorn Priory & Museum** DG8 8PY D & G 95 N10

WALES

- **Aberconwy House** LL32 8AY Conwy 73 N8
- **Aberdulais Tin Works & Waterfall** SA10 8EU Neath 27 J2
- **Beaumaris Castle** LL58 8AP IoA 73 K8
- **Big Pit: National Coal Museum** NP4 9XP Torfn 40 B10
- **Bodnant Garden** LL28 5RE Conwy 73 P9
- **Caerleon Roman Fortress & Baths** NP18 1AE Newpt 28 D4
- **Caernarfon Castle** LL55 2AY Gwynd 72 H11
- **Caldicot Castle & Country Park** NP26 4HU Mons 28 G5
- **Cardiff Castle** CF10 3RB Cardif 28 A7
- **Castell Coch** CF15 7JS Cardif 27 Q6
- **Chirk Castle** LL14 5AF Wrexhm 63 J4
- **Colby Woodland Garden** SA67 8PP Pembks 37 M9
- **Conwy Castle** LL32 8AY Conwy 73 N8
- **Criccieth Castle** LL52 0DP Gwynd 60 H5
- **Dinefwr Park & Castle** SA19 6RT Carmth 38 F7
- **Dolaucothi Gold Mines** SA19 8US Carmth 38 G4
- **Erddig** LL13 0YT Wrexhm 63 K2
- **Ffestiniog Railway** LL49 9NF Gwynd 61 K4
- **Harlech Castle** LL46 2YH Gwynd 61 K6
- **Llanerchaeron** SA48 8DG Cerdgn 48 H8
- **National Showcaves Centre for Wales** SA9 1GJ Powys 39 K8
- **Penrhyn Castle** LL57 4HT Gwynd 73 K9
- **Plas Newydd** LL61 6DQ IoA 73 J9
- **Plas yn Rhiw** LL53 8AB Gwynd 60 C6
- **Portmeirion** LL48 6ER Gwynd 61 K5
- **Powis Castle & Garden** SY21 8RF Powys 62 H11
- **Raglan Castle** NP15 2BT Mons 40 F10
- **Sygun Copper Mine** LL55 4NE Gwynd 61 K2
- **Tintern Abbey** NP16 6SE Mons 28 H2
- **Tudor Merchant's House** SA70 7BX Pembks 37 M10
- **Tŷ Mawr Wybrnant** LL25 0HJ Conwy 61 N2
- **Valle Crucis Abbey** LL20 8DD Denbgs 62 H3

Central London Congestion Charge and Ultra Low Emission Zone

Rail interchange

Index to place names

This index lists places appearing in the main map section of the atlas in alphabetical order. The reference following each name gives the atlas page number and grid reference of the square in which the place appears. The map shows counties, unitary authorities and administrative areas, together with a list of the abbreviated name forms used in the index.

The top 100 places of tourist interest are indexed in **red**, World Heritage sites in **green**, motorway service areas in **blue**, airports in blue *italic* and National Parks in green *italic*.

Scotland

Abers Aberdeenshire
Ag & B Argyll and Bute
Angus Angus
Border Scottish Borders
C Aber City of Aberdeen
C Dund City of Dundee
C Edin City of Edinburgh
C Glas City of Glasgow
Clacks Clackmannanshire (1)
D & G Dumfries & Galloway
E Ayrs East Ayrshire
E Duns East Dunbartonshire (2)
E Loth East Lothian
E Rens East Renfrewshire (3)
Falk Falkirk
Fife Fife
Highld Highland
Inver Inverclyde (4)
Mdloth Midlothian (5)
Moray Moray
N Ayrs North Ayrshire
N Lans North Lanarkshire (6)
Ork Orkney Islands
P & K Perth & Kinross
Rens Renfrewshire (7)
S Ayrs South Ayrshire
S Lans South Lanarkshire
Shet Shetland Islands
Stirlg Stirling
W Duns West Dunbartonshire (8)
W Isls Western Isles (Na h-Eileanan an Iar)
W Loth West Lothian

Wales

Blae G Blaenau Gwent (9)
Brdgnd Bridgend (10)
Caerph Caerphilly (11)
Cardif Cardiff
Carmth Carmarthenshire
Cerdgn Ceredigion
Conwy Conwy
Denbgs Denbighshire
Flints Flintshire
Gwynd Gwynedd
IoA Isle of Anglesey
Mons Monmouthshire
Myr Td Merthyr Tydfil (12)
Neath Neath Port Talbot (13)
Newpt Newport (14)
Pembks Pembrokeshire
Powys Powys
Rhondd Rhondda Cynon Taf (15)
Swans Swansea
Torfn Torfaen (16)
V Glam Vale of Glamorgan (17)
Wrexhm Wrexham

England

BaNES Bath & N E Somerset (18)
Barns Barnsley (19)
BCP Bournemouth, Christchurch and Poole (20)
Bed Bedford
Birm Birmingham
Bl w D Blackburn with Darwen (21)
Bolton Bolton (22)
Bpool Blackpool
Br & H Brighton & Hove (23)
Br For Bracknell Forest (24)
Bristl City of Bristol
Bucks Buckinghamshire
Bury Bury (25)
C Beds Central Bedfordshire
C Brad City of Bradford
C Derb City of Derby
C KuH City of Kingston upon Hull
C Leic City of Leicester
C Nott City of Nottingham
C Pete City of Peterborough
C Plym City of Plymouth
C Port City of Portsmouth
C Sotn City of Southampton
C Stke City of Stoke-on-Trent
C York City of York
Calder Calderdale (26)
Cambs Cambridgeshire
Ches E Cheshire East
Ches W Cheshire West and Chester
Cnwll Cornwall
Covtry Coventry
Cumb Cumbria
Darltn Darlington (27)
Derbys Derbyshire
Devon Devon
Donc Doncaster (28)
Dorset Dorset
Dudley Dudley (29)
Dur Durham
E R Yk East Riding of Yorkshire
E Susx East Sussex
Essex Essex
Gatesd Gateshead (30)
Gloucs Gloucestershire
Gt Lon Greater London
Halton Halton (31)
Hants Hampshire
Hartpl Hartlepool (32)
Herefs Herefordshire
Herts Hertfordshire
IoS Isles of Scilly
IoW Isle of Wight
Kent Kent
Kirk Kirklees (33)
Knows Knowsley (34)
Lancs Lancashire
Leeds Leeds
Leics Leicestershire
Lincs Lincolnshire
Lpool Liverpool
Luton Luton
M Keyn Milton Keynes
Manch Manchester
Medway Medway
Middsb Middlesbrough
N Linc North Lincolnshire
N Som North Somerset
N Tyne North Tyneside (35)
N u Ty Newcastle upon Tyne
N York North Yorkshire
NE Lin North East Lincolnshire
Nhants Northamptonshire
Norfk Norfolk
Notts Nottinghamshire
Nthumb Northumberland
Oldham Oldham (36)
Oxon Oxfordshire
R & Cl Redcar & Cleveland
Readg Reading
Rochdl Rochdale (37)
Rothm Rotherham (38)
Rutlnd Rutland
S Glos South Gloucestershire (39)
S on T Stockton-on-Tees (40)
S Tyne South Tyneside (41)
Salfd Salford (42)
Sandw Sandwell (43)
Sefton Sefton (44)
Sheff Sheffield
Shrops Shropshire
Slough Slough (45)
Solhll Solihull (46)
Somset Somerset
St Hel St Helens (47)
Staffs Staffordshire
Sthend Southend-on-Sea
Stockp Stockport (48)
Suffk Suffolk
Sundld Sunderland
Surrey Surrey
Swindn Swindon
Tamesd Tameside (49)
Thurr Thurrock (50)
Torbay Torbay
Traffd Trafford (51)
W & M Windsor & Maidenhead (52)
W Berk West Berkshire
W Susx West Sussex
Wakefd Wakefield (53)
Warrtn Warrington (54)
Warwks Warwickshire
Wigan Wigan (55)
Wilts Wiltshire
Wirral Wirral (56)
Wokham Wokingham (57)
Wolves Wolverhampton (58)
Worcs Worcestershire
Wrekin Telford & Wrekin (59)
Wsall Walsall (60)

Channel Islands & Isle of Man

Guern Guernsey
Jersey Jersey
IoM Isle of Man

A

Abbas Combe Somset 22 F9
Abberley Worcs 52 D7
Abberley Common Worcs 52 D7
Abberton Essex 46 H8
Abberton Worcs 53 J10
Abberwick Nthumb 109 J7
Abbess Roding Essex 45 Q9
Abbey Devon 9 M3
Abbeycwmhir Powys 50 E6
Abbeydale Sheff 77 Q7
Abbey Dore Herefs 40 E5
Abbey Green Staffs 76 H12
Abbey Hill Somset 21 L9
Abbey St Bathans Border 116 G9
Abbeystead Lancs 83 M4
Abbeytown Cumb 97 N8
Abbey Village Lancs 83 P10
Abbey Wood Gt Lon 33 N6
Abbotrule Border 107 P7
Abbots Bickington Devon 18 H10
Abbots Bromley Staffs 65 K7
Abbotsbury Dorset 10 E7
Abbot's Chair Derbys 77 J6
Abbots Deuglie P & K 124 C10
Abbotsham Devon 18 H8
Abbotskerswell Devon 5 P3
Abbots Langley Herts 44 F11
Abbotsleigh Devon 5 N7
Abbots Leigh N Som 28 H7
Abbotsley Cambs 56 E9
Abbots Morton Worcs 53 J9
Abbots Ripton Cambs 56 E5
Abbot's Salford Warwks 53 K10
Abbotstone Hants 25 J6
Abbotswood Hants 24 F8
Abbots Worthy Hants 24 H7
Abbotts Ann Hants 24 E5
Abbott Street Dorset 11 N5
Abcott Shrops 51 L5
Abdon Shrops 51 P3
Abenhall Gloucs 41 K8
Aberaeron Cerdgn 48 G8
Aberaman Rhondd 27 N2
Aberangell Gwynd 61 P10
Aber-arad Carmth 37 Q3
Aberarder Highld 138 B10
Aberargie P & K 124 D9
Aberarth Cerdgn 48 H8
Aberavon Neath 26 H4
Aber-banc Cerdgn 38 A3
Aberbargoed Caerph 27 R2
Aberbeeg Blae G 40 B11
Abercanaid Myr Td 39 P11
Abercarn Caerph 28 B3
Abercastle Pembks 36 G4
Abercegir Powys 61 P11
Aberchalder Highld 129 K4
Aberchirder Abers 140 F5
Aber Clydach Powys 39 Q7
Abercorn W Loth 115 K5
Abercraf Powys 39 K9
Abercregan Neath 27 K3
Abercwmboi Rhondd 27 N2
Abercych Pembks 37 P2
Abercynon Rhondd 27 P3
Aberdalgie P & K 124 B9
Aberdare Rhondd 39 N11
Aberdaron Gwynd 60 B7
Aberdeen C Aber 133 M3
Aberdeen Airport C Aber 133 L2
Aberdesach Gwynd 60 G2
Aberdour Fife 115 M4
Aberdulais Neath 27 J2
Aberdyfi Gwynd 49 K1
Aberedw Powys 39 P2
Abereiddy Pembks 36 F4
Abererch Gwynd 60 F5
Aberfan Myr Td 27 P2
Aberfeldy P & K 123 L3
Aberffraw IoA 72 F10
Aberffrwd Cerdgn 49 L5
Aberford Leeds 85 N8
Aberfoyle Stirlg 113 Q1
Abergarw Brdgnd 27 L5
Abergarwed Neath 39 J11
Abergavenny Mons 40 D9
Abergele Conwy 74 C8
Aber-giar Carmth 38 D3
Abergorlech Carmth 38 E5
Abergwesyn Powys 49 Q10
Abergwili Carmth 38 C7
Abergwydol Powys 61 N11
Abergwynfi Neath 27 L3
Abergwyngregyn Gwynd 73 L9
Abergynolwyn Gwynd 61 L10
Aberhafesp Powys 50 E2
Aberhosan Powys 49 P1
Aberkenfig Brdgnd 27 L5
Aberlady E Loth 116 B5
Aberlemno Angus 125 K2
Aberllefenni Gwynd 61 N10
Aberllynfi Powys 40 A4
Aberlour, Charlestown of Moray 139 N7
Abermagwr Cerdgn 49 L6
Aber-meurig Cerdgn 49 J9
Abermorddu Flints 75 J12
Abermule Powys 50 G2
Abernant Carmth 37 R6
Abernant Rhondd 39 N11
Abernethy P & K 124 D9
Abernyte P & K 124 E6
Aberporth Cerdgn 48 D10
Abersoch Gwynd 60 E6
Abersychan Torfn 40 C11
Aberthin V Glam 27 N7
Abertillery Blae G 40 B11
Abertridwr Caerph 27 Q4
Abertridwr Powys 62 E8
Abertysswg Caerph 39 Q10
Aberuthven P & K 123 N9
Aberwheeler Denbgs 74 F10
Aberyscir Powys 39 N6
Aberystwyth Cerdgn 49 K4
Abingdon-on-Thames Oxon 31 K3
Abinger Common Surrey 14 G2
Abinger Hammer Surrey 14 F1
Abington Nhants 55 K8
Abington S Lans 106 B5
Abington Pigotts Cambs 45 K3
Abington Services S Lans 106 B5
Abingworth W Susx 14 G7
Ab Kettleby Leics 67 J7
Ab Lench Worcs 53 J10
Ablington Gloucs 42 C10
Ablington Wilts 23 P4
Abney Derbys 77 M7
Above Church Staffs 65 J2
Aboyne Abers 132 E5
Abhainn Suidhe W Isls 152 d5
Abram Wigan 75 Q3
Abriachan Highld 137 P9
Abridge Essex 33 N3
Abronhill N Lans 114 E6
Abson S Glos 29 L7
Abthorpe Nhants 43 N2
Aby Lincs 80 H8
Acaster Malbis C York 86 A6
Acaster Selby N York 85 R7
Accrington Lancs 84 A9
Acha Ag & B 118 G2
Achahoish Ag & B 112 A6
Achalader P & K 124 C4
Achaleven Ag & B 120 H6
Acha Mor W Isls 152 f3
Achanalt Highld 137 J3
Achandunie Highld 145 P10
Achany Highld 145 N5
Acharacle Highld 127 M10
Acharn Highld 120 D3
Acharn P & K 123 K4
Achavanich Highld 151 M8
Achduart Highld 144 C4
Achfary Highld 148 G8
Achgarve Highld 143 N6
A'Chill Highld 126 E3
Achiltibuie Highld 144 C3
Achina Highld 150 C4
Achinhoan Ag & B 103 K6
Achintee Highld 136 C7
Achintraid Highld 135 Q8
Achlyness Highld 148 F6
Achmelvich Highld 148 C11
Achmore Highld 135 Q9
Achmore W Isls 152 f3
Achnacarnin Highld 148 C10
Achnacarry Highld 128 G7
Achnacloich Highld 127 K3
Achnaconeran Highld 137 M12
Achnacroish Ag & B 120 F4
Achnadrish Ag & B 119 M2
Achnafauld P & K 123 M5
Achnagarron Highld 146 C11
Achnaha Highld 126 H10
Achnahaird Highld 144 C2
Achnahannet Highld 138 H10
Achnairn Highld 145 M3
Achnalea Highld 127 Q12
Achnamara Ag & B 112 A4
Achnasheen Highld 136 G4
Achnashellach Highld 136 D6
Achnastank Moray 139 P9
Achosnich Highld 126 H10
Achranich Highld 120 D3
Achreamie Highld 151 J3
Achriabhach Highld 128 G10
Achriesgill Highld 148 F6
Achtoty Highld 149 P4
Achurch Nhants 55 P4
Achvaich Highld 146 C6
Achvarasdal Highld 150 H4
Ackergill Highld 151 Q6
Acklam Middsb 91 R3
Acklam N York 86 E3
Ackleton Shrops 52 E1
Acklington Nthumb 109 L9
Ackton Wakefd 85 N10
Ackworth Moor Top Wakefd 85 N12
Acle Norfk 71 M10
Acock's Green Birm 53 L4
Acol Kent 35 P9
Acomb C York 85 R5
Acomb Nthumb 99 P5
Acombe Somset 21 K10
Aconbury Herefs 40 G5
Acre Lancs 84 B10
Acrefair Wrexhm 63 J3
Acresford Derbys 65 P9
Acton Ches E 64 B2
Acton Dorset 11 N9
Acton Gt Lon 32 H6
Acton Shrops 51 K4
Acton Staffs 64 F4
Acton Suffk 46 F3
Acton Worcs 52 F7
Acton Wrexhm 63 K2
Acton Beauchamp Herefs 52 C10
Acton Bridge Ches W 75 Q8
Acton Burnell Shrops 63 P11
Acton Green Herefs 52 C10
Acton Pigott Shrops 63 P11
Acton Round Shrops 52 B2
Acton Scott Shrops 51 M3
Acton Trussell Staffs 64 H8
Acton Turville S Glos 29 N6
Adbaston Staffs 64 E6
Adber Dorset 22 D9
Adbolton Notts 66 F4
Adderbury Oxon 43 K4
Adderley Shrops 64 C4
Adderstone Nthumb 109 J4
Addiewell W Loth 114 H8
Addingham C Brad 84 G5
Addington Bucks 43 Q6
Addington Gt Lon 33 L9
Addington Kent 34 B10
Addiscombe Gt Lon 33 L9
Addlestone Surrey 32 F9
Addlestonemoor Surrey 32 F9
Addlethorpe Lincs 81 K10
Adeney Wrekin 64 C8
Adeyfield Herts 44 F10
Adfa Powys 62 E12
Adforton Herefs 51 L6
Adisham Kent 35 M11
Adlestrop Gloucs 42 F6
Adlingfleet E R Yk 86 F11
Adlington Ches E 76 G7
Adlington Lancs 75 Q1
Admaston Staffs 65 K7
Admaston Wrekin 64 B9
Admington Warwks 42 E3
Adpar Cerdgn 37 Q2
Adsborough Somset 21 L7
Adscombe Somset 21 J6
Adstock Bucks 43 Q6
Adstone Nhants 54 F10
Adswood Stockp 76 G6
Adversane W Susx 14 F6
Advie Highld 139 L9
Adwalton Leeds 85 K9
Adwell Oxon 31 P2
Adwick le Street Donc 78 E2
Adwick upon Dearne Donc 78 D3
Ae D & G 106 C12
Ae Bridgend D & G 97 K1
Afan Forest Park Neath 27 K3
Affetside Bury 76 D1
Affleck Abers 140 E8
Affpuddle Dorset 11 K6
Affric Lodge Highld 136 H11
Afon-wen Flints 74 F9
Afon Wen Gwynd 60 G5
Afton Devon 5 P4
Afton IoW 12 F7
Agglethorpe N York 90 H9
Aigburth Lpool 75 L6
Aike E R Yk 87 K6

Aiketgate Cumb...98 F9
Aikhead Cumb...97 P8
Aikton Cumb...98 C7
Ailby Lincs...80 H8
Ailey Herefs...51 K11
Ailsworth C Pete...68 C12
Ainderby Quernhow N York...91 N10
Ainderby Steeple N York...91 N8
Aingers Green Essex...47 K7
Ainsdale Sefton...75 K1
Ainsdale-on-Sea Sefton...75 J1
Ainstable Cumb...98 G9
Ainsworth Bury...76 E2
Aintree Sefton...75 L4
Ainville W Loth...115 K8
Aird D & G...111 H1
Aird D & G...94 F6
Aird Highld...127 K4
Aird W Isls...152 h3
Àird a' Mhulaidh W Isls...152 e5
Aird Asaig W Isls...152 e5
Aird Dhubh Highld...135 N8
Airdeny Ag & B...121 J7
Airdrie N Lans...114 D8
Airdriehill N Lans...114 E8
Airds of Kells D & G...96 D4
Àird Uig W Isls...152 d3
Airieland D & G...96 F7
Airmyn E R Yk...124 F3
Airntully P & K...124 C6
Airor Highld...127 N3
Airth Falk...114 G4
Airton N York...84 D3
Aisby Lincs...67 P4
Aisby Lincs...79 L5
Aisgill Cumb...90 C7
Aish Devon...5 L4
Aish Devon...5 P5
Aisholt Somset...21 K6
Aiskew N York...91 M9
Aislaby N York...92 F9
Aislaby N York...92 H5
Aislaby S on T...91 P4
Aisthorpe Lincs...79 N7
Aith Shet...147 i6
Akeld Nthumb...108 F4
Akeley Bucks...43 P4
Akenham Suffk...58 H11
Albaston Cnwll...7 M10
Alberbury Shrops...63 K9
Albourne W Susx...15 J7
Albourne Green W Susx...15 J7
Albrighton Shrops...63 N8
Albrighton Shrops...64 E11
Alburgh Norfk...59 K3
Albury Herts...45 M7
Albury Oxon...43 N10
Albury Surrey...14 F1
Albury End Herts...45 M7
Albury Heath Surrey...14 F2
Alby Hill Norfk...71 J5
Alcaig Highld...137 P4
Alcaston Shrops...51 M3
Alcester Warwks...53 K9
Alciston E Susx...15 P9
Alcombe Somset...20 F4
Alcombe Wilts...18 C6
Alconbury Cambs...56 D5
Alconbury Weald Cambs...56 D5
Alconbury Weston Cambs...56 D5
Aldborough N York...85 N2
Aldborough Norfk...71 J5
Aldbourne Wilts...30 F7
Aldbrough E R Yk...87 N7
Aldbrough St John N York...91 K4
Aldbury Herts...44 D9
Aldcliffe Lancs...83 L3
Aldclune P & K...130 G11
Aldeburgh Suffk...59 P9
Aldeby Norfk...59 N2
Aldenham Herts...44 D10
Alderbury Wilts...24 C8
Aldercar Derbys...66 D3
Alderford Norfk...70 H8
Alderholt Dorset...23 N3
Alderley Gloucs...29 M4
Alderley Edge Ches E...76 F9
Aldermans Green Covtry...54 B4
Aldermaston W Berk...31 M9
Alderminster Warwks...53 N11
Alder Moor Staffs...65 N6
Aldersey Green Ches W...75 M12
Aldershot Hants...25 Q3
Alderton Gloucs...42 B5
Alderton Nhants...43 Q2
Alderton Shrops...63 N7
Alderton Suffk...47 P3
Alderton Wilts...29 N6
Alderwasley Derbys...65 P1
Aldfield N York...85 L1
Aldford Ches W...75 M11
Aldgate Rutlnd...67 N11
Aldham Essex...46 G6
Aldham Suffk...47 J3
Aldingbourne W Susx...14 C9
Aldingham Cumb...82 G1
Aldington Kent...17 J3
Aldington Worcs...42 C3
Aldington Corner Kent...17 J3
Aldivalloch Moray...139 Q10
Aldochlay Ag & B...113 L5
Aldon Shrops...51 M5
Aldoth Cumb...97 M8
Aldreth Cambs...56 H6
Aldridge Wsall...65 K12
Aldringham Suffk...59 N8
Aldro N York...86 F2
Aldsworth Gloucs...42 D9
Aldsworth W Susx...13 M5
Aldunie Moray...139 Q10
Aldwark Derbys...77 N12
Aldwark N York...85 P3
Aldwick W Susx...14 C11
Aldworth W Berk...31 L6
Alexandria W Duns...113 M5
Aley Somset...21 J6
Alfardisworthy Devon...7 K2
Alfington Devon...9 L5
Alfold Surrey...14 E4
Alfold Bars W Susx...14 E4
Alfold Crossways Surrey...14 F4
Alford Abers...132 F1
Alford Lincs...80 H9
Alford Somset...22 E7
Alfreton Derbys...66 C1
Alfrick Worcs...52 D10
Alfrick Pound Worcs...52 D10
Alfriston E Susx...15 P10
Algarkirk Lincs...68 E5
Alhampton Somset...22 E6
Alkborough N Linc...86 G11
Alkerton Gloucs...41 M10
Alkerton Oxon...43 L3
Alkham Kent...17 N2
Alkington Shrops...63 P5
Alkmonton Derbys...65 M4
Allaleigh Devon...5 N5
Allanaquoich Abers...131 L6
Allanbank N Lans...114 F10
Allanton Border...117 J10
Allanton N Lans...114 F10

Allanton S Lans...114 D10
Allaston Gloucs...41 K10
Allbrook Hants...24 G9
All Cannings Wilts...30 C10
Allendale Nthumb...99 N1
Allen End Warwks...53 M1
Allenheads Nthumb...99 N9
Allensford Dur...100 D8
Allen's Green Herts...45 N8
Allensmore Herefs...40 G4
Allenton C Derb...66 B6
Aller Devon...19 P8
Aller Devon...21 N7
Allerby Cumb...97 M10
Allercombe Devon...9 K6
Aller Cross Devon...19 N8
Allerford Somset...20 D4
Allerston N York...92 H10
Allerthorpe E R Yk...86 E6
Allerton C Brad...84 H8
Allerton Highld...138 D3
Allerton Bywater Leeds...85 N9
Allerton Mauleverer N York...85 N4
Allesley Covtry...53 P4
Allestree C Derb...65 Q4
Allet Common Cnwll...3 K5
Allexton Leics...67 K12
Allgreave Ches E...76 H10
Allhallows Medway...34 E7
Allhallows-on-Sea Medway...34 E6
Alligin Shuas Highld...135 Q4
Allimore Green Staffs...64 F8
Allington Dorset...10 C6
Allington Kent...34 D10
Allington Lincs...67 L4
Allington Wilts...23 Q5
Allington Wilts...29 P7
Allington Wilts...30 C9
Allithwaite Cumb...89 K11
Alloa Clacks...114 F3
Allonby Cumb...97 M9
Allostock Ches W...76 D9
Alloway S Ayrs...104 F6
Allowenshay Somset...21 N10
All Saints South Elmham Suffk...59 L4
Allscott Shrops...52 D1
Allscott Wrekin...63 Q9
All Stretton Shrops...51 M2
Alltami Flints...75 J10
Alltchaorunn Highld...121 M3
Alltmawr Powys...39 P2
Alltsigh Highld...137 M12
Alltwalis Carmth...38 C5
Alltwen Neath...38 H11
Alltyblaca Cerdgn...38 D3
Allwood Green Suffk...58 F6
Almeley Herefs...51 K10
Almeley Wooton Herefs...51 K10
Almer Dorset...11 L5
Almholme Donc...78 F2
Almington Staffs...64 C5
Almodington W Susx...13 N6
Almondbank P & K...123 Q7
Almondbury Kirk...85 J12
Almondsbury S Glos...29 J5
Alne N York...85 P2
Alness Highld...145 P11
Alnham Nthumb...108 F7
Alnmouth Nthumb...109 L7
Alnwick Nthumb...109 K7
Alperton Gt Lon...32 H5
Alphamstone Essex...46 F4
Alpheton Suffk...58 C10
Alphington Devon...8 H7
Alport Derbys...77 N10
Alpraham Ches E...75 P11
Alresford Essex...47 J7
Alrewas Staffs...65 M9
Alsager Ches E...64 E1
Alsagers Bank Staffs...64 E3
Alsop en le Dale Derbys...65 M1
Alston Cumb...99 K9
Alston Devon...9 P4
Alstone Gloucs...41 R5
Alstone Somset...21 M4
Alstonefield Staffs...65 L1
Alston Sutton Somset...21 P3
Alswear Devon...19 P9
Alt Oldham...76 H3
Altandhu Highld...143 P3
Altarnun Cnwll...7 J4
Altass Highld...145 M5
Altcreich Ag & B...120 C5
Altgaltraig Ag & B...112 F6
Altham Lancs...84 A8
Althorne Essex...34 G3
Althorpe N Linc...79 L2
Altnabreac Station Highld...150 F7
Altnaharra Highld...149 M9
Altofts Wakefd...85 M10
Alton Derbys...78 B10
Alton Hants...25 M5
Alton Staffs...65 K4
Alton Barnes Wilts...30 C10
Alton Pancras Dorset...10 H4
Alton Priors Wilts...30 C10
Alton Towers Staffs...65 K4
Altrincham Traffd...76 E6
Altskeith Hotel Stirlg...122 D12
Alva Clacks...114 F2
Alvanley Ches W...75 N9
Alvaston C Derb...66 C5
Alvechurch Worcs...53 J6
Alvecote Warwks...65 N11
Alvediston Wilts...23 L8
Alveley Shrops...52 D4
Alverdiscott Devon...19 K8
Alverstoke Hants...13 L5
Alverstone IoW...13 K7
Alverthorpe Wakefd...85 L11
Alverton Notts...67 K4
Alves Moray...139 L3
Alvescot Oxon...42 F10
Alveston S Glos...29 K5
Alveston Warwks...53 N9
Alvingham Lincs...80 G5
Alvington Gloucs...29 J2
Alwalton C Pete...56 C1
Alweston Dorset...22 F2
Alwington Devon...18 H8
Alwinton Nthumb...108 D8
Alwoodley Leeds...85 L7
Alwoodley Gates Leeds...85 L7
Alyth P & K...124 E5
Am Bàgh a Tuath W Isls...152 b13
Amber Hill Lincs...68 E3
Amberley Gloucs...41 M8
Amberley W Susx...14 E8
Amber Row Derbys...78 C12
Amberstone E Susx...15 Q8
Amble Nthumb...109 L9
Amblecote Dudley...52 G3
Ambler Thorn C Brad...84 G9
Ambleside Cumb...89 K6
Ambleston Pembks...37 K5
Ambrosden Oxon...43 M8
Amcotts N Linc...86 F12
America Cambs...56 H5
Amersham Common Bucks...32 D3

Amersham Old Town Bucks...32 D3
Amersham on the Hill Bucks...32 D3
Amerton Staffs...65 J7
Amesbury Wilts...23 P5
Amhuinnsuidhe W Isls...152 d5
Amington Staffs...65 N11
Amisfield D & G...97 K2
Amlwch IoA...72 G5
Ammanford Carmth...38 F9
Amotherby N York...92 F12
Ampfield Hants...24 F8
Ampleforth N York...92 C11
Ampney Crucis Gloucs...42 C11
Ampney St Mary Gloucs...42 C11
Ampney St Peter Gloucs...30 C2
Amport Hants...24 E4
Ampthill C Beds...44 E4
Ampton Suffk...58 C6
Amroth Pembks...37 M9
Amulree P & K...123 M7
Amwell Herts...44 H9
Anaheilt Highld...127 P11
Ancaster Lincs...67 N3
Ancells Farm Hants...25 N2
Anchor Shrops...50 G4
Ancroft Nthumb...117 M10
Ancrum Border...107 Q5
Ancton W Susx...14 D10
Anderby Lincs...81 K8
Anderby Creek Lincs...81 K8
Andersea Somset...21 M6
Andersfield Somset...21 L6
Anderson Dorset...11 L5
Anderton Ches W...76 B8
Anderton Cnwll...4 F6
Andover Hants...24 F4
Andover Down Hants...24 F4
Andoversford Gloucs...42 B8
Andreas IoM...102 e3
Anelog Gwynd...60 B6
Anerley Gt Lon...33 L8
Anfield Lpool...75 L5
Angarrack Cnwll...2 F7
Angarrick Cnwll...3 K7
Angelbank Shrops...51 P5
Angersleigh Somset...21 K9
Angerton Cumb...97 P7
Angle Pembks...36 G10
Anglesey Abbey Cambs...57 K8
Angmering W Susx...14 F10
Angram N York...85 N5
Angram N York...90 E7
Angrouse Cnwll...2 G10
Anick Nthumb...99 Q5
Ankerville Highld...146 E10
Ankle Hill Leics...67 J8
Anlaby E R Yk...87 J9
Anmer Norfk...69 P6
Anmore Hants...13 L3
Annan D & G...97 P5
Annandale Water Services D & G...106 E11
Annaside Cumb...88 D7
Annat Highld...136 B5
Annathill N Lans...114 D7
Anna Valley Hants...24 D4
Annbank S Ayrs...104 G5
Anne Hathaway's Cottage Warwks...53 M9
Annesley Notts...66 E1
Annesley Woodhouse Notts...66 E2
Annfield Plain Dur...100 F8
Anniesland C Glas...113 Q7
Annitsford N Tyne...100 H3
Annscroft Shrops...63 M10
Ansdell Lancs...82 H9
Ansford Somset...22 F7
Ansley Warwks...53 P2
Anslow Staffs...65 M7
Anslow Gate Staffs...65 M7
Anstedbrook Surrey...14 D4
Anstey Hants...25 M5
Anstey Herts...45 M5
Anstey Leics...66 F10
Anstruther Fife...125 L12
Ansty W Susx...15 K6
Ansty Warwks...54 C4
Ansty Wilts...23 L8
Ansty Cross Dorset...11 J4
An Tairbeart W Isls...152 e5
Anthill Common Hants...25 L11
Anthonys Surrey...32 E10
Anthorn Cumb...97 P6
Antingham Norfk...71 K5
An t-Ob W Isls...152 d6
Antonine Wall...114 F5
Anton's Gowt Lincs...68 F3
Antony Cnwll...4 F6
Antrobus Ches W...76 B8
Anvil Corner Devon...7 M4
Anvil Green Kent...35 K12
Anwick Lincs...68 C2
Anwoth D & G...96 C7
Aperfield Gt Lon...33 M10
Apes Dale Worcs...53 J6
Apethorpe Nhants...55 P2
Apeton Staffs...64 F8
Apley Lincs...80 B8
Apperknowle Derbys...78 C8
Apperley Gloucs...41 Q6
Apperley Bridge C Brad...85 J7
Apperley Dene Nthumb...100 D6
Apperset N York...90 D8
Appin Ag & B...120 H4
Appleby N Linc...86 H12
Appleby-in-Westmorland Cumb...90 A3
Appleby Magna Leics...65 P10
Appleby Parva Leics...65 P10
Appleby Street Herts...45 L10
Applecross Highld...135 M7
Appledore Devon...20 C10
Appledore Devon...18 H6
Appledore Kent...16 G5
Appledore Heath Kent...16 G5
Appleford Oxon...31 L4
Applegarth Town D & G...97 M1
Applehaigh Wakefd...85 B1
Applemore Hants...12 F3
Appleshaw Hants...24 E4
Applethwaite Cumb...89 L9
Appleton Halton...75 P7
Appleton Oxon...31 J2
Appleton Warrtn...76 B7
Appleton-le-Moors N York...92 E9
Appleton-le-Street N York...92 F11
Appleton Roebuck N York...85 Q7
Appleton Thorn Warrtn...76 C7
Appleton Wiske N York...91 P6
Appletreehall Border...107 N6
Appletreewick N York...84 H3
Appley Somset...20 G9
Appley Bridge Lancs...75 N2
Apse Heath IoW...13 J8
Apsey Green Suffk...59 J8
Apsley End C Beds...44 G5
Apuldram W Susx...13 N5
Arabella Highld...146 E10
Arbirlot Angus...125 M5
Arborfield Wokham...31 Q9
Arborfield Cross Wokham...31 Q9

Arborfield Green Wokham...31 Q9
Arbourthorne Sheff...78 B6
Arbroath Angus...125 M5
Arbuthnott Abers...133 M9
Arcadia Kent...16 F3
Archddu Carmth...26 C2
Archdeacon Newton Darltn...91 L3
Archencarroch W Duns...113 N5
Archiestown Moray...139 N7
Archirondel Jersey...13 d2
Arclid Ches E...76 E11
Ardallie Abers...141 N8
Ardanaiseig Hotel Ag & B...121 K8
Ardaneaskan Highld...135 Q9
Ardarroch Highld...135 Q8
Ardbeg Ag & B...111 J12
Ardbeg Ag & B...112 G8
Ardbeg Ag & B...112 H5
Ardcharnich Highld...144 F7
Ardchiavaig Ag & B...119 L5
Ardchonnell Ag & B...121 J10
Ardchronie Highld...145 N7
Ardchullarie More Stirlg...122 F10
Arddarroch Ag & B...113 J2
Arddleen Powys...63 J9
Ard Dorch Highld...135 K10
Ardechive Highld...128 G6
Ardeer N Ayrs...104 E2
Ardeley Herts...45 K6
Ardelve Highld...136 B10
Arden Ag & B...113 M4
Ardens Grafton Warwks...53 L9
Ardentallen Ag & B...120 F8
Ardentinny Ag & B...113 J4
Ardentraive Ag & B...112 F6
Ardeonaig Stirlg...122 H4
Ardersier Highld...138 E5
Ardessie Highld...144 D7
Ardfern Ag & B...120 E12
Ardfernal Ag & B...111 M7
Ardgartan Ag & B...121 P12
Ardgay Highld...145 N7
Ardgour Highld...128 E11
Ardgowan Inver...113 J6
Ardhallow Ag & B...112 H6
Ardhasig W Isls...152 e5
Ardheslaig Highld...135 P5
Ardindrean Highld...144 F7
Ardingly W Susx...15 L5
Ardington Oxon...31 J5
Ardington Wick Oxon...31 J5
Ardlamont Ag & B...112 E7
Ardleigh Essex...47 J6
Ardleigh Heath Essex...47 J5
Ardler P & K...124 E5
Ardley Oxon...43 L6
Ardley End Essex...45 P9
Ardlui Ag & B...121 Q9
Ardlussa Ag & B...111 N4
Ardmair Highld...144 D5
Ardmaleish Ag & B...112 G7
Ardminish Ag & B...111 P9
Ardmolich Highld...127 N10
Ardmore Ag & B...113 J6
Ardmore Highld...146 C8
Ardnadam Ag & B...112 H5
Ardnagrask Highld...137 P6
Ardnamurchan Highld...127 K10
Ardnarff Highld...136 B9
Ardnastang Highld...127 P12
Ardpatrick Ag & B...111 Q9
Ardrishaig Ag & B...112 C4
Ardross Highld...145 P10
Ardrossan N Ayrs...104 D3
Ardsley Barns...78 C3
Ardslignish Highld...127 K12
Ardtalla Ag & B...111 K8
Ardtoe Highld...127 L10
Ardullie Highld...137 P3
Ardvasar Highld...127 J4
Ardvorlich P & K...122 G8
Ardvourlie W Isls...152 e5
Ardwell D & G...94 G9
Ardwick Manch...76 G4
Areley Kings Worcs...52 F6
Arevegaig Highld...127 M10
Arford Hants...25 P6
Argoed Caerph...27 P3
Argoed Shrops...63 K8
Argoed Mill Powys...50 D8
Argos Hill E Susx...15 Q5
Argyll Forest Park Ag & B...121 N12
Aribruach W Isls...152 f4
Aridhglas Ag & B...119 J6
Arileod Ag & B...118 G2
Arinacrinachd Highld...135 N4
Arinagour Ag & B...118 G2
Arisaig Highld...127 M7
Arisaig House Highld...127 M7
Arkendale N York...85 M3
Arkesden Essex...45 N5
Arkholme Lancs...89 P12
Arkleby Cumb...97 N10
Arkleton D & G...107 K11
Arkle Town N York...90 H6
Arkley Gt Lon...33 J3
Arksey Donc...78 F2
Arkwright Town Derbys...78 C9
Arle Gloucs...41 Q7
Arlecdon Cumb...88 D3
Arlescote Warwks...54 C10
Arlesey C Beds...44 H4
Arleston Wrekin...64 C10
Arley Ches E...76 C7
Arlingham Gloucs...41 L9
Arlington Devon...19 M5
Arlington E Susx...15 P9
Arlington Gloucs...42 C10
Arlington Beccott Devon...19 M5
Armadale Highld...127 J4
Armadale Highld...150 D4
Armadale W Loth...114 H8
Armaside Cumb...88 F1
Armathwaite Cumb...98 G9
Arminghall Norfk...71 K11
Armitage Staffs...65 K9
Armitage Bridge Kirk...77 Q1
Armley Leeds...85 L8
Armscote Warwks...42 G3
Armshead Staffs...64 H2
Armston Nhants...55 P3
Armthorpe Donc...78 G3
Arnabost Ag & B...118 G2
Arnaby Cumb...88 G10
Arncliffe N York...84 C1
Arncliffe Cote N York...84 C1
Arncroach Fife...125 K11
Arndilly House Moray...139 N6
Arne Dorset...11 N7
Arnesby Leics...54 G1
Arngask P & K...124 C10
Arnisdale Highld...127 M3
Arnish Highld...135 K8
Arniston Mdloth...115 Q8
Arnol W Isls...152 f2
Arnold E R Yk...87 L7
Arnold Notts...66 F3
Arnprior Stirlg...114 B3
Arnside Cumb...89 M11
Aros Ag & B...119 N4
Arowry Wrexhm...63 M4
Arrad Foot Cumb...89 J10

Arran N Ayrs...103 P3
Arrathorne N York...91 K8
Arreton IoW...13 J7
Arrina Highld...135 N4
Arrington Cambs...56 F10
Arrochar Ag & B...121 P12
Arrow Warwks...53 K9
Arrowfield Top Worcs...53 J6
Artafallie Highld...138 B6
Arthington Leeds...85 L6
Arthingworth Nhants...55 J4
Arthog Gwynd...61 L9
Arthrath Abers...141 M8
Arthursdale Leeds...85 M7
Arthurstone P & K...124 E4
Artrochie Abers...141 N9
Arundel W Susx...14 E9
Asby Cumb...88 E3
Ascog Ag & B...112 G8
Ascot W & M...32 D8
Ascott Warwks...42 G5
Ascott Earl Oxon...42 G8
Ascott-under-Wychwood Oxon...42 G8
Asenby N York...91 P11
Asfordby Leics...67 J8
Asfordby Hill Leics...67 J8
Asgarby Lincs...68 C3
Asgarby Lincs...80 F10
Ash Devon...7 P3
Ash Devon...5 P3
Ash Kent...33 R9
Ash Kent...35 N10
Ash Somset...21 L9
Ash Somset...21 P6
Ash Surrey...32 C12
Ashampstead W Berk...31 M7
Ashampstead Green W Berk...31 M7
Ashbocking Suffk...59 J9
Ashbourne Derbys...65 M3
Ashbrittle Somset...20 G9
Ashburnham Place E Susx...16 C8
Ashburton Devon...5 M3
Ashbury Devon...7 P5
Ashbury Oxon...30 F5
Ashby N Linc...79 M2
Ashby by Partney Lincs...80 H10
Ashby cum Fenby NE Lin...80 E2
Ashby de la Launde Lincs...67 P1
Ashby-de-la-Zouch Leics...66 B9
Ashby Folville Leics...66 H9
Ashby Magna Leics...54 E2
Ashby Parva Leics...54 E3
Ashby Puerorum Lincs...80 F9
Ashby St Ledgers Nhants...54 F7
Ashby St Mary Norfk...71 L11
Ashchurch Gloucs...41 Q5
Ashcombe Devon...9 J8
Ashcombe N Som...28 D10
Ashcott Somset...21 N6
Ashdon Essex...45 Q3
Ashdown Forest E Susx...15 N5
Ashe Hants...25 J3
Asheldham Essex...34 G2
Ashen Essex...46 D3
Ashendon Bucks...43 P9
Asheridge Bucks...44 D10
Ashfield Hants...24 F9
Ashfield Herefs...41 J7
Ashfield Stirlg...114 C1
Ashfield cum Thorpe Suffk...59 J8
Ashfield Green Suffk...57 P7
Ashfield Green Suffk...59 K6
Ashfold Crossways W Susx...15 J5
Ashford Devon...19 K6
Ashford Devon...5 K8
Ashford Kent...16 H2
Ashford Surrey...32 F8
Ashford Bowdler Shrops...51 N6
Ashford Carbonell Shrops...51 N6
Ashford Hill Hants...31 L9
Ashford in the Water Derbys...77 M9
Ashgill S Lans...114 E11
Ash Green Surrey...14 C1
Ash Green Warwks...53 Q3
Ashill Devon...9 L2
Ashill Norfk...70 C11
Ashill Somset...21 M10
Ashingdon Essex...34 F3
Ashington BCP...11 N5
Ashington Nthumb...109 L12
Ashington Somset...22 D9
Ashington W Susx...14 H7
Ashkirk Border...107 M5
Ashlett Hants...12 H4
Ashleworth Gloucs...41 N6
Ashleworth Quay Gloucs...41 N6
Ashley Cambs...57 N8
Ashley Ches E...76 E7
Ashley Devon...19 N10
Ashley Dorset...11 Q4
Ashley Gloucs...29 N3
Ashley Hants...12 D6
Ashley Hants...24 F7
Ashley Kent...17 P1
Ashley Nhants...55 K2
Ashley Staffs...64 D5
Ashley Wilts...29 N8
Ashley Green Bucks...44 D10
Ashley Heath Dorset...11 Q4
Ashley Moor Herefs...51 N7
Ash Magna Shrops...63 P4
Ashmanhaugh Norfk...71 L7
Ashmansworth Hants...31 J11
Ashmansworthy Devon...18 H9
Ashmead Green Gloucs...29 M2
Ashmill Devon...7 N4
Ashmore Dorset...23 L9
Ashmore Green W Berk...31 L8
Ashorne Warwks...53 P9
Ashover Derbys...77 Q11
Ashover Hay Derbys...77 Q11
Ashow Warwks...53 P6
Ash Parva Shrops...63 P4
Ashperton Herefs...41 K3
Ashprington Devon...5 N5
Ash Priors Somset...21 J8
Ashreigney Devon...19 M10
Ash Street Suffk...47 J2
Ashtead Surrey...32 H10
Ash Thomas Devon...9 J3
Ashton C Pete...68 B11
Ashton Cnwll...2 F8
Ashton Devon...8 H8
Ashton Hants...25 J10
Ashton Herefs...51 N8
Ashton Inver...113 J6
Ashton Nhants...55 J10
Ashton Nhants...55 P3
Ashton Somset...21 N3
Ashton Common Wilts...29 N10
Ashton Hayes Ches W...75 N10
Ashton Keynes Wilts...30 A4
Ashton under Hill Worcs...42 A4
Ashton-in-Makerfield Wigan...75 P4
Ashton-under-Lyne Tamesd...76 H4

Ashton upon Mersey Traffd...76 E5
Ashurst Hants...12 E3
Ashurst Kent...15 P3
Ashurst Lancs...75 M3
Ashurst W Susx...14 H7
Ashurst Wood W Susx...15 M3
Ash Vale Surrey...32 C12
Ashwater Devon...7 M4
Ashwell Herts...45 K4
Ashwell Rutlnd...67 L9
Ashwell End Herts...45 J4
Ashwellthorpe Norfk...58 H1
Ashwick Somset...22 E4
Ashwicken Norfk...69 N8
Ashwood Staffs...52 F3
Askam in Furness Cumb...88 G11
Askern Donc...78 F1
Askerswell Dorset...10 D6
Askett Bucks...44 B10
Askham Cumb...89 N3
Askham Notts...79 J8
Askham Bryan C York...85 Q6
Askham Richard C York...85 P6
Asknish Ag & B...112 D3
Askrigg N York...90 H8
Askwith N York...85 J5
Aslackby Lincs...68 B6
Aslacton Norfk...58 H2
Aslockton Notts...67 J4
Asney Somset...21 P6
Aspall Suffk...58 H7
Aspatria Cumb...97 N10
Aspenden Herts...45 L6
Aspenshaw Derbys...77 J6
Asperton Lincs...68 E5
Aspley Staffs...64 F5
Aspley Guise C Beds...44 D4
Aspley Heath C Beds...44 D4
Aspley Heath Warwks...53 K6
Aspull Wigan...75 Q2
Aspull Common Wigan...76 B4
Asselby E R Yk...86 E9
Asserby Lincs...81 J8
Asserby Turn Lincs...81 J8
Assington Suffk...46 G4
Assington Green Suffk...58 B10
Astbury Ches E...76 F11
Astcote Nhants...54 H10
Asterby Lincs...80 E8
Asterley Shrops...63 L10
Asterton Shrops...51 L2
Asthall Oxon...42 G9
Asthall Leigh Oxon...42 G9
Astle Highld...146 D7
Astley Shrops...63 N8
Astley Warwks...53 P3
Astley Worcs...52 E7
Astley Abbots Shrops...52 D2
Astley Bridge Bolton...76 D1
Astley Cross Worcs...52 E7
Astley Green Wigan...76 D4
Aston Birm...53 K3
Aston Ches E...63 Q3
Aston Ches W...75 P8
Aston Derbys...77 M7
Aston Flints...75 J10
Aston Herefs...51 M8
Aston Herts...45 K6
Aston Oxon...42 H11
Aston Rothm...78 D6
Aston Shrops...63 N6
Aston Shrops...64 G7
Aston Staffs...64 D3
Aston Staffs...64 G4
Aston Wokham...31 Q5
Aston Wrekin...63 Q10
Aston Botterell Shrops...52 B4
Aston-by-Stone Staffs...64 G5
Aston Cantlow Warwks...53 L8
Aston Clinton Bucks...44 C9
Aston Crews Herefs...41 K7
Aston Cross Gloucs...41 Q5
Aston End Herts...45 K7
Aston Fields Worcs...52 H7
Aston Flamville Leics...54 D2
Aston Heath Ches W...75 P8
Aston Ingham Herefs...41 K7
Aston juxta Mondrum Ches E...76 C12
Aston le Walls Nhants...54 E10
Aston Magna Gloucs...42 E4
Aston Munslow Shrops...51 N3
Aston-on-Carrant Gloucs...41 Q5
Aston on Clun Shrops...51 L4
Aston Pigott Shrops...63 K11
Aston Rogers Shrops...63 K11
Aston Rowant Oxon...31 P3
Aston Sandford Bucks...43 Q9
Aston-sub-Edge Gloucs...42 E3
Aston Tirrold Oxon...31 L5
Aston-upon-Trent Derbys...66 C6
Aston Upthorpe Oxon...31 L5
Astrop Nhants...43 L4
Astrope Herts...44 C8
Astwick C Beds...45 J5
Astwith Derbys...78 D11
Astwood M Keyn...44 D2
Astwood Worcs...52 H8
Astwood Bank Worcs...53 K8
Aswarby Lincs...67 Q4
Aswardby Lincs...80 G8
Atcham Shrops...63 P10
Atch Lench Worcs...53 L10
Athelhampton Dorset...11 J5
Athelington Suffk...59 J6
Athelney Somset...21 M7
Athelstaneford E Loth...116 C6
Atherfield Green IoW...12 H9
Atherington Devon...19 L9
Atherington W Susx...14 E10
Atherstone Somset...21 N10
Atherstone Warwks...53 P1
Atherstone on Stour Warwks...53 M10
Atherton Wigan...76 C3
Atley Hill N York...91 M6
Atlow Derbys...65 N3
Attadale Highld...136 C9
Attenborough Notts...66 E5
Atterby Lincs...79 N4
Attercliffe Sheff...78 B5
Atterley Shrops...52 C2
Atterton Leics...54 B1
Attingham Park Shrops...63 P10
Attleborough Norfk...58 F2
Attleborough Warwks...54 B2
Attlebridge Norfk...70 H8
Attleton Green Suffk...57 P9
Atwick E R Yk...87 M5
Atworth Wilts...29 P9
Auberrow Herefs...40 G3
Aubourn Lincs...79 N11
Auchbreck Moray...139 N10
Auchedly Abers...141 L9
Auchenblae Abers...132 H8
Auchenbowie Stirlg...114 E4
Auchencairn D & G...96 E8
Auchencairn D & G...97 K1
Auchencairn N Ayrs...103 Q4
Auchencrow Border...117 J8

Auchendinny Mdloth...115 N9
Auchengray S Lans...114 H10
Auchenhalrig Moray...140 B3
Auchenheath S Lans...105 Q1
Auchenhessnane D & G...105 P10
Auchenlochan Ag & B...112 E7
Auchenmade N Ayrs...113 L11
Auchenmalg D & G...95 J8
Auchentiber N Ayrs...113 M11
Auchindrain Ag & B...121 K12
Auchindrean Highld...144 F9
Auchininna Abers...140 G6
Auchinleck E Ayrs...105 K5
Auchinloch N Lans...114 B7
Auchinstarry N Lans...114 C6
Auchintore Highld...128 F10
Auchiries Abers...141 P8
Auchlean Highld...130 F5
Auchlee Abers...133 L5
Auchleven Abers...140 F11
Auchlochan S Lans...105 Q2
Auchlossan Abers...132 E4
Auchlyne Stirlg...122 F7
Auchmillan E Ayrs...105 J4
Auchmithie Angus...125 N4
Auchmuirbridge Fife...115 M1
Auchnacree Angus...132 E10
Auchnagatt Abers...141 M7
Auchnarrow Moray...139 M11
Auchnotteroch D & G...94 E6
Auchroisk Moray...139 Q5
Auchterarder P & K...123 N10
Auchterblair Highld...138 G11
Auchtercairn Highld...143 L9
Auchterderran Fife...115 M2
Auchterhouse Angus...124 G5
Auchterless Abers...140 H7
Auchtermuchty Fife...124 E10
Auchterneed Highld...137 N3
Auchtertool Fife...115 M3
Auchtertyre Highld...135 Q10
Auchtubh Stirlg...122 F8
Auckengill Highld...151 Q2
Auckley Donc...78 G3
Audenshaw Tamesd...76 G4
Audlem Ches E...64 C3
Audley Staffs...64 E2
Audley End Essex...45 P4
Audley End Essex...46 C10
Audley End Suffk...58 C10
Audley End House & Gardens Essex...45 P4
Audmore Staffs...64 F8
Audnam Dudley...52 G3
Aughertree Cumb...97 Q10
Aughton E R Yk...86 D7
Aughton Lancs...75 L3
Aughton Lancs...83 M2
Aughton Rothm...78 D6
Aughton Wilts...30 F11
Aughton Park Lancs...75 L2
Auldearn Highld...138 G5
Aulden Herefs...51 M9
Auldgirth D & G...97 J1
Auldhouse S Lans...114 B11
Ault a' chruinn Highld...136 C11
Aultbea Highld...143 M7
Aultgrishin Highld...143 K8
Aultguish Inn Highld...145 J11
Ault Hucknall Derbys...78 D10
Aultmore Moray...140 B5
Aultnagoire Highld...137 N3
Aultnamain Highld...145 P9
Aunby Lincs...67 P9
Aunk Devon...9 K5
Aunsby Lincs...67 P4
Aust S Glos...28 H4
Austendike Lincs...68 E8
Austerfield Donc...78 H5
Austerlands Oldham...76 H3
Austhorpe Leeds...85 M8
Austonley Kirk...77 L3
Austrey Warwks...65 P11
Austwick N York...83 Q1
Authorpe Lincs...80 H7
Authorpe Row Lincs...81 K9
Avebury Wilts...30 C8
Avebury Trusloe Wilts...30 C8
Aveley Thurr...33 Q5
Avening Gloucs...29 P3
Averham Notts...67 J2
Aveton Gifford Devon...5 L7
Aviemore Highld...130 H3
Avington W Berk...31 J9
Avoch Highld...138 C5
Avon Hants...12 B5
Avonbridge Falk...114 G7
Avon Dassett Warwks...54 C10
Avonmouth Bristl...28 G7
Avonwick Devon...5 N6
Awbridge Hants...24 E8
Awkley S Glos...29 J5
Awliscombe Devon...9 L5
Awre Gloucs...41 L10
Awsworth Notts...66 D4
Axborough Worcs...52 F5
Axbridge Somset...21 P3
Axford Hants...25 K5
Axford Wilts...30 F8
Axminster Devon...9 P5
Axmouth Devon...9 P6
Axton Flints...74 F7
Aycliffe Dur...91 M2
Aydon Nthumb...100 C5
Aylburton Gloucs...41 J11
Ayle Nthumb...99 K8
Aylesbeare Devon...9 K6
Aylesbury Bucks...44 B8
Aylesby NE Lin...80 E2
Aylesford Kent...34 C10
Aylesham Kent...35 M11
Aylestone C Leic...66 F12
Aylestone Park C Leic...66 F12
Aylmerton Norfk...71 J4
Aylsham Norfk...71 J6
Aylton Herefs...41 K4
Aylworth Gloucs...42 D7
Aymestrey Herefs...51 M7
Aynho Nhants...43 L5
Ayot Green Herts...45 J8
Ayot St Lawrence Herts...44 H8
Ayot St Peter Herts...45 J8
Ayr S Ayrs...104 F6
Aysgarth N York...90 H9
Ayshford Devon...20 G10
Ayside Cumb...89 K10
Ayston Rutlnd...67 L12
Aythorpe Roding Essex...45 Q8
Ayton Border...117 K9
Azerley N York...91 L11

B

Babbacombe Torbay...5 Q4
Babbington Notts...66 E3
Babbinswood Shrops...63 K6
Babbs Green Herts...45 M8
Babcary Somset...22 D7
Babel Carmth...39 M4
Babel Green Suffk...57 P11
Babell Flints...74 G9
Babeny Devon...8 C9

164 Bablock Hythe – Bickington

Bablock Hythe Oxon 43 J11
Babraham Cambs 57 K10
Babworth Notts 78 H7
Bachau IoA 72 G7
Bache Shrops 51 M4
Bacheldre Powys 50 H2
Bachelor's Bump E Susx 16 E8
Backaland Ork 147 d3
Backbarrow Cumb 89 K10
Backe Carmth 37 P7
Backfolds Abers 141 N5
Backford Ches W 75 L9
Backford Cross Ches W 75 L9
Backies Highld 146 E5
Back of Keppoch Highld 127 M7
Back o' th' Brook Staffs 65 K2
Back Street Suffk 57 P9
Backwell N Som 28 G8
Backworth N Tyne 100 H4
Bacon's End Solhll 53 M3
Baconsthorpe Norfk 70 H5
Bacton Herefs 40 E5
Bacton Norfk 71 L5
Bacton Suffk 58 F7
Bacton Green Suffk 58 F7
Bacup Lancs 84 C10
Badachro Highld 143 L10
Badanloch Highld 150 E10
Badbury Swindn 30 E6
Badby Nhants 54 F9
Badcall Highld 148 F5
Badcaul Highld 144 C7
Baddeley Edge C Stke 64 G2
Baddeley Green C Stke 64 G2
Baddesley Clinton Warwks 53 N6
Baddesley Ensor Warwks 53 P1
Baddidarrach Highld 148 C12
Baddinsgill Border 115 L10
Badenscoth Abers 140 H8
Badentarbet Highld 144 C3
Badenyon Abers 139 Q12
Badersfield Norfk 71 K7
Badgall Cnwll 7 J7
Badgeney Cambs 56 H1
Badger Shrops 64 E12
Badger's Cross Cnwll 2 D8
Badgers Mount Kent 33 P10
Badgeworth Gloucs 41 P8
Badgworth Somset 21 N3
Badharlick Cnwll 7 K7
Badicaul Highld 135 N10
Badingham Suffk 59 L7
Badlesmere Kent 34 H11
Badlieu Border 106 D6
Badlipster Highld 151 N7
Badluarach Highld 144 B6
Badninish Highld 146 D6
Badrallach Highld 144 D7
Badsey Worcs 42 C3
Badshot Lea Surrey 14 B1
Badsworth Wakefd 85 P12
Badwell Ash Suffk 58 E7
Badwell Green Suffk 58 E7
Bagber Dorset 22 G10
Bagby N York 91 Q10
Bag Enderby Lincs 80 G9
Bagendon Gloucs 42 B10
Bagginswood Shrops 52 C4
Baggrow Cumb 97 N10
Bàgh a' Chaisteil W Isls 152 b13
Bagham Kent 35 J11
Bagillt Flints 74 H8
Baginton Warwks 53 Q6
Baglan Neath 26 H4
Bagley Leeds 85 K8
Bagley Shrops 63 L7
Bagley Somset 21 P4
Bagmore Hants 25 L4
Bagnall Staffs 64 H2
Bagnor W Berk 31 K8
Bagshot Surrey 32 C9
Bagshot Wilts 30 G9
Bagstone S Glos 29 L5
Bagthorpe Notts 66 D2
Bagworth Leics 66 D10
Bagwyllydiart Herefs 40 F6
Baildon C Brad 84 H7
Baildon Green C Brad 84 H7
Baile Ailein W Isls 152 f4
Baile a' Mhanaich W Isls 152 c9
Baile Mòr Ag & B 119 J8
Bailey Green Hants 25 L8
Baileyhead Cumb 98 G2
Bailiff Bridge Calder 84 H10
Baillieston C Glas 114 C8
Bailrigg Lancs 83 L4
Bainbridge N York 90 F8
Bainshole Abers 140 F9
Bainton C Pete 68 B11
Bainton E R Yk 86 H5
Bainton Oxon 43 M6
Baintown Fife 124 G12
Bairnkine Border 107 Q6
Baker's End Herts 45 M8
Baker Street Thurr 34 B6
Bakewell Derbys 77 N10
Bala Gwynd 62 C5
Balallan W Isls 152 f4
Balbeg Highld 137 M9
Balbeggie P & K 124 D7
Balblair Highld 137 N7
Balblair Highld 138 C3
Balby Donc 78 F3
Balcary D & G 96 G8
Balchraggan Highld 137 P7
Balchrick Highld 148 E5
Balcombe W Susx 15 K5
Balcombe Lane W Susx 15 K4
Balcomie Links Fife 125 M11
Baldersby N York 91 N11
Baldersby St James N York 91 N11
Balderstone Lancs 83 P8
Balderstone Rochdl 76 G2
Balderton Notts 67 K2
Baldhu Cnwll 3 J6
Baldinnie Fife 124 H10
Baldinnies P & K 123 P9
Baldock Herts 45 J5
Baldock Services Herts 45 J4
Baldovie C Dund 125 J6
Baldrine IoM 102 f5
Baldslow E Susx 16 E8
Baldwin IoM 102 d5
Baldwinholme Cumb 98 D8
Baldwin's Gate Staffs 64 E4
Baldwin's Hill W Susx 15 M3
Bale Norfk 70 E5
Baledgarno P & K 124 F7
Balemartine Ag & B 118 D4
Balerno C Edin 115 L8
Balfarg Fife 124 F12
Balfield Angus 132 E10
Balfour Ork 147 c4
Balfron Stirlg 113 Q3
Balgaveny Abers 140 G7
Balgonar Fife 115 J3
Balgowan D & G 94 G9
Balgowan Highld 130 B5
Balgown Highld 134 G2
Balgracie D & G 94 E6
Balgray S Lans 106 A5
Balham Gt Lon 33 K7
Balhary P & K 124 F3
Balholmie P & K 124 C5
Baligill Highld 150 F3
Balintore Angus 124 F1
Balintore Highld 146 F10
Balintraid Highld 146 D11
Balivanich W Isls 152 c9
Balk N York 91 Q10
Balkeerie Angus 124 G4
Balkholme E R Yk 86 E9
Ballabeg IoM 102 c7
Ballachulish Highld 121 K1
Ballafesson IoM 102 b7
Ballajora IoM 102 f4
Ballakilpheric IoM 102 b6
Ballamodha IoM 102 c6
Ballantrae S Ayrs 94 F2
Ballards Gore Essex 34 F4
Ballards Green Warwks 53 P2
Ballasalla IoM 102 c7
Ballater Abers 132 B5
Ballaugh IoM 102 d3
Ballchraggan Highld 146 D10
Ballencrieff E Loth 116 C6
Ballevullin Ag & B 118 C3
Ball Green C Stke 64 G2
Ball Haye Green Staffs 77 J12
Ball Hill Hants 31 J9
Ballianlay Ag & B 112 F9
Ballidon Derbys 65 M1
Balliekine N Ayrs 103 M2
Balliemore Ag & B 112 G1
Balligmorrie S Ayrs 104 D11
Ballimore Stirlg 122 F9
Ballindalloch Moray 139 M8
Ballindean P & K 124 E7
Ballingdon Suffk 46 F3
Ballinger Common Bucks 44 C11
Ballingham Herefs 41 J5
Ballingry Fife 115 M2
Ballinluig P & K 123 N2
Ballinshoe Angus 124 H2
Ballintuim P & K 124 C2
Balloch Highld 138 D6
Balloch N Lans 114 D6
Balloch P & K 123 L9
Balloch S Ayrs 104 F10
Balloch W Duns 113 M5
Balls Cross W Susx 14 E5
Balls Green E Susx 15 P3
Ball's Green Gloucs 29 P2
Ballygown Ag & B 119 M4
Ballygrant Ag & B 111 J8
Ballyhaugh Ag & B 118 G1
Balmacara Highld 135 P10
Balmaclellan D & G 96 D2
Balmae D & G 96 E9
Balmaha Stirlg 113 N3
Balmalcolm Fife 124 G11
Balmangan D & G 96 D9
Balmedie Abers 141 M12
Balmer Heath Shrops 63 M5
Balmerino Fife 124 G8
Balmerlawn Hants 12 E4
Balmichael N Ayrs 103 N3
Balmore E Duns 114 A6
Balmuchy Highld 146 F9
Balmule Fife 115 M4
Balmullo Fife 124 H8
Balnacoil Highld 146 E3
Balnacra Highld 136 D6
Balnacroft Abers 131 P5
Balnafoich Highld 138 C9
Balnaguard P & K 123 N2
Balnahard Ag & B 119 M6
Balnain Highld 137 M9
Balnakeil Highld 149 J3
Balne N York 86 B11
Balquharn P & K 123 P5
Balquhidder Stirlg 122 F8
Balsall Common Solhll 53 N5
Balsall Heath Birm 53 K4
Balsall Street Solhll 53 N5
Balscote Oxon 42 H3
Balsham Cambs 57 L10
Baltasound Shet 147 k2
Balterley Staffs 64 E2
Balterley Green Staffs 64 E2
Balterley Heath Staffs 64 D2
Baltersan D & G 95 M6
Balthangie Abers 141 K5
Baltonsborough Somset 22 C6
Balvicar Ag & B 120 E9
Balvraid Highld 127 Q1
Balvraid Highld 138 F9
Balwest Cnwll 2 F8
Bamber Bridge Lancs 83 M10
Bamber's Green Essex 45 Q7
Bamburgh Nthumb 109 K3
Bamburgh Castle Nthumb 109 K3
Bamford Derbys 77 N7
Bamford Rochdl 76 F1
Bampton Cumb 89 N3
Bampton Devon 20 E9
Bampton Oxon 42 G11
Bampton Grange Cumb 89 N3
Banavie Highld 128 F9
Banbury Oxon 43 K4
Bancffosfelen Carmth 38 D9
Banchory Abers 132 H5
Banchory-Devenick Abers 133 L4
Bancycapel Carmth 38 C8
Bancyfelin Carmth 37 Q7
Banc-y-ffordd Carmth 38 B4
Bandirran P & K 124 D7
Bandrake Head Cumb 89 J9
Banff Abers 140 G3
Bangor Gwynd 73 K9
Bangor-on-Dee Wrexhm 63 L3
Bangors Cnwll 7 J5
Bangor's Green Lancs 75 L2
Bangrove Suffk 58 D6
Banham Norfk 58 F3
Bank Hants 12 D3
Bankend D & G 97 L4
Bankfoot P & K 124 B6
Bankglen E Ayrs 105 L7
Bank Ground Cumb 89 J7
Bankhead C Aber 133 L2
Bankhead S Lans 114 H12
Bank Newton N York 84 D4
Banknock Falk 114 E5
Banks Cumb 98 H5
Banks Lancs 83 J11
Banks Green Worcs 53 J7
Bankshill D & G 97 P2
Bank Street Worcs 52 B8
Bank Top Calder 84 G10
Bank Top Lancs 75 N2
Banningham Norfk 71 J6
Bannister Green Essex 46 C7
Bannockburn Stirlg 114 E3
Banstead Surrey 33 J10
Bantham Devon 5 L8
Banton N Lans 114 D5
Banwell N Som 28 E10
Bapchild Kent 34 G9
Bapton Wilts 23 L6
Barabhas W Isls 152 g2
Barassie S Ayrs 104 F3
Barbaraville Highld 146 D10
Barber Booth Derbys 77 L7
Barber Green Cumb 89 L10
Barbieston S Ayrs 104 H6
Barbon Cumb 89 Q10
Barbridge Ches E 75 Q12
Barbrook Devon 19 N4
Barby Nhants 54 E6
Barcaldine Ag & B 120 H4
Barcheston Warwks 42 F4
Barclose Cumb 98 F6
Barcombe E Susx 15 M8
Barcombe Cross E Susx 15 M7
Barcroft C Brad 84 F7
Barden N York 91 J8
Barden Park Kent 15 Q2
Bardfield End Green Essex 46 A5
Bardfield Saling Essex 46 B6
Bardney Lincs 80 C10
Bardon Leics 66 D9
Bardon Mill Nthumb 99 M5
Bardowie E Duns 113 R6
Bardown E Susx 16 B5
Bardrainney Inver 113 L6
Bardsea Cumb 89 J11
Bardsey Leeds 85 M6
Bardsey Island Gwynd 60 A8
Bardsley Oldham 76 H3
Bardwell Suffk 58 D6
Bare Lancs 83 K2
Bareppa Cnwll 3 J8
Barfad D & G 95 L5
Barford Norfk 70 G10
Barford Warwks 53 P8
Barford St John Oxon 43 J5
Barford St Martin Wilts 23 N7
Barford St Michael Oxon 43 J5
Barfrestone Kent 35 N12
Bargate Derbys 66 B3
Bargeddie N Lans 114 C8
Bargoed Caerph 27 Q2
Bargrennan D & G 95 L3
Barham Cambs 56 C5
Barham Kent 35 M12
Barham Suffk 58 H10
Bar Hill Cambs 56 G8
Barholm Lincs 68 B10
Barkby Leics 66 G10
Barkby Thorpe Leics 66 G10
Barkers Green Shrops 63 N6
Barkestone-le-Vale Leics 67 K5
Barkham Wokham 31 Q9
Barking Gt Lon 33 N5
Barking Suffk 58 G10
Barkingside Gt Lon 33 N4
Barking Tye Suffk 58 F10
Barkisland Calder 84 G11
Barkla Shop Cnwll 3 J4
Barkston Lincs 67 M4
Barkston Ash N York 85 P8
Barkway Herts 45 M4
Barlanark C Glas 114 B8
Barlaston Staffs 64 G4
Barlavington W Susx 14 D7
Barlborough Derbys 78 D8
Barlby N York 86 B8
Barlestone Leics 66 C11
Barley Herts 45 M4
Barley Lancs 84 B7
Barleycroft End Herts 45 N6
Barley Hole Rothm 78 B4
Barleythorpe Rutlnd 67 L10
Barling Essex 34 G4
Barlings Lincs 79 Q8
Barlochan D & G 96 G7
Barlow Derbys 77 Q9
Barlow Gatesd 100 F6
Barlow N York 86 B9
Barmby Moor E R Yk 86 E5
Barmby on the Marsh E R Yk 86 C9
Barmer Norfk 69 Q5
Barming Heath Kent 34 C11
Barmollack Ag & B 103 L1
Barmouth Gwynd 61 K9
Barmpton Darltn 91 N3
Barmston E R Yk 87 M3
Barnaby Green Suffk 59 P5
Barnacarry Ag & B 112 E2
Barnack C Pete 67 Q11
Barnacle Warwks 54 C4
Barnard Castle Dur 90 H3
Barnard Gate Oxon 43 J9
Barnardiston Suffk 57 N11
Barnbarroch D & G 96 G7
Barnburgh Donc 78 D3
Barnby Suffk 59 P3
Barnby Dun Donc 78 G2
Barnby in the Willows Notts 67 L2
Barnby Moor Notts 78 H7
Barncorkrie D & G 94 F11
Barnehurst Gt Lon 33 P7
Barnes Gt Lon 33 J7
Barnes Street Kent 16 B1
Barnet Gt Lon 33 J3
Barnetby le Wold N Linc 79 Q2
Barnet Gate Gt Lon 33 J3
Barney Norfk 70 E6
Barnham Suffk 58 C5
Barnham W Susx 14 D10
Barnham Broom Norfk 70 G10
Barnhead Angus 125 N1
Barnhill C Dund 125 J6
Barnhill Ches W 63 N1
Barnhill Moray 139 L4
Barnhills D & G 94 E4
Barningham Dur 90 H5
Barningham Suffk 58 E5
Barnoldby le Beck NE Lin 80 E3
Barnoldswick Lancs 84 C6
Barnsdale Bar Donc 78 E1
Barns Green W Susx 14 G5
Barnsley Barns 77 Q2
Barnsley Gloucs 42 C10
Barnsole Kent 35 N11
Barnstaple Devon 19 L7
Barnston Essex 46 B8
Barnston Wirral 75 J7
Barnstone Notts 67 J5
Barnt Green Worcs 53 J6
Barnton C Edin 115 M6
Barnton Ches W 76 B8
Barnwell All Saints Nhants 55 P4
Barnwell St Andrew Nhants 55 P4
Barnwood Gloucs 41 P8
Baron's Cross Herefs 51 N9
Baronwood Cumb 98 G9
Barr S Ayrs 104 E11
Barra W Isls 152 b13
Barra Airport W Isls 152 b12
Barrachan D & G 95 L8
Barraigh W Isls 152 b13
Barrananaoil Ag & B 120 F11
Barrapoll Ag & B 118 C4
Barras Cumb 90 D4
Barrasford Nthumb 99 P4
Barregarrow IoM 102 d4
Barrets Green Ches E 75 Q11
Barrhead E Rens 113 P9
Barrhill S Ayrs 95 J2
Barrington Cambs 56 G10
Barrington Somset 21 N9
Barripper Cnwll 2 G7
Barrmill N Ayrs 113 M11
Barrock Highld 151 N2
Barrow Gloucs 41 P7
Barrow Lancs 83 Q7
Barrow Rutlnd 67 M9
Barrow Shrops 64 C12
Barrow Somset 22 G7
Barrow Suffk 57 P8
Barroway Drove Norfk 69 L11
Barrow Bridge Bolton 76 C1
Barrow Burn Nthumb 108 D7
Barrowby Lincs 67 L5
Barrow Common N Som 28 H9
Barrowden Rutlnd 67 N12
Barrowford Lancs 84 C7
Barrow Gurney N Som 28 H8
Barrow Haven N Linc 87 K10
Barrow Hill Derbys 78 C8
Barrow-in-Furness Cumb 82 F1
Barrow Island Cumb 82 F2
Barrow Nook Lancs 75 M3
Barrow's Green Ches E 76 C12
Barrows Green Cumb 89 N9
Barrow Street Wilts 23 J7
Barrow-upon-Humber N Linc 87 K11
Barrow upon Soar Leics 66 F8
Barrow upon Trent Derbys 66 B6
Barrow Vale BaNES 29 K10
Barry Angus 125 K6
Barry V Glam 27 Q8
Barry Island V Glam 27 Q9
Barsby Leics 66 H10
Barsham Suffk 59 M3
Barston Solhll 53 N5
Bartestree Herefs 40 H4
Barthol Chapel Abers 141 K9
Bartholomew Green Essex 46 C7
Barthomley Ches E 64 E2
Bartley Hants 24 E10
Bartley Green Birm 53 J4
Bartlow Cambs 45 Q3
Barton Cambs 56 H9
Barton Ches W 63 M1
Barton Gloucs 42 C6
Barton Herefs 51 J9
Barton Lancs 75 K2
Barton Lancs 83 L8
Barton N York 91 L5
Barton Oxon 43 L10
Barton Torbay 5 Q3
Barton Warwks 53 L10
Barton Bendish Norfk 69 N11
Barton End Gloucs 29 N3
Barton Green Staffs 65 M8
Barton Hartshorn Bucks 43 N5
Barton Hill N York 86 D2
Barton in Fabis Notts 66 E6
Barton in the Beans Leics 66 C11
Barton-le-Clay C Beds 44 F5
Barton-le-Street N York 92 E12
Barton-le-Willows N York 86 D3
Barton Mills Suffk 57 N6
Barton-on-Sea Hants 12 D6
Barton-on-the-Heath Warwks 42 F5
Barton Park Services N York 91 L5
Barton St David Somset 22 C7
Barton Seagrave Nhants 55 M5
Barton Stacey Hants 24 G5
Barton Town Devon 19 N5
Barton Turf Norfk 71 M7
Barton-under-Needwood Staffs 65 M8
Barton-upon-Humber N Linc 87 J11
Barton upon Irwell Salfd 76 E4
Barton Waterside N Linc 87 J10
Barugh Barns 77 P2
Barugh Green Barns 77 P2
Barvas W Isls 152 g2
Barway Cambs 57 K5
Barwell Leics 54 D1
Barwick Devon 8 B3
Barwick Herts 45 M8
Barwick Somset 22 D10
Barwick in Elmet Leeds 85 N7
Baschurch Shrops 63 M8
Bascote Warwks 54 C8
Bascote Heath Warwks 54 C8
Base Green Suffk 58 F8
Basford Green Staffs 65 J2
Bashall Eaves Lancs 83 Q6
Bashall Town Lancs 83 Q7
Bashley Hants 12 D5
Basildon Essex 34 C4
Basingstoke Hants 25 L3
Baslow Derbys 77 N9
Bason Bridge Somset 21 M4
Bassaleg Newpt 28 C5
Bassendean Border 116 E12
Bassenthwaite Cumb 97 P11
Bassett C Sotn 24 G10
Bassingbourn-cum-Kneesworth Cambs 45 L3
Bassingfield Notts 66 G5
Bassingham Lincs 79 M11
Bassingthorpe Lincs 67 N6
Bassus Green Herts 45 K6
Basted Kent 33 R11
Baston Lincs 68 C9
Bastwick Norfk 71 N8
Batch Somset 21 M2
Batchworth Herts 32 F3
Batchworth Heath Herts 32 F4
Batcombe Dorset 10 F4
Batcombe Somset 22 F5
Bate Heath Ches E 76 C8
Batford Herts 44 G8
Bath BaNES 29 M9
Bath BaNES 29 M9
Bathampton BaNES 29 M9
Bathealton Somset 20 H8
Batheaston BaNES 29 M9
Bathford BaNES 29 M9
Bathgate W Loth 114 H7
Bathley Notts 79 K11
Bathpool Cnwll 7 K9
Bathpool Somset 21 L8
Bath Side Essex 47 N5
Bathville W Loth 114 G8
Bathway Somset 22 D3
Batley Kirk 85 K10
Batsford Gloucs 42 E5
Batson Devon 5 M9
Battersby N York 92 C5
Battersea Gt Lon 33 K7
Battisborough Cross Devon 5 J7
Battisford Suffk 58 F9
Battisford Tye Suffk 58 F10
Battle E Susx 16 D7
Battle Powys 39 N5
Battleborough Somset 21 M3
Battledown Gloucs 41 Q7
Battledykes Angus 125 J2
Battlefield Shrops 63 N9
Battlesbridge Essex 34 D3
Battlesden C Beds 44 D6
Battleton Somset 20 E8
Battlies Green Suffk 58 D8
Battram Leics 66 C10
Battramsley Cross Hants 12 E5
Batt's Corner Hants 25 P5
Baughton Worcs 41 P3
Baughurst Hants 31 M10
Baulds Abers 132 F5
Baulking Oxon 30 G4
Baumber Lincs 80 D9
Baunton Gloucs 42 B10
Baveney Wood Shrops 52 C5
Baverstock Wilts 23 M7
Bawburgh Norfk 70 H10
Bawdeswell Norfk 70 F8
Bawdrip Somset 21 M5
Bawdsey Suffk 47 P4
Bawsey Norfk 69 N8
Bawtry Donc 78 G5
Baxenden Lancs 84 B10
Baxterley Warwks 53 P1
Baxter's Green Suffk 57 P9
Bay Highld 134 E5
Bayble W Isls 152 h3
Baybridge Hants 25 J8
Baybridge Nthumb 99 Q8
Baycliff Cumb 89 J12
Baydon Wilts 30 G7
Bayford Herts 45 K10
Bayford Somset 22 G7
Bayhead W Isls 152 b8
Bay Horse Lancs 83 L5
Bayley's Hill Kent 33 P12
Baylham Suffk 58 G10
Baynard's Green Oxon 43 L6
Baysdale Abbey N York 92 C5
Baysham Herefs 40 H6
Bayston Hill Shrops 63 N10
Baythorne End Essex 46 C3
Bayton Worcs 52 C6
Bayton Common Worcs 52 D6
Bayworth Oxon 31 K2
Beach S Glos 29 L8
Beachampton Bucks 43 Q4
Beachamwell Norfk 69 P11
Beachley Gloucs 28 H4
Beachy Head E Susx 15 Q11
Beacon Devon 9 M4
Beacon End Essex 46 G7
Beacon Hill Kent 16 E4
Beacon Hill Notts 67 K1
Beacon Hill Surrey 14 C3
Beacon's Bottom Bucks 31 R3
Beaconsfield Bucks 32 D4
Beaconsfield Services Bucks 32 D5
Beadlam N York 92 D10
Beadlow C Beds 44 G4
Beadnell Nthumb 109 L4
Beaford Devon 19 L10
Beal N York 85 Q10
Beal Nthumb 108 H1
Bealbury Cnwll 4 E3
Bealsmill Cnwll 7 L9
Beam Hill Staffs 65 N7
Beamhurst Staffs 65 K5
Beaminster Dorset 10 D4
Beamish Dur 100 G7
Beamish Open Air Museum Dur 100 G7
Beamsley N York 84 G5
Bean Kent 33 Q8
Beanacre Wilts 29 P9
Beanley Nthumb 108 H6
Beardon Devon 7 P8
Beardwood Bl w D 83 P9
Beare Devon 9 J4
Beare Green Surrey 14 H2
Bearley Warwks 53 M8
Bearley Cross Warwks 53 M8
Bearpark Dur 100 G9
Bearsden E Duns 113 Q7
Bearsted Kent 34 E11
Bearstone Shrops 64 D4
Bearwood BCP 11 P5
Bearwood Birm 53 J3
Bearwood Herefs 51 L9
Beattock D & G 106 E9
Beauchamp Roding Essex 45 Q9
Beauchief Sheff 77 Q7
Beaudesert Warwks 53 M7
Beaufort Blae G 40 A9
Beaulieu Essex 46 C9
Beaulieu Hants 12 F4
Beaulieu Road Station Hants 12 F3
Beauly Highld 137 P6
Beaumaris IoA 73 K8
Beaumaris Castle IoA 73 K8
Beaumont Cumb 98 D6
Beaumont Essex 47 L7
Beaumont Jersey 13 b2
Beaumont Hill Darltn 91 M3
Beaumont Leys C Leic 66 F10
Beausale Warwks 53 N6
Beauworth Hants 25 K8
Beaworthy Devon 7 N5
Beazley End Essex 46 C6
Bebington Wirral 75 K7
Bebside Nthumb 100 H2
Beccles Suffk 59 N3
Becconsall Lancs 83 K10
Beckbury Shrops 64 E11
Beckenham Gt Lon 33 L8
Beckermet Cumb 88 D5
Beckett End Norfk 69 P12
Beckfoot Cumb 88 G6
Beckfoot Cumb 88 G9
Beck Foot Cumb 89 Q7
Beckfoot Cumb 97 M8
Beckford Worcs 41 R4
Beckhampton Wilts 30 C8
Beck Hole N York 92 G6
Beckingham Lincs 67 L1
Beckingham Notts 79 K6
Beckington Somset 22 H3
Beckjay Shrops 51 L5
Beckley E Susx 16 E6
Beckley Hants 12 C5
Beckley Oxon 43 M9
Beck Row Suffk 57 N5
Becks C Brad 84 F6
Beck Side Cumb 88 H10
Beck Side Cumb 89 K10
Beckton Gt Lon 33 M6
Beckwithshaw N York 85 K4
Becontree Gt Lon 33 N5
Becquet Vincent Jersey 13 c2
Bedale N York 91 M9
Bedburn Dur 100 E12
Bedchester Dorset 23 J10
Beddau Rhondd 27 P5
Beddgelert Gwynd 61 K3
Beddingham E Susx 15 N9
Beddington Gt Lon 33 K9
Beddington Corner Gt Lon 33 K9
Bedfield Suffk 59 J7
Bedfield Little Green Suffk 59 J7
Bedford Bed 55 P10
Bedgebury Cross Kent 16 C4
Bedgrove Bucks 44 B9
Bedham W Susx 14 E6
Bedhampton Hants 13 M3
Bedingfield Suffk 58 H7
Bedingfield Green Suffk 59 J7
Bedlam N York 85 K3
Bedlington Nthumb 100 H2
Bedlinog Myr Td 39 Q11
Bedminster Bristl 29 J8
Bedminster Down Bristl 29 J8
Bedmond Herts 44 G11
Bednall Staffs 64 H8
Bedrule Border 107 P6
Bedstone Shrops 51 L5
Bedwas Caerph 28 A4
Bedwellty Caerph 27 R2
Bedworth Warwks 54 B3
Bedworth Woodlands Warwks 53 Q3
Beeby Leics 66 H10
Beech Hants 25 M5
Beech Staffs 64 F4
Beech Hill W Berk 31 P9
Beechingstoke Wilts 30 C10
Beedon W Berk 31 K7
Beedon Hill W Berk 31 K7
Beeford E R Yk 87 L4
Beeley Derbys 77 P10
Beelsby NE Lin 80 D3
Beenham W Berk 31 M8
Beenham's Heath W & M 32 B7
Beeny Cnwll 6 G6
Beer Devon 9 N7
Beer Somset 21 N7
Beercrocombe Somset 21 M9
Beer Hackett Dorset 10 F2
Beesands Devon 5 N8
Beesby Lincs 81 J7
Beeson Devon 5 N8
Beeston C Beds 56 D11
Beeston Ches W 75 P12
Beeston Leeds 85 L9
Beeston Norfk 70 D9
Beeston Notts 66 E5
Beeston Regis Norfk 70 H4
Beeswing D & G 96 H4
Beetham Cumb 89 M11
Beetham Somset 21 L11
Beetley Norfk 70 E8
Began Cardif 28 B6
Begbroke Oxon 43 K9
Begdale Cambs 69 J11
Begelly Pembks 37 M9
Beggarington Hill Leeds 85 L10
Beggar's Bush Powys 51 J8
Beguildy Powys 50 G5
Beighton Norfk 71 M10
Beighton Sheff 78 D7
Beinn Na Faoghla W Isls 152 c9
Beith N Ayrs 113 L10
Bekesbourne Kent 35 M11
Bekesbourne Hill Kent 35 L11
Belaugh Norfk 71 K8
Belbroughton Worcs 52 G5
Belchalwell Dorset 11 J3
Belchalwell Street Dorset 11 J3
Belchamp Otten Essex 46 E3
Belchamp St Paul Essex 46 D3
Belchamp Walter Essex 46 E3
Belchford Lincs 80 F8
Belford Nthumb 109 J3
Belgrave C Leic 66 F10
Belhaven E Loth 116 F5
Belhelvie Abers 141 M12
Belhinnie Abers 140 C10
Bellabeg Abers 131 Q2
Bellamore Herefs 40 E4
Bellanoch Ag & B 112 B3
Bellasize E R Yk 86 F9
Bellaty Angus 124 E1
Bell Bar Herts 45 J10
Bell Busk N York 84 D4
Belleau Lincs 80 H8
Bell End Worcs 52 H5
Bellerby N York 91 J8
Bellever Devon 8 C9
Belle Vue Cumb 98 D7
Belle Vue Wakefd 85 M11
Bellfield S Lans 105 Q3
Bellfields Surrey 32 E12
Bell Heath Worcs 52 H5
Bell Hill Hants 25 M8
Bellingdon Bucks 44 D10
Bellingham Nthumb 99 N2
Belloch Ag & B 103 J2
Bellochantuy Ag & B 103 J3
Bell o' th' Hill Ches W 63 N3
Bellows Cross Dorset 23 N10
Bells Cross Suffk 58 H10
Bellshill N Lans 114 D9
Bellshill Nthumb 109 J4
Bellside N Lans 114 E9
Bellsquarry W Loth 115 J8
Bells Yew Green E Susx 15 R4
Belluton BaNES 29 J9
Belmaduthy Highld 138 B4
Belmesthorpe Rutlnd 67 P10
Belmont Bl w D 83 P12
Belmont Gt Lon 33 J10
Belmont S Ayrs 104 F6
Belmont Shet 147 j3
Belnacraig Abers 132 B1
Belowda Cnwll 3 N2
Belper Derbys 66 B3
Belper Lane End Derbys 65 Q2
Belph Derbys 78 E8
Belsay Nthumb 100 E2
Belses Border 107 P5
Belsford Devon 5 M5
Belsize Herts 32 E2
Belstead Suffk 47 K3
Belstone Devon 8 B6
Belthorn Bl w D 83 Q10
Beltinge Kent 35 M9
Beltingham Nthumb 99 M5
Beltoft N Linc 79 K2
Belton Leics 66 D8
Belton Lincs 67 M4
Belton N Linc 79 K2
Belton Norfk 71 P11
Belton House Lincs 67 M4
Belton in Rutland Rutlnd 67 K12
Beltring Kent 16 B1
Belvedere Gt Lon 33 P6
Belvoir Leics 67 K5
Bembridge IoW 13 L7
Bemerton Wilts 23 P7
Bempton E R Yk 93 P12
Benacre Suffk 59 P4
Benbecula W Isls 152 c9
Benbecula Airport W Isls 152 c9
Benbuie D & G 105 N10
Benderloch Ag & B 120 G5
Benenden Kent 16 E4
Benfieldside Dur 100 E7
Bengate Norfk 71 L7
Bengeo Herts 45 L9
Bengeworth Worcs 42 B3
Benhall Green Suffk 59 M8
Benhall Street Suffk 59 M8
Benholm Abers 133 K10
Beningbrough N York 85 Q4
Benington Herts 45 K7
Benington Lincs 68 H3
Benington Sea End Lincs 68 H3
Benllech IoA 72 H7
Benmore Ag & B 112 H4
Bennacott Cnwll 7 K6
Bennan N Ayrs 103 Q5
Bennet Head Cumb 89 L2
Bennetland E R Yk 86 F9
Bennett End Bucks 31 Q3
Ben Nevis Highld 128 G10
Benniworth Lincs 80 D7
Benover Kent 16 C1
Ben Rhydding C Brad 84 H6
Benslie N Ayrs 104 F1
Benson Oxon 31 N4
Bentfield Green Essex 45 P6
Benthall Shrops 64 C11
Bentham Gloucs 41 P8
Benthoul C Aber 133 J4
Bentlawnt Shrops 63 K12
Bentley Donc 78 F3
Bentley E R Yk 87 J8
Bentley Hants 25 N4
Bentley Suffk 47 K4
Bentley Warwks 53 P2
Bentley Heath Herts 33 J2
Bentley Heath Solhll 53 M5
Benton Devon 19 M6
Bentpath D & G 107 J11
Bentwichen Devon 19 P6
Bentworth Hants 25 L5
Benvie Angus 124 G6
Benville Dorset 10 E4
Benwick Cambs 56 G3
Beoley Worcs 53 K7
Beoraidbeg Highld 127 M5
Bepton W Susx 25 Q9
Berden Essex 45 N6
Berea Pembks 36 F4
Bere Alston Devon 4 G3
Bere Ferrers Devon 4 G4
Berepper Cnwll 2 G10
Bere Regis Dorset 11 K6
Bergh Apton Norfk 71 L12
Berhill Somset 21 P6
Berinsfield Oxon 31 M3
Berkeley Gloucs 29 K2
Berkeley Heath Gloucs 29 L2
Berkeley Road Gloucs 29 L2
Berkhamsted Herts 44 E10
Berkley Somset 22 H3
Berkswell Solhll 53 N5
Bermondsey Gt Lon 33 L6
Bermuda Warwks 54 B3
Bernera Highld 135 P11
Bernisdale Highld 134 G6
Berrick Prior Oxon 31 N3
Berrick Salome Oxon 31 N4
Berriedale Highld 151 K12
Berrier Cumb 98 E12
Berriew Powys 62 G12
Berrington Nthumb 108 G1
Berrington Shrops 63 N10
Berrington Worcs 51 P7
Berrington Green Worcs 51 P7
Berrow Somset 21 L3
Berrow Worcs 41 M5
Berrow Green Worcs 52 D9
Berry Brow Kirk 84 H12
Berry Cross Devon 19 J10
Berry Down Cross Devon 19 L5
Berryfield Wilts 29 P10
Berryfields Bucks 43 R8
Berry Hill Gloucs 40 H9
Berry Hill Pembks 37 L2
Berryhillock Moray 140 D4
Berryhillock Moray 140 D5
Berrynarbor Devon 19 L4
Berry Pomeroy Devon 5 P4
Berry's Green Gt Lon 33 N10
Bersham Wrexhm 63 J2
Bersted W Susx 14 C10
Berthengam Flints 74 F8
Berwick E Susx 15 P9
Berwick Bassett Wilts 30 C7
Berwick Hill Nthumb 100 F3
Berwick St James Wilts 23 N5
Berwick St John Wilts 23 L9
Berwick St Leonard Wilts 23 K7
Berwick Station E Susx 15 P9
Berwick-upon-Tweed Nthumb 117 M10
Bescaby Leics 67 K7
Bescar Lancs 75 L1
Besford Shrops 63 P7
Besford Worcs 41 Q3
Bessacarr Donc 78 G4
Bessels Leigh Oxon 43 K11
Besses o' th' Barn Bury 76 E3
Bessingby E R Yk 87 M2
Bessingham Norfk 70 H5
Bestbeech Hill E Susx 16 A4
Besthorpe Norfk 58 F2
Besthorpe Notts 79 K10
Bestwood Village Notts 66 F3
Beswick E R Yk 87 J5
Betchcott Shrops 51 M1
Betchworth Surrey 33 J12
Bethania Cerdgn 49 K8
Bethania Gwynd 61 K8
Bethel Gwynd 62 D4
Bethel Gwynd 73 J10
Bethel IoA 72 F9
Bethel Powys 62 F8
Bethersden Kent 16 G3
Bethesda Gwynd 73 K10
Bethesda Pembks 37 L7
Bethlehem Carmth 38 G6
Bethnal Green Gt Lon 33 L6
Betley Staffs 64 D2
Betsham Kent 33 R8
Betteshanger Kent 35 P11
Bettiscombe Dorset 10 B5
Bettisfield Wrexhm 63 M5
Betton Shrops 64 C5
Betton Strange Shrops 63 N10
Bettws Brdgnd 27 L5
Bettws Newpt 28 C4
Bettws Cedewain Powys 50 F1
Bettws Ifan Cerdgn 48 E11
Bettws-Newydd Mons 40 E10
Bettyhill Highld 150 C4
Betws Carmth 38 F9
Betws Bledrws Cerdgn 49 K10
Betws Garmon Gwynd 73 J12
Betws Gwerfil Goch Denbgs 62 E3
Betws-y-Coed Conwy 61 N1
Betws-yn-Rhos Conwy 74 B9
Beulah Cerdgn 48 D11
Beulah Powys 50 C10
Bevendean Br & H 15 L9
Bevercotes Notts 78 H9
Beverley E R Yk 87 J7
Beverston Gloucs 29 P3
Bevington Gloucs 29 K3
Bewaldeth Cumb 97 P11
Bewcastle Cumb 98 H3
Bewdley Worcs 52 E5
Bewerley N York 84 H2
Bewholme E R Yk 87 M5
Bewlbridge Kent 16 B4
Bexhill-on-Sea E Susx 16 C9
Bexley Gt Lon 33 P7
Bexleyheath Gt Lon 33 N7
Bexleyhill W Susx 14 C6
Bexon Kent 34 F10
Bexwell Norfk 69 M11
Beyton Suffk 58 D8
Beyton Green Suffk 58 D8
Bhaltos W Isls 152 e3
Bhatarsaigh W Isls 152 b13
Bibstone S Glos 29 L4
Bibury Gloucs 42 D10
Bicester Oxon 43 M7
Bickenhill Solhll 53 M4
Bicker Lincs 68 E5
Bicker Bar Lincs 68 E4
Bicker Gauntlet Lincs 68 D4
Bickershaw Wigan 76 B3
Bickerstaffe Lancs 75 M3
Bickerton Ches E 63 N2
Bickerton Devon 5 N9
Bickerton N York 85 P5
Bickerton Nthumb 108 G9
Bickford Staffs 64 G9
Bickington Devon 8 E10
Bickington Devon 19 K7

Bickleigh Devon 4 H4
Bickleigh Devon 8 H3
Bickleton Devon 19 K7
Bickley Ches W 63 P2
Bickley Gt Lon 33 M8
Bickley N York 93 J8
Bickley Worcs 52 B6
Bickley Moss Ches W 63 P2
Bicknacre Essex 46 D11
Bicknoller Somset 20 H5
Bicknor Kent 34 F10
Bickton Hants 24 H5
Bicton Herefs 51 M8
Bicton Shrops 51 J4
Bicton Shrops 63 M9
Bidborough Kent 15 Q2
Bidden Hants 25 M3
Biddenden Kent 16 E3
Biddenden Green Kent 16 F2
Biddenham Bed 55 P10
Biddestone Wilts 29 P7
Biddisham Somset 21 N3
Biddlesden Bucks 43 N4
Biddlestone Nthumb 108 F8
Biddulph Staffs 76 G12
Biddulph Moor Staffs 76 G12
Bideford Devon 19 J8
Bideford-on-Avon Warwks 53 L10
Bidston Wirral 75 J6
Bielby E R Yk 86 E6
Bieldside C Aber 133 L4
Bierley IoW 12 H9
Bierton Bucks 44 B8
Big Balcraig D & G 95 M9
Bigbury Devon 5 L7
Bigbury-on-Sea Devon 5 K8
Bigby Lincs 79 Q2
Biggar Cumb 82 F12
Biggar S Lans 106 D2
Biggin Derbys 65 N2
Biggin Derbys 77 M11
Biggin N York 85 Q8
Biggin Hill Gt Lon 33 M10
Biggleswade C Beds 44 H3
Bigholms D & G 98 C2
Bighouse Highld 150 F4
Bighton Hants 25 K6
Biglands Cumb 97 Q7
Bignor W Sus 14 D8
Bigrigg Cumb 88 D4
Big Sand Highld 143 K9
Bigton Shet 147 i9
Bilborough C Nott 66 F4
Bilbrook Somset 20 G5
Bilbrook Staffs 64 G11
Bilbrough N York 85 Q6
Bilbster Highld 151 N6
Bildershaw Dur 91 K2
Bildeston Suffk 58 E11
Billacott Cnwll 7 K6
Billericay Essex 34 B3
Billesdon Leics 67 J11
Billesley Warwks 53 L9
Billingborough Lincs 68 C5
Billinge St Hel 75 N4
Billingford Norfk 58 H5
Billingford Norfk 70 F8
Billingham S on T 91 Q2
Billinghay Lincs 68 C1
Billingley Barns 78 D3
Billingshurst W Sus 14 F6
Billingsley Shrops 52 D4
Billington C Beds 44 D7
Billington Lancs 83 Q8
Billington Staffs 64 G8
Billockby Norfk 71 N9
Billy Row Dur 100 F10
Bilsborrow Lancs 83 L7
Bilsby Lincs 81 J8
Bilsham W Sus 14 D10
Bilsington Kent 17 J4
Bilsthorpe Notts 78 G11
Bilsthorpe Moor Notts 78 G11
Bilston Mdloth 115 N8
Bilston Wolves 52 H1
Bilstone Leics 66 B11
Bilting Kent 17 J2
Bilton E R Yk 87 M8
Bilton N York 85 L4
Bilton Nthumb 109 L7
Bilton Warwks 54 D6
Bilton Banks Nthumb 109 K8
Bilton-in-Ainsty N York 85 P5
Binbrook Lincs 80 D5
Binchester Blocks Dur 100 G11
Bincombe Dorset 10 G8
Binegar Somset 22 E3
Bines Green W Sus 14 H7
Binfield Br For 32 B8
Binfield Heath Oxon 31 Q7
Bingfield Nthumb 100 C4
Bingham Notts 66 H4
Bingham's Melcombe Dorset 11 J4
Bingley C Brad 84 G7
Bings Heath Shrops 63 P8
Binham Norfk 70 E4
Binley Covtry 54 C5
Binley Hants 24 G3
Binley Woods Warwks 54 C5
Binnegar Dorset 11 L7
Binniehill Falk 114 F7
Binscombe Surrey 14 D2
Binsey Oxon 43 K10
Binstead IoW 13 K6
Binsted Hants 25 N5
Binsted W Sus 14 D9
Binton Warwks 53 L10
Bintree Norfk 70 F7
Binweston Shrops 63 J11
Birch Essex 46 G7
Birch Rochdl 76 F2
Birchall Staffs 65 J1
Bircham Newton Norfk 69 P5
Bircham Tofts Norfk 69 P6
Birchanger Essex 45 P7
Birchanger Green Services Essex 45 P7
Birch Cross Staffs 65 L6
Birchencliffe Kirk 84 H11
Bircher Herefs 51 N7
Birchfield Birm 53 K2
Birch Green Essex 46 G8
Birch Green Herts 45 K9
Birch Green Worcs 52 F11
Birchgrove Cardif 28 A6
Birchgrove Swans 26 H3
Birchgrove W Sus 15 M5
Birch Heath Ches W 75 P11
Birch Hill Ches W 75 N9
Birchington-on-Sea Kent 35 N8
Birchley Heath Warwks 53 P2
Birchmoor Warwks 65 N11
Birchmoor Green C Beds 44 D5
Birchover Derbys 77 N11
Birch Services Rochdl 76 F2
Birch Vale Derbys 77 J6
Birchwood Lincs 79 N10
Birchwood Somset 21 K10
Birchwood Warrtn 76 C5
Bircotes Notts 78 G5
Birdbrook Essex 46 C4
Birdforth N York 91 R11
Birdham W Sus 13 N5
Birdingbury Warwks 54 C7

Birdlip Gloucs 41 Q9
Birdoswald Cumb 99 J5
Birdsall N York 86 F2
Birds Edge Kirk 77 M2
Birds Green Essex 45 Q10
Birdsgreen Shrops 52 E4
Birdsmoorgate Dorset 10 B4
Bird Street Suffk 58 E10
Birdwell Barns 77 Q3
Birdwood Gloucs 41 G9
Birgham Border 108 C2
Birichin Highld 146 D6
Birkacre Lancs 83 M12
Birkby N York 91 N6
Birkdale Sefton 82 H12
Birkenbog Abers 140 E3
Birkenhead Wirral 75 K6
Birkenhead (Queensway) Tunnel Lpool 75 K6
Birkenhills Abers 140 H7
Birkenshaw Kirk 85 J9
Birkhall Abers 131 Q5
Birkhill Angus 124 G6
Birkhill D & G 106 G3
Birkholme Lincs 67 N7
Birkin N York 85 Q10
Birks Leeds 85 K10
Birkshaw Nthumb 99 L6
Birley Herefs 51 M10
Birley Carr Sheff 77 Q5
Birling Kent 34 B10
Birling Nthumb 109 L8
Birling Gap E Sus 15 Q11
Birlingham Worcs 41 Q3
Birmingham Birm 53 K3
Birmingham Airport Solhll 53 M4
Birnam P & K 123 Q4
Birness Abers 141 N9
Birse Abers 132 E5
Birsemore Abers 132 E5
Birstall Kirk 85 K10
Birstall Leics 66 F10
Birstwith N York 85 K3
Birthorpe Lincs 68 B5
Birtley Gatesd 100 H7
Birtley Herefs 51 L7
Birtley Nthumb 99 N3
Birts Street Worcs 41 M4
Bisbrooke Rutlnd 67 M12
Biscathorpe Lincs 80 E7
Biscovey Cnwll 3 P4
Bisham W & M 32 B5
Bishampton Worcs 53 J10
Bish Mill Devon 19 P8
Bishop Auckland Dur 91 L1
Bishopbridge Lincs 79 P5
Bishopbriggs E Duns 114 A7
Bishop Burton E R Yk 87 J7
Bishop Middleham Dur 101 J12
Bishopmill Moray 139 N3
Bishop Monkton N York 85 L2
Bishop Norton Lincs 79 N5
Bishopsbourne Kent 35 L11
Bishops Cannings Wilts 30 B9
Bishop's Castle Shrops 51 K3
Bishop's Caundle Dorset 22 F10
Bishop's Cleeve Gloucs 41 Q6
Bishop's Frome Herefs 52 C11
Bishops Gate Surrey 32 D8
Bishop's Green Essex 46 A8
Bishop's Green Hants 31 K9
Bishop's Hull Somset 21 K8
Bishop's Itchington Warwks 54 C9
Bishops Lydeard Somset 21 J7
Bishop's Norton Gloucs 41 N7
Bishop's Nympton Devon 19 P8
Bishop's Offley Staffs 64 E6
Bishop's Stortford Herts 45 N7
Bishop's Sutton Hants 25 K7
Bishop's Tachbrook Warwks 54 C9
Bishopsteignton Devon 8 L7
Bishopstoke Hants 24 H9
Bishopston Swans 26 E4
Bishopstone Bucks 44 A9
Bishopstone E Sus 15 N10
Bishopstone Herefs 51 M8
Bishopstone Kent 35 M8
Bishopstone Swindn 30 E5
Bishopstone Wilts 23 N8
Bishopstrow Wilts 23 J6
Bishop Sutton BaNES 29 J10
Bishop's Waltham Hants 25 J9
Bishopswood Somset 21 L10
Bishop's Wood Staffs 64 F12
Bishopsworth Bristl 28 H8
Bishop Thornton N York 85 K2
Bishopthorpe C York 86 B6
Bishopton Darltn 91 N2
Bishopton Rens 113 M7
Bishopton Warwks 53 M9
Bishop Wilton E R Yk 86 E5
Bishton Newpt 28 E5
Bishton Staffs 65 J6
Bisley Gloucs 41 P10
Bisley Surrey 32 D10
Bisley Camp Surrey 32 D10
Bispham Bpool 82 H7
Bispham Green Lancs 75 N1
Bissoe Cnwll 3 J6
Bisterne Hants 12 B4
Bitchet Green Kent 33 Q11
Bitchfield Lincs 67 N6
Bittadon Devon 19 K5
Bittaford Devon 5 J7
Bittering Norfk 70 D8
Bitterley Shrops 51 Q5
Bitterne C Sotn 24 G10
Bitteswell Leics 54 E4
Bitton S Glos 29 K8
Bix Oxon 31 Q6
Bixter Shet 147 i6
Blaby Leics 66 F12
Blackadder Border 117 J10
Blackawton Devon 5 N6
Blackbeck Cumb 88 D5
Blackborough Devon 9 L3
Blackborough End Norfk 69 M9
Black Bourton Oxon 42 G10
Blackboys E Sus 15 N6
Blackbrook Derbys 65 Q3
Blackbrook St Hel 75 P4
Blackbrook Surrey 14 G5
Blackbrook Staffs 64 E4
Blackburn Abers 133 K2
Blackburn Bl w D 83 Q7
Blackburn Rothm 78 C5
Blackburn W Loth 114 H8
Blackburn with Darwen Services Bl w D 83 Q10
Black Callerton N u Ty 100 F5
Black Carr Norfk 58 G2
Black Corner W Sus 15 K3
Blackcraig E Ayrs 105 L2
Black Crofts Ag & B 120 H6
Black Cross Cnwll 3 M2
Blackden Heath Ches E 76 E9
Blackdog Abers 133 M1
Black Dog Devon 8 F3
Blackdown Devon 7 P9
Blackdown Dorset 10 B3
Blackdyke Cumb 97 N8
Blacker Barns 77 Q2

Blacker Hill Barns 78 B3
Blackfen Gt Lon 33 N7
Blackfield Hants 12 G4
Blackford Cumb 98 E6
Blackford P & K 123 N11
Blackford Somset 21 N4
Blackford Somset 22 B8
Blackfordby Leics 65 Q8
Blackgang IoW 12 H9
Blackhall C Edin 115 M6
Blackhall Colliery Dur 101 L11
Blackhall Mill Gatesd 100 E7
Blackhall Rocks Dur 101 L10
Blackham E Sus 15 P3
Blackhaugh Border 107 L2
Blackheath Essex 46 H7
Blackheath Gt Lon 33 M7
Blackheath Sandw 52 H3
Blackheath Suffk 59 N6
Blackheath Surrey 14 E2
Black Heddon Nthumb 100 D3
Blackhill Abers 141 P5
Blackhill Abers 141 P4
Blackhill Dur 100 E7
Blackhill of Clackriach Abers 141 M6
Blackhorse Devon 9 J6
Blackjack Lincs 68 E4
Blackland Wilts 30 B8
Black Lane Ends Lancs 84 D6
Blacklaw D & G 106 D8
Blackley Manch 76 F3
Blacklunans P & K 131 L12
Blackmarstone Herefs 40 G4
Blackmill Brdgnd 27 M5
Blackmoor Hants 25 N7
Blackmoor N Som 28 G10
Blackmoor Gate Devon 19 M5
Blackmore End Essex 46 C5
Blackmore End Herts 44 H8
Black Mountains 40 H5
Blackness Falk 115 J5
Blacknest Hants 25 P5
Blacknest W & M 32 D8
Black Notley Essex 46 D7
Blacko Lancs 84 C7
Black Pill Swans 26 F4
Blackpool Bpool 82 H8
Blackpool Devon 5 P5
Blackpool Devon 8 F10
Blackpool Gate Cumb 98 G3
Blackpool Zoo Bpool 82 H8
Blackridge W Loth 114 G8
Blackrock Cnwll 2 G7
Blackrock Mons 40 B9
Blackrock Bolton 76 C2
Blackshaw D & G 97 L5
Blackshaw Head Calder 84 D9
Blacksmith's Green Suffk 58 H7
Blacksnape Bl w D 83 Q11
Blackstone W Sus 15 J7
Black Street Suffk 59 P3
Black Tar Pembks 37 J8
Blackthorn Oxon 43 N8
Blackthorpe Suffk 58 D8
Blacktoft E R Yk 86 F10
Blacktop C Aber 133 L3
Black Torrington Devon 7 N4
Blackwall Derbys 65 N3
Blackwater Cnwll 3 J5
Blackwater Hants 32 C10
Blackwater IoW 12 H7
Blackwater Somset 21 L10
Blackwaterfoot N Ayrs 103 N4
Blackwell Cumb 98 E7
Blackwell Darltn 91 M4
Blackwell Derbys 77 Q9
Blackwell Derbys 78 D12
Blackwell Warwks 42 J6
Blackwell Worcs 52 H6
Blackwellsend Green Gloucs 41 M6
Blackwood Caerph 28 A3
Blackwood D & G 106 D12
Blackwood S Lans 105 P1
Blackwood Hill Staffs 64 G1
Blacon Ches W 75 L10
Bladbean Kent 17 L1
Bladnoch D & G 95 M7
Bladon Oxon 43 K9
Blaenannerch Cerdgn 48 D11
Blaenau Ffestiniog Gwynd 61 N3
Blaenavon Torfn 40 C10
Blaenavon Industrial Landscape Torfn 40 C10
Blaencwm Rhondd 27 L3
Blaen Dyryn Powys 39 M4
Blaenffos Pembks 37 M3
Blaengarw Brdgnd 27 L4
Blaengeuffordd Cerdgn 49 L4
Blaengwrach Neath 39 K10
Blaengwynfi Neath 27 L3
Blaenllechau Rhondd 27 M4
Blaenpennal Cerdgn 49 K8
Blaenplwyf Cerdgn 49 K5
Blaenporth Cerdgn 48 D11
Blaenrhondda Rhondd 27 M4
Blaenwaun Carmth 37 P5
Blaen-y-coed Carmth 37 Q5
Blaenycwm Blae G 39 Q9
Blaenycwm Cerdgn 49 N5
Blagdon N Som 28 G10
Blagdon Somset 21 K9
Blagdon Torbay 5 P4
Blagdon Hill Somset 21 K10
Blagill Cumb 99 L9
Blaguegate Lancs 75 M2
Blaich Highld 128 E3
Blaina Blae G 40 B10
Blair Atholl P & K 130 F11
Blair Drummond Stirlg 114 D2
Blairgowrie P & K 124 D4
Blairhall Fife 114 H4
Blairingone P & K 114 H2
Blairlogie Stirlg 114 E2
Blairmore Ag & B 113 J5
Blairmore Highld 148 D5
Blair's Ferry Ag & B 112 E5
Blaisdon Gloucs 41 L8
Blakebrook Worcs 52 F5
Blakedown Worcs 52 G5
Blake End Essex 46 C7
Blakelaw Border 108 F3
Blakeley Lane Staffs 64 H3
Blakemere Herefs 40 E3
Blakemere Ches W 75 N9
Blakenall Heath Wsall 65 J5
Blakeney Gloucs 41 K10
Blakeney Norfk 70 F3
Blakenhall Ches E 64 E3
Blakenhall Wolves 52 H4
Blakesley Nhants 54 H9
Blakey IoW 12 B11
Blanchland Nthumb 100 D8
Blandford Camp Dorset 11 M3
Blandford Forum Dorset 11 L3
Blandford St Mary Dorset 11 L3
Blanefield Stirlg 113 Q5
Bland Hill N York 85 J4
Blanerne Border 117 J9
Blankney Lincs 79 Q11

Blankney Lincs 79 Q11
Blantyre S Lans 114 C9
Blàr a' Chaorainn Highld 128 F1
Blarghour Ag & B 121 J10
Blargie Highld 129 Q5
Blarmachfoldach Highld 128 F10
Blashford Hants 12 B3
Blaston Leics 55 K2
Blatherwycke Nhants 55 N2
Blawith Cumb 89 J9
Blawquhairn D & G 96 C2
Blaxhall Suffk 59 M9
Blaxton Donc 78 H4
Blaydon Gatesd 100 F5
Bleadney Somset 22 B4
Bleadon N Som 28 D11
Bleak Street Somset 22 G7
Blean Kent 35 J9
Bleasby Lincs 80 C7
Bleasby Notts 66 H2
Bleasdale Lancs 83 N6
Bleathwood Herefs 51 P6
Blebocraigs Fife 124 H10
Bleddfa Powys 50 H7
Bledington Gloucs 42 F7
Bledlow Bucks 43 Q11
Bledlow Ridge Bucks 31 R3
Bleet Wilts 29 P10
Blegbie E Loth 116 C9
Blencarn Cumb 99 J12
Blencogo Cumb 97 M8
Blendworth Hants 25 M10
Blenheim Palace Oxon 43 J8
Blennerhasset Cumb 97 N10
Bletchingdon Oxon 43 L8
Bletchingley Surrey 33 L12
Bletchley M Keyn 44 B5
Bletchley Shrops 64 C6
Bletchley Park Museum M Keyn 44 B5
Bletherston Pembks 37 L6
Bletsoe Bed 55 P9
Blewbury Oxon 31 L5
Blickling Norfk 70 H6
Blidworth Notts 66 F1
Blidworth Bottoms Notts 66 F1
Blindburn Nthumb 108 C7
Blindcrake Cumb 97 N11
Blindley Heath Surrey 15 L2
Blisland Cnwll 6 G10
Blissford Hants 24 B3
Bliss Gate Worcs 52 D6
Blisworth Nhants 55 J9
Blithbury Staffs 65 K8
Blitterlees Cumb 97 M8
Blockley Gloucs 42 D5
Blofield Norfk 71 L10
Blofield Heath Norfk 71 L9
Blo Norton Norfk 58 F5
Bloomfield Border 107 P5
Blore Staffs 65 L3
Blore Staffs 65 M2
Blounce Hants 25 M4
Blounts Green Staffs 65 K6
Blowick Sefton 83 J12
Bloxham Oxon 43 J4
Bloxholm Lincs 67 Q1
Bloxwich Wsall 65 J3
Bloxworth Dorset 11 L6
Blubberhouses N York 85 J4
Blue Anchor Cnwll 3 M3
Blue Anchor Somset 20 G5
Blue Bell Hill Kent 34 D10
Blue John Cavern Derbys 77 L7
Blundellsands Sefton 75 J4
Blundeston Suffk 59 Q1
Blunham C Beds 56 C10
Blunsdon St Andrew Swindn 30 C6
Bluntington Worcs 52 G6
Bluntisham Cambs 56 G6
Blunts Cnwll 4 H5
Blunts Green Warwks 53 L7
Blurton C Stke 64 G4
Blyborough Lincs 79 N5
Blyford Suffk 59 N5
Blymhill Staffs 64 F9
Blymhill Lawn Staffs 64 F9
Blyth Border 116 B2
Blyth Notts 78 G6
Blyth Bridge Border 115 L12
Blythburgh Suffk 59 N5
Blythe Border 116 D11
Blythe Bridge Staffs 64 H4
Blythe End Warwks 53 M3
Blythe Marsh Staffs 64 H4
Blyth Services Notts 78 G6
Blyton Lincs 79 L5
Boarhills Fife 125 L10
Boarhunt Hants 13 K3
Boarley Kent 34 D10
Boars Green E Sus 15 P4
Boarsgreave Lancs 84 C11
Boarshead E Sus 15 P4
Boar's Head Wigan 75 P2
Boars Hill Oxon 43 K11
Boarstall Bucks 43 N9
Boasley Cross Devon 7 P6
Boath Highld 145 N10
Boat of Garten Highld 138 H12
Bobbing Kent 34 F9
Bobbington Staffs 52 E2
Bobbingworth Essex 45 P10
Bocaddon Cnwll 4 B5
Bocking Essex 46 D7
Bocking Churchstreet Essex 46 D6
Bockleton Worcs 51 P8
Boconnoc Cnwll 4 A4
Boddam Abers 141 Q7
Boddam Shet 147 i9
Boddington Gloucs 41 P6
Bodedern IoA 72 E7
Bodelwyddan Denbgs 74 D9
Bodenham Herefs 51 P10
Bodenham Wilts 23 N8
Bodenham Moor Herefs 51 P10
Bodewryd IoA 72 F5
Bodfari Denbgs 74 F9
Bodffordd IoA 72 F7
Bodham Norfk 70 H4
Bodiam E Sus 16 D6
Bodicote Oxon 43 J4
Bodieve Cnwll 6 E10
Bodinnick Cnwll 3 R4
Bodle Street Green E Sus 16 B8
Bodmin Cnwll 6 F11
Bodmin Moor Cnwll 6 H9
Bodney Norfk 70 B12
Bodorgan IoA 72 E8
Bodsham Kent 17 K2
Boduan Gwynd 60 F5
Bodwen Cnwll 3 N2
Bodymoor Heath Warwks 53 M1
Bogallan Highld 138 B6
Bogbrae Abers 141 P9
Bogend S Ayrs 104 G3
Boggs Holdings E Loth 116 B7
Boghall Mdloth 115 N8
Boghall W Loth 114 H8
Boghead S Lans 105 N2
Bogmoor Moray 139 Q3
Bogmuir Abers 132 G9
Bogniebrae Abers 140 F6
Bognor Regis W Sus 14 D11
Bogroy Highld 138 G11

Bogue D & G 96 D2
Bohetherick Cnwll 4 H4
Bohortha Cnwll 3 L8
Bohuntine Highld 129 J7
Bojewyan Cnwll 2 C7
Bokiddick Cnwll 3 N3
Bolam Dur 91 K2
Bolam Nthumb 100 E2
Bolberry Devon 5 L9
Bold Heath St Hel 75 P6
Boldmere Birm 53 L2
Boldon Colliery S Tyne 101 J5
Boldre Hants 12 F5
Boldron Dur 90 G4
Bole Notts 79 K6
Bolehill Derbys 65 P1
Bolenowe Cnwll 2 G7
Bolham Devon 20 D11
Bolham Water Devon 21 J11
Bolingey Cnwll 2 H4
Bollington Ches E 76 H8
Bollington Cross Ches E 76 H8
Bollow Gloucs 41 M9
Bolney W Sus 15 J6
Bolnhurst Bed 55 P8
Bolnore W Sus 15 L6
Bolshan Angus 125 M4
Bolsover Derbys 78 D9
Bolsterstone Sheff 77 P4
Boltby N York 91 R9
Bolter End Bucks 31 R4
Bolton Bolton 76 D2
Bolton Cumb 89 Q2
Bolton E Loth 116 C7
Bolton E R Yk 86 E5
Bolton Nthumb 109 J7
Bolton Abbey N York 84 G4
Bolton Bridge N York 84 G4
Bolton-by-Bowland Lancs 84 B6
Boltonfellend Cumb 98 F4
Boltongate Cumb 97 P10
Bolton-le-Sands Lancs 83 L2
Bolton Low Houses Cumb 97 P9
Bolton New Houses Cumb 97 Q9
Bolton-on-Swale N York 91 L9
Bolton Percy N York 85 Q7
Bolton Town End Lancs 83 L2
Bolton upon Dearne Barns 78 D3
Bolventor Cnwll 6 H9
Bomarsund Nthumb 100 H1
Bomere Heath Shrops 63 M8
Bonar Bridge Highld 145 Q7
Bonawe Ag & B 121 J6
Bonby N Lincs 87 J12
Boncath Pembks 37 N3
Bonchester Bridge Border 107 P7
Bonchurch IoW 13 K9
Bondleigh Devon 8 D3
Bonds Lancs 83 L6
Bonehill Devon 8 D9
Bonehill Staffs 65 M11
Bo'ness Falk 114 H5
Boney Hay Staffs 65 K9
Bongate Cumb 89 R2
Bonhill W Duns 113 M5
Boningale Shrops 64 F11
Bonjedward Border 107 Q5
Bonkle N Lans 114 F10
Bonnington Angus 125 L5
Bonnington Kent 17 J4
Bonnybank Fife 124 G12
Bonnybridge Falk 114 E5
Bonnykelly Abers 141 L5
Bonnyrigg Mdloth 115 P8
Bonnyton Angus 124 E6
Bonsall Derbys 77 P12
Bonshaw Tower D & G 97 Q5
Bont Mons 40 D9
Bontddu Gwynd 61 L9
Bont-Dolgadfan Powys 62 B12
Bont-goch Cerdgn 49 L3
Bonthorpe Lincs 81 J9
Bontnewydd Cerdgn 49 K8
Bontnewydd Gwynd 72 H11
Bontuchel Denbgs 74 E12
Bonvilston V Glam 27 Q7
Bon-y-maen Swans 26 G3
Boode Devon 19 K6
Booker Bucks 32 B4
Booley Shrops 63 P7
Boon Border 116 E11
Boon Hill Staffs 64 E2
Boorley Green Hants 24 H10
Boosbeck R & C 92 D3
Boose's Green Essex 46 E5
Boot Cumb 88 G6
Booth Calder 84 G4
Boothby Graffoe Lincs 79 N11
Boothby Pagnell Lincs 67 N5
Boothferry E R Yk 86 D10
Booth Green Ches E 76 G7
Boothstown Salfd 76 D4
Boothtown Calder 84 G10
Boothville Nhants 55 K8
Bootle Cumb 88 E8
Bootle Sefton 75 J5
Boots Green Ches E 76 D9
Boot Street Suffk 59 J6
Booze N York 90 H6
Boraston Shrops 51 R6
Bordeaux Guern 12 d1
Borden Kent 34 F9
Borden W Sus 25 P9
Border Cumb 97 N7
Bordon Hants 25 N6
Boreham Essex 46 D9
Boreham Wilts 23 J4
Boreham Street E Sus 16 B8
Borehamwood Herts 32 H3
Boreland D & G 106 F11
Boreraig Highld 134 C5
Borgh W Isls 152 b13
Borgh W Isls 152 g1
Borghastan W Isls 152 e3
Borgie Highld 149 P5
Borgue D & G 96 C7
Borgue Highld 151 L11
Borley Essex 46 E4
Borley Green Essex 46 E4
Borley Green Suffk 58 D8
Borneskitaig Highld 134 F4
Borness D & G 96 C7
Borough Green Kent 33 R11
Boroughbridge N York 85 M3
Borras Head Wrexhm 63 K2
Borrowash Derbys 66 C5
Borrowby N York 91 R10
Borrowby N York 92 H4
Borrowdale Cumb 88 H6
Borrowstoun Falk 114 H5
Borstal Medway 34 C9
Borth Cerdgn 49 K3
Borthwick Mdloth 115 Q9
Borthwickbrae Border 107 M6
Borthwickshiels Border 107 M5
Borth-y-Gest Gwynd 61 J4
Borve Highld 134 H6
Borve W Isls 152 b9
Borve W Isls 152 e3
Borve W Isls 152 g1

Borwick Lancs 89 N12
Borwick Lodge Cumb 89 J7
Borwick Rails Cumb 88 G10
Bosavern Cnwll 2 B8
Boscastle Cnwll 6 G6
Boscombe Bmouth 11 Q6
Boscombe Wilts 24 C5
Boscoppa Cnwll 3 P4
Bosham W Sus 13 N5
Bosham Hoe W Sus 13 N5
Bosherston Pembks 37 J11
Boskednan Cnwll 2 C7
Boskenna Cnwll 2 C8
Bosley Ches E 76 G10
Bossall N York 86 D3
Bossiney Cnwll 6 F6
Bossingham Kent 17 L1
Bossington Somset 20 B4
Bostock Green Ches W 76 C9
Boston Lincs 68 F3
Boston Spa Leeds 85 N6
Boswarthan Cnwll 2 C7
Boswinger Cnwll 3 N6
Botallack Cnwll 2 B8
Botany Bay Gt Lon 33 L3
Botcheston Leics 66 D11
Botesdale Suffk 58 F5
Bothal Nthumb 100 G1
Bothampstead W Berk 31 K7
Bothamsall Notts 78 H9
Bothel Cumb 97 N10
Bothenhampton Dorset 10 D6
Bothwell S Lans 114 C9
Bothwell Services (southbound) S Lans 114 C9
Botley Bucks 44 D11
Botley Hants 24 H10
Botley Oxon 43 K10
Botolph Claydon Bucks 43 Q7
Botolphs W Sus 14 H9
Botolph's Bridge Kent 17 K4
Bottesford N Linc 79 M2
Bottesford Leics 67 K5
Bottisham Cambs 57 K8
Bottomcraig Fife 124 G8
Bottom of Hutton Lancs 83 L9
Bottom o' th' Moor Bolton 76 C1
Bottoms Calder 84 D11
Bottoms Cnwll 2 B9
Botts Green Warwks 53 N2
Botusfleming Cnwll 4 H4
Botwnnog Gwynd 60 D6
Bough Beech Kent 15 N2
Boughrood Powys 39 Q4
Boughspring Gloucs 28 H3
Boughton Nhants 55 J7
Boughton Norfk 69 N11
Boughton Notts 78 H10
Boughton Aluph Kent 17 J1
Boughton End C Beds 44 E4
Boughton Green Kent 34 D12
Boughton Lees Kent 17 J2
Boughton Malherbe Kent 34 F12
Boughton Monchelsea Kent 34 D12
Boughton Street Kent 35 J10
Boulby R & C 92 F3
Boulder Clough Calder 84 F10
Bouldnor IoW 12 F7
Bouldon Shrops 51 P4
Boulmer Nthumb 109 L7
Boulston Pembks 37 J7
Boultenstone Abers 132 C2
Boultham Lincs 79 N10
Boundary Staffs 64 H4
Bourn Cambs 56 F9
Bournbrook Birm 53 K4
Bourne Lincs 68 B8
Bournebridge Essex 33 P3
Bournemouth BCP 11 Q6
Bournemouth Airport BCP 11 Q5
Bournes Green Gloucs 41 Q10
Bournes Green Sthend 34 F5
Bournheath Worcs 52 G7
Bournmoor Dur 100 H8
Bournstream Gloucs 29 M3
Bournville Birm 53 K4
Bourton Bucks 43 Q6
Bourton Dorset 22 G6
Bourton N Som 28 D9
Bourton Oxon 30 F5
Bourton Shrops 51 Q2
Bourton Wilts 30 B9
Bourton on Dunsmore Warwks 54 D6
Bourton-on-the-Hill Gloucs 42 E5
Bourton-on-the-Water Gloucs 42 E7
Bousd Ag & B 126 D11
Boustead Hill Cumb 98 C6
Bouth Cumb 89 J9
Bouthwaite N York 84 H1
Bouts Worcs 53 J9
Boveney Bucks 32 D7
Boveridge Dorset 23 N10
Bovey Tracey Devon 8 D9
Bovingdon Herts 44 E11
Bovingdon Green Bucks 32 B5
Bovinger Essex 45 P10
Bovington Camp Dorset 11 K7
Bow Devon 8 D4
Bow Gt Lon 33 M5
Bow Ork 147 c6
Bow Brickhill M Keyn 44 D5
Bowbridge Gloucs 41 P10
Bowburn Dur 100 H10
Bowcombe IoW 12 H7
Bowd Devon 9 L7
Bowden Border 107 N4
Bowden Devon 5 P5
Bowden Hill Wilts 29 Q9
Bowdon Traffd 76 E7
Bower Highld 151 N4
Bowerchalke Wilts 23 M8
Bower Hinton Somset 21 N10
Bowermadden Highld 151 N4
Bowers Staffs 64 F6
Bowers Gifford Essex 34 C4
Bowershall Fife 115 K3
Bower's Row Leeds 85 N10
Bowes Dur 90 G4
Bowgreave Lancs 83 L6
Bowhouse D & G 97 L5
Bowithick Cnwll 6 H8
Bowker's Green Lancs 75 M3
Bowland Border 107 M2
Bowland Bridge Cumb 89 L7
Bowley Herefs 51 P10
Bowlhead Green Surrey 14 D3
Bowling C Brad 85 J8
Bowling W Duns 113 N6
Bowling Bank Wrexhm 63 K3
Bowling Green Worcs 52 F10
Bowmanstead Cumb 89 J7
Bowmore Ag & B 110 G9
Bowness-on-Solway Cumb 97 P6
Bowness-on-Windermere Cumb 89 L7
Bow of Fife Fife 124 G10
Bowrfauld Angus 125 K3
Bowscale Cumb 98 D12
Bowsden Nthumb 108 H3
Bowston Cumb 89 M7
Bow Street Cerdgn 49 K4
Bow Street Norfk 58 F1
Bowthorpe Norfk 70 H10
Box Gloucs 29 P2
Box Wilts 29 N8
Boxbush Gloucs 41 K7
Boxbush Gloucs 41 L8
Box End Bed 55 P10
Boxford Suffk 46 G4
Boxford W Berk 31 J8
Boxgrove W Sus 14 C9
Box Hill Surrey 32 H12
Boxley Kent 34 E11
Boxmoor Herts 44 F10
Box's Shop Cnwll 7 J4
Boxted Essex 46 H5
Boxted Essex 46 H5
Boxted Suffk 58 B10
Boxted Cross Essex 46 H5
Boxwell Gloucs 29 N4
Boxworth Cambs 56 F7
Boyden Gate Kent 35 M9
Boyden End Suffk 57 P9
Boylestone Derbys 65 M5
Boyndie Abers 140 G3
Boyndlie Abers 141 L3
Boynton E R Yk 87 L2
Boysack Angus 125 L4
Boys Hill Dorset 10 G2
Boythorpe Derbys 78 C9
Boyton Cnwll 7 J6
Boyton Suffk 47 Q2
Boyton Wilts 23 L7
Boyton Cross Essex 46 B10
Boyton End Suffk 46 C4
Bozeat Nhants 55 M9
Braaid IoM 102 d6
Brabling Green Suffk 59 L8
Brabourne Kent 17 K3
Brabourne Lees Kent 17 K3
Brabstermire Highld 151 P3
Bracadale Highld 134 F8
Braceborough Lincs 67 Q9
Bracebridge Heath Lincs 79 N10
Bracebridge Low Fields Lincs 79 N10
Braceby Lincs 67 P5
Bracewell Lancs 84 C5
Brackenfield Derbys 78 B12
Brackenhirst N Lans 114 D7
Brackenthwaite Cumb 98 C9
Brackenthwaite N York 85 L5
Brackla Brdgnd 27 L6
Bracklesham W Sus 13 P5
Brackletter Highld 128 H8
Brackley Nhants 43 M4
Brackley Hatch Nhants 43 N5
Bracknell Br For 32 B8
Braco P & K 123 L11
Bracobrae Moray 140 D5
Bracon Ash Norfk 71 J12
Bracorina Highld 127 N6
Bradaford Devon 7 M6
Bradbourne Derbys 65 N3
Bradbury Dur 91 N1
Bradden Nhants 54 H11
Braddock Cnwll 4 B4
Bradenham Bucks 32 B3
Bradenstoke Wilts 30 B6
Bradfield Devon 9 K3
Bradfield Essex 47 L5
Bradfield Norfk 71 K5
Bradfield Sheff 77 P5
Bradfield W Berk 31 M8
Bradfield Combust Suffk 58 C9
Bradfield Green Ches E 76 C11
Bradfield Heath Essex 47 L6
Bradfield St Clare Suffk 58 D9
Bradfield St George Suffk 58 D8
Bradford C Brad 84 H8
Bradford Devon 7 M3
Bradford Nthumb 100 D3
Bradford Nthumb 109 J3
Bradford Abbas Dorset 22 D10
Bradford Leigh Wilts 29 N10
Bradford-on-Avon Wilts 29 N10
Bradford-on-Tone Somset 21 J9
Bradford Peverell Dorset 10 G6
Brading IoW 13 L7
Bradley Ches W 63 N3
Bradley Derbys 65 M4
Bradley Hants 25 K5
Bradley N York 90 G10
Bradley NE Lin 80 E2
Bradley Staffs 64 G8
Bradley Wolves 52 H2
Bradley Worcs 53 J8
Bradley Green Somset 21 K6
Bradley Green Warwks 65 P12
Bradley Green Worcs 52 H8
Bradley in the Moors Staffs 65 K4
Bradley Stoke S Glos 29 J6
Bradmore Notts 66 F6
Bradney Somset 21 M5
Bradninch Devon 9 J4
Bradnop Staffs 65 J2
Bradpole Dorset 10 D5
Bradshaw Bolton 76 D1
Bradshaw Calder 84 G10
Bradshaw Kirk 84 G12
Bradstone Devon 7 M8
Bradwall Green Ches E 76 E11
Bradwell Derbys 77 M8
Bradwell Essex 46 E7
Bradwell M Keyn 44 C4
Bradwell Norfk 71 Q11
Bradwell-on-Sea Essex 47 K10
Bradwell Waterside Essex 47 J10
Bradworthy Devon 18 H10
Brae Highld 138 C3
Brae Shet 147 i5
Braeface Falk 114 E5
Braehead Angus 125 N2
Braehead D & G 95 M6
Braehead S Lans 114 H11
Braeintra Highld 136 B9
Braemar Abers 131 L5
Braemore Highld 144 F9
Braemore Highld 151 K8
Brae Roy Lodge Highld 129 K6
Braeside Inver 113 J7
Braes of Coul Angus 124 D1
Braes of Enzie Moray 140 B4

166 Braes of Ullapool – Burnt Houses

Braes of Ullapool Highld 144 E6
Braeswick Ork 147 e2
Braevallich Ag & B 120 H11
Braewick Shet 147 h4
Brafferton Darltn 91 M2
Brafferton N York 85 N1
Brafield-on-the-Green Nhants 55 K9
Bragar W Isls 152 f2
Bragbury End Herts 45 K7
Braidwood S Lans 114 F11
Brailsford Derbys 65 N4
Brailsford Green Derbys 65 N4
Brain's Green Gloucs 41 K10
Braintree Essex 46 D7
Braiseworth Suffk 58 H6
Braishfield Hants 24 F8
Braiswick Essex 46 H6
Braithwaite C Brad 84 F7
Braithwaite Cumb 88 H2
Braithwell Donc 78 E5
Braken Hill Wakefd 85 N12
Bramber W Susx 14 H8
Brambridge Hants 24 H9
Bramcote Notts 66 E5
Bramcote Warwks 54 C3
Bramdean Hants 25 K8
Bramerton Norfk 71 L11
Bramfield Herts 45 K8
Bramfield Suffk 59 M6
Bramford Suffk 47 K2
Bramhall Stockp 76 G7
Bramham Leeds 85 N6
Bramhope Leeds 85 K6
Bramley Hants 31 N10
Bramley Leeds 85 K8
Bramley Rothm 78 D5
Bramley Surrey 14 E2
Bramley Corner Hants 31 N10
Bramley Green Hants 31 N10
Bramley Head N York 84 H4
Bramling Kent 35 M11
Brampford Speke Devon 8 H5
Brampton Cambs 56 D6
Brampton Cumb 89 R2
Brampton Cumb 98 G6
Brampton Lincs 79 L8
Brampton Norfk 71 J7
Brampton Rothm 78 C3
Brampton Suffk 59 N4
Brampton Abbotts Herefs 41 J6
Brampton Ash Nhants 55 K3
Brampton Bryan Herefs 51 L6
Brampton-en-le-Morthen Rothm 78 D6
Bramshall Staffs 65 K5
Bramshaw Hants 24 D10
Bramshill Hants 31 Q10
Bramshott Hants 25 P7
Bramwell Somset 21 P7
Branault Highld 127 J10
Brancaster Norfk 69 P3
Brancaster Staithe Norfk 69 Q3
Brancepeth Dur 100 G10
Branchill Moray 139 K5
Brand End Lincs 68 G3
Branderburgh Moray 147 N11
Brandesburton E R Yk 87 L6
Brandeston Suffk 59 K8
Brand Green Gloucs 41 L6
Brandis Corner Devon 7 M4
Brandiston Norfk 70 H8
Brandon Dur 100 G10
Brandon Lincs 67 M3
Brandon Nthumb 108 G6
Brandon Suffk 57 Q3
Brandon Warwks 54 C5
Brandon Bank Norfk 57 M3
Brandon Creek Norfk 57 L2
Brandon Parva Norfk 70 G10
Brandsby N York 92 C12
Brandy Wharf Lincs 79 P4
Brane Cnwll 2 C9
Bran End Essex 46 B6
Branksome BCP 11 P6
Branksome Park BCP 11 P6
Bransbury Hants 24 G5
Bransby Lincs 79 M8
Branscombe Devon 9 M7
Bransford Worcs 52 E10
Bransgore Hants 12 C5
Bransholme C KuH 87 L8
Bransley Shrops 52 C5
Branson's Cross Worcs 53 K6
Branston Leics 67 K6
Branston Lincs 79 P10
Branston Staffs 65 N8
Branston Booths Lincs 79 Q10
Branstone IoW 13 J8
Brant Broughton Lincs 67 M1
Brantham Suffk 47 K5
Branthwaite Cumb 88 E2
Branthwaite Cumb 98 C10
Brantingham E R Yk 86 H9
Branton Donc 78 G3
Branton Nthumb 108 G6
Branton Green N York 85 N3
Branxton Nthumb 108 E2
Brassey Green Ches W 75 N11
Brasside Dur 100 H9
Brassington Derbys 65 N1
Brasted Kent 33 N11
Brasted Chart Kent 33 N11
Brathens Abers 132 G5
Bratoft Lincs 81 J10
Brattleby Lincs 79 N7
Bratton Somset 20 E4
Bratton Wilts 23 K3
Bratton Wrekin 64 B9
Bratton Clovelly Devon 7 N6
Bratton Fleming Devon 19 M6
Bratton Seymour Somset 22 F7
Braughing Herts 45 M6
Braughing Friars Herts 45 M7
Braunston Nhants 54 E7
Braunston Rutlnd 67 L10
Braunstone Town Leics 66 F11
Braunton Devon 19 J6
Brawby N York 92 E11
Brawl Highld 150 E3
Braworth N York 92 A5
Bray W & M 32 C6
Braybrooke Nhants 55 J4
Braydon Wilts 30 B5
Braydon Brook Wilts 30 A4
Braydon Side Wilts 30 B5
Brayford Devon 19 N6
Bray's Hill E Susx 16 B8
Bray Shop Cnwll 7 L10
Braystones Cumb 88 D5
Braythorn N York 85 K5
Brayton N York 86 B9
Braywick W & M 32 C6
Braywoodside W & M 32 C7
Brazacott Cnwll 7 K6
Breach Kent 17 M1
Breach Kent 34 E9
Breachwood Green Herts 44 G7
Breacleit W Isls 152 e3
Breaclete W Isls 152 e3
Breaden Heath Shrops 63 M5
Breadsall Derbys 66 B4
Breadstone Gloucs 29 L2
Breage Cnwll 2 F9
Breakachy Highld 137 N7
Breakish Highld 135 M11
Brealangwell Lodge Highld 145 M6
Bream Gloucs 41 J10
Breamore Hants 23 P9
Brean Somset 28 D11
Breanais W Isls 152 d4
Brearley Calder 84 F10
Brearton N York 85 L3
Breascleit W Isls 152 f3
Breasclete W Isls 152 f3
Breaston Derbys 66 D5
Brechfa Carmth 38 D6
Brechin Angus 132 F12
Breckles Norfk 58 D2
Brecon Powys 39 P6
Brecon Beacons National Park 39 N7
Bredbury Stockp 76 G5
Brede E Susx 16 E7
Bredenbury Herefs 51 Q9
Bredfield Suffk 59 K10
Bredgar Kent 34 F10
Bredhurst Kent 34 D10
Bredon Worcs 41 Q4
Bredon's Hardwick Worcs 41 P5
Bredon's Norton Worcs 41 Q4
Bredward Herefs 51 J9
Bredwardine Herefs 40 D3
Breedon on the Hill Leics 66 C7
Breich W Loth 114 H9
Breightmet Bolton 76 D2
Breighton E R Yk 86 D8
Breinton Herefs 40 G4
Bremhill Wilts 29 R8
Bremridge Devon 19 N7
Brenchley Kent 16 B2
Brendon Devon 7 L3
Brendon Devon 19 P4
Brendon Hill Somset 20 G6
Brenfield Ag & B 112 B5
Brenish W Isls 152 d4
Brenkley N u Ty 100 G3
Brent Cross Gt Lon 33 J5
Brent Eleigh Suffk 58 D11
Brentford Gt Lon 32 H7
Brentingby Leics 67 K8
Brent Knoll Somset 21 M3
Brent Mill Devon 5 L5
Brent Pelham Herts 45 N5
Brentwood Essex 33 Q4
Brenzett Kent 16 H5
Brenzett Green Kent 16 H5
Brereton Staffs 65 K9
Brereton Green Ches E 76 E10
Brereton Heath Ches E 76 E10
Brereton Hill Staffs 65 K9
Bressay Shet 147 j7
Bressingham Norfk 58 G4
Bressingham Common Norfk 58 G4
Bretby Derbys 65 P7
Bretford Warwks 54 C5
Bretforton Worcs 42 C3
Bretherton Lancs 83 L11
Brettabister Shet 147 j6
Brettenham Norfk 58 D4
Brettenham Suffk 58 E10
Bretton C Pete 68 C12
Bretton Derbys 77 M8
Bretton Flints 75 K11
Brewers End Essex 45 Q7
Brewer Street Surrey 33 L12
Brewood Staffs 64 G10
Briantspuddle Dorset 11 K6
Brick End Essex 45 Q6
Brickendon Herts 45 L10
Bricket Wood Herts 44 G11
Brick Houses Sheff 77 P7
Brickkiln Green Essex 46 C5
Bricklehampton Worcs 41 R3
Bride IoM 102 f2
Bridekirk Cumb 97 M11
Bridell Pembks 37 N2
Bridestowe Devon 7 P7
Brideswell Abers 140 F8
Bridford Devon 8 F7
Bridge Kent 35 L11
Bridge End Cumb 88 G10
Bridge End Cumb 98 D8
Bridge End Devon 5 L7
Bridge End Dur 100 C11
Bridge End Essex 46 B5
Bridge End Lincs 68 C5
Bridgefoot Angus 124 H6
Bridgefoot Cumb 97 L12
Bridge Green Essex 45 N4
Bridgehampton Somset 22 D8
Bridge Hewick N York 85 M1
Bridgehill Dur 100 E8
Bridgehouse Gate N York 84 H2
Bridgemary Hants 13 K4
Bridgemere Ches E 64 D3
Bridgend Abers 140 D8
Bridgend Ag & B 103 L2
Bridgend Ag & B 110 H9
Bridgend Angus 132 E10
Bridgend Brdgnd 27 L6
Bridgend Cerdgn 48 B11
Bridgend Cumb 89 L4
Bridgend D & G 106 E8
Bridgend Devon 5 J7
Bridgend Fife 124 H10
Bridgend Moray 140 B9
Bridgend P & K 124 C8
Bridgend W Loth 115 J6
Bridgend of Lintrathen Angus 124 F2
Bridge of Alford Abers 140 E12
Bridge of Allan Stirlg 114 E2
Bridge of Avon Moray 139 L12
Bridge of Avon Moray 139 M8
Bridge of Balgie P & K 122 F3
Bridge of Brewlands Angus 131 M12
Bridge of Brown Highld 139 L11
Bridge of Cally P & K 124 C3
Bridge of Canny Abers 132 G5
Bridge of Craigisla Angus 124 E2
Bridge of Dee D & G 96 E6
Bridge of Don C Aber 133 M2
Bridge of Dun Angus 125 N1
Bridge of Dye Abers 132 G7
Bridge of Earn P & K 124 C9
Bridge of Ericht P & K 122 E1
Bridge of Feugh Abers 132 H5
Bridge of Gairn Abers 131 Q5
Bridge of Gaur P & K 122 E1
Bridge of Marnoch Abers 140 F6
Bridge of Muchalls Abers 133 L6
Bridge of Orchy Ag & B 121 P5
Bridge of Tilt P & K 130 F11
Bridge of Tynet Moray 140 B4
Bridge of Walls Shet 147 h6
Bridge of Weir Rens 113 M8
Bridge Reeve Devon 19 M10
Bridgerule Devon 7 K4
Bridges Shrops 51 L1
Bridge Sollers Herefs 40 F3
Bridge Street Suffk 58 C10
Bridgetown Cnwll 7 L7
Bridgetown Somset 20 E7
Bridge Trafford Ches W 75 M9
Bridge Yate S Glos 29 K8
Bridgham Norfk 58 E3
Bridgnorth Shrops 52 D2
Bridgwater Somset 21 L6
Bridgwater Services Somset 21 M6
Bridlington E R Yk 87 M2
Bridport Dorset 10 D6
Bridstow Herefs 41 J7
Brierfield Lancs 84 C8
Brierley Barns 78 C2
Brierley Gloucs 41 J8
Brierley Herefs 51 N9
Brierley Hill Dudley 52 G3
Brierlow Bar Derbys 77 K9
Brierton Hartpl 101 L12
Briery Cumb 89 J2
Brigg N Linc 79 P2
Briggate Norfk 71 L7
Briggswath N York 92 H5
Brigham Cumb 89 J2
Brigham Cumb 97 M12
Brigham E R Yk 87 K4
Brighouse Calder 84 H10
Brighstone IoW 12 G8
Brightgate Derbys 77 P11
Brighthampton Oxon 42 H11
Brightholmlee Sheff 77 P5
Brightley Devon 8 B5
Brightling E Susx 16 B6
Brightlingsea Essex 47 K8
Brighton Br & H 15 K10
Brighton Cnwll 3 M4
Brighton City Airport W Susx 14 H9
Brighton le Sands Sefton 75 K4
Brightons Falk 114 G6
Brightwalton W Berk 31 J6
Brightwalton Green W Berk 31 J6
Brightwalton Holt W Berk 31 J7
Brightwell Suffk 47 N3
Brightwell Baldwin Oxon 31 N3
Brightwell-cum-Sotwell Oxon 31 M4
Brightwell Upperton Oxon 31 N3
Brignall Dur 90 H4
Brig o'Turk Stirlg 122 F11
Brigsley NE Lin 80 E3
Brigsteer Cumb 89 M9
Brigstock Nhants 55 N4
Brill Bucks 43 N9
Brill Cnwll 2 H8
Brilley Herefs 51 J11
Brimfield Herefs 51 N7
Brimfield Cross Herefs 51 P7
Brimington Derbys 78 C9
Brimley Devon 8 E9
Brimpsfield Gloucs 41 Q9
Brimpton W Berk 31 L9
Brimpton Common W Berk 31 M9
Brimscombe Gloucs 41 P11
Brimstage Wirral 75 J7
Brincliffe Sheff 77 Q7
Brind E R Yk 86 D9
Brindham Somset 22 C5
Brindister Shet 147 h6
Brindle Lancs 83 N10
Brindley Ches E 63 Q2
Brineton Staffs 64 E9
Bringhurst Leics 55 L2
Bringsty Common Herefs 52 C9
Brington Cambs 56 B5
Brinian Ork 147 c3
Briningham Norfk 70 F5
Brinkely Notts 66 H2
Brinkhill Lincs 80 G9
Brinkley Cambs 57 M9
Brinklow Warwks 54 D5
Brinkworth Wilts 30 B5
Brinscall Lancs 83 N11
Brinscombe Somset 21 P3
Brinsea N Som 28 F10
Brinsley Notts 66 D2
Brinsop Herefs 40 F3
Brinsworth Rothm 78 C6
Brinton Norfk 70 F5
Brisco Cumb 98 E8
Brisley Norfk 70 D8
Brislington Bristl 29 J8
Brissenden Green Kent 16 G3
Bristol Bristl 29 J8
Bristol Airport N Som 28 G9
Bristol Zoo Gardens Bristl 28 H7
Briston Norfk 70 F6
Brisworthy Devon 5 J4
Britannia Lancs 84 C11
Britford Wilts 23 P8
Brithdir Caerph 39 Q11
Brithdir Gwynd 61 N8
British Legion Village Kent 34 C10
Briton Ferry Neath 26 H3
Britwell Salome Oxon 31 N4
Brixham Torbay 5 Q5
Brixton Devon 5 J6
Brixton Gt Lon 33 K7
Brixton Deverill Wilts 23 J5
Brixworth Nhants 55 J6
Brize Norton Oxon 42 G10
Brize Norton Airport Oxon 42 G10
Broad Alley Worcs 52 G7
Broad Blunsdon Swindn 30 D4
Broadbottom Tamesd 77 J5
Broadbridge W Susx 13 P4
Broadbridge Heath W Susx 14 G4
Broad Campden Gloucs 42 D4
Broad Carr Calder 84 G11
Broad Chalke Wilts 23 M8
Broad Clough Lancs 84 C10
Broadclyst Devon 9 J5
Broadfield Inver 113 L6
Broadfield Pembks 37 M9
Broadford Highld 135 L11
Broad Ford Kent 16 C3
Broadford Bridge W Susx 14 G6
Broadgairhill Border 106 G7
Broadgrass Green Suffk 58 E8
Broad Green Cambs 57 N8
Broad Green Essex 46 F7
Broad Green Worcs 52 E9
Broad Green Worcs 53 J6
Broadhaugh Border 117 J10
Broad Haven Pembks 36 G8
Broadheath Traffd 76 E6
Broadhembury Devon 9 L4
Broadhempston Devon 5 N3
Broad Hill Cambs 57 L5
Broad Hinton Wilts 30 C7
Broadholme Lincs 79 M9
Broadland Row E Susx 16 E7
Broadlay Carmth 38 B10
Broad Layings Hants 31 J10
Broadley Essex 45 M10
Broadley Lancs 84 C12
Broadley Moray 140 B3
Broadley Common Essex 45 M10
Broad Marston Worcs 42 D2
Broadmayne Dorset 10 H7
Broad Meadow Staffs 64 F2
Broadmere Hants 25 K4
Broadmoor Gloucs 41 K8
Broadmoor Pembks 37 L9
Broadnymett Devon 8 D4
Broad Oak Carmth 38 E7
Broad Oak Cumb 88 F8
Broadoak Dorset 10 C5
Broad Oak E Susx 15 R6
Broad Oak E Susx 16 E7
Broadoak Gloucs 41 L9
Broad Oak Hants 25 N3
Broad Oak Herefs 40 G7
Broad Oak Kent 35 L10
Broad Oak St Hel 75 P5
Broadoak Wrexhm 75 L12
Broad Road Suffk 59 K5
Broadsands Torbay 5 Q5
Broad's Green Essex 46 C9
Broadstairs Kent 35 Q9
Broadstone BCP 11 N6
Broadstone Mons 40 G11
Broadstone Shrops 51 P3
Broad Street E Susx 16 F7
Broad Street Essex 45 Q8
Broad Street Kent 17 K3
Broad Street Kent 34 E11
Broad Street Medway 34 D8
Broad Street Wilts 30 C10
Broad Street Green Essex 46 F9
Broad Town Wilts 30 C7
Broadwas Worcs 52 D9
Broadwater Herts 45 J7
Broadwater W Susx 14 G10
Broadwaters Worcs 52 F5
Broadway Carmth 37 Q8
Broadway Carmth 38 B10
Broadway Pembks 36 G8
Broadway Somset 21 M10
Broadway Suffk 59 M5
Broadway Worcs 42 C4
Broadwell Gloucs 41 J9
Broadwell Gloucs 42 E6
Broadwell Oxon 42 F10
Broadwell Warwks 54 D7
Broadwey Dorset 10 G8
Broadwindsor Dorset 10 C4
Broadwood Kelly Devon 8 B3
Broadwoodwidger Devon 7 M7
Brobury Herefs 40 D3
Brochel Highld 135 K6
Brochroy Ag & B 121 J6
Brock Lancs 83 L7
Brockamin Worcs 52 E10
Brockbridge Hants 25 K9
Brockdish Norfk 59 J5
Brockencote Worcs 52 G6
Brockenhurst Hants 12 E4
Brocketsbrae S Lans 105 Q2
Brockford Green Suffk 58 G7
Brockford Street Suffk 58 G7
Brockhall Nhants 54 G8
Brockhall Village Lancs 83 Q8
Brockham Surrey 14 H1
Brockhampton Gloucs 41 Q6
Brockhampton Gloucs 42 B7
Brockhampton Hants 13 M3
Brockhampton Herefs 41 J5
Brockhampton Green Dorset 10 H3
Brockholes Kirk 77 M2
Brockhurst Derbys 77 Q10
Brockhurst Warwks 54 D4
Brocklebank Cumb 98 C9
Brocklesby Lincs 80 C1
Brockley N Som 28 G9
Brockley Suffk 58 B6
Brockley Green Suffk 46 C2
Brockley Green Suffk 58 B9
Brockleymoor Cumb 98 F11
Brockmoor Dudley 52 G3
Brockscombe Devon 7 N6
Brock's Green Hants 31 K10
Brockton Shrops 51 K3
Brockton Shrops 51 P2
Brockton Shrops 63 K11
Brockton Shrops 64 D11
Brockton Staffs 64 F6
Brockweir Gloucs 28 H2
Brockwood Park Hants 25 K8
Brockworth Gloucs 41 P8
Brocton Cnwll 6 E11
Brocton Staffs 64 H8
Brodick N Ayrs 103 Q3
Brodie Moray 138 H4
Brodsworth Donc 78 E2
Brogaig Highld 134 H2
Brogborough C Beds 44 D4
Brokenborough Wilts 29 Q4
Broken Cross Ches E 76 G9
Broken Cross Ches W 76 C9
Brokerswood Wilts 23 J3
Bromborough Wirral 75 K7
Brome Suffk 58 H5
Brome Street Suffk 58 H5
Bromeswell Suffk 59 L10
Bromfield Cumb 97 N9
Bromfield Shrops 51 N5
Bromham Bed 55 P10
Bromham Wilts 29 Q9
Bromley Barns 77 Q4
Bromley Dudley 52 G3
Bromley Gt Lon 33 M8
Bromley Shrops 52 D2
Bromley Common Gt Lon 33 M9
Bromley Cross Bolton 76 D1
Bromley Cross Essex 47 J6
Bromley Green Kent 16 H3
Bromlow Shrops 63 K11
Brompton Medway 34 D8
Brompton N York 91 P7
Brompton-by-Sawdon N York 93 J10
Brompton-on-Swale N York 91 L7
Brompton Ralph Somset 20 H7
Brompton Regis Somset 20 E7
Bromsash Herefs 41 K7
Bromsberrow Gloucs 41 L5
Bromsberrow Heath Gloucs 41 L5
Bromsgrove Worcs 52 H6
Bromstead Heath Staffs 64 E8
Bromyard Herefs 52 C9
Bromyard Downs Herefs 52 C9
Bronaber Gwynd 61 M6
Bronant Cerdgn 49 L7
Broncroft Shrops 51 P3
Brongest Cerdgn 48 E11
Bronington Wrexhm 63 N4
Bronllys Powys 39 Q5
Bronwydd Carmth 38 B7
Bronydd Powys 40 B3
Bronygarth Shrops 63 J5
Brook Carmth 37 P8
Brook Hants 24 D10
Brook Hants 24 E7
Brook IoW 12 F8
Brook Kent 17 J2
Brook Surrey 14 D3
Brook Surrey 14 F2
Brooke Norfk 71 K12
Brooke Rutlnd 67 L11
Brookenby Lincs 80 D5
Brook End Bed 55 Q8
Brook End C Beds 56 C11
Brook End Cambs 55 Q6
Brook End M Keyn 44 C3
Brookfield Rens 113 N8
Brookhampton Oxon 31 M3
Brookhampton Somset 22 E8
Brook Hill Hants 24 D10
Brook House Denbgs 74 E10
Brookhouse Lancs 83 M2
Brookhouse Rothm 78 E6
Brookhouse Green Ches E 76 E11
Brookhouses Derbys 77 J6
Brookland Kent 16 H5
Brooklands Traffd 76 E5
Brookmans Park Herts 45 J11
Brooks Powys 62 G12
Brooksby Leics 66 H9
Brooks End Kent 35 N9
Brooks Green W Susx 14 G6
Brook Street Essex 33 Q4
Brook Street Kent 16 G4
Brook Street Suffk 58 B11
Brook Street W Susx 15 K5
Brookthorpe Gloucs 41 N9
Brookville Norfk 57 P1
Brookwood Surrey 32 D11
Broom C Beds 44 H3
Broom Rothm 78 D5
Broom Warwks 53 K10
Broombank Worcs 52 C6
Broome Norfk 59 M2
Broome Shrops 51 L4
Broome Worcs 52 G5
Broomedge Warrtn 76 D6
Broome Park Nthumb 109 J7
Broomer's Corner W Susx 14 G6
Broomershill W Susx 14 F7
Broomfield Essex 46 C9
Broomfield Kent 34 E11
Broomfield Kent 35 M9
Broomfield Somset 21 K7
Broomfields Shrops 63 M8
Broomfleet E R Yk 86 G9
Broom Green Norfk 70 E7
Broomhall W & M 32 D9
Broomhaugh Nthumb 100 C6
Broom Hill Barns 78 C3
Broom Hill Dorset 11 P4
Broom Hill Notts 66 E3
Broomhill Nthumb 109 L9
Broom Hill Worcs 52 G5
Broomhill Green Ches E 64 B3
Broomley Nthumb 100 D6
Broompark Dur 100 G10
Broom's Green Gloucs 41 L5
Broomsthorpe Norfk 70 C6
Broom Street Kent 35 J10
Brora Highld 146 G4
Broseley Shrops 64 C11
Brotherhouse Bar Lincs 68 E9
Brotherlee Dur 99 P10
Brothertoft Lincs 68 E3
Brotherton N York 85 P10
Brotton R & Cl 92 E3
Broubster Highld 151 J5
Brough Cumb 90 C4
Brough Derbys 77 M7
Brough E R Yk 86 H10
Brough Highld 151 M2
Brough Notts 79 L12
Brough Shet 147 j5
Broughall Shrops 63 P4
Brough Lodge Shet 147 k3
Brough Sowerby Cumb 90 C4
Broughton Border 106 E3
Broughton Bucks 44 B9
Broughton Cambs 56 F5
Broughton Flints 75 K11
Broughton Hants 24 E7
Broughton Lancs 83 M8
Broughton M Keyn 44 C4
Broughton N Linc 79 N2
Broughton N York 84 D5
Broughton N York 92 F12
Broughton Nhants 55 L5
Broughton Oxon 43 J4
Broughton Salfd 76 F3
Broughton Staffs 64 E5
Broughton V Glam 27 L8
Broughton Astley Leics 54 E2
Broughton Beck Cumb 89 J10
Broughton Gifford Wilts 29 P9
Broughton Green Worcs 52 H8
Broughton Hackett Worcs 52 G9
Broughton-in-Furness Cumb 88 G9
Broughton Mains D & G 95 N9
Broughton Mills Cumb 88 H8
Broughton Moor Cumb 97 L11
Broughton Poggs Oxon 42 F11
Broughton Tower Cumb 88 G9
Broughty Ferry C Dund 125 J7
Brough with St Giles N York 91 L7
Brow End Cumb 88 H11
Brownber Cumb 90 B5
Brown Candover Hants 25 K5
Brown Edge Lancs 83 J12
Brown Edge Staffs 64 G1
Brown Heath Ches W 75 M10
Brownheath Shrops 63 M6
Brownhill Abers 141 L8
Brownhills Fife 125 K9
Brownhills Wsall 65 K11
Brownieside Nthumb 109 K5
Browninghill Green Hants 31 M10
Brown Lees Staffs 64 G1
Brownlow Heath Ches E 76 F11
Brownrigg Cumb 88 D3
Brownrigg Cumb 97 N7
Brownsea Island Dorset 11 N7
Brown's Green Birm 53 K2
Brownsham Devon 18 F8
Browns Hill Gloucs 41 P11
Brownsover Warwks 54 E5
Brownston Devon 5 L6
Brown Street Suffk 58 F8
Browston Green Norfk 71 P11
Broxa N York 93 J8
Broxbourne Herts 45 L10
Broxburn E Loth 116 F6
Broxburn W Loth 115 K7
Broxfield Nthumb 109 K6
Broxted Essex 45 Q6
Broxton Ches W 63 N1
Broyle Side E Susx 15 N8
Bruan Highld 151 P8
Bruar P & K 130 F11
Bruchag Ag & B 112 G9
Bruera Ches W 75 M11
Bruern Abbey Oxon 42 F7
Bruichladdich Ag & B 110 G9
Bruisyard Suffk 59 L7
Bruisyard Street Suffk 59 L7
Brumby N Linc 79 M2
Brund Staffs 77 L11
Brundall Norfk 71 L10
Brundish Suffk 59 K7
Brundish Street Suffk 59 K6
Brunery Highld 127 N10
Brunnion Cnwll 2 E7
Brunslow Shrops 51 L4
Brunswick Village N u Ty 100 G4
Bruntcliffe Leeds 85 K10
Brunthwaite C Brad 84 F6
Bruntingthorpe Leics 54 G3
Brunton Fife 124 G8
Brunton Nthumb 109 K5
Brunton Wilts 30 F11
Brushford Devon 8 C3
Brushford Somset 20 E8
Bruton Somset 22 F6
Bryan's Green Worcs 52 G7
Bryanston Dorset 11 L3
Bryant's Bottom Bucks 32 B2
Brydekirk D & G 97 N4
Bryher IoS 2 b1
Brymbo Wrexhm 63 J1
Brympton Somset 22 C10
Bryn Carmth 26 E2
Bryn Ches W 75 Q9
Bryn Neath 27 J4
Bryn Shrops 51 J4
Bryn Wigan 75 P3
Brynamman Carmth 38 H9
Brynberian Pembks 37 L3
Brynbryddan Neath 27 J4
Bryn Bwbach Gwynd 61 K5
Bryncae Rhondd 27 N6
Bryncethin Brdgnd 27 L5
Bryncir Gwynd 60 H3
Bryn-côch Neath 26 H2
Bryncroes Gwynd 60 C6
Bryncrug Gwynd 61 K11
Bryn Du IoA 72 E9
Bryn-Eden Gwynd 61 M6
Bryneglwys Denbgs 62 G3
Brynfields Wrexhm 63 K3
Brynford Flints 74 G9
Bryn Gates Wigan 75 Q3
Bryn Golau Rhondd 27 N5
Bryngwran IoA 72 F8
Bryngwyn Mons 40 E10
Bryngwyn Powys 50 G10
Bryn-Henllan Pembks 37 K3
Brynhoffnant Cerdgn 48 E10
Bryning Lancs 83 J9
Brynithel Blae G 28 B2
Brynmawr Blae G 40 B9
Bryn-mawr Gwynd 60 D5
Brynmenyn Brdgnd 27 L5
Brynmill Swans 26 F4
Brynna Rhondd 27 N6
Brynnau Gwynion Rhondd 27 M6
Bryn-penarth Powys 62 F11
Brynrefail Gwynd 73 J11
Brynrefail IoA 72 H6
Brynsadler Rhondd 27 N6
Bryn Saith Marchog Denbgs 62 E2
Brynsiencyn IoA 72 H10
Brynteg IoA 72 H7
Bryn-y-bal Flints 75 J10
Bryn-y-Maen Conwy 73 P8
Bryn-yr-Eos Wrexhm 63 J4
Bualintur Highld 134 G11
Buarth-draw Flints 74 G8
Bubbenhall Warwks 54 B6
Bubwith E R Yk 86 D8
Buccleuch Border 107 J7
Buchanan Smithy Stirlg 113 N3
Buchanhaven Abers 141 Q6
Buchanty P & K 123 N7
Buchany Stirlg 123 J12
Buchlyvie Stirlg 113 Q2
Buckabank Cumb 98 D8
Buckden Cambs 56 D7
Buckden N York 90 F11
Buckenham Norfk 71 M11
Buckerell Devon 9 L5
Buckfast Devon 5 M3
Buckfastleigh Devon 5 M3
Buckhaven Fife 115 Q2
Buckholt Mons 40 G8
Buckhorn Devon 7 M5
Buckhorn Weston Dorset 22 G8
Buckhurst Hill Essex 33 M3
Buckie Moray 140 C3
Buckingham Bucks 43 P5
Buckland Bucks 44 C9
Buckland Devon 5 L8
Buckland Gloucs 42 C4
Buckland Hants 12 E5
Buckland Herts 45 L5
Buckland Kent 17 P2
Buckland Oxon 30 H3
Buckland Surrey 33 J12
Buckland Brewer Devon 18 H9
Buckland Common Bucks 44 C10
Buckland Dinham Somset 22 G3
Buckland Filleigh Devon 7 N3
Buckland in the Moor Devon 8 D10
Buckland Monachorum Devon 4 H3
Buckland Newton Dorset 10 G4
Buckland Ripers Dorset 10 G8
Buckland St Mary Somset 21 L10
Buckland-Tout-Saints Devon 5 M7
Bucklebury W Berk 31 L8
Bucklers Hard Hants 12 G5
Bucklesham Suffk 47 M3
Buckley Flints 75 J11
Buckley Green Warwks 53 M7
Bucklow Hill Ches E 76 D7
Buckminster Leics 67 L7
Bucknall C Stke 64 G3
Bucknall Lincs 80 D10
Bucknell Oxon 43 M6
Bucknell Shrops 51 K6
Buckpool Moray 140 C3
Bucksburn C Aber 133 L2
Buck's Cross Devon 18 G9
Bucks Green W Susx 14 F4
Buckshaw Village Lancs 83 M11
Bucks Hill Herts 32 F2
Bucks Horn Oak Hants 25 P5
Buck's Mills Devon 18 G8
Buckton E R Yk 93 N12
Buckton Herefs 51 L6
Buckton Nthumb 108 H2
Buckworth Cambs 56 C5
Budby Notts 78 G9
Buddileigh Staffs 64 D2
Bude Cnwll 7 J4
Budge's Shop Cnwll 4 E5
Budlake Devon 9 J5
Budle Nthumb 109 J3
Budleigh Salterton Devon 9 K8
Budlett's Common E Susx 15 N6
Budock Water Cnwll 3 J8
Buerton Ches E 64 C3
Bugbrooke Nhants 54 H9
Bugford Devon 5 P6
Buglawton Ches E 76 G11
Bugle Cnwll 3 P3
Bugley Dorset 22 H8
Bugthorpe E R Yk 86 E4
Buildwas Shrops 64 B11
Builth Road Powys 50 D10
Builth Wells Powys 50 E10
Bulbourne Herts 44 D9
Bulbridge Wilts 23 N7
Bulby Lincs 67 Q7
Bulcote Notts 66 G3
Bulford Wilts 23 Q5
Bulford Camp Wilts 24 C5
Bulkeley Ches E 63 P1
Bulkington Warwks 54 C3
Bulkington Wilts 29 Q10
Bulkworthy Devon 18 H10
Bullamoor N York 91 P8
Bull Bay IoA 72 G5
Bullbridge Derbys 66 B2
Bullbrook Br For 32 C8
Bullen's Green Herts 45 J10
Bulley Gloucs 41 M8
Bullgill Cumb 97 M10
Bullingham Herefs 40 G4
Bullinghope Herefs 40 G4
Bullington Hants 24 G5
Bullington Lincs 80 B8
Bullockstone Kent 35 L9
Bull's Green Herts 45 K8
Bull's Green Norfk 59 N2
Bulmer Essex 46 E4
Bulmer N York 86 C2
Bulmer Tye Essex 46 E4
Bulphan Thurr 34 B5
Bulstone Devon 9 M7
Bulstrode Herts 44 E11
Bulverhythe E Susx 16 D9
Bulwark Abers 141 M7
Bulwell C Nott 66 E3
Bulwick Nhants 55 N2
Bumble's Green Essex 45 M10
Bunacaimb Highld 127 M6
Bunarkaig Highld 128 H7
Bunbury Ches E 75 P12
Bunbury Heath Ches E 75 P12
Bunchrew Highld 138 B6
Buncton W Susx 14 G8
Bundalloch Highld 136 B10
Bunessan Ag & B 119 L8
Bungay Suffk 59 L3
Bunker's Hill Lincs 68 E1
Bunnahabhain Ag & B 111 J6
Bunny Notts 66 F6
Buntait Highld 137 L9
Buntingford Herts 45 L6
Bunwell Norfk 58 G2
Bunwell Hill Norfk 58 H2
Bupton Derbys 65 N5
Burbage Derbys 77 K9
Burbage Leics 54 D2
Burbage Wilts 30 F10
Burcher Herefs 51 K8
Burchett's Green W & M 32 B6
Burcombe Wilts 23 N7
Burcot Oxon 31 M3
Burcot Worcs 52 H6
Burcote Shrops 52 D2
Burcott Bucks 44 B8
Burcott Bucks 44 C7
Burdale N York 86 G3
Bures Essex 46 F5
Burford Oxon 42 F9
Burford Shrops 51 P7
Burg Ag & B 119 L4
Burgate Suffk 58 G5
Burgates Hants 25 N7
Burge End Herts 44 G5
Burgess Hill W Susx 15 K7
Burgh Suffk 59 J10
Burgh by Sands Cumb 98 C6
Burgh Castle Norfk 71 P11
Burghclere Hants 31 K10
Burghead Moray 139 L2
Burghfield W Berk 31 N8
Burghfield Common W Berk 31 N9
Burgh Heath Surrey 33 J10
Burgh Hill E Susx 16 C5
Burghill Herefs 40 G3
Burgh Island Devon 5 K8
Burgh le Marsh Lincs 81 J10
Burgh next Aylsham Norfk 71 J7
Burgh on Bain Lincs 80 D6
Burgh St Margaret Norfk 71 N9
Burgh St Peter Norfk 59 P2
Burghwallis Donc 78 E1
Burham Kent 34 C10
Buriton Hants 25 M9
Burland Ches E 63 Q2
Burlawn Cnwll 6 E10
Burleigh Gloucs 41 P11
Burlescombe Devon 20 G10
Burleston Dorset 11 J6
Burlestone Devon 5 N7
Burley Hants 12 C4
Burley Rutlnd 67 L10
Burley Shrops 51 N4
Burleydam Ches E 63 Q4
Burley Gate Herefs 41 J2
Burley in Wharfedale C Brad 84 H6
Burley Lawn Hants 12 C4
Burley Street Hants 12 C4
Burley Wood Head C Brad 84 H6
Burlingham Green Norfk 71 M10
Burlingjobb Powys 51 J9
Burlington Shrops 64 E10
Burlton Shrops 63 M7
Burmarsh Kent 17 K4
Burmington Warwks 42 F4
Burn N York 86 B9
Burnage Manch 76 F5
Burnaston Derbys 65 P6
Burnbanks Cumb 89 N3
Burnbrae N Lans 114 F9
Burn Bridge N York 85 L5
Burnby E R Yk 86 F6
Burn Cross Sheff 77 Q4
Burndell W Susx 14 E10
Burnden Bolton 76 D2
Burnedge Rochdl 76 G2
Burneside Cumb 89 N7
Burneston N York 91 M9
Burnett BaNES 29 K9
Burnfoot Border 107 L7
Burnfoot Border 107 N6
Burnfoot D & G 106 C11
Burnfoot D & G 107 J12
Burnfoot D & G 107 K10
Burnfoot P & K 123 P12
Burnham Bucks 32 D6
Burnham N Linc 87 K11
Burnham Deepdale Norfk 69 Q3
Burnham Green Herts 45 J8
Burnham Market Norfk 70 B4
Burnham Norton Norfk 70 B3
Burnham-on-Crouch Essex 34 G3
Burnham-on-Sea Somset 21 M3
Burnham Overy Norfk 70 B4
Burnham Overy Staithe Norfk 70 C3
Burnham Thorpe Norfk 70 C4
Burnhead D & G 105 Q10
Burnhervie Abers 140 H12
Burnhill Green Staffs 64 E12
Burnhope Dur 100 F8
Burnhouse N Ayrs 113 M11
Burniston N York 93 K8
Burnley Lancs 84 C8
Burnmouth Border 117 L9
Burn Naze Lancs 82 H6
Burn of Cambus Stirlg 123 J12
Burnopfield Dur 100 F7
Burnrigg Cumb 98 F7
Burnsall N York 84 F3
Burnside Angus 124 H1
Burnside Angus 125 K3
Burnside Fife 124 D11
Burnside Moray 147 L11
Burnside W Loth 115 K6
Burnside of Duntrune Angus 125 J6
Burntcommon Surrey 32 E11
Burntheath Derbys 65 N6
Burnt Heath Essex 47 J6
Burnt Hill W Berk 31 M7
Burnthouse Cnwll 3 J7
Burnt Houses Dur 91 J2

Burntisland Fife 115 N4
Burnt Oak E Susx 15 P5
Burnton E Ayrs 105 J8
Burntwood Flints 75 J10
Burntwood Staffs 65 K10
Burntwood Green Staffs 65 K10
Burnt Yates N York 85 K3
Burnworthy Somset 21 K10
Burpham Surrey 32 E12
Burpham W Susx 14 E9
Burradon N Tyne 100 H4
Burradon Nthumb 108 F8
Burrafirth Shet 147 k2
Burras Cnwll 2 H7
Burraton Shet 147 j4
Burravoe Shet 147 j4
Burray Village Ork 147 c5
Burrells Cumb 89 R8
Burrelton P & K 124 D5
Burridge Devon 9 Q3
Burridge Hants 19 L6
Burridge Hants 13 J3
Burrill N York 91 L9
Burringham N Linc 79 L2
Burrington Devon 19 M10
Burrington Herefs 51 M6
Burrington N Som 28 G10
Burrough End Cambs 57 M9
Burrough Green Cambs 57 M9
Burrough on the Hill
  Leics 67 J10
Burrow Lancs 89 Q11
Burrow Somset 20 L5
Burrow Bridge Somset 21 M7
Burrowhill Surrey 32 Q9
Burrows Cross Surrey 14 F2
Burry Green Swans 26 C4
Burry Port Carmth 26 C2
Burscough Lancs 75 M1
Burscough Bridge Lancs 75 M1
Bursea E R Yk 86 E8
Burshill E R Yk 87 K5
Bursledon Hants 12 H3
Burslem C Stke 64 F2
Burstall Suffk 47 K3
Burstock Dorset 10 C4
Burston Norfk 58 H4
Burstow Surrey 15 K3
Burstwick E R Yk 87 N9
Burtersett N York 90 E9
Burthorpe Green Suffk 57 P8
Burthwaite Cumb 98 E8
Burthy Cnwll 3 M3
Burtle Somset 21 N5
Burtoft Lincs 68 E5
Burton BCP 12 B6
Burton Ches W 75 K9
Burton Ches W 75 N11
Burton Dorset 10 G6
Burton Nthumb 109 K3
Burton Pembks 37 J9
Burton Somset 21 K4
Burton Somset 22 C10
Burton Wilts 22 H7
Burton Wilts 29 N6
Burton Agnes E R Yk 87 L3
Burton Bradstock Dorset 10 D7
Burton-by-Lincoln Lincs 79 N10
Burton Coggles Lincs 67 N7
Burton Dassett Warwks 54 C10
Burton End Suffk 45 P7
Burton End Suffk 46 B3
Burton Fleming E R Yk 93 M13
Burton Green Warwks 53 P5
Burton Green Wrexhm 75 K12
Burton Hastings Warwks 54 C3
Burton Hill Wilts 29 Q5
Burton-in-Kendal Cumb 89 N11
Burton-in-Kendal
  Services Cumb 89 N11
Burton in Lonsdale
  N York 89 Q12
Burton Joyce Notts 66 G3
Burton Latimer Nhants 55 M6
Burton Lazars Leics 67 J9
Burton Leonard N York 85 L2
Burton on the Wolds
  Leics 66 F8
Burton Overy Leics 54 H1
Burton Pedwardine Lincs 68 C4
Burton Pidsea E R Yk 87 N9
Burton Salmon N York 85 P9
Burton's Green Essex 46 E6
Burton upon Stather
  N Linc 86 G11
Burton upon Trent Staffs 65 N7
Burton Waters Lincs 79 M9
Burtonwood Warrtn 75 N4
Burtonwood Services
  Warrtn 75 P5
Burwardsley Ches W 75 N12
Burwarton Shrops 52 B4
Burwash E Susx 16 B6
Burwash Common E Susx 16 B6
Burwash Weald E Susx 16 B6
Burwell Cambs 57 L7
Burwell Lincs 80 G8
Burwen IoA 72 G5
Burwick Ork 147 c6
Bury Bury 76 E1
Bury Cambs 56 E4
Bury Somset 20 E8
Bury W Susx 14 E8
Bury End C Beds 45 N7
Bury Green Herts 45 L7
Bury St Edmunds Suffk 58 C8
Burythorpe N York 86 E2
Busby E Rens 113 Q10
Busby Stoop N York 91 P10
Buscot Oxon 30 F3
Bush Abers 133 J11
Bush Cnwll 7 J3
Bush Bank Herefs 51 M10
Bushbury Wolves 64 G11
Bushby Leics 66 G11
Bushey Herts 32 G3
Bushey Heath Herts 32 H3
Bush Green Norfk 59 J3
Bush Green Norfk 58 D9
Bush Hill Park Gt Lon 33 L1
Bushley Worcs 41 P5
Bushley Green Worcs 41 P5
Bushmead Bed 56 C9
Bushmoor Shrops 51 M3
Bushton Wilts 30 B6
Busk Cumb 98 H10
Buslingthorpe Lincs 79 P8
Bussex Somset 21 M6
Butcher's Cross E Susx 15 Q4
Butcombe N Som 28 G10
Bute Ag & B 112 G7
Butleigh Somset 22 C6
Butleigh Wootton Somset 22 C6
Butler's Cross Bucks 44 B10
Butler's Hill Notts 66 E3
Butlers Marston Warwks 53 Q10
Butley Suffk 59 M10
Butley High Corner Suffk 59 M10
Buttercrambe N York 86 D4
Butterknowle Dur 91 J2
Butterleigh Devon 9 J3

Butterley Derbys 66 C2
Buttermere Cumb 88 G3
Buttermere Wilts 30 H10
Butters Green Staffs 64 G2
Buttershaw C Brad 84 H9
Butterstone P & K 123 Q4
Butterton Staffs 65 J2
Butterton Staffs 77 K12
Butterwick Dur 101 K12
Butterwick Lincs 68 G3
Butterwick Lincs 87 J1
Butterwick N York 92 K11
Butt Green Ches E 64 C2
Buttington Powys 62 H10
Buttonbridge Shrops 52 D5
Buttonoak Shrops 52 D5
Buttsash Hants 12 G5
Butt's Green Essex 46 D11
Buxhall Suffk 58 F8
Buxhall Fen Street Suffk 58 F8
Buxted E Susx 15 P6
Buxton Derbys 77 K9
Buxton Norfk 71 J7
Buxton Heath Norfk 71 J8
Buxworth Derbys 77 J7
Bwlch Powys 39 Q2
Bwlchgwyn Wrexhm 63 J2
Bwlchllan Cerdgn 49 K9
Bwlchnewydd Carmth 38 A7
Bwlchtocyn Gwynd 60 E7
Bwlch-y-cibau Powys 62 G9
Bwlch-y-Ddar Powys 62 G8
Bwlchyfadfa Cerdgn 48 G10
Bwlch-y-ffridd Powys 50 B4
Bwlch-y-groes Pembks 37 P3
Bwlchymyrdd Swans 26 E3
Bwlch-y-sarnau Powys 50 D5
Byermoor Gatesd 100 F7
Byers Green Dur 100 G11
Byfield Nhants 54 E10
Byfleet Surrey 32 F10
Byford Herefs 40 E3
Bygrave Herts 45 K4
Byker N u Ty 100 H5
Byland Abbey N York 92 B11
Bylaugh Norfk 70 F8
Bylchau Conwy 74 D10
Byley Ches W 76 D10
Bynea Carmth 26 D4
Byrness Nthumb 108 C9
Bystock Devon 9 J8
Bythorn Cambs 55 Q5
Byton Herefs 51 L8
Bywell Nthumb 100 D6
Byworth W Susx 14 E6

C

Cabbacott Devon 18 H9
Cabourne Lincs 80 C3
Cabrach Ag & B 111 L8
Cabrach Moray 140 B10
Cabus Lancs 83 L5
Cackle Street E Susx 15 N5
Cackle Street E Susx 15 N4
Cackle Street E Susx 16 E7
Cadbury Devon 8 G4
Cadbury Barton Devon 19 N10
Cadbury World Birm 53 K4
Cadder E Duns 114 B7
Caddington C Beds 44 F8
Caddonfoot Border 107 L3
Cadeby Donc 78 E4
Cadeby Leics 66 C11
Cadeleigh Devon 8 G3
Cade Street E Susx 15 R6
Cadgwith Cnwll 2 H11
Cadham Fife 124 F12
Cadishead Salfd 76 D5
Cadle Swans 26 F3
Cadley Lancs 83 M9
Cadley Wilts 24 D3
Cadley Wilts 30 E9
Cadmore End Bucks 31 K4
Cadnam Hants 24 E10
Cadney N Linc 79 P3
Cadole Flints 74 H11
Cadoxton V Glam 27 Q3
Cadoxton Juxta-Neath
  Neath 26 H3
Caeathro Gwynd 72 H11
Caehopkin Powys 39 N9
Caenby Lincs 79 P6
Caerau Cardif 27 K3
Caerau Brdgnd 27 K3
Cae'r-bont Powys 39 N8
Cae'r bryn Carmth 38 F9
Caerdeon Gwynd 61 L8
Caer Farchell Pembks 36 F5
Caergeiliog IoA 72 E8
Caergwrle Flints 75 J12
Caerhun Conwy 73 L9
Caerlanrig Border 107 K9
Caerleon Newpt 28 D4
Caernarfon Gwynd 72 H11
Caernarfon Castle Gwynd 72 H11
Caerphilly Caerph 27 R5
Caersws Powys 50 C4
Caerwedros Cerdgn 48 F9
Caerwent Mons 28 G4
Caerwys Flints 74 F9
Caerynwch Gwynd 61 N8
Caggle Street Mons 40 G8
Caim IoA 73 K7
Caio Carmth 38 G4
Cairnbaan Ag & B 112 H3
Cairnbulg Abers 141 P3
Cairncross Border 117 K8
Cairndow Ag & B 121 N10
Cairneyhill Fife 115 J4
Cairngarroch D & G 94 F7
Cairngorms National
  Park 131 K4
Cairnie Abers 140 D7
Cairnorrie Abers 141 L7
Cairnryan D & G 94 F4
Cairnty Moray 139 P5
Caister-on-Sea Norfk 71 Q9
Caistor Lincs 80 C2
Caistor St Edmund Norfk 71 J11
Cakebole Worcs 52 F6
Cake Street Norfk 58 G2
Calais Street Suffk 46 H4
Calanais W Isls 152 f3
Calbourne IoW 12 G7
Calceby Lincs 80 G8
Calcoed Flints 74 G8
Calcot Gloucs 42 C9
Calcot Row W Berk 31 N8
Calcots Moray 139 N3
Calcott Kent 35 L9
Calcott Shrops 63 M9
Calcutt N York 85 M4
Caldback Cumb 98 C10
Caldbergh N York 91 J9
Caldecote Cambs 56 C9
Caldecote Cambs 56 C2
Caldecote Herts 45 J4

Caldecote Nhants 54 H10
Caldecott Nhants 55 N7
Caldecott Oxon 31 K3
Caldecott Rutlnd 55 L7
Caldecotte M Keyn 44 C5
Calder Cumb 88 D6
Calderbank N Lans 114 D8
Calder Bridge Cumb 88 D5
Calderbrook Rochdl 84 E11
Caldercruix N Lans 114 E7
Calder Grove Wakefd 85 L11
Caldermill S Lans 105 M11
Caldermore Rochdl 84 D12
Calder Vale Lancs 83 R7
Calderwood S Lans 114 B10
Caldey Island Pembks 37 M11
Caldicot Mons 28 G5
Caldwell N York 91 K4
Caldy Wirral 74 H6
Calenick Cnwll 3 K6
Calf of Man IoM 102 a7
Calford Green Suffk 46 C3
Calfsound Ork 147 d2
Calgary Ag & B 119 J2
Califer Moray 139 K4
California Falk 114 G6
California Norfk 71 P9
California Cross Devon 5 L6
Calke Derbys 66 B8
Calke Abbey Derbys 66 B8
Callakille Highld 135 M5
Callander P & K 122 G11
Callanish W Isls 152 f3
Callaughton Shrops 52 B1
Callerton N u Ty 100 F4
Callestick Cnwll 3 J4
Calligarry Highld 127 L4
Callington Cnwll 4 E3
Callingwood Staffs 65 M7
Callow Herefs 40 G5
Callow End Worcs 52 F10
Callow Hill Wilts 30 B5
Callow Hill Worcs 52 D6
Callow Hill Worcs 53 J7
Callows Grave Worcs 51 J7
Calmore Hants 24 E10
Calmsden Gloucs 42 B10
Calne Wilts 30 A8
Calow Derbys 78 C9
Calshot Hants 12 H4
Calstock Cnwll 4 E3
Calstone Wellington
  Wilts 30 B8
Calthorpe Norfk 71 J6
Calthorpe Street Norfk 71 M7
Calthwaite Cumb 98 F10
Calton N York 84 D3
Calton Staffs 65 L2
Calveley Ches E 75 Q2
Calver Derbys 77 N9
Calverhall Shrops 63 Q5
Calver Hill Herefs 51 L11
Calverleigh Devon 8 G4
Calverley Leeds 85 J8
Calver Sough Derbys 77 N8
Calvert Bucks 43 P7
Calverton M Keyn 43 R4
Calverton Notts 66 G2
Calvine P & K 130 E11
Calvo Cumb 97 N7
Calzeat Border 106 E3
Cam Gloucs 29 M2
Camaschoirie Highld 127 P12
Camasine Highld 127 N12
Camas Luinie Highld 136 C10
Camastianavaig Highld 135 J8
Camault Muir Highld 137 N8
Camber E Susx 16 G7
Camberley Surrey 32 C10
Camberwell Gt Lon 33 L7
Camblesforth N York 86 C10
Cambo Nthumb 100 C1
Cambois Nthumb 100 H2
Camborne Cnwll 2 G6
Camborne & Redruth
  Mining District Cnwll 2 G6
Cambourne Cambs 56 F8
Cambridge Cambs 57 J9
Cambridge Gloucs 41 M11
Cambridge Airport
  Cambs 57 J9
Cambrose Cnwll 2 H5
Cambus Clacks 114 F2
Cambuskenneth Stirlg 114 E2
Cambus o' May Abers 132 C5
Cambuswallace S Lans 106 D2
Camden Town Gt Lon 33 K5
Cameley BaNES 29 J11
Camelford Cnwll 6 G8
Camelon Falk 114 F4
Camerory Highld 139 J9
Camer's Green Worcs 41 M5
Camerton BaNES 29 K11
Camerton Cumb 97 L12
Cammachmore Abers 133 L5
Cammeringham Lincs 79 N7
Camore Highld 146 D7
Campbeltown Ag & B 103 K6
Campbeltown Airport
  Ag & B 103 J5
Camperdown N Tyne 100 H4
Cample D & G 106 B11
Campmuir P & K 124 E5
Camps W Loth 115 K7
Campsall Donc 78 E1
Campsea Ash Suffk 59 L9
Camps End Cambs 45 R3
Campton C Beds 44 G4
Camptown Border 107 N5
Camrose Pembks 36 H6
Camserney P & K 123 J6
Camusnagaul Highld 128 F2
Camusnagaul Highld 144 D7
Camusteel Highld 135 N7
Camusterrach Highld 135 N7
Canada Hants 24 D7
Canal Foot Cumb 89 J11
Canaston Bridge Pembks 37 J7
Candacraig Abers 131 Q4
Candlesby Lincs 81 J10
Candle Street Suffk 58 F6
Candover Green Shrops 63 N11
Candy Mill Border 106 F2
Cane End Oxon 31 P6
Canewdon Essex 34 F3
Canford Bottom Dorset 11 P4
Canford Cliffs BCP 11 P7
Canford Heath BCP 11 P6
Canford Magna BCP 11 P5
Canhams Green Suffk 58 F7
Canisbay Highld 151 Q2
Canklow Rothm 78 D5
Canley Covtry 53 P5
Cann Dorset 23 J9
Canna Highld 126 D3
Cann Common Dorset 23 J9
Cannich Highld 137 K9
Cannington Somset 21 K6
Canning Town Gt Lon 33 M6
Cannock Staffs 64 H11
Cannock Chase Staffs 65 J10

Cannock Wood Staffs 65 K9
Cannon Bridge Herefs 40 F3
Canonbie D & G 98 E12
Canon Frome Herefs 41 K3
Canon Pyon Herefs 51 M11
Canons Ashby Nhants 54 F10
Canonstown Cnwll 2 E7
Canterbury Kent 35 L10
Canterbury Cathedral
  Kent 35 L10
Cantley Norfk 71 M11
Cantlop Shrops 63 N11
Canton Cardif 27 R7
Cantraywood Highld 138 E6
Cantsfield Lancs 89 Q12
Canvey Island Essex 34 D6
Canwick Lincs 79 N10
Canworthy Water Cnwll 7 J3
Caol Highld 128 F9
Caolas Scalpaigh W Isls 152 h6
Caoles Ag & B 118 E3
Caonich Highld 128 E6
Capel Kent 16 B2
Capel Surrey 14 H2
Capel Bangor Cerdgn 49 L4
Capel Betws Lleucu
  Cerdgn 49 K9
Capel Coch IoA 72 G7
Capel Curig Conwy 73 M12
Capel Cynon Cerdgn 48 F10
Capel Dewi Carmth 38 C7
Capel Dewi Cerdgn 49 K4
Capel-Dewi Cerdgn 49 K4
Capel Garmon Conwy 61 P1
Capel Green Suffk 59 M11
Capel Gwyn Carmth 38 C7
Capel Gwyn IoA 72 E8
Capel Gwynfe Carmth 38 H7
Capel Hendre Carmth 38 F9
Capel Isaac Carmth 38 E6
Capel Iwan Carmth 37 Q3
Capel-le-Ferne Kent 17 N3
Capelles Guern 12 c1
Capel Llanilltern Cardif 27 P6
Capel Mawr IoA 72 G9
Capel Parc IoA 72 G6
Capel St Andrew Suffk 59 M11
Capel St Mary Suffk 47 K4
Capel Seion Cerdgn 49 L5
Capel Trisant Cerdgn 49 L5
Capeluchaf Gwynd 60 G2
Capelulo Conwy 73 N10
Capel-y-ffin Powys 40 C5
Capel-y-graig Gwynd 73 J10
Capenhurst Ches W 75 L9
Capernwray Lancs 89 N12
Cape Wrath Highld 148 F2
Capheaton Nthumb 100 D2
Caplaw E Rens 113 N9
Capon's Green Suffk 59 K7
Cappercleuch Border 106 H5
Capstone Medway 34 D9
Capton Devon 5 P6
Capton Somset 20 H5
Caputh P & K 124 B5
Caradon Mining District
  Cnwll 7 K10
Caradon Town Cnwll 7 K10
Carbeth Stirlg 113 Q5
Carbis Cnwll 3 N3
Carbis Bay Cnwll 2 E7
Carbost Highld 134 G6
Carbost Highld 134 G9
Carbrook Sheff 78 C6
Carbrooke Norfk 70 D11
Carburton Notts 78 E9
Carclaze Cnwll 3 M4
Car Colston Notts 67 J4
Carcroft Donc 78 E2
Cardenden Fife 115 M2
Cardeston Shrops 63 L9
Cardewlees Cumb 98 D8
Cardhu Moray 139 M7
Cardiff Cardif 27 R7
Cardiff Airport V Glam 27 P9
Cardiff Gate Services
  Cardif 28 B6
Cardiff West Services
  Cardif 27 P6
Cardigan Cerdgn 48 E11
Cardinal's Green Cambs 45 R2
Cardington Bed 56 B11
Cardington Shrops 51 N2
Cardinham Cnwll 4 G12
Cardrain D & G 94 G11
Cardross Ag & B 113 L6
Cardryne D & G 94 G11
Cardurnock Cumb 97 N6
Careby Lincs 67 P9
Careston Angus 132 E12
Carew Pembks 37 K9
Carew Cheriton Pembks 37 K10
Carew Newton Pembks 37 K10
Carey Herefs 40 H5
Carfin N Lans 114 D9
Carfraemill Border 116 C10
Cargate Green Norfk 71 M9
Cargenbridge D & G 97 J2
Cargill P & K 124 C5
Cargo Cumb 98 D6
Cargreen Cnwll 4 F4
Cargurrel Cnwll 3 L7
Carham Nthumb 108 D2
Carhampton Somset 20 F5
Carharrack Cnwll 3 J6
Carie P & K 122 H5
Carinish W Isls 152 c9
Carisbrooke IoW 12 H7
Cark Cumb 89 K11
Carkeel Cnwll 4 F4
Càrlabhagh W Isls 152 e2
Carland Cross Cnwll 3 L4
Carlbury Darltn 91 L4
Carlby Lincs 67 P9
Carlcroft Nthumb 108 D7
Carlecotes Barns 77 M3
Carleen Cnwll 2 G8
Carlesmoor N York 91 K12
Carleton Cumb 98 D5
Carleton Cumb 98 G12
Carleton Lancs 83 J7
Carleton N York 84 E6
Carleton Wakefd 85 N10
Carleton Forehoe Norfk 70 G11
Carleton-in-Craven
  N York 84 E5
Carleton Rode Norfk 58 G2
Carleton St Peter Norfk 71 L11
Carlidnack Cnwll 3 J8
Carlin How R & Cl 92 H4
Carlincott BaNES 29 L11
Carlingcott BaNES 29 L11
Carlin How R & Cl 92 H4
Carlisle Cumb 98 E7
Carlisle Lake District
  Airport Cumb 98 F6
Carloggas Cnwll 3 L2
Carlops Border 115 M9
Carloway W Isls 152 e2
Carlton Barns 78 B2
Carlton Bed 55 N9
Carlton Cambs 57 M10
Carlton Leeds 85 L9
Carlton Leics 66 C11
Carlton N York 86 C10
Carlton N York 91 K9
Carlton N York 92 D11

Carlton Notts 66 G4
Carlton S on T 91 P2
Carlton Suffk 59 M8
Carlton Colville Suffk 59 P3
Carlton Curlieu Leics 54 H1
Carlton Green Cambs 57 M10
Carlton Husthwaite
  N York 92 A11
Carlton-in-Cleveland
  N York 92 A6
Carlton in Lindrick Notts 78 F7
Carlton-le-Moorland
  Lincs 79 M12
Carlton Miniott N York 91 P10
Carlton-on-Trent Notts 79 K11
Carlton Scroop Lincs 67 N3
Carluke S Lans 114 F11
Carlyon Bay Cnwll 3 P4
Carmacoup S Lans 105 P4
Carmarthen Carmth 38 C7
Carmel Carmth 38 E8
Carmel Flints 74 G8
Carmel Gwynd 60 H1
Carmichael S Lans 106 B2
Carmountside C Stke 64 G4
Carmunnock C Glas 114 A9
Carmyle C Glas 114 B9
Carmyllie Angus 125 L4
Carnaby E R Yk 87 L2
Carnbee Fife 125 L11
Carnbo P & K 123 Q12
Carn Brea Cnwll 2 H6
Carnbrogie Abers 141 K10
Carndu Highld 136 B10
Carne Cnwll 3 J9
Carne Cnwll 3 M7
Carne Cnwll 3 N3
Carnell E Ayrs 105 J3
Carnewas Cnwll 6 B11
Carnforth Lancs 83 L1
Carn-gorm Highld 136 C11
Carnhedryn Pembks 36 F5
Carnhell Green Cnwll 2 G6
Carnie Abers 133 K3
Carnkie Cnwll 2 H6
Carnkie Cnwll 2 H7
Carnkiet Cnwll 3 J4
Carno Powys 50 C3
Carnock Fife 115 J3
Carnon Downs Cnwll 3 J6
Carnousie Abers 140 G6
Carnoustie Angus 125 L6
Carnsmerry Cnwll 3 P3
Carnwath S Lans 114 H12
Carnyorth Cnwll 2 B8
Carol Green Solhll 53 N5
Carpalla Cnwll 3 N5
Carperby N York 90 G9
Carr Rothm 78 E6
Carradale Village Ag & B 103 L2
Carragrich W Isls 152 g6
Carrbridge Highld 138 G10
Carrbrook Tamesd 77 J3
Carrefour Jersey 13 b1
Carreglefn IoA 72 F6
Carrhouse N Linc 79 K2
Carrick Ag & B 112 G4
Carrick Castle Ag & B 112 J2
Carriden Falk 115 J5
Carrington Mdloth 115 P9
Carrington Lincs 68 F1
Carrington Traffd 76 F5
Carrog Conwy 61 N3
Carrog Denbgs 62 E3
Carron Falk 114 F5
Carron Moray 139 N7
Carronbridge D & G 105 R10
Carron Bridge Stirlg 114 D4
Carronshore Falk 114 G5
Carr Shield Nthumb 99 M8
Carrutherstown D & G 97 M4
Carr Vale Derbys 78 D9
Carrville Dur 100 H9
Carsaig Ag & B 119 P8
Carscreugh D & G 94 K6
Carsegownie Angus 125 K3
Carseriggan D & G 94 H5
Carsethorn D & G 97 K6
Carshalton Gt Lon 33 K9
Carsington Derbys 65 N2
Carskey Ag & B 103 J8
Carsluith D & G 95 M6
Carsphairn D & G 105 K11
Carstairs S Lans 114 G12
Carstairs Junction S Lans 114 G12
Carswell Marsh Oxon 30 G3
Carter's Clay Hants 24 E8
Carters Green Essex 45 N9
Carterton Oxon 42 G10
Carterway Heads Nthumb 100 D8
Cartington Nthumb 108 G9
Cartland S Lans 114 G12
Cartledge Derbys 77 Q8
Cartmel Cumb 89 L11
Cartmel Fell Cumb 89 L9
Carway Carmth 26 C2
Carwinley Cumb 98 E4
Cashe's Green Gloucs 41 N10
Cashmoor Dorset 23 N10
Casnewydd Newpt 28 B4
Cassington Oxon 43 K9
Cassop Dur 101 J10
Castallack Cnwll 2 D9
Castell Conwy 73 N10
Castell Guern 12 b2
Castell-y-bwch Torfn 28 C3
Casterton Cumb 89 Q11
Castle Cnwll 3 J6
Castle Acre Norfk 70 B9
Castle Ashby Nhants 55 L9
Castlebay W Isls 152 b13
Castle Bolton N York 90 G8
Castle Bromwich Solhll 53 L4
Castle Bytham Lincs 67 P8
Castlebythe Pembks 37 K5
Castle Caereinion Powys 62 G10
Castle Camps Cambs 45 R3
Castle Carrock Cumb 98 G7
Castlecary Falk 114 D6
Castle Cary Somset 22 E6
Castle Combe Wilts 29 P6
Castlecraig Highld 146 E11
Castle Donington Leics 66 D6
Castle Douglas D & G 96 G6
Castle Eaton Swindn 30 D3
Castle Eden Dur 101 L10
Castle Frome Herefs 41 K4
Castle Gate Cnwll 2 D7
Castle Green Surrey 32 D10
Castle Green Cumb 89 N7
Castle Gresley Derbys 65 P9
Castle Hedingham Essex 46 D4
Castlehill Border 106 G3
Castle Hill Kent 16 C2
Castle Hill Suffk 47 K3
Castlehill Highld 151 M3
Castle Kennedy D & G 94 G6
Castle Lachlan Ag & B 112 G2
Castlemartin Pembks 36 H11
Castle Morris Pembks 36 H4

Castlemorton Worcs 41 M4
Castlemorton Common
  Worcs 41 M4
Castle O'er D & G 106 H10
Castle Rising Norfk 69 M7
Castleside Dur 100 D8
Castle Stuart Highld 138 D6
Castlethorpe M Keyn 44 A3
Castlethorpe N Linc 79 N3
Castleton Ag & B 112 C4
Castleton Border 107 N11
Castleton Derbys 77 M7
Castleton N York 92 E5
Castleton Newpt 28 C6
Castleton Rochdl 76 G2
Castleton Ches W 63 M2
Castletown Dur 101 J6
Castletown Highld 151 M3
Castletown IoM 102 c7
Castletown Sundld 101 J6
Castley N York 85 K6
Caston Norfk 58 E1
Castor C Pete 56 C11
Caswell Bay Swans 26 E5
Catacol N Ayrs 112 D11
Catbrain S Glos 29 J6
Catbrook Mons 40 G11
Catch Flints 74 H9
Catchem's Corner Solhll 53 N5
Catchgate Dur 100 F8
Catcliffe Rothm 78 C6
Catcomb Wilts 30 B7
Catcott Somset 21 N5
Caterham Surrey 33 L11
Catfield Norfk 71 M8
Catfield Common Norfk 71 M8
Catford Gt Lon 33 L8
Catforth Lancs 83 L8
Cathcart C Glas 113 Q9
Cathedine Powys 39 Q6
Catherine-de-Barnes
  Solhll 53 M5
Catherine Slack C Brad 84 G9
Catherington Hants 25 M10
Catherston Leweston
  Dorset 10 B6
Catisfield Hants 13 J3
Catley Herefs 41 K3
Catley Lane Head Rochdl 84 C12
Catlodge Highld 130 B6
Catlow Lancs 84 D7
Catlowdy Cumb 98 F3
Catmere End Essex 45 M4
Catmore W Berk 31 K6
Caton Devon 8 D7
Caton Lancs 83 M2
Caton Green Lancs 83 M2
Cator Court Devon 8 C9
Catrine E Ayrs 105 K5
Cat's Ash Newpt 28 E4
Catsfield E Susx 16 C8
Catsfield Stream E Susx 16 C8
Catsgore Somset 22 D6
Catshill Worcs 52 H6
Cattadale Ag & B 103 J3
Cattal N York 85 N4
Cattawade Suffk 47 K5
Catterall Lancs 83 L6
Catteralslane Shrops 63 P4
Catterick N York 91 L7
Catterick Bridge N York 91 L7
Catterick Garrison N York 91 K7
Catterlen Cumb 98 F11
Catterline Abers 133 L8
Catterton N York 85 Q6
Catteshall Surrey 14 D2
Catthorpe Leics 54 E5
Cattistock Dorset 10 F5
Catton Nthumb 99 M7
Catton N York 91 P11
Catwick E R Yk 87 L6
Catworth Cambs 56 B6
Caudle Green Gloucs 41 Q9
Caulcott Oxon 43 L7
Cauldcots Angus 125 N3
Cauldhame Stirlg 114 B3
Cauldmill Border 107 N6
Cauldon Staffs 65 K3
Cauldon Lowe Staffs 65 K3
Cauldwell Derbys 65 N9
Caulkerbush D & G 97 J4
Caulside D & G 98 F2
Caundle Marsh Dorset 22 F10
Caunsall Worcs 52 F4
Caunton Notts 79 J11
Causeway Hants 25 M9
Causeway End Cumb 89 M9
Causeway End D & G 95 M6
Causeway End Essex 46 B8
Causewayhead Cumb 97 M7
Causewayhead Stirlg 114 E2
Causeyend Abers 141 M12
Causey Park Bridge
  Nthumb 109 K10
Cavendish Suffk 46 E2
Cavenham Suffk 57 N7
Caversfield Oxon 43 M6
Caversham Readg 31 N7
Caverswall Staffs 64 H4
Caverton Mill Border 108 B5
Cavil E R Yk 86 E8
Cawdor Highld 138 F5
Cawkwell Lincs 80 F8
Cawood N York 86 A8
Cawsand Cnwll 4 F6
Cawston Norfk 70 H7
Cawston Warwks 54 B6
Cawthorne Barns 77 R3
Cawthorpe Lincs 68 C7
Cawton N York 92 D11
Caxton Cambs 56 F9
Caxton End Cambs 56 F8
Caxton Gibbet Cambs 56 F8
Caynham Shrops 51 P6
Caythorpe Lincs 67 M2
Caythorpe Notts 67 J3
Cayton N York 93 L10
Ceann a Bhaigh W Isls 152 b8
Ceannacroc Lodge Highld 128 H5
Cearsiadar W Isls 152 g4
Ceciliford Mons 40 G11
Cefn Newpt 28 C4
Cefn Berain Conwy 74 D10
Cefn-brith Conwy 62 C2
Cefn Byrle Powys 39 N8
Cefn Canel Powys 62 G6
Cefn Coch Powys 62 F7
Cefn-coed-y-cymmer
  Myr Td 39 N10
Cefn Cribwr Brdgnd 27 K5
Cefn Cross Brdgnd 27 K5
Cefn-ddwysarn Gwynd 62 C5
Cefn-Einion Shrops 51 J4
Cefneithin Carmth 38 F9
Cefngorwydd Powys 50 B11
Cefn-mawr Wrexhm 63 J4

Cefnpennar Rhondd 27 N2
Cefn-y-bedd Flints 63 K1
Cefn-y-pant Carmth 37 N5
Ceint IoA 72 H8
Cellan Cerdgn 49 K10
Cellardyke Fife 125 L12
Cellarhead Staffs 64 H3
Celleron Cumb 89 N2
Celynen Caerph 28 B3
Cemaes IoA 72 F5
Cemmaes Powys 61 P11
Cemmaes Road Powys 61 P11
Cenarth Cerdgn 37 P2
Cerbyd Pembks 36 F5
Ceres Fife 124 H10
Cerne Abbas Dorset 10 G4
Cerney Wick Gloucs 30 C2
Cerrigceinwen IoA 72 G9
Cerrigydrudion Conwy 62 C2
Cess Norfk 71 N8
Ceunant Gwynd 73 J11
Chaceley Gloucs 41 P5
Chacewater Cnwll 3 J5
Chackmore Bucks 43 P4
Chacombe Nhants 43 M3
Chadbury Worcs 42 C3
Chadderton Oldham 76 G3
Chadderton Fold Oldham 76 G2
Chaddesden C Derb 66 C5
Chaddesley Corbett
  Worcs 52 G6
Chaddlehanger Devon 7 N9
Chaddleworth W Berk 31 J7
Chadlington Oxon 42 G7
Chadshunt Warwks 53 Q10
Chadwell Leics 67 K7
Chadwell Shrops 64 E9
Chadwell End Bed 55 Q7
Chadwell Heath Gt Lon 33 N5
Chadwell St Mary Thurr 34 B6
Chadwick Worcs 52 F8
Chadwick End Solhll 53 N6
Chadwick Green St Hel 75 N4
Chaffcombe Somset 9 Q3
Chafford Hundred Thurr 33 R6
Chagford Devon 8 D7
Chailey E Susx 15 M7
Chainbridge Cambs 68 H12
Chainhurst Kent 16 C1
Chalbury Dorset 11 N3
Chalbury Common
  Dorset 11 P3
Chaldon Surrey 33 K11
Chaldon Herring Dorset 11 J8
Chale IoW 12 H9
Chale Green IoW 12 H9
Chalfont Common Bucks 32 E4
Chalfont St Giles Bucks 32 E4
Chalfont St Peter Bucks 32 E4
Chalford Gloucs 41 P11
Chalford Oxon 31 P2
Chalford Wilts 23 J3
Chalgrave C Beds 44 E6
Chalgrove Oxon 31 N3
Chalk Kent 34 B8
Chalk End Essex 46 A9
Chalkhouse Green Oxon 31 P6
Chalkway Somset 10 B3
Chalkwell Kent 34 F9
Challaborough Devon 5 K8
Challacombe Devon 19 N5
Challoch D & G 95 M5
Challock Kent 34 H12
Chalmington Dorset 10 F4
Chalton C Beds 44 E6
Chalton C Beds 56 C10
Chalton Hants 25 M10
Chalvey Slough 32 D6
Chalvington E Susx 15 P9
Chambers Green Kent 16 G2
Chandler's Cross Herts 32 F3
Chandler's Cross Worcs 41 M4
Chandler's Ford Hants 24 G9
Channel's End Bed 56 B9
Channel Tunnel Terminal
  Kent 17 L3
Chantry Somset 22 G4
Chantry Suffk 47 L3
Chapel Cumb 97 P12
Chapel Fife 115 N3
Chapel Allerton Leeds 85 L8
Chapel Allerton Somset 21 N3
Chapel Amble Cnwll 6 E9
Chapel Brampton Nhants 55 J7
Chapelbridge Cambs 57 F2
Chapel Chorlton Staffs 64 E5
Chapel Cross E Susx 15 R7
Chapel End Bed 56 B9
Chapel End C Beds 56 B9
Chapel End Warwks 56 C4
Chapel End Warwks 54 C2
Chapelend Way Essex 46 C4
Chapel-en-le-Frith
  Derbys 77 K7
Chapel Field Bury 76 E2
Chapelgate Lincs 68 H7
Chapel Green Warwks 53 P4
Chapel Green Warwks 54 D8
Chapel Haddlesey N York 86 A10
Chapelhall N Lans 114 E8
Chapel Hill Abers 141 P9
Chapel Hill Lincs 68 D1
Chapel Hill Mons 40 H2
Chapel Hill N York 85 M6
Chapelhope Border 106 H6
Chapelknowe D & G 98 D4
Chapel Lawn Shrops 51 K5
Chapel-le-Dale N York 90 B11
Chapel Leigh Somset 21 J7
Chapel Milton Derbys 77 K7
Chapel of Garioch Abers 140 H11
Chapel Rossan D & G 94 G9
Chapel Row E Susx 16 B8
Chapel Row W Berk 31 M8
Chapels Cumb 88 H11
Chapel St Leonards Lincs 81 L9
Chapel Stile Cumb 89 J6
Chapelton Abers 133 L5
Chapelton Angus 125 M3
Chapelton Devon 19 L8
Chapelton S Lans 114 C11
Chapeltown Bl w D 83 Q12
Chapeltown Moray 139 N11
Chapeltown Sheff 78 B4
Chapmanslade Wilts 23 J4
Chapmans Well Devon 7 L6
Chapmore End Herts 45 L8
Chappel Essex 46 F6
Charaton Cnwll 4 D3
Chard Somset 9 Q3
Chard Junction Somset 9 Q4
Chardleigh Green Somset 9 Q2
Chardstock Devon 9 Q4
Charfield S Glos 29 L4
Chargrove Gloucs 41 Q8
Charing Kent 16 G1
Charing Heath Kent 16 G1
Charing Hill Kent 34 G12
Charingworth Gloucs 42 E4
Charlbury Oxon 42 H8
Charlcombe BaNES 29 M9
Charlcutt Wilts 30 A7
Charlecote Warwks 53 Q9
Charlemont Sandw 53 J2
Charles Devon 19 N7

Charleshill Surrey....14 C2
Charleston Angus....124 H4
Charleston C Aber....133 M4
Charlestown C Brad....84 H7
Charlestown Calder....84 E10
Charlestown Cnwll....3 P4
Charlestown Cnwll....4 P4
Charlestown Derbys....77 J5
Charlestown Dorset....10 G9
Charlestown Fife....115 K4
Charlestown Highld....138 B6
Charlestown Highld....143 L10
Charlestown Salfd....76 E4
Charlestown of Aberlour Moray....139 N7
Charles Tye Suffk....58 F10
Charlesworth Derbys....77 J5
Charlinch Somset....21 K6
Charlottetown Fife....124 F10
Charlton Gt Lon....33 M7
Charlton Hants....24 F4
Charlton Herts....44 H6
Charlton Nthumb....99 M1
Charlton Oxon....31 J5
Charlton Somset....21 L8
Charlton Somset....22 E5
Charlton Somset....22 C7
Charlton Surrey....32 F8
Charlton W Susx....14 C8
Charlton Wilts....23 K9
Charlton Wilts....29 Q4
Charlton Wilts....30 B3
Charlton Worcs....52 F6
Charlton Wrekin....63 Q10
Charlton Abbots Gloucs....42 B7
Charlton Adam Somset....22 C7
Charlton All Saints Wilts....24 B8
Charlton Down Dorset....10 G6
Charlton Hill Shrops....63 P10
Charlton Horethorne Somset....22 F8
Charlton Kings Gloucs....41 Q7
Charlton Mackrell Somset....22 C7
Charlton Marshall Dorset....11 L4
Charlton Musgrove Somset....22 G7
Charlton-on-Otmoor Oxon....43 M8
Charlton on the Hill Dorset....11 L4
Charlton St Peter Wilts....30 D11
Charlwood Hants....25 L7
Charlwood Surrey....15 J3
Charminster Dorset....10 G6
Charmouth Dorset....10 B6
Charndon Bucks....43 P7
Charney Bassett Oxon....30 H3
Charnock Green Lancs....83 M11
Charnock Richard Lancs....83 M12
Charnock Richard Services Lancs....83 M12
Charsfield Suffk....59 K9
Chart Corner Kent....34 D12
Chart Alley Hants....31 M10
Charterhouse Somset....116 H11
Charterhouse Somset....22 C2
Chartershall Stirlg....114 E3
Charterville Allotments Oxon....42 G9
Chartham Kent....35 K11
Chartham Hatch Kent....35 K11
Chart Hill Kent....16 D1
Chartridge Bucks....44 D11
Chart Sutton Kent....16 E1
Chartway Street Kent....34 E12
Charvil Wokham....31 Q7
Charwelton Nhants....54 E9
Chase Terrace Staffs....65 J10
Chasetown Staffs....65 K10
Chastleton Oxon....42 F6
Chasty Devon....7 L4
Chatburn Lancs....84 A6
Chatcull Staffs....64 E5
Chatham Caerph....28 B4
Chatham Medway....34 D9
Chatham Green Essex....46 C8
Chathill Nthumb....109 N4
Chatley Worcs....52 F8
Chatsworth House Derbys....77 N9
Chattenden Medway....34 D8
Chatter End Essex....45 N6
Chatteris Cambs....56 H3
Chatterton Lancs....84 B11
Chattisham Suffk....47 K3
Chatto Border....108 C6
Chatton Nthumb....108 H4
Chaul End C Beds....44 F7
Chawleigh Devon....19 N11
Chawley Oxon....43 K10
Chawston Bed....56 C9
Chawton Hants....25 M6
Chaxhill Gloucs....41 L9
Chazey Heath Oxon....31 P7
Cheadle Staffs....65 J3
Cheadle Stockp....76 F6
Cheadle Heath Stockp....76 G6
Cheadle Hulme Stockp....76 G6
Cheam Gt Lon....32 H9
Cheapside W & M....32 D8
Chearsley Bucks....43 P9
Chebsey Staffs....64 F6
Checkendon Oxon....31 N6
Checkley Ches E....64 D3
Checkley Herefs....41 J4
Checkley Staffs....65 J5
Checkley Green Ches E....64 D3
Chedburgh Suffk....57 Q9
Cheddar Somset....21 P3
Cheddington Bucks....44 D8
Cheddleton Staffs....64 H2
Cheddleton Heath Staffs....65 J2
Cheddon Fitzpaine Somset....21 K8
Chedglow Wilts....29 Q4
Chedgrave Norfk....71 M12
Chedington Dorset....10 D4
Chediston Suffk....59 M5
Chediston Green Suffk....59 M5
Chedworth Gloucs....42 B9
Chedzoy Somset....21 M6
Cheeseman's Green Kent....17 J3
Cheetham Hill Manch....76 F3
Cheldon Devon....19 P10
Chelford Ches E....76 F9
Chellaston C Derb....66 B6
Chellington Bed....55 M9
Chelmarsh Shrops....52 D3
Chelmer Village Essex....46 C10
Chelmick Shrops....51 M2
Chelmondiston Suffk....47 M4
Chelmorton Derbys....77 L9
Chelmsford Essex....46 C10
Chelmsley Wood Solhll....53 M3
Chelsea Gt Lon....33 K6
Chelsfield Gt Lon....33 N9
Chelsham Surrey....33 L10
Chelston Somset....21 J9
Chelsworth Suffk....58 E11
Cheltenham Gloucs....41 Q7
Chelveston Nhants....55 M7
Chelvey N Som....28 G8
Chelwood BaNES....29 K10
Chelwood Common E Susx....15 M5

Chelwood Gate E Susx....15 M5
Chelworth Wilts....29 R3
Chelworth Lower Green Wilts....30 C4
Chelworth Upper Green Wilts....30 C4
Cheney Longville Shrops....51 M4
Chenies Bucks....32 E3
Chepstow Mons....28 H4
Chequerbent Bolton....76 C2
Chequers Corner Norfk....69 J10
Cherhill Wilts....30 B8
Cherington Gloucs....42 G4
Cherington Warwks....42 G4
Cheriton Devon....19 P4
Cheriton Hants....25 J7
Cheriton Kent....17 K7
Cheriton Pembks....37 J11
Cheriton Swans....26 C4
Cheriton Bishop Devon....8 G6
Cheriton Fitzpaine Devon....8 G3
Cherrington Wrekin....64 C8
Cherry Burton E R Yk....87 J7
Cherry Hinton Cambs....57 J9
Cherry Orchard Worcs....52 F10
Cherry Willingham Lincs....79 N9
Chertsey Surrey....32 F9
Cheselbourne Dorset....11 J5
Chesham Bucks....44 D11
Chesham Bury....76 E1
Chesham Bois Bucks....32 D2
Cheshunt Herts....45 L11
Chesil Beach Dorset....10 F9
Chesley Kent....34 E9
Cheslyn Hay Staffs....64 H10
Chessetts Wood Warwks....53 M6
Chessington Gt Lon....32 H9
Chessington World of Adventures Gt Lon....32 H10
Chester Ches W....75 L10
Chesterblade Somset....22 F5
Chesterfield Derbys....78 C9
Chesterfield Staffs....65 L11
Chesterhill Mdloth....115 Q8
Chester-le-Street Dur....100 H8
Chester Moor Dur....100 H8
Chesters Border....107 P5
Chesters Border....107 Q7
Chester Services Ches W....75 L9
Chesterton Cambs....56 C2
Chesterton Cambs....57 J8
Chesterton Gloucs....30 B2
Chesterton Oxon....43 M7
Chesterton Shrops....52 D2
Chesterton Staffs....64 F2
Chesterton Green Warwks....54 B9
Chesterwood Nthumb....99 M6
Chester Zoo Ches W....75 L9
Chestfield Kent....35 K9
Chestnut Street Kent....34 F9
Cheston Devon....5 L5
Cheswardine Shrops....64 D6
Cheswick Nthumb....117 M12
Cheswick Green Solhll....53 L5
Chetnole Dorset....10 F3
Chettiscombe Devon....20 F10
Chettisham Cambs....57 K4
Chettle Dorset....23 L10
Chetton Shrops....52 C3
Chetwode Bucks....43 N6
Chetwynd Wrekin....64 D8
Chetwynd Aston Wrekin....64 D8
Cheveley Cambs....57 N8
Chevening Kent....33 N11
Cheverton IoW....12 G8
Chevington Suffk....57 Q8
Cheviot Hills....108 B8
Chevithorne Devon....20 F10
Chew Magna BaNES....29 J9
Chew Moor Bolton....76 C2
Chew Stoke BaNES....28 H10
Chewton Keynsham BaNES....29 K9
Chewton Mendip Somset....22 D3
Chichacott Devon....8 B5
Chicheley M Keyn....44 C2
Chichester W Susx....14 B10
Chickerell Dorset....10 G8
Chickering Suffk....59 J6
Chicklade Wilts....23 K6
Chicksands C Beds....44 G4
Chickward Herefs....51 J10
Chidden Hants....25 L10
Chiddingfold Surrey....14 E4
Chiddingly E Susx....15 Q8
Chiddingstone Kent....15 P2
Chiddingstone Causeway Kent....15 P1
Chiddingstone Hoath Kent....15 P2
Chideock Dorset....10 C6
Chidham W Susx....13 N4
Chidswell Kirk....85 K10
Chieveley W Berk....31 K9
Chievely Services W Berk....31 K8
Chignall St James Essex....46 B9
Chignall Smealy Essex....46 B9
Chigwell Essex....33 N3
Chigwell Row Essex....33 N4
Chilbolton Hants....24 F7
Chilcomb Hants....24 H7
Chilcombe Dorset....10 E6
Chilcompton Somset....22 E3
Chilcote Leics....65 P10
Childer Thornton Ches W....75 L8
Child Okeford Dorset....23 J10
Childrey Oxon....30 H5
Child's Ercall Shrops....64 C7
Childswickham Worcs....42 C4
Childwall Lpool....75 L6
Childwick Bury Herts....44 G9
Childwick Green Herts....44 G9
Chilfrome Dorset....10 F5
Chilgrove W Susx....25 P10
Chilham Kent....35 J11
Chilla Devon....7 N4
Chillaton Devon....7 N8
Chillenden Kent....35 N11
Chillerton IoW....12 H4
Chillesford Suffk....59 M11
Chillingham Nthumb....108 H4
Chillington Devon....5 P7
Chillington Somset....10 B3
Chilmark Wilts....23 K6
Chilmington Green Kent....16 H3
Chilson Oxon....42 G8
Chilsworthy Cnwll....7 M6
Chilsworthy Devon....7 L3
Chiltern Green C Beds....44 H8
Chiltern Hills....31 Q3
Chilthorne Domer Somset....22 C9
Chilton Bucks....43 P9
Chilton Devon....8 H4
Chilton Dur....100 H12
Chilton Oxon....31 K7
Chilton Suffk....46 H3
Chilton Candover Hants....25 J5
Chilton Cantelo Somset....22 C9
Chilton Foliat Wilts....30 G8
Chilton Polden Somset....21 N5
Chilton Street Suffk....46 D2
Chilton Trinity Somset....21 L5

Chilton Trinity Somset....21 L5
Chilwell Notts....66 E5
Chilworth Hants....24 G9
Chilworth Surrey....14 G1
Chimney Oxon....30 H2
Chineham Hants....25 L2
Chingford Gt Lon....33 M3
Chinley Derbys....77 K7
Chinley Head Derbys....77 K7
Chinnor Oxon....31 Q2
Chipnall Shrops....64 D6
Chippenham Cambs....57 M6
Chippenham Wilts....29 Q7
Chipperfield Herts....44 F11
Chipping Herts....45 L5
Chipping Lancs....83 N6
Chipping Campden Gloucs....42 D4
Chipping Hill Essex....46 E8
Chipping Norton Oxon....42 G6
Chipping Ongar Essex....45 P10
Chipping Sodbury S Glos....29 L6
Chipping Warden Nhants....54 E11
Chipshop Devon....7 N9
Chipstable Somset....20 E8
Chipstead Kent....33 N11
Chipstead Surrey....33 K11
Chirbury Shrops....51 J1
Chirk Wrexhm....63 J5
Chirnside Border....117 J10
Chirnsidebridge Border....117 J10
Chirton Wilts....30 C11
Chisbury Wilts....30 F9
Chiselborough Somset....21 P10
Chiseldon Swindn....30 E6
Chiselhampton Oxon....31 M2
Chiserley Calder....84 F9
Chisholme Border....107 L7
Chislehurst Gt Lon....33 N8
Chislet Kent....35 M9
Chiswell Green Herts....44 G11
Chiswick Gt Lon....33 J7
Chiswick End Cambs....45 L3
Chisworth Derbys....77 J5
Chithurst W Susx....25 P8
Chittering Cambs....57 J7
Chitterne Wilts....23 L5
Chittlehamholt Devon....19 N9
Chittlehampton Devon....19 M8
Chittoe Wilts....29 Q9
Chivelstone Devon....5 N9
Chivenor Devon....19 K6
Chiverton Cross Cnwll....3 J5
Chlenry D & G....94 G6
Chobham Surrey....32 D10
Cholderton Wilts....24 B4
Cholesbury Bucks....44 D10
Chollerford Nthumb....99 P4
Chollerton Nthumb....99 P4
Cholmondeston Ches W....76 B11
Cholsey Oxon....31 M5
Cholstrey Herefs....51 M9
Chop Gate N York....92 B7
Choppington Nthumb....100 H2
Chopwell Gatesd....100 E6
Chorley Ches E....63 P2
Chorley Lancs....83 N11
Chorley Shrops....52 C4
Chorley Staffs....65 K10
Chorleywood Herts....32 E3
Chorleywood West Herts....32 E3
Chorlton Ches E....64 D2
Chorlton-cum-Hardy Manch....76 F4
Chorlton Lane Ches W....63 M3
Choulton Shrops....51 L3
Chowley Ches W....75 N12
Chrishall Essex....45 M4
Chrisswell Inver....113 J6
Christchurch BCP....12 B6
Christchurch Cambs....57 J1
Christchurch Gloucs....40 H9
Christchurch Newpt....28 D4
Christian Malford Wilts....29 R6
Christleton Ches W....75 M10
Christmas Common Oxon....31 N4
Christmas Pie Surrey....32 C12
Christon N Som....28 E11
Christon Bank Nthumb....109 N5
Christow Devon....8 H8
Christ's Hospital W Susx....14 G5
Chuck Hatch E Susx....15 N4
Chudleigh Devon....8 G9
Chudleigh Knighton Devon....8 H9
Chulmleigh Devon....19 N10
Chunal Derbys....77 J5
Church Lancs....83 R9
Churcham Gloucs....41 M8
Church Aston Wrekin....64 D8
Church Brampton Nhants....54 H7
Church Brough Cumb....90 D4
Church Broughton Derbys....65 M5
Church Cove Cnwll....2 H12
Church Crookham Hants....25 P3
Churchdown Gloucs....41 P7
Church Eaton Staffs....64 F8
Church End Bed....55 P9
Church End Bed....55 P8
Church End Bucks....43 Q10
Church End C Beds....44 E5
Church End C Beds....44 E8
Church End C Beds....44 C6
Church End C Beds....44 H4
Church End Cambs....56 C6
Church End Cambs....56 G5
Church End Essex....46 C9
Church End Essex....45 N5
Church End Essex....46 C6
Church End Essex....46 E8
Church End Gloucs....41 P4
Church End Gt Lon....33 J3
Church End Herts....45 J6
Church End Herts....45 L7
Church End Lincs....68 G5
Church End Lincs....81 J8
Church End Suffk....47 M4
Church End Warwks....53 N2
Church End Warwks....53 N2
Church Enstone Oxon....42 H6
Church Fenton N York....91 Q4
Churchfield Sandw....53 J2
Churchgate Herts....45 L11
Churchgate Street Essex....45 N8
Church Green Devon....9 M5
Church Gresley Derbys....65 P8
Church Hanborough Oxon....43 J9
Church Hill Staffs....64 H9
Church Houses N York....92 D7
Churchill Devon....9 M4
Churchill Devon....19 L5
Churchill N Som....28 F10
Churchill Oxon....42 F7
Churchill Worcs....52 G10
Churchill Worcs....52 G5
Churchinford Somset....21 K11
Church Knowle Dorset....11 M8
Church Laneham Notts....79 J9
Church Langton Leics....55 J2
Church Lawford Warwks....54 D5
Church Lawton Ches E....64 F1

Church Lawton Ches E....64 F1
Church Leigh Staffs....65 J5
Church Lench Worcs....53 J10
Church Mayfield Staffs....65 M4
Church Minshull Ches W....76 C11
Church Norton W Susx....14 B11
Churchover Warwks....54 E4
Church Preen Shrops....51 P1
Church Pulverbatch Shrops....63 M11
Churchstanton Somset....21 K10
Churchstoke Powys....51 J2
Churchstow Devon....5 M7
Church Stowe Nhants....54 G9
Church Street Essex....46 D3
Church Street Kent....34 C7
Church Stretton Shrops....51 M2
Churchthorpe Lincs....80 F4
Churchtown Bpool....82 H7
Churchtown Cnwll....6 Q9
Churchtown Derbys....77 P11
Churchtown Devon....19 N4
Churchtown IoM....102 f3
Churchtown Lancs....83 L6
Church Town N Linc....79 K2
Churchtown Sefton....83 J11
Church Village Rhondd....27 P5
Church Warsop Notts....78 F10
Church Wilne Derbys....66 D6
Churnsike Lodge Nthumb....99 K3
Churston Ferrers Torbay....5 Q5
Churt Surrey....25 Q6
Churton Ches W....75 M12
Churwell Leeds....85 K9
Chute Forest Wilts....24 C2
Chwilog Gwynd....60 G4
Chyandour Cnwll....2 D8
Chyanvounder Cnwll....2 G10
Chyeowling Cnwll....3 K6
Chyvarloe Cnwll....2 G11
Cilcain Flints....74 G10
Cilcennin Cerdgn....49 J8
Cilcewydd Powys....62 H11
Cilfrew Neath....27 J2
Cilfynydd Rhondd....27 P4
Cilgerran Pembks....37 N2
Cilgwyn Carmth....38 H6
Cilgwyn Gwynd....60 H1
Ciliau-Aeron Cerdgn....48 H9
Cilmaengwyn Neath....38 H10
Cilmery Powys....50 D10
Cilrhedyn Pembks....37 Q3
Cilsan Carmth....38 F7
Ciltalgarth Gwynd....62 B4
Cilycwm Carmth....38 H4
Cimla Neath....27 J3
Cinderford Gloucs....41 K9
Cinder Hill Wolves....52 H2
Cippenham Slough....32 D5
Cirencester Gloucs....30 B2
Citadilla N York....91 L7
City Gt Lon....33 L6
City V Glam....27 N7
City Airport Gt Lon....33 M6
City Dulas IoA....72 H6
Clabhach Ag & B....118 G1
Clachaig Ag & B....112 G5
Clachan Ag & B....111 Q10
Clachan Ag & B....112 G1
Clachan Ag & B....120 E9
Clachan Ag & B....120 E6
Clachan Highld....135 K8
Clachan-a-Luib W Isls....152 c6
Clachan Mor Ag & B....118 D3
Clachan na Luib W Isls....152 c6
Clachan of Campsie E Duns....114 A5
Clachan-Seil Ag & B....120 E9
Clachnaharry Highld....138 B6
Clachtoll Highld....148 C11
Clackmannan Clacks....114 G3
Clackmannanshire Bridge Fife....114 G4
Clackmarras Moray....139 N4
Clacton-on-Sea Essex....47 L8
Cladich Ag & B....121 L8
Cladswell Worcs....53 K9
Claggan Highld....120 D3
Claigan Highld....134 D5
Clandown BaNES....22 F2
Clanfield Hants....25 M10
Clanfield Oxon....42 G3
Clannaborough Devon....8 G4
Clanville Hants....24 E4
Clanville Somset....22 E7
Claonaig Ag & B....112 C10
Clapgate Dorset....11 N4
Clapgate Herts....45 M7
Clapham Bed....55 P9
Clapham Devon....8 H7
Clapham Gt Lon....33 K7
Clapham N York....83 R1
Clapham W Susx....14 G8
Clapham Green Bed....55 P10
Clap Hill Kent....17 J3
Clappersgate Cumb....89 K6
Clapton Somset....10 C3
Clapton Somset....22 E3
Clapton-in-Gordano N Som....28 G7
Clapton-on-the-Hill Gloucs....42 D8
Clapworthy Devon....19 M9
Clarach Cerdgn....49 K4
Claravale Gatesd....100 E5
Clarbeston Pembks....37 K6
Clarbeston Road Pembks....37 K6
Clarborough Notts....78 J7
Clare Suffk....46 E3
Clarebrand D & G....96 F5
Clarencefield D & G....97 M4
Clarewood Nthumb....100 C4
Clarilaw Border....107 N6
Clark's Green Surrey....14 H3
Clarkston E Rens....113 Q9
Clashmore Highld....146 D7
Clashmore Highld....148 B10
Clashnessie Highld....148 B10
Clashnoir Moray....139 N11
Clathy P & K....123 P8
Clathymore P & K....123 P8
Clatt Abers....140 E10
Clatter Powys....50 D2
Clatterford End Essex....46 A9
Clatworthy Somset....20 F7
Claughton Lancs....83 M2
Claughton Lancs....83 N6
Claughton Wirral....75 J6
Claverdon Warwks....53 M7
Claverham N Som....28 G9
Clavering Essex....45 N5
Claverley Shrops....52 D3
Claverton BaNES....29 M9
Clawdd-coch V Glam....27 P7
Clawdd-newydd Denbgs....62 G2
Clawthorpe Cumb....89 N11
Clawton Devon....7 M5
Claxby Lincs....80 C5
Claxby Lincs....80 F7
Claxton N York....86 C3
Claxton Norfk....71 N11

Claybrooke Magna Leics....54 E3
Clay Common Suffk....59 P4
Clay Coton Nhants....54 E5
Clay Cross Derbys....78 C10
Claydon Oxon....54 D10
Claydon Suffk....58 H10
Clay End Herts....45 K7
Claygate D & G....98 E12
Claygate Kent....16 D3
Claygate Surrey....32 H9
Claygate Cross Kent....33 R11
Clayhall Gt Lon....33 M4
Clayhanger Devon....20 F8
Clayhanger Wsall....65 K11
Clayhidon Devon....21 J10
Clayhill E Susx....16 E6
Clayhill Hants....12 G3
Clayhithe Cambs....57 J8
Clayock Highld....151 L5
Claypit Hill Cambs....45 M10
Claypits Gloucs....41 M10
Claypole Lincs....67 L2
Claythorpe Lincs....80 H8
Clayton C Brad....84 H9
Clayton Donc....78 D2
Clayton W Susx....15 K8
Clayton Green Lancs....83 N10
Clayton-le-Moors Lancs....83 R9
Clayton-le-Woods Lancs....83 N10
Clayton West Kirk....77 N2
Clayworth Notts....79 J6
Cleadale Highld....126 H6
Cleadon S Tyne....101 K5
Cleadon Park S Tyne....101 K5
Clearbrook Devon....4 H4
Clearwell Gloucs....40 H10
Cleasby N York....91 L5
Cleat W Isls....147 c6
Cleatlam Dur....91 J3
Cleator Cumb....88 D4
Cleator Moor Cumb....88 D4
Cleckheaton Kirk....85 J10
Cleedownton Shrops....51 P4
Cleehill Shrops....51 Q5
Cleekhimin N Lans....114 D9
Clee St Margaret Shrops....51 P4
Cleestanton Shrops....51 P5
Cleethorpes NE Lin....80 F2
Cleeton St Mary Shrops....51 Q5
Cleeve N Som....28 F9
Cleeve Oxon....31 N6
Cleeve Hill Gloucs....41 R6
Cleeve Prior Worcs....53 K11
Cleghornie E Loth....116 D5
Clehonger Herefs....40 F4
Cleish P & K....115 K2
Cleland N Lans....114 E2
Clement's End C Beds....44 E8
Clement Street Kent....33 P8
Clenamacrie Ag & B....120 H7
Clench Common Wilts....30 D9
Clenchwarton Norfk....69 L8
Clenerty Abers....141 J4
Clent Worcs....52 H5
Cleobury Mortimer Shrops....52 C5
Cleobury North Shrops....52 B5
Cleongart Ag & B....103 J3
Clephanton Highld....138 F6
Clerkhill D & G....106 H10
Cleuch-head D & G....105 Q9
Clevancy Wilts....30 B7
Clevedon N Som....28 F8
Cleveley Oxon....42 H7
Cleveleys Lancs....82 H6
Cleverton Wilts....29 R5
Clewer Somset....21 P3
Cley next the Sea Norfk....70 F3
Cliburn Cumb....89 P2
Cliddesden Hants....25 J3
Cliff Warwks....53 N1
Cliffe Lancs....83 Q8
Cliffe Medway....34 C7
Cliffe N York....86 C9
Cliffe N York....91 L4
Cliff End E Susx....16 F8
Cliffe Woods Medway....34 C7
Clifford Herefs....40 C3
Clifford Leeds....85 N6
Clifford Chambers Warwks....53 M10
Clifford's Mesne Gloucs....41 L7
Cliffsend Kent....35 P9
Clifton Bristl....28 H7
Clifton C Beds....44 H4
Clifton C York....86 B5
Clifton Calder....84 H10
Clifton Cumb....89 N1
Clifton Derbys....65 M3
Clifton Donc....78 E4
Clifton Lancs....83 L8
Clifton N York....85 L5
Clifton Nthumb....100 G2
Clifton Oxon....43 K5
Clifton Salfd....76 E2
Clifton Worcs....52 F11
Clifton Campville Staffs....65 N10
Clifton Hampden Oxon....31 M3
Clifton Reynes M Keyn....55 M9
Clifton upon Dunsmore Warwks....54 E6
Clifton upon Teme Worcs....52 D8
Cliftonville Kent....35 R8
Climping W Susx....14 F9
Climpy S Lans....114 H8
Clink Somset....22 G4
Clint N York....85 K3
Clinterty C Aber....133 K2
Clint Green Norfk....70 F10
Clintmains Border....107 P3
Clippiau Gwynd....61 P10
Clippesby Norfk....71 N9
Clipsham Rutlnd....67 P8
Clipston Nhants....54 H4
Clipston Notts....66 G5
Clipstone C Beds....44 D6
Clipstone Notts....78 F11
Clitheroe Lancs....83 R7
Clive Shrops....63 P7
Clixby Lincs....80 B3
Cloatley Wilts....29 R4
Clocaenog Denbgs....62 G2
Clochan Moray....140 B4
Clock Face St Hel....75 N5
Cloddiau Powys....62 H10
Clodock Herefs....40 D6
Cloford Somset....22 G5
Clola Abers....141 N7
Clophill C Beds....44 F4
Clopton Nhants....55 Q4
Clopton Suffk....59 J10
Clopton Corner Suffk....59 J10
Clopton Green Suffk....58 B10
Clos du Valle Guern....12 d1
Closeburn D & G....106 B10
Closeburnmill D & G....106 B10
Closeclark IoM....102 c6
Closworth Somset....10 F2
Clothall Herts....45 J5
Clotton Ches W....75 N11
Cloudesley Bush Warwks....54 E3
Clouds Oldham....76 H2
Clough Oldham....76 H2
Clough Foot Calder....84 D9

Clough Head Calder....84 G11
Cloughton N York....93 K8
Cloughton Newlands N York....93 K7
Clousta Shet....147 h6
Clova Angus....131 Q9
Clovelly Devon....18 F8
Clovenfords Border....107 L2
Clovulin Highld....128 D11
Clow Bridge Lancs....84 B9
Clowne Derbys....78 D8
Clows Top Worcs....52 D6
Cloy Wrexhm....63 L4
Cluanie Inn Highld....128 F2
Cluanie Lodge Highld....128 F2
Clubworthy Cnwll....7 L4
Clugston D & G....95 L7
Clun Shrops....51 J4
Clunas Highld....138 G6
Clunbury Shrops....51 L4
Clunderwen Carmth....37 M6
Clune Highld....138 E10
Clunes Highld....128 H6
Clungunford Shrops....51 L5
Clunie P & K....124 C4
Clunton Shrops....51 K4
Cluny Fife....115 N2
Clutton BaNES....29 J10
Clutton Ches W....63 M1
Clutton Hill BaNES....29 K10
Clwt Conwy....74 C11
Clwt-y-bont Gwynd....73 K11
Clydach Mons....26 G2
Clydach Swans....26 G2
Clydach Vale Rhondd....27 M4
Clydebank W Duns....113 P7
Clydey Pembks....37 M8
Clyffe Pypard Wilts....30 C7
Clynder Ag & B....113 K4
Clyne Neath....27 J2
Clynnog Fawr Gwynd....60 G3
Clyro Powys....40 B3
Clyst Honiton Devon....9 J5
Clyst Hydon Devon....9 K4
Clyst St George Devon....9 J7
Clyst St Lawrence Devon....9 K5
Clyst St Mary Devon....9 J6
Cnoc W Isls....152 g3
Cnwch Coch Cerdgn....49 L6
Coad's Green Cnwll....7 K9
Coal Aston Derbys....78 B9
Coalbrookdale Wrekin....64 C10
Coalbrookvale Blae G....80 B10
Coalburn S Lans....105 Q3
Coalburns Gatesd....100 E6
Coaley Gloucs....41 M11
Coalhill Essex....46 D10
Coalmoor Wrekin....64 C10
Coalpit Heath S Glos....29 K6
Coal Pool Wsall....65 J12
Coalport Wrekin....64 D10
Coalsnaughton Clacks....114 G2
Coaltown of Balgonie Fife....115 P1
Coaltown of Wemyss Fife....115 P1
Coalville Leics....66 C9
Coalway Gloucs....40 H9
Coanwood Nthumb....99 K6
Coat Somset....21 P8
Coatbridge N Lans....114 D8
Coatdyke N Lans....114 D8
Coate Swindn....30 D6
Coate Wilts....30 B10
Coates Gloucs....30 B2
Coates Lincs....79 M7
Coates Notts....79 J7
Coatham R & Cl....92 C2
Coatham Mundeville Darltn....91 M3
Cobbaton Devon....19 M8
Coberley Gloucs....41 Q8
Cobhall Common Herefs....40 F4
Cobham Kent....34 B8
Cobham Surrey....32 G10
Cobham Services Surrey....32 G10
Coblers Green Essex....46 C8
Cobley Dorset....23 M9
Cobnash Herefs....51 M8
Cobo Guern....12 c2
Cobridge C Stke....64 F2
Coburby Abers....141 M3
Cock Alley Derbys....78 C9
Cockayne N York....92 D6
Cockayne Hatley C Beds....56 E10
Cock Bank Wrexhm....63 L3
Cock Bevington Warwks....53 K10
Cock Bridge Abers....131 N3
Cock Clarks Essex....46 E11
Cock & End Suffk....57 N10
Cockenzie and Port Seton E Loth....115 R6
Cocker Bar Lancs....83 L10
Cocker Brook Lancs....83 R10
Cockerham Lancs....83 L4
Cockermouth Cumb....97 M12
Cockernhoe Herts....44 H7
Cockersdale Leeds....85 K9
Cockett Swans....26 F3
Cockfield Dur....91 J2
Cockfield Suffk....58 D10
Cockfosters Gt Lon....33 K3
Cock Green Essex....46 C8
Cocking W Susx....14 C7
Cocking Causeway W Susx....14 C7
Cockington Torbay....5 Q4
Cocklake Somset....21 P3
Cockley Beck Cumb....88 H6
Cockley Cley Norfk....69 Q11
Cock Marling E Susx....16 F7
Cockpole Green Wokham....31 Q6
Cocks Cnwll....3 J4
Cockshutford Shrops....51 P3
Cockshutt Shrops....63 M6
Cock Street Kent....34 D12
Cockthorpe Norfk....70 E4
Cockwood Devon....9 J8
Cockyard Herefs....40 F5
Coddenham Suffk....58 H9
Coddington Ches W....63 M1
Coddington Herefs....41 M4
Coddington Notts....67 L1
Codford St Mary Wilts....23 L5
Codford St Peter Wilts....23 L5
Codicote Herts....45 J8
Codmore Hill W Susx....14 F7
Codnor Derbys....66 C3
Codrington S Glos....29 L7
Codsall Staffs....64 F11
Codsall Wood Staffs....64 F11
Coed Darcy Neath....26 H3
Coedely Rhondd....27 N5
Coed Hirwaun Neath....27 K5
Coed Morgan Mons....40 E9
Coedpoeth Wrexhm....63 J2
Coed Talon Flints....75 J11
Coedway Powys....63 K9
Coed-y-Bryn Cerdgn....48 F2
Coed-y-caerau Newpt....28 E4
Coed-y-Cwm Rhondd....27 N4
Coed-y-paen Mons....28 D3

Coed-yr-ynys Powys....39 R7
Coed Ystumgwern Gwynd....61 K7
Coelbren Powys....39 K9
Coffinswell Devon....5 Q3
Coffle End Bed....55 P9
Cofton Devon....8 H8
Cofton Hackett Worcs....53 J5
Cogan V Glam....28 A8
Cogenhoe Nhants....55 L8
Cogges Oxon....42 H9
Coggeshall Essex....46 E7
Coggeshall Hamlet Essex....46 F7
Coggin's Mill E Susx....15 Q5
Coignafearn Highld....138 C12
Coilacriech Abers....131 P5
Coilantogle Stirlg....122 G11
Coillore Highld....134 F8
Coity Brdgnd....27 L6
Col W Isls....152 g3
Colaboll Highld....145 N3
Colan Cnwll....3 J3
Colaton Raleigh Devon....9 K7
Colbost Highld....134 D6
Colburn N York....91 K7
Colby Cumb....89 Q3
Colby IoM....102 c7
Colby Norfk....71 J6
Colchester Essex....46 H6
Colchester Zoo Essex....46 G7
Cold Ash W Berk....31 L8
Cold Ashby Nhants....54 G5
Cold Ashton S Glos....29 M8
Cold Aston Gloucs....42 D8
Coldbackie Highld....149 N5
Coldbeck Cumb....90 B6
Cold Blow Pembks....37 M8
Cold Brayfield M Keyn....55 M10
Cold Cotes N York....83 Q1
Coldean Br & H....15 L9
Coldeast Devon....8 G9
Colden Calder....84 E9
Colden Common Hants....24 H9
Coldfair Green Suffk....59 N8
Coldham Cambs....68 H11
Cold Hanworth Lincs....79 P7
Coldharbour Cnwll....3 J5
Coldharbour Devon....20 H11
Coldharbour Surrey....14 G2
Coldharbour Herts....31 N6
Cold Harbour Wilts....23 M6
Cold Hatton Wrekin....64 B8
Cold Hatton Heath Wrekin....64 B8
Cold Hesledon Dur....101 K9
Cold Hiendley Wakefd....78 B1
Cold Higham Nhants....54 H10
Coldingham Border....117 K8
Cold Kirby N York....92 B10
Cold Newton Leics....66 H11
Cold Northcott Cnwll....7 J7
Cold Norton Essex....46 E11
Cold Overton Leics....67 K10
Coldred Kent....17 N1
Coldridge Devon....8 D3
Coldstream Border....108 D3
Coldwaltham W Susx....14 F8
Coldwell Herefs....40 F4
Coldwells Abers....141 M4
Cold Weston Shrops....51 P4
Cole Somset....22 F6
Colebatch Shrops....51 K3
Colebrook Devon....4 H5
Colebrooke Devon....9 J3
Colebrook Devon....8 E5
Coleby Lincs....79 N11
Coleby N Linc....86 G11
Cole End Warwks....53 M3
Coleford Devon....9 J3
Coleford Gloucs....41 J9
Coleford Somset....22 F4
Coleford Water Somset....20 H8
Colegate End Norfk....59 J3
Cole Green Herts....45 J9
Cole Green Herts....45 M5
Cole Henley Hants....24 H3
Colehill Dorset....11 P4
Coleman Green Herts....44 H5
Coleman's Hatch E Susx....15 N4
Colemere Shrops....63 M6
Colemore Hants....25 M7
Colemore Green Shrops....52 C7
Colenden P & K....124 C7
Coleorton Leics....66 C9
Colerne Wilts....29 N8
Colesbourne Gloucs....41 R9
Cole's Cross Devon....5 N7
Coles Cross Dorset....10 C5
Colesden Bed....56 C9
Coleshill Bucks....32 D3
Coleshill Oxon....30 F4
Coleshill Warwks....53 M3
Colestocks Devon....9 L5
Colgate W Susx....15 J4
Colinsburgh Fife....125 J12
Colinton C Edin....115 M7
Colintraive Ag & B....112 F6
Colkirk Norfk....70 D7
Coll Ag & B....118 H1
Coll W Isls....152 g3
Collace P & K....124 D6
Collafirth Shet....147 i5
Coll Airport Ag & B....118 H1
Collaton Devon....5 M9
Collaton St Mary Torbay....5 P5
College of Roseisle Moray....139 L3
College Town Br For....32 B10
Collessie Fife....124 F10
Colleton Mills Devon....18 N4
Collier Row Gt Lon....33 N3
Collier's Green E Susx....16 D6
Collier's Green Kent....16 C2
Collier Street Kent....16 C2
Colliery Row Sundld....101 J8
Collieston Abers....141 P10
Collin D & G....97 L3
Collingbourne Ducis Wilts....24 D3
Collingbourne Kingston Wilts....24 D2
Collingham Leeds....85 M5
Collingham Notts....79 L11
Collington Herefs....52 C8
Collingtree Nhants....55 J9
Collins Green Warrtn....75 P5
Collins Green Worcs....52 D9
Colliston Angus....125 M4
Colliton Devon....9 L4

Coln St Dennis Gloucs 42 C9
Colonsay Ag & B 111 J2
Colonsay Airport Ag & B 110 H8
Colpy Abers 140 G9
Colquhar Border 107 J1
Colquite Cnwll 6 F10
Colscott Devon 18 G10
Colsterdale N York 91 H10
Colsterworth Lincs 67 M7
Colston Bassett Notts 66 H5
Coltfield Moray 139 L3
Colt Hill Hants 25 N3
Coltishall Norfk 71 K8
Colton Cumb 89 J9
Colton Leeds 85 M8
Colton N York 85 Q6
Colton Norfk 70 G10
Colton Staffs 65 K8
Colt's Hill Kent 16 B2
Columbjohn Devon 8 H5
Colva Powys 50 H10
Colvend D & G 96 H7
Colwall Herefs 41 M3
Colwell Nthumb 99 Q3
Colwich Staffs 65 J8
Colwick Notts 66 G4
Colwinston V Glam 27 N7
Colworth W Susx 14 C10
Colwyn Bay Conwy 73 P8
Colyford Devon 9 N6
Colyton Devon 9 N6
Combe Devon 5 M9
Combe Herefs 51 K8
Combe Oxon 43 J8
Combe W Berk 30 H10
Combe Almer Dorset 11 M5
Combe Common Surrey 14 E4
Combe Down BaNES 29 M10
Combe Fishacre Devon 5 P4
Combe Florey Somset 21 J7
Combe Hay BaNES 29 L10
Combeinteignhead Devon 8 G10
Combe Martin Devon 19 L4
Combe Raleigh Devon 9 M4
Comberbach Ches W 76 B8
Comberford Staffs 65 M10
Comberton Cambs 56 G9
Comberton Herefs 51 N7
Combe St Nicholas Somset 9 P2
Combpyne Devon 9 P6
Combridge Staffs 65 K5
Combrook Warwks 53 P10
Combs Derbys 77 K8
Combs Suffk 58 F9
Combs Ford Suffk 58 F9
Combwich Somset 21 L5
Comers Abers 132 G3
Comeytrowe Somset 21 K8
Comhampton Worcs 52 F7
Commercial End Cambs 57 K8
Commins Coch Powys 61 P11
Commondale N York 92 D5
Common Edge Bpool 82 H8
Common End Cumb 88 D2
Common Moor Cnwll 4 C3
Common Platt Wilts 30 C5
Commonside Ches W 75 P8
Commonside Derbys 65 N4
Common Side Derbys 77 Q8
Commonwood Shrops 63 N6
Commonwood Wrexhm 63 L1
Compass Somset 21 L6
Compstall Stockp 76 H5
Compstonend D & G 96 D8
Compton Devon 5 P4
Compton Hants 24 F7
Compton Hants 24 H8
Compton Staffs 52 F4
Compton Surrey 14 D1
Compton W Berk 31 L6
Compton W Susx 25 N10
Compton Wilts 23 N8
Compton Abbas Dorset 23 J9
Compton Abdale Gloucs 42 C8
Compton Bassett Wilts 30 B8
Compton Beauchamp Oxon 30 F5
Compton Bishop Somset 21 N2
Compton Chamberlayne Wilts 23 M7
Compton Dando BaNES 29 K9
Compton Dundon Somset 22 C7
Compton Durville Somset 21 P10
Compton Greenfield S Glos 28 H5
Compton Martin BaNES 28 H11
Compton Pauncefoot Somset 22 E8
Compton Valence Dorset 10 F6
Comrie Fife 115 J3
Comrie P & K 123 K8
Conaglen House Highld 128 E10
Conchra Highld 136 B10
Concraigie P & K 124 C4
Conder Green Lancs 83 K4
Conderton Worcs 41 Q4
Condicote Gloucs 42 D6
Condorrat N Lans 114 D6
Condover Shrops 63 N11
Coney Hill Gloucs 41 N8
Coneyhurst W Susx 14 G6
Coneysthorpe N York 86 E1
Coneythorpe N York 85 N3
Coney Weston Suffk 58 E5
Conford Hants 25 P7
Congdon's Shop Cnwll 7 P7
Congerstone Leics 66 B11
Congham Norfk 69 M7
Congleton Ches E 76 F11
Congl-y-wal Gwynd 61 L3
Congresbury N Som 28 F9
Congreve Staffs 64 G9
Conheath D & G 97 K4
Conicavel Moray 138 H5
Coningsby Lincs 80 D12
Conington Cambs 56 D3
Conington Cambs 56 F7
Conisbrough Donc 78 F6
Conisholme Lincs 80 H4
Coniston Cumb 89 J7
Coniston E R Yk 87 M8
Coniston Cold N York 84 D3
Conistone N York 84 E2
Connah's Quay Flints 75 J10
Connel Ag & B 120 G6
Connel Park E Ayrs 105 L7
Connor Downs Cnwll 2 F7
Conon Bridge Highld 137 P5
Cononley N York 84 E6
Consall Staffs 64 H4
Consett Dur 100 E7
Constable Burton N York 91 K8
Constable Lee Lancs 84 B10
Constantine Cnwll 6 C10
Constantine Bay Cnwll 6 C10
Contin Highld 137 M4
Conwy Conwy 73 N8
Conwy Castle Conwy 73 N8
Conyer Kent 34 G9
Conyer's Green Suffk 58 C7
Cooden E Susx 16 C9
Cookbury Devon 7 M4
Cookbury Wick Devon 7 M4
Cookham W & M 32 C5
Cookham Dean W & M 32 B5

Cookham Rise W & M 32 C5
Cookhill Worcs 53 K9
Cookley Suffk 59 L5
Cookley Worcs 52 F5
Cookley Green Oxon 31 P4
Cookney Abers 133 L6
Cooksbridge E Susx 15 M8
Cooksey Green Worcs 52 G7
Cook's Green Essex 47 L8
Cooks Green Suffk 58 E10
Cookshill Staffs 64 H3
Cooksland Cnwll 6 F11
Cooksmill Green Essex 46 B10
Cookson Green Ches W 75 P9
Coolham W Susx 14 G6
Cooling Medway 34 D7
Cooling Street Medway 34 D7
Coombe Cnwll 2 K6
Coombe Cnwll 3 M4
Coombe Cnwll 9 L6
Coombe Devon 8 F8
Coombe Devon 9 L6
Coombe Devon 8 H10
Coombe Gloucs 29 M3
Coombe Hants 25 M8
Coombe Wilts 23 P3
Coombe Bissett Wilts 23 P8
Coombe Cellars Devon 8 G10
Coombe Cross Hants 25 L8
Coombe Hill Gloucs 41 P6
Coombe Keynes Dorset 11 K8
Coombe Pafford Torbay 5 Q3
Coombes W Susx 14 H9
Coombe Street Somset 22 F7
Coombeswood Dudley 52 H3
Coopersale Common Essex N11
Coopersale Street Essex 45 N11
Cooper's Corner Kent 33 P12
Cooper's Green E Susx 15 N6
Coopers Green Herts 44 H9
Cooper Street Kent 35 P10
Cootham W Susx 14 F8
Copdock Suffk 47 K3
Copford Green Essex 46 G7
Copgrove N York 85 M3
Copister Shet 147 j4
Cople Bed 56 B11
Copley Calder 84 G10
Copley Dur 90 H2
Copley Tameside 76 H4
Coplow Dale Derbys 77 M8
Copmanthorpe C York 85 Q6
Copmere End Staffs 64 E6
Copp Lancs 83 L6
Coppathorne Cnwll 7 J5
Coppenhall Staffs 64 G8
Coppenhall Moss Ches E 76 D12
Copperhouse Cnwll 2 F7
Coppicegate Shrops 52 D5
Coppingford Cambs 56 C5
Copplestone Devon 8 E4
Coppull Lancs 83 M12
Coppull Moor Lancs 75 P1
Copsale W Susx 14 H6
Copster Green Lancs 83 P8
Copston Magna Warwks 54 C3
Cop Street Kent 35 N10
Copthall Green Essex 33 M2
Copt Heath Solhll 53 M5
Copt Hewick N York 85 M1
Copthorne Cnwll 7 K6
Copthorne W Susx 15 K3
Copt Oak Leics 66 D9
Copy's Green Norfk 70 D4
Copythorne Hants 24 E10
Coram Street Suffk 46 H3
Corbets Tey Gt Lon 33 Q5
Corbière Jersey 13 a3
Corbridge Nthumb 100 C5
Corby Nhants 55 M3
Corby Glen Lincs 67 N7
Corby Hill Cumb 98 F7
Cordon N Ayrs 103 Q4
Cordwell Derbys 77 P8
Coreley Shrops 52 B6
Cores End Bucks 32 C5
Corfe Somset 21 K9
Corfe Castle Dorset 11 M8
Corfe Mullen Dorset 11 N5
Corfton Shrops 51 N4
Corgarff Abers 131 P3
Corhampton Hants 25 K9
Corks Pond Kent 16 B3
Corlae D & G 105 M10
Corley Warwks 53 P4
Corley Ash Warwks 53 P3
Corley Moor Warwks 53 P4
Corley Services Warwks 53 P3
Cormuir Angus 131 P11
Cornard Tye Suffk 46 F3
Corndon Devon 8 C7
Corner Row Lancs 83 K8
Corney Cumb 88 F8
Cornforth Dur 101 J11
Cornhill Abers 140 F4
Cornhill-on-Tweed Nthumb 108 D2
Cornholme Calder 84 D10
Cornish Hall End Essex 46 B4
Cornoigmore Ag & B 118 D3
Cornriggs Dur 99 N9
Cornsay Dur 100 F9
Cornsay Colliery Dur 100 F9
Corntown Highld 137 P5
Corntown V Glam 27 L7
Cornwall Airport Newquay Cnwll 3 L2
Cornwell Oxon 42 F6
Cornwood Devon 5 K5
Cornworthy Devon 5 P5
Corpach Highld 128 F2
Corpusty Norfk 70 G6
Corrachree Abers 132 D3
Corran Highld 127 Q2
Corran Highld 128 E11
Corrany IoM 102 f4
Corrie D & G 97 P1
Corrie N Ayrs 103 Q3
Corriecravie N Ayrs 103 N5
Corriegills N Ayrs 103 Q3
Corriegour Lodge Hotel Highld 129 J6
Corriemoille Highld 137 K3
Corrimony Highld 137 L10
Corringham Lincs 79 L5
Corringham Thurr 34 C5
Corris Gwynd 61 N10
Corris Uchaf Gwynd 61 N10
Corrow Ag & B 113 J1
Corry Highld 135 L11
Corscombe Devon 8 B5
Corscombe Dorset 10 E4
Corse Gloucs 41 M6
Corse Lawn Gloucs 41 N5
Corsham Wilts 29 N6
Corsindae Abers 132 G3
Corsley Wilts 22 H4
Corsley Heath Wilts 22 H4
Corsock D & G 96 G2
Corston BaNES 29 L9
Corston Wilts 29 Q6
Corstorphine C Edin 115 M7
Cors-y-Gedol Gwynd 61 K7

Cortachy Angus 132 B12
Corton Suffk 59 Q1
Corton Wilts 23 K5
Corton Denham Somset 22 E9
Coruanan Highld 128 E10
Corwen Denbgs 62 E3
Coryates Dorset 10 F7
Coryton Devon 7 N8
Coryton Thurr 34 C6
Cosby Leics 54 E2
Coseley Dudley 52 H2
Cosford Shrops 64 E11
Cosgrove Nhants 43 R3
Cosham C Port 13 L4
Cosheston Pembks 37 K10
Coshieville P & K 123 K3
Cossall Notts 66 D4
Cossall Marsh Notts 66 D4
Cossington Leics 66 G9
Cossington Somset 21 M5
Costessey Norfk 70 H9
Costock Notts 66 F7
Coston Leics 67 L8
Coston Norfk 70 F10
Cote Oxon 43 J11
Cote Somset 21 M4
Cotebrook Ches W 75 P10
Cotehill Cumb 98 F8
Cotes Cumb 89 M9
Cotes Leics 66 F8
Cotes Staffs 64 F5
Cotesbach Leics 54 E4
Cotes Heath Staffs 64 F5
Cotford St Luke Somset 21 J8
Cotgrave Notts 66 G5
Cothal Abers 133 L1
Cotham Notts 67 K3
Cothelstone Somset 21 J7
Cotherstone Dur 90 G3
Cothill Oxon 31 K2
Cotleigh Devon 9 N4
Cotmanhay Derbys 66 D3
Coton Cambs 56 H9
Coton Nhants 54 H6
Coton Shrops 63 P5
Coton Staffs 64 G6
Coton Staffs 64 H6
Coton Staffs 65 M11
Coton Clanford Staffs 64 F7
Coton Hayes Staffs 65 J5
Coton Hill Shrops 63 N9
Coton in the Clay Staffs 65 M6
Coton in the Elms Derbys 65 N9
Cotswold Airport Wilts 29 Q3
Cotswold Wildlife Park & Gardens Oxon 42 F10
Cott Devon 5 N4
Cottam E R Yk 87 J2
Cottam Lancs 83 L8
Cottam Notts 79 K8
Cottenham Cambs 57 J7
Cotterdale N York 90 D8
Cottered Herts 45 K5
Cotteridge Birm 53 K5
Cotterstock Nhants 55 P3
Cottesbrooke Nhants 54 H6
Cottesmore Rutlnd 67 M9
Cottingham E R Yk 87 J8
Cottingham Nhants 55 K3
Cottingley C Brad 84 H8
Cottisford Oxon 43 M5
Cotton Suffk 58 G7
Cotton End Bed 44 F3
Cotton Tree Lancs 84 D7
Cottown Abers 133 J1
Cottown Abers 140 D10
Cottown of Gight Abers 141 K8
Cotts Devon 4 H4
Cotwall Wrekin 63 Q8
Cotwalton Staffs 64 H5
Couch's Mill Cnwll 4 D5
Coughton Herefs 41 J7
Coughton Warwks 53 K8
Coulaghailtro Ag & B 111 K6
Coulags Highld 136 D7
Coulby Newham Middsb 92 A4
Coulderton Cumb 88 C5
Coull Abers 132 D4
Coulport Ag & B 113 M3
Coulsdon Gt Lon 33 K10
Coulston Wilts 23 J3
Coulter S Lans 106 D3
Coultershaw Bridge W Susx 14 D7
Coultings Somset 21 K5
Coulton N York 92 D12
Coultra Fife 124 G8
Cound Shrops 63 P11
Coundlane Shrops 63 P11
Coundon Dur 100 G12
Coundon Grange Dur 91 J1
Countersett N York 90 F9
Countess Wilts 23 P5
Countess Cross Essex 46 F5
Countess Wear Devon 8 H7
Countesswells Aber 133 L3
Countesthorpe Leics 54 F2
Countisbury Devon 19 P3
Coupar Angus P & K 124 C5
Coupe Green Lancs 83 N9
Coupland Cumb 90 B3
Coupland Nthumb 108 F4
Cour Ag & B 112 B11
Courance D & G 105 N12
Court-at-Street Kent 17 J4
Courteachan Highld 127 M5
Courteenhall Nhants 55 J10
Court Henry Carmth 38 E7
Courtsend Essex 35 J4
Courtway Somset 21 K6
Cousland Mdloth 115 Q7
Cousley Wood E Susx 16 B4
Cove Ag & B 113 L4
Cove Border 116 H6
Cove Devon 20 E10
Cove Hants 25 Q2
Cove Highld 143 L7
Cove Bay Aber 133 M4
Cove Bottom Suffk 59 P5
Covehithe Suffk 59 Q4
Coven Staffs 64 G11
Coveney Cambs 57 J4
Covenham St Bartholomew Lincs 80 G5
Covenham St Mary Lincs 80 G5
Coven Heath Staffs 64 G11
Coventry Covtry 53 Q5
Coverack Cnwll 3 K8
Coverack Bridges Cnwll 2 G8
Coverham N York 91 J9
Covington Cambs 55 Q6
Covington S Lans 106 C2
Cowan Bridge Lancs 89 Q11
Cowbech E Susx 16 A8
Cowbit Lincs 68 F9
Cowbridge V Glam 27 N7
Cowdale Derbys 77 K9
Cowden Kent 15 N3
Cowdenbeath Fife 115 L4
Cowden Pound Kent 15 N3
Cowden Station Kent 15 N3
Cowers Lane Derbys 65 Q3
Cowes IoW 12 H5
Cowesby N York 91 Q9
Cowesfield Green Wilts 24 C8
Cowfold W Susx 15 J6

Cowgill Cumb 90 C9
Cow Green Suffk 58 F7
Cowhill S Glos 29 J4
Cowie Stirlg 114 F3
Cowlam E R Yk 86 H1
Cowley Devon 8 G5
Cowley Gloucs 41 Q8
Cowley Gt Lon 32 F6
Cowley Oxon 43 L11
Cowling Lancs 83 N11
Cowling N York 84 E6
Cowling N York 91 L9
Cowlinge Suffk 57 N10
Cowmes Kirk 85 J12
Cowpe Lancs 84 C11
Cowpen Nthumb 100 H1
Cowpen Bewley S on T 91 Q2
Cowplain Hants 13 M3
Cowshill Dur 99 N9
Cowslip Green N Som 28 G10
Cowthorpe N York 85 N5
Coxall Herefs 51 L6
Coxbank Ches E 64 C4
Coxbench Derbys 66 B3
Coxbridge Somset 22 C6
Cox Common Suffk 59 M4
Coxford Cnwll 6 H5
Coxford Norfk 70 C6
Coxgreen Staffs 52 E3
Coxheath Kent 34 C12
Coxhoe Dur 101 J11
Coxley Somset 22 C5
Coxley Wakefd 85 K11
Coxley Wick Somset 22 C4
Coxpark Cnwll 7 M10
Coxtie Green Essex 33 Q4
Coxwold N York 92 A11
Coychurch Brdgnd 27 M7
Coylton S Ayrs 104 H6
Coylumbridge Highld 130 G2
Coytrahen Brdgnd 27 L5
Crabbs Cross Worcs 53 K7
Crab Orchard Dorset 11 Q3
Crabtree W Susx 14 H6
Crabtree Green Wrexhm 63 K3
Crackenthorpe Cumb 89 Q2
Crackington Haven Cnwll 6 G5
Crackley Staffs 64 F2
Crackley Warwks 53 P6
Crackleybank Shrops 64 D9
Crackpot N York 90 F7
Cracoe N York 84 E3
Craddock Devon 20 H11
Cradle End Herts 45 N7
Cradley Dudley 52 H4
Cradley Herefs 41 M3
Cradley Heath Sandw 52 H4
Cradoc Powys 50 E9
Crafthole Cnwll 4 G6
Crafton Bucks 44 C8
Crag Foot Lancs 89 M12
Cragg Hill Leeds 85 J8
Craggan Highld 139 J10
Cragganmore Moray 139 M8
Cragg Hill Leeds 85 K8
Cragg Vale Calder 84 F10
Craghead Dur 100 G8
Crai Powys 39 L7
Craibstone Moray 140 D4
Craichie Angus 125 N2
Craig Angus 125 Q2
Craig Highld 136 E6
Craigbank E Ayrs 105 L7
Craigburn Border 115 N9
Craig-cefn-parc Swans 38 G11
Craigcleuch D & G 107 K12
Craigdam Abers 141 K10
Craigdhu Ag & B 120 D7
Craigearn Abers 132 H2
Craigellachie Moray 139 P7
Craigend P & K 123 Q8
Craigend Rens 113 N5
Craigendoran Ag & B 113 L5
Craigends Rens 113 N5
Craighlaw D & G 95 K6
Craighouse Ag & B 111 J5
Craigie P & K 124 C4
Craigie S Ayrs 104 H3
Craigiefold Abers 141 M3
Craigley D & G 96 G6
Craig Llangiwg Neath 38 H10
Craiglockhart C Edin 115 M7
Craigmillar C Edin 115 P7
Craignant Shrops 63 J5
Craigneston D & G 105 N12
Craigneuk N Lans 114 D10
Craigneuk N Lans 114 E9
Craigo Angus 132 H11
Craig Penllyn V Glam 27 M7
Craigrothie Fife 124 H11
Craigruie Stirlg 122 F9
Craig's End Essex 46 C4
Craigton Angus 125 K4
Craigton C Aber 133 L3
Craigton E Rens 113 P10
Craigton of Airlie Angus 124 H2
Craig-y-Duke Neath 38 H11
Craig-y-nos Powys 39 K9
Craik Border 107 J7
Crail Fife 125 M11
Crailing Border 107 M11
Craiselound N Linc 79 J4
Crakehall N York 91 L9
Crakehill N York 85 N1
Crakemarsh Staffs 65 K5
Crambe N York 86 B2
Crambeck N York 86 D2
Cramlington Nthumb 100 H3
Cramond C Edin 115 M6
Cramond Bridge C Edin 115 M6
Crampmoor Hants 24 E8
Cranage Ches E 76 D10
Cranberry Staffs 64 F5
Cranborne Dorset 23 N10
Cranbourne Br For 32 C8
Cranbrook Devon 9 J6
Cranbrook Kent 16 D3
Cranbrook Common Kent 16 D3
Crane Moor Barns 77 Q4
Crane's Corner Norfk 70 D9
Cranfield C Beds 44 D3
Cranford Devon 18 G9
Cranford Gt Lon 32 G6
Cranford St Andrew Nhants 55 M5
Cranford St John Nhants 55 M5
Cranham Gloucs 41 Q9
Cranham Gt Lon 33 Q5
Cranhill Warwks 53 L10
Crank St Hel 75 N4
Cranleigh Surrey 14 G4
Cranmer Green Suffk 58 F6
Cranmore IoW 12 F6
Cranmore Somset 22 E4
Cranoe Leics 55 J1
Cransford Suffk 59 L8
Cranshaws Border 116 H8
Cranstal IoM 102 f2
Cranswick E R Yk 87 J5
Crantock Cnwll 3 J3
Cranwell Lincs 67 N3
Cranwich Norfk 57 P1
Cranworth Norfk 70 E10
Craobh Haven Ag & B 120 E11
Crapstone Devon 4 H4

Crarae Ag & B 112 E2
Crask Inn Highld 149 L11
Crask of Aigas Highld 137 M7
Craster Nthumb 109 L6
Craswall Herefs 40 D4
Crateford Staffs 64 G10
Cratfield Suffk 59 L5
Crathes Abers 133 J5
Crathie Abers 131 N5
Crathie Highld 129 N5
Crathorne N York 91 Q5
Craven Arms Shrops 51 M4
Crawcrook Gatesd 100 E5
Crawford Lancs 75 N3
Crawford S Lans 106 E5
Crawfordjohn S Lans 106 A5
Crawley Hants 24 G6
Crawley Oxon 42 H9
Crawley W Susx 15 J4
Crawley Down W Susx 15 K3
Crawleyside Dur 100 C10
Crawshawbooth Lancs 84 B10
Crawton Abers 133 L8
Craxe's Green Essex 46 G6
Cray N York 90 F10
Cray P & K 131 L11
Crayford Gt Lon 33 P7
Crayke N York 85 R1
Craymere Beck Norfk 70 F6
Crays Hill Essex 34 C4
Cray's Pond Oxon 31 N6
Craythorne Staffs 65 M7
Crazies Hill Wokgm 31 Q6
Creacombe Devon 20 C9
Creagan Inn Ag & B 121 J4
Creag Ghoraidh W Isls 152 c9
Creagorry W Isls 152 c9
Creaguaineach Lodge Highld 129 K10
Creamore Bank Shrops 63 N5
Creaton Nhants 54 H6
Creca D & G 97 P3
Credenhill Herefs 40 F3
Crediton Devon 8 E5
Creebank D & G 95 J4
Creebridge D & G 95 M5
Creech Dorset 11 M8
Creech Heathfield Somset 21 L8
Creech St Michael Somset 21 L8
Creed Cnwll 3 M5
Creekmoor BCP 11 N6
Creekmouth Gt Lon 33 N6
Creeksea Essex 34 F3
Creeting St Mary Suffk 58 G9
Creeton Lincs 67 P8
Creetown D & G 95 N6
Cregneash IoM 102 b7
Creg ny Baa IoM 102 e5
Cregrina Powys 50 F10
Creich Fife 124 G8
Creigiau Cardif 27 P6
Cremyll Cnwll 4 H6
Cressage Shrops 63 Q11
Cressbrook Derbys 77 M9
Cresselly Pembks 37 L9
Cressex Bucks 32 B4
Cressing Essex 46 D7
Cresswell Nthumb 109 M11
Cresswell Pembks 37 K9
Cresswell Staffs 64 H4
Creswell Derbys 78 E9
Creswell Green Staffs 65 K10
Cretingham Suffk 59 J9
Cretshengan Ag & B 111 Q8
Crewe Ches E 64 D1
Crewe-by-Farndon Ches W 63 M2
Crewe Green Ches E 64 D1
Crewkerne Somset 10 C3
Crews Hill Gt Lon 45 K11
Crewton C Derb 66 B5
Crianlarich Stirlg 122 C8
Cribyn Cerdgn 49 J10
Criccieth Gwynd 60 H4
Crich Derbys 65 Q1
Crich Carr Derbys 65 Q1
Crichton Mdloth 115 Q9
Crick Mons 28 G4
Crick Nhants 54 E6
Crickadarn Powys 39 P3
Cricket St Thomas Somset 10 B3
Crickheath Shrops 63 J8
Crickhowell Powys 40 B8
Cricklade Wilts 30 C4
Cricklewood Gt Lon 33 J5
Cridling Stubbs N York 85 Q10
Crieff P & K 123 L8
Criggion Powys 63 J9
Crigglestone Wakefd 85 L12
Crimble Rochdl 76 F1
Crimond Abers 141 P4
Crimplesham Norfk 69 M11
Crimscote Warwks 42 G2
Crinaglack Highld 137 M8
Crinan Ag & B 112 A2
Cringleford Norfk 71 J11
Cringles C Brad 84 G5
Crinow Pembks 37 M7
Cripplesease Cnwll 2 D8
Cripplestyle Dorset 23 N11
Cripp's Corner E Susx 16 D6
Croachy Highld 138 B10
Croanford Cnwll 6 F10
Crockenhill Kent 33 P9
Crocker End Oxon 31 Q5
Crockerhill W Susx 14 C9
Crockernwell Devon 8 E6
Crockerton Wilts 22 H5
Crocketford D & G 96 H3
Crockey Hill C York 86 B6
Crockham Hill Kent 33 N12
Crockhurst Street Kent 16 B2
Crockleford Heath Essex 47 J6
Crock Street Somset 21 M11
Croeserw Neath 27 K3
Croes-goch Pembks 36 F4
Croes-lan Cerdgn 48 F11
Croesor Gwynd 61 K3
Croesyceiliog Carmth 38 B8
Croesyceiliog Torfn 28 C4
Croes-y-mwyalch Torfn 28 C4
Croes-y-pant Mons 28 D2
Croft Leics 54 E1
Croft Lincs 81 K11
Croft Warrtn 76 B4
Croftamie Stirlg 113 P3
Croft Mitchell Cnwll 2 G7
Crofton Cumb 98 C8
Crofton Wakefd 85 L11
Crofton Wilts 30 E9
Croft-on-Tees N York 91 M5
Crofts Moray 139 P6
Crofts Bank Traffd 76 D4
Crofts of Dipple Moray 139 P4
Crofts of Savoch Abers 141 N4
Crofty Swans 26 D3
Crogen Gwynd 62 D5

Croggan Ag & B 120 D7
Croglin Cumb 98 H10
Croick Highld 145 L7
Cromarty Highld 138 E2
Crombie Fife 115 J5
Cromdale Highld 139 K10
Cromer Herts 45 J6
Cromer Norfk 71 J4
Cromford Derbys 77 P12
Cromhall S Glos 29 L4
Cromhall Common S Glos 29 L4
Cromor W Isls 152 g4
Cromra Highld 129 N6
Cromwell Notts 79 K11
Cronberry E Ayrs 105 L5
Crondall Hants 25 N4
Cronk-y-Voddy IoM 102 d4
Cronton Knows 75 N6
Crook Cumb 89 M7
Crook Dur 100 F11
Crookdake Cumb 97 P9
Crooke Wigan 75 P2
Crooked End Gloucs 41 J8
Crookedholm E Ayrs 104 H2
Crooked Soley Wilts 30 G8
Crookhall Dur 100 E8
Crookham Nthumb 108 E3
Crookham W Berk 31 L8
Crookham Village Hants 25 N3
Crook Inn Border 106 E6
Crooklands Cumb 89 N10
Crook of Devon P & K 115 J2
Cropper Derbys 65 N5
Cropredy Oxon 43 K2
Cropston Leics 66 F10
Cropthorne Worcs 42 A3
Cropton N York 92 F9
Cropwell Bishop Notts 66 H5
Cropwell Butler Notts 66 H5
Cros W Isls 152 h1
Crosbost W Isls 152 g4
Crosby Cumb 97 M10
Crosby IoM 102 d5
Crosby N Linc 79 L5
Crosby Sefton 75 K4
Crosby Garret Cumb 90 C6
Crosby Ravensworth Cumb 89 Q4
Crosby Villa Cumb 97 M10
Croscombe Somset 22 D4
Crosemere Shrops 63 M6
Crosland Edge Kirk 77 L1
Crosland Hill Kirk 84 H12
Cross Somset 21 N2
Crossaig Ag & B 112 B11
Crossapol Ag & B 118 D4
Cross Ash Mons 40 F8
Cross-at-Hand Kent 16 D2
Crossbush W Susx 14 E9
Crosscanonby Cumb 97 L10
Cross Coombe Cnwll 2 H5
Crossdale Street Norfk 71 J4
Cross End Bed 55 Q9
Cross End Essex 46 F5
Crossens Sefton 83 J11
Cross Flatts C Brad 84 G7
Crossford Fife 115 J4
Crossford S Lans 114 E12
Crossgate Lincs 68 E7
Crossgate Staffs 64 H5
Crossgatehall E Loth 115 Q7
Crossgates Fife 115 K4
Crossgates N York 93 L10
Cross Gates Leeds 85 M8
Crossgates Powys 50 E8
Crossgill Lancs 83 M3
Cross Green Devon 7 M7
Cross Green Leeds 85 L9
Cross Green Staffs 64 G11
Cross Green Suffk 58 B10
Cross Green Suffk 58 C9
Cross Green Suffk 58 C9
Crosshands Carmth 37 N6
Cross Hands Carmth 38 E8
Crosshands E Ayrs 105 J4
Cross Hands Pembks 37 K7
Cross Hill Derbys 66 C2
Crosshill E Ayrs 104 H7
Crosshill Fife 115 K2
Crosshill S Ayrs 104 G8
Cross Hills N York 84 F6
Crosshouse E Ayrs 104 H2
Cross Houses Shrops 52 C2
Cross Houses Shrops 63 P10
Cross in Hand E Susx 15 P6
Cross Inn Cerdgn 48 G8
Cross Inn Cerdgn 49 J9
Cross Inn Pembks 37 J7
Cross Inn Rhondd 27 P6
Cross Keys Ag & B 113 P3
Crosskeys Caerph 28 B4
Cross Keys Wilts 29 P8
Crosskirk Highld 151 J3
Crosslands Cumb 89 K9
Cross Lane IoW 12 H6
Cross Lane Head Shrops 52 D2
Cross Lanes Cnwll 2 H9
Cross Lanes Cnwll 3 J6
Cross Lanes N York 85 Q2
Cross Lanes Shrops 63 K3
Cross Lanes Wrexhm 63 L3
Crosslee Rens 113 N8
Crossley Kirk 85 J11
Crossmichael D & G 96 G5
Cross Oak Powys 39 Q6
Cross of Jackston Abers 141 J9
Cross o' th' hands Derbys 65 P3
Crosspost W Susx 15 J6
Crossroads Abers 132 H5
Crossroads Abers 133 J6
Cross Roads C Brad 84 F8
Cross Street Suffk 59 J5
Crosston Angus 125 K2
Cross Town Ches E 76 D8
Crossway Mons 40 F9
Crossway Powys 50 F11
Crossway Green Mons 28 H4
Crossway Green Worcs 52 F7
Crossways Dorset 11 J7
Crosswell Pembks 37 M3
Crosthwaite Cumb 89 L8
Croston Lancs 83 L12
Crostwick Norfk 71 L8
Crostwight Norfk 71 L6
Crouch Kent 34 A11
Crouch End Gt Lon 33 K5
Croucheston Wilts 23 N8
Crough House Green Kent 15 N2
Crovie Abers 141 K3
Crow Hants 12 A4
Crowan Cnwll 2 G7
Crowborough E Susx 15 P5
Crowborough Warren E Susx 15 P5
Crowcombe Somset 21 J6
Crowdecote Derbys 77 L10
Crowden Derbys 77 K4
Crowden Devon 7 P3

Crowdhill Hants 24 H9
Crowdleham Kent 33 Q10
Crow Edge Barns 77 M3
Crowell Oxon 31 Q3
Crow End Cambs 56 F9
Crowfield Nhants 43 N3
Crowfield Suffk 58 H9
Crowfield Green Suffk 58 H9
Crowgate Street Norfk 71 L8
Crow Green Essex 33 Q3
Crowhill E Loth 116 H6
Crow Hill Herefs 41 K6
Crowhole Derbys 77 P8
Crowhurst E Susx 16 D8
Crowhurst Surrey 15 M1
Crowhurst Lane End Surrey 15 M1
Crowland Lincs 68 E10
Crowlas Cnwll 2 E8
Crowle N Linc 79 J3
Crowle Worcs 52 G9
Crowle Green Worcs 52 G9
Crowmarsh Gifford Oxon 31 N4
Crown Corner Suffk 59 K6
Crownhill C Plym 4 G5
Crownpits Surrey 14 D2
Crownthorpe Norfk 70 G11
Crowntown Cnwll 2 G8
Crows-an-Wra Cnwll 2 C9
Crow's Green Essex 46 C6
Crowshill Norfk 70 D11
Crow's Nest Cnwll 4 C3
Crowsnest Shrops 63 L11
Crowthorne Wokgm 32 B9
Crowton Ches W 75 P9
Croxall Staffs 65 M9
Croxby Lincs 80 D4
Croxdale Dur 100 H11
Croxden Staffs 65 K4
Croxley Green Herts 32 F3
Croxteth Lpool 75 L4
Croxton Cambs 56 E8
Croxton N Linc 80 B1
Croxton Norfk 58 C3
Croxton Norfk 70 B5
Croxton Staffs 64 E6
Croxtonbank Staffs 64 E6
Croxton Green Ches E 63 Q2
Croxton Kerrial Leics 67 L6
Croy Highld 138 D6
Croy N Lans 114 D6
Croyde Devon 19 J5
Croyde Bay Devon 18 H5
Croydon Cambs 56 F10
Croydon Gt Lon 33 L9
Crubenmore Highld 130 C6
Cruckmeole Shrops 63 M10
Cruckton Shrops 63 M10
Cruden Bay Abers 141 Q8
Crudgington Wrekin 64 C9
Crudie Abers 141 J4
Crudwell Wilts 29 Q4
Crüg Powys 50 G6
Crugmeer Cnwll 6 D10
Crugybar Carmth 38 H4
Crug-y-byddar Powys 50 G4
Crumlin Caerph 28 B3
Crumplehorn Cnwll 4 B6
Crumpsall Manch 76 F3
Crundale Kent 17 J1
Crundale Pembks 37 J7
Crunwere Pembks 37 M8
Cruwys Morchard Devon 20 D11
Crux Easton Hants 31 J11
Cruxton Dorset 11 J5
Crwbin Carmth 38 C9
Cryers Hill Bucks 32 C4
Crymmych Pembks 37 M4
Crynant Neath 39 J10
Crystal Palace Gt Lon 33 L8
Cuaig Highld 135 N4
Cuan Ag & B 120 E10
Cubbington Warwks 53 Q7
Cubert Cnwll 3 J3
Cubley Barns 77 N3
Cublington Bucks 44 B7
Cublington Herefs 40 E4
Cuckfield W Susx 15 K6
Cucklington Somset 22 F8
Cuckney Notts 78 D9
Cuckoo Bridge Lincs 68 D8
Cuckoo's Corner Hants 25 M5
Cuckoo's Nest Ches W 75 L11
Cuddesdon Oxon 43 M11
Cuddington Bucks 43 Q9
Cuddington Ches W 75 Q9
Cuddington Heath Ches W 63 M3
Cuddy Hill Lancs 83 L7
Cudham Gt Lon 33 N10
Cudliptown Devon 7 P9
Cudnell BCP 11 P5
Cudworth Barns 78 B2
Cudworth Somset 10 B2
Cuerdley Cross Warrtn 75 P6
Cufaude Hants 25 L2
Cuffley Herts 45 K11
Cuil Highld 121 J2
Culbokie Highld 137 Q4
Culbone Somset 20 C4
Culburnie Highld 137 N7
Culcabock Highld 138 C7
Culcharry Highld 138 E5
Culcheth Warrtn 76 B4
Culdrain Abers 140 D9
Culduie Highld 135 N8
Culford Suffk 58 B6
Culgaith Cumb 89 Q2
Culham Oxon 31 M3
Culkein Highld 148 B10
Culkein Drumbeg Highld 148 D10
Culkerton Gloucs 29 Q3
Cullen Moray 140 D2
Cullercoats N Tyne 101 J4
Cullerlie Abers 133 J4
Cullicudden Highld 138 B3
Cullingworth C Brad 84 G7
Cuillin Hills Highld 134 H11
Cullipool Ag & B 120 E10
Cullivoe Shet 147 j2
Culloden Highld 138 D7
Cullompton Devon 9 J3
Cullompton Services Devon 20 H11
Culm Davy Devon 20 H10
Culmington Shrops 51 N4
Culmstock Devon 20 H10
Culnacraig Highld 144 C2
Culnaightrie D & G 96 G7
Culpho Suffk 59 J10
Culrain Highld 145 N6
Culross Fife 114 H4
Culroy S Ayrs 104 G7
Culsalmond Abers 140 G9
Culscadden D & G 95 N8
Culshabbin D & G 95 K8
Culswick Shet 147 h7
Cults C Aber 133 L4
Culverstone Green Kent 34 B9
Culverthorpe Lincs 67 P4
Culworth Nhants 43 M3
Culzean Castle & Country Park S Ayrs 104 D8

170 Cumbernauld – Dunnington

Cumbernauld N Lans 114 D6
Cumbernauld Village N Lans 114 D6
Cumberworth Lincs 81 K9
Cumdivock Cumb 98 D8
Cuminestown Abers 141 K6
Cumledge Border 116 H10
Cummersdale Cumb 98 E7
Cummertrees D & G 97 N5
Cummingston Moray 139 L2
Cumnock E Ayrs 105 K6
Cumnor Oxon 43 K11
Cumrew Cumb 98 G8
Cumrue D & G 97 L1
Cumwhinton Cumb 98 F7
Cumwhitton Cumb 98 G8
Cundall N York 91 P12
Cunninghamhead N Ayrs 104 G1
Cunningsburgh Shet 147 i8
Cupar Fife 124 G10
Cupar Muir Fife 124 G10
Curbar Derbys 77 N9
Curbridge Hants 13 J2
Curbridge Oxon 42 G10
Curdridge Hants 25 J10
Curdworth Warwks 53 M2
Curland Somset 21 L10
Curridge W Berk 31 K8
Currie C Edin 115 M8
Curry Mallet Somset 21 M9
Curry Rivel Somset 21 N8
Curteis Corner Kent 16 E3
Curtisden Green Kent 16 C3
Curtisknowle Devon 5 M6
Cury Cnwll 2 H10
Cushnie Abers 132 D2
Cushuish Somset 21 K7
Cusop Herefs 40 C3
Cusworth Donc 78 F3
Cutcloy D & G 95 N11
Cutcombe Somset 20 E5
Cutgate Rochdl 84 C12
Cuthill Highld 146 D7
Cutiau Gwynd 61 L8
Cutler's Green Essex 45 Q5
Cutmadoc Cnwll 3 Q2
Cutmere Cnwll 4 E4
Cutnall Green Worcs 52 G7
Cutsdean Gloucs 42 C6
Cutthorpe Derbys 77 Q9
Cuttivett Cnwll 4 E4
Cuxham Oxon 31 N3
Cuxton Medway 34 C9
Cuxwold Lincs 80 D3
Cwm Blae G 40 B10
Cwm Denbgs 74 E8
Cwmafan Neath 27 J4
Cwmaman Rhondd 27 N2
Cwmann Carmth 38 E2
Cwmavon Torfn 40 C10
Cwmbach Carmth 37 P5
Cwmbach Carmth 38 D11
Cwmbâch Powys 40 A4
Cwmbach Rhondd 39 N11
Cwmbach Llechrhyd Powys 50 E10
Cwmbelan Powys 50 C4
Cwmbran Torfn 28 C3
Cwmbrwyno Cerdgn 49 M4
Cwm Capel Carmth 38 C11
Cwmcarn Caerph 28 B4
Cwmcarvan Mons 40 G10
Cwm-celyn Blae G 40 B10
Cwm-Cewydd Gwynd 61 Q9
Cwm-cou Cerdgn 37 Q2
Cwm Crawnon Powys 39 Q7
Cwmdare Rhondd 39 N11
Cwmdu Carmth 38 F6
Cwmdu Powys 40 A7
Cwmdu Swans 26 F3
Cwmduad Carmth 38 B5
Cwm Dulais Swans 38 F11
Cwmdwr Carmth 38 H5
Cwmfelin Brdgnd 27 K4
Cwmfelin Myr Td 27 P2
Cwmfelin Boeth Carmth 37 N7
Cwmfelinfach Caerph 28 B4
Cwmfelin Mynach Carmth 37 P5
Cwmffrwd Carmth 38 B8
Cwmgiedd Powys 39 J9
Cwmgorse Carmth 38 G9
Cwm Gwaun Pembks 37 K4
Cwmgwili Carmth 38 E9
Cwmgwrach Neath 39 K10
Cwmhiraeth Carmth 37 R3
Cwmifor Carmth 38 G6
Cwm Irfon Powys 49 Q10
Cwmisfael Carmth 38 D8
Cwm Llinau Powys 61 P10
Cwmllynfell Neath 38 H9
Cwmmawr Carmth 38 D9
Cwm Morgan Carmth 37 Q3
Cwmparc Rhondd 27 M3
Cwmpengraig Carmth 37 R3
Cwm Penmachno Conwy 61 N3
Cwmpennar Rhondd 27 N2
Cwmrhos Powys 40 B7
Cwmrhydyceirw Swans 26 G2
Cwmsychbant Cerdgn 38 C2
Cwmtillery Blae G 40 B10
Cwm-twrch Isaf Powys 39 J9
Cwm-twrch Uchaf Powys 38 H9
Cwm-y-glo Carmth 38 E9
Cwm-y-glo Gwynd 73 J11
Cwmyoy Mons 40 D7
Cwmystwyth Cerdgn 49 N6
Cwrt Gwynd 61 M12
Cwrtnewydd Cerdgn 48 H11
Cwrt-y-gollen Powys 40 B8
Cyfarthfa Castle Museum Myr Td 39 P10
Cyffylliog Denbgs 74 E12
Cyfronydd Powys 62 G10
Cylibebyll Neath 38 H11
Cymau Flints 63 J1
Cymmer Neath 27 K3
Cymmer Rhondd 27 N4
Cyncoed Cardif 28 B6
Cynghordy Carmth 39 J4
Cynheidre Carmth 38 D10
Cynonville Neath 27 K3
Cynwyd Denbgs 62 E4
Cynwyl Elfed Carmth 38 B6

D

Daccombe Devon 5 Q3
Dacre Cumb 89 M1
Dacre N York 85 J3
Dacre Banks N York 85 J3
Daddry Shield Dur 99 P10
Dadford Bucks 43 N4
Dadlington Leics 54 C1
Dafen Carmth 26 D2
Daffy Green Norfk 70 E10
Dagenham Gt Lon 33 P5
Daglingworth Gloucs 42 A10
Dagnall Bucks 44 E8
Dagworth Suffk 58 F8
Dail bho Dheas W Isls 152 g1
Dailly S Ayrs 104 E9
Dainton Devon 5 P3
Dairsie Fife 124 H9
Daisy Hill Bolton 76 C3
Daisy Hill Leeds 85 K9
Dalabrog W Isls 152 b11
Dalavich Ag & B 120 H10
Dalbeattie D & G 96 G6
Dalbury Derbys 65 N5
Dalby IoM 102 b5
Dalby Lincs 80 H9
Dalby N York 86 B1
Dalcapon P & K 123 N2
Dalchalm Highld 146 G4
Dalchreichart Highld 129 J2
Dalchruin P & K 123 J9
Dalcrue P & K 123 Q7
Dalderby Lincs 80 E10
Dalditch Devon 9 K8
Dale Cumb 98 G9
Dale Pembks 36 F9
Dale Abbey Derbys 66 C4
Dale Bottom Cumb 89 J2
Dale End Derbys 77 N11
Dale End N York 84 E6
Dale Hill E Susx 16 C5
Dalehouse N York 92 F3
Dalelia Highld 127 N10
Dalgarven N Ayrs 113 K12
Dalgety Bay Fife 115 L4
Dalgig E Ayrs 105 K7
Dalginross P & K 123 K8
Dalguise P & K 123 P3
Dalhalvaig Highld 150 F6
Dalham Suffk 57 N8
Daliburgh W Isls 152 b11
Dalkeith Mdloth 115 Q8
Dallas Moray 139 L5
Dallinghoo Suffk 59 K9
Dallington E Susx 16 B7
Dallington Nhants 55 J8
Dallow N York 91 K12
Dalmally Ag & B 121 M7
Dalmary Stirlg 113 P2
Dalmellington E Ayrs 105 J8
Dalmeny C Edin 115 L6
Dalmore Highld 138 C2
Dalmuir W Duns 113 P7
Dalnabreck Highld 127 M10
Dalnacardoch P & K 130 D10
Dalnahaitnach Highld 138 F11
Dalnaspidal P & K 130 B9
Dalnawillan Lodge Highld 151 J8
Dalqueich P & K 124 B12
Dalquhairn S Ayrs 104 F10
Dalreavoch Highld 146 D3
Dalry N Ayrs 113 K11
Dalrymple E Ayrs 104 F7
Dalserf S Lans 114 E11
Dalsmeran Ag & B 102 H7
Dalston Cumb 98 D8
Dalston Gt Lon 33 L5
Dalswinton D & G 97 J1
Dalton Cumb 89 N11
Dalton D & G 97 M3
Dalton Lancs 75 N2
Dalton N York 91 J5
Dalton N York 91 Q11
Dalton Nthumb 100 E4
Dalton Rothm 78 D5
Dalton-in-Furness Cumb 88 H12
Dalton-le-Dale Dur 101 K8
Dalton Magna Rothm 78 D5
Dalton-on-Tees N York 91 M5
Dalton Parva Rothm 78 D5
Dalton Piercy Hartpl 101 L12
Dalveich Stirlg 122 G8
Dalwhinnie Highld 130 B7
Dalwood Devon 9 N4
Damask Green Herts 45 J6
Damerham Hants 23 N10
Damgate Norfk 71 M10
Dam Green Norfk 58 F4
Damnaglaur D & G 94 G11
Danaway Kent 34 F9
Danbury Essex 46 D10
Danby N York 92 E5
Danby Bottom N York 92 E6
Danby Wiske N York 91 N7
Dandaleith Moray 139 P6
Danderhall Mdloth 115 P7
Danebridge Ches E 76 H10
Dane End Herts 45 L7
Danegate E Susx 15 Q4
Danehill E Susx 15 M5
Dane Hills C Leic 66 F11
Danemoor Green Norfk 70 F11
Danesford Shrops 52 D2
Danesmoor Derbys 78 C11
Dane Street Kent 35 J11
Daniel's Water Kent 16 G3
Danshillock Abers 140 H4
Danskine E Loth 116 D8
Danthorpe E R Yk 87 N8
Danzey Green Warwks 53 L7
Dapple Heath Staffs 65 K7
Darby Green Hants 32 B10
Darcy Lever Bolton 76 D2
Dardy Powys 40 B8
Darenth Kent 33 Q8
Daresbury Halton 75 P7
Darfield Barns 78 C3
Darfoulds Notts 78 F8
Dargate Kent 35 K10
Dargavel Rens 113 N7
Darite Cnwll 4 C3
Darland Medway 34 D9
Darland Wrexhm 75 L12
Darlaston Wsall 52 H1
Darlaston Green Wsall 52 H1
Darley N York 85 J3
Darley Abbey C Derb 66 B4
Darley Bridge Derbys 77 P11
Darley Dale Derbys 77 P11
Darley Green Solhll 53 M6
Darleyhall Herts 44 G7
Darley Head N York 85 J3
Darlingscott Warwks 42 F3
Darlington Darltn 91 M4
Darliston Shrops 63 P5
Darlton Notts 79 K9
Darnford Staffs 65 L10
Darnick Border 107 N3
Darowen Powys 61 P11
Darra Abers 140 H6
Darracott Devon 18 E9
Darracott Devon 19 J5
Darras Hall Nthumb 100 F4
Darrington Wakefd 85 P11
Darsham Suffk 59 N6
Darshill Somset 22 E4
Dartford Kent 33 Q8
Dartford Crossing Kent 33 Q7
Dartington Devon 5 N4
Dartmeet Devon 8 C10
Dartmoor National Park Devon 8 D9
Dartmouth Devon 5 P6
Darton Barns 77 P2
Darvel E Ayrs 105 K2
Darwell Hole E Susx 16 C7
Darwen Bl w D 83 Q10
Datchet W & M 32 E7
Datchworth Herts 45 K8
Datchworth Green Herts 45 K8
Daubhill Bolton 76 C2
Daugh of Kinermony Moray 139 N7
Dauntsey Wilts 30 A6
Dava Highld 139 J8
Davenham Ches W 76 C9
Davenport Stockp 76 G6
Davenport Green Ches E 76 F8
Davenport Green Traffd 76 E6
Daventry Nhants 54 F8
Davidson's Mains C Edin 115 M6
Davidstow Cnwll 7 H7
David Street Kent 34 B9
Davington D & G 106 H9
Davington Hill Kent 34 H10
Daviot Abers 141 J10
Daviot Highld 138 D8
Daviot House Highld 138 D7
Davis's Town E Susx 15 P7
Davoch of Grange Moray 140 D5
Davyhulme Traffd 76 D4
Daw End Wsall 65 J12
Dawesgreen Surrey 15 J1
Dawley Wrekin 64 C10
Dawlish Devon 8 H9
Dawlish Warren Devon 9 J9
Dawn Conwy 73 Q9
Daws Green Somset 21 K9
Daws Heath Essex 34 E5
Daw's House Cnwll 7 L8
Dawsmere Lincs 68 H6
Daybrook Notts 66 F3
Day Green Ches E 76 E12
Dayhills Staffs 64 H5
Dayhouse Bank Worcs 52 H5
Daylesford Gloucs 42 F6
Ddol Flints 74 G9
Ddol-Cownwy Powys 62 D8
Deal Kent 35 Q12
Dean Cumb 88 E2
Dean Devon 5 M4
Dean Devon 19 M4
Dean Devon 19 N4
Dean Dorset 23 L10
Dean Hants 24 G7
Dean Hants 25 J9
Dean Lancs 84 C10
Dean Oxon 42 H7
Dean Somset 22 F5
Dean Bottom Kent 33 Q8
Deanburnhaugh Border 107 K7
Deancombe Devon 5 M4
Dean Court Oxon 43 K10
Deane Bolton 76 C2
Deane Hants 25 J3
Dean End Dorset 23 L10
Dean Head Barns 77 P4
Deanhead Kirk 84 F12
Deanland Dorset 23 M9
Deanlane End W Susx 25 N11
Dean Prior Devon 5 M4
Deanraw Nthumb 99 M6
Dean Row Ches E 76 G7
Deans W Loth 115 J7
Deanscales Cumb 88 E1
Deanshanger Nhants 43 Q4
Deanshaugh Moray 139 Q6
Deanston Stirlg 114 C1
Dean Street Kent 34 D11
Dearham Cumb 97 L11
Dearnley Rochdl 84 D12
Debach Suffk 59 K10
Debden Essex 33 N3
Debden Essex 45 Q5
Debden Green Essex 45 Q5
Debenham Suffk 58 H8
Deblin's Green Worcs 52 E11
Dechmont W Loth 115 J7
Dechmont Road W Loth 115 J7
Deddington Oxon 43 K5
Dedham Essex 47 J5
Dedham Heath Essex 47 J5
Dedworth W & M 32 D7
Deene Nhants 55 N2
Deenethorpe Nhants 55 N2
Deepcar Sheff 77 P4
Deepcut Surrey 32 C11
Deepdale Cumb 90 B9
Deepdale N York 90 E10
Deeping Gate C Pete 68 C10
Deeping St James Lincs 68 C10
Deeping St Nicholas Lincs 68 D9
Deerhurst Gloucs 41 P6
Deerhurst Walton Gloucs 41 P6
Deerton Street Kent 34 H9
Defford Worcs 41 Q3
Defynnog Powys 39 L6
Deganwy Conwy 73 N8
Degnish Ag & B 120 E10
Deighton C York 86 B6
Deighton N York 91 P6
Deiniolen Gwynd 73 K11
Delabole Cnwll 6 F8
Delamere Ches W 75 P10
Delamere Park Ches W 75 P9
Delfrigs Abers 141 M11
Delley Devon 19 K8
Delliefure Highld 139 K9
Dell Quay W Susx 13 P4
Delly End Oxon 42 H9
Delnabo Moray 139 L12
Delny Highld 146 D10
Delph Oldham 77 J2
Delves Dur 100 E8
Delvin End Essex 46 D4
Dembleby Lincs 67 P5
Demelza Cnwll 3 M2
Denaby Donc 78 D4
Denaby Main Donc 78 E4
Denbies Surrey 32 G12
Denbigh Denbgs 74 E10
Denbrae Fife 124 H9
Denbury Devon 5 N3
Denby Derbys 66 C3
Denby Bottles Derbys 66 C3
Denby Dale Kirk 77 N3
Denchworth Oxon 30 H4
Dendron Cumb 82 G1
Denel End C Beds 44 E4
Denfield P & K 123 N9
Denford Nhants 55 N5
Dengie Essex 46 H11
Denham Bucks 32 F5
Denham Suffk 57 P8
Denham Suffk 59 J6
Denham End Suffk 57 P8
Denham Green Bucks 32 F5
Denham Green Suffk 59 J6
Denhead Abers 141 N5
Denhead Fife 125 J10
Denhead of Gray C Dund 124 G6
Denholm Border 107 P6
Denholme C Brad 84 G8
Denholme Clough C Brad 84 G8
Denio Gwynd 60 F5
Denmead Hants 25 L11
Denmore C Aber 133 M2
Denne Park W Susx 14 H5
Dennington Suffk 59 L7
Denny Falk 114 E5
Dennyloanhead Falk 114 E5
Den of Lindores Fife 124 E10
Denshaw Oldham 76 H2
Denside of Durris Abers 133 K5
Densole Kent 17 M2
Denston Suffk 57 P10
Denstone Staffs 65 L4
Denstroude Kent 35 K10
Dent Cumb 90 B9
Denton Cambs 56 C3
Denton Darltn 91 L3
Denton E Susx 15 N10
Denton Kent 17 M1
Denton Kent 34 B7
Denton Lincs 67 L6
Denton N York 84 H5
Denton Nhants 55 L9
Denton Norfk 59 K3
Denton Oxon 43 M11
Denton Tamesd 76 G5
Denver Norfk 69 L11
Denwick Nthumb 109 K7
Deopham Norfk 70 F12
Deopham Green Norfk 70 F12
Depden Suffk 57 P9
Depden Green Suffk 57 P9
Deptford Gt Lon 33 L7
Deptford Wilts 23 M6
Derby C Derb 66 B5
Derby Devon 19 L6
Derbyhaven IoM 102 c7
Derculich P & K 123 M2
Dereham Norfk 70 E9
Deri Caerph 27 Q2
Derril Devon 7 K4
Derringstone Kent 35 M12
Derrington Staffs 64 G7
Derriton Devon 7 L4
Derry Hill Wilts 29 Q8
Derrythorpe N Linc 79 K2
Dersingham Norfk 69 N6
Dervaig Ag & B 119 M2
Derwen Denbgs 62 E2
Derwenlas Powys 61 M12
Derwent Valley Mills Derbys 65 P1
Derwent Water Cumb 88 H3
Derwydd Carmth 38 F8
Desborough Nhants 55 K4
Desford Leics 66 D11
Detchant Nthumb 108 H2
Detling Kent 34 D10
Deuxhill Shrops 52 C3
Devauden Mons 28 G3
Devil's Bridge Cerdgn 49 M5
Devitts Green Warwks 53 P2
Devizes Wilts 30 B10
Devonport C Plym 4 G6
Devonside Clacks 114 G2
Devoran Cnwll 3 K7
Devoran & Perran Cnwll 3 K7
Dewarton Mdloth 115 Q8
Dewlish Dorset 11 J5
Dewsbury Kirk 85 K11
Dewsbury Moor Kirk 85 K10
Deytheur Powys 62 H8
Dial N Som 28 H9
Dial Green W Susx 14 C5
Dial Post W Susx 14 H7
Dibberford Dorset 10 C4
Dibden Hants 12 G3
Dibden Purlieu Hants 12 G3
Dickens Heath Solhll 53 L5
Dickleburgh Norfk 58 H4
Didbrook Gloucs 42 B5
Didcot Oxon 31 L4
Diddington Cambs 56 D7
Diddlebury Shrops 51 N3
Didley Herefs 40 F5
Didling W Susx 25 P9
Didmarton Gloucs 29 N5
Didsbury Manch 76 F5
Didworthy Devon 5 L4
Digby Lincs 67 Q1
Digg Highld 134 H2
Diggle Oldham 77 J2
Digmoor Lancs 75 N3
Digswell Herts 45 J8
Digswell Water Herts 45 J8
Dihewyd Cerdgn 48 H9
Dilham Norfk 71 L7
Dilhorne Staffs 64 H3
Dill Hall Lancs 83 R9
Dillington Cambs 56 C7
Dilston Nthumb 100 C5
Dilton Wilts 23 J4
Dilton Marsh Wilts 23 J3
Dilwyn Herefs 51 L9
Dimple Bolton 83 Q12
Dimple Derbys 77 P11
Dinas Carmth 37 P4
Dinas Cnwll 6 C10
Dinas Gwynd 60 D5
Dinas Gwynd 72 H12
Dinas Rhondd 27 N4
Dinas Cross Pembks 37 K3
Dinas Dinlle Gwynd 72 G12
Dinas-Mawddwy Gwynd 61 Q9
Dinas Powys V Glam 27 R8
Dinder Somset 22 D4
Dinedor Herefs 40 H4
Dingestow Mons 40 F9
Dingle Lpool 75 L6
Dingleden Kent 16 E5
Dingley Nhants 55 K3
Dingwall Highld 137 P4
Dinmael Conwy 62 D3
Dinnet Abers 132 C5
Dinnington N u Ty 100 G4
Dinnington Rothm 78 E6
Dinnington Somset 21 N10
Dinorwic Gwynd 73 K11
Dinton Bucks 43 Q9
Dinton Wilts 23 M7
Dinwoodie D & G 106 E11
Dinworthy Devon 18 F10
Dipford Somset 21 K9
Dipley Hants 31 Q11
Dippen Ag & B 103 L2
Dippenhall Surrey 25 P4
Dippermill Devon 7 N3
Dippertown Devon 7 N8
Dippin N Ayrs 103 Q5
Dipple Moray 139 Q4
Dipple S Ayrs 104 D9
Diptford Devon 5 M5
Dipton Dur 100 F7
Diptonmill Nthumb 99 P6
Dirleton E Loth 116 C4
Dirt Pot Nthumb 99 N9
Discoed Powys 51 J7
Diseworth Leics 66 D7
Dishforth N York 91 P12
Disley Ches E 76 H7
Diss Norfk 58 G4
Disserth Powys 50 E9
Distington Cumb 88 D2
Ditchampton Wilts 23 N7
Ditcheat Somset 22 E6
Ditchingham Norfk 59 L3
Ditchling E Susx 15 L8
Ditherington Shrops 63 N9
Ditteridge Wilts 29 N8
Dittisham Devon 5 P6
Ditton Kent 34 C10
Ditton Green Cambs 57 M9
Ditton Priors Shrops 51 Q3
Dixton Gloucs 41 R5
Dixton Mons 40 G9
Dizzard Cnwll 6 H5
Dobcross Oldham 77 J2
Dobwalls Cnwll 4 C4
Doccombe Devon 8 E7
Dochgarroch Highld 138 B7
Dockenfield Surrey 25 P5
Docker Lancs 89 P11
Docking Norfk 69 P5
Docklow Herefs 51 P9
Dockray Cumb 89 L2
Dockray Cumb 98 B8
Dodbrooke Devon 5 M8
Doddinghurst Essex 33 Q2
Doddington Cambs 56 H3
Doddington Kent 34 G11
Doddington Lincs 79 M9
Doddington Nthumb 108 G3
Doddington Shrops 52 B5
Doddiscombsleigh Devon 8 F7
Dodd's Green Ches E 63 Q3
Doddshill Norfk 69 N6
Doddy Cross Cnwll 4 D4
Dodford Nhants 54 G8
Dodford Worcs 52 H6
Dodington S Glos 29 M6
Dodington Somset 21 J5
Dodleston Ches W 75 K11
Dodscott Devon 19 K9
Dodside E Rens 113 P10
Dod's Leigh Staffs 65 J5
Dodworth Barns 77 P3
Dodworth Bottom Barns 77 Q3
Dodworth Green Barns 77 P3
Doe Bank Birm 53 L1
Doe Lea Derbys 78 D10
Dogdyke Lincs 68 D1
Dogley Lane Kirk 85 J12
Dogmersfield Hants 25 N3
Dogridge Wilts 30 C5
Dogsthorpe C Pete 68 D12
Dog Village Devon 9 J5
Dolanog Powys 62 E9
Dolau Powys 50 G7
Dolaucothi Carmth 38 G3
Dolbenmaen Gwynd 60 H4
Doley Staffs 64 D6
Dolfach Powys 62 B11
Dolfor Powys 50 F3
Dol-för Powys 61 P11
Dolgarrog Conwy 73 N10
Dolgellau Gwynd 61 M8
Dolgoch Gwynd 61 L11
Dol-gran Carmth 38 C5
Doll Highld 146 F4
Dollar Clacks 114 H2
Dollarfield Clacks 114 H2
Dolley Green Powys 51 J7
Dollwen Cerdgn 49 M4
Dolphin Flints 74 H9
Dolphinholme Lancs 83 M4
Dolphinton S Lans 115 K12
Dolton Devon 19 L11
Dolwen Conwy 73 Q9
Dolwyddelan Conwy 61 M2
Dolybont Cerdgn 49 K3
Dolyhir Powys 50 H9
Domgay Powys 63 J8
Donaldson's Lodge Nthumb 108 D1
Doncaster Donc 78 F3
Doncaster Carr Donc 78 F3
Doncaster North Services Donc 78 H1
Doncaster Sheffield Airport Donc 78 G4
Donhead St Andrew Wilts 23 K8
Donhead St Mary Wilts 23 K8
Donibristle Fife 115 L3
Doniford Somset 20 H5
Donington Lincs 68 D5
Donington on Bain Lincs 80 E7
Donington Park Services Leics 66 D7
Donington Southing Lincs 68 D5
Donisthorpe Leics 65 P9
Donkey Street Kent 17 K4
Donkey Town Surrey 32 D10
Donnington Gloucs 42 E6
Donnington Herefs 41 L5
Donnington Shrops 63 P10
Donnington W Berk 31 K8
Donnington W Susx 13 Q4
Donnington Wrekin 64 D9
Donnington Wood Wrekin 64 D9
Donyatt Somset 21 M10
Doomsday Green W Susx 14 H5
Doonfoot S Ayrs 104 F6
Dora's Green Hants 25 P4
Dorback Lodge Highld 131 K1
Dorchester Dorset 10 H6
Dorchester-on-Thames Oxon 31 M3
Dordon Warwks 65 N12
Dore Sheff 77 P7
Dores Highld 137 Q9
Dorking Surrey 14 H1
Dorking Tye Suffk 46 G4
Dormansland Surrey 15 M2
Dormans Park Surrey 15 M3
Dormington Herefs 41 J4
Dormston Worcs 53 J9
Dorn Gloucs 42 E5
Dorney Bucks 32 D6
Dorney Reach Bucks 32 C6
Dornie Highld 136 B10
Dornoch Highld 146 E7
Dornock D & G 98 B5
Dorrery Highld 151 K6
Dorridge Solhll 53 M6
Dorrington Lincs 67 Q2
Dorrington Shrops 63 N11
Dorrington Shrops 64 D4
Dorsington Warwks 53 L10
Dorstone Herefs 40 D3
Dorton Bucks 43 P9
Dosthill Staffs 65 N12
Dothan IoA 72 F9
Dottery Dorset 10 C6
Doublebois Cnwll 4 B4
Doughton Gloucs 29 P4
Douglas IoM 102 e6
Douglas S Lans 105 Q4
Douglas and Angus C Dund 124 H6
Douglas Pier Ag & B 113 J1
Douglastown Angus 124 H3
Douglas Water S Lans 105 R3
Douglas West S Lans 105 Q3
Doulting Somset 22 E5
Dounby Ork 147 b4
Doune Highld 145 L5
Doune Stirlg 114 D1
Dounepark S Ayrs 104 C10
Dounie Highld 145 N7
Dousland Devon 4 H3
Dovaston Shrops 63 K8
Dove Dale Derbys 65 L2
Dove Green Notts 66 D2
Dove Holes Derbys 77 K8
Dovenby Cumb 97 M11
Dover Kent 17 P2
Dover Wigan 75 Q4
Dover Castle Kent 17 P2
Dovercourt Essex 47 N5
Doverdale Worcs 52 F7
Doveridge Derbys 65 L5
Doversgreen Surrey 15 J1
Dowally P & K 123 P3
Dowbridge Lancs 83 K9
Dowdeswell Gloucs 42 B7
Dowlais Myr Td 39 P10
Dowland Devon 7 Q3
Dowlish Ford Somset 21 M10
Dowlish Wake Somset 21 N10
Down Ampney Gloucs 30 C3
Downderry Cnwll 4 D6
Downe Gt Lon 33 M10
Downend Gloucs 29 N3
Downend IoW 13 J7
Downend S Glos 29 K7
Downend W Berk 31 K7
Downfield C Dund 124 H6
Downgate Cnwll 7 K10
Downgate Cnwll 7 L10
Downham Essex 34 C3
Downham Gt Lon 33 M8
Downham Lancs 84 B6
Downham Market Norfk 69 L11
Down Hatherley Gloucs 41 P7
Downhead Somset 22 D8
Downhead Somset 22 F4
Downhill Cnwll 6 B11
Downhill P & K 124 C7
Downholland Cross Lancs 75 L2
Downholme N York 91 J7
Downicarey Devon 7 M7
Downies Abers 133 M5
Downing Flints 74 G8
Downley Bucks 32 B3
Down St Mary Devon 8 D4
Downside Somset 22 E3
Downside Somset 22 E4
Downside Surrey 32 G10
Down Thomas Devon 4 H7
Downton Hants 12 D6
Downton Wilts 24 C9
Dowsby Lincs 68 C6
Dowsdale Lincs 68 F10
Doxey Staffs 64 G7
Doxford Nthumb 109 K5
Doynton S Glos 29 L7
Draethen Caerph 28 B5
Draffan S Lans 114 E12
Dragonby N Linc 79 M1
Dragons Green W Susx 14 G6
Drakeholes Notts 78 H5
Drakelow Worcs 52 F4
Drakemyre N Ayrs 113 K11
Drakes Broughton Worcs 52 H11
Drakewalls Cnwll 7 N10
Draughton N York 84 F5
Draughton Nhants 55 J5
Drax N York 86 C10
Drax Hales N York 86 C10
Draycote Warwks 54 D6
Draycot Foliat Swindn 30 E7
Draycott Derbys 66 D5
Draycott Gloucs 42 E4
Draycott Shrops 52 E2
Draycott Somset 21 Q3
Draycott Somset 22 D9
Draycott Worcs 52 F11
Draycott in the Clay Staffs 65 M6
Draycott in the Moors Staffs 64 H4
Drayford Devon 19 Q10
Drayton C Port 13 L4
Drayton Leics 55 L2
Drayton Lincs 68 E4
Drayton Norfk 71 J9
Drayton Oxon 31 K3
Drayton Oxon 43 J3
Drayton Somset 21 N8
Drayton Somset 21 P10
Drayton Worcs 52 G5
Drayton Bassett Staffs 65 M12
Drayton Beauchamp Bucks 44 C9
Drayton Manor Park Staffs 65 M12
Drayton Parslow Bucks 44 B6
Drayton St Leonard Oxon 31 M3
Drebley N York 84 F3
Dreemskerry IoM 102 f4
Dreen Hill Pembks 36 H7
Drefach Carmth 38 A4
Drefach Carmth 38 D9
Drefach Cerdgn 38 D2
Drefelin Carmth 38 A4
Dreghorn N Ayrs 104 F2
Drellingore Kent 17 M3
Drem E Loth 116 C5
Dresden C Stke 64 G4
Drewsteignton Devon 8 D6
Driby Lincs 80 G9
Driffield E R Yk 87 K4
Driffield Gloucs 30 C2
Driffield Cross Roads Gloucs 30 C3
Drift Cnwll 2 C9
Drigg Cumb 88 E7
Drighlington Leeds 85 K9
Drimnin Highld 119 P2
Drimpton Dorset 10 C4
Drimsallie Highld 128 D8
Dringhouses C York 86 A5
Drinkstone Suffk 58 E8
Drinkstone Green Suffk 58 E8
Drive End Dorset 10 F3
Driver's End Herts 45 J7
Drointon Staffs 65 J7
Droitwich Spa Worcs 52 G8
Dron P & K 124 C9
Dronfield Derbys 78 B8
Dronfield Woodhouse Derbys 77 Q8
Drongan E Ayrs 104 H6
Dronley Angus 124 G6
Droop Dorset 11 J3
Dropping Well Rothm 78 C5
Droxford Hants 25 K9
Droylsden Tamesd 76 G4
Druid Denbgs 62 E3
Druidston Pembks 36 G7
Druimarbin Highld 128 F10
Druimavuic Ag & B 121 J4
Druimdrishaig Ag & B 111 Q7
Druimindarroch Highld 127 M7
Drum Ag & B 112 D6
Drum P & K 115 J1
Drumalbin S Lans 106 B2
Drumbeg Highld 148 D10
Drumblade Abers 140 F8
Drumbreddon D & G 94 F9
Drumbuie Highld 135 P9
Drumburgh Cumb 98 B6
Drumburn D & G 96 H7
Drumburn D & G 97 K6
Drumchapel C Glas 113 Q7
Drumchastle P & K 122 H1
Drumclog S Lans 105 M2
Drumeldrie Fife 125 J12
Drumelzier Border 106 F3
Drumfearn Highld 127 M1
Drumfrennie Abers 132 H5
Drumgley Angus 124 H2
Drumguish Highld 130 E4
Drumin Moray 139 M10
Drumjohn D & G 105 J10
Drumlamford S Ayrs 95 K3
Drumlasie Abers 132 G3
Drumleaning Cumb 98 B8
Drumlemble Ag & B 103 J6
Drumlithie Abers 133 J8
Drummoddie D & G 95 M9
Drummore D & G 94 G11
Drummuir Moray 140 B7
Drumnadrochit Highld 137 N10
Drumnagorrach Moray 140 E5
Drumpark D & G 96 H2
Drumrunie Highld 144 F4
Drumshang S Ayrs 104 E7
Drumuie Highld 134 H6
Drumuillie Highld 138 H11
Drumvaich Stirlg 122 H12
Drunzie P & K 124 C12
Druridge Nthumb 109 M10
Drury Flints 75 J10
Drws-y-coed Gwynd 61 J1
Drybeck Cumb 89 Q4
Drybridge Moray 140 C3
Drybridge N Ayrs 104 G2
Drybrook Gloucs 41 K8
Dryburgh Border 107 P3
Dry Doddington Lincs 67 L3
Dry Drayton Cambs 56 G8
Dryhill Kent 33 P11
Drymen Stirlg 113 P3
Drymuir Abers 141 L6
Drynoch Highld 134 G9
Dry Sandford Oxon 31 K2
Dryslwyn Carmth 38 E7
Dry Street Essex 34 C5
Dryton Shrops 63 P11
Dubford Abers 141 J3
Dublin Suffk 58 H7
Duchally Highld 145 J2
Duck End Bed 44 F3
Duck End Cambs 56 E8
Duck End Essex 46 B5
Duck End Essex 46 B6
Duckend Green Essex 46 C7
Duckington Ches W 63 N2
Ducklington Oxon 42 H10
Duck's Cross Bed 56 B9
Duddenhoe End Essex 45 N4
Duddingston C Edin 115 P7
Duddington Nhants 67 N12
Duddlestone Somset 21 K9
Duddlewell E Susx 15 N5
Duddlewick Shrops 52 C4
Duddo Nthumb 108 F1
Duddon Ches W 75 N11
Duddon Bridge Cumb 88 G9
Duddon Common Ches W 75 N10
Dudleston Shrops 63 K4
Dudleston Heath Shrops 63 L5
Dudley Dudley 52 H3
Dudley N Tyne 100 H3
Dudley Hill C Brad 85 J9
Dudley Port Sandw 52 H2
Dudnill Shrops 52 C6
Dudsbury Dorset 11 P5
Dudswell Herts 44 D9
Duffield Derbys 65 Q3
Duffryn Neath 27 K3
Dufftown Moray 139 P8
Duffus Moray 139 M2
Dufton Cumb 90 A2
Duggleby N York 86 G2
Duirinish Highld 135 P9
Duisdalemore Highld 127 M2
Duisky Highld 128 D9
Dukestown Blae G 39 Q9
Duke Street Suffk 47 J3
Dukinfield Tamesd 76 H4
Dulas IoA 72 H6
Dulcote Somset 22 D4
Dulford Devon 9 K3
Dull P & K 123 K3
Dullatur N Lans 114 D6
Dullingham Cambs 57 M9
Dullingham Ley Cambs 57 M9
Dulnain Bridge Highld 139 J11
Duloe Bed 56 C8
Duloe Cnwll 4 C5
Dulsie Bridge Highld 138 G7
Dulverton Somset 20 E8
Dulwich Gt Lon 33 L7
Dumbarton W Duns 113 M6
Dumbleton Gloucs 42 B4
Dumfries D & G 97 K3
Dumgoyne Stirlg 113 Q5
Dummer Hants 25 K4
Dumpton Kent 35 Q9
Dun Angus 132 G12
Dunalastair P & K 123 J1
Dunan Ag & B 112 H7
Dunan Highld 135 K10
Dunan P & K 122 D1
Dunaverty Ag & B 103 J8
Dunball Somset 21 M5
Dunbar E Loth 116 F5
Dunbeath Highld 151 L10
Dunbeg Ag & B 120 G6
Dunblane Stirlg 114 E1
Dunbog Fife 124 F9
Dunbridge Hants 24 E8
Duncanston Highld 137 Q4
Duncanstone Abers 140 E10
Dunchideock Devon 8 G7
Dunchurch Warwks 54 D6
Duncote Nhants 54 H10
Duncow D & G 97 K2
Duncrievie P & K 124 C11
Duncton W Susx 14 D7
Dundee C Dund 124 H7
Dundee Airport C Dund 124 H7
Dundon Somset 22 B7
Dundonald S Ayrs 104 G3
Dundonnell Highld 144 D7
Dundraw Cumb 97 P8
Dundreggan Highld 129 K1
Dundrennan D & G 96 F8
Dundry N Som 28 H9
Dunecht Abers 133 J2
Dunfermline Fife 115 K4
Dunfield Gloucs 30 D3
Dunford Bridge Barns 77 M3
Dungate Kent 34 G10
Dungavel S Lans 105 M2
Dunge Wilts 23 K2
Dungeness Kent 17 K7
Dungworth Sheff 77 P6
Dunham Massey Traffd 76 D6
Dunham-on-the-Hill Ches W 75 M9
Dunham-on-Trent Notts 79 K9
Dunhampstead Worcs 52 G8
Dunhampton Worcs 52 F7
Dunham Town Traffd 76 E6
Dunham Woodhouses Traffd 76 D6
Dunholme Lincs 79 P8
Dunino Fife 125 K10
Dunipace Falk 114 E4
Dunkeld P & K 123 P4
Dunkerton BaNES 29 L10
Dunkeswell Devon 9 M3
Dunkeswick N York 85 L6
Dunkirk Ches W 75 L9
Dunkirk Kent 35 J10
Dunkirk S Glos 29 M5
Dunkirk Wilts 30 A10
Dunk's Green Kent 33 R11
Dunlappie Angus 132 F10
Dunley Hants 24 G3
Dunley Worcs 52 E7
Dunlop E Ayrs 113 M11
Dunmaglass Highld 137 Q11
Dunmere Cnwll 6 E11
Dunmore Falk 114 G3
Dunnet Highld 151 M2
Dunnichen Angus 125 K3
Dunning P & K 123 P10
Dunnington C York 86 C5
Dunnington E R Yk 87 M5
Dunnington Warwks 53 K10

Dunnockshaw Lancs....84 B9
Dunn Street Kent....34 D10
Dunoon Ag & B....112 H6
Dunphail Moray....139 J6
Dunragit D & G....94 H7
Duns Border....116 H10
Dunsa Derbys....77 N9
Dunsby Lincs....68 B7
Dunscar Bolton....76 D1
Dunscore D & G....96 H1
Dunscroft Donc....78 G2
Dunsdale R & Cl....92 C3
Dunsden Green Oxon....31 Q7
Dunsdon Devon....7 K3
Dunsfold Surrey....14 E4
Dunsford Devon....8 F7
Dunshalt Fife....124 E10
Dunshillock Abers....141 N6
Dunsill Notts....78 D11
Dunsley N York....92 H4
Dunsley Staffs....52 F4
Dunsmore Bucks....44 B10
Dunstable Bridge Lancs....83 P5
Dunstable C Beds....44 E7
Dunstall Staffs....65 M8
Dunstall Common Worcs....41 P3
Dunstall Green Suffk....57 P8
Dunstan Nthumb....109 L6
Dunstan Steads Nthumb....109 L5
Dunster Somset....20 F5
Duns Tew Oxon....43 K6
Dunston Gatesd....100 G6
Dunston Lincs....79 Q11
Dunston Norfk....71 J11
Dunston Staffs....64 H8
Dunstone Devon....5 J6
Dunstone Devon....8 D9
Dunston Heath Staffs....64 G8
Dunsville Donc....78 G2
Dunswell E R Yk....87 K8
Dunsyre S Lans....115 K11
Dunterton Devon....7 M9
Dunthrop Oxon....42 H6
Duntisbourne Abbots Gloucs....41 R10
Duntisbourne Leer Gloucs....41 R10
Duntisbourne Rouse Gloucs....42 A10
Duntish Dorset....10 H3
Duntocher W Duns....113 P7
Dunton Bucks....44 B7
Dunton C Beds....33 J3
Dunton Norfk....70 C6
Dunton Bassett Leics....54 E3
Dunton Green Kent....33 P11
Dunton Wayletts Essex....34 B4
Duntulm Highld....142 D10
Dunure S Ayrs....104 E7
Dunvant Swans....26 F4
Dunvegan Highld....134 D6
Dunwich Suffk....59 P6
Dunwood Staffs....64 H1
Durdar Cumb....98 E8
Durgan Cnwll....3 J9
Durham Dur....100 H9
Durham Cathedral Dur....100 H9
Durham Services Dur....100 H11
Durham Tees Valley Airport S on T....91 P4
Durisdeer D & G....106 A9
Durisdeermill D & G....106 A9
Durkar Wakefd....85 L11
Durleigh Somset....21 L6
Durley Hants....24 J10
Durley Wilts....30 F9
Durley Street Hants....25 J10
Durlock Kent....35 N10
Durlock Kent....35 P9
Durlow Common Herefs....41 K4
Durn Rochdl....84 E12
Durness Highld....149 J3
Durno Abers....140 H10
Duror Highld....121 J2
Durran Ag & B....120 H11
Durrington W Susx....14 G9
Durrington Wilts....23 P4
Dursley Gloucs....29 M3
Dursley Cross Gloucs....41 L7
Durston Somset....21 L7
Durweston Dorset....11 L3
Duston Nhants....55 J8
Duthil Highld....138 H11
Dutlas Powys....50 H5
Duton Hill Essex....45 R6
Dutson Cnwll....7 L7
Dutton Ches W....75 P8
Duxford Cambs....45 N2
Duxford Oxon....30 H3
Duxford IWM Cambs....45 N2
Dwygyfylchi Conwy....73 M8
Dwyran IoA....72 G10
Dyce C Aber....133 L2
Dyer's End Essex....46 C4
Dyfatty Carmth....26 C2
Dyffrydan Gwynd....61 M9
Dyffryn Brdgnd....27 K3
Dyffryn Myr Td....27 P11
Dyffryn V Glam....27 P8
Dyffryn Ardudwy Gwynd....61 K7
Dyffryn Castell Cerdgn....49 N4
Dyffryn Cellwen Neath....39 K9
Dyke Lincs....68 B7
Dyke Moray....138 H4
Dykehead Angus....124 E2
Dykehead Angus....132 B12
Dykehead N Lans....114 F9
Dykehead Stirlg....114 A2
Dykelands Abers....132 H10
Dykends Angus....124 E1
Dykeside Abers....140 H7
Dylife Powys....49 Q2
Dymchurch Kent....17 K5
Dymock Gloucs....41 L5
Dyrham S Glos....29 L7
Dysart Fife....115 P3
Dyserth Denbgs....74 E8

E

Eachway Worcs....53 J5
Eachwick Nthumb....100 E4
Eagland Hill Lancs....83 K6
Eagle Lincs....79 L10
Eagle Barnsdale Lincs....79 L10
Eagle Moor Lincs....79 M10
Eaglescliffe S on T....91 P4
Eaglesfield Cumb....88 E3
Eaglesfield D & G....97 P3
Eaglesham E Rens....113 Q11
Eagley Bolton....76 D1
Eairy IoM....102 d6
Eakring Notts....78 H1
Ealand N Linc....79 K1
Ealing Gt Lon....32 H6
Eals Nthumb....99 K7
Eamont Bridge Cumb....89 N1
Earby Lancs....84 D6
Earcroft Bl w D....83 P10
Eardington Shrops....52 D2
Eardisland Herefs....51 L9
Eardisley Herefs....51 K11
Eardiston Shrops....63 L7
Eardiston Worcs....52 C7
Earith Cambs....56 G6

Earle Nthumb....108 F4
Earlestown St Hel....75 P5
Earley Wokham....31 Q8
Earlham Norfk....71 J10
Earlish Highld....134 E4
Earls Barton Nhants....55 L8
Earls Colne Essex....46 F6
Earls Common Worcs....52 H9
Earl's Croome Worcs....52 H9
Earlsditton Shrops....52 B5
Earlsdon Covtry....53 Q5
Earl's Down E Susx....16 B7
Earlsferry Fife....116 C1
Earlsfield Gt Lon....33 L8
Earlsford Abers....141 K9
Earl's Green Suffk....58 F7
Earlsheaton Kirk....85 K11
Earl Shilton Leics....54 D1
Earl Soham Suffk....59 J8
Earl Sterndale Derbys....77 K10
Earlston Border....107 P2
Earlston E Ayrs....104 G3
Earl Stonham Suffk....58 G9
Earlswood Surrey....15 K1
Earlswood Warwks....53 L5
Earlswood Common Mons....28 F3
Earnley W Susx....13 P5
Earnshaw Bridge Lancs....83 M10
Earsdon N Tyne....101 J4
Earsdon Nthumb....109 K11
Earsham Norfk....59 L3
Earswick C York....86 B4
Eartham W Susx....14 C9
Earthcott S Glos....29 K5
Easby N York....92 C5
Easdale Ag & B....120 D9
Easebourne W Susx....14 C6
Easenhall Warwks....54 C5
Eashing Surrey....14 D2
Easington Bucks....43 P9
Easington Dur....101 L9
Easington E R Yk....87 R11
Easington Nthumb....109 J3
Easington Oxon....31 N3
Easington R & Cl....92 F3
Easington Colliery Dur....101 L9
Easington Lane Sundld....101 K9
Easingwold N York....85 Q1
Easole Street Kent....35 N12
Eassie and Nevay Angus....124 G4
East Aberthaw V Glam....27 N9
East Allington Devon....5 N7
East Anstey Devon....20 D8
East Anton Hants....24 F4
East Appleton N York....91 L7
East Ashey IoW....13 K7
East Ashling W Susx....13 P3
East Aston Hants....24 H4
East Ayton N York....93 K9
East Balsdon Cnwll....7 K5
East Bank Blae G....40 B10
East Barkwith Lincs....80 D7
East Barming Kent....34 C11
East Barnby N York....92 G4
East Barnet Gt Lon....33 K3
East Barns E Loth....116 G6
East Barsham Norfk....70 D5
East Beckham Norfk....70 H4
East Bedfont Gt Lon....32 F7
East Bergholt Suffk....47 J5
East Bierley Kirk....85 J9
East Bilney Norfk....70 D8
East Blatchington E Susx....15 N10
East Bloxworth Dorset....11 L6
East Boldon S Tyne....101 K6
East Boldre Hants....12 F5
East Bolton Nthumb....109 J6
Eastbourne Darltn....91 M4
Eastbourne E Susx....16 A11
East Bower Somset....21 M6
East Bradenham Norfk....70 D10
East Brent Somset....21 M3
Eastbridge Suffk....59 N7
East Bridgford Notts....66 H3
East Briscoe Dur....90 F3
East Buckland Devon....19 N7
East Budleigh Devon....9 J8
Eastburn C Brad....84 F6
East Burnham Bucks....32 D6
East Burton Dorset....11 K7
Eastbury Herts....32 F3
Eastbury W Berk....30 H7
East Butsfield Dur....100 F9
East Butterwick N Linc....79 L2
Eastby N York....84 F4
East Calder W Loth....115 K8
East Carleton Norfk....70 H11
East Carlton Leeds....85 J6
East Carlton Nhants....55 L3
East Chaldon Dorset....11 J8
East Challow Oxon....30 H5
East Charleton Devon....5 N8
East Chelborough Dorset....10 E4
East Chiltington E Susx....15 L8
East Chinnock Somset....22 C10
East Chisenbury Wilts....23 P3
Eastchurch Kent....34 H8
East Clandon Surrey....32 F12
East Claydon Bucks....43 Q6
East Clevedon N Som....28 F8
East Coker Somset....22 C11
Eastcombe Gloucs....41 P10
Eastcombe Somset....21 J7
East Compton Somset....22 E5
East Cornworthy Devon....5 P6
Eastcote Gt Lon....32 G5
Eastcote Nhants....54 H10
Eastcote Solhll....53 M6
Eastcott Cnwll....18 G10
Eastcott Wilts....23 M2
Eastcourt Wilts....29 R4
Eastcourt Wilts....30 F10
East Cowes IoW....12 H5
East Cowick E R Yk....86 C11
East Cowton N York....91 N6
East Cramlington Nthumb....100 H3
East Cranmore Somset....22 F4
East Creech Dorset....11 M8
East Curthwaite Cumb....98 D8
East Dean E Susx....15 Q11
East Dean Gloucs....41 K7
East Dean Hants....24 D8
East Dean W Susx....14 C8
Eastdown Devon....5 P7
East Down Devon....19 L5
East Drayton Notts....79 K8
East Dulwich Gt Lon....33 L7
East Dundry N Som....28 H9
East Ella C KuH....87 K9
East End Bed....56 B9
East End C Beds....32 E3
East End E R Yk....87 L9
East End E R Yk....87 P9
East End Essex....45 M9
East End Essex....47 J11
East End Hants....12 F7
East End Hants....31 J10
East End Herts....45 N6
East End Kent....16 E4
East End Kent....35 J8
East End M Keyn....44 D3

East End Oxon....43 J8
East End Somset....22 F4
East End Suffk....47 L5
East Everleigh Wilts....24 C3
East Farleigh Kent....34 C11
East Farndon Nhants....55 J4
East Ferry Lincs....79 K4
Eastfield N Lans....114 G8
Eastfield N York....93 L10
East Firsby Lincs....79 P6
East Fortune E Loth....116 D6
East Garforth Leeds....85 N8
East Garston W Berk....30 H7
Eastgate Dur....100 B8
Eastgate Lincs....68 B8
Eastgate Norfk....70 H7
East Ginge Oxon....31 J5
East Goscote Leics....66 G9
East Grafton Wilts....30 F10
East Green Suffk....59 M7
East Grimstead Wilts....24 C8
East Grinstead W Susx....15 M3
East Guldeford E Susx....16 H6
East Haddon Nhants....54 H7
East Hagbourne Oxon....31 L5
East Halton N Linc....87 L11
East Ham Gt Lon....33 M5
Eastham Wirral....75 L7
Eastham Ferry Wirral....75 L7
Easthampton Herefs....51 L8
East Hanney Oxon....31 J4
East Hanningfield Essex....34 D2
East Hardwick Wakefd....85 N11
East Harling Norfk....58 E3
East Harlsey N York....91 Q7
East Harnham Wilts....23 P7
East Harptree BaNES....28 H11
East Hartford Nthumb....100 H3
East Harting W Susx....25 M9
East Hatch Wilts....23 K7
East Hatley Cambs....56 F10
East Hauxwell N York....91 K8
East Haven Angus....125 L5
Eastheath Wokham....31 R9
East Heckington Lincs....68 D3
East Hedleyhope Dur....100 F10
East Helmsdale Highld....147 L3
East Hendred Oxon....31 K5
East Heslerton N York....93 J11
East Hewish N Som....28 E9
East Hoathly E Susx....15 P7
East Holme Dorset....11 L8
East Hope Dur....90 H5
Easthope Shrops....51 P2
Easthorpe Essex....46 G7
Easthorpe Notts....66 H1
East Horrington Somset....22 D4
East Horsley Surrey....32 F11
East Horton Nthumb....108 G4
East Howe BCP....11 P6
East Huntspill Somset....21 M4
East Hyde C Beds....44 F8
East Ilkerton Devon....19 N4
East Ilsley W Berk....31 J6
Eastington Devon....8 D2
Eastington Gloucs....41 M10
Eastington Gloucs....42 D9
East Keal Lincs....80 G11
East Kennett Wilts....30 D9
East Keswick Leeds....85 M6
East Kilbride S Lans....114 B10
East Kimber Devon....7 P5
East Kirkby Lincs....80 F11
East Knighton Dorset....11 K7
East Knowstone Devon....20 C8
East Knoyle Wilts....23 J7
East Lambrook Somset....21 P9
East Langdon Kent....17 Q2
East Langton Leics....55 J2
East Lavant W Susx....14 B9
East Lavington W Susx....14 D7
East Layton N York....91 K5
Eastleach Martin Gloucs....42 D10
Eastleach Turville Gloucs....42 E10
East Leake Notts....66 E6
East Learmouth Nthumb....108 D3
East Leigh Devon....5 M5
East Leigh Devon....5 Q5
East Leigh Devon....8 D4
Eastleigh Devon....19 J8
Eastleigh Hants....24 G9
East Lexham Norfk....70 C8
East Linton E Loth....116 E6
East Liss Hants....25 N8
East Lockinge Oxon....31 J5
East Lound N Linc....79 K4
East Lulworth Dorset....11 L8
East Lutton N York....86 H1
East Lydeard Somset....21 J7
East Lydford Somset....22 D7
East Malling Kent....34 C11
East Malling Heath Kent....34 C11
East Marden W Susx....25 P10
East Markham Notts....79 K8
East Martin Hants....23 N9
East Marton N York....84 D4
East Meon Hants....25 L8
East Mere Devon....20 F10
East Mersea Essex....47 J8
East Midlands Airport Leics....66 D7
East Molesey Surrey....32 G9
Eastmoor Norfk....69 P11
East Morden Dorset....11 M6
East Morton C Brad....84 G7
East Morton D & G....106 A9
East Ness N York....92 G11
East Newton E R Yk....87 P9
Eastney C Port....13 J5
Eastnor Herefs....41 L4
East Norton Leics....67 K12
East Oakley Hants....24 H3
Eastoft N Linc....86 E12
East Ogwell Devon....5 P3
Easton Cambs....56 C6
Easton Cumb....98 C8
Easton Cumb....98 F6
Easton Devon....8 F7
Easton Dorset....10 H10
Easton Hants....24 H7
Easton IoW....12 F7
Easton Lincs....67 M7
Easton Norfk....70 H9
Easton Somset....22 D4
Easton Suffk....59 K9
Easton W Berk....31 J7
Easton Wilts....29 R7
Easton Grey Wilts....29 P5
Easton-in-Gordano N Som....28 G7
Easton Maudit Nhants....55 M9
Easton-on-the-Hill Nhants....67 P11

East Orchard Dorset....23 J10
East Ord Nthumb....117 L11
East Panson Devon....7 L6
East Parley BCP....11 Q5
East Peckham Kent....16 B1
East Pennard Somset....22 E6
East Portlemouth Devon....5 M9
East Prawle Devon....5 N10
East Preston W Susx....14 F10
East Pulham Dorset....10 H3
East Putford Devon....18 G10
East Quantoxhead Somset....21 J5
East Rainham Medway....34 E9
East Rainton Sundld....101 J8
East Ravendale NE Lin....80 E4
East Raynham Norfk....70 C6
Eastrea Cambs....56 F1
East Rigton Leeds....85 M6
Eastriggs D & G....97 Q5
East Rolstone N Som....28 E10
Eastrop Swindn....30 E4
East Rounton N York....91 P6
East Rudham Norfk....70 B6
East Runton Norfk....71 J4
East Ruston Norfk....71 L6
Eastry Kent....35 P11
East Saltoun E Loth....116 D8
East Sheen Gt Lon....32 H7
East Shefford W Berk....31 J7
East Sleekburn Nthumb....100 H2
East Somerton Norfk....71 P8
East Stockwith Lincs....79 K5
East Stoke Dorset....11 L7
East Stoke Notts....67 J2
East Stour Dorset....22 H9
East Stour Common Dorset....22 H9
East Stourmouth Kent....35 N10
East Stowford Devon....19 M8
East Stratton Hants....25 J5
East Studdal Kent....17 P1
East Sutton Kent....16 E1
East-the-Water Devon....19 J8
East Thirston Nthumb....109 J10
East Tilbury Thurr....34 B7
East Tilbury Village Thurr....34 B7
East Tisted Hants....25 M7
East Torrington Lincs....80 C7
East Tuddenham Norfk....70 G10
East Tytherley Hants....24 D7
East Tytherton Wilts....29 Q7
East Village Devon....8 E3
Eastville Bristl....29 J7
Eastville Lincs....80 H12
East Wall Shrops....51 N2
East Walton Norfk....69 P9
East Water Somset....22 C5
East Week Devon....8 C6
Eastwell Leics....67 J6
East Wellow Hants....24 E8
East Wemyss Fife....115 Q2
East Whitburn W Loth....114 H8
Eastwick Herts....45 M9
East Wickham Gt Lon....33 N7
East Williamston Pembks....37 L9
East Winch Norfk....69 N9
East Winterslow Wilts....24 C6
East Wittering W Susx....13 M5
East Witton N York....91 J9
Eastwood Notts....66 D3
Eastwood Sthend....34 E5
East Woodburn Nthumb....99 N3
Eastwood End Cambs....56 H1
East Woodhay Hants....31 J9
East Woodlands Somset....22 H4
East Worldham Hants....25 M5
East Worlington Devon....8 D2
East Worthing W Susx....14 H10
East Wretham Norfk....58 C2
East Youlstone Devon....18 F10
Eathorpe Warwks....54 C7
Eaton Ches E....75 P11
Eaton Ches W....75 P11
Eaton Leics....67 K6
Eaton Norfk....71 J10
Eaton Notts....79 J9
Eaton Oxon....43 J11
Eaton Shrops....51 N3
Eaton Shrops....51 L3
Eaton Bishop Herefs....40 F4
Eaton Bray C Beds....44 D7
Eaton Constantine Shrops....63 Q11
Eaton Ford C Beds....56 D9
Eaton Green C Beds....44 D6
Eaton Hastings Oxon....30 F3
Eaton Mascott Shrops....63 P11
Eaton Socon Cambs....56 D9
Eaton upon Tern Shrops....64 C7
Eaves Brow Warrtn....76 C5
Eaves Green Solhll....53 N5
Ebberston N York....92 H10
Ebbesborne Wake Wilts....23 L8
Ebbw Vale Blae G....39 R9
Ebchester Dur....100 F7
Ebdon N Som....28 E9
Ebernoe W Susx....14 D5
Ebford Devon....8 H7
Ebley Gloucs....41 N10
Ebnal Ches W....63 M4
Ebnall Herefs....51 M9
Ebrington Gloucs....42 G4
Ebsworthy Devon....7 P6
Ecchinswell Hants....31 K10
Ecclaw Border....116 G7
Ecclefechan D & G....97 P3
Eccles Border....108 B3
Eccles Kent....34 C10
Eccles Salfd....76 D4
Ecclesall Sheff....77 P5
Ecclesfield Sheff....78 B5
Eccleshall Staffs....64 F6
Eccleshill C Brad....85 J7
Ecclesmachan W Loth....115 K7
Eccles on Sea Norfk....71 N6
Eccles Road Norfk....58 F2
Eccleston Ches W....75 L11
Eccleston Lancs....83 M11
Eccleston St Hel....75 N4
Eccleston Green Lancs....83 M11
Echt Abers....132 H3
Eckford Border....108 B4
Eckington Derbys....78 C8
Eckington Worcs....41 Q4
Ecton Nhants....55 L8
Ecton Staffs....77 L12
Edale Derbys....77 L6
Eday Airport Ork....147 d2
Edburton W Susx....15 J8
Edderside Cumb....97 M9
Edderton Highld....146 C9
Eddington Kent....35 L8
Eddleston Border....115 M12
Eddlewood S Lans....114 C10
Edenbridge Kent....15 N2
Edenfield Lancs....84 B11
Edenhall Cumb....89 N2
Edenham Lincs....67 Q8
Eden Mount Cumb....89 J10
Eden Park Gt Lon....33 L9

Eden Project Cnwll....3 P4
Edensor Derbys....77 N9
Edentaggart Ag & B....113 L3
Edenthorpe Donc....78 G2
Edern Gwynd....60 C5
Edgarley Somset....22 C6
Edgbaston Birm....53 K4
Edgcott Bucks....43 P7
Edgcott Somset....20 C5
Edgcumbe Cnwll....2 H8
Edge Gloucs....41 N9
Edge Shrops....63 L10
Edgebolton Shrops....63 P8
Edge End Gloucs....41 J9
Edgefield Norfk....70 G5
Edgefield Green Norfk....70 G5
Edgefold Bolton....76 C2
Edge Green Ches W....63 N2
Edgehill Warwks....42 H3
Edgeley Shrops....63 Q4
Edgerton Kirk....84 H11
Edgeside Lancs....84 C10
Edgeworth Gloucs....41 Q10
Edgeworthy Devon....20 D10
Edginswell Torbay....5 Q3
Edgiock Worcs....53 K8
Edgmond Wrekin....64 D9
Edgmond Marsh Wrekin....64 D8
Edgton Shrops....51 L3
Edgware Gt Lon....32 H4
Edgworth Bl w D....83 R11
Edinbane Highld....134 F6
Edinburgh C Edin....115 N6
Edinburgh Airport C Edin....115 L6
Edinburgh Castle C Edin....115 N6
Edinburgh Old & New Town C Edin....115 N6
Edinburgh Royal Botanic Gardens C Edin....115 N6
Edinburgh Zoo RZSS C Edin....115 M6
Edingale Staffs....65 N9
Edingham D & G....96 H6
Edingley Notts....66 H1
Edingthorpe Norfk....71 L5
Edingthorpe Green Norfk....71 L5
Edington Border....117 K10
Edington Somset....21 N5
Edington Wilts....23 J3
Edingworth Somset....21 M3
Edistone Devon....18 E9
Edithmead Somset....21 M3
Edith Weston Rutlnd....67 M11
Edlesborough Bucks....44 D8
Edlingham Nthumb....109 J8
Edlington Lincs....80 E8
Edmond Castle Cumb....98 G8
Edmondsham Dorset....11 N2
Edmondsley Dur....100 G8
Edmondthorpe Leics....67 L8
Edmonton Cnwll....6 E11
Edmonton Gt Lon....33 L4
Edmundbyers Dur....100 D8
Ednam Border....108 B2
Ednaston Derbys....65 N3
Edney Common Essex....46 B10
Edradynate P & K....123 M2
Edrom Border....117 J10
Edstaston Shrops....63 N6
Edstone Warwks....53 N8
Edvin Loach Herefs....52 C9
Edwalton Notts....66 F4
Edwardstone Suffk....46 G3
Edwardsville Myr Td....27 L3
Edwinsford Carmth....38 F5
Edwinstowe Notts....78 G10
Edworth C Beds....45 J3
Edwyn Ralph Herefs....52 B9
Edzell Angus....132 F10
Edzell Woods Abers....132 F10
Efail-fach Neath....27 J4
Efail Isaf Rhondd....27 P5
Efailnewydd Gwynd....60 E6
Efail-Rhyd Powys....62 G7
Efailwen Carmth....37 M5
Efenechtyd Denbgs....62 F1
Effgill D & G....107 J1
Effingham Surrey....32 G11
Effingham Junction Surrey....32 G11
Efflinch Staffs....65 M9
Efford Devon....8 G4
Egbury Hants....24 G3
Egdean W Susx....14 E7
Egerton Bolton....83 Q10
Egerton Kent....16 F1
Egerton Forstal Kent....16 F2
Eggborough N York....85 P10
Eggbuckland C Plym....4 H5
Eggesford Devon....8 C2
Egginton C Beds....44 D6
Egginton Derbys....65 P6
Egglescliffe S on T....91 P4
Eggleston Dur....90 G2
Egham Surrey....32 E8
Egham Wick Surrey....32 D8
Egleton Rutlnd....67 L10
Eglingham Nthumb....109 J6
Egloshayle Cnwll....6 E11
Egloskerry Cnwll....7 K7
Eglwysbach Conwy....73 P9
Eglwys-Brewis V Glam....27 N8
Eglwys Cross Wrexhm....63 M4
Eglwys Fach Cerdgn....49 M1
Eglwyswrw Pembks....37 L3
Egmanton Notts....79 J10
Egremont Cumb....88 D8
Egremont Wirral....75 K5
Egton N York....92 G6
Egton Bridge N York....92 G6
Egypt Bucks....32 D6
Egypt Hants....24 H5
Eigg Highld....126 H7
Eight Ash Green Essex....46 G6
Eilanreach Highld....135 P12
Eilean Donan Castle Highld....136 B10
Eisgein W Isls....152 f5
Eishken W Isls....152 f5
Eisteddfa Gurig Cerdgn....49 N6
Elan Valley Powys....50 B7
Elan Village Powys....50 C7
Elberton S Glos....29 J5
Elbridge W Susx....14 C9
Elburton C Plym....4 H6
Elcombe Swindn....30 D6
Elcot W Berk....31 J8
Eldernell Cambs....68 H12
Eldersfield Worcs....41 M5
Elderslie Rens....113 N8
Elder Street Essex....45 P4
Eldon Dur....91 L2
Eldwick C Brad....84 H7
Elfhill Abers....133 L7
Elford Nthumb....109 J4
Elford Staffs....65 M10
Elgin Moray....139 M4
Elgol Highld....135 J7
Elham Kent....17 L2
Elie Fife....116 F1
Elilaw Nthumb....108 F8
Elim IoA....72 E7
Eling Hants....24 F11

Elkesley Notts....78 H8
Elkstone Gloucs....41 R9
Ella Abers....140 G4
Ellacombe Torbay....5 Q4
Elland Calder....84 H11
Elland Lower Edge Calder....84 H11
Ellary Ag & B....111 Q6
Ellastone Staffs....65 L3
Ellel Lancs....83 L4
Ellemford Border....116 H9
Ellenabeich Ag & B....120 D9
Ellenborough Cumb....97 L11
Ellenbrook Salfd....76 D3
Ellenhall Staffs....64 F7
Ellen's Green Surrey....14 G4
Ellerbeck N York....91 R8
Ellerby N York....92 G4
Ellerdine Heath Wrekin....64 B8
Ellerhayes Devon....9 J4
Elleric Ag & B....121 K3
Ellerker E R Yk....86 G9
Ellers N York....84 F6
Ellerton E R Yk....86 E8
Ellerton N York....91 L7
Ellerton Shrops....64 D7
Ellesborough Bucks....44 B10
Ellesmere Shrops....63 L6
Ellesmere Port Ches W....75 L8
Ellingham Hants....11 Q3
Ellingham Norfk....59 M2
Ellingham Nthumb....109 K5
Ellingstring N York....91 K10
Ellington Cambs....56 D6
Ellington Nthumb....109 M11
Elliots Green Somset....22 H4
Ellisfield Hants....25 K4
Ellishader Highld....135 J3
Ellistown Leics....66 C10
Ellon Abers....141 M9
Ellonby Cumb....98 E11
Elloughton E R Yk....86 H9
Ellwood Gloucs....41 J10
Elm Cambs....69 J10
Elmbridge Shrops....52 C6
Elmbridge Worcs....52 H7
Elmdon Essex....45 N4
Elmdon Solhll....53 M4
Elmdon Heath Solhll....53 M4
Elmer W Susx....14 D10
Elmers End Gt Lon....33 L8
Elmer's Green Lancs....75 M2
Elmesthorpe Leics....54 D1
Elm Green Essex....46 D10
Elmhurst Staffs....65 L10
Elmley Castle Worcs....41 R3
Elmley Lovett Worcs....52 G7
Elmore Gloucs....41 M8
Elmore Back Gloucs....41 M8
Elm Park Gt Lon....33 P5
Elmscott Devon....18 E9
Elmsett Suffk....47 J2
Elmstead Heath Essex....47 J7
Elmstead Market Essex....47 J7
Elmstead Row Essex....47 J7
Elmsted Kent....17 J2
Elmstone Kent....35 N10
Elmstone Hardwicke Gloucs....41 Q6
Elmswell E R Yk....87 J3
Elmswell Suffk....58 E8
Elmton Derbys....78 E9
Elphin Highld....144 F3
Elphinstone E Loth....115 R7
Elrick Abers....133 K3
Elrig D & G....95 L8
Elrington Nthumb....99 N5
Elsdon Nthumb....108 E11
Elsecar Barns....78 C4
Elsenham Essex....45 P6
Elsfield Oxon....43 L9
Elsham N Linc....79 P1
Elsing Norfk....70 G8
Elslack N York....84 E5
Elson Hants....13 J4
Elson Shrops....63 L5
Elsrickle S Lans....106 D1
Elstead Surrey....14 C2
Elsted W Susx....25 P9
Elsted Marsh W Susx....25 P9
Elsthorpe Lincs....67 Q7
Elstob Dur....91 N2
Elston Lancs....83 N7
Elston Notts....67 J3
Elstone Devon....19 N10
Elstow Bed....44 F2
Elstree Herts....32 H3
Elstronwick E R Yk....87 N9
Elswick Lancs....83 K7
Elswick N u Ty....100 G5
Elsworth Cambs....56 E8
Elterwater Cumb....89 J6
Eltham Gt Lon....33 N7
Eltisley Cambs....56 E9
Elton Bury....76 E1
Elton Cambs....56 B1
Elton Ches W....75 L8
Elton Derbys....77 M11
Elton Gloucs....41 M8
Elton Herefs....51 M6
Elton Notts....67 J5
Elton S on T....91 P4
Elton Green Ches W....75 M8
Elton-on-the-Hill Notts....67 J4
Eltringham Nthumb....100 D6
Elvanfoot S Lans....106 C6
Elvaston Derbys....66 C5
Elveden Suffk....58 B5
Elvetham Heath Hants....25 P2
Elvingston E Loth....116 D6
Elvington C York....86 C6
Elvington Kent....35 N12
Elwell Devon....19 M7
Elwick Hartpl....101 L11
Elwick Nthumb....109 J3
Elworth Ches E....76 D11
Elworthy Somset....20 H6
Ely Cambs....57 J4
Ely Cardif....27 Q7
Emberton M Keyn....55 M10
Embleton Cumb....97 M11
Embleton Dur....101 L12
Embleton Nthumb....109 L5
Embo Highld....146 E9
Emborough Somset....22 E4
Embo Street Highld....146 E9
Embsay N York....84 F5
Emery Down Hants....12 D4
Emley Kirk....77 N1
Emley Moor Kirk....77 N1
Emmbrook Wokham....31 R9
Emmer Green Readg....31 R7
Emmett Carr Derbys....78 D8
Emmington Oxon....43 P10
Emneth Norfk....69 J10
Emneth Hungate Norfk....69 K10
Empingham Rutlnd....67 M10
Empshott Hants....25 M6
Empshott Green Hants....25 M6
Emsworth Hants....13 M3
Enborne W Berk....31 J9
Enborne Row W Berk....31 J9
Enchmarsh Shrops....51 N1
Enderby Leics....66 E12
Endmoor Cumb....89 N9
Endon Staffs....64 G2
Endon Bank Staffs....64 G1
Enfield Gt Lon....33 L3
Enfield Lock Gt Lon....33 L3
Enfield Wash Gt Lon....33 L3
Enford Wilts....23 P3
Engine Common S Glos....29 L5
England's Gate Herefs....51 P10
Englefield W Berk....31 N7
Englefield Green Surrey....32 E8
Engleseabrook Ches E....64 D2
English Bicknor Gloucs....41 J8
Englishcombe BaNES....29 L9
English Frankton Shrops....63 M6
Engollan Cnwll....6 B9
Enham Alamein Hants....24 F3
Enmore Somset....21 K6
Enmore Green Dorset....23 J8
Ennerdale Bridge Cumb....88 E7
Enniscaven Cnwll....3 N3
Enochdhu P & K....131 K11
Ensay Ag & B....119 K3
Ensbury BCP....11 Q5
Ensdon Shrops....63 L9
Ensis Devon....19 L8
Enson Staffs....64 H6
Enstone Oxon....42 H6
Enterkinfoot D & G....105 Q9
Enterpen N York....91 Q5
Enville Staffs....52 F3
Eochar W Isls....152 b9
Eòlaigearraidh W Isls....152 b12
Eoligarry W Isls....152 b12
Epney Gloucs....41 M9
Epperstone Notts....66 G2
Epping Essex....45 N10
Epping Green Essex....45 N10
Epping Green Herts....45 K10
Epping Upland Essex....45 N10
Eppleby N York....91 K4
Eppleworth E R Yk....87 K8
Epsom Surrey....33 J10
Epwell Oxon....42 H4
Epworth N Linc....79 K3
Epworth Turbary N Linc....79 J3
Erbistock Wrexhm....63 K4
Erdington Birm....53 L2
Eridge Green E Susx....15 Q4
Eridge Station E Susx....15 P4
Erines Ag & B....112 C6
Eriska Ag & B....120 G4
Eriswell Suffk....57 N5
Erith Gt Lon....33 P7
Erlestoke Wilts....23 L3
Ermington Devon....5 K6
Erpingham Norfk....71 J6
Erriottwood Kent....34 G10
Errogie Highld....137 P11
Errol P & K....124 E8
Erskine Rens....113 P7
Erskine Bridge Rens....113 N7
Ervie D & G....94 E5
Erwarton Suffk....47 M5
Erwood Powys....39 Q3
Eryholme N York....91 N5
Eryrys Denbgs....74 H12
Escalls Cnwll....2 B9
Escomb Dur....100 F12
Escott Somset....20 H6
Escrick N York....86 B6
Esgair Carmth....38 C3
Esgair Cerdgn....49 K7
Esgairgeiliog Powys....61 N11
Esh Dur....100 F9
Esher Surrey....32 G9
Esholt C Brad....85 J7
Eshott Nthumb....109 K10
Eshton N York....84 D4
Esh Winning Dur....100 G10
Eskadale Highld....137 M8
Eskbank Mdloth....115 P8
Eskdale Green Cumb....88 G7
Eskdalemuir D & G....106 H10
Eske E R Yk....87 K6
Eskham Lincs....80 G4
Eskholme Donc....86 C11
Esperley Lane Ends Dur....91 J2
Esprick Lancs....83 K8
Essendine Rutlnd....67 Q9
Essendon Herts....45 K10
Essich Highld....138 B8
Esslemont Abers....141 M10
Eston R & Cl....92 B3
Etal Nthumb....108 F3
Etchilhampton Wilts....30 B10
Etchingham E Susx....16 C5
Etchinghill Kent....17 L3
Etchinghill Staffs....65 J9
Etchingwood E Susx....15 N6
Etling Green Norfk....70 F9
Etloe Gloucs....41 K10
Eton W & M....32 D7
Eton Wick W & M....32 D7
Etruria C Stke....64 F3
Etteridge Highld....130 C6
Ettersgill Dur....90 D2
Ettiley Heath Ches E....76 D11
Ettingshall Wolves....52 H2
Ettington Warwks....53 P11
Etton C Pete....67 Q11
Etton E R Yk....87 H6
Ettrick Border....106 H6
Ettrickbridge Border....107 M5
Ettrickhill Border....106 H6
Etwall Derbys....65 P5
Eudon George Shrops....52 C3
Euston Suffk....58 C5
Euximoor Drove Cambs....57 J1
Euxton Lancs....83 M11
Evancoyd Powys....51 J8
Evanton Highld....138 C3
Evedon Lincs....68 B3
Evelith Shrops....52 D1
Evelix Highld....146 D7
Evenjobb Powys....51 J8
Evenley Nhants....43 M5
Evenlode Gloucs....42 F6
Evenwood Dur....91 J2
Evenwood Gate Dur....91 K2
Evercreech Somset....22 F6
Everingham E R Yk....86 F7
Everleigh Wilts....24 C3
Everley N York....93 K9
Eversholt C Beds....44 D5
Evershot Dorset....10 E4
Eversley Hants....31 R10
Eversley Cross Hants....31 R10
Everthorpe E R Yk....86 G8
Everton C Beds....56 D10
Everton Hants....12 E6
Everton Lpool....75 K5
Everton Notts....78 H5
Evertown D & G....98 D3
Evesbatch Herefs....52 C11
Evesham Worcs....42 B3
Evington C Leic....66 G11
Ewden Village Sheff....77 N3
Ewell Surrey....33 J9
Ewell Minnis Kent....17 N2
Ewelme Oxon....31 N4
Ewen Gloucs....30 B3
Ewenny V Glam....27 M7
Ewerby Lincs....68 B3
Ewerby Thorpe Lincs....68 C3

Ewhurst Surrey ...14 F3
Ewhurst Green E Susx ...16 D6
Ewhurst Green Surrey ...14 F3
Ewloe Flints ...75 J10
Ewloe Green Flints ...75 J10
Ewood Bl w D ...83 P10
Ewood Bridge Lancs ...84 B11
Eworthy Devon ...7 N6
Ewshot Hants ...25 P3
Ewyas Harold Herefs ...40 E6
Exbourne Devon ...8 G5
Exbury Hants ...12 G5
Exceat E Susx ...15 P11
Exebridge Somset ...20 E8
Exelby N York ...91 M9
Exeter Devon ...8 H6
Exeter Airport Devon ...9 J6
Exeter Services Devon ...8 H6
Exford Somset ...20 D6
Exfordsgreen Shrops ...63 M11
Exhall Warwks ...53 L9
Exhall Warwks ...54 B3
Exlade Street Oxon ...31 N6
Exley Head C Brad ...84 F7
Exminster Devon ...8 H7
Exmoor National Park ...20 D6
Exmouth Devon ...9 J8
Exning Suffk ...57 M7
Exted Kent ...17 L2
Exton Devon ...9 J7
Exton Hants ...25 K9
Exton Rutlnd ...67 M10
Exton Somset ...20 E6
Exwick Devon ...8 G6
Eyam Derbys ...77 N8
Eydon Nhants ...54 E10
Eye C Pete ...68 E11
Eye Herefs ...51 N8
Eye Suffk ...58 H6
Eye Green C Pete ...68 E11
Eyemouth Border ...117 L8
Eyeworth C Beds ...45 J3
Eyhorne Street Kent ...34 E11
Eyke Suffk ...59 L10
Eynesbury Cambs ...56 D9
Eynsford Kent ...33 P9
Eynsham Oxon ...43 J10
Eype Dorset ...10 C6
Eyre Highld ...134 G5
Eythorne Kent ...17 N1
Eyton Herefs ...51 N8
Eyton Shrops ...51 L3
Eyton Shrops ...63 L9
Eyton Shrops ...63 M7
Eyton Wrexhm ...63 K3
Eyton on Severn Shrops ...63 P11
Eyton upon the Weald Moors Wrekin ...64 C9

F

Faccombe Hants ...30 H10
Faceby N York ...91 R6
Fachwen Powys ...62 E9
Facit Lancs ...84 D11
Fackley Notts ...78 D11
Faddiley Ches E ...63 P2
Fadmoor N York ...92 G9
Faerdre Swans ...26 G2
Faifley W Duns ...113 P6
Failand N Som ...28 G8
Failford S Ayrs ...104 H4
Failsworth Oldham ...76 G3
Fairbourne Gwynd ...61 K9
Fairburn N York ...85 P9
Fairfield Derbys ...77 N9
Fairfield Kent ...16 G5
Fairfield Worcs ...52 H5
Fairfield Park Herts ...44 H5
Fairford Gloucs ...30 D2
Fairford Park Gloucs ...30 D2
Fairgirth D & G ...96 H2
Fair Green Norfk ...69 M8
Fairhaven Lancs ...82 H9
Fair Isle Shet ...147 h10
Fair Isle Airport Shet ...147 h10
Fairlands Surrey ...32 D11
Fairlie N Ayrs ...113 J10
Fairlight E Susx ...16 F8
Fairlight Cove E Susx ...16 F8
Fairmile Devon ...9 L5
Fairmile Surrey ...32 G10
Fairmilehead C Edin ...115 N7
Fairnilee Border ...107 M3
Fair Oak Hants ...24 E5
Fairoak Staffs ...64 E5
Fair Oak Green Hants ...31 N10
Fairseat Kent ...34 A10
Fairstead Essex ...46 D8
Fairstead Norfk ...69 M8
Fairstead Norfk ...71 K7
Fairwarp E Susx ...15 N5
Fairwater Cardif ...27 N7
Fairy Cross Devon ...18 H8
Fakenham Norfk ...70 D5
Fakenham Magna Suffk ...58 D5
Fala Mdloth ...116 B9
Fala Dam Mdloth ...116 B9
Falcut Nhants ...43 M3
Faldingworth Lincs ...79 Q7
Faldouet Jersey ...13 d2
Falfield S Glos ...29 K4
Falkenham Suffk ...47 N4
Falkirk Falk ...114 F5
Falkirk Wheel Falk ...114 F5
Falkland Fife ...124 E11
Fallburn S Lans ...106 C2
Fallgate Derbys ...78 B11
Fallin Stirlg ...114 E3
Falloden Nthumb ...109 K5
Fallowfield Manch ...76 F5
Fallowfield Nthumb ...99 P4
Falmer E Susx ...15 L9
Falmouth Cnwll ...3 K8
Falnash Border ...107 K8
Falsgrave N York ...93 L9
Falstone Nthumb ...108 B12
Fanagmore Highld ...148 E6
Fancott C Beds ...44 E6
Fanellan Highld ...137 N7
Fangdale Beck N York ...92 B8
Fangfoss E R Yk ...86 E4
Fanmore Ag & B ...119 L4
Fannich Lodge Highld ...136 H3
Fans Border ...107 P2
Far Bletchley M Keyn ...44 B5
Farcet Cambs ...56 D2
Far Cotton Nhants ...54 F8
Farden Shrops ...51 P5
Fareham Hants ...13 J3
Farewell Staffs ...65 K10
Far Forest Worcs ...52 D6
Farforth Lincs ...80 F8
Far Green Gloucs ...29 M2
Faringdon Oxon ...30 G3
Farington Lancs ...83 M10
Farlam Cumb ...98 H6
Farleigh N Som ...28 G8
Farleigh Surrey ...33 L10
Farleigh Hungerford Somset ...29 N11
Farleigh Wallop Hants ...25 L4
Farlesthorpe Lincs ...81 J9
Farleton Cumb ...89 N9
Farleton Lancs ...83 N2

Farley Derbys ...77 P11
Farley Staffs ...65 K3
Farley Wilts ...24 C7
Farley Green Suffk ...57 P10
Farley Green Surrey ...14 F2
Farley Hill Wokham ...31 Q9
Farleys End Gloucs ...41 M8
Farlington C Port ...13 M4
Farlington N York ...86 B2
Farlow Shrops ...52 B4
Farmborough BaNES ...29 K9
Farmbridge End Essex ...46 A9
Farmcote Gloucs ...42 C6
Farmcote Shrops ...52 E2
Farmington Gloucs ...42 D8
Farmoor Oxon ...43 K10
Far Moor Wigan ...75 N3
Farms Common Cnwll ...2 H7
Farmtown Moray ...140 D5
Farnah Green Derbys ...65 Q3
Farnborough Gt Lon ...33 N9
Farnborough Hants ...32 C11
Farnborough W Berk ...31 J6
Farnborough Warwks ...54 C10
Farnborough Park Hants ...32 C11
Farncombe Surrey ...14 D2
Farndish Bed ...55 M8
Farndon Ches W ...63 L1
Farndon Notts ...67 J2
Farne Islands Nthumb ...109 L1
Farnell Angus ...125 M2
Farnham Dorset ...23 L10
Farnham Essex ...45 N7
Farnham N York ...85 M3
Farnham Suffk ...59 M8
Farnham Surrey ...25 P4
Farnham Common Bucks ...32 D5
Farnham Green Essex ...45 N6
Farnham Royal Bucks ...32 D5
Farningham Kent ...33 Q9
Farnley Leeds ...85 K8
Farnley N York ...85 J6
Farnley Tyas Kirk ...77 M1
Farnsfield Notts ...78 G12
Farnworth Bolton ...76 D2
Farnworth Halton ...75 N6
Far Oakridge Gloucs ...41 Q11
Farr Highld ...130 F4
Farr Highld ...138 F3
Farr Highld ...150 C4
Farraline Highld ...137 P11
Farringdon Devon ...9 J6
Farrington Gurney BaNES ...22 E2
Far Sawrey Cumb ...89 K7
Farsley Leeds ...85 J8
Farther Howegreen Essex ...34 E2
Farthing Green Kent ...16 E2
Farthinghoe Nhants ...43 L4
Farthingloe Kent ...17 N3
Farthingstone Nhants ...54 E9
Farthing Street Gt Lon ...33 M9
Fartown Kirk ...84 H11
Farway Devon ...9 M6
Fasnacloich Ag & B ...121 J3
Fasnakyle Highld ...137 K10
Fassfern Highld ...128 E8
Fatfield Sundld ...100 H7
Faugh Cumb ...98 G2
Fauld Staffs ...65 M6
Fauldhouse W Loth ...114 G5
Faulkbourne Essex ...46 D8
Faulkland Somset ...22 G2
Fauls Shrops ...63 Q6
Faversham Kent ...34 H10
Fawdington N York ...91 Q12
Fawdon N u Ty ...100 G4
Fawdon Nthumb ...108 G6
Fawfieldhead Staffs ...77 K11
Fawkham Green Kent ...33 Q9
Fawler Oxon ...42 H8
Fawley Bucks ...31 Q5
Fawley Hants ...12 G4
Fawley W Berk ...30 H6
Fawley Chapel Herefs ...41 J6
Fawnog Flints ...74 H10
Fawsley Nhants ...54 F9
Faxfleet E R Yk ...86 F10
Faygate W Susx ...15 J4
Fazakerley Lpool ...75 L4
Fazeley Staffs ...65 M11
Fearby N York ...91 K10
Fearn Highld ...146 E9
Fearnan P & K ...123 J4
Fearnbeg Highld ...135 M4
Fearnhead Warrtn ...76 B5
Fearnmore Highld ...135 M4
Fearnoch Ag & B ...112 D5
Featherstone Staffs ...64 H11
Featherstone Wakefd ...85 N11
Feckenham Worcs ...53 J8
Feering Essex ...46 F7
Feetham N York ...90 G7
Feizor N York ...84 B2
Felbridge Surrey ...15 L3
Felbrigg Norfk ...71 J4
Felcourt Surrey ...15 M3
Felden Herts ...44 F10
Felindre Carmth ...38 A4
Felindre Carmth ...38 H6
Felindre Cerdgn ...49 J9
Felindre Powys ...40 A7
Felindre Powys ...50 G4
Felindre Swans ...38 F11
Felindre Farchog Pembks ...37 L3
Felinfach Cerdgn ...49 J9
Felinfach Powys ...39 P5
Felinfoel Carmth ...38 D11
Felingwmisaf Carmth ...38 D7
Felingwmuchaf Carmth ...38 D7
Felin-newydd Powys ...39 Q4
Felixkirk N York ...91 Q10
Felixstowe Suffk ...47 N5
Felixstowe Ferry Suffk ...47 N4
Felkington Nthumb ...117 L12
Felkirk Wakefd ...78 C1
Felling Gatesd ...100 H6
Fell Lane C Brad ...84 F7
Fell Side Cumb ...98 C10
Felmersham Bed ...55 N9
Felmingham Norfk ...71 K6
Felpham W Susx ...14 D11
Felsham Suffk ...58 D9
Felsted Essex ...46 B7
Feltham Gt Lon ...32 G6
Felthamhill Surrey ...32 G8
Felthorpe Norfk ...70 H8
Felton Herefs ...51 H5
Felton N Som ...28 H9
Felton Nthumb ...109 J9
Felton Butler Shrops ...63 L8
Feltwell Norfk ...57 N1
Fenay Bridge Kirk ...85 J12
Fence Lancs ...84 B8
Fence Rothm ...78 D6
Fence Houses Sundld ...100 H7
Fencott Oxon ...43 M8
Fendike Corner Lincs ...81 J11
Fen Ditton Cambs ...57 J8
Fen Drayton Cambs ...56 H7
Fen End Lincs ...68 E7
Fen End Solhll ...53 M6
Fenham Nthumb ...108 H1
Feniscliffe Bl w D ...83 P10
Feniscowles Bl w D ...83 P10

Feniton Devon ...9 L5
Feniton Court Devon ...9 L5
Fenn Green Shrops ...52 E4
Fenn Street Medway ...34 D7
Fenny Bentley Derbys ...65 M2
Fenny Bridges Devon ...9 L5
Fenny Compton Warwks ...54 C10
Fenny Drayton Leics ...54 B1
Fenny Stratford M Keyn ...44 C5
Fenrother Nthumb ...109 K11
Fenstanton Cambs ...56 F7
Fenstead End Suffk ...57 Q10
Fen Street Norfk ...58 G2
Fen Street Suffk ...58 H8
Fenton C Stke ...64 G3
Fenton Cambs ...56 F5
Fenton Cumb ...98 F6
Fenton Lincs ...67 L2
Fenton Lincs ...79 L8
Fenton Notts ...79 J6
Fenton Nthumb ...108 F3
Fenton Barns E Loth ...116 D11
Fenwick Donc ...78 G1
Fenwick E Ayrs ...104 H1
Fenwick Nthumb ...100 D4
Fenwick Nthumb ...108 H2
Feock Cnwll ...3 K7
Feolin Ferry Ag & B ...111 K7
Fergushill N Ayrs ...104 F1
Feriniquarrie Highld ...134 C6
Fermain Bay Guern ...12 c3
Fern Angus ...132 D12
Ferndale Rhondd ...27 N3
Ferndown Dorset ...11 N4
Ferness Highld ...138 H7
Fernham Oxon ...30 G4
Fernhill Heath Worcs ...52 F9
Fernhurst W Susx ...14 C5
Fernie Fife ...124 F9
Ferniegair S Lans ...114 D10
Fernilea Highld ...134 F9
Fernilee Derbys ...77 J8
Fernwood Notts ...67 K2
Ferrensby N York ...85 M3
Ferriby Sluice N Linc ...86 H11
Ferrindonald Highld ...127 M3
Ferring W Susx ...14 F10
Ferrybridge Wakefd ...85 P10
Ferrybridge Services Wakefd ...85 P10
Ferryden Angus ...125 P2
Ferryhill Dur ...100 H11
Ferryhill Station Dur ...100 H12
Ferry Point Highld ...146 D8
Ferryside Carmth ...38 A9
Fersfield Norfk ...58 F4
Fersit Highld ...129 L8
Feshiebridge Highld ...130 F3
Fetcham Surrey ...32 G11
Fetlar Shet ...147 k3
Fetterangus Abers ...141 N6
Fettercairn Abers ...132 G9
Fewcott Oxon ...43 L6
Fewston N York ...85 J4
Ffairfach Carmth ...38 G3
Ffair Rhos Cerdgn ...49 M7
Ffald-y-Brenin Carmth ...38 G3
Ffarmers Carmth ...38 G3
Ffawyddog Powys ...40 C2
Festiniog Railway Gwynd ...61 K4
Ffordd-las Denbgs ...74 F10
Fforest Carmth ...38 E10
Fforest Gôch Neath ...26 H1
Ffostrasol Cerdgn ...48 F11
Ffrith Flints ...63 J1
Ffrwdgrech Powys ...39 P6
Ffynnonddewi Cerdgn ...48 F10
Ffynnongroyw Flints ...74 H7
Ffynnon-oer Cerdgn ...49 J10
Fickleshole Surrey ...33 M10
Fiddington Gloucs ...41 Q5
Fiddington Somset ...21 K5
Fiddleford Dorset ...22 H10
Fiddlers Green Cnwll ...3 K3
Fiddlers Hamlet Essex ...45 N2
Field Staffs ...65 J5
Field Broughton Cumb ...89 J10
Field Dalling Norfk ...70 E4
Field Head Leics ...66 E10
Fifehead Magdalen Dorset ...22 H9
Fifehead Neville Dorset ...11 J3
Fifehead St Quintin Dorset ...11 J3
Fife Keith Moray ...140 C6
Fifield Oxon ...42 F8
Fifield W & M ...32 C6
Fifield Wilts ...23 P3
Filands Wilts ...29 Q5
Filby Norfk ...71 P9
Filey N York ...93 M10
Filgrave M Keyn ...44 C3
Filkins Oxon ...42 F10
Filleigh Devon ...19 N8
Filleigh Devon ...19 N8
Fillingham Lincs ...79 N6
Fillongley Warwks ...53 P3
Filmore Hill Hants ...25 L8
Filton S Glos ...29 J6
Fimber E R Yk ...86 G3
Finavon Angus ...125 K1
Finberry Kent ...17 J3
Fincham Norfk ...69 N10
Finchampstead Wokham ...31 R9
Finchdean Hants ...25 M10
Finchingfield Essex ...46 B5
Finchley Gt Lon ...33 K4
Findern Derbys ...65 P6
Findhorn Moray ...139 J4
Findhorn Bridge Highld ...138 G10
Findochty Moray ...140 C2
Findo Gask P & K ...123 P9
Findon Abers ...133 M5
Findon W Susx ...14 G9
Findon Mains Highld ...137 Q4
Findon Valley W Susx ...14 G9
Findrack House Abers ...132 G3
Finedon Nhants ...55 M6
Fingal Street Suffk ...59 J6
Fingask P & K ...124 D9
Fingest Bucks ...31 N4
Finghall N York ...91 K9
Fingland Cumb ...98 C6
Fingland D & G ...105 P6
Fingringhoe Essex ...47 J7
Finkle Green Essex ...57 P11
Finkle Street Barns ...77 P4
Finlarig Stirlg ...122 F6
Finmere Oxon ...43 M5
Finnart P & K ...129 N6
Finningham Suffk ...58 G6
Finningley Donc ...78 H4
Finsbay W Isls ...152 e5
Finstall Worcs ...52 H7
Finsthwaite Cumb ...89 J9
Finstock Oxon ...42 H8
Finstown Ork ...147 c4
Fintry Abers ...141 J5
Fintry Stirlg ...114 E2
Finzean Abers ...132 G4
Fionnphort Ag & B ...119 J7
Fionnsbhagh W Isls ...152 e5
Firbank Cumb ...89 N7
Firbeck Rothm ...78 F6

Firby N York ...86 D2
Firby N York ...91 M9
Firgrove Rochdl ...84 D12
Firle E Susx ...15 N9
Firsby Lincs ...81 J11
Firsdown Wilts ...24 C7
Fir Tree Dur ...100 F11
Fishbourne IoW ...13 J6
Fishbourne W Susx ...13 P4
Fishbourne Roman Palace W Susx ...13 P4
Fishburn Dur ...101 K11
Fishcross Clacks ...114 G2
Fisher W Susx ...14 B10
Fisherford Abers ...140 G8
Fisherrow E Loth ...115 Q7
Fisher's Pond Hants ...24 H9
Fisher's Row Lancs ...83 K5
Fisherstreet W Susx ...14 D4
Fisherton Highld ...138 D5
Fisherton S Ayrs ...104 E6
Fisherton de la Mere Wilts ...23 M6
Fishery W Berk ...32 C6
Fishguard Pembks ...37 J3
Fishlake Donc ...78 G1
Fishleigh Devon ...7 Q4
Fishmere End Lincs ...68 E3
Fishnish Pier Ag & B ...120 C4
Fishpond Bottom Dorset ...10 B5
Fishponds Bristl ...29 J7
Fishtoft Lincs ...68 G4
Fishtoft Drove Lincs ...68 F2
Fishwick Lancs ...83 M9
Fiskavaig Highld ...134 F9
Fiskerton Lincs ...79 P9
Fiskerton Notts ...67 J2
Fitling E R Yk ...87 N8
Fittleton Wilts ...23 P3
Fittleworth W Susx ...14 E7
Fitton End Cambs ...68 H9
Fitz Shrops ...63 M9
Fitzhead Somset ...20 H7
Fitzroy Somset ...21 K8
Fitzwilliam Wakefd ...85 N12
Five Ash Down E Susx ...15 N6
Five Ashes E Susx ...15 Q5
Five Bells Somset ...20 G5
Five Bridges Herefs ...41 K2
Fivecrosses Ches W ...75 N8
Five Oak Green Kent ...16 B2
Five Oaks Jersey ...13 c2
Five Oaks W Susx ...14 G5
Five Roads Carmth ...38 C10
Five Wents Kent ...34 E12
Flack's Green Essex ...46 D8
Flackwell Heath Bucks ...32 C4
Fladbury Worcs ...42 A2
Fladdabister Shet ...147 i8
Flagg Derbys ...77 L10
Flamborough E R Yk ...87 N1
Flamborough Head E R Yk ...87 N1
Flamingo Land Theme Park N York ...92 F10
Flamstead Herts ...44 F9
Flamstead End Herts ...45 L10
Flansham W Susx ...14 D10
Flanshaw Wakefd ...85 L11
Flappit Spring C Brad ...84 F7
Flasby N York ...84 E4
Flash Staffs ...77 J10
Flashader Highld ...134 F5
Flaunden Herts ...32 E2
Flawborough Notts ...67 K4
Flawith N York ...85 N1
Flax Bourton N Som ...28 G8
Flaxley Gloucs ...41 K8
Flaxmere Ches W ...75 P9
Flaxpool Somset ...21 J6
Flaxton N York ...86 B2
Fleckney Leics ...54 G2
Flecknoe Warwks ...54 D8
Fledborough Notts ...79 K9
Fleet Hants ...13 M4
Fleet Hants ...25 P2
Fleet Lincs ...68 H7
Fleet Hargate Lincs ...68 H7
Fleetend Hants ...12 H3
Fleet Services Hants ...25 P2
Fleetwood Lancs ...82 H5
Fleggburgh Norfk ...71 N8
Flemingston V Glam ...27 N7
Flemington S Lans ...114 B9
Flempton Suffk ...57 Q7
Fletchersbridge Cnwll ...6 G11
Fletcher's Green Kent ...33 P12
Fletchertown Cumb ...97 P9
Fletching E Susx ...15 M6
Fleur-de-lis Caerph ...27 P3
Flexbury Cnwll ...7 J4
Flexford Surrey ...32 D12
Flimby Cumb ...97 L11
Flimwell E Susx ...16 C4
Flint Flints ...74 H9
Flintham Notts ...67 K3
Flint Mountain Flints ...74 H9
Flinton E R Yk ...87 N8
Flint's Green Solhll ...53 P5
Flishinghurst Kent ...16 D3
Flitcham Norfk ...69 P7
Flitch Green Essex ...46 B7
Flitton C Beds ...44 F4
Flitwick C Beds ...44 F4
Flixborough N Linc ...86 G12
Flixborough Stather N Linc ...86 F12
Flixton N York ...93 L11
Flixton Suffk ...59 L3
Flixton Traffd ...76 D5
Flockton Kirk ...85 K12
Flockton Green Kirk ...85 K12
Flodden Nthumb ...108 F3
Flodigarry Highld ...142 E10
Flookburgh Cumb ...89 J11
Flordon Norfk ...59 J1
Flore Nhants ...54 E8
Flotterton Nthumb ...108 G9
Flowers Green E Susx ...16 B8
Flowton Suffk ...47 K2
Flushdyke Wakefd ...85 L11
Flushing Cnwll ...3 K8
Fluxton Devon ...9 K6
Flyford Flavell Worcs ...52 H10
Fobbing Thurr ...34 C5
Fochabers Moray ...140 B5
Fochriw Caerph ...27 Q3
Fockerby N Linc ...86 F11
Foddington Somset ...22 D7
Foel Powys ...62 D10
Foelgastell Carmth ...38 D9
Foel y Dyffryn Brdgnd ...26 H2
Foggathorpe E R Yk ...86 D7
Fogo Border ...116 H11
Fogwatt Moray ...139 N4
Foindle Highld ...148 E7
Folda Angus ...131 M11
Fole Staffs ...65 K5
Foleshill Covtry ...54 B4
Folke Dorset ...22 E9
Folkestone Kent ...17 M4

Folkingham Lincs ...67 Q5
Folkington E Susx ...15 Q10
Folksworth Cambs ...56 C3
Folkton N York ...93 L10
Folla Rule Abers ...140 H10
Follifoot N York ...85 M5
Folly Gate Devon ...7 Q4
Folly Hill Surrey ...25 P4
Fonmon V Glam ...27 P9
Fonthill Bishop Wilts ...23 L7
Fonthill Gifford Wilts ...23 J10
Fontmell Magna Dorset ...23 J10
Fontmell Parva Dorset ...23 J9
Fontwell W Susx ...14 D9
Foolow Derbys ...77 M8
Foots Cray Gt Lon ...33 N8
Forbestown Abers ...131 Q2
Forcett N York ...91 K4
Ford Ag & B ...120 G2
Ford Bucks ...43 Q10
Ford Devon ...5 K6
Ford Devon ...18 H8
Ford Devon ...5 K6
Ford Nthumb ...108 F2
Ford Shrops ...63 M9
Ford Somset ...20 H7
Ford Somset ...22 C8
Ford Staffs ...77 K12
Ford W Susx ...14 D10
Ford Wilts ...29 P7
Ford Wilts ...30 E10
Forda Devon ...7 P6
Fordcombe Kent ...15 Q2
Fordell Fife ...115 L4
Forden Powys ...62 H12
Ford End Essex ...46 B8
Forder Green Devon ...5 N3
Ford Green Lancs ...83 L6
Fordham Cambs ...57 M6
Fordham Essex ...46 H6
Fordham Norfk ...69 M12
Fordham Heath Essex ...46 H6
Ford Heath Shrops ...63 L10
Fordingbridge Hants ...23 P10
Fordon E R Yk ...93 L11
Fordoun Abers ...133 J9
Ford's Green Suffk ...58 F7
Fordstreet Essex ...46 H6
Ford Street Somset ...21 J10
Fordton Devon ...8 F5
Fordwells Oxon ...42 H9
Fordwich Kent ...35 L10
Fordyce Abers ...140 E3
Forebridge Staffs ...64 H7
Foremark Derbys ...66 B7
Forest Guern ...12 c3
Forest N York ...91 M6
Forest Becks Lancs ...84 B5
Forestburn Gate Nthumb ...108 H10
Forest Chapel Ches E ...76 H9
Forest Coal Pit Mons ...40 C7
Forest Gate Gt Lon ...33 M5
Forest Green Surrey ...14 G3
Forest Hall Cumb ...89 N6
Forest Hall N Tyne ...100 H5
Forest Head Cumb ...98 H6
Forest Hill Gt Lon ...33 L8
Forest Hill Oxon ...43 M10
Forest-in-Teesdale Dur ...99 N12
Forest Lane Head N York ...85 L4
Forest Mill Clacks ...114 H4
Forest of Bowland Lancs ...83 P4
Forest of Dean Gloucs ...41 K9
Forest Row E Susx ...15 M4
Forest Side IoW ...12 H7
Forestside W Susx ...25 N11
Forest Town Notts ...78 F11
Forfar Angus ...125 J3
Forgandenny P & K ...124 B9
Forge Powys ...61 Q12
Forge Hammer Torfn ...28 C3
Forge Side Torfn ...40 C10
Forgie Moray ...140 B5
Forgieside Moray ...140 B5
Forgue Abers ...140 F7
Forhill Worcs ...53 K5
Formby Sefton ...75 J2
Forncett End Norfk ...58 H1
Forncett St Mary Norfk ...58 H2
Forncett St Peter Norfk ...58 H2
Fornham All Saints Suffk ...58 B7
Fornham St Martin Suffk ...58 B7
Fornham St Genevieve Suffk ...58 C7
Fornighty Highld ...138 H6
Forres Moray ...139 J4
Forsbrook Staffs ...64 H4
Forse Highld ...151 N7
Forshaw Heath Warwks ...53 K6
Forsinard Highld ...150 H7
Forss Highld ...151 J3
Forston Dorset ...10 H5
Fort Augustus Highld ...129 L2
Forteviot P & K ...123 Q9
Forth S Lans ...114 G10
Forthampton Gloucs ...41 Q5
Fort Hommet Guern ...12 b2
Forth Rail Bridge C Edin ...115 L5
Forth Road Bridge Fife ...115 L5
Fortingall P & K ...123 J3
Forton Hants ...24 H3
Forton Lancs ...83 L5
Forton Shrops ...63 L9
Forton Somset ...10 B4
Forton Staffs ...64 D8
Fort Richmond Guern ...12 b2
Fortrie Abers ...140 G7
Fortrose Highld ...138 D4
Fortuneswell Dorset ...10 G10
Fort William Highld ...128 G9
Forty Green Bucks ...32 C4
Forty Hill Gt Lon ...33 L3
Forward Green Suffk ...58 G8
Fosbury Wilts ...30 G10
Foscot Oxon ...42 F7
Foscote Nhants ...43 N3
Fosdyke Lincs ...68 F5
Fosdyke Bridge Lincs ...68 F5
Foss P & K ...123 J2
Fossebridge Gloucs ...42 C9
Foss-y-ffin Cerdgn ...48 G8
Fosterhouses Donc ...86 C12
Foster Street Essex ...45 N9
Foston Derbys ...65 M5
Foston Leics ...54 G2
Foston Lincs ...67 M3
Foston N York ...86 B2
Foston on the Wolds E R Yk ...87 L4
Fotherby Lincs ...80 F5
Fothergill Cumb ...97 L11
Fotheringhay Nhants ...55 Q2
Foula Shet ...147 h8
Foula Airport Shet ...147 h8
Foul Anchor Cambs ...69 J8
Foulbridge Cumb ...98 E9
Foulby Wakefd ...85 N11
Foulden Border ...117 K10
Foulden Norfk ...69 P12
Foul Mile E Susx ...16 B8
Foulness Island Essex ...34 H4
Foulridge Lancs ...84 B6
Foulsham Norfk ...70 F6
Fountainhall Border ...116 C11

Four Ashes Solhll ...53 M6
Four Ashes Staffs ...52 E3
Four Ashes Staffs ...64 G10
Four Ashes Suffk ...58 E6
Four Cabots Guern ...12 c2
Four Crosses Powys ...63 J8
Four Crosses Staffs ...64 H10
Four Elms Kent ...15 N1
Four Foot Somset ...22 D7
Four Forks Somset ...21 K6
Four Gates Bolton ...76 B2
Four Gotes Cambs ...69 J9
Four Lane End Barns ...77 P4
Four Lane Ends Ches W ...75 P1
Four Lanes Cnwll ...2 H7
Fourlanes End Ches E ...76 E12
Four Marks Hants ...25 L6
Four Mile Bridge IoA ...72 D8
Four Oaks Birm ...53 L1
Four Oaks Gloucs ...41 L6
Four Oaks Solhll ...53 N4
Fourpenny Highld ...146 E6
Four Points W Berk ...31 M6
Four Roads Carmth ...38 C10
Four Shire Stone Warwks ...34 A12
Fourstones Nthumb ...99 N5
Four Throws Kent ...16 D5
Four Wents Kent ...23 M7
Foveran Abers ...141 N11
Fowey Cnwll ...3 R4
Fowley Common Warrtn ...76 C4
Fowlhall Kent ...16 C2
Fowlis Angus ...124 G6
Fowlis Wester P & K ...123 N8
Fowlmere Cambs ...45 M2
Fownhope Herefs ...41 J5
Foxbar Rens ...113 N9
Foxcombe Devon ...7 P7
Fox Corner Surrey ...32 D11
Foxcote Gloucs ...42 B8
Foxcote Somset ...22 G2
Foxdale IoM ...102 c5
Foxearth Essex ...46 E3
Foxendown Kent ...34 B9
Foxfield Cumb ...88 G9
Foxham Wilts ...29 R6
Fox Hatch Essex ...33 Q3
Foxhills Hants ...24 C2
Foxhole Cnwll ...3 N3
Foxholes N York ...93 K12
Foxley Norfk ...70 F8
Foxley Wilts ...29 Q6
Foxlydiate Worcs ...53 J7
Fox Street Essex ...47 J6
Foxt Staffs ...65 J3
Foxton Cambs ...56 H11
Foxton Dur ...91 N1
Foxton Leics ...54 H3
Foxton N York ...91 P7
Foxup N York ...90 E11
Foxwist Green Ches W ...76 B10
Foxwood Shrops ...52 B5
Foy Herefs ...41 J6
Foyers Highld ...137 N11
Foynesfield Highld ...138 G5
Fraddam Cnwll ...2 F7
Fraddon Cnwll ...3 M3
Fradley Staffs ...65 M9
Fradswell Staffs ...64 H6
Fraisthorpe E R Yk ...87 N2
Framfield E Susx ...15 P7
Framingham Earl Norfk ...71 K11
Framingham Pigot Norfk ...71 K11
Framlingham Suffk ...59 K8
Frampton Dorset ...10 H5
Frampton Lincs ...68 F4
Frampton Cotterell S Glos ...29 J6
Frampton Mansell Gloucs ...41 Q11
Frampton-on-Severn Gloucs ...41 M10
Frampton West End Lincs ...68 F4
Framsden Suffk ...59 J8
Framwellgate Moor Dur ...100 H9
Franche Worcs ...52 F6
Frandley Ches W ...76 B8
Frankaborough Devon ...7 N4
Frankby Wirral ...75 J6
Frankfort Norfk ...71 L7
Franklands Gate Herefs ...40 H2
Frankley Worcs ...52 H4
Frankley Services Worcs ...53 J4
Franksbridge Powys ...50 E9
Frankton Warwks ...54 C6
Frant E Susx ...15 Q4
Fraserburgh Abers ...141 N2
Frating Essex ...47 K7
Frating Green Essex ...47 K6
Fratton C Port ...13 L5
Freathy Cnwll ...4 F6
Freckenham Suffk ...57 M6
Freckleton Lancs ...83 J9
Freebirch Derbys ...77 P9
Freeby Leics ...67 K8
Freefolk Hants ...24 H4
Freehay Staffs ...65 J4
Freeland Oxon ...43 J9
Freethorpe Norfk ...71 N11
Freethorpe Common Norfk ...71 N11
Freiston Lincs ...68 G3
Fremington Devon ...19 K7
Fremington N York ...90 H7
Frenchay S Glos ...29 J7
Frenchbeer Devon ...8 C7
French Street Kent ...33 N11
Frenich P & K ...123 J5
Frensham Surrey ...25 P5
Freshfield Sefton ...75 J2
Freshford Wilts ...29 M10
Freshwater IoW ...12 E7
Freshwater Bay IoW ...12 E7
Freshwater East Pembks ...37 K11
Fressingfield Suffk ...59 K5
Freston Suffk ...47 L5
Freswick Highld ...151 Q3
Fretherne Gloucs ...41 M10
Frettenham Norfk ...71 K8
Freuchie Fife ...124 E11
Freystrop Pembks ...37 J8
Friar Park Sandw ...53 J3
Friars' Gate E Susx ...15 P4
Friar's Hill N York ...92 F8
Friar Waddon Dorset ...10 G7
Friday Bridge Cambs ...68 H11
Friday Street Suffk ...59 L9
Friday Street Suffk ...59 M8
Friday Street Surrey ...14 G2
Fridaythorpe E R Yk ...86 G3
Friden Derbys ...77 M11
Friendly Calder ...84 E10
Friern Barnet Gt Lon ...33 K4
Friesland Ag & B ...118 F3
Friesthorpe Lincs ...79 P7
Frieston Lincs ...67 M3
Frieth Bucks ...31 N4
Frilford Oxon ...31 J3
Frilsham W Berk ...31 L6
Frimley Surrey ...32 C11
Frimley Green Surrey ...32 C11
Frindsbury Medway ...34 C8
Fring Norfk ...69 P5

Fringford Oxon ...43 M6
Frinsted Kent ...34 F11
Frinton-on-Sea Essex ...47 M7
Friockheim Angus ...125 L3
Friog Gwynd ...61 K9
Frisby on the Wreake Leics ...66 H8
Friskney Lincs ...69 J1
Friskney Eaudike Lincs ...69 J1
Friston E Susx ...15 N8
Friston Suffk ...59 N8
Fritchley Derbys ...66 B2
Fritham Hants ...24 C10
Frith Bank Lincs ...68 F3
Frith Common Worcs ...52 C7
Frithelstock Devon ...19 J9
Frithelstock Stone Devon ...19 J9
Frithend Hants ...25 P5
Frithsden Herts ...44 E9
Frithville Lincs ...68 F2
Frittenden Kent ...16 E3
Frittiscombe Devon ...5 N8
Fritton Norfk ...59 J2
Fritton Norfk ...71 P12
Fritwell Oxon ...43 L6
Frizinghall C Brad ...84 H8
Frizington Cumb ...88 D3
Frocester Gloucs ...41 M11
Frodesley Shrops ...63 M12
Frodsham Ches W ...75 N8
Frogden Border ...108 B4
Frog End Cambs ...45 M2
Frog End Cambs ...57 K9
Froggatt Derbys ...77 N8
Froghall Staffs ...65 J3
Frogham Hants ...23 Q10
Frogham Kent ...35 N11
Frogmore Devon ...5 N8
Frognall Lincs ...68 C10
Frogpool Cnwll ...3 J6
Frog Pool Worcs ...52 E7
Frogwell Cnwll ...4 E3
Frolesworth Leics ...54 E2
Frome Somset ...22 H4
Frome St Quintin Dorset ...10 H4
Fromes Hill Herefs ...41 K2
Fron Gwynd ...60 F4
Fron Gwynd ...60 H1
Fron Powys ...50 G1
Fron Powys ...62 H11
Froncysyllte Wrexhm ...63 J4
Fron-goch Gwynd ...62 B4
Fron Isaf Wrexhm ...63 J4
Frostenden Suffk ...59 P4
Frosterley Dur ...100 C11
Froxfield C Beds ...44 D4
Froxfield Wilts ...30 G8
Froxfield Green Hants ...25 M8
Fryern Hill Hants ...24 B4
Fryerning Essex ...34 B2
Fryton N York ...92 F12
Fulbeck Lincs ...67 M1
Fulbourn Cambs ...57 K9
Fulbrook Oxon ...42 F9
Fulflood Hants ...24 H7
Fulford C York ...86 B5
Fulford Somset ...21 K7
Fulford Staffs ...64 H5
Fulham Gt Lon ...33 J7
Fulking W Susx ...15 J8
Fullaford Devon ...19 N6
Fullarton N Ayrs ...104 F2
Fuller's End Essex ...45 P6
Fuller's Moor Ches W ...63 N1
Fuller Street Essex ...46 D8
Fuller Street Kent ...33 Q11
Fullerton Hants ...24 F5
Fulletby Lincs ...80 F9
Fullready Warwks ...42 G2
Full Sutton E R Yk ...86 D4
Fullwood E Ayrs ...113 N11
Fulmer Bucks ...32 E5
Fulmodeston Norfk ...70 E6
Fulnetby Lincs ...80 B8
Fulney Lincs ...68 E7
Fulstone Kirk ...77 M2
Fulstow Lincs ...80 F4
Fulwell Oxon ...42 H7
Fulwood Lancs ...83 M8
Fulwood Notts ...78 D11
Fulwood Sheff ...77 P6
Fulwood Somset ...21 K9
Fundenhall Norfk ...58 H1
Funtington W Susx ...13 N3
Funtley Hants ...13 J3
Funtullich P & K ...123 J7
Furley Devon ...9 P4
Furnace Ag & B ...112 F1
Furnace Carmth ...26 D2
Furnace Cerdgn ...49 L2
Furnace End Warwks ...53 N3
Furner's Green E Susx ...15 M5
Furness Vale Derbys ...77 J7
Furneux Pelham Herts ...45 M6
Further Quarter Kent ...16 F2
Furtho Nhants ...43 P3
Furzehill Devon ...19 P4
Furzehill Dorset ...11 N4
Furzehills Lincs ...80 E9
Furzeley Corner Hants ...13 L3
Furze Platt W & M ...32 C6
Furzley Hants ...24 D10
Fyfett Somset ...21 K10
Fyfield Essex ...45 P9
Fyfield Hants ...24 E4
Fyfield Oxon ...31 J3
Fyfield Wilts ...30 C8
Fyfield Wilts ...30 D10
Fyfield Bavant Wilts ...23 M8
Fylingthorpe N York ...93 J6
Fyning W Susx ...25 P8
Fyvie Abers ...141 J8

G

Gabroc Hill E Ayrs ...113 N11
Gaddesby Leics ...66 H9
Gaddesden Row Herts ...44 F9
Gadfa IoA ...72 G6
Gadgirth S Ayrs ...104 G5
Gadlas Shrops ...63 L5
Gaer Powys ...40 A7
Gaerllwyd Mons ...28 E3
Gaerwen IoA ...72 H9
Gagingwell Oxon ...43 J6
Gailes N Ayrs ...104 F2
Gailey Staffs ...64 G10
Gainford Dur ...91 J4
Gainsborough Lincs ...79 K6
Gainsborough Suffk ...47 L3
Gainsford End Essex ...46 C4
Gairloch Highld ...143 G10
Gairlochy Highld ...128 G7
Gairneybridge P & K ...115 M3
Gaisgill Cumb ...89 Q6
Gaitsgill Cumb ...98 D9
Galashiels Border ...107 M3
Galgate Lancs ...83 L4
Galhampton Somset ...22 D7
Gallanachbeg Ag & B ...120 F3
Gallanachmore Ag & B ...120 F3
Gallantry Bank Ches E ...63 N2
Gallatown Fife ...115 P2

Galley Common – Greensted

173

Galley Common Warwks 53 P2
Galleywood Essex 46 C11
Gallovie Highld 129 P6
Galloway Forest Park 95 N1
Gallowfauld Angus 125 J4
Gallowhill P & K 124 D5
Gallows Green Essex 46 G6
Gallows Green Worcs 52 H8
Gallowstree Common
Oxon 31 P6
Galltair Highld 135 P11
Gallt-y-foel Gwynd 73 K11
Gallypot Street E Susx 15 N4
Galmisdale Highld 127 J7
Galmpton Devon 5 L8
Galmpton Torbay 5 Q5
Galphay N York 91 L12
Galston E Ayrs 105 J2
Gamballs Green Staffs 77 J10
Gamblesby Cumb 99 J10
Gambles Green Essex 46 D8
Gamelsby Cumb 97 Q8
Gamesley Derbys 77 J5
Gamlingay Cambs 56 E10
Gamlingay Cinques
Cambs 56 E10
Gamlingay Great Heath
Cambs 56 D10
Gammersgill N York 90 H10
Gamrie Abers 141 J3
Gamston Notts 66 F5
Gamston Notts 78 H8
Ganarew Herefs 40 H8
Ganavan Bay Ag & B 120 F6
Gang Cnwll 4 D3
Ganllwyd Gwynd 61 M7
Gannachy Angus 132 F10
Ganstead E R Yk 87 L8
Ganthorpe N York 86 C1
Ganton N York 93 K11
Ganwick Corner Herts 33 J2
Gappah Devon 8 G9
Garbity Moray 139 P5
Garboldisham Norfk 58 E4
Garbole Highld 138 D11
Garchory Abers 131 P2
Garden City Flints 75 K10
Gardeners Green Wokham 32 B9
Gardenstown Abers 141 J3
Garden Village Sheff 77 N4
Garderhouse Shet 147 i7
Gardham E R Yk 86 H7
Gare Hill Somset 22 H5
Garelochhead Ag & B 113 J3
Garford Oxon 31 J3
Garforth Leeds 85 N8
Gargrave N York 84 D4
Gargunnock Stirlg 114 C2
Garlic Street Norfk 59 J4
Garlieston D & G 95 N9
Garlinge Kent 35 P8
Garlinge Green Kent 35 K11
Garlogie Abers 133 J3
Garmond Abers 141 K5
Garmouth Moray 139 Q3
Garmston Shrops 63 Q11
Garnant Carmth 38 G9
Garndolbenmaen Gwynd 60 H3
Garnett Bridge Cumb 89 N7
Garnfadryn Gwynd 60 D5
Garnlydan Blae G 39 R9
Garnswllt Swans 38 F9
Garn-yr-erw Torfn 40 B9
Garrabost W Isls 152 h3
Garrallan E Ayrs 105 K6
Garras Cnwll 2 H9
Garreg Gwynd 61 K4
Garrigill Cumb 99 L10
Garriston N York 91 K8
Garroch D & G 96 C2
Garrochtrie D & G 94 G10
Garrochty Ag & B 112 G10
Garros Highld 135 J3
Garsdale Cumb 90 B9
Garsdale Head Cumb 90 C8
Garsdon Wilts 29 Q5
Garshall Green Staffs 64 H5
Garsington Oxon 43 M11
Garstang Lancs 83 L6
Garston Herts 32 G2
Garston Lpool 75 L7
Garswood St Hel 75 P4
Gartachossan Ag & B 110 H9
Gartcosh N Lans 114 C7
Garth Brdgnd 27 K4
Garth Mons 28 D4
Garth Powys 50 C10
Garth Powys 51 J6
Garth Wrexhm 63 J4
Garthamlock C Glas 114 B8
Garthbrengy Powys 39 P5
Gartheli Cerdgn 49 K9
Garthmyl Powys 62 G12
Garthorpe Leics 67 L8
Garthorpe N Linc 86 F11
Garth Row Cumb 89 N7
Garths Cumb 89 N9
Gartly Abers 140 E9
Gartmore Stirlg 113 Q2
Gartness N Lans 114 E8
Gartness Stirlg 113 P4
Gartocharn W Duns 113 N4
Garton E R Yk 87 P8
Garton-on-the-Wolds
E R Yk 86 H3
Gartymore Highld 147 J2
Garva Bridge Highld 129 P5
Garvald Border 115 K11
Garvald E Loth 116 D7
Garvan Highld 128 D9
Garvard Ag & B 111 J3
Garve Highld 137 L3
Garvellachs Ag & B 120 C10
Garvestone Norfk 70 F10
Garvock Inver 113 K7
Garway Herefs 40 F7
Garway Common Herefs 40 G7
Garway Hill Herefs 40 F6
Garynahine W Isls 152 f3
Garyvard W Isls 152 g4
Gasper Wilts 22 G7
Gastard Wilts 29 P8
Gasthorpe Norfk 58 E4
Gaston Green Essex 45 P8
Gatcombe IoW 12 H8
Gatebeck Cumb 89 N9
Gate Burton Lincs 79 L7
Gateford Notts 78 F7
Gateforth N York 85 R9
Gatehead E Ayrs 104 G2
Gate Helmsley N York 86 C4
Gatehouse Nthumb 108 C12
Gatehouse of Fleet D & G 96 C7
Gateley Norfk 70 E7
Gatenby N York 91 N9
Gatesgarth Cumb 88 G4
Gateshaw Border 108 C5
Gateshead Gatesd 100 G6
Gates Heath Ches W 75 M11
Gateside Angus 125 J4
Gateside E Rens 113 P9
Gateside Fife 124 D11
Gateside N Ayrs 113 M10
Gateslack D & G 106 A9
Gathurst Wigan 75 P2
Gatley Stockp 76 F6
Gatton Surrey 33 K11
Gattonside Border 107 N3
Gatwick Airport W Susx 15 K3
Gaufron Powys 50 D7
Gaulby Leics 66 H12
Gauldry Fife 124 H8
Gauldswell P & K 124 E3
Gaulkthorn Lancs 83 R10
Gaultree Norfk 69 J10
Gaunton's Bank Ches E 63 P3
Gaunt's Common Dorset 11 N4
Gaunt's End Essex 45 Q6
Gautby Lincs 80 D9
Gavinton Border 116 H11
Gawber Barns 77 Q2
Gawcott Bucks 43 P5
Gawsworth Ches E 76 G9
Gawthorpe Wakefd 85 K11
Gawthrop Cumb 90 A9
Gawthwaite Cumb 88 H9
Gay Bowers Essex 46 D10
Gaydon Warwks 54 B10
Gayhurst M Keyn 44 B2
Gayle N York 90 D9
Gayles N York 91 J5
Gay Street W Susx 14 F7
Gayton Nhants 54 H9
Gayton Norfk 69 N8
Gayton Staffs 64 H6
Gayton Wirral 75 J7
Gayton le Marsh Lincs 80 H7
Gayton Thorpe Norfk 69 P8
Gaywood Norfk 69 M8
Gazeley Suffk 57 N8
Gear Cnwll 2 H9
Gearraidh Bhaird W Isls 152 g4
Gearraidh na h-Aibhne
W Isls 152 f3
Geary Highld 134 E3
Gedding Suffk 58 D9
Geddington Nhants 55 M4
Gedling Notts 66 G4
Gedney Lincs 68 H7
Gedney Broadgate Lincs 68 H7
Gedney Drove End Lincs 69 J6
Gedney Dyke Lincs 68 H7
Gedney Hill Lincs 68 G10
Gee Cross Tamesd 76 H5
Geeston Rutlnd 67 N11
Geirinis W Isls 152 c10
Geldeston Norfk 59 M2
Gelli Rhondd 27 M3
Gelli Torfn 28 C4
Gellideg Myr Td 39 N10
Gellifor Denbgs 74 F11
Gelligaer Caerph 27 Q3
Gelligroes Caerph 28 A3
Gelligron Neath 38 H10
Gellilydan Gwynd 61 L4
Gellinudd Neath 38 H11
Gelly Pembks 37 L6
Gellyburn P & K 124 C5
Gellywen Carmth 37 P6
Gelston D & G 96 F6
Gelston Lincs 67 M3
Gembling E R Yk 87 L4
Gentleshaw Staffs 65 K10
Georgefield D & G 107 J11
George Green Bucks 32 E6
Georgeham Devon 19 J5
Georgemas Junction
Station Highld 151 L5
George Nympton Devon 19 N8
Georgetown Blae G 39 Q10
Georgia Cnwll 2 D7
Georth Ork 147 c3
Gerinish W Isls 152 c10
Gerlan Gwynd 73 L10
Germansweek Devon 7 N6
Germoe Cnwll 2 F8
Gerrans Cnwll 3 L7
Gerrards Cross Bucks 32 E5
Gerrick R & Cl 92 E4
Gestingthorpe Essex 46 E4
Gethsemane Pembks 37 L2
Geuffordd Powys 62 H9
Gib Hill Ches W 76 B8
Gibraltar Lincs 81 K12
Gibsmere Notts 67 J2
Giddeahall Wilts 29 P7
Giddy Green Dorset 11 K7
Gidea Park Gt Lon 33 P4
Gidleigh Devon 8 C7
Giffnock E Rens 113 Q9
Gifford E Loth 116 C7
Giffordtown Fife 124 F10
Giggleswick N York 84 B2
Gigha Ag & B 111 N11
Gilberdyke E R Yk 86 F9
Gilbert's End Worcs 41 N3
Gilbert Street Hants 25 L7
Gilchriston E Loth 116 C8
Gilcrux Cumb 97 M10
Gildersome Leeds 85 K9
Gildingwells Rothm 78 F6
Gilesgate Moor Dur 100 H9
Gileston V Glam 27 N9
Gilfach Caerph 27 R3
Gilfach Goch Brdgnd 27 M4
Gilfachrheda Cerdgn 48 G9
Gilgarran Cumb 88 D2
Gill Cumb 98 F12
Gillamoor N York 92 D8
Gillan Cnwll 3 J9
Gillen Highld 134 E4
Gillesbie D & G 106 F11
Gilling East N York 92 C11
Gillingham Dorset 22 H8
Gillingham Medway 34 D8
Gillingham Norfk 59 N2
Gilling West N York 91 K6
Gillock Highld 151 M5
Gillow Heath Staffs 76 G12
Gills Highld 151 P2
Gill's Green Kent 16 D4
Gilmanscleuch Border 107 J5
Gilmerton C Edin 115 P7
Gilmerton P & K 123 M8
Gilmonby Dur 90 G4
Gilmorton Leics 54 F3
Gilsland Nthumb 99 J5
Gilson Warwks 53 M3
Gilstead C Brad 84 H7
Gilston Border 116 B10
Gilston Herts 45 N9
Gilston Park Herts 45 N9
Giltbrook Notts 66 D3
Gilwern Mons 40 C9
Gimingham Norfk 71 K5
Ginclough Ches E 76 H8
Gingers Green E Susx 16 A8
Gipping Suffk 58 G8
Gipsey Bridge Lincs 68 F2
Girdle Toll N Ayrs 104 F2
Girlington C Brad 84 H8
Girlsta Shet 147 i7
Girsby N York 91 N5
Girtford C Beds 56 C10
Girthon D & G 96 C7
Girton Cambs 56 H8
Girton Notts 79 K10
Girvan S Ayrs 104 C10
Gisburn Lancs 84 B5
Gisleham Suffk 59 P3
Gislingham Suffk 58 G6
Gissing Norfk 58 H3
Gittisham Devon 9 L5
Givons Grove Surrey 32 H11
Gladestry Powys 50 H9
Gladsmuir E Loth 116 B6
Glais Swans 26 G2
Glaisdale N York 92 F5
Glamis Angus 124 H3
Glanaber Gwynd 61 L2
Glanaman Carmth 38 G9
Glandford Norfk 70 F4
Glan-Duar Carmth 38 D3
Glandwr Pembks 37 N5
Glan-Dwyfach Gwynd 60 H3
Glandy Cross Carmth 37 M5
Glandyfi Cerdgn 49 M1
Glangrwyney Powys 40 C8
Glanllynfi Brdgnd 27 K4
Glanmule Powys 50 G3
Glanrhyd Pembks 37 M2
Glan-rhyd Powys 39 J10
Glanton Nthumb 108 H7
Glanton Pike Nthumb 108 H7
Glanvilles Wootton
Dorset 10 G3
Glan-y-don Flints 74 G8
Glan-y-llyn Rhondd 27 Q5
Glan-y-nant Powys 50 C4
Glan-yr-afon Gwynd 62 B4
Glan-yr-afon Gwynd 62 D4
Glan-yr-afon IoA 73 K7
Glan-yr-afon Swans 38 F10
Glan-y-wern Gwynd 61 K5
Glapthorn Nhants 55 P3
Glapwell Derbys 78 D10
Glasbury Powys 40 A4
Glascoed Denbgs 74 D9
Glascoed Mons 40 D11
Glascote Staffs 65 N11
Glascwm Powys 50 G10
Glasfryn Conwy 62 C2
Glasgow C Glas 113 R8
Glasgow Airport Rens 113 P8
Glasgow Prestwick
Airport S Ayrs 104 G4
Glasgow Science Centre
C Glas 113 Q8
Glasinfryn Gwynd 73 K10
Glasnacardoch Bay
Highld 127 M5
Glasnakille Highld 127 K2
Glasphein Highld 134 C6
Glaspwll Powys 49 M1
Glassenbury Kent 16 D3
Glassford S Lans 114 D12
Glass Houghton Wakefd 85 N10
Glasshouse Gloucs 41 L7
Glasshouse Hill Gloucs 41 L7
Glasshouses N York 85 J2
Glasslaw Abers 141 K4
Glasson Cumb 97 Q6
Glasson Lancs 83 K4
Glassonby Cumb 98 H10
Glasterlaw Angus 125 L3
Glaston Rutlnd 67 M12
Glastonbury Somset 22 C5
Glatton Cambs 56 C3
Glazebrook Warrtn 76 C5
Glazebury Warrtn 76 C4
Glazeley Shrops 52 D3
Gleadless Sheff 78 B7
Gleadsmoss Ches E 76 F10
Gleaston Cumb 82 G1
Glebe Highld 137 N12
Gledhow Leeds 85 L8
Gledpark D & G 96 C8
Gledrid Shrops 63 J5
Glemsford Suffk 58 B11
Glen Achulish Highld 121 K1
Glenallachie Moray 139 N7
Glenancross Highld 127 M6
Glenaros House Ag & B 119 P4
Glen Auldyn IoM 102 f3
Glenbarr Ag & B 103 J2
Glenbarry Abers 140 E5
Glenbeg Highld 127 K11
Glenbervie Abers 133 J8
Glenboig N Lans 114 C7
Glenborrodale Highld 127 L12
Glenbranter Ag & B 112 G2
Glenbreck Border 106 D5
Glenbrittle Highld 134 G11
Glenbuck E Ayrs 105 N4
Glencally Angus 131 Q11
Glencaple D & G 97 K4
Glencarse P & K 124 D8
Glencoe Highld 121 L1
Glencothe Border 106 E4
Glencraig Fife 115 M2
Glencrosh D & G 105 P12
Glendale Highld 134 C6
Glendaruel Ag & B 112 E4
Glendevon P & K 123 P12
Glendoe Lodge Highld 129 L2
Glendoick P & K 124 E8
Glenduckie Fife 124 F9
Glenegedale Ag & B 110 H11
Glenelg Highld 135 P12
Glenerney Moray 139 J6
Glenfarg P & K 124 C10
Glenfield Leics 66 E11
Glenfinnan Highld 128 B8
Glenfintaig Lodge Highld 128 H7
Glenfoot P & K 124 D9
Glenfyne Lodge Ag & B 121 N9
Glengarnock N Ayrs 113 L10
Glengolly Highld 151 K3
Glengorm Castle Ag & B 119 M1
Glengrasco Highld 134 H7
Glenholm Border 106 E3
Glenhoul D & G 105 L12
Glenkin Ag & B 112 H5
Glenkindie Abers 132 C2
Glenlivet Moray 139 M10
Glenlochar D & G 96 E5
Glenlomond P & K 124 D12
Glenluce D & G 94 H7
Glenmassen Ag & B 112 G4
Glenmavis N Lans 114 D8
Glen Maye IoM 102 c5
Glen Mona IoM 102 f4
Glenmore Highld 134 H8
Glenmore Lodge Highld 130 H2
Glen Nevis House Highld 128 G10
Glenochil Clacks 114 F2
Glen Parva Leics 66 F12
Glenquiech Angus 132 C12
Glenralloch Ag & B 112 C7
Glenridding Cumb 89 K3
Glenrothes Fife 115 N1
Glenshero Lodge Highld 129 P6
Glenstriven Ag & B 112 G5
Glentham Lincs 79 P6
Glentrool D & G 95 L3
Glen Trool Lodge D & G 95 M2
Glentruim Highld 130 C5
Glentworth Lincs 79 N6
Glenuig Highld 127 M9
Glenvarragill Highld 134 H8
Glen Vine IoM 102 d5
Glenwhilly D & G 94 H4
Glespin S Lans 105 Q4
Glewstone Herefs 40 H7
Glinton C Pete 68 C11
Glooston Leics 55 J2
Glossop Derbys 77 J5
Gloster Hill Nthumb 109 L9
Gloucester Gloucs 41 N8
Gloucester Services
Gloucs 41 N9
Gloucestershire Airport
Gloucs 41 P7
Glusburn N York 84 F6
Glutt Lodge Highld 150 H9
Gluvian Cnwll 3 M2
Glympton Oxon 43 J7
Glynarthen Cerdgn 48 E11
Glyn Ceiriog Wrexhm 62 H4
Glyncoch Rhondd 27 P4
Glyncorrwg Neath 27 L3
Glynde E Susx 15 N9
Glyndebourne E Susx 15 N8
Glyndyfrdwy Denbgs 62 G4
Glynneath Neath 39 L10
Glynogwr Brdgnd 27 M5
Glyntaff Rhondd 27 P4
Glyntawe Powys 39 K8
Glynteg Carmth 38 A4
Gnosall Staffs 64 F8
Gnosall Heath Staffs 64 F8
Goadby Leics 67 J12
Goadby Marwood Leics 67 K7
Goatacre Wilts 30 B7
Goatham Green E Susx 16 E7
Goathill Dorset 22 F10
Goathland N York 92 G6
Goathurst Somset 21 L6
Goathurst Common Kent 33 P12
Goat Lees Kent 16 H2
Gobowen Shrops 63 J5
Godalming Surrey 14 D2
Goddard's Corner Suffk 59 K7
Goddard's Green Kent 16 E4
Goddards Green W Susx 15 K7
Godden Green Kent 33 Q11
Godford Cross Devon 9 L4
Godington Oxon 43 N6
Godley Tamesd 76 H5
Godmanchester Cambs 56 E6
Godmanstone Dorset 10 G5
Godmersham Kent 35 J12
Godney Somset 22 B5
Godolphin Cross Cnwll 2 F8
Godre'r-graig Neath 38 H10
Godshill Hants 24 B10
Godshill IoW 13 J8
Godstone Staffs 65 J5
Godstone Surrey 33 L12
Godsworthy Devon 7 P9
Godwinscroft Hants 12 C5
Goetre Mons 40 D10
Goff's Oak Herts 45 L11
Gogar C Edin 115 L7
Goginan Cerdgn 49 M4
Golan Gwynd 61 J4
Golant Cnwll 3 R4
Golberdon Cnwll 7 L10
Golborne Wigan 75 Q4
Golcar Kirk 84 G12
Goldcliff Newpt 28 E6
Golden Cross E Susx 15 P8
Golden Green Kent 16 B1
Golden Grove Carmth 38 E8
Goldenhill C Stke 64 F2
Golden Hill Pembks 37 J10
Golden Pot Hants 25 M5
Golden Valley Derbys 66 C2
Golders Green Gt Lon 33 J5
Goldfinch Bottom W Berk 31 L9
Goldhanger Essex 46 F10
Gold Hill Cambs 57 K2
Gold Hill Dorset 23 J10
Golding Shrops 63 P11
Goldington Bed 55 Q10
Goldsborough N York 85 M4
Goldsborough N York 92 G4
Golds Green Sandw 53 J2
Goldsithney Cnwll 2 E8
Goldstone Kent 35 N10
Goldstone Shrops 64 D6
Goldthorpe Barns 78 D3
Goldworthy Devon 18 H9
Golford Kent 16 D3
Golford Green Kent 16 D4
Gollanfield Highld 138 E5
Gollinglith Foot N York 91 K10
Golly Wrexhm 75 K12
Golsoncott Somset 20 G5
Golspie Highld 146 E5
Gomeldon Wilts 24 C6
Gomersal Kirk 85 J10
Gomshall Surrey 14 F1
Gonalston Notts 66 H3
Gonerby Hill Foot Lincs 67 M5
Gonfirth Shet 147 i6
Goodameavy Devon 4 H4
Good Easter Essex 46 A9
Gooderstone Norfk 69 P11
Goodleigh Devon 19 L6
Goodmanham E R Yk 86 G6
Goodmayes Gt Lon 33 N5
Goodnestone Kent 35 J10
Goodnestone Kent 35 N11
Goodrich Herefs 40 H8
Goodrington Torbay 5 Q5
Goodshaw Lancs 84 B10
Goodshaw Fold Lancs 84 B10
Goodstone Devon 8 E10
Goodwick Pembks 37 J3
Goodwood W Susx 14 C9
Goodworth Clatford
Hants 24 F5
Goodyers End Warwks 53 Q3
Goole E R Yk 86 D10
Goole Fields E R Yk 86 E11
Goom's Hill Worcs 53 J9
Goonbell Cnwll 2 H4
Goonhavern Cnwll 3 K4
Goonvrea Cnwll 2 H4
Goosecruives Abers 133 J7
Gooseford Devon 8 C6
Goose Green Essex 47 L6
Goose Green Kent 16 E3
Goose Green Kent 34 B12
Goose Green S Glos 29 K7
Goose Green W Susx 14 G7
Goose Green Wigan 75 P3
Gooseham Cnwll 18 E10
Gooseham Mill Cnwll 18 E10
Goosehill Green Worcs 52 H8
Goose Pool Herefs 40 G4
Goosey Oxon 30 H4
Goosnargh Lancs 83 M8
Goostrey Ches E 76 E9
Gordano Services N Som 28 G7
Gorddinog Conwy 73 L9
Gordon Border 107 Q1
Gordon Arms Hotel
Border 107 J5
Gordonstown Abers 140 E5
Gordonstown Abers 140 H8
Gore Powys 51 J9
Gorebridge Mdloth 115 Q9
Gorefield Cambs 68 H9
Gore Pit Essex 46 F8
Gores Wilts 30 C10
Gore Street Kent 35 N9
Gorey Jersey 13 d2
Goring Oxon 31 M6
Goring-by-Sea W Susx 14 G10
Goring Heath Oxon 31 N6
Gorleston-on-Sea Norfk 71 Q11
Gorrachie Abers 140 H4
Gorran Churchtown
Cnwll 3 N6
Gorran Haven Cnwll 3 P6
Gorran High Lanes Cnwll 3 N6
Gorrig Cerdgn 38 B3
Gors Cerdgn 49 K5
Gorsedd Flints 74 G8
Gorse Hill Swindn 30 D5
Gorseinon Swans 26 F3
Gorseybank Derbys 65 P2
Gorsgoch Cerdgn 48 H10
Gorslas Carmth 38 E9
Gorsley Gloucs 41 K6
Gorsley Common Herefs 41 K6
Gorstage Ches W 75 Q9
Gorstan Highld 137 L3
Gorstella Ches W 75 K11
Gorsten Ag & B 120 D6
Gorst Hill Worcs 52 D6
Gorsty Hill Staffs 65 L6
Gorthleck Highld 137 P11
Gorton Manch 76 G4
Gosbeck Suffk 58 H9
Gosberton Lincs 68 E6
Gosberton Clough Lincs 68 D6
Gosfield Essex 46 D6
Gosford Devon 9 L5
Gosford Oxon 43 K9
Gosforth Cumb 88 E6
Gosforth N u Ty 100 G4
Gosling Street Somset 22 C7
Gosmore Herts 44 H6
Gospel End Staffs 52 G2
Gospel Green W Susx 14 D4
Gosport Hants 13 K5
Gossard's Green C Beds 44 D3
Gossington Gloucs 41 L11
Goswick Nthumb 117 N12
Gotham Notts 66 E6
Gotherington Gloucs 41 Q6
Gotton Somset 21 L7
Goudhurst Kent 16 C3
Goulceby Lincs 80 E8
Gourdas Abers 141 J7
Gourdie C Dund 124 G6
Gourdon Abers 133 K10
Gourock Inver 113 K6
Govan C Glas 113 Q8
Goveton Devon 5 M7
Govilon Mons 40 C9
Gowdall E R Yk 86 B10
Gower Highld 137 N4
Gower Swans 26 D4
Gowerton Swans 26 E3
Gowkhall Fife 115 J3
Gowthorpe E R Yk 86 E4
Goxhill E R Yk 87 M6
Goxhill N Linc 87 L11
Goytre Neath 27 J4
Grabhair W Isls 152 g4
Graby Lincs 68 B6
Grade Cnwll 2 H11
Gradeley Green Ches E 63 Q2
Graffham W Susx 14 C7
Grafham Cambs 56 C7
Grafham Surrey 14 E2
Grafton Herefs 40 G4
Grafton N York 85 N3
Grafton Oxon 30 F2
Grafton Shrops 63 M8
Grafton Worcs 42 A4
Grafton Worcs 51 P8
Grafton Flyford Worcs 52 H9
Grafton Regis Nhants 43 Q2
Grafton Underwood
Nhants 55 M5
Grafty Green Kent 16 F1
Graianrhyd Denbgs 74 H12
Graig Conwy 73 P9
Graig Denbgs 74 F9
Graigfechan Denbgs 62 G1
Grain Medway 34 F7
Grains Bar Oldham 76 H2
Grainsby Lincs 80 E4
Grainthorpe Lincs 80 G4
Grampound Cnwll 3 M5
Grampound Road Cnwll 3 M4
Gramsdal W Isls 152 c9
Gramsdale W Isls 152 c9
Granborough Bucks 43 Q7
Granby Notts 67 J5
Grandborough Warwks 54 E7
Grand Chemins Jersey 13 c2
Grandes Rocques Guern 12 c1
Grandtully P & K 123 M2
Grange Cumb 88 H3
Grange Medway 34 D8
Grange P & K 124 F8
Grange Wirral 74 H6
Grange Crossroads
Moray 140 D5
Grange Hall Moray 139 K4
Grangehall S Lans 106 C1
Grange Hill Essex 33 N4
Grangemill Derbys 77 N12
Grange Moor Kirk 85 J12
Grangemouth Falk 114 G5
Grange of Lindores Fife 124 E9
Grange-over-Sands
Cumb 89 L11
Grangepans Falk 115 J5
Grange Park Nhants 55 J9
Grangetown R & Cl 92 B3
Grangetown Sundld 101 K7
Grange Villa Dur 100 G8
Gransmoor E R Yk 87 L3
Gransmore Green Essex 46 C7
Granston Pembks 36 H4
Grantchester Cambs 56 H9
Grantham Lincs 67 M5
Granton C Edin 115 N6
Grantown-on-Spey
Highld 139 J10
Grantsfield Herefs 51 N8
Grantshouse Border 116 H8
Grappenhall Warrtn 76 B6
Grasby Lincs 80 B3
Grasmere Cumb 89 K5
Grasscroft Oldham 76 H3
Grassendale Lpool 75 L6
Grassgarth Cumb 98 D9
Grass Green Essex 46 C4
Grassington N York 84 F2
Grassmoor Derbys 78 C10
Grassthorpe Notts 79 K10
Grateley Hants 24 D5
Gratwich Staffs 65 J6
Graveley Cambs 56 E8
Graveley Herts 45 J6
Gravelly Hill Birm 53 L3
Gravelsbank Shrops 63 K12
Graveney Kent 35 J9
Gravesend Kent 34 B7
Gravir W Isls 152 g4
Grayingham Lincs 79 M4
Grayrigg Cumb 89 P7
Grays Thurr 34 A7
Grayshott Hants 14 C4
Grayson Green Cumb 88 D2
Grayswood Surrey 14 C4
Graythorpe Hartpl 92 B1
Grazeley Wokham 31 P9
Greasbrough Rothm 78 C4
Greasby Wirral 75 J6
Greasley Notts 66 D3
Great Abington Cambs 57 K11
Great Addington Nhants 55 N5
Great Alne Warwks 53 L8
Great Altcar Lancs 75 K2
Great Amwell Herts 45 L9
Great Asby Cumb 89 R4
Great Ashfield Suffk 58 E7
Great Ayton N York 92 B4
Great Baddow Essex 46 C10
Great Badminton S Glos 29 N6
Great Bardfield Essex 46 B5
Great Barford Bed 56 C10
Great Barr Sandw 53 K2
Great Barrington Gloucs 42 E9
Great Barrow Ches W 75 M10
Great Barton Suffk 58 C7
Great Barugh N York 92 F11
Great Bavington Nthumb 100 C2
Great Bealings Suffk 59 J11
Great Bedwyn Wilts 30 F9
Great Bentley Essex 47 K7
Great Billing Nhants 55 K8
Great Bircham Norfk 69 P6
Great Blakenham Suffk 58 G10
Great Blencow Cumb 98 F11
Great Bolas Wrekin 64 B8
Great Bookham Surrey 32 G11
Great Bosullow Cnwll 2 C8
Great Bourton Oxon 43 K3
Great Bowden Leics 55 J3
Great Bradley Suffk 57 N10
Great Braxted Essex 46 F9
Great Bricett Suffk 58 F10
Great Brickhill Bucks 44 C5
Great Bridgeford Staffs 64 G7
Great Brington Nhants 54 H7
Great Bromley Essex 47 K6
Great Broughton Cumb 97 L12
Great Broughton N York 92 B5
Great Budworth Ches W 76 C8
Great Burdon Darltn 91 N3
Great Burstead Essex 34 B4
Great Busby N York 92 B5
Great Canfield Essex 45 Q8
Great Carlton Lincs 80 H6
Great Casterton Rutlnd 67 P10
Great Chalfield Wilts 29 P9
Great Chart Kent 16 H2
Great Chatwell Staffs 64 E9
Great Chell C Stke 64 F2
Great Chesterford Essex 45 P3
Great Cheverell Wilts 23 L2
Great Chishill Cambs 45 M4
Great Clacton Essex 47 L8
Great Cliffe Wakefd 85 L12
Great Clifton Cumb 97 L12
Great Coates NE Lin 80 E2
Great Comberton Worcs 41 Q3
Great Comp Kent 34 A11
Great Corby Cumb 98 F7
Great Cornard Suffk 46 F4
Great Cowden E R Yk 87 N7
Great Coxwell Oxon 30 F4
Great Cransley Nhants 55 L5
Great Cressingham Norfk 70 C11
Great Crosthwaite Cumb 88 H2
Great Cubley Derbys 65 M4
Great Cumbrae Island
N Ayrs 112 H10
Great Dalby Leics 67 J9
Great Denham Bed 55 P11
Great Doddington Nhants 55 M7
Great Doward Herefs 40 H8
Great Dunham Norfk 70 C9
Great Dunmow Essex 46 A7
Great Durnford Wilts 23 P6
Great Easton Essex 45 R6
Great Easton Leics 55 L2
Great Eccleston Lancs 83 K7
Great Edstone N York 92 E10
Great Ellingham Norfk 58 F1
Great Elm Somset 22 G3
Great Everdon Nhants 54 F9
Great Eversden Cambs 56 G10
Great Fencote N York 91 M8
Greatfield Wilts 30 C5
Great Finborough Suffk 58 F9
Greatford Lincs 68 B10
Great Fransham Norfk 70 C9
Great Gaddesden Herts 44 E9
Greatgate Staffs 65 K4
Great Gidding Cambs 56 C4
Great Givendale E R Yk 86 E4
Great Glemham Suffk 59 L8
Great Glen Leics 54 G1
Great Gonerby Lincs 67 M4
Great Gransden Cambs 56 E9
Great Green Cambs 45 K3
Great Green Norfk 59 K3
Great Green Suffk 58 D7
Great Green Suffk 58 D9
Great Habton N York 92 F11
Great Hale Lincs 68 C4
Great Hallingbury Essex 45 P8
Greatham Hants 25 N7
Greatham Hartpl 91 R1
Greatham W Susx 14 F7
Great Hampden Bucks 32 B2
Great Harrowden Nhants 55 L6
Great Harwood Lancs 83 Q8
Great Haseley Oxon 43 N11
Great Hatfield E R Yk 87 M6
Great Haywood Staffs 65 J7
Great Heck N York 86 B11
Great Henny Essex 46 F4
Great Hinton Wilts 29 P10
Great Hockham Norfk 58 D2
Great Holland Essex 47 M8
Great Hollands Br For 32 B9
Great Horkesley Essex 46 H5
Great Hormead Herts 45 M6
Great Horton C Brad 84 H9
Great Horwood Bucks 43 Q5
Great Houghton Barns 78 C2
Great Houghton Nhants 55 K9
Great Hucklow Derbys 77 M8
Great Kelk E R Yk 87 L3
Great Kimble Bucks 44 B10
Great Kingshill Bucks 32 C3
Great Langdale Cumb 89 J5
Great Langton N York 91 M7
Great Leighs Essex 46 C8
Great Limber Lincs 80 C2
Great Linford M Keyn 44 B3
Great Livermere Suffk 58 C6
Great Longstone Derbys 77 M9
Great Lumley Dur 100 H8
Great Lyth Shrops 63 M10
Great Malvern Worcs 41 M3
Great Maplestead Essex 46 E5
Great Marton Bpool 82 H8
Great Massingham Norfk 69 Q7
Great Melton Norfk 70 H10
Great Meols Wirral 74 H5
Great Milton Oxon 43 N11
Great Missenden Bucks 32 C2
Great Mitton Lancs 83 Q7
Great Mongeham Kent 35 P12
Great Moulton Norfk 58 H3
Great Munden Herts 45 L7
Great Musgrave Cumb 90 C4
Great Ness Shrops 63 L8
Great Notley Essex 46 D7
Great Oak Mons 40 E9
Great Oakley Essex 47 M6
Great Oakley Nhants 55 L3
Great Offley Herts 44 G6
Great Ormside Cumb 90 B3
Great Orton Cumb 98 D7
Great Ouseburn N York 85 P3
Great Oxendon Nhants 55 J4
Great Oxney Green Essex 46 B10
Great Palgrave Norfk 70 B9
Great Park N u Ty 100 G4
Great Parndon Essex 45 N10
Great Pattenden Kent 16 C2
Great Paxton Cambs 56 D8
Great Plumpton Lancs 83 J8
Great Plumstead Norfk 71 L10
Great Ponton Lincs 67 M6
Great Potheridge Devon 19 K10
Great Preston Leeds 85 N9
Great Purston Nhants 43 L4
Great Raveley Cambs 56 E4
Great Rissington Gloucs 42 E8
Great Rollright Oxon 42 G5
Great Ryburgh Norfk 70 E7
Great Ryle Nthumb 108 G7
Great Ryton Shrops 63 N11
Great Saling Essex 46 C6
Great Salkeld Cumb 98 G11
Great Sampford Essex 46 B4
Great Saredon Staffs 64 H10
Great Saughall Ches W 75 K9
Great Saxham Suffk 57 Q8
Great Shefford W Berk 30 H7
Great Shelford Cambs 57 J10
Great Smeaton N York 91 N6
Great Snoring Norfk 70 D5
Great Somerford Wilts 29 Q6
Great Soudley Shrops 64 D6
Great Stainton Darltn 91 N2
Great Stambridge Essex 34 F4
Great Staughton Cambs 56 C7
Great Steeping Lincs 80 H10
Great Stoke S Glos 29 J6
Great Stonar Kent 35 P10
Greatstone-on-Sea Kent 17 K6
Great Strickland Cumb 89 P2
Great Stukeley Cambs 56 E6
Great Sturton Lincs 80 D8
Great Sutton Ches W 75 L8
Great Sutton Shrops 51 N4
Great Swinburne Nthumb 99 P3
Great Tew Oxon 43 J6
Great Tey Essex 46 F6
Great Thurlow Suffk 57 N10
Great Torrington Devon 19 J9
Great Tosson Nthumb 108 G9
Great Totham Essex 46 F9
Great Totham Essex 46 F9
Great Tows Lincs 80 E5
Great Urswick Cumb 88 H11
Great Wakering Essex 34 G5
Great Waldingfield Suffk 46 F3
Great Walsingham Norfk 70 D5
Great Waltham Essex 46 C9
Great Warford Ches E 76 E8
Great Warley Essex 33 Q4
Great Washbourne
Gloucs 42 A5
Great Weeke Devon 8 D7
Great Welnetham Suffk 58 C9
Great Wenham Suffk 47 J4
Great Whittington
Nthumb 100 C4
Great Wigborough Essex 46 G8
Great Wilbraham Cambs 57 K9
Great Wilne Derbys 66 D6
Great Wishford Wilts 23 N6
Great Witchingham Norfk 70 G8
Great Witcombe Gloucs 41 Q8
Great Witley Worcs 52 D7
Great Wolford Warwks 42 F5
Greatworth Nhants 43 L3
Great Wratting Suffk 57 N11
Great Wymondley Herts 45 J6
Great Wyrley Staffs 65 J10
Great Wytheford Shrops 63 P8
Great Yarmouth Norfk 71 Q10
Great Yeldham Essex 46 D4
Grebby Lincs 80 H10
Greeba IoM 102 d5
Green Denbgs 74 E10
Green Bank Cumb 89 K10
Greenbottom Cnwll 3 J5
Greenburn W Loth 114 G9
Greencroft Hall Dur 100 F8
Green Cross Surrey 14 B3
Green Down Somset 22 D3
Green End Bed 55 P11
Green End Bed 55 Q7
Green End Bed 56 B8
Green End Bed 56 C10
Green End Cambs 56 C4
Green End Cambs 56 E6
Green End Cambs 56 G9
Green End Cambs 57 J7
Green End Cambs 57 J8
Green End Herts 45 J5
Green End Herts 45 L5
Green End Herts 45 L7
Greenend Oxon 42 G7
Green End Warwks 53 N3
Greenfield Ag & B 113 K3
Greenfield C Beds 44 F5
Greenfield Flints 74 H8
Greenfield Highld 128 H4
Greenfield Oldham 77 J3
Greenfield Oxon 31 P4
Greenford Gt Lon 32 G6
Greengairs N Lans 114 E7
Greengates C Brad 85 J8
Greengill Cumb 97 M10
Greenhalgh Lancs 83 J8
Greenham Somset 20 H9
Greenham W Berk 31 K9
Green Hammerton N York 85 P4
Greenhaugh Nthumb 108 C12
Green Head Cumb 98 D8
Greenhead Nthumb 99 J5
Green Heath Staffs 65 J9
Greenheys Salfd 76 D3
Greenhill D & G 97 M2
Greenhill Falk 114 E5
Greenhill Herefs 52 D11
Greenhill Kent 35 L9
Greenhill Leics 66 D9
Greenhill S Lans 106 B3
Green Hill Wilts 30 C5
Greenhillocks Derbys 66 C2
Greenhills S Lans 114 B10
Greenhithe Kent 33 Q7
Greenholm E Ayrs 105 K2
Greenholme Cumb 89 P5
Greenhouse Border 107 N5
Greenhow Hill N York 84 H2
Greenland Highld 151 N3
Greenland Sheff 78 C6
Greenlands Bucks 31 Q5
Green Lane Devon 8 E9
Green Lane Worcs 53 K7
Greenlaw Border 116 G12
Greenlea D & G 97 L3
Greenloaning P & K 123 L11
Green Moor Barns 77 P4
Greenmount Bury 84 B12
Green Oak E R Yk 86 E9
Greenock Inver 113 K6
Greenodd Cumb 89 J10
Green Ore Somset 22 D3
Green Park Readg 31 P8
Green Quarter Cumb 89 M6
Greensgate Norfk 70 G9
Greenshields S Lans 106 D1
Greenside Gatesd 100 E6
Greenside Kirk 85 J12
Greens Norton Nhants 54 H10
Greenstead Green Essex 46 E6
Greensted Essex 45 P11

Green Street E Susx ...16 D8
Green Street Gloucs ...35 P10
Green Street Herts ...32 H3
Green Street Herts ...45 N7
Green Street Worcs ...52 G11
Green Street Green
  Gt Lon ...33 N9
Green Street Green Kent ...33 Q8
Greenstreet Green Suffk ...58 F10
Green Tye Herts ...45 N8
Greenway Gloucs ...41 L5
Greenway Somset ...21 M8
Greenway V Glam ...27 Q7
Greenway Worcs ...52 D6
Greenwich Gt Lon ...33 M7
Greenwich Maritime
  Gt Lon ...33 M7
Greete Shrops ...51 P6
Greetham Lincs ...80 F9
Greetham Rutlnd ...67 M9
Greetland Calder ...84 G11
Gregson Lane Lancs ...83 N10
Greinton Somset ...21 N6
Grenaby IoM ...102 c6
Grendon Nhants ...55 L8
Grendon Warwks ...65 P12
Grendon Green Herefs ...51 Q9
Grendon Underwood
  Bucks ...43 P7
Grenofen Devon ...7 P10
Grenoside Sheff ...77 Q5
Greosabhagh W Isls ...152 e6
Gresford Wrexhm ...63 K1
Gresham Norfk ...70 H4
Greshornish Highld ...134 F5
Gressenhall Norfk ...70 E9
Gressenhall Green Norfk ...70 E9
Gressingham Lancs ...83 K6
Gresty Green Ches E ...64 D1
Greta Bridge Dur ...90 H4
Gretna D & G ...98 C5
Gretna Green D & G ...98 C5
Gretna Services D & G ...98 C4
Gretton Gloucs ...42 B5
Gretton Nhants ...55 M2
Gretton Shrops ...51 N2
Grewelthorpe N York ...91 L11
Grey Friars Suffk ...59 P6
Greygarth N York ...91 K12
Grey Green N Linc ...79 K2
Greylake Somset ...21 N6
Greylees Lincs ...67 P3
Greyrigg D & G ...106 I2
Greys Green Oxon ...31 P6
Greysouthen Cumb ...97 L12
Greystoke Cumb ...98 F12
Greystone Angus ...125 K4
Greywell Hants ...25 M3
Gribb Dorset ...10 B4
Gribthorpe E R Yk ...86 E8
Griff Warwks ...54 B3
Griffithstown Torfn ...28 C3
Griffydam Leics ...66 C8
Griggs Green Hants ...25 P7
Grimeford Village Lancs ...76 B1
Grimesthorpe Sheff ...78 B4
Grimethorpe Barns ...78 C2
Grimister Shet ...147 j3
Grimley Worcs ...52 F8
Grimmet S Ayrs ...104 F7
Grimoldby Lincs ...80 G6
Grimpo Shrops ...63 K7
Grimsargh Lancs ...83 N8
Grimsby NE Lin ...80 E2
Grimscote Nhants ...54 G10
Grimscott Cnwll ...7 K3
Grimshader W Isls ...152 g4
Grimshaw Bl w D ...83 Q10
Grimshaw Green Lancs ...75 N1
Grimsthorpe Lincs ...67 P7
Grimston E R Yk ...87 P8
Grimston Leics ...66 H8
Grimston Norfk ...69 Q7
Grimstone Dorset ...10 G6
Grimstone End Suffk ...58 D7
Grinacombe Moor Devon ...7 M6
Grindale E R Yk ...87 L1
Grindle Shrops ...64 D11
Grindleford Derbys ...77 N8
Grindleton Lancs ...84 A6
Grindley Brook Shrops ...63 N4
Grindlow Derbys ...77 M8
Grindon Nthumb ...117 K12
Grindon S on T ...91 P7
Grindon Staffs ...65 J2
Grindon Hill Nthumb ...99 M5
Grindonrigg Nthumb ...108 B12
Gringley on the Hill Notts ...79 J5
Grinsdale Cumb ...98 D6
Grinshill Shrops ...63 N7
Grinton N York ...90 H7
Griomsiadar W Isls ...152 g4
Grishipoll Ag & B ...118 G1
Grisling Common E Susx ...15 N6
Gristhorpe N York ...93 M10
Griston Norfk ...70 D12
Gritley Ork ...147 d5
Grittenham Wilts ...30 B6
Grittleton Wilts ...29 P6
Grizebeck Cumb ...88 H9
Grizedale Cumb ...89 K8
Groby Leics ...66 E10
Groes Conwy ...74 D10
Groes-faen Rhondd ...27 P6
Groesffordd Gwynd ...60 D4
Groesffordd Powys ...39 P6
Groesffordd Marli Denbgs ...74 D9
Groeslon Gwynd ...60 H1
Groeslon Gwynd ...73 J11
Groes-lwyd Powys ...62 H10
Groes-Wen Caerph ...27 Q5
Grogarry W Isls ...152 c10
Grogport Ag & B ...112 B12
Groigearraidh W Isls ...152 c10
Gromford Suffk ...59 M9
Gronant Flints ...74 F7
Groombridge E Susx ...15 P3
Grosebay W Isls ...152 e6
Grosmont Mons ...40 E7
Grosmont N York ...92 G6
Groton Suffk ...46 G3
Grotton Oldham ...76 H3
Grouville Jersey ...13 d3
Grove Bucks ...44 C7
Grove Dorset ...10 H10
Grove Kent ...35 M10
Grove Notts ...79 J8
Grove Oxon ...31 J4
Grove Green Kent ...34 D11
Grovenhurst Kent ...16 C3
Grove Park Gt Lon ...33 M8
Grovesend S Gloucs ...29 K4
Grovesend Swans ...26 C3
Grubb Street Kent ...33 Q8
Gruinard Highld ...143 P7
Gruinart Ag & B ...110 G8
Grula Highld ...134 G10
Gruline Ag & B ...119 P5
Grumbla Cnwll ...2 C8
Grundisburgh Suffk ...59 J10
Gruting Shet ...147 h7
Grutness Shet ...147 i10
Gualachulain Highld ...121 L4
Guanockgate Lincs ...68 G10
Guardbridge Fife ...125 J9

Guarlford Worcs ...41 N3
Guay P & K ...123 P3
Guernsey Guern ...12 c2
Guernsey Airport Guern ...12 b3
Guestling Green E Susx ...16 E8
Guestling Thorn E Susx ...16 E8
Guestwick Norfk ...70 F7
Guestwick Green Norfk ...70 G7
Guide Bridge Tamesd ...76 G4
Guide Post Nthumb ...100 H1
Guilden Morden Cambs ...45 K3
Guilden Sutton Ches W ...75 M10
Guildford Surrey ...14 E1
Guildstead Kent ...34 E10
Guildtown P & K ...124 C6
Guilsborough Nhants ...54 H6
Guilsfield Powys ...62 H10
Guiltreehill S Ayrs ...104 G7
Guineaford Devon ...19 K6
Guisborough R & Cl ...92 C4
Guiseley Leeds ...85 J7
Guist Norfk ...70 E7
Guiting Power Gloucs ...42 C7
Gullane E Loth ...116 C5
Gulling Green Suffk ...58 B9
Gulval Cnwll ...2 D8
Gulworthy Devon ...7 N10
Gumfreston Pembks ...37 L10
Gumley Leics ...54 H3
Gummow's Shop Cnwll ...3 K4
Gunby E R Yk ...86 D8
Gunby Lincs ...67 M8
Gundleton Hants ...25 K7
Gun Green Kent ...16 D4
Gun Hill E Susx ...15 Q8
Gun Hill Warwks ...53 P3
Gunn Devon ...19 M7
Gunnerside N York ...90 F7
Gunnerton Nthumb ...99 Q4
Gunness N Linc ...79 L1
Gunnislake Cnwll ...7 N10
Gunnista Shet ...147 j7
Gunthorpe C Pete ...68 D12
Gunthorpe Norfk ...79 K4
Gunthorpe Norfk ...70 F5
Gunthorpe Notts ...66 H3
Gunton Suffk ...59 Q2
Gunwalloe Cnwll ...2 G10
Gupworthy Somset ...20 F6
Gurnard IoW ...12 H6
Gurnett Ches E ...76 H9
Gurney Slade Somset ...22 E3
Gurnos Powys ...39 J10
Gushmere Kent ...35 J11
Gussage All Saints
  Dorset ...11 N3
Gussage St Andrew
  Dorset ...23 L10
Gussage St Michael
  Dorset ...11 N2
Guston Kent ...17 P2
Gutcher Shet ...147 j3
Guthrie Angus ...125 L3
Guyhirn Cambs ...68 H11
Guyhirn Gull Cambs ...68 G11
Guy's Marsh Dorset ...23 J9
Guyzance Nthumb ...109 K9
Gwaenysgor Flints ...74 E7
Gwalchmai IoA ...72 F8
Gwastadnant Gwynd ...73 K12
Gwaun-Cae-Gurwen
  Carmth ...38 G9
Gwbert on Sea Cerdgn ...48 B10
Gwealavellan Cnwll ...2 F6
Gweek Cnwll ...2 H9
Gwehelog Mons ...40 E10
Gwenddwr Powys ...39 P3
Gwennap Cnwll ...3 J6
Gwennap Mining
  District Cnwll ...3 J6
Gwenter Cnwll ...3 J11
Gwernaffield Flints ...74 H10
Gwernesney Mons ...40 F11
Gwernogle Carmth ...38 D5
Gwernymynydd Flints ...74 H11
Gwersyllt Wrexhm ...63 K2
Gwespyr Flints ...74 F7
Gwindra Cnwll ...3 M4
Gwinear Cnwll ...2 F7
Gwithian Cnwll ...2 F6
Gwredog IoA ...72 G6
Gwrhay Caerph ...28 B3
Gwyddelwern Denbgs ...62 E3
Gwyddgrug Carmth ...38 C4
Gwynfryn Wrexhm ...63 J2
Gwystre Powys ...50 E7
Gwytherin Conwy ...73 Q11
Gyfelia Wrexhm ...63 K3
Gyrn Goch Gwynd ...60 F2

H

Habberley Shrops ...63 L11
Habberley Worcs ...52 E5
Habergham Lancs ...84 B8
Habertoft Lincs ...81 J10
Habin W Susx ...25 P9
Habrough NE Lin ...80 C1
Hacconby Lincs ...68 B7
Haceby Lincs ...67 P5
Hacheston Suffk ...59 L9
Hackbridge Gt Lon ...33 K9
Hackenthorpe Sheff ...78 C7
Hackford Norfk ...70 F11
Hackforth N York ...91 L8
Hack Green Ches E ...64 C3
Hackland Ork ...147 c4
Hackleton Nhants ...55 K9
Hacklinge Kent ...35 P11
Hackman's Gate Worcs ...52 G5
Hackness N York ...93 K8
Hackness Somset ...21 M4
Hackney Gt Lon ...33 L5
Hackthorn Lincs ...79 N7
Hackthorpe Cumb ...89 N2
Hacton Gt Lon ...33 Q5
Hadden Border ...108 C3
Haddenham Bucks ...43 Q10
Haddenham Cambs ...57 J5
Haddington E Loth ...116 C6
Haddington Lincs ...79 M11
Haddiscoe Norfk ...59 N1
Haddon Cambs ...56 C2
Hade Edge Kirk ...77 L3
Hadfield Derbys ...77 J4
Hadham Cross Herts ...45 M8
Hadham Ford Herts ...45 N7
Hadleigh Essex ...34 E5
Hadleigh Suffk ...47 J3
Hadleigh Heath Suffk ...46 H3
Hadley Worcs ...52 F8
Hadley Wrekin ...64 C10
Hadley End Staffs ...65 L8
Hadley Wood Gt Lon ...33 K3
Hadlow Kent ...34 B12
Hadlow Down E Susx ...15 P6
Hadnall Shrops ...63 N8
Hadrian's Wall ...100 B4
Hadstock Essex ...45 Q3
Hadston Nthumb ...109 L10
Hadzor Worcs ...52 G8
Haffenden Quarter Kent ...16 F2
Hafodunos Conwy ...73 Q10
Hafod-y-bwch Wrexhm ...63 K3
Hafod-y-coed Blae G ...28 B2

Hafodyrynys Caerph ...28 B3
Haggate Lancs ...84 C8
Haggbeck Cumb ...98 F3
Haggersta Shet ...147 i7
Haggerston Nthumb ...108 G1
Haggington Hill Devon ...19 L4
Hagley Herefs ...40 H3
Hagley Worcs ...52 G4
Hagmore Green Suffk ...46 G4
Hagnaby Lincs ...80 G11
Hagnaby Lincs ...81 J7
Hagworthingham Lincs ...80 G10
Haigh Wigan ...75 Q2
Haighton Green Lancs ...83 M8
Haile Cumb ...88 D5
Hailes Gloucs ...42 B6
Hailey Herts ...45 L9
Hailey Oxon ...31 N5
Hailey Oxon ...42 H9
Hailsham E Susx ...15 Q9
Hail Weston Cambs ...56 E8
Hainault Gt Lon ...33 N4
Haine Kent ...35 P9
Hainford Norfk ...71 J8
Hainton Lincs ...80 D7
Hainworth C Brad ...84 G7
Haisthorpe E R Yk ...87 L2
Hakin Pembks ...36 H9
Halam Notts ...66 H1
Halbeath Fife ...115 L3
Halberton Devon ...20 F10
Halcro Highld ...151 M4
Hale Cumb ...89 N11
Hale Halton ...75 M7
Hale Hants ...24 C9
Hale Somset ...22 G8
Hale Surrey ...25 P4
Hale Traffd ...76 E6
Hale Bank Halton ...75 M7
Hale Green E Susx ...15 Q8
Hale Nook Lancs ...83 J6
Hales Norfk ...59 M1
Hales Staffs ...64 D5
Hales Green Derbys ...65 M4
Halesowen Dudley ...52 H4
Hales Place Kent ...35 L10
Hale Street Kent ...34 B1
Halesworth Suffk ...59 M5
Halewood Knows ...75 M6
Halford Devon ...8 F10
Halford Shrops ...51 M4
Halford Warwks ...42 H3
Halfpenny Cumb ...89 N9
Halfpenny Green Staffs ...52 F2
Halfpenny Houses N York ...91 L10
Halfway Carmth ...38 F5
Halfway Carmth ...39 K5
Halfway Sheff ...78 C7
Halfway W Berk ...31 J8
Halfway Bridge W Susx ...14 D4
Halfway House Shrops ...63 K10
Halfway Houses Kent ...34 G8
Halifax Calder ...84 G10
Halket E Ayrs ...113 N10
Halkirk Highld ...151 L5
Halkyn Flints ...74 H9
Hall E Rens ...113 N10
Hallam Fields Derbys ...66 D4
Halland E Susx ...15 P7
Hallaton Leics ...55 K1
Hallatrow BaNES ...29 K11
Hallbankgate Cumb ...98 H6
Hall Cliffe Wakefd ...85 L11
Hall Cross Lancs ...83 K9
Hall Dunnerdale Cumb ...88 H6
Hallen S Glos ...28 H6
Hall End Bed ...44 F3
Hall End C Beds ...44 F4
Hallgarth Dur ...101 J9
Hallglen Falk ...114 G5
Hall Green Birm ...53 L4
Hallin Highld ...134 D4
Halling Medway ...34 C9
Hallington Lincs ...80 F6
Hallington Nthumb ...100 C3
Halliwell Bolton ...76 C2
Halloughton Notts ...66 H2
Hallow Worcs ...52 F9
Hallow Heath Worcs ...52 F9
Hallsands Devon ...5 N9
Hall's Green Essex ...45 M10
Hall's Green Herts ...45 K6
Hallthwaites Cumb ...88 G9
Hallworthy Cnwll ...6 H7
Hallyne Border ...106 G2
Halmer End Staffs ...64 E2
Halmond's Frome Herefs ...52 C11
Halmore Gloucs ...41 L11
Halnaker W Susx ...14 C9
Halsall Lancs ...75 L2
Halse Nhants ...43 M4
Halse Somset ...21 J8
Halsetown Cnwll ...2 D7
Halsham E R Yk ...87 P9
Halsinger Devon ...19 K5
Halstead Essex ...46 E5
Halstead Kent ...33 N10
Halstead Leics ...67 J11
Halstock Dorset ...10 E3
Halsway Somset ...21 J6
Haltcliff Bridge Cumb ...98 D11
Haltham Lincs ...80 E11
Haltoft End Lincs ...68 G3
Halton Bucks ...44 C9
Halton Halton ...75 M7
Halton Lancs ...83 L6
Halton Leeds ...85 M8
Halton Nthumb ...100 C5
Halton Wrexhm ...63 J4
Halton East N York ...84 G4
Halton Fenside Lincs ...81 J10
Halton Gill N York ...90 E11
Halton Green Lancs ...83 L6
Halton Holegate Lincs ...80 H10
Halton Lea Gate Nthumb ...99 J6
Halton Quay Cnwll ...4 H4
Halton Shields Nthumb ...100 C5
Halton West N York ...84 C4
Haltwhistle Nthumb ...99 K5
Halvana Cnwll ...7 J7
Halvergate Norfk ...71 N10
Halwell Devon ...5 N5
Halwill Devon ...7 M5
Halwill Junction Devon ...7 N5
Ham Devon ...9 N4
Ham Gloucs ...41 R7
Ham Gt Lon ...33 J7
Ham Kent ...35 P11
Ham Somset ...20 H8
Ham Somset ...21 M7
Ham Somset ...22 E2
Ham Wilts ...30 H9
Hambleden Bucks ...31 R5
Hambledon Hants ...25 L10
Hambledon Surrey ...14 E3
Hamble-le-Rice Hants ...12 H5
Hambleton Lancs ...83 J7
Hambleton N York ...86 B8
Hambleton Moss Side
  Lancs ...83 J7
Hambridge Somset ...21 N9

Hambrook S Glos ...29 K6
Hambrook W Susx ...13 M3
Ham Common Dorset ...22 H8
Hameringham Lincs ...80 F10
Hamerton Cambs ...56 C5
Ham Green Herefs ...41 M3
Ham Green Kent ...16 E5
Ham Green Kent ...34 E8
Ham Green N Som ...28 H7
Ham Green Worcs ...53 J8
Ham Hill Kent ...34 C10
Hamilton S Lans ...114 D10
Hamilton Services
  (northbound) S Lans ...114 C10
Hamlet Dorset ...10 F3
Hammer W Susx ...14 C4
Hammerpot W Susx ...14 F9
Hammersmith Gt Lon ...33 J6
Hammerwich Staffs ...65 K10
Hammerwood E Susx ...15 N3
Hammond Street Herts ...45 L10
Hammoon Dorset ...22 H10
Hamnavoe Shet ...147 i8
Hampden Park E Susx ...15 Q10
Hamperden End Essex ...45 Q5
Hampnett Gloucs ...42 C8
Hampole Donc ...78 E2
Hampreston Dorset ...11 P5
Hampsfield Cumb ...89 L10
Hampson Green Lancs ...83 L4
Hampstead Gt Lon ...33 L5
Hampstead Norreys
  W Berk ...31 L7
Hampsthwaite N York ...85 K3
Hampton C Pete ...56 D2
Hampton Devon ...9 P5
Hampton Gt Lon ...32 G8
Hampton Kent ...35 L8
Hampton Shrops ...52 C4
Hampton Swindn ...30 E4
Hampton Worcs ...42 B3
Hampton Bishop Herefs ...40 H3
Hampton Court Palace
  Gt Lon ...32 H8
Hampton Fields Gloucs ...29 P2
Hampton Green Ches W ...63 N2
Hampton Heath Ches W ...63 N2
Hampton-in-Arden Solhll ...53 N4
Hampton Loade Shrops ...52 D3
Hampton Lovett Worcs ...52 G7
Hampton Lucy Warwks ...53 N9
Hampton Magna Warwks ...53 N8
Hampton on the Hill
  Warwks ...53 N8
Hampton Park Wilts ...23 P7
Hampton Poyle Oxon ...43 L8
Hampton Wick Gt Lon ...32 H8
Hamptworth Wilts ...24 D9
Hamrow Norfk ...70 D7
Hamsey E Susx ...15 M8
Hamsey Green Surrey ...33 L10
Hamstall Ridware Staffs ...65 L8
Hamstead Birm ...53 K2
Hamstead IoW ...12 F6
Hamstead Marshall
  W Berk ...31 J9
Hamsterley Dur ...100 E12
Hamsterley Dur ...100 E7
Hamsterley Mill Dur ...100 E7
Hamstreet Kent ...16 H4
Ham Street Somset ...22 D6
Hamworthy BCP ...11 N6
Hanbury Staffs ...65 M6
Hanbury Worcs ...52 H7
Hanby Lincs ...67 P6
Hanchet End Suffk ...46 B2
Hanchurch Staffs ...64 F4
Handa Island Highld ...148 D7
Handale R & Cl ...92 E4
Hand and Pen Devon ...9 K5
Handbridge Ches W ...75 L10
Handcross W Susx ...15 J5
Handforth Ches E ...76 F7
Hand Green Ches W ...75 M11
Handley Ches W ...75 M12
Handley Derbys ...78 B11
Handley Green Essex ...46 B11
Handsacre Staffs ...65 K9
Handsworth Birm ...53 K3
Handsworth Sheff ...78 C6
Handy Cross Bucks ...32 B4
Hanford C Stke ...64 F3
Hanford Dorset ...22 H9
Hanging Heaton Kirk ...85 K10
Hanging Houghton
  Nhants ...55 J6
Hanging Langford Wilts ...23 M6
Hangleton Br & H ...15 K9
Hangleton W Susx ...14 E9
Hanham S Glos ...29 K8
Hankelow Ches E ...64 C4
Hankerton Wilts ...29 R4
Hankham E Susx ...15 Q9
Hanley C Stke ...64 F3
Hanley Broadheath
  Worcs ...52 C7
Hanley Castle Worcs ...41 N3
Hanley Child Worcs ...52 C7
Hanley Swan Worcs ...41 N3
Hanley William Worcs ...52 C7
Hanlith N York ...84 D1
Hanmer Wrexhm ...63 M4
Hannaford Devon ...19 M7
Hannah Lincs ...81 J8
Hannington Hants ...25 J2
Hannington Nhants ...55 K6
Hannington Swindn ...30 D3
Hannington Wick Swindn ...30 D3
Hanscombe End C Beds ...44 G5
Hanslope M Keyn ...44 B3
Hanthorpe Lincs ...68 B7
Hanwell Gt Lon ...32 H6
Hanwell Oxon ...43 K3
Hanwood Shrops ...63 M10
Hanworth Gt Lon ...32 G8
Hanworth Norfk ...71 J5
Happendon Services
  S Lans ...105 Q3
Happisburgh Norfk ...71 M6
Happisburgh Common
  Norfk ...71 M6
Hapsford Ches W ...75 M9
Hapton Lancs ...84 B9
Hapton Norfk ...58 H2
Harberton Devon ...5 M6
Harbertonford Devon ...5 N6
Harbledown Kent ...35 K10
Harborne Birm ...53 J4
Harborough Magna
  Warwks ...54 D5
Harbottle Nthumb ...108 G8
Harbourneford Devon ...5 M4
Harbours Hill Worcs ...52 H7
Harbridge Hants ...12 B3
Harbridge Green Hants ...12 B3
Harburn W Loth ...115 J9
Harbury Warwks ...53 Q9
Harby Leics ...67 J5
Harby Notts ...79 L9
Harcombe Devon ...9 M7
Harcombe Devon ...9 P6
Harcombe Bottom Devon ...9 N6
Harden C Brad ...84 G7
Harden Wsall ...65 J11

Hardendale Cumb ...89 P4
Hardenhuish Wilts ...29 P7
Hardgate Abers ...133 J4
Hardgate D & G ...96 G5
Hardgate N York ...85 K3
Hardgate W Duns ...113 P7
Hardham W Susx ...14 E7
Hardhorn Lancs ...83 J8
Hardingstone Nhants ...55 J9
Hardington Somset ...22 G4
Hardington Mandeville
  Somset ...10 D2
Hardington Marsh
  Somset ...10 D3
Hardington Moor Somset ...22 C11
Hardisworthy Devon ...18 E9
Hardley Hants ...12 G4
Hardley Street Norfk ...71 M12
Hardmead M Keyn ...55 M11
Hardraw N York ...90 D8
Hardstoft Derbys ...78 D11
Hardway Hants ...13 J4
Hardway Somset ...22 G6
Hardwick Bucks ...44 A8
Hardwick Cambs ...56 G9
Hardwick Nhants ...55 K7
Hardwick Norfk ...59 J3
Hardwick Oxon ...42 H10
Hardwick Oxon ...43 K6
Hardwick Wsall ...53 J1
Hardwicke Gloucs ...41 M9
Hardwicke Gloucs ...41 P6
Hardwick Village Notts ...78 G9
Hardwick Hall Derbys ...78 D11
Hardy's Green Essex ...46 G7
Hare Green Essex ...47 K6
Hare Hatch Wokham ...32 A7
Harehill Derbys ...65 M5
Harehills Leeds ...85 L8
Harehope Nthumb ...108 H5
Harelaw Border ...107 N5
Harelaw D & G ...98 H3
Harelaw Dur ...100 F7
Hareplain Kent ...16 E3
Harescombe Gloucs ...41 N9
Haresfield Gloucs ...41 N9
Hareshaw N Lans ...114 F9
Hare Street Essex ...45 H7
Hare Street Essex ...45 L9
Hare Street Herts ...45 M6
Harewood Leeds ...85 L6
Harewood End Herefs ...40 H6
Harford Devon ...5 K5
Hargate Norfk ...58 G2
Hargatewall Derbys ...77 L9
Hargrave Ches W ...75 M11
Hargrave Nhants ...55 P6
Hargrave Suffk ...57 P9
Harker Cumb ...98 D5
Harkstead Suffk ...47 L5
Harlaston Staffs ...65 N10
Harlaxton Lincs ...67 L5
Harle Syke Lancs ...84 C8
Harlech Castle Gwynd ...61 K6
Harlescott Shrops ...63 N9
Harlesden Gt Lon ...33 J5
Harlesthorpe Derbys ...78 E8
Harleston Devon ...5 N7
Harleston Norfk ...59 K4
Harleston Suffk ...58 F8
Harlestone Nhants ...54 H8
Harley Rothm ...78 B5
Harley Shrops ...63 P11
Harling Road Norfk ...58 E3
Harlington C Beds ...44 E5
Harlington Donc ...78 D3
Harlington Gt Lon ...32 G6
Harlosh Highld ...134 E6
Harlow Essex ...45 N9
Harlow Carr RHS N York ...85 L4
Harlow Hill Nthumb ...100 E5
Harlthorpe E R Yk ...86 D8
Harlton Cambs ...56 G10
Harlyn Cnwll ...6 C10
Harman's Cross Dorset ...11 P7
Harmby N York ...91 K9
Harmer Green Herts ...45 J8
Harmer Hill Shrops ...63 N8
Harmondsworth Gt Lon ...32 F6
Harmston Lincs ...79 N11
Harnage Shrops ...63 P11
Harnham Nthumb ...100 F2
Harnhill Gloucs ...30 C2
Harold Hill Gt Lon ...33 P4
Haroldston West Pembks ...36 G7
Haroldswick Shet ...147 l2
Harold Wood Gt Lon ...33 Q4
Harome N York ...92 D9
Harpenden Herts ...44 G9
Harpford Devon ...9 K6
Harpham E R Yk ...87 K3
Harpley Norfk ...69 Q6
Harpley Worcs ...52 C8
Harpole Nhants ...54 H8
Harpsdale Highld ...151 L4
Harpsden Oxon ...31 Q6
Harpswell Lincs ...79 N6
Harpurhey Manch ...76 F3
Harpur Hill Derbys ...77 K9
Harraby Cumb ...98 E6
Harracott Devon ...19 L8
Harrapool Highld ...135 K11
Harras Cumb ...88 C2
Harrietfield P & K ...123 Q7
Harrietsham Kent ...34 F11
Harringay Gt Lon ...33 L5
Harrington Cumb ...88 C2
Harrington Lincs ...80 G8
Harrington Nhants ...55 K5
Harringworth Nhants ...55 M1
Harris W Isls ...152 d7
Harriseahead Staffs ...64 F1
Harriston Cumb ...97 N10
Harrogate N York ...85 L4
Harrold Bed ...55 L9
Harrop Dale Oldham ...77 J2
Harrow Gt Lon ...32 H5
Harrowbarrow Cnwll ...7 M10
Harrowden Bed ...44 F4
Harrowgate Village
  Darltn ...91 M4
Harrow Green Suffk ...58 C9
Harrow on the Hill Gt Lon ...32 H5
Harrow Weald Gt Lon ...32 H4
Harston Cambs ...56 H10
Harston Leics ...67 K5
Harswell E R Yk ...86 E7
Hart Hartpl ...101 L11
Hartburn Nthumb ...100 F1
Hartburn S on T ...91 P3
Hartest Suffk ...58 B10
Hartfield E Susx ...15 N3
Hartford Cambs ...56 E6
Hartford Ches W ...75 P10
Hartford Somset ...20 E7
Hartfordbridge Hants ...31 Q10
Hartford End Essex ...46 B8

Hartforth N York ...91 K5
Hartgrove Dorset ...23 J9
Harthill Ches E ...63 N1
Harthill N Lans ...114 G8
Harthill Rothm ...78 E6
Hartington Derbys ...77 L11
Hartland Devon ...18 E8
Hartland Quay Devon ...18 E8
Hartlebury Worcs ...52 F6
Hartlepool Hartpl ...101 M11
Hartley Cumb ...90 C5
Hartley Kent ...16 D3
Hartley Kent ...33 R9
Hartley Nthumb ...101 J3
Hartley Green Kent ...33 R9
Hartley Green Staffs ...64 H6
Hartley Wespall Hants ...31 P10
Hartley Wintney Hants ...31 Q10
Hartlip Kent ...34 E9
Hartoft End N York ...92 G7
Harton N York ...86 D3
Harton S Tyne ...101 K5
Harton Shrops ...51 N3
Hartpury Gloucs ...41 M6
Hartshead Kirk ...85 J10
Hartshead Moor
  Services Calder ...85 J10
Hartshead Moor Top Kirk ...85 J10
Hartshill C Stke ...64 F3
Hartshill Warwks ...53 Q2
Hartshorne Derbys ...65 Q8
Hartside Nthumb ...108 F6
Hartsop Cumb ...89 L4
Hart Station Hartpl ...101 M11
Hartswell Somset ...20 H8
Hartwell Nhants ...55 K10
Hartwith N York ...85 L3
Hartwood N Lans ...114 F9
Hartwoodmyres Border ...107 L5
Harvel Kent ...34 B9
Harvington Worcs ...52 H5
Harvington Worcs ...53 K10
Harwell Notts ...78 H5
Harwell Oxon ...31 L5
Harwich Essex ...47 N5
Harwood Bolton ...76 D2
Harwood Dur ...99 M11
Harwood Nthumb ...108 H10
Harwood Dale N York ...93 K7
Harwood Lee Bolton ...76 D2
Harworth Notts ...78 G5
Hasbury Dudley ...52 H4
Hascombe Surrey ...14 E3
Haselbech Nhants ...55 J5
Haselbury Plucknett
  Somset ...10 D3
Haseley Warwks ...53 N7
Haseley Green Warwks ...53 N7
Haseley Knob Warwks ...53 N6
Haselor Warwks ...53 L9
Hasfield Gloucs ...41 N6
Hasguard Pembks ...36 G8
Haskayne Lancs ...75 K2
Hasketon Suffk ...59 L10
Hasland Derbys ...78 C9
Haslemere Surrey ...14 D4
Haslingden Lancs ...84 B10
Haslingfield Cambs ...56 H10
Haslington Ches E ...64 D1
Hassall Ches E ...76 E12
Hassall Green Ches E ...76 E12
Hassell Street Kent ...17 J2
Hassingham Norfk ...71 M11
Hassness Cumb ...88 G3
Hassocks W Susx ...15 K7
Hassop Derbys ...77 N9
Haste Hill Surrey ...14 C4
Haster Highld ...151 P6
Hasthorpe Lincs ...81 J9
Hastingleigh Kent ...17 K2
Hastings E Susx ...16 E9
Hastings Somset ...21 M10
Hastingwood Essex ...45 N10
Hastoe Herts ...44 D9
Haswell Dur ...101 K7
Haswell Plough Dur ...101 K7
Hatch C Beds ...56 D11
Hatch Beauchamp
  Somset ...21 M9
Hatch End Bed ...55 Q8
Hatch End Gt Lon ...32 H4
Hatchet Gate Hants ...12 E4
Hatching Green Herts ...44 G9
Hatchmere Ches W ...75 N9
Hatch Warren Hants ...25 K3
Hatcliffe NE Lin ...80 E3
Hatfield Donc ...78 H2
Hatfield Herefs ...51 Q9
Hatfield Herts ...45 J10
Hatfield Broad Oak Essex ...45 Q8
Hatfield Heath Essex ...45 Q8
Hatfield Peverel Essex ...46 D9
Hatfield Woodhouse
  Donc ...78 H2
Hatford Oxon ...30 H3
Hatherden Hants ...24 G4
Hatherleigh Devon ...7 Q4
Hathern Leics ...66 D7
Hatherop Gloucs ...42 D10
Hathersage Derbys ...77 N7
Hathersage Booths
  Derbys ...77 N7
Hatherton Ches E ...64 C3
Hatherton Staffs ...64 H9
Hatley St George Cambs ...56 E10
Hatt Cnwll ...4 H4
Hattersley Tamesd ...77 J4
Hattingley Hants ...25 L5
Hatton Abers ...141 P8
Hatton Angus ...125 J4
Hatton Derbys ...65 M6
Hatton Gt Lon ...32 G6
Hatton Lincs ...80 E7
Hatton Shrops ...51 M3
Hatton Warrtn ...75 N7
Hatton Warwks ...53 N7
Hatton Heath Ches W ...75 M11
Hatton of Fintray Abers ...133 K1
Haugh E Ayrs ...105 J3
Haugh Lincs ...80 H8
Haugh Rochdl ...76 H1
Haugham Lincs ...80 G7
Haugh Head Nthumb ...108 G4
Haughley Suffk ...58 F8
Haughley Green Suffk ...58 F8
Haugh of Glass Moray ...140 C8
Haugh of Urr D & G ...96 G5
Haughs of Kinnaird
  Angus ...125 M1
Haughton Ches E ...75 P12
Haughton Notts ...78 H9
Haughton Powys ...63 K8
Haughton Shrops ...63 J8
Haughton Shrops ...63 M9
Haughton Shrops ...64 D11
Haughton Staffs ...64 G8
Haughton Green Tamesd ...76 H5
Haughton le Skerne
  Darltn ...91 N4
Haultwick Herts ...45 L7
Haunton Staffs ...65 N10

Hautes Croix Jersey ...13 c1
Hauxton Cambs ...56 H10
Havannah Ches E ...76 F10
Havant Hants ...13 M3
Haven Herefs ...51 L9
Haven Bank Lincs ...68 E2
Haven Side E R Yk ...87 M9
Havenstreet IoW ...13 J6
Havercroft Wakefd ...78 C1
Haverfordwest Pembks ...37 J7
Haverhill Suffk ...46 B3
Haverigg Cumb ...88 F11
Havering-atte-Bower
  Gt Lon ...33 P4
Haversham M Keyn ...44 B3
Haverthwaite Cumb ...89 K10
Haverton Hill S on T ...91 R2
Havyatt N Som ...28 G10
Havyatt Somset ...22 C6
Hawarden Flints ...75 K10
Hawbridge Worcs ...52 G11
Hawbush Green Essex ...46 D7
Hawcoat Cumb ...88 G12
Hawen Cerdgn ...48 E11
Hawes N York ...90 E9
Hawe's Green Norfk ...71 K12
Hawford Worcs ...52 F8
Hawick Border ...107 N7
Hawkchurch Devon ...9 Q5
Hawkedon Suffk ...57 Q10
Hawkenbury Kent ...16 C2
Hawkeridge Wilts ...23 J3
Hawkerland Devon ...9 K7
Hawker's Cove Cnwll ...6 C9
Hawkesbury S Glos ...29 M5
Hawkesbury Warwks ...54 B5
Hawkesbury Upton S Glos ...29 M5
Hawkes End Covtry ...53 P5
Hawk Green Stockp ...76 H6
Hawkhill Nthumb ...109 L7
Hawkhurst Kent ...16 C4
Hawkhurst Common
  E Susx ...15 P7
Hawkinge Kent ...17 M3
Hawkley Hants ...25 N7
Hawkley Wigan ...75 P3
Hawkridge Somset ...20 D7
Hawksdale Cumb ...98 D8
Hawkshaw Bury ...84 A12
Hawkshead Cumb ...89 K7
Hawkshead Hill Cumb ...89 K7
Hawksland S Lans ...105 Q2
Hawkspur Green Essex ...46 B5
Hawkstone Shrops ...63 P7
Hawkswick N York ...84 E1
Hawksworth Leeds ...85 J7
Hawksworth Notts ...67 J3
Hawkwell Essex ...34 E4
Hawkwell Nthumb ...100 E4
Hawley Hants ...25 P1
Hawley Kent ...33 P8
Hawling Gloucs ...42 C7
Hawnby N York ...92 B9
Haworth C Brad ...84 F8
Hawridge Bucks ...44 D10
Hawstead Suffk ...58 C9
Hawstead Green Suffk ...58 C9
Hawthorn Dur ...101 K9
Hawthorn Hants ...25 L6
Hawthorn Rhondd ...27 Q5
Hawthorn Hill Br For ...32 B7
Hawthorn Hill Lincs ...68 D1
Hawthorpe Lincs ...67 P7
Hawton Notts ...67 J2
Haxby York ...86 C4
Haxby Gates C York ...86 B4
Haxey N Linc ...79 K4
Haxey Carr N Linc ...79 J3
Haxted Surrey ...15 M2
Haxton Wilts ...23 P3
Hay Cnwll ...3 N4
Hay Cnwll ...3 P2
Haydock St Hel ...75 P4
Haydon BaNES ...22 F2
Haydon Dorset ...22 F10
Haydon Somset ...21 L8
Haydon Bridge Nthumb ...99 N5
Haydon Wick Swindn ...30 D5
Haye Cnwll ...4 H3
Hayes Gt Lon ...32 F5
Hayes Gt Lon ...33 N8
Hayfield Ag & B ...121 K8
Hayfield Derbys ...77 J5
Hayfield Green Donc ...78 G3
Haygate Wrekin ...64 B10
Hay Green Norfk ...69 K8
Hayhillock Angus ...125 K4
Hayle Cnwll ...2 E7
Hayle Port Cnwll ...2 E7
Hayley Green Dudley ...52 H4
Hayling Island Hants ...13 M4
Haymoor Green Ches E ...64 C3
Hayne Devon ...8 E7
Hayne Devon ...20 E10
Haynes C Beds ...44 G3
Haynes Church End
  C Beds ...44 F3
Haynes West End C Beds ...44 F3
Hay-on-Wye Powys ...40 E3
Hayscastle Pembks ...36 H5
Hayscastle Cross Pembks ...36 H5
Hay Street Herts ...45 M6
Hayton Cumb ...97 M10
Hayton Cumb ...98 F6
Hayton E R Yk ...86 E6
Hayton Notts ...79 J7
Hayton's Bent Shrops ...51 N4
Haytor Vale Devon ...8 ...
Haytown Devon ...18 H10
Haywards Heath W Susx ...15 L6
Haywood Donc ...78 E1
Haywood Oaks Notts ...66 G1
Hazards Green E Susx ...16 C8
Hazelbank S Lans ...114 F12
Hazelbury Bryan Dorset ...11 J3
Hazeleigh Essex ...46 E11
Hazeley Hants ...31 Q10
Hazelford Notts ...67 J2
Hazel Grove Stockp ...76 G6
Hazelhurst Tamesd ...76 H4
Hazelslade Staffs ...65 J9
Hazel Street Kent ...16 C3
Hazel Stub Suffk ...46 B3
Hazelton Walls Fife ...124 G8
Hazelwood Derbys ...66 B3
Hazlemere Bucks ...32 C3
Hazlerigg N u Ty ...100 G4
Hazles Staffs ...65 J3
Hazleton Gloucs ...42 C8
Heacham Norfk ...69 M5
Headbourne Worthy
  Hants ...24 H7
Headbrook Herefs ...51 J9
Headcorn Kent ...16 E1
Headingley Leeds ...85 L8
Headington Oxon ...43 L10
Headlam Dur ...91 K3
Headlesscross N Lans ...114 G9
Headless Cross Worcs ...53 J7
Headley Hants ...25 P5
Headley Hants ...31 L10
Headley Surrey ...32 H11
Headley Down Hants ...25 P5
Headley Heath Worcs ...53 J5
Headon Devon ...7 L4

Headon – Hopwood 175

Headon Notts 79 J8
Heads Nook Cumb 98 G7
Heage Derbys 66 B2
Healaugh N York 85 P6
Healaugh N York 90 G7
Heald Green Stockp 76 F6
Heale Devon 19 M4
Heale Somset 21 K9
Heale Somset 21 N8
Healey N York 91 K10
Healey Nthumb 100 C6
Healey Rochdl 84 D12
Healey Wakefd 85 K11
Healeyfield Dur 100 D8
Healing NE Lin 80 D2
Heamoor Cnwll 2 D8
Heanor Derbys 66 C3
Heanton Punchardon Devon 19 K6
Heapham Lincs 79 L6
Hearn Hants 25 P6
Heart of Scotland Services N Lans 114 G8
Hearts Delight Kent 34 F10
Heasley Mill Devon 19 P7
Heaste Highld 135 L12
Heath Derbys 78 D10
Heath Wakefd 85 M11
Heath and Reach C Beds 44 C6
Heath Common W Susx 14 G8
Heathcote Derbys 77 L11
Heathcote Shrops 64 C6
Heath End Bucks 32 C3
Heath End Hants 31 J10
Heath End Leics 66 B8
Heath End Warwks 53 N8
Heather Leics 66 C10
Heathfield Cambs 45 N2
Heathfield Devon 8 F9
Heathfield E Susx 15 Q6
Heathfield N York 84 H2
Heathfield Somset 21 J8
Heathfield Village Oxon 43 L8
Heath Green Worcs 53 K6
Heath Hall D & G 97 K2
Heath Hayes & Wimblebury Staffs 65 J10
Heath Hill Shrops 64 E9
Heath House Somset 21 P4
Heathrow Airport Gt Lon 32 F7
Heathstock Devon 9 N4
Heathton Shrops 52 E2
Heath Town Wolves 64 H12
Heathwaite N York 91 R6
Heatley Staffs 65 K7
Heatley Warrtn 76 C6
Heaton Bolton 76 C2
Heaton C Brad 84 H8
Heaton Lancs 83 K3
Heaton N u Ty 100 H5
Heaton Staffs 76 H11
Heaton Chapel Stockp 76 G5
Heaton Mersey Stockp 76 F6
Heaton Norris Stockp 76 G5
Heaton's Bridge Lancs 75 L1
Heaverham Kent 33 Q10
Heaviley Stockp 76 G6
Heavitree Devon 8 H6
Hebburn S Tyne 101 J5
Hebden N York 84 F3
Hebden Bridge Calder 84 E9
Hebden Green Ches W 76 B10
Hebing End Herts 45 K7
Hebron Carmth 37 N5
Hebron IoA 72 G7
Hebron Nthumb 109 K11
Heckfield Hants 31 P10
Heckfield Green Suffk 59 J5
Heckfordbridge Essex 46 G7
Heckington Lincs 68 C3
Heckmondwike Kirk 85 J10
Heddington Wilts 30 A9
Heddon-on-the-Wall Nthumb 100 E5
Hedenham Norfk 59 L2
Hedge End Hants 24 H10
Hedgerley Bucks 32 D5
Hedgerley Green Bucks 32 D5
Hedging Somset 21 L7
Hedley on the Hill Nthumb 100 D6
Hednesford Staffs 65 J9
Hedon E R Yk 87 M9
Hedsor Bucks 32 C5
Heeley Sheff 78 B7
Hegdon Hill Herefs 51 Q10
Heglibister Shet 147 i6
Heighington Darltn 91 L2
Heighington Lincs 79 P10
Heightington Worcs 52 E6
Heiton Border 108 B4
Hele Devon 5 M3
Hele Devon 9 J4
Hele Devon 19 K4
Hele Somset 21 J8
Helebridge Cnwll 7 J4
Hele Lane Devon 8 E3
Helensburgh Ag & B 113 K5
Helenton S Ayrs 104 G4
Helford Cnwll 3 J9
Helford Passage Cnwll 3 J9
Helhoughton Norfk 70 C7
Helions Bumpstead Essex 46 B3
Hellaby Rothm 78 E5
Helland Cnwll 6 F10
Hellandbridge Cnwll 6 F10
Hell Corner W Berk 30 H9
Hellescott Cnwll 7 K7
Hellesdon Norfk 71 J9
Hellesveor Cnwll 2 D6
Hellidon Nhants 54 E9
Hellifield N York 84 C4
Hellingly E Susx 15 Q8
Hellington Norfk 71 L11
Helm Nthumb 109 K10
Helmdon Nhants 43 M3
Helme Kirk 77 L1
Helmingham Suffk 59 J9
Helmington Row Dur 100 F11
Helmsdale Highld 147 J2
Helmshore Lancs 84 B11
Helmsley N York 92 C10
Helperby N York 85 N1
Helperthorpe N York 86 H1
Helpringham Lincs 68 C4
Helpston C Pete 68 C11
Helsby Ches W 75 N8
Helsey Lincs 81 K9
Helston Cnwll 2 G9
Helstone Cnwll 6 F8
Helton Cumb 89 N2
Helwith N York 90 H6
Helwith Bridge N York 84 B1
Hemblington Norfk 71 L10
Hembridge Somset 22 D6
Hemel Hempstead Herts 44 F10
Hemerdon Devon 5 J5
Hemingbrough N York 86 C9
Hemingby Lincs 80 E9
Hemingfield Barns 78 C3
Hemingford Abbots Cambs 56 F6
Hemingford Grey Cambs 56 F6
Hemingstone Suffk 58 H10
Hemington Leics 66 D6
Hemington Nhants 56 B4
Hemington Somset 22 G3
Hemley Suffk 47 N3
Hemlington Middsb 92 A4
Hempholme E R Yk 87 K5
Hempnall Norfk 59 K2
Hempnall Green Norfk 59 K2
Hempriggs Moray 139 K3
Hempstead Essex 46 B4
Hempstead Medway 34 D9
Hempstead Norfk 70 G5
Hempstead Norfk 71 N6
Hempsted Gloucs 41 N8
Hempton Norfk 70 D6
Hempton Oxon 43 J5
Hemsby Norfk 71 P8
Hemswell Lincs 79 M5
Hemswell Cliff Lincs 79 N6
Hemsworth Wakefd 78 C1
Hemyock Devon 21 J10
Henbury Bristl 28 H6
Henbury Ches E 76 G9
Hendham Devon 5 M7
Hendomen Powys 50 H1
Hendon Gt Lon 33 J4
Hendon Sundld 101 K7
Hendra Cnwll 2 H7
Hendra Cnwll 6 E9
Hendre Brdgnd 27 M6
Hendre Flints 74 G10
Hendy Carmth 38 E11
Heneglwys IoA 72 G8
Henfield W Susx 15 J7
Henford Devon 7 M6
Henfynyw Cerdgn 48 G8
Henghurst Kent 16 G3
Hengoed Caerph 27 R3
Hengoed Powys 50 H10
Hengoed Shrops 63 J5
Hengrave Suffk 58 B7
Henham Essex 45 Q6
Heniarth Powys 62 F10
Henlade Somset 21 L8
Henley Dorset 10 H4
Henley Gloucs 41 P8
Henley Shrops 51 M3
Henley Shrops 51 P5
Henley Somset 21 P7
Henley Suffk 58 H10
Henley W Susx 14 C6
Henley Green Covtry 54 B4
Henley-in-Arden Warwks 53 M7
Henley-on-Thames Oxon 31 Q6
Henley Park Surrey 32 D11
Henley's Down E Susx 16 C8
Henley Street Kent 34 B9
Henllan Cerdgn 38 B3
Henllan Denbgs 74 D10
Henllan Amgoed Carmth 37 N6
Henllys Torfn 28 C4
Henlow C Beds 44 H4
Henlow Camp C Beds 44 H5
Hennock Devon 8 F8
Henny Street Essex 46 F4
Henryd Conwy 73 N9
Henry's Moat (Castell Hendre) Pembks 37 K5
Hensall N York 86 B10
Henshaw Nthumb 99 L5
Hensingham Cumb 88 C3
Henstead Suffk 59 P3
Hensting Hants 24 H9
Henstridge Somset 22 G9
Henstridge Ash Somset 22 F9
Henstridge Marsh Somset 22 G9
Henton Oxon 43 Q11
Henton Somset 22 C4
Henwick Worcs 52 F9
Henwood Cnwll 7 K10
Henwood Oxon 43 K11
Heolgerrig Myr Td 39 N10
Heol-las Swans 26 G3
Heol Senni Powys 39 L7
Heol-y-Cyw Brdgnd 27 M5
Hepburn Nthumb 108 H5
Hepple Nthumb 108 G9
Hepscott Nthumb 100 G1
Heptonstall Calder 84 E9
Hepworth Kirk 77 M2
Hepworth Suffk 58 E6
Herbrandston Pembks 36 G9
Hereford Herefs 40 G4
Hereson Kent 35 Q9
Heribusta Highld 142 D11
Heriot Border 115 R10
Hermiston C Edin 115 M7
Hermitage Border 107 M10
Hermitage Dorset 10 G3
Hermitage W Berk 31 L8
Hermitage W Susx 13 N4
Hermit Hill Barns 77 Q3
Hermon Carmth 38 A5
Hermon IoA 72 F10
Hermon Pembks 37 N4
Herne Kent 35 L9
Herne Bay Kent 35 L8
Herne Common Kent 35 L9
Herne Hill Gt Lon 33 L7
Herne Pound Kent 34 B11
Herner Devon 19 L8
Hernhill Kent 35 J10
Herodsfoot Cnwll 4 C4
Heronden Kent 35 N11
Herongate Essex 34 A4
Heronsford S Ayrs 94 G2
Heronsgate Herts 32 E3
Herriard Hants 25 L4
Herringfleet Suffk 59 P1
Herring's Green Bed 44 F3
Herringswell Suffk 57 N6
Herringthorpe Rothm 78 D5
Herrington Sundld 101 J7
Hersden Kent 35 M10
Hersham Cnwll 7 K3
Hersham Surrey 32 G9
Herstmonceux E Susx 16 B8
Herston Dorset 11 N9
Herston Ork 147 c6
Hertford Herts 45 L9
Hertford Heath Herts 45 L9
Hertingfordbury Herts 45 K9
Hesketh Bank Lancs 83 K10
Hesketh Lane Lancs 83 N7
Hesket Newmarket Cumb 98 D10
Heskin Green Lancs 83 M12
Hesleden Dur 101 L10
Hesleden N York 90 E11
Hesley Donc 78 G5
Hesleyside Nthumb 99 M2
Heslington C York 86 B5
Hessay C York 85 Q4
Hessenford Cnwll 4 D5
Hessett Suffk 58 D8
Hessle E R Yk 87 J10
Hessle Wakefd 85 N11
Hest Bank Lancs 83 L2
Hestley Green Suffk 58 H7
Heston Gt Lon 32 G7
Heston Services Gt Lon 32 G7
Hestwall Ork 147 b4
Heswall Wirral 75 J7
Hethe Oxon 43 M6
Hethersett Norfk 70 H11
Hethersgill Cumb 98 F5
Hetherside Cumb 98 E5
Hetherson Green Ches W 63 N2
Hethpool Nthumb 108 E4
Hett Dur 100 H11
Hetton N York 84 E3
Hetton-le-Hole Sundld 101 J8
Hetton Steads Nthumb 108 G3
Heugh Nthumb 100 E4
Heughhead Abers 132 B2
Heugh Head Border 117 K9
Heveningham Suffk 59 L6
Hever Kent 15 N2
Heversham Cumb 89 M10
Hevingham Norfk 71 J8
Hewas Water Cnwll 3 N4
Hewelsfield Gloucs 40 H11
Hewenden C Brad 84 G8
Hewish N Som 28 E9
Hewish Somset 10 C3
Hewood Dorset 9 Q4
Hexham Nthumb 99 P5
Hextable Kent 33 P8
Hexthorpe Donc 78 F3
Hexton Herts 44 G5
Hexworthy Cnwll 7 L8
Hexworthy Devon 8 C10
Hey Lancs 84 C6
Heybridge Essex 34 B3
Heybridge Essex 46 E10
Heybridge Basin Essex 46 F10
Heybrook Bay Devon 4 H7
Heydon Cambs 45 N4
Heydon Norfk 70 G7
Heydour Lincs 67 P4
Hey Houses Lancs 82 H9
Heylipoll Ag & B 118 D4
Heylor Shet 147 h4
Heyrod Tamesd 76 H4
Heysham Lancs 83 K3
Heyshaw N York 85 J3
Heyshott W Susx 14 C7
Heyside Oldham 76 G2
Heytesbury Wilts 23 K5
Heythrop Oxon 42 H6
Heywood Rochdl 76 F2
Heywood Wilts 23 J3
Hibaldstow N Linc 79 N3
Hickleton Donc 78 D3
Hickling Norfk 71 N7
Hickling Notts 66 H6
Hickling Green Norfk 71 N7
Hickling Heath Norfk 71 M7
Hickling Pastures Notts 66 H6
Hickmans Green Kent 35 J10
Hicks Forstal Kent 35 L9
Hickstead W Susx 15 K7
Hidcote Bartrim Gloucs 42 E3
Hidcote Boyce Gloucs 42 E3
High Ackworth Wakefd 85 N11
Higham Barns 77 P2
Higham Derbys 78 C12
Higham Kent 15 R1
Higham Kent 34 C8
Higham Lancs 84 B8
Higham Suffk 47 J4
Higham Suffk 57 P7
Higham Dykes Nthumb 100 E3
Higham Ferrers Nhants 55 N7
Higham Gobion C Beds 44 G5
Higham Hill Gt Lon 33 L4
Higham on the Hill Leics 54 C2
Highampton Devon 7 P4
Highams Park Gt Lon 33 M4
High Angerton Nthumb 100 E1
High Ardwell D & G 94 F9
High Auldgirth D & G 106 B12
High Bankhill Cumb 98 H10
High Beach Essex 33 M3
High Bentham N York 83 P1
High Bewaldeth Cumb 97 P11
High Bickington Devon 19 L9
High Biggins Cumb 89 P11
High Birkwith N York 90 C11
High Blantyre S Lans 114 C10
High Bonnybridge Falk 114 E5
High Borrans Cumb 89 L6
High Bradley N York 84 F5
High Bray Devon 19 N6
Highbridge Hants 24 H9
Highbridge Somset 21 M4
Highbrook W Susx 15 L5
High Brooms Kent 15 Q2
High Bullen Devon 19 K9
Highburton Kirk 77 M1
Highbury Gt Lon 33 K5
Highbury Somset 22 F3
High Buston Nthumb 109 L8
High Callerton Nthumb 100 F4
High Casterton Cumb 89 Q11
High Catton E R Yk 86 D4
Highclere Hants 31 J10
Highcliffe BCP 12 C6
High Close Dur 91 K4
High Cogges Oxon 42 H10
High Common Norfk 70 E11
High Coniscliffe Darltn 91 L4
High Crosby Cumb 98 F6
High Cross Cnwll 3 J8
High Cross E Ayrs 113 M12
High Cross Hants 25 M8
High Cross Herts 45 L8
Highcross Lancs 82 H7
High Cross W Susx 15 J7
High Cross Warwks 53 M7
High Drummore D & G 94 G11
High Dubmire Sundld 101 J8
High Easter Essex 46 A8
High Eggborough N York 86 A11
High Ellington N York 91 K10
Higher Alham Somset 22 F5
Higher Ansty Dorset 11 J4
Higher Ballam Lancs 83 J9
Higher Bartle Lancs 83 L8
Higher Berry End C Beds 44 D5
Higher Bockhampton Dorset 10 H6
Higher Brixham Torbay 5 Q6
Higher Burrowton Devon 9 J5
Higher Burwardsley Ches W 75 N12
High Ercall Wrekin 63 Q8
Higher Chillington Somset 10 B3
Higher Clovelly Devon 18 F8
Highercombe Somset 20 D7
Higher Coombe Dorset 10 E6
Higher Disley Ches E 76 H7
Higher Folds Wigan 76 C4
Higherford Lancs 84 C7
Higher Gabwell Devon 5 Q3
Higher Halstock Leigh Dorset 10 D3
Higher Harpers Lancs 84 B7
Higher Heysham Lancs 83 K3
Higher Hurdsfield Ches E 76 H8
Higher Irlam Salfd 76 D5
Higher Kingcombe Dorset 10 E5
Higher Kinnerton Flints 75 K11
Higher Marston Ches W 76 C8
Higher Muddiford Devon 19 L6
Higher Nyland Dorset 22 G9
Higher Ogden Rochdl 76 H1
Higher Pentire Cnwll 2 G9
Higher Penwortham Lancs 83 L9
Higher Prestacott Devon 7 M5
Higher Studfold N York 84 B1
Higher Town Cnwll 3 K5
Higher Town Cnwll 3 N2
Higher Town IoS 2 b1
Higher Tregantle Cnwll 4 F6
Higher Walton Lancs 83 N9
Higher Walton Warrtn 75 Q6
Higher Wambrook Somset 9 P3
Higher Waterston Dorset 10 H5
Higher Whatcombe Dorset 11 K4
Higher Wheelton Lancs 83 N10
Higher Whitley Ches W 76 B7
Higher Wincham Ches W 76 C8
Higher Wraxhall Dorset 10 E4
Higher Wych Ches W 63 N3
High Etherley Dur 91 K1
High Ferry Lincs 68 G2
Highfield E R Yk 86 D8
Highfield Gatesd 100 F6
Highfield N Ayrs 113 L11
Highfields Donc 78 E2
Highfields Caldecote Cambs 56 G9
High Flats Kirk 77 N2
High Garrett Essex 46 D6
Highgate E Susx 15 M4
Highgate Gt Lon 33 K5
Highgate Kent 16 D5
High Grange Dur 100 F12
High Grantley N York 85 K1
High Green Cumb 89 L6
High Green Kirk 85 J12
High Green Norfk 58 H3
High Green Norfk 70 H11
High Green Sheff 77 Q4
High Green Shrops 52 C4
High Green Suffk 58 C8
High Green Worcs 41 P3
Highgreen Manor Nthumb 108 C11
High Halden Kent 16 F3
High Halstow Medway 34 D7
High Ham Somset 21 P7
High Harrington Cumb 88 D2
High Harrogate N York 85 L4
High Haswell Dur 101 K9
High Hatton Shrops 63 Q7
High Hauxley Nthumb 109 M9
High Hawsker N York 93 J5
High Hesket Cumb 98 F9
High Hoyland Barns 77 P2
High Hunsley E R Yk 86 H8
High Hurstwood E Susx 15 P5
High Hutton N York 86 D2
High Ireby Cumb 97 P10
High Kelling Norfk 70 G4
High Kilburn N York 92 B10
High Killerby N York 93 L10
High Knipe Cumb 89 N3
High Lands Dur 91 J2
Highlane Ches E 76 G10
Highlane Derbys 78 C7
High Lane Stockp 76 H6
High Lanes Cnwll 2 F7
High Laver Essex 45 P10
Highlaws Cumb 97 N8
Highleadon Gloucs 41 M7
High Legh Ches E 76 C7
Highleigh W Susx 13 P5
High Leven S on T 91 Q4
Highley Shrops 52 D4
High Littleton BaNES 29 K10
High Lorton Cumb 88 F2
High Marishes N York 92 G11
High Marnham Notts 79 K9
High Melton Donc 78 E3
High Mickley Nthumb 100 D6
Highmoor Cumb 98 B8
Highmoor Oxon 31 P5
Highmoor Cross Oxon 31 P6
Highmoor Hill Mons 28 F4
High Moorsley Sundld 101 J9
Highnam Gloucs 41 M7
High Newport Sundld 101 K7
High Newton Cumb 89 L10
High Newton-by-the-Sea Nthumb 109 L5
High Nibthwaite Cumb 89 J9
High Offley Staffs 64 E7
High Ongar Essex 45 Q11
High Onn Staffs 64 F9
High Park Corner Essex 47 J7
High Pennyvenie E Ayrs 105 J8
High Pittington Dur 101 J9
High Post Wilts 23 P6
Highridge N Som 28 H9
High Roding Essex 45 R8
High Row Cumb 89 K2
High Row Cumb 98 D11
High Salter Lancs 83 N3
High Salvington W Susx 14 G9
High Scales Cumb 97 N9
High Seaton Cumb 97 L12
High Shaw N York 90 E8
High Side Cumb 97 P12
High Spen Gatesd 100 E6
Highstead Kent 35 M9
Highsted Kent 34 F10
High Stoop Dur 100 E10
High Street Cnwll 3 N4
High Street Kent 16 D5
High Street Suffk 35 K10
High Street Suffk 47 Q5
High Street Suffk 59 N6
High Street Suffk 59 N9
Highstreet Green Essex 46 D5
Highstreet Green Surrey 14 D4
Hightae D & G 97 M3
Highter's Heath Birm 53 K5
High Throston Hartpl 101 M11
Hightown Ches E 76 G11
Hightown Hants 12 C4
Hightown Sefton 75 J3
High Town Staffs 65 J10
Hightown Green Suffk 58 E9
High Toynton Lincs 80 E10
High Trewhitt Nthumb 108 G8
High Urpeth Dur 100 G7
High Valleyfield Fife 114 H4
High Warden Nthumb 99 P5
Highway Herefs 51 M10
Highway Wilts 30 B7
Highweek Devon 8 F10
High Westwood Dur 100 E7
Highwood Essex 46 B11
Highwood Staffs 65 L6
Highwood Hill Gt Lon 33 J4
High Woolaston Gloucs 29 J2
High Worsall N York 91 P5
Highworth Swindn 30 E4
High Wray Cumb 89 K7
High Wych Herts 45 N9
High Wycombe Bucks 32 B4
Hilborough Norfk 70 B12
Hilcote Derbys 78 D12
Hilcott Wilts 30 C10
Hildenborough Kent 15 Q1
Hilden Park Kent 15 Q1
Hildersham Cambs 57 K11
Hilderstone Staffs 64 H5
Hilderthorpe E R Yk 87 M2
Hilfield Dorset 10 G4
Hilgay Norfk 57 M1
Hill S Glos 29 K3
Hill Warwks 54 D7
Hillam N York 85 Q9
Hillbeck Cumb 90 C4
Hillborough Kent 35 M8
Hill Brow Hants 25 N8
Hillbutts Dorset 11 N4
Hill Chorlton Staffs 64 E4
Hillcliffelane Derbys 65 P3
Hill Common Norfk 71 N7
Hill Common Somset 21 J8
Hill Deverill Wilts 23 J5
Hilldyke Lincs 68 G3
Hill End Dur 100 C11
Hill End Fife 115 J2
Hillend Fife 115 L4
Hill End Gloucs 41 P4
Hillend Mdloth 115 N8
Hillend N Lans 114 E8
Hillend Swans 26 B4
Hillersland Gloucs 40 H9
Hillerton Devon 8 D5
Hillesden Bucks 43 P6
Hillesley Gloucs 29 M4
Hillfarrance Somset 21 J8
Hill Green Kent 34 E10
Hillgrove W Susx 14 D5
Hillhampton Herefs 41 J2
Hillhead Abers 140 F8
Hillhead Devon 5 Q6
Hill Head Hants 13 J4
Hillhead S Lans 106 C2
Hillhead of Cocklaw Abers 141 Q7
Hilliard's Cross Staffs 65 M10
Hilliclay Highld 151 L4
Hillingdon Gt Lon 32 F6
Hillington C Glas 113 P8
Hillington Norfk 69 N7
Hillis Corner IoW 12 H6
Hillmorton Warwks 54 E6
Hillock Vale Lancs 84 A9
Hill of Beath Fife 115 L3
Hill of Fearn Highld 146 E9
Hillowton D & G 96 F5
Hillpool Worcs 52 G5
Hillpound Hants 25 K10
Hill Ridware Staffs 65 K8
Hillside Abers 133 M5
Hillside Angus 132 H12
Hillside Devon 5 L4
Hill Side Kirk 85 J11
Hill Side Worcs 52 D8
Hills Town Derbys 78 D9
Hillstreet Hants 24 E10
Hillswick Shet 147 h4
Hill Top Dur 90 G2
Hill Top Hants 12 F4
Hill Top Kirk 77 K1
Hill Top Rothm 78 C5
Hill Top Sandw 53 J2
Hill Top Wakefd 85 M12
Hillwell Shet 147 i9
Hilmarton Wilts 30 B8
Hilperton Wilts 29 P10
Hilperton Marsh Wilts 29 P10
Hilsea C Port 13 L4
Hilston E R Yk 87 P8
Hiltingbury Hants 24 G9
Hilton Border 117 K11
Hilton Cambs 56 F7
Hilton Cumb 90 B3
Hilton Derbys 65 N6
Hilton Dorset 11 J4
Hilton Dur 91 K2
Hilton S on T 91 Q4
Hilton Shrops 52 E1
Hilton of Cadboll Highld 146 F10
Hilton Park Services Staffs 64 H11
Himbleton Worcs 52 H9
Himley Staffs 52 G2
Hincaster Cumb 89 N10
Hinchley Wood Surrey 32 H9
Hinckley Leics 54 C2
Hinderclay Suffk 58 F5
Hinderwell N York 92 G4
Hindford Shrops 63 K5
Hindhead Surrey 14 C4
Hindhead Tunnel Surrey 14 C4
Hindle Fold Lancs 83 Q8
Hindley Nthumb 100 D6
Hindley Wigan 76 B3
Hindley Green Wigan 76 C3
Hindlip Worcs 52 G9
Hindolveston Norfk 70 F6
Hindon Wilts 23 K7
Hindringham Norfk 70 E5
Hingham Norfk 70 F11
Hinksford Staffs 52 F3
Hinstock Shrops 64 C7
Hintlesham Suffk 47 K3
Hinton Gloucs 41 K11
Hinton Hants 12 C6
Hinton Herefs 40 D4
Hinton Nhants 54 E10
Hinton S Glos 29 L7
Hinton Shrops 52 C4
Hinton Shrops 63 L10
Hinton Admiral Hants 12 C5
Hinton Ampner Hants 25 K8
Hinton Blewett BaNES 29 J11
Hinton Charterhouse BaNES 29 M10
Hinton Cross Worcs 42 B4
Hinton-in-the-Hedges Nhants 43 M4
Hinton Marsh Hants 25 K8
Hinton Martell Dorset 11 N3
Hinton on the Green Worcs 42 B4
Hinton Parva Swindn 30 F6
Hinton St George Somset 21 P11
Hinton St Mary Dorset 22 H10
Hinton Waldrist Oxon 30 H2
Hints Shrops 51 Q6
Hints Staffs 65 M11
Hinwick Bed 55 M8
Hinxhill Kent 17 J2
Hinxton Cambs 45 P3
Hinxworth Herts 45 J4
Hipperholme Calder 84 H10
Hipsburn Nthumb 109 L7
Hipswell N York 91 K7
Hirn Abers 132 H4
Hirnant Powys 62 E7
Hirst Nthumb 109 M12
Hirst Courtney N York 86 B10
Hirwaen Denbgs 74 F11
Hirwaun Rhondd 39 M10
Hiscott Devon 19 K8
Histon Cambs 56 H8
Hitcham Suffk 58 E10
Hitcham Causeway Suffk 58 E10
Hitcham Street Suffk 58 E10
Hitchin Herts 44 H6
Hither Green Gt Lon 33 M7
Hittisleigh Devon 8 E5
Hive E R Yk 86 F9
Hixon Staffs 65 J7
Hoaden Kent 35 N10
Hoar Cross Staffs 65 L7
Hoarwithy Herefs 40 H6
Hoath Kent 35 M9
Hoathly Kent 16 B3
Hobarris Shrops 51 K5
Hobbles Green Suffk 57 N10
Hobbs Cross Essex 33 N2
Hobbs Cross Essex 45 N9
Hobkirk Border 107 P7
Hobland Hall Norfk 71 P11
Hobsick Notts 66 D2
Hobson Dur 100 F7
Hoby Leics 66 H8
Hoccombe Somset 20 H7
Hockering Norfk 70 G9
Hockerton Notts 79 J12
Hockley Ches E 76 H7
Hockley Covtry 53 P5
Hockley Essex 34 E4
Hockley Staffs 65 N12
Hockley Heath Solhll 53 M6
Hockliffe C Beds 44 D6
Hockwold cum Wilton Norfk 57 P3
Hockworthy Devon 20 G9
Hoddesdon Herts 45 L10
Hoddlesden Bl w D 83 Q10
Hoddom Cross D & G 97 N3
Hoddom Mains D & G 97 N4
Hodgehill Ches E 76 F9
Hodgeston Pembks 37 K10
Hodnet Shrops 63 Q6
Hodsock Notts 78 G6
Hodsoll Street Kent 34 A9
Hodson Swindn 30 E6
Hodthorpe Derbys 78 E8
Hoe Hants 25 J10
Hoe Norfk 70 E9
Hoe Benham W Berk 31 J8
Hoe Gate Hants 25 K10
Hoff Cumb 89 R3
Hogben's Hill Kent 35 J11
Hoggards Green Suffk 58 C9
Hoggeston Bucks 44 A7
Hoggrill's End Warwks 53 N2
Hog Hill E Susx 16 F7
Hoghton Lancs 83 N9
Hoghton Bottoms Lancs 83 N10
Hognaston Derbys 65 N2
Hogsthorpe Lincs 81 K9
Holbeach Lincs 68 G7
Holbeach Bank Lincs 68 G7
Holbeach Clough Lincs 68 G7
Holbeach Drove Lincs 68 F9
Holbeach Hurn Lincs 68 G7
Holbeach St Johns Lincs 68 G8
Holbeach St Mark's Lincs 68 G6
Holbeach St Matthew Lincs 68 H6
Holbeck Notts 78 E9
Holbeck Woodhouse Notts 78 F9
Holberrow Green Worcs 53 J9
Holbeton Devon 5 K6
Holborn Gt Lon 33 K6
Holborough Kent 34 C10
Holbrook Derbys 66 B3
Holbrook Sheff 78 D7
Holbrook Suffk 47 L4
Holbrook Moor Derbys 66 B3
Holbrooks Covtry 53 Q4
Holburn Nthumb 108 G3
Holbury Hants 12 G4
Holcombe Devon 8 H9
Holcombe Somset 22 F3
Holcombe Rogus Devon 20 G9
Holcot Nhants 55 K7
Holden Lancs 84 B5
Holdenby Nhants 54 H7
Holden Gate Calder 84 D10
Holder's Green Essex 46 B6
Holdgate Shrops 51 P3
Holdingham Lincs 67 Q3
Holditch Dorset 9 Q4
Holdsworth Calder 84 G9
Holehouse Derbys 77 J5
Hole-in-the-Wall Herefs 41 J6
Holemoor Devon 7 M4
Hole Street W Susx 14 G8
Holford Somset 21 J5
Holgate C York 86 A5
Holker Cumb 89 K11
Holkham Norfk 70 C3
Hollacombe Devon 7 M4
Holland Fen Lincs 68 E2
Holland Lees Lancs 75 N2
Holland-on-Sea Essex 47 M8
Hollandstoun Ork 147 f1
Hollee D & G 98 B4
Hollesley Suffk 47 P3
Hollicombe Torbay 5 Q4
Hollingbourne Kent 34 E11
Hollingbury Br & H 15 K9
Hollingdon Bucks 44 C6
Hollingrove E Susx 16 C6
Hollingthorpe Leeds 85 M9
Hollington Derbys 65 N4
Hollington Staffs 65 K4
Hollingworth Tamesd 77 J4
Hollins Bury 76 E2
Hollins Derbys 77 Q9
Hollins Staffs 65 J3
Hollinsclough Staffs 77 K10
Hollins End Sheff 78 C7
Hollins Green Warrtn 76 C5
Hollins Lane Lancs 83 L5
Hollinswood Wrekin 64 D10
Hollinwood Shrops 63 N5
Hollocombe Devon 8 B2
Holloway Derbys 77 Q12
Holloway Gt Lon 33 K5
Holloway Wilts 23 J7
Hollowell Nhants 54 H6
Hollowmoor Heath Ches W 75 N10
Hollows D & G 98 E3
Hollybush Caerph 39 R11
Hollybush E Ayrs 104 G7
Hollybush Herefs 41 M4
Holly End Norfk 69 J11
Holly Green Worcs 41 P3
Hollyhurst Ches E 63 P3
Hollym E R Yk 87 Q10
Hollywood Worcs 53 K5
Holmbridge Kirk 77 L2
Holmbury St Mary Surrey 14 G2
Holmbush Cnwll 3 P4
Holmcroft Staffs 64 G7
Holme Cambs 56 D3
Holme Cumb 89 N11
Holme Kirk 77 L2
Holme N Linc 79 M2
Holme N York 91 N10
Holme Notts 79 K11
Holme Chapel Lancs 84 C9
Holme Green N York 85 Q7
Holme Hale Norfk 70 C10
Holme Lacy Herefs 40 H5
Holme Marsh Herefs 51 K9
Holme next the Sea Norfk 69 N3
Holme on the Wolds E R Yk 86 H6
Holme Pierrepont Notts 66 G4
Holmer Herefs 40 G3
Holmer Green Bucks 32 C3
Holme St Cuthbert Cumb 97 M9
Holmes Chapel Ches E 76 E10
Holmesfield Derbys 77 Q8
Holmes Hill E Susx 15 P8
Holmeswood Lancs 83 K12
Holmethorpe Surrey 33 K12
Holme upon Spalding Moor E R Yk 86 E7
Holmewood Derbys 78 C10
Holmfield Calder 84 G9
Holmfirth Kirk 77 L2
Holmgate Derbys 78 C11
Holmhead E Ayrs 105 K6
Holmpton E R Yk 87 Q10
Holmrook Cumb 88 E7
Holmshurst E Susx 16 B6
Holmside Dur 100 G8
Holmwrangle Cumb 98 G8
Holne Devon 5 L3
Holnest Dorset 10 G3
Holnicote Somset 20 E4
Holsworthy Devon 7 L4
Holsworthy Beacon Devon 7 L3
Holt Dorset 11 P4
Holt Norfk 70 G4
Holt Wilts 29 P10
Holt Worcs 52 F8
Holt Wrexhm 63 L1
Holtby C York 86 C4
Holt End Worcs 53 K7
Holt Fleet Worcs 52 F8
Holt Green Lancs 75 L3
Holt Heath Dorset 11 P4
Holt Heath Worcs 52 F8
Holton Oxon 43 M10
Holton Somset 22 F8
Holton Suffk 59 M5
Holton cum Beckering Lincs 80 C7
Holton Heath Dorset 11 M6
Holton Hill E Susx 16 B6
Holton le Clay Lincs 80 F3
Holton le Moor Lincs 79 Q4
Holton St Mary Suffk 47 J4
Holt Street Kent 35 N12
Holtye E Susx 15 N3
Holway Flints 74 G8
Holwell Dorset 10 H2
Holwell Herts 44 H5
Holwell Leics 67 J7
Holwell Oxon 42 F10
Holwick Dur 90 E1
Holworth Dorset 11 J8
Holybourne Hants 25 M5
Holy Cross Worcs 52 G5
Holyfield Essex 45 M11
Holyhead IoA 72 D7
Holy Island IoA 72 D7
Holy Island Nthumb 109 J1
Holy Island Nthumb 109 J1
Holymoorside Derbys 77 Q10
Holyport W & M 32 C7
Holystone Nthumb 108 F9
Holytown N Lans 114 D9
Holywell C Beds 44 E8
Holywell Cambs 56 G6
Holywell Cnwll 3 J3
Holywell Dorset 10 F4
Holywell Flints 74 G8
Holywell Nthumb 101 J4
Holywell Warwks 53 M7
Holywell Green Calder 84 G11
Holywell Lake Somset 20 H9
Holywell Row Suffk 57 N5
Holywood D & G 97 J2
Holywood Village D & G 97 J2
Homer Shrops 64 B12
Homer Green Sefton 75 K3
Homersfield Suffk 59 K3
Homescales Cumb 89 N9
Hom Green Herefs 41 J7
Homington Wilts 23 P8
Honeyborough Pembks 37 J9
Honeybourne Worcs 42 D3
Honeychurch Devon 8 B4
Honey Hill Kent 35 K10
Honeystreet Wilts 30 C10
Honey Tye Suffk 46 G4
Honiley Warwks 53 N6
Honing Norfk 71 L6
Honingham Norfk 70 G10
Honington Lincs 67 N3
Honington Suffk 58 D6
Honington Warwks 42 F3
Honiton Devon 9 M5
Honley Kirk 77 L1
Honnington Wrekin 64 D9
Hoo Kent 35 N9
Hoobrook Worcs 52 F6
Hood Green Barns 77 P3
Hood Hill Rothm 78 B4
Hooe C Plym 4 H6
Hooe E Susx 16 C8
Hoo End Herts 44 H7
Hoo Green Ches E 76 D7
Hoohill Bpool 82 H7
Hook Cambs 56 H2
Hook Devon 10 B3
Hook E R Yk 86 E10
Hook Gt Lon 32 H9
Hook Hants 12 H4
Hook Hants 25 M3
Hook Pembks 37 J8
Hook Wilts 30 C5
Hook-a-Gate Shrops 63 M10
Hook Bank Worcs 41 N3
Hooke Dorset 10 E5
Hook End Essex 33 Q2
Hookgate Staffs 64 D5
Hook Green Kent 16 B4
Hook Green Kent 33 R8
Hook Norton Oxon 42 H5
Hook Street Gloucs 29 K2
Hook Street Wilts 30 C5
Hookway Devon 8 F5
Hookwood Surrey 15 J2
Hooley Surrey 33 K11
Hooley Bridge Rochdl 76 F1
Hoo Meavy Devon 4 H3
Hoo St Werburgh Medway 34 D8
Hooton Ches W 75 L8
Hooton Levitt Rothm 78 E5
Hooton Pagnell Donc 78 D2
Hooton Roberts Rothm 78 D4
Hopcrofts Holt Oxon 43 K6
Hope Derbys 77 M7
Hope Devon 5 L8
Hope Flints 75 K12
Hope Powys 63 J10
Hope Shrops 63 K11
Hope Staffs 65 L1
Hope Bagot Shrops 51 Q6
Hope Bowdler Shrops 51 N2
Hope End Green Essex 45 Q7
Hopehouse Border 107 J6
Hopeman Moray 147 L11
Hope Mansell Herefs 41 J8
Hopesay Shrops 51 L4
Hopetown Wakefd 85 N10
Hope under Dinmore Herefs 51 N10
Hopgrove C York 86 B4
Hopperton N York 85 N4
Hop Pole Lincs 68 D9
Hopsford Warwks 54 C4
Hopstone Shrops 52 E2
Hopton Derbys 65 P1
Hopton Shrops 63 L8
Hopton Shrops 63 P7
Hopton Staffs 64 H7
Hopton Suffk 58 E5
Hopton Cangeford Shrops 51 P4
Hopton Castle Shrops 51 L5
Hoptonheath Shrops 51 L5
Hopton on Sea Norfk 71 Q12
Hopton Wafers Shrops 52 B5
Hopwas Staffs 65 M11
Hopwood Rochdl 76 F2

Hopwood Worcs...53 J5
Hopwood Park Services
  Worcs...53 J6
Horam E Susx...15 Q7
Horbling Lincs...68 C5
Horbury Wakefd...85 L11
Horcott Gloucs...30 D2
Horden Dur...101 L10
Horderley Shrops...51 L3
Hordle Hants...12 D6
Hordley Shrops...63 L6
Horeb Carmth...38 D10
Horeb Cerdgn...38 B3
Horfield Bristl...29 J7
Horham Suffk...59 J6
Horkesley Heath Essex...46 H5
Horkstow N Linc...87 J11
Horley Oxon...43 J3
Horley Surrey...15 K2
Hornblotton Green
  Somset...22 D6
Hornby Lancs...83 N2
Hornby N York...91 L8
Hornby N York...91 N5
Horncastle Lincs...80 E10
Hornchurch Gt Lon...33 P5
Horncliffe Nthumb...117 K11
Horndean Border...117 K11
Horndean Hants...25 M10
Horndon Devon...7 P8
Horndon on the Hill
  Thurr...34 B6
Horne Surrey...15 L2
Horner Somset...20 D4
Horne Row Essex...46 D10
Horners Green Suffk...46 G3
Horney Common E Susx...15 N6
Horn Hill Bucks...32 E4
Horning Norfk...71 L8
Horninghold Leics...55 K1
Horninglow Staffs...65 N7
Horningsea Cambs...57 J8
Horningsham Wilts...22 H5
Horningtoft Norfk...70 D7
Horningtops Cnwll...4 D6
Hornsbury Somset...9 Q3
Hornsby Cumb...98 G8
Hornsbygate Cumb...98 G8
Horns Cross Devon...18 H6
Horns Cross E Susx...16 E6
Hornsea E R Yk...87 N6
Hornsey Gt Lon...33 K4
Horn's Green Gt Lon...33 N10
Horn Street Kent...17 L4
Hornton Oxon...42 H3
Horpit Swindn...30 E5
Horrabridge Devon...4 H3
Horringer Suffk...58 B8
Horringford IoW...13 J7
Horrocks Fold Bolton...76 C1
Horrocksford Lancs...83 R6
Horsacott Devon...7 M9
Horsebridge Devon...7 M9
Horsebridge E Susx...15 Q8
Horsebridge Hants...24 E7
Horsebridge Shrops...63 L11
Horsebridge Staffs...64 H1
Horsebrook Staffs...64 G10
Horsecastle N Som...28 F9
Horsedown Cnwll...2 F7
Horsehay Wrekin...64 C10
Horseheath Cambs...45 R2
Horsehouse N York...90 H10
Horsell Surrey...32 E10
Horseman's Green
  Wrexhm...63 M4
Horsenden Bucks...43 R11
Horsey Norfk...71 P7
Horsey Somset...21 M5
Horsey Corner Norfk...71 N7
Horsford Norfk...71 J9
Horsforth Leeds...85 K7
Horsham W Susx...14 H5
Horsham Worcs...52 D9
Horsham St Faith Norfk...71 J9
Horsington Lincs...80 D10
Horsington Somset...22 F8
Horsley Derbys...66 B3
Horsley Gloucs...29 N3
Horsley Nthumb...100 E5
Horsley Nthumb...108 D10
Horsley Cross Essex...47 K6
Horsleycross Street
  Essex...47 K6
Horsley-Gate Derbys...77 P8
Horsleyhill Border...107 N6
Horsley's Green Bucks...31 R3
Horsley Woodhouse
  Derbys...66 C3
Horsmonden Kent...16 C3
Horspath Oxon...43 M10
Horstead Norfk...71 K8
Horsted Keynes W Susx...15 M5
Horton Bucks...44 C8
Horton Dorset...11 P3
Horton Lancs...84 C5
Horton Nhants...55 K9
Horton S Glos...29 M5
Horton Shrops...63 N6
Horton Somset...21 M10
Horton Staffs...76 H12
Horton Surrey...32 H10
Horton Swans...26 C5
Horton W & M...32 E7
Horton Wilts...30 B9
Horton Wrekin...64 C9
Horton Cross Somset...21 M10
Horton-cum-Studley
  Oxon...43 M9
Horton Green Ches W...63 M2
Horton Heath Hants...24 H10
Horton-in-Ribblesdale
  N York...90 C12
Horton Kirby Kent...33 Q8
Horwich Bolton...76 B1
Horwich End Derbys...77 J7
Horwood Devon...19 K8
Hoscar Lancs...75 M1
Hoscote Border...107 J8
Hose Leics...67 J6
Hosey Hill Kent...33 N11
Hosh P & K...123 L8
Hoswick Shet...147 i9
Hotham E R Yk...86 G8
Hothfield Kent...16 G2
Hoton Leics...66 F7
Hott Nthumb...99 L1
Hough Ches E...64 D2
Hough Ches E...76 F8
Hougham Lincs...67 M3
Hough End Leeds...85 K8
Hough Green Halton...75 M6
Hough-on-the-Hill Lincs...67 M2
Houghton Cambs...56 E6
Houghton Cumb...98 G6
Houghton Hants...24 E7
Houghton Nthumb...100 E5
Houghton Pembks...37 J9
Houghton W Susx...14 E8
Houghton Conquest
  C Beds...44 F3
Houghton Gate Dur...101 H8
Houghton Green E Susx...16 G6
Houghton Green Warrtn...76 B5
Houghton le Side Darltn...91 L2
Houghton-le-Spring
  Sundld...101 J8

Houghton on the Hill
  Leics...66 H11
Houghton Regis C Beds...44 E7
Houghton St Giles Norfk...70 D5
Houlsyke N York...54 F6
Hound Green Hants...31 Q10
Houndslow Border...116 E11
Houndsmoor Somset...20 H8
Houndwood Border...117 J8
Hounslow Gt Lon...32 G7
Househill Highld...138 G5
Houses Hill Kirk...85 J11
Housieside Abers...141 L10
Houston Rens...113 M8
Houstry Highld...151 L9
Houton Ork...147 b5
Hove Br & H...15 K10
Hove Edge Calder...84 H10
Hoveringham Notts...66 H3
Hoveton Norfk...71 L8
Hovingham N York...92 D11
Howbrook Barns...77 Q4
How Caple Herefs...41 J6
Howden E R Yk...86 D9
Howden-le-Wear Dur...100 F11
Howe Highld...151 P4
Howe IoM...102 b7
Howe N York...91 N10
Howe Norfk...71 K12
Howe Bridge Wigan...76 C3
Howegreen Essex...34 E2
Howe Green Essex...46 D11
Howell Lincs...68 C3
How End C Beds...44 E3
Howe of Teuchar Abers...141 J7
Howes D & G...97 P5
How Green Kent...15 P2
How Street Essex...46 C8
Howey Powys...50 E9
Howgate Cumb...88 C2
Howgate Mdloth...115 N9
Howgill Lancs...84 B6
Howick Nthumb...109 L6
Howle Wrekin...64 C7
Howle Hill Herefs...41 J7
Howlett End Essex...45 Q5
Howley Somset...9 P3
Hownam Border...108 C6
Howrigg Cumb...98 D8
Howsham N Linc...79 P3
Howsham N York...86 D3
Howtel Nthumb...108 E3
Howt Green Kent...34 F9
Howton Herefs...40 F6
Howton Cumb...44 G11
How Wood Herts...113 M9
Howwood Rens...113 M9
Hoxa Ork...147 c6
Hoxne Suffk...58 H5
Hoy Ork...147 b5
Hoylake Wirral...74 H6
Hoyland Barns...78 A4
Hoyland Common Barns...78 A4
Hoylandswaine Barns...77 N4
Hoyle W Susx...14 C7
Hoyle Mill Barns...78 B2
Hubberholme N York...90 F11
Hubberston Pembks...36 H9
Hubbert's Bridge Lincs...68 E3
Huby N York...85 K6
Huby N York...85 R2
Huccaby Devon...8 C10
Hucclecote Gloucs...41 P8
Hucking Kent...34 E10
Hucknall Notts...66 E2
Huddersfield Kirk...84 H12
Huddington Worcs...52 H9
Hudnall Herts...44 D9
Hudswell N York...91 K7
Huggate E R Yk...86 G4
Hugglescote Leics...66 C9
Hughenden Valley Bucks...32 B3
Hughley Shrops...51 J1
Hugh Town IoS...2 b2
Huish Devon...19 M9
Huish Wilts...30 D9
Huish Champflower
  Somset...20 G7
Huish Episcopi Somset...21 P8
Hüisinis W Isls...152 d5
Huisinish W Isls...152 d5
Hulcote C Beds...44 D4
Hulcott Nhants...54 H10
Hulcott Bucks...44 B8
Hulham Devon...9 J8
Hulland Derbys...65 N3
Hulland Ward Derbys...65 P3
Hullavington Wilts...29 P6
Hull Bridge E R Yk...87 K7
Hullbridge Essex...34 E3
Hull, Kingston upon
  C KuH...87 K9
Hulme Manch...76 F4
Hulme Staffs...64 H3
Hulme Warrtn...75 Q5
Hulme End Staffs...77 L11
Hulme Walfield Ches E...76 F10
Hulse Heath Ches E...76 D7
Hulton Lane Ends Bolton...76 C3
Hulverstone IoW...12 H7
Hulver Street Norfk...70 D10
Hulver Street Suffk...59 P3
Humber Devon...8 G9
Humber Herefs...51 P9
Humber Bridge N Linc...87 K11
Humberside Airport
  N Linc...80 B2
Humberston NE Lin...80 F3
Humberstone C Leic...66 G12
Humberton N York...85 N1
Humbie E Loth...116 C8
Humbleton E R Yk...87 N8
Humbleton Nthumb...108 E4
Humby Lincs...67 P5
Hume Border...108 A3
Humshaugh Nthumb...99 R4
Huna Highld...151 Q2
Huncoat Lancs...84 B9
Huncote Leics...54 E1
Hundalee Border...107 Q6
Hundall Derbys...78 C8
Hunderthwaite Dur...90 G2
Hundleby Lincs...80 G10
Hundle Houses Lincs...68 E1
Hundleton Pembks...37 J9
Hundon Suffk...57 P11
Hundred End Lancs...83 K10
Hundred House Powys...50 F9
Hungarton Leics...66 H10
Hungerford Hants...23 J11
Hungerford Somset...20 G5
Hungerford W Berk...30 H8
Hungerford Newtown
  W Berk...30 H8
Hunger Hill Bolton...76 C2
Hunger Hill Lancs...75 P1
Hungerstone Herefs...40 F4
Hungerton Lincs...67 L6
Hungryhatton Shrops...64 C7
Hunmanby N York...93 M11
Hunningham Warwks...54 B7
Hunnington Worcs...52 H5
Hunsdon Herts...45 M9
Hunsdonbury Herts...45 M9

Hunsingore N York...85 N4
Hunslet Leeds...85 L9
Hunsonby Cumb...98 H11
Hunstanton Norfk...69 M4
Hunstanworth Dur...99 Q8
Hunsterson Ches E...64 C3
Hunston Suffk...58 E7
Hunston W Susx...13 Q4
Hunston Green Suffk...58 E7
Hunstrete BaNES...29 K10
Hunt End Worcs...53 J8
Hunter's Inn Devon...19 M4
Hunter's Quay Ag & B...112 H5
Huntham Somset...21 M8
Hunthill Lodge Angus...132 D10
Huntingdon Cambs...56 E6
Huntingfield Suffk...59 L6
Huntingford Dorset...22 H7
Huntington C York...86 B4
Huntington Ches W...75 M10
Huntington E Loth...116 C6
Huntington Herefs...40 G3
Huntington Herefs...51 L5
Huntington Staffs...64 H9
Huntingtowerfield P & K...123 Q7
Huntley Gloucs...41 L8
Huntly Abers...140 E8
Hunton Hants...24 H5
Hunton Kent...16 C1
Hunton N York...91 K8
Hunton Bridge Herts...32 F2
Hunt's Corner Norfk...58 F3
Huntscott Somset...20 F4
Hunt's Cross Lpool...75 M6
Hunts Green Bucks...44 C11
Hunts Green Warwks...53 M1
Huntsham Devon...20 F9
Huntshaw Devon...19 K9
Huntington Cross Devon...19 K9
Huntspill Somset...21 L6
Huntworth Somset...21 M6
Hunwick Dur...100 F11
Hunworth Norfk...70 G5
Hurcott Somset...21 N9
Hurdcott Wilts...23 Q6
Hurdsfield Ches E...76 H9
Hurley W & M...32 B5
Hurley Warwks...53 N1
Hurley Bottom W & M...32 B5
Hurley Common Warwks...53 N1
Hurlford E Ayrs...104 H2
Hurlston Green Lancs...75 L1
Hurn BCP...11 Q5
Hurn's End Lincs...68 H2
Hursey Dorset...9 N4
Hursley Hants...24 G8
Hurst Dorset...11 J7
Hurst N York...90 H6
Hurst Somset...21 P9
Hurst Wokham...31 R8
Hurstbourne Priors
  Hants...24 G4
Hurstbourne Tarrant
  Hants...24 F3
Hurst Green E Susx...16 C5
Hurst Green Essex...47 K8
Hurst Green Lancs...83 Q7
Hurst Green Surrey...33 M12
Hurst Hill Dudley...52 H2
Hurstley Herefs...51 K5
Hurstpierpoint W Susx...15 K7
Hurst Wickham W Susx...15 K7
Hurstwood Lancs...84 C9
Hurtiso Ork...147 d5
Hurtmore Surrey...14 D2
Hurworth Burn Dur...101 K11
Hurworth-on-Tees Darltn...91 M5
Hurworth Place Darltn...91 M5
Hury Dur...90 F3
Husbands Bosworth
  Leics...54 G4
Husborne Crawley C Beds...44 D4
Husthwaite N York...92 B11
Hutcherleigh Devon...5 N6
Hut Green N York...85 R10
Huthwaite Notts...78 D11
Hutoft Lincs...81 K8
Hutton Border...117 K10
Hutton Cumb...89 L1
Hutton E R Yk...87 J4
Hutton Essex...34 B3
Hutton Lancs...83 L10
Hutton N Som...28 D10
Hutton Bonville N York...91 M6
Hutton Buscel N York...93 J9
Hutton Conyers N York...91 N12
Hutton Cranswick E R Yk...87 J5
Hutton End Cumb...98 F10
Hutton Henry Dur...101 L11
Hutton-le-Hole N York...92 H8
Hutton Lowcross R & Cl...92 C4
Hutton Magna Dur...91 J4
Hutton Mulgrave N York...92 H5
Hutton Roof Cumb...89 N11
Hutton Roof Cumb...98 D11
Hutton Rudby N York...91 Q5
Hutton Sessay N York...91 Q11
Hutton Wandesley N York...85 Q5
Huxham Devon...8 H5
Huxham Green Somset...22 B6
Huxley Ches W...75 N11
Huyton Knows...75 M5
Hycemoor Cumb...88 D9
Hyde Gloucs...41 P11
Hyde Hants...23 P11
Hyde Tamesd...76 H5
Hyde Heath Bucks...32 D2
Hyde Lea Staffs...64 H8
Hydestile Surrey...14 D2
Hykeham Moor Lincs...79 M10
Hylands House & Park
  Essex...46 B11
Hyndford Bridge S Lans...106 B1
Hynish Ag & B...118 D5
Hyssington Powys...51 J2
Hystfield Gloucs...29 K2
Hythe Hants...12 H4
Hythe Kent...17 L4
Hythe Somset...28 E7
Hythe End W & M...32 E8
Hyton Cumb...88 D9

I

Ibberton Dorset...11 J3
Ible Derbys...77 N12
Ibsley Hants...12 B3
Ibstock Leics...66 C10
Ibstone Bucks...31 Q4
Ibthorpe Hants...24 F3
Iburndale N York...92 H5
Ibworth Hants...24 H3
Icelton N Som...28 E9
Ichrachan Ag & B...121 J4
Ickburgh Norfk...57 R2
Ickenham Gt Lon...32 F5
Ickford Bucks...43 P10
Ickham Kent...35 M10
Ickleford Herts...44 H5
Icklesham E Susx...16 F7
Ickleton Cambs...45 N3
Icklingham Suffk...57 R5

Ickornshaw N York...84 E6
Ickwell Green C Beds...44 G3
Icomb Gloucs...42 E7
Idbury Oxon...42 F8
Iddesleigh Devon...7 L3
Ide Devon...8 G6
Ideford Devon...8 H9
Ide Hill Kent...33 N12
Iden E Susx...16 G6
Iden Green Kent...16 D3
Iden Green Kent...16 E3
Idle C Brad...85 J7
Idless Cnwll...3 K5
Idlicote Warwks...42 G3
Idmiston Wilts...24 C6
Idole Carmth...38 D8
Idridgehay Derbys...65 P2
Idrigill Highld...134 G2
Idstone Oxon...30 F5
Iffley Oxon...43 L11
Ifield W Susx...15 J3
Ifold W Susx...14 E4
Iford BCP...12 B6
Iford E Susx...15 M9
Ifton Heath Shrops...63 K5
Ightfield Shrops...63 Q4
Ightham Kent...33 Q11
Iken Suffk...59 N9
Ilam Staffs...65 L2
Ilchester Somset...22 C9
Ilderton Nthumb...108 G5
Ilford Gt Lon...33 N5
Ilford Somset...21 N10
Ilfracombe Devon...19 K4
Ilkeston Derbys...66 D3
Ilketshall St Andrew
  Suffk...59 M3
Ilketshall St John Suffk...59 M3
Ilketshall St Lawrence
  Suffk...59 M4
Ilketshall St Margaret
  Suffk...59 L4
Ilkley C Brad...84 H6
Illand Cnwll...7 K9
Illey Dudley...52 H4
Illidge Green Ches E...76 E11
Illingworth Calder...84 G9
Illogan Cnwll...2 G6
Illston on the Hill Leics...66 H12
Ilmer Bucks...43 Q10
Ilmington Warwks...42 F3
Ilminster Somset...21 N10
Ilsington Devon...8 D9
Ilsington Dorset...11 J6
Ilston Swans...26 E4
Ilton N York...91 K11
Ilton Somset...21 M10
Imachar N Ayrs...103 M2
Immingham NE Lin...87 M12
Immingham Dock NE Lin...87 M12
Impington Cambs...56 H8
Ince Ches W...75 M8
Ince Blundell Sefton...75 K3
Ince-in-Makerfield
  Wigan...75 Q3
Inchbae Lodge Hotel
  Highld...145 K11
Inchbare Angus...132 F11
Inchberry Moray...139 P5
Incheril Highld...136 E3
Inchinnan Rens...113 P7
Inchlaggan Highld...128 G4
Inchmichael P & K...124 E8
Inchmore Highld...137 P7
Inchnadamph Highld...148 F12
Inchture P & K...124 F7
Inchyra P & K...124 D8
Indian Queens Cnwll...3 M4
Ingatestone Essex...34 B2
Ingbirchworth Barns...77 N3
Ingerthorpe N York...85 L2
Ingestre Staffs...64 H7
Ingham Lincs...79 N7
Ingham Norfk...71 M7
Ingham Suffk...58 C6
Ingham Corner Norfk...71 M7
Ingleborough Norfk...69 J9
Ingleby Derbys...65 Q7
Ingleby Arncliffe N York...91 Q6
Ingleby Barwick S on T...91 Q4
Ingleby Cross N York...91 Q6
Ingleby Greenhow N York...92 C5
Ingleigh Green Devon...8 B2
Inglesbatch BaNES...29 L10
Inglesham Swindn...30 E3
Ingleton Dur...91 K3
Ingleton N York...90 C9
Inglewhite Lancs...83 M7
Ingmanthorpe N York...85 N4
Ingoe Nthumb...100 D3
Ingol Lancs...83 L9
Ingoldisthorpe Norfk...69 N5
Ingoldmells Lincs...81 K10
Ingoldsby Lincs...67 P6
Ingram Nthumb...108 H4
Ingrave Essex...34 A4
Ingrow C Brad...84 F7
Ings Cumb...89 M7
Ingst S Glos...29 J5
Ingthorpe Rutlnd...67 N10
Ingworth Norfk...71 J6
Inkberrow Worcs...53 K9
Inkerman Dur...100 E10
Inkersall Green Derbys...78 C9
Inkhorn Abers...141 M8
Inkpen W Berk...31 J9
Inkstack Highld...151 N3
Inmarsh Wilts...29 Q10
Innellan Ag & B...112 H7
Innerleithen Border...107 J2
Innerleven Fife...115 Q1
Innermessan D & G...94 F6
Innerwick E Loth...116 H6
Innesmill Moray...139 P3
Innsworth Gloucs...41 P7
Insch Abers...140 F10
Insh Highld...130 E4
Inshes Highld...138 D7
Inskip Lancs...83 L7
Inskip Moss Side Lancs...83 K7
Instow Devon...19 J6
Insworke Cnwll...4 F6
Intake Sheff...78 B3
Inver Abers...131 N6
Inver Highld...146 F8
Inver P & K...123 P4
Inverallochy Abers...141 P3
Inveran Highld...145 N5
Inveraray Ag & B...121 L11
Inverarish Highld...135 K8
Inverarity Angus...124 H2
Inverarnan Stirlg...121 Q9
Inverasdale Highld...143 L8
Inverbeg Ag & B...113 L2
Inverbervie Abers...133 K10
Inverboyndie Abers...141 J3
Invercreran Lodge Ag & B...121 J3
Inverdruie Highld...130 D2
Inveresk E Loth...115 Q7
Inveresragan Ag & B...121 J3
Inverey Abers...131 K6
Inverfarigaig Highld...137 Q2
Inverfolla Ag & B...120 H4

Invergarry Highld...129 K4
Invergeldie P & K...123 J7
Invergloy Highld...129 J7
Invergordon Highld...138 C2
Invergowrie P & K...124 G7
Inverguseran Highld...127 N3
Inverhadden P & K...122 H1
Inverherive Highld...121 Q7
Inverie Highld...127 N4
Inverinan Ag & B...121 J8
Inverinate Highld...136 C11
Inverkeilor Angus...125 K3
Inverkeithing Fife...115 L5
Inverkeithny Abers...140 F6
Inverkip Inver...113 J7
Inverkirkaig Highld...148 D1
Inverlael Highld...144 H4
Inverliever Lodge Ag & B...120 G11
Inverlochy Ag & B...121 N7
Invermark Angus...132 E9
Invermoriston Highld...129 M1
Invernaver Highld...150 C4
Inverneill Ag & B...112 B1
Inverness Highld...138 C7
Inverness Airport Highld...138 E5
Invernettie Abers...141 Q7
Invernoaden Ag & B...112 G2
Inveroran Hotel Ag & B...121 P4
Inverquharity Angus...124 H1
Inverquhomery Abers...141 N6
Inverroy Highld...129 J7
Inversanda Highld...128 C12
Invershiel Highld...136 C12
Invershin Highld...145 N6
Invershore Highld...151 N9
Inversnaid Hotel Stirlg...122 B11
Inverugie Abers...141 Q6
Inveruglas Ag & B...121 Q11
Inveruglass Highld...130 E4
Inverurie Abers...141 J11
Inwardleigh Devon...7 Q5
Inworth Essex...46 F8
Iochdar W Isls...152 b9
Iping W Susx...14 C6
iPort Logistics Park Donc...78 F4
Ipplepen Devon...5 Q4
Ipsden Oxon...31 N5
Ipstones Staffs...65 J2
Ipswich Suffk...47 L3
Irby Wirral...75 J6
Irby in the Marsh Lincs...81 J11
Irby upon Humber NE Lin...80 D3
Irchester Nhants...55 M7
Ireby Cumb...97 P10
Ireby Lancs...89 Q11
Ireland C Beds...44 G3
Ireleth Cumb...88 H11
Ireshopeburn Dur...99 N10
Ireton Wood Derbys...65 P3
Irlam Salfd...76 D5
Irnham Lincs...67 P7
Iron Acton S Glos...29 L5
Iron Bridge Cambs...57 J1
Ironbridge Wrekin...64 C11
Ironbridge Gorge Wrekin...64 C11
Iron Cross Warwks...53 K10
Ironmacannie D & G...96 D3
Irons Bottom Surrey...15 J2
Ironville Derbys...66 C2
Irstead Norfk...71 M8
Irthington Cumb...98 G6
Irthlingborough Nhants...55 N6
Irton N York...93 K10
Irvine N Ayrs...104 F2
Isauld Highld...150 H4
Isbister Shet...147 i3
Isbister Shet...147 k5
Isfield E Susx...15 N7
Isham Nhants...55 M6
Isington Hants...25 N5
Islandpool Worcs...52 F4
Islay Ag & B...111 J10
Islay Airport Ag & B...110 H11
Isle Abbotts Somset...21 M9
Isle Brewers Somset...21 N9
Isleham Cambs...57 M6
Isle of Dogs Gt Lon...33 M6
Isle of Grain Medway...34 F7
Isle of Lewis W Isls...152 f3
Isle of Man IoM...102 e4
Isle of Man Ronaldsway
  Airport IoM...102 c7
Isle of Mull Ag & B...119 Q6
Isle of Purbeck Dorset...11 P7
Isle of Sheppey Kent...34 H8
Isle of Skye Highld...134 G8
Isle of Thanet Kent...35 P9
Isle of Walney Cumb...88 G6
Isle of Whithorn D & G...95 N11
Isle of Wight IoW...13 J7
Isleornsay Highld...127 M2
Isles of Scilly IoS...2 b2
Isles of Scilly St Mary's
  Airport IoS...2 b2
Islesteps D & G...97 K4
Islet Village Guern...12 c1
Isleworth Gt Lon...32 H7
Isley Walton Leics...66 C7
Islibhig W Isls...152 d3
Islington Gt Lon...33 K5
Islington Nhants...55 L9
Islip Nhants...55 N6
Islip Oxon...43 L9
Islivig W Isls...152 d3
Isombridge Wrekin...63 Q9
Istead Rise Kent...34 B8
Itchen Abbas Hants...25 J7
Itchen Stoke Hants...25 J7
Itchingfield W Susx...14 G5
Itchington S Glos...29 K5
Itteringham Norfk...70 H6
Itton Devon...7 M11
Itton Mons...28 G5
Itton Common Mons...28 G5
Ivegill Cumb...98 E9
Ivelet N York...90 F7
Iver Bucks...32 E6
Iver Heath Bucks...32 E6
Iveston Dur...100 E8
Ivinghoe Bucks...44 D8
Ivinghoe Aston Bucks...44 D8
Ivington Herefs...51 N9
Ivington Green Herefs...51 N9
Ivybridge Devon...5 M8
Ivychurch Kent...17 J5
Ivy Cross Dorset...23 J8
Ivy Hatch Kent...33 Q11
Ivy Todd Norfk...70 C10
Iwade Kent...34 G9
Iwerne Courtney Dorset...23 J10
Iwerne Minster Dorset...23 J10
Ixworth Suffk...58 D6
Ixworth Thorpe Suffk...58 D6

J

Jack Green Lancs...83 N10
Jack Hill N York...85 J5
Jack-in-the-Green
  Devon...9 J6
Jack's Bush Hants...24 D6
Jacksdale Notts...66 C2
Jackson Bridge Kirk...77 M2
Jackton S Lans...113 Q10
Jacobstow Cnwll...6 G11

Jacobstowe Devon...8 B4
Jacobs Well Surrey...32 E11
Jameston Pembks...37 L11
Jamestown Highld...137 N4
Jamestown W Duns...113 M5
Janetstown Highld...151 M10
Janetstown Highld...151 Q6
Jardine Hall D & G...106 E12
Jarrow S Tyne...101 J5
Jarvis Brook E Susx...15 P5
Jasper's Green Essex...46 C6
Jawcraig Falk...114 F6
Jaywick Essex...47 L9
Jealott's Hill Br For...32 B7
Jedburgh Border...107 Q6
Jeffreston Pembks...37 L9
Jemimaville Highld...138 D4
Jerbourg Guern...12 c3
Jersey Jersey...13 c2
Jersey Airport Jersey...13 b2
Jersey Marine Neath...26 H3
Jerusalem Lincs...79 M9
Jesmond N u Ty...100 H5
Jevington E Susx...15 Q10
Jingle Street Mons...40 G9
Jockey End Herts...44 D9
Jodrell Bank Ches E...76 E9
Jodrell Bank Ches E...76 E9
Johnby Cumb...98 E11
John Lennon Airport
  Lpool...75 M7
John o' Groats Highld...151 Q2
Johns Cross E Susx...16 D6
Johnshaven Abers...133 J11
Johnson Street Norfk...71 M8
Johnston Pembks...36 H8
Johnstone D & G...106 H9
Johnstone Rens...113 N8
Johnstonebridge D & G...106 E11
Johnstown Carmth...38 D8
Johnstown Wrexhm...63 J3
Joppa C Edin...115 P7
Joppa Cerdgn...49 J7
Joppa S Ayrs...104 G6
Jordans Bucks...32 D4
Jordanston Pembks...36 H4
Jordanthorpe Sheff...78 B7
Joyden's Wood Kent...33 P7
Jubilee Corner Kent...16 E1
Jump Barns...78 C3
Jumper's Town E Susx...15 N4
Juniper Nthumb...99 P6
Juniper Green C Edin...115 M7
Jura Ag & B...111 L4
Jurassic Coast Devon...9 Q7
Jurby IoM...102 e3
Jurston Devon...8 D8

K

Kaber Cumb...90 C4
Kaimend S Lans...114 H12
Kames Ag & B...112 E7
Kames E Ayrs...105 M4
Kea Cnwll...3 K6
Keadby N Linc...79 L11
Keal Cotes Lincs...80 G11
Kearby Town End N York...85 M6
Kearsley Bolton...76 D3
Kearsney Kent...17 N2
Kearstwick Cumb...89 P10
Kearton N York...90 G7
Kearvaig Highld...148 G3
Keasden N York...83 R3
Keckwick Halton...75 P7
Keddington Lincs...80 G6
Keddington Corner Lincs...80 G6
Kedington Suffk...57 P11
Kedleston Derbys...65 P4
Keelby Lincs...80 C2
Keele Staffs...64 E3
Keele Services Staffs...64 E3
Keele University Staffs...64 E3
Keeley Green Bed...44 E3
Keelham C Brad...84 G8
Keeres Green Essex...45 Q8
Keeston Pembks...36 H6
Keevil Wilts...29 Q10
Kegworth Leics...66 D7
Kehelland Cnwll...2 G6
Keig Abers...140 F12
Keighley C Brad...84 F7
Keilarsbrae Clacks...114 G2
Keillour P & K...123 N7
Keiloch Abers...131 M6
Keils Ag & B...111 L7
Keinton Mandeville
  Somset...22 C7
Keir Mill D & G...105 Q11
Keirsleywell Row Nthumb...99 L8
Keisley Cumb...90 H3
Keiss Highld...151 Q4
Keith Moray...140 C5
Keithick P & K...124 D4
Keithock Angus...132 F11
Keithtown Highld...137 P4
Kelbrook Lancs...84 D6
Kelby Lincs...67 P4
Keld Cumb...89 N4
Keld N York...90 E6
Keld Head N York...92 F10
Keldholme N York...92 F8
Kelfield N Linc...79 L3
Kelfield N York...86 B7
Kelham Notts...79 J12
Kelhead D & G...97 N4
Kellacott Devon...7 M8
Kellamergh Lancs...83 J9
Kellas Angus...125 J5
Kellas Moray...139 M5
Kellaton Devon...5 N10
Kelleth Cumb...89 R5
Kelling Norfk...70 G3
Kellington N York...85 R10
Kelloe Dur...101 J11
Kelloholm D & G...105 N9
Kells Cumb...88 C3
Kelly Devon...7 L8
Kelly Bray Cnwll...7 L10
Kelmarsh Nhants...55 J5
Kelmscott Oxon...30 F2
Kelsale Suffk...59 M7
Kelsall Ches W...75 N10
Kelshall Herts...45 K4
Kelsick Cumb...97 Q8
Kelso Border...108 A3
Kelstedge Derbys...77 Q11
Kelstern Lincs...80 E5
Kelsterton Flints...75 J9
Kelston BaNES...29 L10
Keltneyburn P & K...123 K3
Kelton D & G...97 K4
Kelty Fife...115 L4
Kelvedon Essex...46 F8
Kelvedon Hatch Essex...33 Q3
Kelynack Cnwll...2 B8
Kemacott Devon...19 M4
Kemback Fife...124 H10
Kemberton Shrops...64 D11
Kemble Gloucs...30 A3
Kemble Wick Gloucs...29 R3
Kemerton Worcs...41 Q4
Kemeys Commander
  Mons...40 D10
Kemnay Abers...132 H1

Kemp's Corner Kent...17 J2
Kempley Gloucs...41 K6
Kempley Green Gloucs...41 K6
Kempsey Worcs...52 F10
Kempsford Gloucs...30 D3
Kemps Green Warwks...53 L6
Kempshott Hants...25 K3
Kempston Bed...55 P11
Kempston Hardwick Bed...44 E3
Kempton Shrops...51 L3
Kemp Town Br & H...15 L10
Kemsing Kent...33 Q10
Kemsley Kent...34 F9
Kemsley Street Kent...34 E10
Kenardington Kent...16 H4
Kenchester Herefs...40 F4
Kencot Oxon...42 F10
Kendal Cumb...89 N8
Kenderchurch Herefs...40 F6
Kendleshire S Glos...29 K6
Kenfig Brdgnd...27 K6
Kenfig Hill Brdgnd...27 K6
Kenilworth Warwks...53 P6
Kenley Gt Lon...33 L10
Kenley Shrops...63 P12
Kenmore Highld...135 N4
Kenmore P & K...123 K4
Kenn Devon...8 H7
Kenn N Som...28 F8
Kennacraig Ag & B...112 B3
Kennall Vale Cnwll...3 J7
Kennards House Cnwll...7 K7
Kenneggy Cnwll...2 F9
Kennerleigh Devon...8 F3
Kennet Clacks...114 G3
Kennethmont Abers...140 E10
Kennett Cambs...57 N7
Kennford Devon...8 H7
Kenninghall Norfk...58 F3
Kennington Gt Lon...33 L6
Kennington Oxon...43 L11
Kennoway Fife...124 G12
Kenny Somset...21 M9
Kenny Hill Suffk...57 M5
Kennythorpe N York...86 D2
Kenovay Ag & B...118 D5
Kensaleyre Highld...134 G5
Kensington Gt Lon...33 J6
Kensington Palace Gt Lon...33 J6
Kenstone Shrops...63 P7
Kensworth C Beds...44 E8
Kensworth Common
  C Beds...44 E8
Kentallen Highld...121 J1
Kentchurch Herefs...40 F6
Kentford Suffk...57 N7
Kent Green Ches E...76 F12
Kentisbeare Devon...9 K3
Kentisbury Devon...19 M4
Kentisbury Ford Devon...19 M4
Kentish Town Gt Lon...33 K5
Kentmere Cumb...89 M6
Kenton Devon...8 H8
Kenton Gt Lon...32 H5
Kenton N u Ty...100 G5
Kenton Suffk...59 J8
Kenton Bankfoot N u Ty...100 G4
Kentra Highld...127 M10
Kents Bank Cumb...89 L11
Kentsboro Hants...24 E5
Kent's Green Gloucs...41 L7
Kent's Oak Hants...24 E8
Kent Street E Susx...16 D7
Kent Street Kent...34 B11
Kenwick Shrops...63 M6
Kenwyn Cnwll...3 K5
Kenyon Warrtn...76 B5
Keoldale Highld...149 J3
Keppoch Highld...136 B11
Kepwick N York...91 Q8
Keresley Covtry...53 Q4
Kermincham Ches E...76 E10
Kernborough Devon...5 N9
Kerne Bridge Herefs...41 J8
Kerrera Ag & B...120 F2
Kerridge Ches E...76 H8
Kerridge-end Ches E...76 H8
Kerris Cnwll...2 C9
Kerry Powys...50 G3
Kerrycroy Ag & B...112 G9
Kersall Notts...78 H11
Kersbrook Devon...9 K8
Kerscott Devon...19 M7
Kersey Suffk...46 G3
Kersey Tye Suffk...46 G3
Kersey Upland Suffk...46 H3
Kershader W Isls...152 f4
Kershopefoot Cumb...98 G2
Kersoe Worcs...42 A4
Kerswell Devon...9 L3
Kerswell Green Worcs...41 P2
Kerthen Wood Cnwll...2 F7
Kesgrave Suffk...47 M3
Kessingland Suffk...59 Q3
Kessingland Beach Suffk...59 Q3
Kestle Cnwll...3 M5
Kestle Mill Cnwll...3 L3
Keston Gt Lon...33 N9
Keswick Cumb...89 J1
Keswick Norfk...71 J11
Keswick Norfk...80 G5
Ketley Wrekin...64 C9
Ketley Bank Wrekin...64 C9
Ketsby Lincs...80 G7
Kettering Nhants...55 L5
Ketteringham Norfk...70 H11
Kettins P & K...124 D4
Kettlebaston Suffk...58 E10
Kettlebridge Fife...124 F11
Kettlebrook Staffs...65 N11
Kettleburgh Suffk...59 K8
Kettleholm D & G...97 N3
Kettleness N York...92 H4
Kettleshulme Ches E...77 J8
Kettlesing N York...85 K4
Kettlesing Bottom N York...85 K4
Kettlestone Norfk...70 E6
Kettlethorpe Lincs...79 L9
Kettletoft Ork...147 e2
Kettlewell N York...90 F12
Ketton Rutlnd...67 N11
Kew Gt Lon...32 H7
Kew Royal Botanic
  Gardens Gt Lon...32 H7
Kewstoke N Som...28 D9
Kexbrough Barns...77 Q3
Kexby Lincs...79 L7
Kexby York...86 C5
Key Green Ches E...76 G11
Key Green N York...92 H6
Keyham Leics...66 H11
Keyhaven Hants...12 E6
Keyingham E R Yk...87 N10
Keymer W Susx...15 L8
Keynsham BaNES...29 K9
Keysoe Bed...55 R8
Keysoe Row Bed...55 R8
Keyston Cambs...55 P5
Key Street Kent...34 F9
Keyworth Notts...66 G6
Kibbear Somset...21 L2
Kibblesworth Gatesd...100 G7
Kibworth Beauchamp
  Leics...54 H2
Kibworth Harcourt Leics...54 H2
Kidbrooke Gt Lon...33 M7
Kidburngill Cumb...88 C7
Kiddemore Green Staffs...64 F10

Kidderminster Worcs 52 F5
Kiddington Oxon 43 J7
Kidd's Moor Norfk 70 G11
Kidlington Oxon 43 K9
Kidmore End Oxon 31 P6
Kidsdale D & G 95 N11
Kidsgrove Staffs 64 F1
Kidstones N York 90 F10
Kidwelly Carmth 38 B10
Kiel Crofts Ag & B 120 G6
Kielder Nthumb 107 Q11
Kielder Forest 107 P12
Kiells Ag & B 111 J7
Kilbarchan Rens 113 M8
Kilbeg Highld 127 M3
Kilberry Ag & B 111 Q8
Kilbirnie N Ayrs 113 L10
Kilbride Ag & B 111 Q5
Kilbride Ag & B 112 F7
Kilbuiack Moray 139 K4
Kilburn Derbys 66 C3
Kilburn Gt Lon 33 J4
Kilburn N York 91 Q8
Kilby Leics 54 G2
Kilchattan Ag & B 112 B9
Kilchattan Ag & B 111 J2
Kilcheran Ag & B 120 F5
Kilchoan Highld 127 J11
Kilchoman Ag & B 110 F8
Kilchrenan Ag & B 121 K8
Kilconquhar Fife 125 K12
Kilcot Gloucs 41 L6
Kilcoy Highld 137 Q5
Kilcreggan Ag & B 113 K5
Kildale N York 92 C5
Kildalloig Ag & B 103 K6
Kildary Highld 146 D10
Kildavaig Ag & B 112 E8
Kildavanan Ag & B 112 F8
Kildonan Highld 146 G11
Kildonan N Ayrs 103 Q5
Kildonan Lodge Highld 150 G12
Kildonnan Highld 127 J7
Kildrochet House D & G 94 F7
Kildrummy Abers 140 D12
Kildwick N York 84 F6
Kilfinan Ag & B 112 D5
Kilfinnan Highld 129 J5
Kilford Denbgs 74 E10
Kilgetty Pembks 37 M9
Kilgrammie S Ayrs 104 E9

Kilgwrrwg Common Mons 28 G3
Kilham E R Yk 87 K2
Kilham Nthumb 108 E3
Kilkenneth Ag & B 118 C4
Kilkenzie Ag & B 103 J5
Kilkerran Ag & B 103 K6
Kilkhampton Cnwll 7 J2
Killamarsh Derbys 78 D7
Killay Swans 26 H4
Killean Stirlg 113 Q4
Killen Highld 138 C4
Killerby Darltn 91 K3
Killerton Devon 9 J5
Killichonan P & K 122 F1
Killiechonate Highld 128 J8
Killiechronan Ag & B 119 P4
Killiecrankie P & K 130 G11
Killilan Highld 136 C10
Killimster Highld 151 P5
Killin Stirlg 122 F6
Killinghall N York 85 L3
Killington Cumb 89 Q9
Killington Devon 19 N4
Killington Lake Services Cumb 89 P8
Killingworth N Tyne 100 H4
Killiow Cnwll 3 K6
Killochyett Border 116 B12
Kilmacolm Inver 113 M7
Kilmahog Stirlg 122 G11
Kilmahumaig Ag & B 112 A3
Kilmalieu Highld 142 E10
Kilmany Fife 124 H8
Kilmarnock E Ayrs 104 H2
Kilmartin Ag & B 112 B2
Kilmaurs E Ayrs 104 G2
Kilmelford Ag & B 120 F10
Kilmersdon Somset 22 F3
Kilmeston Hants 25 K8
Kilmichael Ag & B 103 J5
Kilmichael Glassary Ag & B 112 C3
Kilmichael of Inverlussa Ag & B 112 A4
Kilmington Devon 9 P5
Kilmington Wilts 22 H6
Kilmington Common Wilts 22 H6
Kilmington Street Wilts 22 H6
Kilmorack Highld 137 N7
Kilmore Ag & B 120 G8
Kilmore Highld 127 M3
Kilmory Highld 141 P6
Kilmory Ag & B 112 A7
Kilmory Highld 127 J10
Kilmory N Ayrs 103 P5
Kilmuir Highld 134 D6
Kilmuir Highld 138 C6
Kilmuir Highld 142 D11
Kilmuir Highld 146 D10
Kilmun Ag & B 112 H5
Kilnave Ag & B 110 G7
Kilncadzow S Lans 114 F11
Kilndown Kent 16 C4
Kiln Green Wokham 32 A6
Kilnhill Cumb 97 P11
Kilnhurst Rothm 78 D4
Kilninver Ag & B 120 F8
Kiln Pit Hill Nthumb 100 D7
Kilnsea E R Yk 87 R12
Kilnsey N York 84 E2
Kilnwick E R Yk 86 H5
Kilnwick Percy E R Yk 86 F5
Kilnwood Vale W Susx 15 J4
Kiloran Ag & B 111 J2
Kilpatrick N Ayrs 103 N4
Kilpeck Herefs 40 F5
Kilpin E R Yk 86 E10
Kilpin Pike E R Yk 86 E10
Kilrenny Fife 125 L11
Kilsby Nhants 54 F6
Kilspindie P & K 124 F2
Kilstay D & G 94 G10
Kilsyth N Lans 114 C6
Kiltarlity Highld 137 N7
Kilton R & Cl 92 E3
Kilton Somset 21 J5
Kilton Thorpe R & Cl 92 E3
Kilvaxter Highld 142 D11
Kilve Somset 21 J5
Kilvington Notts 67 K4
Kilwinning N Ayrs 104 E1
Kimberley Norfk 70 G11
Kimberley Notts 66 E3
Kimberworth Rothm 78 C5
Kimblesworth Dur 100 H9
Kimble Wick Bucks 44 A10
Kimbolton Cambs 56 B7
Kimbolton Herefs 51 N8
Kimcote Leics 54 F4
Kimmeridge Dorset 11 M9
Kimmerston Nthumb 108 F3
Kimpton Hants 24 D4
Kimpton Herts 44 H8
Kimworthy Devon 18 F10

Kinbrace Highld 150 F10
Kinbuck Stirlg 123 K11
Kincaple Fife 125 J9
Kincardine Fife 114 G4
Kincardine Highld 145 N1
Kincardine Bridge Fife 114 G4
Kincardine O'Neil Abers 132 F4
Kinclaven P & K 124 C5
Kincorth C Aber 133 M4
Kincorth House Moray 139 J3
Kincraig Highld 130 F3
Kincraigie P & K 123 P3
Kindallachan P & K 123 P3
Kinerarach Ag & B 111 P10
Kineton Gloucs 42 C6
Kineton Warwks 53 Q10
Kinfauns P & K 124 D8
Kingarth Ag & B 112 G10
Kingcausie Abers 133 L4
Kingcoed Mons 40 F10
Kingerby Lincs 79 Q5
Kingford Devon 7 K3
Kingham Oxon 42 F7
Kingholm Quay D & G 97 K3
Kinghorn Fife 115 N4
Kinglassie Fife 115 N2
Kingoodie P & K 124 G7
King's Acre Herefs 40 G3
Kingsand Cnwll 4 G6
Kingsash Bucks 44 C10
Kingsbarns Fife 125 L10
Kingsbridge Devon 5 M8
Kingsbridge Somset 20 F6
Kings Bridge Swans 26 B3
Kingsbrook Bucks 44 B9
Kingsburgh Highld 134 G5
Kingsbury Gt Lon 32 H5
Kingsbury Warwks 53 N1
Kingsbury Episcopi Somset 21 P9
King's Caple Herefs 40 H6
Kingsclere Hants 31 L10
King's Cliffe Nhants 55 P1
Kingscote Gloucs 29 N3
Kingscott Devon 19 K9
King's Coughton Warwks 53 N9
Kingscross N Ayrs 103 Q4
Kingsdon Somset 22 C8
Kingsdown Kent 17 Q1
Kingsdown Swindn 30 D5
Kingsdown Wilts 29 N9
Kingseat Abers 141 L12
Kingseat Fife 115 L3
Kingsey Bucks 43 Q10
Kingsfold W Susx 14 H4
Kingsford E Ayrs 104 H3
Kingsford Worcs 52 F5
Kingsgate Kent 35 Q8
Kings Green Gloucs 41 N5
Kingshall Street Suffk 58 D8
Kingsheanton Devon 19 L6
King's Heath Birm 53 K4
Kings Hill Kent 34 B10
King's Hill Wsall 52 H1
Kings House Hotel Highld 121 P2
Kingshurst Solhll 53 M3
Kingside Hill Cumb 97 N8
Kingskerswell Devon 5 P3
Kingskettle Fife 124 F11
Kingsland Dorset 10 C5
Kingsland Herefs 51 M8
Kingsland IoA 72 D7
Kings Langley Herts 44 F11
Kingsley Ches W 75 P9
Kingsley Hants 25 N6
Kingsley Staffs 65 J3
Kingsley Green W Susx 14 C5
Kingsley Holt Staffs 65 J3
Kingsley Park Nhants 55 J8
Kingslow Shrops 52 E1
Kings Meaburn Cumb 89 Q2
Kingsmead Hants 25 K10
King's Mills Guern 12 b2
King's Moss St Hel 75 N3
King's Newnham Warwks 54 D5
King's Newton Derbys 66 B6
Kingsnorth Kent 16 H3
King's Norton Birm 53 K5
King's Norton Leics 66 H12
King's Nympton Devon 19 N9
King's Pyon Herefs 51 M10
Kings Ripton Cambs 56 E5
King's Somborne Hants 24 F7
King's Stag Dorset 10 H3
King's Stanley Gloucs 41 N11
King's Sutton Nhants 43 K4
Kingstanding Birm 53 K2
Kingsteignton Devon 8 G10
Kingsteps Highld 138 G4
Kingsthorne Herefs 40 G5
Kingsthorpe Nhants 55 J8
Kingston Cambs 56 F9
Kingston Cnwll 7 L9
Kingston Devon 5 N6
Kingston Devon 9 K7
Kingston Dorset 11 J3
Kingston Dorset 11 M9
Kingston E Loth 116 D5
Kingston IoW 12 H8
Kingston Kent 35 M12
Kingston W Susx 14 F10
Kingston Bagpuize Oxon 31 K3
Kingston Blount Oxon 31 Q2
Kingston by Sea W Susx 15 J9
Kingston Deverill Wilts 23 J6
Kingstone Herefs 40 F5
Kingstone Somset 21 N10
Kingstone Staffs 65 K6
Kingston Lacy House & Gardens Dorset 11 N4
Kingston Lisle Oxon 30 G5
Kingston near Lewes E Susx 15 M9
Kingston on Soar Notts 66 E6
Kingston on Spey Moray 139 M3
Kingston Russell Dorset 10 D6
Kingston St Mary Somset 21 K7
Kingston Seymour N Som 28 F8
Kingston Stert Oxon 31 Q2
Kingston upon Hull C KuH 87 K9
Kingston upon Thames Gt Lon 32 H8
King's Walden Herts 44 H7
Kingswear Devon 5 Q6
Kingswells C Aber 133 L3
Kings Weston Bristl 28 H7
Kingswinford Dudley 52 G3
Kingswood Bucks 43 N9
Kingswood Gloucs 29 M4
Kingswood Kent 34 E10
Kingswood Powys 62 H11
Kingswood Somset 20 H6

Kingswood Surrey 33 J11
Kingswood Warwks 53 M6
Kingswood Brook Warwks 53 M6
Kingswood Common Herefs 51 J10
Kingswood Common Staffs 64 F11
Kings Worthy Hants 24 H7
Kingthorpe Lincs 80 C8
Kington Herefs 51 J9
Kington S Glos 29 J4
Kington Worcs 53 J9
Kington Langley Wilts 29 Q7
Kington Magna Dorset 22 G9
Kington St Michael Wilts 29 Q6
Kingussie Highld 130 D4
Kingweston Somset 22 C7
Kinharrachie Abers 141 M9
Kinharvie D & G 97 J3
Kinhrive Highld 146 D11
Kinkell Bridge P & K 123 N9
Kinknockie Abers 141 N7
Kinleith C Edin 115 M8
Kinlet Shrops 52 D4
Kinloch Highld 126 G4
Kinloch Highld 148 F8
Kinloch Highld 149 M6
Kinloch P & K 124 C4
Kinlochard Stirlg 122 D12
Kinlochbervie Highld 148 F5
Kinlocheil Highld 128 D8
Kinlochewe Highld 136 E3
Kinloch Hourn Highld 128 C3
Kinlochlaggan Highld 129 P6
Kinlochleven Highld 128 H12
Kinlochmoidart Highld 127 M9
Kinlochnanuagh Highld 127 L8
Kinloch Rannoch P & K 122 H1
Kinloss Moray 139 K3
Kinmel Bay Conwy 74 D7
Kinmuck Abers 141 K12
Kinmundy Abers 133 L1
Kinnabus Ag & B 102 B1
Kinnadie Abers 141 N7
Kinnaird P & K 123 N1
Kinneff Abers 133 M8
Kinnelhead D & G 106 D9
Kinnell Angus 125 M3
Kinnerley Shrops 63 K8
Kinnersley Herefs 51 L10
Kinnersley Worcs 41 P3
Kinnerton Powys 50 H8
Kinnerton Shrops 51 L1
Kinnerton Green Flints 75 K11
Kinnesswood P & K 124 D12
Kinninvie Dur 90 H2
Kinnordy Angus 124 F3
Kinoulton Notts 67 K6
Kinross P & K 124 C12
Kinrossie P & K 124 D6
Kinsbourne Green Herts 44 G8
Kinsey Heath Ches E 64 C4
Kinsham Herefs 51 K7
Kinsham Worcs 41 Q4
Kinsley Wakefd 85 N12
Kinson BCP 11 P5
Kintail Highld 136 D12
Kintbury W Berk 30 H9
Kintessack Moray 139 J4
Kintillo P & K 124 C9
Kinton Herefs 51 L6
Kinton Shrops 63 L8
Kintore Abers 133 J1
Kintour Ag & B 111 K11
Kintra Ag & B 111 K8
Kintra Ag & B 119 K8
Kintraw Ag & B 120 F11
Kintyre Ag & B 103 K2
Kinveachy Highld 138 Q12
Kinver Staffs 52 F4
Kiplin N York 91 M7
Kippax Leeds 85 N9
Kippen Stirlg 114 B2
Kippford D & G 96 H7
Kipping's Cross Kent 16 B3
Kirbister Ork 147 c5
Kirby Bedon Norfk 71 K11
Kirby Bellars Leics 67 J8
Kirby Cane Norfk 59 N4
Kirby Corner Covtry 53 P5
Kirby Cross Essex 47 M7
Kirby Fields Leics 66 E11
Kirby Green Norfk 59 N4
Kirby Grindalythe N York 86 H2
Kirby Hill N York 85 N2
Kirby Hill N York 91 J4
Kirby Knowle N York 91 Q9
Kirby-le-Soken Essex 47 M7
Kirby Misperton N York 92 F10
Kirby Muxloe Leics 66 E11
Kirby Sigston N York 91 P8
Kirby Underdale E R Yk 86 E3
Kirby Wiske N York 91 N9
Kirdford W Susx 14 G5
Kirk Highld 151 N5
Kirkabister Shet 147 j8
Kirkandrews D & G 96 C8
Kirkandrews upon Eden Cumb 98 D6
Kirkbampton Cumb 98 D6
Kirkbean D & G 97 K6
Kirk Bramwith Donc 78 G1
Kirkbride Cumb 97 P7
Kirkbridge N York 91 L8
Kirkbuddo Angus 125 K4
Kirkburn Border 107 J2
Kirkburn E R Yk 86 H4
Kirkburton Kirk 77 M1
Kirkby Knows 75 L4
Kirkby Lincs 80 D5
Kirkby N York 92 B5
Kirkby Fleetham N York 91 M8
Kirkby Green Lincs 80 B12
Kirkby-in-Ashfield Notts 78 E12
Kirkby in Furness Cumb 88 H10
Kirkby la Thorpe Lincs 68 B3
Kirkby Lonsdale Cumb 89 P11
Kirkby Malham N York 84 D3
Kirkby Mallory Leics 66 D12
Kirkby Malzeard N York 91 L11
Kirkby Mills N York 92 F9
Kirkbymoorside N York 92 F9
Kirkby on Bain Lincs 80 E11
Kirkby Overblow N York 85 L5
Kirkby Stephen Cumb 90 C5
Kirkby Thore Cumb 89 Q2
Kirkby Underwood Lincs 67 Q7
Kirkby Wharf N York 85 N6
Kirkby Woodhouse Notts 78 E12
Kirkcaldy Fife 115 P3
Kirkcambeck Cumb 98 G4
Kirkchrist D & G 96 D8
Kirkcolm D & G 94 E4
Kirkconnel D & G 105 Q4
Kirkconnell D & G 97 K5
Kirkcowan D & G 95 L6
Kirkcudbright D & G 96 D8
Kirkdale Lpool 75 K5
Kirk Deighton N York 85 M4
Kirk Ella E R Yk 87 J9
Kirkfieldbank S Lans 105 R1
Kirkgunzeon D & G 96 H5
Kirk Hallam Derbys 66 D4
Kirkham Lancs 83 M9
Kirkham N York 86 E3
Kirkhamgate Wakefd 85 L10

Kirk Hammerton N York 85 M4
Kirkharle Nthumb 100 C2
Kirkhaugh Nthumb 99 M8
Kirkheaton Kirk 85 J11
Kirkheaton Nthumb 100 C3
Kirkhill Highld 137 P7
Kirkhope S Lans 106 C3
Kirkhouse Cumb 98 H6
Kirkhouse Green Donc 78 G1
Kirkibost Highld 135 K12
Kirkinch P & K 124 F4
Kirkinner D & G 95 M8
Kirkintilloch E Duns 114 B6
Kirk Ireton Derbys 65 P2
Kirkland Cumb 88 E3
Kirkland Cumb 89 N2
Kirkland D & G 105 N7
Kirkland D & G 105 Q4
Kirkland D & G 106 D11
Kirkland Guards Cumb 97 N10
Kirk Langley Derbys 65 P4
Kirkleatham R & Cl 92 C2
Kirklevington S on T 91 Q5
Kirkley Suffk 59 Q2
Kirklington N York 91 N10
Kirklington Notts 78 H12
Kirklinton Cumb 98 E5
Kirkliston C Edin 115 L6
Kirkmabreck D & G 95 N7
Kirkmaiden D & G 94 G11
Kirk Merrington Dur 100 H12
Kirk Michael IoM 102 d4
Kirkmichael P & K 131 K2
Kirkmichael S Ayrs 104 F8
Kirkmuirhill S Lans 105 P1
Kirknewton Nthumb 108 E4
Kirknewton W Loth 115 L8
Kirkney Abers 140 D9
Kirk of Shotts N Lans 114 F8
Kirkoswald Cumb 98 H10
Kirkoswald S Ayrs 104 D8
Kirkpatrick D & G 106 B11
Kirkpatrick Durham D & G 96 F4
Kirkpatrick-Fleming D & G 98 C4
Kirksanton Cumb 88 F10
Kirk Smeaton N York 85 Q12
Kirkstall Leeds 85 K8
Kirkstead Lincs 80 D11
Kirkstile D & G 107 K11
Kirkstone Pass Inn Cumb 89 L4
Kirkstyle Highld 151 P2
Kirkthorpe Wakefd 85 M11
Kirkton Abers 140 G10
Kirkton Abers 140 G11
Kirkton D & G 97 K2
Kirkton Fife 124 H6
Kirkton Highld 135 Q10
Kirkton Highld 136 C7
Kirkton P & K 123 N9
Kirkton of Airlie Angus 124 F3
Kirkton of Auchterhouse Angus 124 G5
Kirkton of Barevan Highld 138 F6
Kirkton of Collace P & K 124 D6
Kirkton of Durris Abers 133 J5
Kirkton of Glenbuchat Abers 132 B1
Kirkton of Glenisla Angus 131 N12
Kirkton of Kingoldrum Angus 124 G2
Kirkton of Lethendy P & K 124 C4
Kirkton of Logie Buchan Abers 141 N10
Kirkton of Maryculter Abers 133 K4
Kirkton of Menmuir Angus 132 E11
Kirkton of Monikie Angus 125 K5
Kirkton of Rayne Abers 140 H10
Kirkton of Skene Abers 133 K3
Kirkton of Tealing Angus 124 H5
Kirkton of Tough Abers 132 F2
Kirktown Abers 141 N4
Kirktown Abers 141 Q5
Kirktown of Alvah Abers 140 G4
Kirktown of Bourtie Abers 141 K10
Kirktown of Deskford Moray 140 D3
Kirktown of Fetteresso Abers 133 K7
Kirktown of Mortlach Moray 139 N8
Kirktown of Slains Abers 141 P8
Kirkurd Border 106 F1
Kirkwall Ork 147 c4
Kirkwall Airport Ork 147 d5
Kirkwelpington Nthumb 100 C1
Kirk Yetholm Border 108 D4
Kirmington N Linc 80 H1
Kirmond le Mire Lincs 80 D5
Kirn Ag & B 112 H6
Kirriemuir Angus 124 H2
Kirstead Green Norfk 59 L1
Kirtlebridge D & G 97 P4
Kirtling Cambs 57 N9
Kirtling Green Cambs 57 N9
Kirtlington Oxon 43 K8
Kirtomy Highld 150 D3
Kirton Lincs 68 F4
Kirton Notts 78 H10
Kirton Suffk 47 M3
Kirton End Lincs 68 F4
Kirton Holme Lincs 68 E4
Kirton in Lindsey N Linc 79 M4
Kirwaugh D & G 95 M7
Kishorn Highld 135 Q9
Kislingbury Nhants 54 H9
Kitebrook Warwks 42 F5
Kite Green Warwks 53 M7
Kites Hardwick Warwks 54 D7
Kit's Coty Kent 34 C10
Kittisford Somset 20 F8
Kittle Swans 26 D4
Kitt Green Wigan 75 P2
Kittybrewster C Aber 133 M4
Kitwood Hants 25 L7
Kivernoll Herefs 40 G5
Kiveton Park Rothm 78 D5
Knaith Lincs 79 L7
Knaith Park Lincs 79 L6
Knap Corner Dorset 22 H8
Knaphill Surrey 32 E10
Knapp Somset 21 L8
Knapp Hill Hants 24 H8
Knapthorpe Notts 79 J12
Knapton N York 86 H2
Knapton Norfk 71 L5
Knapton Green Herefs 51 M10
Knapwell Cambs 56 F8
Knaresborough N York 85 M4
Knarsdale Nthumb 99 L7
Knaven Abers 141 L7
Knayton N York 91 Q9
Knebworth Herts 45 J7
Knedlington E R Yk 86 E9
Kneesall Notts 78 H11
Kneesworth Cambs 45 L3
Kneeton Notts 67 J3

Knelston Swans 26 C4
Knenhall Staffs 64 G5
Knettishall Suffk 58 E5
Knightacott Devon 19 M5
Knightcote Warwks 54 C9
Knightley Staffs 64 F7
Knightley Dale Staffs 64 F7
Knighton BCP 11 P5
Knighton C Leic 66 G12
Knighton Devon 4 H7
Knighton Dorset 10 F2
Knighton Powys 51 J6
Knighton Somset 21 K4
Knighton Staffs 64 D7
Knighton Staffs 64 D10
Knighton Wilts 30 G7
Knighton on Teme Worcs 52 B6
Knightsbridge Gloucs 41 P6
Knightsmill Cnwll 6 H7
Knightwick Worcs 52 D9
Knill Herefs 51 J8
Knipoch Ag & B 120 F8
Knipton Leics 67 M5
Knitsley Dur 100 F9
Kniveton Derbys 65 N3
Knock Cumb 89 R1
Knock Highld 127 M3
Knock Moray 140 E5
Knock W Isls 152 g3
Knockally Highld 151 L11
Knockan Highld 144 F3
Knockando Moray 139 M7
Knockbain Highld 138 B5
Knockbain Highld 137 Q5
Knock Castle N Ayrs 113 J3
Knockdee Highld 151 L4
Knockdow Ag & B 112 G7
Knockdown Wilts 29 N5
Knockeen S Ayrs 104 F10
Knockenkelly N Ayrs 103 Q4
Knockentiber E Ayrs 104 G2
Knockhall Kent 33 Q7
Knockholt Kent 33 N10
Knockholt Pound Kent 33 N10
Knockin Shrops 63 K7
Knockinlaw E Ayrs 104 H2
Knockmill Kent 33 Q10
Knocknain D & G 94 D4
Knockrome Ag & B 111 M7
Knocksharry IoM 102 c4
Knockvennie Smithy D & G 96 C2
Knodishall Suffk 59 N8
Knodishall Common Suffk 59 N8
Knole Somset 22 N8
Knole Park S Glos 28 H6
Knolls Green Ches E 76 E8
Knolton Wrexhm 63 L4
Knook Wilts 23 L5
Knossington Leics 67 K10
Knott End-on-Sea Lancs 83 J5
Knotting Bed 55 N7
Knotting Green Bed 55 N7
Knottingley Wakefd 85 Q10
Knotty Ash Lpool 75 L5
Knotty Green Bucks 32 D4
Knowbury Shrops 51 N6
Knowe D & G 95 K4
Knowehead D & G 105 L11
Knoweside S Ayrs 104 D9
Knowes of Elrick Abers 140 F5
Knowle Bristl 29 J8
Knowle Devon 9 J4
Knowle Devon 9 M8
Knowle Devon 19 J6
Knowle Shrops 51 N6
Knowle Solhll 53 M5
Knowle Somset 20 F6
Knowle Cross Devon 9 K6
Knowle Green Lancs 83 P7
Knowle Hill Surrey 32 E9
Knowlefield Cumb 98 E6
Knowle St Giles Somset 9 J3
Knowle Village Hants 13 J3
Knowle Wood Calder 84 D10
Knowl Green Essex 46 D3
Knowl Hill W & M 32 B7
Knowlton Dorset 11 N3
Knowlton Kent 35 N11
Knowsley Knows 75 M4
Knowsley Safari Park Knows 75 M5
Knowstone Devon 20 C8
Knox N York 85 L4
Knox Bridge Kent 16 D3
Knoydart Highld 127 P4
Knucklas Powys 51 J6
Knuston Nhants 55 M7
Knutsford Ches E 76 D8
Knutsford Services Ches E 76 D8
Krumlin Calder 84 G11
Kuggar Cnwll 2 H11
Kyleakin Highld 135 N10
Kyle of Lochalsh Highld 135 N10
Kylerhea Highld 135 N10
Kylesku Highld 148 F10
Kylesmorar Highld 127 P6
Kylestrome Highld 148 F9
Kynaston Herefs 41 K4
Kynaston Shrops 63 K8
Kynnersley Wrekin 64 C9
Kyre Green Worcs 51 Q8
Kyre Park Worcs 52 B8
Kyrewood Worcs 51 Q7
Kyrle Somset 20 G9

L

La Bellieuse Guern 12 c3
Lacasaigh W Isls 152 f4
Lacasdal W Isls 152 g3
Laceby NE Lin 80 D2
Lacey Green Bucks 32 B3
Lach Dennis Ches W 76 D9
Lackford Suffk 57 Q6
Lacock Wilts 29 Q8
Ladbroke Warwks 54 C9
Laddingford Kent 16 C2
Lade Bank Lincs 68 G2
Ladock Cnwll 3 L4
Lady Ork 147 e2
Ladybank Fife 124 F11
Ladycross Cnwll 7 L5
Ladygill S Lans 106 B4
Lady Hall Cumb 88 F9
Ladykirk Border 117 K11
Ladyridge Herefs 40 H6
Ladywood Birm 53 J3
Ladywood Worcs 52 H8
La Fontenelle Guern 12 c1
La Fosse Guern 12 c3
Laga Highld 127 L10
Lagavulin Ag & B 111 J12
Lagg N Ayrs 103 P5

Laggan Highld 129 K5
Laggan Highld 130 B5
Lagganlia Highld 130 F3
La Grève de Lecq Jersey 13 a1
La Hougue Bie Jersey 13 d2
La Houguette Guern 12 b2
Laid Highld 149 J5
Laide Highld 143 M7
Laig Highld 126 H7
Laigh Clunch E Ayrs 113 N11
Laigh Fenwick E Ayrs 104 H1
Laigh Glenmuir E Ayrs 105 L6
Laindon Essex 34 B4
Lairg Highld 145 N4
Laithes Cumb 98 F11
Lake Devon 7 L3
Lake IoW 13 K8
Lake Wilts 23 N6
Lake District National Park Cumb 88 H4
Lakenheath Suffk 57 N4
Laker's Green Surrey 14 F4
Lakes End Norfk 57 K11
Lakeside Cumb 89 K9
Laleham Surrey 32 F8
Laleston Brdgnd 27 L6
Lamanva Cnwll 3 J8
Lamarsh Essex 46 F4
Lamas Norfk 71 K7
Lamberhurst Kent 16 B4
Lamberhurst Down Kent 16 B4
Lamberton Border 117 L9
Lambeth Gt Lon 33 K6
Lambfair Green Suffk 57 N10
Lambley Notts 66 H4
Lambley Nthumb 99 K6
Lamborne Herefs 33 N3
Lambourn W Berk 30 G7
Lambourne End Essex 33 N3
Lamb Roe Lancs 83 Q8
Lambs Green W Susx 15 J3
Lambston Pembks 36 H7
Lamellion Cnwll 4 F5
Lamerton Devon 7 N9
Lamesley Gatesd 100 G7
Laminess Ork 147 e2
Lamington Highld 146 F9
Lamington S Lans 106 B3
Lamlash N Ayrs 103 Q4
Lamloch D & G 105 J9
Lamonby Cumb 98 E11
Lamorick Cnwll 3 N3
Lamorna Cnwll 2 C9
Lamorran Cnwll 3 M6
Lampen Cnwll 4 B3
Lampeter Cerdgn 49 K11
Lampeter Velfrey Pembks 37 M7
Lamphey Pembks 37 K10
Lamplugh Cumb 88 E3
Lamport Nhants 55 J6
Lamyatt Somset 22 F6
Lana Devon 7 K9
Lana Devon 7 L4
Lanark S Lans 106 A1
Lancaster Lancs 83 L3
Lancaster Services Lancs 83 L5
Lancaut Gloucs 28 H3
Lanchester Dur 100 F9
L'Ancresse Guern 12 c1
Landbeach Cambs 57 J7
Landcross Devon 19 J8
Landerberry Abers 133 J3
Landford Wilts 24 D9
Land-hallow Highld 151 M10
Landimore Swans 26 C4
Landkey Devon 19 L7
Landore Swans 26 G4
Landrake Cnwll 4 E4
Landscove Devon 5 P3
Land's End Cnwll 2 B9
Land's End Airport Cnwll 2 B8
Landshipping Pembks 37 K8
Landue Cnwll 7 L4
Landulph Cnwll 4 F4
Landwade Suffk 57 M7
Landywood Staffs 64 G11
Lane Cnwll 3 K2
Laneast Cnwll 7 J6
Lane Bottom Lancs 84 C8
Lane End Cumb 88 F6
Lane End Hants 24 H8
Lane End Kent 33 P7
Lane End Lancs 84 C6
Lane End Wilts 23 J4
Lane Ends Derbys 65 M5
Lane Ends Lancs 84 B6
Lane Green Staffs 64 G11
Laneham Notts 79 K8
Lane Head Dur 91 J4
Lanehead Dur 99 M10
Lane Head Wigan 76 B4
Lane Head Wsall 64 G11
Lane Heads Lancs 83 K7
Lanercost Cumb 98 H5
Laneshaw Bridge Lancs 84 D7
Lane Side Lancs 84 B10
Langaford Devon 7 M5
Langal Highld 127 L10
Langaller Somset 21 L8
Langar Notts 67 J5
Langbank Rens 113 M6
Langbar N York 84 H4
Langbaurgh N York 92 B4
Langcliffe N York 84 B2
Langdale End N York 93 J8
Langdon Cnwll 7 L2
Langdon Beck Dur 99 N11
Langdon Hills Essex 34 B4
Langdown Hants 12 G4
Langdyke Fife 124 G11
Langenhoe Essex 46 H8
Langford C Beds 44 H3
Langford Devon 9 N5
Langford Essex 46 E9
Langford Notts 79 K12
Langford Oxon 30 F2
Langford Budville Somset 20 H8
Langham Dorset 22 G8
Langham Essex 46 H5
Langham Norfk 70 F3
Langham Rutlnd 67 L9
Langham Suffk 58 E7
Langho Lancs 83 Q8
Langholm D & G 98 D1
Langland Swans 26 E4
Langlee Border 107 M3
Langley Ches E 76 H8
Langley Derbys 66 D3
Langley Gloucs 42 B6
Langley Hants 12 G4
Langley Herts 45 J7
Langley Kent 34 E11
Langley Nthumb 99 M6
Langley Oxon 42 G8
Langley Rochdl 76 G2
Langley Slough 32 F6
Langley Somset 20 G8
Langley Warwks 53 M8
Langley W Susx 25 P9

Langley Warwks 53 M8
Langley Burrell Wilts 29 Q7
Langley Castle Nthumb 99 N6
Langley Common Derbys 65 P5
Langley Green Derbys 65 P4
Langley Green Essex 46 F7
Langley Green Warwks 53 M8
Langley Heath Kent 34 E12
Langley Lower Green Essex 45 N5
Langley Marsh Somset 20 G8
Langley Mill Derbys 66 D3
Langley Moor Dur 100 G9
Langley Park Dur 100 G9
Langley Street Norfk 71 M11
Langley Upper Green Essex 45 N5
Langley Vale Surrey 33 J10
Langney E Susx 16 A10
Langold Notts 78 F6
Langore Cnwll 7 L5
Langport Somset 21 P8
Langrick Lincs 68 E2
Langridge BaNES 29 L8
Langridgeford Devon 19 L8
Langrigg Cumb 97 N9
Langrish Hants 25 M8
Langsett Barns 77 N4
Langside P & K 123 K10
Langstone Hants 13 M4
Langstone Newpt 28 E4
Langthorne N York 91 L8
Langthorpe N York 85 M2
Langthwaite N York 90 G6
Langtoft E R Yk 87 J2
Langtoft Lincs 68 C9
Langton Dur 91 K3
Langton Lincs 80 E10
Langton Lincs 80 G10
Langton N York 86 E2
Langton by Wragby Lincs 80 E8
Langton Green Kent 15 Q3
Langton Green Suffk 58 H6
Langton Herring Dorset 10 F8
Langton Long Blandford Dorset 11 L4
Langton Matravers Dorset 11 N9
Langtree Devon 19 J10
Langtree Week Devon 19 J10
Langwathby Cumb 98 H11
Langwell Highld 144 F4
Langwell House Highld 151 K12
Langwith Derbys 78 E9
Langwith Junction Derbys 78 E10
Langworth Lincs 79 Q8
Lanhydrock House & Gardens Cnwll 3 Q2
Lanivet Cnwll 3 P2
Lanjeth Cnwll 3 N4
Lank Cnwll 6 F9
Lanlivery Cnwll 3 Q3
Lanner Cnwll 2 H6
Lanoy Cnwll 7 K9
Lanreath Cnwll 4 B5
Lansallos Cnwll 4 B6
Lanteglos Highway Cnwll 4 A6
Lanton Border 108 B3
Lanton Nthumb 108 E3
La Passee Guern 12 c1
Lapford Devon 8 D3
Laphroaig Ag & B 111 J12
La Pulente Jersey 13 a2
Lapworth Warwks 53 M6
Larachbeg Highld 120 D3
Larbert Falk 114 F5
Larbreck Lancs 83 K7
Largie Abers 140 F9
Largiemore Ag & B 112 D4
Largoward Fife 125 J12
Largs N Ayrs 113 J9
Largybeg N Ayrs 103 Q5
Largymore N Ayrs 103 R5
Larkbeare Devon 9 K5
Larkfield Inver 113 K6
Larkfield Kent 34 C10
Larkhall S Lans 114 D11
Larkhill Wilts 23 P4
Larling Norfk 58 F3
La Rocque Jersey 13 d3
La Rousaillerie Guern 12 c1
Lartington Dur 90 G3
Lasborough Gloucs 29 M4
Lasham Hants 25 M4
Lashbrook Devon 7 N4
Lashenden Kent 16 E3
Lask Edge Staffs 76 G12
Lasswade Mdloth 115 Q8
Lastingham N York 92 E8
Latcham Somset 21 P4
Latchford Herts 45 M7
Latchford Oxon 31 N2
Latchford Warrtn 76 B6
Latchingdon Essex 34 F2
Latchley Cnwll 7 M7
Lately Common Warrtn 76 C4
Lathbury M Keyn 44 C3
Latheron Highld 151 M10
Latheronwheel Highld 151 M10
Lathom Lancs 75 M2
Lathones Fife 125 J11
Latimer Bucks 32 E3
Latteridge S Glos 29 J5
Lattiford Somset 22 E8
Latton Wilts 30 C3
Lauder Border 116 C11
Laugharne Carmth 37 Q8
Laughterton Lincs 79 L8
Laughton E Susx 15 P8
Laughton Leics 54 H3
Laughton Lincs 67 N5
Laughton Lincs 79 M3
Laughton Common Rothm 78 E4
Laughton-en-le-Morthen Rothm 78 E4
Launcells Cnwll 7 J4
Launcells Cross Cnwll 7 K4
Launceston Cnwll 7 L6
Launton Oxon 43 M7
Laurencekirk Abers 132 H10
Laurieston D & G 96 D5
Lavendon M Keyn 55 M10
Lavenham Suffk 58 D10
Lavernock V Glam 27 Q8
Laverstock Wilts 23 N6
Laverstoke Hants 25 J4
Laverton Gloucs 42 C5
Laverton N York 91 L12
Laverton Somset 22 H3
La Villette Guern 12 c3
Lavister Wrexhm 75 K12
Law S Lans 114 E10
Lawers P & K 122 H6
Lawford Essex 47 J5
Lawford Somset 20 H6
Law Hill S Lans 114 E11
Lawhitton Cnwll 7 L6
Lawkland N York 84 B2
Lawkland Green N York 84 A2
Lawley Wrekin 64 C10

178 Lawnhead – Llangeinor

Lawnhead Staffs 64 F7
Lawrence Weston Bristl 28 H6
Lawrenny Pembks 37 K9
Lawrenny Quay Pembks 37 K9
Lawshall Suffk 58 C10
Lawshall Green Suffk 58 C10
Lawton Herefs 51 M9
Laxay W Isls 152 f4
Laxdale W Isls 152 g3
Laxey IoM 102 f5
Laxfield Suffk 59 L6
Laxford Bridge Highld 148 F7
Laxo Shet 147 j5
Laxton E R Yk 86 E10
Laxton Nhants 55 N1
Laxton Notts 79 J10
Laycock C Brad 84 F7
Layer Breton Essex 46 G8
Layer-de-la-Haye Essex 46 G7
Layer Marney Essex 46 G8
Layham Suffk 47 J4
Laymore Dorset 10 B4
Layter's Green Bucks 32 E4
Laytham E R Yk 86 D7
Laythes Cumb 97 P7
Lazenby R & Cl 92 C3
Lazonby Cumb 98 G10
Lea Derbys 77 Q12
Lea Herefs 41 K7
Lea Lincs 79 L6
Lea Shrops 51 K3
Lea Shrops 63 L10
Lea Wilts 29 Q5
Leachkin Highld 138 B7
Leadburn Border 115 N10
Leadenham Lincs 67 N2
Leaden Roding Essex 45 Q9
Leadgate Cumb 99 K9
Leadgate Dur 100 E8
Leadgate Nthumb 100 E6
Leadhills S Lans 106 A7
Leadingcross Green Kent 34 F12
Leadmill Derbys 77 N7
Leafield Oxon 42 G8
Leagrave Luton 44 F7
Leahead Ches W 76 C10
Lea Heath Staffs 65 J7
Leake N York 91 Q8
Leake Common Side
Lincs 68 H2
Lealholm N York 92 F5
Lealholm Side N York 92 F5
Lealt Highld 135 J4
Leam Derbys 77 N8
Lea Marston Warwks 53 M2
Leamington Hastings
Warwks 54 D7
Leamington Spa Warwks 53 Q7
Leamside Dur 101 J9
Leap Cross E Susx 15 Q9
Learney Abers 132 F4
Leasgill Cumb 89 M10
Leasingham Lincs 67 Q2
Leasingthorne Dur 100 H12
Leatherhead Surrey 32 H11
Leathley N York 85 K6
Leaton Shrops 63 M8
Leaton Wrekin 63 Q10
Lea Town Lancs 83 L9
Leaveland Kent 34 H11
Leavenheath Suffk 46 G4
Leavening N York 86 E3
Leaves Green Gt Lon 33 M10
Lea Yeat Cumb 90 C9
Lebberston N York 93 M10
Le Bigard Guern 12 b3
Le Bourg Guern 12 c3
Le Bourg Jersey 13 d3
Lechlade on Thames
Gloucs 30 E2
Lecht Gruinart Ag & B 110 G7
Leck Lancs 89 Q11
Leckbuie P & K 123 J5
Leckford Hants 24 F6
Leckhampstead Bucks 43 P4
Leckhampstead W Berk 31 J7
Leckhampstead Thicket
W Berk 31 J7
Leckhampton Gloucs 41 Q8
Leckmelm Highld 144 F7
Leckwith V Glam 27 R7
Leconfield E R Yk 87 J6
Ledaig Ag & B 120 G5
Ledburn Bucks 44 C7
Ledbury Herefs 41 L4
Leddington Gloucs 41 L5
Ledgemoor Herefs 51 L10
Ledicot Herefs 51 L8
Ledmore Highld 144 G3
Ledsham Ches W 75 K9
Ledsham Leeds 85 P9
Ledston Leeds 85 N9
Ledstone Devon 5 M7
Ledston Luck Leeds 85 N9
Ledwell Oxon 43 J6
Lee Devon 19 J4
Lee Gt Lon 33 M7
Lee Hants 24 F9
Lee Shrops 63 L6
Leebotwood Shrops 51 N1
Lee Brockhurst Shrops 63 P7
Leece Cumb 82 G1
Lee Chapel Essex 34 C5
Lee Clump Bucks 44 C10
Lee Common Bucks 44 C10
Leeds Kent 34 E11
Leeds Leeds 85 L8
Leeds Bradford Airport
Leeds 85 K7
Leeds Castle Kent 34 E11
Leeds Skelton Lake
Services Leeds 85 M9
Leedstown Cnwll 2 F7
Lee Green Ches E 76 C11
Leek Staffs 77 J12
Leek Wootton Warwks 53 P7
Lee Mill Devon 5 J5
Leeming C Brad 84 F8
Leeming N York 91 M9
Leeming Bar N York 91 M8
Leeming Bar Rest Area
N York 91 M9
Lee Moor Devon 5 J4
Lee-on-the-Solent Hants 13 J5
Lees C Brad 84 F7
Lees Derbys 65 N5
Lees Oldham 76 H3
Lees Green Derbys 65 N5
Leesthorpe Leics 67 K9
Leeswood Flints 75 J11
Leetown P & K 124 E8
Leftwich Ches W 76 C9
Legar Powys 40 B8
Legbourne Lincs 80 G7
Legburthwaite Cumb 89 J3
Legerwood Border 107 P1
Legoland W & M 32 D7
Le Gron Guern 12 b3
Legsby Lincs 80 C6
Le Haguais Jersey 13 c3
Le Hocq Jersey 13 d3
Leicester C Leic 66 F11
Leicester Forest East
Leics 66 E11
Leicester Forest East
Services Leics 66 E11
Leigh Devon 19 P11
Leigh Dorset 10 F3
Leigh Gloucs 41 P6
Leigh Kent 15 Q2
Leigh Shrops 63 K11
Leigh Surrey 15 J1
Leigh Wigan 76 C4
Leigh Wilts 30 C4
Leigh Worcs 52 E10
Leigh Beck Essex 34 E6
Leigh Delamere Wilts 29 P6
Leigh Delamere
Services Wilts 29 P6
Leigh Green Kent 16 F4
Leigh Knoweglass
S Lans 114 B11
Leighland Chapel Somset 20 G6
Leigh-on-Sea Sthend 34 E5
Leigh Park Dorset 11 P5
Leigh Park Hants 13 M3
Leigh Sinton Worcs 52 E10
Leighswood Wsall 65 K12
Leighterton Gloucs 29 N4
Leighton N York 91 K11
Leighton Powys 62 H11
Leighton Shrops 63 Q11
Leighton Somset 22 F4
Leighton Bromswold
Cambs 56 C5
Leighton Buzzard C Beds 44 C6
Leigh upon Mendip
Somset 22 F4
Leigh Woods N Som 28 H8
Leinthall Earls Herefs 51 M7
Leinthall Starkes Herefs 51 M7
Leintwardine Herefs 51 L6
Leire Leics 54 E3
Leiston Suffk 59 N8
Leith C Edin 115 N6
Leitholm Border 108 C1
Lelant Cnwll 2 E7
Lelley E R Yk 87 N8
Lem Hill Worcs 52 D5
Lempitlaw Border 108 C3
Lemreway W Isls 152 g5
Lemsford Herts 45 J9
Lenchwick Worcs 42 B2
Lendalfoot S Ayrs 104 C11
Lendrick Stirlg 122 F11
Lendrum Terrace Abers 141 Q7
Lenham Kent 34 F12
Lenham Heath Kent 34 G12
Lenie Highld 137 N10
Lennel Border 108 D2
Lennox Plunton D & G 96 C8
Lennoxtown E Duns 114 B6
Lent Bucks 32 D6
Lenton C Nott 66 F4
Lenton Lincs 67 P6
Lenwade Norfk 70 G8
Lenzie E Duns 114 B7
Leochel-Cushnie Abers 132 E2
Leomansley Staffs 65 L10
Leominster Herefs 51 N9
Leonard Stanley Gloucs 41 N11
Leoville Jersey 13 a1
Lepe Hants 12 G5
Lephin Highld 134 C6
Leppington N York 86 E3
Lepton Kirk 85 J12
Lerags Ag & B 120 F7
L'Erée Guern 12 b2
Lerryn Cnwll 4 A5
Lerwick Shet 147 j7
Les Arquêts Guern 12 b3
Lesbury Nthumb 109 L7
Les Hubits Guern 12 c3
Leslie Abers 140 F11
Leslie Fife 115 N1
Les Lohiers Guern 12 b2
Lesmahagow S Lans 105 Q2
Les Murchez Guern 12 b3
Lesnewth Cnwll 6 G6
Les Nicolles Guern 12 c3
Les Quartiers Guern 12 c2
Les Quennevais Jersey 13 a2
Les Sages Guern 12 b3
Lessingham Norfk 71 M6
Lessonhall Cumb 97 P8
Lestowder Cnwll 3 K9
Les Villets Guern 12 b3
Leswalt D & G 94 E5
L'Etacq Jersey 13 a1
Letchmore Heath Herts 32 G3
Letchworth Garden City
Herts 45 J5
Letcombe Bassett Oxon 30 H5
Letcombe Regis Oxon 30 H5
Letham Angus 125 K3
Letham Border 107 Q8
Letham Falk 114 G4
Letham Fife 124 F10
Letham Grange Angus 125 M4
Lethenty Abers 140 F11
Lethenty Abers 141 K8
Letheringham Suffk 59 K9
Letheringsett Norfk 70 F5
Lettaford Devon 8 D8
Letterewe Highld 143 P11
Letterfearn Highld 136 B11
Letterfinlay Lodge Hotel
Highld 129 J6
Letters Highld 144 E7
Lettershaw S Lans 106 B6
Letterston Pembks 36 H4
Lettoch Highld 139 J12
Lettoch Highld 139 K9
Letton Herefs 40 D2
Letton Herefs 51 L6
Lett's Green Kent 33 N10
Letty Green Herts 45 K9
Letwell Rothm 78 F6
Leuchars Fife 125 J8
Leumrabhagh W Isls 152 g5
Leurbost W Isls 152 g4
Levalsa Meor Cnwll 3 N5
Levan Inver 113 J6
Levedale Staffs 64 G9
Level's Green Essex 45 N7
Leven E R Yk 87 L6
Leven Fife 115 Q1
Levens Cumb 89 M9
Levens Green Herts 45 L7
Levenshulme Manch 76 G5
Levenwick Shet 147 i9
Leverburgh W Isls 152 d6
Leverington Cambs 68 H10
Leverstock Green Herts 44 F10
Leverton Lincs 68 H3
Le Villocq Guern 12 c2
Levington Suffk 47 M4
Levisham N York 92 G8
Lew Oxon 42 G10
Lewannick Cnwll 7 K8
Lewdown Devon 7 N7
Lewes E Susx 15 M9
Leweston Pembks 36 H6
Lewisham Gt Lon 33 M7
Lewiston Highld 137 N10
Lewistown Brdgnd 27 M5
Lewis Wych Herefs 51 K9
Lewknor Oxon 31 P3
Leworthy Devon 7 L4
Leworthy Devon 19 N6
Lewson Street Kent 34 G10
Lewth Lancs 83 L8
Lewtrenchard Devon 7 N7
Lexden Essex 46 G6
Lexworthy Somset 21 L6
Ley Cnwll 4 B3
Leybourne Kent 34 B10
Leyburn N York 91 J8
Leycett Staffs 64 E3
Leygreen Herts 44 H7
Ley Hill Bucks 44 E11
Leyland Lancs 83 M10
Leyland Green St Hel 75 P4
Leylodge Abers 133 J2
Leys Abers 141 N5
Leys P & K 124 E5
Leysdown-on-Sea Kent 35 J8
Leysmill Angus 125 M3
Leys of Cossans Angus 124 H3
Leysters Herefs 51 P8
Leyton Gt Lon 33 M5
Leytonstone Gt Lon 33 M5
Lezant Cnwll 7 L9
Lezerea Cnwll 2 H8
Leziate Norfk 69 N8
Lhanbryde Moray 139 P4
Libanus Powys 39 N6
Libberton S Lans 106 C1
Libbery Worcs 52 H9
Liberton C Edin 115 N7
Lichfield Staffs 65 L10
Lickey Worcs 53 J5
Lickey End Worcs 52 H6
Lickey Rock Worcs 52 H6
Lickfold W Susx 14 C5
Liddaton Green Devon 7 N8
Liddesdale Highld 127 P12
Liddington Swindn 30 E6
Lidgate Derbys 77 P8
Lidgate Suffk 57 N9
Lidget Donc 78 G4
Lidgett Notts 78 G10
Lidham Hill E Susx 16 E7
Lidlington C Beds 44 E4
Lidsey W Susx 14 D10
Lidsing Kent 34 D10
Liff Angus 124 G6
Lifford Birm 53 K5
Lifton Devon 7 M8
Liftondown Devon 7 L7
Lighthorne Warwks 53 Q9
Lighthorne Heath
Warwks 54 B9
Lightwater Surrey 32 D10
Lightwater Valley Theme
Park N York 91 M11
Lightwood C Stke 64 G4
Lightwood Green Ches E 64 B4
Lightwood Green Wrexhm 63 L4
Lilbourne Nhants 54 F5
Lilburn Tower Nthumb 108 G5
Lilleshall Wrekin 64 D9
Lilley Herts 44 G6
Lilley W Berk 31 J6
Lilliesleaf Border 107 N5
Lillingstone Dayrell
Bucks 43 P4
Lillingstone Lovell Bucks 43 P4
Lillington Dorset 22 E11
Lilliput BCP 11 P7
Lilstock Somset 21 J4
Lilyhurst Shrops 64 D9
Limbrick Lancs 83 N12
Limbury Luton 44 F7
Limebrook Herefs 51 L7
Limefield Bury 76 E1
Limekilnburn S Lans 114 C11
Limekilns Fife 115 K5
Limerigg Falk 114 F7
Limerstone IoW 12 G8
Limestone Brae Nthumb 99 M8
Lime Street Worcs 41 N5
Limington Somset 22 C9
Limmerhaugh E Ayrs 105 L4
Limpenhoe Norfk 71 M11
Limpley Stoke Wilts 29 M10
Limpsfield Surrey 33 M11
Limpsfield Chart Surrey 33 M12
Linby Notts 66 E2
Linchmere W Susx 14 B5
Lincluden D & G 97 K3
Lincoln Lincs 79 N9
Lincomb Worcs 52 F7
Lincombe Devon 5 M6
Lincombe Devon 19 K4
Lindale Cumb 89 L10
Lindal in Furness Cumb 88 H11
Lindfield W Susx 15 L6
Lindford Hants 25 P6
Lindley Kirk 84 H11
Lindley N York 85 K5
Lindores Fife 124 F9
Lindow End Ches E 76 F8
Lindridge Worcs 52 C7
Lindsell Essex 46 B6
Lindsey Suffk 46 H3
Lindsey Tye Suffk 46 H3
Liney Somset 21 N6
Linford Hants 12 C3
Linford Thurr 34 B6
Lingbob C Brad 84 G8
Lingdale R & Cl 92 D3
Lingen Herefs 51 L7
Lingfield Surrey 15 M2
Lingfield Common Surrey 15 M2
Lingwood Norfk 71 M10
Linicro Highld 134 G2
Linkend Worcs 41 N5
Linkenholt Hants 30 H10
Linkhill Kent 16 E5
Linkinhorne Cnwll 7 L10
Linktown Fife 115 N3
Linkwood Moray 139 N4
Linley Shrops 51 K2
Linley Green Herefs 52 C10
Linleygreen Shrops 52 C1
Linlithgow W Loth 114 H6
Linshiels Nthumb 108 E8
Linsidemore Highld 145 M5
Linslade C Beds 44 C7
Linstead Parva Suffk 59 L5
Linstock Cumb 98 E6
Linthurst Worcs 53 J6
Linthwaite Kirk 84 G12
Lintlaw Border 117 J9
Lintmill Moray 140 D3
Linton Border 108 C4
Linton Cambs 46 A3
Linton Derbys 65 P9
Linton Herefs 41 K6
Linton Kent 34 D12
Linton Leeds 85 N6
Linton N York 84 E3
Linton Nthumb 109 L11
Linton Heath Derbys 65 P9
Linton Hill Herefs 41 K7
Linton-on-Ouse N York 85 P3
Linwood Hants 12 C3
Linwood Lincs 80 B6
Linwood Rens 113 N8
Lionacleit W Isls 152 c9
Lional W Isls 152 h1
Lions Green E Susx 15 Q7
Liphook Hants 25 P7
Lipley Shrops 64 D6
Liscard Wirral 75 J5
Liscombe Somset 20 D7
Liskeard Cnwll 4 C4
Lismore Ag & B 120 F4
Liss Hants 25 N8
Lissett E R Yk 87 L4
Liss Forest Hants 25 N7
Lissington Lincs 80 B7
Liston Essex 46 E3
Lisvane Cardif 28 B6
Liswerry Newpt 28 D5
Litcham Norfk 70 C8
Litchborough Nhants 54 G10
Litchfield Hants 24 H3
Litherland Sefton 75 K4
Litlington Cambs 45 K3
Litlington E Susx 15 P10
Little Abington Cambs 57 K10
Little Addington Nhants 55 N6
Little Airies D & G 95 M8
Little Almshoe Herts 44 H6
Little Alne Warwks 53 L8
Little Altcar Sefton 75 J2
Little Amwell Herts 45 L9
Little Asby Cumb 90 A5
Little Aston Staffs 65 K12
Little Atherfield IoW 12 H9
Little Ayton N York 92 B5
Little Baddow Essex 46 D10
Little Badminton S Glos 29 N5
Little Bampton Cumb 98 B7
Little Bardfield Essex 46 B5
Little Barford Bed 56 D9
Little Barningham Norfk 70 H5
Little Barrington Gloucs 42 E9
Little Barrow Ches W 75 M9
Little Barugh N York 92 F10
Little Bavington Nthumb 100 C3
Little Bealings Suffk 59 J11
Littlebeck N York 92 H6
Little Bedwyn Wilts 30 G9
Little Bentley Essex 47 K6
Little Berkhamsted Herts 45 K10
Little Billing Nhants 55 K8
Little Billington C Beds 44 D7
Little Birch Herefs 40 G5
Little Bispham Bpool 82 H7
Little Blakenham Suffk 58 G11
Little Blencow Cumb 98 F11
Little Bloxwich Wsall 65 J11
Little Bognor W Susx 14 E7
Little Bolehill Derbys 65 P1
Little Bollington Ches E 76 D6
Little Bookham Surrey 32 G11
Littleborough Devon 8 F3
Littleborough Notts 79 K7
Littleborough Rochdl 84 D12
Littlebourne Kent 35 M10
Little Bourton Oxon 43 K3
Little Bowden Leics 55 J3
Little Bradley Suffk 57 N10
Little Brampton Herefs 51 J8
Little Brampton Shrops 51 L4
Little Braxted Essex 46 E8
Little Brechin Angus 132 F11
Littlebredy Dorset 10 F7
Little Brickhill M Keyn 44 C5
Little Bridgeford Staffs 64 G7
Little Brington Nhants 54 H8
Little Bromley Essex 47 K6
Little Broughton Cumb 97 M11
Little Budworth Ches W 75 Q10
Littleburn Highld 138 B5
Little Burstead Essex 34 B4
Littlebury Essex 45 P4
Littlebury Green Essex 45 P4
Little Bytham Lincs 67 P8
Little Canfield Essex 45 Q7
Little Carlton Lincs 80 H6
Little Carlton Notts 79 K12
Little Casterton Rutlnd 67 P10
Little Catwick E R Yk 87 L6
Little Catworth Cambs 56 B6
Little Cawthorpe Lincs 80 G7
Little Chalfont Bucks 32 E3
Little Chart Kent 16 G2
Little Chesterford Essex 45 P3
Little Cheveney Kent 16 C2
Little Cheverell Wilts 23 L3
Little Chishill Cambs 45 M4
Little Clacton Essex 47 L8
Little Clanfield Oxon 30 F2
Little Clifton Cumb 88 E1
Little Coates NE Lin 80 E2
Little Comberton Worcs 41 Q3
Little Common E Susx 16 C9
Little Comp Kent 34 B11
Little Compton Warwks 42 F6
Little Corby Cumb 98 F7
Little Cornard Suffk 46 F4
Littlecott Wilts 23 P3
Little Cowarne Herefs 51 Q10
Little Coxwell Oxon 30 G4
Little Crakehall N York 91 L8
Little Cransley Nhants 55 L5
Little Cressingham Norfk 70 C12
Little Crosby Sefton 75 K3
Little Crosthwaite Cumb 88 H1
Little Cubley Derbys 65 M5
Little Dalby Leics 67 K9
Littledean Gloucs 41 K9
Little Dewchurch Herefs 40 H5
Little Ditton Cambs 57 M9
Little Doward Herefs 40 H8
Littledown Hants 30 H10
Little Downham Cambs 57 K4
Little Driffield E R Yk 87 J4
Little Dunham Norfk 70 C9
Little Dunkeld P & K 123 P4
Little Dunmow Essex 46 B7
Little Durnford Wilts 23 P6
Little Easton Essex 45 R7
Little Eaton Derbys 66 B4
Little Ellingham Norfk 70 E12
Little Elm Somset 22 G4
Little Everdon Nhants 54 F9
Little Eversden Cambs 56 G10
Little Faringdon Oxon 30 F2
Little Fencote N York 91 M8
Little Fenton N York 85 Q8
Littleferry Highld 146 E6
Little Fransham Norfk 70 D9
Little Gaddesden Herts 44 E9
Little Garway Herefs 40 F7
Little Gidding Cambs 56 C4
Little Glemham Suffk 59 L9
Little Gorsley Herefs 41 L7
Little Gransden Cambs 56 E9
Little Green Notts 67 J3
Little Green Somset 22 G4
Little Grimsby Lincs 80 F5
Little Gringley Notts 79 J7
Little Habton N York 92 F11
Little Hadham Herts 45 N7
Little Hale Lincs 68 C4
Little Hallam Derbys 66 D4
Little Hallingbury Essex 45 P8
Littleham Devon 9 K8
Littleham Devon 18 H8
Little Hampden Bucks 44 B11
Littlehampton W Susx 14 E10
Little Hanford Dorset 11 K2
Little Harrowden Nhants 55 L6
Little Haseley Oxon 31 N2
Little Hatfield E R Yk 87 M6
Little Hautbois Norfk 71 K7
Little Haven Pembks 36 G8
Littlehaven W Susx 14 H4
Little Hay Staffs 65 L11
Little Hayfield Derbys 77 J6
Little Haywood Staffs 65 J8
Little Heath Staffs 64 G8
Little Heath W Berk 31 N7
Littlehempston Devon 5 N4
Little Hereford Herefs 51 P7
Little Horkesley Essex 46 G5
Little Hormead Herts 45 M6
Little Horsted E Susx 15 N7
Little Horton C Brad 84 H9
Little Horton Wilts 30 B10
Little Horwood Bucks 43 R5
Little Houghton Barns 78 C2
Little Houghton Nhants 55 K8
Littlehoughton Nthumb 109 L6
Little Hucklow Derbys 77 M8
Little Hulton Salfd 76 D3
Little Hungerford W Berk 31 L7
Little Hutton N York 91 Q11
Little Irchester Nhants 55 M7
Little Kelk E R Yk 87 L3
Little Keyford Somset 22 H4
Little Kimble Bucks 44 B10
Little Kineton Warwks 53 Q10
Little Kingshill Bucks 32 C3
Little Knox D & G 96 G6
Little Langdale Cumb 89 J6
Little Langford Wilts 23 N6
Little Laver Essex 45 Q10
Little Leigh Ches W 76 B8
Little Leighs Essex 46 C8
Little Lever Bolton 76 D2
Little Linford M Keyn 44 B3
Little Load Somset 21 P8
Little London Bucks 43 N9
Little London Cambs 56 H1
Little London E Susx 15 Q7
Little London Essex 45 N6
Little London Essex 57 K9
Little London Gloucs 41 L8
Little London Hants 24 F3
Little London Hants 31 N10
Little London Leeds 85 J7
Little London Lincs 68 E8
Little London Lincs 68 H7
Little London Lincs 80 F8
Little London Norfk 69 L8
Little London Powys 50 E3
Little Longstone Derbys 77 M9
Little Madeley Staffs 64 E3
Little Malvern Worcs 41 M4
Little Mancot Flints 75 K10
Little Maplestead Essex 46 E5
Little Marcle Herefs 41 K4
Little Marland Devon 19 K11
Little Marlow Bucks 32 C5
Little Massingham Norfk 69 Q7
Little Melton Norfk 70 H10
Littlemill Abers 131 P5
Littlemill Highld 138 G6
Little Mill Mons 40 D11
Little Milton Oxon 31 N2
Little Missenden Bucks 32 C3
Little Mongeham Kent 35 P12
Littlemoor Derbys 78 B11
Little Moor Somset 21 M7
Littlemore Oxon 43 L11
Little Musgrave Cumb 90 C4
Little Ness Shrops 63 L8
Little Neston Ches W 75 J8
Little Newcastle Pembks 37 J5
Little Newsham Dur 91 J3
Little Norton Somset 21 Q10
Little Oakley Essex 47 M6
Little Oakley Nhants 55 M3
Little Odell Bed 55 N9
Little Offley Herts 44 G6
Little Ormside Cumb 90 B3
Little Orton Cumb 98 D7
Little Ouse Cambs 57 M3
Little Ouseburn N York 85 P3
Littleover C Derb 65 Q5
Little Oxendon Nhants 55 J4
Little Packington Warwks 53 N4
Little Pattenden Kent 16 C2
Little Paxton Cambs 56 D8
Little Petherick Cnwll 6 C10
Little Plumpton Lancs 83 J8
Little Plumstead Norfk 71 L9
Little Ponton Lincs 67 M6
Littleport Cambs 57 L3
Littleport Bridge Cambs 57 L3
Little Posbrook Hants 13 J4
Little Potheridge Devon 19 K10
Little Preston Leeds 85 M9
Little Preston Nhants 54 F10
Littler Ches W 76 B10
Little Raveley Cambs 56 E5
Little Reedness E R Yk 86 E10
Little Ribston N York 85 M4
Little Rissington Gloucs 42 E7
Little Rollright Oxon 42 G6
Little Rowsley Derbys 77 N10
Little Ryburgh Norfk 70 E6
Little Ryle Nthumb 108 G7
Little Ryton Shrops 63 N11
Little Salkeld Cumb 98 H11
Little Sampford Essex 46 B5
Little Sandhurst Br For 32 B10
Little Saredon Staffs 64 H10
Little Saughall Ches W 75 L10
Little Saxham Suffk 57 Q8
Little Scatwell Highld 137 L4
Little Shelford Cambs 57 J10
Little Shrewley Warwks 53 N7
Little Silver Devon 8 G3
Little Singleton Lancs 83 J7
Little Skipwith N York 86 C8
Little Smeaton N York 85 Q11
Little Snoring Norfk 70 D6
Little Sodbury S Glos 29 M6
Little Sodbury End S Glos 29 M5
Little Somborne Hants 24 F7
Little Somerford Wilts 29 Q5
Little Soudley Shrops 64 D6
Little Stainforth N York 84 B2
Little Stainton Darltn 91 N3
Little Stanion Nhants 55 M3
Little Stanney Ches W 75 L9
Little Staughton Bed 56 B8
Little Steeping Lincs 80 H11
Little Stoke Staffs 64 G5
Littlestone-on-Sea Kent 17 K6
Little Stonham Suffk 58 G8
Little Stretton Leics 66 H12
Little Stretton Shrops 51 M2
Little Strickland Cumb 89 P3
Little Stukeley Cambs 56 D5
Little Sugnall Staffs 64 E6
Little Sutton Ches W 75 L8
Little Sutton Shrops 51 N4
Little Swinburne Nthumb 99 Q3
Little Sypland D & G 96 E7
Little Tew Oxon 42 H6
Little Tey Essex 46 F7
Little Thetford Cambs 57 K5
Little Thirkleby N York 91 Q11
Little Thornage Norfk 70 F4
Little Thornton Lancs 83 J7
Little Thorpe Dur 101 L9
Littlethorpe Leics 54 E1
Littlethorpe N York 85 L1
Little Thurlow Suffk 57 N10
Little Thurlow Green
Suffk 57 N10
Little Thurrock Thurr 34 A7
Littleton BaNES 28 H9
Littleton Ches W 75 M10
Littleton D & G 96 D7
Littleton Dorset 11 L4
Littleton Hants 24 G7
Littleton Somset 22 C7
Littleton Surrey 14 D1
Littleton Surrey 32 F8
Littleton Drew Wilts 29 N6
Littleton of Airlie Angus 124 G3
Littleton-on-Severn
S Glos 29 J4
Littleton Panell Wilts 23 M2
Little Torrington Devon 19 J10
Little Totham Essex 46 F9
Little Town Cumb 88 H3
Littletown Dur 101 J9
Little Town Lancs 83 P8
Little Town Warrtn 76 B5
Little Twycross Leics 65 Q11
Little Urswick Cumb 88 H12
Little Wakering Essex 34 G5
Little Walden Essex 45 Q3
Little Waldingfield Suffk 46 G3
Little Walsingham Norfk 70 D5
Little Waltham Essex 46 C9
Little Warley Essex 33 R4
Little Washbourne Gloucs 42 A5
Little Weighton E R Yk 87 J8
Little Welnetham Suffk 58 C8
Little Welton Lincs 80 F6
Little Wenham Suffk 47 K4
Little Wenlock Wrekin 64 C10
Little Weston Somset 22 E8
Little Whitefield IoW 13 K7
Little Whittingham
Green Suffk 59 K5
Little Whittington
Nthumb 100 C4
Littlewick Green W & M 32 B6
Little Wilbraham Cambs 57 K9
Littlewindsor Dorset 10 C4
Little Witcombe Gloucs 41 P8
Little Witley Worcs 52 E8
Little Wittenham Oxon 31 M4
Little Wolford Warwks 42 F5
Littlewood Staffs 64 H10
Little Woodcote Gt Lon 33 K10
Littleworth Bucks 44 C7
Littleworth Oxon 30 G3
Littleworth Staffs 64 H8
Littleworth Staffs 65 J10
Littleworth W Susx 14 H7
Littleworth Worcs 52 G10
Littleworth Worcs 53 J8
Littleworth Common
Bucks 32 D5
Little Wratting Suffk 46 C2
Little Wymington Bed 55 N7
Little Wymondley Herts 45 J6
Little Wyrley Staffs 65 J11
Little Wytheford Shrops 63 P8
Little Yeldham Essex 46 D4
Littley Green Essex 46 C8
Litton Derbys 77 M8
Litton N York 90 E12
Litton Somset 22 D2
Litton Cheney Dorset 10 E6
Liurbost W Isls 152 g4
Liverpool Lpool 75 K5
Liverpool Maritime
Mercantile City Lpool 75 K6
Liversedge Kirk 85 J10
Liverton Devon 8 E9
Liverton R & Cl 92 E4
Liverton Mines R & Cl 92 E3
Liverton Street Kent 34 F12
Livingston W Loth 115 K7
Livingston Village W Loth 115 J8
Lixwm Flints 74 G9
Lizard Cnwll 2 H12
Llaingoch IoA 72 C7
Llaithddu Powys 50 E4
Llan Powys 61 Q12
Llanaber Gwynd 61 K8
Llanaelhaearn Gwynd 60 F3
Llanafan Cerdgn 49 M6
Llanafan-Fawr Powys 50 C9
Llanallgo IoA 72 H6
Llanarmon Gwynd 60 G4
Llanarmon Dyffryn
Ceiriog Wrexhm 62 G6
Llanarmon-yn-Ial Denbgs 74 G12
Llanarth Cerdgn 48 G9
Llanarth Mons 40 E9
Llanarthne Carmth 38 D7
Llanasa Flints 74 F7
Llanbabo IoA 72 F6
Llanbadarn Fawr Cerdgn 49 K4
Llanbadarn Fynydd
Powys 50 F5
Llanbadarn-y-garreg
Powys 50 F11
Llanbadoc Mons 28 E2
Llanbadrig IoA 72 F5
Llanbeder Newpt 28 E4
Llanbedr Gwynd 61 K7
Llanbedr Powys 39 Q2
Llanbedr Powys 40 B7
Llanbedr-Dyffryn-Clwyd
Denbgs 74 G11
Llanbedrgoch IoA 72 H7
Llanbedrog Gwynd 60 E6
Llanbedr-y-Cennin
Conwy 73 N10
Llanberis Gwynd 73 K11
Llanbethêry V Glam 27 N8
Llanbister Powys 50 F6
Llanblethian V Glam 27 N7
Llanboidy Carmth 37 N6
Llanbradach Caerph 27 Q4
Llanbrynmair Powys 62 B11
Llancadle V Glam 27 N8
Llancarfan V Glam 27 P8
Llancayo Mons 40 E11
Llancloudy Herefs 40 G7
Llancynfelyn Cerdgn 49 L2
Llandaff Cardif 27 R7
Llandanwg Gwynd 61 J6
Llandarcy Neath 26 H3
Llandawke Carmth 37 Q8
Llanddaniel Fab IoA 72 H9
Llanddarog Carmth 38 D8
Llanddeiniol Cerdgn 49 J6
Llanddeiniolen Gwynd 73 J10
Llandderfel Gwynd 62 D5
Llanddeusant Carmth 39 J7
Llanddeusant IoA 72 E6
Llanddew Powys 39 P5
Llanddewi Swans 26 C4
Llanddewi Brefi Cerdgn 49 L9
Llanddewi'r Cwm Powys 50 E11
Llanddewi Rhydderch
Mons 40 D9
Llanddewi Velfrey Pembks 37 M7
Llanddewi Ystradenni
Powys 50 F7
Llanddoged Conwy 73 P11
Llanddona IoA 73 J8
Llanddowror Carmth 37 P7
Llanddulas Conwy 74 B8
Llanddwywe Gwynd 61 K8
Llanddyfnan IoA 72 H8
Llandecwyn Gwynd 61 K5
Llandefaelog Powys 39 N5
Llandefaelog-Tre'r-
Graig Powys 39 Q6
Llandefalle Powys 39 Q4
Llandegfan IoA 73 J9
Llandegla Denbgs 62 H2
Llandegley Powys 50 G8
Llandegveth Mons 28 D3
Llandegwning Gwynd 60 D6
Llandeilo Carmth 38 F7
Llandeilo Graban Powys 39 P3
Llandeilo'r Fan Powys 39 L5
Llandeloy Pembks 36 G5
Llandenny Mons 40 F11
Llandevaud Newpt 28 E4
Llandevenny Mons 28 F5
Llandinabo Herefs 40 G6
Llandinam Powys 50 E3
Llandissilio Pembks 37 M6
Llandogo Mons 40 H11
Llandough V Glam 27 N8
Llandough V Glam 27 R8
Llandovery Carmth 39 J5
Llandow V Glam 27 M7
Llandre Carmth 38 G3
Llandre Cerdgn 49 K3
Llandre Isaf Pembks 37 M5
Llandrillo Denbgs 62 E5
Llandrillo-yn-Rhos
Conwy 73 P7
Llandrindod Wells Powys 50 E8
Llandrinio Powys 63 J8
Llandudno Conwy 73 N7
Llandudno Junction
Conwy 73 N8
Llandulas Powys 39 L3
Llandwrog Gwynd 60 G1
Llandybie Carmth 38 F8
Llandyfaelog Carmth 38 B9
Llandyfan Carmth 38 F8
Llandyfriog Cerdgn 37 Q2
Llandyfrydog IoA 72 G6
Llandygai Gwynd 73 K9
Llandygwydd Cerdgn 37 P2
Llandynan Denbgs 62 G3
Llandyrnog Denbgs 74 F10
Llandyssil Powys 50 H2
Llandysul Cerdgn 38 B3
Llanedeyrn Cardif 28 B6
Llanedi Carmth 38 E10
Llaneglwys Powys 39 P4
Llanegryn Gwynd 61 K11
Llanegwad Carmth 38 D7
Llaneilian IoA 72 H5
Llanelian-yn-Rhôs
Conwy 73 Q8
Llanelidan Denbgs 62 F2
Llanelieu Powys 40 A5
Llanellen Mons 40 D9
Llanelli Carmth 26 D2
Llanelltyd Gwynd 61 M8
Llanelly Mons 40 B8
Llanelly Hill Mons 40 B9
Llanelwedd Powys 50 E10
Llanenddwyn Gwynd 61 K7
Llanengan Gwynd 60 E7
Llanerch Gwynd 62 B8
Llanerch Powys 51 J2
Llanerchymedd IoA 72 G7
Llanerfyl Powys 62 E10
Llanfabon Caerph 27 Q4
Llanfachraeth IoA 72 E7
Llanfachreth Gwynd 61 N7
Llanfaelog IoA 72 E9
Llanfaelrhys Gwynd 60 C7
Llanfaenor Mons 40 F8
Llanfaes IoA 73 K8
Llanfaes Powys 39 N6
Llanfaethlu IoA 72 E6
Llanfair Gwynd 61 K6
Llanfair Caereinion
Powys 62 F11
Llanfair Clydogau Cerdgn 49 K10
Llanfair Dyffryn Clwyd
Denbgs 62 F1
Llanfairfechan Conwy 73 L9
Llanfair Kilgeddin Mons 40 D10
Llanfair-Nant-Gwyn
Pembks 37 M3
Llanfairpwllgwyngyll IoA 73 J9
Llanfair Talhaiarn Conwy 74 C9
Llanfair Waterdine
Shrops 50 H5
Llanfairynghornwy IoA 72 E5
Llanfair-yn-Neubwll IoA 72 E8
Llanfallteg Carmth 37 M6
Llanfallteg West Carmth 37 M6
Llanfarian Cerdgn 49 K5
Llanfechain Powys 62 G8
Llanfechan Powys 50 D10
Llanfechell IoA 72 F5
Llanferres Denbgs 74 G11
Llan Ffestiniog Gwynd 61 M4
Llanfflewyn IoA 72 F6
Llanfigael IoA 72 E7
Llanfihangel-ar-arth
Carmth 38 C4
Llanfihangel Glyn Myfyr
Conwy 62 D2
Llanfihangel Nant Bran
Powys 39 M5
Llanfihangel-nant-
Melan Powys 50 G9
Llanfihangel Rhydithon
Powys 50 G7
Llanfihangel Rogiet
Mons 28 F5
Llanfihangel Tal-y-llyn
Powys 39 Q6
Llanfihangel-uwch-
Gwili Carmth 38 D7
Llanfihangel-y-
Creuddyn Cerdgn 49 L5
Llanfihangel-yng-
Ngwynfa Powys 62 E9
Llanfihangel yn Nhowyn
IoA 72 E8
Llanfihangel-y-pennant
Gwynd 61 J3
Llanfihangel-y-pennant
Gwynd 61 L10
Llanfilo Powys 39 Q5
Llanfoist Mons 40 C9
Llanfor Gwynd 62 C5
Llanfrechfa Torfn 28 D4
Llanfrothen Gwynd 61 K4
Llanfrynach Powys 39 P6
Llanfwrog Denbgs 74 F12
Llanfwrog IoA 72 E7
Llanfyllin Powys 62 G8
Llanfynydd Carmth 38 E6
Llanfynydd Flints 75 J12
Llanfyrnach Pembks 37 P4
Llangadfan Powys 62 D10
Llangadog Carmth 38 B10
Llangadog Carmth 38 H6
Llangadwaladr IoA 72 F10
Llangadwaladr Powys 62 G6
Llangaffo IoA 72 G10
Llangain Carmth 38 B8
Llangammarch Wells
Powys 39 M2
Llangan V Glam 27 M7
Llangarron Herefs 40 H7
Llangasty-Talyllyn Powys 39 Q6
Llangathen Carmth 38 E7
Llangattock Powys 40 B8
Llangattock Lingoed
Mons 40 E7
Llangattock-Vibon-Avel
Mons 40 F8
Llangedwyn Powys 62 G7
Llangefni IoA 72 H8
Llangeinor Brdgnd 27 L5

Llangeitho Cerdgn 49 K8
Llangeler Carmth 38 B4
Llangelynin Gwynd 61 K10
Llangennech Carmth 26 C4
Llangenny Powys 40 G8
Llangernyw Conwy 73 Q10
Llangian Gwynd 60 E6
Llangloffan Pembks 36 H4
Llanglydwen Carmth 37 N5
Llangoed IoA 73 K8
Llangoedmor Cerdgn 48 C11
Llangollen Denbgs 62 H4
Llangolman Pembks 37 M5
Llangors Powys 39 G6
Llangorwen Cerdgn 49 K4
Llangovan Mons 40 F10
Llangower Gwynd 62 B6
Llangrannog Cerdgn 48 E10
Llangristiolus IoA 72 G8
Llangrove Herefs 40 H8
Llangua Mons 40 E6
Llangunllo Powys 50 H6
Llangunnor Carmth 38 C7
Llangurig Powys 50 B5
Llangwm Conwy 62 C3
Llangwm Mons 28 F2
Llangwm Pembks 37 J8
Llangwnnadl Gwynd 60 C5
Llangwyfan Denbgs 74 F10
Llangwyllog IoA 72 G8
Llangwyryfon Cerdgn 49 K6
Llangybi Cerdgn 49 K10
Llangybi Gwynd 60 G4
Llangybi Mons 28 E3
Llangyfelach Swans 26 F3
Llangynhafal Denbgs 74 F11
Llangynidr Powys 39 R8
Llangyniew Powys 62 C3
Llangynin Carmth 37 P6
Llangynllo Cerdgn 48 G8
Llangynog Carmth 37 R7
Llangynog Powys 62 G2
Llangynwyd Brdgnd 27 K5
Llanhamlach Powys 39 P6
Llanharan Rhondd 27 L6
Llanharry Rhondd 27 N6
Llanhennock Mons 28 E4
Llanhilleth Blae G 28 B2
Llanidan IoA 72 H10
Llanidloes Powys 50 C4
Llaniestyn Gwynd 60 D5
Llanigon Powys 45 J8
Llanilar Cerdgn 49 K6
Llanilid Rhondd 27 L6
Llanina Cerdgn 48 F8
Llanio Cerdgn 49 L9
Llanishen Cardif 28 A6
Llanishen Mons 40 G11
Llanllechid Gwynd 73 K10
Llanlleonfel Powys 50 C10
Llanllowell Mons 28 E2
Llanllugan Powys 62 E11
Llanllwch Carmth 38 B8
Llanllwchaiarn Powys 62 D4
Llanllwni Carmth 38 D4
Llanllyfni Gwynd 60 H2
Llanmadoc Swans 26 C4
Llanmaes V Glam 27 M8
Llanmartin Newpt 28 E4
Llanmerewig Powys 50 G2
Llanmihangel V Glam 27 M8
Llanmiloe Carmth 37 P9
Llanmorlais Swans 26 D3
Llannefydd Conwy 74 D9
Llannon Carmth 38 E10
Llannor Gwynd 60 F5
Llanon Cerdgn 48 H7
Llanover Mons 40 D10
Llanpumsaint Carmth 38 B6
Llanrhaeadr-ym-
  Mochnant Powys 62 F10
Llanrhian Pembks 36 F4
Llanrhidian Swans 26 D4
Llanrhos Conwy 73 N7
Llanrhychwyn Conwy 73 N11
Llanrhyddlad IoA 72 E6
Llanrhystud Cerdgn 49 J7
Llanrothal Herefs 40 G8
Llanrug Gwynd 73 J11
Llanrumney Cardif 28 B6
Llanrwst Conwy 73 P11
Llansadurnen Carmth 37 Q8
Llansadwrn Carmth 38 G5
Llansadwrn IoA 73 J8
Llansaint Carmth 38 B10
Llansamlet Swans 26 G3
Llansanffraid Glan
  Conwy Conwy 73 P8
Llansannan Conwy 74 C10
Llansannor V Glam 27 L7
Llansantffraed Powys 39 Q7
Llansantffraed-
  Cwmdeuddwr Powys 50 F9
Llansantffraed-in-Elvel
  Powys 50 F9
Llansantffraid Cerdgn 49 J7
Llansantffraid-ym-
  Mechain Powys 62 H8
Llansawel Carmth 38 F4
Llansilin Powys 62 H6
Llansoy Mons 40 F11
Llanspyddid Powys 39 N6
Llanstadwell Pembks 37 J9
Llansteffan Carmth 37 R8
Llanstephan Powys 39 J8
Llantarnam Torfn 28 D4
Llanteg Pembks 37 N8
Llanthewy Skirrid Mons 40 D8
Llanthony Mons 40 D7
Llantilio-Crossenny
  Mons 40 E8
Llantilio Pertholey Mons 40 D8
Llantood Pembks 37 M2
Llantrisant Mons 40 F7
Llantrisant Mons 28 E3
Llantrisant Rhondd 27 M7
Llantrithyd V Glam 27 P7
Llantwit Fardre Rhondd 27 P5
Llantwit Major V Glam 27 M8
Llantysilio Denbgs 62 H3
Llanvaches Newpt 28 H4
Llanvair Discoed Mons 28 H4
Llanvapley Mons 40 E9
Llanvetherine Mons 40 E8
Llanveynoe Herefs 40 D5
Llanvihangel Crucorney
  Mons 40 D7
Llanvihangel Gobion
  Mons 40 D9
Llanvihangel-Ystern-
  Llewern Mons 40 F9
Llanwarne Herefs 40 G6
Llanwddyn Powys 62 D8
Llanwenarth Mons 40 D8
Llanwenog Cerdgn 38 E2
Llanwern Newpt 28 H4
Llanwinio Carmth 37 P4
Llanwnda Gwynd 72 H12
Llanwnda Pembks 36 H4
Llanwnnen Cerdgn 38 E3
Llanwnog Powys 50 D2
Llanwonno Rhondd 27 N3
Llanwrda Carmth 39 H5
Llanwrin Powys 61 N11

Llanwrthwl Powys 50 D8
Llanwrtyd Powys 49 Q11
Llanwrtyd Wells Powys 39 L2
Llanwyddelan Powys 62 E12
Llanybdowd Shrops 62 H7
Llanybri Carmth 37 R8
Llanycefn Pembks 37 L5
Llanychaer Pembks 37 J3
Llanycil Carmth 62 B5
Llanycrwys Carmth 38 F3
Llanymawddwy Gwynd 62 B8
Llanymynech Powys 63 J9
Llanynghenedl IoA 72 E7
Llanynys Denbgs 74 F11
Llan-y-pwll Wrexhm 63 L2
Llanyre Powys 50 E8
Llanystumdwy Gwynd 60 H4
Llanywern Powys 39 Q6
Llawhaden Pembks 37 L7
Llawnt Shrops 62 H6
Llawryglyn Powys 50 B2
Llay Wrexhm 63 K1
Llechcynfarwy IoA 72 F7
Llechfaen Powys 39 P6
Llechrhyd Caerph 39 Q10
Llechryd Cerdgn 37 N2
Llechylched IoA 72 F8
Lledrod Cerdgn 49 L6
Llidiardau Gwynd 61 Q4
Llidiart-y-parc Denbgs 62 F3
Llithfaen Gwynd 60 F4
Lloc Flints 74 G8
Llowes Powys 40 B3
Llwydcoed Rhondd 39 N10
Llwydiarth Powys 62 E9
Llwyn Brecy Dorset 10 E2
Llwyncelyn Cerdgn 48 G8
Llwyndafydd Cerdgn 48 F9
Llwynderw Powys 62 H11
Llwyn-drain Pembks 37 P4
Llwyn-du Mons 40 C8
Llwyndyrys Gwynd 60 F4
Llwyngwril Gwynd 61 K10
Llwynhendy Carmth 26 E2
Llwynmawr Wrexhm 62 H5
Llwyn-on Myr Td 39 N9
Llwyn-y-brain Carmth 37 N7
Llwyn-y-groes Cerdgn 49 K9
Llwynypia Rhondd 27 N4
Llynclys Shrops 63 J7
Llynfaes IoA 72 G7
Llyn-y-pandy Flints 74 H10
Llysfaen Conwy 74 B8
Llyswen Cerdgn 48 G8
Llyswen Powys 39 Q4
Llysworney V Glam 27 M7
Llys-y-frân Pembks 37 K6
Llywel Powys 39 K5
Load Brook Sheff 77 P6
Loan Falk 114 H6
Loanend Nthumb 117 L11
Loanhead Mdloth 115 P8
Loaningfoot D & G 97 J7
Loans S Ayrs 104 F3
Lobb Devon 19 J6
Lobhillcross Devon 7 N7
Lochailort Highld 127 P8
Lochaline Highld 120 C4
Lochans D & G 94 F7
Locharbriggs D & G 97 K2
Lochavich Ag & B 120 H9
Lochawe Ag & B 121 L7
Loch Baghasdail W Isls 152 c11
Lochboisdale W Isls 152 c11
Lochbuie Ag & B 119 Q8
Lochcarron Highld 136 B8
Lochdonhead Ag & B 120 D6
Lochdon Ag & B 120 D6
Lochead Ag & B 112 B11
Lochearnhead Stirlg 122 G8
Loch Eil Highld 128 E6
Locheilside Station
  Highld 128 D8
Lochend Highld 137 Q8
Locheport W Isls 152 c8
Loch Euphort W Isls 152 c8
Lochfoot D & G 97 J2
Lochgair Ag & B 112 D3
Lochgelly Fife 115 M3
Lochgilphead Ag & B 112 C4
Lochgoilhead Ag & B 113 J1
Lochieheads Fife 124 E10
Lochill Moray 139 P3
Lochindorb Lodge
  Highld 138 H9
Lochinver Highld 148 C12
Loch Lomond and The
  Trossachs National
  Park 122 D10
Loch Loyal Lodge Highld 149 N7
Lochluichart Highld 137 K3
Lochmaben D & G 97 M2
Lochmaddy W Isls 152 d8
Loch nam Madadh W Isls 152 d8
Loch Ness Highld 137 P10
Lochore Fife 115 M2
Loch Portain W Isls 152 d8
Lochportain W Isls 152 d8
Lochranza N Ayrs 112 D11
Loch Sgioport W Isls 152 c10
Lochside Abers 132 H11
Lochside D & G 97 J3
Lochside Highld 138 E5
Lochskipport W Isls 152 c10
Lochslin Highld 146 F9
Lochton S Ayrs 95 J2
Lochty Angus 132 E11
Lochty Fife 125 K11
Lochuisge Highld 120 E2
Lochwinnoch Rens 113 L9
Lochwood D & G 97 N2
Lockengate Cnwll 3 P2
Lockerbie D & G 97 N2
Lockeridge Wilts 30 D9
Lockerley Hants 21 Q10
Locking N Som 28 E10
Locking Stumps Warrtn 76 B5
Lockington E R Yk 87 K9
Lockington Leics 66 C6
Lockleywood Shrops 64 C6
Locksbottom Gt Lon 33 N9
Locks Heath Hants 14 F5
Lockton N York 92 G9
Loddington Leics 67 K11
Loddington Nhants 55 K5
Loddiswell Devon 5 M7
Loddon Norfk 71 M12
Lode Cambs 57 M8
Lode Heath Solhll 53 M4
Loders Dorset 10 D6
Lodsworth W Susx 15 R5
Lofthouse Leeds 85 L10
Lofthouse N York 91 J12
Lofthouse Gate Wakefd 85 L10
Loftus R & Cl 92 H3
Logan E Ayrs 105 L6
Loganbeck Cumb 88 H12
Loganlea W Loth 114 H9
Loggerheads Staffs 64 E4
Logie Angus 132 H11
Logie Fife 124 H8
Logie Moray 139 J6

Logie Coldstone Abers 132 C3
Logie Newton Abers 140 G8
Logie Pert Angus 132 G11
Logierait P & K 123 N2
Logierieve Abers 141 M10
Login Carmth 37 M6
Lolworth Cambs 56 F8
Lonbain Highld 135 M5
Londesborough E R Yk 86 F6
London Gt Lon 33 L6
London Apprentice Cnwll 3 N4
London Beach Kent 16 F3
London City Airport
  Gt Lon 33 M6
London Colney Herts 44 H11
Londonderry N York 91 M9
London End Nhants 55 M7
London Gateway
  Services Gt Lon 32 H3
London Gatwick Airport
  W Susx 15 K3
London Heathrow
  Airport Gt Lon 32 F7
London Luton Airport
  Luton 44 G7
London Oxford Airport
  Oxon 43 K8
London Southend
  Airport Essex 34 F4
London Stansted
  Airport Essex 45 Q7
Londonthorpe Lincs 67 N4
London Zoo ZSL Gt Lon 33 L6
Londubh Highld 143 M9
Lonemore Highld 143 L9
Long Ashton N Som 28 H8
Long Bank Worcs 52 E6
Long Bennington Lincs 67 L3
Longborough Gloucs 42 E6
Long Bredy Dorset 10 E7
Longbridge Birm 53 J5
Longbridge Warwks 53 P8
Long Buckby Nhants 54 G7
Longburgh Cumb 98 C6
Longburton Dorset 22 E10
Long Cause Devon 5 N4
Long Clawson Leics 67 J7
Longcliffe Derbys 65 N1
Longcombe Devon 5 P5
Long Common Hants 24 H10
Long Compton Staffs 64 F7
Long Compton Warwks 42 G5
Longcot Oxon 30 F4
Long Crendon Bucks 43 P10
Long Crichel Dorset 11 N3
Longcroft Cumb 97 P6
Longcross Surrey 32 E9
Longden Shrops 63 M11
Longden Common
  Shrops 63 M11
Long Ditton Surrey 32 H9
Longdon Staffs 65 K9
Longdon Worcs 41 N5
Longdon Green Staffs 65 K9
Longdon upon Tern
  Wrekin 63 Q9
Longdown Devon 8 G6
Longdowns Cnwll 3 J7
Long Drax N York 86 C9
Long Duckmanton
  Derbys 78 D9
Long Eaton Derbys 66 C5
Longfield Kent 33 R8
Longford Covtry 54 B4
Longford Derbys 65 N5
Longford Gloucs 41 N7
Longford Gt Lon 32 F7
Longford Kent 33 P11
Longford Shrops 64 B5
Longford Wrekin 64 D8
Longforgan P & K 124 F7
Longformacus Border 116 F10
Longframlington Nthumb 109 J9
Long Green Ches W 75 N9
Long Green Worcs 41 N5
Longham Dorset 11 N5
Longham Norfk 70 D9
Long Hanborough Oxon 43 J9
Longhaven Abers 141 Q7
Long Hedges Lincs 68 G3
Longhirst Nthumb 109 L12
Longhope Gloucs 41 L8
Longhope Ork 147 b6
Longhorsley Nthumb 109 J11
Longhoughton Nthumb 109 L7
Longlands Cumb 98 B11
Longlane Derbys 65 N4
Long Lawford Warwks 54 D5
Longleat Safari &
  Adventure Park Wilts 22 H4
Longlevens Gloucs 41 N8
Longley Calder 84 G10
Longley Green Worcs 52 E9
Longleys P & K 124 F4
Long Load Somset 21 P8
Longmanhill Abers 140 H3
Long Marston Herts 44 C8
Long Marston N York 85 R5
Long Marston Warwks 53 M11
Long Marton Cumb 89 Q2
Long Meadowend Shrops 51 L4
Long Melford Suffk 46 F3
Longmoor Camp Hants 25 M7
Longmorn Moray 139 N4
Long Newnton Gloucs 29 M4
Longnewton Border 107 P4
Long Newton E Loth 116 C9
Longney Gloucs 41 M9
Longniddry E Loth 116 B6
Longnor Shrops 63 M12
Longnor Staffs 77 K10
Longparish Hants 24 G4
Long Preston N York 84 C4
Longridge Lancs 83 M6
Longridge Staffs 64 H8
Longriggend N Lans 114 E7
Long Riston E R Yk 87 L9
Longrock Cnwll 2 D8
Longsdon Staffs 64 H1
Longside Abers 141 Q6
Longslow Shrops 64 C5
Longstanton Cambs 56 F7
Longstock Hants 24 F7
Longstone Pembks 37 M8
Longstowe Cambs 56 E10
Long Stratton Norfk 59 J2
Long Street M Keyn 55 M11
Longstreet Wilts 23 P3
Long Sutton Hants 25 M5
Long Sutton Lincs 68 H7
Long Sutton Somset 21 P8
Longthorpe C Pete 56 C1
Long Thurlow Suffk 58 F7
Longthwaite Cumb 89 J2
Longton C Stke 64 H2
Longton Lancs 83 L10

Longtown Cumb 98 D4
Longtown Herefs 40 D6
Longueville Jersey 13 c3
Longville in the Dale
  Shrops 51 P2
Long Waste Wrekin 64 B9
Long Whatton Leics 66 D7
Longwick Bucks 43 R10
Long Wittenham Oxon 31 L4
Longwitton Nthumb 108 H12
Longwood Shrops 63 Q10
Longworth Oxon 30 G3
Longyester E Loth 116 D8
Lôn-las Swans 26 H3
Lonmay Abers 141 N4
Lonmore Highld 134 E6
Looe Cnwll 4 C6
Loose Kent 34 D12
Loosebeare Devon 8 F4
Loosegate Lincs 68 F7
Loosley Row Bucks 32 B2
Lootcherbrae Abers 140 F5
Lopcombe Corner Wilts 24 D6
Lopen Somset 21 P10
Loppington Shrops 63 M6
Lorbottle Nthumb 108 G8
Lordsbridge Norfk 69 L9
Lordshill C Sotn 24 F10
Lords Wood Medway 34 D10
Lornty P & K 124 D4
Loscoe Derbys 66 C3
Loscombe Dorset 10 D5
Losgaintir W Isls 152 e5
Lossiemouth Moray 147 N11
Lostford Shrops 64 B5
Lostock Gralam Ches W 76 C8
Lostock Green Ches W 76 C8
Lostock Hall Lancs 83 M10
Lostock Hall Fold Bolton 76 C2
Lostock Junction Bolton 76 C2
Lostwithiel Cnwll 3 R3
Lothbeg Highld 146 G3
Lothersdale N York 84 E6
Lothmore Highld 146 H3
Loudwater Bucks 32 C4
Loughborough Leics 66 E8
Loughor Swans 26 E3
Loughton Essex 33 N3
Loughton M Keyn 44 B4
Loughton Shrops 52 B4
Lound Lincs 67 Q8
Lound Notts 78 H6
Lound Suffk 71 P12
Lounston Devon 8 E9
Lount Leics 66 C8
Louth Lincs 80 F6
Loveclough Lancs 84 B9
Lovedean Hants 25 J10
Lover Wilts 24 C9
Loversall Donc 78 F4
Loves Green Essex 46 B10
Lovesome Hill N York 91 N7
Loveston Pembks 37 L9
Lovington Somset 22 D7
Low Ackworth Wakefd 85 N11
Low Angerton Nthumb 100 E1
Lowbands Gloucs 41 M5
Low Barbeth D & G 94 E4
Low Barlings Lincs 80 B9
Low Bell End N York 92 H6
Low Bentham N York 83 P7
Low Biggins Cumb 89 P11
Low Borrowbridge Cumb 89 P6
Low Bradfield Sheff 77 N6
Low Bradley N York 84 F5
Low Braithwaite Cumb 98 E10
Low Burnham N Linc 79 J4
Low Buston Nthumb 109 L8
Lowca Cumb 88 C2
Low Catton E R Yk 86 D4
Low Coniscliffe Darltn 91 L4
Low Crosby Cumb 98 E6
Lowdham Notts 66 H3
Low Dinsdale Darltn 91 N4
Low Ellington N York 91 L10
Lower Aisholt Somset 21 K6
Lower Ansty Dorset 11 J4
Lower Apperley Gloucs 41 P6
Lower Arboll Highld 146 F7
Lower Arncott Oxon 43 N8
Lower Ashton Devon 8 G7
Lower Assendon Oxon 31 Q5
Lower Badcall Highld 148 D8
Lower Ballam Lancs 83 J9
Lower Bartle Lancs 83 L8
Lower Basildon W Berk 31 N6
Lower Bearwood Herefs 51 J9
Lower Beeding W Susx 15 J5
Lower Benefield Nhants 55 N3
Lower Bentley Worcs 52 H7
Lower Beobridge Shrops 52 E2
Lower Birchwood Derbys 66 C2
Lower Boscaswell Cnwll 2 B7
Lower Bourne Surrey 25 N5
Lower Brailes Warwks 42 G4
Lower Breakish Highld 135 M11
Lower Bredbury Stockp 76 H5
Lower Broadheath Worcs 52 F9
Lower Broxwood Herefs 51 J10
Lower Buckenhill Herefs 41 J5
Lower Bullingham Herefs 40 G4
Lower Burgate Hants 23 P10
Lower Burrowton Devon 9 J5
Lower Burton Herefs 51 M9
Lower Caldecote C Beds 44 H2
Lower Cam Gloucs 29 M2
Lower Canada N Som 28 E8
Lower Catesby Nhants 54 E9
Lower Chapel Powys 39 N4
Lower Chicksgrove Wilts 23 J7
Lower Chute Wilts 24 D4
Lower Clapton Gt Lon 33 L6
Lower Clent Worcs 52 G5
Lower Common Hants 25 L4
Lower Compton Wilts 30 B8
Lower Creedy Devon 8 G4
Lower Crossings Derbys 77 J7
Lower Cumberworth Kirk 77 K12
Lower Darwen Bl w D 83 Q10
Lower Dean Bed 55 P8
Lower Denby Kirk 77 M12
Lower Diabaig Highld 135 M3
Lower Dicker E Susx 15 Q8
Lower Dinchope Shrops 51 M4
Lower Down Shrops 51 K4
Lower Dunsforth N York 85 N3
Lower Egleton Herefs 41 J4
Lower Elkstone Staffs 77 J12
Lower Ellastone Staffs 65 L4
Lower End M Keyn 44 D4
Lower End Nhants 55 K7
Lower End Nhants 55 N7
Lower Everleigh Wilts 24 C4
Lower Exbury Hants 14 E6
Lower Eythorne Kent 35 N12
Lower Failand N Som 28 G7
Lower Farringdon Hants 25 M6
Lower Feltham Gt Lon 32 F7
Lower Fittleworth W Susx 15 N5
Lower Foxdale IoM 102 c5

Lower Frankton Shrops 63 L6
Lower Freystrop Pembks 37 J8
Lower Froyle Hants 25 M5
Lower Gabwell Devon 5 Q3
Lower Gledfield Highld 145 N7
Lower Godney Somset 21 N4
Lower Gornal Dudley 52 G2
Lower Gravenhurst
  C Beds 44 G5
Lower Green Herts 44 H5
Lower Green Herts 45 M5
Lower Green Kent 15 R3
Lower Green Norfk 70 E4
Lower Green Staffs 64 G11
Lower Green Suffk 57 Q7
Lower Hacheston Suffk 59 L9
Lower Halstock Leigh
  Dorset 10 E3
Lower Halstow Kent 34 F9
Lower Hamworthy BCP 11 N6
Lower Hardres Kent 35 L11
Lower Harpton Herefs 51 J8
Lower Hartlip Kent 34 E9
Lower Hartshay Derbys 66 C2
Lower Hartwell Bucks 43 R9
Lower Hatton Staffs 64 F4
Lower Hawthwaite Cumb 88 H9
Lower Haysden Kent 15 Q2
Lower Hergest Herefs 51 J9
Lower Heyford Oxon 43 K7
Lower Heysham Lancs 83 J4
Lower Higham Kent 34 C8
Lower Holbrook Suffk 47 L5
Lower Hordley Shrops 63 L6
Lower Horncroft W Susx 14 F4
Lowerhouse Lancs 84 B8
Lower Houses Kirk 84 H12
Lower Howsell Worcs 52 E11
Lower Irlam Salfd 76 D5
Lower Kilburn Derbys 66 B3
Lower Kilcott Gloucs 29 M4
Lower Killeyan Ag & B 102 B11
Lower Kingcombe Dorset 10 E5
Lower Kingswood Surrey 33 J11
Lower Kinnerton Ches W 75 K11
Lower Langford N Som 28 G9
Lower Largo Fife 124 H12
Lower Leigh Staffs 65 J5
Lower Lemington Gloucs 42 E5
Lower Llanfadog Powys 50 E8
Lower Lovacott Devon 19 K8
Lower Loxhore Devon 19 M5
Lower Lydbrook Gloucs 41 J8
Lower Lye Herefs 51 L7
Lower Machen Newpt 28 B5
Lower Maes-coed Herefs 40 D5
Lower Mannington
  Dorset 11 P4
Lower Marston Somset 22 G4
Lower Meend Gloucs 40 H10
Lower Merridge Somset 21 K6
Lower Middleton
  Cheney Nhants 43 L3
Lower Milton Somset 22 C4
Lower Moor Worcs 41 R2
Lower Morton S Glos 29 J5
Lower Nazeing Essex 45 M10
Lower Norton Warwks 53 N8
Lower Nyland Dorset 22 G8
Lower Oddington Gloucs 42 F6
Lower Penarth V Glam 28 A8
Lower Penn Staffs 52 F2
Lower Pennington Hants 12 E6
Lower Penwortham
  Lancs 83 M10
Lower Peover Ches E 76 D9
Lower Place Rochdl 76 D3
Lower Pollicott Bucks 43 R8
Lower Quinton Warwks 42 F2
Lower Rainham Medway 34 E8
Lower Roadwater Somset 20 G5
Lower Salter Lancs 83 N3
Lower Seagry Wilts 29 Q6
Lower Sheering Essex 45 N8
Lower Shelton C Beds 44 E3
Lower Shiplake Oxon 31 Q6
Lower Shuckburgh
  Warwks 54 D8
Lower Slaughter Gloucs 42 D7
Lower Soothill Kirk 85 K10
Lower Soudley Gloucs 41 K9
Lower Stanton St
  Quinton Wilts 29 Q6
Lower Stoke Medway 34 E7
Lower Stondon C Beds 44 H4
Lower Stone Gloucs 29 J4
Lower Stonnall Staffs 65 K11
Lower Stow Bedon Norfk 58 D2
Lower Street E Susx 16 C8
Lower Street Norfk 71 K5
Lower Street Suffk 58 G10
Lower Stretton Warrtn 76 C7
Lower Stroud Dorset 10 C5
Lower Sundon C Beds 44 F6
Lower Swanwick Hants 14 E5
Lower Swell Gloucs 42 E6
Lower Tadmarton Oxon 43 J4
Lower Tale Devon 9 K4
Lower Tasburgh Norfk 59 J1
Lower Tean Staffs 65 J4
Lower Thurlton Norfk 71 N2
Lower Town Cnwll 2 G8
Lower Town Devon 5 M3
Lower Town Herefs 41 K3
Lower Town IoS 2 b1
Lower Town Pembks 37 J3
Lower Trebullett Cnwll 7 J8
Lower Treluswell Cnwll 3 J7
Lower Tysoe Warwks 54 A12
Lower Ufford Suffk 59 L10
Lower Upcott Devon 8 E6
Lower Upham Hants 24 H10
Lower Upnor Medway 34 D8
Lower Vexford Somset 20 H6
Lower Walton Warrtn 76 C6
Lower Waterston Dorset 11 J5
Lower Weare Somset 21 N3
Lower Weedon Nhants 54 F9
Lower Welson Herefs 51 J10
Lower Westmancote
  Worcs 41 Q4
Lower Whatcombe
  Dorset 11 K4
Lower Whatley Somset 22 G4
Lower Whitley Ches W 75 Q8
Lower Wick Gloucs 29 K3
Lower Wick Worcs 52 F10
Lower Wield Hants 25 K5
Lower Willingdon E Susx 15 R10
Lower Withington Ches E 76 F10
Lower Woodend Bucks 31 R5
Lower Woodford Wilts 23 P5
Lower Wraxhall Dorset 10 E4
Lower Wyche Worcs 41 M3
Lower Wyke C Brad 84 H10
Lowesby Leics 67 J10
Lowestoft Suffk 59 R3
Loweswater Cumb 88 F2
Low Fell Gatesd 100 H6
Low Gartachorrans Stirlg 113 P4
Low Gate Nthumb 99 P5

Low Gettbridge Cumb 98 G6
Lowgill Cumb 89 N7
Lowgill Lancs 83 P3
Low Grantley N York 85 K1
Low Green N York 85 K3
Low Habberley Worcs 52 E5
Low Ham Somset 21 P7
Low Harrogate N York 85 L6
Low Hawsker N York 93 J5
Low Hesket Cumb 98 F10
Low Hutton N York 86 E2
Lowick Cumb 89 J9
Lowick Nhants 55 N4
Lowick Nthumb 108 G2
Lowick Bridge Cumb 89 J9
Lowick Green Cumb 89 J9
Low Knipe Cumb 89 N2
Low Laithe N York 85 J3
Lowlands Dur 91 J2
Lowlands Torfn 28 C3
Low Langton Lincs 80 C8
Low Leighton Derbys 77 J6
Low Lorton Cumb 88 F2
Low Marishes N York 92 H11
Low Marnham Notts 79 K10
Low Middleton Nthumb 109 J4
Low Mill N York 92 D7
Low Moor C Brad 84 H10
Low Moorsley Sundld 101 J9
Low Moresby Cumb 88 D3
Low Newton Cumb 89 L10
Low Newton-by-the-
  Sea Nthumb 109 L5
Low Pittington Dur 101 J9
Low Row Cumb 97 P9
Low Row Cumb 98 D11
Low Row Cumb 98 H6
Low Row N York 90 G7
Low Salchrie D & G 94 E4
Low Santon N Linc 79 N1
Lowsonford Warwks 53 M7
Low Street Norfk 71 L7
Low Tharston Norfk 59 J2
Lowther Cumb 89 K3
Lowthorpe E R Yk 87 K3
Lowton Devon 8 F4
Lowton Somset 21 K9
Lowton Wigan 76 B4
Lowton Common Wigan 76 B4
Lowton St Mary's Wigan 76 B4
Low Torry Fife 115 J4
Low Toynton Lincs 80 E9
Low Valley Barns 78 C4
Low Wood Cumb 89 K10
Low Worsall N York 91 N5
Low Wray Cumb 89 K6
Loxbeare Devon 20 E10
Loxhill Surrey 14 E3
Loxhore Devon 19 M5
Loxhore Cott Devon 19 M5
Loxley Warwks 53 N10
Loxley Green Staffs 65 K6
Loxter Herefs 41 L3
Loxton N Som 21 N2
Loxwood W Susx 14 E4
Lubenham Leics 54 H3
Lucasgate Lincs 68 H3
Lucas Green Surrey 32 D10
Luccombe Somset 20 E5
Luccombe Village IoW 14 G11
Lucker Nthumb 109 J4
Luckett Cnwll 7 J9
Lucking Street Essex 46 E5
Luckington Wilts 29 N5
Lucklawhill Fife 124 H8
Lucknam Wilts 29 N6
Luckwell Bridge Somset 20 D5
Lucton Herefs 51 M8
Lucy Cross N York 91 L4
Ludag W Isls 152 c11
Ludborough Lincs 80 F4
Ludbrooke Devon 5 L5
Ludchurch Pembks 37 M8
Luddenden Calder 84 F10
Luddenden Foot Calder 84 F10
Luddenham Court Kent 34 H9
Luddesdown Kent 34 B9
Luddington N Linc 86 F12
Luddington Warwks 53 M10
Luddington in the Brook
  Nhants 56 B4
Ludford Lincs 80 D7
Ludford Shrops 51 N6
Ludgershall Bucks 43 N8
Ludgershall Wilts 24 D4
Ludgvan Cnwll 2 D8
Ludham Norfk 71 M8
Ludlow Shrops 51 N5
Ludney Somset 21 N11
Ludwell Wilts 23 J8
Ludworth Dur 101 J10
Luffenhall Herts 45 J6
Luffincott Devon 7 L6
Luffness E Loth 116 B5
Lugar E Ayrs 105 L5
Luggate Burn E Loth 116 E6
Lugg Green Herefs 51 M8
Luggiebank N Lans 114 D7
Lugton E Ayrs 113 N11
Lugwardine Herefs 40 H4
Luib Highld 135 K10
Luing Ag & B 120 D10
Lulham Herefs 40 F3
Lullington Derbys 65 N9
Lullington E Susx 15 Q10
Lullington Somset 22 G3
Lulsgate Bottom N Som 28 H9
Lulsley Worcs 52 E10
Lulworth Camp Dorset 11 K8
Lumb Calder 84 E10
Lumb Lancs 84 C10
Lumbutts Calder 84 D10
Lumby N York 85 N9
Lumphanan Abers 132 F3
Lumphinnans Fife 115 M3
Lumsden Abers 140 D10
Lunan Angus 125 K2
Lunanhead Angus 132 H12
Luncarty P & K 124 C7
Lund E R Yk 86 H5
Lund N York 86 C8
Lundie Angus 124 E5
Lundin Links Fife 124 H12
Lundin Mill Fife 124 H12
Lundy Devon 18 C4
Lunga Ag & B 120 D8
Lunna Shet 147 J5
Lunsford Kent 34 C10
Lunsford's Cross E Susx 16 C8
Lunt Sefton 75 K3
Luppitt Devon 9 N4
Lupridge Devon 5 M5
Lupset Wakefd 85 K11
Lupton Cumb 89 N10
Lurgashall W Susx 14 D4
Lurley Devon 20 E10
Lusby Lincs 80 E10
Luscombe Devon 5 N5
Luskentyre W Isls 152 e5
Luson Devon 5 L6
Luss Ag & B 113 M3
Lussagiven Ag & B 111 M3
Lusta Highld 134 E4
Lustleigh Devon 8 E8

Luston Herefs 51 N8
Luthermuir Abers 132 G10
Luthrie Fife 124 G9
Lutley Dudley 52 H4
Luton Devon 8 G9
Luton Devon 9 J6
Luton Luton 44 F7
Luton Medway 34 D9
Luton Airport Luton 44 G7
Lutterworth Leics 54 E4
Lutton Devon 5 K5
Lutton Devon 5 L4
Lutton Lincs 68 H7
Lutton Nhants 56 C3
Luxborough Somset 20 E6
Luxulyan Cnwll 3 P3
Luxulyan Valley Cnwll 3 P3
Luzley Tamesd 76 H3
Lybster Highld 151 N10
Lydbury North Shrops 51 K3
Lydcott Devon 19 M6
Lydd Kent 17 J6
Lydd Airport Kent 17 J6
Lydden Kent 17 N2
Lydden Kent 35 P9
Lyddington Rutlnd 55 L1
Lydd-on-Sea Kent 17 K7
Lydeard St Lawrence
  Somset 20 H7
Lyde Green Hants 31 P11
Lydford Devon 7 P8
Lydford on Fosse Somset 22 D7
Lydgate Calder 84 D10
Lydgate Rochdl 84 E12
Lydham Shrops 51 K2
Lydiard Green Wilts 30 C5
Lydiard Millicent Wilts 30 C5
Lydiard Tregoze Swindn 30 C5
Lydiate Sefton 75 L3
Lydiate Ash Worcs 52 H5
Lydlinch Dorset 22 G10
Lydney Gloucs 41 K11
Lydstep Pembks 37 L11
Lye Dudley 52 G4
Lye Cross N Som 28 G10
Lye Green Bucks 44 D11
Lye Green E Susx 15 R4
Lye Green Warwks 53 M7
Lye Head Worcs 52 E6
Lye's Green Wilts 22 H4
Lyford Oxon 30 H3
Lymbridge Green Kent 17 K2
Lyme Regis Dorset 9 R6
Lyminge Kent 17 L3
Lymington Hants 12 E6
Lyminster W Susx 14 E10
Lymm Warrtn 76 C6
Lymm Services Warrtn 76 C7
Lympne Kent 17 K4
Lympsham Somset 21 M2
Lympstone Devon 9 J8
Lynbridge Devon 19 N4
Lynch Highld 130 E4
Lynch Green Norfk 70 H11
Lyndhurst Hants 12 E3
Lyndon Rutlnd 67 M11
Lyndon Green Birm 53 L4
Lyne Border 106 G2
Lyne Surrey 32 E9
Lyne Down Herefs 41 K5
Lyneham Oxon 42 F7
Lyneham Wilts 30 B6
Lyneholmford Cumb 98 G4
Lyne of Skene Abers 133 J2
Lynesack Dur 90 H2
Lyness Ork 147 b6
Lyng Norfk 70 F8
Lyng Somset 21 M7
Lynmouth Devon 19 P3
Lynn Wrekin 63 K11
Lynsted Kent 34 G10
Lynstone Cnwll 7 J4
Lynton Devon 19 N3
Lynton Cross Devon 19 K5
Lyon's Gate Dorset 10 G4
Lyonshall Herefs 51 K9
Lytchett Matravers
  Dorset 11 M6
Lytchett Minster Dorset 11 M6
Lyth Highld 151 N4
Lytham Lancs 83 J10
Lytham St Annes Lancs 82 H10
Lythbank Shrops 63 M10
Lythe N York 92 H4
Lythmore Highld 151 J3

M

Maaruig W Isls 152 e5
Mabe Burnthouse Cnwll 3 J7
Mablethorpe Lincs 81 K7
Macclesfield Ches E 76 G9
Macduff Abers 140 H3
Macharioch Ag & B 103 K8
Machen Caerph 28 B5
Machrie N Ayrs 103 N3
Machrihanish Ag & B 102 G4
Machrins Ag & B 111 J3
Machroes Gwynd 60 E7
Machynlleth Powys 61 N10
Machynys Carmth 26 D3
Mackworth Derbys 65 P5
Macmerry E Loth 116 B7
Maddaford Devon 7 Q6
Madderty P & K 123 N8
Maddington Wilts 23 N4
Maddiston Falk 114 F6
Madehurst W Susx 14 E8
Madeley Staffs 64 E3
Madeley Wrekin 64 C11
Madeley Heath Staffs 64 E3
Madeley Park Wood
  Staffs 64 E4
Madford Devon 9 N4
Madingley Cambs 56 H8
Madley Herefs 40 F4
Madresfield Worcs 52 F11
Madron Cnwll 2 D8
Maenaddwyn IoA 72 G7
Maenan Conwy 73 N10
Maenclochog Pembks 37 K4
Maendy V Glam 27 M7
Maenporth Cnwll 3 K8
Maentwrog Gwynd 61 L4
Maen-y-groes Cerdgn 48 F8
Maer Staffs 64 E4
Maerdy Carmth 38 G6
Maerdy Conwy 62 E3
Maerdy Rhondd 27 L3
Maesbrook Shrops 63 J7
Maesbury Shrops 63 K6
Maesbury Marsh Shrops 63 K6
Maes-glas Newpt 28 C4
Maesgwynne Carmth 37 N6
Maeshafn Denbgs 74 H11
Maesllyn Cerdgn 48 A3
Maesmynis Powys 50 E10
Maesteg Brdgnd 27 K4
Maesybont Carmth 38 E8

Maesycwmmer Caerph....27 R3
Magdalen Laver Essex....45 P10
Maggieknockater Moray....139 P7
Maggots End Essex....45 N6
Magham Down E Susx....15 R8
Maghull Sefton....75 L3
Magna Park Leics....54 E4
Magor Mons....28 F5
Magor Services Mons....28 F5
Maidenbower W Susx....15 K4
Maiden Bradley Wilts....22 H5
Maidencombe Torbay....5 Q3
Maidenhayne Devon....9 P6
Maiden Head N Som....28 H9
Maidenhead W & M....32 C6
Maiden Law Dur....100 F8
Maiden Newton Dorset....10 F5
Maidens S Ayrs....104 D8
Maiden's Green Br For....32 C8
Maidenwell Lincs....80 F8
Maiden Wells Pembks....37 J10
Maidford Nhants....54 G10
Maids Moreton Bucks....43 P4
Maidstone Kent....34 D11
Maidstone Services Kent....34 E11
Maidwell Nhants....55 J5
Mail Shet....147 j7
Maindee Newpt....28 F5
Mainland Ork....147 c4
Mainland Shet....147 b3
Mainsforth Dur....101 J12
Mains of Balhall Angus....132 D11
Mains of Balnakettle Abers....132 F9
Mains of Dalvey Highld....139 L9
Mains of Haulkerton Abers....132 H9
Mains of Lesmoir Abers....140 D10
Mains of Melgunds Angus....125 L2
Mainsriddle D & G....97 J3
Mainstone Shrops....51 J3
Maisemore Gloucs....41 N6
Major's Green Worcs....53 L5
Makeney Derbys....66 B3
Malborough Devon....5 L8
Malcoff Derbys....77 K7
Malden Rushett Gt Lon....32 H10
Maldon Essex....46 E10
Malham N York....84 D3
Maligar Highld....134 H3
Mallaig Highld....127 M5
Mallaigvaig Highld....127 M5
Malleny Mills C Edin....115 L8
Mallows Green Essex....45 N6
Malltraeth IoA....72 G10
Mallwyd Gwynd....61 Q9
Malmesbury Wilts....29 Q5
Malmsmead Devon....20 B4
Malpas Ches W....63 N3
Malpas Cnwll....3 K6
Malpas Newpt....28 C4
Malshanger Hants....25 J3
Malswick Gloucs....41 L7
Maltby Lincs....80 F7
Maltby Rothm....78 E6
Maltby S on T....91 Q4
Maltby le Marsh Lincs....81 J7
Malting Green Essex....46 H7
Maltman's Hill Kent....16 F2
Malton N York....92 F12
Malvern Hills....41 M2
Malvern Hills....41 M3
Malvern Link Worcs....52 E11
Malvern Wells Worcs....41 M3
Mamble Worcs....52 C6
Mamhilad Mons....40 D11
Manaccan Cnwll....3 J9
Manafon Powys....62 F11
Mànais W Isls....152 e6
Manaton Devon....8 E8
Manby Lincs....80 H6
Mancetter Warwks....53 Q1
Manchester Manch....76 F4
Manchester Airport Manch....76 F7
Mancot Flints....75 K10
Mandally Highld....129 K4
Manea Cambs....57 J3
Maney Birm....53 L2
Manfield N York....91 L4
Mangersta W Isls....152 d3
Mangerton Dorset....10 D5
Mangotsfield S Glos....29 K7
Mangrove Green Herts....44 G7
Mangurstadh W Isls....152 d3
Manhay Cnwll....2 H8
Manish W Isls....152 e6
Mankinholes Calder....84 E10
Manley Ches W....75 N9
Manmoel Caerph....40 A11
Mannal Ag & B....118 D3
Manningford Bohune Wilts....30 D10
Manningford Bruce Wilts....30 D10
Manningham C Brad....84 H8
Mannings Heath W Susx....14 H5
Mannington Dorset....11 P4
Manningtree Essex....47 K5
Mannofield C Aber....133 M4
Manorbier Pembks....37 L11
Manorbier Newton Pembks....37 K10
Manordeilo Carmth....38 G6
Manorhill Border....107 G3
Manorowen Pembks....36 H3
Manor Park Gt Lon....33 M5
Mansell Gamage Herefs....40 F3
Mansell Lacy Herefs....40 F3
Mansergh Cumb....89 P10
Mansfield E Ayrs....105 L7
Mansfield Notts....78 E11
Mansfield Woodhouse Notts....78 E11
Mansriggs Cumb....89 J10
Manston Dorset....11 H3
Manston Kent....35 P9
Manston Leeds....85 M8
Manswood Dorset....11 N3
Manthorpe Lincs....67 M5
Manton N Linc....79 M3
Manton Notts....78 G8
Manton Rutlnd....55 M10
Manton Wilts....30 E8
Manuden Essex....45 N6
Manwood Green Essex....45 Q9
Maperton Somset....22 F8
Maplebeck Notts....78 H11
Maple Cross Herts....32 E4
Mapledurham Oxon....31 N7
Mapledurwell Hants....25 J4
Maplehurst W Susx....14 H6
Maplescombe Kent....33 Q9
Mapleton Derbys....65 M3
Mapleton Kent....15 N1
Mapperley Derbys....66 C4
Mapperley Park C Nott....66 F4
Mapperton Dorset....10 D5
Mappleborough Green Warwks....53 K7
Mappleton E R Yk....87 N6
Mapplewell Barns....77 Q2
Mappowder Dorset....10 H3
Màraig W Isls....152 e4
Marazanvose Cnwll....3 K4

Marazion Cnwll....2 E8
Marbhig W Isls....152 g4
Marbury Ches E....63 P3
March Cambs....56 H1
March S Lans....106 C7
Marcham Oxon....31 K3
Marchamley Shrops....63 Q6
Marchamley Wood Shrops....63 Q6
Marchington Staffs....65 L6
Marchington Woodlands Staffs....65 L6
Marchwiel Wrexhm....63 K3
Marchwood Hants....12 F3
Marcross V Glam....27 L8
Marden Herefs....40 H2
Marden Kent....16 D2
Marden Wilts....30 C10
Marden Ash Essex....45 Q11
Marden Beech Kent....16 C2
Marden's Hill E Susx....15 N4
Marden Thorn Kent....16 D2
Mardlebury Herts....45 K8
Mardy Mons....40 D8
Marefield Leics....67 J10
Mareham le Fen Lincs....80 E11
Mareham on the Hill Lincs....80 F10
Marehay Derbys....66 C3
Marehill W Susx....14 F8
Maresfield E Susx....15 N6
Marfleet C KuH....87 L9
Marford Wrexhm....75 K12
Margam Neath....26 H4
Margaret Marsh Dorset....22 H9
Margaret Roding Essex....45 P8
Margaretting Essex....46 B10
Margaretting Tye Essex....34 B2
Margate Kent....35 P8
Margnaheglish N Ayrs....103 Q3
Margrie D & G....96 C8
Margrove Park R & Cl....92 D4
Marham Norfk....69 N10
Marhamchurch Cnwll....7 J4
Marholm C Pete....68 C11
Marian-glas IoA....72 H7
Mariansleigh Devon....19 P9
Marine Town Kent....34 G7
Marionburgh Abers....132 H3
Marishader Highld....135 J3
Maristow Devon....4 G4
Marjoriebanks D & G....97 M2
Mark Somset....21 N4
Markbeech Kent....15 N2
Markby Lincs....81 J8
Mark Causeway Somset....21 N4
Mark Cross E Susx....15 Q4
Markeaton C Derb....65 Q5
Market Bosworth Leics....66 C11
Market Deeping Lincs....68 C10
Market Drayton Shrops....64 C5
Market Harborough Leics....55 J3
Market Lavington Wilts....30 C3
Market Overton Rutlnd....67 M9
Market Rasen Lincs....80 B6
Market Stainton Lincs....80 E7
Market Warsop Notts....78 F10
Market Weighton E R Yk....86 G7
Market Weston Suffk....58 E5
Markfield Leics....66 D10
Markham Caerph....28 A2
Markham Moor Notts....79 J9
Markinch Fife....115 P1
Markington N York....85 L2
Markle E Loth....116 D6
Marksbury BaNES....29 K10
Mark's Corner IoW....12 H6
Marks Tey Essex....46 F7
Markwell Cnwll....4 E5
Markyate Herts....44 E8
Marlborough Wilts....30 E8
Marlbrook Herefs....51 N9
Marlbrook Worcs....52 H6
Marlcliff Warwks....53 L10
Marldon Devon....5 P4
Marle Green E Susx....15 Q7
Marlesford Suffk....59 L9
Marley Kent....35 L12
Marley Kent....35 P11
Marley Green Ches E....63 P3
Marley Hill Gatesd....100 G6
Marlingford Norfk....70 H10
Marloes Pembks....36 F9
Marlow Bucks....32 B5
Marlow Herefs....51 L5
Marlow Bottom Bucks....32 B5
Marlpit Hill Kent....15 N1
Marlpits E Susx....15 N5
Marlpits Kent....16 C6
Marlpool Derbys....66 D3
Marnhull Dorset....22 H9
Marple Stockp....76 H6
Marple Bridge Stockp....76 H6
Marr Donc....78 D3
Marrick N York....90 H7
Marros Carmth....37 N9
Marsden Kirk....77 K1
Marsden S Tyne....101 K5
Marsden Height Lancs....84 C8
Marsett N York....90 G9
Marsh Bucks....44 A10
Marsh C Brad....84 F8
Marsh Devon....9 P3
Marshall's Heath Herts....44 H8
Marshalswick Herts....44 H10
Marsham Norfk....71 J7
Marsh Baldon Oxon....31 M3
Marsh Benham W Berk....31 J9
Marshborough Kent....35 P11
Marshbrook Shrops....51 M3
Marshchapel Lincs....80 G4
Marsh Farm Luton....44 F6
Marshfield Newpt....28 C5
Marshfield S Glos....29 M7
Marshgate Cnwll....6 H6
Marsh Gibbon Bucks....43 Q7
Marsh Green Devon....9 J5
Marsh Green Kent....15 N2
Marsh Green Wrekin....63 Q8
Marshland St James Norfk....69 L10
Marsh Lane Derbys....78 D8
Marshside Sefton....83 J11
Marsh Street Somset....20 D4
Marshwood Dorset....10 B5
Marske N York....90 H6
Marske-by-the-Sea R & Cl....92 D2
Marsland Green Wigan....76 C4
Marston Ches W....76 C8
Marston Herefs....51 L9
Marston Lincs....67 M3
Marston Oxon....43 L10
Marston Staffs....64 G7
Marston Staffs....64 G7
Marston Warwks....53 M3
Marston Wilts....29 Q10
Marston Green Solhll....53 M4
Marston Jabbet Warwks....54 B3
Marston Magna Somset....22 D9
Marston Meysey Wilts....30 D3
Marston Montgomery Derbys....65 L5
Marston Moretaine C Beds....44 D3
Marston on Dove Derbys....65 N6

Marston St Lawrence Nhants....43 L3
Marston Stannett Herefs....51 P9
Marston Trussell Nhants....54 H3
Marstow Herefs....40 H8
Marsworth Bucks....44 C8
Marten Wilts....30 G10
Marthall Ches E....76 E8
Martham Norfk....71 N8
Martin Hants....23 N9
Martin Kent....17 P1
Martin Lincs....80 C11
Martin Lincs....80 E10
Martindale Cumb....89 L3
Martin Dales Lincs....80 C10
Martin Drove End Hants....23 N9
Martinhoe Devon....19 N4
Martinscroft Warrtn....76 C6
Martinstown Dorset....10 G7
Martlesham Suffk....47 M3
Martlesham Heath Suffk....47 M3
Martletwy Pembks....37 K8
Martley Worcs....52 D8
Martock Somset....21 P9
Marton Ches E....76 F10
Marton Ches W....76 B10
Marton Cumb....88 H11
Marton E R Yk....87 N1
Marton E R Yk....87 M7
Marton Lincs....79 K6
Marton Middsb....92 B3
Marton N York....85 N3
Marton N York....92 H10
Marton Shrops....63 J11
Marton Warwks....54 B7
Marton-le-Moor N York....85 M1
Martyr's Green Surrey....32 F11
Martyr Worthy Hants....24 H7
Marwick Ork....147 b3
Marwood Devon....19 K6
Marybank Highld....137 N5
Maryburgh Highld....137 P4
Marygold Border....116 H9
Maryhill C Glas....113 Q7
Marykirk Abers....132 G11
Maryland Mons....40 G8
Marylebone Gt Lon....33 K6
Marylebone Wigan....75 P2
Marypark Moray....139 M8
Maryport Cumb....97 L11
Maryport D & G....94 G11
Marystow Devon....7 N9
Mary Tavy Devon....7 P9
Marywell Abers....132 F5
Marywell Abers....133 M4
Marywell Angus....125 M4
Masham N York....91 L10
Mashbury Essex....46 B9
Masongill N York....89 Q11
Mason N u Ty....100 G3
Mastin Moor Derbys....78 D8
Matching Essex....45 P9
Matching Green Essex....45 P9
Matching Tye Essex....45 P9
Matfen Nthumb....100 D4
Matfield Kent....16 C2
Mathern Mons....28 H4
Mathon Herefs....52 D11
Mathry Pembks....36 G4
Matlask Norfk....70 H5
Matlock Derbys....77 P11
Matlock Bank Derbys....77 P11
Matlock Bath Derbys....77 P12
Matlock Dale Derbys....77 P12
Matson Gloucs....41 N8
Mattersey Notts....78 H5
Mattersey Thorpe Notts....78 H6
Mattingley Hants....25 L2
Mattishall Norfk....70 F10
Mattishall Burgh Norfk....70 F10
Mauchline E Ayrs....105 J4
Maud Abers....141 M6
Maufant Jersey....13 d2
Maugersbury Gloucs....42 F7
Maughold IoM....102 g4
Mauld Highld....137 L8
Maulden C Beds....44 F4
Maulds Meaburn Cumb....90 B6
Maunby N York....91 N9
Maund Bryan Herefs....51 P10
Maundown Somset....20 F8
Mautby Norfk....71 P9
Mavesyn Ridware Staffs....65 L9
Mavis Enderby Lincs....80 G10
Mawbray Cumb....97 L9
Mawdesley Lancs....83 L12
Mawdlam Brdgnd....27 J5
Mawgan Cnwll....2 H9
Mawgan Porth Cnwll....6 B11
Maw Green Ches E....76 D12
Mawla Cnwll....3 J4
Mawnan Cnwll....3 K9
Mawnan Smith Cnwll....3 K9
Mawsley Nhants....55 K5
Mawthorpe Lincs....81 J8
Maxey C Pete....68 C11
Maxstoke Warwks....53 N3
Maxted Street Kent....17 K2
Maxton Border....107 N4
Maxton Kent....17 N3
Maxworthy Cnwll....7 J4
Mayals Swans....26 F4
May Bank Staffs....64 F3
Maybole S Ayrs....104 E8
Maybury Surrey....32 F11
Mayes Green Surrey....14 G3
Mayfield E Susx....15 Q5
Mayfield Mdloth....115 Q8
Mayfield Staffs....65 M3
Mayford Surrey....32 E11
May Hill Mons....41 L7
Mayland Essex....46 F11
Maylandsea Essex....46 F11
Maynard's Green E Susx....15 Q7
Maypole Birm....53 K5
Maypole Kent....35 L8
Maypole Mons....40 G8
Maypole Green Norfk....59 N2
Maypole Green Suffk....58 G8
Maypole Green Suffk....59 M2
May's Green Oxon....31 Q6
May's Green Surrey....32 G11
Mead Devon....18 E9
Meadgate BaNES....29 K10
Meadle Bucks....44 A10
Meadowfield Dur....100 G12
Meadowtown Shrops....63 J11
Meadwell Devon....7 M8
Meaford Staffs....64 G5
Mealabost W Isls....152 g3
Meal Bank Cumb....89 N7
Mealrigg Cumb....97 L10
Mealsgate Cumb....97 N10
Meanwood Leeds....85 L8
Mearbeck N York....84 B3
Meare Somset....21 P5
Meare Green Somset....21 K8
Meare Green Somset....21 M8
Mears Ashby Nhants....55 L7

Measham Leics....65 Q9
Meath Green Surrey....15 K2
Meathop Cumb....89 L10
Meaux E R Yk....87 L7
Meavaig W Isls....152 e3
Meavy Devon....4 H3
Medbourne Leics....55 K2
Medburn Nthumb....100 E5
Meddon Devon....18 F10
Meden Vale Notts....78 F9
Medlam Lincs....68 F1
Medlar Lancs....83 K8
Medmenham Bucks....32 B5
Medomsley Dur....100 E7
Medstead Hants....25 L6
Medway Services Medway....34 E9
Meerbrook Staffs....77 J11
Meer Common Herefs....51 K10
Meesden Herts....45 M5
Meeson Wrekin....64 C8
Meeth Devon....7 Q3
Meeting Green Suffk....57 P9
Meeting House Hill Norfk....71 L6
Meidrim Carmth....37 Q6
Meifod Powys....62 G9
Meigle P & K....124 G3
Meikle Carco D & G....105 P7
Meikle Earnock S Lans....114 C10
Meikle Ferry Highld....146 D7
Meikle Kilmory Ag & B....112 Q5
Meikle Obney P & K....123 Q5
Meikleour P & K....124 D5
Meikle Wartle Abers....140 H9
Meinciau Carmth....38 C9
Meir C Stke....64 H4
Meir Heath Staffs....64 H4
Melbost W Isls....152 g3
Melbourn Cambs....45 M3
Melbourne Derbys....66 C7
Melbourne E R Yk....86 D6
Melbur Cnwll....3 M3
Melbury Devon....18 G10
Melbury Abbas Dorset....23 K9
Melbury Bubb Dorset....10 E3
Melbury Osmond Dorset....10 E3
Melbury Sampford Dorset....10 E4
Melchbourne Bed....55 P7
Melcombe Bingham Dorset....11 J4
Meldon Devon....7 Q5
Meldon Nthumb....100 E1
Meldon Park Nthumb....100 E1
Meldreth Cambs....45 M2
Meldrum Stirlg....114 C1
Melfort Ag & B....120 F10
Meliden Denbgs....74 E7
Melinau Pembks....37 N8
Melin-byrheddyn Powys....61 P12
Melincourt Neath....39 K11
Melin-y-coed Conwy....73 P11
Melin-y-ddol Powys....62 F10
Melin-y-wig Denbgs....62 D2
Melkinthorpe Cumb....89 Q11
Melkridge Nthumb....99 L5
Melksham Wilts....29 P9
Mellangoose Cnwll....2 H9
Mell Green W Berk....31 K7
Mellguards Cumb....98 F9
Melling Lancs....83 N1
Melling Sefton....75 L3
Melling Mount Sefton....75 M3
Mellis Suffk....58 G6
Mellon Charles Highld....143 M7
Mellon Udrigle Highld....143 N6
Mellor Lancs....83 P9
Mellor Stockp....77 J6
Mellor Brook Lancs....83 P9
Mells Somset....22 G4
Mells Suffk....59 M5
Melmerby Cumb....99 J10
Melmerby N York....90 H9
Melmerby N York....91 N11
Melness Highld....149 M4
Melon Green Suffk....58 C9
Melplash Dorset....10 C5
Melrose Border....107 N3
Melsetter Ork....147 b6
Melsonby N York....91 L5
Meltham Kirk....77 L2
Meltham Mills Kirk....77 L2
Melton E R Yk....86 H10
Melton Suffk....59 L10
Meltonby E R Yk....86 E5
Melton Constable Norfk....70 F5
Melton Mowbray Leics....67 J8
Melton Ross N Linc....79 Q2
Melvaig Highld....143 K8
Melverley Shrops....63 K9
Melverley Green Shrops....63 K8
Melvich Highld....150 F4
Membury Devon....9 P4
Membury Services W Berk....30 G7
Memsie Abers....141 N3
Memus Angus....124 H1
Menabilly Cnwll....3 Q4
Menagissey Cnwll....2 H5
Menai Bridge IoA....73 J9
Mendham Suffk....59 K4
Mendip Hills....22 C3
Mendlesham Suffk....58 G7
Mendlesham Green Suffk....58 G8
Menheniot Cnwll....4 D4
Menithwood Worcs....52 D7
Menna Cnwll....3 M4
Mennock D & G....105 Q8
Menston C Brad....85 J6
Menstrie Clacks....114 F1
Menthorpe N York....86 C8
Mentmore Bucks....44 C8
Meoble Highld....127 P7
Meole Brace Shrops....63 N10
Meols Wirral....75 J6
Meonstoke Hants....25 K9
Meon Vale Warwks....42 H2
Meopham Kent....34 B9
Meopham Green Kent....34 B9
Meopham Station Kent....34 B9
Mepal Cambs....56 H4
Meppershall C Beds....44 G5
Merbach Herefs....40 D3
Mere Ches E....76 D7
Mere Wilts....22 H6
Mere Brow Lancs....83 K11
Mereclough Lancs....84 C9
Mere Green Birm....53 L2
Mere Green Worcs....52 H8
Mere Heath Ches W....76 C9
Meresborough Medway....34 E9
Mereworth Kent....34 B11
Meriden Solhll....53 N4
Merkadale Highld....134 G8
Merley BCP....11 N5
Merlin's Bridge Pembks....37 J7
Merrington Shrops....63 M8
Merrion Pembks....36 H11
Merriott Somset....10 C2
Merrivale Devon....7 P11
Merrow Surrey....32 G12
Merry Field Hill Dorset....11 N4
Merryhill Wolves....52 G1
Merry Hill Herts....32 G3
Merry Lees Leics....66 D11
Merrymeet Cnwll....4 C3
Mersea Island Essex....46 H9
Mersey Crossing Halton....75 N7

Mersham Kent....17 J3
Merstham Surrey....33 K11
Merston W Susx....14 C10
Merstone IoW....13 J8
Merther Cnwll....3 L5
Merthyr Carmth....38 A7
Merthyr Cynog Powys....39 M4
Merthyr Dyfan V Glam....27 Q8
Merthyr Mawr Brdgnd....27 J5
Merthyr Tydfil Myr Td....39 P10
Merthyr Vale Myr Td....27 P5
Merton Devon....19 K11
Merton Gt Lon....33 J8
Merton Norfk....70 D12
Merton Oxon....43 M8
Meshaw Devon....19 P9
Messing Essex....46 F8
Messingham N Linc....79 M3
Metal Bridge Dur....100 H11
Metfield Suffk....59 L4
Metherell Cnwll....4 E4
Metheringham Lincs....79 Q11
Methil Fife....115 Q1
Methley Leeds....85 N10
Methley Junction Leeds....85 N11
Methlick Abers....141 L9
Methven P & K....123 P7
Methwold Norfk....57 P2
Methwold Hythe Norfk....57 N2
Mettingham Suffk....59 M3
Metton Norfk....71 J5
Mevagissey Cnwll....3 P5
Mexborough Donc....78 D4
Mey Highld....151 N2
Meysey Hampton Gloucs....30 D2
Miabhaig W Isls....152 e3
Michaelchurch Herefs....40 H6
Michaelchurch Escley Herefs....40 D5
Michaelstone-y-Fedw Newpt....28 C5
Michaelston-le-Pit V Glam....27 Q8
Michaelstow Cnwll....6 F9
Michaelwood Services Gloucs....29 L3
Michelcombe Devon....5 L3
Micheldever Hants....24 H5
Micheldever Station Hants....24 H5
Michelmersh Hants....24 F8
Mickfield Suffk....58 H8
Micklebring Donc....78 E5
Mickleby N York....92 G4
Micklefield Leeds....85 N8
Micklefield Green Herts....32 E3
Mickleham Surrey....32 H11
Mickleover C Derb....65 Q5
Micklethwaite C Brad....84 G8
Micklethwaite Cumb....98 C8
Mickleton Dur....90 G2
Mickleton Gloucs....42 G3
Mickletown Leeds....85 N9
Mickle Trafford Ches W....75 M9
Mickley Derbys....77 Q8
Mickley N York....91 L11
Mickley Green Suffk....58 C9
Mickley Square Nthumb....100 D6
Mid Ardlaw Abers....141 M3
Midbea Ork....147 c2
Mid Beltie Abers....132 G4
Mid Bockhampton BCP....12 B5
Mid Calder W Loth....115 K8
Mid Clyth Highld....151 P9
Mid Culbeuchly Abers....140 G3
Middle Assendon Oxon....31 Q5
Middle Aston Oxon....43 K6
Middle Barton Oxon....43 J6
Middlebie D & G....97 P3
Middlebridge P & K....130 G11
Middle Chinnock Somset....21 Q10
Middle Claydon Bucks....43 P6
Middlecliffe Barns....78 C3
Middlecott Devon....8 D7
Middlecroft Derbys....78 C8
Middle Duntisbourne Gloucs....41 R10
Middleham N York....91 R10
Middle Handley Derbys....78 C8
Middle Harling Norfk....58 F4
Middlehill Cnwll....4 C3
Middlehill Wilts....29 N9
Middlehope Shrops....51 M3
Middle Kames Ag & B....112 D3
Middle Littleton Worcs....42 C3
Middle Madeley Staffs....64 E3
Middle Mayfield Staffs....65 L3
Middle Mill Pembks....36 G5
Middlemoor Devon....4 H3
Middlemoor Highld....91 J12
Middlemuir Abers....141 M3
Middle Rasen Lincs....80 B5
Middle Rocombe Devon....5 Q3
Middle Salter Lancs....83 R1
Middlesbrough Middsb....92 A3
Middlesceugh Cumb....98 E10
Middleshaw Cumb....89 N9
Middlesmoor N York....90 H12
Middlestone Dur....100 G2
Middlestone Moor Dur....100 G11
Middle Stoke Medway....34 E7
Middlestown Wakefd....85 K11
Middle Street Gloucs....41 M10
Middle Taphouse Cnwll....4 B4
Middlethird Border....107 J2
Middleton Ag & B....118 C3
Middleton Derbys....77 P10
Middleton Derbys....65 P2
Middleton Essex....46 F4
Middleton Hants....24 G4
Middleton Herefs....51 P7
Middleton Lancs....83 K3
Middleton Leeds....85 K9
Middleton N York....84 H6
Middleton N York....92 F9
Middleton Nhants....55 L3
Middleton Norfk....69 L9
Middleton Nthumb....100 E1
Middleton Nthumb....108 H2
Middleton P & K....124 C11
Middleton Rochdl....76 G2
Middleton Shrops....51 P5
Middleton Shrops....63 K6
Middleton Suffk....59 N6
Middleton Swans....38 G11
Middleton Warwks....53 M2
Middleton Cheney Nhants....43 K3
Middleton Green Staffs....64 H5
Middleton Hall Nthumb....108 G4
Middleton-in-Teesdale Dur....90 G2
Middleton Moor Suffk....59 N6
Middleton One Row Darltn....91 N5
Middleton-on-Leven N York....91 R5
Middleton-on-Sea W Susx....14 D10
Middleton on the Hill Herefs....51 P7
Middleton on the Wolds E R Yk....86 H5
Middleton Park C Aber....133 M2
Middleton Priors Shrops....52 B3
Middleton Quernhow N York....91 N11
Middleton St George Darltn....91 N4
Middleton Scriven Shrops....52 C3
Middleton Stoney Oxon....43 L7
Middleton Tyas N York....91 L5
Middletown N Som....28 C5
Middletown Powys....63 K9
Middle Town IoS....2 b3
Middle Tysoe Warwks....42 H3
Middle Winterslow Wilts....24 C7
Middlewich Ches E....76 C10
Middle Woodford Wilts....23 P6
Middlewood Cnwll....7 K9
Middlewood Herefs....40 C3
Middlewood Green Suffk....58 G8
Middle Yard Gloucs....41 N11
Middlezoy Somset....21 N7
Middridge Dur....91 L2
Midford BaNES....29 M10
Midge Hall Lancs....83 M9
Midgeholme Cumb....99 J6
Midgham W Berk....31 L9
Midgley Calder....84 F10
Midgley Wakefd....85 K12
Mid Holmwood Surrey....14 H2
Midhopestones Sheff....77 N4
Midhurst W Susx....14 C6
Mid Lavant W Susx....14 C9
Midlem Border....107 N4
Midmar Abers....132 H3
Mid Mains Highld....137 N8
Midney Somset....22 C8
Midpark Ag & B....112 F9
Midsomer Norton BaNES....29 M4
Midtown Highld....149 M4
Midville Lincs....80 G12
Midway Ches E....76 G7
Mid Yell Shet....147 j3
Migdale Highld....145 Q6
Migvie Abers....132 C3
Milborne Port Somset....22 F9
Milborne St Andrew Dorset....11 K5
Milborne Wick Somset....22 F8
Milbourne Nthumb....100 E3
Milbourne Wilts....29 Q5
Milburn Cumb....99 J12
Milbury Heath S Glos....29 K4
Milby N York....85 N2
Milcombe Oxon....43 J5
Milden Suffk....46 F2
Mildenhall Suffk....57 N6
Mildenhall Wilts....30 E8
Milebrook Powys....51 K6
Milebush Kent....16 C2
Mile Elm Wilts....30 A8
Mile End Essex....46 H6
Mile End Gloucs....41 J9
Mile End Suffk....58 D8
Mileham Norfk....70 D8
Mile Oak Br & H....15 J9
Mile Oak Kent....16 B2
Mile Oak Staffs....65 M11
Miles Hope Herefs....51 P7
Milesmark Fife....115 K4
Miles Platting Manch....76 G4
Mile Town Kent....34 G7
Milfield Nthumb....108 G3
Milford Derbys....66 B3
Milford Devon....18 E9
Milford Powys....50 F2
Milford Staffs....64 H7
Milford Surrey....14 D2
Milford Haven Pembks....36 H9
Milford on Sea Hants....12 D6
Milkwall Gloucs....41 J9
Millais Jersey....13 a1
Milland W Susx....25 P8
Milland Marsh W Susx....25 P8
Mill Bank Calder....84 F11
Millbeck Cumb....88 H2
Millbreck Abers....141 N7
Millbridge Surrey....25 P5
Millbrook C Beds....44 E4
Millbrook Cnwll....4 F10
Millbrook C Soton....24 F10
Millbrook Jersey....13 b2
Millbrook Tamesd....76 H4
Mill Brow Stockp....76 H4
Millbuie Abers....133 J2
Millbuie Highld....137 P4
Millcombe Devon....5 N7
Millcorner E Susx....16 E6
Millcraig Highld....145 P11
Mill Cross Devon....5 M4
Milldale Staffs....65 L2
Mill End Bucks....31 R5
Mill End Herts....45 L5
Millerhill Mdloth....115 Q8
Miller's Dale Derbys....77 L9
Miller's Green Derbys....65 Q2
Millers Green Essex....45 Q10
Millerston C Glas....114 B8
Millgate Lancs....84 C11
Mill Green Cambs....57 M11
Mill Green Essex....46 B10
Mill Green Herts....44 H10
Mill Green Herts....45 J8
Mill Green Lincs....68 F6
Mill Green Norfk....58 H4
Mill Green Shrops....64 C6
Mill Green Staffs....65 K12
Mill Green Suffk....46 F2
Mill Green Suffk....58 G7
Mill Green Suffk....58 H8
Mill Green Suffk....59 J6
Millhalf Herefs....51 J11
Millhayes Devon....9 N4
Millhead Lancs....83 L1
Millheugh S Lans....114 D11
Mill Hill E Susx....16 A9
Mill Hill Gt Lon....33 J4
Millhouse Ag & B....112 D7
Millhouse Cumb....98 F11
Millhousebridge D & G....97 M1
Millhouse Green Barns....77 M4
Millhouses Barns....78 C3
Milliken Park Rens....113 N9
Millin Cross Pembks....37 J7
Millington E R Yk....86 F4
Millington Green Derbys....65 P3
Mill Lane Hants....25 M3
Millmeece Staffs....64 F5
Millness Cumb....89 N10
Mill of Drummond P & K....123 P9
Mill of Haldane W Duns....113 M5
Millom Cumb....88 G5
Millook Cnwll....6 H5
Millpool Cnwll....2 G10
Millpool Cnwll....6 G11
Mill Side Cumb....89 M10
Mill Street Kent....34 C11
Mill Street Norfk....70 F8

Mill Street Suffk....58 F6
Millthorpe Derbys....77 P8
Millthrop Cumb....89 Q8
Milltimber C Aber....133 L4
Milltown Abers....131 N2
Milltown Abers....132 D1
Milltown Cnwll....3 Q3
Milltown D & G....98 B11
Milltown Derbys....78 B11
Milltown Devon....19 L5
Milltown Highld....135 N7
Milltown of Auchindoun Moray....139 Q8
Milltown of Campfield Abers....132 G4
Milltown of Edinvillie Moray....139 N8
Milltown of Rothiemay Moray....140 E6
Milnathort P & K....124 C11
Milngavie E Duns....113 Q6
Milnrow Rochdl....76 G1
Milnthorpe Cumb....89 M10
Milnthorpe Wakefd....85 K12
Milovaig Highld....134 C6
Milson Shrops....52 B6
Milstead Kent....34 F10
Milston Wilts....23 Q4
Milthorpe Nhants....43 M2
Milton C Stke....64 G2
Milton Cambs....57 J8
Milton Cumb....98 H6
Milton D & G....95 J7
Milton D & G....96 C6
Milton Derbys....65 P7
Milton Highld....135 Q6
Milton Highld....137 N6
Milton Highld....137 Q6
Milton Highld....146 H8
Milton Inver....113 L7
Milton Kent....34 C8
Milton Moray....139 M12
Milton Moray....140 D3
Milton N Som....28 D10
Milton Newpt....28 E5
Milton Notts....78 H9
Milton Oxon....31 K4
Milton Oxon....43 K5
Milton P & K....123 N4
Milton Pembks....37 K10
Milton Somset....21 P8
Milton Stirlg....113 P1
Milton W Duns....113 N6
Milton Abbas Dorset....11 K4
Milton Abbot Devon....4 E3
Milton Bridge Mdloth....115 N8
Milton Bryan C Beds....44 D6
Milton Clevedon Somset....22 F6
Milton Combe Devon....4 G3
Milton Common Oxon....43 N11
Milton Damerel Devon....7 M3
Milton End Gloucs....30 D2
Milton End Gloucs....41 L9
Milton Ernest Bed....55 P9
Milton Green Ches W....75 M12
Milton Hill Oxon....31 K4
Milton Keynes M Keyn....44 B4
Milton Lilbourne Wilts....30 D10
Milton Malsor Nhants....55 J9
Milton Morenish P & K....122 G5
Milton of Auchinhove Abers....132 E4
Milton of Balgonie Fife....115 P1
Milton of Buchanan Stirlg....113 N3
Milton of Campsie E Duns....114 B6
Milton of Finavon Angus....125 K1
Milton of Leys Highld....138 C7
Milton of Murtle C Aber....133 L4
Milton on Stour Dorset....22 H7
Milton Regis Kent....34 F9
Milton Street E Susx....15 P10
Milton-under-Wychwood Oxon....42 F9
Milverton Somset....20 H8
Milverton Warwks....53 P7
Milwich Staffs....64 H6
Milwr Flints....74 H9
Minard Ag & B....112 E2
Minchington Dorset....23 L10
Minchinhampton Gloucs....29 P2
Mindrum Nthumb....108 E3
Minehead Somset....20 D4
Minera Wrexhm....63 J2
Minety Wilts....30 B3
Minffordd Gwynd....61 K4
Mingarrypark Highld....127 M10
Miningsby Lincs....80 F11
Minions Cnwll....7 K10
Minishant S Ayrs....104 E7
Minllyn Gwynd....61 P8
Minnigaff D & G....95 M5
Minnonie Abers....141 J4
Minshull Vernon Ches E....76 C11
Minskip N York....85 M2
Minstead Hants....12 D3
Minsted W Susx....25 N9
Minster Kent....34 G7
Minster Kent....35 P9
Minsterley Shrops....63 L11
Minster Lovell Oxon....42 G9
Minster-on-Sea Kent....34 G8
Minsterworth Gloucs....41 M8
Minterne Magna Dorset....10 G4
Minterne Parva Dorset....10 G4
Minting Lincs....80 D9
Mintlaw Abers....141 N6
Minto Border....107 N6
Minton Shrops....51 M3
Minwear Pembks....37 K8
Minworth Birm....53 M3
Mirehouse Cumb....88 D4
Mireland Highld....151 P4
Mirfield Kirk....85 K11
Miserden Gloucs....41 Q10
Miskin Rhondd....27 P3
Miskin Rhondd....27 P5
Misson Notts....78 H5
Misterton Leics....54 E4
Misterton Notts....79 J5
Misterton Somset....10 C3
Mistley Essex....47 K5
Mistley Heath Essex....47 K5
Mitcham Gt Lon....33 J8
Mitcheldean Gloucs....41 K8
Mitchell Cnwll....3 K4
Mitchellslacks D & G....106 C10
Mitchel Troy Mons....40 G9
Mitford Nthumb....100 F1
Mithian Cnwll....3 J4
Mitton Staffs....64 G9
Mixbury Oxon....43 M5
Mixenden Calder....84 G9
Moats Tye Suffk....58 F9
Mobberley Ches E....76 E7
Mobberley Staffs....65 J4
Moccas Herefs....40 F3
Mochdre Conwy....73 P8
Mochdre Powys....50 F4
Mochrum D & G....95 L9
Mockbeggar Hants....12 B3
Mockbeggar Kent....16 C1
Mockerkin Cumb....88 E2
Modbury Devon....5 L6
Moddershall Staffs....64 G5
Moelfre IoA....72 H5

Moelfre Powys 62 G6
Moel Tryfan Gwynd 60 H1
Moffat D & G 106 E8
Mogador Surrey 33 J11
Moggerhanger C Beds 56 C10
Moira Leics 53 P9
Molash Kent 35 J12
Mol-chlach Highld 126 H2
Mold Flints 74 H11
Moldgreen Kirk 84 H2
Molehill Green Essex 45 Q7
Molehill Green Essex 46 C7
Molescroft E R Yk 87 J7
Molesden Nthumb 100 F1
Molesworth Cambs 55 Q5
Moll Highld 135 K9
Molland Devon 20 C7
Mollington Ches W 75 L9
Mollington Oxon 54 D11
Mollinsburn N Lans 114 C7
Monachty Cerdgn 43 H8
Mondynes Abers 133 J8
Monewden Suffk 59 K9
Moneydie P & K 123 Q7
Moneyrow Green W & M 32 C7
Moniaive D & G 105 P11
Monifieth Angus 125 K6
Monikie Angus 125 K5
Monimail Fife 124 F10
Monington Pembks 37 M2
Monk Bretton Barns 78 B2
Monken Hadley Gt Lon 33 J3
Monk Fryston N York 85 Q9
Monkhide Herefs 41 J3
Monkhill Cumb 98 D6
Monkhopton Shrops 52 B2
Monkland Herefs 51 M9
Monkleigh Devon 19 J9
Monknash V Glam 27 L8
Monkokehampton Devon 7 J2
Monkseaton N Tyne 101 J4
Monks Eleigh Suffk 58 E11
Monk's Gate W Susx 14 H5
Monks Heath Ches E 76 F9
Monk Sherborne Hants 31 M11
Monkshill Abers 140 H7
Monksilver Somset 20 G6
Monks Kirby Warwks 54 D4
Monk Soham Suffk 59 J7
Monkspath Solhll 53 L5
Monks Risborough Bucks 44 A10
Monksthorpe Lincs 80 H10
Monk Street Essex 45 R6
Monkswood Mons 40 D11
Monkton Devon 9 M4
Monkton Kent 35 N9
Monkton S Ayrs 104 F4
Monkton S Tyne 101 J5
Monkton V Glam 27 M8
Monkton Combe BaNES 29 M10
Monkton Deverill Wilts 23 J6
Monkton Farleigh Wilts 29 N9
Monkton Heathfield Somset 21 L8
Monkton Up Wimborne Dorset 23 M10
Monkton Wyld Dorset 9 Q5
Monkwearmouth Sundld 101 K6
Monkwood Hants 25 L7
Monmore Green Wolves 52 H1
Monmouth Mons 40 G9
Monnington on Wye Herefs 40 E3
Monreith D & G 95 L10
Montacute Somset 22 C10
Montcliffe Bolton 76 C1
Montford Shrops 63 L9
Montford Bridge Shrops 63 M9
Montgarrie Abers 140 E12
Montgomery Powys 50 H1
Montrose Angus 125 P1
Mont Saint Guern 12 b2
Monxton Hants 24 E4
Monyash Derbys 77 L10
Monymusk Abers 132 G1
Monzie P & K 123 M8
Moodiesburn N Lans 114 C7
Moonzie Fife 124 G9
Moor Allerton Leeds 85 L7
Moorbath Dorset 10 C6
Moorby Lincs 80 F11
Moorcot Herefs 51 K9
Moor Crichel BCP 11 N3
Moordown BCP 11 Q6
Moore Halton 75 P7
Moor End C Beds 44 D7
Moor End Calder 84 F9
Moor End Devon 8 C3
Moorend Gloucs 41 L11
Moor End Lancs 83 J6
Moor End N York 86 B7
Moorends Donc 86 C12
Moorgreen Hants 24 H10
Moor Green Herts 45 L6
Moorgreen Notts 66 D3
Moorhall Derbys 77 P8
Moorhampton Herefs 40 E2
Moorhead C Brad 84 H8
Moor Head Leeds 85 K9
Moorhouse Cumb 98 B8
Moorhouse Cumb 98 D7
Moorhouse Donc 78 D2
Moorhouse Notts 79 J10
Moorhouse Bank Surrey 33 M11
Moorland Somset 21 M7
Moorlinch Somset 21 N6
Moor Monkton N York 85 Q4
Moor Row Cumb 88 D4
Moor Row Cumb 98 E7
Moorsholm R & Cl 92 E4
Moorside Dorset 22 H9
Moorside Dur 100 E8
Moor Side Lancs 83 K8
Moor Side Lancs 83 K8
Moor Side Leeds 85 K8
Moor Side Lincs 80 E12
Moorside Oldham 76 H2
Moor Street Medway 34 E8
Moorswater Cnwll 4 C4
Moorthorpe Wakefd 78 D2
Moortown Cnwll 7 P10
Moortown Devon 12 B4
Moortown Hants 12 H3
Moortown IoW 12 G8
Moortown Leeds 85 L7
Moortown Lincs 79 Q4
Moortown Wrekin 63 Q8
Morangie Highld 146 D9
Morar Highld 127 M6
Morborne Cambs 56 C2
Morchard Bishop Devon 8 E3
Morchard Road Devon 8 E4
Morcombelake Dorset 10 B6
Morcott Rutlnd 67 M12
Morda Shrops 63 J6
Morden Gt Lon 33 J8
Morden Dorset 11 M5
Mordiford Herefs 40 H4
Mordon Dur 91 N1
More Shrops 51 K2
Morebath Devon 20 D8
Morebattle Border 108 C5
Morecambe Lancs 83 K8
Moredon Swindn 30 D5
Morefield Highld 144

Morehall Kent 17 M3
Moreleigh Devon 5 M6
Morenish P & K 122 G6
Moresby Parks Cumb 88 D3
Morestead Hants 24 H8
Moreton Dorset 11 K7
Moreton Essex 45 P10
Moreton Herefs 51 N8
Moreton Oxon 43 P9
Moreton Staffs 64 E8
Moreton Staffs 65 L6
Moreton Wirral 75 J6
Moreton Corbet Shrops 63 P7
Moretonhampstead Devon 8 E7
Moreton-in-Marsh Gloucs 42 E5
Moreton Jeffries Herefs 51 G1
Moretonmill Shrops 63 P7
Moreton Morrell Warwks 53 P9
Moreton on Lugg Herefs 40 G3
Moreton Paddox Warwks 53 P9
Moreton Pinkney Nhants 54 F11
Moreton Say Shrops 64 B5
Moreton Valence Gloucs 41 M9
Morfa Cerdgn 48 E10
Morfa Bychan Gwynd 61 J3
Morfa Dinlle Gwynd 72 G12
Morfa Glas Neath 39 K10
Morfa Nefyn Gwynd 60 D4
Morganstown Cardif 27 Q6
Morgan's Vale Wilts 24 C9
Moriah Cerdgn 49 K5
Morland Cumb 89 P2
Morley Ches E 76 F7
Morley Derbys 66 C4
Morley Dur 91 J1
Morley Leeds 85 K9
Morley Green Ches E 76 F7
Morley St Botolph Norfk 70 G12
Mornick Cnwll 7 L10
Morningside C Edin 115 N7
Morningside N Lans 114 E10
Morningthorpe Norfk 59 J2
Morpeth Nthumb 100 G1
Morphie Abers 132 H11
Morrey Staffs 65 L9
Morridge Side Staffs 65 J1
Morriston Swans 26 G4
Morston Norfk 70 E3
Mortehoe Devon 19 J4
Morthen Rothm 78 D6
Mortimer W Berk 31 N9
Mortimer Common W Berk 31 N9
Mortimer's Cross Herefs 51 M8
Mortimer West End Hants 31 N9
Mortlake Gt Lon 32 H7
Morton Cumb 98 C3
Morton Cumb 98 F10
Morton Derbys 78 C11
Morton IoW 13 K7
Morton Lincs 68 B7
Morton Lincs 79 K5
Morton Lincs 79 M11
Morton Notts 67 J2
Morton Shrops 63 J7
Morton-on-Swale N York 91 N8
Morton on the Hill Norfk 70 G9
Morton Tinmouth Dur 91 K2
Morvah Cnwll 2 C6
Morval Cnwll 4 C5
Morvich Highld 136 D11
Morville Shrops 52 C2
Morville Heath Shrops 52 C2
Morwenstow Cnwll 18 D10
Mosborough Sheff 78 C7
Moscow E Ayrs 105 J2
Mose Shrops 52 D3
Mosedale Cumb 98 D11
Moseley Birm 53 K4
Moseley Wolves 52 H1
Moseley Worcs 52 E8
Moses Gate Bolton 76 D2
Moss Ag & B 118 C4
Moss Donc 78 D2
Moss Wrexhm 63 J2
Mossat Abers 140 D12
Mossbank Shet 147 j3
Moss Bank St Hel 75 M4
Mossbay Cumb 88 C1
Mossblown S Ayrs 104 G5
Mossburnford Border 107 Q6
Mossdale D & G 96 D4
Mossdale E Ayrs 105 J9
Moss Edge Lancs 83 K6
Moss End Ches E 76 C6
Mossend N Lans 114 D9
Mosser Mains Cumb 88 F2
Mossley Ches E 76 G11
Mossley Tamesd 76 H3
Mosspaul Hotel Border 107 L10
Moss Side Highld 138 F5
Moss Side Lancs 83 J9
Moss Side Sefton 75 L3
Mosstodloch Moray 139 Q4
Mossy Lea Lancs 75 P1
Mosterton Dorset 10 C4
Moston Manch 76 G3
Moston Shrops 63 P7
Moston Green Ches E 76 D11
Mostyn Flints 74 G7
Motcombe Dorset 23 J8
Mothecombe Devon 5 K6
Motherby Cumb 98 P2
Motherwell N Lans 114 D10
Motspur Park Gt Lon 33 J9
Mottingham Gt Lon 33 M8
Mottisfont Hants 24 E8
Mottistone IoW 12 G8
Mottram in Longdendale Tamesd 77 J5
Mottram St Andrew Ches E 76 G8
Mouilpied Guern 12 c3
Mouldsworth Ches W 75 N10
Moulin P & K 123 N1
Moulsecoomb Br & H 15 J10
Moulsford Oxon 31 M5
Moulsoe M Keyn 44 C3
Moultavie Highld 145 P11
Moulton Ches W 76 C9
Moulton Lincs 68 F7
Moulton N York 91 L6
Moulton Nhants 55 J7
Moulton Suffk 57 N8
Moulton V Glam 27 P8
Moulton Chapel Lincs 68 F8
Moulton St Mary Norfk 71 N10
Moulton Seas End Lincs 68 F6
Mount Cnwll 3 J4
Mount Cnwll 4 A3
Mount Kirk 84 G1
Mountain C Brad 84 G9
Mountain Ash Rhondd 27 L4
Mountain Cross Border 115 L12
Mountain Street Kent 35 J11
Mount Ambrose Cnwll 2 H6
Mount Bures Essex 46 G6
Mountfield E Susx 16 C7

Mountgerald Highld 137 P3
Mount Hawke Cnwll 2 H5
Mount Hermon Cnwll 2 H11
Mountjoy Cnwll 3 L2
Mount Lothian Mdloth 115 N10
Mountnessing Essex 34 A3
Mounton Mons 28 G4
Mount Pleasant Ches E 76 F12
Mount Pleasant Derbys 65 P8
Mount Pleasant Derbys 65 Q2
Mount Pleasant Dur 100 H11
Mount Pleasant E R Yk 87 M1
Mount Pleasant E Susx 15 M7
Mount Pleasant Norfk 58 E2
Mount Pleasant Suffk 57 P11
Mount Sorrel Wilts 23 M8
Mount Tabor Calder 84 G9
Mousehole Cnwll 2 C8
Mow Cop Ches E 76 F12
Mowhaugh Border 108 C5
Mowmacre Hill C Leic 66 F10
Mowsley Leics 54 G3
Moy Highld 129 M8
Moy Highld 138 E9
Moyle Highld 136 B12
Moylegrove Pembks 48 A11
Muasdale Ag & B 103 J2
Muchalls Abers 133 L6
Much Birch Herefs 40 G5
Much Cowarne Herefs 41 J2
Much Dewchurch Herefs 40 G5
Muchelney Somset 21 P8
Muchelney Ham Somset 21 P8
Much Hadham Herts 45 M8
Much Hoole Lancs 83 L10
Much Hoole Town Lancs 83 L10
Muchlarnick Cnwll 4 C5
Much Marcle Herefs 41 K5
Much Wenlock Shrops 64 B12
Muck Highld 126 G8
Mucking Thurr 34 B6
Muckleburgh Collection Norfk 70 G3
Muckleford Dorset 10 G6
Mucklestone Staffs 64 D5
Muckley Shrops 52 B2
Muckton Lincs 80 G7
Muddiford Devon 19 L6
Muddles Green E Susx 15 Q8
Mudeford BCP 12 C6
Mudford Somset 22 D9
Mudford Sock Somset 22 D9
Mudgley Somset 21 P4
Mud Row Kent 34 H8
Mugdock Stirlg 113 Q6
Mugeary Highld 134 H9
Mugginton Derbys 65 P4
Muggintonlane End Derbys 65 P3
Muggleswick Dur 100 D8
Muirden Abers 140 H6
Muirdrum Angus 125 L5
Muiresk Abers 140 H6
Muirhead Angus 124 G6
Muirhead Fife 124 F11
Muirhead N Lans 114 C7
Muirhouses Falk 115 J5
Muirkirk E Ayrs 105 K4
Muirmill Stirlg 114 D4
Muir of Fowlis Abers 132 E2
Muir of Miltonduff Moray 139 M4
Muir of Ord Highld 137 P6
Muirshearlich Highld 128 G8
Muirtack Abers 141 M8
Muirton P & K 123 N10
Muirton Mains Highld 137 M5
Muirton of Ardblair P & K 124 D4
Muker N York 90 E7
Mulbarton Norfk 71 J12
Mulben Moray 139 Q6
Mulfra Cnwll 2 D7
Mull Ag & B 119 Q6
Mullacott Cross Devon 19 K4
Mullardoch Highld 136 H9
Mullion Cnwll 2 H10
Mullion Cove Cnwll 2 G11
Mumby Lincs 81 K9
Munderfield Row Herefs 52 C10
Munderfield Stocks Herefs 52 C10
Mundesley Norfk 71 L5
Mundford Norfk 57 Q2
Mundham Norfk 59 L1
Mundon Essex 46 F11
Mundy Bois Kent 16 F2
Munlochy Highld 138 D12
Munnoch N Ayrs 113 K11
Munsley Herefs 41 K3
Munslow Shrops 51 N3
Murchington Devon 8 C7
Murcot Worcs 42 C4
Murcott Worcs 30 E3
Murcott Wilts 29 Q4
Murkle Highld 151 L3
Murlaggan Highld 128 D6
Murrell Green Hants 25 M2
Murroes Angus 125 J6
Murrow Cambs 68 G10
Mursley Bucks 44 B6
Murston Kent 34 G9
Murthill Angus 125 J4
Murthly P & K 124 C5
Murton Cumb 89 Q3
Murton C York 86 C5
Murton Dur 101 J9
Murton Nthumb 117 L11
Murton Swans 26 E4
Musbury Devon 9 P6
Muscoates N York 92 E10
Musselburgh E Loth 115 Q7
Muston Leics 67 K5
Muston N York 93 M10
Mustow Green Worcs 52 F6
Muswell Hill Gt Lon 33 K4
Mutehill D & G 96 E8
Mutford Suffk 59 P3
Muthill P & K 123 M9
Mutterton Devon 9 J4
Muxton Wrekin 64 D9
Mybster Highld 151 L6
Myddfai Carmth 39 J5
Myddle Shrops 63 N7
Mydroilyn Cerdgn 48 G2
Myerscough Lancs 83 L7
Mylor Cnwll 3 K7
Mylor Bridge Cnwll 3 K7
Mynachlog ddu Pembks 37 M4
Mynydd-Ilan Flints 74 G9
Myndtown Shrops 51 L3
Mynydd Bach Cerdgn 49 M5
Mynydd-bach Mons 28 G8
Mynydd Buch Cerdgn 49 M5
Mynyddgarreg Carmth 38 C10
Mynydd Isa Flints 75 J11
Mynydd Llandygai Gwynd 73 K10
Mynydd Mechell IoA 72 F6
Mynytho Gwynd 60 D5
Myrebird Abers 132 H4

Myredykes Border 107 P10
Mytchett Surrey 32 C11
Mytholm Calder 84 E9
Mytholmroyd Calder 84 F10
Mythop Lancs 83 J8
Myton-on-Swale N York 85 N2

N

Naast Highld 143 M8
Nab's Head Lancs 83 M9
Na Buirgh W Isls 152 d6
Naburn C York 86 B6
Naccolt Kent 17 J2
Nackington Kent 35 L11
Nacton Suffk 47 M4
Nafferton E R Yk 87 K3
Nag's Head Gloucs 29 P3
Nailbridge Gloucs 41 K8
Nailsbourne Somset 21 K8
Nailsea N Som 28 G8
Nailstone Leics 66 C11
Nailsworth Gloucs 29 N2
Nairn Highld 138 E5
Nalderswood Surrey 15 J2
Nancegollan Cnwll 2 G8
Nancledra Cnwll 2 D7
Nanhoron Gwynd 60 D6
Nannerch Flints 74 G9
Nanpantan Leics 66 E8
Nanpean Cnwll 3 N3
Nanquidno Cnwll 2 B8
Nanstallon Cnwll 6 F11
Nant-ddu Powys 39 N8
Nanternis Cerdgn 48 F9
Nantgaredig Carmth 38 D7
Nantgarw Rhondd 27 N6
Nant-glas Powys 50 D7
Nantglyn Denbgs 74 D11
Nantgwyn Powys 50 D5
Nant Gwynant Gwynd 61 L2
Nantile Gwynd 60 H2
Nantmawr Shrops 63 J7
Nantmel Powys 50 D8
Nantmor Gwynd 61 K2
Nant Peris Gwynd 73 K12
Nantwich Ches E 64 C2
Nant-y-Bwch Blae G 39 Q9
Nant-y-derry Mons 40 D10
Nant-y-ffin Carmth 38 D5
Nantyffyllon Brdgnd 27 K4
Nantyglo Blae G 40 B9
Nant-y-gollen Shrops 62 H6
Nant-y-moel Brdgnd 27 K3
Nant-y-pandy Conwy 73 J9
Naphill Bucks 32 B3
Napleton Worcs 52 F11
Nappa N York 84 C4
Napton on the Hill Warwks 54 C8
Narberth Pembks 37 L7
Narborough Leics 54 E11
Narborough Norfk 69 P9
Narkurs Cnwll 4 E5
Nasareth Gwynd 60 H2
Naseby Nhants 54 H5
Nash Bucks 43 Q5
Nash Gt Lon 33 M9
Nash Herefs 51 K8
Nash Newpt 28 D5
Nash Shrops 51 Q6
Nash End Worcs 52 D5
Nash Lee Bucks 44 B10
Nash Street Kent 34 B8
Nassington Nhants 55 Q1
Nastend Gloucs 41 M10
Nasty Herts 45 L7
Nateby Cumb 90 C5
Nateby Lancs 83 L6
National Memorial Arboretum Staffs 65 M9
National Motor Museum (Beaulieu) Hants 12 F4
National Space Centre C Leic 66 F10
Natland Cumb 89 N9
Naughton Suffk 58 F10
Naunton Gloucs 42 D7
Naunton Worcs 41 P4
Naunton Beauchamp Worcs 52 H10
Navenby Lincs 79 N12
Navestock Essex 33 Q3
Navestock Side Essex 33 Q3
Navidale Highld 147 J2
Navity Highld 138 D3
Nawton N York 92 D10
Nayland Suffk 46 H5
Nazeing Essex 45 M10
Nazeing Gate Essex 45 M10
Neacroft Hants 12 C5
Neal's Green Warwks 53 Q4
Neap Shet 147 j6
Near Cotton Staffs 65 K3
Near Sawrey Cumb 89 K7
Neasden Gt Lon 33 J5
Neasham Darltn 91 N5
Neath Neath 26 H3
Neatham Hants 25 M5
Neatishead Norfk 71 L8
Nebo Cerdgn 49 J7
Nebo Conwy 61 P1
Nebo Gwynd 60 H2
Nebo IoA 72 H5
Necton Norfk 70 C10
Nedd Highld 148 D10
Nedderton Nthumb 100 G1
Nedging Suffk 58 E11
Nedging Tye Suffk 58 F10
Needham Norfk 59 J4
Needham Market Suffk 58 G9
Needham Street Suffk 57 N7
Needingworth Cambs 56 G6
Neen Savage Shrops 52 C6
Neen Sollars Shrops 52 B6
Neenton Shrops 52 B3
Nefyn Gwynd 60 E4
Neilston E Rens 113 P6
Nelson Caerph 27 Q3
Nelson Lancs 84 C7
Nemphlar S Lans 105 Q1
Nempnett Thrubwell BaNES 28 H10
Nenthall Cumb 99 Q9
Nenthead Cumb 99 Q9
Nenthorn Border 107 R2
Nep Town W Susx 15 J8
Nercwys Flints 74 H11
Nerston S Lans 114 B10
Nesbit Nthumb 108 H3
Nesfield N York 84 G5
Ness Ches W 75 L8
Nesscliffe Shrops 63 L8
Neston Ches W 75 J8
Neston Wilts 29 P8
Netchwood Shrops 52 B3
Nether Abington S Lans 106 C5
Nether Alderley Ches E 76 F8
Netheravon Wilts 23 N3
Nether Blainslie Border 107 N11
Netherbrae Abers 141 J5

Nether Broughton Leics 66 H7
Netherburn S Lans 114 E11
Netherbury Dorset 10 D5
Netherby Cumb 98 E4
Netherby N York 85 L5
Nether Cerne Dorset 10 G5
Nether Compton Dorset 22 D10
Nethercote Warwks 54 E8
Nethercott Devon 7 L5
Nethercott Devon 19 J5
Nether Crimond Abers 141 K11
Nether Dallachy Moray 139 Q3
Netherend Gloucs 29 J2
Nether Exe Devon 8 H4
Netherfield E Susx 16 C7
Netherfield Leics 66 E6
Netherfield Notts 66 G4
Nether Fingland S Lans 106 B7
Nethergate N Linc 79 L3
Nethergate Norfk 70 G7
Nether Handley Derbys 78 C8
Nether Handwick Angus 124 G4
Nether Haugh Rothm 78 C4
Netherhay Dorset 10 C4
Nether Headon Notts 79 J9
Nether Heage Derbys 66 B2
Nether Heyford Nhants 54 H9
Nether Kellet Lancs 83 L3
Nether Kinmundy Abers 141 P7
Netherland Green Staffs 65 L5
Nether Langwith Notts 78 E8
Netherley Abers 133 K6
Nethermill D & G 106 D12
Nethermuir Abers 141 L7
Netherne-on-the-Hill Surrey 33 K11
Netheroyd Hill Kirk 84 H11
Nether Padley Derbys 77 N8
Nether Poppleton C York 85 R4
Netherseal Derbys 65 P9
Nether Silton N York 91 Q8
Nether Skyborry Shrops 51 J6
Nether Stowey Somset 21 K5
Netherstreet Wilts 29 Q9
Netherthong Kirk 77 L2
Netherthorpe Derbys 78 D9
Netherton Angus 125 L1
Netherton Devon 8 G10
Netherton Dudley 52 H3
Netherton Herefs 40 H6
Netherton Kirk 77 L1
Netherton N Lans 114 E10
Netherton Nthumb 108 H6
Netherton Oxon 31 J2
Netherton P & K 124 C2
Netherton Sefton 75 K4
Netherton Stirlg 113 Q5
Netherton Wakefd 85 L11
Netherton Worcs 52 A3
Nethertown Cumb 88 C8
Nethertown Highld 151 Q1
Nethertown Lancs 83 Q8
Nethertown Staffs 65 L8
Netherurd Border 115 K12
Nether Wallop Hants 24 E6
Nether Wasdale Cumb 88 F6
Nether Welton Cumb 98 E8
Nether Westcote Gloucs 42 E7
Nether Whitacre Warwks 53 M2
Nether Whitecleuch S Lans 105 Q5
Nether Winchendon Bucks 43 Q9
Netherwitton Nthumb 108 H11
Nethy Bridge Highld 139 J11
Netley Hants 24 H5
Netley Marsh Hants 24 E10
Nettlebed Oxon 31 P5
Nettlebridge Somset 22 E4
Nettlecombe Dorset 10 D5
Nettlecombe IoW 13 J9
Nettleden Herts 44 F9
Nettleham Lincs 79 P8
Nettlestead Kent 34 B12
Nettlestead Green Kent 34 B12
Nettlestone IoW 13 K6
Nettlesworth Dur 100 H8
Nettleton Lincs 80 B11
Nettleton Wilts 29 N6
Nettleton Shrub Wilts 29 N7
Netton Devon 5 J7
Netton Wilts 23 N5
Neuadd Carmth 38 G10
Neuadd-ddu Powys 50 C5
Nevendon Essex 34 B3
Nevern Pembks 37 L3
Nevill Holt Leics 55 K2
New Abbey D & G 97 K5
New Aberdour Abers 141 L3
New Addington Gt Lon 33 L9
Newall Leeds 85 J6
New Alresford Hants 25 K7
New Alyth P & K 124 E3
Newark C Pete 68 D12
Newark Ork 147 e2
Newark-on-Trent Notts 67 K2
New Arley Warwks 53 N3
New Arram E R Yk 87 J7
Newarthill N Lans 114 E10
New Ash Green Kent 34 B9
New Balderton Notts 67 K2
New Barn Kent 34 B8
New Barnet Gt Lon 33 J3
New Barton Nhants 55 L8
Newbattle Mdloth 115 Q8
New Bewick Nthumb 108 H6
Newbie D & G 97 P4
Newbiggin Cumb 89 Q2
Newbiggin Cumb 89 G1
Newbiggin Cumb 98 B9
Newbiggin Cumb 98 E12
Newbiggin Cumb 89 Q3
Newbiggin Dur 100 E9
Newbiggin N York 90 G9
Newbiggin N York 90 H7
Newbiggin-by-the-Sea Nthumb 109 M12
Newbigging Angus 124 H4
Newbigging Angus 124 H5
Newbigging S Lans 115 J12
New Bilton Warwks 54 B6
Newbold Derbys 78 B9
Newbold Leics 66 B9
Newbold on Avon Warwks 54 D5
Newbold on Stour Warwks 42 G2
Newbold Pacey Warwks 53 Q9
Newbold Revel Warwks 54 C4
Newbold Verdon Leics 66 C11
Newborough C Pete 68 E11
Newborough IoA 72 G10
Newborough Staffs 65 M8
Newbottle Nhants 43 L4

Newbottle Sundld 101 J8
New Boultham Lincs 79 N10
Newbourne Suffk 47 N4
New Bradwell M Keyn 44 B3
New Brampton Derbys 78 B9
New Brancepeth Dur 100 G10
Newbridge C Edin 115 L7
Newbridge Caerph 28 B3
Newbridge Cerdgn 48 H3
Newbridge Cnwll 2 C8
Newbridge Cnwll 4 E4
Newbridge D & G 97 J2
Newbridge Hants 24 D10
Newbridge IoW 12 G7
Newbridge Oxon 31 K2
Newbridge Green Worcs 41 N4
Newbridge-on-Wye Powys 50 D9
New Brighton Flints 75 J10
New Brighton Wirral 75 K5
New Brinsley Notts 66 D2
New Brotton R & Cl 92 E3
New Buckenham Norfk 58 G2
Newburgh Abers 141 N10
Newburgh Abers 141 L3
Newburgh Fife 124 F9
Newburgh Lancs 75 N2
Newburn N u Ty 100 G5
Newbury Somset 22 E3
Newbury W Berk 31 K8
Newbury Wilts 22 H5
Newby Cumb 89 P2
Newby Lancs 84 C5
Newby N York 83 Q1
Newby N York 89 K8
Newby N York 91 N9
Newby N York 93 K8
Newby Bridge Cumb 89 J8
Newby Cross Cumb 98 D7
Newby East Cumb 98 E7
Newby Head Cumb 89 P2
New Byth Abers 141 K5
Newby West Cumb 98 D7
Newby Wiske N York 91 P9
Newcastle Mons 40 G8
Newcastle Shrops 51 J4
Newcastle Airport Nthumb 100 F4
Newcastle Emlyn Carmth 37 Q3
Newcastleton Border 107 M12
Newcastle-under-Lyme Staffs 64 F3
Newcastle upon Tyne N u Ty 100 G5
Newchapel Pembks 37 M3
Newchapel Staffs 64 F1
Newchapel Surrey 15 L2
Newchurch Blae G 40 A9
Newchurch Carmth 37 Q6
Newchurch IoW 13 J8
Newchurch Kent 17 J4
Newchurch Lancs 84 B10
Newchurch Mons 28 F3
Newchurch Powys 50 H10
Newchurch Staffs 65 L7
Newchurch in Pendle Lancs 84 B7
New Costessey Norfk 71 J10
New Cowper Cumb 97 M9
Newcraighall C Edin 115 P7
New Cross Cerdgn 49 L5
New Cross Gt Lon 33 L7
New Cross Somset 21 P9
New Cumnock E Ayrs 105 L7
New Cut E Susx 16 D6
New Deer Abers 141 L6
New Delaval Nthumb 100 H3
New Delph Oldham 77 J2
New Denham Bucks 32 F4
Newdigate Surrey 14 H2
New Duston Nhants 54 H8
New Earswick C York 86 C4
New Eastwood Notts 66 D3
New Edlington Donc 78 D3
New Elgin Moray 139 M4
New Ellerby E R Yk 87 M7
Newell Green Br For 32 C8
New Eltham Gt Lon 33 N8
New End Worcs 53 L8
Newenden Kent 16 E4
New England C Pete 68 D12
New England Essex 46 H2
Newent Gloucs 41 L6
New Farnley Leeds 85 K9
New Ferry Wirral 75 K6
Newfield Dur 100 F10
Newfield Dur 100 G11
Newfield Highld 146 D10
New Fletton C Pete 56 D2
New Forest National Park Hants 12 D3
Newfound Hants 25 J3
New Fryston Wakefd 85 P10
Newgale Pembks 36 G6
New Galloway D & G 96 D3
Newgate Norfk 70 G4
Newgate Street Herts 45 K10
New Gilston Fife 125 J11
New Grimsby IoS 2 b1
Newhall Ches E 64 C3
Newhall Derbys 65 P9
Newham Nthumb 109 K4
New Hartley Nthumb 100 H3
Newhaven C Edin 115 N6
Newhaven Derbys 77 M11
Newhaven E Susx 15 N10
New Haw Surrey 32 G9
New Hedges Pembks 37 M9
New Herrington Sundld 101 J7
Newhey Rochdl 76 H1
New Holkham Norfk 70 C4
New Holland N Linc 87 K9
Newholm N York 92 H5
New Houghton Derbys 78 E9
New Houghton Norfk 69 Q6
Newhouse N Lans 114 E8
New Houses N York 90 C12
New Houses Wigan 75 Q2
New Hutton Cumb 89 N7
New Hythe Kent 34 B10
Newick E Susx 15 M6
Newingreen Kent 17 K3
Newington Kent 17 L3
Newington Kent 34 E9
Newington Oxon 31 N3
Newington Shrops 51 M4
Newington Bagpath Gloucs 29 N3
New Inn Carmth 38 D4
New Inn Torfn 28 C3
New Invention Shrops 51 J5
New Lakenham Norfk 71 K11
New Lanark S Lans 106 A1
New Lanark Village S Lans 106 A1
Newland Cumb 89 J9
Newland E R Yk 86 E9
Newland Gloucs 40 H9

Newland N York 86 C10
Newland Oxon 42 H9
Newland Somset 20 C6
Newland Worcs 52 E11
Newlandrig Mdloth 115 Q9
Newlands Cumb 98 D10
Newlands Nthumb 100 E7
Newlands of Dundurcas Moray 139 P6
New Lane Lancs 75 M1
New Lane End Warrtn 76 B5
New Langholm D & G 98 D1
New Leake Lincs 80 H12
New Leeds Abers 141 N5
New Lodge Barns 78 B2
New Longton Lancs 83 L10
New Luce D & G 94 H5
Newlyn Cnwll 2 C8
Newmachar Abers 141 L12
Newmains N Lans 114 E10
New Malden Gt Lon 33 J8
Newman's End Essex 45 P9
Newman's Green Suffk 46 F3
Newmarket Suffk 57 M8
Newmarket W Isls 152 g3
New Marske R & Cl 92 C2
New Marston Oxon 43 N10
New Marton Shrops 63 K5
New Mill Abers 133 J5
New Mill Border 107 L7
New Mill Cnwll 2 D7
New Mill Herts 44 C9
New Mill Kirk 77 L2
New Mill Moray 140 C5
Newmillerdam Wakefd 85 L12
Newmill of Inshewan Angus 132 C12
Newmills C Edin 115 L8
New Mills Cnwll 3 L4
New Mills Derbys 77 K6
Newmills Fife 115 J4
Newmills Mons 40 H9
New Mills Powys 62 F12
Newmiln P & K 124 C6
Newmilns E Ayrs 105 K2
New Milton Hants 12 C5
New Mistley Essex 47 K5
New Moat Pembks 37 L5
Newnes Shrops 63 L5
Newney Green Essex 46 B10
Newnham Hants 25 M3
Newnham Herts 45 J4
Newnham Kent 34 G11
Newnham Nhants 54 F9
Newnham Bridge Worcs 52 B7
Newnham on Severn Gloucs 41 L9
New Ollerton Notts 78 H10
New Oscott Birm 53 L2
New Pitsligo Abers 141 L5
New Polzeath Cnwll 6 D9
Newport Cnwll 7 L7
Newport Dorset 11 L6
Newport E R Yk 86 F9
Newport Essex 45 P5
Newport Gloucs 29 L3
Newport Highld 151 L11
Newport IoW 12 H7
Newport Newpt 28 C4
Newport Pembks 37 L3
Newport Wrekin 64 D8
Newport-on-Tay Fife 124 H7
Newport Pagnell M Keyn 44 B3
Newport Pagnell Services M Keyn 44 B3
Newpound Common W Susx 14 F5
New Prestwick S Ayrs 104 F5
New Quay Cerdgn 48 F8
Newquay Cnwll 3 K2
Newquay Zoo Cnwll 3 K2
New Rackheath Norfk 71 K9
New Radnor Powys 50 H8
New Rent Cumb 98 F11
New Ridley Nthumb 100 E6
New Road Side N York 84 E7
New Romney Kent 17 J6
New Rossington Donc 78 G4
New Row Cerdgn 49 M6
New Row Lancs 83 P7
New Sauchie Clacks 114 F3
Newsbank Ches E 76 F10
Newseat Abers 141 L8
Newsham Lancs 83 L8
Newsham N York 91 J5
Newsham N York 91 P10
Newsham Nthumb 100 H3
New Sharlston Wakefd 85 M11
Newsholme E R Yk 86 C4
Newsholme Lancs 84 C5
New Shoreston Nthumb 109 K3
New Silksworth Sundld 101 K7
New Skelton R & Cl 92 D3
Newsome Kirk 84 H12
New Somerby Lincs 67 M4
New Springs Wigan 75 N2
Newstead Border 107 N2
Newstead Notts 66 E2
Newstead Nthumb 109 K4
New Stevenston N Lans 114 E10
New Street Herefs 51 K9
New Swanage Dorset 11 P8
New Swannington Leics 66 C9
Newthorpe N York 85 N9
New Thundersley Essex 34 D4
Newtoft Lincs 79 P6
Newton Ag & B 112 H2
Newton Border 107 P4
Newton Brdgnd 27 J6
Newton C Beds 45 J3
Newton Cambs 45 M2
Newton Cambs 68 H9
Newton Cardif 28 B5
Newton Ches W 75 L10
Newton Ches W 75 N11
Newton Cumb 88 H12
Newton Derbys 78 D11
Newton Herefs 40 H4
Newton Herefs 51 N10
Newton Highld 137 Q6
Newton Highld 138 E3
Newton Highld 151 P7
Newton Lancs 83 L7
Newton Lancs 83 Q1
Newton Lancs 89 P11
Newton Lincs 67 P4
Newton Mdloth 115 P8
Newton Moray 139 N3
Newton N York 92 H12
Newton Nhants 55 L4
Newton Norfk 70 B8
Newton Nthumb 100 D5
Newton S Lans 106 D3
Newton S Lans 114 B8
Newton Sandw 53 J3
Newton Somset 20 H6

Newton Staffs 65 J7
Newton Staffs 46 L3
Newton W Loth 115 K6
Newton Warwks 54 L5
Newton Wilts 24 C9
Newton Abbot Devon 8 F10
Newton Arlosh Cumb 97 P7
Newton Aycliffe Dur 91 M2
Newton Bewley Hartpl 91 Q1
Newton Blossomville M Keyn 55 M10
Newton Bromswold Nhants 55 P7
Newton Burgoland Leics 66 B10
Newton by Toft Lincs 79 P6
Newton Ferrers Devon 5 J7
Newton Ferry W Isls 152 c7
Newton Flotman Norfk 59 J1
Newtongrange Mdloth 115 P8
Newton Green Mons 28 G4
Newton Harcourt Leics 54 G1
Newton Heath Manch 76 G4
Newtonhill Abers 133 L5
Newton Hill Wakefd 85 L10
Newton-in-Bowland Lancs 83 Q5
Newton Kyme N York 85 P6
Newton-le-Willows N York 91 L9
Newton-le-Willows St Hel 75 Q4
Newtonloan Mdloth 115 P8
Newton Longville Bucks 44 B5
Newton Mearns E Rens 113 Q10
Newton Morrell N York 91 M5
Newton Mountain Pembks 37 J9
Newton Mulgrave N York 92 F4
Newton of Balcanquhal P & K 124 D10
Newton of Balcormo Fife 125 K12
Newton of Belltrees Rens 113 M9
Newton-on-Ouse N York 85 Q3
Newton-on-Rawcliffe N York 92 G8
Newton on the Hill Shrops 63 N7
Newton-on-the-Moor Nthumb 109 L9
Newton on Trent Lincs 79 L9
Newton Poppleford Devon 9 L7
Newton Purcell Oxon 43 N5
Newton Regis Warwks 65 P10
Newton Reigny Cumb 98 F12
Newton St Cyres Devon 8 G5
Newton St Faith Norfk 71 J8
Newton St Loe BaNES 29 L8
Newton St Petrock Devon 18 H11
Newton Solney Derbys 65 P7
Newton Stacey Hants 24 C5
Newton Stewart D & G 95 M5
Newton Tony Wilts 24 C5
Newton Tracey Devon 19 K8
Newton under Roseberry R & Cl 92 B4
Newton Underwood Nthumb 100 T1
Newton upon Derwent E R Yk 86 D5
Newton Valence Hants 25 M7
Newton Wamphray D & G 106 E10
Newton with Scales Lancs 83 K9
Newtown BCP 11 P6
Newtown Blae G 40 A9
Newtown Ches W 75 M8
Newtown Cnwll 2 F8
Newtown Cnwll 7 K9
Newtown Cumb 89 N2
Newtown Cumb 97 M8
Newtown Cumb 98 E6
Newtown Cumb 98 G6
Newtown D & G 105 P8
Newtown Derbys 77 J7
Newtown Devon 7 N7
Newtown Devon 19 P8
Newtown Devon 10 D4
Newtown Dorset 11 N3
New Town Dorset 23 L10
New Town Dorset 23 L9
New Town E Susx 15 N7
Newtown Gloucs 41 K11
Newtown Hants 12 D3
Newtown Hants 25 K10
Newtown Hants 31 K9
Newtown Herefs 40 H5
Newtown Herefs 41 J3
Newtown Herefs 51 N9
Newtown Highld 129 L3
Newtown IoW 12 G6
Newtown Nthumb 108 G5
Newtown Nthumb 108 G5
Newtown Nthumb 108 G9
Newtown Powys 50 P2
Newtown Rhondd 27 P3
Newtown Shrops 63 M7
Newtown Shrops 63 N6
Newtown Somset 21 L10
Newtown Staffs 65 J11
Newtown Staffs 76 G11
Newtown Wigan 75 P9
Newtown Wilts 23 K7
Newtown Wilts 30 Q9
Newtown Worcs 52 G9
Newtown Worcs 52 H5
Newtown-in-St Martin Cnwll 3 J10
Newtown Linford Leics 66 E10
Newtown St Boswells Border 107 P3
Newtown Unthank Leics 66 E11
New Tredegar Caerph 39 Q11
New Trows S Lans 105 Q2
New Tupton Derbys 78 C10
Newtyle Angus 124 F5
New Walsoken Cambs 69 J10
New Waltham NE Lin 80 F3
New Whittington Derbys 78 C8
New Winton E Loth 116 B7
New Yatt Oxon 42 H9
Newyears Green Gt Lon 32 F5
Newyork Ag & B 120 H10
New York Lincs 68 E1
New York N Tyne 101 J4
New York N York 85 J3
New Zealand Wilts 30 B7
Nextend Herefs 51 K9
Neyland Pembks 37 J9
Niarbyl IoM 102 b6
Nibley Gloucs 41 K10
Nibley S Gloucs 29 L6
Nibley Green Gloucs 29 L3
Nicholashayne Devon 20 H10
Nicholaston Swans 26 C4
Nickies Hill Cumb 98 G5
Nidd N York 85 L3
Nigg C Aber 133 M4
Nigg Highld 146 E10
Nigg Ferry Highld 146 E11
Nimlet BaNES 29 M8
Ninebanks Nthumb 99 M7
Nine Elms Swindn 30 C5
Nine Wells Pembks 36 F5
Ninfield E Susx 16 C8

Ningwood IoW 12 F7
Nisbet Border 107 Q5
Nisbet Hill Border 116 H11
Niton IoW 12 H9
Nitshill C Glas 113 Q9
Noah's Ark Kent 33 Q10
Noak Bridge Essex 34 C4
Noak Hill Gt Lon 33 P3
Noblethorpe Barns 77 P3
Nobold Shrops 63 M10
Nobottle Nhants 54 H8
Nocton Lincs 79 Q11
Nogdam End Norfk 71 M12
Noke Oxon 43 L9
Nolton Pembks 36 G7
Nolton Haven Pembks 36 G7
No Man's Heath Ches W 64 H2
No Man's Heath Warwks 65 P10
No Man's Land Cnwll 4 G8
Nomansland Devon 20 C10
Nomansland Wilts 24 D10
Noneley Shrops 63 N6
Nonington Kent 35 N11
Nook Cumb 89 N10
Nook Cumb 98 F8
Norbiton Gt Lon 32 G8
Norbreck Bpool 82 H7
Norbridge Herefs 41 L3
Norbury Ches E 63 P3
Norbury Derbys 65 L4
Norbury Gt Lon 33 K8
Norbury Shrops 51 L2
Norbury Staffs 64 E7
Norbury Common Ches E 63 P2
Norbury Junction Staffs 64 E7
Norchard Worcs 52 F7
Norcott Brook Ches W 75 Q7
Norcross Lancs 82 H7
Nordelph Norfk 69 K12
Norden Rochdl 84 C12
Nordley Shrops 52 C2
Norfolk Broads Norfk 71 P10
Norham Nthumb 117 K11
Norland Town Calder 84 G10
Norley Ches W 75 P9
Norleywood Hants 12 F5
Norlington E Susx 15 N8
Normanby E R Yk 92 H9
Normanby N Linc 86 G12
Normanby N York 92 E10
Normanby R & Cl 92 B3
Normanby le Wold Lincs 80 C5
Norman Cross Cambs 56 C2
Normandy Surrey 32 D12
Normans Bay E Susx 16 B9
Norman's Green Devon 9 K4
Normanton C Derb 66 B5
Normanton Leics 67 K4
Normanton Lincs 67 M1
Normanton Notts 67 M11
Normanton Wakefd 85 M10
Normanton Wilts 23 P5
Normanton le Heath Leics 66 B9
Normanton on Cliffe Lincs 67 N3
Normanton on Soar Notts 66 E7
Normanton on the Wolds Notts 66 G5
Normanton on Trent Notts 79 K10
Normoss Lancs 82 H7
Norney Surrey 14 D2
Norrington Common Wilts 29 P9
Norris Green Cnwll 4 F3
Norris Green Lpool 75 L5
Norris Hill Leics 65 Q9
Norristhorpe Kirk 85 J10
Northacre Norfk 58 E1
Northall Bucks 44 D7
Northallerton N York 91 M6
Northall Green Norfk 70 E9
Northam C Sotn 24 G11
Northam Devon 18 H7
Northampton Nhants 55 J8
Northampton Worcs 52 F7
Northampton Services Nhants 55 J8
North Anston Rothm 78 E7
North Ascot Br For 32 C8
North Aston Oxon 43 K6
Northaw Herts 45 K11
Northay Somset 9 P3
North Baddesley Hants 24 F9
North Ballachulish Highld 128 E12
North Barrow Somset 22 E7
North Barsham Norfk 70 D5
Northbay W Isls 152 b13
North Benfleet Essex 34 D4
North Berwick E Loth 116 D4
North Bitchburn Dur 100 F11
North Blyth Nthumb 101 J2
North Boarhunt Hants 13 K3
North Bockhampton BCP 12 B5
Northborough C Pete 68 C10
Northbourne Kent 35 P12
North Bovey Devon 8 D8
North Bradley Wilts 22 H2
North Brentor Devon 7 P8
North Brewham Somset 22 G6
North Bridge Surrey 14 D3
Northbridge Street E Susx 16 C6
Northbrook Hants 24 H6
Northbrook Oxon 43 K7
North Brook End Cambs 45 K3
North Buckland Devon 19 J5
North Burlingham Norfk 71 M10
North Cadbury Somset 22 E8
North Carlton Lincs 79 N8
North Carlton Notts 78 F7
North Cave E R Yk 86 G8
North Cerney Gloucs 42 B10
Northchapel W Susx 14 D6
North Charford Hants 24 C9
North Charlton Nthumb 109 K5
North Cheam Gt Lon 33 J9
North Cheriton Somset 22 F8
North Chideock Dorset 10 C6
Northchurch Herts 44 D10
North Cliffe E R Yk 86 G8
North Clifton Notts 79 K9
North Close Dur 100 H11
North Cockerington Lincs 80 G5
North Connel Ag & B 120 G6
North Cornelly Brdgnd 27 K6
North Corner Cnwll 3 J10
North Cotes Lincs 80 G4
Northcott Devon 7 L6
Northcott Devon 9 L3
Northcott Devon 20 H1
North Country Cnwll 2 G7
Northcourt Oxon 31 L3
North Cove Suffk 59 N4
North Cowton N York 91 M6
North Crawley M Keyn 55 L10
North Cray Gt Lon 33 N8
North Creake Norfk 70 C4
North Curry Somset 21 M8
North Dalton E R Yk 86 H5
North Deighton N York 85 M5
Northdown Kent 35 Q8
North Downs 34 G11
North Duffield N York 86 C8

Northedge Derbys 78 B10
North Elham Kent 17 L2
North Elkington Lincs 80 F5
North Elmham Norfk 70 E8
North Elmsall Wakefd 78 D1
Northend Bucks 31 Q4
North End C Port 13 L4
North End Cumb 98 C6
North End Dorset 23 J7
North End E R Yk 87 M7
North End E R Yk 87 N9
North End Essex 46 B8
North End Hants 23 N10
North End Hants 25 K7
North End Leics 66 F9
North End Lincs 68 E4
North End Lincs 79 P4
North End Lincs 80 F3
North End Lincs 80 H6
North End N Linc 87 L10
North End N Som 28 F9
North End Nhants 55 N7
North End Norfk 58 E2
North End Nthumb 109 J9
North End Sefton 75 J3
North End W Susx 14 D10
North End W Susx 14 G9
Northend Warwks 54 C10
Northenden Manch 76 F6
Northend Woods Bucks 32 C4
North Erradale Highld 143 K9
North Evington C Leic 66 G12
North Fambridge Essex 34 E3
North Featherstone Wakefd 85 N11
North Ferriby E R Yk 87 J10
Northfield Birm 53 J5
Northfield C Aber 133 L5
Northfield E R Yk 87 K10
Northfield Hants 67 P10
Northfleet Kent 34 C7
North Frodingham E R Yk 87 L5
Northgate Lincs 68 C7
North Gorley Hants 12 B2
North Green Norfk 59 J3
North Green Suffk 59 L8
North Greetwell Lincs 79 P9
North Grimston N York 86 H2
North Halling Medway 34 C9
North Hayling Hants 13 M4
North Hazelrigg Nthumb 108 H3
North Heasley Devon 19 P7
North Heath W Susx 14 F7
North Hele Devon 20 E9
North Hill Cnwll 7 K9
North Hillingdon Gt Lon 32 F4
North Hinksey Village Oxon 43 K10
North Holmwood Surrey 14 H1
North Huish Devon 5 L5
North Hykeham Lincs 79 N10
Northiam E Susx 16 E6
Northill C Beds 44 G2
Northington Gloucs 41 L10
Northington Hants 25 J5
North Kelsey Lincs 79 P3
North Kessock Highld 138 B6
North Killingholme N Linc 87 L11
North Kilvington N York 91 P9
North Kilworth Leics 54 G4
North Kingston Hants 12 B4
North Kyme Lincs 68 C2
North Lancing W Susx 14 H9
North Landing E R Yk 93 P12
Northlands Lincs 68 G2
Northleach Gloucs 42 D9
North Lee Bucks 44 B10
North Lees N York 91 M12
Northleigh Devon 9 M5
Northleigh Devon 19 L6
North Leigh Kent 17 K1
North Leigh Oxon 42 H9
North Leverton with Habblesthorpe Notts 79 K7
Northlew Devon 7 P5
North Littleton Worcs 53 K11
Northload Bridge Somset 22 C5
North Lopham Norfk 58 F4
North Luffenham Rutlnd 67 M11
North Marden W Susx 25 P10
North Marston Bucks 43 Q7
North Middleton Mdloth 115 Q9
North Middleton Nthumb 108 G5
North Millbrex Abers 141 M4
North Milmain D & G 94 F7
North Molton Devon 19 N7
Northmoor Oxon 43 J11
North Moreton Oxon 31 M4
Northmuir Angus 124 H2
North Mundham W Susx 14 C10
North Muskham Notts 79 K12
North Newbald E R Yk 86 G8
North Newington Oxon 43 J4
North Newnton Wilts 30 D11
North Newton Somset 21 M4
Northney Hants 13 M4
North Nibley Gloucs 29 L3
North Oakley Hants 25 J2
North Ockendon Gt Lon 33 Q4
Northolt Gt Lon 32 G5
North Ormesby Middsb 92 A3
North Ormsby Lincs 80 F5
Northorpe Lincs 68 B8
Northorpe Lincs 68 D5
Northorpe Lincs 79 M4
North Otterington N York 91 N9
Northover Somset 21 N6
Northover Somset 22 C7
North Owersby Lincs 79 Q5
Northowram Calder 84 H10
North Perrott Somset 10 D3
North Petherton Somset 21 L5
North Petherwin Cnwll 7 K7
North Pickenham Norfk 70 C10
North Piddle Worcs 52 H9
North Poorton Dorset 10 H7
Northport Dorset 11 M7
North Poulner Hants 12 B3
North Queensferry Fife 115 J4
North Radworthy Devon 19 P6
North Rauceby Lincs 67 P2
Northrepps Norfk 71 K4
North Reston Lincs 80 G6
North Rigton N York 85 L5
North Ripley Hants 12 B5
North Rode Ches E 76 G10
North Roe Shet 147 i4
North Ronaldsay Ork 147 f1
North Ronaldsay Airport Ork 147 f1
North Row Cumb 97 H11
North Runcton Norfk 69 M9
North Scale Cumb 82 F1
North Scarle Lincs 79 L10
North Seaton Nthumb 100 H1
North Seaton Colliery Nthumb 100 H1
North Shian Ag & B 120 G4
North Shields N Tyne 101 J4
North Shoebury Sthend 34 G4
North Shore Bpool 82 H8

North Side C Pete 68 E12
North Side Cumb 97 H4
North Skelton R & Cl 92 D3
North Somercotes Lincs 80 H4
North Stainley N York 91 M11
North Stifford Thurr 33 Q5
North Stoke BaNES 29 L8
North Stoke Oxon 31 M5
North Stoke W Susx 14 E8
North Street Cambs 57 L7
North Street Hants 23 N9
North Street Hants 25 L5
North Street Kent 34 H10
North Street Medway 34 E7
North Street W Berk 31 M6
North Sunderland Nthumb 109 K3
North Tamerton Cnwll 7 K5
North Tawton Devon 8 C4
North Third Stirlg 114 D3
North Thoresby Lincs 80 F4
North Togston Nthumb 109 L9
North Tolsta W Isls 152 h2
Northton W Isls 152 d6
North Town Devon 7 P3
North Town Somset 22 D6
North Town W & M 32 C6
North Uist W Isls 152 b8
North Walbottle N u Ty 100 F5
North Walsham Norfk 71 K6
North Waltham Hants 25 J4
North Warnborough Hants 25 M3
Northway Somset 21 J7
North Weald Bassett Essex 45 N11
North Wheatley Notts 79 J6
North Whilborough Devon 5 P3
Northwich Ches W 76 D9
North Wick BaNES 29 J9
Northwick S Glos 28 H5
Northwick Somset 21 M4
Northwick Worcs 52 F9
North Widcombe BaNES 28 H10
North Willingham Lincs 80 C6
North Wingfield Derbys 78 C10
North Witham Lincs 67 M8
Northwold Norfk 57 P1
Northwood C Stke 64 G2
Northwood Derbys 77 P10
Northwood Gt Lon 32 F4
Northwood IoW 12 H6
Northwood Shrops 63 M5
Northwood Worcs 52 E6
Northwood Green Gloucs 41 L8
North Wootton Dorset 22 E10
North Wootton Norfk 69 M7
North Wootton Somset 22 D5
North Wraxall Wilts 29 N5
North Wroughton Swindn 30 D5
Norton Donc 85 Q12
Norton E Susx 15 N10
Norton Gloucs 41 Q6
Norton Halton 75 P7
Norton Hants 24 H5
Norton Herts 45 J5
Norton IoW 12 F7
Norton N Som 40 F7
Norton N Som 28 D9
Norton Nhants 54 F8
Norton Notts 78 F9
Norton Powys 51 J7
Norton S on T 91 Q2
Norton Sheff 78 B7
Norton Shrops 51 M4
Norton Shrops 52 B4
Norton Shrops 63 P10
Norton Suffk 58 D7
Norton Suffk 58 G7
Norton Swans 26 F5
Norton W Susx 14 C9
Norton W Susx 14 C10
Norton Wilts 29 P5
Norton Worcs 52 F10
Norton Worcs 53 K11
Norton Bavant Wilts 23 K5
Norton Bridge Staffs 64 F6
Norton Canes Staffs 65 J10
Norton Canes Services Staffs 65 J10
Norton Canon Herefs 40 G2
Norton Corner Norfk 70 G6
Norton Disney Lincs 79 M11
Norton Ferris Wilts 22 H5
Norton Fitzwarren Somset 21 K8
Norton Green IoW 12 F7
Norton Hawkfield BaNES 29 J9
Norton Heath Essex 45 R10
Norton in Hales Shrops 64 D4
Norton-Juxta-Twycross Leics 65 Q10
Norton-le-Clay N York 85 N1
Norton-le-Moors C Stke 64 G2
Norton Lindsey Warwks 53 N8
Norton Malreward BaNES 29 J9
Norton Mandeville Essex 45 Q10
Norton-on-Derwent N York 86 E1
Norton St Philip Somset 22 G2
Norton Subcourse Norfk 59 N1
Norton sub Hamdon Somset 21 P10
Norton Wood Herefs 51 L11
Norwell Notts 79 K11
Norwell Woodhouse Notts 79 J11
Norwich Norfk 71 J9
Norwich Airport Norfk 71 J9
Norwick Shet 147 k2
Norwood Clacks 114 F4
Norwood Derbys 78 D7
Norwood End Essex 45 Q11
Norwood Green Calder 84 H10
Norwood Green Gt Lon 32 G6
Norwoodside Cambs 56 H1
Noseley Leics 55 J1
Noss Mayo Devon 5 K7
Nosterfield N York 91 M10
Nosterfield End Cambs 46 B3
Nostie Highld 135 Q10
Notgrove Gloucs 42 C7
Nottage Brdgnd 27 K7
Notter Cnwll 4 F4
Nottingham C Nott 66 F4
Nottington Dorset 10 H8
Notton Wakefd 77 N1
Notton Wilts 29 Q8
Nottswood Hill Gloucs 41 L8
Noutard's Green Worcs 52 E7
Nowton Suffk 58 C9
Nox Shrops 63 M9
Nuffield Oxon 31 N5
Nunburnholme E R Yk 86 F6
Nuncargate Notts 66 F2
Nunclose Cumb 98 F9
Nuneaton Warwks 54 B3

Nuneham Courtenay Oxon 31 L2
Nunhead Gt Lon 33 L7
Nunkeeling E R Yk 87 L5
Nun Monkton N York 85 Q4
Nunney Somset 22 G4
Nunney Catch Somset 22 G4
Nunnington Herefs 40 H3
Nunnington N York 92 D11
Nunsthorpe NE Lin 80 E2
Nunthorpe C York 86 B5
Nunthorpe Middsb 92 B4
Nunthorpe Village Middsb 92 B4
Nunton Wilts 23 P8
Nunwick N York 91 N11
Nunwick Nthumb 99 N3
Nupdown S Glos 28 H3
Nup End Bucks 44 B8
Nupend Gloucs 41 M10
Nuptown Br For 32 C7
Nursling Hants 24 F10
Nursted Hants 25 N9
Nursteed Wilts 30 B10
Nurton Staffs 64 F12
Nutbourne W Susx 13 N4
Nutbourne W Susx 14 F7
Nutfield Surrey 33 K12
Nuthall Notts 66 E3
Nuthampstead Herts 45 M5
Nuthurst W Susx 14 H6
Nutley E Susx 15 N4
Nutley Hants 25 K4
Nuttall Bury 84 B12
Nutwell Donc 78 G3
Nybster Highld 151 Q4
Nyetimber W Susx 13 P6
Nyewood W Susx 25 N9
Nymans W Susx 15 K5
Nymet Rowland Devon 8 D3
Nymet Tracey Devon 8 D5
Nympsfield Gloucs 29 N2
Nynehead Somset 21 J8
Nythe Somset 21 N6
Nyton W Susx 14 D9

Oadby Leics 66 G12
Oad Street Kent 34 F10
Oakall Green Worcs 52 E8
Oakamoor Staffs 65 K3
Oakbank W Loth 115 K8
Oak Cross Devon 7 Q5
Oakdale Caerph 28 B3
Oake Somset 21 J8
Oaken Staffs 64 F11
Oakenclough Lancs 83 M6
Oakengates Wrekin 64 C10
Oakenholt Flints 75 J9
Oakenshaw Dur 100 F10
Oakenshaw Kirk 85 J9
Oakerthorpe Derbys 66 C1
Oakford Cerdgn 48 G9
Oakford Devon 20 E7
Oakfordbridge Devon 20 E7
Oakgrove Ches E 76 G10
Oakham Rutlnd 67 L10
Oakhanger Ches E 64 E1
Oakhanger Hants 25 M5
Oakhill Somset 22 E4
Oakington Cambs 56 H8
Oaklands Powys 50 E8
Oakle Street Gloucs 41 M8
Oakley BCP 11 N5
Oakley Bed 55 P10
Oakley Bucks 43 N9
Oakley Fife 115 J3
Oakley Hants 25 J3
Oakley Oxon 31 Q2
Oakley Suffk 58 H5
Oakley Green W & M 32 C7
Oakley Park Powys 50 D3
Oakridge Lynch Gloucs 41 Q11
Oaks Lancs 83 P8
Oaks Shrops 63 M11
Oaksey Wilts 30 A4
Oaks Green Derbys 65 M5
Oakshaw Ford Cumb 98 G3
Oakshott Hants 25 M8
Oakthorpe Leics 65 Q9
Oak Tree Darltn 91 M4
Oakwood C Derb 66 B4
Oakwood Nthumb 99 P5
Oakworth C Brad 84 F7
Oare Kent 34 H9
Oare Somset 20 C4
Oare Wilts 30 D9
Oasby Lincs 67 P4
Oath Somset 21 M8
Oathlaw Angus 125 J2
Oatlands Park Surrey 32 F9
Oban Ag & B 120 G6
Oban Airport Ag & B 120 G6
Obley Shrops 51 K5
Obney P & K 123 P5
Oborne Dorset 22 E9
Obthorpe Lincs 68 B9
Occold Suffk 58 H6
Occumster Highld 151 N9
Ochiltree E Ayrs 105 J5
Ockbrook Derbys 66 C5
Ocker Hill Sandw 52 H2
Ockeridge Worcs 52 E8
Ockham Surrey 32 F11
Ockle Highld 127 K10
Ockley Surrey 14 G3
Ocle Pychard Herefs 41 J3
Octon E R Yk 87 J1
Odcombe Somset 22 C10
Odd Down BaNES 29 M10
Oddendale Cumb 89 P4
Oddingley Worcs 52 G9
Oddington Oxon 43 L9
Odell Bed 55 N9
Odham Devon 7 N4
Odiham Hants 25 M3
Odsal C Brad 84 H9
Odstock Wilts 23 P8
Odstone Leics 66 C11
Offchurch Warwks 54 B7
Offenham Worcs 42 B1
Offerton Stockp 76 G6
Offerton Sundld 101 J6
Offham E Susx 15 M8
Offham Kent 34 B10
Offham W Susx 14 E8
Offleymarsh Staffs 64 E6
Offord Cluny Cambs 56 D8
Offord D'Arcy Cambs 56 D8
Offton Suffk 58 H10
Offwell Devon 9 M5
Ogbourne Maizey Wilts 30 E8
Ogbourne St Andrew Wilts 30 E8
Ogbourne St George Wilts 30 F7
Ogden Calder 84 G10
Ogle Nthumb 100 G2
Oglet Lpool 75 M7
Ogmore V Glam 27 J6
Ogmore-by-Sea V Glam 27 J6
Ogmore Vale Brdgnd 27 M4

Ogwen Bank Gwynd 73 K10
Okeford Fitzpaine Dorset 11 K3
Okehampton Devon 8 B6
Oker Side Derbys 77 P11
Okewood Hill Surrey 14 G3
Olchard Devon 8 G9
Old Nhants 55 K6
Old Aberdeen C Aber 133 M3
Old Alresford Hants 25 J6
Oldany Highld 148 D10
Old Arley Warwks 53 P3
Old Auchenbrack D & G 105 P10
Old Basford C Nott 66 F3
Old Basing Hants 25 L3
Oldberrow Warwks 53 L7
Old Bewick Nthumb 108 H5
Old Bolingbroke Lincs 80 F12
Old Bramhope Leeds 85 K6
Old Brampton Derbys 77 P10
Old Bridge of Urr D & G 96 F5
Old Buckenham Norfk 58 F2
Old Burghclere Hants 31 K10
Oldbury Sandw 53 J3
Oldbury Shrops 52 D2
Oldbury Warwks 53 P2
Oldbury Naite S Glos 29 J4
Oldbury-on-Severn S Glos 29 J4
Oldbury on the Hill Gloucs 29 N5
Old Byland N York 92 B9
Old Cantley Donc 78 G3
Old Cassop Dur 101 J10
Oldcastle Mons 40 D7
Oldcastle Heath Ches W 63 N3
Old Catton Norfk 71 J9
Old Churchstoke Powys 51 J2
Old Clee NE Lin 80 F2
Old Cleeve Somset 20 G5
Old Colwyn Conwy 73 Q8
Oldcotes Notts 78 F8
Old Coulsdon Gt Lon 33 K10
Old Dailly S Ayrs 104 D10
Old Dalby Leics 66 H7
Old Dam Derbys 77 L8
Old Deer Abers 141 N6
Old Ditch Somset 22 C4
Old Edlington Donc 78 E4
Old Eldon Dur 91 L1
Old Ellerby E R Yk 87 M7
Old Felixstowe Suffk 47 N4
Oldfield Worcs 52 F7
Old Fletton C Pete 56 D1
Oldford Somset 22 H3
Old Forge Herefs 40 G7
Old Furnace Herefs 40 G7
Old Glossop Derbys 77 J5
Old Goole E R Yk 86 D10
Old Grimsby IoS 2 b1
Old Hall Green Herts 45 L7
Oldhall Green Suffk 58 C9
Old Hall Street Norfk 71 L5
Oldham Oldham 76 H3
Oldhamstocks E Loth 116 H6
Old Harlow Essex 45 N9
Old Heath Essex 46 H7
Old Hunstanton Norfk 69 N4
Old Hurst Cambs 56 E5
Old Hutton Cumb 89 P9
Old Kea Cnwll 3 L5
Old Kilpatrick W Duns 113 N7
Old Knebworth Herts 45 J7
Old Lakenham Norfk 71 M8
Oldland S Glos 29 K8
Old Langho Lancs 83 Q8
Old Laxey IoM 102 f5
Old Leake Lincs 68 H2
Old Malton N York 92 G12
Oldmeldrum Abers 141 K10
Oldmill Cnwll 4 G6
Old Milverton Warwks 53 P7
Oldmixon N Som 28 D9
Old Newton Suffk 58 F8
Old Oxted Surrey 33 M12
Old Portlethen Abers 133 M5
Old Quarrington Dur 101 J10
Old Radford C Nott 66 F4
Old Radnor Powys 50 H9
Old Rayne Abers 140 G10
Old Romney Kent 17 J5
Old Shoreham W Susx 15 J9
Oldshoremore Highld 148 E4
Old Soar Kent 34 A11
Old Sodbury S Glos 29 M5
Old Somerby Lincs 67 N5
Oldstead N York 92 B9
Old Stratford Nhants 43 Q3
Old Struan P & K 130 E11
Old Swarland Nthumb 109 K9
Old Swinford Dudley 52 G4
Old Tebay Cumb 89 Q6
Old Thirsk N York 91 Q10
Old Town Calder 84 F9
Old Town Cumb 89 P9
Old Town E Susx 15 Q11
Old Town IoS 2 b2
Old Trafford Traffd 76 F4
Old Tupton Derbys 78 C10
Old Wall Cumb 98 F6
Old Warden C Beds 56 C11
Oldways End Somset 20 D8
Old Weston Cambs 55 Q5
Old Wick Highld 151 Q5
Old Windsor W & M 32 D8
Old Wives Lees Kent 35 J11
Old Woking Surrey 32 E11
Old Woodhall Lincs 80 D11
Old Woods Shrops 63 M8
Olgrinmore Highld 151 K6
Olive Green Staffs 65 K8
Oliver's Battery Hants 24 H8
Ollaberry Shet 147 i4
Ollach Highld 135 J11
Ollerton Ches E 76 E8
Ollerton Notts 78 G10
Ollerton Shrops 63 Q7
Olmarch Cerdgn 49 K9
Olmstead Green Cambs 46 B3
Olney M Keyn 55 M10
Olrig House Highld 151 M3
Olton Solhll 53 L4
Olveston S Glos 29 J5
Ombersley Worcs 52 F8
Ompton Notts 78 G10
Onchan IoM 102 e5
Onecote Staffs 65 K1
Onen Mons 40 F9
Ongar Street Herefs 51 L6
Onibury Shrops 51 M5
Onich Highld 128 E12
Onllwyn Neath 39 K9
Onneley Staffs 64 E3
Onslow Green Essex 46 B8
Onslow Village Surrey 14 D1
Onston Ches W 75 P9

Orbost Highld 134 D7
Orby Lincs 81 J10
Orchard Portman Somset 21 K9
Orcheston Wilts 23 N4
Orcop Herefs 40 G6
Orcop Hill Herefs 40 G6
Ord Abers 140 F4
Ordhead Abers 132 G2
Ordie Abers 132 C4
Ordiequish Moray 139 Q4
Ordley Nthumb 99 Q6
Ordsall Notts 78 H8
Ore E Susx 16 E8
Oreleton Common Herefs 51 N7
Oreton Shrops 52 C4
Orford Suffk 47 P3
Orford Warrtn 75 Q5
Organford Dorset 11 M6
Orgreave Staffs 65 L9
Orkney Islands Ork 147 c4
Orkney Neolithic Ork 147 b4
Orlestone Kent 16 H4
Orleton Herefs 51 N7
Orleton Worcs 52 C7
Orlingbury Nhants 55 L6
Ormathwaite Cumb 88 H2
Ormesby R & Cl 92 B3
Ormesby St Margaret Norfk 71 P9
Ormesby St Michael Norfk 71 P9
Ormiscaig Highld 143 M7
Ormiston E Loth 116 A7
Ormsaigmore Highld 126 H11
Ormsary Ag & B 111 Q2
Ormskirk Lancs 75 L2
Ornsby Hill Dur 100 F8
Oronsay Ag & B 110 H3
Orphir Ork 147 b5
Orpington Gt Lon 33 N9
Orrell Sefton 75 K4
Orrell Wigan 75 M3
Orrell Post Wigan 75 M3
Orrisdale IoM 102 d3
Orroland D & G 96 F9
Orsett Thurr 34 B6
Orslow Staffs 64 E9
Orston Notts 67 J4
Orthwaite Cumb 97 Q11
Ortner Lancs 83 M4
Orton Cumb 89 Q5
Orton Nhants 55 K5
Orton Staffs 52 F2
Orton Longueville C Pete 56 D1
Orton-on-the-Hill Leics 65 Q11
Orton Rigg Cumb 98 D6
Orton Waterville C Pete 56 C1
Orwell Cambs 56 G10
Osbaldeston Lancs 83 P8
Osbaldeston Green Lancs 83 P8
Osbaldwick C York 86 B5
Osbaston Leics 66 C11
Osbaston Shrops 63 K7
Osborne IoW 12 H6
Osborne House IoW 13 J6
Osbournby Lincs 67 P4
Oscroft Ches W 75 N10
Ose Highld 134 F7
Osgathorpe Leics 66 C8
Osgodby Lincs 79 Q5
Osgodby N York 86 B8
Osgodby N York 93 L10
Oskaig Highld 135 K8
Oskamull Ag & B 119 M6
Osmaston Derbys 65 M3
Osmington Dorset 10 H8
Osmington Mills Dorset 10 H8
Osmondthorpe Leeds 85 L8
Osmotherley N York 91 Q7
Osney Oxon 43 K10
Ospringe Kent 34 H10
Ossett Wakefd 85 K11
Ossington Notts 79 J11
Ostend Essex 34 G3
Osterley Gt Lon 32 H7
Oswaldkirk N York 92 C11
Oswaldtwistle Lancs 83 Q9
Oswestry Shrops 63 J6
Otairnis W Isls 152 c7
Otford Kent 33 P10
Otham Kent 34 D11
Otham Hole Kent 34 E11
Othery Somset 21 N7
Otley Leeds 85 J6
Otley Suffk 59 J9
Otley Green Suffk 59 J9
Otterbourne Hants 24 H8
Otterburn N York 84 C4
Otterburn Nthumb 108 E11
Otter Ferry Ag & B 112 D4
Otterham Cnwll 7 J6
Otterhampton Somset 21 L5
Otterham Quay Kent 34 E9
Otterham Station Cnwll 7 J6
Otternish W Isls 152 c7
Ottershaw Surrey 32 E9
Otterswick Shet 147 j4
Otterton Devon 9 L7
Otterwood Hants 12 G4
Ottery St Mary Devon 9 L5
Ottinge Kent 17 L2
Ottringham E R Yk 87 P10
Oughterby Cumb 98 D6
Oughtershaw N York 90 E10
Oughterside Cumb 97 M10
Oughtibridge Sheff 77 P5
Oughtrington Warrtn 76 C6
Oulston N York 92 B12
Oulton Cumb 97 Q6
Oulton Leeds 85 M9
Oulton Norfk 70 H6
Oulton Staffs 64 E7
Oulton Staffs 64 H7
Oulton Suffk 59 Q2
Oulton Broad Suffk 59 Q2
Oulton Street Norfk 70 H7
Oundle Nhants 55 P3
Ounsdale Staffs 52 F2
Our Dynamic Earth C Edin 115 N6
Ousby Cumb 99 J11
Ousden Suffk 57 P9
Ousefleet E R Yk 86 F10
Ouston Dur 100 H7
Outchester Nthumb 109 J3
Out Elmstead Kent 35 M12
Outgate Cumb 89 L7
Outhgill Cumb 90 C6
Outlands Staffs 64 E6
Outlane Kirk 84 G11
Out Newton E R Yk 87 R11
Out Rawcliffe Lancs 83 J7
Out Skerries Shet 147 k5
Outwell Norfk 69 K11
Outwood Surrey 15 K2
Outwood Wakefd 85 L10
Outwoods Leics 66 C8
Outwoods Staffs 64 E8
Ouzlewell Green Leeds 85 M10
Ovenden Calder 84 G10
Over Cambs 56 F6
Over Ches W 76 B10
Over Gloucs 41 N8

Over – Pont-ar-Hydfer 183

Over S Glos 29 J6
Over Burrows Derbys 65 N4
Overbury Worcs 41 Q4
Overcombe Dorset 10 H8
Over Compton Dorset 22 D10
Over End Cambs 56 B2
Overgreen Derbys 77 Q9
Over Green Warwks 53 M2
Over Haddon Derbys 77 M10
Over Hulton Bolton 76 C3
Over Kellet Lancs 83 M1
Over Kiddington Oxon 43 J7
Overleigh Somset 22 B6
Overley Staffs 65 M9
Over Monnow Mons 40 G9
Over Norton Oxon 42 G6
Over Peover Ches E 76 E9
Overpool Ches W 75 L8
Overscaig Highld 149 J12
Overseal Derbys 65 P9
Over Silton N York 91 Q8
Oversland Kent 35 J11
Oversley Green Warwks 53 L9
Overstone Nhants 55 K7
Over Stowey Somset 21 J6
Overstrand Norfk 71 K4
Over Stratton Somset 21 P10
Overstreet Wilts 23 N6
Over Tabley Ches E 76 D7
Overthorpe Nhants 43 K4
Overton C Aber 133 L2
Overton Ches W 75 N8
Overton Hants 24 H3
Overton Lancs 83 K4
Overton N York 85 Q4
Overton Shrops 51 N6
Overton Swans 26 C5
Overton Wakefd 85 K12
Overton Wrexhm 63 L4
Overton Bridge Wrexhm 63 K4
Overton Green Ches E 76 E11
Overtown Lancs 84 C9
Overtown Lancs 89 Q11
Overtown N Lans 114 E10
Overtown Swindn 30 D6
Overtown Wakefd 85 M12
Over Wallop Hants 24 D6
Over Whitacre Warwks 53 N2
Over Woodhouse Derbys 78 D9
Over Worton Oxon 43 J6
Overy Oxon 31 M3
Oving Bucks 43 Q7
Oving W Susx 14 C10
Ovingdean Br & H 15 L10
Ovingham Nthumb 100 E5
Ovington Dur 91 J4
Ovington Essex 46 D3
Ovington Hants 25 J7
Ovington Norfk 70 D11
Ovington Nthumb 100 D5
Ower Hants 12 H4
Ower Hants 24 E10
Owermoigne Dorset 11 J7
Owlbury Shrops 51 K2
Owlerton Sheff 77 Q6
Owlpen Gloucs 29 M3
Owl's Green Suffk 59 K7
Owlsmoor Br For 32 B10
Owlswick Bucks 43 R10
Owmby Lincs 79 P6
Owmby Lincs 79 Q3
Owslebury Hants 24 H8
Owston Donc 78 F1
Owston Leics 67 K10
Owston Ferry N Linc 79 K4
Owstwick E R Yk 87 P8
Owthorne E R Yk 87 Q9
Owthorpe Notts 66 H5
Owton Manor Hartpl 101 M12
Oxborough Norfk 69 P11
Oxbridge Dorset 10 D5
Oxcombe Lincs 80 F8
Oxcroft Derbys 78 D9
Oxen End Essex 46 B6
Oxenholme Cumb 89 N9
Oxenhope C Brad 84 F8
Oxen Park Cumb 89 J9
Oxenpill Somset 21 P5
Oxenton Gloucs 41 Q5
Oxenwood Wilts 30 G10
Oxford Oxon 43 L10
Oxford Airport Oxon 43 K8
Oxford Services Oxon 43 N10
Oxgangs C Edin 115 N7
Oxhey Herts 32 G3
Oxhill Dur 100 F8
Oxhill Warwks 42 G2
Oxley Wolves 64 G11
Oxley Green Essex 46 F9
Oxley's Green E Susx 16 C6
Oxlode Cambs 57 J3
Oxnam Border 108 A6
Oxnead Norfk 71 J7
Oxshott Surrey 32 G10
Oxshott Heath Surrey 32 G10
Oxspring Barns 77 P3
Oxted Surrey 33 M11
Oxton Border 116 C10
Oxton N York 85 Q6
Oxton Notts 66 G2
Oxton Wirral 75 J6
Oxwich Swans 26 D5
Oxwich Green Swans 26 D5
Oxwick Norfk 70 D7
Oykel Bridge Highld 145 J5
Oyne Abers 140 G10
Oystermouth Swans 26 F5
Ozleworth Gloucs 29 M4

P

Pabail W Isls 152 h3
Packers Hill Dorset 10 H3
Packington Leics 66 B9
Packmoor C Stke 64 F1
Packmores Warwks 53 P7
Padanaram Angus 124 H2
Padbury Bucks 43 P5
Paddington Gt Lon 33 K6
Paddington Warrtn 76 B6
Paddlesworth Kent 17 M3
Paddlesworth Kent 34 B10
Paddock Wood Kent 16 B2
Paddolgreen Shrops 63 N6
Padfield Derbys 77 J4
Padgate Warrtn 76 B5
Padhams Green Essex 34 B4
Padiham Lancs 84 B8
Padside N York 84 H3
Padstow Cnwll 6 C9
Padworth W Berk 31 M9
Page Bank Dur 100 G11
Pagham W Susx 14 C11
Paglesham Essex 34 G4
Paignton Torbay 5 Q4
Pailton Warwks 54 D4
Paine's Cross E Susx 16 A6
Painleyhill Staffs 65 J5
Painscastle Powys 40 A2
Painshawfield Nthumb 100 D6
Painsthorpe E R Yk 86 F4
Painswick Gloucs 41 P9
Painter's Forstal Kent 34 H10
Paisley Rens 113 P8
Pakefield Suffk 59 Q3
Pakenham Suffk 58 D7
Pale Gwynd 62 D5
Pale Green Essex 46 B3
Palestine Hants 24 D5
Paley Street W & M 32 B7
Palfrey Wsall 53 J1
Palgrave Suffk 58 G5
Pallington Dorset 11 J6
Palmarsh Kent 17 L4
Palmersbridge Cnwll 6 H9
Palmers Green Gt Lon 33 K4
Palmerston E Ayrs 105 J6
Palmerstown V Glam 27 Q8
Palnackie D & G 96 G7
Palnure D & G 95 N5
Palterton Derbys 78 D10
Pamber End Hants 31 M10
Pamber Green Hants 31 M10
Pamber Heath Hants 31 M10
Pamington Gloucs 41 Q5
Pamphill Dorset 11 N5
Pampisford Cambs 57 J11
Panborough Somset 21 Q4
Panbride Angus 125 L6
Pancrasweek Devon 7 K4
Pancross V Glam 27 P8
Pandy Caerph 27 Q5
Pandy Gwynd 61 K11
Pandy Gwynd 61 Q6
Pandy Mons 40 D7
Pandy Powys 62 B11
Pandy Wrexhm 62 H5
Pandy'r Capel Denbgs 62 F2
Pandy Tudur Conwy 73 Q11
Panfield Essex 46 C6
Pangbourne W Berk 31 N7
Pangdean W Susx 15 K8
Panks Bridge Herefs 52 B11
Pannal N York 85 L5
Pannal Ash N York 85 L4
Pant Shrops 63 J8
Pantasaph Flints 74 G8
Panteg Pembks 36 H4
Pantersbridge Cnwll 4 B3
Pant-ffrwyth Brdgnd 27 M5
Pant Glas Gwynd 60 H3
Pantglas Powys 49 N1
Pant-Gwyn Carmth 38 E6
Pant-lasau Swans 26 G2
Pant Mawr Powys 49 P4
Panton Lincs 80 D8
Pant-pastynog Denbgs 74 E11
Pantperthog Gwynd 61 N11
Pantside Caerph 28 B3
Pant-y-caws Carmth 37 M5
Pant-y-dwr Powys 50 D6
Pant-y-ffridd Powys 62 G11
Pantyffynnon Carmth 38 F9
Pantygaseg Torfn 28 C2
Pantygelli Mons 40 D8
Pant-y-gog Brdgnd 27 L4
Pantymwyn Flints 74 H10
Panxworth Norfk 71 M9
Papa Stour Shet 147 g6
Papa Stour Airport Shet 147 g6
Papa Westray Ork 147 d1
Papa Westray Airport Ork 147 d1
Papcastle Cumb 97 M12
Papigoe Highld 151 Q6
Papple E Loth 116 D7
Papplewick Notts 66 F2
Papworth Everard Cambs 56 F8
Papworth St Agnes Cambs 56 E8
Par Cnwll 3 Q4
Paramour Street Kent 35 N10
Parbold Lancs 75 N1
Parbrook Somset 22 D6
Parbrook W Susx 14 F6
Parc Gwynd 62 A6
Parc Llyn Cerdgn 48 D10
Parc Seymour Newpt 28 F4
Pardown Hants 25 K4
Pardshaw Cumb 88 E2
Parham Suffk 59 L8
Park D & G 106 B11
Park Nthumb 99 K6
Park Bottom Cnwll 2 G6
Park Bridge Tamesd 76 H3
Park Corner E Susx 15 P4
Park Corner Oxon 31 P5
Park Corner W & M 32 B6
Park End Bed 55 N10
Parkend Gloucs 41 J10
Park End Nthumb 99 N3
Parker's Green Kent 15 R1
Parkeston Essex 47 M5
Parkeston Quay Essex 47 M5
Park Farm Kent 16 H4
Parkgate Ches W 75 J8
Parkgate Cumb 97 P9
Parkgate D & G 106 D12
Parkgate E Susx 16 C8
Parkgate Essex 46 B6
Park Gate Hants 13 J3
Parkgate Kent 16 F4
Parkgate Kent 33 P9
Park Gate Leeds 85 J7
Parkgate Surrey 14 H2
Park Gate Worcs 52 H6
Park Green Essex 45 N6
Park Green Suffk 58 H8
Parkhall W Duns 113 P7
Parkham Devon 18 H9
Parkham Ash Devon 18 G9
Park Head Derbys 66 B1
Parkhill Dur 101 J11
Park Hill Gloucs 28 H2
Parkhouse Mons 40 G11
Parkmill Swans 26 E4
Park Royal Gt Lon 32 H6
Parkside Dur 101 L8
Parkside N Lans 114 E9
Parkside Wrexhm 63 L1
Parkstone BCP 11 P6
Park Street Herts 44 G11
Park Street W Susx 14 G4
Parkway Herefs 41 L4
Parley Green BCP 11 Q5
Parmoor Bucks 31 R4
Parracombe Devon 19 M4
Parrog Pembks 37 K3
Parsonby Cumb 97 N10
Parson Cross Sheff 77 Q5
Parson Drove Cambs 68 G10
Parson's Heath Essex 46 H6
Parson's Hill Derbys 65 P7
Partick C Glas 113 Q8
Partington Traffd 76 D5
Partney Lincs 80 H10
Parton Cumb 88 C3
Parton D & G 96 E4
Partridge Green W Susx 14 H7
Partrishow Powys 40 C7
Parwich Derbys 65 M1
Paslow Wood Common Essex 45 Q11
Passenham Nhants 43 Q4
Passfield Hants 25 P6
Passingford Bridge Essex 33 P3
Paston C Pete 68 D11
Paston Norfk 71 L5
Pasturefields Staffs 65 J7
Patchacott Devon 7 N5
Patcham Br & H 15 K9
Patchetts Green Herts 32 G3
Patching W Susx 14 F9
Patchole Devon 19 M5
Patchway S Glos 29 J6
Pateley Bridge N York 84 H2
Paternoster Heath Essex 46 G8
Pathe Somset 21 N7
Pathhead Fife 115 P3
Pathhead Mdloth 115 R8
Pathlow Warwks 53 M9
Path of Condie P & K 124 B10
Patmore Heath Herts 45 N6
Patna E Ayrs 104 H7
Patney Wilts 30 C10
Patrick IoM 102 c5
Patrick Brompton N York 91 L8
Patricroft Salfd 76 D4
Patrington E R Yk 87 P10
Patrington Haven E R Yk 87 P11
Patrixbourne Kent 35 L11
Patterdale Cumb 89 L4
Pattingham Staffs 64 F12
Pattishall Nhants 54 H10
Pattiswick Green Essex 46 E7
Patton Shrops 51 P2
Patton Bridge Cumb 89 P7
Paul Cnwll 2 D9
Paulerspury Nhants 43 P3
Paull E R Yk 87 M10
Paulton BaNES 29 K11
Paultons Park Hants 24 E10
Paunton Herefs 52 C10
Pauperhaugh Nthumb 108 H10
Pave Lane Wrekin 64 E9
Pavenham Bed 55 N9
Pawlett Somset 21 L5
Pawston Nthumb 108 D3
Paxford Gloucs 42 E4
Paxton Border 117 L10
Payden Street Kent 34 G11
Payhembury Devon 9 L4
Paynter's Lane End Cnwll 2 G6
Paythorne Lancs 84 B5
Paytoe Herefs 51 L6
Peacehaven E Susx 15 M10
Peak Dale Derbys 77 K8
Peak District National Park 77 M5
Peak Forest Derbys 77 L8
Peak Hill Lincs 68 E9
Peakirk C Pete 68 C11
Pearson's Green Kent 16 C2
Peartree Green Herefs 41 J5
Peasedown St John BaNES 29 L11
Peasehill Derbys 66 C2
Peaseland Green Norfk 70 F9
Peasemore W Berk 31 K7
Peasenhall Suffk 59 M7
Pease Pottage W Susx 15 J4
Pease Pottage Services W Susx 15 J4
Peaslake Surrey 14 F2
Peasley Cross St Hel 75 N5
Peasmarsh E Susx 16 F6
Peasmarsh Somset 21 M11
Peasmarsh Surrey 14 E2
Peathill Abers 141 M3
Peat Inn Fife 125 J11
Peatling Magna Leics 54 F2
Peatling Parva Leics 54 F3
Peaton Shrops 51 P4
Pebmarsh Essex 46 E5
Pebsham E Susx 16 D9
Pebworth Worcs 42 D2
Pecket Well Calder 84 E9
Peckforton Ches E 75 P12
Peckham Gt Lon 33 L7
Peckleton Leics 66 D12
Pedairffordd Powys 62 F7
Pedlinge Kent 17 L4
Pedmore Dudley 52 G4
Pedwell Somset 21 P6
Peebles Border 106 H2
Peel IoM 102 c5
Peel Lancs 83 J9
Peel Common Hants 13 J4
Peene Kent 17 L3
Peening Quarter Kent 16 F5
Peggs Green Leics 66 C8
Pegsdon C Beds 44 G5
Pegswood Nthumb 109 L12
Pegwell Kent 35 Q9
Peinchorran Highld 135 J9
Peinlich Highld 134 G4
Pelcomb Pembks 36 H7
Pelcomb Bridge Pembks 36 H7
Pelcomb Cross Pembks 36 H7
Peldon Essex 46 H8
Pell Green E Susx 16 B4
Pelsall Wsall 65 J11
Pelsall Wood Wsall 65 J11
Pelton Dur 100 G7
Pelton Fell Dur 100 H8
Pelutho Cumb 97 M8
Pelynt Cnwll 4 B6
Pemberton Carmth 26 D2
Pemberton Wigan 75 P3
Pembles Cross Kent 16 F1
Pembrey Carmth 26 C2
Pembridge Herefs 51 L9
Pembroke Pembks 37 J10
Pembroke Dock Pembks 37 J10
Pembrokeshire Coast National Park Pembks 36 G6
Pembury Kent 16 A3
Pen-allt Herefs 40 H6
Penallt Mons 40 H9
Penally Pembks 37 M10
Penare Cnwll 3 N6
Penarth V Glam 28 B8
Penblewin Pembks 37 M7
Pen-bont Rhydybeddau Cerdgn 49 L4
Penbryn Cerdgn 48 E10
Pencader Carmth 38 C4
Pencaenewydd Gwynd 60 G4
Pencaitland E Loth 116 B7
Pencarnisiog IoA 72 F9
Pencarreg Carmth 38 E3
Pencarrow Cnwll 6 G8
Pencelli Powys 39 P7
Penclawdd Swans 26 E3
Pencoed Brdgnd 27 M6
Pencombe Herefs 51 Q10
Pencoyd Herefs 40 G6
Pencraig Herefs 40 H7
Pencraig Powys 62 E7
Pendeen Cnwll 2 B7
Penderyn Rhondd 39 M10
Pendine Carmth 37 P9
Pendlebury Salfd 76 E3
Pendleton Lancs 84 A7
Pendock Worcs 41 M5
Pendoggett Cnwll 6 E9
Pendomer Somset 10 E3
Pendoylan V Glam 27 P7
Penegoes Powys 61 N12
Penelewey Cnwll 3 K6
Pen-ffordd Pembks 37 L6
Pengam Caerph 27 R3
Pengam Cardif 28 B7
Penge Gt Lon 33 L8
Pengelly Cnwll 6 F8
Pengenffordd Powys 40 A6
Pengorffwysfa IoA 72 H5
Pengover Green Cnwll 4 D4
Pen-groes-oped Mons 40 D10
Pengwern Denbgs 74 D8
Penhale Cnwll 2 H10
Penhale Cnwll 3 M3
Penhale Cnwll 3 P5
Penhale Cnwll 4 F6
Penhallow Cnwll 3 J4
Penhalurick Cnwll 2 H7
Penhalvean Cnwll 2 H7
Penhill Swindn 30 D5
Penhow Newpt 28 F4
Penhurst E Susx 16 C7
Peniarth Gwynd 61 K11
Penicuik Mdloth 115 N9
Peniel Carmth 38 C7
Peniel Denbgs 74 E11
Penifiler Highld 135 J7
Peninver Ag & B 103 K5
Penisarwaun Gwynd 73 J11
Penistone Barns 77 N3
Penjerrick Cnwll 3 J8
Penketh Warrtn 75 P6
Penkill S Ayrs 104 D10
Penkridge Staffs 64 H9
Penlean Cnwll 7 J5
Penleigh Wilts 23 J3
Penley Wrexhm 63 L4
Penllergaer Swans 26 F3
Pen-llyn IoA 72 F7
Penllyn V Glam 27 M7
Pen-lôn IoA 72 G10
Penmachno Conwy 61 N2
Penmaen Caerph 28 A3
Penmaen Swans 26 D5
Penmaenan Conwy 73 M8
Penmaenmawr Conwy 73 M8
Penmaenpool Gwynd 61 M8
Penmark V Glam 27 P8
Penmon IoA 73 K7
Penmorfa Gwynd 61 J4
Penmynydd IoA 72 H9
Penn Bucks 32 C4
Penn Wolves 52 G2
Pennal Gwynd 61 M12
Pennan Abers 141 K3
Pennant Cerdgn 48 H8
Pennant Denbgs 62 E5
Pennant Powys 49 Q1
Pennant-Melangell Powys 62 D7
Pennar Pembks 37 J10
Pennard Swans 26 E5
Pennerley Shrops 63 K12
Pennicott Devon 8 G4
Pennines 84 E8
Pennington Cumb 88 H11
Pennington Hants 12 E6
Pennington Green Wigan 76 B2
Pennorth Powys 39 Q6
Penn Street Bucks 32 C3
Pennsylvania S Glos 29 M7
Penny Bridge Cumb 89 J10
Pennycross Ag & B 119 N7
Pennygate Norfk 71 L7
Pennyghael Ag & B 119 N7
Pennyglen S Ayrs 104 E7
Penny Green Derbys 78 E8
Penny Hill Lincs 68 G7
Pennymoor Devon 8 H2
Pennywell Sundld 101 J7
Penparc Cerdgn 48 C11
Penparcau Cerdgn 49 K4
Penpedairheol Caerph 27 Q3
Penpedairheol Mons 40 D11
Penpergwm Mons 40 D9
Penperlleni Mons 40 D10
Penpethy Cnwll 6 F7
Penpillick Cnwll 3 Q3
Penpol Cnwll 3 K7
Penpoll Cnwll 4 A6
Penponds Cnwll 2 G7
Penpont Cnwll 6 F10
Penpont D & G 105 Q11
Penpont Powys 39 M6
Penquit Devon 5 K6
Penrest Cnwll 7 L9
Penrherber Carmth 37 Q3
Pen-rhiw Pembks 37 Q2
Penrhiwceiber Rhondd 27 P3
Pen Rhiwfawr Neath 38 H9
Penrhiwgoch Carmth 38 E8
Penrhiwllan Cerdgn 38 B3
Penrhiwpal Cerdgn 48 E11
Penrhos Gwynd 60 E5
Penrhos IoA 72 D7
Penrhos Mons 40 F9
Penrhos Powys 39 J9
Penrhos garnedd Gwynd 73 J9
Penrhyn Bay Conwy 73 P7
Penrhyn-coch Cerdgn 49 L4
Penrhyndeudraeth Gwynd 61 K4
Penrhyn-side Conwy 73 P7
Penrhys Rhondd 27 N3
Penrice Swans 26 D5
Penrioch N Ayrs 112 C12
Penrith Cumb 98 G12
Penrose Cnwll 6 C10
Penruddock Cumb 89 L1
Penryn Cnwll 3 J8
Pensarn Conwy 74 C8
Pensax Worcs 52 D7
Pensby Wirral 75 J7
Penselwood Somset 22 G7
Pensford BaNES 29 J9
Pensham Worcs 41 Q3
Penshaw Sundld 101 J7
Penshurst Kent 15 P2
Penshurst Station Kent 15 P2
Pensilva Cnwll 4 C3
Pensnett Dudley 52 G3
Penstone Devon 8 E5
Penstrowed Powys 50 E2
Pentewan Cnwll 3 P5
Pentir Gwynd 73 J10
Pentire Cnwll 3 J3
Pentlepoir Pembks 37 M9
Pentlow Essex 46 E3
Pentlow Street Essex 46 E3
Pentney Norfk 69 N9
Pentonbridge Cumb 98 F3
Penton Grafton Hants 24 E4
Penton Mewsey Hants 24 E4
Pentraeth IoA 73 J8
Pentre Denbgs 74 F11
Pentre Flints 75 K10
Pentre Mons 28 E2
Pentre Mons 40 E10
Pentre Powys 50 E3
Pentre Powys 50 H3
Pentre Powys 51 J2
Pentre Rhondd 27 M3
Pentre Shrops 63 L8
Pentre Wrexhm 63 J4
Pentre-bâch Cerdgn 38 E2
Pentre Bach Flints 74 H8
Pentrebach Myr Td 39 P11
Pentre-bach Powys 39 L5
Pentrebeirdd Powys 62 G9
Pentre Berw IoA 72 H9
Pentre-bont Conwy 61 M2
Pentre-cagel Carmth 37 R2
Pentrecelyn Denbgs 62 G2
Pentre-celyn Powys 62 B11
Pentre-chwyth Swans 26 G3
Pentre-clawdd Shrops 63 J6
Pentre-cwrt Carmth 38 B4
Pentredwr Denbgs 62 H3
Pentrefelin Gwynd 61 J4
Pentrefelin IoA 72 G5
Pentre Ffwrndan Flints 75 J9
Pentrefoelas Conwy 61 Q2
Pentregalar Pembks 37 N4
Pentregat Cerdgn 48 F10
Pentre-Gwenlais Carmth 38 F8
Pentre Gwynfryn Gwynd 61 K7
Pentre Halkyn Flints 74 H9
Pentre Hodrey Shrops 51 K5
Pentre Isaf Conwy 74 D9
Pentre Llanrhaeadr Denbgs 74 E11
Pentre Llifior Powys 50 G1
Pentre-llwyn-llwyd Powys 50 C9
Pentre-llyn Cerdgn 49 K6
Pentre-llyn-cymmer Conwy 62 D2
Pentre-Maw Powys 62 B11
Pentre Meyrick V Glam 27 M7
Pentre-piod Torfn 40 C11
Pentre-poeth Newpt 28 C5
Pentre'rbryn Cerdgn 48 F9
Pentre'r-felin Cerdgn 49 K11
Pentre'r Felin Conwy 73 P10
Pentre'r-felin Powys 39 L5
Pentre Saron Denbgs 74 E11
Pentre-tafarn-y-fedw Conwy 73 P11
Pentre ty gwyn Carmth 39 K4
Pentrich Derbys 66 C2
Pentridge Dorset 23 M10
Pen-twyn Caerph 28 B2
Pentwyn Cardif 28 B6
Pen-twyn Mons 40 H10
Pen-twyn Torfn 40 C11
Pentwynmaur Caerph 28 B3
Pentyrch Cardif 27 Q6
Penwithick Cnwll 3 P3
Penwood Hants 31 J10
Penwyllt Powys 39 K8
Penybanc Carmth 38 F7
Penybont Powys 50 F8
Pen-y-bont Powys 62 H7
Penybontfawr Powys 62 F7
Pen-y-bryn Pembks 37 N2
Pen-y-cae Powys 39 K9
Penycae Wrexhm 63 J3
Pen-y-cae-mawr Mons 28 F3
Penycaerau Gwynd 60 C6
Pen-y-cefn Flints 74 F8
Pen-y-clawdd Mons 40 F10
Pen-y-coedcae Rhondd 27 P5
Penycwn Pembks 36 G6
Pen-y-fai Brdgnd 27 L6
Pen-y-felin Flints 74 G10
Pen-y-ffordd Flints 74 G9
Penyffordd Flints 75 J11
Penyffridd Gwynd 72 H12
Pen-y-garn Cerdgn 49 K3
Pen-y-Garnedd Powys 62 F7
Pen-y-graig Gwynd 60 C5
Penygraig Rhondd 27 N4
Penygroes Carmth 38 E9
Penygroes Gwynd 60 H2
Penygroeslon Gwynd 60 E6
Pen-y-Gwryd Gwynd 61 L1
Pen-y-lan V Glam 27 N7
Pen-y-Mynydd Carmth 38 C11
Penymynydd Flints 75 J11
Pen-y-pass Gwynd 61 L1
Pen-yr-Heol Mons 40 F9
Penysarn IoA 72 G5
Pen-y-stryt Denbgs 62 H2
Penywaun Rhondd 39 M10
Penzance Cnwll 2 D8
Peopleton Worcs 52 H10
Peover Heath Ches E 76 E9
Peper Harow Surrey 14 D2
Peplow Shrops 64 B7
Pepper's Green Essex 46 A9
Pepperstock C Beds 44 F8
Perceton N Ayrs 104 F2
Percyhorner Abers 141 M3
Perelle Guern 12 b2
Perham Down Wilts 24 D4
Periton Somset 20 E4
Perivale Gt Lon 32 H6
Perkins Village Devon 9 J6
Perkinsville Dur 100 H7
Perlethorpe Notts 78 G9
Perranarworthal Cnwll 3 J7
Perranporth Cnwll 3 J4
Perranuthnoe Cnwll 2 E8
Perranwell Cnwll 3 J4
Perranwell Cnwll 3 J7
Perran Wharf Cnwll 3 J7
Perranzabuloe Cnwll 3 J4
Perrott's Brook Gloucs 42 B10
Perry Birm 53 K2
Perry Cambs 56 C7
Perry Barr Birm 53 K2
Perry Green Essex 46 E7
Perry Green Herts 45 N8
Perry Green Wilts 29 R4
Perrystone Hill Herefs 41 K6
Perry Street Somset 9 Q4
Pershall Staffs 64 E6
Pershore Worcs 41 Q2
Pertenhall Bed 56 B7
Perth P & K 124 C8
Perthy Shrops 63 L5
Perton Herefs 41 J3
Perton Staffs 64 F12
Pertwood Wilts 23 J6
Peterborough C Pete 68 D12
Peterborough Services Cambs 56 C2
Peterchurch Herefs 40 E4
Peterculter C Aber 133 K4
Peterhead Abers 141 Q6
Peterlee Dur 101 L10
Petersfield Hants 25 N8
Peter's Green Herts 44 G8
Petersham Gt Lon 32 H7
Peters Marland Devon 19 J10
Peterstone Wentlooge Newpt 28 C6
Peterston-super-Ely V Glam 27 P7
Peterstow Herefs 40 H7
Peters Village Kent 34 C9
Peter Tavy Devon 7 P9
Petham Kent 35 K12
Petherwin Gate Cnwll 7 K7
Petrockstow Devon 7 P3
Petsoe End M Keyn 55 M10
Pet Street Kent 17 K1
Pett E Susx 16 F8
Pettaugh Suffk 58 H8
Pett Bottom Kent 35 L12
Petterden Angus 124 H5
Pettinain S Lans 106 C1
Pettistree Suffk 59 L9
Petton Devon 20 G9
Petton Shrops 63 M7
Petts Wood Gt Lon 33 N9
Pettycur Fife 115 N4
Petty France S Glos 29 M5
Pettymuk Abers 141 L11
Petworth W Susx 14 D6
Pevensey E Susx 16 B10
Pevensey Bay E Susx 16 B10
Pewsey Wilts 30 E10
Pewsham Wilts 29 Q8
Pheasant's Hill Bucks 31 R5
Phepson Worcs 52 H8
Philadelphia Sundld 101 J8
Philham Devon 18 E9
Philiphaugh Border 107 L4
Phillack Cnwll 2 F7
Philleigh Cnwll 3 L6
Philpot End Essex 45 R8
Philpstoun W Loth 115 K6
Phocle Green Herefs 41 J6
Phoenix Green Hants 25 N2
Pibsbury Somset 21 P8
Pica Cumb 88 D2
Piccadilly Warwks 53 N1
Piccotts End Herts 44 F9
Pickburn Donc 78 E2
Pickering N York 92 F10
Picket Piece Hants 24 F4
Picket Post Hants 12 C3
Picket Twenty Hants 24 F4
Pickford Covtry 53 P4
Pickford Green Covtry 53 P4
Pickhill N York 91 N10
Picklescott Shrops 63 M12
Pickmere Ches E 76 C8
Pickney Somset 21 K7
Pickstock Wrekin 64 D7
Pickup Bank Bl w D 83 Q10
Pickwell Devon 19 J5
Pickwell Leics 67 K10
Pickwick Wilts 29 P8
Pickworth Lincs 67 P5
Pickworth Rutlnd 67 N9
Picton Ches W 75 M9
Picton Flints 74 F7
Picton N York 91 P5
Piddinghoe E Susx 15 N10
Piddington Bucks 32 A3
Piddington Nhants 55 K9
Piddington Oxon 43 N8
Piddlehinton Dorset 10 H5
Piddletrenthide Dorset 10 H5
Pidley Cambs 56 F5
Piercebridge Darltn 91 L4
Pierowall Ork 147 c1
Piff's Elm Gloucs 41 P6
Pigdon Nthumb 109 J12
Pigeon Green Warwks 53 N8
Pig Oak Dorset 11 N4
Pig Street Herefs 51 L11
Pikehall Derbys 77 M12
Pilford Dorset 11 P4
Pilgrims Hatch Essex 33 Q3
Pilham Lincs 79 L5
Pill N Som 28 H7
Pillaton Cnwll 4 E4
Pillatonmill Cnwll 4 E4
Pillerton Hersey Warwks 53 P11
Pillerton Priors Warwks 53 P11
Pilleth Powys 51 J7
Pilley Barns 77 Q4
Pilley Hants 12 E5
Pilley Bailey Hants 12 E5
Pillgwenlly Newpt 28 D5
Pillhead Devon 19 J8
Pilling Lancs 83 J5
Pilling Lane Lancs 83 J5
Pilning S Glos 28 H5
Pilot Inn Kent 17 K7
Pilsbury Derbys 77 L11
Pilsdon Dorset 10 C5
Pilsgate C Pete 67 Q11
Pilsley Derbys 77 N9
Pilsley Derbys 78 C11
Pilson Green Norfk 71 M9
Piltdown E Susx 15 N6
Pilton Devon 19 L6
Pilton Nhants 55 P4
Pilton Rutlnd 67 M11
Pilton Somset 22 D5
Pilton Green Swans 26 C5
Pimbo Lancs 75 N3
Pimlico Herts 44 F10
Pimlico Lancs 83 R6
Pimlico Nhants 43 N3
Pimperne Dorset 11 L3
Pinchbeck Lincs 68 E7
Pinchbeck Bars Lincs 68 D7
Pincheon Green Donc 86 C11
Pinchinthorpe R & Cl 92 C4
Pincock Lancs 83 M11
Pinfold Lancs 75 L1
Pinford End Suffk 58 C8
Pinged Carmth 38 B11
Pingewood W Berk 31 P8
Pin Green Herts 45 J6
Pinhoe Devon 8 H6
Pinkett's Booth Covtry 53 P4
Pinkney Wilts 29 P5
Pinkneys Green W & M 32 B6
Pinley Covtry 54 B5
Pinley Green Warwks 53 N7
Pin Mill Suffk 47 M4
Pinminnoch S Ayrs 104 C11
Pinmore S Ayrs 104 D11
Pinn Devon 9 L7
Pinner Gt Lon 32 G4
Pinner Green Gt Lon 32 G4
Pinsley Green Ches E 63 P3
Pinvin Worcs 52 H11
Pinwherry S Ayrs 104 D12
Pinxton Derbys 66 D1
Pipe and Lyde Herefs 40 G3
Pipe Aston Herefs 51 M6
Pipe Gate Shrops 64 D4
Pipehill Staffs 65 K10
Piperdam Angus 124 F6
Piperhill Highld 138 F6
Pipers Pool Cnwll 7 J8
Pipewell Nhants 55 L3
Pippacott Devon 19 K6
Pippin Street Lancs 83 N10
Pipton Powys 39 R4
Pirbright Surrey 32 D11
Pirbright Camp Surrey 32 D11
Pirnie Border 107 Q4
Pirnmill N Ayrs 112 C12
Pirton Herts 44 G5
Pirton Worcs 52 G11
Pisgah Cerdgn 49 L5
Pishill Oxon 31 P4
Pistyll Gwynd 60 E4
Pitblae Abers 141 N3
Pitcairngreen P & K 123 Q7
Pitcalnie Highld 146 E10
Pitcaple Abers 140 H10
Pitcarity Angus 131 Q11
Pitchcombe Gloucs 41 N10
Pitchcott Bucks 43 Q7
Pitcher Row Lincs 68 F5
Pitchford Shrops 63 P11
Pitch Green Bucks 43 Q11
Pitch Place Surrey 14 C3
Pitch Place Surrey 32 D11
Pitchroy Moray 139 M8
Pitcombe Somset 22 F7
Pitcot V Glam 27 L7
Pitcox E Loth 116 E6
Pitfichie Abers 132 G1
Pitglassie Abers 140 H7
Pitgrudy Highld 146 E7
Pitlessie Fife 124 G11
Pitlochry P & K 123 N1
Pitmachie Abers 140 G10
Pitmain Highld 130 D4
Pitmedden Abers 141 L10
Pitmedden Garden Abers 141 L10
Pitminster Somset 21 K9
Pitmuies Angus 125 L3
Pitmunie Abers 132 G1
Pitney Somset 21 P7
Pitroddie P & K 124 E8
Pitscottie Fife 124 H10
Pitsea Essex 34 C5
Pitses Oldham 76 H3
Pitsford Nhants 55 J7
Pitstone Bucks 44 D8
Pitt Devon 20 G10
Pitt Hants 24 G8
Pittarrow Abers 132 H9
Pitt Court Gloucs 29 M3
Pittenweem Fife 125 L12
Pitteuchar Fife 115 P1
Pittodrie House Hotel Abers 140 H11
Pitton Wilts 24 C7
Pitt's Wood Kent 33 R12
Pittulie Abers 141 M2
Pityme Cnwll 6 D9
Pity Me Dur 100 H9
Pivington Kent 16 G2
Pixey Green Suffk 59 K5
Pixham Surrey 32 H12
Plains N Lans 114 E8
Plain Street Cnwll 6 E9
Plaish Shrops 51 N1
Plaistow Gt Lon 33 M6
Plaistow W Susx 14 E5
Plaitford Hants 24 D9
Plank Lane Wigan 76 B4
Plas Cymyran IoA 72 E8
Plastow Green Hants 31 L10
Platt Bridge Wigan 75 Q3
Platt Lane Shrops 63 N5
Platts Heath Kent 34 F12
Plawsworth Dur 100 H8
Plaxtol Kent 33 R11
Playden E Susx 16 G6
Playford Suffk 59 J11
Play Hatch Oxon 31 Q7
Playing Place Cnwll 3 K6
Playley Green Gloucs 41 M5
Plealey Shrops 63 M10
Plean Stirlg 114 F4
Pleasance Fife 124 E10
Pleasington Bl w D 83 P10
Pleasley Derbys 78 E10
Pleasleyhill Notts 78 E11
Pleasurewood Hills Suffk 59 Q1
Pleck Dorset 10 H3
Pledgdon Green Essex 45 Q6
Pledwick Wakefd 85 M12
Pleinheaume Guern 12 c1
Plemont Jersey 13 a1
Plemstall Ches W 75 M9
Plenmeller Nthumb 99 K6
Pleshey Essex 46 B9
Plockton Highld 135 P9
Plowden Shrops 51 L3
Plox Green Shrops 63 L11
Pluckley Kent 16 G2
Pluckley Station Kent 16 G2
Pluckley Thorne Kent 16 G2
Plucks Gutter Kent 35 N9
Plumbland Cumb 97 N10
Plumgarths Cumb 89 M8
Plumley Ches E 76 D8
Plump Hill Gloucs 41 K8
Plumpton Cumb 89 J11
Plumpton Cumb 98 G11
Plumpton E Susx 15 L8
Plumpton Nhants 54 F11
Plumpton End Nhants 43 P3
Plumpton Green E Susx 15 L7
Plumpton Head Cumb 98 G11
Plumstead Gt Lon 33 N6
Plumstead Norfk 70 H5
Plumstead Green Norfk 70 H5
Plumtree Notts 66 G5
Plumtree Green Kent 16 E2
Plungar Leics 67 J5
Plurenden Kent 16 G3
Plush Dorset 10 H4
Plusha Cnwll 7 J8
Plushabridge Cnwll 7 K10
Plwmp Cerdgn 48 F10
Plymouth C Plym 4 G6
Plympton C Plym 4 H5
Plymstock C Plym 4 H6
Plymtree Devon 9 K4
Pockley N York 92 D9
Pocklington E R Yk 86 E5
Pode Hole Lincs 68 D8
Podimore Somset 22 C8
Podington Bed 55 N8
Podmore Staffs 64 E5
Point Clear Essex 47 K8
Pointon Lincs 68 C6
Pokesdown BCP 11 Q6
Polbain Highld 144 C3
Polbathic Cnwll 4 E5
Polbeth W Loth 115 J8
Polbrock Cnwll 6 E11
Poldark Mine Cnwll 2 H8
Polebrook Nhants 55 Q3
Pole Elm Worcs 52 F10
Polegate E Susx 15 Q10
Pole Moor Kirk 84 G12
Polesden Lacey Surrey 32 G12
Polesworth Warwks 65 N11
Polgigga Cnwll 2 B9
Polglass Highld 144 C4
Polgooth Cnwll 3 N4
Polgown D & G 105 N9
Poling W Susx 14 F10
Poling Corner W Susx 14 F9
Polkerris Cnwll 3 Q4
Pollard Street Norfk 71 L5
Pollington E R Yk 86 B11
Polloch Highld 127 P10
Pollokshaws C Glas 113 Q9
Pollokshields C Glas 113 Q8
Polmassick Cnwll 3 N5
Polmear Cnwll 3 Q4
Polmont Falk 114 G6
Polnish Highld 127 N8
Polperro Cnwll 4 B6
Polruan Cnwll 3 R4
Polsham Somset 22 C4
Polstead Suffk 46 H4
Polstead Heath Suffk 46 H4
Poltalloch Ag & B 112 B2
Poltescoe Cnwll 2 H11
Poltimore Devon 8 H5
Polton Mdloth 115 P8
Polwarth Border 116 G11
Polyphant Cnwll 7 K8
Polzeath Cnwll 6 D9
Pomathorn Mdloth 115 N9
Pomeroy Derbys 77 L10
Ponde Powys 39 Q4
Pondersbridge Cambs 56 E2
Ponders End Gt Lon 33 L3
Ponsanooth Cnwll 3 J7
Ponsonby Cumb 88 E5
Ponsongath Cnwll 3 J11
Ponsworthy Devon 8 D10
Pont Abraham Services Carmth 38 E10
Pontac Jersey 13 d3
Pontamman Carmth 38 F9
Pontantwn Carmth 38 C9
Pontardawe Neath 38 H11
Pontarddulais Swans 38 E11
Pont-ar-gothi Carmth 38 D7
Pont-ar-Hydfer Powys 39 K6

Pont-ar-llechau Carmth ..38 H7
Pontarsais Carmth ..38 C6
Pontblyddyn Flints ..75 J11
Pont Cyfyng Conwy ..73 M12
Pontcysyllte Aqueduct Wrexhm ..63 J4
Pont Dolgarrog Conwy ..73 N10
Pontdolgoch Powys ..50 D2
Pont-Ebbw Newpt ..28 C5
Pontefract Wakefd ..85 P11
Ponteland Nthumb ..100 F4
Ponterwyd Cerdgn ..49 N4
Pontesbury Shrops ..63 L11
Pontesbury Hill Shrops ..63 L11
Pontesford Shrops ..63 L11
Pontfadog Wrexhm ..62 H4
Pontfaen Pembks ..37 K4
Pont-faen Powys ..39 N5
Pontgarreg Cerdgn ..48 E10
Pontgarreg Pembks ..37 M2
Ponthenri Carmth ..38 C10
Ponthir Torfn ..28 D4
Ponthirwaun Cerdgn ..48 D11
Pontllanfraith Caerph ..28 A3
Pontlliw Swans ..26 C5
Pontllyfni Gwynd ..60 G2
Pontlottyn Caerph ..39 Q10
Pont Morlais Carmth ..38 C10
Pontneddfechan Neath ..39 L10
Pontnewydd Torfn ..28 C3
Pontnewynydd Torfn ..28 C2
Pont Pen-y-benglog Gwynd ..73 L11
Pontrhydfendigaid Cerdgn ..49 M7
Pont Rhyd-sarn Gwynd ..61 Q6
Pont Rhyd-y-cyff Brdgnd ..27 K4
Pontrhydyfen Neath ..27 J3
Pont-rhyd-y-groes Cerdgn ..49 M6
Pontrhydyrun Torfn ..28 D3
Pontrilas Herefs ..40 E6
Pont Robert Powys ..62 F9
Ponts Green E Susx ..16 B7
Pont-rug Gwynd ..72 H11
Pontshaen Cerdgn ..38 C2
Pontshill Herefs ..41 K7
Pontsticill Myr Td ..39 P8
Pont Walby Neath ..39 L10
Pontwelly Carmth ..38 B4
Pontyates Carmth ..38 C10
Pontyberem Carmth ..38 D9
Pont-y-blew Wrexhm ..63 J4
Pontybodkin Flints ..75 J12
Pontyclun Rhondd ..27 N6
Pontycymer Brdgnd ..27 L4
Pontyglasier Pembks ..37 M3
Pontygwaith Rhondd ..27 N3
Pontygynon Pembks ..37 M3
Pontymister Caerph ..28 C4
Pont-y-pant Conwy ..61 N1
Pontypool Torfn ..28 C2
Pontypridd Rhondd ..27 P4
Pont-yr-hafod Pembks ..36 H5
Pont-yr-Rhyl Brdgnd ..27 L4
Pontywaun Caerph ..28 B4
Pool Cnwll ..2 G6
Pool IoS ..b1
Poole BCP ..11 N7
Poole Keynes Gloucs ..30 A3
Poolewe Highld ..143 M9
Pooley Bridge Cumb ..89 M2
Pooley Street Norfk ..58 F4
Poolfold Staffs ..76 G11
Pool Head Herefs ..51 P10
Poolhill Gloucs ..41 L6
Pool in Wharfedale Leeds ..85 K6
Pool of Muckhart Clacks ..114 H1
Pool Quay Powys ..63 J10
Pool Street Essex ..46 D4
Pootings Kent ..15 N9
Popes Hill Gloucs ..41 L9
Popham Hants ..25 J4
Poplar Gt Lon ..33 L6
Poplar Street Suffk ..59 N7
Porchfield IoW ..12 C6
Poringland Norfk ..71 K11
Porkellis Cnwll ..2 H8
Porlock Somset ..20 D4
Porlock Weir Somset ..20 D4
Portachoillan Ag & B ..111 Q9
Port Appin Ag & B ..120 G4
Port Askaig Ag & B ..122 C7
Portavadie Ag & B ..112 G7
Port Bannatyne Ag & B ..112 G8
Portbury N Som ..28 G7
Port Carlisle Cumb ..97 P6
Port Charlotte Ag & B ..110 F9
Portchester Hants ..13 K4
Port Clarence S on T ..91 N4
Port Driseach Ag & B ..112 G6
Port Ellen Ag & B ..110 H12
Port Elphinstone Abers ..141 J11
Portencalzie D & G ..94 E4
Portencross N Ayrs ..112 H11
Port Erin IoM ..102 b7
Portesham Dorset ..10 F7
Portessie Moray ..140 C3
Port e Vullen IoM ..102 f3
Port Eynon Swans ..26 C5
Portfield Gate Pembks ..36 H7
Portgate Devon ..5 N4
Port Gaverne Cnwll ..6 E8
Port Glasgow Inver ..113 M8
Portgordon Moray ..140 B3
Portgower Highld ..146 H2
Porth Cnwll ..3 K2
Porth Rhondd ..27 N4
Porthallow Cnwll ..3 K6
Porthallow Cnwll ..4 C10
Porthcawl Brdgnd ..27 K7
Porthcothan Cnwll ..6 B10
Porthcurno Cnwll ..2 B10
Port Henderson Highld ..143 K10
Porthgain Pembks ..36 F4
Porthgwarra Cnwll ..2 B10
Porthill Staffs ..64 F2
Porthkea Cnwll ..3 K6
Porthkerry V Glam ..27 N9
Porthleven Cnwll ..2 H9
Porthmadog Gwynd ..61 J4
Porthmeor Cnwll ..2 C8
Porth Navas Cnwll ..3 K6
Porthoustock Cnwll ..3 N6
Porthpean Cnwll ..3 Q4
Porthtowan Cnwll ..2 H6
Porthwgan Wrexhm ..63 L3
Porthyrhyd Carmth ..38 D8
Portincaple Ag & B ..113 J4
Portinfer Jersey ..13 a1
Portington E R Yk ..86 E9
Portinnisherrich Ag & B ..121 J10
Portinscale Cumb ..88 H2
Port Isaac Cnwll ..6 E8
Portishead N Som ..28 G7
Portknockie Moray ..140 D2
Portland Dorset ..10 G10
Portlethen Abers ..133 M5
Portling D & G ..96 H7
Portloe Cnwll ..3 M6
Port Logan D & G ..94 G10
Portlooe Cnwll ..4 C6

Portmahomack Highld ..146 G8
Port Mary D & G ..96 F9
Portmeirion Gwynd ..61 K5
Portmellon Cnwll ..3 P6
Portmore Hants ..12 C5
Port Mòr Highld ..126 G8
Portmulgrave N York ..92 G3
Portnacroish Ag & B ..120 H3
Portnaguran W Isls ..152 h3
Portnahaven Ag & B ..110 E10
Portnalong Highld ..134 F9
Portnancon Highld ..149 J5
Port nan Giùran W Isls ..152 h3
Port nan Long W Isls ..152 c7
Port Nis W Isls ..152 h1
Portobello C Edin ..115 P6
Portobello Gatesd ..100 H7
Portobello Wolves ..52 H1
Port of Menteith Stirlg ..113 H11
Port of Ness W Isls ..152 h1
Porton Wilts ..24 G7
Portontown Devon ..4 E7
Portpatrick D & G ..94 E7
Port Quin Cnwll ..6 D8
Port Ramsay Ag & B ..120 G4
Portreath Cnwll ..2 G5
Portreath Harbour Cnwll ..2 G5
Portree Highld ..134 H7
Port Righ Ag & B ..103 L2
Port St Mary IoM ..102 b7
Portscatho Cnwll ..3 L7
Portsea C Port ..13 L5
Portskerra Highld ..150 E3
Portskewett Mons ..28 G5
Portslade Br & H ..15 J9
Portslade-by-Sea Br & H ..15 J9
Portslogan D & G ..94 E6
Portsmouth C Port ..13 L5
Portsmouth Calder ..84 D10
Portsmouth Arms Devon ..19 M9
Portsmouth Dockyard C Port ..13 K4
Port Soderick IoM ..102 d6
Port Solent C Port ..13 L4
Portsonachan Hotel Ag & B ..121 K8
Portsoy Abers ..140 F3
Port Sunlight Wirral ..75 K7
Portswood C Sotn ..24 G10
Port Talbot Neath ..27 J4
Port Tennant Swans ..26 G4
Portuairk Highld ..126 H10
Portway Herefs ..40 G3
Portway Herefs ..40 G3
Portway Sandw ..52 H3
Portway Worcs ..53 K6
Port Wemyss Ag & B ..110 E11
Port William D & G ..95 L9
Portwrinkle Cnwll ..4 E6
Portyerrock D & G ..95 N10
Posbury Devon ..8 F5
Posenhall Shrops ..64 C11
Poslingford Suffk ..57 P11
Posso Border ..106 C3
Postbridge Devon ..8 C9
Postcombe Oxon ..31 P2
Post Green Dorset ..11 M6
Postling Kent ..17 L3
Postwick Norfk ..71 L10
Potarch Abers ..132 F5
Potsgrove C Beds ..44 D6
Potten End Herts ..44 E10
Potter Brompton N York ..93 K11
Pottergate Street Norfk ..58 H2
Potterhanworth Lincs ..79 Q10
Potterhanworth Booths Lincs ..79 Q10
Potter Heigham Norfk ..71 N8
Potterne Wilts ..30 A10
Potterne Wick Wilts ..30 A10
Potter Row Bucks ..44 C11
Potters Bar Herts ..33 J2
Potters Brook Lancs ..83 L5
Potters Corner Kent ..16 H2
Potter's Cross Staffs ..52 F4
Potters Crouch Herts ..44 G10
Potter's Forstal Kent ..16 G2
Potters Green Covtry ..54 B4
Potter's Green E Susx ..15 P6
Potter's Green Herts ..45 L7
Potters Marston Leics ..54 E1
Potter Somersal Derbys ..65 Q3
Potterspury Nhants ..43 Q3
Potter Street Essex ..45 N10
Potterton Abers ..133 M1
Potterton Leeds ..85 N7
Potthorpe Norfk ..70 E7
Pottle Street Wilts ..22 H5
Potto N York ..91 Q6
Potton C Beds ..56 D10
Pott Row Norfk ..69 N8
Pott's Green Essex ..46 F7
Pott Shrigley Ches E ..76 H8
Poughill Cnwll ..7 J3
Poughill Devon ..9 J3
Poulner Hants ..12 B3
Poulshot Wilts ..29 K10
Poulton Gloucs ..30 C2
Poulton Wirral ..75 J5
Poulton-le-Fylde Lancs ..82 H7
Poulton Priory Gloucs ..30 C2
Pound Bank Worcs ..52 D6
Poundbury Dorset ..10 G6
Poundffald Swans ..26 D3
Poundgate E Susx ..15 P5
Pound Green E Susx ..15 P5
Pound Green Suffk ..57 N10
Pound Green Worcs ..52 D5
Pound Hill W Susx ..15 K3
Poundland S Ayrs ..104 E9
Poundon Bucks ..43 N6
Poundsbridge Kent ..15 P2
Poundstock Cnwll ..7 J5
Pounsley E Susx ..15 P6
Pouton D & G ..95 N9
Pouy Street Suffk ..59 M6
Povey Cross Surrey ..15 K2
Powburn Nthumb ..108 H4
Powderham Devon ..8 H8
Powerstock Dorset ..10 D6
Pow Green Herefs ..41 L3
Powhill Cumb ..97 N7
Powmill P & K ..115 J2
Poxwell Dorset ..10 H8
Poyle Slough ..32 F7
Poynings W Susx ..15 J8
Poyntington Dorset ..22 E9
Poynton Ches E ..76 G7
Poynton Wrekin ..63 P8
Poynton Green Wrekin ..63 P8
Poystreet Green Suffk ..58 E9
Praa Sands Cnwll ..2 F9
Pratt's Bottom Gt Lon ..33 N10
Praze-an-Beeble Cnwll ..2 G7
Predannack Wollas Cnwll ..2 H10
Prees Shrops ..63 P6
Preesall Lancs ..83 J5
Prees Green Shrops ..63 P6
Preesgweene Shrops ..63 J6
Prees Heath Shrops ..63 P5

Prees Higher Heath Shrops ..63 P5
Prees Lower Heath Shrops ..63 P5
Prendwick Nthumb ..108 G4
Pren-gwyn Cerdgn ..38 C3
Prenteg Gwynd ..61 K4
Prenton Wirral ..75 J6
Prescot Knowsl ..75 M5
Prescott Devon ..20 H10
Prescott Shrops ..52 C4
Prescott Shrops ..63 M8
Presnerb Angus ..131 M11
Pressen Nthumb ..108 D3
Prestatyn Denbgs ..74 E7
Prestbury Ches E ..76 G8
Prestbury Gloucs ..41 R7
Presteigne Powys ..51 J7
Prestleigh Somset ..22 E5
Preston Border ..116 H10
Preston Br & H ..15 K9
Preston Devon ..8 F10
Preston Dorset ..10 H8
Preston E R Yk ..87 M9
Preston Gloucs ..30 B2
Preston Herts ..44 H7
Preston Kent ..34 H10
Preston Kent ..35 N10
Preston Lancs ..83 M9
Preston Nthumb ..109 K5
Preston Rutlnd ..67 L11
Preston Somset ..20 H6
Preston Torbay ..5 Q4
Preston Wilts ..30 B7
Preston Wilts ..30 F7
Preston Bagot Warwks ..53 M7
Preston Bissett Bucks ..43 N6
Preston Bowyer Somset ..21 J8
Preston Brockhurst Shrops ..63 P7
Preston Brook Halton ..75 N7
Preston Candover Hants ..25 K5
Preston Capes Nhants ..54 E10
Preston Crowmarsh Oxon ..31 M4
Preston Deanery Nhants ..55 K9
Preston Green Warwks ..53 M7
Preston Gubbals Shrops ..63 N8
Preston Montford Shrops ..63 M9
Preston on Stour Warwks ..53 M10
Preston on Tees S on T ..91 N4
Preston on the Hill Halton ..75 P7
Preston on Wye Herefs ..40 E3
Prestonpans E Loth ..115 Q6
Preston Patrick Cumb ..89 N10
Preston Plucknett Somset ..22 C10
Preston St Mary Suffk ..58 D10
Preston Street Kent ..35 N10
Preston-under-Scar N York ..90 H8
Preston upon the Weald Moors Wrekin ..64 C9
Preston Wynne Herefs ..40 H2
Prestwich Bury ..76 F2
Prestwick Nthumb ..100 F4
Prestwick S Ayrs ..104 G3
Prestwick Airport S Ayrs ..104 G4
Prestwood Bucks ..32 C2
Prestwood Staffs ..52 F3
Price Town Brdgnd ..27 M4
Prickwillow Cambs ..57 L4
Priddy Somset ..22 C3
Priestacott Devon ..7 N3
Priestcliffe Derbys ..77 L9
Priestcliffe Ditch Derbys ..77 L9
Priest Hutton Lancs ..89 N12
Priestland E Ayrs ..105 K2
Priestley Green Calder ..84 H10
Priest Weston Shrops ..51 J1
Priestwood Green Kent ..34 B9
Primethorpe Leics ..54 E2
Primrose Green Norfk ..70 G9
Primrose Hill Cambs ..56 G3
Primrosehill Herts ..44 F10
Primrose Hill Dudley ..52 H3
Primrose Hill Lancs ..75 L2
Primsidemill Border ..108 C4
Prince of Wales Bridge Mons ..28 G5
Princes Gate Pembks ..37 M8
Princes Risborough Bucks ..44 A11
Princethorpe Warwks ..54 C6
Princetown Devon ..8 B10
Prinsted W Susx ..13 M4
Prion Denbgs ..74 E11
Prior Rigg Cumb ..98 F4
Priors Halton Shrops ..51 N5
Priors Hardwick Warwks ..54 C10
Priorslee Wrekin ..64 D10
Priors Marston Warwks ..54 C10
Priors Norton Gloucs ..41 P7
Priors Park Gloucs ..41 P5
Priory Wood Herefs ..40 E3
Prisk V Glam ..27 N7
Priston BaNES ..29 L10
Pristow Green Norfk ..58 H3
Prittlewell Sthend ..34 F4
Privett Hants ..25 L8
Prixford Devon ..19 K5
Probus Cnwll ..3 M5
Prora E Loth ..116 C5
Prospect Cumb ..97 M10
Prospidnick Cnwll ..2 G8
Protstonhill Abers ..141 K3
Prudhoe Nthumb ..100 F6
Prussia Cove Cnwll ..2 F9
Publ P & K ..122 D4
Publow BaNES ..29 K9
Puckeridge Herts ..45 M7
Puckington Somset ..21 M10
Pucklechurch S Glos ..29 L7
Puckrup Gloucs ..41 P5
Puddinglake Ches W ..76 D9
Puddington Ches W ..75 K9
Puddington Devon ..8 G2
Puddledock Kent ..16 D1
Puddletown Dorset ..11 J6
Pudleston Herefs ..51 N9
Pudsey Leeds ..85 K8
Pulborough W Susx ..14 F7
Puleston Wrekin ..64 D7
Pulford Ches W ..75 L12
Pulham Dorset ..11 J4
Pulham Market Norfk ..59 J3
Pulham St Mary Norfk ..59 J3
Pullens Green S Glos ..29 J4
Pulloxhill C Beds ..44 F5
Pulverbatch Shrops ..63 M11
Pumpherston W Loth ..115 K7
Pumsaint Carmth ..38 G6
Puncheston Pembks ..37 J4
Puncknowle Dorset ..10 E7
Punnett's Town E Susx ..16 B7
Purbrook Hants ..13 L3
Purfleet-on-Thames Thurr ..33 Q7
Puriton Somset ..21 M4
Purleigh Essex ..46 E11
Purley Gt Lon ..33 K10
Purley on Thames W Berk ..31 N7
Purlogue Shrops ..51 J6
Purlpit Wilts ..29 P9

Purls Bridge Cambs ..57 J3
Purse Caundle Dorset ..22 F10
Purshull Green Worcs ..52 G6
Purslow Shrops ..51 K4
Purston Jaglin Wakefd ..85 N11
Purtington Somset ..10 B3
Purton Gloucs ..41 K10
Purton Gloucs ..41 L11
Purton Wilts ..30 C5
Purton Stoke Wilts ..30 C4
Pury End Nhants ..43 P3
Pusey Oxon ..31 K3
Putley Herefs ..41 K4
Putley Green Herefs ..41 K4
Putloe Gloucs ..41 M9
Putney Gt Lon ..33 J7
Putsborough Devon ..19 J3
Puttenham Herts ..44 D1
Puttenham Surrey ..14 D1
Puttock End Essex ..46 E4
Putton Dorset ..10 G8
Putts Corner Devon ..9 M5
Puxley Nhants ..43 Q4
Puxton N Som ..28 E9
Pwll Carmth ..26 D2
Pwllcrochan Pembks ..36 H10
Pwll-du Mons ..40 C9
Pwll-glas Denbgs ..62 F1
Pwllgloyw Powys ..39 N5
Pwllheli Gwynd ..60 F5
Pwllmeyric Mons ..28 H4
Pwll-trap Carmth ..37 P7
Pwll-y-glaw Neath ..27 J4
Pydew Conwy ..73 P8
Pye Bridge Derbys ..66 D2
Pyecombe W Susx ..15 K8
Pye Corner Newpt ..28 D5
Pye Green Staffs ..65 J9
Pyle Brdgnd ..27 K6
Pyleigh Somset ..20 H7
Pylle Somset ..22 E6
Pymoor Cambs ..57 J3
Pymore Dorset ..10 D6
Pyrford Surrey ..32 F10
Pyrton Oxon ..31 P3
Pytchley Nhants ..55 J6
Pyworthy Devon ..7 K4

Q

Quabbs Shrops ..50 H4
Quadring Lincs ..68 E5
Quadring Eaudike Lincs ..68 E5
Quainton Bucks ..43 Q7
Quaker's Yard Myr Td ..27 P3
Quaking Houses Dur ..100 F8
Quantock Hills Somset ..21 J6
Quarff Shet ..147 i8
Quarley Hants ..24 D5
Quarndon Derbys ..65 Q4
Quarr Hill IoW ..13 J6
Quarrier's Village Inver ..113 M8
Quarrington Lincs ..67 Q3
Quarrington Hill Dur ..101 J10
Quarrybank Ches W ..75 P10
Quarry Bank Dudley ..52 H3
Quarrywood Moray ..139 M3
Quarter N Ayrs ..113 J9
Quarter S Lans ..114 D11
Quatford Shrops ..52 D2
Quatt Shrops ..52 D3
Quebec Dur ..100 F9
Quedgeley Gloucs ..41 M9
Queen Adelaide Cambs ..57 L4
Queenborough Kent ..34 F8
Queen Camel Somset ..22 D9
Queen Charlton BaNES ..29 K9
Queen Elizabeth Forest Park Stirlg ..122 E11
Queen Elizabeth II Bridge Thurr ..33 Q7
Queenhill Worcs ..41 P4
Queen Oak Dorset ..22 G6
Queen's Bower IoW ..13 J8
Queensbury C Brad ..84 G9
Queensferry Flints ..75 K10
Queensferry Crossing Fife ..115 L5
Queen's Head Shrops ..63 K7
Queen's Hills Norfk ..70 H9
Queenslie C Glas ..114 B8
Queen's Park Bed ..55 P10
Queen's Park Essex ..34 B3
Queen's Park Nhants ..55 J8
Queen Street Kent ..16 B2
Queen Street Wilts ..30 B5
Queenzieburn N Lans ..114 C6
Quendon Essex ..45 P6
Queniborough Leics ..66 H9
Quenington Gloucs ..42 D11
Quernmore Lancs ..83 M3
Queslett Birm ..53 J2
Quethiock Cnwll ..4 D4
Quick's Green W Berk ..31 M7
Quidenham Norfk ..58 F4
Quidhampton Hants ..25 J3
Quidhampton Wilts ..23 P7
Quina Brook Shrops ..63 N5
Quinbury End Nhants ..54 G10
Quinton Dudley ..52 H4
Quinton Nhants ..55 K10
Quinton Green Nhants ..55 K10
Quintrell Downs Cnwll ..3 L2
Quixhall Staffs ..65 L4
Quixwood Border ..116 H6
Quoditch Devon ..7 M5
Quoig P & K ..123 L8
Quoisley Ches E ..63 N3
Quorn Leics ..66 E8
Quothquan S Lans ..106 C2
Quoyburray Ork ..147 d5
Quoyloo Ork ..147 b4

R

Raasay Highld ..135 K7
Rabbit's Cross Kent ..16 D1
Rableyheath Herts ..45 J8
Raby Cumb ..97 P8
Raby Wirral ..75 K8
Rachan Mill Border ..106 G3
Rachub Gwynd ..73 K10
Rackenford Devon ..20 C9
Rackham W Susx ..14 F8
Rackheath Norfk ..71 K9
Racks D & G ..97 L3
Rackwick Ork ..147 b5
Radbourne Derbys ..65 P4
Radcliffe Bury ..76 E2
Radcliffe Nthumb ..109 L9
Radcliffe on Trent Notts ..66 G4
Radclive Bucks ..43 N5
Radcot Oxon ..30 G2
Raddery Highld ..138 C5
Raddington Somset ..20 F8
Raddon Devon ..9 J4
Radernie Fife ..125 J11
Radford Covtry ..53 Q4
Radford Semele Warwks ..53 Q8
Radlet Somset ..21 J5
Radlett Herts ..33 J3
Radley Oxon ..31 L3
Radley W Berk ..30 H1

Radley Green Essex ..46 A10
Radmore Green Ches E ..63 Q1
Radnage Bucks ..31 R3
Radstock BaNES ..22 F2
Radstone Nhants ..43 M4
Radway Warwks ..54 B11
Radwell Bed ..55 P9
Radwell Herts ..45 J4
Radwinter Essex ..45 R4
Radwinter End Essex ..45 R4
Radyr Cardif ..27 Q6
RAF College (Cranwell) Lincs ..67 P2
Rafford Moray ..139 K4
RAF Museum Cosford Shrops ..64 E11
RAF Museum Hendon Gt Lon ..33 J4
Ragdale Leics ..66 H8
Ragdon Shrops ..51 M2
Raginnis Cnwll ..2 D9
Raglan Mons ..40 F9
Ragnall Notts ..79 K9
Rainbow Hill Worcs ..52 F9
Rainford St Hel ..75 N3
Rainford Junction St Hel ..75 N3
Rainham Gt Lon ..33 P6
Rainham Medway ..34 E9
Rainhill St Hel ..75 M5
Rainhill Stoops St Hel ..75 N6
Rainow Ches E ..76 H8
Rainsough Bury ..76 F3
Rainton N York ..91 N11
Rainworth Notts ..78 F12
Raisbeck Cumb ..89 Q5
Raise Cumb ..99 Q5
Raithby Lincs ..80 G9
Raithby Lincs ..80 E7
Raithwaite N York ..92 H4
Rake Hants ..25 P8
Rakewood Rochdl ..84 E12
Ralia Highld ..130 C5
Ram Carmth ..38 F6
Ramasaig Highld ..134 C7
Rame Cnwll ..2 H8
Rame Cnwll ..4 F7
Ram Hill S Glos ..29 K6
Ram Lane Kent ..16 H2
Rampisham Dorset ..10 E4
Rampside Cumb ..82 G2
Rampton Cambs ..56 H7
Rampton Notts ..79 K9
Ramsbottom Bury ..84 B11
Ramsbury Wilts ..30 H8
Ramscraigs Highld ..151 L11
Ramsdean Hants ..25 M9
Ramsdell Hants ..25 J2
Ramsden Oxon ..42 H8
Ramsden Worcs ..41 Q2
Ramsden Bellhouse Essex ..34 C3
Ramsden Heath Essex ..34 C3
Ramsey Cambs ..56 F4
Ramsey Essex ..47 M5
Ramsey IoM ..102 f3
Ramsey Forty Foot Cambs ..56 F3
Ramsey Heights Cambs ..56 E3
Ramsey Island Essex ..46 G10
Ramsey Island Pembks ..36 D6
Ramsey Mereside Cambs ..56 F3
Ramsey St Mary's Cambs ..56 F3
Ramsgate Kent ..35 Q9
Ramsgill N York ..84 H1
Ramshaw Dur ..91 J1
Ramshaw Dur ..99 Q3
Ramsholt Suffk ..47 P3
Ramshope Nthumb ..108 E9
Ramshorn Staffs ..65 K3
Ramsley Devon ..8 C6
Ramsnest Common Surrey ..14 D3
Ranby Lincs ..80 E8
Ranby Notts ..78 F6
Rand Lincs ..80 C8
Randwick Gloucs ..41 N10
Ranfurly Rens ..113 M8
Rangemore Staffs ..65 M7
Rangeworthy S Glos ..29 K5
Rankinston E Ayrs ..104 H7
Ranksborough Rutlnd ..67 L10
Rank's Green Essex ..46 D8
Rannoch Station P & K ..122 C4
Ranscombe Somset ..20 E5
Ranskill Notts ..78 G6
Ranton Staffs ..64 G8
Ranton Green Staffs ..64 G8
Ranworth Norfk ..71 M9
Raploch Stirlg ..114 F11
Rapness Ork ..147 d2
Rapps Somset ..21 M10
Rascarrel D & G ..96 G8
Rashfield Ag & B ..112 H5
Rashwood Worcs ..52 G7
Raskelf N York ..85 M1
Rassau Blae G ..39 Q9
Rastrick Calder ..84 H10
Ratagan Highld ..136 C3
Ratby Leics ..66 E11
Ratcliffe Culey Leics ..54 B2
Ratcliffe on Soar Leics ..66 D6
Ratcliffe on the Wreake Leics ..66 G9
Rathen Abers ..141 N4
Rathillet Fife ..124 H8
Rathmell N York ..84 B3
Ratho C Edin ..115 K7
Ratho Station C Edin ..115 K7
Rathven Moray ..140 C3
Ratlake Hants ..24 G8
Ratley Warwks ..42 H2
Ratling Kent ..35 M11
Ratlinghope Shrops ..51 L1
Rattar Highld ..151 N2
Ratten Row Cumb ..98 C10
Ratten Row Cumb ..98 D8
Ratten Row Lancs ..83 K7
Rattery Devon ..5 M4
Rattlesden Suffk ..58 E9
Ratton Village E Susx ..15 Q10
Rattray P & K ..124 C4
Raughton Cumb ..98 D8
Raughton Head Cumb ..98 D8
Raunds Nhants ..55 P5
Ravenfield Rothm ..78 D5
Ravenglass Cumb ..88 F2
Ravenhills Green Worcs ..52 D9
Raveningham Norfk ..59 M1
Ravenscar N York ..93 K6
Ravenscraig N Lans ..114 D10
Ravensdale IoM ..102 e4
Ravensden Bed ..55 P9
Ravenseat N York ..90 E7
Ravenshead Notts ..66 F1
Ravensmoor Ches E ..64 B2
Ravensthorpe Kirk ..85 K10
Ravensthorpe Nhants ..54 H6
Ravenstone Leics ..66 C9
Ravenstone M Keyn ..55 L9
Ravenstonedale Cumb ..90 B7
Ravenstruther S Lans ..114 G12
Ravensworth N York ..91 J7
Raw N York ..93 J6
Rawcliffe C York ..86 A4
Rawcliffe E R Yk ..86 C10
Rawcliffe Bridge E R Yk ..86 C11
Rawdon Leeds ..85 J7
Rawling Street Kent ..34 F10
Rawmarsh Rothm ..78 D4
Rawnsley Staffs ..65 J9
Rawreth Essex ..34 C3
Rawridge Devon ..9 N3
Rawtenstall Lancs ..84 B10
Raydon Suffk ..47 J3
Raylees Nthumb ..108 E11
Rayleigh Essex ..34 E4
Raymond's Hill Devon ..9 Q5
Rayne Essex ..46 D7
Raynes Park Gt Lon ..33 J8
Reach Cambs ..57 L7
Read Lancs ..84 A8
Reading Readg ..31 R8
Reading Services W Berk ..31 P8
Reading Street Kent ..16 G5
Reading Street Kent ..35 Q8
Reagill Cumb ..89 P3
Rearquhar Highld ..146 D6
Rearsby Leics ..66 G9
Rease Heath Ches E ..64 B1
Reawla Cnwll ..2 G7
Reay Highld ..150 H4
Reculver Kent ..35 M8
Red Ball Devon ..20 H10
Redberth Pembks ..37 L9
Redbourn Herts ..44 G8
Redbourne N Linc ..79 N4
Redbrook Wrexhm ..63 N4
Redbrook Street Kent ..16 G3
Redburn Highld ..138 H6
Redburn Nthumb ..99 L5
Redcar R & Cl ..92 C2
Redcastle Ag & B ..96 G5
Redcastle Highld ..137 Q6
Red Dial Cumb ..97 Q9
Redding Falk ..114 G5
Reddingmuirhead Falk ..114 G6
Reddish Stockp ..76 G5
Redditch Worcs ..53 K7
Rede Suffk ..57 P9
Redenhall Norfk ..59 K4
Redenham Hants ..24 D4
Redesmouth Nthumb ..99 N2
Redford Abers ..133 J3
Redford Angus ..125 L4
Redford W Susx ..25 Q8
Redfordgreen Border ..107 K6
Redgate Rhondd ..27 P5
Redgorton P & K ..124 B7
Redgrave Suffk ..58 F5
Redhill Abers ..133 J3
Red Hill BCP ..11 Q5
Redhill Herts ..45 K5
Redhill N Som ..28 H9
Red Hill Warwks ..53 L9
Redhill Surrey ..33 K12
Redisham Suffk ..59 N4
Redland Bristl ..29 J7
Redland Ork ..147 c3
Redlingfield Suffk ..59 J6
Redlingfield Green Suffk ..59 J6
Red Lodge Suffk ..57 N6
Red Lumb Rochdl ..84 C12
Redlynch Somset ..22 F6
Redlynch Wilts ..24 C9
Redmain Cumb ..97 N11
Redmarley Worcs ..52 F6
Redmarley D'Abitot Gloucs ..41 M5
Redmarshall S on T ..91 P3
Redmile Leics ..67 K5
Redmire N York ..90 H8
Redmyre Abers ..133 J9
Rednal Birm ..53 J5
Rednal Shrops ..63 L6
Redpath Border ..107 P3
Redpoint Highld ..135 N2
Red Post Cnwll ..7 K4
Red Rice Hants ..24 D4
Red Rock Wigan ..75 P2
Red Roses Carmth ..37 N8
Red Row Nthumb ..109 L10
Redruth Cnwll ..2 H6
Redstocks Wilts ..29 Q9
Redstone P & K ..124 C7
Redstone Cross Pembks ..37 L7
Redvales Bury ..76 F2
Red Wharf Bay IoA ..72 H6
Redwick Newpt ..28 F5
Redwick S Glos ..28 H5
Redworth Darltn ..91 L3
Reed Herts ..45 K4
Reedham Norfk ..71 N11
Reedness E R Yk ..86 E10
Reeds Beck Lincs ..80 D10
Reeds Holme Lancs ..84 B10
Reepham Lincs ..79 Q9
Reepham Norfk ..70 G7
Reeth N York ..90 H7
Reeves Green Solhll ..53 N5
Regaby IoM ..102 f3
Regil N Som ..28 H9
Reiff Highld ..143 Q2
Reigate Surrey ..33 J12
Reighton N York ..93 N11
Reinigeadal W Isls ..152 f6
Reisque Abers ..141 L11
Reiss Highld ..151 P6
Rejerrah Cnwll ..3 K3
Releath Cnwll ..2 G8
Relubbus Cnwll ..2 F8
Relugas Moray ..139 J6
Remenham Wokham ..31 R6
Remenham Hill Wokham ..31 Q6
Rempstone Notts ..66 F7
Rendcomb Gloucs ..42 B10
Rendham Suffk ..59 M7
Rendlesham Suffk ..59 M9
Renfrew Rens ..113 P8
Renhold Bed ..55 P9
Renishaw Derbys ..78 D8
Rennington Nthumb ..109 L6
Renton W Duns ..113 M6
Renwick Cumb ..98 H9
Repps Norfk ..71 N9
Repton Derbys ..66 B6
Reraig Highld ..135 P10
Rescassa Cnwll ..3 N6
Rescorla Cnwll ..3 Q4
Resipole Burn Highld ..127 N11
Reskadinnick Cnwll ..2 G6
Resolis Highld ..138 C3
Resolven Neath ..39 K11
Rest and be thankful Ag & B ..121 N11
Reston Border ..117 K3
Restronguet Cnwll ..3 K7
Reswallie Angus ..125 K2
Reterth Cnwll ..3 M2
Retford Notts ..78 H7
Retire Cnwll ..3 N2
Rettendon Essex ..34 D3
Retyn Cnwll ..3 L3
Revesby Lincs ..80 E11
Rew Devon ..5 M7
Rew Devon ..8 H5
Rewe Devon ..8 H4
Rew Street IoW ..12 H5
Rexon Devon ..7 M7

Reydon Suffk ..59 P5
Reymerston Norfk ..70 F11
Reynalton Pembks ..37 L9
Reynoldston Swans ..26 D4
Rezare Cnwll ..7 L9
Rhadyr Mons ..40 E11
Rhandirmwyn Carmth ..39 J3
Rhayader Powys ..50 D7
Rheindown Highld ..137 P6
Rhenigidale W Isls ..152 f5
Rhes-y-cae Flints ..74 G9
Rhewl Denbgs ..62 G2
Rhewl Denbgs ..74 F10
Rhewl Mostyn Flints ..74 F7
Rhicarn Highld ..148 C11
Rhiconich Highld ..148 F6
Rhicullen Highld ..146 C10
Rhigos Rhondd ..39 L10
Rhives Highld ..146 E5
Rhiwbina Cardif ..27 R6
Rhiwbryfdir Gwynd ..61 M3
Rhiwderyn Newpt ..28 C5
Rhiwen Gwynd ..73 J11
Rhiwinder Rhondd ..27 N5
Rhiwlas Gwynd ..62 C5
Rhiwlas Gwynd ..73 K10
Rhiwlas Powys ..62 H4
Rhiwsaeson Rhondd ..27 P6
Rhode Somset ..21 K7
Rhoden Green Kent ..16 B2
Rhodesia Notts ..78 E7
Rhodes Minnis Kent ..17 L2
Rhodiad-y-brenin Pembks ..36 E5
Rhonehouse D & G ..96 F9
Rhoose V Glam ..27 P9
Rhos Denbgs ..74 F11
Rhos Neath ..38 H11
Rhosaman Carmth ..38 H9
Rhosbeirio IoA ..72 F5
Rhoscefnhir IoA ..72 D8
Rhoscolyn IoA ..72 C8
Rhoscrowther Pembks ..36 H10
Rhosesmor Flints ..74 H10
Rhos-fawr Gwynd ..60 F4
Rhosgadfan Gwynd ..72 H12
Rhosgoch IoA ..72 G6
Rhosgoch Powys ..50 G11
Rhos Haminiog Cerdgn ..49 J2
Rhoshill Pembks ..37 N2
Rhoshirwaun Gwynd ..60 C5
Rhoslan Gwynd ..60 H4
Rhoslefain Gwynd ..61 K11
Rhosllanerchrugog Wrexhm ..63 J3
Rhôs Lligwy IoA ..72 H6
Rhosmaen Carmth ..38 F7
Rhosmeirch IoA ..72 H8
Rhosneigr IoA ..72 C8
Rhosnesni Wrexhm ..63 K2
Rhôs-on-Sea Conwy ..73 P7
Rhosrobin Wrexhm ..63 K2
Rhossili Swans ..26 B5
Rhostryfan Gwynd ..72 H12
Rhostyllen Wrexhm ..63 K2
Rhosybol IoA ..72 G6
Rhos-y-brithdir Powys ..62 F7
Rhosygadfa Shrops ..63 K5
Rhos-y-garth Cerdgn ..49 L6
Rhos-y-gwaliau Gwynd ..62 C5
Rhos-y-llan Gwynd ..60 D5
Rhosymedre Wrexhm ..63 J4
Rhu Ag & B ..113 K4
Rhuallt Denbgs ..74 E8
Rhubodach Ag & B ..112 F6
Rhuddall Heath Ches W ..75 P11
Rhuddlan Cerdgn ..38 C3
Rhuddlan Denbgs ..74 D8
Rhue Highld ..144 D6
Rhulen Powys ..50 F10
Rhunahaorine Ag & B ..111 Q12
Rhyd Gwynd ..61 L4
Rhydargaeau Carmth ..38 C4
Rhydcymerau Carmth ..38 E5
Rhydd Worcs ..41 N3
Rhyd-Ddu Gwynd ..61 J2
Rhydding Neath ..26 H4
Rhydgaled Conwy ..74 C10
Rhydlanfair Conwy ..61 P1
Rhydlewis Cerdgn ..48 E11
Rhydlios Gwynd ..60 C5
Rhydlydan Conwy ..61 Q2
Rhydowen Cerdgn ..38 C3
Rhydroser Cerdgn ..49 J2
Rhydspence Herefs ..40 C2
Rhydtalog Flints ..62 H1
Rhyd-uchaf Gwynd ..62 C4
Rhyd-y-clafdy Gwynd ..60 F5
Rhydycroesau Shrops ..62 H6
Rhydyfelin Cerdgn ..49 J5
Rhydyfelin Rhondd ..27 P5
Rhyd-y-foel Conwy ..74 C8
Rhydyfro Neath ..38 H11
Rhyd-y-groes Gwynd ..73 K10
Rhydymain Gwynd ..61 Q7
Rhyd-y-meirch Mons ..40 D8
Rhydymwyn Flints ..74 H10
Rhyd-yr-onnen Gwynd ..61 L9
Rhyd-y-sarn Gwynd ..61 M4
Rhyl Denbgs ..74 D7
Rhymney Caerph ..39 Q10
Rhynd P & K ..124 D7
Rhynie Abers ..140 D9
Rhynie Highld ..146 F9
Ribbesford Worcs ..52 E6
Ribbleton Lancs ..83 M9
Ribby Lancs ..83 J9
Ribchester Lancs ..83 P8
Riber Derbys ..77 P11
Riby Lincs ..80 C2
Riccall N York ..86 B9
Riccarton Border ..107 N10
Riccarton E Ayrs ..104 H3
Richards Castle Herefs ..51 N7
Richings Park Bucks ..32 F6
Richmond Gt Lon ..32 H7
Richmond N York ..91 K6
Richmond Sheff ..78 D7
Rich's Holford Somset ..21 J6
Rickerscote Staffs ..64 G8
Rickford N Som ..28 G10
Rickham Devon ..5 M9
Rickinghall Suffk ..58 F5
Rickling Essex ..45 P5
Rickling Green Essex ..45 P6
Rickmansworth Herts ..32 F4
Riddell Border ..107 N5
Riddings Derbys ..66 D2
Riddlecombe Devon ..19 M10
Riddlesden C Brad ..84 G7
Ridge BaNES ..28 H11
Ridge Dorset ..11 M7
Ridge Herts ..33 J3
Ridge Wilts ..23 K7
Ridgebourne Powys ..50 E8
Ridge Green Surrey ..15 L2
Ridge Lane Warwks ..53 M3
Ridge Row Kent ..17 L2
Ridgeway Derbys ..77 P11
Ridgeway Derbys ..78 D8
Ridgeway Worcs ..53 K8
Ridgeway Cross Herefs ..41 L3
Ridgewood E Susx ..15 N7

Riding Mill Nthumb 100 C6
Ridley Kent 34 A9
Ridley Nthumb 99 M5
Ridley Green Ches E 63 P9
Ridlington Norfk 71 L6
Ridlington Rutlnd 67 L11
Ridlington Street Norfk 71 L6
Ridsdale Nthumb 99 P1
Rievaulx N York 92 C9
Rigg D & G 98 C5
Riggend N Lans 114 D7
Righoul Highld 138 G5
Rigmadon Park Cumb 89 P9
Rigsby Lincs 80 H8
Rigside S Lans 105 L9
Riley Green Lancs 83 N10
Rileyhill Staffs 65 L9
Rilla Mill Cnwll 7 K10
Rillaton Cnwll 7 K10
Rillington N York 92 H11
Rimington Lancs 84 B6
Rimpton Somset 22 E9
Rimswell E R Yk 87 P9
Rinaston Pembks 37 J5
Rindleford Shrops 52 D2
Ringford D & G 96 E7
Ringinglow Sheff 77 P7
Ringland Norfk 70 H9
Ringles Cross E Susx 15 N6
Ringlestone Kent 34 F11
Ringley Bolton 76 E3
Ringmer E Susx 15 N8
Ringmore Devon 5 K7
Ringmore Devon 8 H10
Ringorm Moray 139 N7
Ring's End Cambs 68 H11
Ringsfield Suffk 59 M3
Ringsfield Corner Suffk 59 N3
Ringshall Herts 44 E9
Ringshall Suffk 58 F10
Ringshall Stocks Suffk 58 F10
Ringstead Nhants 55 N5
Ringstead Norfk 69 N4
Ringwood Hants 12 B4
Ringwould Kent 17 P1
Rinmore Abers 132 C1
Rinsey Cnwll 2 F9
Rinsey Croft Cnwll 2 F9
Ripe E Susx 15 P9
Ripley Derbys 66 C2
Ripley Hants 12 B5
Ripley N York 85 L3
Ripley Surrey 32 F11
Riplingham E R Yk 86 H9
Riplington Hants 25 L8
Ripon N York 85 L1
Rippingale Lincs 68 B6
Ripple Kent 35 P12
Ripple Worcs 41 P4
Ripponden Calder 84 F11
Risabus Ag & B 102 B1
Risbury Herefs 51 P9
Risby N Linc 86 G12
Risby Suffk 57 Q7
Risca Caerph 28 B4
Rise E R Yk 87 M7
Riseden E Susx 16 A5
Riseden Kent 16 C4
Risegate Lincs 68 D6
Riseholme Lincs 79 N8
Risehow Cumb 97 L1
Riseley Bed 55 P8
Riseley Wokham 31 P9
Rishangles Suffk 58 H7
Rishton Lancs 83 Q9
Rishworth Calder 84 F11
Rising Bridge Lancs 84 B10
Risley Derbys 66 D5
Risley Warrtn 76 C5
Risplith N York 85 K1
Rivar Wilts 30 G10
Rivenhall End Essex 46 E8
River Kent 17 N2
River W Susx 14 D6
River Bank Cambs 57 K7
Riverford Highld 137 P5
Riverhead Kent 33 P11
Rivers Corner Dorset 22 E11
Rivington Lancs 83 N12
Rivington Lancs 76 B1
Roachill Devon 20 C9
Roade Nhants 55 J10
Road Green Norfk 59 K2
Roadhead Cumb 98 G3
Roadmeetings S Lans 114 F11
Roadside E Ayrs 105 K6
Roadside Highld 151 K4
Roadwater Somset 20 G6
Roag Highld 134 E7
Roa Island Cumb 82 F2
Roan of Craigoch S Ayrs 104 E9
Roast Green Essex 45 N5
Roath Cardif 28 B7
Roberton Border 107 L7
Roberton S Lans 106 B4
Robertsbridge E Susx 16 C6
Roberttown Kirk 85 J10
Robeston Wathen
 Pembks 37 L7
Robgill Tower D & G 97 Q4
Robin Hood Lancs 76 G12
Robin Hood Leeds 85 L9
Robinhood End Essex 46 C4
Robin Hood's Bay N York 93 J6
Roborough Devon 4 H4
Roborough Devon 19 L10
Robroyston C Glas 114 B7
Roby Knows 75 M5
Roby Mill Lancs 83 N2
Rocester Staffs 65 L4
Roch Pembks 36 G6
Rochdale Rochdl 76 G11
Roche Cnwll 6 E4
Rochester Medway 34 D8
Rochester Nthumb 108 D10
Rochford Essex 34 F4
Rochford Worcs 52 B7
Roch Gate Pembks 36 G6
Rock Cnwll 6 D9
Rock Neath 27 J4
Rock Nthumb 109 K6
Rock W Susx 14 G8
Rock Worcs 52 D6
Rockbeare Devon 9 J6
Rockbourne Hants 23 P9
Rockcliffe Cumb 98 D6
Rockcliffe D & G 96 G7
Rockcliffe Cross Cumb 98 D6
Rock End Staffs 76 G12
Rockend Torbay 5 Q4
Rock Ferry Wirral 75 K6
Rockfield Highld 146 G8
Rockfield Mons 40 G8
Rockford Devon 19 M4
Rockford Hants 12 B3
Rockgreen Shrops 51 N6
Rockhampton S Glos 29 K4
Rockhead Cnwll 6 H7
Rockhill Shrops 51 J5
Rock Hill Worcs 52 G6
Rockingham Nhants 55 L2
Rockland All Saints Norfk 58 F1
Rockland St Mary Norfk 71 L11
Rockland St Peter Norfk 58 F1
Rockley Notts 78 H8

Rockley Wilts 30 D8
Rockliffe Lancs 84 C10
Rockville Ag & B 113 J3
Rockwell End Bucks 31 R5
Rockwell Green Somset 20 H9
Rodborough Gloucs 41 N10
Rodbourne Swindn 30 D5
Rodbourne Wilts 29 Q6
Rodd Herefs 51 K8
Roddam Nthumb 108 G6
Rodden Dorset 10 F8
Roddymoor Dur 100 F11
Rode Somset 22 H3
Rode Heath Ches E 76 E12
Rode Heath Ches E 76 G10
Rodel W Isls 152 d7
Roden Wrekin 63 P9
Rodhuish Somset 20 F5
Rodington Wrekin 63 Q9
Rodington Heath Wrekin 63 P9
Rodley Gloucs 41 M9
Rodley Leeds 85 K8
Rodmarton Gloucs 29 Q3
Rodmell E Susx 15 M9
Rodmersham Kent 34 G10
Rodmersham Green Kent 34 G10
Rodney Stoke Somset 22 B3
Rodsley Derbys 65 M4
Rodway Somset 21 L5
Roecliffe N York 85 M2
Roe Cross Tamesd 77 J4
Roe Green Herts 45 J10
Roe Green Herts 45 K5
Roe Green Salfd 76 D3
Roehampton Gt Lon 33 J7
Roffey W Susx 14 H4
Rogart Highld 146 C5
Rogate W Susx 25 P8
Roger Ground Cumb 89 K7
Rogerstone Newpt 28 C5
Roghadal W Isls 152 d7
Rogiet Mons 28 F5
Roke Oxon 31 N4
Roker Sundld 101 K6
Rollesby Norfk 71 N9
Rolleston Leics 67 J12
Rolleston Notts 67 J2
Rolleston Notts 23 N4
Rolleston on Dove Staffs 65 N6
Rolston E R Yk 87 N6
Rolstone N Som 28 E10
Rolvenden Kent 16 E4
Rolvenden Layne Kent 16 E4
Romaldkirk Dur 90 G2
Romanby N York 91 N8
Romanno Bridge Border 115 L11
Romansleigh Devon 19 P9
Romden Castle Kent 16 F2
Romesdal Highld 134 G5
Romford Dorset 11 P3
Romford Gt Lon 33 P4
Romiley Stockp 76 H5
Romney Street Kent 33 Q10
Romsey Cambs 57 J9
Romsey Hants 24 F9
Romsley Shrops 52 E5
Romsley Worcs 52 H5
Rona Highld 135 L4
Ronachan Ag & B 111 J10
Rood Ashton Wilts 29 P11
Rookhope Dur 99 P9
Rookley IoW 12 H8
Rookley Green IoW 12 H8
Rooks Bridge Somset 21 N3
Rooks Nest Somset 20 H6
Rookwith N York 91 L9
Roos E R Yk 87 P9
Roose Cumb 82 F1
Roosebeck Cumb 82 G2
Roothams Green Bed 56 B9
Ropley Hants 25 L7
Ropley Dean Hants 25 L7
Ropley Soke Hants 25 L6
Ropsley Lincs 67 N5
Rora Abers 141 Q5
Rorrington Shrops 63 J2
Rosarie Moray 140 B6
Rose Cnwll 3 J4
Roseacre Lancs 83 K8
Rose Ash Devon 20 B9
Rosebank S Lans 114 E11
Rosebush Pembks 37 L5
Rosecare Cnwll 6 H5
Rosecliston Cnwll 3 K3
Rosedale Abbey N York 92 G8
Rose Green Essex 46 G4
Rose Green Suffk 46 G4
Rose Green Suffk 58 E4
Rose Green W Susx 14 C11
Rosehall Highld 145 Q4
Rosehearty Abers 141 M2
Rose Hill E Susx 15 N7
Rose Hill Lancs 84 B9
Rosehill Shrops 63 M9
Roseisle Moray 139 L2
Roselands E Susx 16 A10
Rosemarket Pembks 37 J9
Rosemarkie Highld 138 D4
Rosemary Lane Devon 21 J10
Rosemount P & K 124 D4
Rosenannon Cnwll 6 D11
Rosenithon Cnwll 3 K10
Roser's Cross E Susx 15 Q7
Rosevean Cnwll 3 P3
Rosevine Cnwll 3 L6
Rosewarne Cnwll 2 F7
Rosewell Mdloth 115 P9
Roseworth S on T 91 P2
Roseworthy Cnwll 2 F6
Rosgill Cumb 89 N3
Roskestal Cnwll 2 B10
Roskhill Highld 134 E7
Roskorwell Cnwll 3 K9
Rosley Cumb 98 C9
Roslin Mdloth 115 N8
Rosliston Derbys 65 N9
Rosneath Ag & B 113 K5
Ross D & G 96 D9
Ross Nthumb 109 J2
Rossett Wrexhm 75 L12
Rossett Green N York 85 L5
Rossington Donc 78 G4
Ross-on-Wye Herefs 41 J7
Rosthorne Ches E 76 D7
Rosthwaite Cumb 88 H4
Roston Derbys 65 L4
Rosudgeon Cnwll 2 E9
Rosyth Fife 115 M4
Rothbury Nthumb 108 H9
Rotherby Leics 67 J9
Rotherfield E Susx 15 P5
Rotherfield Greys Oxon 31 P6
Rotherfield Peppard
 Oxon 31 P6
Rotherham Rothm 78 C5
Rothersthorpe Nhants 55 J9
Rotherwick Hants 31 P11
Rothes Moray 139 P6
Rothesay Ag & B 112 G6
Rothiebrisbane Abers 141 J9
Rothiemurchus Lodge
 Highld 130 H5
Rothienorman Abers 140 H8
Rothley Leics 66 F9
Rothley Nthumb 108 G12
Rothmaise Abers 140 H9

Rothwell Leeds 85 M9
Rothwell Lincs 80 C4
Rothwell Nhants 55 K4
Rotsea E R Yk 87 K5
Rottal Lodge Angus 132 B10
Rottingdean Br & H 15 L10
Rottington Cumb 88 C4
Roucan D & G 97 L3
Roud IoW 12 H8
Rougham Norfk 70 B8
Rougham Suffk 58 D8
Roughburgh Cumb 64 G4
Rough Common Kent 35 K10
Rougham Green Suffk 58 D8
Roughlee Lancs 84 C7
Roughpark Abers 131 Q2
Roughton Lincs 80 E10
Roughton Norfk 71 J5
Roughton Shrops 52 D2
Roughway Kent 34 A11
Roundbush Essex 34 F2
Round Bush Herts 32 G3
Roundbush Green Essex 45 Q8
Round Green Luton 44 F8
Roundham Somset 10 C3
Roundhay Leeds 85 M8
Rounds Green Sandw 52 H3
Roundstreet Common
 W Susx 14 F5
Roundswell Devon 19 K7
Roundway Wilts 30 B9
Roundyhill Angus 124 H3
Rousay Ork 147 c3
Rousdon Devon 9 P6
Rousham Oxon 43 K7
Rous Lench Worcs 53 J10
Routenburn N Ayrs 113 J9
Routh E R Yk 87 K7
Rout's Green Bucks 31 N3
Rowanburn D & G 98 E3
Rowardennan Stirlg 113 M2
Rowarth Derbys 77 J6
Row Ash Hants 25 J5
Rowberrow Somset 28 F10
Rowborough IoW 12 H8
Rowde Wilts 29 R10
Rowden Devon 8 C5
Rowen Conwy 73 N9
Rowfield Derbys 65 M2
Rowfoot Nthumb 99 M4
Rowford Somset 21 K6
Rowhedge Essex 47 J7
Rowhook W Susx 14 G4
Rowington Warwks 53 M7
Rowland Derbys 77 N9
Rowland's Castle Hants 13 M3
Rowlands Gill Gatesd 100 F6
Rowledge Surrey 25 P5
Rowley Dur 100 E8
Rowley E R Yk 86 H8
Rowley Shrops 63 J2
Rowley Hill Kirk 85 J12
Rowley Regis Sandw 52 H5
Rowlstone Herefs 40 E6
Rowly Surrey 14 F3
Rowner Hants 13 K4
Rowney Green Worcs 53 K6
Rownhams Hants 24 F10
Rownhams Services
 Hants 24 F9
Rowrah Cumb 88 E3
Rowsham Bucks 44 B8
Rowsley Derbys 77 N10
Rowstock Oxon 31 K4
Rowston Lincs 80 B12
Rowthorne Derbys 78 D10
Rowton Ches W 75 M11
Rowton Shrops 51 L4
Rowton Shrops 63 L9
Rowton Wrekin 63 Q8
Row Town Surrey 32 E9
Roxburgh Border 108 A4
Roxby N Linc 86 G11
Roxby N York 92 F3
Roxton Bed 56 C9
Roxwell Essex 46 B9
Royal Leamington Spa
 Warwks 53 Q7
Royal Oak Darltn 91 L2
Royal Oak Lancs 75 L3
Royal's Green Ches E 64 B4
Royal Sutton Coldfield
 Birm 53 L1
Royal Tunbridge Wells
 Kent 15 Q3
Royal Wootton Bassett
 Wilts 30 C6
Royal Yacht Britannia
 C Edin 115 N6
Roy Bridge Highld 129 J8
Roydhouse Kirk 77 N1
Roydon Essex 45 M9
Roydon Norfk 58 G3
Roydon Norfk 69 Q8
Roydon Hamlet Essex 45 M10
Royston Barns 78 B1
Royston Herts 45 K4
Royton Oldham 77 J3
Rozel Jersey 13 d1
Ruabon Wrexhm 63 J4
Ruaig Ag & B 118 E3
Ruan High Lanes Cnwll 3 L6
Ruan Lanihorne Cnwll 3 L5
Ruan Major Cnwll 2 H11
Ruan Minor Cnwll 2 H11
Ruardean Gloucs 41 J8
Ruardean Hill Gloucs 41 K8
Ruardean Woodside
 Gloucs 41 J8
Rubery Birm 53 J5
Rubha Ban W Isls 152 c12
Ruckcroft Cumb 98 G9
Ruckhall Herefs 40 F4
Ruckinge Kent 17 J4
Ruckland Lincs 80 F8
Ruckley Shrops 63 P12
Rudbaxton Pembks 37 J6
Rudby N York 91 Q5
Ruddington Notts 66 F5
Ruddlemoor Cnwll 3 N3
Rudford Gloucs 41 M7
Rudge Somset 22 H3
Rudgeway S Glos 29 J5
Rudgwick W Susx 14 F4
Rudhall Herefs 41 J6
Rudheath Ches W 76 C9
Rudheath Woods Ches E 76 D9
Rudley Green Essex 46 E11
Rudloe Wilts 29 N8
Rudry Caerph 28 A5
Rudston E R Yk 87 L2
Rudyard Staffs 76 H12
Ruecastle Border 107 P6
Rufford Lancs 83 K12
Rufford Abbey Notts 78 G10
Rufforth C York 85 Q5
Rug Denbgs 62 E3
Rugby Warwks 54 D5
Rugby Services Warwks 54 E5
Rugeley Staffs 65 K10

Ruigsarry W Isls 152 d7
Ruishton Somset 21 L8
Ruisigearraidh W Isls 152 d7
Ruislip Gt Lon 32 F5
Rumbach Moray 140 B5
Rumbling Bridge P & K 115 J2
Rumburgh Suffk 59 L4
Rumby Hill Dur 100 F11
Rumford Cnwll 6 C10
Rumford Falk 114 G6
Rumney Cardif 28 B6
Runcorn Halton 75 N7
Runcton W Susx 14 C10
Runfold Surrey 14 B1
Runhall Norfk 70 G10
Runham Norfk 71 P10
Runnington Somset 20 H9
Runsell Green Essex 46 D10
Runshaw Moor Lancs 83 M11
Runswick N York 92 H3
Runtaleave Angus 131 P10
Runwell Essex 34 D3
Ruscombe Wokham 31 R7
Rushall Herefs 41 K5
Rushall Norfk 59 J4
Rushall Wilts 23 P2
Rushall Wsall 65 K12
Rushbrooke Suffk 58 C8
Rushbury Shrops 51 M2
Rushden Herts 45 K5
Rushden Nhants 55 N7
Rushenden Kent 34 F8
Rusher's Cross E Susx 15 Q5
Rushford Devon 7 N9
Rushford Norfk 58 D4
Rush Green Essex 47 L8
Rush Green Gt Lon 33 P5
Rush Green Herts 45 J7
Rushlake Green E Susx 16 A7
Rushmere Suffk 59 N3
Rushmere St Andrew
 Suffk 47 M2
Rushmoor Surrey 14 B3
Rushock Herefs 51 K9
Rushock Worcs 52 G6
Rusholme Manch 76 F5
Rushton Ches W 75 P11
Rushton Nhants 55 L4
Rushton Shrops 63 Q10
Rushton Spencer Staffs 76 H11
Rushwick Worcs 52 F10
Rushyford Dur 91 M1
Ruskie Stirlg 114 B3
Ruskington Lincs 68 B2
Rusland Cross Cumb 89 K9
Rusper W Susx 14 H3
Ruspidge Gloucs 41 K8
Russell Green Essex 46 D9
Russell's Water Oxon 31 P4
Russel's Green Suffk 59 K6
Russ Hill Surrey 15 J3
Rusthall Kent 15 Q4
Rustington W Susx 14 F10
Ruston N York 93 J10
Ruston Parva E R Yk 87 K3
Ruswarp N York 92 H5
Ruthall Shrops 51 Q3
Rutherford Border 107 Q4
Rutherglen S Lans 114 B9
Ruthernbridge Cnwll 6 E11
Ruthin Denbgs 74 F12
Ruthrieston C Aber 133 M3
Ruthven Abers 140 E6
Ruthven Angus 124 F3
Ruthven Highld 130 D4
Ruthven Highld 138 D7
Ruthvoes Cnwll 6 E9
Ruthwaite Cumb 97 P11
Ruthwell D & G 97 M5
Ruxley Gt Lon 33 N8
Ruxton Green Herefs 40 G7
Ruyton-XI-Towns Shrops 63 L8
Ryal Nthumb 100 D3
Ryall Dorset 10 B6
Ryall Worcs 41 P3
Ryarsh Kent 34 B10
Rycote Oxon 43 P10
Rydal Cumb 89 K5
Ryde IoW 13 K6
Rye E Susx 16 G7
Ryebank Shrops 63 N6
Ryeford Herefs 41 K7
Rye Foreign E Susx 16 F6
Rye Harbour E Susx 16 G7
Ryehill E R Yk 87 N10
Ryeish Green Wokham 31 P9
Rye Street Worcs 41 M4
Ryhall Rutlnd 67 P10
Ryhill Wakefd 85 M12
Ryhope Sundld 101 K7
Rylah Derbys 78 D10
Ryland Lincs 79 P8
Rylands Notts 66 E5
Rylstone N York 84 F4
Ryme Intrinseca Dorset 10 F3
Ryther N York 85 P7
Ryton Gatesd 100 F5
Ryton N York 92 F11
Ryton Shrops 64 D11
Ryton Warwks 54 C3
Ryton-on-Dunsmore
 Warwks 54 C6
Ryton Woodside Gatesd 100 F5
RZSS Edinburgh Zoo
 C Edin 115 M6

S

Sabden Lancs 84 B7
Sabine's Green Essex 33 Q3
Sacombe Herts 45 L8
Sacombe Green Herts 45 L8
Sacriston Dur 100 G9
Sadberge Darltn 91 N3
Saddell Ag & B 103 J3
Saddington Leics 54 H2
Saddlebow Norfk 69 L9
Saddlescombe W Susx 15 K8
Sadgill Cumb 89 M6
Saffron Walden Essex 45 P4
Sageston Pembks 37 L10
Saham Hills Norfk 70 D11
Saham Toney Norfk 70 D11
Saighton Ches W 75 M11
St Abbs Border 117 M11
St Agnes Border 116 F8
St Agnes Cnwll 2 H4
St Agnes IoS 2 b3
St Agnes Mining District
 ....2 H4
St Albans Herts 44 G10
St Allen Cnwll 3 K3
St Andrew Guern 12 c2
St Andrews Fife 125 K9
St Andrews Botanic
 Garden Fife 125 K9
St Andrews Major V Glam 27 Q8
St Andrews Well Dorset 10 D6
St Anne's Lancs 82 H9
St Ann's D & G 106 E11
St Ann's Chapel Cnwll 7 M10
St Ann's Chapel Devon 5 L7
St Anthony-in-Meneage
 Cnwll 3 J9
St Anthony's Hill E Susx 16 A10
St Arvans Mons 28 H3
St Asaph Denbgs 74 E9
St Athan V Glam 27 N9
St Aubin Jersey 13 b2
St Austell Cnwll 3 P4
St Bees Cumb 88 C4
St Blazey Cnwll 3 Q4
St Blazey Gate Cnwll 3 Q4
St Boswells Border 107 P4
St Breock Cnwll 6 D10
St Breward Cnwll 6 G9
St Briavels Gloucs 40 H10
St Brides Pembks 36 F8
St Brides Major V Glam 27 L7
St Brides Netherwent
 Mons 28 F4
St Brides-super-Ely
 V Glam 27 P7
St Brides Wentlooge
 Newpt 28 C6
St Budeaux C Plym 4 G5
Saintbury Gloucs 42 D4
St Buryan Cnwll 2 C9
St Catherine BaNES 29 M8
St Catherines Ag & B 121 L11
St Clears Carmth 37 Q7
St Cleer Cnwll 7 J11
St Clement Cnwll 3 L6
St Clement Jersey 13 d3
St Clether Cnwll 7 J8
St Colmac Ag & B 112 F8
St Columb Major Cnwll 3 M2
St Columb Minor Cnwll 3 K2
St Columb Road Cnwll 3 M3
St Combs Abers 141 P3
St Cross South Elmham
 Suffk 59 L4
St Cyrus Abers 133 J11
St David's P & K 123 N9
St Davids Pembks 36 E5
St Davids Cathedral
 Pembks 36 E5
St Day Cnwll 2 H6
St Decumans Somset 20 G5
St Dennis Cnwll 3 M3
St Devereux Herefs 40 F5
St Dogmaels Pembks 48 B11
St Dogwells Pembks 37 J5
St Dominick Cnwll 4 F3
St Donats V Glam 27 M8
St Edith's Marsh Wilts 29 R9
St Endellion Cnwll 6 D9
St Enoder Cnwll 3 K3
St Erme Cnwll 3 L4
St Erney Cnwll 4 D9
St Erth Cnwll 2 E7
St Erth Praze Cnwll 2 E7
St Ervan Cnwll 6 C10
St Eval Cnwll 6 C11
St Ewe Cnwll 3 N5
St Fagans Cardif 27 Q7
St Fagans: National
 History Museum
 Cardif 27 Q7
St Fergus Abers 141 Q5
St Fillans P & K 122 H8
St Florence Pembks 37 L10
St Gennys Cnwll 6 H5
St George Conwy 74 D8
St Georges N Som 28 E9
St George's V Glam 27 Q7
St George's Hill Surrey 32 F10
St Germans Cnwll 4 D5
St Giles in the Wood
 Devon 19 K9
St Giles-on-the-Heath
 Devon 7 L7
St Gluvia's Cnwll 3 K7
St Harmon Powys 50 D6
St Helen Auckland Dur 91 K1
St Helens Cumb 97 L11
St Helen's E Susx 16 E8
St Helens IoW 13 K7
St Helens St Hel 75 N5
St Helier Gt Lon 33 J8
St Helier Jersey 13 c2
St Hilary Cnwll 2 E8
St Hilary V Glam 27 N8
Saint Hill Devon 9 M4
Saint Hill W Susx 15 M4
St Illtyd Blae G 40 B11
St Ippolyts Herts 44 H6
St Ishmael's Pembks 36 G9
St Issey Cnwll 6 D10
St Ive Cnwll 4 D3
St Ive Cross Cnwll 4 D3
St Ives Cambs 56 F6
St Ives Cnwll 2 E6
St Ives Dorset 11 Q4
St James's End Nhants 55 J8
St James South Elmham
 Suffk 59 L4
St Jidgey Cnwll 6 D10
St John Cnwll 4 F6
St John Jersey 13 b1
St Johns Dur 100 D10
St Johns E Susx 15 P4
St John's IoM 102 b5
St John's Kent 33 P11
St Johns Surrey 32 E10
St Johns Worcs 52 F10
St John's Chapel Devon 19 K7
St John's Chapel Dur 99 Q10
St John's Fen End Norfk 69 K9
St John's Highway Norfk 69 K9
St John's Kirk S Lans 106 C3
St John's Town of Dalry
 D & G 96 D2
St John's Wood Gt Lon 33 K6
St Judes IoM 102 e3
St Just Cnwll 2 B8
St Just-in-Roseland
 Cnwll 3 L7
St Just Mining District
 ....2 B8
St Katherines Abers 141 J9
St Keverne Cnwll 3 K10
St Kew Cnwll 6 E9
St Kew Highway Cnwll 6 E9
St Lawrence Cnwll 6 F11
St Lawrence Essex 46 G11
St Lawrence IoW 13 J9
St Lawrence Jersey 13 c2
St Lawrence Kent 35 Q9
St Leonards Bucks 44 C10
St Leonards Dorset 11 Q4
St Leonard's E Susx 16 E9
St Leonard's Street Kent 34 B11
St Levan Cnwll 2 B9
St Lythans V Glam 27 Q8
St Mabyn Cnwll 6 E9
St Madoes P & K 124 D8
St Margarets Herefs 40 D4
St Margarets Herts 45 L9
St Margaret's at Cliffe
 Kent 17 P2
St Margaret's Hope Ork 147 c6
St Margaret South
 Elmham Suffk 59 L4
St Marks IoM 102 d6
St Martin Cnwll 3 A10
St Martin Cnwll 4 C6
St Martin Guern 12 c2
St Martin Jersey 13 d2
St Martin's IoS 2 c1
St Martin's P & K 124 D7
St Martin's Shrops 63 K5
St Martin's Moor Shrops 63 K5
St Mary Jersey 13 b1
St Mary Bourne Hants 24 G3
St Marychurch Torbay 5 Q3
St Mary Church V Glam 27 N8
St Mary Cray Gt Lon 33 N8
St Mary Hill V Glam 27 M7
St Mary in the Marsh
 Kent 17 J5
St Mary's IoS 2 b2
St Mary's Ork 147 c5
St Mary's Bay Kent 17 K5
St Mary's Hoo Medway 34 E7
St Mary's Platt Kent 34 A11
St Maughans Mons 40 G8
St Maughans Green
 Mons 40 G8
St Mawes Cnwll 3 L8
St Mawgan Cnwll 6 C11
St Mellion Cnwll 4 F4
St Mellons Cardif 28 C6
St Merryn Cnwll 6 C10
St Mewan Cnwll 3 N4
St Michael Caerhays
 Cnwll 3 N6
St Michael Church
 Somset 21 M7
St Michael Penkevil
 Cnwll 3 L6
St Michaels Kent 16 E3
St Michaels Worcs 51 P8
St Michael's Mount Cnwll 2 E8
St Michael's on Wyre
 Lancs 83 K6
St Michael South
 Elmham Suffk 59 L4
St Minver Cnwll 6 D9
St Monans Fife 116 C1
St Neot Cnwll 6 H10
St Neots Cambs 56 D8
St Newlyn East Cnwll 3 K3
St Nicholas Pembks 36 F4
St Nicholas V Glam 27 P7
St Nicholas-at-Wade
 Kent 35 N9
St Ninians Stirlg 114 E3
St Olaves Norfk 71 N12
St Osyth Essex 47 K8
St Ouen Jersey 13 a1
St Owen's Cross Herefs 40 H7
St Paul's Cray Gt Lon 33 N8
St Paul's Walden Herts 44 H7
St Peter Jersey 13 b2
St Peter Port Guern 12 c2
St Peter's Guern 12 b2
St Peter's Kent 35 Q8
St Peter's Hill Cambs 56 E6
St Petrox Pembks 37 J11
St Pinnock Cnwll 4 B4
St Quivox S Ayrs 104 G5
St Ruan Cnwll 2 H11
St Sampson Guern 12 d1
St Saviour Guern 12 b2
St Saviour Jersey 13 c2
St Stephen Cnwll 3 M4
St Stephens Cnwll 4 F5
St Stephens Cnwll 7 L7
St Teath Cnwll 6 F8
St Thomas Devon 9 M6
St Twynnells Pembks 37 J11
St Veep Cnwll 4 B5
St Vigeans Angus 125 M4
St Wenn Cnwll 6 D11
St Weonards Herefs 40 G7
St Winnow Cnwll 3 Q3
St y-Nyll V Glam 27 Q7
Salcombe Devon 5 M9
Salcombe Regis Devon 9 M7
Salcott-cum-Virley
 Essex 46 G9
Sale Traffd 76 E5
Saleby Lincs 81 J8
Sale Green Worcs 52 H9
Salehurst E Susx 16 C6
Salem Carmth 38 F6
Salem Cerdgn 49 L4
Salen Ag & B 119 P4
Salen Highld 127 M11
Salesbury Lancs 83 P8
Salford C Beds 44 D4
Salford Oxon 42 G6
Salford Salfd 76 E4
Salford Priors Warwks 53 K10
Salfords Surrey 15 K2
Salhouse Norfk 71 L9
Saline Fife 115 J3
Salisbury Wilts 23 N7
Salisbury Plain Wilts 23 M5
Salkeld Dykes Cumb 98 G10
Sallachy Highld 145 M3
Salle Norfk 70 G7
Salmonby Lincs 80 F8
Salperton Gloucs 42 C7
Salph End Bed 55 Q10
Salsburgh N Lans 114 E8
Salt Staffs 64 H6
Salta Cumb 97 M9
Saltaire C Brad 84 H7
Saltash Cnwll 4 F5
Saltburn Highld 146 C11
Saltburn-by-the-Sea
 R & Cl 92 D3
Saltby Leics 67 L7
Salt Coates Cumb 97 P7
Saltcoats Cumb 88 E5
Saltcoats N Ayrs 104 D2
Saltcotes Lancs 83 J9
Saltdean Br & H 15 M10
Salterbeck Cumb 88 C3
Salterforth Lancs 84 C6
Salterswall Ches W 76 B10
Saltfleet Lincs 81 J5
Saltfleetby All Saints
 Lincs 81 J5
Saltfleetby St Clement
 Lincs 81 J5
Saltfleetby St Peter Lincs 80 H5
Saltford BaNES 29 K9
Saltmarsh Newpt 28 D6
Saltmarshe E R Yk 86 E10
Saltney Flints 75 L11
Salton N York 92 E10
Saltrens Devon 19 J8
Saltwell Nthumb 100 F2
Saltwick Nthumb 100 G2
Saltwood Kent 17 L4
Salvington W Susx 14 H9
Salwarpe Worcs 52 G8
Salway Ash Dorset 10 C5
Sambourne Warwks 53 K8
Sambrook Wrekin 64 D8
Samlesbury Lancs 83 N9

Samlesbury Bottoms
 Lancs 83 N9
Sampford Arundel
 Somset 20 H10
Sampford Brett Somset 20 H5
Sampford Courtenay
 Devon 8 B4
Sampford Moor Somset 20 H9
Sampford Peverell Devon 20 G10
Sampford Spiney Devon 7 P10
Samson's Corner Essex 47 J8
Samuelston E Loth 116 B7
Sanaigmore Ag & B 110 F7
Sancreed Cnwll 2 C9
Sancton E R Yk 86 G7
Sandaig Highld 127 N4
Sandal Magna Wakefd 85 M11
Sanday Ork 147 e1
Sanday Airport Ork 147 e2
Sandbach Ches E 76 E11
Sandbach Services
 Ches E 76 E11
Sandbank Ag & B 112 H5
Sandbanks BCP 11 Q8
Sanderstead Gt Lon 33 L10
Sandford Cumb 90 B3
Sandford Devon 8 H4
Sandford Dorset 11 M7
Sandford Hants 12 A4
Sandford IoW 13 J8
Sandford N Som 28 F10
Sandford S Lans 105 N1
Sandford Shrops 63 K7
Sandford Shrops 63 P5
Sandford-on-Thames
 Oxon 43 L11
Sandford Orcas Dorset 22 E9
Sandford St Martin Oxon 43 J6
Sandgate Kent 17 M4
Sandhaven Abers 141 M2
Sandhead D & G 94 G8
Sandhill Rothm 78 D4
Sandhills Dorset 10 G3
Sandhills Dorset 10 H2
Sand Hills Leeds 85 M7
Sandhills Oxon 43 L10
Sandhills Surrey 14 D3
Sandhoe Nthumb 100 B5
Sandholme E R Yk 86 F8
Sandholme Lincs 68 G5
Sandhurst Br For 32 B10
Sandhurst Gloucs 41 N7
Sandhurst Kent 16 E5
Sandhurst Cross Kent 16 D5
Sand Hutton N York 86 C3
Sandiacre Derbys 66 D5
Sandilands Lincs 81 K7
Sandiway Ches W 75 Q9
Sandleheath Hants 23 P10
Sandleigh Oxon 31 K2
Sandley Dorset 22 H8
Sandling Kent 34 D10
Sandlow Green Ches E 76 E10
Sandness Shet 147 h6
Sandon Essex 46 D11
Sandon Herts 45 K5
Sandon Staffs 64 H6
Sandon Bank Staffs 64 H6
Sandown IoW 13 K8
Sandplace Cnwll 4 C5
Sandridge Herts 44 H9
Sandringham Norfk 69 N6
Sands Bucks 32 B4
Sandsend N York 92 H4
Sand Side Cumb 89 M10
Sandside Cumb 89 N10
Sandtoft N Linc 79 J2
Sandway Kent 34 E11
Sandwich Kent 35 P10
Sandwich Bay Kent 35 Q10
Sandwick Cumb 89 L3
Sandwick Shet 147 i9
Sandwick W Isls 152 G3
Sandwith Newtown Cumb 88 C4
Sandy C Beds 56 C10
Sandy Bank Lincs 68 E1
Sandycroft Flints 75 K10
Sandy Cross E Susx 15 Q6
Sandy Cross Herefs 52 C9
Sandyford D & G 106 G11
Sandygate Devon 5 Q3
Sandygate IoM 102 e3
Sandy Haven Pembks 36 G9
Sandyhills D & G 96 H7
Sandylands Lancs 83 K3
Sandy Lane C Brad 84 H8
Sandylane Staffs 64 D5
Sandylane Swans 26 E4
Sandy Lane Wilts 29 Q8
Sandy Lane Wrexhm 63 J4
Sandy Park Devon 8 D7
Sandysike Cumb 98 C5
Sandyway Herefs 40 G6
Sangobeg Highld 149 J3
Sangomore Highld 149 J3
Sankey Bridges Warrtn 75 P6
Sankyn's Green Worcs 52 F7
Sanna Highld 126 H10
Sanndabhaig W Isls 152 g3
Sannox N Ayrs 112 E12
Sanquhar D & G 105 P8
Santon Cumb 88 E6
Santon IoM 102 d6
Santon Bridge Cumb 88 F5
Santon Downham Suffk 58 B4
Sapcote Leics 54 D2
Sapey Common Herefs 52 D8
Sapiston Suffk 58 D5
Sapley Cambs 56 D6
Sapperton Derbys 65 M6
Sapperton Gloucs 41 Q11
Sapperton Lincs 67 P5
Saracen's Head Lincs 68 F6
Sarclet Highld 151 Q6
Sarisbury Hants 12 H3
Sarn Brdgnd 27 M6
Sarn Powys 50 H2
Sarnau Carmth 38 A4
Sarnau Cerdgn 48 F9
Sarnau Gwynd 62 D5
Sarnau Powys 39 N5
Sarnau Powys 62 F7
Sarn Bach Gwynd 60 D7
Sarnesfield Herefs 51 L9
Sarn Mellteyrn Gwynd 60 C6
Sarn Park Services
 Brdgnd 27 L6
Sarn-wen Powys 63 J9
Saron Carmth 38 A8
Saron Carmth 38 F7
Saron Gwynd 72 H12
Saron Gwynd 72 H10
Sarratt Herts 32 F2
Sarre Kent 35 N9
Sarsden Oxon 42 G7
Sarson Hants 24 E4
Satley Dur 100 E9
Satmar Kent 17 N3

Satron N York 90 F7
Satterleigh Devon 19 N9
Satterthwaite Cumb 89 K8
Satwell Oxon 31 P6
Sauchen Abers 132 H2
Saucher P & K 124 D6
Sauchieburn Abers 132 G10
Saul Gloucs 41 M10
Saundby Notts 79 K6
Saundersfoot Pembks 37 M9
Saunderton Bucks 44 A11
Saunderton Station Bucks 32 A3
Saunton Devon 19 J6
Sausthorpe Lincs 80 G10
Saverley Green Staffs 64 H4
Savile Town Kirk 85 K11
Sawbridge Warwks 54 E7
Sawbridgeworth Herts 45 N9
Sawdon N York 93 J9
Sawley Derbys 66 D6
Sawley Lancs 84 A9
Sawley N York 85 K2
Sawston Cambs 57 J11
Sawtry Cambs 56 C4
Saxby Leics 67 K8
Saxby Lincs 79 P6
Saxby All Saints N Linc 87 J12
Saxelbye Leics 66 H8
Saxham Street Suffk 58 G8
Saxilby Lincs 79 M8
Saxlingham Norfk 59 J1
Saxlingham Green Norfk 59 K1
Saxlingham Nethergate Norfk 59 J1
Saxlingham Thorpe Norfk 59 J1
Saxmundham Suffk 59 M8
Saxondale Notts 66 H4
Saxon Street Cambs 57 N9
Saxtead Suffk 59 K7
Saxtead Green Suffk 59 K8
Saxtead Little Green Suffk 59 K7
Saxthorpe Norfk 70 G6
Saxton N York 85 P8
Sayers Common W Susx 15 K7
Scackleton N York 92 D12
Scadabay W Isls 152 e6
Scadabhagh W Isls 152 e6
Scafell Pike Cumb 88 G5
Scaftworth Notts 78 H5
Scagglethorpe N York 92 G12
Scalasaig Ag & B 111 J2
Scalby E R Yk 86 F9
Scalby N York 93 K8
Scald End Bed 55 P9
Scaldwell Nhants 55 J6
Scaleby Cumb 98 F5
Scalebyhill Cumb 98 F5
Scale Houses Cumb 98 H9
Scales Cumb 88 H12
Scales Cumb 89 K1
Scalford Leics 67 J7
Scaling N York 92 F4
Scaling Dam R & Cl 92 F4
Scalloway Shet 147 i7
Scalpay Highld 135 L9
Scalpay W Isls 152 h6
Scamblesby Lincs 80 E8
Scammonden Kirk 84 F12
Scamodale Highld 127 Q9
Scampston N York 92 H11
Scampton Lincs 79 N8
Scaniport Highld 138 B8
Scapegoat Hill Kirk 84 G12
Scarba Ag & B 120 D12
Scarborough N York 93 L9
Scarcewater Cnwll 3 M4
Scarcliffe Derbys 78 F7
Scarcroft Leeds 85 M7
Scarfskerry Highld 151 N2
Scargill Dur 90 H4
Scarinish Ag & B 118 E4
Scarisbrick Lancs 75 L1
Scarness Cumb 97 P12
Scarning Norfk 70 D9
Scarrington Notts 67 J4
Scarth Hill Lancs 75 M2
Scarthingwell N York 85 P8
Scartho NE Lin 80 E2
Scatsta Airport Shet 147 i5
Scaur D & G 96 G2
Scawby N Linc 79 N3
Scawsby Donc 78 E3
Scawthorpe Donc 78 E2
Scawton N York 92 B10
Scayne's Hill W Susx 15 L6
Scethrog Powys 39 Q6
Scholar Green Ches E 76 F12
Scholes Kirk 77 M2
Scholes Leeds 85 J10
Scholes Rothm 78 C5
Scholes Wigan 75 Q3
School Aycliffe Dur 91 L2
School Green E Susx 84 H8
School Green Ches W 76 B11
Schoolgreen Wokham 31 N1
School House Dorset 10 H4
Scissett Kirk 77 N2
Scleddau Pembks 36 H4
Scofton Notts 78 G7
Scole Norfk 58 H5
Scone P & K 124 C7
Sconser Highld 135 J9
Scoonie Fife 115 Q6
Scopwick Lincs 79 Q12
Scoraig Highld 144 G6
Scorborough E R Yk 87 J4
Scorrier Cnwll 2 H6
Scorriton Devon 5 H6
Scorton Lancs 83 L5
Scorton N York 91 L7
Sco Ruston Norfk 71 K8
Scotby Cumb 98 F7
Scotch Corner N York 91 L6
Scotch Corner Rest Area N York 91 L6
Scotforth Lancs 83 L3
Scot Hay Staffs 64 E2
Scothern Lincs 79 P8
Scotland Lincs 67 P6
Scotland Gate Nthumb 100 H1
Scotlandwell P & K 115 M1
Scot Lane End Bolton 76 B2
Scotscalder Station Highld 151 K5
Scotsdike Cumb 98 E4
Scot's Gap Nthumb 100 D1
Scotsmill Abers 140 E12
Scotstoun C Glas 113 Q8
Scotswood N u Ty 100 G5
Scotter Lincs 79 L4
Scotterthorpe Lincs 79 L3
Scottish Seabird Centre E Loth 116 D4
Scottish Wool Centre Stirlg 113 Q1
Scottlethorpe Lincs 67 Q8
Scotton Lincs 79 M4
Scotton N York 85 M4
Scotton N York 91 K7
Scottow Norfk 71 K7
Scott Willoughby Lincs 67 Q5
Scoulton Norfk 70 E12
Scounslow Green Staffs 65 K6

Scourie Highld 148 E7
Scourie More Highld 148 D8
Scousburgh Shet 147 i9
Scouthead Oldham 76 H3
Scrabster Highld 151 K3
Scraesburgh Border 107 Q6
Scrafield Lincs 80 F10
Scrainwood Nthumb 108 F8
Scrane End Lincs 68 G4
Scraptoft Leics 66 G11
Scratby Norfk 71 Q9
Scrayingham N York 86 D3
Scrays Lincs 16 D7
Scredington Lincs 68 B4
Scremby Lincs 80 H10
Scremerston Nthumb 117 M11
Screveton Notts 67 J3
Scrivelsby Lincs 80 E10
Scriven N York 85 M3
Scrooby Notts 78 G5
Scropton Derbys 65 M6
Scrub Hill Lincs 68 E1
Scruton N York 91 M8
Scuggate Cumb 98 F3
Scullomie Highld 149 N4
Sculthorpe Norfk 70 C6
Scunthorpe N Linc 79 M2
Scurlage Swans 26 C5
Sea Somset 21 M10
Seaborough Dorset 10 C3
Seabridge Staffs 64 F3
Seabrook Kent 17 L4
Seaburn Sundld 101 K6
Seacombe Wirral 75 K5
Seacroft Leeds 85 M8
Seacroft Lincs 81 L11
Seadyke Lincs 68 F5
Seafield W Loth 115 J8
Seaford E Susx 15 N10
Seaforth Sefton 75 K4
Seagrave Leics 66 G8
Seagry Heath Wilts 29 Q6
Seaham Dur 101 K6
Seahouses Nthumb 109 L3
Seal Kent 33 Q11
Sealand Flints 75 K10
Seale Surrey 14 C1
Seamer N York 91 R5
Seamer N York 93 L9
Seamill N Ayrs 113 J12
Sea Palling Norfk 71 N7
Searby Lincs 79 Q3
Seasalter Kent 35 K9
Seascale Cumb 88 D6
Seathwaite Cumb 88 H4
Seathwaite Cumb 88 H7
Seatle Cumb 89 K10
Seatoller Cumb 88 H4
Seaton Cnwll 4 D6
Seaton Cumb 97 K12
Seaton Devon 9 N6
Seaton Dur 101 K8
Seaton E R Yk 87 M6
Seaton Kent 35 M10
Seaton Nthumb 101 J3
Seaton Rutlnd 55 M1
Seaton Burn N Tyne 100 G3
Seaton Carew Hartpl 101 M12
Seaton Delaval Nthumb 100 H3
Seaton Ross E R Yk 86 E7
Seaton Sluice Nthumb 101 J3
Seatown Dorset 10 C6
Seatown Moray 147 M11
Seave Green N York 92 B7
Seaview IoW 13 K6
Seaville Cumb 97 N7
Seavington St Mary Somset 21 N10
Seavington St Michael Somset 21 N10
Sebastopol Torfn 28 C3
Sebergham Cumb 98 D10
Seckington Warwks 65 N10
Second Severn Crossing Mons 28 G5
Sedbergh Cumb 89 Q8
Sedbury Gloucs 28 H4
Sedbusk N York 90 E8
Sedgeberrow Worcs 42 B4
Sedgebrook Lincs 67 L4
Sedge Fen Suffk 57 M4
Sedgefield Dur 91 N1
Sedgeford Norfk 69 N5
Sedgehill Wilts 23 J8
Sedgemoor Services Somset 21 N3
Sedgley Dudley 52 G2
Sedgley Park Bury 76 F3
Sedgwick Cumb 89 N9
Sedlescombe E Susx 16 D7
Sedrup Bucks 44 A9
Seed Kent 34 G11
Seend Wilts 29 Q10
Seend Cleeve Wilts 29 Q10
Seer Green Bucks 32 D4
Seething Norfk 59 L1
Sefton Sefton 75 K3
Seghill Nthumb 100 H3
Seighford Staffs 64 G7
Seion Gwynd 73 J10
Seisdon Staffs 52 F2
Selattyn Shrops 63 J5
Selborne Hants 25 N6
Selby N York 86 B7
Selham W Susx 14 D7
Selhurst Gt Lon 33 L9
Sellack Herefs 40 H6
Sellafield Station Cumb 88 D6
Sellafirth Shet 147 j3
Sellan Cnwll 2 B9
Sellick's Green Somset 21 K9
Sellindge Kent 17 K3
Selling Kent 35 J11
Sells Green Wilts 29 Q10
Selly Oak Birm 53 K4
Selmeston E Susx 15 P9
Selsdon Gt Lon 33 L10
Selsey W Susx 13 Q6
Selsfield Common W Susx 15 L4
Selside Cumb 89 N7
Selside N York 90 C11
Selsley Gloucs 41 N11
Selsted Kent 17 M2
Selston Notts 66 D2
Selworthy Somset 20 D4
Semer Suffk 46 H2
Semington Wilts 29 P9
Semley Wilts 23 J8
Sempringham Lincs 68 C5
Send Surrey 32 E11
Send Marsh Surrey 32 E11
Senghenydd Caerph 27 N2
Sennen Cnwll 2 B9
Sennen Cove Cnwll 2 B9
Sennybridge Powys 39 L6
Serlby Notts 78 G6
Sessay N York 91 Q11
Setchey Norfk 69 L9
Setley Hants 12 E5
Seton Mains E Loth 116 B6
Settle N York 84 B2
Settrington N York 86 H1
Seven Ash Somset 21 J7
Sevenhampton Gloucs 42 B7
Sevenhampton Swindn 30 E4

Seven Kings Gt Lon 33 N5
Sevenoaks Kent 33 P11
Sevenoaks Weald Kent 33 P12
Seven Sisters Neath 39 K10
Seven Springs Gloucs 41 Q8
Seven Star Green Essex 46 G6
Severn Beach S Glos 28 H5
Severn Bridge S Glos 28 H4
Severn Stoke Worcs 41 P3
Severn View Services S Glos 28 H4
Sevick End Bed 56 B10
Sevington Kent 17 J3
Sewards End Essex 45 Q4
Sewardstonebury Essex 33 M3
Sewell C Beds 44 E7
Sewerby E R Yk 87 M2
Seworgan Cnwll 2 H7
Sewstern Leics 67 M8
Sgabhal W Isls 152 f6
Sgiogarstaigh W Isls 152 h1
Shabbington Bucks 43 N10
Shackerley Shrops 64 F11
Shackerstone Leics 66 B10
Shacklecross Derbys 66 C5
Shackleford Surrey 14 C1
Shade Calder 84 D10
Shader W Isls 152 g1
Shadforth Dur 101 J10
Shadingfield Suffk 59 N4
Shadoxhurst Kent 16 H3
Shadwell Leeds 85 M7
Shadwell Norfk 58 D4
Shaftenhoe End Herts 45 M4
Shaftesbury Dorset 23 J9
Shaftholme Donc 78 F2
Shafton Barns 78 C2
Shafton Two Gates Barns 78 C2
Shakerley Wigan 76 C3
Shalbourne Wilts 30 G9
Shalcombe IoW 12 F7
Shalden Hants 25 M5
Shalden Green Hants 25 M5
Shaldon Devon 8 H10
Shalfleet IoW 12 G7
Shalford Essex 46 C6
Shalford Surrey 14 E1
Shalford Green Essex 46 C6
Shallowford Devon 19 P3
Shalmsford Street Kent 35 K11
Shalstone Bucks 43 N4
Shamley Green Surrey 14 E2
Shandford Angus 132 D11
Shandon Ag & B 113 K4
Shandwick Highld 146 F10
Shangton Leics 55 J1
Shankhouse Nthumb 100 H3
Shanklin IoW 13 K8
Shantron Ag & B 113 L4
Shap Cumb 89 P4
Shapinsay Ork 147 d4
Shapwick Dorset 11 M4
Shapwick Somset 21 P6
Shard End Birm 53 M3
Shardlow Derbys 66 C6
Shareshill Staffs 64 H11
Sharlston Wakefd 85 N11
Sharlston Common Wakefd 85 N11
Sharmans Cross Solhll 53 L5
Sharnal Street Medway 34 D7
Sharnbrook Bed 55 N8
Sharneyford Lancs 84 C10
Sharnford Leics 54 D2
Sharnhill Green Dorset 10 H4
Sharoe Green Lancs 83 M8
Sharow N York 91 M12
Sharpenhoe C Beds 44 F5
Sharperton Nthumb 108 F9
Sharp Green Norfk 71 M8
Sharpness Gloucs 41 K11
Sharpthorne W Susx 15 L4
Sharptor Cnwll 4 H7
Sharpway Gate Worcs 52 H7
Sharrington Norfk 70 F5
Shatterford Worcs 52 E4
Shatterling Kent 35 N10
Shatton Derbys 77 M7
Shaugh Prior Devon 4 H4
Shave Cross Dorset 10 C5
Shavington Ches E 64 C2
Shaw C Brad 84 H2
Shaw Oldham 76 H2
Shaw Swindn 30 D5
Shaw W Berk 31 K8
Shaw Wilts 29 P9
Shawbirch Wrekin 64 B9
Shawbost W Isls 152 f2
Shawbury Shrops 63 P8
Shawclough Rochdl 84 D12
Shaw Common Gloucs 41 L6
Shawdon Hill Nthumb 108 H7
Shawell Leics 54 E4
Shawford Hants 24 H8
Shawforth Lancs 84 D11
Shaw Green Herts 45 K5
Shaw Green Lancs 83 M11
Shaw Green N York 85 M5
Shawhead D & G 96 H3
Shaw Mills N York 85 K3
Shawsburn S Lans 114 E11
Shear Cross Wilts 23 J5
Shearington D & G 97 L5
Shearsby Leics 54 G2
Shearston Somset 21 L7
Shebbear Devon 7 N3
Shebdon Staffs 64 E7
Shebster Highld 151 J4
Shedfield Hants 25 J10
Sheen Staffs 77 L11
Sheepbridge Derbys 78 B9
Sheep Hill Dur 100 F6
Sheepridge Kirk 84 H11
Sheepscar Leeds 85 L8
Sheepscombe Gloucs 41 P9
Sheepstor Devon 5 J3
Sheepwash Devon 7 P3
Sheepwash Nthumb 100 H1
Sheepway N Som 28 H7
Sheepy Magna Leics 65 Q12
Sheepy Parva Leics 65 Q12
Sheering Essex 45 P8
Sheerness Kent 34 G7
Sheerwater Surrey 32 E10
Sheet Hants 25 N8
Sheffield Sheff 78 B6
Sheffield Bottom W Berk 31 N8
Sheffield Green E Susx 15 M6
Sheffield Park E Susx 15 M6
Shefford C Beds 44 G3
Shefford Woodlands W Berk 30 H8
Sheigra Highld 148 E4
Sheinton Shrops 63 Q10
Shelderton Shrops 51 L5
Sheldon Derbys 77 M10
Sheldon Devon 9 M3
Sheldon Birm 53 M4
Sheldwich Kent 34 H11
Sheldwich Lees Kent 34 H11
Shelf Calder 84 H9
Shelfanger Norfk 58 H4
Shelfield Warwks 53 P7
Shelfield Wsall 65 J11
Shelford Notts 66 H4
Shelford Warwks 54 C3
Shellacres Nthumb 108 E11
Shelley Essex 45 Q10
Shelley Kirk 77 M2
Shelley Suffk 47 J4
Shelley Far Bank Kirk 77 M2
Shellingford Oxon 30 G4
Shellow Bowells Essex 45 P9
Shelsley Beauchamp Worcs 52 D8
Shelsley Walsh Worcs 52 D8
Shelton Bed 55 P7
Shelton Norfk 59 K2
Shelton Notts 67 K3
Shelton Shrops 63 M9
Shelton Green Norfk 59 J3
Shelton Under Harley Staffs 64 F4
Shelve Shrops 63 K12
Shelwick Herefs 40 H3
Shenfield Essex 33 R3
Shenington Oxon 42 H3
Shenley Herts 32 H2
Shenley Brook End M Keyn 44 B5
Shenleybury Herts 32 H2
Shenley Church End M Keyn 44 B4
Shenmore Herefs 40 E4
Shennanton D & G 95 L5
Shenstone Staffs 65 K11
Shenstone Worcs 52 F6
Shenstone Woodend Staffs 65 L12
Shenton Leics 66 C11
Shenval Moray 139 N10
Shepeau Stow Lincs 68 H9
Shephall Herts 45 J7
Shepherd's Bush Gt Lon 33 J6
Shepherd's Green Oxon 31 P6
Shepherds Patch Gloucs 41 L10
Shepherdswell Kent 17 N1
Shepley Kirk 77 M2
Shepperdine S Glos 29 J3
Shepperton Surrey 32 F9
Shepperton Green Surrey 32 F9
Shepreth Cambs 56 H11
Shepshed Leics 66 D8
Shepton Beauchamp Somset 21 N9
Shepton Mallet Somset 22 E5
Shepton Montague Somset 22 F7
Shepway Kent 34 D11
Sheraton Dur 101 L11
Sherborne Dorset 22 E10
Sherborne Gloucs 42 D8
Sherborne St John Hants 25 K3
Sherbourne Warwks 53 N8
Sherburn Dur 101 J10
Sherburn N York 93 J10
Sherburn Hill Dur 101 J10
Sherburn in Elmet N York 85 P8
Shere Surrey 14 F1
Shereford Norfk 70 C7
Sherfield English Hants 24 D9
Sherfield on Loddon Hants 31 P10
Sherfin Lancs 84 B10
Sherford Devon 5 N6
Sherford Dorset 11 M6
Sheriffhales Shrops 64 D9
Sheriff Hutton N York 86 C2
Sheringham Norfk 70 H3
Sherington M Keyn 44 C4
Shermanbury W Susx 14 H7
Shernborne Norfk 69 N6
Sherrington Wilts 23 K6
Sherston Wilts 29 P5
Sherwood C Nott 66 F4
Sherwood Forest Notts 78 G11
Shetland Islands Shet 147 i6
Shettleston C Glas 114 B8
Shevington Wigan 75 P2
Shevington Moor Wigan 75 P2
Shevington Vale Wigan 75 P2
Sheviock Cnwll 4 G6
Shibden Head C Brad 84 G9
Shide IoW 12 H7
Shidlaw Nthumb 108 D2
Shiel Bridge Highld 136 C12
Shieldaig Highld 135 P5
Shieldhill D & G 97 L1
Shieldhill House Hotel S Lans 106 C2
Shielfoot Highld 127 M10
Shielhill Angus 124 H2
Shielhill Inver 113 K7
Shifford Oxon 42 F10
Shifnal Shrops 64 D10
Shilbottle Nthumb 109 K8
Shildon Dur 91 L1
Shillford E Rens 113 N10
Shillingford Devon 20 D10
Shillingford Abbot Devon 8 G7
Shillingford St George Devon 8 G7
Shillingstone Dorset 11 J3
Shillington C Beds 44 G5
Shillmoor Nthumb 108 D7
Shilton Oxon 42 F10
Shilton Warwks 54 C4
Shimpling Norfk 58 H4
Shimpling Suffk 58 C10
Shimpling Street Suffk 58 C10
Shincliffe Dur 100 H11
Shiney Row Sundld 101 J8
Shinfield Wokham 31 R8
Shingay Cambs 45 K2
Shingle Street Suffk 59 N4
Shinnersbridge Devon 5 N4
Shinness Highld 145 N2
Shipbourne Kent 33 Q12
Shipdham Norfk 70 D11
Shipham Somset 28 F11
Shiphay Torbay 5 Q4
Shiplake Oxon 31 Q7
Shiplake Row Oxon 31 Q7
Shipley C Brad 84 H8
Shipley Derbys 66 C4
Shipley Shrops 52 F2
Shipley W Susx 14 G6
Shipley Bridge Surrey 15 K2
Shipley Hatch Kent 16 H3
Shipmeadow Suffk 59 M3
Shippea Hill Station Cambs 57 M3
Shippon Oxon 31 K3
Shipston-on-Stour Warwks 42 F4
Shipton Bucks 43 Q6
Shipton Gloucs 42 B8
Shipton N York 86 B3
Shipton Shrops 51 P2
Shipton Bellinger Hants 24 C4
Shipton Gorge Dorset 10 D6
Shipton Green W Susx 13 N3
Shipton Moyne Gloucs 29 P4

Shipton-on-Cherwell Oxon 43 K8
Shiptonthorpe E R Yk 86 F6
Shipton-under-Wychwood Oxon 42 G8
Shirburn Oxon 31 P3
Shirdley Hill Lancs 75 K1
Shire Cumb 99 J11
Shirebrook Derbys 78 E10
Shiregreen Sheff 78 B5
Shirehampton Bristl 28 G7
Shiremoor N Tyne 101 J4
Shirenewton Mons 28 G4
Shire Oak Wsall 65 K11
Shireoaks Notts 78 F7
Shirkoak Kent 16 G4
Shirland Derbys 78 C12
Shirlett Shrops 52 C1
Shirley C Sotn 24 F10
Shirley Derbys 65 N4
Shirley Gt Lon 33 L9
Shirley Solhll 53 L5
Shirl Heath Herefs 51 M8
Shirrell Heath Hants 25 J10
Shirwell Devon 19 L6
Shiskine N Ayrs 112 D6
Shittlehope Dur 100 C10
Shobdon Herefs 51 L8
Shobley Hants 12 L2
Shobrooke Devon 8 G4
Shoby Leics 66 H8
Shocklach Ches W 63 M2
Shocklach Green Ches W 63 M2
Shoeburyness Sthend 34 G5
Sholden Kent 35 P12
Sholing C Sotn 12 G2
Shoot Hill Shrops 63 L9
Shop Cnwll 6 C10
Shop Cnwll 18 G10
Shopwyke W Susx 14 C9
Shore Rochdl 84 D11
Shoreditch Gt Lon 33 L6
Shoreditch Somset 21 K9
Shoreham Kent 33 P10
Shoreham-by-Sea W Susx 15 J10
Shoreswood Nthumb 117 L12
Shorley Hants 25 K8
Shorncote Gloucs 30 B3
Shorne Kent 34 C8
Shortacross Cnwll 4 D5
Shortbridge E Susx 15 N6
Shortfield Common Surrey 25 P3
Shortgate E Susx 15 P8
Short Heath Birm 53 J2
Shortheath Hants 25 N6
Short Heath Wsall 64 H11
Shortlanesend Cnwll 3 K5
Shortlees E Ayrs 104 H3
Shortstown Bed 55 Q10
Shorwell IoW 12 G8
Shoscombe BaNES 29 L11
Shotesham Norfk 71 K12
Shotgate Essex 34 C3
Shotley Suffk 47 M5
Shotley Bridge Dur 100 D7
Shotleyfield Nthumb 100 D7
Shotley Gate Suffk 47 M5
Shottenden Kent 35 J11
Shottermill Surrey 14 C4
Shottery Warwks 53 M9
Shotteswell Warwks 43 J3
Shottisham Suffk 47 P3
Shottle Derbys 65 P2
Shottlegate Derbys 65 P3
Shotton Dur 91 N2
Shotton Dur 101 K10
Shotton Flints 75 K10
Shotton Nthumb 108 D3
Shotton Colliery Dur 101 K10
Shotts N Lans 114 F9
Shotwick Ches W 75 K9
Shougle Moray 139 M5
Shouldham Norfk 69 M10
Shouldham Thorpe Norfk 69 M10
Shoulton Worcs 52 E9
Shover's Green E Susx 16 C4
Shraleybrook Staffs 64 E2
Shrawardine Shrops 63 L9
Shrawley Worcs 52 E8
Shreding Green Bucks 32 E5
Shrewley Warwks 53 N7
Shrewsbury Shrops 63 M9
Shrewton Wilts 23 N5
Shripney W Susx 14 C10
Shrivenham Oxon 30 E5
Shropham Norfk 58 E2
Shroton Dorset 23 J10
Shrub End Essex 46 H7
Shucknall Herefs 41 J3
Shudy Camps Cambs 46 A3
Shuna Ag & B 120 E11
Shurdington Gloucs 41 Q8
Shurlock Row W & M 32 B7
Shurnock Worcs 53 J8
Shurrery Highld 151 J5
Shurrery Lodge Highld 151 J5
Shurton Somset 21 K4
Shustoke Warwks 53 N3
Shute Devon 9 N5
Shute Devon 8 G5
Shutford Oxon 42 H4
Shut Heath Staffs 64 G8
Shuthonger Gloucs 41 P5
Shutlanger Nhants 55 J10
Shutterton Devon 8 H8
Shutt Green Staffs 64 G10
Shuttington Warwks 65 N11
Shuttlewood Derbys 78 D9
Shuttleworth Bury 84 B11
Siabost W Isls 152 f2
Siadar W Isls 152 g1
Sibbertoft Nhants 54 G4
Sibdon Carwood Shrops 51 L4
Sibford Ferris Oxon 42 H4
Sibford Gower Oxon 42 H4
Sible Hedingham Essex 46 C5
Sibley's Green Essex 46 A6
Sibsey Lincs 68 G2
Sibsey Fenside Lincs 68 G2
Sibson Cambs 56 B1
Sibson Leics 66 B12
Sibster Highld 151 P6
Sibthorpe Notts 67 J3
Sibthorpe Notts 79 J9
Sibton Suffk 59 M7
Sicklesmere Suffk 58 D8
Sicklinghall N York 85 M5
Sidbrook Somset 21 L7
Sidbury Devon 9 L6
Sidbury Shrops 52 C3
Sidcot N Som 28 F11
Sidcup Gt Lon 33 N7
Siddick Cumb 97 K12
Siddington Ches E 76 F9
Siddington Gloucs 30 B2
Sidemoor Worcs 52 H6
Sidestrand Norfk 71 K4
Sidford Devon 9 M6
Sidlesham W Susx 13 N3
Sidlesham Common W Susx 13 P5
Sidley E Susx 16 C9

Sidmouth Devon 9 L7
Siefton Shrops 51 N4
Sigford Devon 8 E10
Sigglesthorne E R Yk 87 M6
Sigingstone V Glam 27 M8
Signet Oxon 42 F9
Silchester Hants 31 N10
Sileby Leics 66 G9
Silecroft Cumb 88 F10
Silfield Norfk 70 H12
Silian Cerdgn 49 J10
Silkstead Hants 24 G8
Silkstone Barns 77 N5
Silkstone Common Barns 77 P3
Silk Willoughby Lincs 67 Q3
Silloth Cumb 97 M7
Silpho N York 93 K8
Silsden C Brad 84 F6
Silsoe C Beds 44 F4
Silton Dorset 22 H7
Silverburn Mdloth 115 M9
Silverdale Lancs 89 M11
Silverdale Staffs 64 E3
Silver End Essex 46 E8
Silverford Abers 141 J3
Silvergate Norfk 70 H6
Silverlace Green Suffk 59 L8
Silverley's Green Suffk 59 L5
Silverstone Nhants 43 N3
Silver Street Kent 34 F10
Silver Street Somset 22 C7
Silverton Devon 8 H4
Silverwell Cnwll 3 J5
Silvington Shrops 52 C4
Simister Bury 76 F2
Simmondley Derbys 77 L5
Simonburn Nthumb 99 N5
Simonsbath Somset 19 P5
Simonsburrow Devon 21 J11
Simonstone Lancs 84 B8
Simonstone N York 90 E8
Simprim Border 117 J12
Simpson M Keyn 44 C4
Simpson Cross Pembks 36 H6
Sinclair's Hill Border 116 H11
Sinclairston E Ayrs 105 J6
Sinderby N York 91 N10
Sinderhope Nthumb 99 N8
Sinderland Green Traffd 76 D5
Sindlesham Wokham 31 Q8
Sinfin C Derb 65 Q6
Singleton Kent 16 H3
Singleton Lancs 83 J7
Singleton W Susx 14 C8
Singlewell Kent 34 B8
Sinkhurst Green Kent 16 E2
Sinnahard Abers 132 D2
Sinnington N York 92 G9
Sinton Worcs 52 E9
Sinton Green Worcs 52 E8
Sipson Gt Lon 32 F7
Sirhowy Blae G 39 Q9
Sissinghurst Kent 16 D3
Siston S Glos 29 L7
Sitcott Devon 7 N6
Sithney Cnwll 2 G8
Sithney Common Cnwll 2 G8
Sithney Green Cnwll 34 F9
Sittingbourne Kent 34 F9
Six Ashes Shrops 52 E3
Six Bells Blae G 40 B11
Six Hills Leics 66 G8
Sixhills Lincs 80 D6
Six Mile Bottom Cambs 57 L9
Sixmile Cottages Kent 17 K2
Sixpenny Handley Dorset 23 L10
Six Rues Jersey 13 b1
Sizewell Suffk 59 P8
Skaill Ork 147 d5
Skara Brae Ork 147 b4
Skares E Ayrs 105 K5
Skateraw Abers 133 L6
Skateraw E Loth 116 H6
Skeabost Highld 134 G6
Skeeby N York 91 J11
Skeffington Leics 67 J11
Skeffling E R Yk 87 P11
Skegby Notts 78 E11
Skegby Notts 79 J8
Skegness Lincs 81 L11
Skelbo Highld 146 E9
Skelbo Street Highld 146 E9
Skelbrooke Donc 78 E1
Skeldyke Lincs 68 G5
Skellingthorpe Lincs 79 M9
Skellorn Green Ches E 76 G7
Skellow Donc 78 E2
Skelmanthorpe Kirk 77 N2
Skelmersdale Lancs 75 N2
Skelmorlie N Ayrs 113 J8
Skelpick Highld 150 C5
Skelston D & G 96 G1
Skelton Cumb 98 F10
Skelton E R Yk 86 E10
Skelton N York 91 J11
Skelton R & Cl 92 F4
Skelton on Ure N York 85 M2
Skelwith Bridge Cumb 89 K6
Skendleby Lincs 80 H9
Skene House Abers 133 J2
Skenfrith Mons 40 G7
Skerne E R Yk 87 J4
Skerray Highld 149 N3
Skerricha Highld 148 F5
Skerton Lancs 83 L3
Sketchley Leics 54 C2
Sketty Swans 26 F3
Skewen Neath 26 G3
Skewsby N York 86 C1
Skeyton Norfk 71 K7
Skeyton Corner Norfk 71 K7
Skiall Highld 151 J3
Skidbrooke Lincs 80 H5
Skidbrooke North End Lincs 80 H5
Skidby E R Yk 87 J8
Skigersta W Isls 152 h1
Skilgate Somset 20 D7
Skillington Lincs 67 M7
Skinburness Cumb 97 M7
Skinflats Falk 114 F4
Skinidin Highld 134 D6
Skinners Green W Berk 31 J8
Skinningrove R & Cl 92 H3
Skipness Ag & B 112 D3
Skipper's Bridge D & G 98 D2
Skiprigg Cumb 98 E10
Skipsea E R Yk 87 M4
Skipsea Brough E R Yk 87 M4
Skipton N York 84 D4
Skipton-on-Swale N York 91 N11
Skipwith N York 86 C7
Skirlaugh E R Yk 87 L8
Skirling Border 106 D2
Skirmett Bucks 31 Q5
Skirpenbeck E R Yk 86 D4
Skirwith Cumb 98 H11
Skirwith N York 90 C11
Skirza Highld 151 Q3
Skitby Cumb 98 E5
Skittle Green Bucks 43 Q11
Skokholm Island Pembks 36 E8

Skomer Island Pembks 36 E8
Skulamus Highld 135 M11
Skyborry Green Shrops 51 J6
Skye Green Essex 46 F7
Skye of Curr Highld 138 H11
Skyreholme N York 84 G3
Slack Calder 84 E9
Slackcote Oldham 76 H2
Slack Head Cumb 89 M11
Slackholme End Lincs 81 K9
Slacks of Cairnbanno Abers 141 K7
Slad Gloucs 41 P10
Slade Devon 9 L3
Slade Devon 19 K4
Slade Devon 20 C8
Slade End Oxon 31 M4
Slade Green Gt Lon 33 P7
Slade Heath Staffs 64 G11
Slade Hooton Rothm 78 E6
Sladesbridge Cnwll 6 H9
Slades Green Worcs 41 N5
Slaggyford Nthumb 99 K8
Slaidburn Lancs 83 Q5
Slaithwaite Kirk 84 G12
Slaley Derbys 77 P12
Slaley Nthumb 100 B7
Slamannan Falk 114 F7
Slapton Bucks 44 D7
Slapton Devon 5 N7
Slapton Nhants 43 N2
Slattocks Rochdl 76 G2
Slaugham W Susx 15 J5
Slaughterford Wilts 29 N7
Slawston Leics 55 K2
Sleaford Hants 25 N6
Sleaford Lincs 67 Q3
Sleagill Cumb 89 P4
Sleap Shrops 63 M7
Sleapford Wrekin 64 B9
Sleapshyde Herts 45 H10
Sleasdairidh Highld 145 N4
Slebech Pembks 37 K7
Sledge Green Worcs 41 N5
Sledmere E R Yk 86 H2
Sleetbeck Cumb 98 G3
Sleight Dorset 11 N5
Sleightholme Dur 90 H5
Sleights N York 92 H5
Slepe Dorset 11 M6
Slickly Highld 151 P3
Sliddery N Ayrs 103 P5
Sligachan Highld 135 J10
Sligrachan Ag & B 112 H3
Slimbridge Gloucs 41 L11
Slindon Staffs 64 F6
Slindon W Susx 14 D9
Slinfold W Susx 14 G4
Sling Gloucs 41 J10
Slingsby N York 92 E11
Slip End C Beds 44 F8
Slip End Herts 45 K4
Slipton Nhants 55 N5
Slitting Mill Staffs 65 J9
Slockavullin Ag & B 112 B2
Sloley Norfk 71 K7
Sloncombe Devon 8 D7
Sloothby Lincs 81 J9
Slough Slough 32 D6
Slough Somset 21 P9
Slough Green W Susx 15 K5
Slumbay Highld 136 B8
Slyfield Surrey 32 E12
Slyne Lancs 83 L2
Smailholm Border 107 Q2
Smallbridge Rochdl 84 D12
Smallbrook Devon 8 G5
Smallbrook Gloucs 29 J3
Smallburgh Norfk 71 L7
Smallburn E Ayrs 105 L3
Smalldale Derbys 77 L8
Smalldale Derbys 77 M7
Small Dole W Susx 15 J8
Smalley Derbys 66 C3
Smalley Common Derbys 66 C4
Smalley Green Derbys 66 C4
Smallfield Surrey 15 K2
Small Heath Birm 53 L3
Small Hythe Kent 16 F4
Smallridge Devon 9 P4
Smallthorne C Stke 64 G2
Smallways N York 91 J4
Smallwood Ches E 76 E11
Small Wood Hey Lancs 83 J5
Smallworth Norfk 58 F4
Smannell Hants 24 E4
Smardale Cumb 90 C6
Smarden Kent 16 F2
Smarden Bell Kent 16 F2
Smart's Hill Kent 15 P2
Smeafield Nthumb 108 H1
Smeatharpe Devon 9 M3
Smeeth Kent 17 J3
Smeeton Westerby Leics 54 H2
Smelthouses N York 85 J2
Smerral Highld 151 L10
Smestow Staffs 52 F2
Smethwick Sandw 53 J3
Smethwick Green Ches E 76 E11
Smirisary Highld 127 L9
Smisby Derbys 65 Q8
Smith End Green Worcs 52 E10
Smithfield Cumb 98 F5
Smith Green Lancs 83 L4
Smithies Barns 77 P2
Smith's End Herts 45 M4
Smith's Green Essex 45 Q6
Smith's Green Essex 46 A5
Smithstown Highld 143 L9
Smithton Highld 138 D8
Smithy Bridge Rochdl 84 D12
Smithy Green Ches E 76 D9
Smithy Green Stockp 76 G6
Smithy Houses Derbys 66 C3
Smockington Leics 54 D3
Smoo Highld 149 L3
Smythe's Green Essex 46 G8
Snade D & G 96 G1
Snailbeach Shrops 63 L11
Snailwell Cambs 57 M7
Snainton N York 93 J10
Snaith E R Yk 86 B10
Snake Pass Inn Derbys 77 L5
Snape N York 91 L10
Snape Suffk 59 M9
Snape Green Lancs 83 J12
Snape Street Suffk 59 M9
Snaresbrook Gt Lon 33 N4
Snarestone Leics 65 Q10
Snarford Lincs 79 P7
Snargate Kent 16 H5
Snave Kent 17 J5
Sneachill Worcs 52 G10
Snead Powys 51 K2
Sneath Common Norfk 58 H3
Sneaton N York 92 H5
Sneatonthorpe N York 92 H5
Snelland Lincs 79 Q7
Snelston Derbys 65 M4
Snetterton Norfk 58 E2
Snettisham Norfk 69 N5
Snibston Leics 66 C9

Snig's End Gloucs 41 M6
Snitter Nthumb 108 G9
Snitterby Lincs 79 N5
Snitterfield Warwks 53 N8
Snitton Shrops 51 P5
Snoadhill Kent 16 G2
Snodhill Herefs 40 D4
Snodland Kent 34 C10
Snoll Hatch Kent 16 B1
Snowden Hill Barns 77 N4
Snowdon Gwynd 61 K1
Snowdon Herefs 35 N12
Snowdonia National Park 61 P6
Snow End Herts 45 M5
Snowshill Gloucs 42 C5
Snow Street Norfk 58 G4
Soake Hants 13 L2
Soar Cardif 27 P6
Soar Devon 5 L10
Soar Powys 39 M5
Soay Highld 126 H2
Soberton Hants 25 K10
Soberton Heath Hants 25 K10
Sockbridge Cumb 89 M1
Sockburn Darltn 91 N5
Sodom Denbgs 74 F9
Sodylt Bank Shrops 63 K4
Soham Cambs 57 L6
Soham Cotes Cambs 57 L6
Solas W Isls 152 c7
Solbury Pembks 36 H8
Soldon Devon 7 L3
Soldon Cross Devon 7 L2
Soldridge Hants 25 L6
Sole Street Kent 17 K1
Sole Street Kent 34 B9
Solihull Solhll 53 M5
Sollas W Isls 152 c7
Sollers Dilwyn Herefs 51 M9
Sollers Hope Herefs 41 J5
Sollom Lancs 83 K11
Solva Pembks 36 F6
Solwaybank D & G 98 C3
Somerby Leics 67 K10
Somerby Lincs 79 Q2
Somercotes Derbys 66 C1
Somerford BCP 12 B6
Somerford Keynes Gloucs 30 B3
Somerley W Susx 13 P5
Somerleyton Suffk 59 P1
Somersal Herbert Derbys 65 L5
Somersby Lincs 80 G9
Somersham Cambs 57 G11
Somersham Suffk 58 G11
Somerton Oxon 43 K6
Somerton Somset 22 C7
Somerton Suffk 57 Q10
Somerwood Shrops 63 P9
Sompting W Susx 14 H10
Sompting Abbotts W Susx 14 H9
Sonning Wokham 31 Q7
Sonning Common Oxon 31 P6
Sonning Eye Oxon 31 P6
Sontley Wrexhm 63 K3
Sopley Hants 12 B5
Sopwell Herts 44 H10
Sopworth Wilts 29 N5
Sorbie D & G 95 N9
Sordale Highld 151 L4
Sorisdale Ag & B 126 E11
Sorn E Ayrs 105 K4
Sornhill E Ayrs 105 J3
Sortat Highld 151 N4
Sotby Lincs 80 D8
Sots Hole Lincs 80 C11
Sotterley Suffk 59 N4
Soughton Flints 74 H10
Soulbury Bucks 44 C6
Soulby Cumb 89 M2
Soulby Cumb 90 B4
Souldern Oxon 43 L5
Souldrop Bed 55 N8
Sound Ches E 64 B3
Sound Muir Moray 140 B5
Soundwell S Glos 29 K7
Sourton Devon 5 K3
Soutergate Cumb 88 H10
South Acre Norfk 69 Q9
South Alkham Kent 17 N2
Southall Gt Lon 32 G6
South Allington Devon 5 N9
South Alloa Falk 114 F9
Southam Gloucs 41 R6
Southam Warwks 54 C8
South Ambersham W Susx 14 C7
Southampton C Sotn 24 G11
Southampton Airport Hants 24 G10
South Anston Rothm 78 E7
South Ascot W & M 32 C8
South Ashford Kent 16 H2
South Baddesley Hants 12 F5
South Bank C York 86 B5
South Bank R & Cl 92 B3
South Barrow Somset 22 E8
South Beddington Gt Lon 33 K9
South Beer Cnwll 7 K6
South Benfleet Essex 34 D5
South Bockhampton BCP 12 B5
Southborough Gt Lon 33 M9
Southborough Kent 15 Q2
Southbourne BCP 12 B6
Southbourne W Susx 13 N4
South Bowood Dorset 10 C5
South Bramwith Donc 78 G1
South Brent Devon 5 L5
South Brewham Somset 22 G6
South Broomhill Nthumb 109 L1
Southburgh Norfk 70 G11
South Burlingham Norfk 71 M10
Southburn E R Yk 87 J4
South Cadbury Somset 22 E8
South Carlton Lincs 79 N8
South Carlton Notts 78 F6
South Cave E R Yk 86 G9
South Cerney Gloucs 30 C3
South Chailey E Susx 15 M7
South Chard Somset 9 Q4
South Charlton Nthumb 109 K6
South Cheriton Somset 22 F8
South Church Dur 91 L11
Southchurch Sthend 34 F5
South Cleatlam Dur 91 J3
South Cliffe E R Yk 86 G8
South Clifton Notts 79 K9
South Cockerington Lincs 80 H5
South Cornelly Brdgnd 27 K6
Southcott Cnwll 6 H6
Southcott Devon 8 C8
Southcott Devon 19 J2
Southcott Wilts 30 D10
Southcott Bucks 44 A9
South Cove Suffk 59 P4
South Creake Norfk 70 C5
South Crosland Kirk 77 L1
South Croxton Leics 66 H10
South Dalton E R Yk 86 H6
South Darenth Kent 33 N8
South Dell W Isls 152 g1
South Downs National Park 15 L9

South Duffield N York 86 C8
South Earlswood Surrey 15 K1
Southease E Susx 15 M10
South Elkington Lincs 80 F6
South Elmsall Wakefd 78 D1
Southend Ag & B 103 J8
South End E R Yk 87 R11
South End Hants 24 R10
South End Herefs 41 L3
South End N Linc 87 L11
South End Norfk 58 E3
Southend Wilts 30 E7
Southend Airport Essex 34 F4
Southend-on-Sea Sthend 34 F5
Southernby Cumb 98 D10
Southernden Kent 16 F2
Southerndown V Glam 27 L7
Southerness D & G 97 K7
South Erradale Highld 143 K11
Southerton Devon 9 N4
Southery Norfk 57 M2
South Fambridge Essex 34 F3
South Fawley W Berk 30 H6
South Ferriby N Linc 87 J11
South Field E R Yk 87 J10
Southfield Falk 114 F7
Southfleet Kent 33 B8
Southford IoW 13 J9
Southgate Gt Lon 33 K3
Southgate Norfk 69 N5
Southgate Norfk 70 C5
Southgate Norfk 70 H7
Southgate Swans 26 E5
South Godstone Surrey 15 L1
South Gorley Hants 12 B3
South Gosforth N u Ty 100 G5
South Green Essex 34 B4
South Green Essex 47 J8
South Green Kent 34 E10
South Green Norfk 70 F10
South Green Suffk 58 H5
South Gyle C Edin 115 M7
South Hanningfield Essex 34 C3
South Harting W Susx 25 N9
South Hayling Hants 13 M5
South Hazelrigg Nthumb 108 H3
South Heath Bucks 44 C11
South Heighton E Susx 15 N10
South Hetton Dur 101 K9
South Hiendley Wakefd 78 C1
South Hill Cnwll 7 L10
South Hill Somset 21 Q8
South Hinksey Oxon 43 L11
South Hole Devon 18 E9
South Holmwood Surrey 14 H2
South Hornchurch Gt Lon 33 P5
South Horrington Somset 22 D4
South Huish Devon 5 L8
South Hykeham Lincs 79 M10
South Hylton Sundld 101 J7
Southill C Beds 44 H3
Southington Hants 24 H3
South Kelsey Lincs 79 P4
South Kessock Highld 138 C6
South Killingholme N Linc 87 L12
South Kilvington N York 91 P10
South Kilworth Leics 54 G4
South Kirkby Wakefd 78 D2
South Knighton Devon 5 F10
South Kyme Lincs 68 D2
Southleigh Devon 9 N5
South Leigh Oxon 43 J10
South Leverton Notts 79 K7
South Littleton Worcs 42 C2
South Lopham Norfk 58 F4
South Luffenham Rutlnd 67 M11
South Lynn Norfk 69 M8
South Malling E Susx 15 M8
South Marston Swindn 30 E5
South Merstham Surrey 33 K12
South Middleton Nthumb 108 H5
South Milford N York 85 P9
South Milton Devon 5 L9
South Mimms Services Herts 33 J2
Southminster Essex 34 G2
South Molton Devon 19 N8
South Moor Dur 100 F8
Southmoor Oxon 31 J3
South Moreton Oxon 31 M5
South Mundham W Susx 14 C10
South Muskham Notts 79 K12
South Newbald E R Yk 86 G8
South Newington Oxon 43 J5
South Newton Wilts 23 N6
South Normanton Derbys 78 D12
South Norwood Gt Lon 33 L8
South Nutfield Surrey 15 L2
South Ockendon Thurr 33 N6
Southoe Cambs 56 D8
Southolt Suffk 59 J7
South Ormsby Lincs 80 G8
Southorpe C Pete 56 C11
South Ossett Wakefd 85 L11
Southover Dorset 10 F6
South Owersby Lincs 79 Q5
Southowram Calder 84 H10
South Park Surrey 15 J1
South Perrott Dorset 10 D4
South Petherton Somset 21 P10
South Petherwin Cnwll 7 K8
South Pickenham Norfk 70 C11
South Pill Devon 5 K5
South Pool Devon 5 N8
South Poorton Dorset 10 E5
Southport Sefton 82 H11
South Queensferry C Edin 115 L10
South Radworthy Devon 19 P7
South Rauceby Lincs 67 P3
South Raynham Norfk 70 C7
South Reddish Stockp 76 G5
Southrepps Norfk 71 K5
South Reston Lincs 80 H7
Southrey Lincs 80 D10
Southrop Gloucs 42 E11
Southrope Hants 25 L4
South Runcton Norfk 69 N11
South Scarle Notts 79 L11
Southsea C Port 13 L7
Southsea Wrexhm 63 J2
South Shian Ag & B 120 G4
South Shields S Tyne 101 K5
South Shore Bpool 83 J1
Southside Dur 91 J1
South Somercotes Lincs 80 H5
South Stainley N York 85 L3
South Stifford Thurr 33 Q7
South Stoke Oxon 31 M5
South Stoke BaNES 29 M10
South Stoke W Susx 14 E9
South Stour Kent 17 J3
South Street Kent 35 J10
South Street Kent 35 J9
South Tarbrax S Lans 115 J10
South Tawton Devon 8 C6
South Tehidy Cnwll 2 H6
South Thoresby Lincs 80 H8
South Thorpe Dur 91 J4

South Town Hants 25 L6
Southtown Norfk 71 Q11
Southtown Somset 21 M10
South Uist W Isls 152 c10
Southwaite Cumb 98 F9
Southwaite Services Cumb 98 F9
South Walsham Norfk 71 N9
Southwark Gt Lon 33 L6
South Warnborough Hants 25 M4
Southwater W Susx 14 H5
Southwater Street W Susx 14 H5
Southway C Plym 4 G4
Southway Somset 22 C5
South Weald Essex 33 Q3
Southwell Dorset 10 G10
Southwell Notts 66 H1
South Weston Oxon 31 P3
South Wheatley Cnwll 7 J6
South Wheatley Notts 79 K6
Southwick Hants 13 L4
Southwick Nhants 55 P2
Southwick Somset 21 M4
Southwick Sundld 101 K6
Southwick W Susx 15 J9
Southwick Wilts 23 J2
South Widcombe BaNES 29 J11
South Wigston Leics 54 F1
South Willingham Lincs 80 D7
South Wingate Dur 101 K11
South Wingfield Derbys 66 B1
South Witham Lincs 67 M8
Southwold Suffk 59 P5
South Wonston Hants 24 H6
Southwood Norfk 71 M11
Southwood Somset 22 D6
South Woodham Ferrers Essex 34 E3
South Wootton Norfk 69 M7
South Wraxall Wilts 29 N9
South Zeal Devon 8 C6
Sovereign Harbour E Susx 16 B10
Sowerby Calder 84 F10
Sowerby N York 91 Q10
Sowerby Bridge Calder 84 G10
Sowerby Row Cumb 98 E10
Sower Carr Lancs 83 J4
Sowerhill Somset 20 D8
Sowood Calder 84 G11
Sowton Devon 4 H4
Soyland Town Calder 84 F11
Spa Common Norfk 71 L6
Spain's End Essex 46 B4
Spalding Lincs 68 E7
Spaldington E R Yk 86 E8
Spaldwick Cambs 56 C6
Spalford Notts 79 L10
Spanby Lincs 68 B4
Spanish Green Hants 31 Q10
Sparham Norfk 70 G8
Sparhamill Norfk 70 G8
Spark Bridge Cumb 89 J9
Sparket Cumb 89 L2
Sparkford Somset 22 E8
Sparkhill Birm 53 L4
Sparkwell Devon 5 J5
Sparrow Green Norfk 70 D9
Sparrowpit Derbys 77 K7
Sparrows Green E Susx 16 B4
Sparsholt Hants 24 H5
Sparsholt Oxon 30 H5
Spartylea Nthumb 99 M8
Spath Staffs 65 K5
Spaunton N York 92 F9
Spaxton Somset 21 K6
Spean Bridge Highld 128 H6
Spear Hill W Susx 14 G7
Spearywell Hants 24 F8
Speen W Berk 31 K8
Speen Bucks 32 B2
Speeton N York 93 N11
Speke Lpool 75 M7
Speldhurst Kent 15 Q2
Spellbrook Herts 45 N8
Spelmonden Kent 16 C3
Spelsbury Oxon 42 H7
Spen Kirk 85 J10
Spencers Wood Wokham 31 P9
Spen Green Ches E 76 F11
Spennithorne N York 91 J9
Spennymoor Dur 100 H11
Spernall Warwks 53 K8
Spetchley Worcs 52 G10
Spetisbury Dorset 11 M4
Spexhall Suffk 59 M5
Spey Bay Moray 139 Q3
Speybridge Highld 139 J10
Speyview Moray 139 N7
Spilsby Lincs 80 H9
Spindlestone Nthumb 109 J3
Spinkhill Derbys 78 D8
Spinningdale Highld 146 B3
Spion Kop Notts 78 F10
Spirthill Wilts 30 B6
Spital Wirral 75 K7
Spital Hill Donc 78 G4
Spital in the Street Lincs 79 N6
Spithurst E Susx 15 M7
Spittal E Loth 116 B6
Spittal E R Yk 86 E5
Spittal Highld 151 L6
Spittal Nthumb 117 M11
Spittal Pembks 37 J5
Spittalfield P & K 124 C5
Spittal of Glenmuick Abers 131 P7
Spittal of Glenshee P & K 131 L10
Spittal-on-Rule Border 107 P6
Spixworth Norfk 71 K8
Splatt Cnwll 6 D9
Splatt Cnwll 7 J7
Splatt Devon 8 B4
Splayne's Green E Susx 15 M6
Splott Cardif 28 C4
Spofforth N York 85 L5
Spondon C Derb 66 C5
Spon Green Flints 75 J11
Spooner Row Norfk 58 G11
Sporle Norfk 70 C10
Spott E Loth 116 F6
Spottiswoode Border 116 E11
Spratton Nhants 55 J6
Spreakley Surrey 25 P5
Spreyton Devon 8 D5
Spriddlestone Devon 4 H6
Spridlington Lincs 79 P7
Springburn C Glas 114 A7
Springfield D & G 98 C4
Springfield Essex 46 C10
Springfield Fife 124 G10
Springhill Staffs 64 H11
Springholm D & G 96 K4
Springside N Ayrs 104 G2
Springthorpe Lincs 79 L6
Spring Vale Barns 77 N4
Springwell Sundld 100 H7
Sproatley E R Yk 87 L8
Sproston Green Ches W 76 D10
Sprotbrough Donc 78 C3
Sproughton Suffk 47 K3

Sprouston Border 108 B3
Sprowston Norfk 71 K9
Sproxton Leics 67 L7
Sproxton N York 92 C10
Spunhill Shrops 63 L5
Spurstow Ches E 75 P12
Spyway Dorset 10 E6
Square and Compass Pembks 36 G4
Stableford Shrops 52 D1
Stableford Staffs 64 E4
Stacey Bank Sheff 77 P5
Stackhouse N York 84 B2
Stackpole Pembks 37 J11
Stackpole Elidor Pembks 37 J11
Stacksteads Lancs 84 C11
Staddiscombe C Plym 4 H6
Staddlethorpe E R Yk 86 F9
Stadhampton Oxon 31 M3
Stadhlaigearraidh W Isls 152 b10
Staffield Cumb 98 G9
Staffin Highld 135 J2
Stafford Staffs 64 G7
Stafford Services (northbound) Staffs 64 G6
Stafford Services (southbound) Staffs 64 G6
Stagsden Bed 55 N11
Stainborough Barns 77 Q3
Stainburn Cumb 88 D1
Stainburn N York 85 K5
Stainby Lincs 67 M7
Staincross Barns 77 Q2
Staindrop Dur 91 J3
Staines-upon-Thames Surrey 32 E8
Stainfield Lincs 67 Q7
Stainfield Lincs 80 C9
Stainforth Donc 78 G1
Stainforth N York 84 B2
Staining Lancs 82 H8
Stainland Calder 84 G11
Stainsacre N York 93 J5
Stainsby Derbys 78 D9
Stainton Cumb 89 M1
Stainton Cumb 89 N9
Stainton Cumb 98 D7
Stainton Donc 78 F5
Stainton Middsb 91 Q4
Stainton N York 91 J7
Stainton by Langworth Lincs 79 Q8
Staintondale N York 93 K4
Stainton le Vale Lincs 80 D5
Stainton with Adgarley Cumb 88 H12
Stair Cumb 88 H2
Stair E Ayrs 104 H5
Stairfoot Barns 78 B3
Stairhaven D & G 95 J7
Staithes N York 92 F3
Stakeford Nthumb 100 H1
Stake Pool Lancs 83 K5
Stakes Hants 13 M4
Stalbridge Dorset 22 G10
Stalbridge Weston Dorset 22 G10
Stalham Norfk 71 M7
Stalham Green Norfk 71 M7
Stalisfield Green Kent 34 G11
Stallen Dorset 22 E10
Stallingborough NE Lin 80 D1
Stalling Busk N York 90 E9
Stallington Staffs 64 H5
Stalmine Lancs 83 J6
Stalmine Moss Side Lancs 83 J6
Stalybridge Tamesd 76 H4
Stambourne Essex 46 C4
Stambourne Green Essex 46 C4
Stamford Lincs 67 P10
Stamford Nthumb 109 L6
Stamford Bridge Ches W 75 M10
Stamford Bridge E R Yk 86 D4
Stamfordham Nthumb 100 D4
Stamford Hill Gt Lon 33 L5
Stanah Lancs 83 J6
Stanborough Herts 45 J9
Stanbridge C Beds 44 D7
Stanbridge Dorset 11 M4
Stanbury C Brad 84 F8
Stand N Lans 114 D7
Standburn Falk 114 G6
Standeford Staffs 64 G10
Standen Kent 16 E3
Standen Street Kent 16 E3
Standerwick Somset 22 H4
Standford Hants 25 P4
Standingstone Cumb 97 J11
Standish Gloucs 41 M10
Standish Wigan 75 Q2
Standish Lower Ground Wigan 75 P2
Standlake Oxon 43 J10
Standon Hants 24 G8
Standon Herts 45 M7
Standon Staffs 64 E5
Standon Green End Herts 45 L7
Standwell Green Suffk 58 H6
Stane N Lans 114 F9
Stanfield Norfk 70 D8
Stanford C Beds 44 H3
Stanford Kent 17 L3
Stanford Shrops 63 L9
Stanford Bishop Herefs 52 B11
Stanford Bridge Worcs 52 D7
Stanford Bridge Wrekin 64 D9
Stanford Dingley W Berk 31 M8
Stanford in the Vale Oxon 30 H4
Stanford le Hope Thurr 34 B5
Stanford on Avon Nhants 54 F5
Stanford on Soar Notts 66 E8
Stanford on Teme Worcs 52 D7
Stanford Rivers Essex 33 P2
Stanfree Derbys 78 D8
Stanghow R & Cl 92 D4
Stanground C Pete 56 E11
Stanhill Lancs 83 Q9
Stanhoe Norfk 70 B5
Stanhope Border 106 C6
Stanhope Dur 100 C10
Stanhope Kent 16 H4
Stanhope Bretby Derbys 65 M3
Stanion Nhants 55 M3
Stanklin Worcs 52 G6
Stanley Dur 100 F7
Stanley Derbys 66 D4
Stanley Notts 78 D11
Stanley Staffs 64 H2
Stanley P & K 124 B5
Stanley Wakefd 85 M10
Stanley Common Derbys 66 D4
Stanley Crook Dur 100 F12
Stanley Ferry Wakefd 85 M10
Stanley Gate Lancs 75 M2
Stanley Moor Staffs 64 H2
Stanley Pontlarge Gloucs 42 B5
Stanmer Br & H 15 L8
Stanmore Gt Lon 32 H4
Stanmore Hants 24 H8
Stanmore W Berk 31 K6
Stannersburn Nthumb 99 K2
Stanningfield Suffk 58 C9
Stanningley Leeds 85 K8
Stannington Nthumb 100 G4
Stannington Sheff 77 P6
Stannington Station Nthumb 100 G2
Stansbatch Herefs 51 K9
Stansfield Suffk 57 P10
Stanshope Staffs 65 L1
Stanstead Suffk 58 B11
Stanstead Abbotts Herts 45 L9
Stansted Kent 33 R10
Stansted Airport Essex 45 Q7
Stansted Mountfitchet Essex 45 Q6
Stanton Derbys 65 P8
Stanton Gloucs 42 C5
Stanton Mons 40 D6
Stanton Nthumb 109 J11
Stanton Staffs 65 L3
Stanton Suffk 58 E6
Stanton by Bridge Derbys 66 C6
Stanton by Dale Derbys 66 D4
Stanton Drew BaNES 29 J9
Stanton Fitzwarren Swindn 30 E4
Stanton Harcourt Oxon 43 J10
Stanton Hill Notts 78 D10
Stanton in Peak Derbys 77 N11
Stanton Lacy Shrops 51 N5
Stanton Lees Derbys 77 N11
Stanton Long Shrops 51 L7
Stanton-on-the-Wolds Notts 66 G6
Stanton Prior BaNES 29 K10
Stanton St Bernard Wilts 30 C10
Stanton St John Oxon 43 M10
Stanton St Quintin Wilts 29 P6
Stanton Street Suffk 58 D7
Stanton under Bardon Leics 66 D10
Stanton upon Hine Heath Shrops 63 P7
Stanton Wick BaNES 29 J10
Stantway Gloucs 41 L9
Stanwardine in the Field Shrops 63 L7
Stanwardine in the Wood Shrops 63 M6
Stanway Gloucs 42 C5
Stanway Essex 46 G6
Stanway Green Essex 46 G7
Stanway Green Suffk 59 K6
Stanwell Surrey 32 F7
Stanwell Moor Surrey 32 F7
Stanwick Nhants 55 N6
Stanwick St John N York 91 K4
Stanwix Cumb 98 E6
Staoinebrig W Isls 152 b10
Stape N York 92 G8
Stapehill Dorset 11 P5
Stapeley Ches E 64 C2
Stapenhill Staffs 65 N8
Staple Kent 35 N11
Staple Cross Devon 20 G9
Staplecross E Susx 16 D6
Staplefield W Susx 15 K5
Staple Fitzpaine Somset 21 L9
Stapleford Cambs 57 J10
Stapleford Herts 45 K8
Stapleford Leics 67 K8
Stapleford Lincs 79 L12
Stapleford Notts 66 D5
Stapleford Wilts 23 N6
Stapleford Abbotts Essex 33 P3
Stapleford Tawney Essex 33 P2
Staplegrove Somset 21 K8
Staplehay Somset 21 K9
Staplehurst Kent 16 C2
Staplers IoW 13 H7
Staplestreet Kent 35 J10
Stapleton Cumb 98 G4
Stapleton Leics 54 C1
Stapleton N Som 28 H7
Stapleton Shrops 63 M11
Stapleton Somset 21 P9
Stapley Somset 21 K10
Staploe Bed 56 C8
Staplow Herefs 41 R4
Star Fife 124 F12
Star IoA 72 H9
Star Pembks 37 P3
Star Somset 28 E10
Starbeck N York 85 L4
Starbotton N York 90 F11
Starcross Devon 9 J8
Stareton Warwks 53 Q6
Starkholmes Derbys 77 P12
Starlings Green Essex 45 N5
Starr's Green E Susx 16 D7
Starston Norfk 59 J4
Start Devon 5 N8
Startforth Dur 91 J4
Startley Wilts 29 Q5
Statenborough Kent 35 P11
Statham Warrtn 76 D6
Stathe Somset 21 N7
Stathern Leics 67 J6
Station Town Dur 101 K11
Staughton Green Cambs 56 C7
Staughton Highway Cambs 56 C8
Staunton Gloucs 40 H9
Staunton Gloucs 41 M6
Staunton in the Vale Notts 67 K3
Staunton on Arrow Herefs 51 L8
Staunton on Wye Herefs 40 F3
Staveley Cumb 89 M5
Staveley Derbys 78 D8
Staveley N York 85 M3
Staveley-in-Cartmel Cumb 89 J8
Staverton Devon 5 N4
Staverton Gloucs 41 P7
Staverton Nhants 54 D8
Staverton Wilts 29 N10
Staverton Bridge Gloucs 41 P7
Stawell Somset 21 N6
Stawley Somset 20 H9
Staxigoe Highld 151 Q6
Staxton N York 93 J11
Staylittle Cerdgn 49 L10
Staylittle Powys 50 B3
Staynall Lancs 83 J6
Staythorpe Notts 79 K12
Stead N York 85 J5
Stean N York 90 H12
Stearsby N York 92 D11
Stebbing Essex 46 B6
Stebbing Green Essex 46 B6
Stechford Birm 53 M3
Stedham W Susx 25 N6
Steel Nthumb 99 Q6
Steel Cross E Susx 15 P3
Steelend Fife 115 J4
Steele Road Border 107 N11
Steel Green Cumb 88 G11
Steel Heath Shrops 63 P5
Steen's Bridge Herefs 51 P9
Steep Hants 25 M8
Steephill IoW 13 J9

Steep Lane Calder 84 F10
Steeple Dorset 11 L8
Steeple Essex 46 G11
Steeple Ashton Wilts 29 N11
Steeple Aston Oxon 43 K6
Steeple Barton Oxon 43 K7
Steeple Bumpstead Essex 46 B3
Steeple Claydon Bucks 43 P6
Steeple Gidding Cambs 56 C4
Steeple Langford Wilts 23 M6
Steeple Morden Cambs 45 K3
Steep Marsh Hants 25 N8
Steeton C Brad 84 F6
Stein Highld 134 E4
Stella Gatesd 100 F5
Stelling Minnis Kent 17 L1
Stembridge Somset 21 P9
Stenalees Cnwll 3 Q3
Stenhouse D & G 105 P11
Stenhousemuir Falk 114 F5
Stenigot Lincs 80 E7
Stenscholl Highld 134 H2
Stenson Fields Derbys 65 Q6
Stenton E Loth 116 E6
Steornabhagh W Isls 152 g3
Stepaside Pembks 37 M9
Stepford D & G 96 G2
Stepney Gt Lon 33 L6
Stepping Hill Stockp 76 G6
Steppingley C Beds 44 E4
Stepps N Lans 114 B7
Sternfield Suffk 59 M8
Stert Wilts 30 B10
Stetchworth Cambs 57 M9
Stevenage Herts 45 K6
Stevenston N Ayrs 104 E1
Steventon Hants 25 J3
Steventon Oxon 31 K4
Steventon End Essex 45 Q4
Stevington Bed 55 N10
Stewartby Bed 55 N11
Stewartfield S Lans 114 B10
Stewarton Ag & B 103 J6
Stewarton E Ayrs 113 N12
Stewkley Bucks 44 B6
Stewley Somset 21 M9
Steyne Cross IoW 13 L8
Steyning W Susx 14 H8
Steynton Pembks 36 H9
Stibb Cnwll 7 J4
Stibbard Norfk 70 D7
Stibb Cross Devon 18 H10
Stibb Green Wilts 30 F10
Stibbington Cambs 56 B11
Stichill Border 108 B2
Sticker Cnwll 3 N4
Stickford Lincs 80 G11
Sticklepath Devon 8 C5
Sticklepath Somset 20 G9
Stickling Green Essex 45 N5
Stickney Lincs 80 G12
Stiffkey Norfk 70 E4
Stifford's Bridge Herefs 52 D11
Stileway Somset 21 P5
Stillingfleet N York 86 B6
Stillington N York 86 C2
Stillington S on T 91 P2
Stilton Cambs 56 C3
Stinchcombe Gloucs 29 L3
Stinsford Dorset 10 H6
Stiperstones Shrops 63 L12
Stirchley Birm 53 L4
Stirchley Wrekin 64 C10
Stirling Abers 141 Q7
Stirling Stirlg 114 E7
Stirling Castle Stirlg 114 E7
Stirling Services Stirlg 114 F7
Stirtloe Cambs 56 D7
Stirton N York 84 E4
Stisted Essex 46 D7
Stitchcombe Wilts 30 E8
Stithians Cnwll 2 H7
Stixwould Lincs 80 D10
Stoak Ches W 75 M9
Stobo Border 106 C2
Stoborough Dorset 11 M7
Stoborough Green Dorset 11 M7
Stobs Castle Border 107 N8
Stobswood Nthumb 109 L10
Stock Essex 34 B3
Stock N Som 28 F10
Stockbridge Hants 24 E7
Stockbridge W Susx 13 Q4
Stockbriggs S Lans 105 P6
Stockbury Kent 34 E10
Stockcross W Berk 31 J8
Stockdalewath Cumb 98 E9
Stocker's Head Kent 34 G12
Stockerston Leics 55 L1
Stock Green Worcs 53 J9
Stocking Herefs 41 J5
Stockingford Warwks 53 Q3
Stocking Pelham Herts 45 M6
Stockland Devon 9 N4
Stockland Bristol Somset 21 K4
Stockland Green Kent 15 Q2
Stockleigh English Devon 8 H4
Stockleigh Pomeroy Devon 8 H4
Stockley Wilts 30 A9
Stockley Hill Herefs 40 E4
Stocklinch Somset 21 N10
Stockmoor Herefs 51 L8
Stockport Stockp 76 G5
Stocksbridge Sheff 77 N3
Stocksfield Nthumb 100 D6
Stockton Herefs 51 N8
Stockton Norfk 59 N2
Stockton Shrops 51 M2
Stockton Shrops 64 D12
Stockton Warwks 54 D8
Stockton Wilts 23 L6
Stockton Wrekin 64 D9
Stockton Brook Staffs 64 H2
Stockton Heath Warrtn 75 Q6
Stockton-on-Tees S on T 91 Q4
Stockton on Teme Worcs 52 D7
Stockton on the Forest C York 86 C4
Stockwell End Wolves 64 G12
Stockwell Heath Staffs 65 K8
Stockwood Bristl 29 K8
Stock Wood Worcs 53 J9
Stodday Lancs 83 K3
Stodmarsh Kent 35 M10
Stody Norfk 70 F5
Stoer Highld 148 B10
Stoford Somset 22 D10
Stoford Wilts 23 N6
Stogumber Somset 20 H6
Stogursey Somset 21 K4
Stoke Covtry 54 B5
Stoke Devon 18 E8
Stoke Hants 13 M4
Stoke Hants 24 H2
Stoke Medway 34 E7

Stoke Abbott Dorset 10 C5
Stoke Albany Nhants 55 K3
Stoke Ash Suffk 58 G6
Stoke Bardolph Notts 66 G3
Stoke Bliss Worcs 52 C8
Stoke Bruerne Nhants 54 H11
Stoke-by-Clare Suffk 46 D3
Stoke-by-Nayland Suffk 46 H4
Stoke Canon Devon 8 H5
Stoke Charity Hants 24 H5
Stoke Climsland Cnwll 7 L10
Stoke Cross Herefs 52 B10
Stoke D'Abernon Surrey 32 G10
Stoke Doyle Nhants 55 P3
Stoke Dry Rutlnd 55 L1
Stoke Edith Herefs 41 J3
Stoke Farthing Wilts 23 N8
Stoke Ferry Norfk 69 N12
Stoke Fleming Devon 5 P7
Stokeford Dorset 11 K7
Stoke Gabriel Devon 5 P5
Stoke Gifford S Glos 29 J7
Stoke Golding Leics 54 B3
Stoke Goldington M Keyn 55 L11
Stoke Green Bucks 32 D6
Stokeham Notts 79 K8
Stoke Hammond Bucks 44 B9
Stoke Heath Shrops 64 C6
Stoke Heath Worcs 52 H7
Stoke Holy Cross Norfk 71 J11
Stokeinteignhead Devon 6 B12
Stoke Lacy Herefs 52 B10
Stoke Lyne Oxon 43 M6
Stoke Mandeville Bucks 44 B9
Stokenchurch Bucks 31 Q3
Stoke Newington Gt Lon 33 L5
Stokenham Devon 5 N8
Stoke-on-Trent C Stke 64 G3
Stoke Orchard Gloucs 41 Q6
Stoke Poges Bucks 32 D6
Stoke Pound Worcs 52 H7
Stoke Prior Herefs 51 N9
Stoke Prior Worcs 52 H7
Stoke Rivers Devon 19 N6
Stoke Rochford Lincs 67 M7
Stoke Row Oxon 31 N6
Stoke St Gregory Somset 21 M8
Stoke St Mary Somset 21 L9
Stoke St Michael Somset 22 F4
Stoke St Milborough Shrops 51 P4
Stokesay Shrops 51 M4
Stokesby Norfk 71 N10
Stokesley N York 92 B5
Stoke sub Hamdon Somset 21 Q10
Stoke Talmage Oxon 31 P2
Stoke Trister Somset 22 G7
Stoke-upon-Tern Shrops 64 C7
Stoke Wake Dorset 10 G4
Stoke Wharf Worcs 52 H7
Stolford Somset 21 K4
Stondon Massey Essex 33 Q2
Stone Bucks 43 R9
Stone Gloucs 29 K3
Stone Kent 33 P7
Stone Rothm 78 F6
Stone Somset 22 D6
Stone Staffs 64 G5
Stone Worcs 52 F5
Stonea Cambs 57 K1
Stone Allerton Somset 21 N3
Ston Easton Somset 22 E3
Stonebridge N Som 28 E10
Stonebridge Norfk 58 D2
Stonebridge Warwks 53 N4
Stone Bridge Corner C Pete 68 E12
Stonebroom Derbys 78 C11
Stone Chair Calder 84 H9
Stone Cross E Susx 15 P5
Stone Cross E Susx 15 R10
Stone Cross Kent 16 B4
Stone Cross Kent 17 P3
Stone Cross Kent 35 P11
Stonecross Green Suffk 58 B9
Stonecrouch Kent 16 C4
Stone-edge-Batch N Som 28 G8
Stoneferry C KuH 87 L9
Stonefield Castle Hotel Ag & B 112 C7
Stonegate E Susx 16 C5
Stonegate N York 92 F5
Stonegrave N York 92 D10
Stonehall Worcs 52 H11
Stonehaugh Nthumb 99 M3
Stonehaven Abers 133 L7
Stonehenge Wilts 23 P5
Stone Hill Donc 78 H2
Stonehouse C Plym 4 G6
Stonehouse Gloucs 41 N10
Stonehouse S Lans 114 D12
Stone in Oxney Kent 16 G5
Stoneleigh Warwks 53 Q6
Stoneley Green Ches E 63 Q2
Stonely Cambs 56 C7
Stoner Hill Hants 25 M8
Stonesby Leics 67 K7
Stonesfield Oxon 43 J8
Stones Green Essex 47 L6
Stone Street Kent 33 Q11
Stone Street Suffk 46 H3
Stone Street Suffk 59 N4
Stonestreet Green Kent 17 J3
Stonethwaite Cumb 88 H4
Stonewells Moray 139 P3
Stonewood Kent 33 P7
Stoneybridge W Isls 152 b10
Stoneyburn W Loth 114 H8
Stoney Cross Hants 12 E3
Stoneygate C Leic 66 G11
Stoneyhills Essex 34 G3
Stoneykirk D & G 94 G7
Stoney Middleton Derbys 77 N8
Stoney Stanton Leics 54 D2
Stoney Stoke Somset 22 G6
Stoney Stratton Somset 22 F6
Stoney Stretton Shrops 63 L11
Stoneywood C Aber 133 L2
Stonham Aspal Suffk 58 H8
Stonnall Staffs 65 K11
Stonor Oxon 31 N5
Stonton Wyville Leics 55 J2
Stonybreck Shet 147 h10
Stony Cross Herefs 51 P7
Stony Cross Herefs 52 C10
Stony Houghton Derbys 78 E10
Stony Stratford M Keyn 43 R4
Stonywell Staffs 65 K9
Stoodleigh Devon 19 M9
Stoodleigh Devon 19 N6
Stop 24 Services Kent 17 K3
Stopham W Susx 14 E7
Stopsley Luton 44 F7
Stoptide Cnwll 6 D9
Storeton Wirral 75 J7
Storeyard Green Herefs 41 L3

Storey Arms Powys ... 39 M7
Stornoway W Isls ... 152 g3
Stornoway Airport W Isls ... 152 g3
Storridge Herefs ... 52 D11
Storrington W Susx ... 14 F8
Storth Cumb ... 89 M10
Storwood E R Yk ... 86 D6
Stotfield Moray ... 147 M11
Stotfold C Beds ... 52 J4
Stottesdon Shrops ... 66 G11
Stoughton Leics ... 66 G11
Stoughton Surrey ... 32 D12
Stoughton W Susx ... 13 P2
Stoulton Worcs ... 52 G10
Stourbridge Dudley ... 52 G4
Stourhead Wilts ... 22 H6
Stourpaine Dorset ... 11 L3
Stourport-on-Severn Worcs ... 52 E6
Stour Provost Dorset ... 22 H9
Stour Row Dorset ... 22 H9
Stourton Leeds ... 85 L9
Stourton Staffs ... 52 F4
Stourton Warwks ... 22 H6
Stourton Wilts ... 22 H6
Stourton Caundle Dorset ... 21 P7
Stout Somset ... 21 P7
Stove Shet ... 147 i9
Stoven Suffk ... 59 N4
Stow Border ... 116 B12
Stow Lincs ... 79 L7
Stow Bardolph Norfk ... 69 M11
Stow Bedon Norfk ... 58 E1
Stowbridge Norfk ... 69 L10
Stow-cum-Quy Cambs ... 57 K8
Stowe Gloucs ... 40 H10
Stowe Shrops ... 51 K6
Stowe-by-Chartley Staffs ... 65 J7
Stowehill Nhants ... 54 G9
Stowell Somset ... 29 J10
Stowey BaNES ... 7 N5
Stowford Devon ... 7 N5
Stowford Devon ... 8 C9
Stowford Devon ... 9 L7
Stowford Devon ... 19 M5
Stowlangtoft Suffk ... 58 E7
Stow Longa Cambs ... 56 E6
Stow Maries Essex ... 34 E2
Stowmarket Suffk ... 58 F9
Stow-on-the-Wold Gloucs ... 42 E6
Stowting Kent ... 17 K2
Stowting Common Kent ... 17 K2
Stowupland Suffk ... 58 G8
Straad Ag & B ... 112 F9
Straanruie Highld ... 139 J1
Strachan Abers ... 132 G6
Strachur Ag & B ... 112 G1
Stradbroke Suffk ... 59 J6
Stradbrook Wilts ...
Stradishall Suffk ... 57 P10
Stradsett Norfk ... 69 M11
Stragglethorpe Lincs ... 67 M2
Stragglethorpe Notts ... 66 G5
Straight Soley Wilts ... 30 G8
Straiton Mdloth ... 115 N8
Straiton S Ayrs ... 104 G8
Straloch Abers ... 141 L11
Straloch P & K ... 131 J11
Stramshall Staffs ... 65 K5
Strang IoM ... 102 e6
Strangeways Salfd ... 76 F4
Strangford Herefs ... 41 J6
Stranraer D & G ... 94 F6
Strata Florida Cerdgn ... 49 N7
Stratfield Mortimer W Berk ... 31 N9
Stratfield Saye Hants ... 31 P10
Stratfield Turgis Hants ... 31 P10
Stratford C Beds ... 56 D11
Stratford Gt Lon ... 33 M5
Stratford St Andrew Suffk ... 59 M8
Stratford St Mary Suffk ... 47 J5
Stratford sub Castle Wilts ... 23 P7
Stratford Tony Wilts ... 23 N8
Stratford-upon-Avon Warwks ... 53 M9
Strath Highld ... 143 L9
Strath Highld ... 144 D1
Strathan Highld ... 149 M4
Strathaven S Lans ... 114 C12
Strathblane Stirlg ... 113 Q5
Strathcanaird Highld ... 144 E3
Strathcarron Highld ... 136 C7
Strathcoil Ag & B ... 120 C7
Strathdon Abers ... 131 Q2
Strathkinness Fife ... 125 J9
Strathloanhead W Loth ... 114 G7
Strathmashie House Highld ... 129 Q6
Strathmiglo Fife ... 124 E11
Strathpeffer Highld ... 137 N4
Strathtay P & K ... 123 M2
Strathwhillan N Ayrs ... 103 Q3
Strathy Highld ... 150 E4
Strathy Inn Highld ... 150 E4
Strathyre Stirlg ... 122 F9
Stratton Cnwll ... 7 J3
Stratton Dorset ... 10 G6
Stratton Gloucs ... 42 B11
Stratton Audley Oxon ... 43 M6
Stratton-on-the-Fosse Somset ... 22 f3
Stratton St Margaret Swindn ... 30 E5
Stratton St Michael Norfk ... 59 J2
Stratton Strawless Norfk ... 71 J8
Stream Somset ... 20 G5
Streat E Susx ... 15 L8
Streatham Gt Lon ... 33 K8
Streatley C Beds ... 44 F6
Streatley W Berk ... 31 M6
Street Devon ... 9 M9
Street Lancs ... 83 M6
Street N York ... 92 E6
Street Somset ... 22 B6
Street Ashton Warwks ... 54 D4
Street Dinas Shrops ... 63 K6
Street End Kent ... 15 K6
Street End E Susx ...
Street End Kent ... 35 L11
Street End W Susx ... 13 P5
Street Gate Gatesd ... 100 G6
Streethay Staffs ... 65 L10
Street Houses N York ... 85 G6
Streetlam N York ... 91 M7
Street Lane Derbys ... 66 C3
Streetly Wsall ... 53 K1
Streetly End Cambs ... 57 L11
Street on the Fosse Somset ... 22 E5
Strefford Shrops ... 63 M3
Strelitz P & K ... 124 D5
Strelley Notts ... 66 E4
Strensall York ... 86 B3
Strensham Worcs ... 41 Q4
Strensham Services (northbound) Worcs ... 41 P3
Strensham Services (southbound) Worcs ... 41 P4
Stretcholt Somset ... 21 L4
Strete Devon ... 5 P7
Stretford Herefs ... 51 M9
Stretford Herefs ... 51 N9
Stretford Traffd ... 76 E5
Strethall Essex ... 45 L11

Stretham Cambs ... 57 K6
Strettington W Susx ... 14 Q9
Stretton Ches W ... 63 M2
Stretton Derbys ... 78 C11
Stretton Rutlnd ... 67 N9
Stretton Staffs ... 64 G10
Stretton Staffs ... 64 G10
Stretton Warrtn ... 76 B7
Stretton en le Field Leics ... 65 P10
Stretton Grandison Herefs ... 41 K3
Stretton-on-Dunsmore Warwks ... 54 C6
Stretton on Fosse Warwks ... 42 G4
Stretton Sugwas Herefs ... 40 G3
Stretton under Fosse Warwks ... 54 D4
Stretton Westwood Shrops ... 51 Q1
Strichen Abers ... 141 M5
Strines Stockp ... 76 H6
Stringston Somset ... 21 J5
Strixton Nhants ... 55 M8
Stroat Gloucs ... 28 H3
Strollamus Highld ... 135 K10
Stroma Highld ... 151 Q1
Stromeferry Highld ... 136 B9
Stromness Ork ... 147 b4
Stronaba Highld ... 128 H7
Stronachlachar Stirlg ... 122 C10
Stronafian Ag & B ... 112 F5
Stronchrubie Highld ... 144 G1
Strone Ag & B ... 113 J5
Strone Highld ... 128 G8
Strone Highld ... 137 P10
Stronmilchan Ag & B ... 121 M7
Stronsay Ork ... 147 e3
Stronsay Airport Ork ... 147 e3
Strontian Highld ... 127 P12
Strood Kent ... 16 E4
Strood Medway ... 34 C8
Strood Green Surrey ... 14 H1
Strood Green W Susx ... 14 E6
Stroud Gloucs ... 41 N10
Stroud Hants ... 25 M8
Stroude Surrey ... 32 E8
Stroud Green Essex ... 34 F4
Stroud Green Gloucs ... 41 N10
Stroxton Lincs ... 67 M6
Struan Highld ... 134 F8
Struan P & K ... 130 E11
Strubby Lincs ... 81 J7
Strumpshaw Norfk ... 71 M10
Strutherhill S Lans ... 114 D11
Struthers Fife ... 124 H11
Struy Highld ... 137 L8
Stryd-y-Facsen IoA ... 72 E7
Stryt-issa Wrexhm ... 63 J3
Stuartfield Abers ... 141 M7
Stubbers Green Wsall ... 65 K11
Stubbington Hants ... 13 J4
Stubbins Lancs ... 84 B11
Stubbs Cross Kent ... 16 H3
Stubbs Green Norfk ... 59 K1
Stubhampton Dorset ... 23 N10
Stubley Derbys ... 77 Q8
Stubshaw Cross Wigan ... 75 Q4
Stubton Lincs ... 67 L2
Stuckton Hants ... 23 Q10
Studfold N York ... 84 B1
Stud Green W & M ... 32 C7
Studham C Beds ... 44 E8
Studholme Cumb ... 98 B7
Studland Dorset ... 11 P8
Studley Warwks ... 53 K8
Studley Wilts ... 29 Q8
Studley Common Warwks ... 53 K8
Studley Roger N York ... 85 L1
Studley Royal N York ... 85 K1
Studley Royal Park & Fountains Abbey N York ... 85 K2
Stuntney Cambs ... 57 K5
Stunts Green E Susx ... 16 A8
Sturbridge Staffs ... 64 F6
Sturgate Lincs ... 79 L6
Sturmer Essex ... 46 C3
Sturminster Common Dorset ... 22 H11
Sturminster Marshall Dorset ... 11 M5
Sturminster Newton Dorset ... 22 H10
Sturry Kent ... 35 L10
Sturton N Linc ... 79 N3
Sturton by Stow Lincs ... 79 M7
Sturton le Steeple Notts ... 79 K7
Stuston Suffk ... 58 H5
Stutton N York ... 85 P7
Stutton Suffk ... 47 L5
Styal Ches E ... 76 F7
Stydd Lancs ... 83 P8
Stynie Moray ... 139 Q4
Styrrup Notts ... 78 H4
Succoth Ag & B ... 121 P11
Suckley Worcs ... 52 D10
Suckley Green Worcs ... 52 D10
Sudborough Nhants ... 55 N4
Sudbourne Suffk ... 59 N10
Sudbrook Lincs ... 67 N3
Sudbrook Mons ... 28 G5
Sudbrooke Lincs ... 79 P8
Sudbury Derbys ... 65 M6
Sudbury Gt Lon ... 32 H5
Sudbury Suffk ... 46 F3
Sudden Rochdl ... 76 G1
Sudgrove Gloucs ... 41 Q10
Suffield N York ... 93 K8
Suffield Norfk ... 71 J5
Sugdon Wrekin ... 63 Q9
Sugnall Staffs ... 64 E6
Sugwas Pool Herefs ... 40 G3
Suisnish Highld ... 127 K1
Sulby IoM ... 102 e3
Sulgrave Nhants ... 43 L3
Sulham W Berk ... 31 N7
Sulhamstead W Berk ... 31 N8
Sulhamstead Abbots W Berk ... 31 N9
Sulhamstead Bannister W Berk ... 31 N8
Sullington W Susx ... 14 F8
Sullom Shet ... 147 i5
Sullom Voe Shet ... 147 i5
Sully V Glam ... 27 Q8
Sumburgh Airport Shet ... 147 i10
Summerbridge N York ... 85 J3
Summercourt Cnwll ... 3 L4
Summerfield Norfk ... 69 P4
Summerfield Worcs ... 52 F6
Summer Heath Bucks ... 31 Q4
Summerhill Pembks ... 37 M9
Summerhill Staffs ... 65 K11
Summer Hill Wrexhm ... 63 K1
Summerhouse Darltn ... 91 K3
Summerlands Cumb ... 89 N8
Summerley Derbys ... 77 Q8
Summersdale W Susx ... 14 B9
Summerseat Bury ... 76 F1
Summertown Oxon ... 43 L10
Summit Oldham ... 76 H1
Summit Rochdl ... 84 E11
Sunbiggin Cumb ... 89 Q5
Sunbury-on-Thames Surrey ... 32 G8
Sundaywell D & G ... 96 G1

Sunderland Ag & B ... 110 F8
Sunderland Cumb ... 97 N11
Sunderland Lancs ... 83 K4
Sunderland Sundld ... 101 K7
Sunderland Bridge Dur ... 100 H10
Sundhope Border ... 107 J5
Sundon Park Luton ... 44 F6
Sundridge Kent ... 33 N11
Sunk Island E R Yk ... 87 P11
Sunningdale W & M ... 32 D9
Sunninghill W & M ... 32 D9
Sunningwell Oxon ... 31 K5
Sunniside Dur ... 100 F10
Sunniside Gatesd ... 100 G6
Sunny Brow Dur ... 100 F11
Sunnyhill C Derb ... 65 Q6
Sunnyhurst Bl w D ... 83 P10
Sunnylaw Stirlg ... 114 E2
Sunnymead Oxon ... 43 L9
Surbiton Gt Lon ... 32 H9
Surfleet Lincs ... 68 E6
Surfleet Seas End Lincs ... 68 E6
Surlingham Norfk ... 71 L11
Surrex Essex ... 46 F7
Sustead Norfk ... 71 J5
Susworth Lincs ... 79 L3
Sutcombe Devon ... 7 L2
Sutcombemill Devon ... 7 L3
Suton Norfk ... 70 G12
Sutterby Lincs ... 80 G9
Sutterton Lincs ... 68 E5
Sutton C Beds ... 45 J2
Sutton C Pete ... 68 B12
Sutton Cambs ... 56 H5
Sutton Devon ... 5 L8
Sutton Devon ... 8 D4
Sutton Donc ... 78 F1
Sutton E Susx ... 15 P11
Sutton Gt Lon ... 33 J9
Sutton Kent ... 35 P12
Sutton N York ... 85 P10
Sutton Norfk ... 71 M7
Sutton Notts ... 67 J5
Sutton Pembks ... 36 H7
Sutton Shrops ... 52 D3
Sutton Shrops ... 63 K7
Sutton Shrops ... 64 C6
Sutton St Hel ... 75 P5
Sutton Staffs ... 64 D8
Sutton Suffk ... 47 P2
Sutton W Susx ... 14 D8
Sutton Abinger Surrey ... 14 G2
Sutton-at-Hone Kent ... 33 Q8
Sutton Bassett Nhants ... 55 J3
Sutton Benger Wilts ... 29 Q6
Sutton Bingham Somset ... 10 H2
Sutton Bonington Notts ... 66 D8
Sutton Bridge Lincs ... 69 J8
Sutton Cheney Leics ... 66 C12
Sutton Coldfield Birm ... 53 L1
Sutton Courtenay Oxon ... 31 L3
Sutton Crosses Lincs ... 68 H8
Sutton cum Lound Notts ... 78 H7
Sutton Fields Notts ... 66 C7
Sutton Green Surrey ... 32 E11
Sutton Green Wrexhm ... 63 L3
Sutton Heath Suffk ... 59 L11
Sutton Howgrave N York ... 91 M11
Sutton-in-Ashfield Notts ... 78 E11
Sutton-in-Craven N York ... 84 F6
Sutton in the Elms Leics ... 54 E2
Sutton Lane Ends Ches E ... 76 H9
Sutton Maddock Shrops ... 64 D12
Sutton Mallet Somset ... 21 N6
Sutton Mandeville Wilts ... 23 L7
Sutton Manor St Hel ... 75 N5
Sutton Marsh Herefs ... 40 H3
Sutton Montis Somset ... 22 E8
Sutton-on-Hull C KuH ... 87 L8
Sutton on Sea Lincs ... 81 K7
Sutton-on-the-Forest N York ... 86 A2
Sutton on the Hill Derbys ... 65 N5
Sutton on Trent Notts ... 79 K10
Sutton Poyntz Dorset ... 10 H8
Sutton St Edmund Lincs ... 68 G9
Sutton St James Lincs ... 68 H8
Sutton St Nicholas Herefs ... 40 H3
Sutton Scotney Hants ... 24 H5
Sutton Street Kent ... 34 D10
Sutton-under-Brailes Warwks ... 42 G4
Sutton-under-Whitestonecliffe N York ... 91 Q10
Sutton upon Derwent E R Yk ... 86 D6
Sutton Valence Kent ... 16 E1
Sutton Veny Wilts ... 23 K5
Sutton Waldron Dorset ... 23 J8
Sutton Weaver Ches W ... 75 P9
Sutton Wick BaNES ... 29 Q9
Sutton Wick Oxon ... 31 K3
Swaby Lincs ... 80 G9
Swadlincote Derbys ... 65 P8
Swaffham Norfk ... 70 B10
Swaffham Bulbeck Cambs ... 57 L8
Swaffham Prior Cambs ... 57 L8
Swafield Norfk ... 71 K6
Swainby N York ... 91 Q6
Swainshill Herefs ... 40 G3
Swainsthorpe Norfk ... 71 J12
Swainswick BaNES ... 29 M8
Swalcliffe Oxon ... 42 H4
Swalecliffe Kent ... 35 J8
Swallow Lincs ... 80 D3
Swallow Beck Lincs ... 79 N10
Swallowcliffe Wilts ... 23 L8
Swallowfield Wokham ... 31 P9
Swallownest Rothm ... 78 D6
Swallows Cross Essex ... 33 R3
Swampton Hants ... 24 G3
Swanage Dorset ... 11 P9
Swanbourne Bucks ... 44 A6
Swanbridge V Glam ... 27 Q8
Swancote Shrops ... 52 D2
Swanland E R Yk ... 87 J9
Swanley Kent ... 33 P9
Swanley Village Kent ... 33 P8
Swanmore Hants ... 25 K10
Swannington Leics ... 66 D9
Swannington Norfk ... 70 H9
Swanpool Lincs ... 79 N10
Swanscombe Kent ... 33 R7
Swansea Swansea ... 26 G4
Swansea Airport Swans ... 26 E4
Swansea West Services Swans ... 26 F2
Swan Green Ches W ... 76 D9
Swanton Abbot Norfk ... 71 K7
Swanton Morley Norfk ... 70 F8
Swanton Novers Norfk ... 70 F6
Swanton Street Kent ... 34 F10
Swan Valley Nhants ... 54 F9
Swan Village Sandw ... 53 J2
Swanwick Derbys ... 66 C2
Swanwick Hants ... 13 J4
Swarby Lincs ... 67 N4
Swardeston Norfk ... 71 J11
Swarkestone Derbys ... 66 B7
Swarland Nthumb ... 109 K9

Swarraton Hants ... 25 J6
Swartha C Brad ... 84 F6
Swarthmoor Cumb ... 88 H10
Swaton Lincs ... 68 C5
Swavesey Cambs ... 56 G7
Sway Hants ... 12 D5
Swayfield Lincs ... 67 N7
Swaythling C Sotn ... 24 G10
Sweet Green Worcs ... 52 C8
Sweetham Devon ... 8 G5
Sweethaws E Susx ... 15 P5
Sweetlands Corner Kent ... 16 D2
Sweets Cnwll ... 6 H5
Sweetshouse Cnwll ... 3 Q2
Swefling Suffk ... 59 L8
Swepstone Leics ... 66 B10
Swerford Oxon ... 42 H5
Swettenham Ches E ... 76 E10
Swffryd Blae G ... 28 B3
Swift's Green Kent ... 16 F2
Swilland Suffk ... 59 J10
Swillbrook Lancs ... 83 L8
Swillington Leeds ... 85 M9
Swimbridge Devon ... 19 M7
Swimbridge Newland Devon ... 19 L7
Swinbrook Oxon ... 42 G9
Swincliffe Kirk ... 85 J5
Swincliffe N York ... 85 K4
Swincombe Devon ... 19 N5
Swinderby Lincs ... 79 L11
Swindon Gloucs ... 41 Q7
Swindon Nthumb ... 108 F10
Swindon Staffs ... 52 F3
Swindon Swindn ... 30 D5
Swine E R Yk ... 87 L8
Swinefleet E R Yk ... 86 E10
Swineford S Glos ... 29 L8
Swineshead Bed ... 55 b13
Swineshead Lincs ... 68 E4
Swineshead Bridge Lincs ... 68 E4
Swiney Highld ... 151 M9
Swinford Leics ... 54 C9
Swinford Oxon ... 43 J10
Swingfield Minnis Kent ... 17 M2
Swingfield Street Kent ... 17 M2
Swingleton Green Suffk ... 46 G2
Swinhoe Nthumb ... 109 K4
Swinhope Lincs ... 80 E4
Swinithwaite N York ... 90 H7
Swinmore Common Herefs ... 41 K3
Swinscoe Staffs ... 65 L3
Swinside Cumb ... 88 H2
Swinstead Lincs ... 67 P7
Swinthorpe Lincs ... 79 Q7
Swinton Border ... 117 J11
Swinton N York ... 91 L10
Swinton N York ... 92 F12
Swinton Rothm ... 78 D4
Swinton Salfd ... 76 E3
Swiss Valley Carmth ... 38 D11
Swithland Leics ... 66 F10
Swordale Highld ... 137 Q3
Swordland Highld ... 127 N6
Swordly Highld ... 150 D4
Sworton Heath Ches E ... 76 C7
Swyddffynnon Cerdgn ... 49 M7
Swyncombe Oxon ... 31 P4
Swynnerton Staffs ... 64 F5
Swyre Dorset ... 10 E7
Sycharth Powys ... 62 H7
Sychnant Powys ... 50 D12
Sychtyn Powys ... 62 D10
Syde Gloucs ... 41 Q9
Sydenham Gt Lon ... 33 L8
Sydenham Oxon ... 43 Q10
Sydenham Damerel Devon ... 7 M9
Sydenhurst Surrey ... 14 D4
Syderstone Norfk ... 70 B6
Sydling St Nicholas Dorset ... 10 F5
Sydmonton Hants ... 31 K10
Sydnal Lane Shrops ... 64 E11
Syerston Notts ... 67 J3
Syke Rochdl ... 84 D12
Sykehouse Donc ... 86 B11
Syleham Suffk ... 59 J5
Sylen Carmth ... 38 D10
Symbister Shet ... 147 j6
Symington S Ayrs ... 104 G3
Symington S Lans ... 106 C3
Symondsbury Dorset ... 10 C6
Symonds Yat (East) Herefs ... 40 H8
Symonds Yat (West) Herefs ... 40 H8
Sympson Green C Brad ... 85 J7
Synderford Dorset ... 10 B4
Synod Inn Cerdgn ... 48 F9
Syre Highld ... 150 G5
Syreford Gloucs ... 42 B7
Syresham Nhants ... 43 M3
Syston Leics ... 66 G10
Syston Lincs ... 67 M4
Sytchampton Worcs ... 52 F8
Sywell Nhants ... 55 K7

T

Tabley Hill Ches E ... 76 D8
Tackley Oxon ... 43 K7
Tacolneston Norfk ... 58 H2
Tadcaster N York ... 85 P6
Taddington Derbys ... 77 L9
Taddington Gloucs ... 42 C5
Taddiport Devon ... 19 J9
Tadley Hants ... 31 M10
Tadlow Cambs ... 56 F11
Tadmarton Oxon ... 42 H4
Tadpole Swindn ... 30 C5
Tadwick BaNES ... 29 L8
Tadworth Surrey ... 33 J11
Tafarnaubach Blae G ... 39 Q9
Tafarn-y-bwlch Pembks ... 37 L4
Tafarn-y-Gelyn Denbgs ... 74 G11
Taff's Well Rhondd ... 27 Q6
Tafolwern Powys ... 62 B11
Taibach Neath ... 27 J6
Tain Highld ... 146 D8
Tain Highld ... 151 N3
Tai'r Bull Powys ... 39 N6
Tairgwaith Neath ... 38 H4
Takeley Essex ... 45 Q7
Takeley Street Essex ... 45 Q7
Talachddu Powys ... 39 N5
Talacre Flints ... 74 G7
Talaton Devon ... 9 K6
Talbenny Pembks ... 36 G8
Talbot Green Rhondd ... 27 N7
Talbot Village BCP ... 11 P6
Taleford Devon ... 9 L5
Talerddig Powys ... 62 C12
Talgarreg Cerdgn ... 48 G10
Talgarth Powys ... 39 N4
Talisker Highld ... 134 F10
Talke Staffs ... 64 F2
Talke Pits Staffs ... 64 F2
Talkin Cumb ... 98 F6
Talladale Highld ... 143 N11
Talla Linnfoots Border ... 106 F6
Tallaminnoch S Ayrs ... 104 G10
Tallarn Green Wrexhm ... 63 M3
Tallentire Cumb ... 97 M11
Talley Carmth ... 38 F5
Tallington Lincs ... 68 B10
Tallwrn Wrexhm ... 63 J3
Talog Carmth ... 37 Q5
Talsarn Cerdgn ... 49 J9
Talsarnau Gwynd ... 61 K5
Talskiddy Cnwll ... 6 C11
Talwrn IoA ... 72 H8
Talwrn Wrexhm ... 63 L3
Tal-y-bont Cerdgn ... 49 L3
Talybont-on-Usk Powys ... 39 Q7
Tal-y-bont Conwy ... 73 N10
Tal-y-bont Gwynd ... 61 K8
Tal-y-bont Gwynd ... 73 K9
Tal-y-Cafn Conwy ... 73 N9
Tal-y-coed Mons ... 40 F8
Tal-y-garn Rhondd ... 27 N6
Tal-y-llyn Gwynd ... 61 M10
Talysarn Gwynd ... 60 H2
Tal-y-Waun Torfn ... 40 C10
Talywern Powys ... 61 P12
Tamer Lane End Wigan ... 76 B3
Tamerton Foliot C Plym ... 4 E4
Tamworth Staffs ... 65 N11
Tamworth Services Warwks ... 65 N12
Tancred N York ... 85 P3
Tancredston Pembks ... 36 G5
Tandridge Surrey ... 33 L12
Tanfield Dur ... 100 F7
Tanfield Lea Dur ... 100 F7
Tangasdale W Isls ... 152 b13
Tangiers Pembks ... 37 J7
Tangley Hants ... 24 C3
Tangmere W Susx ... 14 C9
Tan Hill N York ... 90 E5
Tankerness Ork ... 147 d4
Tankersley Barns ... 77 Q4
Tankerton Kent ... 35 K9
Tannach Highld ... 151 P7
Tannachie Abers ... 133 J7
Tannadice Angus ... 125 J1
Tanner's Green Worcs ... 53 K6
Tannington Suffk ... 59 K7
Tannochside N Lans ... 114 C9
Tansley Derbys ... 77 Q11
Tansor Nhants ... 55 Q2
Tantobie Dur ... 100 F7
Tanton N York ... 92 B5
Tanwood Worcs ... 52 G6
Tanworth in Arden Warwks ... 53 L6
Tan-y-Bwlch Gwynd ... 61 L4
Tan-y-fron Wrexhm ... 63 J2
Tan-y-grisiau Gwynd ... 61 M3
Tan-y-groes Cerdgn ... 48 D10
Taobh Tuath W Isls ... 152 d6
Taplow Bucks ... 32 C6
Tarbert Ag & B ... 111 P11
Tarbert Ag & B ... 112 C7
Tarbert W Isls ... 152 e5
Tarbet Ag & B ... 121 Q12
Tarbet Highld ... 127 N6
Tarbet Highld ... 148 E7
Tarbock Green Knows ... 75 M6
Tarbolton S Ayrs ... 104 H4
Tarbrax S Lans ... 115 J10
Tardebigge Worcs ... 53 J7
Tarfside Angus ... 132 D8
Tarland Abers ... 132 D3
Tarleton Lancs ... 83 K11
Tarlscough Lancs ... 83 K12
Tarlton Gloucs ... 29 Q2
Tarnock Somset ... 21 M3
Tarns Cumb ... 97 M8
Tarnside Cumb ... 89 L8
Tarporley Ches W ... 75 P11
Tarr Somset ... 20 G7
Tarrant Crawford Dorset ... 11 M4
Tarrant Gunville Dorset ... 23 M10
Tarrant Hinton Dorset ... 11 M2
Tarrant Keyneston Dorset ... 11 M4
Tarrant Launceston Dorset ... 11 M3
Tarrant Monkton Dorset ... 11 M3
Tarrant Rawston Dorset ... 11 M3
Tarrant Rushton Dorset ... 11 M4
Tarring Neville E Susx ... 15 N10
Tarrington Herefs ... 41 K3
Tarves Abers ... 141 L9
Tarvin Ches W ... 75 N10
Tarvin Sands Ches W ... 75 N10
Tasburgh Norfk ... 59 J2
Tasley Shrops ... 52 C2
Taston Oxon ... 42 H7
Tatenhill Staffs ... 65 N7
Tathall End M Keyn ... 44 B2
Tathwell Lincs ... 80 G6
Tatsfield Surrey ... 33 M11
Tattenhall Ches W ... 75 N12
Tatterford Norfk ... 70 C6
Tattersett Norfk ... 70 C6
Tattershall Lincs ... 80 D12
Tattershall Bridge Lincs ... 80 D11
Tattershall Thorpe Lincs ... 80 D11
Tattingstone Suffk ... 47 K4
Tattingstone White Horse Suffk ... 47 L4
Tatton Park Ches E ... 76 D7
Tatworth Somset ... 9 Q4
Tauchers Moray ... 140 B6
Taunton Somset ... 21 K9
Taunton Deane Services Somset ... 21 K9
Taverham Norfk ... 70 H9
Taverners Green Essex ... 45 Q8
Tavernspite Pembks ... 37 M8
Tavistock Devon ... 7 N10
Taw Green Devon ... 8 F6
Tawstock Devon ... 19 K8
Taxal Derbys ... 77 J8
Taychreggan Hotel Ag & B ... 121 K8
Tay Forest Park P & K ... 130 E12
Tayinloan Ag & B ... 111 P12
Taynish Ag & B ...
Taynton Gloucs ... 41 M7
Taynton Oxon ... 42 F9
Taynuilt Ag & B ... 121 J6
Tayock Angus ... 125 L2
Tayport Fife ... 125 K8
Tayvallich Ag & B ... 111 Q4
Tealby Lincs ... 80 D5
Tealing Angus ... 125 J4
Team Valley Gatesd ... 100 G6
Teangue Highld ... 127 M2
Teanord Highld ... 137 Q3
Tebay Cumb ... 89 P5
Tebay Services Cumb ... 89 P5
Tebworth C Beds ... 44 D6
Tedburn St Mary Devon ... 8 F6
Teddington Gloucs ... 41 Q5
Teddington Gt Lon ... 32 H8
Tedstone Delamere Herefs ... 52 C9

Tedstone Wafer Herefs ... 52 C9
Teesport R & Cl ... 92 C2
Teesside Park S on T ... 91 Q3
Teeton Nhants ... 54 H6
Teffont Evias Wilts ... 23 L7
Teffont Magna Wilts ... 23 L7
Tegryn Pembks ... 37 P4
Teigh Rutlnd ... 67 L9
Teigncombe Devon ... 8 C7
Teigngrace Devon ... 8 H10
Teignmouth Devon ... 8 H10
Teindside Border ... 107 L8
Telford Wrekin ... 64 C10
Telford Services Shrops ... 64 D10
Telham E Susx ... 16 D8
Tellisford Somset ... 22 H2
Telscombe E Susx ... 15 M10
Telscombe Cliffs E Susx ... 15 M10
Tempar P & K ... 122 H1
Templand D & G ... 97 M2
Temple Cnwll ... 6 H10
Temple Mdloth ... 115 P9
Temple Balsall Solhll ... 53 N5
Temple Bar Cerdgn ... 49 J10
Temple Cloud BaNES ... 29 J10
Templecombe Somset ... 22 F9
Temple End Suffk ... 57 N2
Temple Ewell Kent ... 17 N2
Temple Grafton Warwks ... 53 L9
Temple Guiting Gloucs ... 42 C6
Temple Herdewyke Warwks ... 54 C10
Temple Hirst N York ... 86 B10
Temple Normanton Derbys ... 78 C10
Temple of Fiddes Abers ... 133 K8
Temple Sowerby Cumb ... 89 Q1
Templeton Devon ... 20 D10
Templeton Pembks ... 37 M8
Templetown Dur ... 100 E8
Tempsford C Beds ... 56 D10
Tenbury Wells Worcs ... 51 Q7
Tenby Pembks ... 37 M10
Tendring Essex ... 47 L6
Tendring Green Essex ... 47 L6
Tendring Heath Essex ... 47 L6
Ten Mile Bank Norfk ... 57 L1
Tenpenny Heath Essex ... 47 K7
Tenterden Kent ... 16 F4
Terling Essex ... 46 D8
Tern Wrekin ... 64 B9
Ternhill Shrops ... 64 B6
Terregles D & G ... 97 J3
Terrington N York ... 86 C1
Terrington St Clement Norfk ... 69 K8
Terrington St John Norfk ... 69 K9
Terry's Green Warwks ... 53 L6
Teston Kent ... 34 C11
Testwood Hants ... 24 D10
Tetbury Gloucs ... 29 P3
Tetbury Upton Gloucs ... 29 P3
Tetchill Shrops ... 63 L5
Tetcott Devon ... 7 L5
Tetford Lincs ... 80 F8
Tetney Lincs ... 80 F3
Tetney Lock Lincs ... 80 F3
Tetsworth Oxon ... 43 P11
Tettenhall Wolves ... 64 G12
Tettenhall Wood Wolves ... 64 G12
Teversal Notts ... 78 D11
Teversham Cambs ... 57 J9
Teviothead Border ... 107 L8
Tewel Abers ... 133 K7
Tewin Herts ... 45 K8
Tewin Wood Herts ... 45 K8
Tewkesbury Gloucs ... 41 P5
Teynham Kent ... 34 G9
Thackley C Brad ... 85 J7
Thackthwaite Cumb ... 88 F2
Thackthwaite Cumb ... 89 L2
Thainstone Abers ... 141 J12
Thakeham W Susx ... 14 G7
Thame Oxon ... 43 P10
Thames Ditton Surrey ... 32 H9
Thamesmead Gt Lon ... 33 N6
Thamesport Medway ... 34 F7
Thanington Kent ... 35 L11
Thankerton S Lans ... 106 C2
Tharston Norfk ... 59 J2
Thatcham W Berk ... 31 K9
Thatto Heath St Hel ... 75 N5
Thaxted Essex ... 45 R5
Theakston N York ... 91 M9
Thealby N Linc ... 86 G11
Theale Somset ... 21 P4
Theale W Berk ... 31 M8
Thearne E R Yk ... 87 K7
The Bank Ches E ... 76 F12
The Beeches Gloucs ... 42 B11
Theberton Suffk ... 59 N7
The Blythe Staffs ... 65 J6
The Bog Shrops ... 51 K3
The Bourne Worcs ... 52 H9
The Braes Highld ... 135 J10
The Bratch Staffs ... 52 F2
The Bridge Kent ... 33 Q7
The Broad Herefs ... 51 N8
The Broads ... 71 P10
The Brunt E Loth ... 116 F6
The Bryn Mons ... 40 D9
The Bungalow IoM ... 102 e4
The Burf Worcs ... 52 F7
The Camp Gloucs ... 41 Q9
The Chequer Wrexhm ... 63 N4
The City Bed ... 56 B9
The City Bucks ... 31 R3
The Common Oxon ... 42 G6
The Common Wilts ... 30 D5
The Common Wilts ... 24 B7
The Corner Kent ... 16 C2
The Cronk IoM ... 102 d3
Theddingworth Leics ... 54 G4
Theddlethorpe All Saints Lincs ... 81 J6
Theddlethorpe St Helen Lincs ... 81 J6
The Deep C KuH ... 87 L9
The Den N Ayrs ... 113 L11
The Forge Herefs ... 51 K9
The Forstal Kent ... 17 J3
The Fouralls Shrops ... 64 B6
The Green Cumb ... 88 G10
The Green Essex ... 46 C7
The Green N York ... 92 F5
The Grove Dur ... 100 E8
The Grove Worcs ... 41 P4
The Haven W Susx ... 14 F4
The Haw Gloucs ... 41 P6
The Headland Hartpl ... 101 M11
The Hendre Mons ... 40 F7
The Hill Cumb ... 88 G10
The Holt Wokham ... 31 Q7
The Hundred Herefs ... 51 N8
Thelbridge Cross Devon ... 19 R10
The Leacon Kent ... 16 H4
The Lee Bucks ... 44 C10
The Lhen IoM ... 102 e2
Thelnetham Suffk ... 58 F5
The Lochs Moray ... 139 P3
Thelveton Norfk ... 58 H4
Thelwall Warrtn ... 76 C6
The Marsh Shrops ... 51 K1
Themelthorpe Norfk ... 70 G7
The Middles Dur ... 100 G8
The Moor Kent ... 16 D6
The Mumbles Swans ... 26 F5

The Murray S Lans ... 114 B10
The Mythe Gloucs ... 41 P5
The Narth Mons ... 40 H10
The Neuk Abers ... 132 H5
Theobald's Green Wilts ... 30 B8
The Quarry Gloucs ... 41 L2
The Quarter Kent ... 16 E2
The Reddings Gloucs ... 41 P7
Therfield Herts ... 45 L4
The Rhôs Powys ... 40 A5
The Ross P & K ... 123 K8
The Sands Surrey ... 14 C2
The Shoe Wilts ... 29 N7
The Smithies Shrops ... 52 C1
The Spring Warwks ... 53 P6
The Square Torfn ... 28 C3
The Stair Kent ... 15 K5
The Stocks Kent ... 16 G5
The Strand Wilts ... 29 Q10
Thetford Norfk ... 58 C4
Thetford Forest Park ... 57 Q3
Thethwaite Cumb ... 98 D9
The Towans Cnwll ... 2 F5
The Vauld Herefs ... 51 P10
The Wyke Shrops ... 64 D10
Theydon Bois Essex ... 33 N2
Theydon Mount Essex ... 33 N2
Thicket Priory N York ... 86 C6
Thickwood Wilts ... 29 N8
Thimbleby Lincs ... 80 E8
Thimbleby N York ... 91 Q7
Thingwall Wirral ... 75 J7
Thirkleby N York ... 91 Q11
Thirlby N York ... 91 Q10
Thirlestane Border ... 116 D11
Thirn N York ... 91 L9
Thirsk N York ... 91 Q10
Thirtleby E R Yk ... 87 L7
Thistleton Lancs ... 83 K7
Thistleton Rutlnd ... 67 M8
Thistley Green Suffk ... 57 M5
Thixendale N York ... 86 F3
Thockrington Nthumb ... 99 Q2
Tholomas Drove Cambs ... 68 H11
Tholthorpe N York ... 85 P2
Thomas Chapel Pembks ... 37 L8
Thomas Close Cumb ... 98 E10
Thomastown Abers ... 140 E8
Thompson Norfk ... 58 D1
Thomshill Moray ... 139 M4
Thong Kent ... 34 B8
Thongsbridge Kirk ... 77 M2
Thoralby N York ... 90 G9
Thoresby Notts ... 78 G9
Thoresthorpe Lincs ... 81 J9
Thoresway Lincs ... 80 D4
Thorganby Lincs ... 80 D3
Thorganby N York ... 86 C7
Thorgill N York ... 92 F7
Thorington Suffk ... 59 N6
Thorington Street Suffk ... 46 H5
Thorlby N York ... 84 E5
Thorley Herts ... 45 N8
Thorley IoW ... 12 F7
Thorley Houses Herts ... 45 N7
Thorley Street IoW ... 12 F7
Thormanby N York ... 91 Q11
Thornaby-on-Tees S on T ... 91 Q3
Thornage Norfk ... 70 F5
Thornborough Bucks ... 43 Q5
Thornborough N York ... 91 M10
Thornbury C Brad ... 85 J8
Thornbury Devon ... 7 M3
Thornbury Herefs ... 51 Q9
Thornbury S Glos ... 29 J4
Thornby Cumb ... 98 C6
Thornby Nhants ... 54 H5
Thorncliff Staffs ... 77 J12
Thorncombe Dorset ... 10 B4
Thorncombe Street Surrey ... 14 E2
Thorncott Green C Beds ... 56 C11
Thorncross IoW ... 12 G8
Thorndon Suffk ... 58 H7
Thorndon Cross Devon ... 7 P6
Thorne Donc ... 78 H1
Thorne Coffin Somset ... 22 C10
Thornecroft Devon ... 5 N3
Thornehillhead Devon ... 18 H10
Thorner Leeds ... 85 L7
Thornes Staffs ... 65 K11
Thornes Wakefd ... 85 L11
Thorne St Margaret Somset ... 20 H9
Thorney Bucks ... 32 F5
Thorney C Pete ... 68 F11
Thorney Notts ... 79 L9
Thorney Somset ... 21 P8
Thorney Hill Hants ... 12 C5
Thorney Island W Susx ... 13 N4
Thorney Toll Cambs ... 68 H11
Thornfalcon Somset ... 21 K9
Thornford Dorset ... 22 E11
Thorngrafton Nthumb ... 99 M5
Thorngrove Somset ... 21 N7
Thorngumbald E R Yk ... 87 N10
Thornham Norfk ... 69 P3
Thornham Magna Suffk ... 58 G6
Thornham Parva Suffk ... 58 G6
Thornhaugh C Pete ... 67 Q12
Thornhill C Sotn ... 24 H10
Thornhill Caerph ... 27 P6
Thornhill Cumb ... 88 D8
Thornhill D & G ... 105 Q10
Thornhill Derbys ... 77 M7
Thornhill Kirk ... 85 K11
Thornhill Stirlg ... 114 B1
Thornhill Lees Kirk ... 85 K11
Thornholme E R Yk ... 87 L2
Thornicombe Dorset ... 11 L4
Thornington Nthumb ... 108 E10
Thornley Dur ... 100 E10
Thornley Dur ... 100 B11
Thornly Park Rens ... 113 N9
Thornliebank E Rens ... 113 Q9
Thorns Suffk ... 57 P9
Thornsett Derbys ... 77 J6
Thorns Green Ches E ... 76 E7
Thornthwaite Cumb ... 88 H2
Thornthwaite N York ... 85 J3
Thornton Angus ... 124 H3
Thornton Bucks ... 43 Q4
Thornton C Brad ... 84 G8
Thornton Fife ... 115 P1
Thornton Lancs ... 82 H7
Thornton Leics ... 66 D11
Thornton Lincs ... 80 E10
Thornton Middsb ... 91 Q4
Thornton Nthumb ... 117 L11
Thornton Pembks ... 36 H7
Thornton Sefton ... 75 K3
Thornton Curtis N Linc ... 87 K10
Thorntonhall S Lans ... 113 Q9
Thornton Heath Gt Lon ... 33 L9
Thornton Hough Wirral ... 75 L7
Thornton-in-Craven N York ... 84 D6
Thornton in Lonsdale N York ... 89 R12
Thornton-le-Beans N York ... 91 P8
Thornton-le-Clay N York ... 86 C2
Thornton-le-Dale N York ... 92 H9

Thornton le Moor Lincs ...79 P4
Thornton-le-Moor N York ...91 P9
Thornton-le-Moors Ches W ...75 M9
Thornton-le-Street N York ...91 P9
Thorntonloch E Loth ...116 G6
Thornton Rust N York ...90 F9
Thornton Steward N York ...90 F9
Thornton Watlass N York ...91 L9
Thornwood Common Essex ...45 N10
Thornydykes Border ...116 E13
Thornythwaite Cumb ...89 L2
Thoroton Notts ...67 J4
Thorp Arch Leeds ...85 N6
Thorpe Derbys ...65 M2
Thorpe E R Yk ...87 J6
Thorpe Lincs ...81 J7
Thorpe N York ...84 F3
Thorpe Norfk ...59 N1
Thorpe Notts ...67 J2
Thorpe Surrey ...32 E8
Thorpe Abbotts Norfk ...59 J5
Thorpe Acre Leics ...66 E8
Thorpe Arnold Leics ...67 K8
Thorpe Audlin Wakefd ...85 P12
Thorpe Bassett N York ...92 H12
Thorpe by Water Rutlnd ...55 M1
Thorpe Common Rothm ...78 C5
Thorpe Constantine Staffs ...65 N10
Thorpe End Norfk ...71 K10
Thorpe Green Essex ...47 L7
Thorpe Green Lancs ...83 N10
Thorpe Green Suffk ...58 D9
Thorpe Hesley Rothm ...78 B4
Thorpe in Balne Donc ...78 F2
Thorpe Langton Leics ...55 J2
Thorpe Larches Dur ...91 N3
Thorpe Lea Surrey ...32 E8
Thorpe le Fallows Lincs ...79 M7
Thorpe-le-Soken Essex ...47 L7
Thorpe le Street E R Yk ...86 F6
Thorpe Malsor Nhants ...55 L5
Thorpe Mandeville Nhants ...43 L3
Thorpe Market Norfk ...71 K5
Thorpe Marriot Norfk ...70 H9
Thorpe Morieux Suffk ...58 D10
Thorpeness Suffk ...59 P8
Thorpe on the Hill Leeds ...85 L10
Thorpe on the Hill Lincs ...79 M10
Thorpe Park Surrey ...32 E8
Thorpe St Andrew Norfk ...71 K10
Thorpe St Peter Lincs ...81 J11
Thorpe Salvin Rothm ...78 E7
Thorpe Satchville Leics ...67 J10
Thorpe Thewles S on T ...91 P2
Thorpe Tilney Lincs ...80 C12
Thorpe Underwood N York ...85 P3
Thorpe Underwood Nhants ...55 K4
Thorpe Waterville Nhants ...55 P4
Thorpe Willoughby N York ...86 A9
Thorpland Norfk ...69 M10
Thorrington Essex ...47 K7
Thorverton Devon ...8 H4
Thrales End Beds ...44 G8
Thrandeston Suffk ...58 G5
Thrapston Nhants ...55 P5
Threapland Cumb ...97 M10
Threapland N York ...84 E3
Threapwood Ches W ...63 M3
Threapwood Staffs ...65 J4
Threapwood Head Staffs ...65 J4
Threave S Ayrs ...104 F8
Three Ashes Herefs ...40 G7
Three Bridges W Susx ...15 K3
Three Burrows Cnwll ...3 J5
Three Chimneys Kent ...16 E3
Three Cocks Powys ...40 A4
Three Crosses Swans ...26 E3
Three Cups Corner E Susx ...16 B7
Three Gates Worcs ...52 C8
Threehammer Common Norfk ...71 L8
Three Hammers Cnwll ...7 J7
Three Holes Norfk ...69 K12
Threekingham Lincs ...68 B5
Three Leg Cross E Susx ...16 B4
Three Legged Cross Dorset ...11 Q4
Three Mile Cross Wokhm ...31 P9
Threemilestone Cnwll ...3 J5
Threemiletown W Loth ...115 K6
Three Oaks E Susx ...16 E8
Threlkeld Cumb ...89 J2
Threshers Bush Essex ...45 P10
Threshfield N York ...84 E2
Thrigby Norfk ...71 P9
Thringarth Dur ...90 H3
Thringstone Leics ...66 D8
Thrintoft N York ...91 N8
Thriplow Cambs ...45 N2
Throapham Rothm ...78 E6
Throckenhalt Lincs ...68 G10
Throcking Herts ...45 K6
Throckley N u Ty ...100 F5
Throckmorton Worcs ...52 H10
Throop BCP ...11 Q6
Throop Dorset ...11 K6
Throphill Nthumb ...100 E1
Thropton Nthumb ...108 G9
Throsk Stirlg ...114 F3
Througham Gloucs ...41 Q10
Throughgate D & G ...96 H1
Throwleigh Devon ...8 C6
Throwley Kent ...34 H11
Throwley Forstal Kent ...34 H11
Thrumpton Notts ...66 E6
Thrumpton Notts ...78 H7
Thrumster Highld ...151 P7
Thrunscoe NE Lin ...80 F2
Thrunton Nthumb ...108 H7
Thrup Oxon ...30 G3
Thrupp Gloucs ...41 P11
Thrupp Oxon ...43 K8
Thrushelton Devon ...7 N7
Thrussington Leics ...66 G9
Thruxton Hants ...24 D4
Thruxton Herefs ...40 F7
Thrybergh Rothm ...78 D5
Thulston Derbys ...66 C6
Thundersley Essex ...34 D5
Thurcaston Leics ...66 F10
Thurcroft Rothm ...78 E6
Thurdon Cnwll ...7 K3
Thurgarton Norfk ...71 J5
Thurgarton Notts ...67 H2
Thurgoland Barns ...77 P3
Thurlaston Leics ...66 E12
Thurlaston Warwks ...54 D6
Thurlbear Somset ...21 L9
Thurlby Lincs ...68 B9
Thurlby Lincs ...79 M11
Thurlby Lincs ...81 J8
Thurleigh Bed ...44 G3
Thurlestone Devon ...5 N7
Thurloxton Somset ...21 L7
Thurlstone Barns ...77 N3
Thurlton Norfk ...59 N1

Thurlwood Ches E ...76 E12
Thurmaston Leics ...66 G10
Thurnby Leics ...66 G11
Thurne Norfk ...71 M9
Thurnham Kent ...34 E10
Thurning Nhants ...56 B4
Thurning Norfk ...70 G6
Thurnscoe Barns ...78 D3
Thurrock Services Thurr ...33 Q6
Thursby Cumb ...98 G8
Thursden Lancs ...84 D8
Thursford Norfk ...70 E5
Thursley Surrey ...14 C3
Thurso Highld ...151 K3
Thurstaston Wirral ...74 H7
Thurston Suffk ...58 D7
Thurston Clough Oldham ...76 H2
Thurstonfield Cumb ...98 C7
Thurstonland Kirk ...77 M2
Thurston Planche Suffk ...71 L12
Thurton Norfk ...71 L12
Thurvaston Derbys ...65 N5
Thuxton Norfk ...70 F10
Thwaite N York ...90 F7
Thwaite Suffk ...58 G7
Thwaite Head Cumb ...89 K8
Thwaites C Brad ...84 G7
Thwaite St Mary Norfk ...59 L1
Thwaites Brow C Brad ...84 G7
Thwing E R Yk ...87 K1
Tibbermore P & K ...123 Q8
Tibbers D & G ...105 Q10
Tibberton Gloucs ...41 M7
Tibberton Worcs ...52 G9
Tibberton Wrekin ...64 C8
Tibenham Norfk ...58 H3
Tibshelf Derbys ...78 D11
Tibshelf Services Derbys ...78 D11
Tibthorpe E R Yk ...86 H4
Ticehurst E Susx ...16 C5
Tichborne Hants ...25 J7
Tickencote Rutlnd ...67 N10
Tickenham N Som ...28 H8
Tickford End M Keyn ...44 C3
Tickhill Donc ...78 E5
Ticklerton Shrops ...51 N2
Ticknall Derbys ...66 B7
Tickton E R Yk ...87 K7
Tidbury Green Solhll ...53 L5
Tidcombe Wilts ...30 G10
Tiddington Oxon ...43 N10
Tiddington Warwks ...53 N9
Tiddleywink Wilts ...29 P7
Tidebrook E Susx ...15 R5
Tideford Cnwll ...4 E5
Tideford Cross Cnwll ...4 E4
Tidenham Gloucs ...28 H3
Tideswell Derbys ...77 M8
Tidmarsh W Berk ...31 N7
Tidmington Warwks ...42 H4
Tidpit Hants ...23 N9
Tidworth Wilts ...24 D4
Tiers Cross Pembks ...36 H8
Tiffield Nhants ...54 H10
Tigerton Angus ...132 E11
Tigh a' Ghearraidh W Isls ...152 b8
Tigharry W Isls ...152 b8
Tighnabruaich Ag & B ...112 E7
Tigley Devon ...5 M4
Tilbrook Cambs ...55 Q7
Tilbury Thurr ...34 B7
Tilbury Dock Thurr ...34 B7
Tilbury Green Essex ...46 D3
Tilbury Juxta Clare Essex ...46 D4
Tile Cross Birm ...53 M3
Tile Hill Covtry ...53 P5
Tilehouse Green Solhll ...53 M5
Tilehurst Readg ...31 N7
Tilford Surrey ...14 B2
Tilgate W Susx ...15 K4
Tilgate Forest Row W Susx ...15 J4
Tilham Street Somset ...22 D6
Tillers Green Gloucs ...41 L5
Tillicoultry Clacks ...114 E12
Tillietudlem S Lans ...114 E12
Tillingham Essex ...46 H11
Tillington Herefs ...40 G3
Tillington W Susx ...14 D6
Tillington Common Herefs ...40 F3
Tillybirloch Abers ...132 G3
Tillyfourie Abers ...132 G2
Tillygreig Abers ...141 L11
Tillyrie P & K ...114 C11
Tilmanstone Kent ...35 N12
Tilney All Saints Norfk ...69 L8
Tilney High End Norfk ...69 L8
Tilney St Lawrence Norfk ...69 K9
Tilshead Wilts ...23 M4
Tilstock Shrops ...63 P5
Tilston Ches W ...63 M2
Tilstone Bank Ches W ...75 P11
Tilstone Fearnall Ches W ...75 P11
Tilsworth C Beds ...44 D7
Tilton on the Hill Leics ...67 J11
Tiltups End Gloucs ...29 N3
Tilty Essex ...45 Q6
Timberland Lincs ...80 C12
Timbersbrook Ches E ...76 G11
Timberscombe Somset ...20 E5
Timble N York ...85 J4
Timewell Devon ...20 E8
Timpanheck D & G ...98 C3
Timperley Traffd ...76 E6
Timsbury BaNES ...29 K10
Timsbury Hants ...24 E8
Timsgarry W Isls ...152 d3
Timsgearraidh W Isls ...152 d3
Timworth Suffk ...58 C7
Timworth Green Suffk ...58 C7
Tincleton Dorset ...11 J6
Tindale Cumb ...99 M6
Tingewick Bucks ...43 L8
Tingrith C Beds ...44 E8
Tingwall Ork ...147 c4
Tingwall Airport Shet ...147 i7
Tinhay Devon ...7 M7
Tinker's Hill Hants ...24 F4
Tinkersley Derbys ...77 P10
Tinsley Sheff ...78 C5
Tinsley Green W Susx ...15 K3
Tintagel Cnwll ...6 F7
Tintern Mons ...28 G2
Tintinhull Somset ...22 C9
Tintwistle Derbys ...77 K4
Tinwald D & G ...97 K2
Tinwell Rutlnd ...67 P11
Tippacott Devon ...19 P4
Tipp's End Norfk ...57 L3
Tiptoe Hants ...12 D5
Tipton Sandw ...52 H2
Tipton Green Sandw ...52 H2
Tipton St John Devon ...9 L6
Tiptree Essex ...46 F8
Tiptree Heath Essex ...46 F8
Tirabad Powys ...39 L3
Tircoed Swans ...26 F2
Tiree Ag & B ...118 C7
Tiree Airport Ag & B ...118 D7
Tiretigan Ag & B ...111 Q8
Tirley Gloucs ...41 N6
Tiroran Ag & B ...119 J7
Tirphil Caerph ...39 Q11
Tirril Cumb ...89 N2
Tir-y-fron Flints ...75 J11

Tisbury Wilts ...23 L7
Tisman's Common W Susx ...14 F4
Tissington Derbys ...65 M2
Titchberry Devon ...18 E8
Titchfield Hants ...13 J4
Titchfield Common Hants ...13 J4
Titchmarsh Nhants ...55 P5
Titchwell Norfk ...69 P3
Tithby Notts ...66 H5
Titley Herefs ...51 K8
Titmore Green Herts ...45 J6
Titsey Surrey ...33 M11
Tittensor Staffs ...64 G4
Tittleshall Norfk ...70 D8
Titton Worcs ...52 F6
Tiverton Ches W ...75 P11
Tiverton Devon ...20 E10
Tivetshall St Margaret Norfk ...58 H3
Tivetshall St Mary Norfk ...58 H3
Tivington Somset ...20 E4
Tivy Dale Barns ...77 P2
Tixall Staffs ...64 H7
Tixover Rutlnd ...67 P11
Toab Shet ...147 i10
Toadhole Derbys ...78 C12
Toadmoor Derbys ...65 Q2
Tobermory Ag & B ...119 N2
Toberonochy Ag & B ...120 D11
Tobha Mòr W Isls ...152 b10
Tocher Abers ...140 H9
Tockenham Wilts ...30 B6
Tockenham Wick Wilts ...30 B6
Tockholes Bl w D ...83 P10
Tockington S Glos ...29 J5
Tockwith N York ...85 P5
Todber Dorset ...22 H9
Todburn Nthumb ...109 J10
Toddington C Beds ...44 E6
Toddington Gloucs ...42 B5
Toddington Services C Beds ...44 E6
Todds Green Herts ...45 J6
Todenham Gloucs ...42 F4
Todhills Angus ...124 H5
Todhills Cumb ...98 D6
Todhills Dur ...100 G11
Todhills Rest Area Cumb ...98 D6
Todmorden Calder ...84 D10
Todwick Rothm ...78 E7
Toft Cambs ...56 G9
Toft Ches E ...76 E8
Toft Lincs ...67 Q8
Toft Shet ...147 i5
Toft Warwks ...54 D6
Toft Hill Dur ...91 K3
Toft Hill Lincs ...80 D11
Toft Monks Norfk ...59 N2
Toft next Newton Lincs ...79 P6
Toftrees Norfk ...70 C6
Toftwood Norfk ...70 E10
Togston Nthumb ...109 L9
Tokavaig Highld ...127 L2
Tokers Green Oxon ...31 P7
Tolastadh bho Thuath W Isls ...152 h2
Toldish Cnwll ...3 M3
Tolland Somset ...20 H7
Tollard Farnham Dorset ...23 L10
Tollard Royal Wilts ...23 L10
Toll Bar Donc ...78 F2
Tollbar End Covtry ...54 B5
Toller Fratrum Dorset ...10 F5
Toller Porcorum Dorset ...10 F5
Tollerton N York ...85 Q2
Tollerton Notts ...66 G5
Toller Whelme Dorset ...10 D4
Tollesbury Essex ...46 G9
Tolleshunt D'Arcy Essex ...46 G9
Tolleshunt Knights Essex ...46 G8
Tolleshunt Major Essex ...46 G9
Tollingham E R Yk ...86 F8
Toll of Birness Abers ...141 N9
Tolpuddle Dorset ...11 J6
Tolworth Gt Lon ...32 H9
Tomatin Highld ...138 D10
Tomchrasky Highld ...129 J2
Tomdoun Highld ...128 G4
Tomich Highld ...137 P10
Tomich Highld ...137 P6
Tomich Highld ...145 N4
Tomich Highld ...146 C11
Tomintoul Moray ...139 M12
Tomlow Warwks ...54 D8
Tomnacross Highld ...137 N7
Tomnavoulin Moray ...139 M10
Tompkin Staffs ...64 H2
Ton Mons ...28 C3
Ton Mons ...28 E3
Tonbridge Kent ...15 Q2
Tondu Brdgnd ...27 J11
Tonedale Somset ...20 H9
Tonfanau Gwynd ...61 J11
Tong C Brad ...85 J8
Tong Kent ...34 G11
Tong Shrops ...64 E11
Tong W Isls ...152 g3
Tonge Leics ...66 C7
Tong Green Kent ...34 H11
Tongham Surrey ...14 C1
Tongland D & G ...96 E7
Tong Norton Shrops ...64 E11
Tongue Highld ...149 M5
Tongue End Lincs ...68 C9
Tongwynlais Cardif ...27 Q6
Tonmawr Neath ...27 J3
Tonna Neath ...26 H3
Ton-teg Rhondd ...27 P5
Tonwell Herts ...45 K8
Tonypandy Rhondd ...27 N4
Tonyrefail Rhondd ...27 N5
Toot Baldon Oxon ...31 M2
Toot Hill Essex ...45 P10
Toothill Hants ...24 F10
Toothill Swindn ...30 D6
Tooting Gt Lon ...33 K8
Tooting Bec Gt Lon ...33 K8
Topcliffe N York ...91 P11
Topcroft Norfk ...59 K2
Topcroft Street Norfk ...59 K2
Top End Beds ...55 P8
Topham Donc ...86 B11
Top of Hebers Rochdl ...76 F2
Toppesfield Essex ...46 C4
Toprow Norfk ...58 H1
Topsham Devon ...8 H7
Top-y-rhos Flints ...75 J11
Torbeg N Ayrs ...103 N4
Torboll Highld ...146 E6
Torbreck Highld ...138 B8
Torbryan Devon ...5 N3
Torcastle Highld ...128 G9
Torcross Devon ...5 N8
Tore Highld ...137 Q4
Torfrey Cnwll ...3 Q4
Torinturk Ag & B ...112 B9
Torksey Lincs ...79 L8
Torlundy Highld ...128 G8
Tormarton S Glos ...29 M6
Tormore N Ayrs ...103 N3
Tornagrain Highld ...138 E6
Tornaveen Abers ...132 F3
Torness Highld ...137 Q10

Toronto Dur ...100 G12
Torpenhow Cumb ...97 P10
Torphichen W Loth ...114 H7
Torphins Abers ...132 F4
Torpoint Cnwll ...4 G6
Torquay Torbay ...5 Q4
Torquhan Border ...116 B11
Torr Devon ...5 J6
Torran Highld ...135 K6
Torrance E Duns ...114 B6
Torranyard N Ayrs ...104 F2
Torre Somset ...20 G5
Torridon Highld ...136 C5
Torridon House Highld ...136 B4
Torrin Highld ...135 K11
Torrisdale Ag & B ...103 L3
Torrisdale Highld ...149 P4
Torrish Highld ...146 H1
Torrisholme Lancs ...83 K2
Torroble Highld ...145 N4
Torry C Aber ...133 M3
Torryburn Fife ...115 J4
Torteval Guern ...12 b3
Torthorwald D & G ...97 L3
Tortington W Susx ...14 E10
Torton Worcs ...52 F6
Tortworth S Glos ...29 L4
Torvaig Highld ...135 J7
Torver Cumb ...89 J8
Torwood Falk ...114 F4
Torwoodlee Border ...107 M2
Torworth Notts ...78 G7
Tosberry Devon ...18 E9
Toscaig Highld ...135 N8
Toseland Cambs ...56 E8
Tosside Lancs ...84 A4
Tostock Suffk ...58 D8
Totaig Highld ...134 C6
Tote Highld ...134 G6
Tote Highld ...135 J6
Tote Hill W Susx ...14 B6
Totford Hants ...25 J6
Tothill Lincs ...80 H7
Totland IoW ...12 F7
Totley Sheff ...77 P8
Totley Brook Sheff ...77 P7
Totnes Devon ...5 N5
Toton Notts ...66 E5
Totronald Ag & B ...118 G2
Totscore Highld ...134 G3
Tottenham Gt Lon ...33 L4
Totteridge Gt Lon ...33 J3
Totternhoe C Beds ...44 D7
Tottington Bury ...76 E1
Totton Hants ...24 F10
Touchen End W & M ...32 C7
Toulston N York ...85 P6
Toulton Somset ...21 K7
Toulvaddie Highld ...146 F9
Tovil Kent ...34 D11
Towan Cnwll ...3 P5
Towan Cnwll ...6 C10
Toward Ag & B ...112 H7
Toward Quay Ag & B ...112 G7
Towcester Nhants ...54 H11
Towednack Cnwll ...2 D7
Tower of London Gt Lon ...33 L6
Towersey Oxon ...43 Q10
Towie Abers ...132 C2
Tow Law Dur ...100 E10
Town End Cambs ...56 H2
Town End Cumb ...89 K5
Town End Cumb ...89 L6
Town End Cumb ...89 L12
Townend W Duns ...113 M6
Towngate Cumb ...98 G8
Towngate Lincs ...68 C10
Town Green Lancs ...75 L3
Town Green Norfk ...71 M9
Townhead Barns ...77 M3
Town Head Cumb ...89 L6
Townhead Cumb ...97 N10
Townhead Cumb ...99 J11
Townhead D & G ...106 C12
Town Head N York ...84 B3
Townhead of Greenlaw D & G ...96 F5
Townhill Fife ...115 K3
Town Kelloe Dur ...101 J11
Townlake Devon ...7 M9
Town Lane Wigan ...76 C4
Town Littleworth E Susx ...15 M7
Town of Lowton Wigan ...75 Q4
Town Row E Susx ...15 Q5
Towns End Hants ...31 M10
Townsend Somset ...21 N10
Townshend Cnwll ...2 F7
Town Street Suffk ...57 P3
Townwell S Glos ...29 L4
Town Yetholm Border ...108 E4
Towthorpe C York ...86 B5
Towthorpe E R Yk ...86 H3
Towton N York ...85 P7
Towyn Conwy ...74 D8
Toxteth Lpool ...75 K6
Toynton All Saints Lincs ...80 H11
Toynton Fen Side Lincs ...80 H11
Toynton St Peter Lincs ...80 H11
Toy's Hill Kent ...33 N12
Trabboch E Ayrs ...104 H5
Trabbochburn E Ayrs ...104 H5
Traboe Cnwll ...3 J11
Tracebridge Somset ...20 F9
Tradespark Highld ...138 D5
Trafford Park Traffd ...76 E5
Trallong Powys ...39 M6
Tranent E Loth ...115 P7
Tranmere Wirral ...75 K6
Trantelbeg Highld ...150 D6
Trantlemore Highld ...150 D6
Tranwell Nthumb ...100 F1
Trapp Carmth ...38 F9
Traprain E Loth ...116 D6
Trap's Green Warwks ...53 L7
Trapshill W Berk ...30 H9
Traquair Border ...107 J3
Trash Green W Berk ...31 N8
Trawden Lancs ...84 D7
Trawscoed Cerdgn ...49 L6
Trawsfynydd Gwynd ...61 M5
Trealaw Rhondd ...27 N4
Treales Lancs ...83 J8
Trearddur Bay IoA ...72 B9
Treator Cnwll ...6 D10
Trebanog Rhondd ...27 N4
Trebanos Neath ...38 H11
Trebartha Cnwll ...7 J7
Trebarwith Cnwll ...6 F7
Trebeath Cnwll ...7 J7
Trebetherick Cnwll ...6 D10
Treborough Somset ...20 F6
Trebudannon Cnwll ...3 L2
Trebullett Cnwll ...7 K8
Treburgett Cnwll ...6 E7
Treburley Cnwll ...7 K8
Treburrick Cnwll ...6 B10
Trebyan Cnwll ...3 Q3
Trecastle Powys ...39 K6
Trecogo Cnwll ...7 K8
Trecott Devon ...8 D4
Trecwn Pembks ...37 J4
Trecynon Rhondd ...27 L3
Tredavoe Cnwll ...2 C8

Tredegar Blae G ...39 Q10
Tredethy Cnwll ...6 F10
Tredington Gloucs ...41 Q6
Tredington Warwks ...42 F3
Tredinnick Cnwll ...4 B3
Tredinnick Cnwll ...4 C5
Tredinnick Cnwll ...4 D5
Tredinnick Cnwll ...4 H5
Tredinnick Cnwll ...6 C6
Tredomen Powys ...39 Q5
Tredrissi Pembks ...37 L2
Tredunnock Mons ...28 C3
Tredustan Powys ...39 Q5
Treen Cnwll ...2 B10
Treen Cnwll ...2 C7
Treesmill Cnwll ...3 Q3
Treeton Rothm ...78 C5
Trefasser Pembks ...36 G3
Trefdraeth IoA ...72 G9
Trefecca Powys ...39 Q5
Trefechan Myr Td ...39 N10
Trefeglwys Powys ...50 C3
Trefenter Cerdgn ...49 K7
Treffgarne Pembks ...36 H5
Treffgarne Owen Pembks ...36 G5
Treffynnon Pembks ...36 G5
Trefil Blae G ...39 Q9
Trefilan Cerdgn ...49 J9
Trefin Pembks ...36 G4
Treflach Shrops ...63 J6
Trefnanney Powys ...62 H9
Trefnant Denbgs ...74 E9
Trefonen Shrops ...63 J7
Trefor Gwynd ...60 F3
Trefor IoA ...72 F7
Treforest Rhondd ...27 P4
Trefrew Cnwll ...6 G8
Trefriw Conwy ...73 N11
Tre-gagle Mons ...40 H10
Tregaian IoA ...72 G8
Tregare Mons ...40 F7
Tregarne Cnwll ...3 J10
Tregaron Cerdgn ...49 L8
Tregarth Gwynd ...73 K10
Tregaswith Cnwll ...3 L2
Tregatta Cnwll ...6 F7
Tregawne Cnwll ...3 P2
Tregeare Cnwll ...7 J7
Tregeiriog Wrexhm ...62 G5
Tregele IoA ...72 F5
Tregellist Cnwll ...6 E9
Tregenna Cnwll ...3 N2
Tregeseal Cnwll ...2 B8
Tregew Cnwll ...3 K7
Tre-Gibbon Rhondd ...39 N10
Tregidden Cnwll ...3 J10
Tregiskey Cnwll ...3 P5
Treglemais Pembks ...36 F5
Tregole Cnwll ...6 H5
Tregolls Cnwll ...3 J7
Tregonce Cnwll ...6 D10
Tregonetha Cnwll ...3 N2
Tregony Cnwll ...3 M5
Tregoodwell Cnwll ...6 G8
Tregorrick Cnwll ...3 P4
Tregoss Cnwll ...3 N2
Tregoyd Powys ...40 A4
Tregreenwell Cnwll ...6 H7
Tregullon Cnwll ...3 P3
Tregunna Cnwll ...6 D10
Tregunnon Cnwll ...7 J8
Tregurrian Cnwll ...3 B11
Tregynon Powys ...50 F1
Tre-gynwr Carmth ...38 B8
Trehafod Rhondd ...27 N4
Trehan Cnwll ...4 F5
Treharris Myr Td ...27 N3
Treharrock Cnwll ...6 E9
Trehemborne Cnwll ...6 C10
Treherbert Carmth ...38 E2
Treherbert Rhondd ...27 M3
Trehunist Cnwll ...4 D4
Trekenner Cnwll ...7 K8
Treknow Cnwll ...6 F7
Trelan Cnwll ...3 J10
Trelash Cnwll ...6 H6
Trelassick Cnwll ...3 L4
Trelawne Cnwll ...4 C6
Trelawnyd Flints ...74 E8
Treleague Cnwll ...3 K10
Treleaver Cnwll ...3 J11
Trelech Carmth ...37 Q4
Tre-lech a'r Betws Carmth ...37 Q5
Treleddyd-fawr Pembks ...36 E5
Trelewis Myr Td ...27 N3
Treligga Cnwll ...6 E8
Trelights Cnwll ...6 D9
Trelill Cnwll ...6 E9
Trelinnoe Cnwll ...7 K8
Trelion Cnwll ...3 M4
Trelissick Cnwll ...3 K7
Trellech Mons ...40 H10
Trelleck Grange Mons ...28 G2
Trelogan Flints ...74 F7
Trelow Cnwll ...6 C10
Trelowarren Cnwll ...2 H9
Trelowia Cnwll ...4 D5
Treluggan Cnwll ...3 L5
Trelystan Powys ...51 J2
Tremadog Gwynd ...61 J4
Tremail Cnwll ...6 G7
Tremain Cerdgn ...48 C11
Tremaine Cnwll ...7 J7
Tremar Cnwll ...4 D4
Trematon Cnwll ...4 F5
Trembraze Cnwll ...4 D4
Tremeirchion Denbgs ...74 E9
Tremethick Cross Cnwll ...2 C8
Tremore Cnwll ...3 P3
Tre-Mostyn Flints ...74 F8
Trenance Cnwll ...3 K10
Trenance Cnwll ...6 C10
Trenance Cnwll ...3 L2
Trenarren Cnwll ...3 P5
Trench Wrekin ...64 C9
Trench Green Oxon ...31 P7
Trencreek Cnwll ...3 L2
Trendeal Cnwll ...3 L4
Trendrine Cnwll ...2 D7
Treneague Cnwll ...6 E10
Trenear Cnwll ...2 H8
Treneglos Cnwll ...7 J7
Trenerth Cnwll ...2 F7
Trenewan Cnwll ...4 C6
Trenewth Cnwll ...6 F8
Trengune Cnwll ...6 H6
Treninnick Cnwll ...3 K3
Trenoweth Cnwll ...3 K7
Trent Dorset ...22 C10
Trentham C Stke ...64 G4
Trentishoe Devon ...19 N3
Trent Port Lincs ...79 L8
Trent Vale C Stke ...64 G4
Treoes V Glam ...27 M6
Treorchy Rhondd ...27 M3
Trequite Cnwll ...6 E9
Tre'r-ddol Cerdgn ...49 L2
Trerhyngyll V Glam ...27 N7
Trerulefoot Cnwll ...4 E5
Tresaith Cerdgn ...48 D8

Tresawle Cnwll ...3 L5
Trescott Staffs ...52 F1
Trescowe Cnwll ...2 E8
Tresean Cnwll ...3 J3
Tresham Gloucs ...29 M4
Treshnish Isles Ag & B ...118 L5
Tresillian Cnwll ...3 L5
Tresinney Cnwll ...6 G8
Treskinnick Cross Cnwll ...7 J5
Tresmeer Cnwll ...7 J7
Tresparrett Cnwll ...6 G6
Tressait P & K ...130 E12
Tresta Shet ...147 i6
Tresta Shet ...147 k3
Treswell Notts ...79 K8
Treswithian Cnwll ...2 G7
Tre Taliesin Cerdgn ...49 L2
Trethevey Cnwll ...6 F7
Trethewey Cnwll ...2 B9
Trethomas Caerph ...28 B7
Trethosa Cnwll ...3 M4
Trethurgy Cnwll ...3 P3
Tretio Pembks ...36 D5
Tretire Herefs ...40 G7
Tretower Powys ...39 R8
Treuddyn Flints ...75 J12
Trevadlock Cnwll ...7 J8
Trevalga Cnwll ...6 F7
Trevalyn Wrexhm ...75 L12
Trevanger Cnwll ...6 D9
Trevanson Cnwll ...6 D10
Trevarrack Cnwll ...2 D8
Trevarren Cnwll ...3 M2
Trevarrian Cnwll ...3 B11
Trevarrick Cnwll ...3 N6
Tre-vaughan Carmth ...37 N7
Tre-vaughan Carmth ...38 B7
Treveal Cnwll ...2 D6
Treveighan Cnwll ...6 F9
Trevellas Downs Cnwll ...3 J4
Trevelmond Cnwll ...4 B4
Trevemper Cnwll ...3 K3
Treveor Cnwll ...3 N6
Treverbyn Cnwll ...3 P3
Treverbyn Cnwll ...3 P5
Treverva Cnwll ...3 J7
Trevescan Cnwll ...2 B9
Trevethin Torfn ...40 C11
Trevia Cnwll ...6 G8
Trevigro Cnwll ...4 E3
Trevilla Cnwll ...3 L7
Trevilson Cnwll ...3 L3
Treviscoe Cnwll ...3 M3
Treviskey Cnwll ...3 M6
Trevithick Cnwll ...3 L3
Trevithick Cnwll ...3 N5
Trevone Cnwll ...6 C9
Trevor Wrexhm ...63 J3
Trevorgans Cnwll ...2 C9
Trevorrick Cnwll ...6 C10
Trevose Cnwll ...6 B9
Trewalder Cnwll ...6 F8
Trewalkin Powys ...39 R5
Trewarmett Cnwll ...6 F7
Trewassa Cnwll ...6 H7
Trewavas Mining District Cnwll ...2 F9
Treween Cnwll ...7 J8
Trewellard Cnwll ...2 B8
Trewen Cnwll ...7 J8
Trewennack Cnwll ...2 H8
Trewent Pembks ...37 K11
Trewern Powys ...63 J9
Trewetha Cnwll ...6 E8
Trewethern Cnwll ...6 E9
Trewidland Cnwll ...4 D5
Trewint Cnwll ...3 J11
Trewint Cnwll ...7 J8
Trewithian Cnwll ...3 L7
Trewoodloe Cnwll ...7 L10
Trewoon Cnwll ...2 H9
Trewoon Cnwll ...3 N4
Treworga Cnwll ...3 L5
Treworgan Cnwll ...3 K4
Treworld Cnwll ...6 G6
Treworthal Cnwll ...3 L6
Tre-wyn Mons ...40 D7
Treyarnon Cnwll ...6 B10
Treyford W Susx ...25 P9
Trickett's Cross Dorset ...11 Q4
Triermain Cumb ...98 H5
Triffleton Pembks ...37 J6
Trillacott Cnwll ...7 K7
Trimdon Dur ...101 K11
Trimdon Colliery Dur ...101 K11
Trimdon Grange Dur ...101 K11
Trimingham Norfk ...71 K4
Trimley Lower Street Suffk ...47 N4
Trimley St Martin Suffk ...47 N4
Trimley St Mary Suffk ...47 N4
Trimpley Worcs ...52 E6
Trimsaran Carmth ...38 C10
Trims Green Herts ...45 N8
Trimstone Devon ...19 K5
Trinafour P & K ...130 D11
Trinant Caerph ...28 B2
Tring Herts ...44 C9
Tringford Herts ...44 C9
Tring Wharf Herts ...44 C9
Trinity Angus ...132 F12
Trinity Jersey ...13 c1
Trinity Gask P & K ...123 N2
Triscombe Somset ...21 J6
Trislaig Highld ...128 F9
Trispen Cnwll ...3 L4
Tritlington Nthumb ...109 K11
Troan Cnwll ...3 L3
Trochry P & K ...123 P5
Troedrhiwfuwch Caerph ...39 Q10
Troedyraur Cerdgn ...48 E11
Troedyrhiw Myr Td ...39 P11
Trois Bois Jersey ...13 b2
Troon Cnwll ...2 H7
Troon S Ayrs ...104 F4
Tropical World Roundhay Park Leeds ...85 L7
Trossachs Stirlg ...122 C2
Trossachs Pier Stirlg ...122 E11
Troston Suffk ...58 C6
Troswell Cnwll ...7 J6
Trotshill Worcs ...52 G9
Trottiscliffe Kent ...34 B9
Trotton W Susx ...25 P9
Trough Gate Lancs ...84 D11
Troutbeck Cumb ...89 L5
Troutbeck Cumb ...89 L6
Troutbeck Bridge Cumb ...89 L6
Troway Derbys ...78 C8
Trowbridge Wilts ...22 H3
Trowell Notts ...66 D4
Trowell Services Notts ...66 D4
Trowle Common Wilts ...29 N10
Trowley Bottom Herts ...44 F8
Trowse Newton Norfk ...71 K10
Troy Leeds ...85 J7
Trudoxhill Somset ...22 G5

Trull Somset ...21 K9
Trumfleet Donc ...78 F1
Trumpan Highld ...134 D4
Trumpet Herefs ...41 K5
Trumpington Cambs ...56 H9
Trumpsgreen Surrey ...32 E9
Trunch Norfk ...71 K5
Trunnah Lancs ...82 H6
Truro Cnwll ...3 K7
Truscott Cnwll ...7 K7
Trusham Devon ...8 F8
Trusley Derbys ...65 N5
Trusthorpe Lincs ...81 K7
Trysull Staffs ...52 F2
Tubney Oxon ...31 J4
Tuckenhay Devon ...5 N5
Tuckhill Shrops ...52 E3
Tuckingmill Cnwll ...2 G6
Tuckingmill Wilts ...23 L7
Tuckton BCP ...12 B6
Tucoyse Cnwll ...3 M5
Tuddenham Suffk ...57 P6
Tuddenham Suffk ...59 J11
Tudeley Kent ...16 A2
Tudhoe Dur ...100 H11
Tudorville Herefs ...41 J7
Tudweiliog Gwynd ...60 D5
Tuesley Surrey ...14 D2
Tuffley Gloucs ...41 N8
Tufton Hants ...24 H3
Tufton Pembks ...37 K5
Tugby Leics ...67 J12
Tugford Shrops ...51 P3
Tughall Nthumb ...109 K4
Tullibody Clacks ...114 F2
Tullich Abers ...132 B5
Tullich Highld ...138 B10
Tullich Highld ...146 B10
Tulliemet P & K ...123 P2
Tulloch Abers ...141 J9
Tullochgorm Ag & B ...112 A2
Tulloch Station Highld ...129 L8
Tullymurdoch P & K ...124 D2
Tullynessle Abers ...140 E12
Tulse Hill Gt Lon ...33 L8
Tumble Carmth ...38 E9
Tumbler's Green Essex ...46 E6
Tumby Lincs ...80 E11
Tumby Woodside Lincs ...80 E12
Tummel Bridge P & K ...123 K1
Tunbridge Wells Kent ...15 Q3
Tundergarth D & G ...97 N2
Tunga W Isls ...152 g3
Tungate Norfk ...71 K6
Tunley BaNES ...29 L10
Tunstall E R Yk ...87 P9
Tunstall Kent ...34 F9
Tunstall Lancs ...89 P12
Tunstall N York ...91 L7
Tunstall Norfk ...71 N10
Tunstall Staffs ...64 B7
Tunstall Suffk ...59 M9
Tunstall Sundld ...101 J1
Tunstead Derbys ...77 L8
Tunstead Norfk ...71 L7
Tunstead Milton Derbys ...77 J7
Tupsley Herefs ...40 H4
Tupton Derbys ...78 C10
Turgis Green Hants ...31 P10
Turkdean Gloucs ...42 C8
Tur Langton Leics ...54 H2
Turleigh Wilts ...29 N10
Turleygreen Shrops ...52 E4
Turn Lancs ...84 B11
Turnastone Herefs ...40 E4
Turnberry S Ayrs ...104 D8
Turnchapel C Plym ...4 H6
Turnditch Derbys ...65 P3
Turner Green Lancs ...83 N9
Turner's Green E Susx ...16 B7
Turner's Green Warwks ...53 M7
Turners Hill W Susx ...15 L4
Turners Puddle Dorset ...11 K6
Turnford Herts ...45 L10
Turnhouse C Edin ...115 L7
Turnworth Dorset ...11 K3
Turriff Abers ...140 H6
Turton Bottoms Bl w D ...83 Q12
Turves Cambs ...56 G1
Turvey Bed ...55 N10
Turville Bucks ...31 Q4
Turville Heath Bucks ...31 Q4
Turweston Bucks ...43 M4
Tushielaw Inn Border ...107 J6
Tutbury Staffs ...65 N6
Tutnall Worcs ...53 J6
Tutshill Gloucs ...28 H3
Tuttington Norfk ...71 J7
Tutts Clump W Berk ...31 M8
Tutwell Cnwll ...7 M9
Tuxford Notts ...79 J9
Twatt Ork ...147 b4
Twatt Shet ...147 i6
Twechar E Duns ...114 C6
Tweedbank Border ...107 N3
Tweedmouth Nthumb ...117 M10
Tweedsmuir Border ...106 E5
Twelveheads Cnwll ...3 J6
Twelve Oaks E Susx ...16 B6
Twemlow Green Ches E ...76 E10
Twenty Lincs ...68 C8
Twerton BaNES ...29 L9
Twickenham Gt Lon ...32 H7
Twigworth Gloucs ...41 N7
Twineham W Susx ...15 J7
Twineham Green W Susx ...15 J7
Twinhoe BaNES ...29 M10
Twinstead Essex ...46 E4
Twitchen Devon ...20 B7
Twitchen Shrops ...51 L5
Twitham Kent ...35 N11
Two Bridges Devon ...8 B9
Two Dales Derbys ...77 P11
Two Gates Staffs ...65 M12
Two Mile Ash W Susx ...14 G5
Two Mile Oak Cross Devon ...5 P3
Two Pots Devon ...19 K4
Two Waters Herts ...44 E9
Twycross Leics ...65 Q11
Twycross Zoo Leics ...65 P11
Twyford Bucks ...43 N6
Twyford Hants ...24 H8
Twyford Leics ...67 J10
Twyford Lincs ...67 M7
Twyford Norfk ...70 F7
Twyford Wokhm ...31 Q7
Twyford Common Herefs ...40 G5
Twyn-carno Caerph ...39 Q9
Twynholm D & G ...96 D7
Twyning Gloucs ...41 P4
Twyning Green Gloucs ...41 P4
Twynllanan Carmth ...38 H7
Twyn-yr-Odyn V Glam ...27 P7
Twyn-y-Sheriff Mons ...40 F10
Twywell Nhants ...55 N5
Tyberton Herefs ...40 E4
Tyburn Birm ...53 L2
Tycroes Carmth ...38 F9
Tycrwyn Powys ...62 F9
Tydd Gote Lincs ...69 J8
Tydd St Giles Cambs ...68 H8
Tydd St Mary Lincs ...68 H8
Tye Hants ...13 M4
Tye Green Essex ...45 P7
Tye Green Essex ...46 B6
Tye Green Essex ...45 Q4

Tye Green Essex...46 D7
Tyersal C Brad...85 J8
Tyldesley Wigan...76 C3
Tyler Hill Kent...35 L10
Tylers Green Bucks...32 C3
Tyler's Green Essex...45 P10
Tylers Green Surrey...33 L12
Tylorstown Rhondd...27 N3
Tylwch Powys...50 D5
Ty-nant Conwy...62 D3
Ty-nant Gwynd...62 B7
Tyncelyn Cerdgn...49 L8
Tyndrum Stirlg...121 Q6
Tyn-dwr Denbgs...62 H4
Tyneham Dorset...11 L8
Tynemouth N Tyne...101 K4
Tyne Tunnel S Tyne...101 J5
Tynewydd Rhondd...27 M3
Tyninghame E Loth...116 F5
Tynron D & G...105 P11
Ty'n-y-bryn Rhondd...27 N5
Ty'n-y-coedcae Caerph...28 B5
Tyn-y-nant IoA...72 H7
Tyn-y-graig Cerdgn...49 M7
Ty'n-y-Groes Conwy...73 N9
Tyn-y-nant Rhondd...27 P5
Tyrie Abers...141 M4
Tyringham M Keyn...43 B2
Tyseley Birm...53 L4
Tythegston Brdgnd...27 K6
Tytherington Ches E...76 G8
Tytherington S Glos...29 K5
Tytherington Somset...23 H4
Tytherington Wilts...23 K5
Tytherleigh Devon...9 Q7
Tytherton Lucas Wilts...29 Q7
Tytherhanger Herts...44 H10
Tywardreath Cnwll...3 Q4
Tywardreath Highway Cnwll...3 Q3
Tywyn Conwy...73 N8
Tywyn Gwynd...61 K12

U
Ubbeston Green Suffk...59 L6
Ubley BaNES...28 H10
Uckerby N York...91 L6
Uckfield E Susx...15 N6
Uckinghall Worcs...41 P4
Uckington Gloucs...41 Q7
Uckington Shrops...63 P10
Uddingston S Lans...114 C9
Uddington S Lans...105 Q3
Udimore E Susx...16 F7
Udny Green Abers...141 L10
Udny Station Abers...141 L10
Uffcott Wilts...30 D7
Uffculme Devon...20 G10
Uffington Lincs...67 Q10
Uffington Oxon...30 G4
Uffington Shrops...63 N9
Ufford C Pete...68 B11
Ufford Suffk...59 L11
Ufton Warwks...54 C8
Ufton Nervet W Berk...31 N9
Ugadale Ag & B...103 L4
Ugborough Devon...5 L5
Uggeshall Suffk...59 N5
Ugglebarnby N York...92 H5
Ughill Sheff...77 N5
Ugley Essex...45 P6
Ugley Green Essex...45 P6
Ugthorpe N York...92 G4
Uibhist A Deas W Isls...152 c10
Uibhist A Tuath W Isls...152 b8
Uig Ag & B...118 G2
Uig Highld...134 C5
Uig Highld...134 G3
Uig W Isls...152 d3
Uigshader Highld...134 H6
Uisken Ag & B...119 L9
Ulbster Highld...151 P8
Ulcat Row Cumb...89 L2
Ulceby Lincs...80 H9
Ulceby N Linc...87 L12
Ulceby Skitter N Linc...87 L12
Ulcombe Kent...16 E1
Uldale Cumb...97 Q10
Uley Gloucs...29 M3
Ulgham Nthumb...109 L11
Ullapool Highld...144 E6
Ullenhall Warwks...53 L7
Ullenwood Gloucs...41 Q8
Ulleskelf N York...85 Q7
Ullesthorpe Leics...54 E3
Ulley Rothm...78 D6
Ullingswick Herefs...51 Q10
Ullinish Lodge Hotel Highld...134 F8
Ullock Cumb...88 E2
Ullswater Cumb...89 L3
Ullswater Steamers Cumb...89 L3
Ulnes Walton Lancs...83 L11
Ulpha Cumb...88 G8
Ulpha Cumb...89 M10
Ulrome E R Yk...87 M4
Ulsta Shet...147 j4
Ulting Wick Essex...46 E10
Ulva Ag & B...119 L3
Ulverley Green Solhll...53 L4
Ulverston Cumb...89 J11
Ulwell Dorset...11 N8
Ulzieside D & G...105 P8
Umberleigh Devon...19 M8
Unapool Highld...148 F10
Underbarrow Cumb...89 M8
Under Burnmouth Border...98 F2
Undercliffe C Brad...85 J8
Underdale Shrops...63 N5
Underling Green Kent...16 D2
Underriver Kent...33 Q12
Underwood Newpt...28 E5
Underwood Notts...66 D2
Undley Suffk...57 M4
Undy Mons...28 F5
Union Mills IoM...102 d6
Union Street E Susx...16 C4
Unst Shet...147 k2
Unstone Derbys...78 B8
Unstone Green Derbys...78 B8
Unthank Cumb...98 D7
Unthank Cumb...98 F7
Unthank Cumb...98 H10
Unthank Derbys...77 P8
Unthank Nthumb...117 M11
Upavon Wilts...23 P2
Up Cerne Dorset...10 G4
Upchurch Kent...34 E9
Upcott Devon...19 P7
Upcott Herefs...51 K10
Upend Cambs...57 N9
Up Exe Devon...8 H4
Upgate Norfk...70 H8
Upgate Street Norfk...58 G2
Upgate Street Norfk...59 K2
Uphall Dorset...10 E4
Uphall W Loth...115 J7
Upham Devon...8 H4
Upham Hants...25 J9
Uphampton Herefs...51 L8
Uphampton Worcs...52 F8
Uphill N Som...28 D10
Up Holland Lancs...75 N3

Uplawmoor E Rens...113 N10
Upleadon Gloucs...41 M6
Upleatham R & Cl...92 D3
Uplees Kent...34 H9
Uploders Dorset...10 D6
Uplowman Devon...20 F10
Uplyme Devon...9 Q6
Up Marden W Susx...25 L10
Up Mudford Somset...22 D9
Up Nately Hants...25 M3
Upottery Devon...9 N3
Upper Affcot Shrops...51 M4
Upper Arley Worcs...52 E4
Upper Arncott Oxon...43 M8
Upper Astrop Nhants...43 L4
Upper Badcall Highld...148 E8
Upper Basildon W Berk...31 M7
Upper Batley Kirk...85 K10
Upper Beeding W Susx...14 H8
Upper Benefield Nhants...55 N3
Upper Bentley Worcs...53 J7
Upper Bighouse Highld...150 F5
Upper Birchwood Derbys...66 D1
Upper Boat Rhondd...27 Q5
Upper Boddington Nhants...54 D10
Upper Borth Cerdgn...49 K3
Upper Brailes Warwks...42 G4
Upper Breinton Herefs...40 G4
Upper Broadheath Worcs...52 F9
Upper Broughton Notts...66 H7
Upper Bucklebury W Berk...31 L8
Upper Burgate Hants...23 P10
Upper Bush Medway...34 C9
Upperby Cumb...98 E7
Upper Caldecote C Beds...56 E11
Upper Canada N Som...28 E10
Upper Canterton Hants...24 E9
Upper Catesby Nhants...54 E9
Upper Catshill Worcs...52 H6
Upper Chapel Powys...39 N4
Upper Cheddon Somset...21 J7
Upper Chicksgrove Wilts...23 L7
Upper Chute Wilts...24 E4
Upper Clapton Gt Lon...33 L5
Upper Clatford Hants...24 F5
Upper Coberley Gloucs...41 R8
Upper Cotton Staffs...65 K3
Upper Cound Shrops...63 N1
Upper Cudworth Barns...78 C2
Upper Cumberworth Kirk...77 N2
Upper Dallachy Moray...139 Q3
Upper Deal Kent...35 Q12
Upper Dean Bed...55 N7
Upper Denby Kirk...77 N2
Upper Denton Cumb...99 J5
Upper Dicker E Susx...15 Q9
Upper Dinchope Shrops...51 M4
Upper Dounreay Highld...150 H3
Upper Dovercourt Essex...47 M5
Upper Drumbane Stirlg...122 H11
Upper Dunsforth N York...85 N3
Upper Eashing Surrey...14 D2
Upper Eathie Highld...138 E3
Upper Egleton Herefs...41 J11
Upper Elkstone Staffs...77 K12
Upper Ellastone Staffs...65 L4
Upper End Derbys...77 K8
Upper Enham Hants...24 F3
Upper Farmcote Shrops...52 E2
Upper Farringdon Hants...25 M6
Upper Framilode Gloucs...41 M9
Upper Froyle Hants...25 N5
Upper Godney Somset...22 B5
Upper Gravenhurst C Beds...44 G4
Upper Green Mons...40 E7
Upper Green Suffk...57 P7
Upper Green W Berk...30 H9
Upper Grove Common Herefs...40 H6
Upper Hackney Derbys...77 P11
Upper Hale Surrey...25 P3
Upper Halliford Surrey...32 F8
Upper Halling Medway...34 C9
Upper Hambleton Rutlnd...67 M10
Upper Hardres Court Kent...35 L12
Upper Hardwick Herefs...51 L9
Upper Hartfield E Susx...15 N4
Upper Hartshay Derbys...66 C2
Upper Hatherley Gloucs...41 Q7
Upper Hatton Staffs...64 F5
Upper Haugh Rothm...78 C4
Upper Hayton Shrops...51 N4
Upper Heaton Kirk...85 J11
Upper Helmsley N York...86 C4
Upper Hergest Herefs...51 J9
Upper Heyford Nhants...54 H8
Upper Heyford Oxon...43 K6
Upper Hill Herefs...51 M10
Upper Hockenden Kent...33 P8
Upper Hopton Kirk...85 J11
Upper Howsell Worcs...52 E11
Upper Hulme Staffs...77 J11
Upper Ifold Surrey...14 E4
Upper Inglesham Swindn...30 E3
Upper Kilcott Gloucs...29 M5
Upper Killay Swans...26 E3
Upper Kinchrackine Ag & B...121 M7
Upper Knockando Moray...139 M7
Upper Lambourn W Berk...30 G6
Upper Landywood Staffs...64 H11
Upper Langford N Som...28 E9
Upper Langwith Derbys...78 E9
Upper Largo Fife...124 H12
Upper Leigh Staffs...65 J4
Upper Littleton N Som...28 H9
Upper Lochton Abers...132 H5
Upper Longdon Staffs...65 K9
Upper Ludstone Shrops...52 E2
Upper Lybster Highld...151 N9
Upper Lydbrook Gloucs...41 J8
Upper Lye Herefs...51 L7
Upper Maes-coed Herefs...40 E3
Upper Marham Norfk...69 N10
Upper Midhope Sheff...77 J3
Upper Milton Worcs...52 E6
Upper Minety Wilts...30 B4
Upper Moor Worcs...52 H11
Upper Moor Side Leeds...85 K9
Upper Mulben Moray...139 Q5
Upper Netchwood Shrops...52 B2
Upper Nobut Staffs...65 K5
Upper Norwood W Susx...14 E7
Upper Oddington Gloucs...42 E6
Upper Padley Derbys...77 N8
Upper Pennington Hants...12 E5
Upper Pollicott Bucks...43 Q9
Upper Poppleton C York...85 Q4
Upper Quinton Warwks...42 E4
Upper Ratley Hants...24 E8
Upper Rissington Gloucs...42 E7
Upper Rochford Worcs...52 B7
Upper Ruscoe D & G...95 N5
Upper Sapey Herefs...52 B8
Upper Saxondale Notts...66 H4
Upper Seagry Wilts...29 Q6
Upper Shelton C Beds...44 E4
Upper Sheringham Norfk...70 H4

Upper Skelmorlie N Ayrs...113 J8
Upper Slaughter Gloucs...42 D7
Upper Soudley Gloucs...41 K9
Upper Spond Herefs...51 K10
Upper Standen Kent...17 M3
Upper Staploe Bed...56 C8
Upper Stoke Norfk...71 K11
Upper Stondon C Beds...44 G4
Upper Stowe Nhants...54 F9
Upper Street Hants...23 P9
Upper Street Norfk...58 H5
Upper Street Norfk...71 L8
Upper Street Norfk...71 M9
Upper Street Suffk...47 L5
Upper Street Suffk...58 G10
Upper Strensham Worcs...41 P4
Upper Sundon C Beds...44 F6
Upper Swell Gloucs...42 C6
Upper Tankersley Barns...77 Q4
Upper Tean Staffs...65 J4
Upperthong Kirk...77 L2
Upperthorpe Derbys...78 D7
Upperthorpe N Linc...79 J4
Upper Threapwood Ches W...63 M3
Upperton W Susx...14 D6
Upper Town Derbys...77 Q10
Upper Town Derbys...77 N11
Upper Town Herefs...51 P11
Upper Town Highld...151 Q1
Upper Town N Som...28 H9
Upper Town Suffk...58 D7
Upper Tumble Carmth...38 C9
Upper Tysoe Warwks...42 H3
Upper Ufford Suffk...59 K10
Upperup Gloucs...30 B3
Upper Upham Wilts...30 F7
Upper Upnor Medway...34 D8
Upper Victoria Angus...125 K5
Upper Vobster Somset...22 F4
Upper Wardington Oxon...43 K3
Upper Weald M Keyn...44 A4
Upper Weedon Nhants...54 G9
Upper Welland Worcs...41 M3
Upper Wellingham E Susx...15 N8
Upper Weston BaNES...29 L9
Upper Weybread Suffk...59 J5
Upper Wick Worcs...52 F10
Upper Wield Hants...25 K5
Upper Winchendon Bucks...43 Q9
Upperwood Derbys...77 P12
Upper Woodford Wilts...23 P6
Upper Wootton Hants...25 K2
Upper Wraxall Wilts...29 N7
Upper Wyche Herefs...41 M3
Uppincott Devon...8 G4
Uppingham Rutlnd...67 L12
Uppington Dorset...11 N3
Uppington Shrops...63 Q10
Upsall N York...91 Q9
Upsettlington Border...117 K12
Upshire Essex...33 M2
Up Somborne Hants...24 F7
Upstreet Kent...35 M9
Up Sydling Dorset...10 F4
Upthorpe Suffk...58 E6
Upton Bucks...43 Q9
Upton C Pete...68 B12
Upton Cambs...56 C6
Upton Ches W...75 L10
Upton Cnwll...7 J4
Upton Cnwll...7 K10
Upton Cnwll...98 C10
Upton Devon...5 L8
Upton Devon...9 L6
Upton Dorset...10 H8
Upton Dorset...11 M6
Upton E R Yk...87 L4
Upton Halton...75 N6
Upton Hants...24 F10
Upton Hants...24 F2
Upton Leics...66 B12
Upton Lincs...79 L6
Upton Nhants...55 J8
Upton Norfk...71 M9
Upton Notts...67 J1
Upton Notts...79 J8
Upton Oxon...31 L6
Upton Oxon...42 F9
Upton Pembks...37 K9
Upton R & Cl...92 F3
Upton Slough...32 D6
Upton Somset...20 E7
Upton Somset...21 P8
Upton Wakefd...78 D1
Upton Warrtn...53 J6
Upton Wilts...23 J6
Upton Bishop Herefs...41 J6
Upton Cheyney S Glos...29 L8
Upton Cressett Shrops...52 C2
Upton Crews Herefs...41 K6
Upton Cross Cnwll...7 K10
Upton End C Beds...44 G5
Upton Grey Hants...25 M4
Upton Heath Ches W...75 L9
Upton Hellions Devon...8 H4
Upton Lovell Wilts...23 L5
Upton Magna Shrops...63 P9
Upton Noble Somset...22 F6
Upton Pyne Devon...8 H5
Upton St Leonards Gloucs...41 P8
Upton Scudamore Wilts...23 J4
Upton Snodsbury Worcs...52 H9
Upton Towans Cnwll...2 F7
Upton-upon-Severn Worcs...41 N4
Upton Warren Worcs...52 H7
Upwaltham W Susx...14 D8
Upware Cambs...57 K6
Upwell Norfk...69 J11
Upwey Dorset...10 G7
Upwick Green Herts...45 N7
Upwood Cambs...56 E4
Urchfont Wilts...30 B11
Urdimarsh Herefs...51 N11
Ure Bank N York...91 N12
Urlay Nook S on T...91 P4
Urmston Traffd...76 E5
Urpeth Dur...100 G7
Urquhart Moray...139 P3
Urquhart Castle Highld...137 P10
Urra N York...92 B6
Urray N York...137 N5
Uryside Abers...141 J11
Usan Angus...125 Q2
Ushaw Moor Dur...100 G9
Usk Mons...28 E2
Usselby Lincs...80 B5
Usworth Sundld...100 H7
Utkinton Ches W...75 P10
Utley C Brad...84 F6
Uton Devon...8 G5
Utterby Lincs...80 F5
Uttoxeter Staffs...65 K5
Uwchmynydd Gwynd...60 B7
Uxbridge Gt Lon...32 F5
Uyeasound Shet...147 k3
Uzmaston Pembks...37 J7

V
Vale Guern...12 c1
Valley IoA...72 D8
Valley End Surrey...32 D9
Valley Truckle Cnwll...6 H6
Valtos Highld...135 J3
Valtos W Isls...152 e3
Vange Essex...34 C5
Varteg Torfn...40 C10
Vatsetter Shet...147 j3
Vatten Highld...134 E7
Vaynor Myr Td...39 P9
Vazon Bay Guern...12 b2
Veensgarth Shet...147 i7
Velindre Powys...40 B4
Velly Devon...18 F8
Venngreen Devon...7 M2
Vennington Shrops...63 K10
Venn Ottery Devon...9 K6
Venny Tedburn Devon...8 G5
Venterdon Cnwll...7 L10
Ventnor IoW...13 J9
Venton Devon...5 L5
Vernham Dean Hants...30 H11
Vernham Street Hants...30 H11
Vernolds Common Shrops...51 N4
Verwood Dorset...11 Q3
Veryan Cnwll...3 M6
Veryan Green Cnwll...3 M6
Vicarage Devon...9 N7
Vickerstown Cumb...82 F1
Victoria Barns...77 M3
Victoria Blae G...40 A10
Victoria Cnwll...3 N2
Vidlin Shet...147 j5
Viewfield Moray...139 P3
Viewpark N Lans...114 C9
Vigo Kent...34 B10
Village de Putron Guern...12 c3
Ville la Bas Jersey...13 a1
Villiaze Guern...12 b3
Vinehall Street E Susx...16 D7
Vines Cross E Susx...15 Q7
Virginia Water Surrey...32 E9
Virginstow Devon...7 M6
Vobster Somset...22 F4
Voe Shet...147 i5
Vowchurch Herefs...40 E4
Vulcan Village St Hel...75 N5

W
Waberthwaite Cumb...88 E8
Wackerfield Dur...91 K2
Wacton Norfk...58 H2
Wadborough Worcs...52 G11
Waddesdon Bucks...43 Q8
Waddeton Devon...5 P5
Waddicar Sefton...75 L4
Waddingham Lincs...79 N4
Waddington Lancs...83 Q6
Waddington Lincs...79 N11
Waddon Devon...8 G9
Waddon Dorset...10 F7
Waddon Gt Lon...33 K9
Wadebridge Cnwll...6 G10
Wadeford Somset...21 N11
Wadenhoe Nhants...55 P4
Wadesmill Herts...45 L8
Wadhurst E Susx...16 C4
Wadshelf Derbys...77 P9
Wadswick Wilts...29 N8
Wadworth Donc...78 F4
Waen Denbgs...74 F11
Waen Denbgs...74 F10
Waen Powys...62 H8
Waen Powys...62 H8
Waen Fach Powys...62 H8
Waen-pentir Gwynd...73 K10
Waen-wen Gwynd...73 K10
Wagbeach Shrops...63 L11
Wainfelin Torfn...28 C2
Wainfleet All Saints Lincs...81 J12
Wainfleet Bank Lincs...81 J11
Wainfleet St Mary Lincs...81 J11
Wainford Norfk...59 L3
Wainhouse Corner Cnwll...6 H4
Wainscott Medway...34 C8
Wain's Hill N Som...28 D8
Wainstalls Calder...84 F9
Waitby Cumb...90 B5
Waithe Lincs...80 F4
Wakefield Wakefd...85 M11
Wake Green Birm...53 K4
Wakerley Nhants...67 N12
Wakes Colne Essex...46 F6
Walberswick Suffk...59 P6
Walberton W Susx...14 D9
Walbottle N u Ty...100 F5
Walbutt D & G...96 F5
Walby Cumb...98 F6
Walcombe Somset...22 D4
Walcot Lincs...67 Q5
Walcot N Linc...86 D10
Walcot Shrops...63 J6
Walcot Swindn...30 D8
Walcot Warwks...53 L9
Walcote Leics...54 F3
Walcot Green Norfk...58 H4
Walcott Lincs...80 D10
Walcott Norfk...71 M5
Walden N York...90 G10
Walden Head N York...90 G10
Walden Stubbs N York...85 R12
Walderslade Medway...34 D9
Walderton W Susx...13 M3
Walditch Dorset...10 D6
Waldley Derbys...65 L5
Waldridge Dur...100 G8
Waldringfield Suffk...47 M3
Waldron E Susx...15 P7
Wales Rothm...78 D6
Wales Somset...22 D8
Walesby Lincs...80 D5
Walesby Notts...78 H9
Walford Herefs...40 G5
Walford Herefs...41 J6
Walford Shrops...63 M7
Walford Staffs...64 F6
Walford Heath Shrops...63 M8
Walgherton Ches E...64 C2
Walgrave Nhants...55 K6
Walhampton Hants...12 H5
Walkden Salfd...76 D3
Walker N u Ty...100 H5
Walker Fold Lancs...83 P7
Walkeringham Notts...79 J5
Walkerith Lincs...79 J5
Walkern Herts...45 K6
Walker's Green Herefs...51 N11
Walker's Heath Birm...53 K5
Walkerton Fife...115 N1
Walkford BCP...12 C6
Walkhampton Devon...4 H3
Walkington E R Yk...87 J8
Walkley Sheff...77 P5
Walk Mill Lancs...84 C9
Walkwood Worcs...53 J7

Wall Nthumb...99 P4
Wall Staffs...65 L11
Wallacetown S Ayrs...104 E5
Wallacetown S Ayrs...104 F5
Wallands Park E Susx...15 M8
Wallasey Wirral...75 J5
Wallasey (Kingsway) Tunnel Wirral...75 K6
Wall End Cumb...88 H10
Wall End Herefs...51 M9
Wallend Medway...34 F7
Wall Heath Dudley...52 G3
Wallhead Cumb...98 F6
Wallingford Oxon...31 M4
Wallington Gt Lon...33 K9
Wallington Hants...13 J3
Wallington Herts...45 K5
Wallington Heath Wsall...65 J10
Wallis Pembks...37 K5
Walliswood BCP...11 P6
Wall Houses Nthumb...100 D4
Walloch Cumb...89 K1
Wall under Haywood Shrops...51 N2
Wallyford E Loth...115 Q7
Walmer Kent...35 Q12
Walmer Bridge Lancs...83 L10
Walmersley Bury...76 E1
Walmley Birm...53 L2
Walmsgate Lincs...80 G8
Walpole Somset...21 M5
Walpole Suffk...59 M6
Walpole Cross Keys Norfk...69 K8
Walpole Highway Norfk...69 K9
Walpole St Andrew Norfk...69 K8
Walpole St Peter Norfk...69 J9
Walrow Somset...21 M4
Walsall Wsall...53 J1
Walsall Wood Wsall...65 J10
Walsden Calder...84 D11
Walsgrave on Sowe Covtry...54 C4
Walsham le Willows Suffk...58 E6
Walshaw Bury...76 E1
Walshford N York...85 N4
Walsoken Norfk...69 J10
Walston S Lans...115 K12
Walsworth Herts...44 H5
Walter's Ash Bucks...32 C3
Walters Green Kent...15 P3
Walterston V Glam...27 Q8
Walterstone Herefs...40 D6
Waltham Kent...17 K1
Waltham NE Lin...80 E3
Waltham Abbey Essex...33 M2
Waltham Chase Hants...25 J10
Waltham Cross Herts...33 L2
Waltham on the Wolds Leics...67 K7
Waltham St Lawrence W & M...32 B7
Waltham's Cross Essex...46 C5
Walthamstow Gt Lon...33 L4
Walton C Pete...68 D11
Walton Cumb...98 G6
Walton Derbys...78 B10
Walton Leeds...85 N6
Walton Leics...54 F4
Walton M Keyn...44 C4
Walton Powys...51 J9
Walton Shrops...51 M5
Walton Somset...22 C6
Walton Staffs...64 F6
Walton Staffs...64 E6
Walton Suffk...47 N4
Walton W Susx...13 M3
Walton Wakefd...85 M11
Walton Warwks...53 P9
Walton Wrekin...64 C10
Walton Cardiff Gloucs...41 P5
Walton East Pembks...37 K6
Walton Elm Dorset...22 F9
Walton Grounds Nhants...43 L5
Walton Highway Norfk...69 J9
Walton-in-Gordano N Som...28 F7
Walton-le-Dale Lancs...83 M9
Walton-on-Thames Surrey...32 G9
Walton-on-the-Hill Staffs...64 H8
Walton-on-the-Hill Surrey...33 J10
Walton-on-the-Naze Essex...47 N7
Walton on the Wolds Leics...66 F8
Walton-on-Trent Derbys...65 N8
Walton Park Pembks...37 J5
Walton West Pembks...36 G8
Walwen Flints...74 G9
Walwen Flints...74 H9
Walwick Nthumb...99 P4
Walworth Darltn...91 M4
Walworth Gt Lon...33 L7
Walworth Gate Darltn...91 L3
Walwyn's Castle Pembks...36 G8
Wambrook Somset...9 P3
Wampool Cumb...97 P7
Wanborough Surrey...14 D1
Wanborough Swindn...30 E6
Wandon End Herts...44 G7
Wandsworth Gt Lon...33 J7
Wangford Suffk...59 N5
Wanlip Leics...66 F10
Wanlockhead D & G...105 K2
Wannock E Susx...15 Q10
Wansford C Pete...68 D12
Wansford E R Yk...87 K4
Wanshurst Green Kent...16 D2
Wanstead Gt Lon...33 M5
Wanstrow Somset...22 F5
Wanswell Gloucs...29 K2
Wantage Oxon...31 J5
Wants Green Worcs...52 E9
Wapley S Glos...29 L7
Wappenbury Warwks...54 B7
Wappenham Nhants...43 M3
Warbleton E Susx...15 R7
Warborough Oxon...31 M4
Warboys Cambs...56 F4
Warbreck Bpool...82 H7
Warbstow Cnwll...7 J4
Warburton Traffd...76 C6
Warcop Cumb...90 C4
Warden Kent...34 H8
Warden Nthumb...99 P5
Ward End Birm...53 L3
Ward Green Suffk...58 F8
Warden Green Cross Suffk...58 F8
Wardhedges C Beds...44 F4
Wardington Oxon...43 K3
Wardle Ches E...64 B1
Wardle Rochdl...84 D12
Wardley Gatesd...101 J5
Wardley Rutlnd...67 L12
Wardley Salfd...76 E3

Wardlow Derbys...77 M8
Wardsend Ches E...76 H7
Wardy Hill Cambs...57 J4
Ware Herts...45 L9
Wareham Dorset...11 M7
Warehorne Kent...16 H4
Warenford Nthumb...109 J4
Waren Mill Nthumb...109 J3
Warenton Nthumb...109 J4
Wareside Herts...45 M8
Waresley Cambs...56 E9
Waresley Worcs...52 F6
Ware Street Kent...34 D11
Warfield Br For...32 C8
Warfleet Devon...5 P7
Wargate Lincs...68 E6
Wargrave Wokham...31 N7
Warham Herefs...40 G4
Warham Norfk...70 D4
Wark Nthumb...108 D2
Wark Nthumb...99 M5
Warkleigh Devon...19 M9
Warkton Nhants...55 L5
Warkworth Nhants...43 K4
Warkworth Nthumb...109 L8
Warlaby N York...91 N8
Warland Calder...84 E11
Warleggan Cnwll...4 B3
Warleigh BaNES...29 M9
Warley Town Calder...84 G10
Warlingham Surrey...33 L10
Warmbrook Derbys...65 P1
Warmfield Wakefd...85 M11
Warmingham Ches E...76 D11
Warmington Nhants...55 Q3
Warmington Warwks...54 C11
Warminster Wilts...23 J4
Warmley S Glos...29 L8
Warmsworth Donc...78 E4
Warmwell Dorset...11 J7
Warndon Worcs...52 G9
Warner Bros. Studio Tour Herts...32 F2
Warnford Hants...25 M8
Warnham W Susx...14 G4
Warnham Court W Susx...14 G4
Warningcamp W Susx...14 E9
Warninglid W Susx...15 J5
Warren Ches E...76 G9
Warren Pembks...36 H11
Warrenby R & Cl...92 C2
Warrenhill S Lans...106 B2
Warren Row W & M...32 A6
Warren's Green Herts...45 K6
Warren Street Kent...34 G11
Warrington M Keyn...55 M10
Warrington Warrtn...75 Q6
Warriston C Edin...115 N6
Warsash Hants...12 H3
Warslow Staffs...77 K12
Warsop Vale Notts...78 E10
Warter E R Yk...86 G5
Warthermaske N York...91 L11
Warthill N York...86 C4
Wartling E Susx...16 B9
Wartnaby Leics...66 H7
Warton Lancs...83 L10
Warton Lancs...89 M12
Warton Nthumb...108 H8
Warton Warwks...53 P11
Warwick Warwks...53 Q8
Warwick Bridge Cumb...98 F7
Warwick Castle Warwks...53 P7
Warwick-on-Eden Cumb...98 F7
Warwick Services Warwks...53 Q9
Wasbister Ork...147 c1
Wasdale Head Cumb...88 G5
Wash Derbys...77 K7
Washall Green Herts...45 N6
Washaway Cnwll...6 G10
Washbourne Devon...5 N6
Washbrook Suffk...47 K3
Washfield Devon...20 D10
Washfold N York...90 H6
Washford Somset...20 G5
Washford Pyne Devon...8 E2
Washingborough Lincs...79 P10
Washington Sundld...101 J7
Washington W Susx...14 G8
Washington Services Gatesd...100 H7
Washwood Heath Birm...53 L3
Wasing W Berk...31 M9
Waskerley Dur...100 D8
Wasperton Warwks...53 P9
Wasps Nest Lincs...79 Q10
Wass N York...92 B11
Wast Water Cumb...88 F5
Watchet Somset...20 H4
Watchfield Oxon...30 F4
Watchfield Somset...21 M4
Watchgate Cumb...89 N7
Watchill Cumb...89 Q8
Watcombe Torbay...5 Q3
Watendlath Cumb...89 J3
Water Devon...8 E8
Water Lancs...84 C10
Waterbeach Cambs...57 J7
Waterbeck D & G...97 Q3
Waterden Norfk...70 C5
Water Eaton Oxon...43 L9
Water Eaton Oxon...64 G10
Water End Bed...56 B10
Water End C Beds...44 F3
Water End E R Yk...86 E7
Water End Essex...45 Q4
Water End Herts...44 G9
Water End Herts...45 J10
Waterfall Staffs...65 J2
Waterfoot Ag & B...103 L3
Waterfoot Lancs...84 C11
Waterford Herts...45 K9
Water Fryston Wakefd...85 P10
Watergate Cnwll...6 G8
Waterhead Cumb...89 K6
Waterheads Border...115 N11
Waterhouses Dur...100 F10
Waterhouses Staffs...65 J2
Wateringbury Kent...34 B11
Waterlane Gloucs...41 Q10
Waterloo Derbys...78 C11
Waterloo Highld...135 M11
Waterloo N Lans...114 E10
Waterloo Norfk...71 J8
Waterloo P & K...123 R6
Waterloo Pembks...37 J10
Waterloo Sefton...75 K4
Waterloo Cross Devon...20 G10
Waterloo Port Gwynd...72 H11
Waterlooville Hants...13 L3
Watermead Bucks...44 C8
Watermillock Cumb...89 M2
Water Newton Cambs...56 C2
Water Orton Warwks...53 M3
Waterperry Oxon...43 N9
Waterrow Somset...20 G8
Watersfield W Susx...14 E7
Waterside Bl w D...83 Q10

Waterside Bucks...32 D2
Waterside Cumb...97 P9
Waterside Donc...86 C12
Waterside E Ayrs...104 H8
Waterside E Ayrs...105 J1
Waterside E Duns...114 C6
Water's Nook Bolton...76 C3
Waterstein Highld...134 C7
Waterstock Oxon...43 N10
Waterston Pembks...36 H9
Water Stratford Bucks...43 N5
Water Street Neath...27 J6
Waters Upton Wrekin...64 B8
Water Yeat Cumb...89 J9
Watford Herts...32 G3
Watford Nhants...54 G7
Watford Gap Services Nhants...54 F7
Wath N York...84 H2
Wath N York...91 N11
Wath upon Dearne Rothm...78 C3
Watlington Norfk...69 M10
Watlington Oxon...31 P3
Watnall Notts...66 E3
Watten Highld...151 N6
Wattisfield Suffk...58 E6
Wattisham Suffk...58 E10
Watton Dorset...10 C6
Watton E R Yk...87 J5
Watton Norfk...70 D12
Watton-at-Stone Herts...45 K8
Watton Green Norfk...70 D12
Wattons Green Essex...33 P3
Wattston N Lans...114 D7
Wattstown Rhondd...27 M4
Wattsville Caerph...28 B4
Wauldby E R Yk...86 H9
Waulkmill Abers...132 G6
Waunarlwydd Swans...26 F3
Waun Fach Powys...40 B6
Waunfawr Cerdgn...49 K4
Waunfawr Gwynd...73 J11
Waungron Swans...38 E11
Waunlwyd Blae G...40 A10
Wavendon M Keyn...44 C4
Waverbridge Cumb...97 P8
Waverton Ches W...75 M11
Waverton Cumb...97 P9
Wawne E R Yk...87 K8
Waxham Norfk...71 N7
Waxholme E R Yk...87 R9
Way Kent...35 P9
Waye Devon...8 E10
Wayford Somset...10 B3
Waytown Dorset...10 D5
Way Village Devon...8 G3
Way Wick N Som...28 E10
Weacombe Somset...20 H5
Weald Oxon...42 G11
Wealdstone Gt Lon...32 H4
Weardley Leeds...85 L6
Weare Somset...21 N4
Weare Giffard Devon...19 J8
Wearhead Dur...99 N10
Wearne Somset...21 P8
Weasdale Cumb...90 A6
Weasenham All Saints Norfk...70 C8
Weasenham St Peter Norfk...70 C7
Weaste Salfd...76 E4
Weatheroak Hill Worcs...53 K6
Weaverham Ches W...75 Q9
Weaverslake Staffs...65 L9
Weaverthorpe N York...86 H1
Webbington Somset...21 N2
Webb's Heath S Glos...29 K7
Webheath Worcs...53 J7
Webton Herefs...40 F4
Wedderlairs Abers...141 K9
Wedding Hall Fold N York...84 E6
Weddington Warwks...54 B2
Wedhampton Wilts...30 C11
Wedmore Somset...21 P4
Wednesbury Sandw...53 J2
Wednesfield Wolves...64 H12
Weecar Notts...79 J10
Weedon Bucks...44 B8
Weedon Bec Nhants...54 G9
Weedon Lois Nhants...43 M2
Weeford Staffs...65 L11
Week Devon...5 N4
Week Devon...19 L8
Week Devon...19 P10
Weeke Devon...8 E3
Weeke Hants...24 H7
Weekley Nhants...55 M4
Week St Mary Cnwll...7 J4
Weel E R Yk...87 K7
Weeley Essex...47 L7
Weeley Heath Essex...47 L7
Weem P & K...123 J4
Weeping Cross Staffs...64 H8
Weethley Warwks...53 K9
Weeting Norfk...57 P3
Weeton E R Yk...87 R10
Weeton Lancs...83 J8
Weeton N York...85 L5
Weetwood Leeds...85 K7
Weir Lancs...84 C10
Weirbrook Shrops...63 K7
Weir Quay Devon...4 F4
Weisdale Shet...147 i6
Welborne Norfk...70 F10
Welbourn Lincs...79 M12
Welburn N York...86 D2
Welbury N York...91 P6
Welby Lincs...67 N4
Welches Dam Cambs...57 J3
Welcombe Devon...18 E9
Weldon Nhants...55 M3
Weldon Bridge Nthumb...109 J10
Welford W Berk...31 J8
Welford Nhants...54 G4
Welford-on-Avon Warwks...53 L10
Welham Leics...55 J2
Welham Notts...79 J7
Welham Bridge E R Yk...86 E8
Welham Green Herts...45 J10
Well Hants...25 N4
Well Lincs...81 J8
Well N York...91 M10
Welland Worcs...41 M4
Wellbank Angus...125 J5
Well End Bucks...32 C5
Well End Herts...32 H3
Wellesbourne Mountford Warwks...53 P9
Well Head Herts...44 H6
Well Hill Kent...33 N9
Wellhouse W Berk...31 L8
Welling Gt Lon...33 N7
Wellingborough Nhants...55 L7
Wellingham Norfk...70 C7
Wellingore Lincs...79 N12
Wellington Cumb...88 E6
Wellington Herefs...51 N11
Wellington Somset...20 H9
Wellington Wrekin...64 B9
Wellington Heath Herefs...41 L3
Wellington Marsh Herefs...51 N11
Wellow BaNES...29 L10
Wellow IoW...12 F7

Wellow Notts 78 H10
Wellpond Green Herts 45 M7
Wells Somset 22 D4
Wellsborough Leics 66 B11
Wells Green Ches E 64 C1
Wells Head C Brad 84 G8
Wells-next-the-Sea Norfk 70 D3
Wellstye Green Essex 46 B8
Well Town Devon 9 J4
Welltree P & K 123 J8
Wellwood Fife 115 K3
Welney Norfk 57 K2
Welshampton Shrops 63 M5
Welsh Bicknor Herefs 41 J8
Welsh End Shrops 63 N5
Welsh Frankton Shrops 63 K5
Welsh Hook Pembks 36 H5
Welsh Newton Herefs 40 G8
Welshpool Powys 62 H10
Welsh St Donats V Glam 27 N7
Welton Cumb 98 D9
Welton E R Yk 86 H9
Welton Lincs 79 P8
Welton Nhants 54 F7
Welton le Marsh Lincs 81 J10
Welton le Wold Lincs 80 G6
Welwick E R Yk 87 Q11
Welwyn Herts 45 J8
Welwyn Garden City Herts 45 J9
Wem Shrops 63 N6
Wembdon Somset 21 L6
Wembley Gt Lon 32 H5
Wembury Devon 4 H7
Wembworthy Devon 8 C3
Wemyss Bay Inver 113 J7
Wenallt Cerdgn 49 L6
Wendens Ambo Essex 45 P4
Wendlebury Oxon 43 M8
Wendling Norfk 70 D9
Wendover Bucks 44 B10
Wendron Cnwll 2 H8
Wendron Mining District Cnwll 2 H8
Wendy Cambs 56 F11
Wenfordbridge Cnwll 6 F9
Wenhaston Suffk 59 N5
Wennington Cambs 56 E5
Wennington Gt Lon 33 P6
Wennington Lancs 83 N1
Wensley Derbys 77 N11
Wensley N York 90 H9
Wentbridge Wakefd 85 F11
Wentnor Shrops 51 L2
Wentworth Cambs 57 J5
Wentworth Rothm 78 C4
Wentworth Castle Barns 77 Q3
Wenvoe V Glam 27 Q8
Weobley Herefs 51 L10
Weobley Marsh Herefs 51 L10
Wepham W Susx 14 F9
Wereham Norfk 69 N11
Wergs Wolves 64 F12
Wern Gwynd 61 J4
Wern Powys 49 Q8
Wern Powys 63 J9
Wern Powys 63 J5
Wern Shrops 63 J5
Werneth Low Tamesd 76 H5
Wernffrwd Swans 26 D3
Wern-Gifford Mons 40 D7
Wern-y-gaer Flints 74 H10
Werrington C Pete 68 C11
Werrington Cnwll 7 L7
Werrington Staffs 64 H3
Wervin Ches W 75 M9
Wesham Lancs 83 K8
Wessington Derbys 78 B12
West Aberthaw V Glam 27 N8
West Acre Norfk 69 P9
West Allerdean Nthumb 117 L12
West Alvington Devon 5 M8
West Amesbury Wilts 23 P5
West Anstey Devon 20 C8
West Appleton N York 91 L8
West Ashby Lincs 80 E9
West Ashling W Susx 13 P3
West Ashton Wilts 23 J2
West Auckland Dur 91 K2
West Ayton N York 93 K9
West Bagborough Somset 21 J6
West Bank Blae G 40 B10
West Bank Halton 75 N7
West Barkwith Lincs 80 C7
West Barnby N York 92 G4
West Barns E Loth 116 F6
West Barsham Norfk 70 D5
West Bay Dorset 10 D6
West Beckham Norfk 70 H4
West Bedfont Surrey 32 F7
Westbere Kent 35 M10
West Bergholt Essex 46 G6
West Bexington Dorset 10 E7
West Bilney Norfk 69 N9
West Blatchington Br & H 15 K9
West Boldon S Tyne 101 J6
Westborough Lincs 67 L3
Westbourne BCP 11 P6
Westbourne W Susx 13 N3
West Bourton Dorset 22 G7
West Bowling C Brad 85 J9
West Brabourne Kent 17 K2
West Bradenham Norfk 70 D10
West Bradford Lancs 83 R6
West Bradley Somset 22 D6
West Bretton Wakefd 77 P1
West Bridgford Notts 66 F3
West Briscoe Dur 90 F3
West Bromwich Sandw 53 J1
Westbrook Kent 35 P8
Westbrook W Berk 31 J8
Westbrook Wilts 29 Q7
West Buckland Devon 19 M7
West Buckland Somset 21 J8
West Burrafirth Shet 147 h6
West Burton N York 90 G9
West Burton W Susx 14 E8
Westbury Bucks 43 N4
Westbury Shrops 63 K10
Westbury Wilts 23 J3
Westbury Leigh Wilts 23 J3
Westbury-on-Severn Gloucs 41 J9
Westbury-on-Trym Bristl 28 H7
Westbury-sub-Mendip Somset 22 C3
West Butsfield Dur 100 F1
West Butterwick N Linc 79 L3
Westby Lancs 83 K8
West Byfleet Surrey 32 F10
West Cairngaan D & G 94 G12
West Caister Norfk 71 P10
West Calder W Loth 115 J8
West Camel Somset 22 D8
West Chaldon Dorset 11 K8
West Challow Oxon 30 H5
West Charleton Devon 5 M8
West Chelborough Dorset 10 E4
West Chevington Nthumb 109 L10
West Chiltington W Susx 14 F7
West Chinnock Somset 21 P10
West Chisenbury Wilts 23 P3
West Clandon Surrey 32 F11
West Cliffe Kent 17 Q2
West Clyst Devon 8 H6
West Coker Somset 22 C10

West Combe Devon 5 M4
Westcombe Somset 22 F5
West Compton Somset 22 D5
West Compton Abbas Dorset 10 E6
Westcote Gloucs 42 E7
Westcote Barton Oxon 43 J6
Westcott Bucks 43 P8
Westcott Devon 9 J4
Westcott Surrey 14 G1
West Cottingwith N York 86 C7
West Cowick E R Yk 86 C11
West Cross Swans 26 F4
West Curry Cnwll 7 K6
West Curthwaite Cumb 98 C8
West Dean Gloucs 41 J9
West Dean W Susx 13 P3
West Dean Wilts 24 B8
West Deeping Lincs 68 B10
West Down Devon 19 J4
Westdown Camp Wilts 23 M4
Westdowns Cnwll 6 F8
West Drayton Gt Lon 32 F6
West Drayton Notts 78 H8
West Dunnet Highld 151 M2
West Ella E R Yk 87 J9
West End Bed 55 N10
West End Br For 32 D8
West End Caerph 28 B3
West End Cumb 98 D7
West End E R Yk 86 G9
West End E R Yk 87 M9
West End E R Yk 87 P9
West End Hants 24 H10
West End Herts 25 L6
West End Herts 45 J10
West End Lancs 45 L10
West End Leeds 85 K7
West End Lincs 80 F6
West End N Som 28 F8
West End N York 84 H1
West End Norfk 70 D10
West End Norfk 71 P10
West End Oxon 31 M5
West End S Glos 29 J8
West End Somset 22 F6
West End Surrey 32 D10
West End Surrey 32 G9
West End W & M 32 B7
West End W Susx 14 H7
West End Wilts 23 K8
West End Wilts 23 L8
West End Green Hants 31 Q8
Westenhanger Kent 17 K3
Wester Aberchalder Highld 137 P11
Westerdale Highld 151 L6
Westerdale N York 92 D5
Westerfield Suffk 58 H11
Westergate W Susx 14 D10
Westerham Kent 33 N11
Westerhope N u Ty 100 F5
Westerland Devon 5 P4
Westerleigh S Glos 29 L6
Western Isles W Isls 152 e6
Wester Ochiltree W Loth 115 J6
Wester Pitkierie Fife 125 L11
Wester Ross Highld 143 P9
Westerton W Susx 14 C9
Westerton of Rossie Angus 125 N2
Westerwick Shet 147 h7
West Ewell Surrey 32 H9
West Farleigh Kent 34 C11
West Farndon Nhants 54 E10
West Felton Shrops 63 K7
Westfield BaNES 22 F3
Westfield Cumb 88 C1
Westfield E Susx 16 E8
Westfield Highld 151 J4
Westfield N Lans 114 D6
Westfield Norfk 70 E10
Westfield Surrey 32 E11
Westfield W Loth 114 G7
Westfields Dorset 10 G3
Westfields Herefs 40 G3
Westfields of Rattray P & K 124 D3
Westfield Sole Kent 34 D10
West Flotmanby N York 93 M11
Westford Somset 21 J8
Westgate Dur 99 P10
Westgate N Linc 79 K2
Westgate Norfk 70 D2
Westgate Hill C Brad 85 J9
Westgate-on-Sea Kent 35 P8
Westgate Street Norfk 71 J8
West Ginge Oxon 31 J5
West Grafton Wilts 30 D10
West Green Hants 31 Q11
West Grimstead Wilts 24 C8
West Grinstead W Susx 14 H6
West Haddlesey N York 85 R10
West Haddon Nhants 54 G6
West Hagbourne Oxon 31 L5
West Hagley Worcs 52 G4
Westhall Suffk 59 N4
West Hallam Derbys 66 C4
West Hallam Common Derbys 66 C4
West Halton N Linc 86 G11
Westham Dorset 10 G9
Westham E Susx 16 B10
West Ham Gt Lon 33 M5
Westham Somset 21 N4
Westhampnett W Susx 14 C9
West Handley Derbys 78 C8
West Hanney Oxon 31 J4
West Hanningfield Essex 34 C2
West Harnham Wilts 23 P7
West Harptree BaNES 28 H11
West Harting Somset 21 L9
West Hatch Somset 21 L9
West Hatch Wilts 23 K8
West Haven Angus 125 L11
Westhead Lancs 75 M2
West Heath Norfk 53 J5
West Heath Norfk 71 J5
West Helmsdale Highld 147 J2
West Hendred Oxon 31 J5
West Heslerton N York 93 J11
West Hewish N Som 28 F8
Westhide Herefs 41 J3
Westhill Abers 133 K3
West Hill Devon 9 K6
Westhill Highld 138 D7
West Hoathly W Susx 15 L4
West Holme Dorset 11 L7
Westholme Somset 22 D4
Westhope Herefs 51 M10
Westhope Shrops 51 M3
West Horndon Essex 34 A5
Westhorpe Lincs 68 D5
Westhorpe Suffk 58 F7
West Horrington Somset 22 D4

West Horsley Surrey 32 F11
West Horton Nthumb 108 G4
West Hougham Kent 17 N3
Westhoughton Bolton 76 C2
Westhouse N York 89 R12
Westhouses Derbys 78 C12
West Howe BCP 11 P5
West Howetown Somset 20 E6
Westhumble Surrey 32 H12
West Huntingtower P & K 124 B8
West Huntspill Somset 21 M4
West Hyde C Beds 44 G8
West Hyde Herts 32 E4
West Hythe Kent 17 L6
West Ilkerton Devon 19 N4
West Ilsley W Berk 31 K6
West Itchenor W Susx 13 P4
West Keal Lincs 80 G11
West Kennett Wilts 30 C8
West Kilbride N Ayrs 113 J11
West Kingsdown Kent 33 Q9
West Kington Wilts 29 N6
West Kirby Wirral 74 H6
West Knapton N York 92 H11
West Knighton Dorset 10 H7
West Knoyle Wilts 23 J7
West Kyloe Nthumb 108 H2
Westlake Devon 5 L6
West Lambrook Somset 21 P9
Westland Green Herts 45 M7
West Langdon Kent 17 P1
West Lavington W Susx 14 C7
West Lavington Wilts 23 M3
West Layton N York 91 J5
West Leake Notts 66 E7
West Learmouth Nthumb 108 D2
West Lees N York 91 Q6
West Leigh Devon 8 C4
Westleigh Devon 19 J7
Westleigh Devon 20 G10
West Leigh Somset 20 H7
Westleton Suffk 59 N7
West Lexham Norfk 70 B8
Westley Shrops 51 L10
Westley Suffk 58 B8
Westley Waterless Cambs 57 M9
West Lilling N York 86 C2
Westlington Bucks 43 Q9
West Linton Border 115 L11
West Littleton S Glos 29 M7
West Lockinge Oxon 31 J5
West Lulworth Dorset 11 K8
West Lutton N York 86 H1
West Lydford Somset 22 D7
West Lyn Devon 19 P4
West Lyng Somset 21 M7
West Lynn Norfk 69 L8
West Malling Kent 34 B10
West Malvern Worcs 41 M2
West Marden W Susx 25 N11
West Markham Notts 79 J9
Westmarsh Kent 35 N10
West Marsh NE Lin 80 E2
West Marton N York 84 D5
West Melbury Dorset 23 J9
West Melton Rothm 78 C3
West Meon Hants 25 L8
West Meon Hut Hants 25 L8
West Meon Woodlands Hants 25 L8
West Mersea Essex 46 H9
Westmeston E Susx 15 L8
West Mickley Nthumb 100 D6
West Midland Safari Park Worcs 52 E5
Westmill Herts 45 L6
Westmill Herts 45 L8
West Milton Dorset 10 D5
Westminster Gt Lon 33 L5
Westminster Abbey & Palace Gt Lon 33 K6
West Molesey Surrey 32 G8
West Monkton Somset 21 L7
West Moors Dorset 11 M4
West Morden Dorset 11 L6
West Morriston Border 107 P2
West Morton C Brad 84 G8
West Mudford Somset 22 D9
Westmuir Angus 124 G2
West Ness N York 92 E11
West Newbiggin Darltn 91 N3
West Newton E R Yk 87 M7
West Newton Norfk 69 N6
West Newton Somset 21 L7
West Norwood Gt Lon 33 L7
Westoe S Tyne 101 K5
West Ogwell Devon 5 N3
Weston BaNES 29 L9
Weston Ches E 64 D2
Weston Ches E 76 D3
Weston Devon 9 M7
Weston Devon 10 C5
Weston Halton 75 N7
Weston Hants 25 M9
Weston Herefs 51 L9
Weston Herts 45 J5
Weston Lincs 68 F7
Weston N York 85 J6
Weston Notts 79 K10
Weston Shrops 51 L6
Weston Shrops 51 Q2
Weston Shrops 63 J8
Weston Staffs 64 H7
Weston W Berk 31 J7
Weston by Welland Nhants 55 K2
Weston Colley Hants 24 H5
Weston Colville Cambs 57 L10
Weston Corbett Hants 25 L4
Weston Coyney C Stke 64 H3
Weston Favell Nhants 55 K8
Weston Green Cambs 57 M10
Weston Heath Shrops 64 E9
Weston Hills Lincs 68 E8
Weston in Arden Warwks 54 C3
Westoning C Beds 44 E8
Weston-in-Gordano N Som 28 F7
Westoning Woodend C Beds 44 E8
Weston Jones Staffs 64 E7
Weston Longville Norfk 70 G9
Weston Lullingfields Shrops 63 M7
Weston-on-Avon Warwks 53 M10
Weston-on-the-Green Oxon 43 L8
Weston Park Staffs 64 E10
Weston Patrick Hants 25 L4
Weston Rhyn Shrops 63 J5
Weston-sub-Edge Gloucs 42 C4
Weston-super-Mare N Som 28 D9
Weston Turville Bucks 44 B9
Weston-under-Lizard Staffs 64 E10
Weston under Penyard Herefs 41 K7
Weston-under-Redcastle Shrops 63 P6

Weston under Wetherley Warwks 54 B7
Weston Underwood Derbys 65 P4
Weston Underwood M Keyn 55 L10
Weston-upon-Trent Derbys 66 C6
Westonzoyland Somset 21 M6
West Orchard Dorset 22 H10
West Overton Wilts 30 D9
Westow N York 86 D2
West Panson Devon 7 K5
West Park Abers 133 J5
West Parley Dorset 11 Q5
West Peckham Kent 34 B11
West Peeke Devon 7 K5
West Pelton Dur 100 G7
West Pennard Somset 22 D5
West Pentire Cnwll 3 J2
West Pinchbeck Lincs 68 D7
West Porlock Somset 20 D4
Westport Somset 21 N9
West Pulham Dorset 10 H3
West Putford Devon 18 G10
West Quantoxhead Somset 20 H5
Westquarter Falk 114 G6
Westra V Glam 27 Q8
West Raddon Devon 8 H4
West Rainton Dur 101 J7
West Rasen Lincs 79 P6
West Ravendale NE Lin 80 E4
Westray Ork 147 E2
Westray Airport Ork 147 c1
West Raynham Norfk 70 C7
West Retford Notts 78 H7
Westridge Green W Berk 31 M6
Westrigg W Loth 114 G8
Westrop Swindn 30 E4
West Rounton N York 91 P6
West Row Suffk 57 N5
West Rudham Norfk 70 B6
West Runton Norfk 71 J4
Westruther Border 116 E11
Westry Cambs 56 H1
West Saltoun E Loth 116 B8
West Sandford Devon 8 G4
West Sandwick Shet 147 j4
West Scrafton N York 90 H10
West Sleekburn Nthumb 100 H1
West Somerton Norfk 71 P8
West Stafford Dorset 10 H7
West Stockwith Notts 79 K5
West Stoke W Susx 13 P3
West Stonesdale N York 90 E6
West Stoughton Somset 21 P4
West Stour Dorset 22 G8
West Stourmouth Kent 35 N9
West Stow Suffk 57 Q6
West Stowell Wilts 30 D10
West Stratton Hants 25 J5
West Street Kent 34 F11
West Street Kent 34 G10
West Street Medway 34 C7
West Street Suffk 58 E6
West Tanfield N York 91 M11
West Taphouse Cnwll 4 A4
West Tarbert Ag & B 112 C8
West Tarring W Susx 14 G10
West Thirston Nthumb 109 K10
West Thorney W Susx 13 N4
Westthorpe Derbys 78 D8
West Thorpe Notts 66 G7
West Thurrock Thurr 33 Q7
West Tilbury Thurr 34 B7
West Tisted Hants 25 L7
West Torrington Lincs 80 C7
West Town BaNES 28 G8
West Town Hants 13 M5
West Town Herefs 51 M8
West Town N Som 28 G8
West Town Somset 22 C6
West Town Somset 22 F5
West Tytherley Hants 24 D7
West Walton Norfk 69 J9
Westward Cumb 98 C9
Westward Ho! Devon 18 H7
Westwell Kent 16 H2
Westwell Oxon 42 E9
Westwell Leacon Kent 16 G1
West Wellow Hants 24 D9
West Wembury Devon 4 H7
West Wemyss Fife 115 Q1
Westwick Cambs 56 H7
Westwick Dur 90 H4
West Wick N Som 28 E10
West Wickham Cambs 57 L10
West Wickham Gt Lon 33 M9
West Williamston Pembks 37 K9
West Winch Norfk 69 M9
West Winterslow Wilts 24 C7
West Wittering W Susx 13 N5
West Witton N York 90 H9
Westwood Devon 9 J5
Westwood Kent 35 R8
Westwood Nthumb 99 M5
Westwood Wilts 29 N10
West Woodburn Nthumb 108 E12
West Woodhay W Berk 31 J9
Westwood Heath Covtry 53 P5
West Woodlands Somset 22 H4
Westwoodside N Linc 79 J4
West Worldham Hants 25 M6
West Worthing W Susx 14 G10
West Wratting Cambs 57 M10
West Wycombe Bucks 32 B3
West Wylam Nthumb 100 F6
Westwick Highld 29 P7
West Yoke Kent 33 Q9
West Youlstone Cnwll 18 E10
Wetham Green Kent 34 E8
Wetheral Cumb 98 F7
Wetherby Leeds 85 N5
Wetherby Services Leeds 85 N5
Wetherden Suffk 58 F8
Wetheringsett Suffk 58 H7
Wethersfield Essex 46 C5
Wethersta Shet 147 i6
Wetherup Street Suffk 58 H8
Wetley Rocks Staffs 64 H3
Wettenhall Ches E 76 B11
Wetton Staffs 77 M12
Wetwang E R Yk 86 H3
Wetwood Staffs 64 E6
Wexcombe Wilts 30 F10
Wexham Slough 32 E6
Wexham Street Bucks 32 E6
Weybourne Norfk 70 G4
Weybourne Surrey 25 P3
Weybread Suffk 59 J5
Weybread Street Suffk 59 K5
Weybridge Surrey 32 F9
Weycroft Devon 9 Q5
Weydale Highld 151 M3
Weyhill Hants 24 D4
Weymouth Dorset 10 G9
Whaddon Bucks 43 Q5
Whaddon Cambs 45 J2
Whaddon Gloucs 41 M9
Whaddon Wilts 24 B9
Whaddon Wilts 29 N9
Whale Cumb 89 P2
Whaley Derbys 78 E9

Whaley Bridge Derbys 77 J7
Whaley Thorns Derbys 78 E9
Whaligoe Highld 151 P8
Whalley Lancs 83 Q8
Whalley Banks Lancs 83 Q8
Whalsay Shet 147 k5
Whalton Nthumb 100 F2
Whaplode Lincs 68 F7
Whaplode Drove Lincs 68 F9
Wharf Warwks 54 C10
Wharfe Lancs 83 N5
Wharles Lancs 83 K8
Wharley End C Beds 44 D3
Wharncliffe Side Sheff 77 P5
Wharram-le-Street N York 86 F2
Wharton Ches W 76 B10
Wharton Herefs 51 N9
Whashton N York 91 K5
Whasset Cumb 89 N3
Whatcote Warwks 42 G3
Whateley Warwks 65 N12
Whatfield Suffk 47 J3
Whatley Somset 10 B3
Whatley Somset 22 G4
Whatley's End S Glos 29 K6
Whatlington E Susx 16 C7
Whatsole Street Kent 17 K2
Whatstandwell Derbys 65 Q1
Whatton-in-the-Vale Notts 67 J4
Whauphill D & G 95 M8
Whaw N York 90 G6
Wheal Peevor Cnwll 2 H5
Wheal Rose Cnwll 2 H5
Wheatacre Norfk 59 P2
Wheatfield Oxon 31 P2
Wheathampstead Herts 44 H9
Wheathill Shrops 52 B4
Wheathill Somset 22 D7
Wheatley Hants 25 N6
Wheatley Oxon 43 M10
Wheatley Hill Dur 101 K10
Wheatley Hills Donc 78 F3
Wheatley Lane Lancs 84 C7
Wheaton Aston Staffs 64 F9
Wheddon Cross Somset 20 E5
Wheelbarrow Town Kent 17 L2
Wheeler End Bucks 32 B3
Wheeler's Green Wokham 31 Q8
Wheelerstreet Surrey 14 D3
Wheelock Ches E 76 D2
Wheelock Heath Ches E 76 D12
Wheelton Lancs 83 N11
Wheldale Wakefd 85 P10
Wheldrake C York 86 C6
Whelford Gloucs 30 D3
Whelpley Hill Bucks 44 D9
Whelpo Cumb 98 C10
Whelston Flints 75 J9
Whempstead Herts 45 K7
Whenby N York 86 B1
Whepstead Suffk 58 B9
Wherstead Suffk 47 L3
Wherwell Hants 24 F5
Wheston Derbys 77 M9
Whetsted Kent 34 B12
Whetstone Gt Lon 33 J4
Whetstone Leics 54 F11
Wheyrigg Cumb 97 P8
Whicham Cumb 88 D4
Whichford Warwks 42 G5
Whickham Gatesd 100 G6
Whiddon Devon 7 N5
Whiddon Down Devon 8 D6
Whigstreet Angus 125 J4
Whilton Nhants 54 F8
Whimble Devon 7 L4
Whimple Devon 9 J6
Whimpwell Green Norfk 71 M6
Whinburgh Norfk 70 E10
Whin Lane End Lancs 83 J6
Whinnieliegate D & G 96 E8
Whinnow Cumb 98 C8
Whinnyfold Abers 141 P9
Whinny Hill S on T 91 P3
Whippingham IoW 12 H6
Whipsnade C Beds 44 E8
Whipsnade Zoo ZSL C Beds 44 E8
Whipton Devon 8 H6
Whisby Lincs 79 M10
Whissendine Rutlnd 67 K9
Whissonsett Norfk 70 D8
Whistlefield Ag & B 113 J3
Whistlefield Inn Ag & B 112 H3
Whistley Green Wokham 31 P7
Whiston Knows 75 N5
Whiston Nhants 55 L8
Whiston Rothm 78 D6
Whiston Staffs 64 G9
Whiston Staffs 65 J3
Whiston Cross Shrops 64 E11
Whiston Eaves Staffs 64 H3
Whitacre Fields Warwks 53 N2
Whitbeck Cumb 88 D4
Whitbourne Herefs 52 D9
Whitburn S Tyne 101 K6
Whitburn W Loth 114 H8
Whitby Ches W 75 L8
Whitby N York 92 G4
Whitbyheath Ches W 75 L9
Whitchurch BaNES 28 H9
Whitchurch Bucks 43 Q7
Whitchurch Cardif 27 R6
Whitchurch Devon 7 P10
Whitchurch Hants 24 H3
Whitchurch Herefs 40 H7
Whitchurch Oxon 31 N7
Whitchurch Pembks 36 D6
Whitchurch Shrops 63 P4
Whitchurch Canonicorum Dorset 10 B6
Whitchurch Hill Oxon 31 N7
Whitcombe Dorset 10 H7
Whitcott Keysett Shrops 51 L3
Whiteacre Kent 17 K1
Whiteacre Heath Warwks 53 N3
Whiteash Green Essex 46 D5
White Ball Somset 20 G9
Whitebridge Highld 129 N1
Whitebrook Mons 40 H8
Whitebushes Surrey 15 K1
Whitecairns Abers 141 M2
Whitechapel Gt Lon 33 L5
White Chapel Lancs 83 M7
Whitechurch Pembks 37 M3
Whitecliffe N York 85 N4
Whitecraig E Loth 115 Q7
Whitecroft Gloucs 41 J10
Whitecrook D & G 94 H7
Whitecross Cnwll 3 J4
Whitecross Cnwll 6 D10
Whitecross Falk 114 G7
White End Worcs 41 M5
Whitefarland N Ayrs 103 M1
Whitefaulds S Ayrs 104 D6
Whitefield Bury 76 E3
Whitefield Somset 20 G6
Whitefield Somset 21 L9

Whitefield Lane End Knows 75 M6
Whitefield Abers 140 H10
Whitegate Ches W 76 B10
Whitehall Hants 25 N3
Whitehall Ork 147 e3
Whitehall W Susx 14 G6
Whitehaven Cumb 88 C3
Whitehill Kent 34 H10
Whitehill Leics 66 C10
Whitehills Abers 140 G3
Whitehouse Abers 132 F11
Whitehouse Ag & B 112 B9
Whitehouse Common Birm 53 L1
White Kirkley Dur 100 C11
White Lackington Dorset 10 H5
Whitelackington Somset 21 N10
White Ladies Aston Worcs 52 Q3
Whiteleaf Bucks 44 B10
White-le-Head Dur 100 F7
Whiteley Hants 13 J3
Whiteley Bank IoW 12 J8
Whiteley Green Ches E 76 G8
Whiteley Village Surrey 32 F10
White Mill Carmth 38 C7
Whitemire Moray 138 H5
Whitemoor C Nott 66 E14
Whitemoor Cnwll 3 N3
Whitemoor Derbys 66 B3
Whitemoor Staffs 76 G11
Whiteness Shet 147 i7
White Notley Essex 46 D8
Whiteoak Green Oxon 42 H9
White Ox Mead BaNES 29 L10
Whiteparish Wilts 24 D8
White Pit Lincs 80 G8
Whiterashes Abers 141 K11
White Roding Essex 45 Q9
Whiterow Highld 151 Q7
Whiterow Moray 139 J4
Whiteshill Gloucs 41 N10
Whitesmith E Susx 15 P8
White Stake Lancs 83 M10
Whitestaunton Somset 9 P3
Whitestone Devon 8 G6
White Stone Herefs 40 H3
Whitestone Warwks 54 C3
Whitestone Cross Devon 8 H7
Whitestreet Green Suffk 46 H4
Whitewall Corner N York 86 E1
White Waltham W & M 32 B7
Whiteway BaNES 29 L9
Whitewell Lancs 83 P6
Whiteworks Devon 5 K4
Whitfield C Dund 125 J6
Whitfield Kent 17 N2
Whitfield Nhants 43 M4
Whitfield Nthumb 99 M7
Whitfield S Glos 29 K4
Whitfield Hall Nthumb 99 M7
Whitford Devon 9 P5
Whitford Flints 74 G8
Whitgift E R Yk 86 F10
Whitgreave Staffs 64 G6
Whithorn D & G 95 M10
Whiting Bay N Ayrs 103 Q4
Whitkirk Leeds 85 M9
Whitland Carmth 37 N7
Whitlaw Border 107 M7
Whitletts S Ayrs 104 G5
Whitley N York 85 R11
Whitley Readg 31 Q8
Whitley Sheff 77 Q5
Whitley Wilts 29 P9
Whitley Bay N Tyne 101 J4
Whitley Chapel Nthumb 99 P7
Whitley Heath Staffs 64 F7
Whitley Lower Kirk 85 J11
Whitley Row Kent 33 P11
Whitlock's End Solhll 53 L5
Whitminster Gloucs 41 M10
Whitmore Dorset 11 P3
Whitmore Staffs 64 F4
Whitnage Devon 20 G10
Whitnash Warwks 53 Q8
Whitney-on-Wye Herefs 40 C2
Whitrigg Cumb 97 P10
Whitrigg Cumb 97 P7
Whitsbury Hants 23 Q10
Whitsome Border 117 J11
Whitson Newpt 28 E6
Whitstable Kent 35 K9
Whitstone Cnwll 7 K5
Whittingham Nthumb 108 H10
Whittingslow Shrops 51 M3
Whittington Derbys 78 C8
Whittington Gloucs 42 B7
Whittington Lancs 89 P11
Whittington Norfk 69 N12
Whittington Shrops 63 K6
Whittington Staffs 52 F4
Whittington Staffs 65 M10
Whittington Warwks 65 P12
Whittington Moor Derbys 78 B9
Whittlebury Nhants 43 P3
Whittle-le-Woods Lancs 83 N10
Whittlesey Cambs 56 E1
Whittlesford Cambs 57 K11
Whittlestone Head Bl w D 83 Q11
Whitton N Linc 86 G10
Whitton Nthumb 108 H11
Whitton Powys 51 J7
Whitton S on T 91 P2
Whitton Shrops 51 N6
Whitton Suffk 58 H11
Whittonditch Wilts 30 F7
Whittonstall Nthumb 100 D7
Whitway Hants 31 K11
Whitwell Derbys 78 E9
Whitwell Herts 44 H7
Whitwell IoW 12 H9
Whitwell N York 91 M7
Whitwell Rutlnd 67 M10
Whitwell-on-the-Hill N York 86 D2
Whitwell Street Norfk 70 G8
Whitwick Leics 66 C10
Whitwood Wakefd 85 N10
Whitworth Lancs 84 C11
Whixall Shrops 63 N5
Whixley N York 85 M4
Whorlton Dur 91 J4
Whorlton N York 91 P6
Whyle Herefs 51 N8
Whyteleafe Surrey 33 L10
Wibdon Gloucs 28 H4
Wibsey C Brad 84 H9
Wibtoft Warwks 54 D4
Wichelstowe Swindn 30 C5
Wichenford Worcs 52 E8
Wichling Kent 34 G11
Wick BCP 11 Q6
Wick Devon 9 P4
Wick Highld 151 Q6
Wick S Glos 29 L7
Wick Somset 21 L4
Wick Somset 21 N4
Wick V Glam 27 M7
Wick W Susx 14 E10
Wick Wilts 23 Q9

Wick Wilts 23 Q9
Wick Worcs 41 Q3
Wicken Cambs 57 L6
Wicken Nhants 43 Q4
Wicken Bonhunt Essex 45 P5
Wickenby Lincs 80 B7
Wick End Bed 55 N10
Wicken Green Village Norfk 70 B6
Wickersley Rothm 78 D5
Wicker Street Green Suffk 46 H3
Wickford Essex 34 D3
Wickham Hants 13 K4
Wickham W Berk 31 J8
Wickham Bishops Essex 46 E9
Wickhambreaux Kent 35 M10
Wickhambrook Suffk 57 P9
Wickhamford Worcs 42 C4
Wickham Green Suffk 58 G7
Wickham Green W Berk 31 J8
Wickham Heath W Berk 31 J8
Wickham Market Suffk 59 L9
Wickhampton Norfk 71 N11
Wickham St Paul Essex 46 E4
Wickham Skeith Suffk 58 G7
Wickham Street Suffk 57 P10
Wickham Street Suffk 58 G7
Wick Hill Wokham 31 Q9
Wicklewood Norfk 70 G11
Wickmere Norfk 70 H5
Wick St Lawrence N Som 28 E9
Wicksteed Park Nhants 55 L5
Wickstreet E Susx 15 P9
Wickwar S Glos 29 L5
Widdington Essex 45 P5
Widdop Calder 84 D8
Widdrington Nthumb 109 L10
Widdrington Station Nthumb 109 L11
Widecombe in the Moor Devon 8 D9
Widegates Cnwll 4 D5
Widemouth Bay Cnwll 7 J4
Wide Open N Tyne 100 G4
Widford Essex 46 C10
Widford Herts 45 M8
Widham Wilts 30 C5
Widley Hants 13 L3
Widmer End Bucks 32 C3
Widmerpool Notts 66 G6
Widmore Gt Lon 33 M8
Widnes Halton 75 N6
Widworthy Devon 9 N5
Wigan Wigan 75 P3
Wigborough Somset 21 P10
Wiggaton Devon 9 L6
Wiggenhall St Germans Norfk 69 L9
Wiggenhall St Mary Magdalen Norfk 69 L10
Wiggenhall St Mary the Virgin Norfk 69 L9
Wiggenhall St Peter Norfk 69 L9
Wiggens Green Essex 46 B3
Wiggenstall Staffs 77 K11
Wigginton C York 86 B3
Wigginton Herts 44 D9
Wigginton Oxon 42 H5
Wigginton Staffs 65 M11
Wigginton Bottom Herts 44 D10
Wigglesworth N York 84 B4
Wiggonby Cumb 98 C7
Wiggonholt W Susx 14 F7
Wighill N York 85 P6
Wighton Norfk 70 D4
Wightwick Wolves 52 F1
Wigley Derbys 77 P9
Wigley Hants 24 E10
Wigmore Herefs 51 L7
Wigmore Medway 34 D9
Wigsley Notts 79 L9
Wigsthorpe Nhants 55 P4
Wigston Leics 54 G1
Wigston Fields Leics 54 F12
Wigston Parva Leics 54 D3
Wigthorpe Notts 78 E5
Wigtoft Lincs 68 E5
Wigton Cumb 98 C8
Wigtown D & G 95 N7
Wigtwizzle Sheff 77 N4
Wike Leeds 85 M7
Wilbarston Nhants 55 K3
Wilberfoss E R Yk 86 D5
Wilburton Cambs 57 J6
Wilby Nhants 55 L7
Wilby Norfk 58 F3
Wilby Suffk 59 K6
Wilcot Wilts 30 D10
Wilcott Shrops 63 L8
Wilcove Cnwll 4 F5
Wilcrick Newpt 28 E5
Wilday Green Derbys 77 P8
Wildboarclough Ches E 76 H10
Wilden Bed 56 B9
Wilden Worcs 52 F6
Wilde Street Suffk 57 N5
Wildhern Hants 24 E3
Wildhill Herts 45 J10
Wildmanbridge S Lans 114 E10
Wildmill Brdgnd 27 L6
Wildmoor Hants 25 L2
Wildmoor Worcs 52 H5
Wildsworth Lincs 79 K4
Wilford C Nott 66 F4
Wilkesley Ches E 64 B4
Wilkhaven Highld 146 G8
Wilkieston W Loth 115 L8
Wilkin's Green Herts 44 H10
Wilksby Lincs 80 F11
Willand Devon 9 K3
Willards Hill E Susx 16 C6
Willaston Ches E 64 C2
Willaston Ches W 75 K8
Willen M Keyn 44 C3
Willenhall Covtry 54 B5
Willenhall Wsall 52 H1
Willerby E R Yk 87 J9
Willerby N York 93 K11
Willersey Gloucs 42 C4
Willersley Herefs 40 D2
Willesborough Kent 17 J2
Willesborough Lees Kent 17 J2
Willesden Gt Lon 33 J5
Willesleigh Devon 19 L7
Willesley Wilts 29 N5
Willett Somset 20 H7
Willey Shrops 52 C2
Willey Warwks 54 D4
Willey Green Surrey 32 D12
Williamscot Oxon 43 K3
Williamstown Rhondd 27 N4
Willian Herts 45 J5
Willicote Herefs 53 M10
Willingale Essex 45 Q9
Willingdon E Susx 15 Q10
Willingham Cambs 56 H6
Willingham by Stow Lincs 79 L7
Willingham Green Cambs 57 M10
Willingham St Mary Suffk 59 N4
Willington Bed 56 C10
Willington Derbys 65 P6

Willington Dur 100 G11
Willington Dur 34 D11
Willington N Tyne 101 J5
Willington Warwks 42 F4
Willington Corner
Ches W 75 N10
Willitoft E R Yk 86 D5
Williton Somset 20 G5
Willoughby Lincs 81 J9
Willoughby Warwks 54 E7
Willoughby Hills Lincs 68 G3
Willoughby-on-the-
Wolds Notts 66 G2
Willoughby Waterleys
Leics 54 F2
Willoughton Lincs 79 M5
Willow Green Ches W 75 Q8
Willows Green Essex 46 C8
Willsbridge S Glos 29 K8
Willsworthy Devon 7 P8
Willtown Somset 21 N8
Wilmcote Warwks 53 M9
Wilmington BaNES 29 L10
Wilmington E Susx 9 N5
Wilmington G t Lon 15 Q10
Wilmington Kent 33 P8
Wilmslow Ches E 76 F7
Wilnecote Staffs 65 N12
Wilpshire Lancs 83 G8
Wilsden C Brad 84 G8
Wilsford Lincs 67 P4
Wilsford Wilts 23 P5
Wilsford Wilts 30 C11
Wilsham Devon 19 P4
Wilshaw Kirk 77 L2
Wilsill N York 85 J2
Wilsley Green Kent 16 D3
Wilsley Pound Kent 16 D3
Wilson Herefs 40 H7
Wilson Leics 66 C7
Wilsontown S Lans 114 H10
Wilstead Bed 44 F3
Wilsthorpe Lincs 68 B9
Wilstone Herts 44 C9
Wilstone Green Herts 44 C9
Wilton Cumb 88 D4
Wilton Herefs 41 J7
Wilton N York 92 H10
Wilton R & Cl 92 C3
Wilton Wilts 23 N7
Wilton Wilts 30 F10
Wilton Dean Border 107 M7
Wimbish Essex 45 Q4
Wimbish Green Essex 45 R5
Wimbledon Gt Lon 33 J8
Wimblington Cambs 56 H2
Wimboldsley Ches W 76 C11
Wimborne Minster
Dorset 11 N5
Wimborne St Giles
Dorset 11 P2
Wimbotsham Norfk 69 M11
Wimpole Cambs 56 G10
Wimpstone Warwks 53 N11
Wincanton Somset 22 G7
Winceby Lincs 80 F10
Wincham Ches W 76 C8
Winchburgh W Loth 115 K6
Winchcombe Gloucs 42 B6
Winchelsea E Susx 16 F7
Winchelsea Beach E Susx 16 G7
Winchester Hants 24 H7
Winchester Services
Hants 25 J6
Winchet Hill Kent 16 C3
Winchfield Hants 25 N2
Winchmore Hill Bucks 32 D3
Winchmore Hill Gt Lon 33 K3
Wincle Ches E 76 H10
Wincobank Sheff 78 C5
Winder Cumb 88 D3
Windermere Cumb 89 L7
Windermere Jetty Cumb 89 L7
Winderton Warwks 42 G3
Windhill Highld 137 P6
Windlehurst Stockp 76 H6
Windlesham Surrey 32 D9
Windmill Cnwll 6 C9
Windmill Staffs 77 M8
Windmill Hill E Susx 16 B8
Windmill Hill Somset 21 M10
Windrush Gloucs 42 E9
Windsole Abers 140 E4
Windsor W & M 32 D7
Windsor Castle W & M 32 D7
Windsoredge Gloucs 29 N2
Windsor Green Suffk 58 D9
Windygates Fife 115 Q1
Windyharbour Ches E 76 F9
Windy Hill Wrexhm 63 J1
Wineham W Susx 15 J7
Winestead E R Yk 87 P10
Winewall Lancs 84 D7
Winfarthing Norfk 58 G4
Winford IoW 13 J8
Winford N Som 28 H9
Winforton Herefs 40 E4
Winfrith Newburgh
Dorset 11 K8
Wing Bucks 44 C7
Wing Rutlnd 67 M11
Wingate Dur 101 K11
Wingates Bolton 76 C2
Wingates Nthumb 108 H10
Wingerworth Derbys 78 C10
Wingfield C Beds 44 E6
Wingfield Suffk 59 J5
Wingfield Wilts 23 N11
Wingham Kent 35 M11
Wingland Lincs 69 J7
Wingmore Kent 17 L2
Wingrave Bucks 44 B8
Winkburn Notts 78 H12
Winkfield Br For 32 C8
Winkfield Row Br For 32 C8
Winkhill Staffs 65 K2
Winkhurst Green Kent 15 P1
Winkleigh Devon 8 B3
Winksley N York 85 K1
Winkton BCP 12 B5
Winlaton Gatesd 100 F6
Winlaton Mill Gatesd 100 F6
Winless Highld 151 P6
Winmarleigh Lancs 83 L6
Winnall Hants 24 H8
Winnersh Wokham 31 Q8
Winnington Ches W 76 B9
Winscales Cumb 88 D2
Winscombe N Som 28 F11
Winsford Ches W 76 C10
Winsford Somset 20 D6
Winsham Devon 19 L5
Winsham Somset 10 B3
Winshill Staffs 65 P7
Winshwen Swans 26 G3
Winskill Cumb 98 H11
Winslade Hants 25 L4
Winsley Wilts 29 M10
Winslow Bucks 43 Q6
Winson Gloucs 42 C10
Winsor Hants 24 E10
Winster Cumb 89 L8
Winster Derbys 77 N11
Winston Dur 91 J3
Winston Suffk 58 H8
Winstone Gloucs 41 Q9
Winston Green Suffk 58 H8
Winswell Devon 19 J10
Winterborne Came
Dorset 10 H7
Winterborne Clenston
Dorset 11 K4
Winterborne
Herringston Dorset 10 H7
Winterborne Houghton
Dorset 11 K4
Winterborne Kingston
Dorset 11 L5
Winterborne Monkton
Dorset 11 K4
Winterborne Stickland
Dorset 11 K4
Winterborne Tomson
Dorset 11 L5
Winterborne
Whitechurch Dorset 11 K5
Winterborne Zelston
Dorset 11 L5
Winterbourne S Glos 29 K6
Winterbourne W Berk 31 K8
Winterbourne Abbas
Dorset 10 F6
Winterbourne Bassett
Wilts 30 C7
Winterbourne Dauntsey
Wilts 24 B6
Winterbourne Earls Wilts 24 B6
Winterbourne Gunner
Wilts 24 B6
Winterbourne Monkton
Wilts 30 C8
Winterbourne
Steepleton Dorset 10 F7
Winterbourne Stoke
Wilts 23 N5
Winterbrook Oxon 31 M5
Winterburn N York 84 D3
Winteringham N Linc 86 H10
Winterley Ches E 76 D12
Wintersett Wakefd 85 M12
Winterslow Wilts 24 C7
Winterton N Linc 86 H11
Winterton-on-Sea Norfk 71 P8
Winthorpe Lincs 81 L10
Winthorpe Notts 79 K12
Winton BCP 11 Q6
Winton Cumb 90 C5
Winton E Susx 15 P10
Winton N York 91 P7
Wintringham Cambs 56 D8
Wintringham N York 92 H10
Winwick Cambs 56 B4
Winwick Nhants 54 G6
Winwick Warrtn 75 Q5
Wirksworth Derbys 65 P1
Wirral 75 J6
Wirswall Ches E 63 P3
Wisbech Cambs 69 J10
Wisbech St Mary Cambs 68 H10
Wisborough Green
W Susx 14 G5
Wiseman's Bridge
Pembks 37 M9
Wiseton Notts 79 J6
Wishanger Gloucs 41 Q9
Wishaw N Lans 114 E10
Wishaw Warwks 53 M2
Wisley Surrey 32 F10
Wisley Garden RHS
Surrey 32 F10
Wispington Lincs 80 D9
Wissenden Kent 16 F3
Wissett Suffk 59 M5
Wissington Norfk 57 M1
Wissington Suffk 46 G5
Wistanstow Shrops 51 M4
Wistaston Ches E 64 C1
Wistaston Green Ches E 64 C1
Wisterfield Ches E 76 F9
Wiston Pembks 37 K7
Wiston S Lans 106 C3
Wiston W Susx 14 G8
Wistow Cambs 56 E4
Wistow Leics 54 G2
Wistow N York 86 B8
Wiswell Lancs 83 R7
Witcham Cambs 57 J5
Witchampton Dorset 11 N3
Witchford Cambs 57 J6
Witcombe Somset 21 Q9
Witham Essex 46 E9
Witham Friary Somset 22 G5
Witham on the Hill Lincs 67 P9
Witham St Hughs Lincs 79 M11
Withcall Lincs 80 F7
Withdean Br & H 15 K9
Witherenden Hill E Susx 16 B5
Witheridge Devon 20 C10
Witherley Leics 53 Q1
Withern Lincs 80 H7
Withernsea E R Yk 87 Q9
Withernwick E R Yk 87 N7
Withersdale Street Suffk 59 K4
Withersfield Suffk 57 M11
Witherslack Cumb 89 L10
Withiel Cnwll 6 E11
Withiel Florey Somset 20 F7
Withielgoose Cnwll 6 E11
Withington Gloucs 42 B8
Withington Herefs 40 H3
Withington Manch 76 F5
Withington Shrops 63 P9
Withington Staffs 65 J5
Withington Green Ches E 76 F9
Withington Marsh Herefs 40 H3
Withleigh Devon 20 D10
Withnell Lancs 83 P10
Withnell Fold Lancs 83 N10
Withybed Green Worcs 53 J6
Withybrook Warwks 54 D4
Withycombe Somset 20 F5
Withyham E Susx 15 P4
Withy Mills BaNES 29 K11
Withypool Somset 20 C6
Withywood Bristl 28 H8
Witley Surrey 14 D3
Witnesham Suffk 59 J10
Witney Oxon 42 H9
Wittering C Pete 67 Q11
Wittersham Kent 16 F5
Witton Birm 53 K3
Witton Norfk 71 L10
Witton Norfk 71 L10
Witton Gilbert Dur 100 G8
Witton le Wear Dur 100 F11
Witton Park Dur 100 F12
Wiveliscombe Somset 20 F8
Wivelrod Hants 25 L6
Wivelsfield E Susx 15 L7
Wivelsfield Green E Susx 15 L7
Wivelsfield Station
W Susx 15 L7
Wivenhoe Essex 47 J7
Wivenhoe Cross Essex 47 J7
Wiveton Norfk 70 F4
Wix Essex 47 L6
Wixams Bed 44 F3
Wixford Warwks 53 K9
Wix Green Essex 47 L6
Wixhill Shrops 63 Q6

Wixoe Suffk 46 C3
Woburn C Beds 44 D5
Woburn Safari Park
C Beds 44 D5
Woburn Sands M Keyn 44 C4
Wokefield Park W Berk 31 N9
Woking Surrey 32 E10
Wokingham Wokham 32 A8
Wolborough Devon 8 F10
Woldingham Surrey 33 L11
Wold Newton E R Yk 93 L12
Wold Newton NE Lin 80 F4
Wolfclyde S Lans 106 D3
Wolferlow Herefs 52 C8
Wolferton Norfk 69 M6
Wolfhampcote Warwks 54 E7
Wolfhill P & K 124 C6
Wolf Hills Nthumb 99 K6
Wolf's Castle Pembks 37 J5
Wolfsdale Pembks 36 H6
Wollaston Dudley 52 G4
Wollaston Nhants 55 M8
Wollaston Shrops 63 K9
Wollaton Wolves 66 E4
Wollaton Hall & Park
C Nott 66 E4
Wolleigh Devon 8 F8
Wollerton Shrops 64 B6
Wollescote Dudley 52 H4
Wolseley Bridge Staffs 65 J7
Wolsingham Dur 100 D10
Wolstanton Staffs 64 F2
Wolstenholme Rochdl 84 C12
Wolston Warwks 54 C5
Wolsty Cumb 97 M8
Wolvercote Oxon 43 K9
Wolverhampton Wolves 64 G12
Wolverhampton
Halfpenny Green
Airport Staffs 52 F2
Wolverley Shrops 63 M6
Wolverley Worcs 52 F5
Wolverton Hants 31 L10
Wolverton Kent 17 N2
Wolverton M Keyn 44 B3
Wolverton Warwks 53 N8
Wolverton Wilts 22 H7
Wolverton Common
Hants 31 M10
Wolvesnewton Mons 28 F7
Wolvey Warwks 54 C3
Wolvey Heath Warwks 54 D3
Wolviston S on T 91 Q2
Wombleton N York 92 D10
Wombourne Staffs 52 G2
Wombwell Barns 78 C3
Womenswold Kent 35 M12
Womersley N York 85 Q11
Wonastow Mons 40 G9
Wonersh Surrey 14 E2
Wonford Devon 8 H6
Wonson Devon 8 B7
Wonston Dorset 10 H3
Wonston Hants 24 H5
Wooburn Bucks 32 C5
Wooburn Green Bucks 32 C5
Wooburn Moor Bucks 7 M3
Woodacott Devon 7 F7
Woodale N York 90 G11
Woodall Rothm 78 D7
Woodbank Ches W 75 K9
Woodbastwick Norfk 71 L9
Woodbeck Notts 79 K8
Wood Bevington Warwks 53 K10
Woodborough Notts 66 G3
Woodborough Wilts 30 C10
Woodbridge Devon 9 M6
Woodbridge Dorset 23 J9
Woodbridge Suffk 59 K10
Wood Burcote Nhants 43 N2
Woodbury Devon 9 J7
Woodbury Salterton
Devon 9 J7
Woodchester Gloucs 41 N11
Woodchurch Kent 16 G4
Woodchurch Wirral 75 J6
Woodcombe Somset 20 E4
Woodcote Gt Lon 33 K10
Woodcote Oxon 31 N6
Woodcote Wrekin 64 D9
Woodcott Hants 24 G2
Woodcroft Gloucs 28 H4
Woodcutts Dorset 23 L10
Wood Dalling Norfk 70 F7
Woodditton Cambs 57 M9
Woodeaton Oxon 43 L9
Wood Eaton Staffs 64 F8
Wooden Pembks 37 M9
Wood End Bed 44 E4
Wood End Bed 56 B7
Wood End C Beds 44 E6
Wood End Cambs 56 G5
Wood End Gt Lon 32 G6
Wood End Herts 45 L6
Woodend Highld 127 P12
Woodend Nhants 54 G11
Wood End Warwks 65 L4
Woodend W Loth 114 G7
Wood End W Susx 13 P5
Wooden Nthumb 37 M9
Wood End Warwks 53 L6
Wood End Warwks 53 N1
Wood End Warwks 65 H12
Wood Enderby Lincs 80 E11
Woodend Green Essex 45 Q6
Woodfalls Wilts 24 B9
Woodford Cnwll 18 E10
Woodford Devon 5 N6
Woodford Gloucs 29 J3
Woodford Nhants 55 M5
Woodford Gt Lon 33 M4
Woodford Bridge Gt Lon 33 M4
Woodford Green Gt Lon 33 M4
Woodford Halse Nhants 54 E10
Woodford Wells Gt Lon 33 M4
Woodgate Birm 53 J4
Woodgate Devon 20 H10
Woodgate Norfk 70 F9
Woodgate Norfk 70 H9
Woodgate Worcs 52 H7
Woodgate W Susx 14 D10
Wood Green Gt Lon 33 K3
Woodgreen Hants 24 B10
Woodgreen Oxon 42 H9
Woodhall Herts 45 J7
Woodhall N York 90 F8
Woodhall Hill Leeds 85 K8
Woodhall Spa Lincs 80 D11
Woodham Bucks 43 M9
Woodham Dur 91 M1
Woodham Surrey 32 F9
Woodham Ferrers Essex 34 D2
Woodham Mortimer
Essex 46 E10
Woodham Walter Essex 46 E10
Wood Hayes Wolves 64 H11
Woodhead Abers 141 J8
Woodhey Shrops 52 D4
Woodhill Shrops 52 D4
Woodhill Somset 21 M8
Woodhorn Nthumb 109 M12
Woodhouse Leeds 85 L8
Woodhouse Leics 66 E8
Woodhouse Sheff 78 D7

Woodhouse Wakefd 85 M11
Woodhouse Eaves Leics 66 E9
Woodhouse Green Staffs 76 G11
Woodhouselee Mdloth 115 N8
Woodhouselees D & G 98 E3
Woodhouse Mill Sheff 78 C6
Woodhouses Cumb 98 C8
Woodhouses Oldham 76 H3
Woodhouses Staffs 65 M8
Woodhurst Cambs 56 F5
Woodingdean Br & H 15 L9
Woodkirk Leeds 85 K10
Woodland Abers 141 L11
Woodland Devon 5 K5
Woodland Devon 5 N3
Woodland Dur 90 H1
Woodland Kent 17 L3
Woodland S Ayrs 104 C10
Woodland Head Devon 8 E5
Woodlands Donc 78 E2
Woodlands Dorset 11 N3
Woodlands Hants 12 E2
Woodlands Kent 33 Q10
Woodlands N York 85 K4
Woodlands Somset 21 J5
Woodlands of Durris
Abers 133 J5
Woodlands Park W & M 32 B6
Woodlands St Mary
W Berk 30 G7
Woodland Street Somset 22 D6
Woodland View Sheff 77 Q6
Wood Lane Shrops 63 L5
Wood Lane Staffs 64 E2
Woodleigh Devon 5 M7
Woodlesford Leeds 85 M9
Woodley Stockp 76 H5
Woodley Wokham 31 Q7
Woodmancote Gloucs 29 M3
Woodmancote Gloucs 41 R6
Woodmancote Gloucs 42 B10
Woodmancote W Susx 13 N3
Woodmancote W Susx 15 M8
Woodmancote Worcs 41 J5
Woodmancott Hants 25 J5
Woodmansey E R Yk 87 K7
Woodmansgreen W Susx 25 Q8
Woodmansterne Surrey 33 K10
Woodmanton Devon 9 J7
Woodmarsh Wilts 23 J3
Woodmill Staffs 65 L8
Woodminton Wilts 23 M9
Woodnesborough Kent 35 P11
Woodnewton Nhants 55 P2
Woodnook Notts 66 D2
Wood Norton Norfk 70 E6
Woodplumpton Lancs 83 L8
Woodrising Norfk 70 E11
Wood Row Leeds 85 M9
Woodrow Worcs 52 G5
Wood's Corner E Susx 16 B7
Woods Eaves Herefs 51 J11
Woodseaves Shrops 64 C6
Woodseaves Staffs 64 E7
Woodsend Wilts 30 E7
Woodsetts Rothm 78 F7
Woodsford Dorset 11 J6
Wood's Green E Susx 16 B4
Woodside Br For 32 D8
Woodside Cumb 97 L11
Woodside Essex 45 N11
Woodside Fife 124 H11
Woodside Gt Lon 33 L9
Woodside Hants 12 E6
Woodside Herts 45 J10
Woodside P & K 124 D5
Woodside Green Kent 34 F11
Woodstock Oxon 43 J8
Woodstock Pembks 37 K5
Wood Street Norfk 71 M8
Wood Street Village
Surrey 32 D12
Woodthorpe Derbys 78 D9
Woodthorpe Leics 66 E9
Woodthorpe Lincs 80 H7
Woodton Norfk 59 M2
Woodtown Devon 18 H8
Woodvale Sefton 75 K2
Woodville Derbys 65 P8
Woodwall Green Staffs 64 E6
Wood Walton Cambs 56 C4
Woodyates Dorset 23 M9
Woody Bay Devon 19 N4
Woofferton Shrops 51 N7
Wookey Somset 22 C4
Wookey Hole Somset 22 C4
Wool Dorset 11 K7
Woolacombe Devon 19 J5
Woolage Green Kent 17 M1
Woolage Village Kent 35 M12
Woolaston Gloucs 29 J2
Woolaston Common
Gloucs 29 J2
Woolavington Somset 21 M5
Woolbeding W Susx 14 C6
Woolcotts Somset 20 E7
Wooldale Kirk 77 M4
Wooler Nthumb 108 G4
Woolfardisworthy Devon 20 H12
Woolfardisworthy Devon 18 H9
Woolfold Bury 76 E1
Woolfords S Lans 115 J10
Woolhampton W Berk 31 M9
Woolhope Herefs 41 J4
Woolland Dorset 11 J3
Woollard BaNES 29 K9
Woollensbrook Herts 45 L9
Woolley BaNES 29 M8
Woolley Cambs 56 C6
Woolley Cnwll 18 E10
Woolley Derbys 78 B11
Woolley Wakefd 77 Q5
Woolley Bridge Derbys 77 J5
Woolley Edge Services
Wakefd 85 L12
Woolmere Green Worcs 52 H8
Woolmer Green Herts 45 J8
Woolminstone Somset 10 C3
Woolpack Kent 16 E3
Woolpit Suffk 58 E8
Woolpit Green Suffk 58 E8
Woolscott Warwks 54 E7
Woolsgrove Devon 8 E4
Woolsington N u Ty 100 F4
Woolstaston Shrops 51 M1
Woolsthorpe by Belvoir
Lincs 67 L5
Woolsthorpe-by-
Colsterworth Lincs 67 M7
Woolston C Sotn 12 G3
Woolston Devon 5 M8
Woolston Devon 5 M8
Woolston Shrops 51 M1
Woolston Shrops 63 K6
Woolston Somset 20 H5
Woolston Somset 22 D7
Woolston Warrtn 76 C6
Woolstone Gloucs 41 Q6
Woolstone M Keyn 44 C4
Woolstone Oxon 30 G4
Woolston Green Devon 5 N3

Woolton L pool 75 M6
Woolton Hill Hants 31 J10
Woolverstone Suffk 47 L4
Woolverton Somset 22 H3
Woolwich Gt Lon 33 N6
Woonton Herefs 51 P8
Woonton Herefs 108 G6
Woore Shrops 64 D4
Wooton Green Suffk 59 J6
Wootten Bed 44 E3
Wootten Dur 12 C5
Wootton Herefs 51 K10
Wootton IoW 13 H7
Wootton Kent 17 M2
Wootton N Linc 87 K12
Wootton Nhants 55 J9
Wootton Oxon 43 K11
Wootton Shrops 63 K6
Wootton Staffs 64 F7
Wootton Staffs 65 L3
Wootton Bassett Wilts 30 C5
Wootton Bridge IoW 13 H6
Wootton Broadmead Bed 44 E3
Wootton Common IoW 13 H6
Wootton Courtenay
Somset 20 E5
Wootton Fitzpaine Dorset 10 B5
Wootton Rivers Wilts 30 E9
Wootton St Lawrence
Hants 25 K3
Wootton Wawen Warwks 53 M8
Worcester Worcs 52 F9
Worcester Park Gt Lon 33 J9
Wordsley Dudley 52 G3
Worfield Shrops 52 D1
Worgret Dorset 11 L7
Workhouse End Bed 56 B10
Workhouse Green Suffk 46 F4
Workington Cumb 88 D1
Worksop Notts 78 H8
Worlaby Lincs 80 G8
Worlaby N Linc 87 K11
World's End Bucks 44 B10
World's End Hants 25 L11
World's End W Berk 31 K7
World's End W Susx 15 L7
Worle N Som 28 E9
Worleston Ches E 76 C12
Worlingham Suffk 59 N3
Worlington Devon 19 P10
Worlington Suffk 57 N6
Worlingworth Suffk 59 J7
Wormald Green N York 85 L2
Wormbridge Herefs 40 F5
Wormegay Norfk 69 M10
Wormelow Tump Herefs 40 G6
Wormhill Derbys 77 L9
Wormhill Herefs 40 F4
Worminghall Bucks 43 N10
Wormington Gloucs 42 B4
Worminster Somset 22 D5
Wormit Fife 124 H7
Wormleighton Warwks 54 D10
Wormley Herts 45 L10
Wormley Surrey 14 D3
Wormleybury Herts 45 L10
Wormley Hill Donc 86 C12
Wormshill Kent 34 E11
Wormsley Herefs 51 M11
Worplesdon Surrey 32 D11
Worrall Sheff 77 P5
Worrall Hill Gloucs 41 J8
Worsbrough Barns 78 B3
Worsbrough Bridge
Barns 78 B3
Worsbrough Dale Barns 78 B3
Worsley Salfd 76 D4
Worstead Norfk 71 L7
Worsthorne Lancs 84 C8
Worston Lancs 84 A6
Worth Kent 35 P11
Worth Somset 22 C4
Worth W Susx 15 K4
Wortham Suffk 58 G5
Worthen Shrops 63 K11
Worthenbury Wrexhm 63 M3
Worthing Norfk 70 E8
Worthing W Susx 14 G10
Worthington Leics 66 C8
Worth Matravers Dorset 11 N9
Worthing Hants 25 K3
Wortley Barns 77 P4
Wortley Gloucs 29 M4
Wortley Leeds 85 K8
Worton N York 90 H8
Worton Wilts 29 N11
Wortwell Norfk 59 K4
Wotherton Shrops 63 J12
Wothorpe C Pete 67 P11
Wotter Devon 5 J4
Wotton Surrey 14 G2
Wotton-under-Edge
Gloucs 29 M4
Wotton Underwood
Bucks 43 P8
Woughton on the Green
M Keyn 34 C9
Wouldham Kent 34 C9
Woundale Shrops 52 E2
Wrabness Essex 47 L5
Wrafton Devon 19 J6
Wragby Lincs 80 D8
Wragby Wakefd 85 N11
Wramplingham Norfk 70 H11
Wrangaton Devon 5 L5
Wrangbrook Wakefd 78 D1
Wrangle Lincs 68 H1
Wrangle Common Lincs 68 H1
Wrangle Lowgate Lincs 68 H1
Wrangway Somset 20 H9
Wrantage Somset 21 M9
Wrawby N Linc 80 D2
Wraxall Somset 28 G8
Wraxall Somset 22 E6
Wray Lancs 83 N2
Wray Castle Cumb 89 K6
Wraysbury W & M 32 E7
Wrayton Lancs 89 P22
Wrea Green Lancs 83 J9
Wreaks Cumb 88 H9
Wreay Cumb 89 M1
Wreay Cumb 89 N3
Wrecclesham Surrey 25 P4
Wrekenton Gatesd 100 H6
Wrelton N York 92 F9
Wrenbury Ches E 63 Q3
Wrench Green N York 93 K9
Wreningham Norfk 70 H1
Wrentham Suffk 59 P4
Wrenthorpe Wakefd 85 L10
Wrentnall Shrops 63 M11
Wressle E R Yk 86 D9
Wressle N Linc 79 N1
Wrestlingworth C Beds 56 E11
Wrexham Wrexhm 69 N12
Wrexham Industrial
Estate Wrexhm 63 K2
Wribbenhall Worcs 52 E5
Wrickton Shrops 52 B3
Wrightington Bar Lancs 75 P1
Wright's Green Essex 45 P8

Wrinehill Staffs 64 D3
Wrington N Som 28 G9
Writhlington BaNES 22 F2
Writtle Essex 46 B10
Wrockwardine Wrekin 64 B9
Wroot N Linc 78 H3
Wrose C Brad 85 J8
Wrotham Kent 33 P10
Wrotham Heath Kent 34 B10
Wrottesley Staffs 64 F12
Wroughton Swindn 30 D6
Wroxall IoW 13 J9
Wroxall Warwks 53 N6
Wroxeter Shrops 63 P10
Wroxham Norfk 71 L8
Wroxton Oxon 43 J3
Wyaston Derbys 65 M4
Wyatt's Green Essex 33 Q2
Wyberton Lincs 68 F4
Wyboston Bed 56 C9
Wybunbury Ches E 64 C2
Wychbold Worcs 52 G7
Wych Cross E Susx 15 M4
Wychnor Staffs 65 M9
Wychwood Ches E 64 D2
Wyck Hants 25 N5
Wyck Rissington Gloucs 42 E7
Wycliffe Dur 91 J4
Wycoller Lancs 84 D7
Wycomb Leics 67 K7
Wycombe Marsh Bucks 32 C4
Wyddial Herts 45 L5
Wye Kent 17 J1
Wyesham Mons 40 G9
Wyfordby Leics 67 K8
Wyke C Brad 84 H10
Wyke Devon 8 F6
Wyke Devon 22 H8
Wyke Shrops 64 D7
Wyke Surrey 32 C12
Wyke Champflower
Somset 22 F6
Wykeham N York 93 K10
Wyken Covtry 54 B4
Wyken Shrops 52 D2
Wyke Regis Dorset 10 G9
Wykey Shrops 63 L7
Wykin Leics 54 C2
Wylam Nthumb 100 G6
Wylde Green Birm 53 L2
Wyllie Caerph 27 N3
Wylye Wilts 23 M6
Wymeswold Leics 66 G7
Wymington Bed 55 N8
Wymondham Leics 70 G12
Wymondham Leics 67 L9
Wyndham Brdgnd 27 M4
Wynford Eagle Dorset 10 F5
Wynyard Park S on T 91 P1
Wynyard Village S on T 91 P1
Wyre Piddle Worcs 52 H11
Wysall Notts 66 G7
Wyson Herefs 51 N7
Wythall Worcs 53 K5
Wytham Oxon 43 K10
Wythburn Cumb 89 J4
Wythenshawe Manch 76 F6
Wythop Mill Cumb 97 K3
Wyton Cambs 56 E6
Wyton E R Yk 87 M8
Wyverstone Suffk 58 F7
Wyverstone Street Suffk 58 F7
Wyville Lincs 67 L6

Yeo Vale Devon 18 H8
Yeovil Somset 22 D10
Yeovil Marsh Somset 22 C9
Yeovilton Somset 22 D9
Yerbeston Pembks 37 L8
Yesnaby Ork 147 b4
Yetlington Nthumb 108 G8
Yetminster Dorset 10 F3
Yetson Devon 5 N5
Yettington Devon 9 K7
Yetts o'Muckhart Clacks 115 J1
Yews Green C Brad 84 G9
Yew Tree Sandw 53 J3
Y Felinheli Gwynd 73 J10
Y Ferwig Cerdgn 48 C10
Y Ffôr Gwynd 60 F5
Yielden Bed 55 P6
Yieldshields S Lans 114 F11
Yiewsley Gt Lon 32 F6
Y Nant Wrexhm 63 J2
Ynys Gwynd 61 K5
Ynysboeth Rhondd 27 P3
Ynysddu Caerph 28 A4
Ynysforgan Swans 26 G2
Ynyshir Rhondd 27 N4
Ynyslas Cerdgn 49 K2
Ynysmaerdy Rhondd 27 N5
Ynysmeudwy Neath 38 H10
Ynystawe Swans 26 G2
Ynyswen Powys 39 K9
Ynyswen Rhondd 27 M3
Ynysybwl Rhondd 27 P3
Ynysymaengwyn Gwynd 61 K11
Yockenthwaite N York 90 E11
Yockleton Shrops 63 L9
Yokefleet E R Yk 86 F10
Yoker C Glas 113 P7
York C York 86 B5
York Lancs 83 Q8
Yorkletts Kent 35 K9
Yorkley Gloucs 41 K10
Yorkshire Dales
National Park 90 E11
York Town Surrey 32 B10
Yorton Heath Shrops 63 N7
Youlgreave Derbys 77 N11
Youlthorpe E R Yk 86 E4
Youlton N York 85 P3
Young's End Essex 46 C8
Yoxall Staffs 65 L8
Yoxford Suffk 59 M7
Y Rhiw Gwynd 60 C6
Ysbyty Cynfyn Cerdgn 49 N5
Ysbyty Ifan Conwy 61 P2
Ysbyty Ystwyth Cerdgn 49 M6
Ysceifiog Flints 74 G9
Ysgubor-y-Coed Cerdgn 49 L2
Ystalyfera Neath 39 J10
Ystrad Rhondd 27 M3
Ystrad Aeron Cerdgn 49 J9
Ystradfellte Powys 39 M9
Ystrad Ffin Carmth 39 J2
Ystradgynlais Powys 39 J9
Ystrad Meurig Cerdgn 49 M7
Ystrad Mynach Caerph 27 P2
Ystradowen V Glam 27 N7
Ystumtuen Cerdgn 49 M5
Ythanbank Abers 141 M6
Ythanwells Abers 140 G8
Ythsie Abers 141 L7

Z

Zeal Monachorum Devon 8 D4
Zeals Wilts 22 H7
Zelah Cnwll 3 K4
Zennor Cnwll 2 D7
Zoar Cnwll 3 J10
Zouch Notts 66 E7
ZSL London Zoo Gt Lon 33 K6
ZSL Whipsnade Zoo
C Beds 44 E8